Financial Accounting

Second Edition

Financial Accounting

Serge Matulich, Ph.D., C.P.A.
Roy E. Crummer Graduate School of Business
Rollins College

Lester E. Heitger, Ph.D., C.P.A.
Graduate School of Business
Indiana University

McGraw-Hill Book Company
New York St. Louis San Francisco Auckland Bogotá Hamburg
Johannesburg London Madrid Mexico Montreal New Delhi Panama
Paris São Paulo Singapore Sydney Tokyo Toronto

FINANCIAL ACCOUNTING

1234567890 DOCDOC 8987654

ISBN 0-07-040912-9

This book was set in Caledonia by Ruttle, Shaw & Wetherill, Inc.
The editors were Jim DeVoe, Barbara Brooks, Gail Gavert, Scott Amerman, and Philip E. McCaffrey;
the designer was Merrill Haber;
the production supervisor was Charles Hess.
New drawings were done by J & R Services, Inc.
R. R. Donnelly & Sons Company was printer and binder.

Library of Congress Cataloging in Publication Data

Matulich, Serge.
    Financial accounting.

    Includes index.
    1. Accounting.   I. Heitger, Lester E.   II. Title.
HF5635.M4325   1985   657'.042   84-14348
ISBN 0-07-040912-9

Material from Uniform CPA Examination Questions and Unofficial Answers, Copyright © 1960, 1961,
1962, 1963, 1964, 1965, 1966, 1967, 1968, 1969, 1970, 1971, 1972, 1973, 1974, 1975, 1976, 1977, 1978,
1979, 1980, 1981, 1982, 1983 by the American Institute of Certified Public Accountants, Inc., is
reprinted (or adapted) with permission.

Material from the Certificate in Management Accounting Examinations, Copyright © 1972, 1973, 1974,
1975, 1976, 1977, 1978, 1979, 1980, 1981, 1982 by the National Association of Accountants, is reprinted
(or adapted) with permission.

Contents in Brief

v

Contents

PART 2   ACCOUNTING FOR BUSINESS OPERATIONS

Preface

Our primary objective with the first edition of this book was to write a comprehensive, flexible text that was easy to use by both instructors and students. This second edition is intended to continue the same theme while responding to the changing business environment that accounting serves. In writing this second edition, we have listened carefully to adopters, reviewers, editors, and our students, and have also taken into account our own experiences with the book. As a result, we have been able to streamline the writing style, rearrange some of the material, and improve the level of the book by eliminating some topics that are too complex for an introductory textbook. In addition we also have enhanced an already strong support package available to students and instructors using this book.

The basic philosophy of the first edition is unchanged. The book is suitable for introductory courses at either the undergraduate or graduate levels. The coverage of material is designed to satisfy the needs of potential accounting majors as well as those who will not continue with advanced accounting courses. A careful balance between conceptual and technical material is maintained because we believe that a combination of basic concepts and practical application of techniques is essential if students are to retain the body of accounting knowledge they will need in other courses and in their future business experiences.

The book deliberately contains more material than is typically covered in a single semester or quarter. Most instructors like the flexibility afforded by a book that covers the basic financial accounting concepts and allows them to select additional topics to satisfy their particular course objectives.

Although we have made substantial revisions in the second edition, we have retained the desirable and successful features of the first edition.

ORGANIZATION OF THE TOPICS

The basic organization of the book satisfied most users of the first edition and remains unchanged in this second edition. The book is divided into four parts. **Part 1, The Reporting Function,** introduces the basic accounting concepts, procedures, and statements that provide students with the foundation needed for further study. This part is an overview of principles and techniques that result in the reporting of financial position and results of operations at the end of each accounting cycle.

With the foundation obtained from Part 1, students are ready for a detailed look at the components of financial statements in Parts 2 and 3. **Part 2, Accounting for Business Operations,** is a traditional discussion of accounting and control of day-to-day operations that require decisions about assets and liabilities. **Part 3, Investments by Creditors, Owners, and Businesses,** emphasizes the way a business accounts for the funds invested in the organization by creditors and owners, and also for the funds the organization invests in other businesses. The five chapters in Part 3 cover accounting for bonds payable, capital, and long-term investments, including investments in consolidated subsidiaries.

The many separate concepts and topics discussed in Parts 2 and 3 are brought together in **Part 4, The Synthesis of Financial Accounting.** In this part of the book, students are introduced to the statement of changes in financial position, analysis of financial statements, and the latest issues on inflation accounting.

NEW ORGANIZATIONAL FEATURES

Although the basic organization of topics is unchanged from the first edition, many improvements have been made in the presentation of the material.

a. The entire text has been improved by smoothing out the writing, by deleting material that proved to be too complex or difficult for beginning students, and by shifting some of the material among the early chapters.

b. Numeric examples in the chapters have been revised to make them easier to comprehend and to relate to one another.

c. Accounting for owners' equity has been divided into two chapters. Chapter 13 now includes an expanded coverage of partnership accounting and basic concepts of corporate capital. Chapter 14 covers the more complex issues of corporate capital, such as treasury stock, stock conversions, and earnings per share.

d. The last chapter on accounting for the effects of inflation has been completely revised, and not-for-profit accounting has been deleted from the book.

SPECIAL FEATURES OF THE BOOK

The most desirable special features of the first edition have been retained. These include the presentation of basic accounting concepts in a setting familiar to individual students, permitting them to grasp fundamentals of the accounting equation easily in Chapter 2. This innovative chapter has proven successful in providing students with the background that makes the study of subsequent chapters easier.

The time value of money is covered at the beginning of Part 2, as it is in the first edition. Most users of the book found that early coverage of this topic enhanced the teaching of subsequent topics, such as imputed interest, bond investments, installment notes, leases, and bonds payable.

The more complex accounting topics, such as earnings per share and deferred taxes, are discussed in simple enough terms to make them clear to beginning students, but are nevertheless treated in sufficient detail to provide an adequate background. The text material is supported and complemented with numerous diagrams, tables, and illustrations to clarify complex topics and concepts.

To make the teaching of the statement of changes in financial position as easy and flexible as possible, the topic is divided into two chapters. Chapter 17 covers the conceptual and interpretive aspects of the statement of changes; Chapter 18 deals with the technical aspects of statement preparation. This two-chapter approach has been much appreciated by users of the first edition.

NEW FEATURES AND IMPROVEMENTS

In response to comments of reviewers, adopters, and students, we have incorporated the following improvements in the second edition.

a. The concepts of revenue and expense, originally discussed in Chapter 2, have been moved to Chapter 3 and placed in a better context.

b. Closing the books has been shifted from Chapter 5 to Chapter 4 to complement the discussion of temporary accounts and to reduce the complexity of Chapter 5, which discusses adjusting entries.

c. Reversing entries have been placed in an appendix to Chapter 5.

d. The depreciation discussion in Chapter 10 has been updated to include the accelerated cost recovery system (ACRS) now required for tax reporting.

e. Accounting for partnership capital has been expanded to include admission and retirement of a partner.

f. Accounting for capital has been divided into two chapters, with the second one treating the more advanced issues of corporate capital.

g. The comprehensive treatment of many complex topics in the first edition has been simplified to make the material more suitable for introductory students. This includes topics such as tax allocations, bonds payable, consolidations, statement of changes, and price level adjustments.

h. Compound interest tables have been expanded to five decimal places and cover more periods and interest rates than the first edition.

LEARNING AIDS

The learning aids that we introduced in the first edition have now become standard features of good accounting textbooks. These have been retained and improved in the second edition. The learning aids include a brief **chapter overview** and list of **learning objectives** at the beginning of each chapter. **Marginal notes** throughout the book focus the student's attention on important terms, concepts, or ideas. Wide margins allow students to insert their own marginal notes. All figures include an explanatory legend, and the text refers to and explains each figure. A comprehensive **summary** at the end of each chapter reinforces important material, reviews new terminology, and provides an excellent review of the chapter. The summary is followed by a list of **key terms** introduced in the chapter, each referenced to the page number where it was first used. A complete **glossary** is included at the end of the book, with each entry referenced to the chapter where it was first used. The use of **boldface** type and various type styles help students identify and recognize important materials.

END-OF-CHAPTER MATERIAL

The questions, exercises, and problems at the end of each chapter are arranged in the same sequence as the chapter material, and they cover all topics in the chapter. Each chapter also contains one or two cases. To the extent possible, the exercises and problems are also arranged in the order of difficulty, with the shorter and easier problems occurring first, and the more demanding ones found in the later part of the chapter.

The exercises are generally short and relatively easy, and they typically cover a single topic or concept. The problems are longer and more challenging, usually integrating several topics or concepts. Far more end-of-chapter material is provided than can be assigned in a single course, making the book very flexible. Assignment material can be suited to any class level and the book may be used with a different set of assignments in each successive term.

All questions, exercises, problems, and cases are thoroughly coordinated with chapter material, enabling students to obtain guidance from the chapter when attempting a solution. All end-of-chapter material has been designed by the authors and is thoroughly compatible with the text material.

It ranges over a wide variety of topics, presents interesting and realistic rather than artificial situations, and offers a variety of learning experiences. Solutions to exercises, problems, and cases have been class tested and thoroughly checked by two independent accounting instructors.

NEW FEATURES IN ASSIGNMENT MATERIAL

As suggested by users of the first edition, several improvements have been added to the end-of-chapter material.

a. A greater variety of exercises and problems is included in the second edition than in the first.

b. Material from CPA and CMA examinations is included in the questions, exercises, and problems where such material is suitable for an introductory course and compatible with the text.

c. The exercises and problems retained from the first edition have been revised and improved, many have been replaced with new materials, and many new items have been added.

d. One or two cases have been added to each chapter. The cases expose students to a relatively complex business situation that incorporates a number of accounting concepts. Cases typically ask students to provide some interpretation, and they may integrate concepts from earlier chapters. The opportunity for classroom discussion of many accounting topics is afforded by the cases.

INSTRUCTOR'S SUPPLEMENTS

No accounting textbook offers as much help to the instructor as this one. A comprehensive **Solutions Manual** contains solutions to all questions, exercises, problems, and cases. But the really significant part of this manual is the wealth of information designed to enhance the planning of courses, selection of assignment material, and presentation of lectures. The manual contains comments on each chapter, suggestions on the teaching approach, and suggested assignment material for a variety of course goals. A brief description of each exercise, problem, and case is provided, together with the time required to complete the solution, the level of difficulty, and the availability of a transparency of the solution.

A **problem-topic-grid** in the Solutions Manual offers a complete cross-reference between all exercises, problems, and cases and the topics covered in the chapter, enabling instructors to identify topic coverage of assigned materials. This problem-topic grid is invaluable in planning class assignments and in advising students who request additional practice materials.

A major new innovation in the second edition is the inclusion of a complete set of **lecture notes** for each chapter, covering all chapter topics in outline form, and including illustrations and examples of critical issues. The lecture notes are accompanied by **teaching transparencies** for use in class lectures and presentations. They contain examples that emphasize and complement text material, without duplicating the examples and figures available to students in the text. With these lecture notes, instructors can prepare polished and professional class presentations in a minimum of time.

Also available is a comprehensive set of **transparencies** of selected exercise, problem, and case solutions, suitable for use with overhead projectors. The very comprehensive book of **examination questions** contains over 1,000 multiple choice, true-false, and matching objective questions with solutions and more than 150 test problems with solutions and indications of time estimates and difficulty levels. The objective test questions are computerized for retrieval and test generation by the Examiner System. All examination material is arranged by chapter and is in a form suitable for duplication directly from the book of examination questions. The quantity of test material far exceeds the requirements of a single course, allowing the instructor to design many different tests on any topic in the book to suit a variety of class levels and goals.

STUDENT SUPPLEMENTS

An excellent study guide is available to students as a supplement to the textbook. The **Study Guide** is carefully planned and designed to give students a maximum learning experience with a minimum of effort, focusing on the important aspects of each chapter and reinforcing chapter material by means of objective and practical exercises and self-tests. This supplement truly guides students through the most appropriate learning process and enables them to assess their progress and ensure mastery of the materials. Students are given suggestions on how to approach problems and what steps to take to arrive at the correct solutions. Complete answers and explanations are provided in the study guide to all self-test materials and exercises.

A separate volume of **Working Papers** is available for all problems in the text. The working papers are prenumbered and labeled, and where appropriate, partially filled in with data that students would otherwise have to copy from the textbook. **Key figures** are provided at the end of the text for all problems for which one or two check figures can be given to enable students to determine if their solution for exercises, problems, and cases is correct.

Two practice sets are available with this book and may be used to strengthen the knowledge of procedural materials studied in the first six chapters. The **Service Firm Practice Set,** which is computerized, covers one month of operations of a business that provides engineering services. The set contains all necessary forms and instructions to enable students to obtain a solution by means of a personal computer. The computerized practice set is ideal to help acquaint students with electronic data processing in an accounting system. The **Merchandising Firm Practice Set**, in a printed format, covers a month's operation of a retail business and contains all forms and instructions necessary to enable students to complete the set manually.

One of the major advantages of the teaching and learning package contained with this book is the complete integration and coordination of all elements of the package, made possible because each item was developed, written, and tested by the authors.

FLEXIBILITY

We have tried to make the book as flexible as possible, so that it may be adapted to a variety of course objectives. The material is arranged in a sequence that we found to be logical for a first course in financial accounting. It is unlikely, however, that all 20 chapters will be covered in a single semester or quarter. However, the instructor may select any number of topics or entire chapters to omit from a course without loss of continuity, as discussed in the Solutions Manual.

Instructors who arrange their course differently from the chapter sequence in the book will find the book very adaptable and flexible. The quantity of available material permits users to choose those topics that best satisfy specific course objectives and to omit topics that are deemed less important for a particular class. The combination of textbook, instructor's supplements, and student supplements makes the book suitable for many class situations and levels. The material constitutes a complete package that should appeal to the experienced instructor, and it is equally suitable for schools that use student teachers. The book is also suitable for self study, and this leaves room for an instructor to digress, elaborate, and discuss supplementary topics in the classroom. As used in this book, the pronoun "he" embraces both genders when used without reference to a specific person.

ACKNOWLEDGMENTS

A large number of individuals have contributed to the preparation of this book and supplementary materials. We are grateful to many professors, students, and others for their help, advice, and guidance. Special thanks to Hobart W. Adams, University of Akron College of Business Administration; Rosie Bukics, Lafayette College; Harold L. Cannon, S.U.N.Y. at Albany; and Barbara Zarkowski, Bellevue Community College. Our special appreciation to Joseph T. Guy, Georgia State University and Marshall Richter, Brooklyn College for their help in checking our materials for accuracy. The editorial staff of McGraw-Hill whose help was invaluable in preparation of the book and supplements includes Don Mason, Jim DeVoe, Barbara Brooks, Gail Gavert, Mel Haber, and Dennis Conroy. Members of the authors' families contributed much with their work, suggestions, patience, and sacrifices. We are grateful to the many other people who have helped us to produce the manuscripts and supplements and to make the necessary corrections in the final proofs of the books. Any remaining errors are the sole responsibility of the authors.

Serge Matulich
Lester E. Heitger

The Reporting Function

part 1

Accounting as practiced today has evolved over many centuries in response to the economic, social, and political environments that it served. But the changes that have taken place are small in comparison to those fundamental accounting characteristics that have remained unchanged for the past five centuries. The strength of accounting lies in the stability of the basic features described in the following six chapters.

Your thorough understanding of these features is essential for success in your study of the more important aspects of accounting. A sound knowledge of the basic functions of collecting, processing, and reporting accounting information gives you the foundation on which to develop the skills you need to analyze, interpret, and use accounting information in business decision making.

Accounting Information for Economic Decisions

1

This chapter provides a broad overview of the discipline of accounting. When you have completed studying the chapter, you should understand:

1 Why accounting is useful in decision making.

2 The definition of accounting and its characteristics.

3 What is meant by the accounting entity.

4 Who uses accounting information.

5 How accounting developed in ancient and more recent times.

6 What professional accountants do and what is required to enter the accounting profession.

7 Why organizations developed to influence accounting.

You are about to start the study of one of the most essential elements of business decision making. Most business decisions cannot be made without careful analysis of relevant information. The nature and purpose of accounting is to provide that information.

Limited resources require choosing among alternatives

Whether you go into business for yourself, work for a small or large company, enter professional practice, or benefit from an independent income, many of your decisions in life will be economic in nature, and you will want accounting information to help you make those decisions. How many people should you hire? Is your departmental budget adequate?

Should you rent or buy office space? Which of several investments is best for your needs? There are countless other decisions. All involve economic alternatives. We live in a world of limited resources; thus, we frequently find ourselves choosing among alternatives to make the most efficient use of available resources.

Seldom is an important economic decision made that does not depend on accounting information. Accounting is the language of economic activity, and any organization that earns or spends money, regardless of its size, relies on accounting for effective and efficient management. In fact, accounting developed as a natural, logical response to the need for information that could be used to make decisions involving economic alternatives.

The purpose of this chapter is to acquaint you with accounting. First we provide some definitions of accounting and describe its basic characteristics. Next we look at the types of businesses and organizations that accounting serves and the variety of decision makers for whom accounting information is prepared. Then we review the evolution of accounting and discuss the environment in which accounting operates. Finally we discuss the accounting profession and some of the organizations that have been influential in shaping accounting thought.

THE DISCIPLINE OF ACCOUNTING

Accounting is a comprehensive discipline. Any simple definition tends to be incomplete, but definitions can serve as a convenient starting point.

> Accounting is the art of recording, classifying, and summarizing in a significant manner and in terms of money, transactions and events which are, in part at least, of a financial character, and interpreting the results thereof.[1]

This definition reveals accounting as the practice of **recording** information as it becomes available when an economic event measurable in financial terms—that is, a business **transaction**—takes place. The information is **classified** according to whether the transaction affects cash, land, debts, or shares of stock. Because there are many such transactions generating a huge amount of financial data, it is necessary to **summarize** the information into a **significant** form. This means the summaries of accounting information must be in the form of reports that serve specific decision-making purposes. The recording, classifying, and summarizing are all done **in terms of money,** which means that financial transactions must be measured in dollar amounts. Finally, **interpreting** the results of accounting information involves communicating and explaining the information to decision makers. To accomplish all these goals, accounting must be based

---

[1]American Institute of Certified Public Accountants, *Accounting Terminology Bulletin No. 1–Review and Resume,* (New York: AICPA, 1953) p. 1.

on rules and standards that are understood by users of financial information. You will study such rules and standards throughout this book.

Now examine another definition:

Accounting is the process of identifying, measuring, and communicating economic information to permit informed judgments and decisions by users of the information.[2]

Accounting information is important in decision making

This definition of accounting places less emphasis on the information processing aspects and more on the decision-making aspects of accounting. Decisions and judgments are required in order to identify, measure, and communicate accounting information, just as judgment is needed to interpret and use the information to arrive at an economic decision. The second definition places more emphasis on accounting as a decision-making science; the first definition regards accounting as an art. Accounting is an art to the extent that it requires judgment, insight, and talent developed through intensive study. It is a science to the extent that it is rigorous, deals with measurement, and is related to other sciences such as statistics and economics.

Many people confuse bookkeeping with accounting. **Bookkeeping** consists of the day-to-day recording of business data and is generally work of a routine, clerical nature. Bookkeepers usually need only a rudimentary knowledge of accounting to perform their tasks, and many of their duties can be performed automatically by computers. On the other hand, accountants must be qualified in the analysis and interpretation of many complex economic events, financial advising, systems design, and business management.

Basic Characteristics of Accounting

Accounting information must have at least three basic characteristics in order to be useful to decision makers: relevance, timeliness, and accuracy.

Relevance means that accounting information must address the specific problem or decision at hand. Information on the cost of materials used in last week's production may be relevant to a factory supervisor who must control the costs of a product, but it would probably not be relevant to investors who must decide whether or not to risk their money in the company. Investors would find total profit relevant, although the same information might be of little value to the factory supervisor. Consequently, accountants must be capable of presenting economic information in reports that can serve a variety of purposes. Each report may be relevant for some decision-making situations and not for others.

---

[2]American Accounting Association, *A Statement of Basic Accounting Theory*, (Evanston, Ill.: AAA, 1966) p. 1.

Timeliness refers to the need for accounting information to be current. Many types of information lose value rapidly, and financial information is particularly sensitive to the passage of time. For example, last week's interest rate may be of little value to a manager who must borrow money this week, because interest rates often change rapidly. Knowing how much a business is earning today may help an investor to decide whether or not to invest in the business. If the information is old, the investor's decision may not be wise. It is sometimes more important to have approximate financial information immediately than to have precise information later. As you will learn, some degree of precision may have to be sacrificed to achieve timely reporting of relevant information.

Accurate information now is better than precise information later

Accuracy is a major prerequisite of timely and relevant accounting information. Accuracy is not the same as precision, however, and it is important to distinguish between the two. A report that states a company earned $560,000 last year can be considered accurate although the precise amount of earnings may be $560,384. On the other hand, earnings reported at $846,932.17 may appear precise, but the information is of no value if the actual amount is $150,000. Many people mistakenly believe that accounting information is always correct to the nearest penny. In fact, accounting information includes some estimates and approximations. Within the constraints imposed by the methods of measurement and the standards applied, the information produced should reflect the facts fairly.

In addition to relevance, timeliness, and accuracy, accounting information must have a number of other characteristics. It sould be understandable to the user; it should be objective and unbiased so that the user can rely on the information. Accounting information is communicated by means of reports, and a wide variety may be used. Below we present some definitions, discuss specific characteristics of accounting, and describe some of the organizations and individuals that accounting serves.

NATURE OF ACCOUNTING REPORTS

Financial and managerial accounting reports

All accounting reports can be classified into two broad categories: internal reports and external reports. **Internal** reports are referred to as **managerial accounting** reports because they are oriented toward the specific information needs of managers. Typically, management accounting information deals with functions such as planning, control, and coordination of operations—matters relevant for decisions made by the internal management of organizations. Managerial accounting reports typically are more detailed and are prepared more frequently than external reports. They often deal with segments of the organization rather than the whole business. Managerial accounting is discussed extensively in the second volume of this series.[3]

[3]Lester E. Heitger and Serge Matulich, *Managerial Accounting*, 2d ed. (New York: McGraw-Hill, 1985).

External reports, usually called **financial accounting** reports, are more general in nature than internal reports because they serve a wider variety of information users **outside** the business—investors, lenders, and owners. Because they are used for a much broader spectrum of decisions, financial accounting reports are more uniform and more condensed than managerial reports. Financial accounting is the primary focus of this book.

All organizations in our society need both financial and managerial accounting information in order to measure their performance and manage their operations. In addition, most organizations must prepare external reports on management's stewardship of the organization. **Stewardship** is the function of safeguarding the property turned over by investors to the managers of a business venture. Although we deal primarily with accounting for private businesses, we sometimes discuss accounting for public organizations such as hospitals, universities, or governmental agencies.

THE ACCOUNTING ENTITY

The accounting entity—an important accounting concept

An accounting report must relate to a specific accounting entity. An **accounting entity** is any legal or economic unit whose functions and financial affairs can be viewed as distinct from the functions and affairs of other such units. Accounting entities may be classified broadly into four categories: businesses, not-for-profit organizations, individuals, and fiduciaries. More specific examples include manufacturers, retailers, schools, school districts, governments, a branch of a business, or any other type of organization or segment of an organization. The accountant must define carefully the limits of the accounting entity and must keep its financial affairs separate from the affairs of other entities so that users of accounting information know precisely whose affairs are described in finanical reports. Although this book focuses primarily on business entities, much of the discussion applies to all accounting entities.

Businesses

Businesses are accounting entities which operate for the purpose of earning a profit. The major forms of business organizations include sole proprietorships; partnerships; corporations; and other more specialized entities. Figure 1-1 shows the relationship among the number of businesses of each type and the volume of business they handle.

Sole proprietorships are businesses owned by one individual. They represent the realization of the American dream of being "one's own boss" and are by far the most numerous form of business in the United States. Almost 80 percent of all business enterprises are sole proprietorships; however, they represent only slightly more than 10 percent of the dollar volume of business activity because most of them are relatively small operations. It is easy to start a business as a sole proprietorship even with limited financial resources. There are few legal restrictions, and the indi-

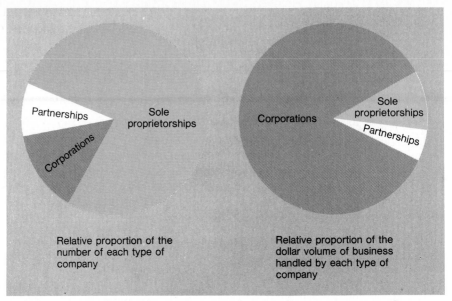

Relative proportion of the
number of each type of
company

Relative proportion of the
dollar volume of business
handled by each type of
company

**Figure 1-1   Sole proprietorships, partnerships, and corporations are the most
common types of business organizations. Although the number of corporations is
relatively small, they handle most of the business in the United States.**

vidual owner can make all business decisions, usually without being accountable to anyone else.

Because most individuals have limited resources, a sole proprietorship
often is limited in size. Investment in the business is restricted to the
amounts the owner can save and borrow. The owner is personally responsible for all the debts and obligations of the business, and such responsibility extends to the entire wealth of the owner, regardless of the amount
invested in the business.

Sole proprietorships are viewed as accounting entities whose financial
affairs must be kept separate from the owner's affairs. The reason is simple:
The owner is usually interested in the accomplishments of the business
as a distinct operation. For example, a proprietor who owns a theater and
a sporting goods store normally would want to know how each separate
business is doing and would not want to have their financial affairs mixed
together. Similarly, the owner's personal affairs should not be mixed with
business affairs. By defining the sole proprietorship as a separate accounting entity, the accountant can supply the owner with measurements, reports, and evaluations that provide maximum benefit in operating the
business.

Although sole proprietorships are viewed as separate accounting entities, they are not legally separate from their owners. When the owner
retires, dies, or sells the business, the accounting entity is terminated and
ceases to exist. Since it is not a legal entity, a sole proprietorship is not
subject to taxation on the income it earns. Instead, the owner is taxed on

the income of the business together with any income from other sources. For example, if a sole proprietorship earns \$20,000 income in one year and the owner of the business earns an additional \$4,000 from sources not connected with the business, the owner must pay income taxes on \$24,000. The taxes must be paid on all earnings even if the owner does not receive all of the business income but leaves it in the business as an additional investment.

Partnerships are businesses that have two or more owners who have agreed to carry on a business as co-owners and to share the profits or losses of the business in some agreed-upon proportion. Partnerships comprise less than 10 percent of all businesses in the United States, and they generate about 5 percent of the total dollar volume of all business. Like proprietorships, partnerships are easily formed with few legal restrictions. A written agreement among the partners is not necessary but is highly desirable so that all partners clearly understand their duties, obligations, and privileges.

Mutual trust is necessary in a partnership

Mutual trust must exist among partners because each is personally and individually responsible for all business debts and obligations to the full extent of their wealth. The actions of any one partner are binding on all other partners, so it is important that each partner have a clear understanding of what the business may or may not do. For example, if one partner buys some equipment for the partnership, and the business subsequently cannot pay for the equipment, the seller may demand full payment from any one of the partners who has sufficient wealth to satisfy the debt. It does not matter how much the partner invested in the business or what share of the business he happens to own.

Partnerships exist as long as the partners wish to continue in business. If one partner dies, retires, or disposes of his interest in the business, however, the partnership is immediately terminated. The remaining partners may, of course, form a new partnership and continue in business, but in that case a new business entity comes into existence. The dissolution of a partnership requires a careful accounting of the affairs of the business so that all business debts can be paid and any remaining business property divided among the partners equitably.

Accountants view partnerships as business entities whose affairs are distinct from the financial affairs of each partner. Each owner is interested in the financial accomplishments and operations of the business but usually is not especially concerned with the separate affairs of the other partners. Mixing personal affairs with business affairs would make it impossible to measure properly the partnership income that is to be divided among the owners. Therefore, the accounting entity must be carefully defined to ensure that only partnership affairs are reported in the financial statements of the partnership.

Like sole proprietorships, partnerships are not taxed on their business income, but the partners are responsible for taxes on their shares of income from the partnership together with any other personal income they may have. For example, if two partners share profits equally and the business earns $30,000 of income in one year, each partner's share is $15,000. If one partner has, in addition, $8,000 of income from other sources, he must pay taxes on $23,000 even if he does not receive all of his share of partnership income but leaves it invested in the business. The other partner may have no other source of income, in which case she must pay taxes on $15,000 even if none or only part of that amount was received from the partnership.

Partnerships and sole proprietorships pay no income tax

Accountants are frequently called upon to prepare financial statements for partnerships. Although accounting reports of partnerships are usually not provided to the public, they may be needed for tax purposes, for lenders, for prospective buyers of the business, or for the partners' use in managing the business. Many partnerships are very large and complex organizations, requiring elaborate accounting systems for their operations. Professionals such as attorneys and accountants have traditionally operated as partnerships. Some accounting firms, for example, have in excess of 1,000 partners and operate hundreds of offices throughout the world.

Corporations are legal entities created by state law, usually having all the rights, privileges, and obligations that people have. From a legal point of view, corporations may be viewed as artificial persons. Only about 15 percent of all businesses in the United States are corporations, yet they account for almost 85 percent of the dollar volume of all business. Forming a corporation is more complicated than forming a sole proprietorship or a partnership. Persons who want to incorporate a business must request a **corporate charter** from the state in which the business is to operate. The charter is a document approved by the state, indicating that a legal corporate entity has been created. Obtaining a charter requires considerable paperwork. Legal fees usually must be paid, and stock certificates must be printed. **Stock certificates** represent shares of ownership which are given to investors when they acquire an interest in the business and become **shareholders**. Many more characteristics of corporations are discussed in Chapter 13; at this point we discuss only the main aspects of a corporation as an accounting entity.

Corporations are artificial persons

Despite the complexities and costs of forming a corporation, this form of business organization offers many advantages:

1. The corporation has continued existence, despite changes, retirement, or death of owners.

2. Ownership is easily transferrable by shareholders, who may sell or exchange all or part of their stock in the corporation without affecting the business.

3. The shareholders are not responsible for the obligations of the corporation. Their responsibility is limited to their investment, which is the maximum amount they can lose if the business is not successful.

4. The ability to distribute shares to many owners provides the corporation with access to large amounts of money and other resources.

5. The management of the corporation can be turned over to professional managers, and the owners are left free to pursue their personal interests.

Corporations are distinct entities for both legal and accounting purposes. A corporation may have a few owners who do not plan to dispose of their stock certificates, or it may have many owners who trade their stock among one another in stock markets. Frequently the owners leave the management of the corporation to professional managers who must report periodically and inform the owners what the business is accomplishing. Periodic reporting is necessary so that managers can account for the way they are discharging their stewardship function. To ensure that reports prepared by management are fair and reliable, accountants may be hired by the corporation to perform an audit and express an opinion on the fairness of the financial statements. Such audits are very important to shareholders since they must rely on the financial statements as their primary source of information about their corporation.

Tax laws in the United States require corporations to pay taxes on the income they earn. Corporate tax rates are different from tax rates imposed on individuals, and the taxation of corporate income may have advantages as well as disadvantages. In some cases, corporate tax rates are lower than individual tax rates. Wealthy individuals, who may have to pay high taxes on income from partnerships or proprietorships, may be able to reduce their tax burden by incorporating their businesses. The disadvantage of corporate taxation occurs when corporations distribute to the owners the income that remains after corporate taxes are paid. When the shareholders receive these distributions, called **dividends**, they must report them as income and pay taxes on them together with any other income they may have from other sources.

Other business entities include specialized business organizations such as mutual funds, joint ventures, cooperatives, and syndicates. **Mutual funds** are businesses whose primary purpose is to own stocks of a large number of corporations. The shareholders of mutual funds indirectly invest in the operations of many different corporations and thereby avoid the risk of buying shares of a company that operates one type of business which may or may not be successful.

Joint ventures are similar to partnerships except that they are formed only for a specific project and their operations terminate when the project is completed. The owners of joint ventures may be other accounting entities such as corporations, governments, or individuals. For example, several companies may form a joint venture for the purpose of developing a new noncorrosive alloy needed in space exploration. Any one company may be unwilling or unable to risk the resources necessary for such a project, but if several companies pool their resources and talents, the project becomes feasible.

Cooperatives are businesses that normally do not operate for the purpose of making a profit but instead offer their owners some advantage, such as lower prices, coordinated marketing of products, or pooling of many small producers' products into large quantities for ease of distribution. Many farming businesses belong to cooperatives. Farmers in a particular community may join together to form a cooperative for the purpose of operating a large grain storage facility. Each farmer can use the facility and share the cost of operations, which is normally less than the cost of operating many separate smaller facilities. Sometimes cooperatives are formed by consumers for the purpose of buying large volumes of goods at prices lower than individuals have to pay.

Syndicates are organizations of several businesses that join together for a brief time in order to handle a specific business transaction, such as buying all the stock issued by a corporation and then selling the stock to the public at a profit. Syndicates usually involve financial businesses, such as banks and insurance companies, rather than manufacturing or merchandising businesses.

Not-for-Profit Organizations

Businesses control only abut 60 percent of all economic resources in the United States. The remaining 40 percent is controlled by organizations that do not operate primarily for the purpose of earning profits. These include governments; various governmental agencies; and nongovernmental organizations such as schools, universities, hospitals, foundations, and charitable organizations. Although this text does not emphasize the accounting practices of not-for-profit organizations, the basic principles discussed apply to them as well as to all other accounting entities.

Individuals

Individuals are accounting entities for whom accountants frequently prepare financial reports, but their affairs are seldom a subject of public interest. Most individuals like to keep their financial affairs private. However, it may be necessary for them to prepare financial reports for the use of lenders and for income tax purposes. In some cases political candidates must disclose their financial affairs to be eligible to run for office.

Fiduciaries

A **fiduciary** is a person entrusted with property belonging to others for the purpose of managing or safeguarding that property. Fiduciary entities include estates and trusts. An **estate** is the property left for disposal according to a will. The fiduciary of the estate, known as an **executor,** has the responsibility of managing the property and distributing it to those named in the will as recipients. Once the property is disposed of, the fiduciary's function terminates.

A **trust** is an entity created by a living person or by the will of a deceased person to hold property for the benefit of another person or for some other purpose. The fiduciary in charge of the trust is called a **trustee** and is responsible for managing the trust property in accordance with the wishes of the trust creator. Fiduciaries have specific legal and contractual obligations regarding the safekeeping of the property entrusted to them.

Some fiduciaries, like businesses, operate for profit, and others are not-for-profit organizations, such as charities or foundations. The accounting for fiduciary entities does not differ significantly from accounting for other types of entities, except that special types of reports may be required to ensure that fiduciaries are discharging their obligations properly.

USERS OF ACCOUNTING INFORMATION

Almost everyone uses accounting information

Accounting serves virtually every segment of society. Whenever economic activity takes place and wherever property exists, accounting can measure and report vital information necessary for making sound economic decisions. What this means, of course, is that someone wants such information and uses it to make important decisions. Let us, therefore, look briefly at the users of accounting information.

Since users of financial accounting information are many and diverse, it is impossible to provide information precisely suitable for each one. Financial accounting reports are therefore general purpose statements intended to serve the various needs of general groups, such as owners, creditors, managers, governments, employees, financial analysts, and investors. Let us examine some of the reasons why these users need accounting information.

Owners have an obvious interest in the information provided by the financial accounting system. They assume the primary risk of business by investing their money. They are naturally interested in obtaining accounting information that tells them something about the operation of their business and how much it is earning. Owners use accounting information to measure performance, compare their company with others, and make decisions to increase or decrease their ownership.

Creditors are individuals or institutions that provide part of a company's resources by lending it money. Although creditors are not owners of the business to which they lend, they earn interest income on the resources provided to businesses, so their activities represent investments. Creditors are interested in analyzing the company's financial statements to determine that their investment is safe, that interest due to them can be paid, and that their money can be repaid when due.

Managers must ensure that the company satisfies its long-range goal of producing profits. In addition to external financial statements, managers need more detailed internal reports broken down by operating divisions within the company, areas of responsibility, product lines, and other subdivisions of business operations. Managers depend heavily on these internal financial and managerial reports to help them manage operations intelligently and to justify the results of their business decisions, which are eventually reflected in reports issued to the public. Consequently, internal reports for managers are prepared much more frequently than external reports and are usually available only within the organization.

Governments and numerous government agencies use financial statements to ensure that businesses are meeting their legal obligations to pay taxes, contribute social security benefits for their employees, and satisfy federal and state regulations such as those concerning the registration and trading of their stock. Some types of business are granted special privileges by governments because the services they provide can best be offered by a single large company rather than by many small competing companies. Examples of such **regulated businesses** are electric utility companies and gas transmission companies. These businesses are allowed to operate without competition, and they could easily charge exorbitant prices since users of their services cannot obtain similar services from other companies.

To prevent abuses that may occur when special privileges are granted, governmental agencies like the Federal Aviation Administration and the Federal Energy Regulatory Commission monitor companies in certain industries such as airlines, utilities, and railroads. Companies in regulated industries must provide their regulatory agencies with accounting reports, and they also use accounting information to substantiate requests for rate increases as well as to report to their owners.

Employees of large organizations are vitally interested in the company's performance. They use financial statements to determine whether they are obtaining a fair share of the resources distributed by the company, to bargain for wages and fringe benefits, and to counter management's claims during such bargaining. Prospective employees frequently investigate a company prior to accepting a position by examining its financial statements in order to learn something about the company's operations, growth prospects, and profitability. Many companies contribute money for their employees' retirement pensions and either invest the contributions on behalf of the employees or turn the contributions over to pension trusts for investment by trustees. Financial statements that report on these pension funds are of vital interest to employees.

Financial analysts are experts in analyzing financial reports. Many investment decisions are made on their advice. Security analysts employed by stock brokerage firms frequently advise clients on buying and selling stocks of corporations. Banks, pension trusts, university endowment funds, and other institutional investors may employ their own financial staffs who analyze financial statements and express their judgment on the performance of businesses. Institutional investors, such as mutual funds or insurance companies, buy all types of investments in large quantities in contrast to individual investors, whose resources tend to be much more limited. Security analysts provide both institutional and individual investors with services that involve the use and interpretation of accounting information.

Investors depend on accounting information when they make investment decisions, whether or not they employ security analysts for investment advice. Before they commit their money to a business in the form of loans or ownership interests, investors need to make a careful investigation to determine that a particular business represents an investment appropriate for their needs. The most significant aspect of such an investigation is an analysis of the business's financial statements.

Clearly, accounting is a vital part of today's society and stands at the center of its economic activity. To understand how modern accounting practice has evolved, we describe below how accounting developed to suit the environment in which it operated and the users whom it served.

DEVELOPMENT OF ACCOUNTING

Accounting has developed over the ages in response to the financial information needs of decision makers in business, government, and private life. Decision makers operate in a complex economic environment that is constantly changing. Their information needs change with the environment, and accounting must adapt to satisfy these changing needs. Accounting must be as vital and dynamic as the society that it serves, and to function well it must adapt to the requirements of organizations and to changes in modern technology.

Consider this example: The industrial revolution created the need for detailed cost information for the manufacture of many different types of products using complex machinery and production facilities. Previously, accounting had served small businesses that produced only a limited number of products by hand and in small quantities. In the nineteenth century large businesses provided accounting reports to their owners every 2 years, accounting records were maintained by hand, and reports consisted only of highly summarized sales and cost data. Today many owners expect and receive quarterly reports on the operations of their businesses, and managers receive detailed monthy, weekly, and sometimes even daily reports on all types of business activity.

To handle even larger volumes of information, accounting adapted first to mechanical, then to electrical, and finally to electronic means of

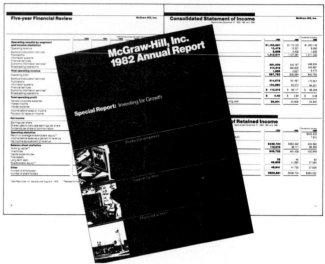

Figure 1-2   (*left*) **Many cuneiform tablets, such as this one from Babylon, have been discovered in excellent condition and have provided much insight into the history of ancient times. Scribes recorded transactions on tablets of clay, then impressed their seal on the clay and baked the tablet in order to preserve the records. The seal served as assurance that the record was correct. (*right*) The accountant's opinion and signature on modern financial reports serves the same function.**

data processing. Although accounting has evolved to meet the needs of decision makers, its basic framework and underlying concepts remain unchanged since the fifteenth century.

Early History

In earliest recorded history, it was the need for accounting information that actually brought about the development of writing. The history of accounting dates back to ancient Mesopotamian and Egyptian times. Ancient rulers controlled most of the wealth and employed scribes, who were trained in writing and record keeping. Scribes also performed services for private citizens who required evidence of business transactions. Archaeologists have discovered many ancient clay tablets, such as the one shown in Figure 1-2. These tablets describe such transactions as the exchange of two goats for a given quantity of wheat, or an agreement to deliver a future grain harvest to the army.

Scribes—the accountants of ancient times

Until the fifteenth century, accounting was not clearly defined but evolved slowly in response to the needs of business, government, and society. During the fifteenth century, however, trade flourished among the independent city-states of what is now Italy. The economic and political environment of that time gave rise to the accounting system that we use today. The system evolved during the Renaissance and was first formally described in the appendix of a now famous book[4] on arithmetic and geometry, written in 1494 by a Franciscan monk and scholar named Frater Luca Paciolo, a contemporary and friend of Leonardo da Vinci.

A number of factors helped to influence the formal development of accounting methods. The church and the government of that time were strongly interrelated, and many civil laws were influenced by religious beliefs. For example, it was illegal to pay or accept interest, because payment for the use of money was considered sinful usury. **Usury** is the practice of extracting interest payments beyond what the law permits. Because interest on money was prohibited, there was no incentive to lend money, and large business ventures requiring substantial investment could be organized only by inviting investors to become partners.

Typically the merchant or craftsman who worked alone needed to know only how much money he earned. With the formation of partnerships, however, it became necessary to account not only for the profits of the venture but also for the separate investment of each partner. When the venture terminated and its goods were divided among the partners, each partner naturally wanted to receive his original investment in addition to a fair share of the profits. But often the original investment consisted of some type of merchandise, and the final distribution consisted of gold or silver or a different type of merchandise and required some agreement about the value of goods. Differentiating and measuring business profits as distinct from owners' investments and assigning value in terms of a specific commodity were very early ideas in accounting.

In some cases all partners in the venture could not participate in the business. Often the operation of the venture was turned over to some of the partners who then became **accountable** to the others for their actions. The managers assumed the role of stewards entrusted with the goods to be traded. The managers became responsible for the proper operations of the business and for reporting their accomplishments to all the partners. Such an accounting by the managers usually took place when the venture terminated. The reporting function of accounting has early roots, and it came about because the owners were separated from the management of the business.

The roots of modern accounting are 5 centuries old

Although the accounting system used during the fifteenth century continued to evolve, its essential features remain the same today as they were in Paciolo's time. A system that has survived virtually intact for five centuries, from the Renaissance to the age of computers, is indeed impressive. Its strength lies in its basic simplicity, its flexibility, its ability to express and communicate a tremendous amount of information in a very compact form, and its verifiability. Accounting has truly become the language of business.

---

[4]Frater Luca Paciolo, *Summa de Arithmetica, Geometria, Proportioni et Proportionalita,* 1494. Translated freely, the title is *A Comprehensive Summary of Arithmetic, Geometry, Proportions, and Proportionality.*

Recent History

The Italian accounting system soon spread throughout Europe and the rest of the world. The industrial revolution brought about the need for more precise and timely measurement of accounting data. Accounting information was important not only to investors but also to managers, who found such information invaluable in the operation of businesses. Accounting was therefore developed and refined further to suit internal management needs as well as external investor needs.

The growth of the corporate form of business focused attention on the need for reporting to large numbers of public shareholders who often traded their shares of corporate stock with one another. Such trading was eventually organized into stock markets that required regulation, which in turn further affected the development of accounting. The rapid growth of railroads in this country brought about the need to account for vast amounts of property that required huge investments and had a very long life. The passage of income tax legislation forced accountants to examine more carefully their methods of income measurement. International corporations developed, creating the need to account for foreign operations. The revolution in electronic data processing (EDP) caused by the development of large-scale computers resulted in many changes and new developments in the design of accounting systems.

Although business conditions today are vastly different from those in the fifteenth century, the accounting system described by Paciolo was easily adapted to serve modern business. As a result, the profession of accounting gained respect and stature.

THE ACCOUNTING PROFESSION

As professionals, accountants have traditionally been concerned with maintaining the integrity of financial reports. Their work has always been characterized by a high level of ethical and moral standards. Competence, integrity, high ethical standards, and dedication to serve society are professional characteristics that accountants guard jealously.

Professional Accounting Practice

Accountants who offer professional services to the public must meet qualifications required by the state in which they practice. A person satisfying the qualifications is certified by the state and becomes a **certified public accountant,** or **CPA.** Certified public accountants perform a variety of services generally classified as auditing, taxation, and management advisory services. Some accounting firms perform all these services; others specialize only in some of them.

Auditing consists of examining financial statements and testing accounting records to determine that the correct procedures have been followed in preparing the statements and to ensure that the statements are fair and not misleading. Financial statements are accounting reports issued by a business to describe its financial affairs and the results of its operations. Contrary to popular opinion, the typical audit is not intended to uncover deliberate fraud. Instead, the function of the audit is to verify that records have been maintained properly so that statements prepared from the records are complete and fair representations of financial affairs.

The CPA can be relied upon to judge the fairness of financial reports

Certified public accountants who perform audits are **independent** practitioners who may not have financial interests in the businesses they audit, and their reports are intended for the public. Their examination is performed so that they can express an **opinion** about the fairness and adequacy of the financial statements. The opinion of the CPA is an important part of financial reports and is required by law on the statements of many companies whose shares are bought or sold by the public. Only a CPA may express an opinion about the fairness of financial statements. The CPA's opinion is highly respected and heavily relied upon because individuals outside the business have no other way of determining that the financial statements provided by a business are fair and reliable.

Tax services constitute an important part of the CPA's functions, because virtually all corporations and individuals are subject to the taxes of federal, state, and local governments. The accountant not only helps with the preparation of tax returns but also performs tax research and planning. Because federal tax laws are extremely complex, many businesses and individuals rely on accountants specializing in taxation to ensure compliance with tax laws and to minimize their tax burden.

Management advisory services may constitute a large portion of an accounting firm's work. Such services include advising and participating in virtually every aspect of business activity. Businesses may seek the assistance of CPAs when their own personnel do not have the time or expertise to work on a particular problem. Some common management advisory services include development and implementation of computer accounting systems, development of systems for managing important business resources such as merchandise or equipment, and development of employee incentive plans. The CPA firm is usually very familiar with the business of its clients and often can provide advice and expertise quickly and efficiently in order to help managers make appropriate decisions.

Private Sector Accounting

Private businesses employ many accountants in cost accounting, internal auditing, and other accounting functions. A large number of accountants employed by businesses have professional certification, although many who are not CPAs provide valuable accounting services.

Who needs accountants?

Cost accounting is the measurement and control of costs incurred in manufacturing products or providing services. Many manufacturing firms employ cost accountants to provide data to managers who must decide which products to produce, which expenses to trim, and how best to operate the business.

Internal auditing is the examination of the accounting and other records and operations of a business by a staff of internal accountants who perform audits throughout the year in order to uncover errors, implement administrative controls, and ensure the reliability of numerous accounting reports. One of the functions of internal auditors is to ensure that the accounting records of their company are in proper order and readily accessible to CPAs who perform independent audits of the entire business.

Businesses also employ accountants to perform many accounting functions such as preparing financial reports, planning and budgeting business operations, maintaining accounting systems, and supervising bookkeeping staffs. Accountants who provide the many managerial services described above can obtain a **Certificate in Management Accounting (CMA)** by passing a rigorous professional examination. Some accountants earn both the CPA and CMA, although neither certificate is a prerequisite for the other.

Public Sector Accounting

Nonbusiness organizations such as universities, foundations, and hospitals employ accountants who perform services similar to those required by businesses. Federal, state, and local government agencies all employ accountants to enable them to perform their regulatory functions. For example, the General Accounting Office (GAO) is the federal government's auditing organization. The GAO hires accountants to audit other governmental agencies and businesses that perform services for the government. The Internal Revenue Service (IRS) administers the tax laws and is the government's tax collection agency. Its accountants audit business and individual tax reports to ensure compliance with the law. Other agencies that hire accountants include the Securities and Exchange Commission (SEC), Interstate Commerce Commission (ICC), Federal Energy Regulatory Commission (FERC), Federal Bureau of Investigation (FBI), and many more.

Entry into the Accounting Profession

To qualify as a profession, a discipline must define and demand rigorous standards. These include:

1. A common body of knowledge which members of the profession are expected to attain.

2. A well-defined code of ethics to which members are expected to adhere.

3. A dedication to serve society rather than special interests.

4. Acceptance and recognition as a profession by society.

Accounting is a relatively young profession, but its standards and stature compare with those of medicine and law. A prospective accountant must obtain a college degree with specialization in accounting. The curriculum is demanding and requires intensive study of a wide variety of accounting topics. In addition, a broad general education, including the study of law, statistics, mathematics, and economics, is also expected in most accounting programs. In most states a 4-year baccalaureate degree is sufficient, but now more and more accountants have graduate degrees.

After graduation, the prospective accountant must exhibit a satisfactory degree of proficiency by passing a rigorous 2½-day professional examination. Only about 10 percent of those who take the examination manage to pass all parts on their first attempt. The examination may be repeated by candidates who are not successful. Either the CPA or the CMA examination, or both, may be taken, depending on the certification desired.

Professional accountants must pass rigorous examinations

The CPA examination tests candidates on their knowledge of auditing, accounting theory, business law, and accounting practice. It includes questions on financial and cost accounting, taxation, statistics, quantitative methods, and electronic data processing. It also tests the candidate's ability to write coherently. Passing the CPA examination is not sufficient to obtain the CPA certificate. The candidate must also satisfy experience requirements imposed by the state in which certification is to be obtained. Such requirements range from 1 to 5 years of practical accounting experience. In addition, many states require a specified number of hours of continuing education each year in order to maintain the certificate.

The CMA examination tests candidates on their knowledge of economics, finance, financial and managerial accounting, taxation, organization and behavior theory, quantitative methods, and ethics. To obtain the Certificate in Management Accounting, a candidate must not only pass the examination but must also satisfy educational and experience requirements of the Institute of Management Accounting, an organization established to administer the CMA. In addition, each certificate holder must meet continuing education requirements in order to maintain certification.

Obtaining either the CPA or CMA has many rewards. The work of the accountant is challenging, exciting, and interesting. Advancement in the accounting profession tends to be rapid, and many accountants easily move into high administrative levels in a variety of industries.

ORGANIZATIONS INFLUENCING ACCOUNTING DEVELOPMENT

Many factors have influenced the development of accounting. The demands of financial analysts for meaningful and complete information, the passage of tax legislation, and the results of research by professional and governmental bodies all help to change the way accounting information is reported. In this section, we briefly describe some of the organizations that have had a major influence in the development of accounting thought.

American Institute of Certified Public Accountants

The **American Institute of Certified Public Accountants (AICPA)** was organized early in this century and has become the largest organization of accountants in the United States. All members are certified public accountants. The AICPA designs and grades the uniform CPA examination that is given twice a year in every state. It publishes *The Journal of Accountancy*, a monthly professional periodical, and other professional literature. As a major accounting organization, the AICPA has had a tremendous impact on the development of accounting theory and the principles, concepts, and standards that you will study in subsequent chapters.

Perceiving the need to formalize accounting rule making, the AICPA decided that a rule-making body should be created to issue pronouncements on important accounting topics. These pronouncements helped to define a number of significant accounting principles and addressed individual accounting problems that had developed in practice, but they did not constitute a complete body of accounting theory. The rule-making organization, whose pronouncements are binding on the accounting profession, is called the Financial Accounting Standards Board.

Financial Accounting Standards Board

Formal accounting rules can have a strong impact on the accounting profession, on firms issuing accounting reports, and on users of accounting information. Therefore the rules should be developed only after careful research and in an environment free from the influence of special interests. To achieve such an environment the AICPA created the Financial Accounting Foundation which is financed by contributions from AICPA members.

The FASB makes accounting rules

The foundation is charged with funding and overseeing the **Financial Accounting Standards Board (FASB)**, a completely independent rule-making body whose members are required to sever all relations with businesses, accounting firms, government, or other organizations upon accepting appointment to the board. The FASB consists of seven paid members who are appointed for a period of 5 years. The board is answerable only to the Financial Accounting Foundation, which is an autonomous body managed by a group of trustees. The FASB has issued numerous pronouncements, called accounting **standards**, dealing with a variety of accounting subjects. The standards are based on research and are subject to public hearings prior to becoming binding rules. Many FASB standards are mentioned or discussed in this book.

American Accounting Association

The **American Accounting Association (AAA)** is an organization made up primarily of college and university accounting professors, although many practitioners also are members. The AAA is a research-oriented organization concerned primarily with promoting good accounting practice. The AAA publishes theoretical statements describing accounting as its members believe it should be, rather than as it is. Its quarterly publication, *The Accounting Review,* contains research articles on accounting and accounting education. The association's pronouncements do not have any authority over the accounting profession, but the profession is influenced by the AAA's research, and many of its recommendations have found their way into practice.

Securities and Exchange Commission

In 1934 Congress created the **Securities and Exchange Commission (SEC)** to regulate corporations whose shares are issued to the public and to oversee the operations of markets in which shares of corporations are traded by the public. Much stock trading takes place on stock exchanges, which are organized auction markets in which prices of stocks are established by bidding for shares offered for sale. Stock exchanges establish criteria that must be met by corporations whose shares are accepted for trading. Companies whose shares are traded on stock exchanges are required to file accounting reports with the SEC, and the reports must be audited by CPAs.

Corporations under SEC jurisdiction must obtain SEC approval prior to issuing stock to the public. The commission also has the power to prescribe the form and content of financial reports of companies under its jurisdiction and on some occasions has taken the lead in issuing rules on accounting. Generally, however, the SEC has cooperated closely with the AICPA and has allowed the accounting profession to develop its own accounting principles and practices. It has often influenced the development of accounting, however, by exerting pressure on the profession to improve its accounting rules.

National Association of Accountants

The **National Association of Accountants (NAA)** is an organization interested mainly in the internal reporting process. Its primary objectives are to promote research in managerial accounting, provide educational opportunities to its members, and foster interest in management accounting. The NAA publishes a monthly professional journal called *Management Ac-*

counting. The organization's interests encompass a wide range of reporting on social and economic matters. To give its members the opportunity to earn professional certification, the NAA formed the Institute of Management Accounting, whose function is to administer the CMA examination that is given twice a year in each state.

SUMMARY

Whether viewed as an art or a science, **accounting** must satisfy the need for relevant, timely, and accurate information. Such information is provided to users in the form of **internal,** or **managerial accounting,** reports intended primarily for business managers, and **external,** or **financial accounting,** reports intended for users outside a business organization. To be useful, accounting reports must inform the user of the economic activities of a specific **accounting entity.** We are concerned primarily with business entities, but accounting also serves other entities such as **not-for-profit organizations, individuals,** and **fiduciary** entities.

Typically business entities are classified as **sole proprietorships, partnerships,** and **corporations.** Unincorporated businesses, such as partnerships and sole proprietorships, are the most numerous types of businesses, but they handle only a small fraction of the dollar volume of business. They are owned by individuals or groups of individuals who are fully responsible for all obligations of the business. These businesses do not pay income taxes, but the owners must pay the tax on business income together with any other income they may have from other sources. Corporations are accounting entities that have a legal existence of their own. They operate under a **corporate charter** issued by a state and issue **stock certificates** to their owners in exchange for the owners' investment in the business. The owners are not responsible for the obligations of the corporation, and they pay taxes only on the income distributed to them by the business. The corporation, however, must also pay taxes on its income before it can make distributions to its **shareholders.**

Users of accounting information include owners, creditors, managers, governments, employees, financial analysts, and investors. Each has important reasons for requiring accounting information, because all make economic decisions of some sort. Consequently, there is virtually no segment of society that is not served by accounting information.

The field of accounting developed in response to the need for economic information in decision making. As the nature of business and economic decisions changed, accounting evolved to serve the needs of decision makers. Many political, social, religious, and other influences had an impact on the development of accounting thought, yet the basic system that was developed in the fifteenth century still serves society today. The evolution that occurred in the system did not affect the basic form which gives accounting its stability and strength.

Today the accounting profession is characterized by respect and integrity, and it is relied upon to provide essential information to all of society. Professional accounting organizations, as well as governmental bodies, have been influential in the development of modern accounting theory, and the accounting system we know today continues to adapt to current business conditions and new technology.

KEY TERMS

Many new terms commonly used in business and accounting have been introduced in this chapter. Most of these terms are used and explained in subsequent parts of the book. You should become familiar with the ones in the list that follows. The italic numbers in parenthesis indicate the pages on which the terms first appear.

accounting (*4-5*)
American Accounting Association (AAA) (*23*)
American Institute of Certified Public Accountants (AICPA) (*22*)
auditing (*18*)
bookkeeping (*5*)
Certificate in Management Accounting (CMA) (*20*)
certified public accountant (CPA) (*18*)
corporate charter (*10*)
corporation (*10*)
cost accounting (*20*)
creditor (*13*)
entity (*7*)
external reports (*7*)
fiduciary (*12*)
financial accounting (*7*)
Financial Accounting Standards Board (FASB) (*22*)

independent CPA (*19*)
internal auditing (*20*)
internal reports (*6*)
management advisory services (*19*)
managerial accounting (*6*)
National Association of Accountants (NAA) (*23*)
not-for-profit organization (*12*)
opinion of auditor (*19*)
partnership (*9*)
regulated business (*14*)
Securities and Exchange Commission (SEC) (*23*)
shareholder (*10*)
sole proprietorship (*7*)
stewardship (*7*)
stock certificate (*10*)
tax services (*19*)
transaction (*4*)
usury (*17*)

QUESTIONS

1. Every individual and organization is confronted with decisions regarding economic resources. What is the function of accounting information in making such decisions?
2. Briefly describe the difference between accounting and bookkeping.
3. Describe the difference between financial accounting and managerial accounting.
4. What is the meaning of the term **accounting entity**? Describe some entities.
5. Briefly discuss some of the advantages and disadvantages of the proprietorship, partnership, and corporate forms of business.

6. What is a regulated industry? Why are companies in regulated industries under the jurisdiction of governmental agencies?

7. Discuss the users of accounting information that are listed in the text and the reasons they need the information.

8. Ancient scribes recorded business transactions and then impressed the record with a seal. What similar actions exist today in the accounting profession?

9. The idea of businesses managed by professional managers rather than by owners is common in modern times. How did the concept of separation of owners and managers first come about?

10. Describe some of the services that certified public accountants perform for their clients.

11. What are the main differences between being employed as an accountant by an organization and being an independent certified public accountant?

12. What is the significance of the term **public** in the title **CPA**?

13. Why is the opinion expressed by a CPA on the financial statements of a business important to users of the statements?

EXERCISES

Ex. 1-1   **Characteristics of accounting entities.**   Listed below are some characteristics of business organizations.

a. Only one owner

b. Ownership easily transferred

c. Owner responsible for business debts

d. Created by operation of law

e. Ability to raise large amounts of money

f. Few restrictions to starting business

g. Continuity of existence

h. May undertake any type of business

i. More than one owner

j. Double taxation of income

k. Financial affairs separate from owners'

l. Income tax paid by entity

m. One owner can obligate all others

n. May have large number of owners

o. Organized for purpose of earning profits

Required: List the letters *a* through *o* on a sheet of paper. For each item above, indicate by initials *C*, *P*, and *S* which characteristic describes corporations, partnerships, and sole proprietorships.

Ex. 1-2   **Information needs of a business.**   Martin Brown has just received his college degree in history. He is having some difficulty in obtaining a job. Over the past few years, he has acquired some experience in clipping and grooming his two poodles, so he has decided to start a dog-grooming business. He rents a small shop near a busy street and opens a dog-grooming service. In addition to charging fees for bathing, grooming, and clipping dogs, he sells pet supplies such as collars, leashes, and dishes. All of his business is done for cash. His equipment consists of brushes and hair clippers, a telephone and desk, and some supplies such as soap and flea powder.

Required: Describe what sort of information Martin may want to collect and record in order to keep informed of his business's progress. Use your imagination and your current knowledge of business operations.

Ex. 1-3   **Two accounting entities.**   James Barton lives in a small town where he operates a service station owned by himself and his neighbor, Bill Wharton. Below is a list of events that occurred during a 3-month period.

    a.   James writes a check to pay for 6,000 gallons of gasoline delivered to the station yesterday.

    b.   Bill sends a personal check to his bank to pay his credit card bill.

    c.   James uses his credit card to purchase a new refrigerator for his home.

    d.   After a discussion with Bill, James invests some of the service station's money by buying 100 shares of Scallop Oil Company stock.

    e.   Realizing that the oil stock is a good investment, James buys another 100 shares with his personal funds.

    f.   James takes $1,000 of the service station's money for his own use, something the partners do each month.

    g.   Bill also withdraws $1,000 of the station's money for his own use.

    h.   James pays his income tax which includes the tax on his share of the service station's profit.

    i.   Bill uses part of the $1,000 he withdrew from the business to buy a coat for his wife.

    j.   James sells half of his Scallop Oil Company stock.

    k.   James buys a new compressor for the service station with money borrowed from the bank.

    l.   The service station sells its old compressor to James at a profit of $200.

Required: List the letters *a* through *l* on a sheet of paper. Indicate by initial letter whether the events should be accounted for by James Barton as an individual entity, *I*; by the service station as a partnership, *P*; by both, *B*; or by neither, *N*.

Ex. 1-4   **Distinguishing among entities.**   Jack Zahn and George Parme operate a business known as the Parme-Zahn Company. They share profits and losses equally. George runs the business full time, but Jack only works for the partnership on weekends, because he has a full-time job with Cheeze Corporation. During 1985 the following transactions occurred:

    a.   Jack signed a contract with an auto dealer to acquire a new pickup truck for the partnership to be used for delivery of merchandise to customers.

    b.   George made a down payment of $2,000 on the new truck and took delivery of the vehicle.

c. Jack received his paycheck from Cheeze Corporation.

d. George paid for the truck license from his own funds, expecting to be reimbursed later.

e. Cheeze Corporation gave Jack a check for $300 as payment for merchandise bought from Parme-Zahn.

f. George borrowed $20 from Jack to buy a gift for his wife's birthday.

g. Jack made an income tax payment of $3,000 to the Internal Revenue Service because his share of partnership income was $9,000.

h. George borrowed $20,000 from the bank to be used to buy a small computer for the partnership.

i. George received a tax refund from the Internal Revenue Service for a tax overpayment he made last year on partnership income.

Required: For each item above, decide whether the partner is acting as an individual entity or as the partnership entity.

Ex. 1-5   **Information for different types of users.**   The accountant of a small corporation whose shares are owned by the public has collected several items of accounting information about the company's operations.

a. Dividends to be distributed to shareholders

b. Overtime rate paid for work in excess of 40 hours per week

c. Total sales for 1 year of operations

d. Cost of factory maintenance in June compared with cost in May

e. Profit on the sale of land held by the company as an investment

f. Income earned by the employee pension fund

g. Amount received from sale of raw materials sold as scrap from last month's production

h. Total wages paid to secretarial staff

i. Total wages paid to production employees

j. Total wages and salaries for the year

k. Amount of money obtained by issuing additional shares of stock last week

l. Amount offered by a customer to have the company produce a custom-made product that will require 3 weeks of work

Required: On a sheet of paper list the letters *a* through *l*. Indicate which items you consider especially relevant to one of the company's shareholders, *S*; its manager, *M*; and one of its production workers, *W*. Any one item may be relevant in more than one category.

Ex. 1-6   **Distinguishing the accounting entity.**   Lungubu lives in a remote African village. All his life he has saved his money, and last year when his savings amounted to $5,000, he was finally able to buy a car. Having the only car in the village, he stays very busy operating as a taxi service. At the rate he uses his car, it will last 4 years. When he has occasion to drive someone to a distant town, Lungubu sometimes buys tools and utensils that he sells in his village. At the end of the year, however, he finds that he has very little money. To find out why he has done so badly, he prepares the following accounting of his operations:

Money spent:		
To buy car	$4,600	
For gas and oil	900	
Movies while in city	95	
For car repairs	150	
For tools and utensils	320	
For ferryboat fares	60	
Food and living expenses	2,600	$8,725
Money received:		
From customers	4,520	
Sale of tools and utensils	640	
Sale of worn-out car parts	60	5,220
Loss		$3,505

Required: Revise the above accounting report to explain to Lungubu what his taxi service has accomplished.

PROBLEMS

P. 1-1   **Defining the accounting entity.**   Janet Faltas recently started a business selling swimming pool chemicals. She kept records of her spending and after the first month of operations, she collected the following data, which she tried to arrange into an accounting report.

	Money Paid	Money Received
Deposited personal funds in business bank account	$5,000	
Paid rent on store	200	
Borrowed from bank to buy merchandise		$1,000
Paid for merchandise	2,400	
Paid for store fixtures	600	
Paid apartment rent	330	
Paid for gasoline and oil for car	60	
Paid part-time employee	280	
Monthly car payment	150	
Collected from customers		3,000
Paid for food and clothing	300	
Totals	$9,320	$4,000

a.   Faltas does not use her car in her business, as her apartment is within walking distance of her store.

b.   At the end of the month, 25 percent of the merchandise is on hand.

c.   The store fixtures are expected to last 5 years.

d.   All payments were made by check from the business bank account.

Required: Revise the accounting report in order to determine as closely as possible how much Janet's business earned in the first month of operations.

P. 1-2   **Defining the accounting entity.**   Bartholomew Francescatti is a cobbler. He has just finished his apprenticeship and, having saved 900 dinars, decides to open his own shop. He finds a location that he can rent for 25 dinars per month. His workbench cost 480 dinars, his tools cost 240 dinars, and both are expected to last 20 years. He purchased leather, thread, nails, and other supplies for 40 dinars. During the first 2 months of business, customers paid him a total of 150 dinars for repair work and 90 dinars for new shoes that he made for them. He spent 60 dinars for food and gave 65 dinars to his mother, with whom he lives. He bought a present costing 20 dinars for his fiancé. Bartholomew used leather and other supplies costing 15 dinars in performing his customers' repair work and making their new shoes. He keeps 10 dinars in his shop to make change but considers all other money his personal property and not part of his business. All the money he collects from customers, except for the 10-dinar change fund, he takes home. When he needs to buy anyting for his shop or to pay the rent, he does so from his personal funds.

Required: Prepare an accounting for Francescatti's shop for the first 2 months of operations. Be careful in defining the accounting entity.

P. 1-3   **Dividing partnership property and profits.**   Durbin works as a bricklayer in the southwestern United States. During his spare time he makes artificial fireplace logs from sawdust and wax. He produces the logs throughout the year and stores them in his garage. In the fall he sells his accumulation of logs to retail outlets in the county where he lives.

Just prior to this year's selling season, the county passed an emergency ordinance prohibiting the use of fireplaces because of high levels of air pollution. Durbin was unable to sell the logs that he had manufactured all year at a cost of $10,000. Durbin's neighbor, Etler, suggests shipping the logs to another part of the country where the weather has been unusually cold. Etler's friend, Filmer, owns a tractor and trailer and agrees to transport the logs. The three form a temporary partnership and agree to share profits equally.

Durbin contributes his logs and Filmer provides the use of his vehicle, on the condition that the partnership pay for the cost of fuel and $1,500 vehicle rental. Etler invests $8,000 to buy merchandise for the return trip so that Filmer does not have to travel without cargo. The logs are loaded, and Filmer drives off.

Several days later Filmer is able to sell half his cargo for $9,500. Using the proceeds and the money contributed by Etler, he buys a load of frozen meat for $15,000 and proceeds further. At his next stop he sells the meat and the rest of the logs for $28,000 and buys a cargo of frozen lobsters for $24,000. When Filmer returns home, the partners sell the lobsters for $31,000 and decide to terminate the partnership. Filmer spent $1,500 on fuel and had to replace a tire for $160 while on the trip.

Required: Decide how the money is to be divided among the partners.

P. 1-4   **Accounting for and dividing venture property.**   Captain Abdul owns a ship. Bagatella the merchant owns merchandise consisting of cloth and wine that costs 2,000 florins (fl). Mayor Caputto has considerable gold, some of which he wishes to invest. The three form a partnership. Abdul agrees to provide his ship for the duration of the venture, provided the partnership pays his crew and 500 florins rent for the ship. Bagatella contributes his merchandise, and Caputto contributes 2,500 gold florins. They decide to share profits equally when the venture is terminated. Captain Abdul is entrusted with the responsibility of trading the goods at several distant ports. The merchandise and gold are loaded on the ship and Abdul sails off.

At the first port Captian Abdul buys 100 sheep for fl 200 and sells half the wine for fl 1,600. In the second port he exchanges all of the cloth for 500 liters of oil and buys herbs for fl 1,000. In the third port he sells the remaining wine for fl 1,200 and 50 sheep for fl 450 and buys copper utensils for fl 2,000. In the fourth port he sells half the oil and half the utensils for fl 1,800 and buys spices for fl 900.

When Abdul returns home, the spices and herbs are sold by Bagatella for fl 3,500, and the sheep are sold for fl 600. The remaining oil brings only fl 50 because it has become rancid. Bagatella agrees to accept the copper utensils at their cost as part of his share of the venture. The crew of the ship has fl 1,500 wages due them.

Required: Decide how the venture property is to be divided among the partners when the venture is terminated.

P. 1-5   **Interpreting an accounting report.**   Following is a report prepared by the owner of a small proprietorship that employs two workers.

Jean Bryson Company
Operations for the Month of March 1985

Sales of merchandise for cash	$ 8,700	
Sales of merchandise on credit, not yet collected	7,300	$16,000
Cost of sold merchandise, paid for in cash		8,500
Gross profit		7,500
Salaries paid in cash	1,800	
Rent paid in cash	300	
Supplies used, bought for cash	220	
Supplies used, bought on credit, not yet paid for	400	
Other expenses paid by check	1,900	4,620
Profit		$ 2,880

Required: Examine the report carefully, and respond to the questions that follow by indicating whether they are true or false.
1. This statement reports the operations for the year 1985.
2. The business obtains most of its profit by selling merchandise.
3. The business appears to be profitable.
4. The amount of cash received by the business from customers is less than the gross profit.
5. The company evidently does not own its premises.
6. The business earned a profit of $7,500.
7. The business entity will have to pay taxes on its income.

8. The owner of the business must divide the profit with the two employees since they contributed to making the profit.
9. The company used $620 of supplies in its operations.

P. 1-6   **Interpreting a financial statement.**   A public utility reported the following financial statement to its shareholders:

Statement of Income
For the 2 Years Ended December 31, 1985

	1985	1984
	(Thousands of dollars)	
Operating Revenue		
Electric	$621,864	$533,185
Gas	143,896	131,238
Total	765,760	664,423
Operating Expenses		
Operation and Maintenance:		
Fuel for electric generation	133,557	128,472
Purchased gas	96,695	81,371
Purchased power and interchange-net	65,292	38,727
Other production expense	14,831	12,622
Transmission and distribution	16,464	14,010
Maintenance	51,565	48,338
Other operating expenses	54,482	48,443
Total	432,886	371,983
Depreciation and amortization	64,412	57,021
Taxes, other than income	81,677	70,993
Income taxes	17,209	13,556
Total	596,184	513,553
Operating Income	169,576	150,870
Interest deductions:		
Interest on long-term debt	78,403	57,609
Interest on short-term debt	8,624	5,912
Total	87,027	63,521
Net Income	$ 82,549	$ 87,349

Required: Respond to the following questions by indicating whether they are true or false.

a. The company charged its customers more for electricity in 1985 than in 1984.
b. The company spent more than $48 million for maintenance in 1984.
c. The company has to pay taxes on its net income of $82,549 million in 1985.
d. Profit in 1984 was $150,870.
e. Expenses in 1985 were larger than in 1984, therefore the company earned less profit in 1985.
f. The utility operates with large amounts of borrowed money.
g. Most of the company's profit comes from the sale of gas.
h. Fuel cost was lower in 1984 than in 1985.

Fundamental Accounting Concepts | 2

This chapter is the foundation for the entire course in financial accounting. It contains many new concepts, but if you master the information here, you are less likely to encounter serious problems with future chapters. Study this chapter until you understand:

1 How financial information is recorded in accounts.

2 The debit and credit rules.

3 What assets and equities are and how they are measured.

4 The accounting equation.

5 What a balance sheet is and why it balances.

6 How owners' equity changes.

7 How accounts reflect economic events.

In ordinary English the term **account** means a narrative, statement, report, description, or methodical enumeration. **To account** means to give a rational explanation, narrate, report, or describe an event. In accounting, these terms have much more specific meanings, but they are not far removed from ordinary English. The term **account** means a record consisting of specific information. **To account** means to communicate that information. These basic definitions form the foundation of accounting, but they only hint at the scope of the discipline. Like these definitions, Chapter 2 is basic and forms the foundation for your study of accounting. By examining the account as a single unit of a complete accounting system, we set the stage for a thorough understanding of accounting and the information it can provide to decision makers.

An **accounting system** is an orderly combination of accounts and other financial records arranged according to some rational principles. The accounting system you will study here is part of a larger **information system**

33

that provides decision makers with financial and managerial accounting data as well as other types of useful information.

We begin the chapter by examining the form and function of an account and the way it is used to accumulate data and provide information. To communicate and use information, it is necessary first to accumulate, measure, classify, and summarize data according to fundamental concepts and principles. These concepts and principles of accounting make it the language of business, and they enable users of accounting information to understand and interpret the reports produced by the accounting system. The remainder of this chapter, and many of the following chapters, discuss the concepts and principles used to obtain, measure, classify, and disseminate accounting information.

Most accounting concepts pertain to all accounting entities

Although this book deals primarily with accounting for business enterprises, this chapter is devoted to the financial accounts of an individual. The funamental concepts of accounting pertain to **all** accounting entities, but you will find these concepts easier to understand when placed in a familiar context as we have done here.

FORM AND FUNCTION OF AN ACCOUNT

An **account** may have a variety of forms. The following example illustrates several: Marc Johnson, a college student, has decided to keep an account of his money in order to manage his spending better. He arrives at college with $575 and his automobile. Following is a verbal account of Marc's finances:

A verbal account

Started the week of September 8 with $575 cash. Bought five textbooks for $89.85 on September 9. Exchanged chemistry text for math text on September 12, paying the difference of $3.15, leaving a balance of $482 at the end of the week. Received $90 wages from part-time job on September 20. Spent $57.50 for auto tune-up and $24.50 on a dinner date, leaving $490 on September 23.

This verbal account of Marc's cash transactions contains the information he needs in order to keep track of the money he receives and spends. But it is not very systematic, and the information is hard to assimilate. Marc may decide to improve the form of his cash account by maintaining it as follows:

9/8	Beginning balance	$575.00
9/9	Bought textbooks	− 89.85
		485.15
9/12	Exchanged texts	− 3.15
		482.00
9/20	Received wages	+ 90.00
		572.00
9/23	Auto tune-up	− 57.50
		514.50
9/23	Dinner date	− 24.50
9/23	Ending balance	$490.00

This account is much more systematic and is therefore more informative as well. The numbers are separated from the verbal description. The written information can easily be associated with a particular number, and each item can be identified with a specific date. The **account balance**—that is, the amount left at any time—is readily available. Nevertheless, this form of the account is still cumbersome and can be improved.

The Three-Column Account

In Figure 2-1, cash receipts have been separated from cash payments. Note how the information presented previously becomes clearer by using this format. The form of the account in Figure 2-1 is commonly used by businesses. This type of account is called a **three-column account** because it has three money columns. The account balance is available after each entry. Businesses frequently maintain such accounts not only for their cash records but also for amounts they owe to their creditors and for amounts owed to them by customers. A copy of the account serves as a monthly statement to their customers. Figure 2-2 shows an example of such a statement sent by a physician to her patient. The first money column is used to record charges for services, the second is for collections from the patient, and the third is the account balance that the patient is to pay.

Formal accounts are systematic and logical

Account of Cash

Figure 2-1
A three-column account, with a column for increases, decreases, and the remaining balance.

Date		Receipts	Payments	Balance
9/8	Beginning balance	$575.00		$575.00
9/9	Bought textbooks		$89.85	485.15
9/12	Exchanged texts		3.15	482.00
9/20	Received wages	90.00		572.00
9/23	Auto tune-up		57.50	514.50
9/23	Dinner date		24.50	490.00

Banks provide similar accounts to their customers in the form of monthly statements of the customers' checking accounts. An example of such a statement is shown in Figure 2-3. The depositor's beginning balance is shown at the upper right. Like the accounts in Figures 2-1 and 2-2, this one also has three money columns. They list the checks that Margaret Greene wrote and the bank paid from her account, all the deposits it has received from her, and a daily balance. Note that the statement in Figure 2-2 is prepared by hand, whereas the bank statement is prepared by a computer.

Purpose of the account.   Let us return to Marc's cash account. Why should Marc want to keep track of his cash in an account? In fact, he probably does not maintain a formal cash account, but he certainly wants to know what amounts he has spent, for what purposes, and what amount is available for future spending. Like Marc, businesses also need this type of

STATEMENT

BARBARA A. FANNIX, M.D.
WEDGWOOD
113 HULEN STREET
FORT WORTH. TEXAS 76138

Deborah Jones
2354 Blueberry St.
Ft. Worth, TX 76123

DATE	NAME	DESCRIPTION - CODE	CHARGE		PAYMENT		CURRENT BALANCE	
8/23	OV		8	00			8	00
8/23	LAB		29	00			37	00
9/7	OV		8	00			45	00
9/7	INJ.		6	00	51	00	0	00
10/18	IM		N	C				
10/18	OV		8	00			8	00
10/18	XR		23	00			31	00

CODE: **PLEASE PAY THE LAST FIGURE IN THIS COLUMN** ☚
  OV—OFFICE VISIT, EXAM OR TREATMENT   XR—X-RAY
  INJ—INJECTION   SURG—SURGERY   NC—NO CHARGE
  IM—IMMUNIZATION   ER—EMERGENCY ROOM   HC—HOUSE CALL
  LAB—LABORATORY   HOSP—HOSPITAL CARE   INS—INSURANCE
NOTE:_____

Figure 2-2
A three-column account maintained by a physician for each patient. A copy of the account serves as a statement for billing the patient.

information in order to make sound economic decisions. Marc may be able to remember how much cash he has on hand, but businesses must rely on recorded information to keep track of their money. They maintain accounts as part of an **accounting information system,** whose purpose is to collect, organize, and summarize information in a systematic manner so that it is available when needed for making decisions and for accounting to those who need financial information.

The T Account

The three-column account is convenient for maintaining business records. The third column, which shows the balance, is important to the decision maker. For purposes of studying accounting, however, a simpler form of the account is often used.

 Examine Marc's Cash account, shown again in Figure 2-4. Whenever Marc obtains money, he enters the amount in the first money column.

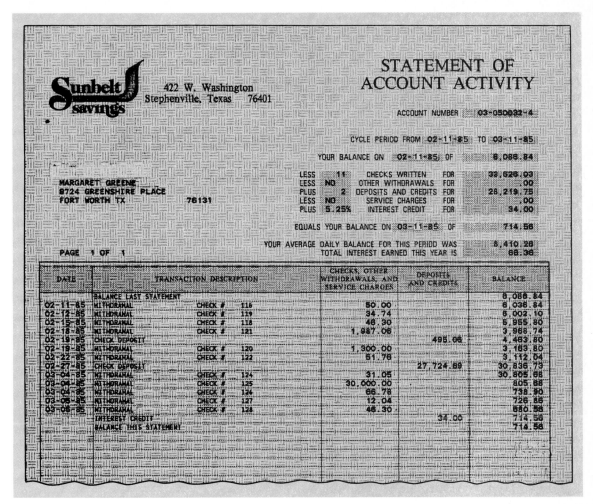

Figure 2-3   A checking account statement from a bank is essentially a three-column account.

Whenever he spends money, he enters the amount in the second column. These two columns are used for recording changes in the account. The third column shows the effect of these changes. The balance in the third column is simply the difference between the totals of the first two columns.

Figure 2-4
The T account is made up of the two columns from the three-column account in which account changes are recorded. The left side shows increases in cash; the right side shows decreases in cash.

Account of Cash

Date		Receipts	Payments	Balance
9/8	Beginning balance	$575.00		$575.00
9/9	Bought textbooks		$89.85	485.15
9/12	Exchanged texts		3.15	482.00
9/20	Received wages	90.00		572.00
9/23	Auto tune-up		57.50	514.50
9/23	Dinner date		24.50	490.00

At this point we emphasize primarily the increases and decreases in cash. Figure 2-4 is identical to Marc's three-column Cash account in Figure 2-1, but it shows the first two columns separated by a heavy line in the form of the letter T. The left side of the T contains all the cash increases, and the right side contains all the cash decreases. These two columns of the three-column account make up the **T account** which is used throughout this book to illustrate information in accounting records.

The meaning of debit and credit

Debit and credit are important terms understood and accepted by the business community and users of accounts. Just as the + sign is universally understood to denote addition, the terms *debit* and *credit* are universally understood in business to denote the left and right side of T accounts. The term **charge** has the same meaning as debit and is often used in its place.

The left side of the T account is called the **debit** side. Amounts shown on the left side are called **debits.** The right side of the T account is called the **credit** side and the amounts shown on the right side are called **credits.** Debit and credit are abbreviated *dr* and *cr*.[1]

To debit an account means to enter an amount on the left side. To credit an account means to enter an amount on the right side. No negative or positive meanings are implied by the terms debit and credit. They mean no more than left and right. The concept is simple, but we cannot over-emphasize the importance of your understanding debit and credit termi-nology. Become familiar with these terms, and your grasp of the many accounting concepts that follow will be stronger.

Figure 2-5 illustrates Marc's Cash account in formal T account form. Each side of the account contains the date of the entry, an explanation,

Cash

Date		Dr.	Date		Cr.
9/8	Balance	575.00	9/9	Textbooks	89.85
9/20	Wages	90.00	9/12	Exchanged texts	3.15
			9/23	Auto tune-up	57.50
			9/23	Dinner date	24.50
				Total	175.00
			9/23	Balance	490.00
	Total	665.00			665.00
9/23	Balance	490.00			

Figure 2-5 **The formal T account. Finding and recording the account balance involves finding total debits and credits, entering a credit large enough to make credits equal to debits, finding total credits to verify the equality, and then entering a debit as the ending balance.**

---

[1]The abbreviations derive from the Latin terms *debitur* and *creditur*.

and the amount of debit or credit. The balance of the account is obtained by adding each side and finding the difference. If the sum of the debit entries exceeds the sum of the credit entries, the account has a debit balance, which is recorded on the debit side. If the sum of the debits is less than the sum of the credits, the account has a credit balance. Cash accounts normally have debit balances.

Note that dollar signs are omitted in the T account since the numeric information in accounts is always in terms of money. All the information shown in Figure 2-5 is included in accounts in a formal information system of a business. But for purposes of studying accounting, it is often sufficient to show only the debits and credits, along with a date or other reference if needed. The account must, of course, have a title.

The balance of the account can be calculated at any time by finding the difference between total debits and total credits. The balance can be shown in the appropriate column after drawing a line under the last entry in the account. This simple version of the T account, which is used throughout this book, is shown for Marc's cash in Figure 2-6. In addition to the Cash account, many other accounts can be maintained. There are, in fact, several major categories of accounts. Cash belongs in the category called assets, which we now discuss.

Figure 2-6
The simplified T account, showing only debits and credits, is especially useful for the study of accounting.

	Cash		
Bal.	575.00		89.85
	90.00		3.15
			57.50
			24.50
Bal.	490.00		

ASSETS

Assets are future economic benefits

Assets are economic resources from which benefits can be obtained by their owner, now or in the future. Cash is only one of many assets owned by businesses and individuals. The majority of an entity's assets is in the form of noncash resources such as land, buildings, equipment, materials, patents, and any other tangible or intangible property that has value. Owners obtain benefits from assets by using them to satisfy various needs. For example, you use oil to lubricate your car. Although you no longer have the oil, you have the benefit of a smoothly operating car from which you get benefits in the form of transportation. Eventually the car wears out. But until the car wears out completely, it is an asset because it can provide future transportation. Assets can be exchanged for one another. You may exchange money for a car or land for money when you believe that the benefit available from the asset you are receiving is more important than the benefit available from the asset you are giving up.

Asset Accounts

Marc's cash account enables him to keep track of one of his assets. Marc's other assets can also be accounted for in a similar way. A separate account can be used for every type of asset or for major categories of assets. Businesses must account for all their assets and must, therefore, maintain numerous separate asset accounts. To understand how assets are accounted for, we now examine some other asset accounts that Marc might maintain.

When Marc bought five textbooks for $89.85, he merely exchanged one of his assets, cash, for a new asset, textbooks. The transaction was shown on the credit side of his Cash account, representing the reduction in cash when he paid for the books. This exchange resulted from an economic decision. Marc decided that having the textbooks was more important than having the cash, and he was therefore willing to give up the cash asset in order to obtain the textbook asset. The textbooks are assets because Marc can obtain benefits from them in the future.

Because Marc's money is in the form of dollars, the numbers in the Cash account represent dollars. How should the textbooks be represented? There are several ways to describe textbooks. The account might describe the books according to their color or size, or Marc might decide that describing the subjects of the books is a more satisfactory approach, as shown in the following account:

Textbooks

1 psychology
2 history
1 chemistry
1 accounting

The problem is that, unlike the numbers in the Cash account, the descriptions in the Textbooks account have nothing in common with one another. The subjects cannot be added up to arrive at an account balance. If we assume that the balance is 5, representing the number of volumes in the account, we know little about the asset. We need a description of the textbooks that makes the Textbooks account comparable to other asset accounts.

Assets are measured in terms of money

Money measurement.   In an economy in which goods are paid for with money, it is convenient to describe assets in terms of money. As a common measure, money describes assets in a way that is economically meaningful. Accounting has therefore developed the concept of **money measurement,** which requires expressing all accounts in terms of money. Marc can assign to each textbook the amount of money he paid—that is, its cost—in which case the Textbooks account might appear as follows:

Textbooks

	17.90
	25.00
	24.45
	22.50
Bal.	89.85

Earlier you saw that when cash is received, the amount is recorded on the left side of the cash account, and when cash is paid, the amount is recorded on the right side. This means that increases in cash are recorded by debits, and decreases are recorded by credits. The same rule applies to all assets. When Marc obtains textbooks, the **change** in the textbook asset is recorded by debiting the Textbooks account to record the increase in the asset as shown above. When the chemistry textbook is returned to the bookstore and the mathematics text is acquired in its place, the Textbooks account can be reduced, or credited, by the amount representing the chemistry text, and increased, or debited, by the amount representing the mathematics text. The account then appears as follows:

Textbooks

Purchasing math book increases the asset account →	17.90	24.45 ← **Returning chemistry book reduces the asset account**
	25.00	
	24.45	
	22.50	
	27.60	
Bal.	93.00	

Notice that we have applied specific rules to record changes in the textbook asset in the same way as we did with cash. Increases in assets are recorded as debits and decreases as credits.

Asset Valuation

Expressing assets in money terms is not without problems. The money measurement concept does not tell us what dollar amount should be assigned to the assets. Consider the following situation: Before he left for college, Marc had an opportunity to purchase a used car from a friend. The friend wanted $4,600, a price Marc thought was fair. However, when Marc offered to buy the automobile for $4,300, his offer was accepted. Marc had only $800. With the help of his parents, he obtained a bank loan of $3,500, with which he paid the rest of the purchase price. He agreed to repay his obligation to the bank over a period of 2 years. By the time Marc brought his car to college, a similar automobile could be obtained from an auto dealer for about $4,500.

Marc's car is an asset for which an account can be established. What amount should be recorded in the asset account for the car? Should the Automobile account be debited $4,600, a fair value in Marc's opinion; $4,500, the cost of replacing the car; or $4,300, Marc's purchase price? Would $800, representing Marc's own cash outlay for the car, be a more appropriate amount to record in the account? In order for asset accounts to be meaningful, it is necessary to agree on the dollar amount to be assigned to each asset. If one accountant records assets at their fair value, another at their replacement cost, and yet another at their cost or purchase price, accounting information would not be especially useful, because there would be no valid basis for comparing financial reports.

The cost concept.   Accounting information is most useful if **assets are recorded at their cost** to the owner. This **cost concept** is an important one in accounting for several reasons. Costs can be measured *objectively* because they are determined in market transactions. If such transactions are between independent parties, costs represent the fair market value of the assets at the time they are exchanged. It is relatively easy to verify the cost of an asset. On the other hand, Marc's opinion of fair value or the amount required to replace the asset are subjective estimates of value. It is important to understand, however, that as time passes the costs of assets recorded in accounts do not necessarily represent amounts for which the asset can be sold or replaced.

Cost is an objective measure of value

According to the cost concept, Marc's Automobile account should be debited $4,300, which is Marc's cost. The fact that Marc borrowed part of the money and has not yet repaid it does not affect the asset's cost, although it does affect some other accounts discussed later. The Automobile account therefore appears as follows:

Automobile

| 4,300 | |

The stable dollar concept.   Recording the cost of assets in terms of money as required by the cost and money measurement concepts implies that the dollar is a stable measuring unit. The **stable dollar concept** used in accounting is based on the assumption that a dollar available today is worth as much as a dollar used for buying assets in the past. But we know that changing price levels cause the value of money to change. Unfortunately, accountants have not agreed on a method of accounting for the change in the value of money. Although the stable dollar assumption is not entirely valid, it enables the efficient operation of accounting systems and is therefore an accepted feature of accounting practice.

The asset account is a basic accounting record and assets are a major category of accounts in any accounting system. Now that you are familiar with assets, we turn our attention to another category of accounts, known as equities.

EQUITIES

Equities defined and described

The concept of equity derives from property ownership. In our economic system, the ownership of property carries with it the right to the benefits provided by the property or a claim on the property. There is no doubt that Marc's cash and textbook assets belong to him. He has the right to decide how to use the books and how to spend his money. We refer to these rights as the **equity** the owner has in his assets.

Now when Marc bought his car, he did not have sufficient assets to pay the full price. Marc provided $800 of his own money, and a bank provided $3,500 in the form of a loan. Since Marc was unable to acquire the car by paying with his own assets, he also was unable to acquire the entire equity in the car. By lending some of its money to Marc, the bank also acquired some claims or equity rights. As Marc's creditor, the bank has an equity in Marc's assets: It has the right to be paid. Marc's obligation to repay the debt is the bank's equity.

Measurement of Equities

As an owner of assets, Marc has rights called **owners' equities,** also known as **capital, net worth,** or **proprietorship.**[2] Because his ownership is not complete, his creditors have claims called creditors' equities. Creditors' equities are known as **liabilities.** Liabilities include such obligations as amounts payable to banks to repay loans, mortgages on real estate, taxes payable to governments, and many others. You can see that the term equities can mean either liabilities or capital. When we refer to liabilities and owners' equity in general, we use the term equities; when we refer to a specific category of equities we use the more specific terms.

To account for assets, we assigned to them some measures of value. We must also be able to measure equities if we are to account for them. Because we equate equities with claims against assets, and express assets in terms of dollars, we can equate Marc's assets and the equities in his assets on September 23 in the following manner:

$$\$490 = \text{Marc's equity in his cash}$$
$$\$\ 93 = \text{Marc's equity in his textbooks}$$

We cannot say, however, that $4,300 equals Marc's equity in his automobile. He had to borrow money to acquire the automobile, and his

---

[2]The terms *net worth* and *proprietorship* are becoming obsolete. We mention them because they are still occasionally found in use. The term *owners' equity* is used in this text whether the entity is a sole proprietorship, a partnership, or a corporation.

equity is not complete. Until he repays the loan, his equity in the car is measured as follows:

$$\$3,500 = \text{Bank's equity in the automobile}$$
$$\$ \ \ 800 = \text{Marc's equity in the automobile}$$

This does not mean that the bank owns part of the automobile.[3] The equation simply shows that Marc's equity is limited to the amount of assets he provided to obtain the car. The bank was willing to lend $3,500 to Marc only because he agreed to repay the money. His agreement was probably given in the form of a note that he signed, promising to repay the debt and to pay, in addition, interest for the use of the bank's money. **Interest is the cost of using borrowed money** and is the bank's compensation for providing the loan to Marc. For the time being, however, we shall not be concerned with the interest. Marc has an automobile, but he also has a liability of $3,500. He can acquire the entire equity in the automobile only by repaying his liability to the bank. Until he does so, the bank retains some equity rights.

We now review these concepts by looking again at Marc's assets and the related equities on September 23.

Marc's cash:	$ 490 =	Marc's equity:	$ 490	
Marc's textbooks:	93 =	Marc's equity:	93	
Marc's automobile:	4,300 =	{ Bank's equity:	3,500	
		{ Marc's equity:	800	
Total assets:	$4,883	Total equities:	$4,883	

You see that **for every dollar of assets, there is a dollar of equities.** Owners' equity is measured by the amounts recorded in asset accounts. Liabilities, on the other hand, can be measured independently of assets, because there is an agreement between the creditor and the borrower as to the amount owed. The automobile cost $4,300, and Marc owes $3,500 to the bank; therefore, his owners' equity in the car is measured as the **residual** of $800—that is, the amount remaining after the liability is deducted from the cost.[4]

Equities are claims against assets in general

Now that you see how the concept of equities is derived, it is important to emphasize that equities are not related to any *specific* assets. Liabilities are equities that convey to creditors the right to be repaid from the assets *in general,* not from any specific assets; and owners' equities are the **residual** claims of the owner on all assets remaining after the liabilities have been deducted. Therefore, Marc's equity in his assets does not consist of several separate figures but is instead measured by the sum of $490,

---

[3]The bank may have legal rights, including the right to repossess and sell the automobile if the loan is not repaid. Here we are concerned only with the accounting concept of equities.

[4]For the sake of simplicity, we ignore any other assets and liabilities Marc may have.

$93, and $800 and is expressed as the single value of $1,383, summarized as follows:

Assets		=	Equities	
Cash	$ 490		Liabilities	$3,500
Textbooks	93			
Automobile	4,300		Marc's equity	1,383
Total assets	$4,883		Total equities	$4,883

THE ACCOUNTING EQUATION

In our economic system, all property is owned by someone, either an individual, a group of persons, a business, or some other type of organization. Ownership is represented by equities, which are claims that derive from a fundamental concept in our economic existence: the right to enjoy the benefits of private property. In some cases these are the claims of owners, and in some cases they are the claims of creditors, but whether they represent owners' or creditors' equities, they always equal the amount of assets. We can express the relationship between assets and equities as the fundamental **accounting equation**:

$$ASSETS = EQUITIES$$
or
$$A = E$$

The accounting equation is a conceptual representation of economic facts. Accounting presents such facts in the form of financial information by expressing assets and equities in terms of money. The numbers in accounts are used to translate the possession of assets into wealth. In economic terms, **wealth** is all property that has utility or monetary value. Numbers in accounts represent economic well-being. A person's property, or assets, has economic value, and the extent of his wealth is his equity in the assets. However, it is important to bear in mind that the accounting numbers themselves are *not* wealth; they are only records that *represent* economic facts.

Because the accounting equation represents economic facts, there is an implication that the numbers in accounts describe these facts. This is true only to the extent that the numbers we assign to assets, liabilities, and capital are valid. For example, had we assigned to Marc's automobile the replacement cost of $4,500 instead of the $4,300 cost, his total equity would appear to be $200 greater. Since accountants choose to assign to assets their cost rather than some other value, the accounting equation measures equities in terms of asset costs. Amounts other than cost are subject to bias or are too difficult to measure objectively. For example, Marc may think that the automobile has a fair value of $4,600, but it may not be possible to find a buyer for more than $4,400. Marc may be so attached to the car that he would not part with it for less than $5,000. Each value has relevance but none is objective. Cost is an objective measure, but it is not always the best representation of value. For example, a parcel of land purchased 3 years ago for $50,000 may have a market value of $80,000 today.

The accounting equation cannot be out of balance

Given the concepts of assets and equities and the method of measuring them, there is no way that one side of the accounting equation can be different from the other side. Total assets must equal total equities. Both are measured in terms of money, and the amounts assigned to assets and liabilities can be independently determined. Because owners' equity is a *residual* claim on assets, its amount completes the accounting equation at all times, regardless of the values assigned to assets or liabilities.

The accounting equation can be expanded to the following form:

$$Assets = Creditor's\ equity + Owners'\ equity$$

or

$$A = L + C$$

The right side of the equation represents equities divided into two components: creditors' equities, or liabilities (L), and owners' equity or capital (C). The residual nature of capital can be emphasized by expressing the equation in the form shown below.

$$Assets - Liabilities = Capital$$

or

$$A - L = C$$

This equation shows that **capital** is a **residual** consisting of **net assets**, or all assets remaining after all liabilities have been deducted. Regardless of the form used, the accounting equation represents a single accounting entity. We now look at the way the information about Marc's assets, liabilities, and capital can be reported in a financial statement that represents Marc's accounting equation.

Financial Position

Financial information from Marc's asset accounts and the equities developed in the previous discussion can be summarized in an accounting report known as the **statement of financial position.** In Figure 2-7, the statement represents Marc's accounting equation, and is composed of his assets and equities, and their totals at a particular *point in time.* The assets and their balances are on the left side of the statement, and the equities and their

Figure 2-7
Statement of
financial position,
also called a
balance sheet,
shows a balance
between assets
and equities.

Marc Johnson
Statement of Financial Position
September 23, 1985

Assets		Equities	
Cash	$ 490	Payable to bank	$3,500
Textbooks	93		
Automobile	4,300	Capital	1,383
Total assets	$4,883	Total equities	$4,883

balances are on the right side. The total dollar amount of equities, and both sides of the statement, are in balance. For this reason, the statement of financial position is commonly referred to as a **balance sheet,** and the accounting equation that it represents is often called the balance sheet equation. This balance sheet is a financial report summarizing the data contained in separate accounts.

The balance
sheet represents
the accounting
equation

As a representation of the accounting equation, the balance sheet must always show the assets and equities in balance by showing total assets equal to total liabilities and capital. Since it is prepared from the balances of individual accounts, it is convenient to maintain the same balance among accounts as is reported in the balance sheet. You already know the procedure for increasing and decreasing asset accounts. Now we examine how individual liability and capital accounts are maintained.

Equity Accounts

By convention Marc's separate asset accounts normally have debit balances. If we record data in equity accounts so that they normally have credit balances, then the total debit balances of assets should equal the total credit balances of equities, because assets equal equities in the accounting equation and in the balance sheet. The convention of recording assets with debits and equities with credits provides a system for maintaining the separate asset and equity accounts as components of a balance sheet, and therefore as individual representations of the accounting equation. The balances of assets and equities, taken from Marc's balance sheet in Figure 2-7, appear as follows recorded in T accounts:

Assets   =   Equities

Cash	Textbooks	Automobile	Payable to Bank	Capital
490	93	4,300	3,500	1,383

Total Debits   =   Total Credits

We said earlier that assets are recorded as debits, and asset accounts can be increased by debits and decreased by credits. By analogy, since equities are recorded as credits, an equity account can be increased by crediting the account and decreased by debiting it. For example, if Marc reduces his liability by paying the bank $100, this reduction in cash is shown in the Cash account as a credit, denoting a decrease in his cash balance. The repayment of part of the loan reduces the amount owed to the bank and is shown in the Payable to Bank account as a debit, leaving a balance of $3,400 in that account. This $100 transaction is shown in the following T accounts:

Assets   =   Equities

Cash		Textbooks		Automobile		Payable to Bank		Capital	
490	100	93		4,300		100	3,500		1,383

Total Debits   =   Total Credits

Total debits always equal total credits

The payment of cash to the bank resulted in a credit entry in the Cash account and a debit entry in the liability account, reducing each of them by $100. The transaction is recorded by a debit and a credit that are equal in amount, leaving the total dollar amount of debits equal to the total dollar amount of credits, and leaving total assets still equal to total equities. The accounting equation is still in balance.

RECORDING TRANSACTIONS IN ACCOUNTS

The accounting equation states that assets equal equities. No financial transaction can destroy this equality. Whenever an account is debited, some other account must be credited, and the total dollar amount of all the debits must equal the total dollar amount of all the credits. In summary, the three major categories of accounts—assets, liabilities, and capital—are increased or decreased in the following way:

Assets   =   Equities

Assets		Liabilities		Owners' Equity	
Increases	Decreases	Decreases	Increases	Decreases	Increases
+	−	−	+	−	+

Changes in Assets and Liabilities

If assets always equal equities and debits always equal credits, an economic decision resulting in a financial transaction can be expressed in one or more of the following ways:

1. An increase in one asset (dr) equals a decrease in another asset (cr).
2. An increase in an asset (dr) equals an increase in an equity (cr).
3. A decrease in an asset (cr) equals a decrease in an equity (dr).
4. An increase in one equity (cr) equals a decrease in another equity (dr).

Let us look now at some examples that illustrate each type of transaction listed above.

1. **An asset increases and another asset decreases.** You saw this type of transaction when Marc bought his textbooks for cash. The textbook asset increased and the cash asset decreased. This type of transaction is very common and occurs whenever assets are purchased for cash.

2. **An asset increases and an equity increases.** The second type of transaction occurred when Marc borrowed money from the bank for the purpose of buying his automobile. His automobile account increased and his liability to the bank increased. Part of the automobile purchase occurs as the first type of transaction. The increase in the automobile asset of $4,300 simultaneously decreased cash by $800 and increased liabilities by $3,500.

3. **An asset decreases and an equity decreases.** The third basic type of transaction is illustrated by the repayment of part of the bank loan. The cash asset decreased and the liability also decreased. Most repayments of debts are accompanied by decreases in cash because creditors seldom accept other assets as payment.

4. **An equity increases and another equity decreases.** The fourth type of transaction may occur if Marc finds himself short of money when one of his bank payments comes due. If he asks a friend to make the payment for him, and promises to repay the friend later, Marc's liability to the bank will be reduced, but he will increase his liability to his friend.

None of these transactions had any effect on owners' equity. Why did Marc's total equity remain the same after he repaid part of his liability? If the bank's equity in Marc's assets is reduced, does not Marc's equity increase? No, because the increase in Marc's equity in his car is offset by a simultaneous decrease in capital, resulting from the decrease in cash (transaction 3) or from the increase in another debt (transaction 4), leaving his total equity balance the same as before. Since the balance in owners' equity is a measure of wealth, changes in the capital account are especially significant financial information. Owners' equity is an indication of economic well-being and is very important in accounting for the affairs of individuals and businesses. Therefore, it is necessary to examine carefully the types of transactions that result in changes in owners' equity.

Changes in Owners' Equity

Of the four types of transactions just described, the last three involve equities. All three can affect capital, much as they affected liabilities in Marc's case. The effect on capital is of special interest, because capital represents wealth and we are interested in measuring changes in wealth. One very important use of accounting information is to enable decision makers to increase owners' equity. We are particularly interested in owners' equity changes called revenues and expenses.

Revenues.   An increase in owners' equity that occurs as a result of an earning process is called **revenue.** Typically revenue cannot be earned without expending some effort. Businesses earn revenue by providing goods or services. Most individuals earn revenue by supplying services in the form of work to someone willing to pay for the work done. In exchange for work an individual obtains money, increasing assets and owners' equity at the same time. In most cases when revenue is earned, the increase in capital is accompanied by an increase in assets, but earning revenue can also result in a liability decrease. Revenue occurs in the form of the following basic transactions:

Revenues increase owners' equity

1. An asset increases (dr) and owners' equity increases (cr).
2. A liability decreases (dr) and owners' equity increases (cr).

Revenue obtained by reducing liabilities is not as common as revenue earned by increasing assets. The examples below illustrate increases in owners' equity by describing how Marc earned revenue to increase his capital. Similar examples for businesses are discussed in later chapters.

1. Upon arriving at college, Marc obtained a part-time job and on September 20 received his first wages of $90. As you saw earlier, there was a $90 increase in Marc's Cash account. This increase in cash did not require Marc to give up another asset, nor did it create an obligation that he would have to repay. Instead, the increase in cash made Marc better off—that is, there was a corresponding increase in capital.

2. Let us assume that Marc borrowed $15 from his friend Janet in order to buy gasoline for his car. A week later Janet needed to have a term paper typed. She suggested to Marc that he could repay his debt by typing the paper for her. When Marc did the work, he earned revenue. However, instead of increasing his assets, his work

resulted in the decrease of a liability. In other words, Marc's effort caused him to be better off. The reduction in his liability, which caused an increase in his capital, is called revenue.

Expenses.   The using up of wealth is a common occurrence in everyday life. All accounting entities consume goods and services. Such consumption results in decreases in owners' equity called **expenses.** Businesses must incur expenses in order to operate. Individuals incur expenses to satisfy basic needs. Expenses occur when assets are consumed or used up, or when liabilities are incurred in order to consume goods or services. In both cases owners' equity decreases. Expenses occur in the form of the following basic transactions:

Expenses decrease owners' equity

1. An asset decreases (cr) and owners' equity decreases (dr).
2. A liability increases (cr) and owners' equity decreases (dr).

Both types of expenses are common for businesses and individuals. Examples of Marc's expense transactions are discussed below.

1. The first type of expense transaction generally occurs when an asset is used up, rather than exchanged for another asset. If Marc spends money to buy a lunch, his cash asset decreases. One might argue that the cash has been exchanged for food, another asset, but if the food is immediately consumed, it no longer exists. In either case, whether eating a lunch is viewed as the using up of food or money, an asset has decreased and there is a corresponding decrease in owners' equity. Similarly, when Marc spends money to have his automobile serviced, the consumption of the services decreases his cash asset and his capital. If Marc buys fuel for the automobile, the gasoline he obtains can be viewed as an asset, but as soon as this asset is consumed, Marc's net worth also declines. There is no corresponding increase in another asset or a decrease in a liability resulting from using up the gasoline. As an asset is used up, or consumed, an expense occurs, reducing owners' equity, whether that asset is used to obtain a service which is consumed immediately, or the asset itself is consumed some way by the owner.

2. Expenses can easily occur in the form of liability increases. For example, if Marc has his automobile serviced and the serviceman agrees to accept payment next week, Marc incurs a liability. Whether the service is paid for now or later, as soon as Marc receives it, he is less well-off financially. The increase in his liability causes a decrease in his capital. Later when he pays the debt, there will be a reduction in cash and a corresponding reduction in the liability, but the payment of the liability will not have any effect on capital. The reduction of capital occurs when the service is received.

Revenues and expenses can be included in the accounting equation as part of owners' equity.

$$\text{Assets} = \qquad\qquad\qquad \text{Equities}$$

$$\text{Assets} = \text{Liabilities} \quad + \quad \text{Capital}$$

$$\text{Assets} = \text{Liabilities} + \text{Capital} + (\text{Revenues} - \text{Expenses})$$

Revenues and expenses together represent the **net change in capital.** If revenues are greater than expenses, the difference is **net income.** If expenses are greater than revenues, the difference is **net loss.** It is important for you to remember that changes in capital must be accompanied by changes in assets or liabilities. Capital is the residual measure that results when liabilities are deducted from assets. Net income is the increase in capital that occurs because there is a net increase in assets. Capital is only a measure of how well-off Marc is; it exists only as a concept or a number in an account. Marc's wealth is really in the form of assets that he has and can use. The primary goal of businesses is to earn income, or profit. The accounting system must provide business managers with adequate information about assets, liabilities, capital, revenues, and expenses to enable them to manage the business profitably.

Review of Accounts and Their Changes

To reinforce your understanding of the concepts we have discussed so far, let us examine Marc's asset and equity accounts at the time he arrived at college on September 8. We shall trace the changes in these accounts resulting from Marc's financial transactions. The accounts and their balances on September 8 are shown below:

A		=	L	+	C
Cash	**Automobile**		**Payable to Bank**		**Capital**
575	4,300		3,500		1,375
Debits		=		Credits	

The balance in the capital account is a residual amount obtained by subtracting the $3,500 liability from total assets. The information in these accounts is summarized in Marc's balance sheet, shown in Figure 2-8. Note the date of this balance sheet.

Bear in mind that this statement does not represent all Marc's goods, obligations, and wealth. At this point, however, it serves to illustrate the fundamental nature of accounts. More elaborate details are covered in later chapters.

Marc Johnson
Statement of Financial Position
September 8, 1985

Assets		Equities	
Cash	$ 575	Payable to bank	$3,500
Automobile	4,300	Capital	1,375
Total assets	$4,875	Total equities	$4,875

Figure 2-8
Marc's balance
sheet when he
arrived at college.

Assume that after Marc arrived at college, the following events, which have already been described, took place:

a. Marc bought textbooks for $89.85 on September 9.

b. On September 12 Marc exchanged his chemistry textbook for a mathematics textbook, paying the $3.15 difference in cash. The chemistry text had cost $24.45 and the math text cost $27.60.

c. He received $90 wages on September 20 from his part-time job.

d. He spent $57.50 to have his automobile tuned up on September 23.

e. He spent $24.50 on a dinner date on September 23.

f. He made a $100 payment on his automobile loan on September 27.

Transactions
change the
accounting
equation

These events affect Marc's assets and equity accounts and therefore change his balance sheet. After recording the transactions in T accounts, we can prepare a new balance sheet and compare it with the previous one.

The purchase of textbooks (item *a*) is an exchange of one asset for another. The accounts in the September 8 balance sheet do not include a textbook asset. This does not pose a problem because it is easy to create an account as needed for any asset or equity. The Textbooks account is established and is increased with a debit of $89.85 to indicate the acquisition of the books. At the same time the Cash account is credited the same amount to indicate a decrease in cash. These debit and credit entries are coded in the accounts with the small letter *a* so that each debit can be matched with its credit counterpart, as illustrated in Figure 2-9.

When Marc exchanges his textbooks (*b*), the cost of the chemistry text is removed from the Textbooks account by a credit of $24.45, and the cost of the mathematics text is debited to the same account in the amount of $27.60. At this point the debits do not equal the credits. The equality is established by the credit of $3.15 in the Cash account, which is the additional cash Marc had to pay to the bookstore when he exchanged the book. Note that this transaction results in one debit and two credits labeled *b* in the Cash and Textbooks accounts, but the amount of the debit still equals the total amount of the credits.

Assets

Liabilities

Cash

Debits		Credits	
Bal.	575.00	a.	89.85
c.	90.00	b.	3.15
		d.	57.50
		e.	24.50
		f.	100.00
Bal.	390.00		

Payable to Bank

Debits		Credits	
f.	100.00	Bal.	3,500.00
		Bal.	3,400.00

Automobile

Debits		Credits
Bal.	4,300.00	

Owners' Equity

Textbooks

Figure 2-9
**A complete set of
T accounts with
entries coded to
match each debit
with its credit
counterpart.**

Debits		Credits	
a.	89.85	b.	24.45
b.	27.60		
Bal.	93.00		

Capital

Debits		Credits	
d.	57.50	Bal.	1,375.00
e.	24.50	c.	90.00
		Bal.	1,383.00

Item *c* is a *revenue* transaction. The $90 cash received as wages is recorded as a debit in the Cash account, because cash increased when Marc received the money. This increase in money is a revenue that increased Marc's wealth. The increase in his equity is indicated by a credit to the Capital (Owners' Equity) account.

Item *d* is an *expense* transaction. The decrease in cash of $57.50 for automobile maintenance is recorded by a credit in the Cash account. Expenses reduce owners' equity, and the decrease is indicated by a debit of $57.50 in the Capital account.

The $24.50 date (*e*) is an expense that reduces owners' equity and is recorded as a debit in the Capital account. The corresponding reduction in cash is a credit in the Cash account.

The payment of $100 (*f*) on the automobile loan decreases cash and is shown as a credit in the Cash account. The corresponding decrease in the liability is a debit.

REVIEW OF FINANCIAL POSITION

The preceding descriptions illustrate the effect of financial transactions on accounts and the process of maintaining accounts. Before a new balance sheet is prepared, we must compute the ending balance in each account as shown in Figure 2-9. The balance sheet in Figure 2-10 contains the title and balance of each account from Figure 2-9. This simple balance sheet has several characteristics worth noting. The title of the report indicates the name of the accounting entity, the name of the statement, and the date. The assets are expressed in terms of their cost measured in dollars, and the equality between assets and equities is shown by their total amounts. The double underlining of the totals is a traditional method of terminating accounting reports.

Figure 2-10
The balance sheet always shows total assets equal to total equities. Note the difference between this statement and the one in Figure 2-8.

Marc Johnson
Statement of Financial Position
September 30, 1985

Assets		Equities	
Cash	$ 390	Payable to bank	$3,400
Textbooks	93		
Automobile	4,300	Capital	1,383
Total assets	$4,783	Total equities	$4,783

Compare this balance sheet with the one in Figure 2-8. Each transaction changed Marc's financial position slightly, and the difference between the two statements is the net result of several transactions. Note that Marc's capital changed from $1,375 to $1,383. The change occurred as follows:

Beginning capital, September 8	$1,375
Add revenue	90
Total	1,465
Less expenses ($57.50 + $24.50)	82
Ending capital, September 30	$1,383

It is not convenient to prepare balance sheets frequently, especially for individuals. Usually they are prepared at the end of each year and reflect a large number of changes resulting from an entire year's transactions. This important accounting statement is discussed in more detail in the next chapter.

The discussion in this chapter of changes in assets, liabilities, and owners' equity contains many new ideas and many difficult concepts. These ideas and concepts are very important, and they will be discussed and elaborated upon in subsequent chapters. You should not proceed to the next chapter until you feel completely familiar and comfortable with the principles summarized on the next page.

SUMMARY   **Accounts** are records of financial information, maintained in a systematic manner. The T account form is most suitable for a study of accounting. The left side of the T account is the **debit** side, and amounts shown on the left side are known as **debits.** The right side of the T account is the **credit** side, and amounts shown on the right side are known as **credits.** To debit an account means to enter an amount on the left side. To credit an account means to enter an amount on the right side. The term **charge** means debit.

Assets are valuable economic resources and are accounted for at their cost in terms of money. The **money measurement concept** enables accountants to describe all assets in common terms. The **cost concept** is adopted for accounting because costs can be measured objectively. The **stable dollar concept,** while imperfect, implies that the value of money does not change significantly.

Equities represent the rights to obtain benefits from assets. The rights may be those of the asset's owner in which case they are known as **owners' equity,** or **capital.** Equities also represent the claims of creditors who, by providing the necessary money or credit, have made it possible for the owners to obtain the assets. The rights of creditors terminate when the owners discharge their obligation by repaying the debt. Creditor's equities are known as **liabilities.**

For every asset there is a corresponding equity. This is expressed by the fundamental accounting equation **Assets = Equities.** The equation expresses economic facts if we assign to assets and equities amounts that have economic relevance. The basic equation can be expanded in the following form:

$$Assets = Liabilities + Capital$$

If the equation is intended to emphasize owners' equity, it can be converted to the form:

$$Assets - Liabilities = Capital$$

In this form the equation shows that capital is a **residual** obtained by deducting liabilities from assets—that is, **Capital = Net assets.**

The accounting equation can be represented by a report called the **statement of financial position,** or **balance sheet.** In the balance sheet all assets, liabilities, and owners' equities are listed in a way that shows the equality between assets and equities. A balance sheet is a description of financial position at a **point in time.** As financial transactions are undertaken, the balance sheet accounts change, reflecting the changing financial position. The changes may occur in assets, liabilities, or owners' equity.

Owners' equity increases when **revenues** are earned. Revenues usually increase assets, but they can also decrease liabilities. Owners' equity decreases when **expenses** are incurred. Expenses occur when assets are used up. The difference between revenues and expenses is **net income** or **net loss.** Net income or net loss changes the amount of owners' equity.

Increases in assets and decreases in equities are recorded by debits. Decreases in assets and increases in equities are recorded by credits. Every financial transaction results in a dollar amount of debits that is equal to the dollar amount of credits. In an accounting system in which assets equal equities, debits must always equal credits.

One of the primary functions of accounting is to provide information for economic decision making. Good accounting information facilitates control of revenues and expenses as well as of assets and equities, enabling decision makers to increase owners' equity over time.

KEY TERMS

Following are important terms that have been defined and discussed in this chapter. You should be thoroughly acquainted with the meaning of these terms before proceeding to the next chapter.

account *(33, 34)*	liability *(43)*
account balance *(35)*	money measurement *(40)*
accounting equation *(45)*	net assets *(46)*
accounting system *(33, 36)*	net income *(52)*
asset *(39)*	net loss *(52)*
balance sheet *(47)*	net worth *(43)*
capital *(43, 46)*	owners' equity *(43)*
charge *(38)*	proprietorship *(43)*
cost *(42)*	residual *(44, 46)*
credit *(38)*	revenue *(50)*
debit *(38)*	stable dollar *(42)*
equity *(43)*	statement of financial position *(46)*
expense *(51)*	T account *(38)*
interest *(44)*	wealth *(45)*

QUESTIONS

1. What kinds of information are found in a three-column account? What is the purpose of the account?

2. What does it mean to make a debit entry in a T account?

3. "I just paid $9,000 for my new car," said Tim to Shirley. "What a big expense that was," she commented. "Yes, I'm now $9,000 poorer." Explain why the last two statements are incorrect.

4. Describe the accounting concept of money measurement.

5. Why do accountants choose to measure assets in terms of cost rather than another value? Does cost represent economic reality?

6. In connection with the accounting equation Assets = Equities, it is sometimes said the equities represent the source of assets. Discuss how equities can be viewed as sources of assets.

7. When an individual applies for a bank loan, the bank usually requests a list of the person's assets and liabilities, and their amounts. Why doesn't the bank ask for the borrower's capital?

8. What kind of information is found in a statement of financial position? Why does this statement represent the accounting equation A = L + C?

9. What are revenues and what effect do they have on capital? What are expenses and how do they affect capital?

10. What is the primary function of accounting?

11. What is net income? Try to express net income in the form of an equation? Do the same for net loss.

12. An accounting system is made up of many parts. Name one component of the system. What is the purpose of such a system?

EXERCISES

Ex. 2-1 **Recording debits and credits in accounts.** Following are four T accounts maintained by Westcliff Hardware and some of the company's transactions:

Cash				Nails			
8/1	2,600	8/4	548	8/1	460		
8/9	309	8/22	118	8/14	220		

Paint				Payable to Suppliers			
8/1	1,000			8/22	118	8/1	396
8/13	212					8/14	220
8/22	300						

a. On August 24 $150 was paid to suppliers for paint bought earlier.

b. On August 26 $340 of paint was purchased, $100 of which was paid for in cash.

c. Purchased nails on August 28 for $130 cash.

d. On August 30 $505 of paint was purchased but was not paid for.

e. On August 31 $220 was paid to suppliers.

Required:
   a. Find the balance of each account at the end of the day on August 22.
   b. Record the transactions for August 24 through August 31 in the T accounts.
   c. Find the balance of each account on August 31.

Ex. 2-2   **Recording debits and credits in accounts.**   Following are some accounts maintained by Charles Metcalf and a list of several transactions:

Cash			Stamp Collection			
6/1	3,000	6/14	600	6/1	1,800	6/9	300
6/9	900					

Owed to Bank			
6/14	700	6/1	500
		6/5	200

a.   On June 18 Charles bought stamps for his collection for $400 cash.

b.   On June 20 he borrowed $750 from the bank.

c.   On June 25 he sold for $200 cash half the stamps that he bought on June 18.

d.   On June 28 he repaid $500 of the bank loan.

Required:
   a.   Find the balance of each account on June 15.
   b.   Record the transactions in the accounts.
   c.   Find the balance of each account on June 30.

Ex. 2-3   **Understanding a three-column account.**   At the end of August, Renee received a bank statement that was improperly printed by a computer. All items were processed correctly, but some of the figures were left off the statement in the printing process. Provide the missing figures indicated by the small letters.

Twilite City Bank
November 30, 1985

Bank Statement for
Renee Penn

Balance at beginning of month $ a

Date	Deposits	Checks	Balance
8/02		2,750	b
8/03		908	15,682
		1,550	c
8/05	10,000	2,300	d
8/10		e	11,032
8/15	f	1,542	12,090
8/20		2,000	g
8/25		h	6,250
8/31	3,100		i

Required: Provide the missing figures indicated by letters a through i.

Ex. 2-4   **Recording data in accounts.**   Carver manages a government motor pool. He wants to keep track of the gasoline, oil, and tires that his office buys and uses for official cars. This is his log.

Nov. 1	Cost of gasoline on hand	$2,575
	Cost of oil on hand	632
	Cost of tires on hand	3,091
3	Gasoline purchased	300
4	Gasoline dispensed	182
	Oil dispensed	52
5	Gasoline dispensed	359
6	Tires purchased	212
8	Tires dispensed	543
	Oil dispensed	79
9	Tires stolen	350
	Gasoline purchased	760
10	Oil dispensed	198
	Gasoline dispensed	257
13	Gasoline purchased	500
16	Gasoline leaked from broken pipe	118
21	Oil purchased	145
26	Gasoline dispensed	485
	Oil dispensed	10

Required: Establish T accounts for each of the three assets and record the above events in the accounts. Then find the balance of each account.

Ex. 2-5   **Preparation of a simple balance sheet.**   On February 7, 1985, Robert Crandal applied for a personal loan at his bank. He supplied the bank with the following data:

Cash on hand and in bank	$ 4,800
Monthly salary	1,900
Lot and home	85,000
Furniture	16,000
Car	9,000
Owed on lot and home	54,000
Owed on car	4,200

On February 9, after verifying the data, the bank agreed to lend Robert $4,000.

Required: Prepare Robert's balance sheet after he obtained the loan.

Ex. 2-6   **Application of the cost concept.**   Patricia Hall operates a small typing service and needs a bank loan. When she applied for the loan, the bank asked her to prepare a statement of financial position. Below is the statement as prepared by Patricia on March 31. She based her figures on her own estimate of the current market value of her assets.

Cash		$1,950
Typewriter, purchased for $700	$700	
Amount still owed	300	400
Desk provided by landlord as part of rented office		400
Chairs, purchased for $600		600
Accounting and law books, purchased for $225 at estate sale		1,000
Calculators, purchased for $250		300
Miscellaneous office supplies purchased for $80		80
Total assets		4,730
Amount owed to furniture store		350
Total		$4,380

Required: Using appropriate accounting principles and concepts, prepare a balance sheet for Patricia.

Ex. 2-7 **Preparation of a simple balance sheet.** Melissa Gonzales wanted to borrow $1,000 from her bank in order to buy some furniture for her apartment. At the bank's request, she made the following list on July 30, 1985.

Cash in checking and savings accounts	$2,250
Investments	1,200
Car purchased last week for	5,000
Monthly salary	1,150
Furniture	850

After asking Melissa some questions, the loan officer discovered that she owed $4,500 to the car dealer and $300 to a friend. The remaining information was verified as correct, and the bank agreed to lend Melissa $1,000 on July 31.

Required: Use the above data to prepare a balance sheet for Melissa after she has obtained the bank loan.

Ex. 2-8 **Use of the accounting equation.** Below is part of the balance sheet of Traylor Typewriter Company.

Traylor Typewriter Company
Balance Sheet
June 10, 1985

Assets

Cash	$20,000
Furniture	10,000
Equipment	60,000
Total	$90,000

Required:
a. What is the total of the company's equities?
b. Suppose that the company's only liability is a $40,000 bank loan. What is the company's capital?
c. If the company borrows $9,500 to buy some machinery, how will the company's capital change?

Ex. 2-9   **Use of the accounting equation.**   The balance sheet of Kartell Corporation contains the following list of assets:

Cash	$ 8,500,000
Merchandise	9,800,000
Land	4,700,000
Buildings	25,000,000
Other assets	4,500,000

The corporation owes $6,700,000 to a bank and $9,300,000 to a mortgage company.

Required:
a. What is the company's total equity?
b. What is the company's total capital?
c. How will equities change when the company buys equipment for $2,500,000 cash?
d. How will equities change when one of the other assets, which cost $400,000, is destroyed in a fire?
e. Describe the change in equities when the company borrows $3,000,000 to buy equipment.

Ex. 2-10   **Using T account data.**   Emily Steward prepared the following T accounts, which include beginning asset and equity balances and some of last week's transactions.

		Cash					Mortgage on Cabin		
Bal.		2,500	a.		1,000	e.		55	a.
c.		250	b.		100				
			d.		60				
			e.		150				

(Mortgage on Cabin, a. = 15,000)

		Cabin					Payable to Dad		
a.		16,000				b.		100	Bal.

(Payable to Dad, Bal. = 200)

		Owners' Equity		
d.		60	Bal.	2,300
e.		95	c.	250

Required: Explain how the changes labeled *a* through *d* might have occurred by describing the transactions that would cause the changes.

Ex. 2-11   Recording data in T accounts.   Mohammed works in the supply room of a small factory. Whenever he receives a shipment of supplies, he must record their cost in the following accounts: Paints, Varnishes, Solvents, and Resins. Whenever he issues supplies, he must record the reduction in the same accounts. The following data are available:

Mar. 1	Cost of paint on hand	$2,100
	Cost of varnish on hand, 360 gal.	2,880
	Cost of solvent on hand	900
	Cost of resin on hand	0
2	Issue paint	450
5	Received resin, 600 gal. at $12 per gal.	
	Received varnish, 300 gal.	2,400
6	Issued red paint	390
7	Received resin, 300 gal. at $12 per gal.	
12	Issued solvent	225
	Issued varnish, 90 gal.	
14	Received white paint	3,000
15	Received solvent	1,200
	Issued solvent	420
16	Issued varnish, 150 gal.	
19	Issued resin, 210 gal.	
20	Received green paint	1,800
21	Issued resin, 480 gal.	
23	Issued resin, 120 gal.	
25	Notified purchasing department to order 1,200 gal. of resin	
27	Issued solvent	660

Required: Establish T accounts for the four assets, and record the above events. Then find the balances of the accounts.

Ex. 2-12   Changes in balance sheet.   Below is a statement of financial position for James Elkabong, and a list of February transactions:

James Elkabong
Balance Sheet
January 31, 1985

Cash	$ 900		Credit card liability	$ 600
Furniture	2,000		Mortgage on land	6,000
Land	9,000			
Gun collection, at cost	3,500		Capital	8,800
Total assets	$15,400		Total equities	$15,400

a.   On February 5 James bought furniture for $500, paying $100 cash with an agreement to pay the remainder in 30 days.

b.   On February 9 he sold a gun from his collection to a friend for $100 cash. The cost of the gun was $120.

c.   On February 15 he paid $300 cash on his credit card liability.

d.   On February 20 he bought a new gun for his collection for $150, and charged the purchase on his credit card.

e.   On February 28 James received a $700 salary check.

Required: Prepare a balance sheet for James on February 28.

PROBLEMS

P. 2-1   **Balance sheet from account balances.**   Following is a list of T account balances of Bud Bailey:

	Debits	**Credits**
Cash	$ 3,700	
Savings bonds	10,000	
Automobile	9,700	
House	105,000	
Furniture	22,600	
Jewelry	4,000	
Paintings	9,000	
Note payable on automobile		$ 7,800
Mortgage payable on house		80,000
Owed to brother		1,600
Capital		?

Required: Use the above data to prepare Bud's balance sheet on December 31, 1985.

P. 2-2   **Effect of transactions on the accounting equation.**   Following are some transactions of Archie Stover during the month of November:

a.   Bought used boat for $1,750 cash.

b.   Received $500 prize in sweepstakes contest.

c.   Bought new car for $9,000 to use on vacation and tow boat. Paid $200 cash and gave a note for the balance to the bank that provided the loan.

d.   Borrowed $3,000 from bank to spend on vacation next month.

e.   Archie's boat, which was not insured, was stolen and could not be recovered.

f.   Paid taxes on home, $700 cash.

g.   Received November paycheck for $1,950.

h.   To increase his vacation fund, Archie went to the horse races, where he lost $5,500 cash.

i.   The bank repossessed Archie's new car and cancelled the debt.

j.   Archie borrowed $5,000 from a friend and used part of it to repay the $3,000 bank loan.

k.   He bought a new boat for $4,000 cash.

Required: Establish a schedule as illustrated below. Enter each transaction and show the changes in Archie's accounting equation. The first transaction, in which one asset increases and another decreases, is given as an example.

Transaction	Assets	=	Liabilities	+	Capital
a. Bought used boat	+1,750 −1,750				

P. 2-3   **Effect of transaction on the accounting equation.**   Martha Bergman decided to establish a hair-styling service. The following events and transactions took place in her new business:

a.   Martha opened a bank account for her business by depositing $8,000.

b.   She bought hair-styling equipment for $1,500 cash.

c.   Martha spent a week looking for a location that she could use for her business, but none of those advertised were suitable.

d.   Arrangements were made for the hair-styling service to occupy a booth of an established beauty parlor. Martha's rent was set at 10 percent of her total revenue.

e.   Martha bought furniture for $2,800, paying $500 in cash with the balance due in 30 days.

f.   An advertisement placed in a newspaper to run for 1 week cost $285, which Martha paid by check.

g.   A payment of $400 was made on the furniture.

h.   During the first month of operations, Martha collected $900 in fees.

i.   The required rent was paid to the beauty parlor.

j.   An item of equipment costing $200 was found to be defective. Martha returned it to the supplier and received a cash refund.

k.   Martha had a broken piece of equipment repaired. She received a bill for $19 but did not pay it.

l.   Martha paid $25 for telephone service for the month.

Required: Establish a schedule as illustrated below. Enter each transaction and show the changes in Martha's accounting equation. Entry *a* is given as an example.

Transaction	Assets	=	Liabilities	+	Capital
a. Investment of cash by owner	+8,000				+8,000

P. 2-4   **Balance sheets and their changes.**   Jane Little has $500 cash on June 1, 1984, and owns two horses that are boarded at Beck Riding Stables. The horses cost $900 each when she bought them last year. The stable rents these and other horses to its customers. At the end of each month, it pays to Jane the rent from her horses, after deducting the amounts it charges her for their upkeep. During June the two horses were rented for a total of 85 hours at $4 per hour. They consumed $75 of feed each, and the stable rent for each horse was $42. Jane bought a saddle for $180 in June for her own use when she rides. The stable charged her $18 in June for veterinary fees.

Required:

a. Prepare a balance sheet for Jane on June 1, using only the information provided.

b. Prepare a balance sheet for Jane on June 30, using only the information provided.

c. Show how you calculate the change in Jane's equity from June 1 to June 30.

P. 2-5 Preparation of a balance sheet.   David Miller owns Miller's Carpet Cleaners. On February 1, 1985, the company had $1,886 cash in its checking account, and customers owed $937 to the company. The carpet-cleaning machine that the company owns cost $1,739, and its estimated fair value is $800. The company has soap and cleaning fluids on hand that cost $551. Other cleaning equipment and accessories owned by the company cost $1,287. David originally invested $2,000 when he started the business 1 year ago. The company owes $1,785 to one of David's friends who loaned the company the money in January, and it owes $315 to its suppliers.

Required: Prepare a balance sheet for the company on February 1, 1985.

P. 2-6 Two balance sheets.   John Smith owns a home which cost $60,000 and on which he has a mortgage of $48,000. The home was recently appraised at $95,000. He has furniture and other personal property that cost $20,000 and could be sold for about $11,000. His car cost $8,200 and has a fair value of $5,500. He still owes $5,000 on the car. Smith owns stocks and bonds which he bought for $9,500 and which have a market value of $11,300. His bank account balance is $2,700 and he has an additional $450 in currency. His collection of United States coins, which he has saved over the past 10 years, cost $780, but the collection could be sold for about $1,300. Property taxes on Smith's home are due in the amount of $1,700.

Required:

a. Prepare two simple balance sheets for John Smith, one based on cost and the other on fair values.

b. Explain the difference in Smith's equity in the two balance sheets. Which do you prefer? Provide reasons for your preference.

P. 2-7 Balance sheet changes.   When Mike and Jean decided to get married, they made a list of all their property and obligations so that they could make plans for their future. Following is the list they put together on July 1, 1985:

	Mike	**Jean**
Cash	$3,000	$8,000
Car	5,000	4,000
Furniture	1,500	
Stock investment	4,500	
Bank loan		3,000
Car loan	2,300	

The following events occurred during July, after Jean and Mike were married:

a. Paid $300 expenses of wedding ceremony.

b. Sold Mike's car for $5,000 cash and used part of the money to repay the car loan.

c. Spent $2,200 on food, gasoline, motels, and entertainment during honeymoon.

d. Bought house for $60,000 paying $5,000 cash and giving a mortgage note payable for the balance.

e. Received $160 dividend on Mike's stock investment.

f. Jean received her salary check of $1,600.

g. Paid $1,200 for furniture.

h. Paid utility bills, $180 cash.

i. Received Mike's salary of $1,780 at the end of July.

Required: Prepare a single balance sheet for Mike and Jean on July 31, 1985.

P. 2-8   **Changes in balance sheet.**   Below is Bill Adams' balance sheet and a list of transactions that occurred during March.

Bill Adams
Balance Sheet
March 1, 1985

Cash	$ 13,250	Car loan	$ 4,690
Stock investments	18,500	Home mortgage	76,850
Bond investments	44,000		
Car	14,600		
Home	138,000	Capital	146,810
Total assets	$228,350	Total equities	$228,350

a. Bill bought more stock as an investment for $8,000 cash.

b. He received a check for $2,300 interest on his bonds.

c. Paid phone bill of $60.

d. Paid $320 for car repairs.

e. Paid $270 on his car loan, including $90 interest.

f. Bill sold half of his bond investments for $22,000 cash.

g. Received $2,000 dividend check.

h. Paid $1,480 property tax on his home.

i. Received $3,200 salary check at end of March.

Required: Prepare a balance sheet for Bill Adams on March 31.

P. 2-9   **Sole proprietor's balance sheet.**   On October 1 Walter Hollandsworth decided to open a printing shop. Before he opened for business, the following transactions occurred:

Oct. 1 Walter deposited $7,000 of his own money in the business's checking account.

2 He obtained a $12,000 loan from Continental National Bank for the business, for which he signed a note.

4 Walter bought used printing equipment for $6,100 cash and new binding and cutting equipment for $5,700 cash.

7 He purchased paper for $3,000, to be paid in 30 days.

7 Ink, chemicals, and supplies cost $1,950 cash.

9 Walter purchased used furniture for $790 cash.

After posting these transactions, Walter shows you a balance sheet he prepared. "Assets are more than liabilities, so I've already made money, right?" asks Walter. Walter explains further that he did not include the bank loan or the purchase of equipment in his Cash account because "they balance each other pretty close." He forgot to record a cash refund for returning $80 of chemicals. He did not like the furniture, so he valued it at only $650. But the used equipment was really a good buy, so he recorded that at what he thought was closer to its fair value. He estimated the paper and supplies on the basis of how much he would receive if he were to sell them. The statement that Walter prepared is shown below.

Hollandsworth Printing
October 10, 1985

Assets		Liabilities	
Cash	$ 4,260	Due to paper supplier	$ 3,000
Paper	2,500	Bank loan	12,000
Supplies	1,000	Total liabilities	$15,000
Furniture	650		
Equipment	13,200		
Total assets	$21,650		

Required: Prepare a correct balance sheet for the printing shop.

P. 2-10 **Reconstruction of lost records.** Ben Buzby started a storm-window installation business in October. He kept notes on his transactions, which his wife used to prepare T accounts and a balance sheet on October 31. Ben accidentally spilled coffee on the records, and many portions became illegible.

The legible portions of the balance sheet, T accounts, and other records are reproduced below.

Buzby's Storm Windows
Balance Sheet
October 31, 1985

Cash	$	Accounts payable	$ 993
Receivable	726	Note payable	
Supplies			
Equipment			
Van	4,135	Owners' equity	
Total assets	$	Total equities	$9,721

a. Deposited $_____ into checking account, $5,000 of which was borrowed from the bank on a note.

b. Bought van for $4,135 cash.

c. Bought tools, ladders, and other equipment for $_____ cash.

d. Spent $134 cash on supplies such as putty, screws, etc.

e. Paid $_____ cash to have broken ladder repaired.

f. Spent $184 for _____.

g. Windows bought and used in October cost $_____.

h. _____ for $2,966.

i. At the end of October, $_____ had been collected from customers' accounts.

j. Supplies used in October cost $_____.

k. Amount still owed on windows at the end of October is $_____.

Cash			
a.	8,050	b.	4,135
		d.	134
		f.	184
Bal.			

Accounts Payable		
	g.	2,074
	Bal.	993

Receivable from Customers	
h.	2,966
Bal.	726

Note Payable		
	a.	5,000
	Bal.	5,000

Supplies	
Bal.	0

Equipment	
c.	987
f.	
Bal.	1,171

Van	
Bal.	4,135

Owners' Equity			
e.	80	a.	3,050
		h.	2,966
		Bal.	

Required: Reconstruct the above records by supplying the missing information.

P. 2-11   **Preparing a corrected balance sheet.**   On May 1 Jerry started a business printing designs on T-shirts. He maintained his records in T accounts. After the first month of operation, he prepared the following statement:

Prints by Jerry
May 30, 1985

Cash	$3,150	Note payable	$4,000
Dyes	480		
Designs	1,680		
Supplies	350		
Press	1,500	Owners' equity	1,740
Total	$7,160	Total	$5,740

Jerry knows something is wrong with the statement so he asks you for help. While going over the above statement and some of Jerry's records, you discover the following errors:

a.   The total amount earned for printing was $1,190 and was recorded in the Cash account but was not recorded elsewhere.

b.   When dye was purchased for $800 cash, the Cash account was credited $800, but the Dyes account was debited for $880.

c.   When salaries amounting to $510 were paid in cash to employees, Owners' Equity was debited $510, but Cash was credited $560.

d.   Furniture was purchased for $630 cash but was recorded as an expense.

e.   When designs were purchased, the Designs account was debited for the regular price of $1,680, but Cash was credited for only $1,480, the amount paid, because the price had been reduced for a special sale.

f.   Jerry owes $100 for ink and other supplies. The purchase of these items has not been recorded.

g.   A $4,000 note is owed to the West Bank of Westcreek. Part of the loan had been used to buy the press.

Required: Prepare a corrected balance sheet on May 30, 1985.

P. 2-12   **Recording transactions that change the balance sheet.**   The balance sheet of Thomas Goldsmith is given below for June 1, 1985. During June, Thomas had the following financial transactions:

a.   Thomas made a $95 payment on his bank loan.

b.   He drove his car over some glass, destroying a tire, so he bought a new tire for $90 cash.

c.   He bought a tape recorder for $86 and two tapes for $17 and charged them all on his credit card.

d.   He spent $20 for gasoline for his car.

e.   Food consumed during June cost $170.

f.   Thomas made a $150 payment on his credit-card bill.

g. His room rent for June was $92, which he paid in cash.

h. When Thomas received his June paycheck for $700, he sent $100 to his parents to repay part of his loan.

i. He paid $82 cash to the motorcycle shop: $30 for repairs and $52 for a new luggage rack.

j. Thomas accidentally ruined one of his tapes that had cost $7.

Thomas Goldsmith
Balance Sheet
June 1, 1985

Assets		Equities	
Cash	$ 350	Bank loan	$ 900
Car	5,200	Credit card account	250
Motorcycle	1,500	Car loan	2,100
Tape collection	300	Owed to parents	600
Personal property	1,800	Capital	5,300
Total assets	$9,150	Total equities	$9,150

Required:

a. Set up a T account for each of Thomas's assets and equities, and enter in each account the beginning balance from the balance sheet.

b. Enter the June transaction in the T accounts. Do not add any new accounts.

c. Find the balance in each account.

d. Prepare a new balance sheet for Thomas on June 30, 1985.

Case 2-1 **Balance sheet preparation and interpretation.**

Jane Rand is working her way through college and is applying for a loan from the school's financial aid office. At the request of the school, she provides the following statement about her personal finances:

"I work part-time as a cashier in a nearby grocery store, earning $300 per month during the 9-month school year and $700 per month during the summer. Most of my summer salary is saved for the next year's school expenses. Annual tuition and fees are $2,580, and my monthly living expenses are $250. In addition, I pay about $60 per month on my credit-card purchases. Following is the cost of my assets and amount of debts on August 31:

Cash in savings account	$1,500
Bicycle	160
Books and school supplies	600
Stereo set	450
Personal clothing and other items	800
Owed to bicycle shop	100
Owed to credit card	30

"By supplementing my savings and salary, a loan will enable me to complete my education without excessive hardship."

Gary Sables also works to finance his college studies, and in applying for a loan from the school, he makes the following statement:

"My job at a nearby service station pays $350 per month, and I work 10 months of the year, leaving 2 months of the summer for travel and vacation. My payments amount to $2,520 per year for tuition and fees, about $275 per month for living expenses, and $230 per month for car payments and other debts. The cost of my assets and my debts amounts to the following:

Cash	$ 200
Books and school supplies	400
Clothing and personal supplies	1,000
Car	7,200
Stereo and television	1,450
Record collection	700
Car loan	6,800
Owe to television dealer	900
Owe to brother	500

"Without a loan from the school, I will have difficulty meeting my obligations and completing my education at the same time."

The college has received many similar applications and its loan funds are limited. The loan officer decides that Gary is in more financial difficulty than Jane and makes a loan to Gary while rejecting Jane's application.

Required:
a. Prepare a balance sheet for each of the students.
b. Prepare a schedule showing each student's expected receipts of cash and expected cash payments for the year.
c. Which student is more likely to have the ability to repay the school debt?
d. Assess the soundness of the decision made by the loan officer.

The Balance Sheet

3

This chapter discusses the balance sheet and some accounting principles that pertain to it. When you have completed the chapter, you should understand:

1 Concepts underlying the organization of balance sheets.

2 Form and function of the balance sheet of corporations and unincorporated businesses.

3 Some basic aspects of changes in owners' equity.

4 How transactions are handled in an accounting system, and their effects on the balance sheet.

5 Accounting for the operations of a small business.

6 The economic relationship among many accounting entities.

Maintaining accounts according to the concepts discussed in Chapter 2 is not a common practice among individual persons. Individuals usually do not maintain personal accounts, and often they do not know the exact amount or cost of their property. On the other hand, businesses are responsible for reporting to their owners the amounts of each asset and liability, so they must keep accurate accounts. When the balances of these accounts are organized and summarized in a **balance sheet**, the result is a presentation of the **financial position** of a business.

The accounting equation developed and examined in Chapter 2 is the basis for the balance sheet. Now that you understand how this statement is made up, what it represents, and why it balances, you are ready to examine the principles governing the reporting of financial position. In this chapter we present and describe a complete balance sheet and discuss several concepts that affect its preparation. We also develop a detailed example of business operations that illustrates how business transactions affect the balance sheet and change it over a period of time.

BALANCE SHEET CONCEPTS AND ORGANIZATION

Financial statements communicate information; therefore, they must be prepared in accordance with rules and concepts understood by their users. These rules and concepts are called **generally accepted accounting principles (GAAP).** You are already familiar with some of them: the accounting entity, money measurement, and the cost concepts, which all apply to the preparation of the balance sheet. Other concepts that affect preparation of this statement include the going concern concept and the periodicity concept.

Businesses are going concerns whose life span is indefinite

The going concern concept.   When people invest in a business, they usually expect it to survive for a long time. The business often enters into long-term contracts such as rental agreements, and it acquires assets such as warehouses and machinery that can be expected to provide benefits for many years. The **going concern concept** requires accountants to prepare financial statements on the assumption that the business will complete its contracts, that it will not dispose of its assets immediately, and that it will, indeed, continue to exist indefinitely.

The going concern concept, also known as the **continuity** assumption, relates to the cost concept introduced in Chapter 2. It is reasonable to report assets on the balance sheet at their cost rather than at amounts for which the assets can be sold. Aside from being an objective measure, the cost of assets is the amount of resources committed by the business to its future operations. As time passes, the value of assets may change, but their cost still remains relevant as a measure of resources committed to future operations and expected to provide future benefits.

Periodicity.   A business that expects to continue in existence for a long time must issue periodic reports to keep owners, managers, creditors, and others informed about its economic performance and financial condition. The **periodicity concept** means that the life of a going concern is divided into specific time intervals for periodic reporting. The traditional **accounting period** is 1 year, at the end of which time financial statements are prepared. If the accounting period ends on December 31, the business is said to be on a **calendar year.** If the accounting year ends on some other date, the business is said to be on a **fiscal year.**

The balance sheet is a static statement

The periodicity concept ensures timely accounting information but its use also results in the sacrifice of some accuracy. In any accounting period, some information may not be available and may have to be estimated. And so, while the business described by the balance sheet continues to operate over time, the balance sheet indicates the financial position of a business at a single **point in time.** The date on the statement is important: It indicates the account balances that existed at the balance sheet date. Note the heading of the balance sheet of Jupiter Corporation in Figure 3-1. It includes the name of the company, the title of the statement, and the date. A necessary part of the balance sheet, and indeed of any financial state-

Jupiter Corporation
Statement of Financial Position
December 31, 1985

Assets			Liabilities and Owners' Equity		
Current assets:			Current liabilities:		
Cash		$ 38,570	Notes payable		$ 12,000
Temporary investments		18,000	Accounts payable		49,800
Notes receivable		2,500	Taxes payable		36,600
Accounts receivable	$ 96,280		Salaries payable		18,200
Less allowance for			Current portion of		
uncollectible accounts	5,000	91,280	mortgage payable		4,000
Merchandise inventory		78,800	Total current liabilities		120,600
Prepaid expenses		6,200	Long-term liabilities:		
Total current assets		235,350	Mortgage payable, 9%	$42,000	
Investments:			Less current portion	4,000	38,000
Bond retirement fund		42,000	Bonds payable, 10%,		
Investment in securities		82,000	due 1998		100,000
Total investments		124,000	Total long-term liabilities		138,000
Fixed assets:			Other liabilities:		
Land		50,000	Employee pension		
Buildings	1,095,000		obligation		23,500
Less accumulated			Deferred income taxes		7,500
depreciation	480,500	614,500	Total other liabilities		31,000
Furniture and			Total liabilities		289,600
equipment	1,129,700		Owners' equity		
Less accumulated			Contributed capital		
depreciation	425,600	704,100	Preferred stock, 6%,		
Total fixed assets		1,368,600	$100 par, 1,000		
Intangibles:			shares outstanding		100,000
Patents		32,000	Common stock, 80,000		
Trademarks		8,150	shares outstanding		864,000
Total intangibles		40,150	Total contributed capital		964,000
			Retained earnings		514,500
			Total owners' equity		1,478,500
			Total liabilities and		
Total assets		$1,768,100	owners' equity		$1,768,100

Figure 3-1   **Balance sheet of a corporation, with assets and equities classified into categories. This statement is in account form.**

ment, is the designation of the monetary unit. Dollar signs are used at the top and bottom of the statement, and appropriate single and double underlining designates subtotals and totals.

Balance Sheet Organization

Various asset and liability accounts reported in a balance sheet are usually classified into several categories used to group accounts with similar characteristics. The classifications discussed in connection with Jupiter Corporation's balance sheet are typical, but some variation in classification and account titles is found in practice.

You should not expect to understand fully all the account descriptions that follow. Many are discussed in greater detail in later chapters. The intent for now is to expose you to the various types of accounts reported in the balance sheet so that you have a general understanding of the information it contains.

Assets

Assets are usually classified into current assets, investments, fixed assets, and other assets. Not all classifications are always used, and sometimes balance sheets are not classified at all. Current and fixed asset classifications are most commonly reported.

Current assets. As shown in Figure 3-1, **current assets** consist of those normally used in the firm's operating cycle or 1 year, whichever is longer. The **operating cycle** is the time period required for a business to convert cash into merchandise, sell the merchandise, convert the customers' accounts receivable back into cash, and pay its accounts payable. The cycle varies for different businesses, but since it is usually shorter than 1 year, most businesses use an operating cycle of 1 year for the purpose of classifying current assets.

Assets are presented in order of liquidity

Current assets are usually listed in the order of their relative liquidity. **Liquidity** is a measure of the speed with which an asset can be converted into cash, or liquidated. Cash is shown first, followed by temporary, or short-term, investments. **Temporary investments** consist of government bonds, corporate bonds, or other securities that can be converted into cash quickly. Customers sometimes give the firm promissory notes that indicate the amount, the interest rate, and the time that payment is to be made for purchases of goods or services. These signed documents are called **notes receivable.** Sales of goods or services to steady customers are usually made on **open account,** which means that the company bills customers periodically for purchases. Such open accounts are called **accounts receivable,** and they represent amounts owed to the company by its customers. Accounts receivable are often referred to as **trade accounts.**

Not all receivables can be collected from customers

When a company grants credit to customers, it assumes that customers will pay their bills. However, it is unlikely that every dollar of receivables will be collected. The amount that may become uncollectible is estimated and deducted from the balance of trade receivables on the balance sheet to show the net amount expected to be collected. The amount deducted is called the **allowance for uncollectible accounts.**

Merchandise inventory is an asset consisting of the goods held by a business for sale to its customers. A firm that primarily sells services, such as dental treatment or hair styling, usually has little or no merchandise inventory. However, such a firm may have an inventory of supplies necessary for providing the service. A dentist, for example, needs gauze pads, gold, silver, medications, and X-ray film, none of which are sold but instead are used in providing the service.

Manufacturing firms maintain several inventory categories. Products that are completed and available for sale to customers are classified as **finished goods.** Those still in the process of being manufactured are classified as **work in process.** In addition, a manufacturer maintains an inventory of **raw materials** that will be used in production and converted to finished goods. If Jupiter Corporation were a manufacturer, the balance sheet in Figure 3-1 might report inventories as follows:

Finished goods	$16,800	
Work in process	42,000	
Raw materials	20,000	
Total inventories		$78,800

Prepaid expenses are assets, not expenses

Prepaid expenses are assets that have been purchased and will be used in the normal course of business within the accounting year. Do not let the term confuse you. In Chapter 2 you learned that expenses are reductions of owners' equity and occur when assets or services are used up. Prepaid expenses, on the other hand, are assets that have been paid for but have not yet been used. They will be used and will become expenses within a relatively short time. They include such items as rent paid in advance, insurance premiums, and supplies. As time passes the company's occupancy of the rented premises uses up the prepaid rent, the insurance protection expires, and supplies are used up. Prepaid expenses are assets as long as future benefits can be obtained from them.

Investments.   Assets that the company intends to hold for investment purposes and does not plan to liquidate within the next year are classified as **investments.** Such assets may include the stock of other corporations, bonds, cash held in savings accounts for specific purposes such as retirement of debts or for construction of a new plant, and the cash value of life insurance policies. Long-term investments generally earn some revenue such as interest, but for most companies this is not a major source of income.

Fixed assets.   Tangible property that a firm uses in its operations and does not sell to customers is reported in the category of **fixed assets,** or **long-lived assets.** These include land, buildings, machinery, equipment, furniture, fixtures, and other tangible property. Fixed assets have a useful life that extends beyond the operating cycle of the company. Most fixed assets wear out, deteriorate, or become obsolete as they are used, which means that they are subject to **depreciation.** The benefits of the asset are consumed over the asset's useful life, and therefore a portion of the cost is reduced each year that the asset is in service. This depreciation of the asset is recorded in an account known as **accumulated depreciation.** The accumulated depreciation account has a credit balance that is deducted from the debit balance representing the original cost of the asset on the balance sheet.

Contra-asset accounts have credit balances

Accounts like accumulated depreciation and allowance for uncollectible accounts, which are deducted from asset accounts, are known as **contra assets.** They are so named because they have credit balances which are contra, or opposite, to the debit balances of the related assets. The contra asset is used because there is a need to preserve information about the cost of the asset. The net amount obtained by deducting the contra-asset balance from the assets' cost is known as the assets' **book value,** which is the original cost less the reductions in cost that have taken place. Jupiter Corporation's buildings, for example, have a book value of $614,500. Book value is also known as **carrying value.** It is the cost of the asset still remaining to be used in the future.

Intangible assets. Long-lived assets that have no tangible existence but rather are rights conferred upon the owner are called **intangible assets.** Examples of intangible assets include patents, trademarks, copyrights, and franchises, all discussed in Chapter 10. Like fixed assets, intangibles are not kept for sale but are used in the operation of the business.

Other assets. In some balance sheets, a category called **other assets** may be found, which includes assets that do not fit into other classifications. Sometimes long-term investments or long-term insurance policies are classified as other assets. Fixed assets that are no longer in use, such as obsolete machinery awaiting disposal, are also reported here.

Liabilities

The most common classifications of an entity's obligations are current liabilities, long-term liabilities, and other liabilities.

Liabilities are debts of the accounting entity

Current liabilities. Obligations that are due within the next operating cycle are classified as **current liabilities.** As shown in Figure 3-1, they include **accounts payable** to suppliers for purchases of merchandise, short-term **notes payable** to banks, officers, or other lenders, and **taxes payable** on property, income, or wages and salaries. Also included are **wages and salaries payable,** and **interest payable** on notes. Those portions of specific long-term liabilities that will come due within the next operating cycle of the business are classified as current liabilities. An example is that portion of the mortgage that Jupiter Corporation will repay during the next accounting period.

Long-term liabilities. Obligations that the business will not repay during the next operating cycle are classified as **long-term liabilities.** They include the remainder of **mortgages payable,** long-term **notes payable,** and **bonds payable,** all of which are issued by the company for the purpose of obtaining funds from lenders. Repayment of some of these liabilities, such as mortgages, may be made in monthly installments over a period of many years. Others, such as bonds payable, may be due in one lump sum at some specified date.

Other liabilities.   Company obligations to customers under warranty or guarantee agreements and pension obligations to employees may be classified among long-term liabilities or may be listed in a separate category called **other liabilities. Deferred credits** are accounts with credit balances which may become future obligations but which are not liabilities on the balance sheet date.

Owners' Equity

Owners' equity is the residual of assets less liabilities

When the assets and liabilities of an entity have been determined, owners' equity, or capital, can be found as a residual. This way of determining owners' equity is suitable for an individual or a business with a single owner. If a business has more than one owner, each may own a different share of the business. Accounting for owners' equity therefore requires the use of more than a single residual account. In addition, legal requirements and changes in capital further complicate accounting for owners' equity. Owners' equity changes because owners contribute assets to the business or receive assets from the business. It also changes because business operations may result in net income or losses.

Corporate owners' equity consists of several accounts

Owners' equity of corporations.   When owners contribute assets to a corporation, the company issues shares of stock to them in the form of certificates as evidence of their ownership interests. Such shares represent **contributed capital,** as shown in Figure 3-1, and may consist of preferred stock or common stock. **Preferred stock** provides assurance to owners that if the company earns income, the preferred shareholders will be entitled to a specified but limited amount prior to any distributions to other owners. **Common stock** is issued to owners willing to take the risk of not getting anything in return in order to have the right to all income earned by the corporation, without limitations, after payments to preferred shareholders. Common stock and preferred stock together are known as **capital stock.**

When a corporation earns net income, it may distribute part of it to its shareholders. Such distributions are called **dividends.** Laws prohibit distributions of assets that reduce contributed capital; therefore, corporations do not record earnings as part of contributed capital accounts. Instead, as assets increase from earnings, the corresponding increase on the equity side of the accounting equation is recorded in an account called **retained earnings.** When dividends are paid to shareholders, the cash account and the retained earnings account are reduced. If the company has no earnings, it may not pay dividends. Usually all earnings are not distributed to owners, and the amounts not distributed are reinvested in the business so that the company may grow and expand its operations. The retained earnings account is part of owners' equity, together with contributed capital accounts.

Owners' equity of unincorporated businesses.   Whether assets are contributed by owners or earned by the business, the increase in assets is also an increase in owners' equity. If the business is a sole proprietorship or a partnership, changes in owners' equity are not recorded in separate retained earnings accounts. For unincorporated businesses there is no legal requirement to limit distributions of assets to amounts earned, and owners may withdraw amounts earned as well as amounts they originally contributed. Distributions of assets to owners of unincorporated businesses are called **drawings** or **withdrawals**, rather than dividends.

Usually a single capital account is shown in the balance sheet for each owner, indicating the owner's total interest in the business. A separate account is necessary for each partner because one partner may invest or withdraw more than the others. The balance in each capital account includes amounts invested in the business by the partner, plus the partner's share of business earnings, less any drawings made by the partner. Figure 3-2 illustrates the balance sheet of a partnership. Sole proprietors and partners do not receive any evidence of ownership from their company. Their ownership is represented by balances in their capital accounts.

FORM AND FUNCTION OF THE BALANCE SHEET

You should remember from Chapter 2 that the balance sheet is a representation of the accounting equation

$$\text{Assets} = \text{Liabilities} + \text{Capital}$$

Businesses own assets, owners own businesses

The assets reported on the balance sheet equal the rights or claims of those who provided the assets to the entity. If the accounting entity is an individual, capital represents actual ownership of assets. If the entity is a business, the assets belong to the business firm. Capital represents the owners' interest in the business. The owners do not own the assets; they own the business entity itself. The business entity owns the assets and communicates information about its assets and equities by means of a balance sheet.

The two forms of the balance sheet

The balance sheet of Jupiter Corporation in Figure 3-1 shows the assets on the left side and the equities on the right side. This form of the balance sheet is known as the **account form.** The balance sheet of Bellmar Company in Figure 3-2 is in **report form**, with assets reported above equities. Both the account form and report form are commonly used by all types of business entities. The choice depends mainly on convenience.

Function of the Balance Sheet

The function of the balance sheet is to communicate vital information to the reader efficiently. By organizing the balance sheet into categories of assets and equities, important relationships are disclosed which may not be evident from a simple listing of account balances. The relationship between total assets and total liabilities, for example, may tell the reader

Bellmar Company
Balance Sheet
December 31, 1985

Assets

Current assets:			
Cash		$ 3,350	
Marketable securities		4,000	
Accounts receivable	$6,110		
Less allowance for bad debts	250	5,860	
Materials and supplies		6,300	
Prepaid expenses		780	
Total current assets			$20,290
Investments:			
Cash surrender value of life insurance		1,300	
Land held for future development		12,000	
Total investments			13,300
Fixed assets:			
Furniture and fixtures		10,800	
Equipment		4,500	
Total		15,300	
Less accumulated depreciation		5,100	
Total fixed assets			10,200
Total assets			$43,790

Liabilities and Owners' Equity

Current liabilities:			
Accounts payable		$ 3,600	
Interest payable		450	
Salaries payable		910	
Total current liabilities			$ 4,960
Long-term debt:			
Notes payable 13%		6,000	
Mortgage payable, 9%, due 1998		7,200	
Total long-term debt			13,200
Total liabilities			18,160
Owners' equity:			
Capital, Belling		14,230	
Capital, Martin		11,400	
Total capital			25,630
Total liabilities and owners' equity			$43,790

Figure 3-2   **Classified balance sheet of a partnership, presented in report form. Note the two capital accounts.**

something about the riskiness of the business. If the amount of assets is twice the amount of liabilities in one company and three times the liabilities in another, an investor may find the second company to be a more desirable investment than the first. Similarly, the relationship between current assets and current liabilities offers information about the company's liquidity, as we discuss next.

Working capital.   Current assets and current liabilities are used in the day-to-day operations of a business. Their quantities are constantly changing as the company sells merchandise, collects receivables, and pays its current debts. The difference between current assets and current liabilities is called **net working capital,** or simply **working capital,** and is the net amount of current resources not needed to meet current obligations.

Working capital and the current ratio are measures of liquidity

Evaluating the amount of working capital is essential in assessing the financial position and liquidity of a business entity. Working capital is related to the size of the business and the amount of business activity. As the business grows or as business activity increases, the amount of working capital must also increase if the company is to maintain normal operations without difficulty. For example, an increase in the sale of merchandise usually means that accounts receivable also increase. Increased purchases of merchandise become necessary so accounts payable increase and must be paid with larger quantities of cash. A shortage of working capital in growing businesses can cause critical problems, such as insufficient inventory or a lack of cash for the payment of obligations when they come due.

Current ratio.   Another item of information obtained from working capital accounts is the **current ratio,** which is current assets divided by current liabilities. The current ratio is an indicator of how well the entity is able to meet its current obligations as they come due. If the current ratio is too low, the company may have difficulty paying its current liabilities. If it is too high, the company may be losing the opportunity to improve its earnings. Current assets are needed for operations, but because they produce little or no revenue, a high concentration of current assets is wasteful.

The working capital and current ratio of Jupiter Corporation are calculated as follows:

$$\text{Working capital} = \text{Current assets} - \text{Current liabilities}$$
$$= \$235{,}350 - \$120{,}600$$
$$= \$114{,}750$$

$$\text{Current ratio} = \text{Current assets/Current liabilities}$$
$$= \$235{,}350/\$120{,}600$$
$$= 1.95$$

A current ratio of about 2 is often considered adequate for many businesses, but there is considerable variation in what is appropriate. Jupiter Corporation should have no difficulty meeting its current obligations. On the other hand, the current ratio of Bellmar Company is about 4 ($20,290/$4,960), which indicates that the company may not be managing its current assets and current liabilities efficiently.

CHANGES IN OWNERS' EQUITY

Now we examine financial transactions that affect owners' equity. Transactions that increase or decrease capital are particularly significant for businesses because businesses exist for the purpose of increasing the capital section of the balance sheet by earning income. In order to observe how capital changes, let us review again the accounting equation:

$$A = L + C$$

which we write here as

$$A - L = C$$

A − L is also known as **net assets.** Obviously the quantity of net assets is equal to the amount of capital.

Owners benefit from a business when it increases net assets through business operations. Owners' equity may also increase as a result of contributions of assets to the business by owners. It is important to distinguish carefully between such changes in owners' equity and changes that result from operating the business.

Owners' equity increases from revenues and from owners' investments

In Chapter 2 we noted that owners' equity is increased by earning revenue and decreased by incurring expenses. Earning revenue means an increase in net assets, and incurring expenses means a decrease in net assets. These changes in net assets are reflected on the equities side of the equation as changes in owners' equity.

From the accounting equation, you can see that if an asset increases without a corresponding decrease in another asset or a change in liabilities, capital must also increase. For example, assume that assets increase by $10. Then,

$$(A + \$10) - L = C + \$10$$

The $10 change on the right side of the equation is **revenue** if it is earned as a result of business operations. Revenue also occurs if a liability decreases without a corresponding change in another liability or in assets. For example,

$$A - (L - \$10) = C + \$10$$

To illustrate decreases in owners' equity, we again use the accounting equation:

$$A - L = C$$

We note that a change in one of the components on the left side of the equation, without any other changes on the same side, must have an equal effect on the right side of the equation. For example, if assets decrease by $7 without any change in other assets or in liabilities, capital must also decrease by $7 as follows:

$$(A - \$7) - L = C - \$7$$

Similarly, if liabilities increase by $7 without any other changes on the left side of the equation, capital must decrease.

$$A - (L + \$7) = C - \$7$$

Expenses decrease owners' equity

The $7 change on the right side of the equation, resulting from a decrease in assets or an increase in liabilities, is an **expense** if it occurs as a result of business operations. Owners' equity may also decrease as a result of distribution of assets to owners by the business. The two types of decreases must be carefully distinguished.

If business operations result in more revenues than expenses the business earns **net income.** If expenses exceed revenues the business incurs a **net loss.** Net income is the excess of revenues over expenses, and using the example above we have:

$$\text{Revenues} - \text{Expenses} = \text{Net income}$$
$$\$10 \quad - \quad \$7 \quad = \quad \$3$$

Businesses are operated in order to earn profits

In order to earn revenue, a business must usually incur expenses as well. If a business sells products, it must pay its salespeople. If it earns rent by providing office space to tenants, it must pay for maintenance and taxes on the property it owns and rents. Therefore, expenses are an essential part of earning revenue. Note that contributions by owners are not revenue, and dividends or drawings are not expenses of a business. Dividends are voluntary distributions to owners that decrease assets but do not generate revenue.

Revenues and expenses occur continuously during the life of a business, but the periodicity concept requires reporting of financial position and net income at regular time intervals. Note that net income is measured **over a period of time** and covers the interval between two balance sheets reported at different **points in time.** Every transaction changes the balance sheet in some way; net income is a summary of those transactions that change owners' equity as a result of operating the business.

THE ACCOUNTING SYSTEM

To trace the effect of transactions on accounts over a period of time, we now illustrate an accounting system by describing the operation of a business. The company used in our example is a small corporation, which we follow from its inception to the end of the first month of operations.

Illustrative Example of a Business Entity

For many years Robert Barewood worked as a cabinet maker for a small furniture manufacturing company. In his spare time, he pursued his hobby of refinishing antique furniture for his home. During the past few years, several friends who admired his work asked him to refinish items of furniture for them. When the number of such requests grew fairly large, Robert decided to quit his job and establish a furniture refinishing service. He withdrew some money from a savings account and started Barewood's Furniture Refinishing Company, which he organized as a corporation.

A number of events took place during the company's first month of operations. In almost every situation, the company's activities involve a financial transaction of some sort. Services are performed for a fee, cash changes hands, goods are exchanged, credit is extended, and so on. As a business owner, Robert has to keep track of the various transactions if he hopes to manage his business well and to determine how it is doing. To keep records properly, he needs to analyze each transaction, preferably as it occurs, to determine its effect on the accounting equation. He can keep track of changes in the accounting equation by recording the transactions in asset, liability, and capital accounts.

There are two sides to every transaction

You know from previous discussion that each transaction affects at least two accounts. Whenever one or more accounts is debited, one or more accounts must also be credited. This **dual aspect** of financial transactions must be reflected in the accounting records in order to maintain the equality of assets and equities. Any change in total assets is accompanied by a corresponding change in total equities. For example, if the company earns revenue, assets increase and capital also increases by the same amount—the accounting equation, A = E, remains in balance and the balance is maintained in the accounting records.

Businesses record the dual aspect of each transaction by maintaining a **double-entry accounting system.** Basically, this is a system that reflects the accounting equation of the business in its accounting records. In the double-entry system, the amount of money involved in each transaction is recorded twice—once as a debit and once as a credit.

We now analyze the transactions of Barewood's Furniture Refinishing Company for the month of March in detail and show the effect each transaction has on the asset, liability, and capital accounts that make up the balance sheet. At all times the analysis must meet the requirement that assets equal equities, and debits equal credits.

  a. On March 1 Robert Barewood opened a bank account for his business and deposited $5,000 of his personal funds in exchange for which he received shares of stock in his company.

The increase in cash is recorded as a debit in the Cash account. The cash is an asset belonging to the company. The owner's interest in the company's assets is recorded as a credit in the Capital Stock account. Only these two accounts have balances at this time. Visualize what the balance sheet of the company looks like.

Cash		Capital Stock	
a. 5,000			a. 5,000

  b. The company rented a small shop where Robert could operate his new business. The rent was $240 per month, and Robert paid the first 2 months' rent on March 1 by writing a check on the company's bank account.

The payment of rent is a reduction of the cash asset and is recorded by a credit in the Cash account. Prepaid rent is an asset that will be used up as time passes. As it is used it will become an expense. The increase in the Prepaid Rent account is recorded by a debit of $480.

Cash		Prepaid Rent	
a. 5,000	b. 480	b. 480	

  c. Arrangements were made on March 4 with the Plasticote Paint and Varnish Company to enable the firm to buy materials on open account, and Robert took delivery of materials costing $1,200. The bill required payment within 30 days.

The Materials asset account is debited to record the cost of materials. The company has an obligation to pay for the materials within 30 days, and this obligation is recorded by crediting a liability. The liability is the source of the materials asset. As with all transactions, the debit equals the credit; therefore, the accounts reflect the fact that assets equal equities.

Materials		Accounts Payable	
c. 1,200			c. 1,200

d. On March 7 the company bought lumber for $900 cash and also had a telephone installed in the shop. Two customers brought furniture to the shop for refinishing.

Lumber is classified as materials, and its acquisition requires a debit in the Materials account to indicate an increase in the asset. The corresponding decrease in cash is recorded by a credit in the Cash account. The remaining items on this date are not recorded in the accounting system. Ordering a telephone does not have any effect on either assets, liabilities, or owners' equity. Neither does the acquisition of future work for the firm. When the work on furniture is performed, the business will have earned some revenue. After the telephone is installed, the business will incur telephone expenses. But the aspects of these transactions that are recognized in accounting—the financial effects—will take place only in the future and do not affect the accounts now.

Cash				Materials	
a. 5,000	b.	480	c. 1,200		
	d.	900	d. 900		

e. On March 11 the company bought tools and equipment from Standard Machinery Corporation for $3,500. Robert paid $1,500 by check and signed a 20 day 14.4 percent note for the balance.

The accounting equation is always in balance

The equipment acquisition had two sources: the decrease in cash and the increase in a liability. The Equipment account is debited for the cost of equipment. The $3,500 debit must be matched by an equal amount of credits. Cash was reduced by $1,500 and is credited. The remaining credit of $2,000 is an increase in the Notes Payable, a liability. Although three accounts are affected by this transaction, the dollar amount of debits equals the dollar amount of credits. Assets had a net increase of $2,000 ($3,500 increase in equipment and $1,500 decrease in cash), and liabilities increased by $2,000, so the accounting equation is still in balance.

Cash				Equipment	
a. 5,000	b.	480	e. 3,500		
	d.	900			
	e.	1,500			

Notes Payable	
	e. 2,000

f. Robert needed a workbench for his shop but was too busy with his customers' projects to build one. He therefore hired a man to build the workbench. The man completed the job in 2 days, using up lumber and other materials that had cost $260. Robert paid the man $200 for his work. A similar workbench can be bought for $650.

This transaction affects only asset accounts. The business gave up some of its cash and materials in exchange for a workbench. The cost of the workbench is equal to the cost of the assets given up. Cash is reduced by a $200 credit, and the Materials account is reduced by a $260 credit. The workbench is classified as equipment, and the increase in the Equipment account is recorded by a debit of $460. Note that this transaction involves application of the cost concept. The fact that the company could have bought a similar workbench for $650 is not relevant in the analysis of the transaction that took place.

	Cash				Materials		
a.	5,000	b.	480	c.	1,200	f.	260
		d.	900	d.	900		
		e.	1,500				
		f.	200				

	Equipment	
e.	3,500	
f.	460	

g. Since more work was brought to the shop, Robert agreed to hire full-time the worker who built the workbench. He will be paid $850 per month to do sanding, paint stripping, and general cleaning in the shop, starting on March 18.

Hiring an employee is, in itself, not a financial transaction. An agreement has been made, but at this time no financial effects can be recorded.

h. By March 25 all the refinishing projects were completed. During the month Robert collected $1,280 cash from his customers and sent bills in the amount of $290 to Mrs. Brown and $400 to Mr. Hall. Both had open accounts with the company.

The receipt of cash is recorded by a debit in the Cash account, because cash increased by $1,280. Amounts owed by customers for completed work are assets and are debited to Accounts Receivable. Both the increase in cash and the increase in receivables resulted from the company performing services for customers and thereby earning revenue. The revenue in-

Revenues and expenses change the retained earnings account

creases owners' equity by $1,970 and is recorded by a credit in the Retained Earnings account. This is a new capital account used to record capital increases and decreases from operating the business. The increase in assets is accompanied by an increase in equities, leaving the accounting equation in balance.

Cash					Accounts Receivable	
a.	5,000	b.	480		h.	690
h.	1,280	d.	900			
		e.	1,500			
		f.	200			

Retained Earnings	
h.	1,970

    i. Robert made a $600 payment on his account with Plasticote on March 28.

    This transaction reduces both an asset and a liability. The debt owed to Plasticote is reduced by the $600 payment, and the decrease in cash is recorded by a credit in the Cash account. The decrease in the liability is recorded by a debit in Accounts Payable. Both sides of the accounting equation are reduced by an equal amount.

Cash					Accounts Payable			
a.	5,000	b.	480		i.	600	c.	1,200
h.	1,280	d.	900					
		e.	1,500					
		f.	200					
		i.	600					

    j. On March 29 the company received a check for $290 from Mrs. Brown in payment of her account.

    The receipt of a check from a customer increases cash and is recorded with a debit of $290 in the Cash account. The customer now no longer owes the money to the company, and the account receivable must be reduced. The decrease in Accounts Receivable is recorded by a credit of $290. There is no effect on equities from this transaction. Remember that revenue earned from this customer was already recorded in transaction *h* as an increase in Accounts Receivable and an increase in Retained Earnings.

	Cash					Accounts Receivable		
a.	5,000	b.	480		h.	690	j.	290
h.	1,280	d.	900					
j.	290	e.	1,500					
		f.	200					
		i.	600					

k. On March 30 the note to Standard Machinery was paid in full, including interest.

Interest is usually expressed in annual terms. Interest of 14.4 percent per year for 20 days on $2,000 is $16 ($2,000 × .144 × 20/360). Therefore, the amount of cash needed to discharge the obligation is $2,016 which is recorded by a credit to show the decrease in the Cash account. The Notes Payable liability is reduced by a debit of $2,000. Nothing is left in the account since the entire obligation has been repaid. The interest of $16 is an expense incurred for the use of the money. The expense is a reduction in owners' equity and is recorded by a debit in the retained earnings account. Each part of the equation A = L + C decreased, and the equation remains in balance.

	Cash					Notes Payable		
a.	5,000	b.	480		k.	2,000	e.	2,000
h.	1,280	d.	900					
j.	290	e.	1,500					
		f.	200					
		i.	600					
		k.	2,016					

	Retained Earnings		
k.	16	h.	1,970

l. By the end of the month, the company had used up lumber and other materials costing $470, in addition to the materials used to build the workbench.

The amount of materials used can be determined by counting the amount remaining at the end of the month. The reduction is recorded by a credit to the Materials account. The goods were used in the production of revenue and represent expenses for the business. Since expenses are decreases in owners' equity, they are recorded by debits in the Retained Earnings account.

Materials				Retained Earnings			
c.	1,200	f.	240	k.	16	h.	1,970
d.	900	l.	470	l.	470		

m. Bills for telephone and electricity for March were received in the amount of $90. Robert decided to pay these bills in April.

Expenses reduce owners' equity whether or not they are paid

Although the utility bills are not yet paid, they represent services that have been used during the month. It would not have been possible to operate the business and earn revenue without these services, and the eventual payment for the service will consume part of the cash asset. Using services is an expense in the month the benefit is obtained rather than at the time the bill is paid. Therefore, this $90 expense is recorded as a debit reducing owners' equity at this time. Since the services have already been used, the company has an obligation to pay for them. This obligation is recorded as an increase in Accounts Payable, which is credited for $90.

Accounts Payable				Retained Earnings			
i.	600	c.	1,200	k.	16	h.	1,970
		m.	90	l.	470		
				m.	90		

n. Robert gave a check for $425 to his employee.

Wages are expenses of operating a business. The company obtains services from the employee, and the expense is incurred over the period of employment but is usually recorded at the time it is paid. The payment reduces cash and is recorded as a credit in the Cash account. It also reduces owners' equity, and the same amount is recorded as a debit in the Retained Earnings account. As always, the accounting equation remains in balance.

Cash				Retained Earnings			
a.	5,000	b.	480	k.	16	h.	1,970
h.	1,280	d.	900	l.	470		
j.	290	e.	1,500	m.	90		
		f.	200	n.	425		
		i.	600				
		k.	2,016				
		n.	425				

o. Estimated life of the tools and equipment is 10 years. A full month's use is assumed for calculating depreciation.

The total cost of the equipment is $3,960. If the company is going to benefit from using the equipment for 10 years, it should recognize that a portion of the cost applies to each period. The company was able to earn its revenues by using the equipment, so depreciation is a necessary expense of operating the business. Since the equipment was used for 1 month and there are 120 months of expected useful life, the amount of asset cost assigned to each month is 1/120th of the cost, or $33. A new account is established in which accumulated depreciation is recorded. Depreciation decreases owners' equity each month that the equipment is in use. The credit of $33 recorded in the Accumulated Depreciation account is equal to the debit of $33 recorded as depreciation expense that decreases the Retained Earnings account. Together, the Equipment account and the Accumulated Depreciation account represent the equipment, one containing the original cost and the other the amount of cost used up. The Accumulated Depreciation contra asset account's credit balance is deducted from the asset account debit balance to arrive at the equipment's book value.

	Equipment			**Retained Earnings**		
e.	3,500		k.	16	h.	1,970
f.	460		l.	470		
			m.	90		
			n.	425		
			o.	33		

	Accumulated Depreciation	
	o.	33

p. At the end of the month, the corporation paid Robert $150 from the company's bank account as a dividend.

Distributions of assets to the owner reduce assets and also reduce owners' equity. However, such reductions are not expenses because they are not necessary for generating revenues. The credit to the Cash account records the reduction of cash and is matched by a corresponding debit in the Retained Earnings account. Because the business entity is a corporation, this reduction in retained earnings is called a dividend. The dividend can be paid because the company has a credit balance in retained earnings, indicating that it has earned income which may be distributed to the owner.

	Cash				Retained Earnings			
a.	5,000	b.	480	k.	16	h.	1,970	
h.	1,280	d.	900	l.	470			
j.	290	e.	1,500	m.	90			
		f.	200	n.	425			
		i.	600	o.	33			
		k.	2,016	p.	150			
		n.	425					
		p.	150					

q. Since a month had passed, half of the rent paid earlier was now used up.

A prepaid expense becomes an expense when it is used up

On March 1 the company paid rent for 2 months in advance. This was properly recorded as a prepaid expense. Now half this asset has been used up and no longer exists. It is therefore necessary to remove the portion used from the Prepaid Rent account by crediting the account $240. The expiration of this asset is recorded with a debit of $240 in the Retained Earnings account. Note that no transaction occurred at the end of the month because the rent was paid at the beginning of the month. Expenses should be recorded at the time they are incurred, regardless of the time of payment. It would be impractical to record the use of a prepaid expense day by day, however, and the one entry at the end of the month records the expense for the entire month.

	Prepaid Rent				Retained Earnings		
b.	480	q.	240	k.	16	1,970	
				l.	470		
				m.	90		
				n.	425		
				o.	33		
				p.	150		
				q.	240		

The trial balance is an accounting tool

The trial balance.   Although only 16 transactions have been recorded for the month, the accounts of the company have undergone many changes. Before a balance sheet for the company is prepared, it is convenient to determine whether the debit and credit equality has been maintained in the accounts. To do so we prepare a **trial balance,** which is a complete listing of the balances in all accounts. The trial balance is not a financial statement. It is simply a list which proves the equality of total debits and credits. If an error has been made in analyzing a transaction and the dollar amount of debits does not equal the dollar amount of credits, the trial balance will show an imbalance, which will make it necessary to locate the error. It is possible, of course, that debits equal credits in the accounts but that an amount was recorded in the wrong account. Other counterbalancing errors may have occurred, or entire transactions may have been omitted. The trial balance does not disclose these kinds of errors.

All the accounts of Barewood's Furniture Refinishing Company are shown in Figure 3-3 in which account balances have been calculated. The trial balance in Figure 3-4 is constructed from these account balances. It

Figure 3-3
In a double-entry accounting system, the collection of all accounts of a business should always be in balance.

Assets

Cash

a.	5,000	b.	480
h.	1,280	d.	900
j.	290	e.	1,500
		f.	200
		i.	600
		k.	2,016
		n.	425
		p.	150
Bal.	299		

Accounts Receivable

h.	690	j.	290
Bal.	400		

Materials

c.	1,200	f.	260
d.	900	l.	470
Bal.	1,370		

Prepaid Rent

b.	480	q.	240
Bal.	240		

Equipment

e.	3,500	
f.	460	
Bal.	3,960	

Accumulated Depreciation

	o.	33

Liabilities

Accounts Payable

i.	600	c.	1,200
		m.	90
		Bal.	690

Notes Payable

k.	2,000	e.	2,000

Owners' Equity

Capital Stock

	a.	5,000

Retained Earnings

k.	16	h.	1,970
l.	470		
m.	90		
n.	425		
o.	33		
p.	150		
q.	240		
		Bal.	546

**Barewood's Furniture Refinishing Company
Trial Balance
March 31, 1985**

	Debits	Credits
Cash	$ 299	
Accounts receivable	400	
Materials	1,370	
Prepaid rent	240	
Equipment	3,960	
Accumulated depreciation		$ 33
Accounts payable		690
Capital stock		5,000
Retained earnings		546
Totals	$6,269	$6,269

Figure 3-4
A trial balance is a list of all accounts and their balances, showing the balance of debits and credits. Accounts with zero balances are not included.

indicates that total debits equal total credits. Notice that the Notes Payable account is not included in the trial balance because its balance is zero.

Calculating the change in owners' equity.   The balance sheet for the company is presented in Figure 3-5. The Capital account has the original credit of $5,000 representing the owner's investment. The Retained Earnings account has a credit balance of $546. This account changed during the month as a result of business operations and the cash dividend paid to the owner. The amount of net income can be calculated by deducting all the expenses from total revenues for the month as recorded in the Retained Earnings account. The computation of net income follows on page 96.

**Barewood's Furniture Refinishing Company
Balance Sheet
March 31, 1985**

Assets			Liabilities and Owners' Equity		
Current assets:			Current liabilities:		
Cash	$ 299		Accounts payable		$ 690
Accounts receivable	400				
Materials	1,370		Owners equity:		
Prepaid rent	240		Capital stock	$5,000	
Total current assets		$2,309	Retained earnings	546	
Fixed assets:			Total capital		5,546
Equipment	3,960				
Less accumulated					
depreciation	33				
Total fixed assets		3,927	Total liabilities and		
Total assets		$6,236	owners' equity		$6,236

Figure 3-5   A balance sheet prepared from the accounts illustrated in Figure 3-3 and listed in the trial balance in Figure 3-4.

Total revenue		$1,970
Less expenses:		
Interest	$ 16	
Materials used	470	
Utilities	90	
Wages	425	
Depreciation	33	
Rent	240	
Total expenses		1,274
Net income		$ 696

Dividends are not expenses

Robert Barewood originally invested $5,000 cash in the business, and by the end of the month the business had earned $696 from operations. The company paid a $150 dividend, leaving a $546 net increase in total capital. The change in capital is shown in the following calculation:

Original investment		$5,000
Add net income	$696	
Less dividend	150	546
New capital balance		$5,546

The Business as a Sole Proprietorship

If Robert Barewood were to operate his business as a sole proprietorship, there would be some differences in accounting for owners' equity. For example, in return for his investment of $5,000 cash, the business entity would not issue stock to Barewood, and would maintain only one capital account for recording all changes in owners' equity.

Cash		Capital	
a. 5,000			a. 5,000

Other transactions are recorded the same way as already shown, until transaction *h*, which resulted in earning revenue. The entity records revenues and expenses in the Capital account instead of using a Retained Earnings account:

Cash		Accounts Receivable	
a. 5,000	b. 480	h. 690	
h. 1,280	d. 900		
	e. 1,500		
	f. 200		

	Capital
	a. 5,000
	h. 1,970

Proprietorships need only one capital account

Any expenses that previously affected the Retained Earnings account are recorded in the Capital account if the business is a sole proprietorship. For example, transactions *k, l,* and *m* cause the Capital account to change as follows:

Capital

k.	16	a.	5,000
l.	470	h.	1,970
m.	90		

The owner may withdraw assets from the business whether or not the business is profitable. Instead of recording a dividend in the Retained Earnings account as before, Barewood records withdrawals as a reduction of the Capital account. By the end of the accounting period, the owners' equity account appears as shown below. All other accounts are exactly the same as before.

Capital

k.	16	a.	5,000
l.	470	h.	1,970
m.	90		
n.	425		
o.	33		
p.	150		
q.	240		
		Bal.	5,546

Note that total owners' equity is still $5,546, and net income of the business is $696, just as before. In the balance sheet, the owners' equity section would appear as a single account, with the rest of the balance sheet identical to the one shown in Figure 3-5.

ECONOMIC RELATIONSHIP OF THE ACCOUNTING EQUATION

Financial statements are meaningful and useful because the accounting rules on which they are based are known and generally accepted by the business community and users of accounting information. The accounting equation applies not only to business entities that prepare financial statements, but also to individuals, governments, and the entire economy.

Figure 3-6 illustrates parts of balance sheets for a number of entities, including individuals, businesses, and governments, Note the relationship among the various assets and equities. The Account Payable of Able Corporation is an Account Receivable of Baker Company. Baker Company owns investments in the common stock of Security Bank, which the bank reports as owners' equity. A note receivable reported by the bank as an asset is the liability of Tom Jones, who borrowed the money to finance the purchase of an automobile. Tom Jones owns stock in Able Corporation. This is reported in his balance sheet as an asset and is an equity in Able Corporation's statement. Able Corporation owes income taxes reported in its balance sheet as taxes payable. This is a tax receivable for the United States government. The government's obligations, reported as bonds payable, are owned by Security Bank which reports them as an asset. The government's salaries payable liability is due to its employee Bob Smith, who has a corresponding salary receivable.

The accounting equation of the economy is in balance

As we follow such examples in the economy, we see that there is a great deal of double counting. The assets of some entities are the equities of others. Tom Jones' ownership of Able Corporation stock is really his indirect ownership of part of Able Corporation's assets. The accounting equation theoretically balances throughout the economy. When the double counting is eliminated, we see that the worldly goods in the economy

Figure 3-6 In a free enterprise economy, all balance sheets are related and the entire economy maintains a theoretical balance among accounts.

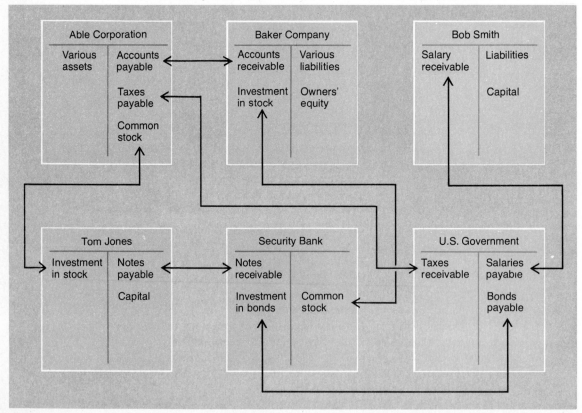

really exist for the benefit of individuals in a society. Businesses and other organizations are only intermediaries through which benefits are passed on to people in the form of payments such as rents, salaries, interest, and distributions of profits.

SUMMARY

The balance sheet presents the financial position of a business at a point in time. Business organizations are considered to be **going concerns** that will continue to operate indefinitely. This **continuity assumption** leads to the **periodicity** concept in accounting. The life of a business is divided into **accounting periods** so that timely financial reports can be provided. At the end of each period, financial statements are presented. The most common accounting period is 1 year, which may be a **calendar year** or a **fiscal year.**

The balance sheet reports the cost of assets, because costs can be objectively determined and are considered relevant for a going concern. In applying the accounting equation, accountants assume that the business is an **entity** separate from its owners, and only the affairs of the business are reported in financial statements.

Balance sheet accounts may be classified into groups of similar items so that the information provided is meaningful. The following categories of assets, liabilities, and owners' equity are usually reported by corporations:

Assets	**Liabilities**
Current assets	Current liabilities
Investments	Long-term liabilities
Fixed assets	Other liabilities
Intangible assets	**Owners' Equity**
Other assets	Contributed capital
	Retained earnings

If the business entity is not a corporation, the owners' equity section of the balance sheet usually lists one capital account for each owner, indicating the owners' entire interest in the business.

Current assets and **current liabilities** are classifications of assets and obligations used in one **operating cycle** of the business. **Working capital** is defined as current assets less current liabilities. The **current ratio** is defined as current assets divided by current liabilities. These measures provide information on the liquidity of the business and are examples of information contained in the balance sheet but not found in the individual accounts.

The owners' equity of a business can increase as a result of earnings or from the investment of owners. It can decrease as a result of expenses or the distribution of assets to owners. Distributions by corporations to their shareholders are called **dividends.** If the business is not a corporation, distributions to owners are called **drawings.** Dividends and drawings are **not** expenses because they do not contribute to the generation of revenues.

In the **double-entry accounting system**, every transaction has a **dual** effect on the accounting records. The equality of the accounting equation is always maintained in the accounting records by recording an equal amount of debits and credits for each transaction.

At the end of an accounting period, the balances in all accounts are found and listed in a **trial balance**, which shows whether or not debits equal credits. A trial balance is usually taken prior to preparation of financial statements.

The accounting equation is a universal concept and applies to the entire economy. One entity's equities are another entity's assets. The balance sheet represents the accounting equation of an entity, but it is only one of several financial statements prepared to provide complete financial information.

KEY TERMS   Much new terminology is introduced in this chapter. The list below consists of terms that you should understand before proceeding to the next chapter. Other new terms introduced in this chapter are discussed more thoroughly in later chapters.

accounting period *(74)*
book value *(78)*
capital stock *(79)*
continuity *(74)*
contra asset *(78)*
contributed capital *(79)*
current assets *(76)*
current liabilities *(78)*
current ratio *(82)*
depreciation *(77)*
dividend *(79)*
double-entry system *(85)*
drawings *(80)*

fiscal year *(74)*
fixed assets *(77)*
generally accepted accounting principles (GAAP) *(74)*
going concern *(74)*
intangible assets *(78)*
liquidity *(76)*
operating cycle *(76)*
periodicity *(74)*
retained earnings *(79)*
trial balance *(93)*
working capital *(82)*

QUESTIONS

1. Discuss how the cost concept and the going concern concept are related.

2. What does the accounting concept of periodicity mean?

3. The entity concept means that the affairs of the business are not mixed with the affairs of the owners. When is an owner also an accounting entity?

4. Why does the balance sheet contain more information than can be found in all the separate individual accounts?

5. Describe the meaning of the operating cycle. Why do most companies use an operating cycle of 1 year?

6. What is a contra asset? Why is it so called?

7. Define working capital and the current ratio.

8. What is contributed capital? In a partnership balance sheet, the classification contributed capital does not exist. Does that mean that there is no contributed capital in partnerships?

9. Who is the residual equity holder in a sole proprietorship? What is meant by the term "residual"?

10. What is the difference between dividends and drawings? What is their effect on owners' equity? On assets? On liabilities?

11. What is the difference between expenses and prepaid expenses? Where are prepaid expenses reported?

12. What is meant by the dual aspect of business transactions? How is the dual aspect reflected in the accounting records?

13. Describe the capital accounts of a corporation, and compare them to the capital accounts of a partnership. Why does each partner have a separate capital account?

EXERCISES

Ex. 3-1 **Calculation of current ratio and working capital.**   The current accounts from the balance sheets of Barber Tool Company and Schaver Blades, Inc., are shown below:

	Barber	Schaver
Current assets:		
Cash	$ 780	$ 790
Temporary Investments	1,000	950
Notes receivable	400	190
Accounts receivable	1,802	1,050
Merchandise inventory	800	1,036
Prepaid expenses	250	950
Current liabilities:		
Notes payable	600	1,170
Taxes payable	320	320
Accounts payable	970	1,360
Salaries payable	760	970

Required:
  a. Calculate the current ratio and the amount of working capital for each company.
  b. Discuss which company will find it easier to meet its current obligations. State your reasons.

Ex. 3-2 **Simple balance sheet for a partnership.**   Bill and Jane decided to form a partnership and open a lemonade stand. They each invested $5 and agreed to share profits equally. They bought lemons for $5 and sugar for $3. Jane built a stand from materials she found, and Bill made the lemonade. By the end of the day, they had sold three-quarters of their lemonade and planned to sell the rest the next day. They found that they had a total of $9.60 in cash, and Bill's father still owed them $.40 for lemonade he had bought.

Required: Prepare a balance sheet for the partnership at the end of the day.

Ex. 3-3   **Retained Earnings account.**   Burry Corporation constructs underground storage tanks. It has credit balances of $120,000 in its Capital Stock account and $40,000 in its Retained Earnings account at the end of June 1985. During July it earned revenues of $67,000, of which $32,000 was collected in cash. Salaries were $17,500, and materials used in construction of tanks cost $23,400. The company bought land for $9,000 and paid dividends of $3,000 in July.

Required:
  a.   Establish a Retained Earnings T account for the company and enter the beginning balance.
  b.   Record the July revenues, expenses, and dividends in the Retained Earnings account and find the ending balance.

Ex. 3-4   **Changes in capital of a sole proprietorship.**   Joan Peterson operates a beauty shop. The credit balance in her owners' equity account at the beginning of May was $14,800. During the month she collected revenues in the amount of $10,300 and paid $4,500 of salaries. Rent and utilities were $350 and $120, respectively. Interest expense of $80 was paid in cash, and Joan withdrew $1,500 from the business.

Required:
  a.   Set up the owners' equity account at the beginning of May and record the above information.
  b.   Calculate the net income for the month.

Ex. 3-5   **Working capital and current ratio.**   The current assets and current liabilities taken from the balance sheets of three companies are presented below:

	Company		
	A	B	C
Current assets:			
Cash	$2,460	$1,640	$10,200
Temporary investments		3,500	7,900
Accounts receivable	3,780	3,650	12,650
Merchandise inventory	8,860	4,300	16,760
Prepaid expenses	2,900	910	3,490
Current liabilities:			
Notes payable	3,500	3,400	1,900
Accounts payable	2,740	1,980	7,380
Taxes payable	1,000	600	4,200
Rent payable	1,200		300
Salaries payable	560	1,020	

Required:
    a. Compute working capital and the current ratio for each company.
    b. Discuss each company's ability to meet its current obligation and comment on their current ratios.

Ex. 3-6   **Changes in the accounting equation.** Following are transactions undertaken by a corporation which was established in January:

    a. Shareholders invest $15,000 cash in the business and receive shares of common stock from the company.
    b. The company bought land for $4,000 cash plus a $13,000 mortgage.
    c. Merchandise is bought on open account for $3,000.
    d. Equipment is obtained in exchange for $9,000 of preferred stock.
    e. $3,200 is paid on the mortgage, including $200 interest.
    f. The land bought in **b** is sold for $17,000 cash.
    g. The mortgage on the land, plus $150 interest, is paid with the cash obtained from the land sale.
    h. Services are performed for $7,000, of which $2,500 is on open account.
    i. Accounts receivable of $500 are collected.
    j. $1,500 of dividends are paid in cash.
    k. Salaries of $2,400 are paid in cash.
    l. $1,000 is paid on accounts payable.

Required: Prepare a schedule as illustrated below. For each transaction indicate the effect on assets, liabilities, and owners' equity. The first transaction is given as an example.

Transactions	Assets	=	Liabilities	+	Owners' Equity
a. Common stock issued for cash	+$15,000				+$15,000

Ex. 3-7   **Dual aspect of business transactions.** Below is a list of transactions, each of which affects two accounts.

    a. The owner invests personal money in a sole proprietorship.
        Debit—Cash
        Credit—Owners' Equity
    b. The business borrows money from a bank and gives the bank a note.
    c. Equipment is purchased on open account.
    d. A building is purchased and the price is paid by check.
    e. Supplies are bought for cash.
    f. An account payable is paid by check.
    g. The owner withdraws money from the business.
    h. Services are performed for cash.
    i. Salary is paid to an employee.

    j.   An account receivable is collected.

    k.   Services are performed on account.

    l.   Equipment is acquired in exchange for land.

Required: For each transaction indicate which account is debited and which is credited. Always indicate first the account debited. The first transaction is solved as an example.

Ex. 3-8   **Understanding the accounting equation.** Benson Corporation, a manufacturer of mechanical adding machines, is going out of business. It has $5,000 cash. The owners' equity section of the balance sheet appears below.

Owners' equity:	
Common stock, 40,000 shares	$ 7,000
Retained earnings	1,000
Total capital	8,000
Total liabilities and owners' equity	$17,000

In preparation for terminating operations of the company, all the noncash assets are sold for two-thirds of their book value, and all the liabilities are paid off.

Required:
    a.   Calculate the amount of cash available for distribution to shareholders when the company is liquidated.
    b.   How much money will the owner of 100 shares of stock receive when the company is liquidated?

Ex. 3-9   **Dual aspect of business transactions.** Below is a list of independent transactions, each affecting at least two accounts of a corporation.

    a.   Equipment is purchased, half with cash and half on account.
        Debit—Equipment
        Credit—Cash
        Credit—Accounts Payable

    b.   Stock is issued to shareholders for cash.

    c.   An account receivable is collected.

    d.   Merchandise is bought on open account.

    e.   Rent expense is paid in cash.

    f.   Land is sold for cash at a profit.

    g.   A cash dividend is paid.

    h.   A piece of equipment and cash are received in exchange for land.

    i.   A patent is bought, and a 60-day note is given to the seller in payment.

    j.   Services are performed for customers, half for cash and half on open account.

    k.   A note is paid with cash including principal and interest.

    l.   The patent is sold for cash, at a price less than it cost.

Required: For each transaction indicate the accounts to be debited and credited. Always show first the accounts debited. The first transaction is solved as an example.

Ex. 3-10 **Changes in the capital account of a sole proprietorship.** Fred operates a TV repair shop. The balance of his Capital account on April 1 is $1,100. The following transactions took place in April:

    a. Parts are purchased for $670 on open account.

    b. Customers are billed $5,540 for work performed in April.

    c. Employees are paid $2,350 for wages.

    d. Accounts payable of $420 are paid by check.

    e. Equipment is bought for $300 cash.

    f. Gasoline used during April cost $160.

    g. Fred withdrew $850 from the business.

    h. Customers paid $2,020 on accounts receivable.

    i. Electronic parts used in April cost $440.

    j. Used $2,000 cash to buy temporary investments.

    k. Performed services for $400 cash.

Required:
    a. Set up Fred's Capital account, enter the beginning balance, and enter the transactions that affected the account.
    b. Calculate net income for April and the balance of the Capital account at the end of April.

Ex. 3-11 **Partnership capital.** Joyce and John formed a partnership to operate a clothing store. Joyce contributed $12,000 cash, and John contributed $14,000 cash, but they agreed to share profits equally. The store opened on April 1. Below are summaries of the first 3 months of operations:

April	Revenues	$4,780
	Expenses	6,900
	Joyce, drawings	450
	John, drawings	600
May	Revenues	6,750
	Expenses	5,450
	Joyce, drawings	500
	John, drawings	425
June	Revenues	7,360
	Expenses	5,220
	Joyce, additional investment	1,500
	John, drawings	270

Required: Set up a capital account for each partner and enter each month's revenues, expenses, drawings, and investments. Calculate the balance in each account at the end of each month.

Ex. 3-12 **Trial balance.** Following in alphabetical order are accounts and account balances of Copler Company on June 30, 1985:

Accounts payable	$2,060
Accounts receivable	950
Accumulated depreciation	2,300
Allowance for uncollectible accounts	60
Capital stock	2,400
Cash	430
Equipment	7,500
Merchandise	2,500
Mortgage payable	4,270
Notes payable, current	1,800
Patents	2,500
Retained earnings	990

Required: Prepare a trial balance for the company.

Ex. 3-13 **Balance sheet preparation.** Refer to the data in Exercise 3-12 about Copler Company.

Required: Prepare a classified balance sheet for the company.

Ex. 3-14 **Solving a cash-shortage problem.** Bob and Emily are partners operating a small flower and plant shop. They have a number of steady customers who buy on open account, although some sales are for cash. The store is profitable, but it always seems to be short of cash and the partners sometimes have difficulty meeting their payables on time. "What we need is an increase in sales," Bob said one day. "Let's advertise some specials at reduced prices next week and build up a cash reserve so that we're not always short of working capital." Emily thought this was a good idea and said, "I'll order the additional inventory we'll need for the sale, and you arrange for the advertising. We'll also need to hire some part-time help for the extra volume."

The sale was successful, but at the end of the week, Bob and Emily found that, despite the profit increase from the sale, they had even more trouble meeting their current obligations.

Required: Discuss the possible reasons the increase in sales did not help solve the problems of the business.

Ex. 3-15 **Preparations of trial balance.** Fredrick Lawson operates a legal practice in a small town. Following is a list of accounts and account balances, in alphabetical order, taken from the company's books on October 31, 1985:

Accounts payable	$ 2,490
Accounts receivable	5,120
Accumulated depreciation, library	3,050
Accumulated depreciation, furniture	2,690
Advances from clients	5,080
Advances to employees	370

Capital, Lawson	$37,600
Cash	6,830
Furniture and equipment	6,270
Notes payable, long term	21,470
Office supplies	790
Pension investment, cash value	33,500
Professional library	18,750
Rent deposit	750

Required: Arrange the above data into a trial balance. (*Hint*: Advances from clients are current liabilities.)

Ex. 3-16   **Balance sheet preparation.**   Refer to the list of accounts and account balances in Exercise 3-15.

Required: Prepare a classified balance sheet for the business on October 31, 1985. (*Hint*: Advances from clients are current liabilities.)

PROBLEMS

P. 3-1   **Working capital and current ratio analysis.**   Following is part of the consolidated balance sheet of Chronology Reflector Company as reported in the company's annual report to shareholders. The company is engaged in newspaper publishing, newsprint and forest products operations, book publishing, information services, and broadcasting.

Chronology Reflector Company and Subsidiaries
Consolidated Balance Sheet
(In thousands of dollars)

Assets	December 31 1985	December 31 1984
Current assets:		
Cash	$ 22,548	$ 19,783
Marketable securities	4,607	83,536
Accounts receivable, less allowance for doubtful accounts (1985: $31,578; 1984: $27,903)	245,785	225,164
Inventories	133,285	130,964
Prepaid expenses	37,330	27,304
Total current assets	$443,555	$486,751

Liabilities		
Current liabilities:		
Accounts payable	$162,069	$135,720
Employees' compensation	43,225	36,738
Income taxes	23,344	40,312
Other taxes	9,949	7,723
Dividends payable	12,219	10,166
Current portion of long-term debt	24,886	8,288
Total current liabilities	$275,692	$238,947

Required:
  a. Compute the company's working capital for the 2 years.
  b. Compute the company's current ratio for the 2 years.
  c. Compute the amount of accounts receivable actually owed to the company by its customers.
  d. Discuss the change in your findings from one year to the next and the company's ability to meet its current obligations.

P. 3-2   **Balance sheet preparation.**   James Norbeck, owner of Norbeck Chemical Company, a sole proprietorship, has just hired a new treasurer and asked him to prepare a statement of financial position for the company. Norbeck needs the statement to show to the bank when he applies for a loan. The treasurer came up with the following:

Norbeck Chemical Company
September 30, 1985

Accumulated depreciation	$ 53,470
Cash	21,490
Owed to suppliers	27,650
Due from customers	53,720
Note payable to Clemson Bank	48,000
Machinery	51,550
Chemicals on hand for sale	84,960
Land	54,000
Note payable to State Bank	117,000
Building	198,660
Office furniture and equipment	11,250
Note payable to Wright Bank	26,900
Mortgage payable	70,000
Supplies on hand	9,240
Note receivable from Hirt Company	30,500
Total	$858,390

The treasurer proudly reported that the company had gone well beyond the three-quarter-million-dollar mark. After Norbeck fired him he hires you to take over the position. You discover that the note payable to the Wright Bank is long term, the accounts listed are correct, and temporary investments of $18,000 are not included in the list.

Required: Rearrange the above summary into a statement of financial position. Add the owner's capital account to complete the statement.

P. 3-3   Balance sheet preparation.   The bookkeeper of Malone Corporation was asked to prepare a balance sheet and he offered the following:

Malone Corporation
Statement of Account Balances
December 31, 1985

Debits		Credits	
Cash	$ 25,740	Notes payable	$ 26,390
Accounts receivable	15,640	Accounts payable	28,490
Notes receivable	15,300	Taxes payable	14,350
Merchandise	49,560	Allowance for doubtful	
Temporary investments	10,000	accounts	350
Land	34,500	Bonds payable, long-term	40,000
Equipment	47,550	Accumulated depreciation	13,150
Patents	9,900	Mortgage payable	15,260
		Deferred credits	900
		Common stock	15,000
		Retained earnings	54,300
Total debits	$208,190	Total credits	$208,190

Required: Recast the above information into a balance sheet.

P. 3-4   Preparation of a classified balance sheet.   Boyd Corporation was organized on June 1, 1985. It issued common stock to its shareholders in exchange for $150,000 cash. The company used $50,000 cash to buy land and buildings at a total cost of $125,000, giving a 10-year mortgage for the balance. $25,000 of the purchase price is assigned to the land. The company bought equipment for $35,000, paying $5,000 cash and a 90-day note for the balance. It bought merchandise for $120,000, paying ⅓ cash and ⅔ on open account. Merchandise costing $14,000 was sold for $22,000 cash. The above events took place in the first week of the company's existence.

Required:
   a.   Prepare a balance sheet for the company at the end of the week.
   b.   Compute the company's working capital and current ratio.

P. 3-5   Balance sheet preparation.   Listed below in alphabetical order are the accounts and account balances of Hovell and Schakke Construction Company, a partnership, on August 31, 1985.

Accounts payable	$12,550
Accounts receivable	6,900
Accumulated depreciation	8,750
Bank loan payable, long-term	6,000
Building and equipment	44,140
Capital, Hovell	17,715
Capital, Schakke	18,535
Cash	9,530
Franchise	2,000
Interest payable	380

Continued

Land	9,860
Mortgage payable	17,600
Note payable to Schakke	8,500
Notes receivable	14,320
Receivable from officers	200
Temporary investments	4,500
Wages payable	1,420

Required:
a. Use the data to prepare a properly classified balance sheet for the company in good accounting form. (*Hint:* Total assets = $82,700)
b. Compute the company's working capital and current ratio.

P. 3-6   **Business operations.**   Below is the trial balance of Bensen Corporation on July 31, 1985, and also a list of transactions that took place in August 1985.

Bensen Corporation
Trial Balance
July 31, 1985

	Debits	Credits
Cash	$13,820	
Accounts receivable	14,230	
Supplies	1,150	
Equipment	24,000	
Accumulated depreciation		$11,500
Accounts payable		13,600
Installment note payable		14,000
Common stock		5,000
Retained earnings		9,100
Totals	$53,200	$53,200

August transactions:
a. Bought equipment for $4,000 cash.
b. Received $8,600 cash for services performed in August.
c. Bought supplies for $2,000 cash.
d. Collected $4,500 of accounts receivable.
e. Billed customers $3,800 for services performed in August and not yet collected.
f. Paid August and September rent, $900 total.
g. Paid August salaries, $5,850.

h. Paid $3,500 on accounts payable and $160 for utilities.

i. Received a bill for $800 for legal services performed for the company in August.

j. Paid $360 installment on note, including $60 interest.

k. Used supplies costing $890.

l. Depreciation for August is $380.

Required:

a. Establish a T account for each item in the trial balance.

b. Record the August transactions in the T accounts. Establish new accounts if necessary.

c. Find the balances of the accounts.

d. Prepare a trial balance on August 31.

P. 3-7   Partnership balance sheet from a trial balance.   The trial balance of Black and White Company, a partnership, is provided below.

Black and White Company
Trial Balance
August 31, 1985

	Debits	Credits
Cash	$ 90,450	
Accounts receivable	331,200	
Estimated uncollectible accounts		$ 6,300
Merchandise inventory	432,940	
Life insurance cash value	13,500	
Retirement fund	65,000	
Equipment	165,600	
Accumulated depreciation, equipment		41,160
Buildings	168,360	
Accumulated depreciation, buildings		37,950
Land	55,890	
Notes payable		248,900
Accounts payable		342,330
Salaries payable		10,800
Loan payable, due 1989		100,000
Capital, Black		286,340
Capital, White		249,160
	$1,322,940	$1,322,940

Required: Prepare a properly classified balance sheet for the partnership on August 31, 1985.

P. 3-8   **Balance sheet from a corporation's trial balance.**   The following trial balance was taken from the books of Chromatica Company.

Chromatica Company
Trial Balance
December 31, 1985

	Debits	Credits
Cash	$ 75,950	
Temporary investments	25,000	
Accounts receivable	230,200	
Less estimated uncollectible accounts		$ 5,800
Merchandise inventory	402,900	
Supplies	8,600	
Common stock investment, long-term	23,500	
Retirement fund	85,000	
Land	40,000	
Buildings	160,500	
Less accumulated depreciation		37,900
Equipment	165,600	
Less accumulated depreciation		41,200
Notes payable		130,000
Accounts payable		220,300
Salaries payable		44,750
Mortgage payable		96,800
Common stock		300,000
Retained earnings		340,500
Totals	$1,217,250	$1,217,250

Required: Prepare a classified balance sheet on December 31, 1985.

P. 3-9   **Balance sheet from incomplete records.**   On July 2, 1985 Willy Frandic invests $8,000 to start an appliance repair service. By the end of July he finds that he has only $5,000 cash. Willy has kept records of all cash payments and disbursements and, thinking the business has not done well, he prepares the following statement and asks you to tell him what the business is accomplishing.

Willy's Appliance Service
Balance Sheet
July 31, 1985

Assets		Equities	
Cash	$ 5,000	Note payable	$ 6,000
Equipment	7,000	Owners' equity	6,000
Total assets	$12,000	Total equities	$12,000

While examining his checkbook, you find the following information:

Date			Checks	Deposits
July	2	Investment by owner		$8,000
	2	Three months' rent	$ 900	
	5	Bought supplies	380	
	11	Telephone service	80	
	19	Withdrawal by Frandic	650	
	24	Cash from customers		1,200
	26	Wages to part-time help	910	
	30	Bought equipment for $7,000	1,000	
	30	Cleaning services	280	
	31	Balance		$5,000

In addition, you find that the company has billed customers for services in the amount of $1,700 which has not yet been collected and has bills from suppliers for purchases of supplies of $100 which is still owed. There are unused supplies on hand that cost $290.

Required:

    a. Prepare a revised balance sheet for the company, taking into account all available data.

    b. Explain to the owner how much income he earned in July.

    c. Show a calculation to explain the change in owners' equity.

P. 3-10   **Balance sheet from cash records.**   After investing $10,000 in a television repair business, Orville Bailey found that he had only $3,300 cash at the end of June, his first month of operations. Thinking that perhaps he made a mistake starting the business, he asks you for advice about quitting. He shows you the following checkbook records:

Date			Checks	Deposits
June	1	Investment by owner		$10,000
	3	Bought equipment for $8,000	$2,500	
	3	Rent on workshop for 3 months	1,200	
	4	Bought supplies	900	
	10	Collected from customers		850
	14	Bought insurance for 1 year	2,400	
	18	Wages for part-time help	950	
	20	Withdrawal by owner	600	
	24	Collected from customers		1,400
	27	Utility bills	180	
	28	Cleaning services	220	
	31	Balance		$ 3,300

In addition to the checkbook record, you find that Orville has billed customers for services in the amount of $1,950 which has not yet been collected and that he owes $300 for purchases of supplies. An inventory shows that supplies costing $430 are on hand. The unpaid portion of the equipment is a 60-day open account. Depreciation on the equipment for the month is $80.

Required:
a. Prepare a balance sheet for the company at the end of June, taking into account all available data.
b. Explain to the owner how much income he earned in June.

P. 3-11   **Classified balance sheet.**   The following trial balance was taken from the books of the Wyoming Banana Plantation.

Wyoming Banana Plantation
Balance Sheet
October 31, 1985

	Debits	Credits
Cash	$ 395,470	
Temporary investments	89,830	
Accounts receivable	245,610	
Allowance for doubtful accounts		$ 8,000
Receivables from employees	3,000	
Merchandise inventory	954,360	
Supplies	194,430	
Prepaid insurance	17,170	
Office equipment	852,000	
Accumulated depreciation		360,500
Processing equipment	1,705,260	
Accumulated depreciation		580,830
Buildings	2,100,760	
Accumulated depreciation		753,360
Land	2,908,800	
Notes payable		315,310
Accounts payable		814,600
Wages payable		45,670
Interest payable		38,420
Notes payable, due 3/31/90		500,000
Bonds payable, 9%, due 1999		2,100,000
Common stock		2,500,000
Retained earnings		1,450,000
Totals	$9,466,690	$9,466,690

Required:
a. Use the data in the trial balance to prepare a classified balance sheet.
b. Compute the company's working capital and current ratio on October 31.

P. 3-12 **Business operations and balance sheets.** Below is a trial balance taken from the books of Rainbow Painters on May 31, 1985. The company is operated as a sole proprietorship. In addition, a summary of the company's June 1985 transactions is provided.

Rainbow Painters
Trial Balance
May 31, 1985

	Debits	Credits
Cash	$ 2,369	
Accounts receivable from customers	3,630	
Paint	1,856	
Equipment	2,670	
Accumulated depreciation, equipment		$ 400
Trucks	9,030	
Accumulated depreciation, trucks		3,780
Accounts payable to suppliers		1,504
Installment note payable		5,150
Capital, Jones		8,721
Totals	$19,555	$19,555

June transactions:

June   5 Purchased paint for $294 cash.

7 Purchased gasoline for $48. All the gasoline was used in June.

7 Used paint costing $730.

10 Billed customers $2,430 for work performed in June.

13 Collected $1,860 owed by customers on account.

20 Paid $280 for June installment on note owed to bank, including $80 interest.

25 Purchased new equipment for $600 cash.

26 Used paint costing $364.

27 Paid $350 owed to suppliers.

27 Billed customers $987 for work done in June.

28 Paid employee $702 cash for wages.

28 Collected $690 of accounts receivable.

30 Depreciation expense for June is $200 on the truck and $70 on the equipment.

30 Jones withdrew $300 from the business for personal use.

Required:
   a. Prepare a balance sheet on May 31, 1985.
   b. Set up T accounts, enter the beginning balances, and enter the June transactions.
   c. Prepare a balance sheet on June 30, 1985.

P. 3-13   **Business operations and the balance sheet.**   George Vickers operates a tree pruning and cutting service as a sole proprietor. Below is his company's balance sheet on May 31, 1985 and a description of June transactions.

Vickers Pruning and Cutting
Balance Sheet
May 31, 1985

Assets

Current assets:		
Cash	$ 5,920	
Accounts receivable	2,340	
Supplies	1,300	
Prepaid insurance	1,100	$10,660
Fixed assets:		
Equipment and trucks	24,540	
Accumulated depreciation	9,560	14,980
Total assets		$25,640

Liabilities and Capital

Current liabilities:		
Accounts payable	$ 2,810	
Taxes payable	210	$ 3,020
Long-term liabilities:		
Installment notes payable		14,040
Total liabilities		17,060
Capital, Vickers		8,580
Total liabilities and capital		$25,640

June transactions:

June 3 The company bought a used truck for $8,500, paying $1,500 cash and a 15 percent installment note for the balance.

5 Supplies costing $50 were used on a job removing dead branches from several trees on a private estate.

6 A two-way radio was installed in the new truck for $200 cash.

7 Billed customer $380 for branch removal.

10 Paid $130 cash for truck repairs.

11 Paid $2,280 of accounts payable.

12 The company contracted to remove from a park several trees that had been uprooted by a tornado. Supplies costing $450 were used on the job.

14 Wood removed from the park was sold as firewood for $980 cash.

17 The park was billed $2,700 for tree removal.

18 Supplies costing $700 were purchased on open account.

20 Accounts receivable of $2,190 were collected.

24 A tree was removed from a construction site to make room for a new home. The company collected $400 for the job and sold the tree trunk to a veneer manufacturer for $900 cash.

26 Paid $80 cash for utilities.

28 The owner withdrew $1,000 cash from the business.
29 Paid employees $2,100 wages for June.
29 Depreciation expense on trucks and equipment for June is $260. Insurance expense for June is $100.
30 Mailed checks for $930 in payment of installment notes, including $230 interest.

Required:
   a. Establish a T account for each item in the balance sheet and enter the beginning balances.
   b. Enter the June transactions in the T accounts and find the ending balance of each account.
   c. Prepare a trial balance at the end of June.
   d. Prepare a classified balance sheet on June 30.

P. 3-14   **Business operations and the balance sheet.**   The Everts Landscaping Company performs gardening and landscaping services. The company's balance sheet on April 30, 1985, and a list of May transactions are provided below:

Everts Landscaping Company
Balance Sheet
April 30, 1985

Assets

Current assets:		
Cash	$ 9,860	
Accounts receivable	2,480	
Supplies	2,180	
Prepaid insurance	1,240	$15,760
Fixed assets:		
Vehicles and equipment	24,840	
Accumulated depreciation	10,800	14,040
Total assets		$29,800

Liabilities and Capital

Current liabilities:		
Accounts payable	$ 1,920	
Wages payable	120	
Notes payable, current portion	3,600	$ 5,640
Long-term liabilities:		
Notes payable	17,640	
Less current portion	3,600	14,040
Total liabilities		19,680
Capital:		
Common stock		2,000
Retained earnings		8,120
Total liabilities and capital		$29,800

May transactions:

May   1 Employees are paid $120 owed to them from last month.
      2 $1,120 of accounts payable are paid in cash.
      6 Supplies costing $1,480 are purchased on account.
      7 Customers are billed $1,940 for work done in May.
      8 Accounts receivable of $3,060 are collected.
      9 The entire balance of accounts payable is paid in cash.
     13 Paid Gomez Garage $120 in cash, of which $40 is for gasoline and the remainder for repairs.
     15 New equipment is purchased for $260 on account.
     16 Salaries and wages are paid in cash, $1,660.
     16 Customers are billed $1,740 for work done in May.
     20 An employee drove the company truck over a piece of new equipment, destroying an item that had cost $560. He refuses to pay for the damage and is fired.
     22 Supplies are purchased for $1,360 cash.
     23 A check of $260 is sent to supplier on account.
     27 Accounts receivable of $760 are collected.
     31 Depreciation expense for May is $760.
     31 Cost of unused supplies is $2,300. Insurance that had cost $140 has expired.
     31 Installment payments are made on the current portions of the notes payable, $840, which includes $260 interest.
     31 The company paid a $1,000 cash dividend to its owners.

Required:
   a. Enter the April 30 balances in T accounts, and record the May transactions. Find the ending balances.
   b. Prepare a trial balance and a balance sheet on May 31, 1985.
   c. Calculate the amount of net income for May.

Case 3-1   **Analysis of current assets and liabilities.**
The accompanying balance sheets are taken from the annual report of Peako Instrument Corporation which operates subsidiaries in power supply, semiconductor, and industrial equipment industries. The statements contain several items that you will study in later chapters.

Required:
   a. Compute the company's working capital and current ratio for the 2 years.
   b. Compute the amount of trade receivables actually owed to the company by its customers.
   c. Determine what percentage of total assets was contributed by creditors and what percentage was contributed by shareholders. (*Hint:* Include minority interest in total capital.)
   d. Discuss the company's current position based on your findings and the company's ability to meet its current obligations. Compare and contrast with the previous year.

Peako Instrument Corporation and Subsidiaries
Consolidated Balance Sheets
As of September 30, 1985 and 1984

Assets	1985	1984
Current Assets:		
Cash	$ 2,276,000	$ 1,977,000
Certificate of deposit	2,271,000	2,840,000
Trade notes and accounts receivable less allowance for uncollectibles:		
$371,000 (1985) and $330,000 (1984)	18,632,000	14,718,000
Inventories	20,131,000	15,984,000
Prepaid expenses and other current assets	928,000	629,000
Total Current Assets	44,238,000	36,148,000
Other Assets	598,000	688,000
Property, plant and equipment—at cost	22,612,700	18,839,800
Less accumulated depreciation and amortization	(8,582,700)	(7,196,800)
Excess of cost over net assets of subsidiaries	1,486,000	1,545,000
Total Assets	$60,352,000	$50,024,000

Liabilities and Shareholders' Equity

	1985	1984
Current Liabilities:		
Notes payable—banks	$ 268,000	$ 290,000
Trade notes and accounts payable	7,037,000	5,832,000
Accrued expense and sundry liabilities	7,167,000	5,793,000
Federal, foreign, and local income taxes	2,386,000	2,378,000
Current installments of long-term debt	754,000	812,000
Total Current Liabilities	17,612,000	15,105,000
Long-term Debt	4,388,000	4,507,000
Deferred Compensation		595,000
Deferred Taxes	1,312,000	714,000
Total Liabilities	23,312,000	20,921,000
Minority Interest in Subsidiary	711,000	427,000
Shareholders' Equity:		
Common stock	2,966,000	2,961,000
Paid-in capital	2,569,000	2,555,000
Retained earnings	30,794,000	23,160,000
Total Shareholders' Equity	36,329,000	28,676,000
Total Equities	$60,352,000	$50,024,000

Case 3-2   **Balance sheet preparation and analysis.** George Biltmore, chairman of the board of Overbilt Corporation, appointed his son-in-law, Wilbur Overberen, as president and instructed him to arrange for a bank loan to finance expansion of operations. The loan officer told Wilbur the bank would lend the funds as long as the total liabilities of the corporation did not exceed 45 percent of total assets at any time while the loan was outstanding. Wilbur then hired the chairman's son, Charles Biltmore, as vice president of finance and instructed him to prepare a balance sheet to support the bank loan. Young Charles prepared the following:

119

Financial Condition of Overbilt Corporation
December 31, 1985

Working capital:		
Cash	$ 219,300	
Merchant accounts:		
Receivable	278,050	
Payable	325,270	
Allowance for doubtful accounts	11,400	$ 160,680
Interest accounts:		
Interest receivable	9,300	
Interest payable	13,700	(4,400)
Other working capital assets:		
Merchandise inventory	587,600	
Receivable from banks	17,150	
Savings accounts	11,380	616,130
Other working capital liabilities:		
Current portion of long-term note	25,000	
Notes payable	180,000	
Wages payable	10,000	
Payable to suppliers	20,130	
Taxes payable	25,900	(261,030)
Net working capital		511,380
Investments and long-term liabilities:		
Buildings	3,528,300	
Less accumulated depreciation	293,400	
	3,234,900	
Finance by bonds payable, due 1993	1,300,000	1,934,900
Furniture and equipment	924,600	
Less accumulated depreciation	49,500	
	875,100	
Financed by note payable, due 1997	365,000	510,100
Other investments:		
Long-term:		
Certificates of deposit	200,000	
Investment in LP Co. common stock	174,000	
Investment in PU Co. common stock	376,000	
Temporary investments in bonds	28,620	778,620
Other liabilities:		
Notes payable	130,000	
Less current portion	25,000	(105,000)
Net investments and liabilities		3,118,620
Capital:		
Retained earnings	495,000	
Preferred stock	635,000	
Common stock	2,500,000	
Total capital		3,630,000
Grand total		$7,260,000

Required:

a. Use the data available to construct a properly classified balance sheet for the company.

b. Compute the company's working capital and current ratio.

c. Determine the maximum amount the company can borrow and still satisfy the bank's requirement.

d. Determine the amount of current liabilities the company has to repay prior to making the bank loan in order to increase its current ratio to 2.

The Income Statement and the Books of Account

4

In Chapter 3, we discussed the way balance sheet accounts change as a result of financial transactions. Some of the most important and frequent changes occur in the form of revenues and expenses that change the balance of owners' equity. In this chapter we look more closely at the concept of income, the process of income measurement, and the manner of reporting income in the income statement. The chapter also illustrates the way businesses manage information in the double-entry accounting system by maintaining books of account. When you have completed this chapter, you will understand:

---

1   The form and function of the income statement and statement of retained earnings.

2   The difference between temporary and permanent accounts.

3   The form and function of two types of accounting records maintained by organizations for the purpose of analyzing and summarizing accounting information.

4   Preparation of the trial balance from information contained in the ledger.

5   The process of closing the books of account.

6   The effect of temporary accounts on the ending balance of the retained earnings account.

In the course of doing business, owners' equity changes frequently as an entity earns revenue and incurs expenses. The change for any given period of time is measured as the difference between total revenues and total expenses, called net income, or profit. In this chapter we focus on income, its measurement, and the way it is reported.

Because a major purpose of business is to earn a profit, business managers maintain careful records of all revenues and expenses in their effort to produce a satisfactory net income. The way accounting information is collected, recorded, and maintained so that it can be used to prepare financial statements is also explained in this chapter.

INCOME MEASUREMENT PRINCIPLES AND CONCEPTS

Businesses earn revenue by selling goods and services. The revenues of service businesses such as repair shops and barber shops as well as physicians' and lawyers' offices are called **fees.** The revenues of businesses that sell products are called **sales revenue.** Business entities cannot earn revenue without incurring expenses. Expenses are incurred to provide the facilities and resources that are necessary prerequisites to offering a service or selling a product.

For example, a physician needs an office in which to practice. The expenses of operating the office include rent, utilities, and maintenance. Staff must be hired to help with patients and record keeping, so salaries must be paid. Without these various expenses, the physician could not perform the services required by patients. Similarly, all businesses must incur expenses in order to have the facilities and resources to carry on business operations and to earn revenue. The relationship between revenues and expenses is reflected in net income by applying several accounting rules to income measurement. These rules include the realization principle, the matching principle, and the accrual concept.

Revenue Realization

The periodicity concept discussed in Chapter 3 requires revenue to be recognized in the period in which it is earned. Accountants have developed rules to enable them to recognize when the earning process has taken place. The **realization principle** in accounting states that before revenue can be recognized, an exchange or performance must usually take place. Service revenue is not realized, and cannot be recognized, until a service is performed.

Revenue is recognized at the time it is realized

For example, if a prospective buyer of a building pays to have the building appraised, the appraiser has not earned any revenue until the appraisal is performed. The performance of the service must take place to satisfy the principle of revenue realization. Sales revenue is usually realized when an exchange of goods takes place. If goods are delivered, revenue is recognized, because a sale has taken place, even if the customer has not yet paid for the goods. In most situations performance of service or delivery of goods satisfies the revenue realization principle.

In some special situations, the realization concept does not apply. Revenue may be recognized prior to the time of exchange or well after the exchange has taken place. For example, a company that undertakes the construction of a project requiring several accounting periods to complete may recognize revenue in each period of construction based on the percentage of the project's completion. The earning process takes place in each period as construction proceeds, even though delivery of the finished project occurs in a subsequent period. Sometimes goods are sold in one period, but the buyer pays for the goods in installments over several subsequent periods. It may be appropriate for the seller to recognize revenue on such installment sales in the periods in which the payments are collected rather than at the time of sale.[1] This book deals primarily with revenues recognized at the time of performance or delivery.

Matching

The **matching principle** in accounting requires that the expenses incurred in producing revenues be matched with the revenues earned in order to arrive at a proper measurement of income. For example, if a business sells merchandise in March, the cost of the merchandise and the salesperson's commission must be considered an expense in March, even though the commission may not be paid until April, and the cost of the merchandise was paid in February. In this way the sales revenue and the sales commission are properly matched in the same time period in which the selling effort was expended and the sale was accomplished. When the revenue and expense are matched, the income measure is a fair representation of the net amount earned during the accounting period.

Expenses are matched with revenues

Sometimes it is difficult to associate a particular expense with specific revenues. For example, if salesclerks wait in the store for customers but no one comes in to buy, are the clerks' wages expenses? Whether or not customers make purchases, it is necessary for the clerks to be available. The wage expense is incurred in the period in which the clerks were employed, and it is matched with the revenue earned in the same period.

Period costs are expenses

Expenses of a period are often matched with revenues of the same period even though there is no clear-cut relationship between them. Many expenses such as taxes or maintenance cannot be related directly to specific revenues. It is assumed, however, that they are a necessary part of doing business, and they are simply matched with the revenues that are earned in the same accounting period in which the expenses are incurred. Costs that are incurred in business operations but that cannot be matched with specific revenues are called **period costs**, and they become expenses which are matched with all revenues earned in the period.

---

[1] Accounting for long-term construction projects and for installment sales are not covered in this book.

The Accrual Concept

Accrual is a timing concept

The need to recognize revenues when earned, whether or not cash is collected, and to match the revenues with the expenses incurred, whether or not they are paid, makes necessary the application of the **accrual concept in accounting.** This concept consists of the following rules: Revenues are recorded at the time they are earned, in accordance with the principle of revenue realization, regardless of the time payment is received; expenses are recorded at the time they are incurred, in accordance with the matching principle, regardless of the time payment is made. The revenue realization principle and the matching principle, coupled with the accrual concept, ensure that income is measured accurately in each accounting period.

Other Accounting Principles

We pointed out in Chapter 1 that one of the primary requirements of accounting information is *relevance*. The various principles and concepts developed by accountants are intended to ensure relevance of reported income and financial position. In addition to the rules already discussed, accountants apply the principles of consistency, conservatism, objectivity, and materiality to ensure the relevance of the information reported.

Consistency.   The wide variety of economic activities with which accounting deals has given rise to accounting rules and methods that permit more than one way of measuring and reporting income and financial position. Accountants must use their judgment in deciding which alternative is appropriate in a given situation. Once an alternative has been selected, the **consistency principle** requires its consistent use from one period to the next so that financial statements of different periods can be compared meaningfully. If a change in method is required, special procedures must be followed to disclose the effects of the change. Examples of accounting alternatives that require application of the consistency principle are discussed in later chapters.

Conservatism.   Accountants must often decide among alternatives and must sometimes interpret the variety of accounting theories that exist. They must use their judgment in applying accounting principles and concepts. The **conservatism principle** guides accountants in applying accounting rules in a way that is least likely to overstate income. This does not mean that income should be understated or that assets should be undervalued. Rather, the principle is intended to prevent financial reports from creating an overly optimistic impression.

The conservatism principle is not without problems because conservatism in one period may cause the opposite condition in another period. For example, if the estimate of the useful life of a fixed asset is too conservative, depreciation expense is excessive and understates net income. In later periods, when the asset still produces revenue but no more depreciation expense can be recorded, net income will be overstated because there is no more depreciation expense to be matched with the revenue earned by the asset.

Objectivity.   To be objective, accounting information should be based on verifiable evidence and should not be biased. The **objectivity principle** requires accountants to prepare financial statements so as to appear neither more nor less favorable than is warranted. For this reason the accountant seeks to verify the correctness of amounts to be reported by examining evidence that provides objective information.

Application of accounting principles leads to objective accounting information

For example, the cost of an asset can be verified by reference to objective evidence such as the canceled check written in payment, or a note signed as evidence of an obligation to pay for the asset. Cost is therefore more objective than the asset's appraised value, which depends on someone's opinion rather than on verifiable evidence. Similarly, in selecting an alternative accounting method, the accountant should select the one that results in the most relevant measure of net income and asset value, not the one that gives the most favorable impression of management's ability. The accounting profession has developed a reputation for objectivity, and the objectivity of accounting reports is relied upon by users of accounting information.

Materiality.   The large amount of detailed information contained in the records of a business must be summarized into understandable form in the financial statements. If too many details are reported, the statements can become confusing. The **materiality principle** states that information should be summarized to eliminate trivial details and to report financial information in a way that will not be misleading. For example, reporting information to the nearest cent or even to the nearest dollar is trivial, and financial statement figures are often rounded to the nearest $100 or $1,000. That way they are easier to comprehend and still useful for making decisions. Similarly, information from several accounts that may be significant to managers may be combined into a single figure for reporting purposes. Instead of reporting separate figures for telephone, electricity, water, and fuel expenses, the accountant may combine them all into one category called utility expense. Deciding what is and what is not material requires judgment which comes with experience.

Cash Flow and Expenditures

Many people confuse revenues and expenses with cash inflows and cash outflows and believe that net income is the same as the net amount of cash collected. These are not the same concepts at all, although they are related. During most of the accounting period, the revenues earned are also collected, and the expenses incurred are also paid, although there is usually

Cash flow is not income

a time lag between earnings or expenses and the related cash flows. At the end of the accounting period, however, this time lag results in reporting of revenues and expenses that may not have been collected or paid but were earned and incurred, making net income different from net cash flows.

The cash basis of accounting.   Most individuals and some businesses view their revenues and expenses only in terms of cash received and spent. This view of income is known as the **cash basis** of accounting and is not as accurate as the accrual basis. Under the cash basis of accounting, revenues are recorded only when money is received, and expenses are recorded only when money is paid. For example, a physician may perform services for his patients and bill them at the end of the month. The earning process takes place when the service is performed, not when the patient pays the bill; but if the physician maintains his records on a cash basis, revenue would be recognized at the time money is received from the patient. Similarly, expenses may occur prior to payment for the use of goods or services, as when a company uses electricity during the month but pays its electric bill only in the following month. In a cash basis system, the expense is recorded only when the bill is paid.

All expenditures are not expenses
    Under the cash basis of accounting most receipts of money are revenue and most expenditures of money are expenses. The accrual basis, on the other hand, distinguishes between expenses and expenditures. **Expenditures** occur when cash is paid which may be for expenses such as salaries, for repayment of debts such as notes payable, or for purchases of assets such as equipment. Unlike the cash basis of accounting, the accrual basis recognizes the substance of each economic event, whether or not a cash flow occurs.

    Some cash payments clearly involve important economic events that cannot be considered expenses even if a business uses the cash basis of accounting. Examples include purchases of assets and repayments of debts. Businesses that do not use accrual accounting therefore usually use a **modified cash basis,** which allows the timing of revenues and expenses as cash receipts and payments take place but recognizes that some receipts and payments constitute economic events that are not revenues and expenses.

    Many small businesses, notably professional service firms, are served adequately by the modified cash basis of accounting. The timing lags that cause errors at the end of one accounting period are partially offset by similar timing lags at the beginning of the period, so the net errors in measuring income and financial position are relatively small. Such errors are viewed as immaterial for businesses that do not have to prepare financial reports for public use. Sound accounting theory, however, does not permit such errors for businesses that issue financial reports to the public and therefore requires use of the accrual basis of accounting. In this book we seldom deal with cash basis accounting systems.

Income Statement Equation

The accounting principles and concepts discussed above and in previous chapters apply to measurements of financial position as well as to measurements of income. When the principles are applied by the accountant in income measurement, the resulting report is a fair representation of the results of a period's operations. In Chapter 3 we calculated net income by deducting expenses from revenues, implying the following definition of net income:

$$\text{Net income} = \text{Revenues} - \text{Expenses}$$

Actually, this equation describes only income from the normal operations of a business. In addition to revenues earned and expenses incurred by a business in its normal operations, other revenues and expenses may occur which are not a part of normal business operations and which are usually reported in the form of gains or losses.

Gains and Losses

Sometimes businesses sell assets not normally kept for sale. Manufacturing equipment that is no longer needed or property held for investment purposes may be sold occasionally, even if such selling is not a usual part of business operations. If owners' equity increases from such sales, the increase is considered a **gain.** If owners' equity decreases from such transactions, the result is considered a **loss.** Gains and losses are **net** measures of changes in owners' equity that result from nonoperating activities of a business.

Gains and losses are net changes in owners' equity

For example, a company owns a parcel of land which cost $10,000 and which the company keeps for future expansion. Due to a change in plans, the company decides it no longer needs the land, and the parcel is sold for $18,000. This is not a part of normal business operations, because the company is not in the business of buying and selling land. The selling price of $18,000 and the cost of the land of $10,000 are netted to arrive at the gain of $8,000, which is the increase in owners' equity from the land transaction. Losses sometimes occur involuntarily, as when property is destroyed by fire or flood. Losses also occur when assets are sold for less than book value. If land costing $10,000 is sold for $9,000, a loss of $1,000 is recorded.

When gains and losses are included in the definition of income, the income statement equation becomes

$$\text{Net income} = \text{Revenues} - \text{Expenses} + \text{Gains} - \text{Losses}$$

Note that this equation is actually part of the balance sheet equation $A = L + C$, with net income or net loss representing the net change in capital over a period of time. The accounting equation can therefore be expanded as follows to include financial position plus the results of operating the entity:

$$\text{Assets} = \text{Liabilities} + (\text{Capital} + \text{Revenue} + \text{Gains} - \text{Expenses} - \text{Losses})$$

Business operations change owners' equity and the results of operations are reported in the income statement. We are now ready to examine in detail the complete income statement of a corporation.

THE INCOME STATEMENT

The **income statement** is a financial report that summarizes the results of business activities of an accounting period. Business activities include operations and other events that result in recording of revenues, expenses, gains, and losses. The income statement may take the form of a multiple-step or a single-step report.

The Multiple-Step Income Statement

The **multiple-step income statement** has revenues, gains, expenses, and losses classified into several categories. Classification allows you to interpret the information more easily. An example is shown in Figure 4-1, which illustrates the classified income statement of Beatrix Corporation, a business that derives most of its revenues from service fees.

Income statements may be classified

The income statement of Beatrix Corporation is divided into several distinct sections, each reporting some aspect of the company's activities during the past accounting period. Note that the date in the heading indicates the period of time covered by the statement, in this case a year. The different parts of the statement are discussed below.

Operating income.   Most of the revenues and expenses of a business are earned and incurred as a result of normal business operations—those activities for which the business is primarily organized. The revenues earned from these usual business operations are called **operating revenues,** and the expenses incurred in normal business operations are called **operating expenses.** The difference between operating revenues and operating expenses is called **operating income** and is the primary measure of business success. Therefore, operating income is usually identified separately in the income statement. Beatrix Corporation earned $47,800 of operating income during 1985.

Other revenues and expenses.   Revenues and expenses not connected with the primary operations of the business are reported in a separate section following operating income. This section may also include gains and losses. Examples of other revenues include incidental rent revenue, dividends received from stock investments, or interest earned from bond investments. Often these items are referred to as income rather than revenue if there are no expenses to be matched with them. Interest expense is reported here, because it is not considered an operating expense; rather it is classified as a financing expense. Operating income and other income make up the company's income subject to income taxation. Beatrix Corporation had $780 of other income in 1985.

Beatrix Corporation
Income Statement
For the Year Ended December 31, 1985

Operating income:			
Fees for services			$135,340
Less operating expenses:			
Salaries		$73,400	
Office rent		5,200	
Materials and supplies		4,665	
Depreciation		1,400	
Legal and professional fees		1,600	
Property taxes		610	
Maintenance and repairs		390	
Bad debts		275	87,540
Total operating income			47,800
Other income:			
Investment income	$ 680		
Gain on sale of investments	1,200	1,880	
Interest expense	980		
Loss on sale of equipment	120	(1,100)	
Total other income			780
Income before income taxes			48,580
Less applicable income taxes			10,780
Income after tax and before extraordinary items			37,800
Extraordinary items:			
Loss from riot damage (net of tax)			2,100
Net income			$ 35,700
Earnings per share on ordinary income			$1.26
Extraordinary items			(.07)
Earnings per share (on 30,000 shares outstanding)			$1.19

Figure 4-1
A multiple-step, or classified, income statement of a corporation. Note the division into operating income, other income, extraordinary items, and earnings per share.

Corporations must pay income taxes

Income taxes.   Operating income and other income are added together to arrive at **income before taxes.** On rare occasions there may be extraordinary items that are not included in this figure, as in our example in Figure 4-1. The income of corporations is taxed by the federal and many state governments. The income tax is deducted from income before tax to arrive at **net income.** Only corporate businesses are taxed as separate entities. Partnerships and sole proprietorships do not pay taxes on their income. Rather, the owners are taxed directly on their share of business income, whether or not the income is withdrawn from the business. Consequently, noncorporate businesses do not report income taxes on their income statements.

    There seems to be no special justification for reporting income taxes separately from other expenses, except that taxes are a major expense, and businesses wish to emphasize to their shareholders how much of their money goes to governments.

Extraordinary items.   Occasionally a special category is reported on the income statement following income after taxes. **Extraordinary items** arise from events that are both **unusual** and **nonrecurring,** such as certain natural catastrophes. Examples of extraordinary items may include losses from flood damage in an area not normally subject to flooding or losses from riots or civil disturbances. If such losses are insured and the company receives insurance proceeds greater than the amount of the loss, it would report extraordinary gains. FASB pronouncements on income classification restrict this category so that it is not often found on income statements.[2] Some situations, however, must be reported as extraordinary items, as you will see in later chapters.

Any income taxes that apply to gains or losses from extraordinary items are not reported in the income tax expense that applies to ordinary income. Instead, such taxes are reported with the extraordinary item, usually showing only the net extraordinary item after tax. Beatrix Corporation incurred an extraordinary loss of $2,100 in 1985, as shown in Figure 4-1.

Earnings per share.   Probably the most significant figure on the income statement, and one on which users of statements tend to focus their attention, is **earnings per share (EPS).** EPS is derived by dividing net income by the average number of common shares of stock held by the company's owners. Beatrix Corporation had 30,000 shares of stock outstanding, so the earnings per share figure is obtained by dividing net income of $35,700 by 30,000 shares. The resulting EPS is $1.19. If the company reports extraordinary items, EPS must be calculated for these and for net income before extraordinary items as well. In practice the calculation of earnings per share can be an extremely complex task. Some of its more important aspects are discussed in Chapter 14.

EPS—the single most important accounting figure

Note that the term net income is used for the last figure of the income statement prior to the EPS figures. Net income is often referred to as the **bottom line,** and EPS for this figure must always be provided. Partnerships and sole proprietorships do not issue stock—therefore they cannot report earnings per share—and their income statements end with net income. There is no other significant difference between the income statements of corporations and unincorporated businesses.

The Single-Step Income Statement

In the **single-step income statement,** there is no attempt to classify operating income apart from other income. All ordinary revenues and gains are reported together, and all ordinary expenses, including income taxes, are deducted to arrive at net income. Figure 4-2 illustrates the single-step income statement of Beatrix Corporation, which like the multiple-step statement, shows net income before extraordinary items.

---

[2] APB Opinion No. 30, as amended by FASB Statements No. 4 and No. 16, describes the criteria for reporting extraordinary items.

Beatrix Corporation
Income Statement
For the Year Ended December 31, 1985

Revenues and gains:		
Fees for services		$135,340
Investment income		680
Gain on sale of investments		1,200
Total revenues and gains		137,220
Less expenses and losses:		
Salaries	$73,400	
Office rent	5,200	
Materials and supplies	4,665	
Depreciation	1,400	
Legal and professional fees	1,600	
Property taxes	610	
Maintenance and repairs	390	
Bad debts	275	
Interest expense	980	
Loss on sale of equipment	120	
Income tax expense	10,780	
Total expenses and losses		99,420
Income before extraordinary items		37,800
Extraordinary loss from riot damage (net of tax)		2,100
Net income		$ 35,700
Earnings per share on ordinary income		$1.26
Extraordinary items		(.07)
Earnings per share (on 30,000 shares outstanding)		$1.19

Figure 4-2
A single-step, or unclassified, income statement of a corporation. Note that extraordinary items are separated from other revenues and expenses.

Notice that extraordinary items and earnings per share are still re-ported as separate categories in the single-step income statement, just as in the classified statement. Of course, extraordinary items seldom exist, and earnings per share are reported only for corporations, so the single-step income statement often is a simple report, as its name implies.

ACCOUNTING FOR INCOME

We now discuss how the accounting system accumulates the data used to produce the income statement. In Chapters 2 and 3 we recorded such data in the capital account or the retained earnings account of the entity in order to emphasize the idea that net income is a change in owners' equity. Now let us see how capital or retained earnings are subdivided into rev-enues and expenses to make income measurement efficient and accurate.

Subdividing Owners' Equity

Remember that if a business is a sole proprietorship or a partnership, changes in owners' equity are recorded in the capital accounts. If the business is a corporation, the capital accounts are divided into contributed capital and retained earnings. All changes from business operations and dividend distributions are recorded in the retained earnings account. In this chapter we use the retained earnings account to illustrate accounting for changes in owners' equity. The same rules apply to capital accounts of unincorporated businesses.

Revenues and expenses are owners' equity accounts

The balance of the retained earnings account consists of all net income of past periods less any dividends that the company distributed to its owners. Reductions of owners' equity are recorded by debits; therefore, all expenses and dividends are entered on the debit side of the account. Conversely, all revenues are recorded on the credit side since they increase owners' equity.

As you saw in Figure 4-1, accountants classify revenues and expenses into various categories on the income statement. Such classifications satisfy the information needs of managers who must have meaningful information about revenues and expenses in order to make a variety of operating decisions concerning production, marketing, advertising, hiring, and many other activities.

To classify revenues and expenses into meaningful categories, accountants divide the retained earnings account into a number of separate accounts, each of which accumulates data on a specific category of revenue or expense. The number of accounts into which retained earnings is divided depends on the information needs of managers. When the two sides of the retained earnings account are divided into revenues, expenses, and dividends, the account might then appear as in Figure 4-3.

Figure 4-3
The Retained Earnings account may be subdivided into several categories for recording increases and decreases in owners' equity.

Retained Earnings

Dividends	Bal. 1/1/85 3,580
Salaries expense	Service revenue
Rent expense	Sales revenue
Supplies expense	Interest income
Tax expense	Gains
Depreciation expense	
Losses	

Whenever a transaction affects retained earnings, it can be classified into its proper category. However, to use the retained earnings account itself to keep track of all the categories of revenues and expenses would be cumbersome indeed. Instead, we can temporarily assign separate T accounts to each category for one accounting period. Figure 4-4 illustrates graphically that dividends, expenses, and revenues are subdivisions of Retained Earnings. Each of these accounts is maintained separately and becomes part of the Retained Earnings account only at the end of the accounting period when financial statements are prepared.

Figure 4-4
Graphic subdivision of Retained Earnings into temporary accounts that are maintained separately during the accounting period.

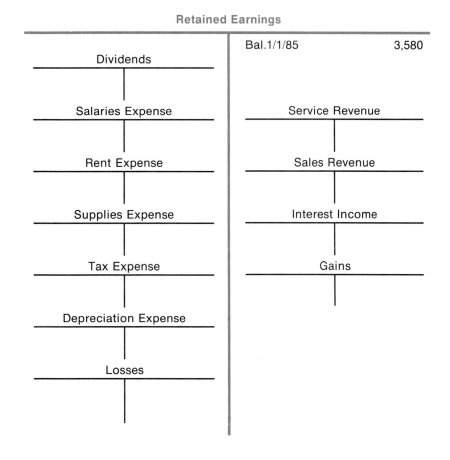

Retained Earnings

Dividends	Bal.1/1/85 3,580
Salaries Expense	Service Revenue
Rent Expense	Sales Revenue
Supplies Expense	Interest Income
Tax Expense	Gains
Depreciation Expense	
Losses	

Temporary and permanent accounts.   The accounts shown above as subdivisions of retained earnings are called **temporary accounts,** or **nominal accounts.** They are temporary because they are maintained only for one accounting period at a time and are never shown on the balance sheet. By contrast, asset, liability, and owners' equity accounts that make up the balance sheet are called **permanent accounts,** or **real accounts.** They are maintained permanently as long as the business is in existence. Permanent accounts are used to measure an entity's financial position, and their balances are reported on the balance sheet. Temporary accounts are used to measure periodic income, and their balances are reported on the income statement.

The balance sheet reports only permanent account balances

You have already seen in previous chapters how transactions affect accounts. Recording transactions in accounts as they occur would be tedious and inefficient and could result in errors. Fortunately the double-entry accounting system consists of books of account that make the process efficient and minimize the chance of errors.

The income statement is made up of temporary accounts

THE BOOKS OF ACCOUNT

The books of account— journal and ledger

The double-entry accounting system consists of two basic types of records called the **journal** and the **ledger.** Together they are called the **books of account** in which all aspects of business transactions are recorded systematically. The books of account serve as a check on each other, making errors easy to locate by providing a clear trail for tracing each transaction and the way it affects the books and, eventually, the financial statements.

Most large businesses do not maintain their books of account by entering transactions in them by hand. Computers have replaced most of the manual bookkeeping techniques that we discuss here. Even the most sophisticated electronic systems, however, use the principles and procedures used in the manual system that we illustrate. A manual record-keeping system still represents the best method of teaching the accounting principles and procedures that you need to know in order to understand accounting and the financial statements that the system produces. And, although microcomputers are appearing in more and more small businesses, many still use manual accounting systems today.

The ledger is a collection of accounts

The ledger.   Many individual accounts are necessary to maintain the records of even a small business. The collection of all permanent and temporary accounts maintained by a business is known as the **general ledger,** and the individual accounts are often referred to as **ledger accounts.** As you know, every financial transaction affects two or more ledger accounts at the same time. If you examine the transactions recorded in one T account, you generally cannot determine what other T accounts have been affected by the same transaction. It would be difficult to maintain a ledger accurately and trace transactions or locate errors if transactions were recorded in the ledger as we did in Chapter 3. Therefore, a procedure called **posting** has been developed for recording transactions in ledger accounts. Posting can take place only after a transaction is recorded in the journal.

The journal.   The journal is known as the **book of original entry** because it is the place where a transaction is first recorded in the accounting system. Transactions are recorded in the journal in chronological order, which makes the journal a sort of business diary. One of the important advantages of the journal is that it contains in one place a complete record of each financial transaction, including the date of the transaction, the accounts affected, and the amounts involved.

Any type of transaction can be recorded in the **general journal.** When a transaction takes place, some sort of document is usually prepared. This might be a check, an invoice, a purchase order, a receipt, or any one of the many documents generated in the course of business activities. Such papers are known as **source documents,** and they are the source of information for recording transactions in the journal. The information in the source documents is first **analyzed** by the accountant to determine which accounts are affected by the transaction and in what amounts. Then the information is **journalized** as a systematic entry in the journal.

Form of the General Journal Entry

*The journal
entry is the
shorthand of
business*

The general journal consists of a date column at the left margin and two money columns at the right. The space in between is for the names of accounts affected by each transaction. In most accounting systems, ledger accounts are assigned a reference number, and a reference column is therefore provided in the journal for entering this number when necessary.

The date in the journal is very important for tracing each transaction and relating it to past business events. Each transaction affects at least two accounts and involves an equal dollar amount of debits and credits. The accounts to be debited are listed in the journal first, with the amounts of the debits entered in the left money column. The accounts to be credited are listed next and indented to indicate credits, with the amount of the credit entered in the right money column. Following the debit and credit entries is a memorandum explaining the entry, identifying the source document from which the entry derived, or showing how the amounts debited or credited are calculated. When the entry is complete, it contains all the information necessary to describe a transaction.

An example of a **journal entry** is illustrated below. It describes a transaction consisting of a purchase of equipment for $300 cash on May 8. The transaction is **analyzed** and recorded as follows:

Date	Explanation	Ref	Debit	Credit
May 8	Equipment	300		
	Cash			3 00
	Purchased collating machine.			
	Purchase order no. 437.			

Note carefully the form of this journal entry. It indicates which ledger account is to be debited, which is to be credited, and the dollar amount of the debits and credits. Nothing pertaining to this transaction has yet been recorded in the ledger. Journal entries are the shorthand of business. Each entry contains a tremendous amount of information in a very compact form. Even the form of the entry communicates information, because the indentation and location of account titles and amounts indicates which are to be debited and which are to be credited. The memorandum at the bottom of the entry explains details of the transaction that are not obvious in the entry itself. Although the memorandum is usually included in the general journal, it may be omitted in routine transactions when the entry is clear without it.

When more than two accounts are affected by a transaction, the result is a **compound journal entry.** For example, if on April 28 a company acquires land for $6,000 by making a $900 cash payment and assuming a mortgage liability of $5,100, the following journal entry is recorded:

Date	Explanation	Ref	Debit	Credit
apr. 28	Land		6000	
	Cash			900
	Mortgage payable			5100
	Issued check no. 1103 and 5-year			
	9% mortgage note for 1.2 acre lot.			

Because the complete transaction is recorded in one place, a good audit trail is provided. The **audit trail** is the information that enables the accountant to trace each transaction to its source to determine that it has been properly recorded. This facilitates the correcting of errors when they occur and provides the business with good control over its records and property. In addition, the journal entry contains the instructions needed for recording the transaction in the ledger with a minimum of errors.

The above entry tells the bookkeepers to record in the general ledger a $6,000 debit in the Land account, a $900 credit in the Cash account, and a $5,100 credit in the Mortgage Payable account. Accounts that do not exist in the ledger are created as needed. For instance, if the company did not have any mortgage liabilities previously, a new ledger account for this liability is established when the land is purchased.

Posting to the Ledger

Information collected in the journal is periodically **posted** by transferring it to the ledger. The account reference number or a check mark is usually placed in the reference column of the journal to indicate that the entry has been posted, so that it is neither omitted nor posted twice. A reference indicating the journal page from which the entry came is usually made in the ledger account in order to complete the audit trail.

In a complex accounting system with a large number of accounts, the use of reference numbers for each account becomes a necessity. For example, an account numbering system might consist of a three-digit number

Journal entries are posted to ledger accounts

assigned to each ledger account. The first digit identifies a general classification—1 for assets, 2 for liabilities, and so on. The second digit identifies accounts within a classification—for instance, 0 for current assets, 1 for investments, and 3 for fixed assets. The third digit identifies a specific account within a classification. Cash may have account number 101, accounts receivable may have number 102, and land may have number 131.

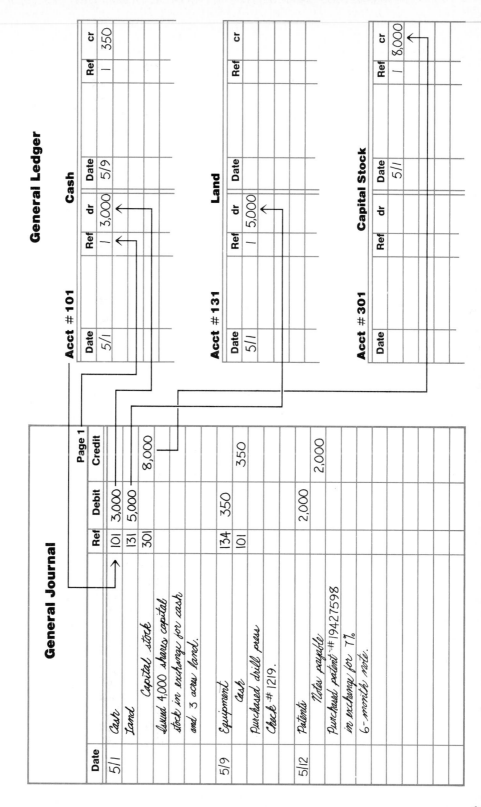

Figure 4-5 The general journal showing entries posted to the general ledger.

An account numbering system simplifies bookkeeping, so account numbers are very useful in practice, especially if the accounting system is computerized. Because account numbers are not essential for studying accounting, however, they are seldom used in this text.

Figure 4-5 illustrates a general journal and the manner in which the journal entries are posted to ledger accounts. Note the use of account numbers to show that an entry has been posted. The entries dated May 1 and May 9 have been posted because the account number is entered in the reference column in the journal. The entry dated May 12 has not yet been posted because the reference column is blank. Many journal entries are discussed in the remainder of this chapter and throughout this book, and you will become very familiar with this method of communication.

ILLUSTRATIVE EXAMPLE

In the following example, we demonstrate how business transactions are analyzed, recorded in the general journal, and posted in T accounts. We also show how the balances in the T accounts are used to prepare financial statements at the end of the accounting period.

Evergreen Corporation is a small company that provides landscaping services to homeowners and home builders. The May 31, 1985, balance sheet and the general ledger in Figure 4-6 contain all the permanent accounts of the business. At the beginning of the accounting period, there are no temporary account balances. We now demonstrate how transactions affect the permanent and temporary accounts by journalizing and posting purchases of goods and services, sales of goods and services, and some miscellaneous transactions.

Buying Goods and Services

Remember that some purchases result in expenses while others represent acquisitions of assets. Some cash expenditures are expenses while others are not. A careful analysis of each transaction determines how it is to be recorded.

TRANSACTION *a.*   The company purchases two power mowers, one for $180 and the other for $270, on open account.

a.	Equipment	450	
	Accounts payable		450
	Purchased two mowers from Reliable		
	Garden Equipment Company. Purchase		
	order no. 3857.		

Evergreen Corporation
Balance Sheet
May 31, 1985

Assets		Liabilities and Owners' Equity	
Cash	$1,100	Notes payable	$1,000
Accounts receivables	2,700	Accounts payable	1,250
Materials and supplies	400	Owners' Equity	
Equipment	6,400	Capital stock	4,000
Accumulated depreciation	(1,600)	Retained earnings	2,750
		Total liabilities and	
Total assets	$9,000	owners' equity	$9,000

General Ledger

Assets	Liabilities

Cash

Bal.	1,100		

Notes Payable

		Bal.	1,000

Accounts Receivable

Bal.	2,700		

Accounts Payable

		Bal.	1,250

Materials and Supplies

Bal.	400		

Owners' Equity

Equipment

Bal.	6,400		

Capital Stock

		Bal.	4,000

Accumulated Depreciation

		Bal.	1,600

Retained Earnings

		Bal.	2,750

Figure 4-6 The balance sheet is made up of permanent account balances, each of which is found in the general ledger.

This transaction represents the purchase of new assets. A debit is recorded in the Equipment account in the amount of $450, the cost of the assets. A liability increased by the same amount when this equipment was bought, and the increase is recorded by a credit. There is no effect on owners' equity from this transaction.

TRANSACTION *b*. A garden tractor owned by the company requires repairs that cost $65, paid in cash.

b.	Repairs expense	65	
	Cash		65
	Tractor repairs paid by check no. 1003.		

Transaction **b** is the purchase of services for cash. When the service was obtained, owners' equity decreased, because the consumption of services is an expense. The service was paid for in cash, and therefore the Cash account decreases also. The decrease in owners' equity is recorded by a debit. The decrease in cash is recorded by a credit. But now, instead of debiting a permanent owners' equity account, we debit an expense account that is a temporary subdivision of Retained Earnings. Refer again to Figure 4-4 to make sure you understand that the debit to Repairs Expense has the same effect as a debit to Retained Earnings.

TRANSACTION *c*. Fuel is purchased on open account for $32 for the operation of the company's equipment.

c.	Materials and supplies	32	
	Accounts payable		32
	Purchased gasoline from Benzine Oil Co.		
	Invoice no. 3991.		

There is more than one way to record a transaction

In this transaction an asset was acquired that will be used in the operation of the business. The increase in the asset is recorded by a debit, and the obligation to pay for the asset is recorded by a credit. When the fuel is used, it will become an expense whether or not payment for it has been made. The company may even find it practical to record purchase of the fuel as an expense rather than as an asset, on the assumption that the fuel will be used almost immediately and will certainly become an expense before the end of the accounting period.

TRANSACTION *d*. Accounts payable in the amount of $700 are paid by check.

d.	Accounts payable	700	
	Cash		700
	Issued checks as follows:		
	No, 1004 to Palmer Supply Co., $250.		
	No. 1005 to Reliable Garden Co., $450.		

This transaction represents the reduction of a liability and a corresponding reduction in cash. There is no effect on owners' equity.

Selling Goods and Services

In analyzing and recording transactions, we must take into account the timing of economic events such as the sales of goods and services in order to decide if a transaction has resulted in the earning of revenue. Some cash receipts are revenues while others are not. Some revenues are earned even though no cash is received.

TRANSACTION *e*. The company landscapes a newly built home and upon completion of the work sends the builder a bill for $420.

e.	Accounts receivable	420	
	Service revenue		420
	Performed landscaping for Condor		
	Construction Co. Job order no. 317.		

In this transaction a service was performed and completed; therefore, the company earned revenue. Owners' equity has increased even though the money has not yet been collected. Instead of the money, the company has an account receivable, which is an asset. To record the increase in assets, Accounts Receivable is debited for $420. The corresponding increase in owners' equity is recorded in a revenue account, a temporary subdivision of Retained Earnings.

TRANSACTION *f*. A pruning and spraying job is completed for a homeowner who pays $30 cash for the work.

f.	Cash	30	
	Service revenue		30
	Completed work on job order no. 318		
	for cash.		

The performance of the service increases owners' equity because the company earned revenue. The increase in cash is recorded by a debit and the increase in owners' equity by a credit.

TRANSACTION g. The builder for whom landscaping services were performed makes a $150 payment on his account.

g.	Cash	150	
	Accounts receivable		150
	Received payment on account from		
	Condor Construction Co.		

This transaction has no effect on owners' equity. The customer's check increased the Cash account and reduced the customer's obligation to the company. This money was earned earlier; consequently, revenue already had been recorded at the time the service was performed. When the cash is collected later, the receipt should not be recorded as revenue again.

TRANSACTION h. An old power mower is no longer suitable for the company's needs. A customer offers to buy the mower for $100 cash, and the company accepts the offer. The mower cost $750, and accumulated depreciation of $670 was recorded on it.

Some assets have more than one account; a transaction may affect both

h.	Cash	100	
	Accumulated depreciation	670	
	Equipment		750
	Gain on sale of equipment		20
	Sold old mower with a book value of $80		
	for cash.		

This transaction results in an increase in owners' equity because an asset that had a book value of $80 was sold for $100, resulting in a gain. The company is not in the business of selling lawn mowers; therefore, the gain is not classified as revenue from normal operations. The receipt of cash is recorded as a debit in the Cash account. The increase in owners' equity, recorded as a credit, is calculated by finding the difference between the amount received and the book value of the mower. The mower becomes the property of the buyer, and the disposal of the assets is recorded in the Equipment and Accumulated Depreciation accounts. The Equipment account contained the $750 cost of the asset as a debit, and the Accumulated Depreciation contra asset account contained a $670 credit representing the cost of the mower that had been assigned as expense to previous periods. When the equipment is sold, both accounts must be reduced in order to remove the mower from the company's books.

TRANSACTION *i*. Mr. Alfonzo, a customer going on vacation, pays $90 in advance to the company in June for mowing and watering his lawn during the first 3 weeks in July.

i.	Cash	90	
	Unearned revenue		90
	Received advance payment on job		
	order no. 319.		

Sometimes money is received prior to the performance of services. The company cannot recognize revenue unless it has performed the services that represent the earning process. When customers pay for services in advance, the company has an obligation to them, and this obligation is recorded as a liability. The increase in cash is recorded as a debit, and the increase in liabilities is recorded as a credit. The obligation will eventually be discharged by the performance of services rather than by the payment of money. Note that the account title Unearned Revenue is not a revenue but a liability. It is a permanent account. Do you see a parallel here with the title Prepaid Expenses, which is also a permanent account?

Other Transactions

Some transactions have no source documents

Not all events affecting the business result in source documents from which journal entries are prepared. The accountant must carefully examine the accounts prior to preparing financial statements to ensure that all effects on assets, liabilities, and owners' equity are reflected in the accounting period.

TRANSACTION *j*. Depreciation expense for one month is $45. Depreciation of fixed assets is an example of a situation that does not provide a source document.

j.	Depreciation expense	45	
	Accumulated depreciation		45
	Depreciation of equipment for 1 month.		

The using up of fixed assets reduces owners' equity and must be recorded as an expense in the period in which the use takes place. However, no one writes a check for depreciation, and there is often no physical evidence that provides a source for the necessary journal entry. Depreciation expense is recorded by a debit to a temporary account, which reduces owners' equity, and a credit to the contra asset account Accumulated Depreciation, which reduces the book value of the equipment.

TRANSACTION *k*. Previously the company acquired some fuel and added the cost to the cost of other materials and supplies it had on hand. At the end of the month, the company determined that materials and supplies costing $56 had been used during the month.

k.	Materials and supplies expense	56	
	Materials and supplies		56
	To record use of prepaid expenses		
	for June.		

Although no document is available for this event, the expense must be recorded and the asset account reduced. Materials and supplies are prepaid expenses whose use reduces owners' equity, and the reduction is recorded as an expense.

TRANSACTION *l*. Evergreen Corporation declares and pays a cash dividend of $50.

l.	Dividends	50	
	Cash		50
	Declared and paid dividend of $.05		
	per share.		

This transaction reduces owners' equity but is not an expense. Dividends are distributions of company assets to owners and are reductions of assets and retained earnings. Cash and owners' equity are reduced. The reduction in owners' equity is recorded in the Dividends account, which is a subdivision of Retained Earnings.

Posting the T Accounts

Journalizing occurs continuously as transactions take place. Periodically, journalized transactions must be posted to the ledger. The debit and credit data in each journal entry are transferred to the appropriate ledger accounts, and consequently the account balances change. If any journal entry requires the creation of a new ledger account, the needed account is then simply added to the general ledger.

The ledger shown in Figure 4-6, with beginning balances of permanent accounts, is reproduced in Figure 4-7, with all the journal entries posted. Note that a new liability account, Unearned Revenue, has been created as a result of transaction **i**. In addition, six temporary accounts now exist as part of owners' equity. These accounts were opened at the beginning of the accounting period so that revenues and expenses of the period

Figure 4-7
A complete general ledger including permanent and temporary accounts, prior to taking a trial balance.

Assets

Cash

Bal.	1,100	b.	65
f.	30	d.	700
g.	150	l.	50
h.	100		
i.	90		
Bal.	655		

Accounts Receivable

Bal.	2,700	g.	150
e.	420		
Bal.	2,970		

Materials and Supplies

Bal.	400	k.	56
c.	32		
Bal.	376		

Equipment

Bal.	6,400	h.	750
a.	450		
Bal.	6,100		

Accumulated Depreciation

h.	670	Bal.	1,600
		j.	45
		Bal.	975

Liabilities

Notes Payable

		Bal.	1,000

Accounts Payable

d.	700	Bal.	1,250
		a.	450
		c.	32
		Bal.	1,032

Unearned Revenue

		i.	90

Owners' Equity

Capital Stock

		Bal.	4,000

Retained Earnings

		Bal.	2,750

Service Revenue

		e.	420
		f.	30
		Bal.	450

Gain on Sale of Equipment

		h.	20

Repairs Expense

b.	65		

Materials and Supplies Expense

k.	56		

Depreciation Expense

j.	45		

Dividends

l.	50		

could be recorded. At the end of the accounting period, these accounts must be closed so that their balances are reflected as changes in the retained earnings account, which at present still contains the balance it had at the beginning of the accounting period.

Accounts are **opened** simply by posting an initial entry in them; accounts are **closed** by eliminating their debit or credit balances, which are transferred to the permanent owners' equity account, thus leaving a balance of zero in the closed account. While any account may be opened at any time, only temporary accounts are closed. Closing temporary accounts changes the retained earnings account to its proper balance at the end of the accounting period.

Trial Balance

After all journal entries have been posted, new account balances are found. To ensure that all dollar amounts of debits and credits are equal in the ledger, we can take a trial balance by listing all the accounts and their balances in two columns and finding the totals of debits and credits. If the trial balance contains both permanent and temporary accounts, it is called a **pre-closing trial balance.** If the temporary accounts have been closed, their balances no longer exist in the ledger, and a **post-closing trial balance** is taken.

The trial balance is an accounting tool, not a statement

The pre-closing trial balance taken from the ledger of Evergreen Corporation on June 30 is shown in Figure 4-8. Note that the balance of Retained Earnings is still $2,750, unchanged from the beginning of the

Figure 4-8
Trial balance made up from the ledger accounts in Figure 4-7. This is called a pre-closing trial balance because it contains temporary accounts.

Evergreen Corporation
Trial Balance
June 30, 1985

	Debits	Credits
Cash	$ 655	
Accounts receivable	2,970	
Materials and supplies	376	
Equipment	6,100	
Accumulated depreciation		$ 975
Notes payable		1,000
Accounts payable		1,032
Unearned revenue		90
Capital stock		4,000
Retained earnings, 5/31/85		2,750
Service revenue		450
Gain on sale of equipment		20
Repairs expense	65	
Materials and supplies expense	56	
Depreciation expense	45	
Dividends	50	
Totals	$10,317	$10,317

period. Of course, we know that retained earnings changed during the period, but these changes have all been recorded in temporary accounts.

The balances of the temporary revenue and expense accounts are used to calculate net income, which is the **net** change in retained earnings resulting from the period's operations. Retained earnings also changed as a result of dividend payments, but dividends are capital transactions and have nothing to do with the determination of income. **Capital transactions** are transactions between the company and its owners affecting capital. Issuance of stock to shareholders or payment of dividends are examples.

The Income Statement

Earlier you saw how revenues and expenses are organized into an income statement. Now you see that the amounts reported in the income statement are actually account balances taken from temporary accounts. When an account is maintained for each category of revenue and expense needed by management, it becomes easy to organize the income statement into classifications with the details necessary to provide meaningful information about the period's operations. The income statement of Evergreen Corporation is shown in single-step form in Figure 4-9. Note the heading, which shows the period of time covered. Note also that the temporary account, Dividends, does not appear on the statement.

Figure 4-9
Income statement containing the temporary revenue and expense accounts from Figure 4-7. The Dividends account is not included in the income statement.

Evergreen Corporation		
Income Statement		
For the Month Ended June 30, 1985		
Revenues and gains:		
Service revenue	$450	
Gain on sale of equipment	20	
Total revenues and gains		$470
Less expenses:		
Repairs expense	65	
Materials and supplies expense	56	
Depreciation expense	45	
Total expenses		166
Net income		$304

Changes in Retained Earnings

Temporary accounts change retained earnings when the books are closed

If all the expenses, revenues, and dividends had been recorded directly in the Retained Earnings account, the balance in the account would have increased by $254. The revenues and gain of $470 would have increased Retained Earnings, and the expenses of $166 and dividends of $50 would have decreased it, for a net increase of $254. The June 30 balance of the Retained Earnings account should be $3,004, which is the correct balance to be reported on the June 30 balance sheet. But the balance in the account is still the beginning balance of $2,750. To bring the retained earnings balance to its correct amount, it is necessary to close the temporary accounts.

Closing the Books

Remember that revenue and expense accounts are subdivisions of retained earnings. At the beginning of the accounting period, the revenue and expense accounts are opened, as illustrated at the top of Figure 4-10. Changes in owners' equity are recorded in these temporary accounts during the accounting period. At the end of the period, all the temporary account balances are summarized in the income statement, and the resulting net income must be added to the retained earnings account to bring its balance up to date. The middle part of Figure 4-10 shows each temporary account becoming part of the retained earnings account as it is closed.

After closing, the retained earnings account contains the changes previously recorded in the temporary accounts, and its ending balance is correct. If the business is not a corporation the capital account is used to record the net change in owners' equity. Closing the books is a systematic procedure of journalizing and posting that transfers the temporary account balances to the appropriate owners' equity account.

Income summary account.   Transferring the balances of temporary accounts to owners' equity is a two-step process. First, all the revenue and expense account balances are transferred to a new temporary account called **income summary,** or **revenue and expense summary,** or **profit and loss summary.** When all revenue and expense accounts have zero balances, they are closed. But the income summary account remains open. The balance in this account is, of course, net income. The second step is to close the income summary account by transferring net income from income summary to retained earnings or to capital if the business is not a corporation.

Closing entries.   Like other entries, **closing entries** are first recorded in the journal and then posted to the ledger. Only temporary accounts are closed. The asset, liability, and permanent owners' equity accounts remain open.

Closing entries affect only owners' equity accounts

The Service Revenue account has a credit balance of $450, which is to be transferred to the Income Summary account. The following entry creates, or opens, the Income Summary account and transfers the Service Revenue balance to it, leaving Service Revenue with a zero balance:

1.	Service revenue	450	
	Income summary		450
	To close Service Revenue account.		

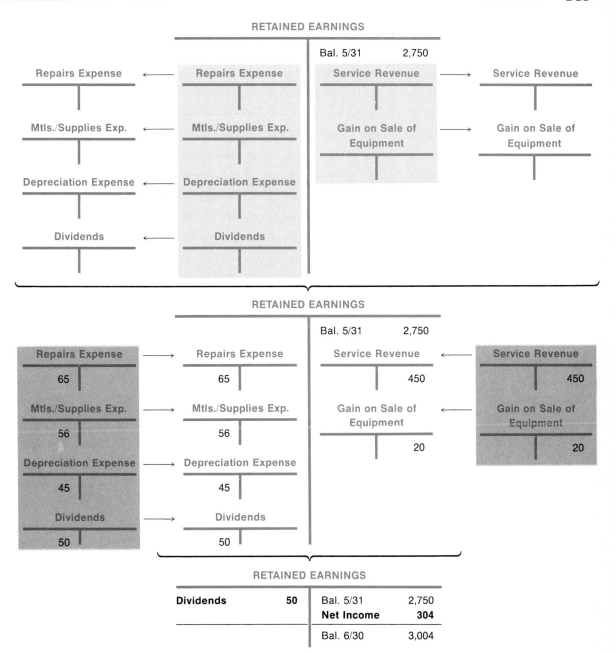

Figure 4-10   The Retained Earnings account collects all changes in owners' equity resulting from operations of the business and the payment of dividends. At the beginning of the period the account is subdivided into various temporary accounts that are maintained separately from the Retained Earnings account, as depicted in the top part of the figure. At the end of the accounting period, these temporary accounts have balances that must be transferred to the Retained Earnings account, as depicted in the middle part of the figure. The temporary accounts become part of the Retained Earnings account with a new balance as depicted in the bottom part of the figure. Now the Retained Earnings account reflects the changes that took place in temporary accounts during the accounting period.

When this entry is posted, the Service Revenue account is closed, and the two accounts appear as follows:

Service Revenue				Income Summary		
1.	450	Bal.	450		1.	450

The Gain on Sale of Equipment account has a credit balance of $20. To create a zero balance in this account, we must debit it $20. The corresponding credit goes to Income Summary.

2.	Gain on sale of equipment	20	
	Income summary		20
	To close gain account.		

When entry 2 is posted, the Income Summary account contains two credits: the $450 service revenue and the $20 gain. It is not necessary to close each account separately. We can close both the revenue and gain accounts with one entry, by debiting these accounts and crediting Income Summary for the total of $470. We use separate entries here for clarity. Next, we close the expense accounts. Repairs Expense has a debit balance of $65. To transfer this balance to Income Summary and create a zero balance in Repairs Expense, we prepare the following closing entry:

3.	Income summary	65	
	Repairs expense		65
	To close Repairs expense.		

The remaining expenses are closed in the same way, as shown below.

4.	Income summary	56	
	Materials and supplies expense		56
	To close Materials and supplies expense.		

5.	Income summary	45	
	Depreciation expense		45
	To close Depreciation expense.		

Look at Figure 4-7, which shows the ledger of Evergreen Corporation prior to closing the books. The company's temporary accounts are repro-

Figure 4-11
Closing entries posted to Income Summary. The Income Summary and Dividend accounts are now ready to be closed to Retained Earnings.

Service Revenue			
		e.	420
		f.	30
1.	450	Bal.	450

Gain on Sale of Equipment			
2.	20	h.	20

Repairs Expense			
b.	65	3.	65

Materials and Supplies Expense			
k.	56	4.	56

Depreciation Expense			
j.	45	5.	45

Dividends	
l.	50

Retained Earnings			
		Bal.	2,750

Income Summary			
3.	65	1.	450
4.	56	2.	20
5.	45		
		Bal.	304

duced in Figure 4-11, which also contains the Income Summary and Retained Earnings accounts. When entries 1 through 5 are posted as shown in Figure 4-11, the only temporary accounts with balances remaining in the books are Income Summary and Dividends. The balance in Income Summary is $304, which is the net income for the period.

Net income is credited to retained earnings

To transfer net income to Retained Earnings, we simply close the Income Summary account. It has a credit balance, so we debit the account to create a zero balance. The corresponding credit increases Retained Earnings by the amount of net income earned during the period.

6.	Income summary	304	
	Retained earnings		304
	To close Income summary.		

The Dividends account is neither an expense nor a revenue. It does not enter into the determination of net income. Therefore it is not closed to Income Summary. This account is closed directly to Retained Earnings as follows:

7.	Retained earnings	50	
	Dividends		50
	To close Dividends account.		

Closing the dividend or drawings account

If the business is not a corporation there is no Dividends account. Instead a Drawings account is used for each owner, and it is closed directly to the owner's Capital account. The income summary account is also closed to the owner's capital accounts, with each owner's share of the net income credited.

The posting of entries 6 and 7 is illustrated in Figure 4-12, in which the Retained Earnings account balance is changed from the beginning balance of $2,750 to the new ending balance of $3,004. Closing temporary accounts is a simple mechanical process, yet it confuses many students who do not have a complete understanding of the difference between temporary and permanent accounts. If you are having difficulty at this time, review Chapters 2, 3, and 4.

Figure 4-12
Income Summary and Dividend accounts closed to Retained Earnings. The results of the period's operations are now reflected in the new Retained Earnings balance.

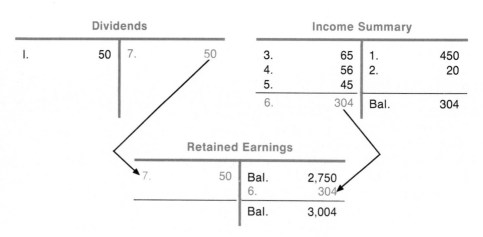

Only temporary accounts are closed

Now that all temporary accounts are closed, a new trial balance can be taken. The post-closing trial balance is illustrated in Figure 4-13. It does not contain any temporary accounts. The accounts in the post-closing trial balance are used to prepare the balance sheet at the end of the accounting period.

Evergreen Corporation
Trial Balance
June 30,1985

	Debits	Credits
Cash	$ 655	
Accounts receivable	2,970	
Materials and supplies	376	
Equipment	6,100	
Accumulated depreciation		$ 975
Notes payable		1,000
Accounts payable		1,032
Unearned revenue		90
Capital stock		4,000
Retained earnings		3,004
Totals	$10,101	$10,101

Figure 4-13
The post-closing trial balance contains only permanent accounts because the temporary accounts have been closed and have zero balances.

The balance sheet on June 30, 1985, is shown in Figure 4-14. All permanent accounts and their balances are included. The temporary account balances no longer exist. The changes in owners' equity, previously recorded in the temporary accounts, are now reflected in the new balance of the Retained Earnings account, which has increased by $254 since May 31. This increase results from the net income of $304 less the dividends of $50 paid during June.

Evergreen Corporation
Balance Sheet
June 30, 1985

Assets		Liabilities and Owners' Equity	
Cash	$ 655	Notes payable	$1,000
Accounts receivable	2,970	Accounts payable	1,032
Materials and supplies	376	Unearned revenue	90
Equipment	6,100	Capital stock	4,000
Accumulated depreciation	(975)	Retained earnings	3,004
		Total liabilities and	
Total assets	$9,126	owners' equity	$9,126

Figure 4-14
Balance sheet containing all accounts in the post-closing trial balance from Figure 4-13.

STATEMENT OF RETAINED EARNINGS

The primary goal of a business is to earn income for the benefit of its owners. Because income is reflected in the retained earnings account, changes in this account are very important to users of financial statements.

Figure 4-15
The retained
earnings
statement
explains the
change in
retained earnings
from one period
to the next.

Evergreen Corporation
Statement of Retained Earnings
For the Month Ended June 30, 1985

Retained earnings, May 31, 1985	$2,750
Add net income	304
	3,054
Less dividends	50
Retained earnings, June 30, 1985	$3,004

---

*A basic
financial
statement found
in the annual
report*

Therefore, a **statement of retained earnings** is prepared as part of the total package of financial statements. This statement shows how retained earnings changed from one period to the next. The statement of retained earnings of Evergreen Corporation for the month of June shows how the beginning balance of the Retained Earnings account increased as a result of net income that the company earned and decreased as a result of dividends that it paid. The new balance of Retained Earnings resulting from these changes is reported in the balance sheet at the end of June. Figure 4-15 illustrates the statement of retained earnings.

Figure 4-16   **The financial statements of an accounting entity are interrelated and show the financial position and the results of one period's operations.**

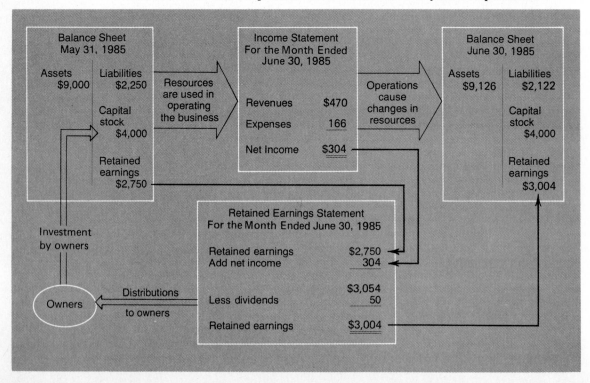

The beginning and ending balance sheets, the income statement, and the statement of retained earnings are shown graphically in Figure 4-16, which illustrates the relationships among these statements. Note that the balance sheet shows the financial position at one point in time, whereas the other two statements show the results of operations over a period of time—in our example, the month of June 1985.

ACCOUNTING WITH EDP SYSTEMS

In most large organizations, the journalizing, posting, closing, and statement preparation procedures discussed in this chapter are performed by computers. **Electronic data processing (EDP)** of accounting information follows basically the same procedures as the manual operations described here. The primary difference is that the original data from source documents are input into the computer and all the remaining tasks are done automatically.

The advantages of EDP include speed, accuracy, volume, and timeliness of information. Once data are input, processing by the computer is extremely rapid and error-free. One item of data may be used in many ways to produce information. For example, information from a sales receipt showing that a customer purchased an item of merchandise may be used by the computer to generate the journal entry for the transaction, post accounts receivable, post a revenue account, reduce the merchandise inventory account, increase the customer's individual account receivable, check to see that the customer has not exceeded his credit limit, and decide if the merchandise item needs to be reordered. The computer can be relied upon to do all this without computational errors, and can be instructed to produce reports for managers on the day's sales, collections of receivables, orders for merchandise, statements for customers, and many other types of information needed for the daily operation of the business. By using computers to process accounting data, ledger accounts can be maintained up-to-date on a daily basis and financial and managerial reports can be prepared quickly whenever needed.

Data input and output for EDP. Providing accounting data to a computer is accomplished in several ways. Data from source documents are usually input by an operator using the keyboard of a computer terminal. This type of processing requires checks and controls to prevent or catch human errors. In many operations, data are transmitted to the computer electronically, eliminating or reducing the possibility of human error. For example, electronic cash registers may transmit data on sales directly to the computer and may read prices and product codes electronically from a product label or magnetically coded price tag. In addition to printing a cash register tape for the customer, the computer can immediately record the transaction and update the customer's account and inventory records. In some cases a customer can communicate directly with a computer by means of a touch-tone telephone whose signals tell the computer to use funds in the customer's bank account for the payment of bills or to transfer funds from one account to another.

The ability of the computer to manipulate vast amounts of data with extreme accuracy and speed has been used to great advantage in many kinds of information processing. The computer is especially beneficial in payroll processing because this accounting function, discussed in Chapter 11, requires huge amounts of detailed record keeping. Maintenance of inventory records and management of investments are other areas that have benefitted greatly. With vast amounts of accounting and other data available in the computer, managers can now obtain statistical analyses of operations, forecasts and projections that allow the evaluation of alternative actions, and simulations that give managers an insight into the future course of business. Computers provide such information either directly on a television-type screen, in printed form, or by talking to users. The amount and quality of information available to management now is far greater than was ever possible in the past.

EDP Control

While the computer has solved many data processing problems and enhanced many business operations and decision making, it has also created some new problems in safeguarding information, controlling its use, and ensuring proper control of resources. Auditors must use new techniques to examine financial reports and test the accuracy of the underlying information. Computers have been used by unscrupulous managers to manipulate records and hide illegal transactions and fraud from auditors. There have been many cases of fraud and theft using computers.

A bank customer once left blank deposit slips coded with his account number on the bank's counters and other customers used them to make deposits, not knowing that the money would go into the wrong account. The customer withdrew the money from his account and disappeared before steps could be taken to prevent a recurrence of his scheme. In another case a computer programmer altered a program to allow him to write checks on his account when there was no money in it. Another programmer had a bank computer deposit in his account all amounts that were dropped from a calculation when interest on savings accounts was rounded to the nearest cent. A customer of an auto parts supplier used the supplier's computer codes to order parts delivered to his business without charging his account, then sold the parts back to the supplier. Programming and operator errors have caused computers to print million-dollar social security checks, bill customers thousands of dollars for a $5 purchase, and pay salaries and dividends to nonexisting employees and shareholders. The detection and prevention of computer errors and abuses is discussed in Chapter 8.

SUMMARY

Revenue increases owners' equity and is earned by selling goods or services. **Expenses** are incurred by consuming assets or services, and they are a necessary part of doing business.

The **revenue realization principle** determines when revenues can be recognized and states that revenue usually occurs when services are performed or goods are delivered. In some cases revenue may be recognized during construction of a project that requires several years to complete. In the case of some installment sales, revenue may be realized only when cash is collected well after delivery of goods.

The **matching principle** requires that expenses incurred to earn revenue are matched with revenues. **Period costs** cannot be associated with specific revenues and are matched with the revenues earned in the period in which the expense occurs. Matching of expenses with revenues is accomplished by applying the **accrual concept,** which states that revenues are recorded when earned, regardless of the time the money is collected; and expenses are recorded when incurred, regardless of the time they are paid.

Other rules that ensure relevance of accounting information are consistency, conservatism, objectivity, and materiality. **Consistency** requires the application of the same accounting method in each accounting period. **Conservatism** requires application of methods that are least likely to overstate net income or financial position. **Objectivity** requires that financial statements be based on objective evidence and not favor any one user of information. **Materiality** requires avoiding the reporting of trivial items and details.

Net income is not the same as the amount of cash collected by the business because sometimes there are time lags between recording of revenues and expenses and the receipts and payments of cash. Some businesses use the **cash basis** of accounting, in which revenues and expenses are recorded at the time of receipt or payment rather than when earned or incurred. Cash basis accounting serves many small businesses well but does not always produce accurate financial information. In a cash basis system, expenditures are treated as expenses; in **accrual basis** accounting, however, **expenditures** occur when cash is paid, whether for expenses, for the purchase of assets, or for the payment of debts.

The **income statement** is a report of business operations covering a specific period of time. Revenues, expenses, gains, and losses may be classified into several categories in the income statement to make it easier to interpret. The income statement equation may be expressed as

$$\text{Net income} = \text{Revenues} - \text{Expenses}$$

and in this form represents the results of normal business operations. Business transactions that are not part of daily operations may result in **gains** or **losses,** which are the **net** change in owners' equity from the transaction. Revenues and expenses as well as gains and losses are reported in the income statement.

In a service concern, the income statement is divided into **operating income** and **other income.** A corporation reports the **income tax** levied against its income. Unincorporated businesses do not report income taxes in the income statement, because such taxes are levied directly on the owners. Unusual and nonrecurring events are reported in the income statement under a separate classification called **extraordinary items.** One of the most significant figures in the income statement of a corporation is **earnings per share (EPS).** It indicates how much income was earned for each share of common stock outstanding.

In order to account for revenues and expenses efficiently, the retained earnings account is subdivided into separate revenue and expense accounts in which changes in owners' equity are recorded during the accounting period. Such accounts are called **temporary,** or **nominal,** accounts, because they exist only for one accounting period. Asset, liability, and owners' equity accounts are called **permanent,** or **real,** accounts, and they exist as long as the business exists. The income statement is made up of temporary accounts. The balance sheet contains all the permanent accounts of a business.

The **books of account** are the **journal,** which is a chronological record of all financial transactions, and the **ledger,** which is a collection of all permanent and temporary accounts. The journal is the **book of original entry** in which all business transactions are analyzed and described completely in the form of **journal entries.** The information in journal entries is **posted** in ledger accounts whose balances are reported in the financial statements. A **statement of retained earnings** is prepared to explain how the balance in retained earnings changed from one period to the next.

A trial balance may be taken at any time to determine if the total dollar amount of all debits equals the total dollar amount of all credits in the accounts. If the trial balance contains temporary accounts, it is called a **pre-closing trial balance;** if it contains only permanent accounts, it is a **post-closing trial balance.** At the end of the accounting period the temporary accounts are closed in order to eliminate their balances. **Closing** the books consists of transferring the balances of temporary accounts to retained earnings. If the business is not a corporation, the temporary accounts are closed to capital. Revenue and expense accounts are first transferred to **income summary,** whose balance, representing net income, is then transferred to retained earnings. Dividends are closed directly to retained earnings, because dividends do not affect income. Drawings are similarly closed directly to the proprietor's or each partner's capital account.

Most accounting information is processed using **electronic data processing (EDP).** Computers are able to prepare journals, ledgers, trial balances, and financial and managerial reports with incredible speed and accuracy. Data are input into computers manually from a keyboard or electronically from cash registers, telephones, and other devices. Output is produced by computers in the form of printed reports or on television screens. The use of computers has benefitted businesses greatly, and has also created the need for new procedures to control errors and prevent fraud.

KEY TERMS

accrual *(124)*
audit trail *(136)*
book of original entry *(134)*
books of account *(134)*
capital transactions *(147)*
cash basis *(126)*
closing entry *(148)*
compound journal entry *(135)*
conservatism *(124)*
consistency *(124)*
earnings per share (EPS) *(130)*
electronic data processing
  (EDP) *(155)*
expenditure *(126)*
extraordinary items *(130)*
fee revenue *(122)*
gain *(127)*
general journal *(134)*
general ledger *(134)*
income statement *(128)*
income summary *(148)*
income tax *(129)*
journal *(134)*
journal entry *(135)*
journalize *(135)*
ledger *(134)*
loss *(127)*

matching *(123)*
materiality *(125)*
multiple-step income
  statement *(128)*
net income *(129)*
nominal account *(133)*
objectivity *(125)*
operating expense *(128)*
operating income *(128)*
operating revenue *(128)*
permanent account *(133)*
post-closing trial balance *(146)*
posting *(136)*
pre-closing trial balance *(146)*
profit and loss summary *(148)*
real account *(133)*
realization principle *(122)*
revenue and expense
  summary *(148)*
revenue realization *(122)*
sales revenue *(122)*
single-step income
  statement *(130)*
source document *(134)*
statement of retained
  earnings *(154)*
temporary account *(133)*

QUESTIONS

1. What term describes distributions of assets by corporations to their owners? What term is used when such distributions are made by unincorporated businesses? Why are such distributions not classified as expenses?

2. How does the income statement indicate the period of time it covers? What does the statement report?

3. What is the difference between the single-step and the multiple-step income statement? If a company prepared each of these statements for the same time period, would net income be the same in the two statements? Why or why not?

4. Describe the classifications of accounts reported in the income statement.

5. What are the main differences between the income statement of a corporation and that of a partnership?

6. Some increases in owners' equity are classified as revenues and others as gains. What is the difference between them?

7. Describe the matching principle in accounting.

8. State the accrual concept precisely and in a concise manner.

9. Describe the principle of revenue realization.

10. What kinds of transactions cause increases in owners' equity? What kinds cause decreases? Give some examples of each.

11. What are temporary accounts, and how do they differ from permanent accounts?

12. Why is the journal called the book of original entry?

13. Describe the form of the general journal and the way transactions are recorded in it.

14. What is the posting process? What does it accomplish?

15. Most journal entries are supported by source documents. Why are journal entries sometimes made when there is no source document?

16. On Monday Bill contracted to mow his neighbor's lawn for $10. On Tuesday he mowed the lawn. On Wednesday the neighbor paid him $30, part for mowing the lawn this week and part for doing it for the next 2 weeks. How much revenue did Bill earn this week? When should the revenue be recognized? How is any additional amount classified?

17. Increases in assets and increases in expenses are both recorded by debits. Does this mean that assets are the same as expenses? If not, what is the difference, and why are they recorded the same way?

18. Describe the method used to close a temporary account. What is the purpose of the income summary account? Before this account is closed, what does its balance represent?

19. What does the statement of retained earnings report?

20. What is the difference between cash basis accounting and accrual basis accounting? What is meant by the modified cash basis?

EXERCISES

Ex. 4-1   **Classifying transactions into revenues and expenses.**   Following are transactions entered into by Fargo Drydock Company in May.

a. The company collected $25 cash for lifting a boat out of the water and loading it on the owner's trailer.

b. Collected $1,680 of accounts receivable.

c. Paid rent for May, $380.

d. Agreed to buy a crane next month for $1,200 less than the normal factory price.

e. Paid $900 wages to employees.

f. An employee accidentally smashed the starboard side of a customer's boat with a forklift. The repairs cost $1,970.

g. Billed customers $5,280 for repairs performed in May.

h. The company received a bill for $182 for oil used in May.

i. The owner of the company estimates that he will need $250 of engine oil next month.

j. A customer agreed to pay $600 for repairs on her boat to be done next week.

k. The owner of the company withdrew $750 cash.

l. A steady customer paid $360 for maintenance on her boat from next June through August.

m. The company received the electric bill for $160 but will not pay it until next month.

n. The owner received an offer to sell the business for $36,000. His capital balance is $31,000, but he declined the offer.

o. Anchors, chains, and other merchandise are sold to customers for $560.

Required: On a sheet of paper, list the letters *a* through *o*. Indicate next to each letter whether the transaction requires recording a revenue, *R*; an expense, *E*; or neither, *N*.

Ex. 4-2   **Classifying changes in owners' equity.**   Faraday Company operates cocktail lounges in well-known restaurants, serving the restaurant's dinner guests and customers at the lounge. Following are some of the company's transactions for the month of June:

a. Sold beverages to customers for $8,600 cash.

b. Purchased new chairs for $9,800 cash.

c. Paid salaries to bartenders, $2,400.

d. Sold ice-making machine that had a book value of $300 for $380 cash.

e. Billed restaurants for beverages served to diners, $6,100.

f. Paid $950 cash for 1-year insurance policy to start on July 1.

g. Glassware broken in the normal course of business cost $32.

h. Fire in one lounge destroyed furniture that had just been purchased for $800.

i. Paid June rent $675 cash.

j. Beverages used in June, $3,700.

k. Sold stock held as investment for $9,000. The cost of the stock was $7,300.

l. Paid June utility bills in the amount of $150.

m. Received $200 interest on bonds held as investment.

n. Paid $1,000 dividend to owners.

o. Received $125 bill for June bookkeeping services.

p. Paid $73 interest on loan used to install new mahogany bar.

Required: For each item above, indicate how it should be classified on the income statement of the company. Use the following classifications: Operating revenue, Operating expense, Other revenue, Other expense, Gain, Loss, and None if the item cannot be classified on the income statement.

Ex. 4-3 **Multiple-step income statement.** Following is an income statement prepared for Alpha Gum Company by its controller:

Alpha Gum Company Income Statement For the Quarter Ended June 30, 1985		
Revenue from fees		$11,150
Interest income		120
Gain on sale of land		580
Total revenues		11,850
Less expenses:		
Salaries	$4,790	
Rent	1,840	
Utilities	470	
Interest	680	
Loss on sale of equipment	200	
Income tax	1,370	
Total expenses and losses		9,350
Net income		$ 2,500
Earnings per share		$.04

When the controller found out that the president of the company wanted a multiple-step statement he asks you to prepare one.

Required:
    a. Recast the above statement into multiple-step form.
    b. Determine the number of common shares the company has outstanding.

Ex. 4-4 **Calculating earnings per share.** The net income of Walter Manufacturing Company was $476,000 in 1985. At the end of the year its retained earnings balance was $1,260,000, and it had 280,000 shares of common stock outstanding. It plans to issue 100,000 additional shares in 1986.

Required: Compute the company's earnings per share for 1985.

Ex. 4-5 **Calculating earnings per share.** When Stresslab Corporation started operation in 1983, it issued 80,000 shares of common stock. During 1984 it issued an additional 160,000 shares of common stock and used the proceeds to buy a new plant. The company had total revenues of $1,421,300 and total expenses of $984,500 for the year ended December 31, 1985. After paying a cash dividend of $68,000 in 1985, the company had a credit balance of $1,632,000 in retained earnings at the end of the year.

Required:
    a. Calculate earnings per share for 1985.
    b. Determine the retained earnings balance at the beginning of 1985.

Ex. 4-6   **Effect of transactions on retained earnings.**   Below is a list of transactions, some of which affect retained earnings.

a. Received telephone bill for $340.   **Answer: $ − 340**

b. Issued stock for $112,000 cash to shareholders.   **Answer: 0**

c. Billed customers $8,290 for services rendered.

d. Paid $1,177 of accounts payable.

e. Paid $580 for legal services.

f. Sold land that cost $3,000 for $500 cash and a $4,000 note receivable.

g. Received $6,575 payment on note receivable, $1,100 of which is interest.

h. Used supplies costing $760.

i. Recorded depreciation expense of $270.

j. Received $2,156 owed by customers on accounts receivable.

k. $370 cash taken in robbery. The robber was caught but only $70 was recovered. The robbery is not covered by insurance.

l. Paid employees' salaries, $7,210 cash.

m. Paid $5,000 in settlement of note payable, none of it interest.

n. Paid dividends of $6,100 cash.

o. Received $9,500 cash for services to be performed next year.

p. Purchased insurance coverage for next 4 years, paying $1,900 cash.

q. Sold, for $850 cash, equipment that cost $1,000 and had $200 accumulated depreciation recorded on it.

r. Purchased supplies costing $1,190 on account.

s. Recorded commissions payable to salespeople of $3,800 for sales made this month.

t. Recorded this period's income tax of $2,350, all of which will be paid next period.

u. Awarded $5,000 by court in legal action, of which $2,000 is owed to attorney.

Required: For each item indicate how the transaction described affects retained earnings. The first two transactions are solved as examples.

Ex. 4-7   **Purchase and sale of fixed asset.**   On July 15 Phrozen Vegetable Farms bought a tractor for $26,580 cash, planning to use it to cultivate its fields. The new machine proved unsuitable so the company sold it on July 23 to Stye Construction Company for $7,500 cash, a $7,000 90-day note, and a $10,500 2-year note.

Required:
a. In the general journal of Phrozen Vegetable Farms prepare the entries to record the purchase and sale of the tractor.
b. Prepare the journal entry to record the purchase of the tractor by Stye Construction Company in its general journal.

Ex. 4-8   **Purchase and sale of land.**   On March 15, 1985, Martinus Company purchased 150 acres of land for $450,000 as an investment. The company normally does not buy and sell land as part of its business operations. On August 1 Martinus sold 50 acres of this land for $180,000, receiving $40,000 cash and a mortgage for the balance. On October 1 the company received a payment of $3,200 on its mortgage, including $2,100 interest. On the same date the company sold another 50 acres of its land for $145,000 cash.

Required: Record the above transactions in Martinus Company's general journal.

Ex. 4-9   **Preparation of retained earnings statement.**   On December 31, 1984, Hoddington Corporation had a credit balance in retained earnings of $1,535,800. Net income after tax for 1985 was $390,100. Expenses and taxes for the year totaled $113,200. In 1985 the company declared and paid cash dividends of $83,500.

Required: Prepare the statement of retained earnings on December 31, 1985.

Ex. 4-10   **Preparation of retained earnings statement.**   The December 31, 1983 balance of Bolton Corporation's Retained Earnings account was $9,566,000. In 1984 the company paid $4,200,000 of cash dividends, and had an ending balance in retained earnings of $19,822,000. The company had total revenues of $85,902,000 and total expenses of $73,360,000 for the year ending December 31, 1985. It declared and paid dividends of $4,800,000 in 1985.

Required: Prepare statements of retained earnings on December 31, 1985 for the current and previous accounting period.

Ex. 4-11   **Retained earnings statement and owners' equity.**   The owners' equity of Starling Corporation consisted of $1,000,000 of common stock, and $410,000 of retained earnings on January 1, 1985. In April the company issued preferred stock for $400,000 cash. In October the company declared and paid $4,500 of cash dividends on its preferred stock and $12,000 of cash dividends on its common stock. Net income for 1985 was $358,000.

Required:
  a.   Prepare a statement of retained earnings at the end of 1985.
  b.   Prepare the owners' equity section of the balance sheet for the company on December 31, 1985.

Ex. 4-12   **Differentiating between income and cash flows.**   Irving Clippem recently started a poodle grooming service. At the end of 2 months of operations he shows you the following figures:

	June	July
Cash collected from customers	$ 800	$1,400
Expenses paid by check	1,000	600
Profit or (loss)	$(200)	$ 800

Clippem says, "I'm really doing great. At this rate I should make a good profit by the end of the year." You, of course, know there's more here than meets the eye. After asking a few questions you find out that at the end of each month the following situation existed:

	June	July
Amounts still owed by customers	$130	$200
Unpaid utility bills	50	240

In addition you find that I. Clippem has not paid his July rent of $300 and that his fixed assets cost $2,400 and will last 5 years.

Required: Prepare condensed income statements for June and July for I. Clippem, and explain which accounting principles and concepts he violated.

Ex. 4-13   **Accounting principles and concepts.**   Below are several statements describing the application of accounting principles and concepts discussed in the chapter.

a. Alpha Company computed depreciation expense last year in accordance with tax laws, which is also acceptable for accounting purposes. This year the company plans to use the same method of computing depreciation.

b. Beta Corporation's field sales personnel are paid a commission based on the amount of sales they produce. The company's store salespeople are paid a salary, and records are not kept on the amount of sales they make. The store personnel salaries are recorded in the period in which they work, but the field personnel commissions are recorded as expenses in the period in which the sold goods are delivered.

c. Gamma Company's sales revenue for the year was $23,705,032.17 but the company reported sales revenue as $23,705,000. Its salary expenses were $646,974.69 and wages paid to office workers were $1,102,004.22, but the company reported these as compensation expense of $1,749,000.

d. The controller of Delta Company is concerned that reporting the company's temporary investments at their cost of $85,000 will overstate financial position, because the investments' market value is only $71,000. After consulting with the company's CPA firm, the investments are reported at their market value.

e. Epsilon Corporation collected $46,000 of fees, but it reported fee revenue of $63,500 because it performed work for which it has not yet been paid.

f. Eta Company has a large amount of prepaid insurance carried as an asset. At the end of each accounting period, the company examines its policies to see how much of the insurance has expired, and it records this portion as an expense.

g. The auditor examining the statements of Theta Company notices that some expenses which should have been reported in 1985 are recorded in 1986 instead. Although reporting these expenses in 1985 makes the net income for the year unsatisfactory, the auditor insists that the expenses be shifted to the proper period.

Required: For each item discuss which accounting principles or concepts are being applied. Some items may involve more than one principle or concept.

Ex. 4-14   **Retained earnings statements and owners' equity.** Dormouse Corporation issued common stock for $2,500,000 on June 10, 1984, when it started in business. By December 31, 1984, the company had incurred a net loss of $740,000. In February 1985, the company issued preferred stock for $1,000,000. Net income for 1985 was $1,390,000, and before the end of the year, the company declared and paid dividends of $120,000.

Required:
   a.   Prepare the retained earnings statements at the end of 1984 and 1985.
   b.   Prepare the owners' equity section of the company's balance sheet on December 31, 1984 and 1985.

Ex. 4-15   **Calculating income from cash records.** "I can't understand it," complains Laura, who operates a physical fitness center. "Ever since I opened in August, I've been attracting more and more customers, but I'm losing more and more money." You ask her to explain what has taken place during the last 3 months, and she prepares the following schedule:

	August	September	October
Cash received from customers	$5,000	$5,000	$6,000
Cash paid for expenses	4,000	4,500	6,500
Income (loss)	$1,000	$ 500	$(500)
Due from customers at end of month	–0–	$1,000	$2,000
Due to suppliers at end of month	2,000	2,500	–0–

All supplies and services are used in the month of purchase, and no supplies are on hand at the end of a month.

Required:
   a.   From the above data, calculate net income for each month.
   b.   Respond to Laura's comment and explain the situation to her.

Ex. 4-16   **Closing entries for a sole proprietorship.** The pre-closing trial balance of a sole proprietorship operated by J. P. Barber, who provides tax consulting services, is located at the top of p. 167.

Required: Prepare the necessary closing entries in the general journal. Use an income summary account.

J. P. Barber, Tax Consultant
Trial Balance
December 31, 1985

	Debits	Credits
Cash	$ 652	
Accounts receivable	243	
Land	5,000	
Building	40,000	
Accumulated depreciation		$12,000
Accounts payable		600
Mortgage payable		30,000
Capital, J. P. Barber		4,000
Fee revenue		1,005
Rent revenue		480
Drawings	90	
Salary expense	600	
Depreciation expense	1,500	
Totals	$48,085	$48,085

Ex. 4-17 Closing entries for a corporation. Following are selected accounts in the ledger of Dendrite Corporation on December 31.

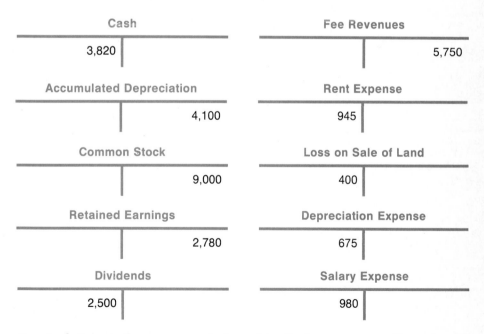

Required: Prepare the necessary closing entries for the company on December 31. Use an income summary account.

Ex. 4-18   **Using income statement data.**   The following statement is taken from the annual report of Hallfrank Insurance Company, an international insurance brokerage firm specializing in insuring business assets and operations. The company, whose stock trades on a major stock exchange, reported a retained earnings balance of $63,142,000 on December 31, 1983.

Hallfrank Insurance Company
Statements of Consolidated Income

Year ended December 31, (thousands of dollars, except per share data)	1985	1984
Net commissions and fees	$237,902	$186,058
Other income (principally interest income)	20,969	11,531
Total revenues	258,871	197,589
Operating expenses:		
Salaries and employee benefits	116,978	89,460
Other operating expenses	78,549	56,927
Interest expense	6,513	1,889
Total expenses	202,040	148,276
Income before income taxes	56,831	49,313
Provision for income taxes	29,397	26,234
Net income	$ 27,434	$ 23,079
Net income per share of common stock	$2.90	$2.45
Dividends declared and paid, per share	$1.30	$1.05

Required: Prepare the statements of retained earnings for the company for the years 1984 and 1985 and determine how many shares of common stock the company issued in 1985.

Ex. 4-19   **(AICPA, CMA) Accounting principles and concepts.**   Select the proper response to the following multiple-choice questions taken from CPA and CMA examinations.

1.   (AICPA) During the lifetime of an entity, accountants produce financial statements at arbitrary points in time in accordance with which basic accounting concept?
   a. Objectivity.   b. Periodicity.   c. Conservatism.   d. Matching.

2. (CMA) The concept referred to by the term "matching" principle is:
   a. that net income should be reported on an annual basis.
   b. that all transactions must refer to a statement of the Financial Accounting Standards Board (FASB).
   c. that all cash receipts for a period be related to the cash disbursements for the period.
   d. that, where possible, the expenses included in the income statement were incurred to produce the revenues.
   e. the current liabilities have the same period of existence as the current assets.

3. (AICPA) What is the underlying concept that supports the immediate recognition of a loss?
   a. Conservatism.   b. Consistency.   c. Judgment.   d. Matching.

4. (CMA) The consistency concept as used in accounting requires that
   a. related revenues and expenses be recognized in the same accounting period.
   b. a business entity must continue to use the same reporting or valuation methods once a method has been adopted.
   c. like transactions be treated in the same manner in different periods.
   d. a business entity report events in a manner which minimizes current income.
   e. a business entity use the same independent auditor each year.

PROBLEMS

P. 4-1   **Income statement of a sole proprietorship.**   Listed below, in alphabetical order, are the temporary accounts and account balances of Seymore X-Ray Laboratory, a sole proprietorship. The accounts represent a month of operations ending on October 31, 1985.

Depreciation expense, laboratory	$ 460
Gain on sale of equipment	1,600
Insurance expenses	283
Office supplies and expenses	325
Rent expense	500
Repairs expense	750
Salaries and wages	5,738
Telephone expense	68
Utilities expense	130
X-ray fees	16,054

Required: Prepare a single-step income statement for the month of October, 1985.

P. 4-2   **Single-step income statement from trial balance.**   Sparkette Company provides consulting services to hospitals. It also earns some incidental income from royalties on a patent it owns. The following trial balance was taken from the company's books on December 31, 1985 after a year of operations:

Sparkette Company
Trial Balance
December 31, 1985

	Debits	Credits
Cash	$ 18,420	
Receivables	14,630	
Prepaid expenses	1,760	
Equipment	49,500	
Accumulated depreciation		$ 4,310
Patents	19,600	
Notes payable		18,000
Unearned revenue		1,500
Capital stock, 10,000 shares		40,000
Retained earnings		27,600
Service revenue		41,710
Royalty income		2,150
Salary expense	11,600	
Rent expense	5,800	
Utility expense	2,260	
Depreciation expense	1,780	
Interest expense	1,400	
Loss on sale of equipment	950	
Gain on sale of investment		430
Income tax expense	8,000	
Total	$135,700	$135,700

Required: Prepare a single-step income statement for the company.

P. 4-3   **Classified income statement from trial balance.**   Refer to the trial balance of Sparkette Company in Problem 4-2.

Required: Use the data in the trial balance to prepare a classified income statement for the company.

P. 4-4   **Income statement preparation.**   The following trial balance is taken from the books of Polaris Service Company at the end of its accounting period:

Polaris Service Company
Trial Balance
December 31, 1985

	Debits	Credits
Cash	$ 41,100	
Temporary investments	52,000	
Receivables	68,900	
Equipment	88,600	
Accumulated depreciation		$ 16,700
Notes payable		35,800
Taxes payable		3,600
Common stock (20,000 shares)		100,000
Retained earnings		82,500
Operating revenue		77,780
Interest income		2,830
Gain on sale of equipment		1,300
Dividends	8,000	
Salaries expense	35,640	
Rent expense	7,200	
Insurance expense	1,120	
Office supplies expense	642	
Utilities expense	968	
Depreciation expense	3,560	
Interest expense	4,680	
Income tax expense	8,100	
Totals	$320,510	$320,510

Required: Prepare an income statement for the company.

P. 4-5   **Income statement preparation.**   Below is a list of temporary accounts, in alphabetical order, taken from the ledger of Waco Broadcasting Company whose fiscal year ends on June 30, 1985. The company has outstanding two million shares of common stock.

Administrative wages and salaries	$ 6,370,800
Depreciation of equipment	1,036,500
Depreciation of office building	739,000
Gain on sale of radio station	1,810,000
Income tax expense	9,200,000
Interest expense	328,000
Legal and professional fees expense	870,800
Loss on sale of equipment	35,000
Maintenance and repairs expense	2,045,100
Production salaries and wages	18,340,400
Revenue from advertising	65,385,600
Royalties and film rental expense	5,825,000
Telephone and other utilities	1,905,000
Transportation expense	3,800,000

Required: Use the above data to prepare a classified income statement for the company for the year ending June 30, 1985.

P. 4-6   Classified income statement.   The trial balance below is taken from the books of Roadrunner Moving Company at the end of 1985:

Roadrunner Moving Company
Trial Balance
December 31, 1985

	Debits	Credits
Cash	$ 19,660	
Temporary investments	45,000	
Accounts receivable	30,050	
Land	50,000	
Buildings	205,400	
Accumulated depreciation, buildings		$ 42,920
Trucks and equipment	480,300	
Accumulated depreciation, equipment		150,840
Accounts payable		13,650
Unearned revenue		11,400
Wages and salaries payable		4,210
Notes and bonds payable		350,000
Common stock, 100,000 shares		150,000
Retained earnings, 12/31/84		48,390
Trucking fees		370,800
Wages and salaries	162,500	
Fuel expense	67,200	
Repairs and maintenance expense	11,340	
Insurance expense	6,290	
Depreciation expense	26,600	
Licenses and fees	1,970	
Gain on early bond retirement (net of tax)[1]		4,000
Investment income		6,000
Interest expense	14,000	
Loss on sale of truck	4,300	
Income tax expense	27,600	
Totals	$1,152,210	$1,152,210

[1]FASB rules require classification of this item as extraordinary.

Required: Using the data in the trial balance, prepare a classified income statement in good form for the year.

P. 4-7   Journal entries for a business.   The following transactions were undertaken by the Falkon Company after its formation:

a.   The company issued 10,000 shares of common stock for $40,000 cash.

b.   Purchased operating supplies for $7,000 on open account.

c. The company rented an office for $450 per month, paying 3 months' rent in advance. Occupancy is to start at the beginning of next month.

d. Equipment costing $9,000 was purchased for $2,500 cash and a 90-day 12 percent note payable for the balance.

e. The company bought a parcel of land for $7,500, paying $1,200 cash and a 15 percent long-term mortgage for the balance.

f. Services were performed for $3,400 on open account.

g. Accounts payable in the amount of $2,400 were paid by check.

h. Services were performed for $4,750, of which $1,000 was received in cash and the remainder was on open account.

i. Payment of $250 was made on the 90-day note, including $110 interest.

j. Collected $2,000 of accounts receivable.

Required: Journalize the above transactions in the general journal.

P. 4-8 **Reconstruction of journal entries from the ledger.**   Charlie Wibb started a business offering heating and air conditioning services to homeowners. He maintained a double-entry accounting system and by the end of his first month of operations had the ledger accounts shown below:

Required: Prepare the general journal entries that must have been used to post the accounts, including memorandum explanations of the entries.

Cash				Accounts Receivable				Prepaid Rent			
a.	20,000	b.	1,200	e.	950	g.	2,400	b.	1,200	i.	600
f.	1,380	c.	1,500	f.	1,970						
g.	2,400	h.	500								
		i.	450								

Supplies				Equipment				Accumulated Depreciation			
d.	800	j.	540	c.	4,800					k.	90

Accounts Payable				Notes Payable				Capital, Wibb			
h.	500	d.	800	i.	400	c.	3,300			a.	20,000

Service Revenue				Rent Expense				Supplies Expense			
		e.	950	i.	600			j.	540		
		f.	3,350								

Depreciation Expense				Interest Expense			
k.	90			l.	50		

P. 4-9   **Journalizing transactions of a partnership.**   Following are transactions of the Gomez & Antonini Company, a partnership formed in February 1985 for the purpose of performing surveying services for building contractors.

a. Gomez and Antonini each contribute $3,000 cash to the partnership.

b. The company bought surveying equipment for $2,860, of which $1,000 is paid in cash and the remainder is on open account.

c. A pickup truck is purchased for $8,700, for which the partnership signs a note payable.

d. Clients are billed $3,250 for services performed.

e. Utility bills for $65 are received and paid in cash.

f. Collected $2,400 cash on accounts receivable.

g. Salaries of $750 are paid to employee.

h. Paid $1,400 cash on accounts payable.

i. The credit card statement is received, listing $70 charged for equipment and $110 for miscellaneous expenses.

j. Depreciation expense on the equipment and pickup is $140.

k. Gomez withdraws $700 cash, and Antonini withdraws $680.

Required: Prepare journal entries to record the above transactions.

P. 4-10   **Journal entries for a business.**   Rolita Corporation was established on March 1 for the purpose of buying tracts of land as investments, subdividing them into smaller parcels, and selling them at a gain. The following transactions occurred during the first month of the company's operations:

a. The company received $50,000 cash from shareholders in exchange for which it issued 10,000 shares of common stock.

b. Office space was rented at $800 per month. The company paid for 1 month's rent by check and recorded rent expense.

c. Office supplies were acquired for $500 on open account. The company maintains supplies as an asset.

d. A parcel of land was bought for $32,000. The company paid $4,000 cash and gave a 2-year note on the balance.

e. The parcel of land was divided into four equal pieces by a surveyor. The surveying fee of $1,500 is recorded as an expense and is payable within 30 days.

f. One of the four parcels of land was sold for $12,300 cash.

g. $1,000 was paid on open account.

h. The company paid $7,320 to repay a quarter of the 2-year note, including $320 interest.

i. A second parcel of land was sold for $7,800, of which $3,000 was received in cash and the balance as a note receivable.

j. At the end of the month the company found that it has $120 of office supplies still on hand and the rest had been used up.

Required: Journalize the above transactions in the general journal.

P. 4-11   **Journalizing, closing, and statement preparation.**   Following is the condensed trial balance of Rodriguez Corporation:

Rodriguez Corporation Trial Balance June 30, 1985		
	Debits	**Credits**
Cash	$ 5,000	
Receivables	8,000	
Fixed assets	25,000	
Accumulated depreciation		$ 4,000
Accounts payable		6,500
Bonds payable		10,000
Common stock		7,000
Retained earnings		10,500
Totals	$38,000	$38,000

During the following 3 months, these events took place:

a.   Billed customers for services of $19,300.

b.   Bought prepaid expenses for $3,400 on open account.

c.   Paid $8,300 cash for salaries.

d.   Collected $16,400 of receivables.

e.   Paid $6,100 of accounts payable.

f.   Paid $400 cash for bond interest.

g.   Sold for $1,220 cash a fixed asset which cost $2,000 and had $900 of accumulated depreciation recorded.

h.   Used $3,000 of prepaid expenses for operations.

i.   Paid a cash dividend of $4,500.

j.   Depreciation expense for the period was $720.

k.   The company paid taxes at the rate of 20 percent of income before tax. The tax for the quarter was computed and paid in cash.

Required:
   a.   Journalize the transactions in the general journal.
   b.   Establish a general ledger, enter the beginning balances, post the journal entries, and find ending balances.
   c.   Prepare an income statement and a statement of retained earnings for the 3 months ending September 30, 1985.
   d.   Prepare closing entries in the general journal.

P. 4-12   **Journalizing, closing, and statement preparation.**   Following is the condensed trial balance of Tobayami Corporation:

	Tobayami Corporation **Trial Balance** **March 31, 1985**		
		Debits	**Credits**
Cash		$19,000	
Receivables		9,500	
Fixed assets		25,000	
Accumulated depreciation			$ 4,000
Accounts payable			9,000
Bonds payable			10,000
Common stock			17,000
Retained earnings			13,500
Totals		$53,500	$53,500

During the following 3 months, these events took place:

a.   Billed customers for services of $18,000.

b.   Bought equipment for $5,400, of which $1,400 was paid in cash and the balance was on open account.

c.   Paid $11,300 cash for operating expenses.

d.   Paid $9,100 of accounts payable.

e.   Paid $520 cash for bond interest.

f.   Collected $17,400 of accounts receivable.

g.   Sold for $1,400 cash a fixed asset which cost $3,000 and had $1,250 of accumulated depreciation recorded.

h.   Paid a cash dividend of $7,200.

i.   Depreciation expense for the period was $630.

j.   The company pays taxes at the rate of 30 percent of income before tax. The tax for the quarter was computed and paid in cash.

Required:
a.   Journalize the transactions in the general journal.
b.   Establish a general ledger, enter the beginning balances, post the journal entries, and find ending balances.
c.   Prepare an income statement and a statement of retained earnings for the 3 months ending June 30, 1985.
d.   Prepare closing entries in the general journal.

P. 4-13   **Business operations and statements.**   Caroline Greenhill owns Greenhill Upholstery, which repairs and recovers furniture. The trial balance on November 30, 1985 is shown below, and the December transactions are listed.

Greenhill Upholstery
Trial Balance
November 30, 1985

	Debits	Credits
Cash	$ 2,820	
Accounts receivable	1,750	
Supplies inventory	1,020	
Tools	3,860	
Accumulated depreciation		$ 950
Notes payable		900
Accounts payable		830
Capital, Greenhill, 12/31/84		4,200
Service revenue		26,150
Wages and salaries	12,500	
Supplies expense	3,080	
Rent expense	6,050	
Utilities expense	940	
Advertising expense	590	
Depreciation expense	420	
Totals	$33,030	$33,030

December transactions:

a.   Purchases of supplies on open account, $600.

b.   December rent paid in cash, $550.

c.   Salaries paid in December, $800.

d.   Customers billed for December work, $1,800.

e.   Payments on accounts payable, $1,200.

f.   Collection of accounts receivable, $1,560.

g.   Utilities paid for December, $120.

h.   Drawings by owner, $750.

i.   Depreciation expense for December, $50.

j.   Supplies used during December, $540.

Required:
   a.   Journalize the December transactions.
   b.   Establish the general ledger and enter the balances from the trial balance. Post the journal entries to the ledger and create any new accounts required. Find the ending balances.
   c.   Prepare a trial balance on December 31, 1985.
   d.   Prepare an income statement and a balance sheet at the end of the year.

Case 4-1   Business operations and statements.

Following is the April 30 balance sheet for Vicki's Art Appraisals and a summary of transactions for May 1985.

Vicki's Art Appraisals
Statement of Financial Position
April 30, 1985

Assets

Current assets:			
Cash		$3,300	
Accounts receivable		5,625	
Total current assets			$ 8,925
Fixed assets:			
Professional library	$ 6,360		
Accumulated depreciation	3,525	2,835	
Automobile	10,185		
Accumulated depreciation	2,730	7,455	
Total fixed assets			10,290
Total assets			$19,215

Equities

Current liabilities:		
Accounts payable	$3,195	
Unearned revenue	2,340	
Total current liabilities		$ 5,535
Long-term notes payable		7,500
Total liabilities		13,035
Capital, Vinson		6,180
Total equities		$19,215

May transactions:

May 2 Paid May rent, $420 cash.

 3 Paid $1,170 owed to Chicago Air airline on account payable.

 6 Purchased art books for $150 cash.

 8 Billed clients for services, $4,500.

 9 Collected $9,150 of accounts receivable.

 13 Paid $1,500 on accounts payable.

 16 Paid cash for gasoline used in May, $70.

 17 Sold to a book collector two volumes from the professional library for $380 cash. The books originally cost $200 and had a book value of $110.

 20 Bought office supplies for $75 on account. All were used in May.

 21 Billed clients for services, $3,975.

 23 Received American Express bill, $1,245 for transportation in May.

 27 Customer entertainment charged on open account, $375.

 28 Paid salaries of $975 to secretary and $1,590 to assistant.

 29 Performed services in the amount of $2,000 for clients who had paid for the work in advance last month.

 29 Cash withdrawn by owner for personal use, $3,200.

 30 Collected advance fees of $2,225 for services to be performed in June.

31 Paid $2,120 on notes payable, of which $620 was for interest and the balance repayment of principal.

31 Depreciation expense for May: library, $120; automobile, $165.

Required:

a. Prepare journal entries to record the above transactions.

b. Post the beginning balances from the balance sheet in T accounts and also post the May journal entries. Find the ending balances.

c. Prepare a trial balance on May 31, 1985.

d. Prepare an income statement and a balance sheet for May 1985.

e. Prepare journal entries to close all temporary accounts at the end of May.

f. The owner asks you to explain why the money received on May 30 is not included in income for May. She also wants to know why depreciation expense is recorded when it did not require the payment of any money. Refer to appropriate accounting principles in your explanation.

Case 4-2 **Operation and financial statements of a corporation.**

The following transactions occurred during May 1985, the first month of operations of Mike's Film Shop, Inc.

May 2 The company issued 1,000 shares of common stock to Mike in exchange for $6,000.

3 Office furniture and equipment were purchased for $1,290 cash.

4 Chemicals, paper, and other supplies were purchased for $520 on open account.

6 The company purchased film processing equipment for $3,500, paying $1,000 in cash and a note for $2,500 payable in 2 years.

8 Paid $360 for advertising.

13 Accounts payable of $400 were paid.

13 Supplies costing $370 were bought on account.

14 Cash collected from customers for film processing, $115.

16 Employees are paid $180 cash.

17 More equipment was purchased for $680 cash.

17 Collected $420 cash from customers for film processing.

20 Paid May rent, $200 cash.

27 Paid $300 on accounts payable.

28 Collected $515 cash from customers for film processing.

31 During May supplies costing $620 were used.

31 Depreciation for May was $80 on processing equipment and furniture.

31 Mike wanted to withdraw $600 from the corporation as a dividend but was told by an accountant that he could not do so.

Required:

a. Journalize the above transactions in the general journal.

b. Post the journal entries to the general ledger.

c. Find the balances of the accounts and prepare a trial balance on May 31.

d. Prepare an income statement, a statement of retained earnings, and a balance sheet for May.

e. Prepare closing entries in the general journal to close all temporary accounts.

f. Discuss briefly why Mike was told that the corporation could not pay a dividend.

The Accounting Cycle and Periodic Adjustments

5

Much of the daily record keeping that takes place during an accounting period consists of routine bookkeeping which increasingly is performed by computers. When accountants are asked to provide information for decision making, they must ensure that their reports are relevant, timely, and accurate. Simply using the information routinely accumulated by the accounting system is not enough because some of the information may not be correct. At the end of each accounting period, accountants must examine the accounting records thoroughly and employ their professional knowledge to ensure that the data will yield a proper measure of income and financial position. This chapter explains the procedures performed at the end of each accounting period. It will help you to understand:

1 How adjusting entries satisfy the accrual concept and the matching principle in accounting.

2 How to record several different types of adjustments.

3 How to prepare a worksheet.

4 The complete accounting cycle.

You are now familiar with three of the basic reports that make up the financial statements of a business entity: the balance sheet, or statement of financial position, the income statement, and the retained earnings statement. You also understand a number of accounting principles and concepts used in preparing these statements. In this chapter we discuss some of the accounting procedures that take place at the end of each accounting period to ensure that the statements are accurate and satisfy generally accepted accounting principles. We illustrate some special journal entries used for adjusting account balances and we also introduce the worksheet, a convenient accounting tool used in the end-of-period accounting process. At the end of the chapter, you will find a complete set of financial statements of a corporation, as well as a summary of the important principles and concepts we have covered up to this point.

THE NEED FOR PERIODIC ADJUSTMENTS

The periodicity concept requires income measurements for specific time periods, such as a year or a quarter. The measurement has to be accurate to present fairly the financial position and the results of operations of a business. **Fair presentation** of financial statements can be accomplished only if the revenue realization and matching principles are satisfied. These principles require the reporting of revenues in the period in which they are earned and expenses in the period in which they are incurred.

The measurement of revenues and expenses is closely related to cash receipts and expenditures. However, important timing differences exist between the recognition of revenue or expense and the exchange of money or cash flow. Income may be earned even though it has not been received. Expenses may be incurred even though payment has not yet been made. It is also possible to receive money for goods or services before they are provided, and to spend money for goods and services before they are used or received. In each case the revenues and expenses must be recognized in the period in which they are earned or incurred, which is not always the period when the cash flow takes place.

During the accounting period, most transactions are recorded from source documents. In some cases source documents are not available until some time after earnings or expenses occur. In a few cases, source documents are not prepared at all. Consequently, some events are not recorded by the end of the accounting period, and incorrect balances exist in some accounts. If some accounts have incorrect balances at the time financial statements are to be prepared, those accounts need to be adjusted to their correct balances. The incorrect balances in some accounts are not the result of mistakes or improper accounting procedures. Rather, they occur because the passage of time causes changes that are not yet reflected in the records. At the end of each accounting period the accountant must examine the accounts and determine which ones need adjusting.

The passage of time causes the need for adjustments

Adjusting Entries

Journal entries, commonly known as **adjusting entries,** are used to bring incorrect account balances to their correct amounts. Financial statements can be prepared only when all accounts have correct balances. The adjusting process, while consisting largely of mechanical record-keeping techniques, is a crucial part of end-of-period procedures. It enables accountants to arrive at proper measures of income and financial position.

*Adjusting
entries correct
incorrect
balances*

The process is both simple and logical. First, for each account it is necessary to determine what *is* in the account, i.e., its balance. Next, it is necessary to determine what *should be* in the account. Finally, if there is a difference, the account is either debited or credited so that the final balance becomes correct. A corresponding credit or debit entry must be made to one or more accounts so that the adjusting entry balances.

Adjustments can be made at any time it is determined that an account has an improper balance. If such an entry is made to correct an error that was made in the books, the entry is referred to as a **correcting entry.** The term *adjusting entry* is usually used for adjustments that are made at the end of an accounting period.

Basically there are five types of adjustments. Two are classified as accruals, and two are classified as deferrals; the remaining type is classified as an allocation. Accruals and deferrals are discussed first, and allocations are treated later.

ACCRUALS AND DEFERRALS

*Accruals and
deferrals
defined*

Simply defined, **accruals** are adjustments that must be made for events that require a cash payment or receipt, but the payment or receipt has not yet occurred. **Deferrals** are adjustments that must be made for events that were recorded when a cash payment or receipt took place. Accruals and deferrals are timing concepts.

To **accrue** means to accumulate, or build up, as a result of the passage of time. For example, a savings account accumulates, or accrues, interest even though the payment of the interest may take place only monthly or quarterly. The earning of interest is continuous. To **defer** means to postpone, or leave until a later time. For example, a company may buy coal to heat its plant. Heating the plant uses up the coal and is an expense. However, the company may buy the coal in the summer and postpone, or defer, burning the coal until winter.

Accruals and deferrals may be related to the timing of asset exchanges. Virtually all exchanges of assets eventually result in the payment or receipt of cash, although cash is not always paid immediately when goods or services are bought or sold. You will find it much easier to understand accruals and deferrals if you think of them in terms of the timing of cash payments, and for this purpose it is convenient to assume that every exchange of assets is made for cash.

In the case of the savings account on which interest accrues with the passage of time, at the end of some time period the interest is actually paid, and cash changes hands. The receipt or payment of cash takes place after the accrual of interest. In the coal example, on the other hand, cash was paid first (when the coal was acquired), and then the deferral of the expense occurred.

Accrual adjustments are required when:

1. Revenue is earned but not recorded because payment has not been received.
2. Expense is incurred but not recorded because payment has not been made.

Deferral adjustments depend on the way a payment or receipt is initially recorded. Such adjustments are required when:

3a. Payment is made and recorded as an asset, but some or all of the asset has expired, or
3b. Payment is made and recorded as an expense, but all the expense is not incurred.
4a. Payment is received and recorded as revenue, but all the revenue is not earned, or
4b. Payment is received and recorded as unearned revenue (a liability) but some or all of the revenue is earned.

A discussion and detailed examples for each case are provided below. In summary, however, if no cash flow has taken place, the required adjustments are accruals. If a cash flow has taken place, the required adjustments are deferrals. These concepts are summarized in Figure 5-1, to which we refer in the following discussion.

Figure 5-1
Relationship between accruals and deferrals and the timing of asset exchanges.

	Assets have been acquired	Liabilities have been incurred
Cash flow has not yet taken place	1 Revenues have **accrued** (accumulated) and must be recorded as receivables	2 Expenses have **accrued** (accumulated) and must be recorded as payables
Cash flow has taken place	3 Expenses are **deferred** (postponed) and must be recorded as prepaid expenses	4 Revenues are **deferred** (postponed) and must be recorded as unearned revenues

Accrued Revenues (Receivables)

Earning is a flow process that occurs when effort is expended. If no payment takes place during the effort, revenue still accrues (accumulates). The situation described in Box 1 of Figure 5-1 is illustrated by a service that has been performed by a company whose client has not yet been billed. For example, an engineering company completes a land survey. Until the bill is prepared to be sent to the client, the revenue is not recorded because the source document does not exist. The company has nevertheless earned revenue and should recognize the existence of assets in the form of receivables by recording the asset and accruing the revenue.

Accrued revenues are assets

Some revenues are earned merely with the passage of time. A company may invest some of its money in government bonds that pay interest every 6 months. The interest is earned continuously as long as the money is invested, although interest is received only every 6 months. The receipt of the interest payment does not always coincide with the end of the accounting period. If interest on bond investments has been earned but not received, it should be recorded and reported in the financial statements.

For example, on May 1 a company buys $10,000 of 9 percent bonds that pay interest on May 1 and November 1. By November 1 the company has earned and received $450. This income is recorded as a debit in the Cash account and a credit in the Interest Income account when it is received. By December 31 when the company's accounting period ends, an additional 2 months' interest income of $150 has been earned. Because the cash has not yet been received, however, the income is not yet recorded in the accounts. To report income accurately, the company should record the 2 months' interest income in the current period, even though the money will be received later. The following entry adjusts the accounts:

Dec. 31	Interest receivable	150	
	Interest income		150
	To accrue interest on bond investment.		
	$10,000 × .09 × 60/360 days = $150		

The interest receivable, often recorded as accrued interest, is an asset that appears on the balance sheet. The credit to Interest Income increases the balance in the revenue account to the correct amount of $600. After the adjusting entry is posted, the two accounts appear as follows:

Interest Receivable			**Interest Revenue**	
Dec. 31 150			Nov. 1	450
			Dec. 31	150
			Bal.	600

Accrued Expenses (Payables)

Box 2 in Figure 5-1 represents the situation in which the cash flow has not occurred, but the company has incurred an obligation because it has received goods or services. For example, the firm's employees provide labor

Accrued expenses are liabilities

for the company. Periodically the company pays for the labor and records wages expense. If the end of the period does not coincide with a payment date, the company accrues (accumulates) the labor expenses and recognizes the existence of its obligation in the form of payables. The labor services received are expenses in the period in which the work is performed even though payment has not been made. For example, a company may have a policy of paying its hourly employees every other Friday. Whenever wages are paid, an entry is made to record the payment, as shown in the following entry:

Dec. 28	Wages expense	7,000	
	Cash		7,000
	To record payroll for 2 weeks.		

The next payment of wages will normally take place on Friday, January 11, but the accounting period ends on December 31. The company receives the services of its employees from December 28 to December 31, and it should record these services as expenses even though it will pay for them in January. Otherwise, wages expense appearing on the income statement will be incorrect. Assuming that wages of $600 have been earned by employees since their last payday, the following adjusting entry is made:

Dec. 31	Wages expense	600	
	Wages payable		600
	To accrue payroll from December 28		
	to end of year.		

The debit to Wages Expense increases the expense account so that the proper balance will appear on the income statement. The credit to Wages Payable, also commonly called accrued wages, creates the liability account that will appear on the balance sheet. The fact that the cash outflow for these wages will occur later does not change the amount of services obtained during the current accounting period. After the adjustment is posted, the two accounts appear as follows:

Wages Payable			Wages Expense		
	Dec. 31	600	Bal.	120,600	
			Dec. 28	7,000	
			Dec. 31	600	
			Bal.	128,200	

Prepaid (Deferred) Expenses

Prepaid expenses are assets, not expenses

Spending money does not necessarily result in an expense. Often it results in the exchange of cash for another asset. The expense occurs when the acquired asset is used. For example, when coal is burned, the using up of the coal stockpile is an expense. The company no longer has the coal available as a resource, nor has it exchanged the coal for another asset. But if the coal is not used in this period, the company has an asset whose use is deferred to the next period. Box 3 of Figure 5-1 indicates that assets have been bought but not yet used. When they are used later, they will become expenses. The recognition of these expenses is deferred (postponed) until a future period.

It is possible to record some transactions in more than one way; the method chosen depends on what is most suitable for a particular business. For example, a business uses office supplies continuously in its operations. If most supplies are used shortly after they are acquired, it may be convenient to record the acquisition of supplies as an expense. Another business may record the purchase of office supplies as the acquisition of an asset called supplies, a prepaid expense.

Whichever method is adopted, accounts must be adjusted if some of the supplies are used and some still remain on hand at the end of the year. To illustrate, assume that supplies costing $800 have been purchased during the accounting period, and a physical count of the inventory discloses that supplies costing $75 are on hand. This means that $725 of supplies have been used.

Purchase recorded as expense.   If purchases of supplies are recorded as expenses, the purchase entry appears as follows:

May 17	Office supplies expense	800	
	Cash (or Accounts payable)		800
	Purchased office supplies.		

At the end of the period, the Office Supplies Expense account has a debit balance of $800. The correct balance in this account is $725. The remaining $75 of supplies on hand have not been used and are therefore not an expense of this period but an asset whose use is deferred until the next period. The following adjusting entry is needed:

Dec. 31	Office supplies	75	
	Office supplies expense		75
	To adjust expense account based on		
	physical count of supplies on hand.		

*Adjusting
entries may
create
permanent
accounts*

The debit of $75 to Office Supplies creates a prepaid expense account, which appears in the December 31 balance sheet as an asset. The credit to the Office Supplies Expense account reduces the $800 balance of this account to the correct balance of $725. After the adjusting entry is posted, the two accounts appear as follows:

Office Supplies				Office Supplies Expense		
Dec. 31	75			Bal.	800	Dec. 31	75
				Bal.	725		

The asset account, Office Supplies, did not exist previously and is created with the adjusting entry so that this asset may appear in the balance sheet. The Office Supplies Expense account balance appears in the income statement. If the adjusting entry had not been made, assets would be understated and expenses would be overstated.

*Sometimes
there is more
than one way to
record a
transaction*

Purchase recorded as asset. If a purchase of supplies is originally recorded as a prepaid expense, an asset, the entry is as follows:

May 17	Office supplies	800	
	Cash		800
	Purchased office supplies.		

At the end of the period, the asset account has a debit balance of $800. Only $75 of supplies are on hand, however, so the account should have a balance of $75. The following journal entry is made to adjust the Office Supplies account:

Dec. 31	Office supplies expense	725	
	Office supplies		725
	To reduce office supplies to the amount		
	of supplies on hand as per physical		
	count.		

The debit to Office Supplies Expense creates the expense account which will appear in the income statement. The credit to Office Supplies reduces the asset account so that its proper balance appears in the balance sheet. When the adjusting entry is posted, the two accounts appear as follows:

Office Supplies				Office Supplies Expense		
Bal.	800	Dec. 31	725	Dec. 31	725	
Bal.	75					

Note that the ending balances in the two accounts after adjustment are the same regardless of how supplies purchases are recorded. This occurs because the accounting system reports economic facts no matter how the records are maintained. The economic facts are that the company has supplies on hand costing $75, and it used $725 of supplies during the past accounting period. If the financial statements are to be accurate, they should report these amounts. The asset account is a deferred expense; that is, the using up of the asset is postponed until the next accounting period although the payment of cash for supplies has already been made in the current period. Because the payment for the supplies is made before the expense occurs, these assets are classified as prepaid expenses in the balance sheet.

Unearned (Deferred) Revenue

Unearned revenues are liabilities, not revenues

A company may collect money before it performs services. In Box 4 of Figure 5-1, the cash flow has already taken place, but the earning process is postponed until a future accounting period. For example, when rent is collected in advance, there is a resulting obligation to provide the rented facilities to the tenant during the following month. This obligation is properly recorded as a liability that will be discharged as time passes. The rent will be earned next month as the tenant occupies the rented facility.

There are two ways to record the rent receipt. It is possible to make the entry for the June rent as follows:

May 28	Cash	250	
	Unearned rent revenue		250
	Received rent for June.		

At the end of June when the rent has been earned, the revenue is recorded and the liability eliminated.

June 30	Unearned rent revenue	250	
	Rent revenue		250
	To record rent revenue received earlier.		

However, by the end of June, another rent payment is received for the next month, so the first entry has to be repeated again. Since the earning process is completed shortly after collection of the rent, it is more convenient to record the revenue when the cash is received. Instead of recording unearned revenue each time rent is received, the entry is

May 28	Cash	250	
	Rent revenue		250
	Received rent for June.		

Receipt recorded as revenue.   If the rent receipt is recorded as revenue, the Rent Revenue account may contain some unearned rent at the end of the accounting period. For example, if a total of $2,000 of rents has been collected, this is the credit balance in the Rent Revenue account. On December 31 it is necessary to remove from the account any rent that has been collected for the following year. If the tenant made a $250 rent payment in December for January occupancy, the payment must be removed from the revenue account with the following adjusting entry:

Dec. 31	Rent revenue	250	
	Unearned rent revenue		250
	To remove January rent receipt		
	from rent revenue.		

The debit reduces the balance in the Rent Revenue account to $1,750, which is the amount of rent actually earned during the accounting period. The Unearned Rent Revenue represents an obligation that the company owes to its tenant. This obligation is properly shown in the balance sheet as a liability. Prior to closing the books, the two accounts appear as follows:

Unearned Rent Revenue		**Rent Revenue**		
Dec. 31	250	Dec. 31 250	Bal.	2,000
			Bal.	1,750

The accounting system must adapt to the business, not the business to the accounting system

Receipt recorded as liability.   When frequent collection of revenue is made in advance, it may be convenient to credit a revenue account. In some cases, however, it may be more appropriate to credit a liability account and to record the revenue only at the end of the accounting period. For example, if magazine subscriptions are sold for periods of one or more years, or if long-term lease payments are received in advance, it may be more appropriate to record these transactions as liabilities than as revenues. The accounting system should be designed to serve the user efficiently, and the nature of the business often dictates which method should be adopted.

For example, instead of collecting rent revenues monthly, the company has a lease arrangement that requires the tenant to pay an entire year's rent in advance. On June 1 the tenant pays $3,000 for the next 12 months' rent, and the receipt of cash is recorded as follows:

June 1	Cash	3,000	
	Unearned rent revenue		3,000
	Received 12 months' rent in advance.		

On December 31 part of the rent received in June has been earned, and part is still an obligation to the tenant. However, no revenue has been recorded, and the Unearned Rent Revenue account is now overstated. The amount earned must be removed from the liability account and recorded as revenue. The entry is as follows:

Dec. 31	Unearned rent revenue	1,750	
	Rent revenue		1,750
	To record rent earned for 7 months.		

The Rent Revenue and Unearned Rent Revenue accounts now have correct balances as shown below.

Unearned Rent Revenue					Rent Revenue		
Dec. 31	1,750	June 1	3,000			Dec. 31	1,750
		Bal.	1,250				

ALLOCATIONS

Definition of allocation

Allocation is the process of assigning costs and expenses to specific accounting periods. Two common examples are depreciation and uncollectible accounts. Adjustments requiring allocations are not specifically related to cash flows. Moreover, the amounts of such adjustments must be estimated and are not as precise as accruals and deferrals.

Depreciation

When a firm buys fixed assets such as buildings or machinery, it expects to use them for a number of accounting periods. The assets are expected to provide the firm with some benefits, such as facilitating the earning process or generating revenues. Because the useful life of a fixed asset is longer than one accounting period, the entire cost of the asset cannot be recorded as an expense of the period in which it is purchased. The entire cost is recorded as an asset at the time of purchase, whether or not all of it was paid in cash. To satisfy the matching principle, the company must spread the cost of the asset over its useful life and must allocate the cost to each period of the asset's life.

For example, on January 1 an office machine expected to last for 10 years is acquired for $820. Each year that the machine is used, one-tenth of its cost, or $82, may be recorded as an expense for that year. Recording an equal amount of depreciation each year is known as straight-line depreciation. On December 31 the following adjusting entry is made:

Dec. 31	Depreciation expense	82	
	Accumulated depreciation		82
	To record depreciation on office		
	machine for 1 year.		

Accumulated depreciation is a contra asset

The original cost of the machine remains in the asset account. The depreciation is credited to Accumulated Depreciation, a contra asset account, and the two accounts together indicate the book value of the asset. The depreciation expense reported in the income statement is the portion of the office machine's original cost that is allocated to the current year. After the adjusting entry is posted, these accounts appear as follows:

Office Machinery			Accumulated Depreciation	
Jan. 1	820		Dec. 31	82

Depreciation Expense	
Dec. 31	82

The depreciation expense of $82 appears in the income statement. The Office Machinery account and its related Accumulated Depreciation account are both permanent accounts and appear together in the balance sheet. The Accumulated Depreciation account accumulates the amount of cost assigned to each period in which the asset was used. Therefore, the balance of the Accumulated Depreciation account increases over time. On the other hand, Depreciation Expense is a temporary account and is closed at the end of the period, so it starts each period with a zero balance.

At the end of the second year of use, the same adjusting entry will be made. The balance of the Accumulated Depreciation account will then be $164, indicating that this much of the original cost of the asset has been expensed. The depreciation expense of $82 will again appear in the income statement, showing the amount of expense allocated to the second year. Depreciation is discussed further in Chapter 10. Here we are concerned only with the concept of depreciation adjustments.

Uncollectible Accounts

Occasionally when firms sell goods and services on credit, the customer fails to pay the account. The amount not collected is an uncollectible account, also called a bad debt. At the end of the accounting period, some of the accounts receivable may not be collectible. The receivables resulted from revenues earned in the current period. If some of the receivables cannot be collected, the loss of these revenues should be reported in the current period also. Moreover, if some of the accounts receivable are uncollectible, assets are overstated and must be adjusted to reflect the amount that is expected to be collectible. Recording the bad debts in the period in which the revenues are earned satisfies the matching principle. Reducing the book value of the accounts receivable with the adjusting entry satisfies the conservatism principle.

Allocation adjustments require estimates

It is necessary to estimate the amount of receivables that will not be collectible in order to make the adjusting entry for bad debts. Methods of making such estimates are discussed in a later chapter. Here we are concerned only with the adjustment itself. For example, a company has $6,500 of accounts receivable at year-end. If $300 of the receivables are expected to become uncollectible, the following adjusting entry is made:

Dec. 31	Bad debts expense	300	
	Allowanced for uncollectible		300
	accounts		
	To record uncollectible accounts.		

The debit to Bad Debts Expense increases expenses reported in the current period's income statement. This represents the allocation of expected bad debts to the period in which the revenue is reported. The credit to Allowance for Uncollectible Accounts reduces the book value of the accounts receivable asset. The balance of the accounts receivable account is not reduced because the total amount of receivables owed to the company by customers has not changed. Instead, the credit is posted to the contra asset account. The asset and its related contra asset are reported together in the balance sheet, the net amount representing net realizable value, or the total amount of current receivables expected to be collected in the future.

Sometimes the Allowance for Uncollectible Accounts already has a balance before the adjusting entry is made. In this case it is simply changed to the correct balance. For example, if the allowance account already has a $30 credit balance, the entry above would be for $270, which would bring the balance of the allowance account to the desired $300 credit.

Accumulated depreciation and the allowance for doubtful accounts are both contra-asset accounts. Each time depreciation expense is recorded, accumulated depreciation builds up so that it grows over the asset's life. On the other hand, when bad debts expense is recorded, the allowance for doubtful accounts also builds up, but this balance then declines during the following year as accounts receivable are found to be bad and are written off. The writing off of accounts receivable is discussed in Chapter 8; here you need only understand that the balance of the allowance account does not accumulate over a period of years.

Summary of Accruals, Deferrals, and Allocations

Note that every adjusting entry involves both temporary and permanent accounts and therefore affects both the income statement and the balance sheet. Accruals and deferrals that require recording expenses reduce assets or increase liabilities; if they require recording revenues, they increase assets or reduce liabilities.

Timing of cash flows affects accruals and deferrals, but not allocations

Allocations differ from accruals and deferrals because they necessitate estimating the amount of the adjustment. Depreciation expense is based on an estimate of expected useful life of the asset. Bad debts expense is based on an estimate of uncollectible amounts of receivables. In addition, allocations are not related to the timing of cash flows. On the other hand, accruals and deferrals can be calculated precisely and are directly related to cash flows.

Figure 5-2 summarizes and explains these adjustments, gives examples, and shows the balance sheet and income statement treatment of deferrals, accruals, and allocations.

THE WORKSHEET

The **worksheet** is an accounting tool designed to facilitate the completion of the end-of-period processes of adjusting accounts, closing the books, and preparing financial statements. It is a columnar form with debit and credit columns for the unadjusted trial balance, the adjusting entries, the adjusted trial balance, the income statement, and the balance sheet. Sometimes columns for retained earnings are also provided. Having all of these items in one place is very useful.

Because of the volume of work in the end-of-period procedures, occasional errors are bound to occur in the adjustments, trial balances, or financial statements. The worksheet is not part of the formal accounting system, and therefore any changes or corrections can be made on the worksheet prior to journalizing the adjusting and closing entries and preparing financial statements. A portion of a worksheet, with a trial balance entered, is shown in Figure 5-3.

Steps in Worksheet Preparation

We demonstrate and explain worksheet procedures and at the same time illustrate a complete set of adjusting and closing entries using Pathmaker Company as an example. On December 31, 1985, the company's trial

	Balance Sheet Treatment	Explanation	Examples	Income Statement Treatment
A C C R U A L S	**Assets** are recorded as prepaid expenses.	Cash outflow has occurred. Goods or services have been received but not yet used.	Prepaid insurance, office supplies, or prepaid rent.	An **expense** is recorded for the portion of the asset used during the period. The unused portion is an asset and will become an expense in future periods.
	Liabilities are recorded as unearned revenues.	Cash inflow has occurred. Payment has been received for goods and services that have not yet been delivered.	Rent received in advance or subscriptions collected in advance.	**Revenue** is recorded for the portion of goods and services delivered. The portion not delivered is a liability which will become revenue in future periods.
D E F E R R A L S	**Assets** are recorded as receivables.	Cash inflow has not occurred. The earning process is complete, but no assets have been received.	Interest on bond investments or unbilled services.	**Revenues** are recognized and recorded in the period in which the earning process is complete.
	Liabilities are recorded as payables.	Cash outflow has not occurred. Benefits have been used or received, but no cash has been paid.	Interest on bonds payable, salaries payable, or taxes payable.	**Expenses** are recognized and recorded in the period in which benefits are consumed.
A L L O C A T I O N S	Recorded as reduction in asset or increase in contra asset.	Cash outflow occurred when the asset was bought, or it continues to occur if periodic payments are made on installment purchase. The cost of the asset is allocated to each period of its expected useful life.	Depreciation of equipment, amortization of intangibles, or depletion of natural resources.	**Expense** is recognized in each period in which the asset is used. Timing of cash flows does not affect the income statement. The expense does not result in any payments. The amount must be estimated.
		Services or goods have been provided, but payment has not been received. Payment is expected in future period but may not take place.	Bad debts on credit sales.	**Expense** is recorded in the period in which sales takes place for amounts which are expected to be uncollectible. The amount must be estimated.

Figure 5-2   **Accruals, deferrals, and allocations are end of period adjustments that affect the balance sheet and the income statement.**

balance shown in Figure 5-3 is prepared from the general ledger. The preparation of the worksheet involves the following steps which are illustrated in Figure 5-4, the completed worksheet of Pathmaker Company. Each step is explained in the order performed.

Pathmaker, Inc.
Worksheet
December 31, 1985

	Trial Balance Debit	Trial Balance Credit	Adjustments Debit	Adjustments Credit	Adjusted Trial Balance Debit	Adjusted Trial Balance Credit	Income Statement Debit	Income Statement Cre
Cash	2,200							
Accounts receivable	1,600							
Prepaid insurance	180							
Land	4,000							
Building	30,000							
Accumulated depreciation		3,600						
Accounts payable		980						
Mortgage payable		22,000						
Capital stock		5,000						
Retained earnings, 1/1/85		4,200						
Fees earned		47,910						
Rent revenue		1,300						
Dividends	16,000							
Salaries expense	28,000							
Interest expense	1,920							
Office supplies expense	480							
Utilities expense	610							
Totals	84,990	84,990						

Figure 5-3 Unadjusted trial balance in a worksheet, ready for adjusting and extending into financial statements.

Steps in worksheet preparation

Step 1. The unadjusted trial balance is entered in the first two columns of the worksheet. It is important that the debits and credits balance before proceeding.

Step 2. Each of the adjusting entries is entered in the adjustments columns as it would be in the journal. The amount to be debited is entered in the left column, and the amount to be credited in the right column. If the account already exists, the adjustment is placed on the same line as the previous balance. If the account does not exist, a new line is used to list the new account and enter the adjustment. The adjustments are coded with a letter or number so that they can be traced later if an error occurs. Each of the adjusting entries is discussed below.

a. Pathmaker Company rents one of the offices in its building to a typing service for $100 per month. Rent Income is credited whenever rent is received, and the Rent Income account balance of $1,300 includes the receipt of the January 1985 rent. Rent Income account is overstated because all the rent in this account has not been earned. The unearned portion is transferred to a liability account by means of a $100 debit to Rent Income and a $100 credit to a new account called Unearned Rent Income.

b. Since the last payroll date, salaries amounting to $1,150 have been earned by employees and are not yet paid. The $28,000 balance in

Pathmaker, Inc.
Worksheet
For the Year Ended December 31, 1985

	(1)		(2)		(3)		(4)		(5)	
Cash	2,200				2,200				2,200	
Accounts receivable	1,600				1,600				1,600	
Prepaid insurance	180			d. 90	90				90	
Land	4,000				4,000				4,000	
Building	30,000				30,000				30,000	
Accum. depreciation		3,600		e. 1,200		4,800				4,800
Accounts payable		980				980				980
Mortgage payable		22,000				22,000				22,000
Capital stock		5,000				5,000				5,000
Retained earnings		4,200				4,200				(4,200)
Fees earned		47,910				47,910		47,910		
Rent revenue		1,300	a. 100			1,200		1,200		
Dividends	16,000				16,000				(16,000)	
Salaries expense	28,000		b. 1,150		29,150		29,150			
Interest expense	1,920		f. 165		2,085		2,085			
Office supplies expense	480			c. 70	410		410			
Utilities expense	610				610		610			
Totals	84,990	84,990								
Unearned rent revenue				a. 100		100				100
Salaries payable (2)				b. 1,150		1,150				1,150
Supplies inventory			c. 70		70				70	
Insurance expense			d. 90		90		90			
Depreciation expense			e. 1,200		1,200		1,200			
Interest payable				f. 165		165				165
Totals			2,775	2,775	87,505	87,505	33,545	49,110		
Net income							15,565	(5)		(15,565)
Totals							49,110	49,110	53,960	53,960
										(6)

Figure 5-4 **Completed 10-column worksheet. The end-of-period procedures can be performed in the worksheet without disturbing the books. In the balance sheet columns the three marked amounts together make up the new Retained Earnings balance. The colored numbers in circles indicate the steps described in the text.**

Salaries Expense is the amount actually paid to employees. Salaries that have been earned by employees but not yet paid must be debited to Salaries Expense. The credit for the accrual is entered in a new Salaries Payable liability account that is created on a new line in the worksheet.

c. A physical count of office supplies indicates that supplies costing $70 are on hand. The purchase of office supplies was recorded as an expense. The expense account is overstated and must be reduced. The credit of $70 to this account is matched by a debit to a new prepaid expense account called Supplies Inventory.

d. The Prepaid Insurance account represents the payment on a 1-year fire insurance policy. The policy was purchased on June 30, 1985. Half a year has elapsed since the insurance policy was bought; therefore, half the policy has expired. The asset account Prepaid Insurance must be reduced by $90, and Insurance Expense is created and debited.

e. The building is estimated to have a useful life of 25 years and no salvage value. Straight-line depreciation is used, which means that the amount of depreciation expense is the same each year. The annual depreciation is 1/25, or 4 percent, of the original cost of the building. The Depreciation Expense account is debited, and the Accumulated Depreciation account is credited $1,200.

f. The mortgage payable carries an interest rate of 9 percent per year. Payments on principal and interest are made monthly. The last payment was made on December 1, 1985. Nine percent interest per year on $22,000 is $1,980 ($22,000 × .09). Only 1 month's interest has accrued, however, since the last payment was made on December 1; therefore, only 1/12 of $1,980, or $165, is the interest expense for December. This amount is debited to Interest Expense and credited to Interest Payable, a new liability account.

The adjustment columns must be added. If the debits do not equal the credits, an error exists and must be found and corrected before proceeding further.

Step 3. An adjusted trial balance is now prepared by combining and extending the figures in the old trial balance and the adjustments columns. This is analogous to finding the new balance in each account. For example, if an asset account has been debited by an adjustment, its balance increases. If it has been credited, its balance decreases. The adjusted trial balance contains the new accounts created by the adjusting process. The totals of the two columns are found before going to the next step.

You need to recognize permanent and temporary accounts by their titles

Step 4. Extending the trial balance into the financial statements columns must be done carefully to ensure that each number is in its proper place and none is omitted. The permanent account balances are extended into the balance sheet columns; assets are entered as debits, and equities and contra assets as credits. All temporary accounts except Dividends are extended into the income statement columns, with expenses entered as debits and revenues as credits. Dividends are extended into the balance sheet debit column, because dividends are not involved in income determination.

Step 5. The revenue and expense columns are added and their totals entered at the bottom of the income statement columns. Now we treat these two columns exactly as we do the two sides of the Income Summary account when the books are closed. The credit balance of $15,565, which represents net income, must be transferred to Retained Earnings by closing the Income Summary account. To do so, we enter a debit in the income statement columns beneath total expenses and a credit in the balance sheet columns. This is done on the line labeled net income. The final balances in the two income statement columns show by their equality that the difference between revenues and expenses, or net income, has been transferred to Retained Earnings.

The balance sheet columns contain all the asset, liability, and capital account balances, as well as the beginning Retained Earnings balance, Dividends, and net income. The last three items, circled in the worksheet, will be combined and will appear in the statement of retained earnings. Only the new Retained Earnings balance of $3,765 will appear in the formal balance sheet when it is prepared from the worksheet.

It is also possible to have a pair of retained earnings columns in the worksheet, as shown in Figure 5-5. This is the same example as that shown in Figure 5-4. Here, however, retained earnings, dividends, and net income are extended into the columns labeled Retained Earnings. The new retained earnings balance is calculated in these columns as the difference between total debits and total credits and is extended into the balance sheet columns. When the retained earnings columns consist only of three items, most accountants extend these three items directly into the balance sheet columns as we did in Figure 5-4. For more complicated retained earnings statements, the retained earnings columns can be very convenient.

Pathmaker, Inc.
Worksheet
For the Year Ended December 31, 1985

	Trial Balance		Adjustments		Adjusted Trial Balance		Income Statement		Retained Earnings		Balance Sheet	
	Debit	Credit	Debit	Credit	Debit	Credit	Debit	Credit	Debit	Credit	Debit	Credit
Cash	2,200				2,200						2,200	
Accounts receivable	1,600				1,600						1,600	
Prepaid insurance	180			d. 90	90						90	
Land	4,000				4,000						4,000	
Building	30,000				30,000						30,000	
Accum. depreciation		3,600		e. 1,200		4,800						4,800
Accounts payable		980				980						980
Mortgage payable		22,000				22,000						22,000
Capital stock		5,000				5,000						5,000
Retained earnings		4,200				4,200				4,200		
Fees earned		47,910				47,910		47,910				
Rent revenue		1,300	a. 100			1,200		1,200				
Dividends	16,000				16,000				16,000			
Salaries expense	28,000		b. 1,150		29,150		29,150					
Interest expense	1,920		f. 165		2,085		2,085					
Office supplies expense	480			c. 70	410		410					
Utilities expense	610				610		610					
Totals	84,990	84,990										
Unearned rent revenue				a. 100		100						100
Salaries payable				b. 1,150		1,150						1,150
Supplies inventory			c. 70		70						70	
Insurance expense			d. 90		90		90					
Depreciation expense			e. 1,200		1,200		1,200					
Interest payable				f. 165		165						165
Totals			2,775	2,775	87,505	87,505	33,545	49,110				
Net income							15,565			15,565		
Totals							49,110	49,110	16,000	19,765		
Retained earnings									3,765			3,765
Totals									19,765	19,765	37,960	37,960

Figure 5-5 **The 12-column worksheet has an additional pair of columns for the retained earnings statement. Compare the numbers in the retained earnings columns with the circled amounts in the 10-column worksheet in Figure 5-4.**

Step 6. Everything that was in the adjusted trial balance has been summarized and recorded in the two balance sheet columns. Therefore, they should balance, and we prove that they do by adding them and comparing the totals.

Notice that except for the three circled amounts that must be combined, the balance sheet columns are really the post-closing trial balance. Once the worksheet is completed, it is used as the source of the adjusting and closing entries that are made if the books are actually to be closed. The financial statements can now be prepared by organizing the information in the financial statement columns of the worksheet into formal reports. Because the worksheet organizes the end-of-period work in one place and makes the entire process easier, it is a very practical accounting tool.

THE ACCOUNTING CYCLE

An **accounting cycle** consists of the accounting procedures that take place during an accounting period. The cycle begins with the first transaction of each period and ends with the preparation of financial statements. Although the accounting period is usually 1 year, for convenience we frequently use monthly periods in this textbook. The accounting cycle is repeated in each accounting period and consists of several specific steps in the processing of financial information:

A trial balance may be taken at any time in the accounting cycle

1. Identifying economic events to be recorded
2. Journalizing transactions from source documents
3. Posting journal entries to the ledger
4. Preparing a trial balance
5. Adjusting accounts at the end of the period
6. Preparing the adjusted trial balance
7. Preparing financial statements
8. Closing temporary accounts at the end of the period
9. Preparing reversing entries and opening temporary accounts at the beginning of the following period in order to start the cycle again

The first three steps—identifying, journalizing, and posting transactions—take place throughout the accounting period. The next five steps are commonly known as end-of-period procedures; they involve preparing the unadjusted trial balance, adjusting accounts, preparing the adjusted trial balance, closing accounts, and preparing financial statements. These five steps are often accomplished in the worksheet before the adjusting and closing entries are journalized and posted. The last step, consisting of

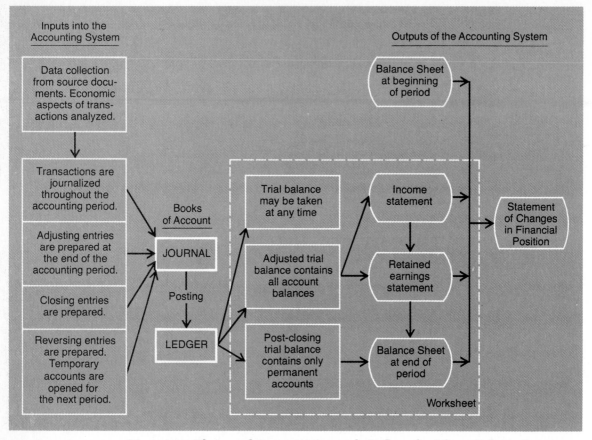

Figure 5-6   The complete accounting cycle in flow chart form. Information goes into the books of account in the form of raw data. It comes out of the system in the form of financial statements.

reversing entries, is purely a mechanical bookkeeping process and has no effect on financial reports. Reversing entries are designed only to facilitate routine bookkeeping; they are discussed in the appendix to this chapter.

The accounting cycle is illustrated in the diagram in Figure 5-6. The input into the accounting system consists mainly of data that must be collected and analyzed. The books of account containing these financial data are arranged systematically so that the necessary output can be extracted. The end-of-period procedures require accountants to use expertise and judgment to ensure that all adjustments are made and the resulting financial statements are complete and accurate. The output of the system consists of the condensation of thousands of events and transactions into concise summaries of financial information that can be used by managers, owners, investors, and others who make economic decisions regarding the business entity that provides the statements.

A Complete Set of Financial Statements

To clarify further the output of the accounting system, we present on pages 202–215 the financial statements taken from the 1983 annual report of Rangaire Corporation. An **annual report** usually contains a letter from the company's president to its shareholders as well as photographs, highlights, and descriptions of the company's operations, in addition to the financial statements. You are not expected to understand everything in these financial statements. Note that the statements are consolidated—that is, they are the combined statements of Rangaire Corporation and other companies owned by the reporting entity. Consolidations are discussed in Chapter 16.

Rangaire Corporation does not have a statement of retained earnings in its annual report. Instead, it provides a more comprehensive statement of stockholders' equity, which includes the retained earnings information as well as data about changes in other capital accounts.

Examine the various titles and classifications of accounts in the statements, and the many notes that accompany the report. The notes to financial statements are an integral part of the annual report. They are needed to satisfy the requirements of the **full disclosure** principle, which states that all pertinent information should be provided so that the statements do not mislead the users.

Users of financial statements rely on the auditor's opinion

Carefully read the accountant's report on page 202 certifying that the statements have been audited. This report expresses the opinion that the staements present fairly the financial position and results of operations. This certification is very important and means that the statements can be relied upon because they have been examined by an auditor and certified as fair presentations of financial condition.

Examine the statement of changes in financial position on page 206. This statement explains what caused the financial position to change from one period to the next by indicating the sources from which the company obtained working capital and the uses to which it put the working capital during the period. The preparation of this statement is discussed in Chapters 17 and 18.

Interim Reports

In addition to the annual report, which contains the complete set of four financial statements, most companies provide interim reports to their shareholders. An **interim report** consists of the income statement, which is usually prepared at quarterly intervals. Some companies' managers require financial statements every month. Because of the speed and efficiency of computers, even weekly statements are now possible. The adjusting entries needed at the end of each interim period must be reflected in the interim statements. To avoid having to adjust and close the books at frequent intervals, the accountant uses the worksheet to prepare interim reports. The adjusting and closing entries in the interim worksheet are not journalized.

RANGAIRE Corporation and Subsidiaries

Auditors' Report

PEAT MARWICK
Certified Public Accountants

The Board of Directors and Stockholders
Rangaire Corporation:

We have examined the consolidated balance sheets of Rangaire Corporation and subsidiaries as of July 31, 1983 and 1982, and the related consolidated statements of earnings, stockholders' equity and changes in financial position for each of the years in the three-year period ended July 31, 1983. Our examinations were made in accordance with generally accepted auditing standards and, accordingly, included such tests of the accounting records and such other auditing procedures as we considered necessary in the circumstances. In connection with our examination of the consolidated financial statements, we also examined the supporting Schedules 1, 2 and 3.

In our opinion, the aforementioned consolidated financial statements present fairly the financial position of Rangaire Corporation and subsidiaries at July 31, 1983 and 1982 and the results of their operations and the changes in their financial position for each of the years in the three-year period ended July 31, 1983, in conformity with generally accepted accounting principles applied on a consistent basis. Also, in our opinion, the related supporting schedules, when considered in relation to the basic consolidated financial statements taken as a whole, present fairly in all material respects the information set forth therein.

Peat, Marwick, Mitchell & Co.

Dallas, Texas
October 7, 1983

RANGAIRE Corporation and Subsidiaries

Consolidated Statements of Earnings

Years ended July 31, 1983, 1982 and 1981

	1983	1982	1981
Revenues:			
Manufacturing	$41,827,664	41,692,310	54,487,491
Lime operations	30,723,544	36,083,118	23,925,430
Construction	14,479,475	18,475,500	19,483,680
	87,030,683	96,250,928	97,896,601
Costs and expenses:			
Manufacturing	34,799,033	34,811,710	45,035,260
Lime operations	26,478,718	29,057,411	18,937,515
Construction	13,477,664	16,943,950	17,840,964
	74,755,415	80,813,071	81,813,739
Gross profit	12,275,268	15,437,857	16,082,862
Selling, general and administrative expenses	9,506,679	11,805,596	11,556,136
Operating profit	2,768,589	3,632,261	4,526,726
Other deductions (income):			
Interest expense	2,642,575	2,971,878	2,567,046
Gain on disposal of assets	(1,251,357)	(363,394)	(2,227)
Other—net	(583,453)	(478,573)	(194,764)
	807,765	2,129,911	2,370,055
Earnings before income taxes and extraordinary item	1,960,824	1,502,350	2,156,671
Federal and state income taxes:			
Current	(128,299)	280,065	97,567
Deferred	232,277	80,732	22,514
	103,978	360,797	120,081
Earnings before extraordinary item	1,856,846	1,141,553	2,036,590
Extraordinary item (less applicable income taxes of $818,800) - gain on termination of pension plan	961,200	—	—
Net earnings	$ 2,818,046	1,141,553	2,036,590
Earnings per share of common stock:			
Earnings before extraordinary item	$.49	.30	.54
Extraordinary item	.25	—	—
Net earnings	$.74	.30	.54

See accompanying Financial Review and Summary of Significant Accounting Policies.

RANGAIRE Corporation and Subsidiaries

Consolidated Balance Sheets

July 31, 1983 and 1982

Assets		1983	1982
	Current assets:		
	Cash	$ 1,067,347	1,155,523
	Accounts receivable, principally trade—net of allowance for doubtful receivables of $90,000 in 1983 and $110,000 in 1982	12,934,592	14,322,073
	Refundable Federal and state income taxes	—	136,203
	Prepaid Federal income taxes	284,259	435,922
	Inventories, at the lower of cost (principally first-in, first-out) or market:		
	Raw materials	6,580,185	8,785,996
	Work in process	744,733	1,080,752
	Finished goods	3,947,991	5,972,335
	Total inventories	11,272,909	15,839,083
	Prepaid expenses	1,479,969	687,434
	Total current assets	27,039,076	32,576,238
	Property, plant and equipment, at cost—partially pledged:		
	Land	2,298,161	2,253,715
	Buildings and building improvements	4,198,485	6,680,442
	Machinery and equipment	42,447,710	44,982,787
	Furniture and fixtures	904,430	939,444
	Automotive equipment	786,229	869,403
		50,635,015	55,725,791
	Less accumulated depreciation and depletion	23,456,708	24,183,521
	Net property, plant and equipment	27,178,307	31,542,270
	Proceeds from industrial revenue bonds held in escrow	—	1,400,768
	Other assets and deferred charges, at cost less applicable amortization	606,927	1,191,349
		$54,824,310	66,710,625

See accompanying Financial Review and Summary of Significant Accounting Policies.

RANGAIRE Corporation and Subsidiaries

Liabilities and Stockholders' Equity		1983	1982
Current liabilities:			
	Notes payable to banks—unsecured	$ 1,400,000	2,375,000
	Current installments of long-term debt	2,160,000	1,229,700
	Accounts payable—trade	7,619,902	9,452,854
	Federal income taxes payable	316,423	—
	Accrued expenses:		
	Salaries and wages	284,702	519,250
	Taxes, other than on income	207,506	240,226
	Interest and other	1,280,696	1,666,410
	Total current liabilities	13,269,229	15,483,440
	Long-term debt, excluding current installments	10,370,000	22,180,700
	Deferred credits	277,689	442,037
	Deferred Federal income taxes	625,886	545,272
	Stockholders' equity:		
	Common stock of $.10 par value. Authorized 6,000,000 shares; issued 3,821,382 in 1983 and 3,503,978 shares in 1982	382,138	350,398
	Additional paid-in capital	14,339,470	12,089,870
	Retained earnings	15,559,898	15,618,908
	Total stockholders' equity	30,281,506	28,059,176
	Commitments and Contingencies		
		$54,824,310	66,710,625

RANGAIRE Corporation and Subsidiaries

Consolidated Statements of Changes in Financial Position

Years ended July 31, 1983, 1982 and 1981

	1983	1982	1981
Sources of working capital:			
Net earnings before extraordinary item	$ 1,856,846	1,141,553	2,036,590
Items which do not use (provide) working capital:			
Depreciation and depletion	5,334,063	4,602,006	3,990,084
Amortization and reduction of deferred credits and charges	(114,419)	28,720	12,633
Deferred Federal income taxes	80,614	287,327	140,196
Working capital provided from operations, exclusive of extraordinary item	7,157,104	6,059,606	6,179,503
Working capital provided by extraordinary item - gain on termination of pension plan	961,200	—	—
Working capital provided from operations	8,118,304	6,059,606	6,179,503
Decrease in other assets	534,493	—	87,615
Decrease in industrial revenue bonds held in escrow	1,400,768	—	—
Proceeds from long-term debt	—	5,200,000	8,800,000
Issuance of common stock	271,937	—	61,243
Proceeds from sale of property, plant and equipment	4,295,113	478,009	32,579
Increase in deferred credits	—	365,881	—
Decrease in working capital	3,322,951	1,577,623	—
	$17,943,566	13,681,119	15,160,940
Uses of working capital:			
Additions to property, plant and equipment	5,265,213	6,906,032	7,435,439
Acquisition of Corson Lime Company	—	2,895,998	—
Cash dividends declared	862,269	840,954	816,365
Reduction in long-term debt	11,810,700	1,394,700	893,700
Increase in other assets	—	242,667	—
Cash payments in lieu of fractional shares of stock dividend	5,384	—	4,179
Proceeds from industrial revenue bonds held in escrow	—	1,400,768	—
Increase in working capital	—	—	6,011,257
	$17,943,566	13,681,119	15,160,940
Changes in components of working capital:			
Increase (decrease) in current assets:			
Cash	(88,176)	(10,302)	(270,957)
Accounts receivable	(1,387,481)	3,925,505	(843,444)
Federal and state income taxes	(287,866)	(323,941)	675,071
Inventories	(4,566,174)	501,690	(6,120,701)
Prepaid expenses	792,535	163,220	358,029
	(5,537,162)	4,256,172	(6,202,002)
Increase (decrease) in current liabilities:			
Notes payable to banks	(975,000)	2,375,000	(10,350,000)
Current installments of long-term debt	930,300	336,000	10,000
Accounts payable	(1,832,952)	2,832,489	(1,588,459)
Federal income taxes	316,423	—	(60,181)
Accrued expenses	(652,982)	290,306	(224,619)
	(2,214,211)	5,833,795	(12,213,259)
Increase (decrease) in working capital	$ (3,322,951)	(1,577,623)	6,011,257

See accompanying Financial Review and Summary of Significant Accounting Policies.

RANGAIRE Corporation and Subsidiaries

Consolidated Statements of Stockholders' Equity

Years ended July 31, 1983, 1982 and 1981

	Common stock		Additional paid-in capital	Retained earnings	Total
	Shares	Amount			
Balances at July 31, 1980	3,356,593	$335,659	$11,196,657	$14,948,972	$26,481,288
Exercise of common stock options	13,253	1,325	59,918	—	61,243
Dividends:					
Cash ($.24 per share)	—	—	—	(816,365)	(816,365)
Stock (4%)	134,132	13,414	833,295	(850,888)	(4,179)
Net earnings	—	—	—	2,036,590	2,036,590
Balances at July 31, 1981	3,503,978	350,398	12,089,870	15,318,309	27,758,577
Cash dividend ($.24 per share)	—	—	—	(840,954)	(840,954)
Net earnings	—	—	—	1,141,553	1,141,553
Balances at July 31, 1982	3,503,978	350,398	12,089,870	15,618,908	28,059,176
Dividends:					
Cash ($.24 per share)	—	—	—	(862,269)	(862,269)
Stock (8%)	279,569	27,957	1,981,446	(2,014,787)	(5,384)
Stock contribution to ESOP	37,835	3,783	268,154	—	271,937
Net earnings	—	—	—	2,818,046	2,818,046
Balances at July 31, 1983	3,821,382	$382,138	$14,339,470	$15,559,898	$30,281,506

See accompanying Financial Review and Summary of Significant Accounting Policies.

RANGAIRE Corporation and Subsidiaries

Supporting Schedules

**Schedule 1 —
Valuation Accounts**

In Thousands of Dollars

Year ended July 31, 1983:	Balance at beginning of period	Additions charged to earnings	Deductions	Balance at end of period
Allowance for doubtful receivables	$110	6	26	90
Year ended July 31, 1982:				
Allowance for doubtful receivables	$ 90	127	107	110
Year ended July 31, 1981:				
Allowance for doubtful receivables	$ 81	136	127	90

RANGAIRE Corporation and Subsidiaries

**Schedule 2—
Property, Plant and Equipment**

In Thousands of Dollars

Year ended July 31, 1983:	Balance at beginning of period	Additions	Acquisition (sale) of subsidiary	Retirements or sales	Balance at end of period
Land	$ 2,254	78	—	(34)	2,298
Buildings and building improvements	6,680	95	(2,293)	(283)	4,199
Machinery and equipment	44,983	4,891	(7,218)	(208)	42,448
Furniture and fixtures	939	142	(138)	(39)	904
Automotive equipment	869	59	(6)	(136)	786
	$55,725	5,265	(9,655)	(700)	50,635
Year ended July 31, 1982:					
Land	$ 1,761	27	466	—	2,254
Buildings and building improvements	5,547	28	1,169	(64)	6,680
Machinery and equipment	38,499	6,643	1,205	(1,364)	44,983
Furniture and fixtures	909	26	16	(12)	939
Automotive equipment	756	182	40	(109)	869
	$47,472	6,906	2,896	(1,549)	55,725
Year ended July 31, 1981:					
Land	$ 1,680	81	—	—	1,761
Buildings and building improvements	5,555	150	—	(158)	5,547
Machinery and equipment	31,922	6,961	—	(384)	38,499
Furniture and fixtures	839	86	—	(16)	909
Automotive equipment	774	157	—	(175)	756
	$40,770	7,435	—	(733)	47,472

RANGAIRE Corporation and Subsidiaries

**Schedule 3—
Accumulated Depreciation
and Depletion of Property,
Plant and Equipment**

In Thousands of Dollars

Year ended July 31, 1983:	Balance at beginning of period	Additions charged to earnings	Sale of subsidiary	Retirements, renewals and replacements	Balance at end of period
Depletion	$ 356	20	—	—	376
Depreciation:					
Buildings and building improvements	2,429	264	(896)	(36)	1,761
Machinery and equipment	20,413	4,836	(4,726)	(210)	20,313
Furniture and fixtures	590	95	(85)	(35)	565
Automotive equipment	395	119	—	(72)	442
	23,827	5,314	(5,707)	(353)	23,081
	$24,183	5,334	(5,707)	(353)	23,457

Year ended July 31, 1982:					
Depletion	$ 334	22	—	—	356
Depreciation:					
Buildings and building improvements	2,177	266	—	(14)	2,429
Machinery and equipment	17,281	4,112	—	(980)	20,413
Furniture and fixtures	515	88	—	(13)	590
Automotive equipment	345	114	—	(64)	395
	20,318	4,580	—	(1,071)	23,827
	$20,652	4,602	—	(1,071)	24,183

Year ended July 31, 1981:					
Depletion	$ 314	20	—	—	334
Depreciation:					
Buildings and building improvements	2,140	195	—	(158)	2,177
Machinery and equipment	14,074	3,590	—	(383)	17,281
Furniture and fixtures	445	85	—	(15)	515
Automotive equipment	389	100	—	(144)	345
	17,048	3,970	—	(700)	20,318
	$17,362	3,990	—	(700)	20,652

RANGAIRE Corporation and Subsidiaries

Financial Review and Summary of Significant Accounting Policies

Principles of Consolidation

The consolidated financial statements include the accounts of Rangaire Corporation (Company) and all of its subsidiaries. All material intercompany accounts and transactions have been eliminated in consolidation.

Property, Plant and Equipment

A subsidiary of the Company has entered into a sale and leaseback transaction covering substantially all of its equipment and limestone reserves. Accordingly, this lease obligation has been recorded as a direct liability and the related assets have been capitalized and are being depreciated over their estimated useful lives.

Depreciation of property, plant and equipment is being provided by the straight-line and declining-balance methods over estimated useful lives as follows:

Buildings and
  building
  improvements _____ 3-40 years
Machinery and
  equipment _____ 3-20 years
Furniture and
  fixtures _____ 3-10 years
Automotive
  equipment _____ 3-8 years

Depletion of the cost of limestone quarries (included in land in the accompanying consolidated balance sheets) is being provided by the unit-of-production method based upon estimates of recoverable limestone reserves as determined by independent engineering studies.

Maintenance and repairs are charged to expense as incurred; renewals and betterments are capitalized. When units of property are retired or otherwise disposed of, their cost and related accumulated depreciation are cleared from the accounts and any resulting gain or loss is credited or charged to earnings.

The Company capitalizes interest on capital expenditures incurred on projects during their construction period. Total interest costs for 1983, 1982 and 1981 were $2,738,881, $3,503,252 and $2,892,888, of which $96,306, $531,374 and $325,842, respectively, has been capitalized.

During fiscal year 1983, the Company recognized gains totaling $382,854, net of federal income tax and investment tax credit recapture, on the cash sale of various fixed assets which were not necessary for its operations.

Acquisition

On September 1, 1981, the Company acquired substantially all of the assets and certain of the obligations of G. & W. H. Corson, Incorporated and its wholly-owned subsidiary Calcite Quarry Corporation for approximately $4,200,000 in cash. Corson Lime Company, a wholly-owned subsidiary, was formed to operate the two limestone operations located in Pennsylvania.

The acquisition was accounted for as a purchase and the accompanying consolidated statements of earnings include the operations of Corson Lime Company for the eleven months ended July 31, 1982 and the year ended July 31, 1983.

The following summarizes the estimated consolidated results of operations assuming Corson Lime Company had been acquired August 1, 1980:

Sale of Operating Assets of Subsidiary

Effective June 30, 1983, the Company sold substantially all the operating assets of Chambers Corporation (Chambers), a wholly-owned subsidiary in the business of manufacturing built-in cooking equipment, to Hobart Corporation (Hobart) for approximately $11,650,000 in cash. The Company recognized a gain on the sale of Chambers of approximately $73,000, net of federal income tax and recapture of investment tax credits.

The Chambers sale agreement stipulated that Hobart assumed accrued Chambers' brand service warranties, accrued vacation pay, interest accrued applicable to long-term debt, long-term debt on building and accrued property taxes aggregating approximately $950,000. The Company retained liabilities, if any, arising from current litigation and product liabilities (other than for warranty claims) relating to products sold prior to June 30, 1983. Additionally, the Company guaranteed the collection of accounts receivable balances sold to Hobart on June 30, 1983.

The remaining assets and liabilities of Chambers were retained by Induction Corporation (formerly Chambers) which is involved solely in the manufacture of induction cooktops.

Revenues attributable to the operating assets sold to Hobart were approximately $15,385,000 in 1983, $16,344,000 in 1982 and $18,913,000 in 1981.

	1982	1981
Revenues _____	$97,500,000	113,700,000
Net income _____	$ 1,200,000	2,300,000
Earnings per share of common stock _____	$.31	.61

RANGAIRE Corporation and Subsidiaries

Employee Benefit Plans

The Company has noncontributory defined benefit pension plans covering two groups of union employees and, until July 31, 1983, all non-union employees. As of July 31, 1983, the Company terminated its defined benefit pension plan for non-union employees and effective August 1, 1983 commenced a defined contribution retirement savings plan for these employees. Total pension expense for the years ended July 31, 1983, 1982 and 1981 was $51,649, $369,791 and $292,292, respectively, which includes amortization of prior service costs over a twenty-year period. The Company funded $51,649, $169,791 and $292,292 of pension costs in 1983, 1982 and 1981, respectively. No contribution was required and no expense was recorded in 1983 for the new retirement savings plan.

At the date of the termination of the pension plan for non-union employees, accumulated plan assets and liabilities were approximately $4,250,000 and $2,470,000, respectively. The resulting $961,200 gain, net of $818,800 of Federal income taxes is included in the 1983 consolidated statement of earnings as an extraordinary item. Distribution of plan net assets to the participants and the Company is pending approval of the pension plan termination by the Pension Benefit Guaranty Corporation. The actuarially computed present value of accumulated vested and unvested benefits of the non-union pension plan, utilizing a weighted average assumed rate of return of 6.5%, aggregated approximately $1,871,000 and $461,000 in 1982 and $1,710,000 and $432,000 in 1981, respectively. Net assets available for benefits were approximately $2,939,000 in 1982 and $2,482,000 in 1981.

At August 1, 1982 and January 1, 1983, the latest actuarial valuation dates of the union pension plans, the actuarially computed present value of accumulated vested and unvested benefits, utilizing a weighted average assumed rate of return of 6.5%, aggregated approximately $340,000 and $80,000 in 1983, $259,000 and $54,000 in 1982 and $150,000 and $28,000 in 1981, respectively. Net assets available for benefits were approximately $787,000 in 1983, $672,000 in 1982 and $628,000 in 1981.

The Company contributes to an employee stock ownership plan which covers substantially all full-time non-union employees. The plan is designed to invest primarily in the Company's common stock. Contributions to the plan are made at the option of the Company and aggregated $271,940 in 1983 and $80,000 in 1981. The 1983 contribution consisted of 37,835 shares of the Company's common stock and the 1981 contribution consisted of cash.

Notes Payable to Banks and Long-term Debt

At July 31, 1983 the Company had lines of credit aggregating $9,000,000 with two banks. The terms of the lines of credit call for interest rates at prime (10½% at July 31, 1983). The lines of credit may be withdrawn at the option of the lenders. The average amount of the short-term debt outstanding for the years ended July 31, 1983, 1982 and 1981 was approximately $2,522,000, $3,890,000 and $10,168,000, respectively, with a related weighted average interest rate of 11½% in 1983 and 17% in 1982 and 1981. The maximum amount of short-term debt outstanding under lines of credit at any month-end during the fiscal year was $3,950,000 in 1983, $6,675,000 in 1982 and $12,050,000 in 1981.

The loan agreements relating to long-term debt require maintenance of certain financial ratios, restrict further borrowings and restrict payment of cash dividends and the redemption and retirement of stock. Unrestricted retained earnings available for the aforementioned purposes at July 31, 1983 approximated $6,046,000.

The aggregate maturities of long-term debt for the four years ending July 31, 1988 are as follows:

1985	$795,000
1986	810,000
1987	986,250
1988	986,250

RANGAIRE Corporation and Subsidiaries

Following is a summary of long-term debt at July 31, 1983 and 1982:

	1983	1982
8⅝% note, payable in annual installments of $52,700 to 1983 and $367,000 thereafter through 1987, with a final installment of $57,700 due on July 31, 1987, plus interest payable quarterly (repaid in July 1983)	$ —	1,578,400
6¾% note, payable in annual installments of $286,000, with a final installment of $282,000 paid on September 1, 1982, plus interest payable semi-annually	—	282,000
9⅞% note, payable in annual installments of $250,000 to 1986, and $656,250 thereafter to 1994, plus interest payable quarterly	6,000,000	6,250,000
Term note - payable in three quarterly installments of $225,000 and a final quarterly installment of $50,000, plus interest at ½% above prime rate payable quarterly	725,000	4,500,000
Term note - payable in two quarterly installments of $250,000 and a final quarterly installment of $150,000, plus interest at ½% above prime rate payable quarterly	650,000	4,500,000
Industrial revenue bonds, payable in semi-annual serial maturities of $165,000 to 1991 and a final maturity of $1,865,000 on December 31, 1991, plus interest at 65% of prime rate (with 10% minimum and 15% maximum)	4,505,000	4,835,000
Capitalized lease obligations: Payable in annual installments in varying amounts from $205,000 in 1984 to a maximum of $230,000 in 1986, plus interest at 6% payable semi-annually	650,000	840,000
Payable in annual installments of $125,000 to 1987, plus interest at 5½% payable semi-annually (assumed by purchaser of subsidiary)	—	625,000
	12,530,000	23,410,400
Less current installments	2,160,000	1,229,700
Long-term debt, excluding current installments	$10,370,000	22,180,700

RANGAIRE Corporation and Subsidiaries

Construction Contracts

Profit on long-term construction contracts is recorded on the basis of the Company's estimates of the percentage of completion of individual contracts, commencing when progress reaches a point where experience is sufficient to estimate final results with reasonable accuracy. That portion of the total contract price is accrued which is allocable, on the basis of the Company's engineering estimates of the percentage of completion, to contract expenditures and work performed. At the time a loss on any contract becomes known, the entire amount of the estimated ultimate loss is accrued.

Stockholders' Equity

At July 31, 1983, 500,000 shares of $5.00 par value preferred stock are authorized and none issued.

On August 1, 1983, the Company issued an additional 37,835 shares of common stock with a market value of $269,574 to the employee stock ownership plan as a contribution for the year ended July 31, 1984.

Earnings Per Share of Common Stock

Earnings per share of common stock are based on the weighted average number of shares outstanding during each year after giving retroactive effect to stock dividends. Common stock equivalents (an immaterial number of options which expired prior to July 31, 1981) have not been included in determining earnings per share of common stock because their inclusion would not materially reduce the per share amounts shown in the consolidated statements of earnings and retained earnings.

Federal Income Taxes

Federal and state income taxes on earnings before income taxes and extraordinary item for the years ended July 31, 1983 ($103,978), July 31, 1982 ($360,797) and July 31, 1981 ($120,081) result in effective tax rates of 5.3%, 24.0% and 5.6%, respectively. The reasons for the differences between Federal income tax expense computed by applying the statutory Federal income tax rate to earnings before income taxes and extraordinary item and income tax expense at the effective tax rates are as follows:

	1983 Amount	1983 Percent of pretax earnings	1982 Amount	1982 Percent of pretax earnings	1981 Amount	1981 Percent of pretax earnings
Computed "expected" tax expense	$901,978	46.0%	$691,081	46.0%	$992,069	46.0%
Increases (reductions) in taxes resulting from:						
Excess of statutory depletion over cost depletion	(111,287)	(5.7)	(142,180)	(9.5)	(156,631)	(7.3)
Investment tax credits	(633,773)	(32.3)	(226,268)	(15.1)	(644,157)	(29.9)
Jobs tax credit	—	—	(810)	—	(7,315)	(.3)
State income taxes, net of Federal income tax benefit	31,382	1.6	84,351	5.6	23,640	1.1
Internal Revenue Service settlement	—	—	(193,251)	(12.8)	—	—
Other	(84,322)	(4.3)	147,874	9.8	(87,525)	(4.0)
Taxes on earnings before extraordinary item	103,978	5.3%	$360,797	24.0%	$120,081	5.6%
Tax on extraordinary item	818,800					
	$922,778					

RANGAIRE Corporation and Subsidiaries

Federal income taxes for the year ended July 31, 1982 were reduced by $193,251 as a result of an agreement with the Internal Revenue Service primarily concerning investment tax credits.

State income taxes for the years ended July 31, 1983, 1982 and 1981, were approximately $58,115, $156,205 and $43,778, respectively.

Investment tax credits are recorded as a reduction of the provision for Federal income taxes in the year realized. The Company has investment tax credit carry-forwards that will expire in 1998 if unused, of approximately $43,850 for tax purposes and $-0- for financial statement purposes.

Deferred Federal income taxes have been provided for timing differences between financial statement earnings and those earnings reported for tax purposes. The sources and tax effect of the components of timing differences are listed as follows:

	Year ended July 31,		
	1983	1982	1981
Warranty reserves	$ **10,122**	(33,092)	(111,242)
Bad debt deduction	**9,200**	(9,200)	(4,140)
Depreciation method	**350,169**	239,028	136,082
Investment tax credits	**(153,196)**	(109,350)	—
Sale of operating assets of subsidiary	**17,133**	—	—
Other	**(1,151)**	(6,654)	1,814
	$232,277	80,732	22,514

Commitments

The Company maintains its warehouses and certain of its other facilities on leased premises and leases some of the automobiles, trucks and equipment used in its operations. Generally, the leases are for periods varying from one to eleven years and are renewable at the option of the Company.

Total rent expense for the years ended July 31, 1983, 1982 and 1981 was $1,020,824, $1,441,401 and $1,300,441, respectively. Rent expense includes $751,694 in 1983, $353,607 in 1982 and $545,693 in 1981 of vehicle rental payments which were based upon a constant weekly rate in 1983 and upon the number of miles certain leased trucks were driven in 1982 and 1981. Of the $1,020,824 total 1983 rent expense, $857,652 was paid under noncancellable leases.

At July 31, 1983, future minimum lease payments under noncancellable operating leases are as follows:

Years ending:	Future minimum rentals
1984	$ 776,000
1985	685,000
1986	636,000
1987	488,000
1988	467,000
	$3,052,000

The Chairman of the Board owns the patent for induction cooktops manufactured by the Company. Pursuant to a royalty agreement entered into in June 1979, the Company pays the Chairman of the Board fifteen dollars for each induction cooktop manufactured and sold until 100,000 units have been sold. The royalty paid in 1983, 1982 and 1981 was not significant; however, the royalty could become significant in future periods.

RANGAIRE Corporation and Subsidiaries

Contingencies

The Company and its wholly-owned subsidiary, Induction Corporation (formerly Chambers Corporation), are defendants in lawsuits pending in U.S. District Court and U.S. Court of Appeals. The plaintiffs, one of which is a former distributor of Chambers' products, allege damages arising out of the Company's alleged violation of Federal antitrust laws, breach of contract, unfair competition, interference with prospective advantage and wrongful termination of franchise. The plaintiffs seek aggregate damages of not less than $7,100,000, trebled as a result of alleged antitrust violations; $14,200,000 in state law compensatory damages, plus punitive damages of not less than $9,000,000; court costs and attorneys' fees. The Company is vigorously contesting these lawsuits and has filed answers denying any unlawful conduct. In one suit (representing $2,500,000 of the $7,100,000 being sought as

damages) Induction Corporation moved for summary judgment as to the plaintiff's claims. The motion was granted by the district court and plaintiff has appealed the ruling to the U.S. Court of Appeals. Due to the inherent uncertainty of both the outcome of these cases and the estimated amount or range of potential loss, provisions for losses, if any, have not been recorded on the Company's books. However, management believes the resolution of these lawsuits will not have a material impact on the financial position of the Company.

Supplementary Earnings Statement Information

	1983	1982	1981
Maintenance and repairs	$2,269,797	3,564,089	2,324,491
Depreciation and depletion	5,334,063	4,602,006	3,990,084
Taxes, other than on income (principally payroll related taxes)	2,055,947	2,169,688	1,726,849
Rental expense	1,020,824	1,441,401	1,300,441
Advertising expense	394,417	785,693	1,031,575

Related Party

A certified common carrier, which is owned by a former member of the Company's board of directors, transported limestone products for the Company during the periods that the owner served as a director. The Company paid approximately $1,277,000 in 1982 and $2,367,000 in 1981 to the carrier for transportation services.

RANGAIRE Corporation and Subsidiaries

Summary of Quarterly Financial Data (Unaudited)

The following quarterly financial information is unaudited; however, in the opinion of management all adjustments necessary to a fair statement of the results of operations for the interim periods

have been included, except that certain adjustments, related primarily to adjustment of inventory to physical count and actual cost, adjustments of inventory to net realizable value, adjustment of pension expense and revision of the estimated tax provision, increased net income in the fourth quarter by

approximately $558,000 in 1983, $750,000 in 1982 and $737,000 in 1981. It is not practicable to determine the effect, if any, that the adjustments had on the results of operations for the three previous quarters (000 omitted except per share amounts):

	Three months ended			
Year ended July 31, 1983:	October 31, 1982	January 31, 1983	April 30, 1983	July 31, 1983
Revenue	$25,554	20,096	20,464	20,917
Gross profit	$ 4,101	2,656	3,021	2,497
Net earnings before extraordinary item	$ 529	248	278	802
Net earnings	$ 529	248	278	1,763
Net earnings per share of common stock before extraordinary item	$.14	.07	.07	.21
Net earnings per share of common stock	$.14	.07	.07	.46

SUMMARY   **Adjusting entries** are made necessary by the periodicity concept, which requires preparation of financial statements at regular intervals. In order to measure income and financial position properly, accruals and deferrals must be recorded by means of adjusting entries that bring the account balances up to date. **Accruals** occur when expenses or revenues have materialized but no exchange has taken place. **Deferrals** occur when an exchange of assets has taken place, but the related expense or revenue has not yet materialized. In addition to accruals and deferrals, **allocation** adjustments must be made to assign costs such as depreciation and uncollectible accounts to each accounting period. After all adjustments are made and posted, the books can be closed.

A **worksheet** may be used to facilitate the end-of-period procedures and to avoid making adjusting and closing entries at interim periods. The worksheet consolidates adjusting entries, closing entries, trial balances, and financial statements into a single form. In order not to disturb the bookkeeping routine, **reversing entries** may be made at the end of the period after the books have been closed.

The sequence of accounting procedures repeated during each accounting period is known as the **accounting cycle.** It consists of journalizing transactions, posting ledger accounts, making adjusting entries, preparing trial balances and financial statements, closing the books, and reversing certain adjusting entries.

The output of the accounting information system consists of an **annual report** that contains the basic financial statements and includes notes that explain alternative accounting principles used by the reporting company. Before an independent accountant certifies that the statements are fair, they must be audited. Companies frequently issue **interim reports** at quarterly intervals in addition to annual financial statements.

SUMMARY OF ACCOUNTING PRINCIPLES AND CONCEPTS

The principles and concepts discussed in the last few chapters are part of the generally accepted accounting principles used in the determination of income and financial position. You should be familiar with these principles and concepts and keep them in mind throughout your study of accounting.

GAAP   **Principles** are rules adopted by the accounting profession. Some are derived from certain basic assumptions about business entities and the business environment in which the entities operate. Some are conventions agreed upon by the profession and by users of accounting information. In order to apply the principles, accountants have developed a number of accounting **concepts,** some of which derive from the principles, and some of which are themselves assumptions or conventions adopted by the profession. The distinction between principles and concepts is not always clear, and the labels are not important. What *is* important, however, is that you understand the purpose and use of the principles and concepts because they constitute the standards that are applied by accountants and are generally accepted and understood by users of accounting reports.

Principles

Objectivity. Accounting measurements must be based on verifiable evidence and be as objective as possible. Accounting reports should not be biased in favor of or against a specific entity or user.

Revenue Realization. Revenue is realized when an exchange takes place in an arm's-length transaction—that is, between independent parties—or when the earning process is completed by performance.

Matching. If income is to be measured properly, expenses incurred during a period for the purpose of earning revenue should be matched with the revenue earned in the same period.

Consistency. Once an accounting principle or method is adopted, it should be applied consistently from one period to the next so that valid comparisons between financial statements of different periods can be made.

Conservatism. When judgment is required in deciding how to apply accounting principles, concepts, and conventions, the accountant should choose the approach that is least likely to overstate net income or financial position.

Full Disclosure. Accounting reports should disclose financial information fairly and completely to ensure that they are not misleading.

Materiality. Financial reporting is concerned only with significant information. Trivial details need not be reported and precise figures may be rounded to make them more easily readable.

Industry Practices. Exceptions to principles sometimes occur due to the specialized nature of some entities. In those cases industry practices constitute generally accepted principles.

Concepts

Entity. The business is viewed as an economic unit separate from its owners. Accountants report on the affairs of the entity.

Money Measurement. Financial accounting is concerned with economic events that can be expressed in terms of money.

Cost. Assets are valued at cost since cost is objectively measurable and verifiable.

Stable Dollar. It is assumed that the monetary unit is stable, i.e., that the dollar always maintains the same value.

Going Concern. The business entity is expected to remain in existence indefinitely.

Periodicity. The life of the business entity is divided into time periods at the end of which financial statements are prepared. Accruals and deferrals are required because of the periodicity concept.

Accrual. Revenues are recorded when earned regardless of the time payment is received. Expenses are recorded when incurred regardless of the time payment is made.

KEY TERMS

accounting cycle *(199)*
accrual *(182)*
adjusting entry *(181)*
allocation *(180)*
annual report *(201)*
correcting entry *(182)*

deferral *(182, 186)*
fair presentation *(181)*
full disclosure *(201)*
interim report *(201)*
reversing entry *(200, 218)*
worksheet *(193)*

APPENDIX: REVERSING ENTRIES

Reversing entries facilitates bookkeeping

Certain types of journal entries are routinely made and posted at the end of the accounting period *after the books are closed* in order to facilitate bookkeeping procedures and avoid disturbing the normal routine of recording transactions. These **reversing entries** are the opposite of some adjusting entries made previously. In effect, they open some temporary accounts for the new accounting period before any transactions take place. For example, the following journal entry has been made to adjust a revenue account at the end of a period:

Dec. 31	Prepaid rent	1,600	
	Rent expense		1,600

In order to reverse this entry, a new journal entry is made at a later time. This new entry cancels the previous one, as follows:

Jan. 2	Rent expense	1,600	
	Prepaid rent		1,600

Why should anyone want to reverse a previous entry if it was correct in the first place? To answer this question, we first look at some routine accounting procedures without reversing entries. For example, whenever Pathmaker Company pays salaries, the bookkeeper makes the following journal entry for the appropriate amount:

	Salaries expense	4,860	
	Cash		4,860

Remember that this is a routine entry which is made many times in each accounting period although the amount may differ each time. At the end of the accounting period, salaries are accrued and recorded by the accountant as illustrated in the worksheet.

Dec. 31	Salaries expense	1,150	
	Salaries payable		1,150

The Salaries Payable account is created at the end of the accounting period so that the liability may be reported in the balance sheet. The liability will be eliminated when salaries are paid in the next accounting period, and the following entry will have to be made:

Jan. 9	Salaries expense	3,400	
	Salaries payable	1,150	
	Cash		4,550

Part of the $4,550 cash payment is for last period's salaries, and it eliminates the accrued liability of $1,150. But this entry requires a change from the usual way of recording salaries. Remember that the usual entry has only a debit to Salaries Expense and a credit to Cash. If the entry is recorded routinely by a computer, a special program has to be written to have the computer record the January 9 salary payment because it is different from the usual entry.

If the entry is recorded by hand, the bookkeeper has to change the routine followed with all other salary payments. This problem, and the likelihood of errors it can cause, can be eliminated with reversing entries. After the books are closed, the adjusting entry that created the Salaries Payable account at the end of the period is reversed in the next period. The reversing entry appears below.

Jan. 1	Salaries payable	1,150	
	Salaries expense		1,150

The entry eliminates the liability from the books and transfer its balance to the expense account. But the expense account has been closed and has a zero balance. The reversing entry opens the Salaries Expense account for the new accounting period, and when the reversing entry is posted the expense account contains a credit balance of $1,150. This credit balance now makes possible the routine recording of the first salary payment of the new period, as follows:

Jan. 9	Salaries expense	4,550	
	Cash		4,550

When this entry is posted, the expense account contains a $3,400 debit balance, precisely the amount of salary expense incurred so far in the new accounting period. Reversing the previous entry eliminates the need to change the normal bookkeeping routine. The above example, with and without reversing entries, is illustrated in the T accounts in Figure 5-7.

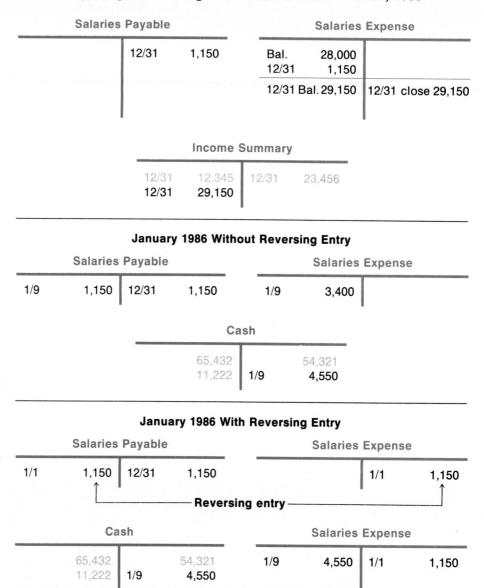

Figure 5-7   Salaries are accrued on December 31 and paid on January 9. If reversing entries are made on January 1, the January 9 entry is the same as all other entries for salary payments throughout the accounting period. Without reversing entries, the normal routine cannot be followed. Note, however, that on January 9 the balances of all accounts are the same with reversing entries as they are without reversing entries.

Not all adjusting entries need to be reversed. The adjusting entry to accrue salaries created a salaries payable account. But the company does not need a salaries payable account on its books during the accounting period. It needs it only at the end of the period when financial statements are to be prepared. The reversing entry eliminates this unneeded account. In general, the rule for reversing adjusting entries is simple:

Rules for making reversing entries

If a permanent account was created by an adjusting entry, reverse the entry. Otherwise do not reverse.

Some permanent accounts are not maintained in the books, because they are not needed until the end of the accounting period. Examples are accrued salaries, interest receivable, and interest payable. Some permanent accounts are not maintained because the company has a policy of recording certain transactions in temporary accounts.

For example, unearned rent is usually recorded as rent revenue since it becomes revenue within a short time. Supplies may be recorded as expenses since they are used shortly after they are acquired. In these cases the permanent account comes into existence only when the adjustment is made: for example, to accrue salaries, to remove unused supplies from supplies expense, or to record a liability for the rent revenue that has not been earned. Reversing entries eliminate these permanent accounts, and the books are left ready for the next period's transactions.

In rare cases an adjusting entry creates a permanent account that is not reversed. For example, if depreciation is recorded for the very first time, the accumulated depreciation account is created. Once created, it is used each year, and its balance grows. The intent, of course, is to leave this account on the books and not to eliminate it by a reversing entry.

QUESTIONS

1. Why is it necessary to prepare adjusting entries at the end of the accounting period?

2. Describe a transaction that could be recorded either as an expense or as the purchase of an asset. How is the asset classified?

3. What are accruals, and how are they related to cash flows? What are deferrals, and how are they related to cash flows?

4. Describe a transaction that could be recorded either as a revenue or as a liability. How is the liability classified?

5. Give an example of an allocation that is made by an adjusting entry.

6. Is it necessary to prepare a worksheet at the end of the accounting period? What purpose does the worksheet serve?

7. Describe the first two steps of the accounting cycle.

8. Name the three basic financial statements found in the annual report and describe the function of each.

9. What is an interim report and when is it issued?

10. "We collected $160,000 cash from our customers this year and wrote $110,000 of checks to pay for expenses. Therefore, our net income is $50,000." Explain why this statement is not necessarily true.

11. List at least three of the six accounting principles described, and explain what they mean.

12. List at least four of the accounting concepts described, and explain what they mean.

*13. What is a reversing entry, and why is it made?

EXERCISES

Ex. 5-1   **Correcting journal entries.**   The bookkeeper of Plano Company prepared the following journal entries when the company bought office supplies on open account. None of the payables have yet been paid.

Mar. 5	Office supplies	3,400	
	Cash		3,400
Mar. 15	Office supplies	4,500	
	Accounts payable		4,500
Mar. 19	Office expense	1,700	
	Accounts payable		1,700
Mar. 27	Office supplies	2,100	
	Accounts receivable		2,100
Mar. 29	Office expenses	600	
	Supplies payable		600

Required: Prepare the entries needed to correct the bookkeeper's errors.

Ex. 5-2   **Correcting incorrect entries.**   At the end of the year, two adjustments were recorded as follows by the bookkeeper of Zelda Corporation:

Dec. 31	Depreciation expense	37,200	
	Accumulated depreciation		37,200
Dec. 31	Bad debts expense	7,350	
	Accounts receivable		7,350

The accountant who examined the records found that depreciation for the year should have been $29,200 instead of the amount recorded, and Bad Debts Expense should have been $8,350.

---

*Questions marked with asterisks are based on information in the appendix of this chapter.

Required:

    a. Prepare the entries to correct the accounts assuming that the books have not yet been closed.

    b. Prepare the entries to correct the accounts assuming that the temporary accounts have been closed to Income Summary, but the Income Summary account is still open.

Ex. 5-3   **Journalizing a deferral and a correction.**   The Supplies Inventory account of Belamore Corporation has a debit balance of $5,640 on December 31. A physical count of supplies on this date indicates that supplies costing $850 are on hand. While examining the journal, the bookkeeper notices that a July 2 purchase of supplies costing $620 was erroneously recorded as a purchase of equipment. Depreciation was recorded on this nonexistent equipment in the amount of $40.

Required: Prepare the necessary adjusting entries to correct the accounts.

Ex. 5-4   **Explaining adjusting entries.**   Partec Company charges purchases of food for the company cafeteria to Employee Benefits Expense. Cleaning supplies used in the cafeteria are charged to Prepaid Expenses when purchased. Cafeteria employees' pay is charged to Wage Expense. At the end of the year, the accountant prepared the following adjusting entries:

Dec. 31	Food inventory	1,815	
	Employee benefits expense		1,815
	Supplies expense	1,980	
	Prepaid expenses		1,980
	Wage expense	2,340	
	Wages payable		2,340

Required: Give a brief written explanation for each of the above adjusting entries.

Ex. 5-5   **Accruals of expenses and revenues.**   Endora Investment Company borrows money from private investors by selling them 1-year notes payable. It then uses the money to buy government securities and municipal bonds. On December 31, the company has outstanding $325,000 of notes payable, on which $18,560 of interest is accrued. It holds investments of $298,600 on which $20,320 of interest is accrued. In addition the company owes $2,100 of accrued salaries and $3,230 of accrued taxes, all of which will be paid in January.

Required: Record all of the accruals in the general journal.

Ex. 5-6   **Deferrals of expenses and revenues.**   Phoxie Company stores its fuel oil in underground tanks and records the purchases as assets. It keeps all office supplies in one storage room and records their purchases as expenses. The company collects rent on its warehouse every 6 months in accordance with the terms of the lease and records the receipts as unearned rent revenue. It accepts retainers from customers before it agrees to perform services for them and records the receipts as service revenue. On December 31 the following account balances exist in the ledger:

	Debit	Credit
Fuel oil inventory	$9,860	
Office supplies expense	4,520	
Unearned rent revenue		$11,550
Service revenue		49,870

The accountant provides you with the following list of adjustment data:

Fuel oil on hand	$ 1,500
Office supplies on hand	750
Unearned rent revenue	3,540
Unearned service revenue	2,110

Required: Prepare the necessary adjusting entries on December 31.

Ex. 5-7 **Deferred and accrued expense and revenue.** Monteverdi Theatrical Agency sponsors monthly performances of concerts, operas, and plays. It credits unearned ticket revenue when it collects money from patrons for season tickets. At the end of 1985, the Unearned Ticket Revenue account has a balance of $84,600, of which $42,800 is for performances that will take place during 1986 and the balance for performances that have already taken place. The Ticket Revenue account is credited for tickets sold at each performance, and it has a balance of $123,400.

The company owes $2,250 to its employees for December salaries that will be paid in January. It owns a municipal bond, bought as a temporary investment from the city when it built a parking lot near the company's theater. Interest of $900 is accrued on the bond and will be paid by the city on January 15.

The company's theater is rented to other users between the performances that it sponsors. Amounts collected from these users are credited to a Rent Revenue account which now has a $22,500 balance. $1,200 of this was paid in December by a group which will use the theater in January for a revival meeting.

Required: Prepare the necessary adjusting entries on December 31, 1985.

Ex. 5-8 **Prepaid expense adjustment.** On September 1, 1984, Haplos Company purchased a 2-year liability insurance policy. The premium for the policy was $4,800, which the company decided to charge to prepaid insurance.

On December 16, 1985, the company had to pay $1,285 for damage to a customer's car caused by one of its employees. The payment was recorded as follows:

Dec. 16	Casualty loss	1,285	
	Cash		1,285

The insurance company agreed that the liability policy covers the damage and had indicated it would send $1,285 to the Haplos Company to reimburse it in January 1986. The check arrived on January 5, 1986.

Required: Record the purchase of the insurance in 1984. Prepare the adjusting entries on December 31, 1984, and on December 31, 1985, to record the insurance expense for each year and the amount receivable from the insurance company. Record the collection of the cash in 1986.

Ex. 5-9   **Recording deferrals and accruals.**   Fenestra Cleaners operates a window washing service. The company charges all purchases of cleaning supplies to supplies expense. On December 31, 1985, a physical count reveals that supplies costing $4,010 are on hand.

The company buys insurance to pay for any windows broken by employees. The Prepaid Insurance account has a debit balance of $900, which represents the premium of a 2-year policy bought on June 30, 1985.

Wages were last paid on December 23. By December 31 $1,750 of wages are accrued and not paid.

The company frequently signs contracts to clean windows on multistory buildings, and collects part of the revenue in advance, which it records as unearned cleaning revenue. The Unearned Cleaning Revenue account has a credit balance of $5,780, but $2,360 of this amount has already been earned.

Required: Prepare the adjusting entries needed to bring the accounts up to date on December 31, 1985.

Ex. 5-10   **Deferred revenues and expenses.**   During 1985 Literatea Publishing Company collected $146,300 for magazine subscriptions and credited the receipts to Subscriptions Payable. On December 31, 1985, an audit reveals that $97,800 of magazines have not yet been delivered to subscribers.

The company rents a warehouse for which it pays rent of $500 per month. Rent payments are recorded as expenses. The last payment for January 1986 rent was made on December 23, 1985.

Purchases of ink, paper, and other printing supplies are recorded as supplies inventory. The Supplies Inventory account has a debit balance of $59,200, and a physical count indicates that $3,720 of supplies are on hand.

The company records sales revenue for magazines sold to book stores and newsstand dealers. These customers have the privilege of returning unsold magazines at the end of each month for a credit to their accounts. The Sales Revenue account has a credit balance of $188,600 but the return of $2,790 of magazines at the end of December has not yet been recorded.

Required: Prepare the necessary adjusting entries on December 31, 1985.

Ex. 5-11   **Uncollectible accounts adjustment.**   On December 31, 1985, Holotex Company had a debit balance of $59,680 in accounts receivable and a credit balance of $160 in the Allowance for Doubtful Accounts. The company's accountant estimates that the balance in the allowance account should be $2,800 if it is to reflect properly the amount of receivables that are expected to be collected.

On December 31, 1986, the company had $85,400 of accounts receivable and the Allowance for Doubtful Accounts had a debit balance of $130. The accountant estimates that the allowance account should have a credit balance of $3,000 when the books are closed.

After the expense accounts have been closed to income summary—but before the Income Summary account is closed—the accountant realizes he made a mistake in making his estimate of bad debts for 1986. The estimate should be $3,500 instead of $3,000.

Required:

  a. Prepare the necessary adjusting entry to correct the account balances on December 31, 1985.
  b. Prepare the adjusting entry on December 31, 1986, as originally estimated.
  c. Close the expense account at the end of 1986.
  d. Prepare the entry to correct the error.

Ex. 5-12   **Calculating and recording depreciation.**   Juniper Company bought a building for $200,000 in 1975 with an estimated useful life of 20 years. The company owns $120,000 of equipment with a 10-year useful life. On June 1, 1985, it bought another building for $45,000 with an estimated useful life of 25 years. The company uses straight-line depreciation computed to the nearest whole month.

Required:

  a. Prepare the adjusting entries to record depreciation at the end of 1985.
  b. If the old building was originally bought on April 1, what is the balance of accumulated depreciation for this building after entry **a** is posted?

Ex. 5-13   **Allocation adjustments.**   Following are selected account balances from the ledger of Troyka Corporation:

	Debit	Credit
Accounts receivable	$ 44,300	
Allowance for doubtful accounts		$ 200
Buildings	135,000	
Accumulated depreciation, buildings		24,500
Equipment	80,000	
Accumulated depreciation, equipment		14,600

Depreciation is recorded at the rate of 5 percent of cost on the building and 10 percent of cost on the equipment each year. The company estimates that the Allowance for Doubtful Accounts should have a credit balance of $2,500.

Required:

  a. Prepare the necessary adjusting entries to record depreciation and bad debts expense on December 31.
  b. Prepare the closing entries to close temporary accounts.

*Ex. 5-14   **Deferrals and reversing entries.**   Moxie Corporation records the purchase of heating oil as an asset and of office supplies as expenses. The company records the rent it receives on part of its office building every quarter as unearned lease revenue. It collects the rents on its parking spaces monthly and records the receipts as parking rent income. On December 31, 1985, the following account balances exist in the ledger:

Heating oil inventory	$7,500	
Office supplies expense	4,500	
Unearned lease revenue		$42,000
Parking rent income		12,000

The accountant provides you with the following list of adjustment data:

Heating oil on hand	$ 1,750
Office supplies on hand	600
Unearned lease revenue	4,500
Unearned parking income	1,000

Required:
   a. Prepare the necessary adjusting entries on December 31, 1985.
   b. Prepare the necessary reversing entries on January 1, 1986.
   c. Explain what is accomplished with the reversing entry.

*Ex. 5-15   **Interest accrual with reversing entry.**   Newberry Corporation owns $10,000 of 12 percent U.S. Treasury bonds that pay interest on April 30 and October 31 each year.

Required:
   a. Record the receipt of interest on October 1.
   b. Prepare the necessary adjusting entry to accrue interest on December 31.
   c. Record the necessary reversing entry on January 1 and the April 1 receipt of interest.
   d. Assume that reversing entries are not prepared, and record the April 1 collection of interest.
   e. Briefly discuss the advantage of the reversing entry.

*Ex. 5-16   **Adjustments and reversing entries.**   Noreen Company records purchases of maintenance supplies as an asset. When it pays rent it records rent expense. The company's Maintenance Supplies account has a debit balance of $8,500 and its Rent Expense account has a debit balance of $9,600 on December 31, 1985. Depreciation of equipment for the year is $1,560. $1,200 of maintenance supplies are on hand, and $850 of the rent expense is for January 1986 rent. The cost of the equipment is $14,900. Salaries in the amount of $1,840 are accrued at the end of the year and not paid.

Required:
   a. Prepare the necessary adjusting entries on December 31, 1985.
   b. Prepare the appropriate reversing entries on January 1, 1986.

Ex. 5-17   **Calculation of income from cash flows.**   During 1985 Lani Corporation received $15,000 cash from all sources. Of this amount, $3,000 was a loan from a bank, and the remainder was from customers. There were no accounts receivable at the beginning of the year. At the end of the year the company made this adjusting entry:

Dec. 31	Accounts receivable	2,000	
	Service revenue		2,000

Cash payments during the year amounted to $8,000, including $3,000 for the purchase of equipment and the rest for operating expenses. At the end of the year the company made the following adjusting entries:

---

* Exercises marked with asterisks are based on information in the appendix of this chapter.

Dec. 31	Depreciation expense	1,500	
	Accumulated depreciation		1,500
	Salaries expense	2,500	
	Accrued salaries		2,500

The company is subject to an income tax of 20 percent of income.

Required: Calculate Lani Corporation's net income for 1985.

Ex. 5-18 **Interpretation of financial statements.** Examine the financial statements of Rangaire Corporation reproduced at the end of the chapter. Based on your observations, indicate whether each of the following statements is true or false.

a. The company uses the calendar year for its accounting period.

b. There were 3,808,170 shares outstanding on July 31, 1983.

c. Depreciation is not reported separately in the income statement, but it is possible to determine that depreciation expense for the 1983 fiscal year was $5,314,000.

d. The company's approximate tax rate on earnings before extraordinary is 5.3 percent for 1983.

e. The company reported extraordinary gains in 1982 and 1983.

f. The current ratio on July 31, 1983 was 2.04.

g. The allowance for doubtful accounts is reported for 1983 but not for 1982.

h. Working capital on July 31, 1983 is $13,769,847, which is a decrease of $3,322,951 from 1982.

i. There are 500,000 shares of preferred stock issued.

j. The number of common shares issued is not the same as the average number of shares used to calculate EPS.

k. The change in working capital is reported in the statement of changes in financial position.

l. The owner of 100 shares of Rangaire common stock received $24 of cash dividends in the 1983 fiscal year.

m. The name of the company's auditor is Arthur Andersen.

n. The company acquired $5,265,213 of new equipment in 1983.

o. The inventory of raw materials decreased by $2,205,811 from 1982 to 1983.

p. From the balance sheet and the statement of changes in financial position, it is possible to determine that accounts receivable amounted to $10,396,568 on July 31, 1981.

q. The company uses straight-line depreciation for all of its fixed assets.

r. Although the company does some manufacturing, it obtains most of its revenues from retailing operations.

s. The interim reports of the company have been audited by a CPA firm.

t. The auditor's report indicates that the financial statements of the company were examined and the accounting records were tested as necessary.

u. Because the statements are consolidated, they include data on more than one accounting entity; the other entities consist of companies owned by Rangaire Corporation.

v. The second paragraph of the auditor's report specifically mentions the realization principle.

w. The company's rent expense for 1983 was $1,020,824.

x. In 1981 the company acquired a subsidiary that quarries limestone.

y. The company terminated a pension plan during 1983.

z. Almost 50 percent of the company's inventory consisted of work in process on July 1983.

PROBLEMS

P. 5-1 **Year-end adjusting entries.** Oolita Company provides maintenance services for industrial robots. Following are data for adjustments needed in the company's books on June 30, the end of the fiscal year.

a. On April 1 the company bought a 1-year casualty insurance policy for $1,440 and recorded it as prepaid insurance.

b. The company pays rent on a leased computer and records the payments as rent expense. The $475 payment for the July rent was made on June 20.

c. At the end of June $1,200 of salaries are accrued.

d. To enable one of its suppliers to build a special order of maintenance parts, the company loaned the supplier $29,600 on May 1, in exchange for which it received a 15 percent 90-day note. Interest on the note for 60 days is accrued by June 30.

e. The company collected $5,000 from one of its customers in March as payment in advance for maintenance services on newly installed painting robots. The receipt of the deposit was recorded as unearned revenue. By June 30 Oolita Company had performed all but $400 of the services.

f. The allowance for doubtful accounts has a credit balance of $10. The company's management estimates that the allowance account should have a $500 credit balance.

g. Depreciation on equipment is $1,000.

Required: Prepare the necessary adjusting entries at the end of June.

P. 5-2   **Accruals, deferrals, and allocations.**   Algipond Construction Company builds residential and commercial swimming pools. Its accounting period ends on November 30. The following data are available for adjustments:

a.   The company owns $10,000 of corporate bonds as a temporary investment. Interest on the bonds in the amount of $460 is accrued by November 30.

b.   Materials and supplies in the amount of $9,400 are recorded as an asset. A physical count indicates that materials and supplies costing $1,300 are on hand.

c.   On July 1 the company bought a 1-year liability insurance policy for $3,600 and recorded the payment as insurance expense. The Prepaid Insurance account has a debit balance of $1,200, which represents the premium on a 1-year fire and casualty policy which the company bought on December 1 of last year.

d.   The balance in Accounts Receivable is $46,400. Construction of a pool was completed in November. The owner was billed during construction for the portion of the pool completed. The last bill for $3,600 has not yet been sent.

e.   The Allowance for Uncollectible Accounts has a credit balance of $160. The company estimates that 2 percent of receivables should be reported in the allowance account on November 30.

f.   Salaries in the amount of $3,200 are accrued on November 30.

g.   The company has received an advance payment of $5,000 on a new pool to be completed by February 28. The deposit was credited to Unearned Revenue. Work was started in late November and $3,000 of the deposit has been earned by the end of November.

h.   Interest of $350 is accrued on notes payable owed to banks.

i.   Depreciation on construction equipment is $2,200.

Required:
a.   Prepare the necessary adjusting entries in the general journal.
b.   If you have studied the appendix to the chapter, indicate which of your adjusting entries should be reversed.

P. 5-3   **Accruals, deferrals, and allocations.**   Silas Company specializes in the construction of silos. Its accounting period ends on December 31. The following data are available for adjustments:

a.   Materials and supplies in the amount of $19,400 are recorded as an expense. A physical count indicates that materials and supplies costing $2,680 are on hand.

b.   The company owns $40,000 of bonds as a temporary investment. Interest on the bonds in the amount of $1,460 accrued by December 31.

c.   On June 1 the company bought a 1-year liability insurance policy for $3,600 and recorded the payment as prepaid insurance.

d.   The balance in accounts receivable is $96,400. Construction of a silo completed in December is not yet billed in the amount of $23,600.

e.   The Allowance for Uncollectible Accounts has a debit balance of $660. The company estimates that 3 percent of receivables should be reported in the allowance account on December 31.

f.   During the year the company collected advance payment of $18,000 on new silos. The deposits are credited to construction revenue. By the end of the year $3,000 of this revenue had not been earned.

g.   Interest of $1,350 is accrued on notes payable owed to banks.

h.   Salaries in the amount of $6,200 are accrued on December 31.

i.   Depreciation on construction equipment is $4,200.

Required:

a.   Prepare the necessary adjusting entries in the general journal.

b.   If you have studied the appendix to the chapter, indicate which of your adjusting entries should be reversed.

P. 5-4   **Adjusting accounts in a trial balance.**   The following trial balance was taken from the books of Holotex Company at the end of the company's accounting period:

**Holotex Company
Trial Balance
December 31, 1985**

	Debits	Credits
Cash	$ 12,500	
Notes receivable	15,000	
Accounts receivable	20,600	
Allowance for uncollectible accounts		$ 400
Prepaid expenses	5,000	
Equipment	55,000	
Accumulated depreciation		9,400
Accounts payable		27,800
Notes payable, long term		25,000
Common stock		10,000
Retained earnings		24,600
Service revenues		95,000
Rent expense	18,000	
Salary expense	49,500	
Maintenance expense	8,900	
Utility expense	4,700	
Other operating expenses	3,000	
Totals	$192,200	$192,200

Information for adjustments is provided below.

a.   Interest of $900 is accrued on notes receivable.

b.   Revenues in the amount of $3,400 have been earned but not billed or recorded.

c.   Prepaid expenses consist of supplies on hand with a cost of $1,200. The rest have been used in operations.

d.   Depreciation on equipment for the year is $4,300.

e.   The allowance for uncollectible accounts should be 3 percent of the ending balance of accounts receivable.

f.   Interest of $1,680 is accrued on notes payable.

g. Rent expense includes $360 paid for January 1986.

h. Salaries of $2,700 are accrued.

i. Income tax expense, payable in April 1986, is $1,000.

Required:

    a. Prepare the necessary adjusting entries in the general journal.

    b. If you have studied the appendix to the chapter, prepare reversing entries on January 1, 1986.

P. 5-5 **Six-column worksheet.** The adjusted trial balance of Miraloma Corporation on December 31, 1985, is provided below.

Miraloma Corporation
Trial Balance
December 31, 1985

	Debits	Credits
Cash	$ 4,420	
Temporary investments	5,000	
Accounts receivable	7,100	
Allowance for doubtful accounts		$ 400
Materials	7,300	
Prepaid expenses	880	
Equipment	16,300	
Accumulated depreciation		6,100
Patents	10,500	
Notes payable		500
Accounts payable		4,600
Salaries payable		1,000
Interest payable		300
Bonds payable, due 1998		14,000
Common stock		10,000
Retained earnings, 12/31/84		7,100
Revenue from fees		82,390
Dividend revenue		100
Interest revenue		160
Gain on sale of investments		120
Salaries expense	60,800	
Materials expense	8,000	
Rent expense	2,800	
Interest expense	1,380	
Depreciations expense	1,130	
Bad debts expense	410	
Maintenance expense	750	
Totals	$126,770	$126,770

Required:

    a. Enter the trial balance in a six-column worksheet. (Note: This is already done for you if you are using working papers available with the textbook.)

Extend the account balances to the income statement and balance sheet columns.

b. Prepare a single-step income statement and a balance sheet. Ignore income taxes.

P. 5-6   **Worksheet and adjustments.**   The following trial balance was taken from the books of Simplicia Corporation prior to making year-end adjusting entries. The data for adjustments are provided below.

Simplicia Corporation
Trial Balance
December 31, 1985

	Debits	Credits
Cash	$ 3,400	
Notes receivable	1,500	
Accounts receivable	2,000	
Supplies	300	
Equipment	10,000	
Accumulated depreciation		$ 1,700
Accounts payable		3,200
Notes payable, long term		4,000
Common stock		5,000
Retained earnings 12/31/84		1,400
Dividends	900	
Revenues		9,000
Salary expense	3,000	
Advertising expense	1,100	
Rent expense	1,300	
Utilities expense	740	
Interest expense	60	
Totals	$24,300	$24,300

a. An inventory count discloses that supplies costing $30 are on hand.

b. Interest of $80 is accrued on notes receivable.

c. Interest of $160 is accrued on notes payable.

d. Rent Expense includes $100 of rent paid for January 1986.

e. Services performed in December and not yet billed amount to $280.

f. Depreciation expense for the year is $300.

Required: Enter the trial balance into a 10-column worksheet. (Note: This is already done in the working papers available with the textbook.) Make the adjusting entries and prepare an adjusted trial balance. Extend the adjusted trial balance to the income statement and balance sheet columns of the worksheet.

P. 5-7   **Worksheet with adjustments.**   Following are the trial balance and data for adjustment for the Geddem Collection Agency for the fiscal year ending June 30, 1985.

Geddem Collection Agency
Trial Balance
June 30, 1985

	Debits	Credits
Cash, checking account	$ 12,580	
Accounts receivable	8,000	
Office supplies	2,350	
Prepaid insurance	3,000	
Automobiles and equipment	36,000	
Accumulated depreciation		$ 9,000
Notes payable, current		6,500
Installment note payable		15,000
Capital stock		10,000
Retained earnings, 6/30/84		6,800
Dividends	3,000	
Collection fees		98,400
Wages and salaries expenses	49,000	
Travel expense	13,630	
Maintenance expense	5,740	
Telephone and utilities	2,100	
Legal fees	6,400	
Rent expense	2,600	
Office expense	1,300	
Totals	$145,700	$145,700

Data for adjustments:

a. Accounts receivable in the amount of $3,690 have not yet been recorded; they arise from services performed but not yet billed.

b. All the automobiles and equipment were purchased late in May, 1983. They have an estimated useful life of 4 years with no salvage value. Straight-line depreciation is used.

c. When the June payment was made on the installment note, the entire amount paid, including principal and interest, was charged to installment notes payable. Interest included in the payment was $180. The payment was made on June 30.

d. Interest of $200 is accrued on the short-term note payable.

e. A physical count of office supplies indicated that supplies costing $110 are on hand.

f. On June 30 wages and salaries payable amounted to $900.

g. On January 4, 1985, a 1-year liability insurance policy was purchased for $3,000.

h. Rent expense includes $200 paid for July 1985 rent.

Required: Enter the above trial balance in a six-column worksheet. (Note: This is already done in the working papers available with the textbook.) **Make adjusting entries, and prepare the adjusted trial balance in the worksheet.**

P. 5-8   Worksheet adjustments.

Anderson and Miller Company
Trial Balance
December 31, 1985

	Debits	Credits
Cash	$ 17,330	
Accounts receivable	8,590	
Allowance for doubtful accounts		$ 100
Notes receivable	10,000	
Office supplies	2,760	
Prepaid insurance	850	
Equipment	35,500	
Accumulated depreciation		8,920
Accounts payable		11,500
Installment note payable		16,000
Capital, Linda Anderson		7,000
Capital, Lori Miller		6,000
Drawings, Linda Anderson	13,200	
Drawings, Lori Miller	12,800	
Service fees		95,700
Interest income		400
Salaries expense	34,100	
Supplies expense	1,800	
Rent expense	3,900	
Maintenance	2,800	
Interest expense	1,990	
Totals	$145,620	$145,620

Above is the trial balance of Anderson and Miller Company on December 31, 1985. The following adjustments are required at the end of the year prior to preparing financial statements:

a. The rent expense account contains $300 of rent paid in advance for January 1986.

b. Notes receivable consists of a 60-day 12 percent note received from a customer on December 1, 1985.

c. The allowance for doubtful accounts should be increased by $320.

d. Salaries in the amount of $1,780 are accrued.

e. Mortgage note interest of $140 is accrued.

f. Straight-line depreciation is used on the equipment, which is estimated to have a useful life of 10 years and no salvage value.

g. On December 23 a customer sent a check to the company in payment of his $80 account, but the bookkeeper forgot to record the transaction.

h. Service fees in the amount of $280 were received in advance and are not yet earned.

Required:

a. Enter the trial balance in a six-column worksheet. (Note: This is already done in the working papers available with the textbook.) Prepare the adjusting entries in the worksheet, and complete the adjusted trial balance.

b. If you have studied the appendix to the chapter, indicate which of the adjusting entries should be reversed.

P. 5-9 **Difference between income and cash flow.** Following are the beginning balance sheet and the current year's income statement, in condensed form, for the India Ink Corporation:

India Ink Corporation
Balance Sheet
December 14, 1984

Cash	$ 4,000	Salaries payable	$11,000
Fixed assets	41,000	Note payable	10,000
Accumulated depreciation	(5,000)	Owners' equity	19,000
Total assets	$40,000	Total equities	$40,000

India Ink Corporation
Income Statement
For the Year Ended December 31, 1985

Revenues		$55,000
Less expenses:		
Salaries	$22,000	
Rent and utilities	3,000	
Other expenses	4,000	
Depreciation	2,000	21,000
Net income		$24,000

At the end of the year, the company had $9,000 cash and no other current assets. Salaries payable amounted to $14,000, and the note payable had been paid in full. There were no dividends paid during the year, and the company bought some new equipment for cash.

Required:

a. Prepare the December 31, 1985, balance sheet.

b. Calculate how much cash was paid for the new equipment.

c. Determine how much cash the company obtained and spent during the year by operating the business, and explain the difference beween net income and net cash inflow from operations.

P. 5-10   **Financial statements from cash records.**   Presented below is the condensed balance sheet of Kullen Company, as prepared by the owner, Harry Kullen:

Kullen Company
Position Sheet
December 31, 1985

Cash	$11,500
Fixed assets	26,000
Total assets	37,500
Liabilities	14,000
Capital	$23,500

Mr. Kullen started the business in January 1984. He maintained only a check-book record during the past 2 years. Following is a summary of this record for the year 1985:

Balance at beginning of year		$10,000
Add deposits:		
Collections from customers		37,000
Personal funds invested		10,000
Borrowed from friend		5,000
Total		62,000
Deduct payments:		
Salaries	$15,000	
Rent and utilities	4,000	
Supplies	3,500	
Loan payments (includes $1,000 interest)	18,000	
Purchase of equipment	10,000	
Total payments		50,500
Balance at the end of year		$11,500

Mr. Kullen believes that his business is not doing well because cash increased by only $1,500 since the beginning of the year. When you question him about the balance sheet, he says, "I wrote down what I have and what I owe. The money is in the bank. The equipment cost $26,000, and I still owe $9,000 on it. The rest I owe to my friend, and I have to pay him back in January. There are almost no supplies left to speak of, so I ignored them. I'll have some more money when I collect from my customers, but that will be next year. This year is a disaster. I can't go on if all I make is $1,500 a year." He asks you to explain why the business is doing so badly. In going over his bills and invoices, you determine the following:

	December 31	
	1985	**1984**
Money owed to the company by customers	$7,500	$1,000
Money owed by the company to suppliers	3,000	0
Depreciation expense on equipment for 1 year	2,200	1,600
Interest accrued on debts	300	100
Supplies on hand	500	0

There are no other accruals or deferrals.

Required:
  a. Prepare the company's income statement for 1985.
  b. Prepare a corrected balance sheet on December 31, 1985.
  c. Explain to the owner why net income is different from cash inflow from operations.

P. 5-11   **Income statement from balance sheets and cash data.**   Below are comparative balance sheets for Qubik Corporation and data on the company's cash receipts and disbursements.

Qubik Corporation
Balance Sheet

	December 31	
	1985	1984
Assets		
Cash	$20,360	$12,000
Marketable securities	20,000	20,000
Accounts receivable	17,500	15,000
Interest receivable	240	200
Equipment	27,500	25,000
Accumulated depreciation	(13,200)	(10,200)
Total assets	$72,400	$62,000
Liabilities and Capital		
Accounts payable	$ 7,800	$ 7,400
Salaries payable	9,000	8,000
Taxes payable	600	1,600
Common stock	25,000	25,000
Retained earnings	30,000	20,000
Total liabilities and capital	$72,400	$62,000

Following are data summarized from the checkbook records:

Beginning cash balance, Jan. 1, 1985		$12,000
Add cash receipts:		
From customers	$72,000	
Interest on investments	1,460	73,460
		85,460
Less cash disbursements:		
Salaries	29,000	
For services received on open account	19,600	
For taxes	9,000	
For dividends	5,000	
For new equipment	2,500	65,100
Ending cash balance		$20,360

Required: Use the data provided to prepare the company's income statement for 1985.

P. 5-12   **Reconstruction of past balance sheet.**   Below are the balance sheet and income statement of Falcon Corporation and some information about the company's activities during 1985.

Falcon Corporation
Balance Sheet
December 31, 1985

Assets

Cash	$ 7,020
Investments	8,000
Accounts receivable	7,000
Interest receivable	30
Equipment	11,000
Accumulated depreciation	(5,600)
Total assets	$27,450

Liabilities and Capital

Accounts payable	$ 3,000
Wages payable	3,400
Taxes payable	100
Common stock	13,000
Retained earnings	7,950
Total liabilities and capital	$27,450

Falcon Corporation
Income Statement
For the Year Ended December 31, 1985

Fees earned	$29,800	
Interest income	600	
Total		$30,400
Expenses:		
Wages	12,200	
Services and repairs	8,800	
Depreciation	1,100	
Taxes	3,500	
Total expenses		25,600
Net income		$ 4,800

---

a.   In 1985 the company bought new equipment for $1,000 cash.

b.   The company paid $2,000 of cash dividends in 1985.

c.   The company collected $620 of interest during the year.

d.   There was no change in the Investment account.

e.   The company paid $3,600 cash to the government for taxes.

f.   The actual amount of cash paid for wages in 1985 was $12,000.

g. All services and repairs are obtained on open account. During 1985 the company issued checks of $8,800 for payment of open accounts.

h. Accounts receivable increased by $1,000 since last year.

Required: From the above data, reconstruct the December 31, 1984, balance sheet. (Hint: You may find T accounts helpful.)

P. 5-13   **Worksheet, journal entries, and statements.**   The trial balance of Organic Publications, Inc., is given for December 31, 1985. The company publishes a magazine on organic gardening, which is sold on newsstands and by subscription. In addition you are provided with information necessary to adjust the accounts prior to preparing financial statements.

Organic Publications, Inc.
Trial Balance
December 31, 1985

	Debits	Credits
Cash	$ 82,820	
Notes receivable	3,600	
Accounts receivable	47,500	
Allowance for bad debts		$ 100
Prepaid insurance	880	
Land	16,000	
Building	240,000	
Furniture and equipment	12,000	
Accumulated depreciation		20,300
Accounts payable		17,000
Subscriptions received in advance		19,000
Bonds payable		50,000
Common stock, 20,000 shares		200,000
Retained earnings		31,000
Magazine revenues		280,000
Rent income		2,600
Dividends	10,000	
Bond interest expense	4,000	
Salaries expense	190,000	
Office supplies expense	6,300	
Utilities expense	3,100	
Maintenance expense	3,800	
Totals	$620,000	$620,000

a. Interest of $300 is accrued on the notes receivable.

b. Prepaid insurance represents the cost of a 2-year insurance policy bought on July 1, 1985.

c. The company rents a portion of its building to an advertising agency for $350 per month. On December 27 the advertising agency paid the January 1986 rent, which was recorded as rent income.

d.   Office supplies are purchased frequently and recorded as expenses. A physical count at the end of the year revealed that supplies costing $650 were on hand.

e.   By the end of the year, salaries in the amount of $9,500 were accrued and not yet paid.

f.   Interest of $6,080 is accrued on the bonds payable.

g.   Whenever a subscription payment is received, it is recorded as subscriptions received in advance. By December 1985 the company earned $8,200 of the subscriptions by delivery of magazines.

h.   The land and building were bought on January 2, 1978, and the building is estimated to have a useful life of 25 years. Annual depreciation on furniture and equipment is 10 percent of original cost.

i.   The company estimates that 4 percent of accounts receivable will be uncollectible.

j.   Federal income taxes for 1985 are estimated at $12,000.

Required:
a.   Prepare a 10-column worksheet, enter the above trial balance, and complete the worksheet by entering the adjustments, and extending the adjusted trial balance. You may also use a 12-column worksheet.
b.   Prepare adjusting and closing entries in the general journal.
c.   Prepare a multistep income statement, a statement of retained earnings, and a classified balance sheet.
d.   If you have studied the appendix to the chapter journalize the necessary reversing entries.

P. 5-14   **Worksheet, journal entries, and statements.**   Kettermann and Arnold are partners providing paralegal services for attorneys and courts. They share profits and losses equally. The trial balance on page 242 was taken at the end of the accounting period prior to making adjusting entries, and the following data for adjustments are also provided.

a.   On December 30 a client paid $750 owed on account, but the receipt of cash was not recorded.

b.   Office supplies costing $220 are on hand.

c.   Depreciation expense for the year is $1,450.

d.   The partnership performed work for its own attorney in the amount of $200. Instead of billing the attorney, the partners asked him to cancel a $200 account they owed him. The attorney agreed but the transaction has not yet been recorded.

e.   The company has not paid the December rent of $300 because the landlord has not made necessary repairs. The repairs will be made in January, at which time the rent will be paid.

f.   Interest on the note payable has accumulated in the amount of $180 and will be paid when the note matures.

g.   Salaries of $480 are accrued at the end of the year.

h.   Travel and entertainment expense includes $320 paid for an airline ticket which will be used by Arnold in January to visit a client in another city.

Kettermann and Arnold
Trial Balance
December 31, 1985

	Debits	Credits
Cash	$10,900	
Accounts receivable	6,400	
Office supplies	900	
Office equipment	4,500	
Furniture and fixtures	9,800	
Accumulated depreciation		$ 3,700
Accounts payable		2,100
Notes payable, long term		4,000
Capital, Kettermann		5,360
Capital, Arnold		5,360
Drawings, Kettermann	2,100	
Drawings, Arnold	1,500	
Fees earned		49,600
Rent expense	2,900	
Salaries expense	23,800	
Utilities expense	1,600	
Travel expense	3,000	
Maintenance expense	1,470	
Licenses and fees expense	400	
Miscellaneous expenses	250	
Loss on sale of equipment	600	
Totals	$70,120	$70,120

Required:
    a. Prepare a worksheet for the company, enter the trial balance and adjustments, and complete the worksheet.
    b. Prepare adjusting and closing entries in the general journal.
    c. Prepare a balance sheet and income statement for the partnership.
    d. If you have studied the appendix to the chapter, prepare reversing entries on January 1, 1986.

Case 5-1   **Examination of an annual report.**

Refer to the financial statements of Rangaire Corporation reproduced on pages 202–215. Below are questions that pertain to these statements. Although the questions are arranged in groups relating to different parts of the annual report, you may have to refer to several parts of the report to answer some of the questions.

A. Income statement

    1. Is the company on a fiscal year or a calendar year? Explain.
    2. From what activities does the company obtain most of its revenues?
    3. What were net income and earnings per share in 1983?

4. Multiply EPS in 1978 by the common shares issued as reported in the balance sheet. Why is the result not equal to net income? How many shares were used to calculate EPS?

5. Is depreciation expense reported separately on the income statement? How much is depreciation expense for 1983?

6. What is the company's approximate tax rate as calculated from the $103,978 tax reported in the income statement? Where does the company explain why its tax rate is different from the 46 percent corporate tax rate?

B. Balance sheet

7. What was the current ratio in 1982 and 1983?

8. How much did customers owe to the company on July 31, 1983?

9. What contra asset accounts can you find in the balance sheet?

10. How much does the company owe in income taxes to the federal government, and where is the amount reported?

11. How many shares of common and preferred stock are issued at the end of the 1983 fiscal year?

12. What percentage of owners' equity is made up of retained earnings?

13. By what amount did long-term debt increase or decrease in 1983?

14. Use the balance sheet data to calculate working capital for 1982 and 1983. By how much did working capital increase or decrease in 1983?

C. Statement of changes in financial position

15. Does the change in working capital reported in the statement of changes match your calculation in item 13 above?

16. According to the statement of changes, what was depreciation and depletion for 1983? Is the amount consistent with your answer for item 4? How much was depreciation expense for 1983?

17. How much did the company spend on new plant and equipment in 1983?

18. How much working capital did the company obtain by issuing new stock in 1983?

19. What was the decrease in inventories from 1982 to 1983 according to the statement of changes? Does this amount match the difference between 1982 and 1983 inventories reported in the balance sheet?

20. Did prepaid expense increase or decrease from 1982 to 1983? What was the balance of prepaid expenses on July 31, 1981?

D. Statement of stockholders' equity.

21. How many shares of stock were outstanding when the company paid its 1982 cash dividend?

22. How much cash did an investor who owns 1,000 shares of the company's common stock receive from the company from July 31, 1980 to July 31, 1983?

23. How many shares of stock did the company pay as a dividend in 1983?

24. How large a dividend did the company pay on its preferred stock in 1982?

E. Notes to financial statements

25. In what type of assets was the majority of plant, property, and equipment invested in 1983?

26. What method of depreciation is used for financial reporting?

27. What is the difference in accounting between maintenance and repairs of fixed assets and betterments and renewals?

28. During 1983 the company disposed of a major portion of its assets. What did the company sell, to whom, and for how much? What was the book value of the sold assets?

29. How is the company's treatment of union employees different from its treatment of nonunion employees?

30. Describe briefly the nature of the company's long-term liabilities.

31. Do you perceive any trend in earnings according to the quarterly reports for 1983?

32. Are the interim reports audited?

F. Auditor's report

33. Where can you find the name of the company's independent auditors?

34. What term do the auditors use to describe the way financial statements are presented? Does the auditor's report say the statements are accurate?

35. What accounting principle is mentioned in the second paragraph of the auditor's report?

36. Do the auditors say that the audit included an examination of the company's books of account? What was examined?

Case 5-2   **Accounting cycle of a business.***

Superlative Service Company provides maintenance and repair service for heavy road-grading equipment. As a Subchapter S corporation, the company is not subject to income taxes. The company prepares financial statements monthly. The last trial balance, taken on April 30 after the books had been closed, is presented below.

---

* This comprehensive case allows you to review materials from Chapters 2 to 5.

Superlative Service Company
Post-Closing Trial Balance
April 30, 1985

	Debits	Credits
Cash	$ 35,900	
Accounts receivable	39,770	
Allowance for doubtful accounts		$ 1,040
Supplies inventory	3,940	
Spare parts inventory	26,300	
Prepaid insurance	1,200	
Office equipment	16,880	
Machinery and equipment	96,600	
Accumulated depreciation		30,250
Notes payable		25,000
Accounts payable		18,500
Bonds payable		50,000
Capital stock		40,000
Retained earnings		55,800
Totals	$220,590	$220,590

The following transactions took place during May 1985:

a. Services were performed on open account, and customers were billed for $36,310. Services performed for cash amounted to $6,870.

b. Accounts payable of $14,800 were paid by check.

c. Supplies costing $1,690 were purchased on account.

d. Spare parts costing $5,400 were purchased on open account.

e. Collection of accounts receivable amounted to $35,400.

f. The company sold for $5,000 cash a piece of equipment that had become obsolete. The original cost of the equipment was $9,000 and it had $2,500 of accumulated depreciation.

g. Salaries paid by check amounted to $16,900.

h. Other expenses paid during May were as follows: rent, $4,000; travel, $8,100; maintenance, $480; utilities, $320.

i. A check for $5,170 was issued in payment of notes payable, including $170 of interest.

j. The company entered into a contract to buy advertising for $2,400 during the following 4 months. The amount of $600 for May advertising was paid by check.

k. The company bought new equipment for $4,600 cash.

l. During May the company declared and paid a dividend of $4,000.

   At the end of May, the following information was available for preparing adjusting entries:

m. Revenues earned but not billed by the end of May amounted to $15,320.

n. On May 31 supplies costing $2,120 were on hand.

o. Spare parts costing $6,840 were used during the month.

p. Depreciation expense for May is $4,360.

q. Interest of $240 is accrued on notes payable at the end of May. The interest accrued on bonds payable is $1,000.

r. Prepaid insurance represents a 1-year fire insurance policy bought on April 30, 1985.

s. Management decided to increase the allowance for doubtful accounts to $2,500.

t. Salaries and wages in the amount of $920 are accrued.

u. Monthly rent is $2,000. The payment in May was for May and June rent.

Required:

a. Use the April 30 trial balance to establish a general ledger for the company. Enter the beginning balances in each ledger account. (Note: This is already done in the working papers available with the textbook.)

b. Journalize and post the May transactions, and find the balance of each ledger account at the end of May.

c. Prepare a trial balance on May 31 in a 10- or 12-column worksheet. Enter the adjusting entries in the worksheet, and prepare an adjusted trial balance. Extend the adjusted trial balance to the financial statement columns.

d. Journalize the adjusting and closing entries at the end of May, and post them to close the books.

e. Prepare the company's income statement, statement of retained earnings, and balance sheet in good accounting form on May 31.

Merchandising Operations

6

The primary objective of merchandising firms is to buy goods in quantity and resell them at a profit. These firms typically have a large investment in their merchandise inventory, an asset which requires some special accounting treatment. When you have completed your study of the chapter, you should understand:

1   The difference between the income statements of a merchandising business and a service business.

2   The difference between perpetual and periodic inventory systems.

3   The end-of-period procedures used by merchandising businesses to close books and prepare statements.

4   The nature of several new contra accounts reported in the income statement of a merchandising business.

5   The calculation of cost of goods sold and gross margin.

6   Worksheets for merchandising businesses.

7   The meaning and use of special journals and subsidiary ledgers.

In previous chapters, we discussed fundamental accounting principles and concepts mainly in connection with service-oriented businesses. These principles and concepts apply to merchandising and manufacturing businesses as well as to other types of accounting entities. However, merchandising and manufacturing businesses require special treatment because they have large amounts of resources invested in inventories of goods. Such inventories require accounting procedures not needed in service operations. In this chapter we focus on the operations of merchandising businesses. Manufacturing operations are discussed in the managerial volume of this series.

We first examine the income statement of a merchandising business and contrast it with the income statement of a service firm. Then we look at the types of inventory systems that a merchandising business may use and the revenues and expenses related to the business of selling merchandise. Later we examine some of the special records that businesses maintain to help process a mass of financial data, and we also look at worksheet procedures for merchandising businesses. After completing this chapter, you should have a good understanding of merchandising operations and their accounting procedures. The chapter also reinforces the concepts you learned earlier, because they apply to merchandising firms as well.

MERCHANDISING OPERATIONS

Merchandising businesses such as the local grocery store, the large department store, the hardware store, and the specialty clothing store are familiar retail outlets that sell goods to final consumers. Others include the wholesale distributors that supply goods to retailers and other businesses. Merchandisers buy products at one price and sell them to customers at a higher price. The selling price of the product must be high enough to cover the cost of the products plus operating expenses and to provide a satisfactory profit. Merchandise transactions require recording merchandise purchases at cost and merchandise sales at selling prices. The difference between the cost and selling price is the **gross margin**, or **gross profit.** The gross margin earned by the business is used to pay operating expenses; any remainder is net income.

Cost of goods sold is an expense

Recording revenue at the time merchandise is sold satisfies the revenue realization principle, and matching expenses with related sales revenue satisfies the matching principle. The sale of merchandise reduces the merchandise inventory, and the cost of the sold product represents the expense to be matched with sales revenue. This expense is frequently referred to as a product expense and is called **cost of goods sold (CGS)** in the income statement where it is deducted from sales to arrive at gross margin. Note that gross margin is nothing more than the difference between the purchase price and the selling price of the merchandise. The purchase price is the cost of merchandise to the business. When the merchandise is sold, this asset expires and its cost becomes an expense.

Income Statement

Figure 6-1 shows the income statement of Jupiter Corporation, a merchandising firm whose balance sheet you saw in Chapter 3. This income statement is somewhat different from the income statements of service firms. The first item in any income statement is revenue from operations. Merchandising firms call such revenue **sales**; service firms refer to it as **service revenue.** The primary difference between the income statements of merchandising and service businesses is that merchandising firms include in

Merchandising firms have product expenses

Jupiter Corporation
Income Statement
For the Year Ended December 31, 1985

Sales			$1,547,200
Less cost of goods sold			618,800
Gross margin			928,400
Selling expenses:			
Sales salaries and commissions	$213,750		
Advertising	75,000		
Transportation and travel	23,400		
Telephone	7,950		
Total selling expenses		$320,100	
Administrative expenses:			
Wages and salaries	257,600		
State and local taxes	35,270		
Telephone	5,800		
Depreciation	87,000		
Amortization of intangibles	4,500		
Insurance	9,220		
Bad debts	4,410		
Total administrative expenses		403,800	
Total operating expenses			723,900
Operating income			204,500
Other revenues and expenses:			
Interest expense	(12,200)		
Less interest revenue	6,800	(5,400)	
Gain on sale of land	9,000		
Less loss on sale of equipment	(1,600)	7,400	
Total other income			2,000
Income before income tax			206,500
Less income tax			82,000
Net income after tax			$ 124,500
Earnings per common share			$1.48

Figure 6-1
Classified income statement of merchandising business. Note the cost of goods sold section and subsection for selling and administrative expenses.

the income statement product expense, which is the cost of the products they sell. The cost of goods sold identifies the **product expense** that is deducted from sales revenue to arrive at gross margin for the period. Operating expenses are subtracted from gross margin to arrive at operating income.

The operating expense section of a merchandising firm's income statement is similar to that of a service firm, although some of the expenses may be different. For example, a merchandising firm may have selling expenses such as commissions, advertising, and shipping. Therefore, the operating expense portion of the merchandising income statement may be divided into two parts: selling and administrative expenses.

Cost of goods sold is a very significant expense in a merchandising business. In our example, this expense is almost as large as all other operating expenses combined. Often it is much larger than all other expenses. The measurement of cost of goods sold therefore requires some care. To a great extent the method of measuring cost of goods sold depends on the type of merchandise that the business sells and the accounting system used for this asset. The two basic types of inventory systems are the perpetual and the periodic systems. The perpetual system is discussed first, and the periodic system is covered later in the chapter.

PERPETUAL INVENTORY SYSTEM

A perpetual inventory account is always up to date

In a **perpetual inventory system,** a continuous record is maintained of all inventory transactions. Each inventory purchase is recorded as an increase in the merchandise account, and each sale is recorded as a decrease in the account. Merchandising businesses that sell large, differentiated products such as pianos, automobiles, or major appliances, or unique items such as jewelry or works of art, usually use a perpetual inventory system. Firms also use the perpetual inventory system if they require timely inventory cost data. Figure 6-2 shows a perpetual inventory record of the type used by businesses to maintain inventory information on a continuous basis.

Most manufacturing firms use a perpetual inventory system because it permits timely and accurate determination of the cost of manufactured

PERPETUAL INVENTORY RECORD

Description 21" color T.V.   **Minimum Stock** 5

Code or Brand W 205   **Location** Warehouse   **Maximum Stock** 25

Date	Explanation	Purchases			Sales			Balance		
		No. of Units	Cost per Unit	Total Cost	No. of Units	Cost per Unit	Total Cost	No. of Units	Cost per Unit	Total Cost
Jan. 1	Balance							12	260	3,120
7	Sale				3	260	780	9	260	2,340
18	Purchase	10	260	2,600				19	260	4,940
22	Sale				2	260	520	17	260	4,420
25	Sales return				(1)	260	(260)	18	260	4,680

Figure 6-2   Inventory record showing details of a specific class of items in inventory.

products. Perpetual inventory systems can be costly because they require more record keeping than periodic systems. For this reason, perpetual systems are usually maintained only when required by the nature of the merchandise sold or by the type of business operated. However, recent advances in computer systems have enabled many more firms to use perpetual inventories.

A company may maintain a single perpetual inventory record for many items of identical goods, such as refrigerators of the same model. Another record is maintained for a different model of refrigerator, which may have a different cost. On the other hand, if each item of inventory is different from all others, such as automobiles with different equipment options or different costs, the company must specifically identify each item and maintain a separate inventory record of it. In this case a **specific identification** inventory method is used, which is a type of perpetual inventory system. Whenever an item is sold, it must be identified so that its cost may be removed from the inventory and charged to cost of goods sold.

Purchases and Sales

To illustrate the operation of a perpetual inventory system, we use the example of Silvertone Pianos, Inc., a piano dealer whose accounting period ends on December 31. At the beginning of 1985, the company had on hand the following inventory:

5 Grand pianos	@ $3,500 each =	$17,500
10 Upright pianos	@ 900 each =	9,000
Total cost of inventory		$26,500

The Merchandise Inventory account appears as follows:

Merchandise Inventory

1/1/85 Bal. 26,500	

On January 7 the company bought six spinet pianos at $740 each, including delivery costs. The purchase is recorded with the following journal entry:

Jan. 7	Merchandise inventory	4,440	
	Accounts payable		4,440
	Purchased six spinets at $740 each from		
	Chase Piano Manufacturing Company.		
	Purchase order no. 1102.		

On January 12 one of the grand pianos is sold for $4,500 cash. The sale requires the following **two** entries:

Jan. 12	Cash	4,500	
	Sales		4,500
	Sold grand piano. Sales		
	invoice no. 1931.		
Jan. 12	Cost of goods sold	3,500	
	Merchandise inventory		3,500
	To remove the cost of grand piano from		
	the inventory account.		

The first entry records the sales revenue. The second entry reduces the asset account Merchandise Inventory and transfers the cost of the piano to the expense account Cost of Goods Sold. The merchandise account is thus perpetually kept up to date and reflects the cost of merchandise actually on hand and available for sale.

Purchase Returns and Allowances

A company sometimes finds it necessary to return some of the goods it has purchased to the supplier, or **vendor.** The vendor may take the goods back or allow a price reduction to compensate for damaged or undesirable items. For example, Silvertone receives a shipment of six baby grand pianos costing $2,900 each and makes the following entry:

Jan. 25	Merchandise inventory	17,400	
	Accounts payable		17,400
	Received six baby grand pianos from		
	Stoneway Piano Company. Purchase		
	order no. 1105.		

When the company discovers that one of the new pianos is a style that was not ordered, it informs the supplier that it wants to return the piano. The supplier agrees to an allowance of $250 if Silvertone keeps the piano. Silvertone makes the following entry to record the allowance:

Jan. 28	Accounts payable	250	
	Merchandise inventory		250
	Received credit from Stoneway Piano		
	Company for wrong-style piano.		

When this specific piano is sold, the company has to reduce the Merchandise Inventory account by the piano's actual cost, which is now $2,650—the original cost of $2,900 less the $250 allowance.

Merchandise is sometimes returned to the vendor

If the merchandise is actually returned, the original transaction recording the purchase is simply reversed. For example, when a second piano is found defective and returned to the vendor, the return is recorded by Silvertone as follows:

Jan. 25	Accounts payable	2,900	
	Merchandise inventory		2,900
	Returned baby grand to Stoneway for		
	credit on account.		

Sales Returns and Allowances

In order to maintain customer satisfaction and satisfy warranty agreements, businesses often allow customers to return merchandise if it is unsatisfactory or damaged. Sometimes a business allows customers to pay less than the original price if they agree to keep damaged merchandise. To illustrate the recording of such sales returns and allowances, consider a spinet piano that was sold for $1,290 on January 15 on open account. The journal entries for the sale are:

Jan. 15	Accounts receivable	1,290	
	Sales		1,290
	Sold spinet to C. Brown.		
	Invoice no. 1934.		
Jan. 15	Cost of goods sold	740	
	Merchandise inventory		740
	To remove spinet from inventory.		

The piano is found to be defective, and it is returned by the customer. The transaction is recorded as follows:

Sales returns and allowances is a contra revenue account

Jan. 22	Sales returns and allowances	1,290	
	Accounts receivable		1,290
	Spinet sold on invoice no. 1934 to C.		
	Brown returned because of defective		
	pedal action.		
Jan. 22	Merchandise inventory	740	
	Cost of goods sold		740
	To replace returned spinet to inventory.		

The Cost of Goods Sold entry recorded at the time of sale is reversed, returning the cost of the merchandise back into the inventory account. The Sales entry, however, is not reversed. Instead, the **Sales Returns and Allowances** account is debited, and Sales remains recorded at the **gross** amount. The sales returns and allowances account provides managers with valuable information about the volume of returns and allowances. If the balance in this account is excessive, managers can analyze the reasons and take appropriate action to eliminate the cause of customer dissatisfaction with the merchandise. When the income statement is prepared, the balance of sales returns and allowances is deducted from sales revenue to yield **net sales.** Sales Returns and Allowances is, therefore, a **contra revenue** account related to Sales, and it is maintained for control purposes.

End-of-Period Procedures

Remember that the balance of the merchandise account at the beginning of the period consists of the cost of all merchandise on hand. The account balance represents the totals recorded on separate inventory cards for each different type of piano. The merchandise account is charged each time pianos are purchased, and is credited each time one is sold. The transactions with customers resulted in establishing three temporary accounts: Sales revenue; Cost of Goods Sold, an expense; and Sales Returns and Allowances, a contra revenue. By the end of the accounting period, the balances in these three temporary accounts and in the permanent Merchandise Inventory account appear as follows for Silvertone Pianos, Inc.:

Merchandise Inventory		Cost of Goods Sold	
18,700		156,200	

Sales		Sales Returns and Allowances	
	243,500		2,130

After the books are closed, the balances of the temporary accounts appear in the income statement as shown in Figure 6-3. Note that the balance of sales returns and allowances is used to calculate net sales in the gross margin portion of the income statement.

PERIODIC INVENTORY SYSTEM

A business that sells many diverse small items of merchandise such as groceries, small appliances, cosmetics, clothing, hardware, or office supplies generally do not keep track of the cost of each item as it is sold, because there are too many items. In such cases a **periodic inventory**

Silvertone Pianos, Inc.
Income Statement
For the Year Ended December 31, 1985

Gross sales			$243,500
Less sales returns and allowances			2,130
Net sales			241,370
Less cost of goods sold			156,200
Gross margin			85,170
Less operating expenses:			
Selling expenses:			
Sales commissions	$12,160		
Advertising	3,780		
Depreciation	14,000	$29,940	
Administrative expenses:			
Salaries and wages	14,400		
Utilities	7,940		
Depreciation	17,000		
Office supplies	3,320	42,660	
Total expenses			72,600
Operating income			$ 12,570

Figure 6-3
Merchandising income statement, showing gross margin section, with cost of goods sold reported as a single figure rather than a computation. Compare this statement with the one in Figure 6-4.

A periodic physical count of inventory must be taken in a periodic inventory system

system is maintained in which purchases of inventory are recorded, but cost of goods sold is not recorded as sales take place. The cost of goods sold is calculated and recorded periodically, usually at the end of the accounting year. To compute cost of goods sold, it is first necessary to take a physical count of inventory to determine the quantity of goods remaining on hand and to assign to the counted goods their original cost. Cost of goods sold is then computed by adding together the beginning inventory and all purchases made during the year, to arrive at the amount of goods available for sale. The cost of ending inventory is subtracted from the goods available for sale to get the cost of goods sold. The cost of goods sold is thus obtained indirectly by finding the difference between the goods available for sale and the amount left unsold at the end of the accounting period.

In a periodic inventory system the merchandise account is not affected by purchases or sales

To illustrate a periodic inventory system we use the example of Bellcroft Sporting Goods. The company starts the accounting period with merchandise inventory costing $28,000. The beginning inventory is, of course, the ending inventory of the previous period. The account appears as follows:

Merchandise Inventory

12/31/84 Bal. 28,000

Purchases and Sales

In a periodic system, the balance of the Merchandise Inventory account is not changed throughout the accounting period. The purchases of the period are recorded in a **Purchases** account, a temporary account in which all the period's merchandise purchases are recorded as follows:

Jan. 8	Purchases	6,500	
	Accounts payable		6,500
	Received sporting goods from Wilsy		
	Manufacturing Company. Purchase		
	order no. 687.		

When a sale takes place, it is recorded as follows:

Jan. 14	Cash (or Accounts receivable)	280	
	Sales		280
	Sold golf clubs to J. Miller.		

Notice that only the sale is recorded. No transfer of cost is made from the Merchandise Inventory account to a cost of goods sold account at the time of sale.

Purchase Returns and Allowances

As we explained before, goods are sometimes returned to the vendor for credit, or the vendor may make an allowance for goods that are not as ordered. The entry to record purchase returns and allowances is not the same as that in a perpetual system, because different accounts are maintained in a periodic system. For example, if Bellcroft Sporting Goods returns to the vendor merchandise purchased for $135, the entry is:

Jan. 17	Accounts payable	135	
	Purchase returns and allowances		135
	Returned merchandise purchased from		
	Wilsy Manufacturing Company.		
	Purchase order no. 878.		

The account **Purchase Returns and Allowances** is a **contra expense** account related to Purchases. It is used to accumulate all the purchase returns and allowances for the current period. Purchase Returns and Allowances is a temporary account. The company could, of course, credit the Purchases account directly to cancel a previous purchase when the goods are returned. In that case, however, valuable information would be lost.

The total cost of purchases is the balance of several accounts

The company would be unable to determine how much of its merchandise had to be returned to vendors. Buying and returning goods is costly and yields no profit for the business, so managers want to know the amount of their purchase returns and allowances. If a particular vendor consistently supplies goods that must be returned, the company may either try to resolve the problem or look for another supplier.

The amount of net purchases is calculated by deducting the balance of Purchase Returns and Allowances from the balance of purchases. **Net purchases** are the net total of goods added to the inventory of merchandise on hand at the beginning of the year. The beginning balance of merchandise plus net purchases is the total amount of goods available for sale during the accounting period.

Sales Returns and Allowances

With a periodic inventory system, a single entry is required to record sales returns and allowances. If a customer returns goods bought for $28, the following entry is recorded:

Jan. 19	Sales returns and allowances	28	
	Cash (or Accounts receivable)		28
	Merchandise returned by J. Smythe.		

Neither the sales nor the sales returns are identified with a specific item of inventory. The returned merchandise becomes part of the inventory on hand, but because the cost of the returned goods was not deducted from the inventory account at the time of sale, the merchandise and the purchases accounts are not affected by the sales returns.

End-of-Period Procedures

The income statement of a merchandising business reports cost of goods sold, but with a periodic inventory system a cost of goods sold account is not maintained. This expense can be computed by using information obtained from the accounting records and from the physical count of inventory on hand. Let's assume that at the end of an accounting period the periodic inventory records of Bellcroft Sporting Goods are:

Merchandise Inventory		Sales	
12/31/84 Bal. 28,000			238,900

Purchases		Sales Returns and Allowances	
167,400		2,980	

The periodic count of inventory is used to find CGS

The Merchandise Inventory account still contains the balance it had at the beginning of the year. All the merchandise purchases during the year have been recorded in the Purchases account. The total of the balances of these two accounts constitutes the **goods available for sale** during the period. If all the merchandise has been sold, there is no inventory on hand at the end of the period, and the cost of goods sold is equal to the cost of goods available for sale. But that is unlikely. Businesses typically maintain some merchandise on hand at all times. When the cost of unsold inventory is deducted from the cost of goods available for sale, the result is the cost of the goods that have been sold.

A physical count of merchandise on hand must be taken at the end of the period to determine the number of units in ending inventory. Next, the cost of each unit must be determined. The physical count of inventory for Bellcroft Sporting Goods indicates that goods costing $30,300 are on hand. The following calculation determines cost of goods sold:

Beginning inventory	$ 28,000
Add purchases	167,400
Goods available for sale	195,400
Less ending inventory	30,300
Cost of goods sold	$165,100

The above calculation appears in the cost of goods sold section of the income statement in Figure 6-4. Compare this statement with the one in Figure 6-3. In Figure 6-4 the cost of goods sold section is more elaborate

Bellcroft Sporting Goods
Income Statement
For the Year Ended December 31, 1985

Gross sales		$238,900
Less sales returns and allowances		2,980
Net sales		235,920
Less cost of goods sold		
Beginning inventory	$ 28,000	
Add purchases	167,400	
Goods available for sale	195,400	
Less ending inventory	30,300	
Cost of goods sold		165,100
Gross margin		70,820
Less operating expenses:		
Selling and administrative expenses:		
Salaries and wages	12,400	
Sales commissions	10,150	
Advertising	3,780	
Utilities	7,940	
Depreciation	20,600	
Total expenses		54,870
Operating income		$ 15,950

Figure 6-4
Merchandising income statement showing gross margin section with cost of goods sold computed as the difference between goods available for sale and ending inventory.

and shows the determination of cost of goods sold, not as an account balance, but rather as a calculation. In practice, companies usually report cost of goods sold as a single amount in their annual reports, regardless of the inventory system used. Managers, on the other hand, are more interested in the complete calculation.

The beginning inventory account balance remains in the merchandise inventory account until the end of the accounting period, and the purchases account reflects the merchandise purchased during the period. After the inventory count at the end of the period, the inventory cost and expense accounts are adjusted. This is accomplished by:

1. Entering the physical inventory count into the inventory account
2. Closing the purchases account
3. Eliminating the beginning inventory balance
4. Opening the cost of goods sold account

In our example the entry is as follows:

A special type of journal entry

Dec. 31	Merchandise inventory (ending)	30,300	
	Cost of goods sold	165,100	
	Merchandise inventory (beginning)		28,000
	Purchases		167,400
	To close Purchases and adjust inventory.		

Study the above entry carefully. The cost of the ending inventory is debited to the Merchandise Inventory account so that the amount determined by the physical count is recorded in the ledger. The beginning inventory balance is written off completely with a credit. The Purchases account is a temporary account, and it is closed by writing off its balance with a credit. The debit to Cost of Goods Sold is the amount needed to balance the entry. Notice that this entry accomplishes exactly what we already verified by the cost of goods sold calculation made previously and included in the income statement. The beginning inventory and the purchases are combined into goods available for sale, which are divided between the goods sold (an expense) and the goods remaining on hand (an asset). The Cost of Goods Sold account can now be closed to income summary together with all other temporary accounts.

COMPARISON OF PERPETUAL AND PERIODIC SYSTEMS

The main differences between the perpetual and periodic inventory systems are illustrated in the journal entries in Figure 6-5, which shows how the same transactions are recorded in each system. In the perpetual system, the Merchandise Inventory account is used to record acquisitions of merchandise. The Cost of Goods Sold account is used during the entire accounting period to record the expiration of inventory as it is sold. Cost of

Goods Sold, Sales, Sales Returns and Allowances, and other temporary accounts are closed to income summary as usual.

In the periodic inventory system, the acquisition of goods is recorded in a purchases account. At the end of the period the Cost of Goods Sold account is created by closing the Purchases account and adjusting the merchandise account. If contra purchases accounts exist—Purchase Returns and Allowances, for example—they are also closed in the same entry, as you will see later. Regardless of the inventory system used, the purchase price of merchandise is not the only cost of acquiring inventory. Below we discuss shipping costs and purchase discounts, which also affect the cost of goods held for sale by a business.

Perpetual Inventory System			Periodic Inventory System		
Merchandise	2,000		Purchases	2,000	
Accounts payable		2,000	Accounts payable		2,000
To record purchase of merchandise.			To record purchase of merchandise.		
Accounts payable	150		Accounts payable	150	
Merchandise		150	Purchase returns and		
To record return of merchandise.			allowances		150
			To record return of merchandise.		
Accounts receivable	1,000		Accounts receivable	1,000	
Sales		1,000	Sales		1,000
Cost of goods sold	600		To record sales of merchandise.		
Merchandise		600			
To record sale of merchandise.					
Sales returns and allowances	80		Sales returns and allowances	80	
Accounts receivable		80	Accounts receivable		80
Merchandise	50		To record goods returned by customer.		
Cost of goods sold		50			
To record goods returned by customer.					

Figure 6-5 **Comparison of entries in perpetual and periodic inventory systems.**

FREIGHT-IN

The cost of merchandise includes not only its purchase price but also the cost of shipping and any other cost required to make the goods ready for sale. The amount paid by a business for shipping when it receives merchandise from a supplier is usually recorded in a temporary account called **Freight-in**, or Transportation-in, as follows:

May 7	Freight-in	78	
	Cash		78
	Paid common carrier for shipping goods.		

Freight-in is a cost of buying goods

Freight-in is maintained as a separate account because many different items may be included in a shipment, and it is usually difficult to allocate the shipping cost among different goods, even in a perpetual inventory system. However, freight-in is a cost of acquiring goods and must eventually become part of the cost of goods sold. At the end of the accounting period, the balance of the Freight-in account is closed directly to the Cost of Goods Sold account.

CASH DISCOUNTS

Many companies offer **cash discounts** to their customers in order to encourage prompt payment of open accounts. Such cash discounts are stated on the invoice and tell the customer how much may be deducted from the invoice price. For example, **invoice terms** of 2/10, n/30 mean that 2 percent may be deducted from the amount due if payment is made within 10 days of the invoice date; otherwise, the net amount due must be paid within 30 days. Two examples of invoice terms without discounts are n/EOM, which means that the net amount is due at the end of the month, and n/30, which means that the net amount is due in 30 days.

Cash discounts are inducements for quick payment

A cash discount is a strong inducement to pay the bill within the discount period, and most well-managed businesses do so even if it means borrowing money from a bank in order to make the payment. For example, if the terms for a purchase are 2/10, n/30 on a $1,000 invoice, the cost of waiting the last 20 days before paying the bill is 2 percent of $1,000, or $20. This represents an annual interest rate of 36 percent,[1] and most businesses can borrow from their banks at lower rates.

Cash discounts may be available to a business on its merchandise purchases; they may also be offered by the business to its customers. The business accounts separately for discounts on purchases and on sales.

Purchase Discounts

Cash discounts offered to a business by vendors are called **purchase discounts** and may be accounted for in two ways. Purchases may be recorded either at net invoice cost or at gross invoice cost. The gross invoice method is used by most businesses.

Gross invoice method.   A purchase of merchandise with an invoice price of $1,000 is made on June 1. The terms of the invoice are 2/10, n/30. When purchases are recorded at their gross amount, discounts do not have to be calculated until payment is made. The June 1 purchase is recorded at gross as follows:

---

[1] Interest of 36 percent per year on $1,000 for 20 days is computed as follows: $1,000 × .36 × 20/360 = $20. Chapter 7 contains a discussion of interest calculation.

June 1	Purchases	1,000	
	Accounts payable		1,000
	Received merchandise from Acme Supply. Purchase order no. 894. Terms 2/10, n/30.		

When the payment is made in time to take the discount, the entry is:

June 10	Accounts payable	1,000	
	Cash		980
	Purchase discounts taken		20
	Paid Acme Supply and deducted 2 percent discount. Check no. 1504.	.	

If the payment is not made in time, the entry to record the payment without the discount is:

June 28	Accounts payable	1,000	
	Cash		1,000
	Paid Acme Supply. Check no. 1519.		

A discount taken is not revenue; it is a cost reduction

The discounts taken account has a credit balance and therefore looks like a revenue, but it is actually a contra expense account. **Purchase Discounts Taken** is an account contra to purchases, and it should be deducted from purchases in the calculation of cost of goods sold. When the discount is taken, the cost of the merchandise purchased is less than originally recorded. Purchase discounts taken are sometimes incorrectly reported among other revenues in the income statement. However, a business cannot earn income by buying goods; it does so by selling them. If discounts are not taken, the gross invoice method does not disclose the amount of discounts lost. Lost discounts are really interest expense, but they are buried in the purchases account and overstate the cost of merchandise.

Net invoice method.   If purchases are recorded at net invoice cost, the discount must be calculated and deducted from the invoice price. Using the same example, the $1,000 purchase on June 1 and the June 10 payment are recorded at their net amounts as follows:

June 1	Purchases	980	
	Accounts payable		980
	Received merchandise from Acme Supply. Purchase order no. 894.		
	Terms 2/10, n/30.		

June 10	Accounts payable	980	
	Cash		980
	Paid Acme Supply. Check no. 1504.		

If the payment is not made in time to take advantage of the cash discount, the full amount of the invoice must be paid because the discount has been lost. The entry is:

June 28	Accounts payable	980	
	Purchase discounts lost	20	
	Cash		1,000
	Paid Acme Supply. Check no. 1519.		

A discount lost is interest expense

Typically the **Purchase Discounts Lost** account is a financing expense and appears in the income statement among administrative or interest expenses. If this account becomes large, it alerts managers that a problem may exist. Someone may not be paying the bills in time, or the arrangements may not have been made to have the necessary cash available when needed. Whatever the cause of lost discounts, managers have accounting data that indicate a problem may exist, and they can analyze the data to determine if measures are necessary to change the situation.

The above illustrations of purchase discounts apply to periodic inventory systems. There is no Purchases account in a perpetual system, so any discounts taken reduce the balance of the Merchandise Inventory account. Notice that Purchase Discounts Taken and Purchase Discounts Lost are both purchase discounts accounts. The former is used with the gross invoice method and the latter with the net invoice method. The two methods are illustrated in Figure 6-6, where they can be compared using the same example discussed above.

In a perpetual inventory system, the disadvantage of the net invoice method is that unit prices often change into amounts difficult to deal with. For example, if purchases are recorded at net, and a discount of 3 percent is available on an item priced at $78.65, the item must be recorded at $76.2905 ($78.65 − .03 × $78.65).

Sales Discounts

Cash discounts offered by businesses to their customers are called **sales discounts.** They may also be accounted for by recording sales either at net or gross.

Sales recorded at gross.   If a sale of $700 is made on June 1 with terms of 3/10, n/30, the following entry is used to record the sale at the gross invoice amount:

Gross Invoice Method			Net Invoice Method		
Purchases	1,000		Purchases	980	
Accounts payable		1,000	Accounts payable		980
Purchase on terms			Purchase on terms		
2/10, n/30.			2/10, n/30.		
Accounts payable	1,000		Accounts payable	980	
Cash		980	Cash		980
Purchase discount taken		20	Payment within		
Payment within			discount period.		
discount period.					
Accounts payable	1,000		Accounts payable	980	
Cash		1,000	Purchase discounts lost	20	
Payment after discount			Cash		1,000
period.			Payment after discount		
			period.		

Figure 6-6 **Comparison of purchases and subsequent payment with the gross invoice method and the net invoice method.**

June 1	Accounts receivable	700	
	Sales		700
	Sold merchandise to Apex Corporation.		
	Invoice no. 4666.		

When the customer pays the invoice within the discount period, the receipt of cash is recorded as follows:

June 10	Cash	679	
	Sales discounts	21	
	Accounts receivable		700
	Received payment from Apex		
	Corporation.		

Sales discounts are contra revenues

Sales Discounts is a contra revenue account related to Sales. When the contra sales accounts are deducted from gross sales in the income statement, the result is net sales. If the account is not paid within the discount period, the full amount is collected, as follows:

June 28	Cash	700	
	Accounts receivable		700
	Received payment from Apex		
	Corporation.		

When cash discounts are offered to customers, a financing charge is actually included in the invoice price of the goods sold. The problem with the gross sales method is that if discounts are not taken, what really amounts to interest income is buried in the sales revenue account. Usually the amounts are insignificant and, if they do not distort gross margin in the income statement, the method does not pose serious problems.

Sales recorded at net.   The net invoice method of recording sales is demonstrated with the same example. The following entries are used to record the $700 sale and the subsequent collection of the receivable within the discount period:

June 1	Accounts receivable	679	
	Sales		679
	Sold merchandise to Apex Corporation.		
	Invoice no. 4666.		
June 10	Cash	679	
	Accounts receivable		679
	Received payment from Apex Corpora-		
	tion.		

If payment is received later, however, when the discount can no longer be taken by the customer, the following entry is made:

June 28	Cash	700	
	Sales discounts earned		21
	Accounts receivable		679
	Received payment from Apex		
	Corporation.		

Sales discounts earned are interest income

The **sales discount earned** is a revenue, usually reported as interest income. It is the amount earned by allowing the customer to postpone the payment of debt. This income is often combined with other interest income when reported in the income statement. The gross and net methods of recording sales are summarized in Figure 6-7 using the above examples.

You see now that in addition to the basic entries for purchases and sales, many other accounts affecting the determination of gross margin may be maintained by a merchandising company. Much of the effort of maintaining such accounts has been eliminated by computers, which make inventory accounting efficient and timely and improve greatly the type of information available from inventory records.

Gross Invoice Method			Net Invoice Method		
Accounts receivable	700		Accounts receivable	679	
Sales		700	Sales		679
Sale on terms 3/10, n/30.			Sale on terms 3/10, n/30.		
Cash	679		Cash	679	
Sales discounts	21		Accounts receivable		679
Accounts receivable		700	Receipt within discount period.		
Receipt within discount period.					
Cash	700		Cash	700	
Accounts receivable		700	Sales discounts earned		21
Receipt after discount period.			Accounts receivable		679
			Receipt after discount period.		

Figure 6-7   **Comparison of sales and subsequent collection with the gross invoice method and the net invoice method.**

To illustrate how the various merchandising accounts may appear in the income statement, the gross margin portion of Saturn Supply Company's income statement is shown in Figure 6-8. In this illustration, sales and purchases are assumed to be recorded at gross invoice price, and a periodic inventory system is used.

The journal entry needed to eliminate the purchases-related account balances of Saturn Supply Company and to create the Cost of Goods Sold account is made as follows on page 267:

Saturn Supply Company
Income Statement
For the Year Ended November 30, 1985

Gross sales			$2,734,160
Less sales discounts		$ 32,800	
Sales returns and allow- ances		16,390	49,190
Net sales			2,684,970
Less cost of goods sold:			
Beginning inventory		119,270	
Purchases	$1,640,641		
Add freight-in	42,880		
Less purchase discounts	(21,511)		
Less purchase returns and allowances	(7,300)		
Total purchases		1,654,710	
Goods available for sale		1,773,980	
Less ending inventory		122,720	
Cost of goods sold			1,651,260
Gross margin			1,033,710

Figure 6-8   **Calculation of cost of goods sold and gross margin in detail. The rest of the statement is omitted.**

Dec. 31	Merchandise (ending)	122,720	
	Purchase discounts	21,511	
	Purchase returns and allowances	7,300	
	Cost of goods sold	1,651,260	
	Purchases		1,640,641
	Freight-in		42,880
	Merchandise (beginning)		119,270
	To adjust Merchandise and create Cost		
	of goods sold account prior to		
	closing books.		

If the company uses a perpetual inventory system, Freight-in is closed either to Cost of Goods Sold or to Income Summary. Purchases, Purchase Discounts, and Purchase Returns and Allowances accounts do not exist in a perpetual system, and the Merchandise account usually does not need adjusting. With either system the gross margin section of the income statement can be shown fully detailed, as in Figure 6-8.

The Sales, Sales Discounts, and Sales Returns and Allowances are simply closed to Income Summary:

	Sales	2,734,160	
	Sales discounts		32,800
	Sales returns and allowances		16,390
	Income summary		2,684,970
	To close Sales and contra sales accounts.		

ILLUSTRATIVE EXAMPLE WITH WORKSHEETS

Worksheets are time-saving tools

We use Benbrook Company to illustrate the worksheet procedures for a merchandising business for both a perpetual and periodic inventory system. The unadjusted trial balance on December 31, 1985, for the perpetual system appears in the worksheet in Figure 6-9 and for the periodic system in Figure 6-10. Unlike the worksheet in Chapter 5, these worksheets do not contain an adjusted trial balance. There are only a few simple adjustments, so they are extended together with the original trial balance amounts directly into the financial statement columns. To keep the worksheet simple, many accounts are not shown individually but are instead combined into broad categories such as other current assets and liabilities. All sales are on credit and the company records sales and purchases at gross invoice amount.

The following data are available for adjusting the accounts at the end of the year:

a. Depreciation of equipment used in selling is $13,000. Depreciation of other equipment is $40,000.

b. It is estimated that .5 percent of net sales will become uncollectible.

c. A $120 check paid for freight-in was erroneously debited to a prepaid expense account.

d. A physical count of inventory at year-end discloses that merchandise costing $82,800 is on hand.

e. The corporate income tax rate is 40 percent of pretax income.

Perpetual Inventory Worksheet

For purposes of discussing the worksheet in Figure 6-9, we present each of the adjusting entries in general journal form. Depreciation on equipment is divided between selling and administrative expenses. The adjustment increases each of these expenses by a debit to Depreciation Expense, and it also increases the Accumulated Depreciation account.

a.	Depreciation expense (selling)	13,000	
	Depreciation expense (administrative)	40,000	
	Accumulated depreciation		53,000
	To record depreciation of equipment.		

Various methods are available for estimating the amount of uncollectible accounts. The estimate made here requires increasing the allowance for doubtful accounts by .5 percent of net sales, calculated as follows:

Gross sales	$985,800
Less sales returns and allowances	9,800
Net sales	$976,000

.5 percent of net sales: $976,000 × .005 = $4,880

The amount to be recorded as Bad Debts Expense is $4,880, which is the portion of this period's sales revenue that is expected to be uncollectible. The expense could be recorded as part of selling expenses. We show it as a separate account.

b.	Bad debts expense	4,880	
	Allowance for doubtful accounts		4,880
	To record bad debts as .5 percent of net sales.		

The Cost of Goods Sold account is understated because Freight-in is still recorded separately. In addition, part of Freight-in expense was recorded as an asset, making current assets overstated. The first entry below eliminates this error, and the next entry closes Freight-in to CGS.

c.	Freight-in	120	
	Prepaid expense		120
	To correct error in recording freight-in.		
d.	Cost of goods sold	2,180	
	Freight-in		2,180
	To close Freight-in to Cost of Goods Sold.		

In a perpetual system, the physical count of merchandise verifies the correctness of the balance in the merchandise account. Cost of Goods Sold is recorded as sales take place. If necessary the CGS balance is adjusted before it is extended to the income statement columns as shown. The merchandise is extended to the balance sheet columns.

In the income statement columns, we find that the difference between revenues and expenses is $142,000 ($985,800 − $843,800). This is the income subject to income tax. The estimated tax liability and the tax expense are recorded as follows:

e.	Income tax expense	56,800	
	Estimated income tax payable		56,800
	To record income tax for the period.		
	.40 × $142,000 = $56,800		

Finally, net income is transferred to retained earnings. The beginning balance of retained earnings and the net income are both extended to the balance sheet columns. Of course, when the formal balance sheet is prepared, these two amounts are combined into one figure representing the ending balance of retained earnings.

Periodic Inventory Worksheet

With a periodic inventory system, the unadjusted trial balance is somewhat different from the trial balance for a perpetual system, as shown in Figure 6-10. The Cost of Goods Sold account does not exist, the Merchandise account contains the beginning inventory balance, and there is a Purchases account, a Purchase Returns and Allowances account, and a Purchase Discounts account as well as Freight-in. A physical count of merchandise must be taken to determine the amount of ending inventory.

Benbrook Company
Worksheet
For the Year Ended December 31, 1985

	Trial Balance		Adjustments		Income		Balance Sheet	
	Debit	Credit	Debit	Credit	Debit	Credit	Debit	Credit
Cash	66,640						66,640	
Accounts receivable	192,860						192,860	
Allowance for doubtful accounts		340		b. 4,880				5,220
Merchandise	82,800						82,800	
Other current assets	13,420			c. 120			13,300	
Plant and equipment	615,000						615,000	
Accumulated depreciation		95,200		a. 53,000				148,200
Accounts payable		131,080						131,080
Other current liabilities		26,100						26,100
Long-term debt		225,000						225,000
Capital stock		175,000						175,000
Retained earnings		118,000						118,000
Sales		985,800				985,800		
Sales returns and allowances	9,800				9,800			
Cost of goods sold	516,530		d. 2,180		518,710			
Freight-in	2,060		c. 120	d. 2,180				
Selling expenses	171,100		a. 13,000		184,100			
Administrative expenses	86,310		a. 40,000		126,310			
Totals	1,756,520	1,756,520						
Bad debts expense			b. 4,880		4,880			
			60,180	60,180	843,800	985,800		
Estimated income tax					56,800			56,800
Net income					85,200			85,200
Totals					985,800	985,800	970,600	970,600

Figure 6-9 Worksheet for merchandising business using perpetual inventory system. Note treatment of merchandise and cost of goods sold.

Benbrook Company
Worksheet
For the Year Ended December 31, 1985

	Trial Balance		Adjustments		Income		Balance Sheet	
Cash	66,640						66,640	
Accounts receivable	192,860						192,860	
Allowance for doubtful accounts		340		b. 4,880				5,220
Merchandise	74,300		d. 82,800	d. 74,300			82,800	
Other current assets	13,420			c. 120			13,300	
Plant and equipment	615,000						615,000	
Accumulated depreciation		95,200		a. 53,000				148,200
Accounts payable		131,080						131,080
Other current liabilities		26,100						26,100
Long-term debt		225,000						225,000
Capital stock		175,000						175,000
Retained earnings		118,000						118,000
Sales		985,800				985,800		
Sales returns and allowances	9,800				9,800			
Purchases	533,830			d. 533,830				
Purchase returns		6,350	d. 6,350					
Purchase discounts		2,450	d. 2,450					
Freight-in	2,060			d. 2,180				
Selling expenses	171,100		a. 13,000		184,100			
Administrative expenses	86,310		a. 40,000		126,310			
Totals	1,765,320	1,765,320						
Bad debts expense			b. 4,880		4,880			
Cost of goods sold			d. 518,710		518,710			
			668,310	668,310	843,800	985,800	970,600	
Estimated income tax					56,800			56,800
Net income					85,200			85,200
Totals					985,800	985,800	970,600	970,600

Figure 6-10 Worksheet for merchandising business using periodic inventory system. Note treatment of merchandise and accounts related to purchases.

Adjusting entries **a, b, c,** and **e** are exactly the same as those already illustrated for a perpetual inventory system. Look at these entries again and see how they are entered in the worksheet in Figure 6-10. The only difference between the two worksheets is the treatment of the inventory accounts that determine cost of goods sold.

In entry **d** Merchandise is credited $74,300 to write off the beginning inventory, and it is debited $82,800 to enter the ending balance as determined by the physical count of inventory. Purchases and Freight-in are credited to write them off, and Purchase Returns and Allowances and Purchase Discounts are debited, eliminating their balances. This leaves Cost of Goods Sold as the debit needed to balance the entry.

d.	Merchandise (ending)	82,800	
	Purchase returns	6,350	
	Purchase discounts	2,450	
	Cost of goods sold	518,710	
	Merchandise (beginning)		74,300
	Purchases		533,830
	Freight-in		2,180

Cost of goods sold is a balancing item in the worksheet entry

The above entry creates the Cost of Goods Sold account, which can now be extended to the income statement columns. Carefully examine the entry on the worksheet to make sure you understand it. We have shown only one of a number of ways to prepare the worksheet in this situation. Some accountants prefer to extend both the beginning and ending inventory balances and purchases to the income statement columns without creating the Cost of Goods Sold account. Purchase Returns, Purchase Discounts, and Freight-in are similarly extended. The net result is still the same amount of net income. The important thing is not the mechanical procedure but the resulting financial statements and your understanding of the process.

ADDITIONAL MERCHANDISING TOPICS

In addition to the topics discussed above, many other aspects of accounting for merchandising operations exist. For example, we have not discussed how cost is assigned to the goods on hand after a physical count of merchandise is taken at the end of the accounting period. Assigning costs to inventory and estimating the amount of inventory when a physical count is not taken are topics discussed in Chapter 9. Below we discuss inventory losses, trade discounts, and freight-out.

Inventory Losses

There are many reasons for inventory shrinkage

When large amounts of inventory flow through a business, inventory losses are bound to occur due to breakage, spoilage, deterioration, pilferage, and obsolesence. If a perpetual inventory system is used, the amount of inventory loss is determined when the physical count of merchandise discloses that fewer goods are on hand than perpetual inventory records show. If the discrepancy is large, management may try to discover the cause in order to prevent future losses. All losses cannot be prevented, of course. Some goods may spoil due to the passage of time, some become shopworn when they are put on display and handled by customers, and some breakage may occur as a result of accidents. When inventory losses are discovered, the entry to record the loss is made as follows:

Dec. 30	Inventory loss	189	
	Merchandise inventory		189
	To record inventory losses.		

Inventory losses, or **inventory shrinkage,** may be reported separately as a deduction from gross margin to arrive at adjusted gross margin in the income statement. Although such losses are reported separately to managers, they are included with cost of goods sold in the financial statements of the company. Moreover, when a periodic inventory system is used, it is usually not possible to determine precisely the amount of shrinkage that occurs in inventory during the accounting period. This is because the cost of goods sold is a residual determined by a physical count of inventory, and all goods not on hand are assumed to have been sold, although some may have been stolen, misplaced, or somehow lost. The losses become buried in the cost of goods sold figure. Special estimating techniques are available that can be used to determine if significant losses have occurred, but these methods cannot disclose small amounts of lost merchandise. Such inventory estimating procedures are discussed in Chapter 9.

Trade Discounts

Trade discounts are not recorded in the books

It is a common practice of many businesses to quote all prices of merchandise at retail. The practice facilitates printing catalogs and price lists with only one price. When selling to another business that must resell the goods at a higher price to earn a profit, the supplier offers a **trade discount** stated as a percentage of the retail price. A retailer who gets a trade discount of 40 percent on merchandise quoted at $3,000 retail knows that his cost will be $1,800 if he makes the purchase. When the purchase is made, it is recorded at the cost of $1,800; the $3,000 retail price does not affect the books. Trade discounts are information to the buyer, but they do not enter into the accounting system.

Freight-Out

Freight-out is a selling expense

The cost of delivering merchandise to customers is called freight-out and is not a cost of acquiring merchandise. **Freight-out** is an expense of selling merchandise and is reported among other selling expenses in the income statement. Freight-out and freight-in are two entirely different accounts, and only the latter enters into the calculation of cost of goods sold.

Special Accounting Records

In this book, we use the general journal and the general ledger to record all types of business transactions and to communicate many kinds of accounting information. In practice, however, many other special records are used to record accounting information. Some of these special records are discussed below. The appendix to this chapter contains a more complete discussion and illustrations of special accounting records.

Special journals make record keeping efficient

Special journals.   The general journal may be used to record any financial transactions that can occur in any business. It is, however, not very efficient for recording repetitive transactions such as purchases of merchandise, payments of wages, and sales of merchandise that may occur hundreds or even thousands of times in an accounting period. For such routine, repetitive transactions, **special journals** are used to make the journalizing process efficient. Special journals have columns for a variety of accounts, and they may be designed in many different ways to suit individual businesses.

Control accounts.   In addition to special journals, businesses employ other types of specialized records such as the inventory record illustrated in Figure 6-2. Businesses that buy and sell goods and services on credit must maintain careful individual records of their suppliers' and customers' accounts. Accounts receivable and accounts payable in the general ledger are not sufficiently detailed to keep track of individual customers or suppliers because these accounts contain the totals of all individual amounts owed to or by the business. These totals act as controls over the separate amounts owed by individual customers or to individual suppliers; therefore, accounts receivable and accounts payable in the general ledger are called **control accounts.** The individual, detailed accounts are maintained in a subsidiary ledger.

Subsidiary accounts show the details of control accounts

Subsidiary ledgers.   A control account in the general ledger is supported by individual accounts in the subsidiary ledger. A **subsidiary ledger** is a collection of individual accounts of a specific type, such as individual accounts receivable. A separate subsidiary account is assigned to each supplier and to each customer. These individual **subsidiary accounts** are subdivisions of the control accounts and are not part of the general ledger. The subsidiary accounts receivable ledger may consist of hundreds of separate accounts. The total of the accounts receivable balances in the subsidiary ledger equals the total balance in the accounts receivable control account. Similarly, the total of all the individual account balances in

Account Receivable

Deborah Jones
2345 Blueberry St.
Fort Worth, TX 76123

Acct. No. 1114
Credit Limit $ 500.00

Date	Explanation	Ref.	Charges	Payments	Current Balance
June 21	Ladies' Wear	53	27.67		27.67
26	Housewares	54	19.16		46.83
29	Patio Shop	54	162.80		209.63
July 7	Misc. Merchandise	56	41.37		251.00
9	Payment	R2		200.00	51.00
19	Misc. Merchandise	58	38.45		89.45

Please pay last amount in this column.

Figure 6-11
Subsidiary account receivable. A copy may be used as a statement for billing customer.

Figure 6-12   **The subsidiary ledger and its relationship to the control account.**

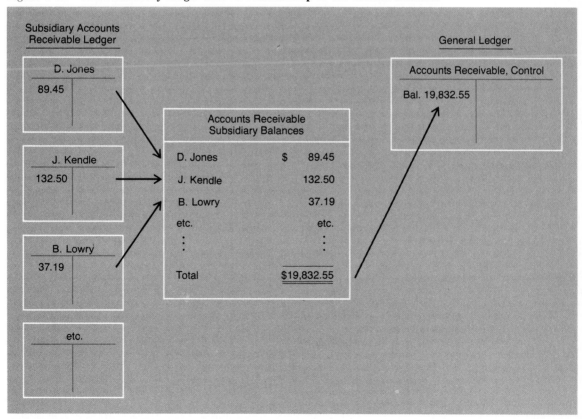

the accounts payable subsidiary ledger must equal the balance in the accounts payable control account in the general ledger.

Figure 6-11 is an example of a customer's three-column subsidiary account. A copy of such an account may be sent to the customer periodically as a statement requesting payment. The relationship of the subsidiary accounts to the control account is illustrated in Figure 6-12.

Many other general ledger accounts have subsidiary records in which details of the control account are maintained. The individual merchandise record in Figure 6-2 is an example. Individual records are also maintained for each piece of equipment in fixed assets, and temporary investments are subdivided into various categories of stock and bond investments that are maintained individually in order to keep track of their separate costs. Although we seldom use subsidiary accounts in this book, they are an important part of the accounting system.

SUMMARY

The main source of revenue for merchandising businesses is from sales of merchandise. Often the main expense of operating such businesses is the cost of merchandise sold. The difference between **sales revenue** and **cost of goods sold** is called **gross margin.**

The operating portion of the income statement of a merchandising business is divided into three main parts. There is a section for the calculation of gross margin, a section for selling expenses, and a section for administrative expenses. The remainder of the statement is generally the same for all types of businesses.

With a **perpetual inventory system,** each time a purchase is made, it is recorded as an increase in merchandise inventory. When a sale takes place, the sales revenue is immediately matched with the cost of goods sold, the merchandise account is reduced, and the cost of goods sold is increased. A perpetual inventory system with **specific identification** ties the cost of each item directly to the item when it is sold.

For some types of merchandise inventories it is impractical to keep track of the cost of goods sold on a continuous basis. In such cases a **periodic inventory system** is used. In a periodic system, cost of goods sold cannot be determined until a physical count of inventory is made. The merchandise inventory account contains the beginning balance of merchandise. Any additions during the accounting period are recorded as **purchases.** Together the beginning balance of inventory and the purchases account balance represent the amount of **goods available for sale** during the period. Cost of goods sold is calculated by deducting the ending inventory from goods available for sale.

When customers return merchandise that they had previously bought, the seller debits **sales returns and allowances.** The balance in sales returns and allowances is deducted from **gross sales** to arrive at **net sales** in the income statement. When the business returns merchandise to its suppliers, it credits merchandise if it uses a perpetual inventory system and **purchase returns and allowances** if it uses a periodic system. The balance in purchase returns and allowances is deducted from gross purchases to arrive at net purchases. **Freight-in,** the cost of shipping merchandise purchases, is a **product cost** and is added to purchases in calculating cost of goods sold. **Freight-out** is a selling expense.

Cash discounts are sometimes offered to buyers to induce them to pay for their purchases promptly. If cash discounts are offered for purchases, the acquisition of merchandise may be recorded at net or gross invoice amount. When purchases are recorded at gross, **purchase discounts taken** are deducted from purchases in calculating cost of goods sold. When purchases are recorded at net, **purchase discounts lost** are considered a financing expense. Purchase discounts taken and purchase returns and allowances are **contra expense** accounts.

A business may offer cash discounts to its customers and record sales at net or gross invoice amount. When sales are recorded at net, **sales discounts earned** represent interest income. When sales are recorded at gross, **sales discounts** are deducted from gross sales in the income statement to arrive at net sales. Sales discounts and sales returns and allowances are **contra revenue** accounts. **Trade discounts** are not recorded in the accounting books.

Inventory losses may occur as a result of breakage, spoilage, or theft. If a perpetual inventory system is used, losses are found when the inventory records do not match the periodic count of inventory. If a periodic system is used, inventory losses are buried in cost of goods sold.

Businesses maintain a number of special records to make record keeping more efficient. **Special journals** are used to record routine, repetitive transactions such as sales, purchases, and cash collections and payments. **Subsidiary accounts** are maintained in the **subsidiary ledger** for receivables and payables in order to keep separate records for each individual supplier and credit customer. The total of the subsidiary account balances equal the balance in the **control account.**

KEY TERMS

cash discount *(261)*	**periodic inventory system** *(254)*
contra expense accounts *(256)*	**perpetual inventory system** *(250)*
contra revenue accounts *(254)*	**purchases** *(256)*
control account *(274)*	**purchase discounts** *(261)*
cost of goods sold (CGS) *(248)*	**purchase returns and**
discounts earned *(265)*	**allowances** *(256)*
discounts lost *(263)*	**sales** *(248)*
discounts taken *(262)*	**sales discounts** *(263)*
freight-in *(260)*	**sales returns and**
freight-out *(274)*	**allowances** *(254)*
goods available for sale *(258)*	**special journals** *(274)*
gross invoice method *(261)*	**specific identification**
gross margin *(248)*	**method** *(251)*
gross profit *(248)*	**subsidiary account** *(274)*
inventory shrinkage *(273)*	**subsidiary ledger** *(274)*
net invoice method *(262)*	**terms of invoice** *(261)*
net purchases *(257)*	**trade discount** *(273)*
net sales *(254)*	**vendor** *(252)*

APPENDIX: SPECIAL JOURNALS

Special journals are designed to simplify the journalizing and posting of repetitive transactions. Most of the repetition occurs in the recording of cash receipts, cash disbursements, purchases, and sales. Although businesses may have special journals for other kinds of transactions, the four types described here are the most common.

Purchases Journal

In the general journal, the entry for purchases requires a debit entry, a credit entry, and a memorandum from which subsidiary accounts can be posted. The credit part of the entry is used for posting the control account, and the memorandum indicates which subsidiary account must be posted, as shown in the following entry:

July 9	Purchases (or merchandise)	470	
	Accounts payable		470
	Purchased merchandise from General		
	Supply. Purchase order no. 47113.		

Instead of using the general journal, the business can record this same transaction on one line by using the special purchases journal illustrated in Figure 6-13. When the journal is posted to the ledger, the total of the single column is posted as a debit to purchases and a credit to accounts

PURCHASES JOURNAL
Page P2

Date		Purchase Order no.	Account title	Terms	Ref.	Amount
July	7	47113	General Supply	n/30	✓	4 7 0 00
	9	47116	Acme Corporation	n/30	✓	1 2 3 5 00
	13	47117	Apex Industries	2/10, n/30	✓	6 8 5 00
	22	47118	General Supply	n/30	✓	1 9 8 2 00
		.	.			.
		.	.			.
		.	.			.
July	31		Posted			1 4 8 3 2
						(201)(504)

Figure 6-13 **A special journal for recording purchases. The single amount column is for debits to purchases and credits to accounts payable.**

payable. Many purchases, therefore, can be posted at once, and as a result much work is eliminated and the chance of errors is reduced. The individual items on each line of the purchases journal also can easily be posted to the subsidiary accounts payable ledger, and since the subsidiary account balances must equal the accounts payable control balance, a check is provided to ensure that all accounts have been posted correctly. A check mark in the reference column indicates that the subsidiary account is posted, and the account numbers in parentheses under the total indicate the control accounts to which the total is posted.

Sales Journal

The total of many purchases or sales is posted only once

Very similar to the purchases journal, the sales journal in Figure 6-14 contains all credit sale transactions. Cash sales do not involve accounts receivable and are recorded in the cash receipts journal. The total of the single column in the sales journal is posted as a debit to accounts receivable control and as a credit to sales. Each subsidiary account receivable is posted individually. Customers' accounts are usually posted daily so that the latest balance is available in the event customers wish to make a payment or inquire about their accounts. Check marks in the reference column and account numbers at the bottom of the money column indicate that posting has taken place.

SALES JOURNAL

Page S1

Date		Invoice No.	Account debited	Terms	Ref.	Amount
July	7	3116	D. Jones	n/30		41 37
	9	3117	M. Smith	n/30		1 73 42
	12	3118	C. Kittle	n/30		1 32 50
			etc.			
			.			
			.			
			.			
July	31		Posted			21 06 2 00
						(103) (401)

Figure 6-14   A special journal for recording credit sales. The single amount column is for debits to accounts receivable and credits to sales revenue.

Cash Receipts Journal

Most cash receipts are either from cash sales or from collections of accounts receivable. The cash receipts journal in Figure 6-15 has a separate credit column for each of these cash collections in addition to the cash debit

CASH RECEIPTS JOURNAL   Page R2

Date	Explanation	Cash Debit	Account Title	Ref.	Accounts Receivable Credit	Cash Sales Credit	Account	Ref.	Credit
July 6	Cash sales	387 19				387 19			
7	Cash sales	4 13 88				4 13 88			
7	Invoice no. 3110	360 00	Superior Corp.	✓	360 00				
7	acct. no. 1114	200 00	D. Jones	✓	200 00				
8	Bank loan	1 000 00					Note payable	302	1 000 00
9	.	.	.		.	.			.
	.	.	.		.	.			.
	.	.	.		.	.			.
31	Cash sales	4 36 03				4 36 03			
	Posted	1 8 862 00			8 22 0 00	9 382 00			1 2 60 00
		(101)			(103)	(401)			NA

Figure 6-15 **A special journal for recording cash receipts. Such journals may be designed in many forms to suit the needs of a particular business.**

column. Other cash receipts can be journalized in the third credit column, which is accompanied by a space for indicating the account to be credited. The cash, accounts receivable, and cash sales columns are posted in total to the general ledger periodically. The individual accounts receivable are posted to the subsidiary accounts receivable ledger, usually daily. The total of the third credit column is not posted, as indicated by the letters NA (not applicable), because it does not pertain to any one account. Each account in this column is posted individually. The totals of the four columns are used to check on the equality of debits and credits in the cash receipts journal.

Cash Disbursements Journal

Figure 6-16 illustrates the cash disbursements journal, often called the check register. It is similar to the cash receipts journal and is treated in a similar way. Most of the cash credits have corresponding debits for payments on accounts payable. If cash purchases are made frequently, a column for these is also provided. Other debits are recorded for individual accounts as necessary. Some cash receipts and cash disbursements may be impractical to record in the special journals because they involve complex entries. Examples are the sale of fixed assets at a gain or loss, exchanges of stock for cash and other assets, and purchases of assets for cash and a note payable. Such transactions are recorded in the general journal, which can be used to record any type of transaction.

The journals illustrated here are typical of the kinds of special journals found in businesses. However, there is no standard form for special journals. Usually they are specifically designed to fit the needs of each business

CASH DISBURSEMENTS JOURNAL   Page D5

Date	Explanation	Check No.	Cash Credit	Account Title	Ref.	Accounts Payable Debit	Other Accounts	Ref.	Debit (Credit)
July 11	July rent	719	2 8 0 00				Rent expense	507	2 8 0 00
12	Electric bill	720	5 8 80				Utilities expense	509	5 8 80
14	Purch. order no. 47116	721	4 7 0 00	General Supply	✓	4 7 0 00			
16	Freight-in	722	3 1 30				Freight-in	503	3 1 30
17	Purch. order no. 47117	723	6 7 1 30	Apex Industries	✓	6 8 5 00	Discount taken	551	(1 3 70)
	.	.	.	.		.	.		.
	.	.	.	.		.	.		.
	.	.	.	.		.	.		.
31	Purch. order no. 47131	742	6 0 0 00	ICU Corp.		6 0 0 00			
	Posted		1 2 7 1 2 00			6 9 3 2 00			5 7 8 0 00
			(101)			(201)			NA

Figure 6-16   A special journal for recording cash payments. Many versions of this journal may be found in practice.

and may have fewer or more columns than the forms illustrated here. Because much of the data in larger companies is processed by computers, a large variety of specialized coding forms may be required.

QUESTIONS

1. What are the most important differences between the income statement of a service business and that of a merchandising business?

2. What is the purpose of taking a physical count of inventory when a perpetual inventory system is maintained? What is the purpose of the physical count if the business maintains a periodic inventory system?

3. What information is provided to managers when Sales Returns and Purchase Returns accounts are maintained?

4. Explain how use of the Cost of Goods Sold account differs in the perpetual and periodic inventory systems.

5. An error occurred in the counting of inventory at the end of the accounting period, and the result was an understatement of ending inventory. If the company maintains a periodic inventory system, what is the effect of the error on cost of goods sold, gross margin, and net income of the current period?

6. Two companies in the same line of business typically buy merchandise on terms 2/10, n/30. One company maintains a Discounts Lost account and the other a Discounts Taken account. Explain the difference between these accounts.

7. What is the difference between a trade discount and a purchase discount?

8. The manager of Bleeker Company says, "You must have made a mistake in the financial statements. The amounts for total assets and total equities shown

on the balance sheet are different from the amounts on the worksheet for the same period." Respond to the manager's comment.

9. Describe the function of subsidiary ledgers and their relation to control accounts.

10. Discuss some advantages of maintaining special journals in comparison to recording all transaction in the general journal.

EXERCISES

Ex. 6-1   Purchase and sale of merchandise.   The beginning inventory balance of Slater Company on November 1 was as follows:

10 units Overseal	@ $15 per unit	$150
15 units Underseal	@ 18	270
20 units Everseal	@ 20	400
Total		$820

The following transactions took place during November:

Nov. 5 The company purchased five units of Everseal on open account for $20 each.

7 The company sold two units of Overseal for cash at $22 each.

11 Three units of Underseal were sold on account for $28 each.

Required:

a.   Assuming a perpetual inventory system, journalize the above transactions.

b.   Assuming a periodic inventory system, journalize the above transactions.

Ex. 6-2   Perpetual and periodic systems.   The beginning inventory balance on June 1 consisted of two types of products:

13 generators	@ $200 per unit	$2,600
16 transformers	@ 260	4,160
Total		$6,760

The following transactions took place in June:

June 10 Bought three generators on account at $200 each and three transformers at $260 each.

20 Sold five generators on account at $420 each.

25 Customer returned one generator because it was defective. Credited customer's account for the sales price.

27 Returned the defective unit to supplier for credit on account.

Required:

a.   Journalize the above transactions assuming that the company maintains a perpetual inventory system.

b.   Journalize the above transactions assuming that the company maintains a periodic inventory system.

Ex. 6-3   **Gross margin computation.**   Blehasco Corporation, a maker of furniture, reported the following information taken from its annual report at the end of 1985:

	1985	**1984**
Sales	$747,100	$712,517
Cost of goods sold	584,167	566,333
Inventories	124,716	128,424

Required: Prepare the gross margin section of the company's 1985 income statement in detail.

Ex. 6-4   **Calculation and reporting of gross margin.**   Following are some data for a company that uses a periodic inventory system:

Sales	$159,275
Beginning inventory	23,185
Purchases	82,620
Ending inventory	25,840

Required:
    a. Prepare the journal entry at the end of the accounting period to adjust the accounts and establish the correct balance in Cost of Goods Sold.
    b. Show how gross margin is reported in the income statement.

Ex. 6-5   **Purchase and sales returns, periodic inventory.**   Pilgrim Company purchases merchandise from Mirglip Company on open account with terms n/30. Both companies use a periodic inventory system. On July 12 Pilgrim purchased goods for $3,700 from Mirglip and on July 16 returned goods costing $400 because they were defective. On August 10 Pilgrim paid its account.

Required:
    a. Record the above transactions in the journal of Pilgrim Company.
    b. Record the above transactions in the journal of Mirglip Company.

Ex. 6-6   **Purchases and sales returns, perpetual inventory.**   Refer to the data on the purchases and sales described in Exercise 6-5. Assume that both companies use a perpetual inventory system and that Mirglip's cost of goods sold is 60 percent of its selling price.

Required:
    a. Record the transactions in the journal of Pilgrim Company.
    b. Record the transactions in the journal of Mirglip Company.

Ex. 6-7   **Gross margin calculation.**   Garth Corporation uses a periodic inventory system. During the year it had total sales of $543,210. The beginning inventory balance was $58,200, and purchases during the year amounted to $325,900. A physical count of inventory disclosed that goods costing $63,100 are on hand at the end of the fiscal year on November 30.

Required: Prepare the gross margin section of Garth Corporation's income statement at the end of its fiscal year. Show all details of the costs of goods sold calculation.

Ex. 6-8   **Gross margin calculation with returns and allowances.**   Poliglot Company uses a perpetual inventory system. During the year it had gross sales of $3,450,000 and sales return and allowances of $14,300. The beginning inventory balance was $350,000, purchases during the year amounted to $2,100,000, and purchase returns were $12,000. The ending balance in the inventory account was $380,000, and this was verified by a physical count. The fiscal year ends on November 30.

Required: Prepare the gross margin section of Poliglot Company's income statement at the end of its fiscal year. Detail the cost of goods sold calculation.

Ex. 6–9   **Gross margin with inventory loss.**   Milton Company had merchandise on hand costing $600,000 at the beginning of the year. During the year it acquired additional merchandise for $2,954,000 and sales amounted to $4,500,000. Also, merchandise costing $4,500 was stolen by employees, but the company did not know about the thefts. A physical count of inventory disclosed goods costing $612,000 on hand at the end of the year. The company uses a perpetual inventory system and the ending balance in the merchandise inventory account was $616,500.

Required:
   a.   Prepare the cost of goods sold section of the income statement for management. Show the calculation of cost of goods sold.
   b.   Discuss where the cost of the stolen merchandise would be reported with a periodic and a perpetual inventory system.

Ex. 6-10   **Cost of goods sold calculation.**   Following are selected account balances of Latimer Company on December 31, 1985. A physical count of inventory disclosed that merchandise costing $75,500 is on hand.

Inventory, 1/1/85	$ 68,100
Purchases	479,800
Freight-in	7,450
Purchase returns and allowances	10,850
Purchase discounts	9,000
Freight-out	8,200
Accounts payable	64,000
Accounts receivable	81,900

Required:
   a.   Calculate the cost of goods sold for the year.
   b.   Does the company use a perpetual or periodic inventory system? Explain.

Ex. 6-11   **Recording cash discounts at gross.**   On October 1, 1985, Cactus Lumber Company was billed $50,000 for purchases of merchandise from Desert Timber Company. On October 8 the company received a bill for $60,000 for additional purchases. The terms of the invoices were 2/15, n/30. Both companies record sales and purchases at gross and use a periodic inventory system. Cactus Lumber Company paid both bills on October 21.

Required:
   a.   Record the purchases and the payments in the journal of Cactus Lumber Company. Make a separate entry for each invoice.
   b.   Record the sale and the receipts in the journal of Desert Timber Company. Make a separate entry for each invoice.

Ex. 6-12 **Cash discounts and net invoice method.** Refer to the data in Exercise 6-11 on the transactions between Cactus Lumber Company and Desert Timber Company. Assume that both companies record purchases and sales using the net invoice method.

Required:
    a. Record the purchases and the payments in the journal of Cactus Lumber Company. Make a separate entry for each invoice.
    b. Record the sale and the receipts in the journal of Desert Timber Company. Make a separate entry for each invoice.

Ex. 6-13 **Cash discounts with net invoice method.** On October 2, 1985, Nebraska Pineapple Farm sold merchandise for $12,000 to Hawaiian Markets, Inc., on open account. Terms of the invoice were 2/10, n/30. Both companies use the periodic inventory system and record sales and purchases at net invoice cost. On October 10 Hawaiian Markets paid half the account, and on October 29 it paid the other half.

Required:
    a. Journalize the sale and collection of cash in the books of Nebraska Pineapple Farm.
    b. Journalize the purchase and payment of cash in the books of Hawaiian Markets, Inc.

Ex. 6-14 **Cash discounts with gross invoice method.** Refer to the data in Exercise 6-13 on the transactions between Nebraska Pineapple Farm and Hawaiian Markets, Inc. Assume that both companies use the gross invoice method to record sales and purchases.

Required:
    a. Journalize the sale and collection of cash in the books of Nebraska Pineapple Farm.
    b. Journalize the purchase and payment of cash in the books of Hawaiian Markets, Inc.

Ex. 6-15 **Gross margin calculation.** The table below shows some data from the income statements of several different companies.

Company

	a	b	c	d	e	f
Sales	$7,000	$	$	$4,000	$6,000	$4,500
Beginning inventory	400	600	450	400		700
Purchases		4,400	6,000		4,500	5,000
Purchase discounts	1,600			100	240	200
Freight-in	240	150	0	200	360	100
Goods available for sale	4,400	4,800	6,300		4,650	
Ending inventory			600	450		700
Cost of goods sold	3,800	4,150	5,700	2,050		
Gross margin	$	$ 350	($150)	$	$2,025	$

Required: Provide the missing values in order to complete each statement.

Ex. 6-16   **Purchases and returns with net invoice method.**   Northwest Utilities Company purchases its electric meters with terms 2/10, n/30. On May 15 the company received 300 220-volt meters and 500 110-volt meters with an invoice cost of $65 and $60 respectively. Ten 110-volt and 20 220-volt meters were issued on May 19 from inventory for installation. Whenever meters are issued from inventory Service Installation Expense is debited for their cost. On May 21 two 110-volt meters were returned by installers because they were defective. The company issued two new meters and returned the defective ones to the supplier for credit. The company maintains a perpetual inventory system and records all purchases at net invoice cost.

Required:
    a.   Record the above events in the general journal.
    b.   Record payment of the invoice assuming the payment is made on May 23.
    c.   Record payment of the invoice assuming the payment is made on June 10.

Ex. 6-17   **Purchases and returns with gross invoice method.**   Refer to the information in Exercise 6-16 but assume that the company records all purchases at gross invoice cost.

Required:
    a.   Record the events that took place in May in the general journal.
    b.   Record payment of the invoice assuming the payment is made on May 23.
    c.   Record payment of the invoice assuming the payment is made on June 10.

*Ex. 6-18   **Subsidiary ledger.**   Below is a special journal maintained by Cride Company which makes most of its purchases and sales on credit. The company's accounts receivable and accounts payable balances on June 1 are $6,980 and $5,100 respectively.

Sales Journal

Date	Invoice	Account Name	Ref	Amount
June 3	1014	Hollis Corporation		2,590
6	1015	Dodd Company		1,985
9	1016	Zuni Company		2,145
12	1017	Parvin Company		5,160
13	1018	Hollis Corporation		1,680
15	1019	Dodd Company		985
17	1020	Apterix Company		3,280
19	1021	Dodd Company		860
20	1022	Zuni Company		3,490
22	1023	Barnet & Sons		2,500
28	1024	Zuni Company		2,470

*Exercises marked with asterisks are based on information in the appendix of this chapter.

The company did not make or receive any payments on account during June. Following are beginning balances in the subsidiary ledger on June 1:

Apterix Company	$2,400	Hollis Corporation	$1,000
Barnet & Sons	0	Parvin Corporation	0
Dodd Company	580	Zune Company	3,000

Required: Establish a subsidiary ledger with one account for each company listed in the journal. Post the information in the journal to the subsidiary ledger and the appropriate control account.

*Ex. 6-19   Special journal.   Below is a special journal maintained by Soldi Sales Company.

Date	Explanation	Cash Cr	Name	Ref	A/P Dr	Other Accounts	Ref	Dr (Cr)
4/3	April rent	600	Martin			Rent Expense		600
4	On account	1,500	Adam Company		1,500			
13	Delivery	90	Sloe Express			Freight-in		90
15	Cash purchase	2,300	Odom Co.			Purchases		2,300
18	On account	3,000	Dodd Corp.		3,000			
30	Electric bill	190	City Electric			Utilities		190
		7,680			4,500			3,180

Required: Describe the purpose of the journal and explain how the various items in the journal should be posted to control and subsidiary accounts.

PROBLEMS

P. 6-1   **Merchandising transactions.**   The Wright Bicycle Shop uses the perpetual inventory system and records purchases and sales at gross. It buys bicycles from various suppliers and sells them at retail. Below are some transactions related to the purchase and sale of one model that costs $80 and sells at retail for $120.

Oct. 1 Purchased 20 units on open account, terms 2/10, n/30.
   2 Sold four units for cash and three on open account, terms n/30.
   7 Paid cash refund to a customer for return of defective bicycle.
   8 Returned defective bicycle to supplier, receiving credit on account.
   9 Sold two units on open account with terms n/30 and six for cash.
  13 Purchased 15 units on open account, terms 2/10, n/30.
  14 Collected $480 of accounts receivable.
  15 Paid $1,600 for October 1 purchase.
  20 Customers returned two defective bicycles. One was exchanged for a new bicycle, and credit was given on account for the other.
  21 Notified supplier of defective bicycle, and supplier offered a $25 allowance. The company accepted the allowance on account and kept the bicycle.
  22 Paid for October 13 purchase in full, less discount.
  23 Paid shipping charges of $200 for delivery of merchandise to the company.
  26 Collected $360 of accounts receivable.

Required: Record the above transactions in general journal form.

P. 6-2   **Merchandising income statement.**   The adjusted trial balance of Shubik Company is provided below. The company uses a periodic inventory system. On December 31, 1985, a physical count of inventory revealed that merchandise costing $58,700 was on hand.

Shubik Company
Trial Balance
December 31, 1985

	Debits	Credit
Cash	$ 40,700	
Accounts receivable	75,900	
Inventory, 1/1/85	48,150	
Prepaid expenses	4,200	
Furniture, fixtures, and equipment	50,000	
Accumulated depreiation		$ 8,600
Accounts payable		18,560
Notes payable, long term		15,000
Capital, J. Shubik		107,340
Sales		741,800
Sales returns and allowances	11,200	
Purchases	528,700	
Purchase discounts		7,350
Freight-in	19,500	
Freight-out	2,180	
Salaries	92,190	
Rent	18,350	
Depreciation	2,800	
Supplies	3,580	
Interest	1,200	
Totals	$898,650	$898,650

Required: Prepare the company's income statement for the year 1985.

P. 6-3   **Merchandising operations with perpetual system.**   Marvis Furniture Outlet operates a retail furniture store. It uses a perpetual inventory system and records all purchases and sales at gross. The company's inventory of reclining armchairs consists of eight units costing $100 and ten units costing $120 each. Transactions pertaining to the inventory of chairs during May are listed below.

May 2 Four chairs costing $120 were sold for $160 each, one for cash and three on open account.

4 Six chairs were purchased on account at $150 each, on terms 2/10, n/30.

8 The customer who bought a chair on open account on May 2 notified the company that the item has a defect, and he wanted to exchange it for another one. The company offered a $20 allowance instead and the customer agreed. His account was credited for $20.

10 Received shipment of four chairs costing $100 each, purchased on open account, with terms 2/10, n/30.

11 Collected $850 of accounts receivable from customers.

12 One of the chairs received on May 10 was damaged beyond repair when unpacked. It was returned to the supplier for credit.

17 Paid for the May 4 purchase.
20 Paid for the May 10 purchase.
22 Sold three chairs costing $100 for $130 cash each, and two chairs costing $120 on account for $160 each.
25 Paid $180 cash for freight in on merchandise shipments from suppliers to the company, and $40 cash for freight out on shipments from company to customers.
28 A small fire in the warehouse destroyed one chair costing $100.

Required: Record the above transactions in the general journal.

P. 6-4 **Reconstructing merchandising transactions.** Selected accounts from the ledger of Bermuda Company are provided below. The company uses a periodic inventory system.

Cash			
Bal.	5,000	b.	2,600
d.	3,300	i.	800
e.	5,100	j.	4,000
h.	1,800		
Bal.	5,800		

Sales			
		c.	2,500
		d.	3,300
		h.	4,700
		Bal.	10,500

Accounts Receivable			
Bal.	6,000	e.	5,100
c.	2,500		
h.	2,900		
Bal.	6,300		

Sales Returns and Allowances			
i.	800		

Merchandise			
Bal.	3,600	k.	3,600
k.	4,600		

Purchases			
a.	4,800		
g.	3,900		
Bal.	8,700	k.	8,700

Accounts Payable			
b.	2,600	Bal.	3,200
f.	600	a.	4,800
j.	4,000	g.	3,900
		Bal.	4,700

Purchase Returns and Allowances			
k.	600	f.	600

Cost of Goods Sold			
k.	7,100		

Required: Reconstruct the journal entries posted above, and explain each entry by means of a memorandum.

P. 6-5 **Reconstructing journal entries.** Hunt & Peck Auto Supply uses a perpetual inventory system. Entries for some of the company's transactions have been posted in the T accounts below and coded with a small letter.

Cash						Accounts Payable				
Bal.	3,020	b.	2,600		d.	1,625	a.		3,250
e.	1,600	d.	1,625		f.	425			
g.	1,100	f.	425				Bal.		1,200
h.	1,700								
Bal.	2,770								

Accounts Receivable						Sales			
c.	2,500	g.	1,100			c.		2,500
h.	800					e.		1,600
Bal.	2,200					h.		2,500
						Bal.		6,600

Merchandise						Cost of Goods Sold		
a.	3,250	c.	1,625		c.	1,625	
b.	2,600	e.	1,040		e.	1,040	
		h.	1,625		h.	1,625	
Bal.	1,560				Bal.	4,290	

Required: Reconstruct the journal entries posted above, and explain each of the transactions by means of memorandum entries.

P. 6-6 **Merchandising transactions and gross margin.** Following are the May transactions of Villi's Variety Store. The company uses a periodic inventory system and records purchases and sales using the gross invoice method. The beginning inventory balance on May 1 was $19,800.

May 2 Merchandise costing $4,730 was purchased on open account with terms 2/10, n/30.

7 Sales of merchandise to date amounted to $6,160, of which $2,600 was on open account with terms n/30.

8 The company issued a check for $5,488 as payment on account for purchases made in late April. A 2 percent discount was taken with this payment.

10 A customer returned an item that had been sold for $110 and received a cash refund.

15 The company received a credit for returning several items of merchandise bought on May 2 for $300 gross and damaged in shipment.

16 Collections of accounts receivable amounted to $1,010.

19 Merchandise costing $3,800 was bought on account with terms n/30, and the company paid the $82 freight bill in cash.

20 A customer wanted to return a defective item that had been sold for $140 cash. The company offered an allowance of $30, which the customer accepted in cash.

21 A check was issued for the May 2 purchase less the May 15 returns.

22 An allowance of was granted by a supplier for merchandise costing $40 gross that was defective. The retail price of the merchandise was reduced.

29 Sales of merchandise since May 7 amounted to $4,650, of which $1,600 was on account with terms 2/10, n/30.

30 A physical count of merchandise indicated that goods costing $20,800 were on hand.

Required:

a. Journalize the above transactions in the general journal.

b. Prepare the gross margin section of the income statement for May.

P. 6-7 **Merchandising operations and gross margin.** Miniature Model Mart, a small hobby store, maintains a periodic inventory system for its merchandise and records purchases and sales using the gross invoice method. The cost of inventory on September 1 was $24,600. The following transactions occurred in September:

Sept. 1 Merchandise costing $1,500 was purchased on account, with terms 3/10, n/30.

7 Merchandise sold last month for $60 cash was returned by a customer for a cash refund.

8 Merchandise costing $4,500 was purchased on account with terms 2/10, n/30.

10 Sales for the first 10 days in September amounted to $3,500. All sales were cash.

14 A customer returned a defective item that had been sold for $180 on September 3 and was given a cash refund.

16 The defective item was returned to the supplier for a credit on account. The invoice cost of the item was $100 when purchased on Sept. 1.

17 Paid for September 8 purchase in full less cash discount.

26 Cash sales were $9,800.

28 Paid for Sept. 1 purchase in full less item returned on Sept. 16.

30 Merchandise on hand at the end of September cost $22,650.

Required:

a. Journalize the above transactions in the general journal.

b. Prepare the gross margin section of the income statement at the end of September.

P. 6-8 **Periodic inventory with net invoice method.** Elikai Company uses a periodic inventory system and records purchases and sales using the net invoice method. On February 1, 1985, it had merchandise on hand with a cost of $15,340. Following are February transactions:

Feb. 1 Bought merchandise on open account. Invoice cost is $8,000 and terms are 2/10, n/30.

2 Merchandise is sold for $1,600 cash and $5,000 on open account with terms n/30.

4 Bought merchandise on open account. Invoice cost is $3,000 and terms are 2/10, n/30.

5 Merchandise sold for $70 was returned for a cash refund.

7 Cash collections of open accounts amounted to $4,800.

11 Paid accounts payable by check for the February 1 purchase.

14 Merchandise found unsuitable was returned to the vendor for credit. Original invoice cost was $500 with 2 percent discount which had been taken.

18 Merchandise is sold for $2,950 cash and $4,650 on open account with terms n/30.

25 Issued a check for the February 4 purchase of merchandise.

27 Collected $4,600 of accounts receivable.

28 Paid operating expenses by check, $2,160. Depreciation expense for the month is $1,900.

28 A physical count of inventory reveals that merchandise costing $14,870 is on hand.

Required:

a. Record the February transactions in the general journal.

b. Prepare the income statement on February 29, 1985.

P. 6-9   **Perpetual inventory with net invoice method.**   Hollis Company maintains a perpetual inventory system and records all purchases and sales using the net invoice method. Beginning inventory, on March 1, was $6,450. The following transactions occurred during March:

March 1 Merchandise was bought on open account on terms 2/10, n/30. The invoice cost was $14,000.

3 Goods costing $7,470 net were sold for $2,880 cash and $9,000 of open accounts with terms n/30.

4 Merchandise was bought on open account on terms 2/10, n/30. The invoice cost was $6,000.

5 Goods costing $80 net and sold for $130 were returned for a cash refund.

6 Goods purchased on March 1 with an invoice cost of $1,000 were returned to the vendor for credit.

9 Accounts receivable of $8,640 were collected.

13 Issued check in payment of accounts payable for the March 1 purchase.

14 Issued check in payment of accounts payable for the March 4 purchase.

17 Goods costing $7,900 net were sold for $5,310 cash and $8,370 of open accounts with terms n/30.

27 Collected $8,280 of accounts receivable.

30 Paid operating expenses of $3,910 by check. Depreciation expense for the month is $3,420.

31 A physical count of inventory revealed that goods costing $9,730 are on hand. Inventory losses are reported as part of cost of goods sold.

Required:

a. Journalize the March transactions in the general journal.

b. Prepare the company's income statement at the end of March.

P. 6-10 **Merchandising worksheet with periodic system.** The trial balance of Minoa Corporation at the end of the 1985 fiscal year is shown below. The company uses a periodic inventory system.

Minoa Corporation
Trial Balance
November 30, 1985

	Debits	Credits
Cash	$ 3,410	
Temporary investments	4,000	
Accounts receivable	13,600	
Merchandise inventory	15,600	
Prepaid expenses	2,700	
Furniture and fixtures	32,000	
Accumulated depreciation		$ 9,700
Accounts payable		13,200
Long-term debt		9,500
Capital stock		12,000
Retained earnings, 11/30/84		16,800
Sales		149,940
Sales returns	2,400	
Purchases	77,900	
Purchase returns		300
Freight-in	3,700	
Expenses	56,130	
Totals	$211,440	$211,440

The following adjustments are required at the end of the period:

a. Merchandise costing $16,500 is on hand.

b. A physical count indicates that prepaid expenses costing $900 have not been used.

c. An analysis of accounts receivable indicates that an allowance for doubtful accounts should be established in the amount of $270.

d. Interest of $60 is accrued on temporary investments.

e. Depreciation for the year is $2,000.

Required: Prepare and complete a worksheet for the company.

P. 6-11 **Merchandising worksheet for a perpetual system.** Below is the trial balance of Irina Company, taken at the end of the company's fiscal year. The company uses the perpetual inventory system.

Irina Company
Trial Balance
December 31, 1985

	Debits	Credits
Cash	$ 4,200	
Temporary investments	7,500	
Accounts receivable	12,000	
Merchandise inventory	21,550	
Supplies	1,800	
Equipment	37,500	
Accumulated depreciation		$ 10,610
Accounts payable		23,000
Bonds payable		12,000
Common stock		15,000
Retained earnings		8,700
Sales		205,000
Sales discounts	3,000	
Cost of goods sold	108,960	
Operating expenses	77,800	
Totals	$274,310	$274,310

The following data are provided at the end of the period for adjustments:

a. Interest of $300 has accrued on bonds payable.

b. A sale of goods costing $1,300 was recorded but the cost of the goods was not removed from the merchandise account.

c. The allowance for doubtful accounts should be 2 percent of ending receivables.

d. Wages in the amount of $900 are accrued.

e. Depreciation on equipment is $2,500 for the year.

Required: Prepare a worksheet for the company on December 31, 1985.

P. 6-12 **Income statement from balance sheets and cash data.** Below are data on Qubeb Corporation cash receipts and disbursements. The company's comparative balance sheets are on page 295.

Beginning cash balance January 1, 1985		$ 12,200
Add cash receipts:		
Collection of receivables		70,000
Cash sales		22,500
		104,700
Less cash disbursements:		
Salaries	$ 13,400	
For merchandise bought on open account	57,300	
For operating expenses	7,000	
For dividends	6,000	83,700
Ending cash balance		$ 21,000

Qubeb Corporation
Balance Sheet

| | December 31 | |
	1985	1984
Assets:		
Cash	$ 21,000	$ 12,200
Accounts receivable	17,500	15,000
Merchandise	22,700	20,000
Equipment	25,000	25,000
Accumulated depreciation	(13,200)	(10,200)
Total assets	$ 73,000	$ 62,000
Liabilities and capital:		
Accounts payable	$ 15,800	$ 15,400
Salaries payable	2,600	2,000
Long-term debt	9,600	9,600
Common stock	15,000	15,000
Retained earnings	30,000	20,000
Total liabilities and capital	$ 73,000	$ 62,000

Required: Use the data to prepare the company's 1985 income statement.

*P. 6-13 **Cash disbursement and purchases journals.** Topaz Company maintains a number of special journals to facilitate its bookkeeping. It records all purchases at gross. Following is a list of cash payments to be journalized in the cash disbursements journal in January:

Date	Check No.	Explanation
Jan. 2	153	Paid $800 office rent for January.
4	154	Apex Company account payable, $1,500.
10	155	Zuni Company account payable, $3,260.
13	156	State Express for delivery of merchandise, $90.
15	157	Ubid Auction for purchase of merchandise, $4,300.
18	158	Holli Corporation account payable, $3,000.
23	159	Zee Rocks Company for used office copier, $2,400.
30	160	City Electric Company for electric bill, $190.

The following purchases of merchandise are to be journalized in the purchases journal:

Jan. 3	Holli Corporation, $4,580, terms n/30.
12	Parvin Company, $5,140, terms 2/10, n/30.
17	Apex Company, $1,280, terms n/EOM.
24	Zuni Company, $2,290, terms n/30.

Required:
a. Establish a cash disbursements journal and a purchases journal similar to the ones shown in the text. Enter the transactions in the journals and find the totals in the journals at the end of the month.

* Problems marked with asterisks require information in the appendix of this chapter.

b. Explain how the various items in the two journals should be posted to control and subsidiary accounts.

*P. 6-14   **Use of special journals and ledgers.**   Shindler Company uses special journals for cash receipts, cash disbursements, purchases, and sales. The company records purchases and sales using the gross invoice method. The cash balance on March 1 was $3,600. Following are data on the company's transactions for March.

1. Subsidiary accounts payable beginning balances are:
   a. Baker Corporation, $3,000.
   b. Giant Distributors, Inc., $1,900.

2. Subsidiary accounts receivable beginning balances are:
   a. Drummond Company, $1,250.
   b. Quatro & Sons, $1,900.
   c. Otto Corporation, $910.

3. Purchases made during March:

Mar.   4 Little Supply Company, $1,600; terms 2/10, n/30.
      12 Giant Distributors, Inc., $600; terms n/30.
      15 Baker Corporation, $1,200; terms n/30.
      18 Little Supply Company, $1,000; terms 2/10, n/30.

4. Credit sales were made at terms n/60 as follows:

Mar.   5 Acme Company, $1,210.
      11 Drummond Company, $650.
      27 Quatro & Sons, $1,050.

5. Cash disbursements were made as follows:

Mar.   1 Store rent, $400. Check no. 553.
       4 Giant Distributors, Inc., $1,000. Check no. 554.
      13 Largo Delivery Service, $260, for freight-in. Check no. 555.
      13 Little Supply Company, $1,568, for March 4 purchase less 2 percent discount. Check no. 556.
      15 Baker Corporation, $2,000. Check no. 557.
      18 Purchased equipment for $3,000. Check no. 558.
      30 Little Supply Company, $1,000. Check no. 559.
      30 Jones, $1,790, for employee's salary. Check no. 560.

6. Receipts of cash during the month were as follows:

Mar.   7 Otto Corporation, $800.
      15 Cash sales, $4,380.
      19 Drummond Corporation, $1,250.
      28 Quatro & Sons, $2,000.
      29 Cash sales, $5,100.
      31 Collection of $5,050 including $5,000 note plus $50 interest.

Required:

   a. Establish special journals similar to those illustrated in the appendix for cash receipts, cash disbursements, purchases and sales. Also establish control accounts for cash, receivables, and payables, and subsidiary accounts receivable and payable.

   b. Enter the beginning balance in the subsidiary and control accounts.

   c. Record the transactions in the journals and find totals in the special journals.

   d. Post only cash, accounts receivable, and accounts payable, including subsidiary accounts.

   e. Prepare schedules of subsidiary accounts to prove the balances in the control accounts.

Case 6-1   **Accounting cycle of a business.**[2]

Boltek's Hobby Shop, Inc., operates a retail store in a major shopping center. Financial statements are prepared quarterly, but the books are closed only on June 30, the end of the company's fiscal year. The trial balance after closing the books on June 30, 1985 is provided on page 298.

The company uses the periodic inventory system and records purchases and sales using the gross invoice method. During the July-September quarter of operations the following transactions took place:

   a. Merchandise purchases on account amounted to $52,500 gross with terms 2/10, n/30.

   b. Checks in the amount of $58,400 were issued in payment of accounts payable of $59,460 with the difference recorded as purchase discounts taken.

   c. Freight-in of $610 on merchandise purchases was paid by check.

   d. Sales on open account were $66,840 with terms n/30. Cash sales were $16,100.

   e. Collections of receivables amounted to $69,130.

   f. On July 20 the $18,000 note payable was paid in full, including $630 interest, of which $420 was accrued at the end of the last period.

   g. Cash refunds of $1,900 were paid for merchandise returned by customers.

   h. The company declared and paid dividends of $3,000.

   i. Wages and salaries paid in cash, including those accrued in the last year, amounted to $9,800.

   j. On September 1 the company borrowed $9,000 from its bank by signing a 60-day 16 percent note.

   k. Rent expense was paid by checks in the amount of $4,000.

   l. Merchandise returned to vendors for credit amounted to $1,260.

   m. On September 30 the company repaid $5,000 of the long-term note payable by issuing a $5,150 check which included interest.

   n. Expenses were paid as follows during the quarter: utilities, $1,400; insurance, $3,600; accounting services, $480.

---

[2] This comprehensive case allows you to review materials from Chapters 1–6.

Boltek's Hobby Shop, Inc.
Post-Closing Trial Balance
June 30, 1985

	Debits	Credits
Cash	$ 32,390	
Accounts receivable	46,790	
Allowance for doubtful accounts		$ 900
Merchandise inventory	104,380	
Supplies inventory	1,800	
Furniture and fixtures	65,280	
Accumulated depreciation		14,980
Notes payable		18,000
Accounts payable		26,100
Accrued wages		2,160
Interest payable		420
Notes payable, long-term		30,000
Capital stock		100,000
Retained earnings, 6/30/85		58,080
Totals	$250,640	$250,640

At the end of the quarter, the following items require adjustments:

o. A physical count of inventory on September 30 reveals that merchandise costing $102,600 is on hand.

p. Supplies costing $690 have not been used.

q. It is estimated that 4 percent of the ending balance of accounts receivable will become uncollectible.

r. Depreciation on furniture and equipment is $1,700.

s. Accrued wages amount to $1,160.

t. Interest of $1,140 is accrued on notes payable.

u. Rent expense includes payments for July, August, September, and October.

v. The insurance policy was bought on August 1 and provides protection against fire for 1 year.

Required:

a. Journalize and post the transactions for the July-September quarter.

b. Establish a ledger from the trial balance, enter the beginning balances, and post the transactions from the journal. Find the ending account balances.

c. Enter the ending account balances into a 10-column worksheet. Make sure the trial balance balances, then enter the adjustments in the worksheet. Prepare an adjusted trial balance, and extend it to the financial statement columns. Ignore income taxes.

d. Use the worksheet data to prepare an income statement, balance sheet, and retained earnings statement in good accounting form for the quarter. Show cost of goods sold in detail.

Accounting for Business Operations

The operations of a business involve thousands of transactions: Working capital cycles from merchandise to receivables, from receivables to cash, from cash to payables, and from payables to merchandise. Accompanying this constant cycle are other activities that require the use of labor and equipment. A significant part of managing a profit-oriented organization is accounting for working capital; for the use of machinery and equipment; and for the payment of salaries, taxes, and other expenses and liabilities.

You now have a general background on financial statements and the accounting procedures that go into their preparation. The next five chapters are devoted to a discussion of how accountants and managers deal with the accounting and managerial issues of daily business operations. Each chapter examines a small part of the balance sheet and the related income concepts. After considering the time value of money in Chapter 7, we analyze the balance sheet by looking first at current assets in Chapters 8 and 9, then at fixed assets and depreciation in Chapter 10, and finally at liabilities in Chapter 11.

Time Value of Money

7

Like all assets, money has value, and the value of a sum of money at any point in time may be different from the value of the same quantity of money at another time. The difference is determined by the timing of payments or receipts of money and the interest rate at which money can be borrowed or invested. When you have completed this chapter, you should understand:

1   What interest is and how it is computed.

2   The use of simple interest calculations.

3   The concepts of compound interest and its effect on the growth of money.

4   The meaning of future value and present value.

5   The meaning of annuities and rents.

6   The use of future value and present value tables to solve a variety of problems dealing with the time value of money.

7   The effect that time has on the value of money, and how the time value of money affects decision making.

Businesses and individuals are constantly faced with decisions involving the timing of money payments and receipts. A company has $3 million—should it build a new plant today, or should it invest the money to earn interest and build the plant 2 years from now? Or should the company borrow additional money today and pay interest so that it can build a larger plant now? Should a couple buy a home with a 14 percent mortgage, or should they rent instead and wait for mortgage rates to decrease?

In each case interest is paid by the borrower and earned by the lender. In addition to providing compensation for the use of money, interest must also compensate for the risk of a possible loss of money. A well-established, reputable business can borrow money at a lower interest rate than a business that has not established a good credit reputation. Investing in federal government bonds is safer than investing in the bonds of a company that buys, develops, and sells land. Therefore, the government is able to borrow money at a lower interest rate than the land-development company. Because risk varies with different investments, many varieties of interest rates exist. A good place to start the study of the time value of money is to discuss the concept of simple interest and show how it is calculated.

SIMPLE INTEREST

Interest is the cost of using borrowed money

Money available today is more valuable than money available at some future time because money received today can be invested or spent. Money received in the future requires the sacrifice of waiting before it can be used or invested. The compensation for waiting is the time value of money, called **interest**. The money lent, borrowed, or invested is called **principal**. Interest rates are normally expressed as a percentage of the principal, usually as annual rates, such as 14 percent per year. Federal law requires interest rates to be stated in annual terms in all contracts.

Simple interest is the cost of money for a single period of time—a year or a quarter, for example. The formula for simple interest is

$$\text{Interest} = \text{Principal} \times \text{interest rate} \times \text{time period}$$

or

$$I = P \times r \times t$$

The rate and time components of the formula must be expressed in common terms: If the interest rate is yearly, time must also be stated in years. If the rate is in monthly terms, time must be in monthly terms too. For example, simple interest of 1 percent per month is the same as 12 percent per year. If you borrow $1,000 for 6 months at 1 percent per month, you may calculate the interest in monthly terms.

$$I = \$1,000 \times .01 \times 6 \text{ months} = \$60$$

The calculation can also be made in annual terms.

$$I = \$1,000 \times .12 \times 6/12 \text{ year} = \$60$$

Definition of a business year

For interest calculations in business, it is common practice to assume that the year has 360 days and each month has 30 days. Interest is payable for the day money is repaid but not for the day it is borrowed. For example, a 60-day 6 percent $1,000 note dated July 1 is due 60 days later on August 30. The interest is calculated as

$$\$1,000 \times .06 \times 60/360 = \$10$$

Simple interest is generally used for short-term debts or investments of 1 year or less. Short-term notes on which both principal and interest are repaid together at one time are common in business. But many loans and investments are for periods of time longer than a year. In such cases the lender or investor generally is not satisfied with simple interest but wants the interest revenue to be available for further investment so that additional income may be earned. When earned interest is invested to earn more interest, compounding of interest takes place.

COMPOUND INTEREST

When the interest earned during one period earns interest in the next and subsequent periods, compounding of interest takes place. **Compound interest** is interest that is earned and is allowed to accumulate. For example, if you invest $1,000 in a savings account paying 6 percent interest per year, interest accumulates as follows:

Principal invested in first year	$1,000.00
Interest for first year, $1,000 × .06 × 1	60.00
Amount available at end of first year	1,060.00
Interest for second year, $1,060 × .06 × 1	63.60
Amount available at end of second year	$1,123.60

The interest earned in the second year is greater than $60 because it is earned on the principal **plus** the first year's interest, which remains invested in the account.

Compounding of interest may take place more frequently than once a year. For example, if your savings account pays 6 percent interest compounded quarterly, 1.5 percent interest is added to the account every 3 months, as follows:

Principal invested in first year	$1,000.00
Interest for first quarter, $1,000 × .06 × 1/4	15.00
Amount available at end of first quarter	1,015.00
Interest for second quarter, $1,015 × .06 × 1/4	15.23
Amount available at end of second quarter	1,030.23
Interest for third quarter, $1,030.23 × .06 × 1/4	15.45
Amount available at end of third quarter	1,045.68
Interest for fourth quarter, $1,045.68 × .06 × 1/4	15.69
Amount available at end of first year	$1,061.37

Compounding of interest is a growth process

The more frequent the compounding, the more interest is earned, as shown in Figure 7-1. Many savings accounts compound interest daily. The limit is reached with continuous compounding, which is the fastest way that money can grow. Calculation of continuous compounding requires the use of calculus and is not discussed in this text.

Compound interest affects many decisions involving the timing of money receipts and payments. Consider these examples. What is the re-

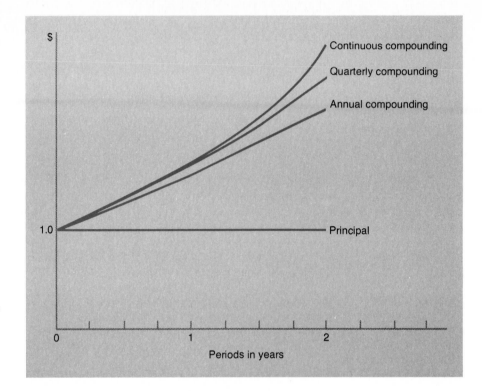

Figure 7-1
**Comparable rate
of growth with
annual, quarterly,
and continuous
compounding.
Scale is
exaggerated for
clarity.**

quired monthly loan payment including interest and principal that is necessary to repay a loan in 20 years? When a baby is born, her parents invest
some money at compound interest to provide for her college education.
What will be the amount of the investment when she turns 18? A company
pays money into a retirement fund for its employees. How much must be
paid each month to ensure that a sufficiently large fund is available for
retired employees? To answer these and similar questions, we need to
apply the principles of compound interest.

To deal with compound interest problems, we define the following
terms:

P = the principal sum that earns interest.

i = the interest rate per period. This is equivalent to $r \times t$ in the simple
interest formula. For annual interest, $i = r$; for monthly interest, $i =
r \times 1/12$; for quarterly interest, $i = r \times 1/4$, etc.

n = the number of periods during which compounding takes place. A
period can be any length of time.

Future Value of $1

A sum of money invested today at compound interest accumulates to a
larger sum at the end of some future time period. The sum that accumu-

Investments grow to a larger amount over time

lates in the future is called the **future value**, or the **amount**. For example, the future value of $1,000 invested at 6 percent compounded annually for 2 years is $1,123.60, as shown in a previous example. The amount includes original principal and the accumulated interest. Using the formula for simple interest, the amount of interest, I, at the end of 1 year on $1,000 at 6 percent is

$$
\begin{aligned}
I &= P \times r \times t \\
&= P \times i \\
&= \$1,000 \times .06 \\
&= \$60
\end{aligned}
$$

The future value, abbreviated fv, includes the principal and the accumulated interest, as shown below.

$$
\begin{aligned}
fv &= P + (P \times i) \\
&= P + Pi \\
&= P\,(1 + i) \\
&= \$1,000\,(1 + .06) \\
&= \$1,060
\end{aligned}
$$

The future value varies with the interest rate, the compounding frequency, the number of periods, and the size of the principal. If we know the future value of a $1 principal investment, we can use it to calculate the future value of any investment. It is easy to construct a table of future values of a $1 investment for a variety of interest rates and time periods. For example, at 8 percent interest per period, $1 accumulates as follows:

Future value of $1 at 8% for 1 period = $1.00   × 1.08 = $1.08000
Future value of $1 at 8% for 2 periods = 1.08   × 1.08 = $1.16640
Future value of $1 at 8% for 3 periods = 1.1664   × 1.08 = $1.25971
Future value of $1 at 8% for 4 periods = 1.25971 × 1.08 = $1.36049

The above table can be diagramed as follows:

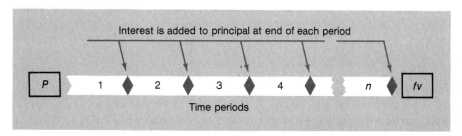

Interest is added to principal at end of each period

P | 1 | 2 | 3 | 4 | *n* | *fv*

Time periods

Future value includes the original principal plus accumulated interest

The end of each period is designated by a small diamond (◇).The arrows pointing to the end of each period indicate that interest payments are added to the investment. Later you will see diagrams that show payments taken out of the investment, a process illustrated by arrows pointing away from the end of the period. Diagrams of this type can help you visualize and solve compound interest problems.

Formula for Future Value of $1

The computations made above show that at the end of the first period, the future value of $1 is simply 1.08; at the end of the second period, it is 1.08 × 1.08, or 1.08^2; at the end of the third period, it is 1.08^3, and so on. From this we derive the following general formula for the future value of $1, with n representing the number of compounding periods:

$$fv = (1 + i)^n$$

Using the formula for the future value of $1, a computer can easily calculate future values for any interest rate and for any number of time periods, as shown in Table I at the end of this book (page 882). To obtain the future value of any principal other than $1, it is necessary only to multiply the principal by the factor found in the future value of $1 table.

$$fv = P(1 + i)^n$$
$$\text{or}$$
$$fv = Pf$$

where f is the factor in the future value of $1 table with interest rate, i, and the number of periods, n. Computations using this equation are illustrated next.

Use of Future Value of $1 Table

The following problems and solutions illustrate the use of the future value of $1 table.

Problem 1.   Mrs. Raman deposits $2,500 in a savings account that earns 6 percent interest per year, compounded quarterly. What is the future value of this investment at the end of 3 years?

Solution 1.   With quarterly compounding for 3 years, the number of quarters is 12. The quarterly interest rate is one quarter of the annual rate, or 1.5 percent. The problem can be diagramed as follows:

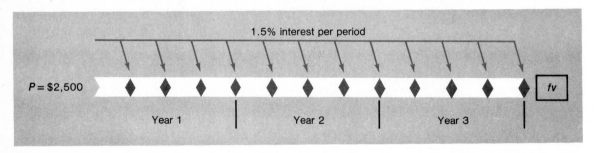

Using Table I with $i = 1.5\%$ and $n = 12$, we look down the 1.5% column. Where $n = 12$, the factor f in the table of future values of $1 is 1.19562.

$$fv = P \times f\,(n = 12, \, i = 1.5\%)$$
$$= \$2,500 \times 1.19562$$
$$= \$2,989.05$$

If you set up each problem in this way, the variable on the left side of the equal sign tells you to use the future value of $1 table, and the variables in parentheses tell you which row and column in the table to use.

Problem 2. Five years ago Sable Company invested some money at 7 percent interest compounded semiannually. The investment has grown to a current total of $70,530. What was the original investment?

Solution 2. In this problem we know the future value instead of the original principal. With semiannual compounding during the 5 years, $n = 10$ and $i = 3.5\%$.

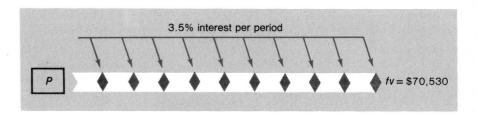

The equation to be solved is:

$$fv = P \times f\,(n = 10, \, i = 3.5\%)$$

This tells us that we must locate the factor, f, in Table I, where we find the value 1.41060. Because fv is known we solve for the principal, P, and obtain

$$\$70,530 = P \times 1.41060$$
$$P = \$70,530/1.41060$$
$$= \$50,000$$

Sable Company originally invested $50,000 that grew in 5 years at 7 percent compounded semiannually to $70,530.

COMPOUND DISCOUNT

Present value is the value today of money available in the future

Often an investment decision hinges on how much future receipts are worth today. Finding the **present value** of future receipts involves discounting the future value to the present in order to determine the amount that should be invested or whether an investment should be made. **Discounting** is the opposite of compounding. Instead of finding how interest accumulates, we find the present value of some future amount of money that is assumed to include accumulated interest.

Discounting is the reciprocal of compounding   From the discussion of compound interest, you know that the future value of $1 at 8 percent for one period is $1.08. Therefore, the present value of $1.08 discounted for one period at 8 percent is $1. We can obtain the present value, abbreviated *pv*, as follows:

$$pv = \frac{fv}{(1 + i)} = \frac{\$1.08}{(1 + .08)} = \$1$$

Present Value of $1

Knowing the present value of $1 is useful because it enables us to find the present value of any future payment. Assuming 8 percent interest per period, we can construct a table of present values of $1 as follows:

Present value of $1 discounted at 8% for 1 period = $1.00/1.08 = $.92593
Present value of $1 discounted at 8% for 2 periods = .92593/1.08 = .85734
Present value of $1 discounted at 8% for 3 periods = .85734/1.08 = .79384
Present value of $1 discounted at 8% for 4 periods = .79384/1.08 = .73503

Formula for Present Value of $1

The first value is obtained by dividing $1 by 1.08. The second value is obtained by dividing $1 by 1.08^2, and so on. Thus the general formula for the present value of $1 is

$$pv = \frac{1}{(1 + i)^n}$$

Table II (page 886) is constructed using this formula. To find the present value of any future amount, the appropriate factor from the table is multiplied by the future value.

Present value tells us the value today of some future payment, and the future value tells us the value in the future of some payment today. The two concepts are closely related, as indicated by the following diagram:

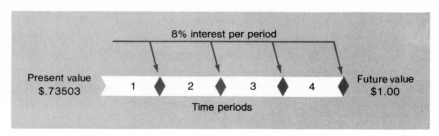

$1 in the future has a present value today of only $.73503, or $.73503 has a future value of $1 if compounding or discounting takes place over four periods at 8 percent.

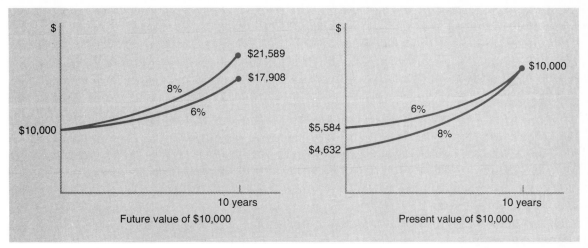

Figure 7-2   **Graphic illustration of future value and present value. An investment of $10,000 grows faster with a higher interest rate. A future receipt of $10,000 is worth more today if the interest rate is low and less if the interest rate is high. With a high interest rate the investment needed today to grow to $10,000 in 10 years is smaller than the investment needed if the interest rate were lower.**

The difference between present value and future value is the time value of money

The point is, more money is required in the future to be worth as much as less money today. The price of waiting is the interest cost. Figure 7-2 shows how the present and future values are related for two different interest rates over a 10-year period. Note that the higher interest rate compounds to a greater future value, but discounts to a smaller present value, because the higher the interest rate, the faster the growth of the investment.

The general equation for solving future value problems was given earlier as $fv = P \times f$, but from the above you see that P is really the present value of the principal. Therefore the following general equations can be used to solve either future value or present value of $1 problems:

$$fv = pv \times f \text{ (from Table I)}$$
$$pv = fv \times f \text{ (from Table II)}$$

Use of Present Value of $1 Table

The present value of $1 and the future value of $1 are reciprocals of each other. They are so closely related, Tables I and II can be used to solve either type of problem. For example, Problem 2 describes Sable Company's investment which grew to $70,530 after 5 years at 7 percent compounded semiannually. This is really a present value problem, because we have the future value and want to know the present value. Earlier the problem was solved by dividing the future value of $1 factor into the known future value. The same solution is obtained by multiplying the known future value by the appropriate present value factor from Table II as follows:[1]

$$pv = fv \times f\,(n = 10,\, i = 3.5)$$
$$= \$70{,}530 \times .70892$$
$$= \$50{,}000.13$$

Following are additional problems involving present values.

Problem 3. Albert Company can invest at 12 percent compounded annually. Baker Company can invest at 12 percent compounded semiannually. Each company will need $75,000 4 years from now. How much must each invest today?

Solution 3. With annual compounding, $n = 4$ and $i = 12\%$. With semiannual compounding, $n = 8$ and $i = 6\%$. Both situations are diagramed below.

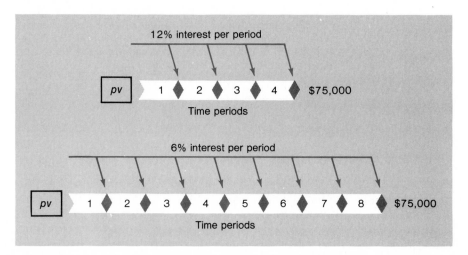

Using Table II, we find the present value factor and multiply by the future value to obtain the present value of $75,000 for each case. For Albert Company

$$pv = fv \times f\,(n = 4,\, i = 12\%)$$
$$= \$75{,}000 \times .63552$$
$$= \$47{,}664$$

For Baker Company

$$pv = fv \times f\,(n = 8,\, i = 6\%)$$
$$= \$75{,}000 \times .62741$$
$$= \$47{,}056$$

---

[1] The difference of $.13 between the two answers is due to rounding of the tables to five decimal places. If the more precise present value factor of .70891881 is used, the error is smaller.

Once again, the more frequent the compounding, the smaller the present value. In other words, an investment grows faster with more frequent compounding; therefore, Baker Company needs to invest less than Albert Company.

Problem 4.   Preval Corporation bought a small computer in exchange for a 3-year $7,000 non-interest-bearing note. A non-interest-bearing note pays the face value on maturity, with no interest added. The current interest rate on loans for computer purchases is 14 percent per year. The computer should be recorded at its cost, which is the present value of the note. What is the cost of the computer?

Solution 4.   The problem is diagramed below, followed by the solution.

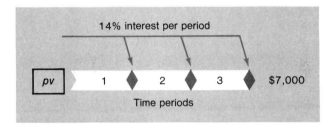

From Table II we find the factor .67497 for $n = 3$ and $i = 14\%$. Multiplying by $7,000, we get the present value, which is the cost of the computer.

$$pv = fv \times f (n = 3, i = 14\%)$$
$$= \$7,000 \times .67497$$
$$= \$4,724.79$$

The difference between the present value of $4,724.79 and the $7,000 face value is the interest that is implied in the non-interest-bearing note. The face value of the note is viewed as consisting of both principal and interest. The interest is said to be imputed in such notes. Because the note will be paid 3 years from now, the $7,000 future payment includes the present cost of the computer and the cost of financing the purchase. If Preval Corporation paid $4,724.79 in cash for the computer, the seller could invest the cash at 14 percent interest, and the investment would accumulate to a future value of $7,000 in 3 years. The present value of the note tells us the cost of the computer if it had been bought for cash.

ANNUITIES

Not all investments are made with a single payment. Money may be added to an investment periodically, or withdrawn from an investment at specific intervals. Tables of present and future values may be used to evaluate investments that include periodic additions or withdrawals.

*Definition of
ordinary
annuity*

An **annuity** is a series of equal payments made at equal time intervals, with compounding or discounting taking place at the time of each payment or withdrawal. Each periodic payment is called a **rent**. There are several different types of annuities, but here we discuss only ordinary annuities. In an **ordinary annuity,** each rent is paid or received at the **end** of each period. There are as many periods as there are rents. Rents may be viewed either as payments into an annuity or as receipts from an annuity. As with single investments, the future value or the present value of annuities may be calculated.

An example of an annuity is a contract with an insurance company that provides for future income in exchange for a single lump-sum investment today. The buyer of the annuity pays a given sum of money to an insurance company, and in return the insurance company guarantees the buyer a specified income each year or each month for a specified number of years or months or for the remainder of the buyer's life. In this case the rents are the periodic income from the insurance company, and the initial lump-sum investment is the present value of the annuity.

*Annuities are
periodic
payments or
receipts*

Another example of an annuity is an arrangement made by parents to accumulate a college fund for their new child. They agree to pay an insurance company a specified annual payment for the next 18 years, at the end of which time the insurance company will guarantee a certain amount of money to be used for the child's college education. In this case the college fund is the future value of the annuity, which accumulates as a result of the rent payments and the interest they earn. Although many people think of annuities in terms of insurance contracts, annuities have much wider application. Installment purchases, long-term bonds, and pension plans all involve annuities.

Future Value of Annuity of $1

If you open a savings account that compounds interest each month, and at the end of each month you deposit $100 in the account, your deposits represent the rents of an annuity. After 1 year you will have made 12 deposits of $100 each, or a total of $1,200, but the account will have more than $1,200 in it because each deposit earns interest. The total sum of the account at the time the last rent is paid is called the **future value,** or the **amount of the annuity**—the sum accumulated in the future from all the rents paid and the interest earned by the rents. The abbreviation *FV* is used for the future value of an annuity to differentiate it from the lowercase *fv* for the future value of $1.

To obtain a table of future values of annuities, we assume payments of $1 each period into a fund that earns 8 percent interest compounded each period. The diagram at the top of page 313 illustrates an annuity of four rents of $1, each paid at the end of each period, with interest of 8 percent compounded each period.

Notice that there are four rents and four periods, and each rent is paid at the **end** of each period. At the end of the first period, $1 is deposited and starts earning interest. The interest earned on this dollar is added to

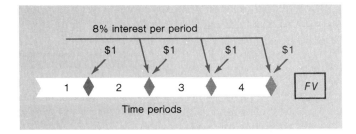

the fund one period after the initial deposit and starts earning interest at the same time that the second rent is deposited. The first dollar earns interest for three periods, the second dollar earns interest for two periods, and so on. The future value at the end of the fourth period can be calculated by finding the future value of each individual deposit using the future value of $1 table (Table I) as follows:

Future value of $1 at 8% for 3 periods = $1.25971
Future value of $1 at 8% for 2 periods = 1.16640
Future value of $1 at 8% for 1 period = 1.08000
The fourth rent of $1 earns no interest = 1.00000
Total for four rents   = $4.50611

The future value of an annuity is always larger than the sum of the rents

At the end of 4 years, the four separate $1 deposits grow to $4.50611, which includes the four deposits plus $.50611 in interest. The four individual future values together make up the future value of the annuity, which is $4.50611. The future value of the above annuity is illustrated in Figure 7-3, which shows how each dollar grows to accumulate an amount that includes the four $1 investments plus compound interest.

Formula for Future Value of Annuity of $1

Using the approach described above, the future value of any annuity may be computed, but this approach is not very efficient. The formula for the future value of an annuity of $1 can be used to produce tables for a variety

Figure 7-3
Future value of an annuity of $1 for four periods, with each rent paid at the end of a period. The first rent earns interest for more periods than the others and therefore grows to a larger amount. The last rent earns no interest at all.

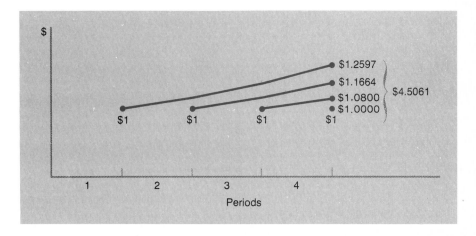

of periods and interest rates. Without elaborating on its derivation, we present the formula here.

$$FV = \frac{(1 + i)^n - 1}{i}$$

It is not necessary to memorize this formula. Table III (page 890) is derived from it, and you should just know how to use the tables to solve annuity problems. The table assumes rents of $1. To find the future value of an annuity with larger rents, it is necessary only to multiply the rent R by the factor in the tables as follows:

$$FV = Rf$$

where R is the periodic rent and f is the future value of an annuity of $1 with interest rate i and number of periods n.

Use of Future Value of Annuity of $1 Table

Problem 5.   For Sybil's first birthday, and for each one thereafter, her parents deposited $450 in a savings account for her college education. The savings account pays 5 percent interest compounded annually. The last deposit was made on Sybil's 18th birthday. How large is the account on this date?

Solution 5.   The first deposit was made at the end of the first year on the first birthday. There is a total of 18 rents, the last of which earns no interest. This is an ordinary annuity with $n = 18$ and $i = 5\%$. It can be diagramed as follows:

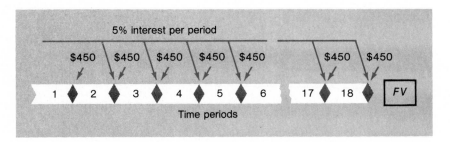

The general equation for the future value of an annuity is used to solve the problem. From Table III we find that the factor f is 28.13238. Then

$$FV = R \times f\,(n = 18, i = 5\%)$$
$$= \$450 \times 28.13238$$
$$= \$12,659.57$$

Problem 6.   At the beginning of 1985, the directors of Annabel Corporation decided that they will have to expand their plant facilities in a few years. The estimated cost of a new plant is $18,500,000. This amount will be needed on January 1, 1988. The company plans to invest an equal sum each quarter to accumulate the needed funds. Starting on April 1, 1985, it will deposit money into a trust fund that earns interest at the rate of 10 percent per year, compounded quarterly. How much must the company deposit each quarter to accumulate the amount needed by January 1, 1988?

Solution 6. In this problem we have the future value and not the rent. There are 12 quarters in 3 years, and 10 percent interest is 2.5 percent per quarter. The problem is diagramed as follows:

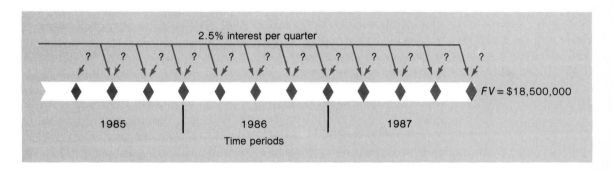

To find the future value of this annuity, we use the general equation for the future value of an annuity and substitute into it the known values. From Table III we find the factor with $n = 12$ and $i = 2.5\%$.

$$FV = R \times f\,(n = 12,\, i = 2.5\%)$$
$$\$18,500,000 = R \times 13.79555$$

The equation is solved for the rent as follows:

$$R = \$18,500,000/13.79555$$
$$= \$1,341,012.14$$

The company has to deposit $1,341,012.14 each quarter in order to accumulate $18,500,000 by January 1988.

Present Value of Annuity of $1

The **present value of an annuity** is the amount today that must be invested at compound interest in order to obtain periodic rents over some future time. For example, Bixby Corporation will need $10,000 at the end of each of the next 3 years for new office equipment. At the beginning of the first year, the company invests $25,771 in a fund that earns 8 percent interest compounded annually. The initial investment is the present value of the annuity; the $10,000 annual withdrawals from the fund are the rents, each occurring at the end of each period. The following diagram illustrates the annuity. The last rent will exhaust the fund, leaving nothing on deposit. Notice that we use the abbreviation *PV* for the present value of an annuity to differentiate it from the lowercase *pv* for the present value of $1. This is how the annuity works:

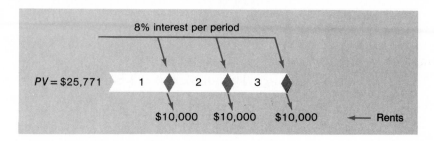

Initial investment at beginning of first year *(PV)*	$25,771.00
Add interest earned by end of first year ($25,771 × .08)	2,061.68
Total available at end of first year	27,832.68
Less first rent withdrawn from fund	10,000.00
Balance	17,832.68
Add interest earned by end of second year ($17,832.68 × .08)	1,426.61
Total available at end of second year	19,259.29
Less second rent withdrawn from fund	10,000.00
Balance	9,259.29
Add interest earned by end of third year ($9,259.29 × .08)	740.74
Total available at end of third year	10,000.03
Less third rent withdrawn from fund	10,000.00
Balance	$ .03

The balance of $.03 is due to rounding of interest to the nearest cent. How did we know what the initial investment must be in order to obtain the three equal rents? By using the present value of $1, we can obtain a table for the present value of an annuity of $1. We can then use the table to solve problems dealing with the present value of annuities. The present value of an annuity of $1 can be illustrated as follows:

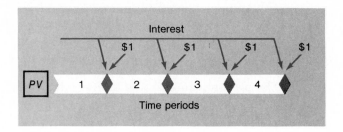

With each rent paid or received at the **end** of each period when compounding takes place, the number of rents is the same as the number of periods. By discounting each individual future rent to the present using Table II, we find the present value of the entire annuity.

Present value of first $1 discounted at 8% for 1 period	=	$ .92593
Present value of second $1 discounted at 8% for 2 periods	=	.85734
Present value of third $1 discounted at 8% for 3 periods	=	.79383
Present value of fourth $1 discounted at 8% for 4 periods	=	.73503
Present value of annuity of 4 rents at 8%	=	$3.31213

The present value of an annuity is smaller than the sum of the rents

The above tells us that a $3.31 investment is needed at the beginning in order to be able to withdraw $1 at the end of four consecutive periods. The first rent is worth more than the others because it is received earlier. Table IV at the end of the book may be used to solve problems involving the present value of annuities. The formula used to construct the table is

$$PV = \frac{1 - \dfrac{1}{(1 + i)^n}}{i}$$

The above annuity is illustrated graphically in Figure 7-4, which shows that the more distant future payments are worth less today than the ones paid or received earlier.

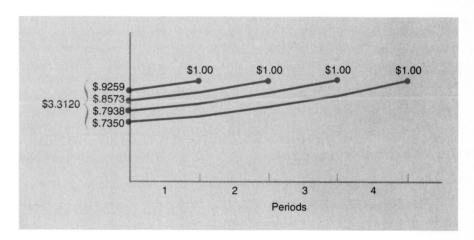

Figure 7-4
Present value of annuity of $1 for four periods with each $1 rent paid at the end of a period. The farther in the future the payment, the less it is worth today.

Use of Present Value of Annuity of $1 Table

The future value and the present value of annuities are not related as nicely as the future value and present value of single investments. The relationship is complex because the principal consists of rents paid at different times. The following problems illustrate the use of Table IV.

Problem 7.   Harold is about to retire and wants to provide himself with an income of $8,000 per year for the rest of his life. An insurance company calculates that his life expectancy is 24 more years and offers him an annuity that yields 9 percent compounded annually. How much will the insurance company collect from Harold in exchange for the future annuity payments?

Solution 7. The investment by Harold today is the present value of an annuity of $8,000 per year with $n = 24$ and $i = 9\%$.

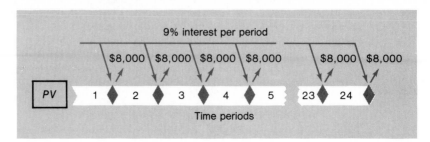

The general equation for solving present value of annuity problems is given below. Using Table IV, the factor 9.70661 is found for the value of f.

$$PV = R \times f\,(n=24,\ i=9\%)$$
$$= \$8,000 \times 9.70661$$
$$= \$77,652.88$$

To assure himself an income of $8,000 per year, Harold must pay the insurance company $77,652.88 today. He will receive rents at the end of the first year and each year thereafter. What happens if Harold lives longer than 24 years?[2]

Problem 8. Lawrence Corporation bought a new machine for $68,900 and agreed to pay $10,000 per year including interest of 11 percent until the equipment is fully paid for. The first payment starts 1 year from today. How many payments will the company have to make?

Solution 8. In this problem we know the present value and the rent. We know that $i = 11\%$, but n is unknown. From the data given, however, we can diagram the problem and calculate the factor as follows:

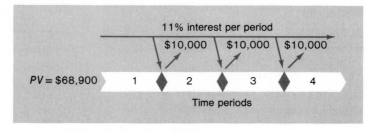

$$PV = R \times f\,(n = ?,\ i = 11\%)$$
$$\$68,900 = \$10,000 \times f$$

Solving for f yields the factor which can be looked up in the present value of annuity table to determine the number of periods.

---

[2] The insurance company keeps making the payments. Its calculations are based on probabilities. What it pays to those living longer than expected, it makes up from those who die earlier than expected.

$$f = \$68,900/\$10,000$$
$$= 6.89000$$

In Table IV we look down the 11 percent column until we find the factor closest to 6.89000. This is 6.89081, from which we find that $n = 15$ periods. Therefore, it will take 15 years to repay the debt at the rate of $10,000 per year.

TIME VALUE OF MONEY IN DECISION MAKING

Compound interest and compound discount concepts can be applied in many accounting situations. In this section we explore some general applications of these concepts. More specific problems are discussed in other parts of this book and its companion volume.

The solution of complex compound interest and compound discount problems is usually easy if the problems are broken down into their components. Often there are several possible approaches to the solution. But all problems can be solved by using one or more of the following general equations and its associated compound interest table:

Table I: $fv = pv \times f(n= , i=)$

Table II: $pv = fv \times f(n= , i=)$

Table III: $FV = R \times f(n= , i=)$

Table IV: $PV = R \times f(n= , i=)$

In all cases the variable on the left of the equal sign tells you which compound interest table to use. To solve any equation you can have only one unknown variable. Before attempting a solution, you should:

Approach to solving compound interest problems

1. Determine the problem requirements and decide whether the problem involves a single payment or more than one payment. For a single payment, use Tables I and II, which deal with future values and present values of $1. If there is more than one equal payment, you may use annuity tables.

2. Diagram the problem to help you visualize what data you have and what you need to determine.

3. Determine n and i in order to obtain the appropriate factor from the table.

4. Decide whether the problem involves money in the future or money in the present. This tells you whether to use tables for future values or for present values.

Some compound interest and discount problems may require the use of more than one table. The best way to learn this material is to become

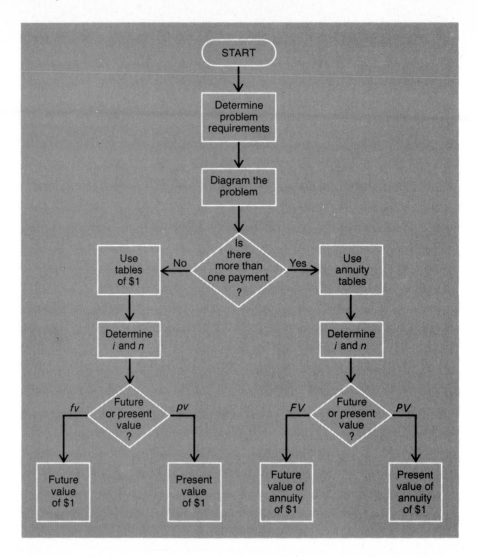

Figure 7-5
**Flowchart for
selecting the
appropriate
compound
interest or present
value table.**

familiar with the tables and their use by solving problems. Figure 7-5 illustrates in flowchart form the approach to basic problem solving. Some of the examples below demonstrate the use of tables in a variety of situations.

Problem 9.   For 5 years starting with 1986, Miller plans to invest $10,000 on each September 1. On September 1, 1991, his two children start college, and he plans to start withdrawing four equal, annual installments from this investment fund to finance their education. How much can he withdraw in order to exhaust the fund, if the interest rate is 9 percent compounded annually?

Solution 9.   The five $10,000 deposits are the five rents of an annuity whose future value can be determined on September 1, 1990, when the last investment is made. This future value represents the present value of an annuity of four rents, the first of which is available on September 1, 1991. In both cases $i = 9\%$. The problem is diagramed below.

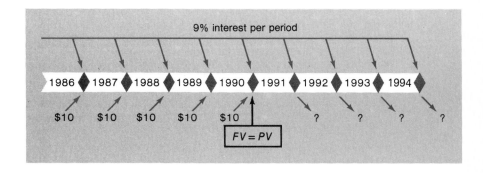

First, we obtain the future value of the annuity on September 1, 1990.

$$
\begin{aligned}
FV &= R \times f\,(n=5,\, i=9\%) \\
&= \$10{,}000 \times 5.98471 \\
&= \$59{,}847.10 \\
&= PV \text{ of next annuity}
\end{aligned}
$$

Next, we use the first solution to find the rents of the second annuity, whose present value we now have.

$$
\begin{aligned}
PV &= R \times f\,(n=4,\, i=9\%) \\
\$59{,}847.10 &= R \times 3.23972 \\
R &= \$59{,}847.10/3.23972 \\
&= \$18{,}472.92
\end{aligned}
$$

Miller can withdraw four annual rents of $18,472.92 each, with the first rent available on September 1, 1991.

Problem 10. A vintner can invest his money at 14 percent compounded annually. He has a choice of selling his wine now for $20,000 or aging it in storage and selling it 3 years from now for $30,000. What should he do?

Solution 10. There are two approaches to this problem. We can discount the future receipt of $30,000 at 14 percent to the present to find out how it compares with $20,000 today. Or we can assume $20,000 is invested today at 14 percent and compare its future value with $30,000 3 years from now.

In either case we are dealing with one payment; therefore, Tables I and II are appropriate. For the first approach, we need the present value of $30,000, with $n = 3$ and $i = 14\%$. From Table II we find the factor .67497 which we multiply by the amount.

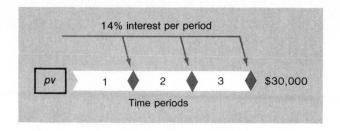

$$pv = fv \times f\,(n=3,\ i=14\%)$$
$$= \$30,000 \times .67497$$
$$= \$20,249.10$$

Since the present value of the future payment is more than $20,000 today, the vintner should store his wine. We verify this conclusion by finding the future value of $20,000 invested today at 14 percent for 3 years.

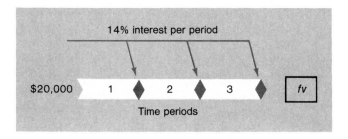

$$fv = pv \times f\,(n=3,\ i=14\%)$$
$$= \$20,000 \times 1.48154$$
$$= \$29,630.80$$

The future value is less than $30,000, so it is clear that the vintner is better off storing the wine. The value of the wine grows faster than the value of the money. Would the decision be the same if interest were compounded quarterly?

Problem 11.   Payments on an installment note are $100 per month for the next 3 months, and $150 per month for the following 6 months, at the end of which the note will be fully paid. The first payment starts 1 month from now. George would like to buy this note as an investment in order to earn a 12 percent annual return compounded monthly. How much should he pay for the note?

Solution 11.   There is more than one payment, so the problem involves annuities. But the definition of annuities requires all payments to be equal. Before the problem can be solved, it must be converted to annuities with equal rents. We need to find the value of the note today; therefore, we are dealing with present values. The problem is diagramed as follows.

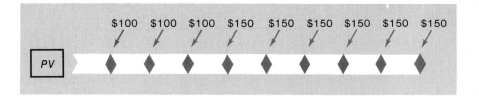

*Annuities may
be added or
subtracted*   As usual, several approaches are possible. The simplest is to find the present value of an annuity of $150 as if all rents are equal. The first three rents lack $50 each, however; therefore, we can deduct the present value of a $50 annuity of three rents. With monthly compounding, $i = 1\%$.

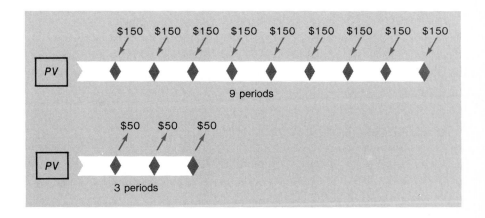

$$PV = R \times f\,(n = 9, i = 1\%)$$
$$= \$150 \times 8.56602 \qquad = \$1,284.90$$
$$\text{Less } PV = R \times f\,(n = 3, i = 1\%)$$
$$= \$50 \times 2.94099 \qquad = \underline{147.05}$$

Present value of note $\underline{\underline{\$1,137.85}}$

Problem 12. A savings and loan association pays 6 percent interest compounded quarterly on a certain type of savings account. Judy deposits $300 in such an account each quarter for 2 years. How much money will be in her account 3 years after the last deposit?

Solution 12. The problem involves two future values. First the deposits accumulate to a future value, which is then left in the account. This earns interest and accumulates to a larger future value. The problem is diagramed on page 324.

First, we find the future value of an annuity of $300 with $n = 8$ and $i = 1.5\%$. Next, we view this future value as a single investment that will remain in the account for 3 years. We find its future value with $n = 12$ and $i = 1.5\%$.

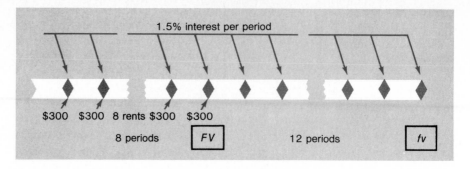

$$
\begin{aligned}
FV &= R \times f\,(n=8,\ i=1.5\%) \\
&= \$300 \times 8.43284 \\
&= \$2{,}529.85 = \text{new principal sum } P \\
fv &= P \times f\,(n=12,\ i=1.5\%) \\
&= \$2{,}529.85 \times 1.19562 \\
&= \$3{,}024.74
\end{aligned}
$$

The savings account will grow to $3,024.74 three years after Judy's last deposit.

Simple Interest Applications

In the beginning of this chapter, we discussed simple interest in single-period situations. Compound interest tables can be used to solve simple interest problems, as illustrated in the examples below. Remember that interest is always expressed in annual terms, and if a period is less than a year long, the rate must be adjusted accordingly.

Simple interest is interest for a single period

Problem 13.   Sadler Company often accepts notes receivable in exchange for merchandise and charges 10 percent interest on them. A customer offers a $23,650 non-interest-bearing 9-month note for merchandise that normally sells for $22,300. Should the company accept the note? If the company accepts the note and assumes its present value is the same as the selling price of the merchandise, how much interest will the note earn?

Solution 13.   If the company charges 10 percent interest, it should discount the non-interest-bearing note at 10 percent. The note is for 9 months, or 3/4 of the year, so the appropriate rate is 7.5 percent (10% × 9/12 year). The future value of the note is $23,650, which is to be received 9 months from now. The present value of the note is calculated as

$$
\begin{aligned}
pv &= fv \times f\,(n=1,\ i=7.5\%) \\
&= \$23{,}650 \times .93023 \\
&= \$21{,}999.94
\end{aligned}
$$

The note is worth $22,000, which is less than the selling price of the merchandise. This does not mean, however, that the company should reject the offer. By accepting the note. the company may make a profit on the sale, which would otherwise be lost, although the profit would be $300 less than normal. The solution does not provide an answer; it merely provides information so that a rational decision can be made. The final decision depends on many factors in addition to the present value of the note.

Management may decide to accept the note in order to sell the goods and view the note as yielding less than 10 percent interest. The selling price of the merchandise is then viewed as the present value of the note. The interest yield can be found as follows:

$$fv = pv \times f\,(n=1,\ i=?\%)$$
$$\$23,650 = \$22,300 \times f$$
$$f = \$23,650/\$22,300$$
$$= 1.06054$$

The answer 1.06054 is the future value of $1 and includes the $1 principal and interest for one 9-month period. If interest for three-quarters of a year is .06054, interest for the whole year is .06054 × ⁴⁄₃ = .08072. By accepting the $23,650 noninterest 9-month note, the company would be earning 8.072 percent interest per year.

Problem 14.   Joe sold his car to a friend for a $2,000 2-year 2 percent note on which the friend pays the interest every quarter. The last interest payment and all the principal are due in 3 months. Joe needs money now, so he offers to sell the note to Harry, who agrees to buy it only if he can earn 10 percent annual interest on his money. How much should Harry pay for the note?

Solution 14.   When the note matures in 3 months, its owner will collect the $2,000 principal plus interest at 2 percent per year for 3 months. The interest will amount to

$$\$2,000 \times .02 \times 3/12\ \text{year} = \$10$$

The future value of the note is therefore $2,010, and we have to discount this at 10 percent interest to find the note's present value. Because only 3 months are left, which is a quarter of a year, we use a quarter of 10 percent interest, or 2.5 percent.

$$pv = fv \times f\,(n=1,\ i=2.5\%)$$
$$= \$2,010 \times .97561$$
$$= \$1,960.98$$

To earn 10 percent interest per year on the note, Harry should pay $1,960.98 to Joe. Although the note is interest bearing, it is worth less than its face value because the interest rate on the note is below normal.

SUMMARY   The time value of money is called **interest.** It is the cost of using someone else's money, or the price someone charges for waiting to receive money. Interest rates vary because, in addition to the compensation that must be paid for waiting, the interest must also compensate for the risk assumed.

The original sum of money that earns interest is called the **principal.** **Simple interest** is calculated by multiplying the principal by the interest rate and by the time period. The interest rate and the time period must be expressed in common terms.

Compound interest is interest paid for more than one period, with each successive payment including interest on the principal and on all previous interest earned. The more frequent the compounding, the greater the growth rate of money.

A sum of money invested at compound interest grows to a **future value,** or an **amount.** The formula for the future value of $1 can be used to construct a table of future values. The table can be used to calculate future values of any principal investment for a variety of interest rates and time periods.

Compound discount is the reverse of compound interest. By discounting some future payment of money to the present, we find its **present value.** The present value is the sum that would accumulate to the future payment if invested at a given rate of compound interest. The formula for the present value of $1 can be used to construct a table of present values. Such a table can be used to find present values of future receipts of money for a variety of interest rates and time periods.

An **annuity** is a series of equal payments or receipts called **rents.** Rents may be either payments or receipts of money. In an **ordinary annuity,** each rent is paid or received at the **end** of each period when interest is compounded. The **amount,** or **future value,** of an annuity is the sum to which the annuity rents will accumulate at some future time, with compound interest. The **present value of an annuity** is the value today of rents that will be paid or received in future time periods, with compound interest. Formulas for future values and present values of annuities of $1 can be used to construct tables of future values and present values of annuities.

Future values and present values are used to solve many business problems and to make business decisions. Such problems and decisions often involve combinations of future and present values and may include annuities or single payments. The present and future value of $1 tables and concepts are applicable to simple interest situations as well as to problems involving compound interest.

KEY TERMS

amount *(305)*
amount of annuity *(312)*
annuity *(312)*
compound discount *(307)*
compound interest *(303)*
discount *(307)*
future value *(305)*
future value of annuity *(312)*

interest *(302)*
ordinary annuity *(312)*
present value *(307)*
present value of annuity *(365)*
principal *(302)*
rent *(312)*
simple interest *(302)*

QUESTIONS

1. What is the distinction between simple interest and compound interest?
2. Why does more frequent compounding result in faster investment growth?
3. Explain what is meant by the future value of $1.
4. George calculates the compound discount of a future payment by using a 5 percent interest rate. Jane calculates the compound discount on the same future payment by using a 7 percent interest rate. Who will find the greater present value for the investment? Why?
5. Explain what an ordinary annuity is.
6. What elements comprise the future value of an annuity? Explain completely.
7. Does the future value of $1 table or the future value of annuity of $1 table have the larger value for any given interest rate and number of periods?
8. Explain the concept of the present value of an annuity.
9. For any given number of periods and any given interest rate, does the table of present value of annuity of $1 or the table of the present value of $1 contain the larger factor? Explain.
10. "If I have a choice between getting $1,000 now or $1,200 2 years from now, obviously I am better off with the larger amount." Explain to the person making this statement why the reasoning may be faulty.
11. Will discounting future rent payments at 6 percent or 8 percent yield the smaller present value?

EXERCISES

Ex. 7-1 **Simple interest computation and accrual.** Celestial Corporation received a $9,600 90-day 9 percent note on December 1, 1985. The note and interest are due on February 28, 1986. The company's accounting period ends on December 31.

Required:
a. Compute the interest to be accrued on December 31, 1985.
b. How much will the company collect when the note matures?

Ex. 7-2 **Simple interest computations.** Trydent Company received a $6,000 90-day 10 percent note and a $14,300 60-day 12 percent note in exchange for merchandise. The company bought some equipment by giving to the seller a $31,500 60-day 11 percent note.

Required: Calculate the amount of interest that will be paid on each note when it matures.

Ex. 7-3 **Present value and implied interest of non-interest note.** Barket Company is offered a $30,000 6-month non-interest-bearing note in exchange for merchandise normally selling for $28,169. The company usually expects to earn 12 percent interest per year on its notes receivable.

Required:
a. What is the present value of the note based on the company's expected interest rate?
b. What is the implied interest rate on the note based on the value of the merchandise?
c. Should the company accept the note in exchange for the merchandise? Explain.

Ex. 7-4   Calculating the term of a simple interest note.   A $15,600 12 percent note made today will require payment of $15,834 when it matures.

Required: How many days will pass from the time the note is made to the time it matures?

Ex. 7-5   Use of future value of $1 table.   Using the future value of $1 table, find the future value of $9,600 at 8 percent interest for:

a. 2 years   b. 4 years   c. 10 years   d. 12 years

Ex. 7-6   Use of future value of $1 table.   Use the future value of $1 table to find the future value of $5,200 for 10 periods at:

a. 3 percent   b. 5 percent   c. 10 percent   d. 15 percent

Ex. 7-7   Use of future value of $1 table.   Calculate the future value of $4,000 invested at 12 percent interest for 3 years with interest compounded:

a. annually   b. semiannually   c. quarterly   d. monthly

Ex. 7-8   Relation of future value and present value of $1.   Christopher withdrew the entire balance of $5,491.54 from a savings account that paid 5 percent interest compounded semiannually. The account was established 5 years earlier. Calculate how much was originally deposited in the account by using:

a. the future value of $1 table.   b. the present value of $1 table.

Ex. 7-9   Finding the number of periods.   For his retirement, Little invested $25,000 in a pension fund that earned interest at 14 percent compounded annually. The fund grew to $785,237 when Little retired at the age of 65. How old was he when he made the original investment?

Ex. 7-10   Use of present value of $1 table.   Use the present value of $1 table to find the present value of $9,300 at 9 percent to be received in:

a. 3 years   b. 5 years   c. 10 years   d. 14 years

Ex. 7-11   Use of present value of $1 table.   Using the present value of $1 table, find the present value of $6,500 to be paid 5 years from now at:

a. 2 percent   b. 6 percent   c. 10 percent   d. 20 percent

Ex. 7-12   Use of present value of $1 table.   Calculate the present value of $8,500 at 18 percent interest for 4 years with discount compounded:

a. annually   b. semiannually   c. quarterly   d. monthly

Ex. 7-13   Finding the interest and term of notes.   Qubique Corporation had two long-term notes. One note was a $7,000 10 percent note for which the company just received $15,005.13. The other was a $5,000 3-year note whose maker paid the company $6,838.15 when the note matured. Interest compounded annually on both notes.

Required:
    a.   How long did the company hold the $7,000 note?
    b.   What was the interest rate on the $5,000 note?

Ex. 7-14   **Use of future value of annuity table.**   Use the future value of annuity of $1 table to find the future value of an annuity of six rents of $300 each at:

    a. 3 percent **b.** 6 percent **c.** 7 percent **d.** 12 percent

Ex. 7-15   **Finding *n* and *i* for an annuity.**   At the end of each year, James deposited $500 into a fund until it grew to $5,720 including the last deposit and compound interest on all previous deposits.

Required:
    a.   If 10 deposits were made, what was the approximate rate of interest earned?
    b.   If the fund earned 10 percent interest, how many deposits did James make?

Ex. 7-16   **Finding the rent of annuities.**   An annuity of 10 rents earning 9 percent interest per period accumulates to $3,038.59. Another annuity which has 15 rents and earns interest at the rate of 10 percent per period accumulates to $6,354.50.

Required: Compute the size of the rents for each annuity.

Ex. 7-17   **Use of present value of annuity table.**   Find the present value of an annuity of 12 rents of $400 each at:

    a. 7 percent **b.** 8 percent **c.** 15 percent **d.** 20 percent

Ex. 7-18   **Finding the rent of an annuity.**   The present value of an annuity of 16 rents at 2 percent interest is $58,655.71. The present value of an annuity of 22 rents at 6 percent interest is $43,349.69.

Required: Find the size of the rent for each annuity.

Ex. 7-19   **Finding the number of rents of an annuity.**   Samuel Company bought a warehouse for $85,000, paying $15,000 cash and financing the balance with a 12 percent mortgage. The monthly payment on the mortgage, including principal and interest, is $2,049. The company also makes a monthly payment of $1,800 on another mortgage whose interest rate is 6 percent and whose principal balance is $59,168.

Required: Calculate how long it will take to repay each mortgage.

PROBLEMS

P. 7-1   **Simple interest computations.**   Barstow Company accepts notes from its customers in exchange for merchandise which it sells. Today it received the following notes:

$3,000 60-day 10 percent note.
$1,500 90-day 9 percent note.

The company also collected from customers the following notes which matured today:

$4,500 30-day note for which the company received $4,541.25.
$6,000 10 percent note for which the company received $6,125.

Required:
    a. How much will the company collect when the notes it received today mature?
    b. What was the interest rate of the $4,500 note?
    c. How long did the company hold the $6,000 note?

P. 7-2   **Choosing between simple interest notes.** Jimmy Baker is selling his yacht because its operating cost is too high. He advertises the yacht for $50,000 but is willing to accept less as long as the offer is reasonable. He receives the following offers from three prospective buyers:

1. Cash payment of $47,000.

2. Cash payment of $7,000 plus a $46,000 1-year non-interest-bearing note.

3. A 6-month 3 percent note for $50,000.

Jimmy feels that 12 percent interest is reasonable, and therefore he wants to reject the offers that include the notes. Before deciding, however, he comes to you for advice.

Required:
    a. Using 12 percent interest per year, evaluate the three offers and decide which is the highest.
    b. What other factors should Jimmy consider in arriving at a decision?

P. 7-3   **Valuation of a simple interest note.** Prandos Company is selling a tractor to Morris, a farmer who wants to pay for it with a 6-month 8 percent note because he cannot pay cash until he sells his crop. The current rate of interest is 14 percent, but, knowing Morris, the company realizes that he would never agree to more than 8 percent. The price of the tractor is $9,600. To make up the difference in interest rates, the company can increase the selling price of the tractor and receive a larger 8 percent note.

Required:
    a. What should the price of the tractor be in order for the company to earn 14 percent annual interest on its 8 percent note?
    b. If the company accepts the $9,600 8 percent note but assumes the present value of the note must be based on 14 percent interest, what is the sales price of the tractor?

P. 7-4   **Accumulation of a retirement fund.** When George was 30 years old he inherited $15,000. He had an adequate income from his job so he decided to invest the money in a retirement fund with the hope that he could retire earlier than usual. The fund earns 9 percent interest per year, compounded semiannually. At the age of 35, George received a $5,000 bonus from his employer and added it to his retirement fund. George retired from his job at 50 in order to travel around the world.

Required: Compute the amount in George's fund at the time of his retirement.

P. 7-5   **Accumulation of a fund.**   When Julie was born her grandfather gave her $10,000, stipulating that her parents must invest it and that the investment may not be used until Julie reached her 25th birthday. Her parents invested the money in a trust fund that earned 8 percent interest per year, compounded annually. On Julie's 15th birthday her parents were notified that in the future the trust fund would earn 8 percent interest compounded quarterly. On Julie's 25th birthday, Julie withdrew all the money from the trust fund.

Required: Compute the amount available in the trust fund when Julie became 25 years old.

P. 7-6   **Deciding between alternatives.**   Loggo Corporation owns a stand of timber that currently will yield revenue of $880,000 from log sales. Cutting costs would be $100,000 if the timber is cut now. The company expects that if it cuts the timber 5 years from now, revenues from log sales will be $2,200,000, and cutting costs will amount to $200,000. The company normally requires an annual return of 20 percent.

Required:
  a. Decide whether the timber should be cut now or 5 years from now, assuming that the company requires **quarterly** compounding. Support your answer with calculations.
  b. Would your answer be different if the company's rate of return required **annual** compounding? Support your answer with figures.

P. 7-7   **Choosing among alternatives.**   Sylvia Corporation wishes to sell one of its subsidiaries. It has received the following offers from three prospective buyers:

  a. 100,000 shares of common stock whose market value is $15 per share, plus a note promising to pay one lump-sum payment of $500,000 in 5 years.
  b. A down payment of $300,000 and 10 payments of $250,000 at the end of each year for the next 10 years.
  c. Two lump-sum payments of $1,500,000 each. The first payment is to be made 3 years from now, and the second payment, 5 years from now.

Required: Compare the three offers, using a 10 percent interest rate compounded annually, and decide which should be accepted. Support your answer with computations.

P. 7-8   **Accumulating a fund.**   Betty wants to buy a car when she is 18 and starts college. During the last 2 years in high school, she will have a part-time job and will be able to save $150 per month, which she will deposit in a savings account each month. The account pays 6 percent interest compounded monthly. Betty will make a total of 24 deposits.

Required:
  a. How much will be available in the account after the last deposit?
  b. How much would Betty have to deposit each month in order to have $4,500 when she goes to college?
  c. How much would she have to invest now in a single lump sum to accumulate $4,500?

P. 7-9   Future and present value of annuity.   Ferris Corporation plans to make five equal annual investments of $5,000 in a fund that will earn 9 percent per year compounded annually. The first investment will be made on April 1, 1985. From the fund that accumulates, the company will make three equal annual withdrawals starting on April 1, 1990. The last withdrawal is to exhaust the fund completely.

Required: Calculate the size of each annual withdrawal.

P. 7-10   Bond repayment fund.   Bolder Company has $600,000 of bonds payable outstanding. The sum of $200,000 has to be repaid on June 1 of 1990, 1991, and 1992. To provide a fund for repayment, the company plans to make five equal annual deposits in a fund that will earn 9 percent interest compounded annually. The first deposit will be made on June 1, 1985.

Required: Calculate how much the company must deposit each year so that there is enough to make all three bond payments when they are due.

P. 7-11   Retirement fund with interruption.   Benny Lopov is a professional pickpocket. He decides to invest part of his income for his retirement by depositing $8,000 in a savings account every year on his birthday. The account pays 9 percent interest compounded annually. After the fourth deposit, Benny is arrested and spends 45 months in jail, during which time he makes no further investments. After his release, he continues the retirement plan, but with only $6,000 invested on each birthday. He plans to retire 2 years after he has made ten $6,000 deposits.

Required: Calculate how much Benny will have in his retirement fund when he retires.

P. 7-12   Future value with journal entries.   Columbia Electric Company estimates that it will have to replace one of its electric generators in 3 years. Generators now cost $350,000 but the company expects prices to increase, so on December 31, 1985, the company invests $350,000 in a savings account that earns 6 percent interest compounded quarterly. The following journal entry is recorded:

Dec. 31	Time deposit	350,000	
1985	Cash		350,000
	Deposited funds at 6% compounded		
	quarterly for 3 years, to replace		
	electric generator.		

Required:
   a.   Calculate how much will be available for the purchase of the new generator on December 31, 1988.
   b.   Prepare the journal entries on December 31, 1986, 1987, and 1988, to record the increase in the time deposit.
   c.   Verify that the interest added to the account and the original principal add up to the amount you computed in part **a.**

P. 7-13   **Present value with journal entries.**   Pork Hollow City estimates that if the present rate of crime continues, it will need an addition to its jail in 3 years. The city expects to require a total of $550,000 for the addition which should be started in January 1989. On December 31, 1985, the city plans to deposit money in a savings account that earns interest at 6 percent compounded quarterly, in order to accumulate the required amount by December 31, 1988. When the funds are deposited an entry will be made debiting Time Deposit and crediting Cash. Each year on December 31, the interest accumulated in the time deposit is to be credited to interest revenue.

Required:
    a.   Calculate how much must be deposited on December 31, 1985 and prepare the journal entry to record the deposit.
    b.   Prepare journal entries on December 31, 1986, 1987, and 1988, to record interest income.
    c.   Verify that the initial deposit plus the accumulated interest add up to the required amount for the jail addition.

P. 7-14   **Accumulating two college funds.**   Meredith Culpepper plans to establish a fund for the college education of her two daughters. She plans to invest a sum of money on June 1, 1985, to provide the following future payments:

    a. Starting on June 1, 1989, $6,000 each year for 5 years to be paid to her older daughter.
    b. Starting on June 1, 1991, $8,000 each year for 4 years to be paid to her younger daughter.

Required: Calculate how much Meredith Culpepper needs to invest on June 1, 1985, assuming the fund earns 5 percent interest compounded annually.

P. 7-15   **Evaluating life insurance.**   Dave McCrary and Mike Welmer are both 20 years old and married, and each has one child. They wish to provide for their families in case they die and at the same time to start building a nest egg for their future.

    Dave talked to an insurance agent who said, "I have the ideal policy for you. If you die any time before you are 40, your family will receive $50,000. If you live to be 40, the policy pays you $50,000. The annual premium is $2,200 for 20 years. You pay a total of $44,000 over the 20-year period, so the insurance actually costs you nothing. The insurance company pays the $50,000 whether you live or die." Dave bought the policy, paying the first year's premium.

    Mike also investigated various insurance policies. He finally decided on a 20-year $50,000 term policy with annual premiums of $230. The policy pays $50,000 to Mike's family if he dies during the next 20 years, but if he survives he gets nothing from the policy. Total premiums over the 20-year period are $4,600. Mike also plans to invest $1,970 in a savings account each year when he pays the insurance premium. The account pays 5.5 percent interest, but Mike figures that since the interest is taxable, the account will effectively yield 4 percent compounded annually. Mike buys the term policy and deposits $1,970 in the savings account.

Required:

    a. How much money will each family have 20 years from now if both men survive?

    b. How much money will each family have if both men die next week?

    c. How much money will each family have if both men die at the age of 38?

P. 7-16   **Variable interest retirement fund.** Paul Bennet plans to invest $1,000 per year starting on January 15, 1986, in an Individual Retirement Account (IRA) to provide for his retirement. He selects a plan that has the following terms: Interest is compounded annually at 8 percent as long as the fund balance is below $10,000. Thereafter, interest is compounded annually at 9 percent. Paul plans to make a total of 16 payments into the IRA plan and withdraw all the money from the plan 1 year after the last payment.

Required:

    a. How many payments are required before the fund starts earning 9 percent interest?

    b. How much will be available when Paul withdraws the funds from the trust?

Case 7-1   **Alternative uses of investment fund.**

Aunt Brunhilda just died and left money in a foundation which includes an inheritance for George as follows: On December 31 of each of the next 5 years the foundation will pay $2,000 to George. George plans to invest the money immediately in a fund that earns 12 percent interest per year, compounded annually. The first payment will be made on December 31, 1986, and George will leave the money invested until December 31, 1992, so that it will be available when he is ready to buy the sailing yacht which he always wanted.

A lending company has offered George a single payment of $7,391.80 on December 31, 1985, in exchange for his rights to the inheritance. George is giving serious thought to the offer since he could invest all of the money at 12 percent immediately.

Required:

    a. How much will be available on December 31, 1992 if George invests the inheritance as he plans?

    b. Should George accept the offer from the lending company? Support your answer with figures.

    c. At what interest rate is the lending company discounting the annuity?

Cash and Other Liquid Assets

8

The liquid, or quick, assets of a business include cash, temporary investments, and receivables. The latter two can be converted quickly into cash, which is used to pay obligations as they come due. When you have finished studying this chapter, you should understand:

1   Accounting for cash in general.

2   Preparation of bank reconciliations.

3   The difference between equity securities and debt securities.

4   Accounting for temporary investments and their use in managing a business.

5   Accounting for notes receivable, accounts receivable, and bad debts.

6   Important aspects of control over current assets.

Effective working capital management is crucial for successful business operations. The availability, use, and control of each current asset should be carefully planned and managed. Merchandise must be available in quantities to satisfy customers' needs without excessive investment of resources. As merchandise is converted to accounts or notes receivable, managers can plan the timing of account collection so that cash is available for paying accounts and notes payable. The amount of working capital must increase as the volume of business increases. That is, an increase in sales usually requires a larger merchandise inventory, more money invested in accounts receivable, and an increase in payables, requiring greater amounts of cash to meet current obligations. Finally, an effective system of internal control is vital for safeguarding assets and ensuring that business operations proceed according to plans and in keeping with the goals of the business entity.

    Working capital is defined as current assets less current liabilities; the working capital accounts are often referred to as **circulating capital** because

Figure 8-1
The current assets and liabilities circulate continuously in the course of business operations. Cash flows from the customer to the business and from the business to suppliers of merchandise. Receivables arise from credit sales of merchandise, which is obtained by increasing accounts payable.

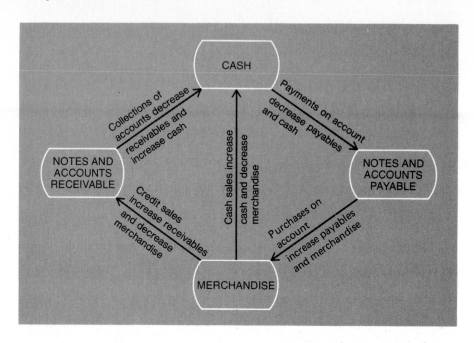

of the continuous cycle of activity caused by daily business transactions. As illustrated in Figure 8-1, maintaining a proper balance among the components of working capital is one of management's important functions and is facilitated by proper accounting procedures.

In this chapter we examine accounting for the asset portion of working capital, which consists of cash, temporary investments, notes receivable, and accounts receivable. These are the liquid assets of the business. At the end of the chapter we discuss some aspects of internal control designed to safeguard an organization's current assets. Merchandise, which often constitutes a very large part of current assets, is not as liquid because two steps are usually required to convert it to cash. Merchandise is first converted to accounts receivable by means of sales, and the receivables are then converted to cash. Accounting for merchandise is discussed in Chapter 9.

Liquid assets can be converted to cash easily and quickly

CASH

Cash is an unproductive asset

Businesses need an adequate supply of cash to pay salaries, payables, and other obligations as they come due. A business that cannot pay its obligations on time is **insolvent** and can be forced into bankruptcy. Many profitable businesses experience serious cash shortages during periods of expanding sales, tight money supplies, additions of new plants or stores, or other business expansions. During such times, managers must be particularly diligent in planning cash flows to have adequate cash available. Cash, however, is an unproductive asset unless invested, and a well-managed business avoids keeping excessive amounts on hand or in banks. To ensure that sufficient cash is available when needed and that too much cash is not idle, managers must plan and control carefully the cash needs of the business. In addition, because cash is universally desirable, a business must maintain careful control over its cash to ensure that it is not lost through fraud or embezzlement.

Definition of Cash

Cash consists of demand deposits, currency, coins, money orders, and checks awaiting deposit. **Demand deposits** are bank checking accounts. Savings accounts are called **time deposits.** Time deposits are usually considered cash although they are in reality temporary investments. Things that are sometimes mistakenly viewed as cash, and are not, include postage stamps, which are actually prepaid expenses; items that should be classified as receivables, including postdated checks; checks returned by the bank for lack of sufficient funds; and IOUs of employees and officers for small amounts borrowed from the company.

Cash Planning and Budgeting

There is a time lag between earning of revenue and collection of cash

Proper cash planning is part of the overall budgeting function and is discussed thoroughly in the *Managerial Accounting* volume of this series. Here we discuss only the rudiments of cash planning to acquaint you with its usefulness. To ensure that sufficient cash is on hand when payments need to be made, managers must allow for a lag between the earning of revenue and its collection. A wholesale distributor of consumer goods, for example, may experience heavy sales prior to the holiday season. But the collection of receivables from these sales occurs some 30 to 60 days later. The distributor's payables to suppliers may be due prior to the sale of the goods, and the company must plan to have large amounts of cash on hand, perhaps in August, to pay for the goods that will be sold in September. The cash flow from the sales may take place in November, at which time there is little need for the company to have large amounts of cash.

Budgets are plans of future activities

Planning of cash receipts and payments is typically done by means of a **budget** which is a formal, detailed plan prepared by managers as much as a year in advance. With proper cash budgeting, the company can arrange in advance to borrow the cash needed to pay for merchandise in August. Then it can use the November receipts to repay the loan and invest any excess cash in temporary investments until the next time a large outflow must occur. In some cases the company may liquidate temporary investments to pay bills rather than borrow the money from a bank. Other aspects of cash management include the periodic preparation of a bank reconciliation and the maintenance of various cash funds for specific purposes.

The Bank Reconciliation

A bank sends its depositors monthly statements describing the activity in the depositor's account. The statement includes the cash balance in the account at the beginning of the month, a list of deposits made during the month, a list of checks paid by the bank for the depositor, and the ending balance in the account. The bank also lists any service charges that it has deducted from the account and other transactions that may have taken place, such as the collection of a note by the bank on behalf of the depositor.

When the depositor receives the monthly statement, a reconciliation should be prepared to explain any difference between the bank statement and the cash account in the ledger. The reconciliation provides data for correcting any errors that were made by the bank or in the ledger.

The bank reconciliation helps to control cash

The **bank reconciliation** is a simple schedule that can take several forms. The most convenient is the two-column reconciliation that contains one column for the bank balance and one column for the book balance. For example, the Cash account of Polara Corporation at the end of June 1985 appears in the books as follows:

Cash

Bal. 6/1	14,890.00	Checks paid in June	13,001.30
Deposits	8,095.10		
Bal. 6/30	9,983.80		

On July 2 the company receives the bank statement shown in Figure 8-2. The ending balance in the bank statement is $9,561.40, which differs from the ending balance in the cash account by $422.40. The bank statement contains two items that the company cannot know about until it receives the statement. One is the $7 service charge which the bank removed from the checking account as payment for its services. The second is the debit memo for $34 for a check that was deposited by the company and which the bank could not collect.

Checks that bounce are marked NSF and returned to the depositor

When a depositor sends customers' checks to the bank for deposit, the bank credits the depositor's account for the total amount of the checks. It then forwards the checks to the banks on which they are drawn for payment by the makers of the checks. The makers' banks reduce each maker's checking account and pay the bank from which the checks were received. If the maker does not have sufficient money in the account to cover the check, his bank will return the check to the depositor's bank. Polara Company's bank was unable to collect on the $34 check which bounced. Such checks are marked **NSF** (not sufficient funds) by the bank and returned to the depositor. But this check was credited to the account as part of a deposit made earlier by the company. The bank must therefore remove this amount by debiting Polara's checking account $34. The bank returns the NSF check and a debit memo to the depositor to let him know that it was unable to collect the check, and that the depositor's account has been debited, or decreased, by the amount of the check.

Figure 8-3 shows a schedule prepared to reconcile the cash account with the bank statement. The first column starts with the ending bank

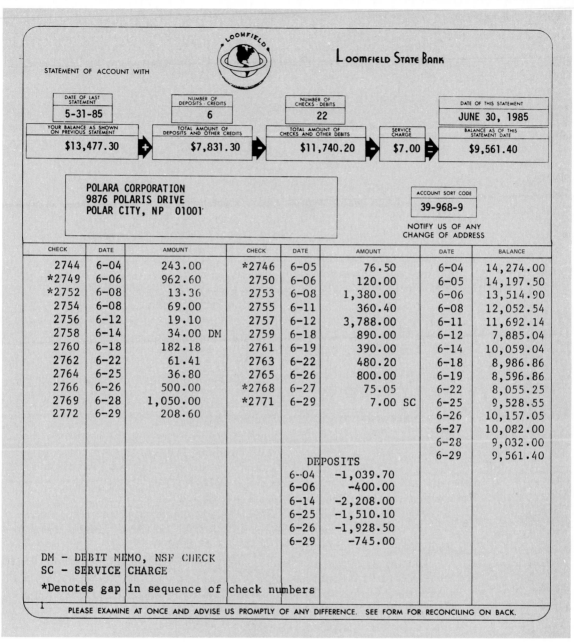

Figure 8-2 **A bank statement representing cash in the form of a demand deposit.**

balance of $9,561.40 from the bank statement. The second column starts with the ending balance from the cash account. The reconciliation is accomplished by summarizing in the schedule information from the bank statement and the cash account. All differences between the bank statement and the book balance are explained, and a correct cash balance is obtained. By examining the statement in our example, we find that the bank has not yet recorded a deposit of $1,703.50 mailed by the company to the bank. In addition, an examination of the check record indicates that the following checks written by the company have not yet been presented to the bank for payment:

No. 1146	$ 136.60
1149	802.00
1150	55.00
1152	301.50
	$1,295.10

Polara Corporation
Bank Reconciliation
June 30, 1985

Balance per bank statement	$ 9,561.40	Balance per books			$9,983.80
Add deposit in transit	1,703.50	Less service charge	$ 7.00		
	11,264.90	NSF check	34.00		41.00
Less outstanding checks					9,942.80
No. 1146	$136.60				
No. 1149	802.00	Add transposition error			27.00
No. 1150	55.00				
No. 1152	301.50	1,295.10			
Corrected bank balance	$ 9,969.80	Corrected book balance			$9,969.80

Figure 8-3
Two-column bank reconciliation.

The deposit in transit is added to the bank balance because the bank will add this amount as soon as it receives the funds. The outstanding checks are deducted from the bank balance. The bank will deduct these from the account as it pays them. Since the statement seems to contain no errors, and no other adjustments appear to be necessary, the total is found, indicating a corrected bank balance of $9,969.80.

The NSF check returned by the bank is not really cash, but it is still owed by the customer who made the check, because it did not clear the bank; therefore, it should be classified as an account receivable. Typically businesses attempt to deposit returned checks a second time, on the assumption that the maker of the check may have increased his bank balance, and the check will clear. If the check does not clear, the company notifies the maker of the NSF check and asks for payment. Some companies record NSF checks as notes receivable rather than accounts receivable.

The NSF check and the service charge are deducted from the cash balance. During the reconciliation process, all checks paid by the bank are compared to the check record to ensure that an error did not occur in recording the payments. In this case an error exists, because the statement does not reconcile with the books. A check written to the telephone company in the amount of $36.80 was recorded in the cash account as $63.80. The bank paid the proper amount since the check was correctly made.

This transposition error[1] reduced the cash account excessively, and the difference must be added to the cash balance. When the adjusted cash balance is the same as the adjusted bank balance, the bank reconciliation is complete. Now it is necessary to prepare adjusting entries to correct the balance in the cash account. These can be prepared from the data in the right column of the reconciliation.

The NSF check is taken out of cash and placed into accounts receivable; the service charge is recorded as an expense; the transposition error understated cash and overstated telephone expense. The Cash account is credited because the cash balance in the ledger contains more cash than the company owns and must be reduced to the correct amount. The correcting entry is

June 30	Accounts receivable	34	
	Bank service charge	7	
	Telephone expense		27
	Cash		14
	To adjust as required by bank		
	reconciliation.		

Note that no adjusting entries are needed for the bank side of the reconciliation. The bank is a different entity, and we do not maintain its records. If a bank error is found, we notify the bank. For example, the bank may have neglected to record a deposit, or it may have paid a check in the wrong amount. Items such as deposits in transit and checks outstanding are taken care of in the normal course of business.

Petty Cash

Petty cash is used for small, incidental cash payments

It is usually impractical for a company to write checks for all small expenditures that occur in everyday business. Incidental items like taxi fares, postage-due mail, and parking meter payments are best made from a fund especially designated for this purpose. The **petty cash fund** is used to control minor expenditures that cannot easily be paid by check and to limit the loss of cash that would be possible if large amounts were kept on hand. The petty cash fund is usually established in some relatively small amount and is turned over to a petty cash custodian. The custodian is responsible for making cash payments from the fund.

When the petty cash custodian pays money from the fund, a record is prepared, briefly describing the reasons for the expenditure. Periodically, or when the fund is almost depleted, the custodian lists the items paid and requests cash to replenish the fund. If a policy of surprise audits exists, the petty cash custodian can expect the fund to be inspected at any time.

---

[1] Errors caused by transpositions are evenly divisible by 9. This fact can often be used to determine if a transposition error was made.

Such a policy helps to prevent unauthorized use of the money, such as borrowing of small amounts for private use or accepting employees' IOUs in exchange for petty cash.

To establish a petty cash fund of $200, a company issues a check to the petty cash custodian, who cashes the check and obtains currency. The entry is as follows:

Feb. 4	Petty cash	200	
	Cash		200
	To establish petty cash fund.		

Each time money is removed from the fund, the custodian records the amount on a petty cash ticket or voucher. The voucher is a preprinted form with spaces for the date, amount, and explanation of the transaction. For example, if $4.80 is taken from the fund for taxi fare, the custodian pays the money and prepares a petty cash voucher for $4.80. At any time the total of the cash and vouchers in the fund equals $200. When the cash runs low, or at the end of some period such as a month, the vouchers are presented for reimbursement. The entry to replenish the fund might be

Feb. 28	Office expense	82.58	
	Postage	17.40	
	Transportation expense	79.22	
	Cash		179.20
	Reimbursed petty cash vouchers and		
	replenished the fund.		

The check is again issued to the petty cash custodian, who uses it to replenish the fund. Often the fund is replenished at the end of the accounting period, so that all expenses and prepayments paid for by the fund can be reported in the financial statements. The petty cash fund remains on the books, and its balance is included in the cash balance in the financial statements.

Cash Short or Over

Even with careful control of cash, errors may occur in the handling of cash. If control is adequate, such errors are small, but nevertheless they must be accounted for. For example, if errors occur as a result of making change for cash sales to customers, the amount of cash available at the end of the day is different from the amount recorded on the cash register tapes. If the cash register records indicate that sales for the day amounted to $2,478.50, and cash on hand amounts to $2,483.70, the day's sales are recorded as follows:

Mar. 6	Cash	2,483.70	
	Cash short or over		5.20
	Sales		2,478.50
	To record cash sales for the day.		

If a cash shortage occurred, it would be recorded as a debit to the Cash Short or Over account. The balance of this account is reported at the end of the accounting period among miscellaneous revenues and expenses in the income statement.

TEMPORARY INVESTMENTS

Marketable securities can be liquidated on short notice

Earlier we stated that savings accounts, or time deposits, may be used as temporary investments of cash. However, savings account balances are usually reported as cash rather than as temporary investments. Specifically, **temporary investments** are current assets consisting of marketable securities acquired for the purpose of investing idle cash for short periods of time such as a few weeks or months. Whether an investment is temporary or long term depends entirely on management's intentions. If managers intend to hold the investment for more than a year, the investment should not be classified as temporary. But if the intent is to liquidate the investment in less than a year, it is considered temporary.

Market prices of securities are readily available.

The collection of all marketable securities owned by an investor is called a **portfolio.** The term **marketable** means that the securities can be traded readily in a securities market, and the **market value** of the entire portfolio can be determined readily as well. Because securities are traded frequently, the latest price is always available. Temporary or **short-term investments** fall into two classifications: **marketable equity securities** and **marketable debt securities**.

Marketable Equity Securities

Equity securities consist of common and preferred stock, representing owners' equity of a company. If such companies pay dividends, the owner of the equity securities obtains dividend income. If such companies do not pay dividends, investors buy their stock in the hope that it will increase in price and then can be sold at a gain.

Recording purchases and sales.   When temporary equity investments are purchased, they are recorded at their cost. For example, on February 6, Temco Company buys 500 shares of Linden Corporation common stock at $12.50 per share and pays a commission of $150. The entry to record the purchase is as follows:

Feb. 6	Temporary investments	6,400	
	Cash		6,400
	Bought 500 shares Linden common at		
	$12.50 per share plus $150 commission.		

In April of the same year, Linden Corporation declares and pays a dividend of $.20 per share on its common stock. When Temco Company receives the dividend, it makes the following entry:

Apr. 16	Cash	100	
	Dividend income		100
	Received $.20 per share dividend on		
	Linden common.		

On July 3 Temco sells 200 shares of its Linden Corporation common stock at $15 per share, paying a commission of $80. The total cost of the stock and the net proceeds from the sale are used to calculate the gain or loss on the transaction. All 500 shares cost $6,400, so the cost per share is $12.80 ($6,400/500 shares). The cost of the sold shares of $2,560.00 (200 shares × $12.80 per share) must be removed from the Temporary Investments account. The net proceeds consist of the amount received from the transaction, $2,920 in this case. The proceeds and the gain on the sale are calculated as follows:

Selling price, 200 shares at $15 per share	$3,000
Less commission	80
Net proceeds	2,920
Less original cost of 200 shares	2,560
Gain	$ 360

The commissions on the purchase and sale of securities are not treated as expenses, but instead enter into the calculation of the cost of the securities and the proceeds from their sale. The entry to record the sale is as follows:

July 3	Cash	2,920	
	Gain on sale of stock		360
	Temporary investments		2,560
	Sold 200 shares Linden common at $15		
	per share less commission of $80.		

Pay particular attention to the cash flow aspects of the above transaction. Although $2,920 of cash flowed into the business, the income statement will report only $360 of gain added to net income. Your understanding of these relationships will be very important later when you study the statement of changes in financial position.

A loss may be recognized before equity securities are sold

Valuation of equity securities.   FASB Statement no. 12 requires marketable equity securities to be carried in the balance sheet at cost, or if the aggregate market value of the equities portfolio is lower than cost, the securities must be carried at their market value. This **lower of cost or market (LCM)** rule means that if the aggregate market value of the portfolio declines below its cost, a loss must be recognized in the period in which the decline takes place, even if the loss is not realized by a sale. Statement no. 12 is therefore in conflict with the realization principle. Conflicts between accounting principles are not unusual. Sometimes a choice must be made among the principles; sometimes room is left for judgment and interpretation.[2]

At the end of the accounting period, the entire portfolio must be valued at cost and at market to determine the amount to be reported in the balance sheet. On December 31, 1985, the equity portfolio of Temco Company consists of three securities with the following costs and market values:

	Cost	Market Price/Share	Market Value
300 shares Linden Corporation common	$ 3,840	$16	$ 4,800
100 shares Marsten Company 8% preferred	6,000	47	4,700
800 shares Norma Corporation common	31,200	36	28,800
Totals	$41,040		$38,300

The market value is less than cost, so the market value must be reported. The following adjusting entry is made at the end of the accounting period in order to recognize the unrealized loss:

Dec. 31	Loss from decline in market value		
	of temporary equity investments	2,740	
	Allowance for decline in market		
	value of temporary investments		2,740
	To reduce equity portfolio to market		
	value.		

The loss is reported in the income statement among other revenues and expenses. Note that the loss does not result in a cash outflow. The allowance account is a contra asset account reported in the balance sheet together with the marketable securities, as follows:

Temporary investments:
Marketable equity securities at cost $41,040
Less allowance for decline in market value   2,740 $38,300

[2] In this particular case, the Financial Accounting Standards Board felt that the conservatism principle should have precedence, because the information on the decline in market value can be objectively determined, and it is important enough to require disclosure even if the temporary investments have not been sold.

If, by the end of the next accounting period, the value of the investment portfolio increases, Temco Company may recover part or all of the previously recorded loss. The increase in market value can be recognized only up to the original cost of the portfolio. Any value above cost can be realized only if the securities are sold. For example, if the market value of the portfolio on December 31, 1986, is $40,000, then $1,700 of the previous loss in market value has been recovered. The company recognizes the increase in market value as follows:

Dec. 31	Allowance for decline in market value		
	of temporary investments	1,700	
	Recovery of unrealized loss		1,700
	Reduced allowance account to report		
	equity securities at LCM.		

By reducing the allowance account, the company again reports marketable equity securities at their market value, which is still below the original cost. On the other hand, if the market value at the end of 1986 is $42,000, the entire loss of $2,740 has been recovered. In this case, however, the book value of the portfolio may be increased only up to the original cost, as follows:

Dec. 31	Allowance for decline in market value		
	of temporary investments	2,740	
	Recovery of unrealized loss		2,740
	Eliminated allowance account to report		
	equity portfolio at cost.		

Equity securities may not be reported above their cost

After this entry is posted, the allowance account has a zero balance, and the marketable equity portfolio is again reported in the balance sheet at cost. The recovery of the loss incurred in 1985 is reported in 1986 as if it were a gain, among miscellaneous revenues in the income statement.

The allowance for decline in market value does not apply to any specific security in the portfolio, but to the aggregate portfolio. If a security is sold while this contra account exists, the sale is recorded exactly as before, without regard to the allowance account. The allowance account is adjusted only at the end of the accounting period when financial statements are prepared. If the allowance account does not exist because the market value of securities is above their cost, it is appropriate to disclose the market value in the balance sheet by means of a footnote.

Marketable Debt Securities

Debt securities consist of corporate and government bonds, notes, and bills. They represent business and government debt on which the borrower pays interest. Debt securities mature on specified dates, at which time the borrower is required to repay the borrowed funds. Bonds are issued in $1,000 denominations and usually pay interest every 6 months.

Bond interest is expressed as a percentage of the face value of the bond, and the rate is fixed for the life of the bond contract. Market interest rates change, however, after a bond is issued. If 12 percent interest is available to investors in the bond market, and a company issues a 12 percent bond, investors will be willing to pay the full face value for it. Later if the market rate of interest rises to 14 percent, the 12 percent bond will no longer be as attractive to investors because they can buy other bonds that yield more interest. Consequently, to sell the 12 percent bond, the seller will have to offer it at a price lower than $1,000, and the bond will trade at a **discount.** Similarly, if interest rates decrease to 10 percent in the market, investors will find the 12 percent bond quite attractive and will bid up its price above its face value in an attempt to buy it. The bond will then sell at a **premium.** Bond prices are quoted as a percentage of their face value. For example, a price of 98 means that each bond may be bought for 98 percent of $1,000, or $980, and a price of 101 1/2 means that each bond may be bought or sold for $1,015. The amount of discount or premium can be determined by finding the present values of the future interest payments and principal repayment, as discussed in more detail in Chapter 12.

Market rates of interest determine discounts and premiums

According to FASB pronouncements, marketable debt securities are reported at cost unless there has been a permanent impairment in their value, in which case they should be written down to their market price. If the market price is less than cost, but the reduction in value is not viewed as permanent, no write-down is necessary. This is logical because the face value of bonds will be received when they mature, regardless of the current price. Therefore, the lower of cost or market rule usually does not apply to marketable debt securities.

Bonds traded on interest payment dates. On April 1, 1985, Temco Company bought $10,000 face value of Rose Corporation's 12 percent bonds at 95 as a temporary investment. The bonds mature in 1992 and pay interest on April 1 and October 1. Temco Company paid a total of $9,600 including $100 commission for the bonds. With semiannual interest, the bonds will pay 6 percent of the face value every 6 months.

Bonds are bought to earn interest

To record the purchase of the ten bonds, the company makes the following entry:

Apr. 1	Temporary investments	9,600	
	Cash		9,600
	Bought $10,000 Rose Corp. 12% bonds,		
	due 1992, at 95 plus $100 commission.		

If Temco holds the bonds for one year, it will receive $1,200 on its investment of $9,600. Therefore, the current yield on the bonds is 12.5 percent interest ($1,200/$9,600) compounded semiannually. **Current yield** is the return on an investment for a single period, such as one year. Compounding is semiannual in this case because the investor can reinvest the interest received every 6 months and can earn additional interest.

Short-term investors are interested in current yield

On October 1 Temco Company receives the semiannual interest payment on its bond investment. The receipt of interest is recorded as follows:

Oct. 1	Cash	600	
	Interest income		600
	Received semiannual interest on Rose		
	Corp. bonds.		
	$10,000 × .12 × 6/12 = $600.		

The calculation of interest is the face value of the bond times the interest rate times time expressed as a fraction of the year. The interest rate is annual so time must also be in annual terms.

When the company needs cash, it can sell some of its marketable securities. On October 1 the company sells eight of the Rose bonds at 94 1/2 less $80 commission. The net proceeds of the sale amount to $7,480 ($945 × 8 bonds less $80 commission). The sold bonds must be removed from the investment account to record the sale.

Oct. 1	Cash	7,480	
	Loss on sale of temporary investment	200	
	Temporary investments		7,680
	Sold $8,000 face value of Rose Corp.		
	bonds at 94 1/2 less $80 commission.		

The credit of $7,680 is the cost of the eight bonds which have been sold. The loss on the sale is the difference between the cost of the investment and the net proceeds from its sale. By holding the bonds 6 months the company earned a net amount of $400—$600 as interest income less a $200 loss on the sale of the bonds. The remaining two bonds will continue earning interest until they are sold. By December 31, the end of the accounting period, 3 months' interest accrues on the two remaining bonds, and an adjusting entry must be made.

Dec. 31	Interest receivable	60	
	Interest income		60
	To accrue interest on Rose Corp. bonds.		
	$2,000 × .12 × 3/12 = $60.		

Bonds traded between interest payments. When bonds are traded between interest payment dates, the buyer must pay to the seller the interest accrued on the bonds since the last interest payment was made. Then at the next interest payment date, the new owner of the bonds receives the full 6 months' interest, regardless of the length of time that the bonds have been owned. The seller can obtain his share of the interest only by collecting it from the buyer at the time of sale, because the company issuing the bonds does not keep track of the length of time each owner holds the bonds.

For example, Temco Company buys six Daisy Corporation 14 percent bonds on May 1 for $5,820 plus accrued interest. The bonds pay interest on June 30 and December 31. The following entry is recorded:

May 1	Temporary investments	5,820	
	Interest receivable	280	
	Cash		6,100
	Bought $6,000 face value Daisy Corp.		
	14% bonds with 4 months' accrued		
	interest.		
	$6,000 × .14 × 120/360 = $280.		

The investor must buy interest accrued on bonds

When the above entry is posted, the Interest Receivable account appears as follows:

Interest Receivable

5/1	280	

On June 30 when the interest payment is received, it is recorded by a debit to Cash, a credit to Interest Income, and a credit to Interest Receivable, as follows:

June 30	Cash	420	
	Interest income		140
	Interest receivable		280
	Received semiannual interest on Daisy		
	Corp. bonds, $140 of which was accrued		
	earlier.		
	$6,000 × .14 × 60/360 = $140.		

After posting, the Interest Receivable and Interest Income accounts appear as follows:

Interest Receivable					Interest Income		
5/1	280	6/30	280			6/30	140

It is also possible to record the above transactions without use of an interest receivable account. For example, the bond purchase and interest receipt could be recorded as follows:

May 1	Temporary investments	5,820	
	Interest income	280	
	Cash		6,100
	Bought $6,000 face value Daisy Corp.		
	14% bonds with 60 days accrued		
	interest.		
	$6,000 × .14 × 120/360 = $280.		

June 30	Cash	420	
	Interest income		420
	Received semiannual interest on Daisy		
	Corp. bonds.		
	$6,000 × .14 × 6/12 = $420.		

By using only the Interest Income account, the June 30 entry does not require writing off the accrued interest. The Interest Income account automatically has the correct balance of $140 after posting on June 30 as shown below.

Interest Income			
5/1	280	6/30	420

When bond investments are sold between interest payment dates, the seller receives the proceeds of the sale and the interest that has accrued since the last interest payment. For example, on September 30 Temco Company sells four of its Daisy bonds at 98 plus accrued interest. The company originally paid $970 for each of its six $1,000 bonds. To record the sale of four bonds, the company makes the following entry:

Sept. 30	Cash	4,060	
	Temporary investments		3,880
	Interest income		140
	Gain on sale of investments		40
	Sold $4,000 of Daisy Corp. bonds at 98		
	plus 3 months' accrued interest.		
	$4,000 × .14 × 3/12 = $140		
	Gain = (4 × $980) − (4 × $970)		
	= $3,920 − $3,880 = $40		

Certificates of Deposit and Treasury Bills

Discounted securities are non-interest bearing

Businesses often invest their idle cash in short-term, temporary investments such as treasury bills (T bills) or large **certificates of deposit (CDs)**. CDs typically are available from banks. Although CDs can be purchased in $1,000 and $10,000 denominations, many are for $100,000. They earn interest for investors and usually mature within a short time such as 30, 60, 90 days, or a year. **Treasury bills** are known as **discounted securities**. They do not earn interest but are instead sold for less than face value and are redeemed by the United States Treasury for their face value when they mature. Maturities range from 30 days to a year. The difference between the issue price and the face value is the discount, which represents interest to the buyer. Treasury bills sell in minimum amounts of $10,000. In most cases the buyers of CDs and treasury bills keep the securities until they mature. If on June 5 Temco Company buys $100,000 of 90-day United States Treasury bills for $98,500, the investment is recorded as follows:

June 5	Temporary investments	98,500	
	Cash		98,500
	Acquired 90-day T bills.		

Ninety days later when the bills mature, the entry is

Sept. 5	Cash	100,000	
	Temporary investments		98,500
	Interest income		1,500
	Treasury bills matured.		

Identification of Marketable Securities

When identical marketable securities are acquired on different dates, the investor has two ways of identifying the securities when they are sold.

Specific identification may be used to record the sale if a record is maintained on the certificates and if the ones being sold can be identified with a specific purchase. Otherwise, it is assumed that the first securities bought are the first ones sold. For example, Temco Company makes the following purchases:

Date	Description	Price/Share	Cost
Apr. 5	100 shares Bellco Corp., common	$15	$1,500
Apr. 29	200 shares Bellco Corp., common	19	3,800

On May 20 the company sells 100 shares at $18 per share. If the company uses specific identification of securities, it may choose to deliver stock bought on April 29 and record a loss of $100. Or it may prefer to record a gain of $300 by delivering the stock acquired on April 5. If the company cannot identify the shares sold because it does not keep track of the purchase date of specific shares' certificates, it must use the **first in, first out** method for recording the sale. In that case the sale would result in a gain.

It is also possible to calculate gains or losses on sales on the basis of an average price, but since this method is not permitted for tax purposes, it is seldom found in practice.

NOTES RECEIVABLE

Promissory notes are negotiable instruments

A **promissory note** is a legal document signed by the maker, or borrower, promising to pay to the lender, or payee, the principal amount of the note plus interest at a stated rate. A date when the note is to be paid is indicated. Notes are **negotiable instruments,** which means they may be sold by the owner. Frequently businesses accept notes from their customers in exchange for merchandise or for accounts receivable that the customer does not pay when due. The business may accept the note to accommodate the customer or to make the sale, which might be lost if cash payment were required. Sometimes the business decides not to keep the note because it needs cash in its working capital. In this case the note may be sold to a bank or other institution. When a note is sold, the payee endorses the note by signing it on the back and transfers it to the next holder.

To illustrate the accounting for notes receivable, we use the example of Beylor Company, which sometimes accepts notes from its customers as payment for services. On May 13 the company received a $5,000 60-day 12 percent note from Mendoza Company for services performed. The transaction is recorded as follows:

May 13	Notes receivable	5,000	
	Service revenue		5,000
	Received 60-day 12% note from		
	Mendoza.		

Sixty days later when the note is collected, the entry is

July 12	Cash	5,100	
	Notes receivable		5,000
	Interest income		100
	Collected note.		
	$5,000 × .12 × 60/360 = $100		

Sometimes when a note matures, the customer does not pay the debt. At that time the note is in **default** and should be transferred from Notes Receivable to a special account for dishonored notes. If Mendoza Company does not pay the note when due, the entry to record such transfer is

July 13	Notes receivable past due	5,100	
	Notes receivable		5,000
	Interest income		100
	To record note in default.		
	$5,000 × .12 × 60/360 = $100		

The interest income has been earned and is therefore recorded. If, however, the company is not successful in collecting the note, or if it collects only a part of the note, a loss is incurred. For example, Beylor Company may turn the defaulted note over to a collection agency. If the agency collects the note and charges a fee of 40 percent of the amount collected, the entry is

July 29	Cash	3,060	
	Loss on defaulted note	2,040	
	Notes receivables past due		5,100
	Received proceeds of past-due note from		
	collection agency.		

The loss may also be recorded as a collection expense.

Discounting Notes Receivable

Discount on notes receivable is calculated on their maturity value

If a business needs cash and does not wish to hold its notes to maturity, it can discount notes with a bank in exchange for cash. The bank buys the notes and holds them to maturity, earning interest on its investment.

When a bank discounts a note receivable, it first calculates the maturity value of the note. **Maturity value** is the total amount paid on the note when it matures. Using its own discount rate, the bank then calculates the amount of interest that it will charge for the note. The interest charged by the bank is calculated on the maturity value of the note and is deducted from the maturity value to arrive at the amount of proceeds, which the bank pays to the seller of the note. If Beylor discounts the Mendoza note immediately upon receiving it, and the bank charges a 15 percent discount rate, the following calculation is made by the bank:

Maturity value of note (principal + interest):	
$5,000 + ($5,000 × .12 × 60/360)	$5,100.00
Less discount ($5,100 × .15 × 60/360)	127.50
Proceeds to seller	$4,972.50

Upon receiving the proceeds, Beylor makes the following entry:

May 13	Cash	4,972.50	
	Interest expense	27.50	
	Notes receivable		5,000.00
	Discounted Mendoza note at 15%.		

The interest expense is the cost of obtaining cash today, rather than waiting until the note matures. The bank's discount rate is higher than the interest rate of the note; therefore, Beylor must make up the difference to the bank.

If Beylor had waited 30 days before discounting the note, the bank would have calculated its discount as before, except that the discount would have been for a shorter time period because only 30 days must pass for the note to mature. The calculation is

Maturity value of note	$5,100.00
Less discount ($5,100 × .15 × 30/360)	63.75
Proceeds to seller	$5,036.25

In this case Beylor records the sale of the note as follows:

June 12	Cash	5,036.25	
	Notes receivable		5,000.00
	Interest income		36.25
	Discounted Mendoza note at 15%.		

By waiting 30 days before discounting the note, Beylor earned some interest income instead of incurring interest expense.

When the bank computes the discount on a note and deducts it from the maturity value, it is actually charging more than the stated rate of interest. In the above example, $63.75 is interest on $5,100, but the bank provides only $5,036.25 to the seller of the note, making the true interest rate slightly higher than 15 percent.

Selling notes receivable creates contingent liabilities

When a note is discounted with the bank, the seller of the note is liable to the bank for the proceeds on the note if the maker does not pay. Such a **contingent liability** may materialize in the future but is not owed at the time financial statements are prepared. A contingent liability arising from discounting of notes must be disclosed in the financial statements. This is usually accomplished by means of a footnote indicating the amount of the discounted notes and explaining that there is a contingent liability for this amount. In our example, if the maker of the note does not pay the bank at maturity, Beylor will have to pay the bank $5,100. Beylor may disclose its contingent liability in its June 30 balance sheet with the following footnote:

> The company is contingently liable in the amount of $5,100 for notes receivable discounted that are due after June 30.

If the maker of the discounted note defaults on the note, the bank returns the note to the endorser and demands payment. For example, assume that the Mendoza note was discounted on June 12, as previously illustrated. On July 12 the note is not paid as promised. The bank returns the note to Beylor Company and collects the maturity value. Beylor Company records the transaction as follows:

July 12	Notes receivable past due	5,100	
	Cash		5,100
	To record payment of defaulted note.		

Beylor will now attempt to collect the note from Mendoza Company. If it succeeds in collecting only part of the note, the remainder is written off as a loss.

Imputed Interest on Notes Receivable

Interest may be buried in the face value of a note

Promissory notes are sometimes written without any provision for the payment of interest. The payee accepts such notes with the understanding that the face amount of the note will be collected on the due date. For example, Beylor Company has the opportunity to sell $9,000 of merchandise to Mr. Carr, who offered a $9,000, 6-month non-interest note in exchange. In accepting the offer, Beylor's management knows that the present value of the note is less than $9,000. The sale nevertheless results in a profit, and if the note is not accepted, the sale may be lost.

Non-interest-bearing notes may not be recorded at their face value because the future receipt consists of principal and interest.[3] The interest

---

[3] "Interest on Receivables and Payables," *Opinions of the Accounting Principles Board no. 21* (New York: AICPA, August 21, 1971).

is implied and must be **imputed** when the note is recorded, which means that the amount of implied interest must be extracted and recorded separately as a discount. When the note is collected, the imputed interest is recorded as interest income. The imputed interest must be calculated by using an interest rate that is reasonable under the circumstances. If the usual rate of interest for similar transactions is 12 percent per year, the 6-month note must be discounted at 6 percent to find its present value. For notes whose term is longer than one year, it is appropriate to use compound discount. For short-term notes, simple interest discounting may be used. The present value of the note is calculated as follows:

$$\text{Present value} = \frac{\text{Face amount of note}}{1 + \text{interest rate}} = \frac{\$9,000}{1.06} = \$8,490.57$$

If Beylor Company accepts Mr. Carr's 6-month note on March 1, the sale is recorded with the following journal entry:

Mar. 1	Notes receivable	9,000.00	
	Discount on notes receivable		509.43
	Sales		8,490.57
	Received non-interest 6-month note from		
	Mr. Carr. Imputed interest at 12%.		

The discount is the difference between the present value and face value of the note and is recorded as a contra asset. It is deducted from the face value of the note in the balance sheet. As time passes, interest is earned on the note. When the interest revenue is recorded, the discount is written off. For example, when the note is collected 6 months later, the entry is

Sept. 1	Cash	9,000.00	
	Discount on notes receivable	509.43	
	Notes receivable		9,000.00
	Interest income		509.43
	Collected Carr note.		

If the end of the accounting period occurs before the note is collected, the imputed interest earned must be recorded. In this case, interest does not accrue, because the note is not interest bearing. The interest is earned on the book value of the note and is recorded by reducing the discount. For example, if Beylor Company prepares financial statements on March 31, it would record interest income as follows:

Mar. 31	Discount on notes receivable	84.91	
	Interest income		84.91
	$8,490.57 × .12 × 30/360		

The interest recorded is precisely 1/6 of the discount. The remaining 5/6 will be recorded 5 months later when the note matures. Unlike the discount recorded on notes sold to a bank, imputed interest is based on a true interest rate, resulting in a precise calculation.

Interest should also be imputed on notes that pay interest at a rate that is clearly lower than is warranted under the circumstances. For example, a $16,000, 1-year 3 percent note has a present value less than its face value if the normal interest rate is 10 percent. The imputed interest is calculated by discounting the maturity value of the note. The maturity value is

$$\$16,000 \times 1.03 = \$16,480$$

The maturity value discounted at 10 percent for one year is the present value of the note:

$$\$16,480/1.10 = \$14,981.82$$

The note is recorded at its face value of $16,000 with a contra account of $1,018.18, for a book value of $14,981.82. Interest income is computed by multiplying the book value times 10 percent interest.

ACCOUNTS RECEIVABLE

When merchandise or services are sold on credit, an **account receivable** is charged for the amount of the sale. Accounts receivable generally consist of such **trade accounts**. A company may have other receivables—from employees or from the sale of fixed assets, for example—but these are usually classified as special receivables and are not mixed with trade accounts.

Merchandising companies often have significant amounts of accounts receivable, and the proper measurement and control of these accounts is therefore of prime importance. Some control is achieved by separating the duties of bookkeepers who maintain control accounts from those who maintain the subsidiary ledgers. In addition, proper control of receivables includes an adequate credit investigation prior to granting credit to customers, limits on the amounts that customers can charge on their accounts, and timely billing to assist in early collection of the accounts. Follow-up of past-due accounts is also important in ensuring collection of receivables to the fullest extent possible.

Recording bad debts in the period of sale satisfies the matching principle

Even with careful investigation of customers' credit ratings, and careful control over receivables, a small number of accounts will become uncollectible. The **allowance for uncollectible accounts** is maintained so that the balance sheet reports the amounts expected to be collected. The allowance is a contra asset account that is credited when the bad debt expense is recorded. This procedure satisfies the conservatism principle and the matching principle. Reporting the net realizable value of accounts receivable results in a more conservative—and more realistic—amount than the full balance of receivables. At the same time, the loss from not collecting a receivable is matched with the sales revenue that was recorded when the receivable was created. Both the revenue and the bad debt expense are reported in the same accounting period although the company will only discover later which specific accounts are uncollectible.

Accounts receivable are reported at net realizable value

Several methods are available for making estimates of the bad debts expense for a period. In all cases past experience helps companies arrive at the most appropriate figure for the allowance account. Some companies assume that a certain percentage of the ending accounts receivable balance will be uncollectible. Others base the estimate on a percentage of credit sales. Probably the best estimates are obtained by aging the accounts receivable.

Aging Accounts Receivable

Aging receivables is a simple process that often provides the most reliable estimate of uncollectible accounts. The account balances in the subsidiary ledger are categorized according to the length of time they have been outstanding. The company estimates the probability of loss for each category based on its past experience and uses the estimate to calculate the amount expected to be lost. An aging schedule prepared by Trammel Corporation is illustrated in Figure 8-4.

Based on previous experience, Trammel Corporation knows that about .5 of 1 percent of current accounts eventually become uncollectible, but about 2 percent are uncollectible if they are overdue up to 30 days. Such percentages estimated for each category are shown in Figure 8-4. The percentages are multiplied by the total owed in each category to arrive at the uncollectible amounts shown at the bottom of the schedule. On December 31, 1985, this estimate is $1,181. For Trammel Corporation, the control accounts appear as follows on that date:

Accounts Receivable, Control		Allowance for Uncollectible Accounts	
Bal. 12/31 45,000			Bal. 12/31 140

To record the bad debts expense and bring the balance of the allowance for uncollectible accounts up to the current estimated amount of $1,181, Trammel Corporation makes the following entry:

Dec. 31	Bad debts expense	1,041	
	Allowance for uncollectible accounts		1,041
	To record bad debts based on		
	aging schedule.		

Trammel Corporation
Schedule of Accounts Receivable Aging and Uncollectible Amounts
December 31, 1985

Name	Account Balance	Not Due	Past Due 1–30 Days	Past Due 31–60 Days	Past Due 61–90 Days	Past Due Over 90 Days
Arnold	$ 1,200	$ 1,200				
Baker	4,200			$ 4,200		
Davis	420		$ 420			
Farias	1,000	800	100	100		
Heitger	800			300	$ 300	$200
Justin	9,980	9,980				
Kaler	2,600			2,600		
Limpit	5,000		5,000			
Martin	240				240	
Russell	7,680		7,680			
Simkin	1,610				1,610	
Tabor	6,500	6,100	300		100	
Welshe	3,770	2,170		900		700
Total	45,000	20,250	13,500	8,100	2,250	900
Percent estimated uncollectible		.5%	2%	5%	10%	20%
Amount estimated uncollectible	$ 1,181	$ 101	$ 270	$ 405	$ 225	$180

Figure 8-4   **Accounts receivables may be aged to obtain an accurate estimate of uncollectible accounts.**

Uncollectibles as a Percentage of Receivables

Uncollectibles may be estimated as a percentage of receivables . . .

Instead of preparing an aging schedule, the managers may decide that they can get a reasonable estimate of uncollectible accounts by calculating a percentage of the ending accounts receivable balance. For example, if the company estimates that 2.5 percent of its accounts receivable balance will become uncollectible, its allowance for uncollectible accounts balance should be reported at 2.5 percent of $45,000, or $1,125. The allowance account already has a credit balance of $140, so the adjusting entry to bring this balance up to the estimated amount is

Dec. 31	Bad debts expense	985	
	Allowance for uncollectible accounts		985
	To record uncollectible accounts at		
	2.5 percent of accounts receivable.		

Uncollectibles as a Percentage of Sales

... or as a percentage of credit sales

It is also possible to estimate uncollectibles as a percentage of credit sales. Estimates are usually based on the company's past collection experience. For example, Trammel Corporation estimates that .5 percent of its credit sales will prove to be uncollectible. With credit sales of $235,000, the company's estimate of bad debts expense for the year is $1,175 (.005 × $235,000). In this case the amount already recorded in the Allowance for Uncollectible Accounts does **not** affect the adjusting entry. The two previous methods were used to estimate the amount that should be in the allowance account. This method estimates the amount of bad debts expense. Because the full amount of sales has been recorded in the period, the entire portion of sales deemed to be uncollectible must also be reported in the same period as bad debts expense to satisfy the matching principle, as illustrated in the following entry:

Dec. 31	Bad debts expense	1,175	
	Allowance for uncollectible accounts		1,175
	To record bad debts as .5 percent of		
	credit sales.		

Writing Off Uncollectible Accounts

During the following year, the company will find that some of its accounts are not collectible. When all efforts to collect an account fail, the account is written off. This is done by reducing the balance of accounts receivable and the allowance account. The uncollectible account balance is thus removed from the control account. At the same time, the customer's account is removed from the subsidiary accounts receivable ledger and placed in a separate file of defaulted accounts. If the company decides to write off Martin's $240 past-due account, for example, the following entry is made:

Feb. 6	Allowance for uncollectible accounts	240	
	Accounts receivable		240
	To write off Martin's account, found		
	to be uncollectible.		

Writing off accounts receivable does not affect owners' equity

Notice that writing off a bad debt does not affect owners' equity, nor does it change the net amount of accounts receivable or the amount of working capital. The reduction in owners' equity occurred when the bad debt estimate was made and recorded at the end of last year. Here we are using part of the allowance account that was provided for the purpose of writing off uncollectible accounts. The net realizable value of accounts receivable before and after the write-off remains the same, as shown in the following example:

	Before Writing Off $240 Account	After Writing Off $240 Account
Accounts receivable	$45,000	$44,760
Allowance for uncollectible accounts	(1,181)	(941)
Book value of accounts receivable	$43,819	$43,819

If the estimate of doubtful accounts was a good one, most of the allowance account will be used up by the end of the next accounting period. The amount remaining in this account at the end of the year, whether a debit or a credit, represents the estimation error. The balance of the allowance account is again adjusted when a new estimate is made.

Collecting Written-Off Accounts

Occasionally an account that was written off is later collected. For example, Trammel Corporation collects a $40 account that was written off last year. The entry to record the collection is made as follows:

Mar. 11	Accounts receivable	40	
	Allowance for uncollectible accounts		40
	To restore Palmer's account, previously		
	written off.		
11	Cash	40	
	Accounts receivable		40
	Collected Palmer's account.		

The first entry restores the account balance in Accounts Receivable and informs the bookkeeper that the subsidiary account must be transferred from the file of bad accounts to the subsidiary accounts receivable ledger. The second entry then records the collection of the account.

Direct Write-Off of Receivables

Some businesses do not maintain an allowance for doubtful accounts. Instead they write off uncollectible accounts directly to Bad Debts Expense. When an account becomes uncollectible, the following entry is made:

June 6	Bad debts expense	140	
	Accounts receivable		140
	To write off Smith account.		

At the end of the accounting period, no adjusting entry is made. The accounts written off during the period make up the balance in the Bad Debts Expense account, which is reported on the income statement.

The direct write-off method is permitted for income tax purposes, and a small number of businesses therefore also use it for reporting purposes. However, the method does not match revenues and expenses properly, and the accounts receivable amount in the balance sheet is overstated because the entire balance probably will not be collected. Therefore the direct write-off method is not consistent with generally accepted accounting principles.

Pledging and Factoring

Receivables may be converted to cash prior to their due date

Companies with large amounts of accounts receivable may find that they need cash and cannot wait for the accounts to be collected. The accounts receivable may be **pledged** as security for a bank loan. Alternatively the accounts may be **factored,** which is a term used for the selling of receivables. A factor is a finance company which purchases the receivables outright, usually paying an amount smaller than the total balance in the accounts. The difference between the account balance and the amount received represents interest expense. The interest rate for factoring accounts is usually high because the factor must assume the loss from uncollectible accounts, but many companies routinely factor their accounts receivable immediately after making a sale on open account. By doing so, they immediately convert receivables to cash and avoid bad debts and record-keeping costs.

CONTROL OVER ASSETS

Good accounting systems provide good control

Proper accounting for current assets is only one segment of the entire control system that is essential for the proper operation of a business. A system of **internal control** is the set of procedures and rules established by a business to ensure that all assets are used as intended by management for legitimate business purposes. The accounting system itself is a significant part of the internal control system. Control over assets can be achieved by applying three important principles:

1. Separate duties
2. Assign responsibilities
3. Establish specific routines in the operation of the business

Separate Duties

An essential element of good internal control is the separation of the key operating and record-keeping functions in a business. Employees with access to assets should not have access to accounting records pertaining to the assets. For example, employees who receive merchandise shipments should not record the receipts in the merchandise accounts. Instead, they should prepare a receiving report that can be used by the merchandise bookkeeper to debit the Purchases account and by the accounts payable bookkeeper to credit the accounts payable. By separating the duties of these employees, an error by any one shows up immediately as an imbalance in the accounts or as a discrepancy between invoices and receiving reports. Moreover, any attempt at theft would require the cooperation of several employees, so merchandise losses are less likely to occur.

Assign Responsibilities

With the separation of duties achieved, employees should be assigned specific responsibilities. For example, if several bookkeepers are responsible for accounts receivable, not all should have access to the entire subsidiary ledger. Instead, each bookkeeper should be assigned specific accounts and sole responsibility for them. If an employee is responsible for specific assets, far better control is likely than if no one were responsible and all employees had equal access to these records.

Establish Specific Routines

If specific procedures are established for most aspects of business operations, errors are much less likely to occur, and good control is achieved. Examples of established routines include:

1. Requiring employees to initial a designated space on source documents when they are prepared, approved, or journalized
2. Requiring approval of all disbursements by an officer
3. Depositing all cash receipts intact, on a daily basis
4. Preparing certain documents in triplicate

Surprise audits are good control devices

One control procedure that is very effective simply because it does *not* follow an established routine is a system of surprise audits of segments of the business. An internal auditing staff performs these audits and reports directly to the board of directors. All assets must be protected by adequate control procedures, but the most elaborate controls are usually necessary to safeguard cash because it is universally desired, unidentifiable as to ownership, and probably used more often than any other asset. Below we discuss the control of cash receipts and cash disbursements.

Control of receipts.   An excellent way of safeguarding cash is to deposit intact all cash receipts in a bank account. When cash is received by a business, a record of receipts is maintained. For example, cash sales are recorded on the cash register tape. At the end of the day, all the cash should be deposited so that the daily cash receipt totals from the cash register tapes match the bank's deposit records. A business should avoid using part of the daily cash receipts for the payment of expenses, purchases of assets, or repayment of liabilities.

All cash receipts should be deposited intact

Cash received by mail should be the responsibility of individuals authorized to open the mail. Most such receipts are checks or money orders. As the mail is opened, cash receipts should be tabulated, with an indication of who made the payment, and turned over to the individual responsible for making bank deposits. The list of receipts and the payors should be given to bookkeepers who record the receipts in the appropriate accounting records. The individuals who open the mail and who make bank deposits should not have access to any accounting records.

If the accounts receivable bookkeeper has no access to cash receipts, and the cashier has no access to the accounts receivable ledger, any theft of cash received from customers requires the cooperation of at least two individuals because a theft by one person would immediately cause a discrepancy in the records of another. Similarly, the person having access to cash should not receive the monthly bank statement. The responsibility for reconciling the bank statement with the cash record should belong to someone who does not have access to cash. These procedures and the division of responsibility provide good control over cash receipts.

Control of disbursements.   Control of cash disbursements is accomplished by ensuring that substantially all cash payments are made by check. The person authorized to approve cash payments should not also be authorized to sign checks. The person authorized to sign checks should have no access to the accounting records. Cash disbursements should be recorded by someone who does not have access to cash. Then, if an error or theft occurs, it will show up in the records immediately. A **voucher system** is an additional safeguard over cash disbursements and requires the approval and recording of all cash disbursements in a voucher register prior to making payments. Vouchers are discussed in the appendix to this chapter.

All cash disbursements should be made by check

The receipt and the disbursement of cash should also be separate functions handled by different persons. Any cash that must be kept on hand, such as change funds for cash registers or petty cash funds, must be under the strict control of an individual who has sole responsibility for safeguarding such funds. Routine cash disbursements, such as periodic payment of payrolls, may be made from demand deposits maintained only for that purpose. Often a single check for the entire payroll is drawn on the company's main bank account and deposited in a special payroll account from which individual payroll checks are paid.

Control procedures can be costly, and the cost must be weighed carefully against the benefits obtained. For example, a small company with only two or three office employees obviously cannot afford the same separation of duties as a company with 200 employees.

Control of EDP Operations

Electronic data processing of accounting information creates the need for control procedures designed specifically to ensure the correctness of computer data and to prevent theft or other abuse of company resources by use of the computer. Separation of duties, assignment of responsibilities, and establishment of specific procedures apply to EDP control. EDP also requires control of data input and the design of program controls.

Control of data input.   Input of data into the computer may be electronic or manual. Electronic input occurs when data are transmitted by one computer to another over telephone lines or by a direct wire hookup, when data are read by the computer directly from forms printed with magnetic ink, or when printed material is read by optical character recognition equipment (OCR) into the computer's core. Computer systems have internal devices such as verification of input by multiple reading designed to prevent input errors.

Most source documents are input manually by means of a keyboard. One way to ensure input accuracy is to have two operators input the same data and have the computer compare the inputs and indicate any discrepancies. Another way to check for human errors is by use of check totals. The total amount in a batch of source documents is calculated prior to sending the data into the computer. The computer calculates the total and compares it with the check total. Any discrepancy indicates the possibility of an input error. The computer program that accepts input data is usually designed to check for input errors as well. For example, the program may accept only numeric information for some data and only alphabetic information for others; it warns the operator if the wrong type of data is input. The program may also accept data only within a certain range of values, such as a maximum and minimum amount for salaries, or a specific number of digits for social security numbers.

Design of program controls.   Computer programs are usually designed to maintain control over information processing. The computer may be instructed to warn computer operators that an item of information being processed may be illogical. Programs may be designed, for example, to question the logic of having an employee whose age is given as 6 or 130; to warn if an account receivable has a balance in excess of a reasonable limit; and to reject instructions to print salary checks in excess of a specified amount. Similar devices check the logic and accuracy of internal computations performed by the computer.

In addition to checking that data are within reasonable limits, computer programs are also designed to perform a count of items that are processed. For example, the count of payroll checks should match the number of employees, and a count of payables input by an operator should match the number of invoices submitted to the operator for processing. Programs may be designed to warn operators during processing and also to print reports on item counts, limits exceeded, and other data for use by managers responsible for ensuring adequate controls. Computer programs can also be designed to keep track of accounting information and to generate reports on items that need attention. For example, if a receivable is past due or exceeds the credit limit allowed to a customer, the computer generates a letter asking the customer for payment.

The information contained in a company's computer, and the programs used to process the information are valuable resources over which careful control must be maintained. Loss of information is prevented by having duplicate sets of data and programs stored in safe locations. Control over access to computer information is achieved by assigning computer accounts to employees, requiring the use of passwords to use the accounts, and by limiting the type of information that account users may access.

SUMMARY

Proper control over working capital accounts, sometimes called **circulating capital,** is important for the smooth operation of a business. Managers must maintain a careful balance among working capital components and must ensure that the amount of working capital increases with increasing business volume.

A **bank reconciliation** is a schedule used to reconcile any difference between the cash records and the **demand deposits** maintained at banks. The bank statement provides information for the bank reconciliation, such as the amount of service charges paid to the bank, and any **NSF** checks returned by the bank because the maker did not have sufficient funds to enable the bank to pay the check. Good cash management requires making virtually all cash payments by check. For small amounts for which writing checks is not practical, a **petty cash fund** may be established.

Idle cash may be invested in marketable securities. **Marketable equity securities** are usually accounted for separately from **marketable debt securities.** Equity securities consist of common and preferred stock. Such investments may provide dividend income to the investor. At the end of the accounting period, the equity **portfolio** is reported at the **lower of cost or market** value in the balance sheet. If the **market value** of the aggregate portfolio is lower than cost, the **unrealized loss** is reported in the income statement, and the market value of the portfolio is reported in the balance sheet. Subsequent increases in market value permit recovery of previous unrealized losses, but such recovery is limited to the balance in the allowance account in which the decline in market value is recorded.

The portfolio of marketable debt securities is usually valued at cost. Debt securities consist of corporate and government bonds, **treasury bills, certificates of deposit**, and other debt instruments, all of which yield interest income to the investor. The price of **discounted securities,** such as treasury bills, increases as they approach maturity, and the difference between the price at one date and the price at a later date constitutes interest income.

Bonds may be bought at a **discount** or at a **premium.** The **current yield** on a bond is the return on investment for a single period. When bonds are purchased between interest payment dates, in addition to the price of the bond, the accrued interest must be paid to the seller.

Notes receivable are **negotiable instruments** and may be converted to cash by discounting them with a bank. The bank calculates the discount on the note's **maturity value** and deducts the amount from the proceeds, which it pays to the seller of the note. The seller is contingently liable to the bank for the note until the note is paid. The **contingent liability** must be disclosed in a footnote to the financial statements.

Notes receivable are usually recorded at face value. However, when they do not bear a reasonable amount of interest, they must be reported at their present value, which is calculated by **imputing** a reasonable interest rate.

When accounts receivable are reported in the balance sheet, a reasonable deduction must be made for the accounts expected to be uncollectible. Estimating **uncollectible accounts** may be done by **aging** the receivables, or by calculating a percentage of receivables or credit sales. When a receivable is found to be uncollectible, it is written off against the **allowance for uncollectible accounts.** This allowance is established at the end of each accounting period when bad debts are estimated. Sometimes a written-off account is subsequently collected. Uncollectible accounts are written off directly to bad debts expense by some businesses, but the direct write-off method does not match revenues and expenses properly.

Receivables may be used to obtain cash by **pledging** them as security for a loan, or they may be **factored** by selling them outright, usually for an amount lower than their face value.

Control of cash and other current assets is accomplished by separating the duties of employees, assigning specific responsibilities, and establishing routines for operating the business. A **voucher system,** discussed in the appendix to this chapter, may be used to obtain a high degree of control over cash. Control procedures required for electronic data processing include verification of data input into the computer, design of computer programs to check on the accuracy and logic of data and computations, and limitations on access to computer information.

KEY TERMS

accounts receivable   *(357)*
aging of receivables   *(358)*
bank reconciliation   *(338)*
budget   *(337)*
cash short or over   *(342)*
certificates of deposit (CD)   *(351)*
circulating capital   *(335)*
contingent liability   *(355)*
current yield   *(348)*
default   *(353)*
demand deposit   *(337)*
discount   *(347)*
discounted security   *(351)*
factor   *(362)*
first in, first out   *(352)*
imputed interest   *(356)*
insolvent   *(336)*
internal control   *(362)*
lower of cost or market
  (LCM)   *(345)*
marketable debt security   *(343)*

marketable equity security   *(343)*
market value   *(343)*
maturity value   *(353)*
negotiable instrument   *(352)*
non-interest-bearing notes   *(355)*
NSF check   *(338)*
petty cash   *(341)*
pledge   *(362)*
portfolio   *(343)*
premium   *(347)*
promissory notes   *(352)*
short-term investments   *(343)*
temporary investments   *(343)*
time deposit   *(337)*
trade accounts   *(357)*
treasury bills   *(351)*
uncollectible accounts   *(358)*
voucher   *(367)*
voucher register   *(369)*
voucher system   *(364)*

APPENDIX: VOUCHER SYSTEM

Good control over cash disbursements can be obtained by use of a **voucher system** which requires the preparation and verification of vouchers for all payments. A **voucher,** as illustrated in Figure 8-5, is a document used for authorizing all cash disbursements. Although the form varies, it usually

Veronica Corporation
Voucher

Voucher no. 4182

Pay to   TRAMMEL CORP.
         1234 FIFTH ST.   Date _____ Oct. 4, 1985 _____
         FOGTOWN, N.D.   Date due Oct. 18, 1985 _____

Date of invoice ___ 10/8/85 ___   Amount $ 3850 _____
Invoice no.   3133 _____   Less discount   77 _____
                                         Net amount   3773 _____

Accounts   **Amount**

Purchases $ 3850 _____
Freight-in   _____
Utilities   _____   **Payment**
Salaries   _____

_____   _____   Check no.   _____
Total credit to   Date   _____
vouchers payable $ 3850 _____   Amount $ _____

Verification and Approval

	Date	**Initials**
Footings and extensions	10/5	SM
Prices	10/9	JP
Quantities	10/9	LH
Accounts	10/8	SM
Payment		

Figure 8-5
A voucher. When payment is made, the remaining blank spaces will be completed.

contains spaces for the date of the voucher, the due date for the cash payment, and the date payment is actually made. Also included is the amount of the payment, the discount available, and the accounts to be debited. The credit is always to vouchers payable. In addition, the voucher contains spaces for several types of verification, including authorization to make the payment.

Operating a voucher system may be thought of as the setting up of an artificial liability by the company to itself. For example, instead of making the entry

Sept. 2	Utilities expense	138	
	Cash		138
	Paid electric company.		

the company makes the following entries for a cash payment:

Sept. 2	Utilities expense	138	
	Vouchers payable		138
	Approved payment of utilities.		
Sept. 6	Vouchers payable	138	
	Cash		138
	Issued check to electric company.		

The September 2 entry is made when the expenditure is authorized, at which time a voucher is prepared and recorded. The second entry is made when the check is prepared to pay for the expenditure.

The **voucher register** is a special journal used for recording all authorized expenditures. Often it replaces the purchases journal. An example of a voucher register is illustrated in Figure 8-6. When all payments are made through the voucher register, the cash disbursements journal contains only three money columns: one for cash (cr), one for cash discounts taken (cr) or cash discounts lost (dr), and one for vouchers payable (dr). The voucher register may have many columns: one for vouchers payable (cr), and one for each expense or other account to be debited when an expenditure takes place. Entries in the voucher register are made as follows:

	Purchase (or Expense)	3,850	
	Vouchers payable (instead of		
	Accounts payable)		3,850

The above entry is, of course, made in the voucher register and not in the general journal. When payment is made, the entry in the cash disburse-

Voucher Register

Voucher No.	Date	Name	Payment Made Check No.	Payment Made Date	Vouchers Payable cr.	Purchases dr.	Utilities dr.	Salaries dr.	Other Accounts Account	Other Accounts Amount dr. (cr.)
4180	10/1	Trammel	630	10/11	1,100	1,100				
4181	10/4	Jones	631	10/4	380				Rent	380
4182	10/4	Trammel			3,850	3,850				
4183	10/7	W.C. Field			18				Supplies	18
4184	10/12	D.C. Electric	632	10/13	195		195			

Figure 8-6   **Example of a voucher register.**

ment journal is as follows:

	Vouchers payable	3,850	
	Cash		3,773
	Discounts taken		77

At the same time, the check number and the date of payment are recorded in the voucher register in the spaces provided, indicating that the voucher has been paid.

Use of the voucher system provides strong control over all purchases and cash payments since considerable verification and authorization can be required in order to process a purchase and its subsequent payment.

QUESTIONS

1. A company sells $20,000 of merchandise each month. Explain why working capital would have to increase if the company's sales increased to $30,000 a month. Discuss the effect of increased sales on various working capital accounts.

2. What steps should a company take when the bank returns a deposited customer's check marked NSF?

3. Explain how a company can use the purchase and sale of temporary investments in its cash planning.

4. If a petty cash fund in the amount of $300 is established, why might the petty cash custodian ask for reimbursement of only $243 at the end of the month?

5. You are examining a corporation's investment portfolio and find that it consists of some common stocks, some short-term treasury bills, and some long-term corporate bonds. On what basis would you decide whether to classify the investments as temporary or long term?

6. By the end of the year, your company's marketable equity securities portfolio has declined in value to $4,500 below cost. How should the decline be reported? What should be reported when the portfolio value rises to $1,400 above cost by the end of the following year?

7. Under what conditions should marketable debt securities be valued below their cost? Why are they treated differently from equity investments?

8. What is a discount on bond investments? How would a bond price be quoted if the bond traded at a discount of $150 below face value?

9. What is a premium on bond investments? How much above face value is a bond trading if it is quoted at a price of 102?

10. When bonds are purchased, the buyer often must pay interest on the bond in addition to the purchase price. Explain the reason for this, and describe how the interest payment is recorded.

11. What is a discounted security? How is interest earned on investments in discounted securities?

12. Is it possible to record interest income when a note receivable with 12 percent interest is discounted with a bank that charges 13 percent interest? Explain.

13. Explain what is meant by "the maturity value of a note."

14. What is a contingent liability? How might it arise in connection with notes receivable?

15. Why is interest imputed on a note that bears no interest? What accounting principles are involved?

16. Discuss what accounting principles and concepts are involved in estimating bad debts and recording an allowance for uncollectible accounts. Why does writing off an uncollectible account not affect owners' equity or working capital?

17. The mail clerk opens the mail, makes a record of the cash received, and then turns this record and the cash over to the accounts receivable bookkeeper. The bookkeeper records customers' payments in their accounts and deposits the cash with the bank. Once a month the bookkeeper prepares a bank reconciliation. Discuss how this company's control procedures might be improved.

EXERCISES

Ex. 8-1   Bank deposit in transit.   The balance in Himrick Company's Cash account is $12,430. The bank statement shows a balance of $14,200 and a service charge of $34. There are 35 checks outstanding, totaling $2,860.

Required: Calculate the amount of deposits in transit.

Ex. 8-2   Reconciling outstanding checks.   "I need this bank reconciliation, but at the moment we don't have our record of checks written. Do as much as you can and plug in the checks outstanding. We'll find out later if the amount is correct." You look at the information and determine the following:

Balance per bank	$42,150
Balance per books	41,700
Deposits in transit	1,730
Bank service charge	45

Required: Calculate the amount of checks outstanding.

Ex. 8-3   Bank reconciliation.   Muriel Cross, owner of the Cross House of Books, received her bank statement for September. Following is information on the statement and on her cash balance as of September 30:

a. The cash balance per books was $10,548, and the balance per bank statement was $9,783.

b. September 30 cash receipts in the amount of $1,329 were not deposited until October 1.

c. The bank statement included a service charge of $42.

d. A customer's check in the amount of $179 was marked NSF and returned by the bank.

e. Checks outstanding were: no. 2234 for $95, no. 2235 for $106, no. 2238 for $470, no. 2239 for $50, and no. 2241 for $64.

Required: Prepare a bank reconciliation as of September 30.

Ex. 8-4   **Petty cash.**   On June 7 Marston Company established a petty cash fund of $100. During the rest of the month, the petty cash custodian recorded the following payments in petty cash vouchers:

COD postage	$ 9.60
Delivery charges for merchandise	42.10
Cab fare and parking fees	23.40
Replacing glass in a broken window	19.00

On June 30, the petty cash fund contained $5.90, and the custodian requested that the fund be replenished.

Required: Prepare the entries in the general journal to establish the petty cash fund and to replenish it at the end of the month.

Ex. 8-5   **Petty cash with discrepancy.**   Blue Bell Company established a petty cash fund of $150 on May 4. The petty cash custodian made a number of payments from the fund, and it contained $26.40 on May 31, at which time she submitted the following vouchers for reimbursement:

Taxi fares and parking fees	$64.50
Lawn mowing and shrub clipping	30.00
Repair front door lock	19.60
Postage due	9.30

Required: Prepare the entries to establish the petty cash fund and to restore it at the end of the month to its original amount.

Ex. 8-6   **Identification of temporary investments.**   Bittner Company has the following stocks in its portfolio of equity securities:

No. of Shares	Company	Date Bought	Purchase Price	Total Cost*
200	General Avionics common	7/5/84	$15	$ 3,050
100	Consolidated Scrap common	3/1/85	82	8,275
600	General Avionics common	4/9/85	20	12,120
400	General Avionics common	6/6/85	22	8,880

* Total cost includes commission.

On September 5, 1985, the company sold 500 shares of its General Avionics common stock at $21 per share, paying a commission of $100.

Required:
a. Assume that 100 shares bought on April 9 and 400 shares bought on June 6 were sold, and record the sale of the stock.
b. Assume that the company does not identify which shares are sold, and record the sale of the stock.

Ex. 8-7 **Marketable equity securities.** Geronika Company had idle funds and decided to invest in marketable equity securities. The following transactions took place:

July   1 Purchased 1,000 shares Bolo Corporation common stock for cash at $40.00 per share and paid a commission of $180.
        31 Received a dividend of $.80 per share on the Bolo stock.
Sept.   3 Sold 600 shares of Bolo common for $42.50 per share and paid a commission of $100.
Dec. 31 At the end of the accounting period, Bolo common stock is trading in the market at $39.50 per share.

Required:
  a. Record the above transactions in the general journal.
  b. Prepare the necessary adjusting entry on December 31.
  c. Show how the marketable securities would be reported in the balance sheet on December 31.

Ex. 8-8 **Valuation of equity securities.** Flapper Company's portfolio of marketable equity securities contains the stocks of two corporations, whose costs and market prices per share were as follows:

	Cost	Market Value Per Share on December 31		
		1985	1986	1987
200 shares Flip Corp.	$2,600	$12.00	$11.50	$16.00
400 shares Flupp Corp.	6,250	15.00	15.75	14.25

Required: Prepare adjusting entries on December 31, 1985, 1986, and 1987.

Ex. 8-9 **Purchase and sale of debt securities.** On March 1, 1985, Moomaw Company bought $10,000 face value of Didrickson Corporation's 5-year 12 percent bonds as a temporary investment. The bonds pay interest on March 1 and September 1. Moomaw Company paid $9,600 for the bonds. On September 1, 1985, Moomaw Company received the semiannual interest payment on the bond investment, and on the same date sold $4,000 of the bonds at 95.

Required: Record the above transactions in the general journal.

Ex. 8-10 **Bond investment with interest accrual.** Martin Company acquired $10,000 face value of 12 percent bonds on March 1, 1985, as a temporary investment. The bonds cost $9,650 and pay interest on March 1 and September 1. The company closes its books on December 31. On March 1, 1986, after the company received the interest on its bond investment, Martin sold $6,000 of the bonds at 98.

Required: Record the bond purchase, collection of interest, interest accrual on December 31, and sale of the bonds.

Ex. 8-11   **Debt investment with accrued interest.**   On March 1 Slusher Company bought $50,000 face value of 15 percent bonds for $52,000 plus accrued interest as a temporary investment. The bonds pay interest on August 1 and February 1. On October 1 the company sold $20,000 face value of these bonds for $19,800 plus accrued interest.

Required: Record the above transactions including interest receipt on August 1 and interest accrual on December 31.

Ex. 8-12   **Discounted debt securities.**   Mattson Company acquired $100,000 face amount of treasury bills on June 10 for $98,500 cash. On June 28 the company sold $40,000 face value of the bills, receiving $39,870. The remaining bills were held until July 25 when they matured.

Required: Journalize the purchase, sale, and maturity of the treasury bills.

Ex. 8-13   **Accounting for notes receivable.**   Hollorim Corporation accepts notes from its customers in exchange for merchandise. On October 1 it received a $3,500, 60-day 12 percent note from Selma Company, and on November 1 it received a $5,000, 90-day 10.5 percent note from Trimble Company. The company closes its books on December 31. Both notes were collected when they matured.

Required: Record receipt of the two notes, their collection, and interest accrual on December 31.

Ex. 8-14   **Defaulted note receivable.**   On August 1, Manola Company received a $4,000, 60-day 9 percent note from Barber Company for merchandise that Barber purchased. Sixty days later Barber had not paid the note. On November 18 Manola Company was notified that Barber Company had been declared bankrupt, and the note could not be collected.

Required: Prepare all journal entries related to the note receivable.

Ex. 8-15   **Discounting a note receivable.**   Barton Company sold merchandise to Morris Company and received a $4,800, 60-day 8 percent note on March 15. Barton needs cash to pay its rent, so on March 30 it discounts the note with its bank. The bank discounts notes using a 12 percent interest rate.

Required:
     a.   Journalize the above transactions for Barton Company.
     b.   Prepare a note for the company's financial statements to report the contingent liability.

Ex. 8-16   **Finding discount rate charged by bank.**   Humler Company received a $6,000, 90-day 10 percent note from a customer. After holding the note for 30 days, the company discounted it and obtained $6,006.50 proceeds from the bank.

Required: Compute the discount rate used by the bank.

Ex. 8-17 **Imputed interest.** Morning Manufacturing Company sold merchandise to Roberts Corporation in exchange for a $14,000, 1-year non-interest-bearing note on March 31, 1985. The normal interest rate for such transactions is 16 percent.

Required:
- **a.** Record receipt of the note with imputed interest.
- **b.** Prepare the necessary adjusting entry on December 31, 1985.
- **c.** Prepare the entry to record the collection of the note on March 31, 1986.

Ex. 8-18 **Imputed interest on low-interest note.** Dr. Smith performed surgery and as payment received a $6,000, 6-month 4 percent note on April 10. The normal rate of interest for such notes is 15 percent.

Required: Record the receipt and collection of the note.

Ex. 8-19 **Uncollectible accounts.** On December 31, 1985, Sam's Sportswear Store had a balance of $27,400 in accounts receivable, and the Allowance for Uncollectible Accounts balance was zero. From past experience Sam estimates that 4 percent of the accounts receivable will not be collected. During 1986 Sam wrote off $986 of accounts that he could not collect. On December 31, 1986, the balance in accounts receivable was $30,700.

Required:
- **a.** Prepare the journal entry to record estimated bad debts on December 31, 1985.
- **b.** Journalize the write-off of defaulted accounts in 1986.
- **c.** Prepare the entry on December 31, 1986, to bring the Allowance for Uncollectible Accounts up to date. (Hint: T accounts may be helpful.)

Ex. 8-20 **Accounting for bad debts.** Malone Company had credit sales of $320,000 in 1985. Its accounts receivable balance on December 31 is $44,500 and the Allowance for Uncollectible Accounts has a debit balance of $200. On January 17, 1986, the company wrote off a $320 account that could not be collected.

Required:
- **a.** Record bad debts expense for 1985 assuming the company estimates bad debts at 1 percent of credit sales.
- **b.** Record bad debts expense for 1985 assuming the company estimates bad debts as 7 percent of ending accounts receivable.
- **c.** Record the January 17 entry.

Ex. 8-21 **Collecting a written-off account.** On September 17, 1985, Goodley Company wrote off a $350 past-due account receivable of a customer who could not be located during the past 8 months. On December 12 the company received a check and the following note from the customer: "Enclosed is a check for $250 in partial payment of my account. I shall send you the remainder next month. This debt was overlooked after my move to Pittsburgh and I apologize for the delay."

Required: Record the September 17 entry to write off the account and the December 12 entry to record its collection.

PROBLEMS

P. 8-1   **Bank reconciliation.**   The following information is available for the preparation of a bank reconciliation for Janet Corporation on May 31.

a.   The bank statement, dated May 28, shows a balance of $15,354.70.

b.   The balance per books of Janet Corporation is $14,364.48.

c.   The bank returned a customer's check for $395.48 which was marked NSF.

d.   Checks outstanding as of May 31 were: no. 578 for $1,509.47; no. 580 for $345.83; no. 581 for $216.50; no. 583 for $1,102.00; and no. 586 for $713.80.

e.   A deposit of $2,487.90 was in transit because it was mailed to the bank on May 30.

f.   When recording a $543.00 cash receipt from a customer, Janet Company's accountant erroneously listed the collection as $534.00.

g.   The bank service charge for May was $23.00.

Required: Prepare a bank reconciliation for Janet Corporation as of May 31.

P. 8-2   **Bank reconciliation.**   The owner of Romar Company has just received the June bank statement shown below.

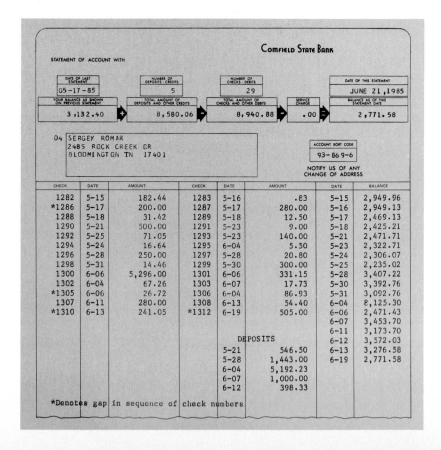

The company's cash account has a balance of $5,520.02 on June 25, and the check register shows 36 checks and 7 deposits. A tick mark next to a check indicates that the check was found in the previous month's bank statement. Following is a summary of data taken from the check register.

Date	Check	Amount	Deposit	Date	Check	Amount	Deposit
5/10	1281	30.18✔		6/01	1299	300.00	5,192.23
5/11	1282	182.44		6/01	1300	5,296.00	
5/11	1283	.83		6/01	1301	331.15	
5/11	1284	448.38✔		6/01	1302	67.26	
5/11	1285	17.08✔		6/01	1303	17.73	
5/14	1286	200.00		6/01	1304	34.42	
5/14	1287	280.00		6/01	1305	26.72	
5/14	1288	31.42		6/05	1306	86.93	1,000.00
5/17	1289	12.50		6/07	1307	280.00	
5/18	1290	500.00	546.50	6/07	1308	54.40	
5/18	1291	9.00		6/08			398.33
5/20	1292	71.05		6/08	1309	17.00	
5/21	1293	140.00		6/08	1310	241.05	
5/22	1294	16.64		6/15	1311	32.09	
5/24	1295	5.50		6/15	1312	505.00	
5/25	1296	250.00		6/18	1313	VOID	
5/25	1297	20.80		6/19	1314	100.00	423.79
5/28	1298	14.46	1,443.00	6/20	1315	5.87	
				6/25	1316	2,015.00	4,494.61

Required: Prepare a bank reconciliation for Romar Company on June 25.

P. 8-3   **Accounting for temporary equity investments.**   On January 1, 1985, the Cor-ind Company held the following common stocks as temporary investments:

Corporation	No. of Shares	Total Cost
A	200	$ 2,000
B	800	19,200
C	500	9,000

The following transactions occurred in 1985:

May 22 Acquired 400 shares of D Corporation common stock at $18 per share plus a commission of $80.

July 10 Received a cash dividend of $.50 per share on C Corporation common stock.

Aug. 9 Sold 500 B Corporation common shares for $22 per share, paying a commission of $190.

Sept. 12 Sold 100 shares D Corp. common at $23 per share less $50 commission.

Dec. 31 The quoted market prices per share were:

Corporation	Price/Share
A	$ 9.00
B	21.00
C	15.25
D	19.50

Required:
   a. Give the appropriate journal entry on each date.
   b. Show how these investments would be reported on the balance sheet of Corind Company on December 31, 1985.

P. 8-4   **Valuation of marketable equity securities.**   Lindsey Company's portfolio of marketable equity securities contains the stocks of three corporations, whose costs and market prices per share were as follows:

	Cost	**Market Value Per Share on December 31**			
		1985	**1986**	**1987**	**1988**
500 shares Slan Corp.	$11,250	$23.00	$23.00	$24.50	$25.00
800 shares Willy Corp.	12,400	15.00	15.00	15.25	15.50
300 shares Coby Corp.	6,400	20.00	21.00	22.00	19.50
Total cost	$30,050				

Required: Prepare adjusting entries, if required, on December 31, 1985, 1986, 1987, and 1988.

P. 8-5   **Accounting for bond investments.**   Melissa Corporation owns $15,000 face value of 12 percent government bonds which it purchased at par and holds as a temporary investment. The bonds pay interest on June 30 and December 31. The company's cash needs fluctuate and it plans its temporary investments and liquidations to suit its needs. The following transactions occurred during the accounting period which ends on December 31:

   On March 1 the company purchased $20,000 face value of 7.5 percent bonds at 87 plus accrued interest. The bonds pay interest on February 1 and August 1.
   On April 30 the company sold $8,000 face value of its 12 percent bonds at 101 plus accrued interest.
   On September 30 the remaining $7,000 face value of 12 percent bonds were sold at 98.5 plus accrued interest.

Required: Record the above transactions, including semiannual interest collections and year-end interest accrual.

P. 8-6   **Marketable security transactions.**   Harold Corporation's accounting period ends on December 31. The company's portfolio of marketable securities on January 1, 1985, consisted of the following temporary investments recorded at cost:

1. Armand Company 10 percent bonds, $10,000 face value, due March 31, 1986, purchased for $9,900. Interest is payable on June 30 and December 31 of each year.
2. Mason Corporation common stock, 3,000 shares, purchased for $21,000.

The following transactions occurred during 1985:

Jan. 25 Acquired 900 shares of Brightglow Company common stock at $14 per share and paid $90 commission.

Feb. 29 Sold $6,000 face value of Armand bonds at 101 plus accrued interest.

May 31 Bought $40,000 face value of Cubique Corporation 12 percent bonds at 102 plus accrued interest. Interest is payable on Jan. 31 and July 31.

June 30 Received semiannual interest on Armand bonds.

July 15 Received $.50 per share cash dividend on Brightglow common.

July 22 Sold 2,000 shares Mason common at $7.50 per share less $90 commission.

July 31 Received semiannual interest on Cubique bonds.

Sept. 30 Sold $4,000 face value of Armand bonds at 97 plus accrued interest.

Dec. 31 Interest is accrued on Cubique bonds, and the following market prices of securities are obtained:

Armand bonds	98
Cubique bonds	101
Brightglow common	$11.75 per share
Mason common	8.00 per share

Required: Journalize the above transactions in the general journal.

P. 8-7 **Discounting notes receivables.** Kathy's Kitchenware Company sells all its merchandise in exchange for 90-day 10 percent notes. On January 31, 1985, the company received one such note for $10,000 from Mrs. Dukesi. On March 1, 1985, it received a $5,000 note from Mr. Kraus. On March 31, 1985, the company discounted both notes with its bank at a discount rate of 16 percent.

Required: Prepare a separate journal entry to record the discounting of each note on March 31.

P. 8-8 **Discounting notes receivable.** The Notes Receivable account of Montini Corporation includes a $10,000, 90-day 11 percent note dated June 1, 1985, and a $7,000, 60-day 9 percent note dated July 31, 1985. On July 1, 1985, Montini Corporation discounted the $10,000 note with its bank at 12 percent interest. On August 15 the company discounted the $7,000 note with the same bank.

On September 1, 1985, the bank notified Montini Corporation that the $10,000 note was not paid, and payment was requested from Montini. Montini Corporation issued a check to the bank in exchange for the defaulted note. On September 30, Montini Corporation collected the defaulted note in full, including 11 percent interest from the date of default.

Required: Record the above transactions in the general journal.

P. 8-9 **Understanding imputed interest.** Reliable Industrial Equipment Company sells new and used machinery. Typically, its merchandise is priced to yield a 40 percent gross margin, but the price on used equipment is usually negotiable. Company policy is not to accept less than a 30 percent gross margin, because below that level operations become unprofitable. A used digital drill press which cost $8,400 is priced at $14,000, and Mr. Marich, who just opened a small machine shop, has offered to buy the press in exchange for a 1-year $13,400 non-interest note. The manager of Reliable thinks the note is probably not enough to meet the minimum margin requirement, but he wants to sell the drill press to Marich in order to gain a satisfied customer for future sales. He decides that if the note does not have a large enough present value, he will ask Marich to add enough interest to make it acceptable. The company normally discounts notes at 15 percent interest.

Required:

    a. Compute the present value of the non-interest note and decide whether it should be accepted.

    b. Find the interest rate, rounded to the nearest whole percentage, that would have to be added to the note to make it acceptable.

P. 8-10   **Accounts receivable transactions.** Jason Company sells merchandise on terms 2/10, n/30 and records sales and receivables at gross. Account balances on June 1 were $6,400 debit in Accounts Receivable and $710 credit in Allowance for Uncollectible Accounts. Following are transactions for the month of June:

June 3 Collected $3,800 of receivables within the discount period.

      5 Sold merchandise for $1,200 on account to Barris Company.

      6 Sold merchandise for $1,950 on account to Farrel Corporation.

    10 Received payment from Barris Company.

    16 Sold merchandise for $2,200 on account to Jamison Company.

    18 A customer who made a $2,000 purchase on May 19 could not pay his account and offered a $2,000, 90-day 12 percent note in exchange. The company accepted the note and credited the account.

    21 A $600 account is determined to be uncollectible and is written off.

    23 Received payment in full from Farrel Corporation.

    25 Received payment from Jamison Company.

    26 An account of $250, written off last March, was collected.

    27 Several credit sales were made for a total of $6,500.

    30 The allowance for uncollectible accounts was increased to $800.

Required: Record the above transactions in the general journal.

P. 8-11   **Aging accounts receivable.** Boatler Corporation sells merchandise on terms n/30. Its accounts receivable consist of the following accounts on July 31:

Customer	Date of Purchase	Amount	Customer	Date of Purchase	Amount
Abbot	Jan. 5	$680	Elmire	June 12	$450
Bitner	Mar. 2	590	Feidaux	June 21	290
Calgore	Mar. 16	220	Calgore	July 9	180
Drapper	Apr. 13	340	Abbot	July 17	100
Abbot	Apr. 28	285	Elmire	July 21	230
Drapper	May 18	400	Drapper	July 28	205
Bitner	June 6	290			

The company estimates bad debts by aging receivables according to the following schedule:

Account Status	Percent Estimated Uncollectible
Current	1%
1–60 days past due	3%
61–90 days past due	5%
Over 90 days past due	10%

Required:
    a. Prepare an aging schedule similar to the one illustrated in the chapter, and calculate the required balance for Allowance for Uncollectible Accounts on July 31.
    b. Assume that Allowance for Uncollectible Accounts has a debit balance of $15.70 prior to the adjustment, and prepare the entry to record bad debts expense on July 31.

P. 8-12 **Adjusting current accounts.** Following are some of the account balances found in the trial balance of Milton Corporation on December 31, 1985:

Account	Debit	Credit
Cash	$30,000	
Temporary Investments	60,000	
Accounts Receivable	86,350	
Allowance for Doubtful Accounts		$1,606
Notes Receivable	20,000	
Merchandise	97,480	

You are conducting the company's internal audit of current assets. In your examination of the above accounts, you discover the following:

a. Cash includes a check in the amount of $300 received from a customer and returned by the bank, marked NSF. Also included in Cash is a demand deposit of $27,680 and currency of $1,900.

b. Included in Temporary Investments is a $1,000, 90-day 12 percent note receivable given by the company president for a loan he received from the company. The note is dated December 1, 1985.

c. Accounts Receivable includes a $950 account that is 8 months past due and should be written off because the customer is bankrupt. The company normally estimates that 4 percent of the ending balance of Accounts Receivable will be uncollectible.

d. Interest on notes receivable has been properly accrued except for the president's note found in the investment account.

Required: Prepare the necessary adjusting entries to bring the current asset accounts to their proper balances.

*P. 8-13 **Voucher register.** Bellini Company maintains a voucher system to control expenditures. Checks are issued only for payments approved by vouchers. The company uses a periodic inventory system. The last voucher recorded in February was no. 411. Following are selected transactions for March:

Mar. 6 Approved payment of utility bill for $384.
      9 Purchased merchandise from Torro Company for $7,200, terms n/30.
    11 Approved payment of parking lot paving repairs to Greene Asphalt Company in the amount of $1,750.

* Problems marked with an asterisk are based on materials in the appendix to the chapter.

15 Issued check no. 321 for semimonthly payroll in the amount of $12,400.
18 Issued check no. 322 for the March 9 purchase.
20 Purchased merchandise from Sable, Inc., for $2,300 on terms n/30.
22 Paid for utilities with check no. 323.
30 Issued check no. 324 to Greene Asphalt Company.
31 Approved payment of telephone bill for $165.

Required:
a. Establish a voucher register, similar to Figure 8-6, with debit columns for purchases, repairs, utilities, and wages, and a two-column cash disbursement journal with a cash credit and a vouchers payable debit column.
b. Record the above transactions in the two special journals, total the journals, and verify the equality of debits and credits in each.

Case 8-1 Operations with current accounts.

Compusoft, Inc., provides software development services. It employs several programmers and buys computer time from a computer service company. Computer time is billed monthly and is payable in 30 days. The company bills its clients on terms n/30 whenever a job is completed. To minimize its investment in unproductive assets, Compusoft tries to maintain a relatively small cash balance and invests its excess cash in marketable securities. A portion of the company's trial balance at the end of May is shown below:

Partial Trial Balance
May 31

	Debits	Credits
Cash	6,972	
Temporary investment in debt securities	19,910	
Accounts receivable	67,200	
Allowance for doubtful accounts		750
Notes receivable	16,000	
Accounts payable		23,500

The accounts receivable subsidiary ledger contains the following unpaid balances on May 31, including the billing dates and amounts of outstanding accounts:

Algeryafi Corporation

April 14	4,800
May 24	3,100
Balance	7,900

Dedbete Company

Feb. 25	340
March 9	660
Balance	1,000

Leyter Company

March 28	4,200

Izzo & Sons

March 16	6,000
May 19	8,600
Balance	14,600

Uther Enterprises

March 21	13,000
April 11	5,200
May 5	7,900
Balance	26,100

Mavis Company

May 17	13,400

During June the following events occurred:

June 1 The company called Leyter's manager and asked for payment on its past due account. The manager stated that a cash shortage prevented payment just then, but he offered to give Compusoft a $4,346 6-month non-interest note in exchange for the account. Leyter has been a good customer, so Compusoft accepted the offer, imputed interest on the note at 12 percent, and wrote off the difference between the present value of the note and the receivable against the Allowance for Doubtful Accounts.

June 5 After numerous attempts to collect the account of Dedbete Company, Compusoft finally decided that collection is not possible and wrote off the account against the Allowance for Doubtful Accounts. Several days later, Mr. Geddem, who operates a collection agency, approached the company and offered its services to Compusoft. The manager of Compusoft agreed to let Geddem try to collect the Dedbete account for a fee of 25 percent of all amounts collected.

June 11 The company's temporary investments consist of a $20,000 face value treasury bill which matured today.

June 15 The company's notes receivable consist of a $16,000, 90-day 9 percent note obtained from a customer on May 30. The manager decided to sell the note and invest in marketable securities with a higher yield. The note was therefore discounted with the company's bank which charges a 12 percent discount rate. The company then bought $30,000 face value of 14 percent bonds at 96 plus accrued interest and paid a commission of $200. The bonds pay interest on March 15 and September 15.

June 16 The remainder of the excess cash was invested on this date in 1,000 shares of Upmobile Corporation common stock which was purchased in the market at $9 per share plus a $300 commission.

June 22 The company received a check for $750 from Geddem Collection Agency, which had succeeded in collecting the Dedbete account in full. Compusoft therefore restored the account receivable and recorded its collection, including a debit of $250 to collection expense.

June 27 The company billed its clients for services performed in June: Algeryafi, $11,500; Izzo & Sons, $9,450; and Uther Enterprises, $17,700.

June 28 Cash collections of open accounts during June were as follows: Izzo & Sons, $6,000; Mavis Company, $13,400; and Uther Enterprises, $13,000.

June 29 In order to meet its payroll and pay accounts payable, the company sold 600 shares of its Upmobile common stock at $8 per share, and paid a commission of $160.

June 30 The company paid salaries of $15,400 and accounts payable of $21,600. Adjusting entries are required to record interest income on the non-interest note and bond investments and to adjust the stock investment to lower of cost or market. The market value of Upmobile common is $8.50 per share. The company estimates bad debts by aging accounts receivable. Current accounts result in 1 percent of losses, accounts past due 1 to 30 days result in 2 percent of losses, and accounts past due more than 30 days result in 4 percent of losses. The manager of the company wants a report on the status of current assets at the end of June.

Required:
    a. Journalize the June transactions in the general journal.
    b. Prepare the current asset portion of the company's balance sheet, including the note describing the contingent liability.

Inventory Valuation and Estimation

9

The subject of this chapter is accounting for merchandise inventories. Merchandise often makes up a large part of a company's current assets. We discuss several methods of measuring inventory values, assigning costs to inventories, and estimating the amount of inventory on hand. You should understand Chapter 6 before you start studying Chapter 9 because the topics covered in the two chapters are closely related. When you have completed your study of this chapter, you should have a good understanding of:

1   Who owns inventory while it is in transit.

2   The costs that are included in inventory.

3   Several different methods of inventory valuation, their advantages and disadvantages, and their effects on the balance sheet and the income statement.

4   Reporting of inventories at lower of cost or market value.

5   Inventory estimation when a physical count is not taken.

6   The effect of inventory errors on the income statement and balance sheet.

Merchandise is a large part of the working capital of many businesses, and it often poses significant measurement and valuation issues. The accounting system must provide the business with appropriate information about the cost of merchandise sold and the cost of merchandise on hand; it must also give managers the ability to control merchandise inventories. Proper control and valuation of inventories are crucial for profitable business operations:

    1. To meet the demands of customers, sufficient inventory must be available.

2. To avoid excessive investment of resources in inventory that may deteriorate or become obsolete.

3. To minimize misuse and theft.

4. To avoid errors in valuation which can seriously affect the financial statements.

We first turn to the issue of determining inventory ownership and which costs should be included in inventory. Next we discuss the valuation of perpetual and periodic inventories to determine what dollar amounts should be reported for goods in the balance sheet and for cost of goods sold in the income statement. We also examine the inventory estimation methods used when a physical count of inventory is not possible. Finally we show how inventory errors can affect the financial statements and the procedures used to find and correct such errors.

TRANSFER OF OWNERSHIP

Transfer of merchandise ownership generally occurs when a sale of goods results in an exchange of goods or money. If the buyer pays for goods to be delivered next week, the sale has taken place, and the goods no longer belong to the seller even though they are in his possession. If the buyer orders goods, and the seller delivers them, the sale has taken place although payment has not yet been made. There is no sale, however, if a customer orders goods to be shipped next week but does not pay for them. Remember that goods belong to the seller until shipment takes place or money is received from the buyer.

The owner has title to goods

Transfer of ownership, or title to the goods, also depends on the terms of shipment. Goods in transit may belong either to the buyer or to the seller. If goods are shipped **f.o.b. shipping point,** they belong to the buyer as soon as they are loaded and are in possession of the common carrier providing the transportation. When the seller has placed the merchandise "free **on board**" the common carrier, the buyer is responsible for the freight and insurance on the goods and assumes the risk of loss.

Terms of shipment determine ownership

If goods are shipped **f.o.b. destination,** they belong to the seller until they are unloaded from the common carrier. The seller assumes the risk of loss and pays for the freight and insurance. A business must maintain its records carefully in order to determine the amount of goods in transit and their ownership and to ensure that all merchandise owned is included in inventory.

Consignments

Merchandise may be shipped without a transfer of title taking place. A business can send merchandise to a dealer who does not buy the merchandise but instead agrees to accept it **on consignment** and sell it if possible. The business that owns the merchandise is called the **consignor.** The dealer who has possession of the goods is the **consignee.** Title to the goods remains with the consignor until the consignee sells them. At that time the consignee must pay the consignor the selling price less any commission earned on the sale.

Holders of goods are not always owners

Merchandise on consignment is part of the inventory of the consignor even though it is not on hand. The consignee is responsible for safeguarding the merchandise and must return the unsold portion. At the end of an accounting period, merchandise on consignment must be included in the ending inventory of the consignor. On the other hand, a consignee must take care not to include in ending inventory merchandise held on consignment. Art studios and antique dealers often operate on consignment. An art studio may display artwork belonging to several artists. When a piece is sold, the studio retains a portion of the sales price as a commission and remits the remainder to the artist.

COSTS INCLUDED IN INVENTORY

There is more to inventory cost than the price of the merchandise. Determining the costs that should be included in inventory is the first step in inventory valuation. Such **inventoriable costs** include all costs necessary to make the inventory ready for sale: the purchase price of goods, freight-in, and insurance on the inventory while it is in transit. In addition, the cost of assembly or packaging may be considered inventoriable. Inventoriable costs are **product costs** because they can be associated directly with a product. Such costs become expenses when the product is sold, at which time they are recorded as cost of goods sold.

Distinction between product costs and period costs

Although product costs are clearly inventoriable, there are many product-related costs whose treatment is not so clear. For example, should the salary of the purchasing agent be included as part of inventory cost, or is it an expense of the period in which the salary is earned? Should the cost of inventory storage or insurance be considered a cost of the merchandise? Such indirect costs might seem like product costs, but they are usually treated as **period costs** for convenience. Period costs can be associated with a specific accounting period. They are expenses of that period and are matched with revenues earned in the same period. Period costs do not affect the inventory accounts. Deciding whether a particular cost is an inventoriable product cost or a period cost is often a matter of judgment. Similar costs, however, should always receive the same treatment.

FLOW OF INVENTORY

The physical flow of inventory in and out of the business parallels a similar flow of costs through the accounting records. When a business obtains title to inventory, the cost of the goods must be recorded in the accounting records. When the goods are sold, their cost becomes an expense, and the accounting records must eventually reflect the cost expiration.

Physical Flow of Inventory

The physical flow of business inventories may occur in a variety of ways. Some businesses find it necessary to "rotate" their stock of inventory so that fresh goods are always available. For example, in a paint store, the oldest cans of paint are placed at the front of the shelves so that they sell first and thus do not spoil or deteriorate with age. The usual rule for moving inventory is first in, first out. Some inventories, however, follow a last in, first out pattern. For example, if coal is stored in a pile, the inventory removed from the pile is the latest inventory purchased because coal obtained earlier is at the bottom of the pile.

Cost-Flow Assumptions

The physical movement of inventory usually does not concern the accountant. The flow of inventory **costs**, however, is of considerable interest. Inventory cost flows directly affect the value of ending inventory and the amount charged to cost of goods sold. Consequently, inventory cost flows affect both the balance sheet and the income statement.

Accounting for inventory cost flows is relatively simple if the purchase price of inventory does not fluctuate. However, it is common for inventory costs to vary, sometimes significantly. The accountant must decide which of the various purchase prices paid for merchandise should be assigned to ending inventory and which should be charged to cost of goods sold. A

FIFO and LIFO are cost-flow assumptions

number of costing alternatives can be used. It is possible to assign the most recent costs to the unsold merchandise on the assumption that **first in, first out (FIFO)** is the appropriate flow of costs. On the other hand it is also possible to assign the most recent costs to cost of goods sold. In this case a **last in, first out (LIFO)** flow of costs occurs in the business.

It is, of course, also possible to make other assumptions about cost flows, and use, for example, average prices. There is no need for the cost flow to follow the physical movement of inventory unless costs are identified with specific inventory items. The decision to use FIFO, LIFO, or an average cost depends on the assumptions made about the flow of costs, and the method chosen should be the one that best satisfies the matching concept.

A particular cost-flow assumption applied to perpetual inventories may give different results when applied to periodic inventories. Perpetual and periodic inventory systems are discussed in Chapter 6 and are used in this chapter to illustrate various cost-flow assumptions.

The effects of various inventory valuation methods are illustrated by Boltek Corporation's inventory for the month of July. The beginning balance consists of 20 units that cost $10.00 per unit. During July the company purchased 80 additional units as follows:

July	1	beginning balance	20 units @ $10.00	$ 200.00
	3	purchase	12 units @ 10.40	124.80
	11	purchase	28 units @ 10.70	299.60
	23	purchase	24 units @ 10.90	261.60
	30	purchase	16 units @ 12.00	192.00
Totals			100 units	$1,078.00

From the 100 units available for sale during the month, the company sold 70 units, leaving an ending inventory of 30 units on hand on July 31. Sales occurred as follows:

July	9 sale	16 units
	19 sale	36 units
	27 sale	18 units
	Total sales	70 units

In order to prepare financial statements, Boltek Corporation must assign a cost to the 30 units in ending inventory. The cost depends on the inventory method used by the company and on the cost-flow assumption adopted. To illustrate valuation concepts, we first discuss periodic inventories.

Valuation of Periodic Inventories

In a **periodic inventory system,** cost of goods sold is calculated at the end of the period by deducting the cost of ending inventory from the total cost of goods available for sale. To obtain the cost of ending inventory, the company must count the goods remaining on hand at the end of the period and assign a cost to each item. The cost to be assigned to the ending inventory depends on the cost-flow assumption adopted.

First in, first out (FIFO).   FIFO is logically appealing as a costing technique because it follows the actual physical movement of many inventory items. If the beginning inventory is $200 and purchases during July total an additional $878, we know that total cost of goods available for sale is $1,078. The physical count of inventory reveals 30 units remaining on hand. Using FIFO valuation, we assume that these 30 units in ending inventory are the latest units purchased. The ending inventory is made up of the last two purchases, as follows:

16 units @ $12.00	$192.00
14 units @ $10.90	152.60
30 units on hand	$344.60

Valuing the 30 remaining units at $344.60 assumes that when sales took place, the earliest units purchased were the first sold. Cost of goods sold can therefore be calculated on this assumption as follows:

July 3 sale of	16 units @ $10.00	$160.00
July 19 sale of 36 units	4 10.00	40.00
	12 10.40	124.80
	20 10.70	214.00
July 27 sale of 18 units	8 10.70	85.60
	10 10.90	109.00
Total sales	70 units	$733.40

We know, however, that cost of goods sold is simply the difference between goods available for sale and ending inventory. Therefore when the ending inventory is known, it is simple to compute cost of goods sold as follows:

Goods available for sale	$1,078.00
Less ending inventory	344.60
Cost of goods sold	$ 733.40

Last in, first out (LIFO).   Using LIFO inventory valuation in a periodic system, we assume that the 30 units remaining on hand were the earliest units purchased. These units consist of the beginning balance and part of the first purchase of the month as follows:

20 units @ $10.00	$200.00
10 units @ $10.40	104.00
30 units on hand	$304.00

Cost of goods sold is calculated by deducting the ending inventory from goods available for sale, as follows:

Goods available for sale	$1,078.00
Less ending inventory	304.00
Cost of goods sold	$ 774.00

Weighted average.   The weighted average cost of the inventory available in July is obtained by dividing the total cost of inventory, including the beginning balance and purchases, by the total units available for sale. In our example the calculation is

$$\frac{\text{Cost of goods available for sale}}{\text{Number of units for sale}} = \frac{\$1,078}{100 \text{ units}} = \$10.78/\text{unit}$$

Average cost falls between FIFO and LIFO

The cost of ending inventory is obtained by assigning the average cost of $10.78 to each unit in ending inventory. With 30 units remaining on hand, the ending inventory is valued at $323.40 (30 × $10.78). The cost of the 70 sold units is $754.60 (70 × $10.78). Note that the average cost of ending inventory and cost of goods sold fall between the value obtained using FIFO and LIFO cost.

Valuation of Perpetual Inventories

In a **perpetual inventory system,** the inventory account contains a current record of all inventory transactions. Each purchase and each sale is recorded in the inventory account as soon as the transactions occur. The inventory account is kept up to date, hence the name perpetual.

As in a periodic system, purchases in a perpetual system are recorded at their invoice cost. Recording sales requires making two entries: one to record the sales revenue, as in the periodic system; and one to transfer the product cost from the inventory account to cost of goods sold. If the purchase price of inventories varies, some cost-flow assumption must be made. Perpetual systems may be maintained using specific identification, FIFO, LIFO, or moving average.

Some types of inventories are suitable for specific identification

Specific identification.   The specific identification method of inventory valuation requires an ability to follow the physical flow of each inventory item and its cost from acquisition through sale. The method is appropriate when each item of inventory can be separately identified and therefore has a cost that applies only to that item. Specific identification is used with unique and costly items such as automobiles, houses, or fine jewelry.

First in, first out (FIFO).   The flow of costs with perpetual FIFO is illustrated in Figure 9-1. Notice that the units remaining in inventory are always assumed to be those purchased most recently. For example, after the July 9 sale of 16 units, the 16 units remaining on hand consist of the most recent 12 units purchased on July 3, and 4 units from the beginning balance. The units removed from inventory are always assigned the oldest costs. Similarly the sale of 36 units on July 19 first exhausts the 4 remaining units from the beginning balance, then the next 12 units purchased, and finally 20 units from the most recent purchase. By the end of the month, you see that ending inventory consists of 30 units with a cost of $344.60. Cost of goods sold of $733.40 can be obtained by adding the total cost column of the sold units.

Perpetual and periodic FIFO yield the same results

If you compare perpetual FIFO with the previous calculation for periodic FIFO, you will note the two are the same. With FIFO valuation, periodic and perpetual systems both give the same ending inventory cost and cost of goods sold.

Last in, first out (LIFO).   With a perpetual LIFO system, when a sale takes place, the cost of the most recent purchase as of the date of sale is transferred from inventory to cost of goods sold. Figure 9-2 illustrates how perpetual LIFO is maintained. The July 9 sale of 16 units comes first from the July 3 purchase of 12 units and then reduces the initial balance by 4, to 16 units. The July 19 sale of 36 units consists of the 28 units purchased on July 11 plus 8 units from the beginning balance. From the original 20 units, the cost of 8 units still remains in inventory at the end of the period. The ending inventory consists of 30 units with a cost of $337.40. Cost of goods sold of $740.60 is obtained by adding the total cost column of the sold units. This figure can be verified by subtracting the ending inventory of $337.40 from the goods available for sale of $1,078.

Boltek Corporation
FIFO Perpetual Inventory Record

Date	Explanation	Purchases			Sales			Balance	
		No. of Units	Unit Cost	Total Cost	No. of Units	Unit Cost	Total Cost	No. of Units	Total Cost
July 1	Balance	20	$10.00	$200.00				20	$200.00
3	Bought 12 units	12	10.40	124.80				32	324.80
9	Sold 16 units				16	$10.00	$160.00	16	164.80
11	Bought 28 units	28	10.70	299.60				44	464.40
19	Sold 36 units				4	10.00	40.00		
					12	10.40	124.80		
					20	10.70	214.00	8	85.60
23	Bought 24 units	24	10.90	261.60				32	347.20
27	Sold 18 units				8	10.70	85.60		
					10	10.90	109.00	14	152.60
30	Bought 16 units	16	12.00	192.00				30	344.60

Figure 9-1   **Inventory valuation assuming first in, first out flow of costs and a perpetual inventory system.**

Perpetual and periodic LIFO usually yield different results

Notice the difference between perpetual LIFO and periodic LIFO. The cost of ending inventory with the periodic LIFO system is $304 because the cost of all units sold is removed from the inventory account at the end of the period, after all purchases of the period are recorded. With the perpetual system, the cost of ending inventory is $337.40, because some of the units on hand are valued at the most recent purchase prices. Perpetual LIFO and periodic LIFO often produce different inventory valuations.

Boltek Corporation
LIFO Perpetual Inventory Record

Date	Explanation	Purchases			Sales			Balance	
		No. of Units	Unit Cost	Total Cost	No. of Units	Unit Cost	Total Cost	No. of Units	Total Cost
July 1	Balance	20	$10.00	$200.00				20	$200.00
3	Bought 12 units	12	10.40	124.80				32	324.80
9	Sold 16 units				12	$10.40	$124.80		
					4	10.00	40.00	16	160.00
11	Bought 28 units	28	10.70	299.60				44	459.60
19	Sold 36 units				28	10.70	299.60		
					8	10.00	80.00	8	80.00
23	Bought 24 units	24	10.90	261.60				32	341.60
27	Sold 18 units				18	10.90	196.20	14	145.40
30	Bought 16 units	16	12.00	192.00				30	337.40

Figure 9-2   **Inventory valuation assuming last in, first out flow of costs and a perpetual inventory system.**

Moving average. To maintain a perpetual inventory using average costs, a company must calculate the average cost for the units on hand each time a purchase occurs. A moving average is calculated by computing a new weighted average of the units on hand after each purchase. The procedure is illustrated in Figure 9-3. For example, the average cost of the units on hand after the July 3 purchase is based on 20 units at $10 each and 12 units at $10.40 each. The average cost is $10.15, calculated by dividing the total cost of $324.80 ($200 + $124.80) by 32 units. The ending inventory of 30 units is valued at $343.20.

Boltek Corporation
Moving Average Perpetual Inventory Record

		Purchases			Sales			Balance		
Date	Explanation	No. of Units	Unit Cost	Total Cost	No. of Units	Unit Cost	Total Cost	No. of Units	Unit Cost	Total Cost
July 1	Balance	20	$10.00	$200.00				20	$10.00	$200.00
3	Bought 12 units	12	10.40	124.80				32	10.15	324.80
9	Sold 16 units				16	$10.15	$162.40	16	10.15	162.40
11	Bought 28 units	28	10.70	299.60				44	10.50	462.00
19	Sold 36 units				36	10.50	378.00	8	10.50	84.00
23	Bought 24 units	24	10.90	261.60				32	10.80	345.60
27	Sold 18 units				18	10.80	194.40	14	10.80	151.20
30	Bought 16 units	16	12.00	192.00				30	11.44	343.20

Calculation of average costs:
July 3 $324.80 / 32 units = $10.15 per unit
July 11 $462.00 / 44 units = $10.50 per unit
July 23 $345.60 / 32 units = $10.80 per unit
July 30 $343.20 / 30 units = $11.44 per unit

Figure 9-3 **Inventory valuation in a perpetual inventory system using moving average costs.**

The units removed from inventory are valued at the weighted average cost at the time of sale. The total amount charged to cost of goods sold is $734.80, obtained from the total column of sold units. If costs increase over time, the moving average cost also increases, but it always lags somewhat behind the current cost of purchases. As with periodic systems, the average cost valuation and cost of goods sold are somewhere between those obtained with FIFO and LIFO valuation.

Summary and Comparison of Inventory Valuation Methods

The six inventory values obtained in the previous example are summarized in Figure 9-4. If total sales are $1,000, gross margin varies from $226 to $266.60, depending on the inventory system and the cost-flow assumption applied in valuing the ending inventory.

Boltek Corporation
Gross Margin Calculations

Periodic Inventory Systems

	FIFO	Weighted Average	LIFO
Sales	$1,000.00	$1,000.00	$1,000.00
Beginning inventory	200.00	200.00	200.00
Purchases	878.00	878.00	878.00
Goods available for sale	1,078.00	1,078.00	1,078.00
Less ending inventory	344.60	323.40	304.00
Cost of goods sold	733.40	754.60	774.00
Gross margin	$ 266.60	$ 245.40	$ 226.00

Perpetual Inventory Systems

	FIFO	Moving Average	LIFO
Sales	$1,000.00	$1,000.00	$1,000.00
Beginning inventory	200.00	200.00	200.00
Purchases	878.00	878.00	878.00
Goods available for sale	1,078.00	1,078.00	1,078.00
Less ending inventory	344.60	343.20	337.40
Cost of goods sold	733.40	734.80	740.60
Gross margin	$ 266.60	$ 265.20	$ 259.40

Figure 9-4
Summary of results of inventory valuation with different cost-flow assumptions. Sales, purchases, and quantities are identical in each example.

It is clear that the selection of an inventory valuation method can have a significant effect on net income. If managers could select an inventory method at will and change methods whenever they wished, they could easily manipulate reported income. For this reason, and to assure comparable financial statements from one period to another, accountants have adopted the **consistency principle.** It requires that any accounting method, once selected, be applied consistently from one accounting period to the next. In addition, the **full disclosure principle** is satisfied by disclosing the method used for valuing inventories in the financial statements, usually by means of footnotes.

The inventory method used should be disclosed

To understand the impact of inventory method on financial statements, you should be aware of the strengths and weaknesses of each inventory valuation method as described below.

Specific identification.   The advantage of specific identification is that it provides good matching of cost of goods sold with sales revenue. The disadvantage is the possibility of income manipulation. Managers may choose the amount of gross profit by deciding which item to deliver when merchandise is sold. Moreover, the method does not lend itself to many different types of products and is generally limited to a few businesses that deal in expensive or unique items.

First in, first out.   By far the most popular method, FIFO has the advantage of being easy to apply. It tends to conform to the physical movement of inventory and results in reporting inventories on the balance sheet at a cost that is close to current market prices. But during periods of rising prices, net income is higher than with other valuation methods because old, lower inventory costs are matched with the latest, high selling prices. When prices are rising, the higher net income results in a higher tax expense.

Use of FIFO may result in reporting inventory profits

FIFO valuation has several disadvantages. Current revenues tend to be matched with old prices and thus imply that the company is able to earn a higher profit than is actually possible with current economic conditions. The higher profits reported by matching current revenues with older costs are known as **inventory profits.** During periods of rising prices, inventory profits make a company seem more profitable than it actually is.

Last in, first out.   As you might expect, the biggest advantage of LIFO is lower tax expense during periods of rising prices. Net income tends to be stated more nearly in current terms because revenues are matched with current rather than old product costs. The lower tax expense results in improved cash flows.

LIFO results in lower taxes if prices are rising

LIFO has some serious disadvantages. If it is used for a number of years while prices are rising, balance sheet inventory values become grossly understated since inventories are reported at costs that existed several years before. If the company has to reduce its inventory below the amount normally on hand, it is selling merchandise that is valued at very old costs. This has happened in the steel industry and in the plywood industry when inventories were depleted by strikes. In such cases high profits result from the artificially low product costs, requiring the payment of high income taxes. In addition, the depleted inventories must be replaced at the latest high prices.

During periods of rising prices, net income is lower with LIFO. Although this results in a tax advantage, reduced earnings per share tend to be viewed unfavorably. The Internal Revenue Code requires that companies choosing LIFO for tax purposes must also use it for external reporting purposes. A company has no choice but to report the lower income if it wants the tax savings offered by LIFO.

Average cost methods.   Inventory valuation at average cost is one of the least popular methods for merchandising companies. However, many public utilities use the method. Average cost methods are the middle ground in terms of the comparative advantages and disadvantages of FIFO and LIFO. Neither net income nor ending inventories are shown at current values.

LOWER OF COST OR MARKET VALUATION (LCM)

Like other assets, inventory normally is reported in the balance sheet at cost. However, under the conservatism principle, it is sometimes necessary to report inventories at amounts lower than cost if a permanent decline in value has occurred. This happens when part of the inventory becomes obsolete, shopworn, or damaged, or if a general price decline occurs. For example, when electronic calculators became popular, mechanical or electric adding machines could only be sold for less than they cost.

The conservatism principle dictates use of LCM

If the market value is lower than cost, inventories should be reported at market value. The problem is that there is no single market price that can be used for valuing inventories. Companies buy merchandise in one market and sell it in another market. Prices in the market in which a company buys merchandise are lower than prices in the market in which it sells. In most cases prices in the buying market are considered the most appropriate for inventory valuation at **lower of cost or market**. If the cost of replacing an inventory item is less than the item's original cost, the replacement cost should be reported as the value of that inventory item. **Replacement cost** is the market price in the company's buying market.

Replacement cost is not always the appropriate market price to use for comparing cost and market values of merchandise. AICPA has rules for deciding whether to use replacement cost, net realizable value, or net realizable value less a normal profit margin as the appropriate market value.

Net realizable value, obtained from the company's selling market, is the selling price less the cost of marketing the product. It is the highest amount that may be used in determining inventory market values because it is the most that can be realized from selling an inventory item. If replacement cost is greater than net realizable value, the latter acts as a ceiling and is the appropriate market price to be compared with cost when choosing the lower of cost or market.

Choosing the appropriate market price for inventory valuation

Net realizable value less a normal profit margin is the lowest amount that may be used to determine market values. If replacement cost is below net realizable value less a normal profit, replacement cost should not be used for determining the market value of inventory, because net realizable value less a normal profit margin is a floor below which inventory should not be valued. There are then three possibilities in choosing an appropriate market price to compare with cost: replacement cost, net realizable value, or net realizable value less a normal profit. Of the three market prices from which to choose, the correct one is always the middle value.

For example, if a company has 1,000 items of inventory which cost $10 each, and there appears to be a loss in the utility of these items, they must be valued at lower of cost or market. To compare the cost with the market value in order to arrive at LCM valuation, consider the following:

Cost	$10
Replacement cost	8
Selling price	12
Marketing expense	3
Normal profit	4

At what amount should the inventory be reported? Before we can compare the cost and market, we need to find the three relevant market values and choose one of them. Replacement cost is given at $8 per unit. Net realizable value is the selling price of $12 less the $3 expense needed to market the product, or $9. Net realizable value of $9 less a normal profit of $4 is $5. Cost must therefore be compared with one of the following market prices:

Replacement cost	$8
Net realizable value	9 (maximum limit)
Net realizable value less normal profit	5 (minimum limit)

Since replacement cost is neither above the maximum nor below the minimum, it is the relevant market price. If replacement cost happened to be $9.50, the relevant market price would be $9. Figure 9-5 illustrates several examples of inventory valuation at lower of cost or market. Note that the middle market value is always used.

Figure 9-5
Examples of lower of cost or market inventory valuation for five products. Boldface figures represent the relevant market price to be compared with cost.

		Market			Lower of Cost or Market (LCM)
Product	Cost	Replacement Cost	Net Realizable Value	Net Realizable Value Less Normal Profit Margin	
A	$12	$ 8	$ 9	$5	$ 8
B	10	9	8	6	8
C	10	11	12	7	10
D	12	8	13	9	9
E	11	13	12	8	11

Recording Declines in Inventory Value

With the market value determined, it is easy to compare with cost. Because the replacement cost of $8 is less than the $10 original cost, the inventory has to be reduced to market value. This is accomplished with the following journal entry:

Dec. 31	Loss from decline in inventory value	2,000.	
	Allowance for decline in inventory		
	value		2,000
	To write down the cost of 1,000 units of		
	merchandise from $10 per unit to $8 per		
	unit.		

Inventory is reduced to market with a contra asset account

Use of lower of cost or market for inventory valuation is an application of the conservatism principle. The decline in inventory value means that the inventory is worth less than its cost, but it also means that it will probably be sold for less. Consequently, failure to write down the inventory that has declined in value overstates assets in the balance sheet and the current period's income and also penalizes the income of a subsequent period when the merchandise is sold at its lower price. To keep from misleading users of financial statements, the decline in inventory values should be reported in the period in which it occurs. The loss is reported in the income statement, and the allowance account is reported in the balance sheet as a contra asset, as follows:

In the Income Statement

Sales	$111,000
Cost of goods sold	63,000
Gross margin	48,000
Less loss from decline in inventory value	2,000
Adjusted gross margin	$ 46,000

In the Balance Sheet

Merchandise inventory, at cost	$10,000
Less allowance for decline in value	2,000
Merchandise inventory, at market	$ 8,000

There are several ways to handle the Allowance for Decline in Inventory Value account when the written-down inventory is sold in a future accounting period. One method is simply to ignore the account until the end of the period and adjust it up or down when the inventory is again valued at lower of cost or market. An upward adjustment is treated as recovery of a previous loss, and a downward adjustment is an additional loss. As was the case with temporary investments, inventories may not be reported above their cost; therefore, a gain in a subsequent period from increases in inventory market values may not exceed the balance in the allowance account.

Application of LCM to Inventories

When more than one type of inventory is to be valued, the accountant must decide whether to apply lower of cost or market to individual items, to different classes of inventories, or to the inventory as a whole. Figure 9-6 illustrates these three ways of applying LCM valuations.

Applying LCM to individual items of inventory results in the most conservative (lowest) inventory valuation. If LCM is applied to groups of items or to the entire inventory, the decline in value of some items may be offset by other items whose market value is above cost, and the valuation that results is closer to actual cost. Accountants must use their judgment in deciding how to apply lower of cost or market in order to obtain the

Application of LCM Valuations

	Cost	Market	Valuation at Lower of Cost or Market		
			Individual Items	Major Classes	Total Inventory
Refrigerators					
Model 22AS	$ 6,400	$ 6,100	$ 6,100		
Model 24AS	10,500	11,000	10,500		
Model 24AR	8,100	6,900	6,900		
Totals	25,000	24,000		$24,000	
Stoves					
Model 311T	5,200	5,000	5,000		
Model 311N	7,300	7,200	7,200		
Model 314N	9,000	9,400	9,000		
Totals	21,500	21,600		21,500	
Total Inventory	$46,500	$45,600	$44,700	$45,500	$45,600

Figure 9-6   **Lower of cost or market applied to individual inventory items, classes of inventory, and the entire inventory.**

most appropriate valuation and measure of income. Whichever method is selected should, of course, be used in accordance with the consistency principle.

INVENTORY ESTIMATION

Physical counts of inventory are time-consuming and expensive. Consequently, inventories are usually counted only once a year. To prepare interim financial statements, it is necessary to estimate the amount of inventory in order to arrive at interim net income. In addition, inventory estimation may be required if merchandise has been stolen, destroyed by fire, or otherwise lost, since physical counts are impossible when these events occur.

Gross Margin Method of Estimation

Past gross margin may be used to estimate inventory cost

Gross margin divided by sales revenue is called **gross margin ratio,** or **gross margin percentage.** It represents the percentage of selling price that is available to the business for operating expenses and profit. A company whose gross margin ratio is consistent from period to period can use it to arrive at fairly accurate estimates of inventory. For example, Sarnel Corporation's gross margin for the year 1985 is shown below.

Sales		$200,000	100%
Beginning inventory	$ 30,000		
Purchases	130,000		
Goods available for sale	160,000		
Less ending inventory	32,000		
Cost of goods sold		128,000	64%
Gross margin		$ 72,000	36%

$$\text{Gross margin ratio} = \frac{\text{Gross margin}}{\text{Sales}} = \frac{\$72,000}{\$200,000} = .36$$

With a gross margin ratio of 36 percent, the cost of goods sold is 64 percent of sales. If these relationships persist from period to period, the company may use them to estimate ending inventory. For example, on June 30, 1986, Sarnel Corporation prepares interim financial statements without taking a physical count of inventory. The gross margin calculation is as follows:

Sales		$120,000	100%
Beginning inventory	$ 32,000		
Purchases	70,000		
Goods available for sale	102,000		
Less ending inventory	?		
Cost of goods sold ($120,000 × 64%)		76,800	64%
Gross margin ($120,000 × 36%)		$ 43,200	36%

Gross margin and cost of goods sold are estimated on the basis of relationships existing in previous periods. It is now a simple matter to obtain an estimate of ending inventory by deducting the cost of goods sold from the goods available for sale. The ending inventory for the quarter is estimated as follows:

Goods available for sale	$102,000
Less estimated cost of goods sold	76,800
Estimated ending inventory	$ 25,200

The gross margin method of estimating ending inventory may be used when merchandise has been destroyed and an insurance claim is to be filed. Auditors may use the method to ensure that the physical count of inventory is reasonable. If different gross margin rates apply to different classes of merchandise, a separate calculation should be made for each class in order to arrive at the most accurate estimates.

Retail Inventory Method

Companies that sell merchandise at retail usually have all inventory items marked at the retail selling price. When a physical count of inventory is taken, it is much simpler to find the inventory value at retail than to determine the cost of each item counted. The **retail inventory method** is a procedure used to convert the retail value of inventory to cost so that the inventory can be reported in the balance sheet. In addition, the retail inventory method is also used to estimate the amount of inventory at retail and at cost when a physical count of inventory is not taken.

To use the retail inventory method, companies must maintain records of purchases at cost and at retail value. The relationship between the cost and retail value of the beginning inventory and purchases is used to calculate the cost of ending inventory. The procedure is:

Steps in the retail inventory method

1. Find goods available for sale at cost and at retail value.
2. Calculate the ratio of cost to retail value.
3. Find the ending inventory at retail.
4. Multiply the ending inventory at retail by the cost to retail ratio.

To illustrate the above steps, we use the following example of a company whose cost and retail inventory data are given below:

	Cost	Retail
Beginning inventory	$ 21,550	$ 35,000
Purchases	181,370	321,000
Sales		316,000

The calculation to obtain an estimate of the ending inventory at retail and to convert it to cost is as follows:

Retail Inventory Calculation		
	Cost	**Retail**
Beginning inventory	$ 21,550	$ 35,000
Purchases	181,370	321,000
Goods available for sale	202,920	356,000
Cost to retail ratio, $202,920/$356,000	57%	
Less sales		316,000
Ending inventory at retail		$ 40,000
Ending inventory at cost, $40,000 × .57	$ 22,800	

The cost of goods available for sale, $202,920, is divided by the retail value of goods available for sale, $356,000, to find the cost to retail ratio, which is nothing more than 1 minus the gross margin percentage for the current period. Note that the retail inventory method depends on the current gross margin percentage, whereas the gross margin method of inventory estimation depends on the gross margin percentage of previous periods. In our example the cost to retail ratio is .57, which means that 57 percent of the retail value of inventory is the cost of the inventory.

If a physical count of inventory is taken at retail, the figure obtained is multiplied by the cost-to-retail ratio to obtain the cost of the inventory. An estimate of ending inventory may also be made, however, to verify the physical count and to determine any discrepancies between the amount of merchandise on hand and the amount that should be on hand based on the estimate.

If a physical count is not taken, the retail value of ending inventory is estimated using the goods available for sale and the sales figures. Sales for the period are deducted from the retail value of goods available for sale. This leaves the retail value of the unsold inventory. The ending inventory at retail is multiplied by the cost to retail ratio to arrive at ending inventory at cost. In our example the ending inventory is estimated at a retail value of $40,000, which is converted to a cost of $22,800 ($40,000 × .57).

Maintaining inventory records at both cost and retail may be complicated since retail prices sometimes change frequently. For example, a company may reduce prices for a sale, or it may increase prices when it finds replacement costs increasing. When retail price changes take place during an accounting period, the retail inventory method of estimation is somewhat more complicated than illustrated here.

A physical count of inventory is needed for the annual report

Typically an auditor will not certify financial statements unless a physical count of inventory is taken. If a count is taken at retail, the cost of inventory obtained by the retail inventory method will be accepted by the auditor as a verifiable estimate. On the other hand, inventory cost obtained by the gross margin method is not acceptable for certified financial statements because a physical count is usually not taken and, even if taken, the cost to retail ratio is calculated on the basis of past periods rather than current-period gross margin percentage.

EFFECT OF INVENTORY ERRORS

Our discussion of inventory valuation and estimation indicates some of the complexities of accounting for merchandise inventories. With the large volume of inventory that many businesses handle and the difficulty of accounting for and controlling these assets, inventory errors can occur easily. Errors can be made during the physical count, in determining the timing of ownership transfer, and in the costing of merchandise, as well as at other times.

Inventory errors distort income and financial position

Misstatements of inventories can have a serious effect on income. If the ending inventory is overstated, cost of goods sold is understated, and net income is therefore overstated. The opposite is true if ending inventory is understated. Since ending inventory of one period is the beginning inventory of the next period, errors in inventory valuation affect income of at least two consecutive periods. The accountant must pay particular attention to the physical count of inventory, cutoff dates for purchases and sales of merchandise, and valuation of ending inventory to ensure the proper determination of income.

The way an inventory error affects the income statement is illustrated in Figure 9-7, which shows incorrect gross margin calculations in the years 1985 and 1986 that result from a $200 overstatement of the 1985 ending inventory. If the correct figure of $6,000 had been used in the 1985 statement, gross margin would be reported as $11,200 instead of $11,000. Because the incorrect ending inventory in 1985 is used as the beginning inventory in the following year, 1986 gross margin is also incorrect. It should be $12,600 instead of the $12,400 amount reported in the 1985 statement.

Figure 9-7
Gross margin is misstated in two periods because of an error in the ending inventory in one period. The correct gross margin is $11,000 in 1985, and $12,600 in 1986. The incorrect 1985 ending inventory is the 1986 beginning inventory, so an error occurs in both years.

Gross Margin Calculation				
	1985		**1986**	
Sales		$60,000		$71,600
Beginning inventory	$ 5,000		$ 6,200	
Purchases	50,000		60,000	
Goods available for sale	55,000		66,200	
Less ending inventory	6,200*		7,000	
Cost of goods sold		48,800		59,200
Gross margin		$11,200		$12,400

* Based on physical count that was incorrect and resulted in an overstatement of $200 in the 1985 ending inventory.

In the following example, we discuss some common types of inventory errors and their correction. The example is fairly simple, but it provides some idea of the problems posed by inventories.

Illustrative Example

To illustrate the effect of inventory errors on various account balances, let us examine the records of Melissa Company, whose accounting period ends on December 31. At year-end the company is audited, and a staff accountant is assigned to audit inventories. The company uses a perpetual inventory system.

If few accounts are involved, use a vertical worksheet

A physical count of inventory reveals that goods costing $32,400 are on hand on December 31, 1985. This figure and the account balances for merchandise, receivables, payables, sales, and cost of goods sold are entered at the top of the vertical worksheet illustrated in Figure 9-8. An examination and analysis of the underlying records discloses the following:

a. On December 28, 1985, a credit sale of $1,400 was recorded for goods that cost $900. The goods were shipped f.o.b. destination and reached the customer on January 6. The merchandise was not included in the physical count of inventory.

Melissa Company
Worksheet
For the Year Ending December 31, 1985

	Physical Count	Accounts Receivable	Merchandise	Accounts Payable	Sales	Cost of Goods Sold
Beginning balances	$32,400	$30,500	$35,700	($18,400)	($218,000)	$161,000
a. Sale of next period	900	(1,400)	900		1,400	(900)
b. Goods in transit	3,000					
c. Goods held for customer	(200)					
d. Purchase of next period			(600)	600		
e. Unrecorded purchase			100	(100)		
Ending balances	$36,100	$29,100	$36,100	($17,900)	($216,600)	$160,100

Figure 9-8   **Example of a vertical worksheet used for adjusting account balances that are incorrect because of inventory errors. Included is a column for the physical count of inventory.**

Analysis: When goods are shipped f.o.b. destination, the transfer of title occurs when the shipment reaches the customer. The sale of $1,400 should be recorded in the 1986 accounting period, and the goods should be included in the ending inventory at cost because they belong to Melissa Company on December 31. To reverse the sale transaction when a perpetual inventory system is used, the following entries must be made.

a.	Sales	1,400	
	Accounts receivable		1,400
	Merchandise	900	
	Cost of goods sold		900

The above entries are the exact opposite of the entries that were made when the sale was recorded. Because we are using a worksheet, these entries are not made in the books. They are illustrated here only to explain the adjustments that must be entered in the worksheet. The necessary adjustments are made in the books only after the worksheet is completed and all adjustment data are available. In addition to adjusting the account balances, we must increase the physical count in the worksheet by $900. The adjustments are coded with the letter **a** in Figure 9-8.

b. A credit purchase of $3,000 was recorded on December 27 when the invoice was received. The supplier shipped the goods f.o.b. shipping point. Because the merchandise did not arrive by December 31, it was not included in the physical count of ending inventory.

Analysis: Goods that are shipped f.o.b. shipping point belong to the buyer while they are in transit. The purchase of $3,000 was properly recorded, but the goods are not included in the physical count. In the worksheet, the physical count of inventory is increased, but no other adjustment is made.

c. Goods that were sold in December for cash were included in the physical count of inventory at their cost of $200. The customer had requested that the company hold the merchandise until it could be picked up sometime in January.

Analysis: When the customer paid for goods in cash, an exchange occurred, and title to the goods was transferred. Although the goods have not yet been delivered, they do not belong to the company and should not be included in the physical count of inventory. In the worksheet, the physical count is reduced by the cost of $200, but no other adjustment is required since the sale was recorded properly.

d. A purchase of $600 on open account was recorded on December 30 when the invoice was received. The goods were shipped f.o.b. destination by the supplier and were not included in the physical count of inventory since they arrived after December 31.

Analysis: Because of the terms of shipment, the $600 purchase did not occur until 1986. The entry to record the purchase should not have been made, and the merchandise should not be included in the physical count. The physical count is correct with respect to the merchandise in transit, but the entry to record the purchase must be corrected as follows:

d.	Accounts payable	600	
	Merchandise		600

e. The bookkeeper failed to record a November 1985 credit purchase of merchandise in the amount of $100 because the invoice got lost behind a desk. The omission was discovered during the audit when the supplier indicated that the account was past due. The merchandise had been received in early December and was included in the physical count of inventory. A check was sent to the supplier on January 4, 1986.

Analysis: When a purchase is not recorded, merchandise and accounts payable are understated. To record the purchase, we make the following entry in the worksheet:

e.	Merchandise	100	
	Accounts payable		100

Item **e** in the worksheet completes the adjustments, and the new account balances can now be calculated and entered in the worksheet columns. When this has been done, we see that the physical count of inventory is the same as the new balance in the merchandise account, as it should be in a perpetual inventory system. The beginning and ending balances of the accounts are now compared, and an adjusting entry is journalized and posted. This brings the accounts to their proper balances.

Dec. 31	Merchandise	400	
	Accounts payable	500	
	Sales	1,400	
	Accounts receivable		1,400
	Cost of goods sold		900
	To adjust accounts in accordance with		
	worksheet.		

A single adjusting entry can be used to adjust many accounts

The data for this compound adjusting entry are taken directly from the worksheet after all the adjustments have been analyzed. Although using a worksheet is not required, it provides documentation for the audit, and the single journal entry requires less work than making each adjustment separately.

SUMMARY

Merchandise inventories constitute a major portion of many companies' working capital, and good accounting and control procedures must be in effect to avoid inventory losses and to ensure proper inventory valuation. Sales and purchases of merchandise should be recorded when transfer of title takes place. Title is transferred when an exchange takes place, that is, when payment is received or the goods are delivered. Goods may be shipped **f.o.b. destination** or **f.o.b. shipping point.** The former transfers title when the goods reach their destination. The latter transfers title at the time the goods are placed on the common carrier.

Goods on **consignment** belong to the **consignor** but are in the possession of the **consignee,** who is selling the goods without taking title to them. Although goods may be consigned, they must be included in the inventory of the consignor at the end of the accounting period.

Inventoriable costs are the costs necessary to make merchandise saleable. They include the purchase price of merchandise, shipping and insurance costs, and, in some cases, the cost of assembly or packaging. Such costs are considered **product costs,** and they become expenses when the product is sold. Costs such as salaries of employees who order or handle merchandise and other costs associated with the acquisition and sale of merchandise are treated as **period costs,** which become expenses in the period in which they are incurred.

The valuation of inventories and calculation of cost of goods sold depend on the cost-flow assumption used in measuring inventory costs. **First in, first out (FIFO)** valuation assumes that the goods purchased first are sold first, and the ending inventory consists of the goods valued at the most recent prices paid. **Last in, first out (LIFO)** valuation assumes that the goods purchased most recently are sold first, and the ending inventory consists of goods valued at the earliest prices paid. It is also possible to adopt an **average** cost-flow assumption or to value inventories on a **specific identification** basis.

FIFO valuation produces the same results whether perpetual or periodic inventory systems are used. With LIFO valuation, there can be a difference in value between periodic and perpetual systems. During periods of rising prices, LIFO results in a closer match between costs and revenues and produces a lower gross margin than FIFO. On the other hand, balance sheet valuation of inventory is usually out of date. FIFO produces balance sheet valuations that are close to market values, but the method does not produce a good match between current costs and current revenues in the income statement and results in the reporting of **inventory profits.**

To satisfy the principles of **consistency** and **full disclosure,** the inventory valuation method selected by a business should be applied consistently from period to period. In addition, the method used should be disclosed in the financial statements.

When the value of inventories has declined due to obsolescence or market conditions, reporting the costs of inventory in the balance sheet may be inappropriate. Inventories should be reported at **lower of cost or market (LCM),** and any loss incurred should be reported in the period in which the value of inventory declined. When costs and market values are compared, any one of three market values may be appropriate: **replacement cost, net realizable value,** or **net realizable value less a normal profit.** LCM may be applied to inventories as a whole, to different classes of merchandise, or to individual items.

Ending inventory balances may be estimated using the **gross margin method** or the **retail inventory method.** The gross margin method depends on the gross margin percentage of prior periods. The retail inventory method depends on the gross margin percentage of the current period and requires the business to keep track of purchases at both cost and retail. Estimates of inventory costs may be used for interim reporting. For audited financial statements a physical inventory count must be taken. The gross margin method of inventory estimation may not be used for audited statements.

Inventory errors can cause distortions in the balance sheet and income statement. The accountant must examine inventory transactions carefully and must be satisfied with the physical count and valuation of inventories in order to ensure the proper recording of income and correct balance sheet valuation.

KEY TERMS

average cost *(389)*	inventoriable cost *(386)*
consignee *(386)*	inventory profits *(394)*
consignment *(385)*	last in, first out (LIFO) *(387)*
consignor *(386)*	lower of cost or market (LCM) *(395)*
consistency *(393)*	moving average *(392)*
first in, first out (FIFO) *(387)*	net realizable value *(395)*
f.o.b. destination *(385)*	period cost *(386)*
f.o.b. shipping point *(385)*	product cost *(386)*
full disclosure *(393)*	replacement cost *(395)*
gross margin method *(398)*	retail inventory method *(400)*
gross margin percentage *(398)*	specific identification *(390)*
gross margin ratio *(398)*	weighted average *(389)*

QUESTIONS

1. What are inventoriable costs? Give some examples.

2. What is the difference between period costs and product costs? How does each satisfy the matching principle of accounting?

3. Describe how the terms of merchandise shipment affect the timing of ownership transfer.

4. Describe the cost-flow assumptions underlying FIFO and LIFO inventory valuation methods. Is it the intent of these methods to simulate the physical flow of merchandise? Explain.

5. Compare the effect of LIFO and FIFO inventory valuation on the income statement and balance sheet in periods of rising and falling prices.

6. What is the difference between periodic LIFO and perpetual LIFO? Why can they yield different inventory values?

7. The weighted average method of inventory valuation may be used with periodic inventories. With perpetual inventories, the moving average method is used instead. Why?

8. Zitco Corporation has a number of high-priced, identical inventory items acquired at varying prices. The company uses specific identification for recording the sale of these items. What might the company do in order to lower its income tax expense?

9. Describe how the lowest market price (floor) is calculated in arriving at lower of cost or market inventory valuation.

10. What is the highest market value (ceiling) that should be used in valuing inventories at lower of cost or market?

11. Under what conditions will the gross margin method of inventory estimation provide the most reliable results?

12. Marlin Company uses the retail inventory method each quarter without taking a physical count of inventories. At the end of the year, the company again estimates inventories, using the retail inventory method, but it also takes a physical count of inventories. Why should inventories be estimated when a physical count is taken?

13. The ending inventory of Davis Corporation was overstated by $5,000 at the end of 1985. What effect will the error have on the 1985 income statement and balance sheet? What effect will the error have on the 1986 income statement and balance sheet?

EXERCISES

Ex. 9-1 Transfer of title to inventory. Following is a summary of Newton Corporation's merchandise orders shipped and received during July:

Shipments of Merchandise Sold			
Invoice Price	f.o.b. Terms	Date Shipped	Date Delivered
$12,000	Destination	July 2	July 9
16,000	Shipping point	19	22
8,000	Destination	21	23
14,000	Destination	28	Aug. 3
11,000	Shipping point	29	6

Receipts of Merchandise Purchased			
Invoice Cost	f.o.b. Terms	Date Shipped	Date Received
$ 3,000	Destination	June 26	July 2
9,000	Shipping point	30	3
8,000	Destination	July 11	14
7,000	Shipping point	16	19
10,000	Destination	29	Not yet received
6,000	Shipping point	30	Net yet received

Required: Calculate the amount of sales revenue and purchase cost for July.

Ex. 9-2 Transfer of title to merchandise. The following information pertains to the April operations of Globus Company which records all sales and purchases at gross invoice amount:

April 2 Received notification from Acme Company that merchandise shipped f.o.b. destination by Globus on March 28 arrived today. The invoice price was $1,800 with terms n/30.

3 Received merchandise on terms 2/10, n/30. Invoice cost is $2,100. The goods were shipped f.o.b. shipping point on March 26.

4 Received merchandise on terms 3/10, n/60. Invoice cost is $2,500. The goods were shipped f.o.b. destination on March 29.

5 Received notification from Miller Company that merchandise shipped to them on March 30 arrived on April 3 in order. The $4,700 sale to Miller was made on terms 2/10, n/30 and shipped f.o.b. shipping point.

6 Received check of $8,722 from Kyler Company as payment in full for merchandise it received on April 4. The goods had been shipped to Kyler on March 29, f.o.b. destination, terms 2/10, n/30.

12 Merchandise ordered on April 3 arrived accompanied by an invoice for $18,500 with terms 2/15, EOM. The shipment was sent f.o.b. shipping point.

27 Merchandise shipped f.o.b. shipping point during April was billed to customers in the amount of $25,000 with terms 2/10, n/30.

28 Received invoice for goods purchased from Melon Company for $2,200 terms n/30. Goods were shipped this date by Melon, f.o.b. shipping point, and should arrive by May 3.

29 Received invoice for goods purchased from Cramer Corporation for $3,000 with terms 2/10, n/30. The shipment was made by Cramer on this date, f.o.b. destination. Transit time is expected to require 9 days.

30 Shipped goods to Flora Corporation, f.o.b. destination. Invoice cost is $1,200 with terms 2/10, n/30. Transit time is 6 days.

Required: Calculate the amount to be recorded for sales and purchases in April.

Ex. 9-3 **Periodic FIFO, LIFO, and average.** The beginning inventory balance of a certain item on February 1 and the purchases of this item during February were as follows:

Date		No. of Units	Cost Per Unit	Total Cost
Feb. 1	Beginning inventory	45	$1.80	$ 81.00
4	Purchase	60	1.90	114.00
11	Purchase	25	2.00	50.00
17	Purchase	100	2.02	202.00
25	Purchase	50	2.08	104.00

The company uses a periodic inventory system. On February 28 ending inventory consisted of 125 units.

Required: Determine ending inventory and cost of goods sold using:
   a. FIFO inventory valuation.
   b. LIFO inventory valuation.
   c. Weighted average inventory valuation.

Ex. 9-4 **Valuation of perpetual inventory.** The inventory account for quart cans of indoor house paint showed the following at the end of July:

Date		Cans	Cost /Can
July 1	Beginning inventory	70	$3.00
10	Purchase	50	3.05
12	Sale	100	
19	Purchase	90	3.15
27	Sale	50	

Required: Assuming a perpetual inventory system, determine the cost of goods sold and the cost of ending inventory using:
   a. FIFO.
   b. LIFO.

Ex. 9-5 **Inventory valuation with a periodic system.** Cheyenne Company uses a periodic inventory system. It maintained the following record of purchases and sales of the 16.5V dual-phase transformer:

Jan.	1	Beginning inventory	120 @	$18.00	$2,160.00
Mar.	3	Purchases	30	18.50	555.00
May	22	Sold 80 units			
June	1	Purchases	60	19.20	1,152.00
Aug.	8	Sold 90 units			
Oct.	18	Purchases	40	21.00	840.00

Required: Compute the cost of ending inventory and cost of goods sold using:
a. First in, first out.
b. Last in, first out.
c. Weighted average.

Ex. 9-6   **Periodic and perpetual inventory valuation.**   Following is Grinn Company's inventory record of a specific item for March:

March	1	Beginning balance	20 units @ $125	$2,500
	6	Sold 8 units		
	17	Purchases	10 units @ 130	1,300
	27	Sold 6 units		

Required:
a. Assuming that the company maintains a periodic inventory system, calculate the cost of ending inventory and cost of goods sold using FIFO and LIFO.
b. Assuming that the company maintains a perpetual inventory system, calculate the cost of ending inventory and cost of goods sold using FIFO and LIFO.

Ex. 9-7   **Specific identification.**   Modular Furniture Company sells executive chairs which are made to order by a local manufacturer. The company uses a perpetual inventory system with specific identification. On hand are the following inventory items on May 1:

Model No.	No. of Units	Cost Per Unit	Total Cost
K 301	2	$280	$560
L 401	3	320	960
M 501	2	200	400
N 601	1	240	240

The following transactions took place during May:

May 2 Purchased two chairs, model N 601, at $250 each on account.
4 Sold two chairs, model L 401, for $500 cash each.
5 Sold one chair, model K 301, for $480 on account.
9 Purchased three chairs, model M 501, at $190 each on account.
12 Sold one chair, model N 601, purchased on May 2 on account.
16 Purchased two chairs, model K 301, for $285 each on account.
22 Sold one chair, model M 501, for cash, delivering a chair purchased prior to May.
24 Purchased two chairs, model L 401, for $325 each on account.

Required: Calculate the amount of ending inventory on May 31.

Ex. 9-8   **Lower of cost or market valuation.**   Bokke Corporation has the following data on several of its inventory items:

Inventory Item	Units on Hand	Cost	Replacement Cost	Net Realizable Value	Net Realizable Value Less Normal Profit
A	1,000	$ 36	$38	$ 38	$ 30
B	800	64	58	69	62
C	750	9	8	7	5
D	1,200	108	98	120	100
E	1,000	75	76	79	70
F	500	20	20	18	13

Required: Indicate which market price is used for deciding whether each inventory item should be valued at cost or market and show the amount that should be reported for each item on the balance sheet, using item-by-item LCM.

Ex. 9-9   **Gross margin method of inventory estimation.**   Flambis Company recently lost all its inventory in a fire. The following information is available:

Sales	$52,400
Beginning inventory	12,750
Purchases	30,590
Normal gross margin	40%

Required: Use the gross margin method to determine the amount of ending inventory destroyed by fire.

Ex. 9-10   **Inventory estimation with gross margin method.**   Bartok Corporation's gross margin has typically been 42 percent of net sales. Recently a substantial amount of inventory was lost in a flood. The following information was recovered from the company's records:

Gross sales	$168,600
Sales returns and allowances	4,750
Gross purchases	100,550
Purchase returns and allowances	2,167
Beginning inventory	18,450

Required: Estimate the amount of ending inventory using the gross margin method.

Ex. 9-11   **Retail inventory method.**   The following information about inventory is available from the books of Funk Music Company:

	Cost	Retail
Beginning inventory	$ 74,000	$110,000
Purchases	108,000	170,000
Goods available for sale	$182,000	$280,000
Sales for the period		$195,000

Required: Estimate the cost of ending inventory by using the retail inventory method.

Ex. 9-12 **Retail inventory method of loss estimation.** Millikan Company has just completed a physical count of inventory which revealed that goods with a retail value of $101,700 are on hand. Management suspects that some inventory is missing and decides to use the retail inventory method to estimate what the cost of its ending inventory should be based on the following data:

	Cost	Retail
Beginning inventory	$ 48,000	$ 80,000
Purchases	356,150	605,000
Sales for the period		573,000

Required: Estimate the cost of the actual ending inventory and determine the cost of the missing inventory.

Ex. 9-13 **Inventory error.** Milo Company reported the following income during a 4-year period:

	1982	1983	1984	1985
Sales	$220,000	$250,000	$260,000	$240,000
Cost of goods sold	122,000	118,000	118,000	121,000
Gross margin	98,000	132,000	142,000	119,000
Expenses	72,000	85,000	87,000	82,000
Net income	$ 26,000	$ 47,000	$ 55,000	$ 37,000

The company uses a periodic inventory system. The ending inventory in 1982 was understated by $20,000. The ending inventory in 1984 was overstated by $5,000.

Required:
    a. Revise the above statements to reflect the correct amounts.
    b. Explain the effect of the error on total income for the 4 years.

Ex. 9-14 **Effect of inventory errors.** Matilda Company uses a perpetual inventory system. A physical count of inventory at the end of the year indicates that goods costing $48,500 are on hand. During the year-end audit the following items were discovered:

    a. Goods on consignment with another company, costing $1,000, are not included in the physical count.

    b. Goods costing $1,200 are in transit and are not included in the physical count. They were shipped on December 27 f.o.b. shipping point, and the purchase has not been recorded.

    c. Merchandise costing $300, and sold to a customer who paid $500 cash on December 28, has not yet been shipped and is included in the physical count of inventory. The sale was recorded at the time of cash receipt but the Merchandise account was not reduced at the time of sale.

Required:
    a. Compute the corrected ending inventory balance.
    b. Prepare the necessary adjusting entry in the general journal assuming that the books have not been closed.
    c. Discuss what the effect would be on net income of the year if none of the corrections were made.

Ex. 9-15   **(AICPA) Average inventory valuation.**   The following information was obtained from the inventory records of the Alexander Company for January:

	Units	Unit Cost	Total Cost
Balance at January 1	2,000	$ 9.775	$19,550
Purchases			
January 6	1,500	10.300	15,450
January 16	3,400	10.750	36,550
Sales			
January 7	(1,800)		
January 31	(3,200)		
Balance at January 31	1,900		

Required: Assuming that Alexander maintains perpetual inventory records, what is the inventory at January 31, using the moving average inventory method, rounded to the nearest dollar?

a. $19,523   **b.** $19,702   **c.** $19,950   **d.** $19,998

Assuming that Alexander does *not* maintain perpetual inventory records, what is the inventory at January 31, using the weighted average inventory method, rounded to the nearest dollar?

a. $19,523   **b.** $19,702   **c.** $19,950   **d.** $19,998

PROBLEMS

P. 9-1   **Perpetual inventory system.**   Mooglie Company sells musical instruments. Following is the company's record on the purchases and sales of one type of electronic synthesizer. The company maintains a perpetual inventory system.

April	1	Beginning balance	12 @	$3,200	$38,400
	6	Sold 5 units			
	10	Purchases	3	3,450	10,350
	19	Sold 3 units			
	23	Purchases	6	3,500	21,000
	24	Sold 4 units			
	27	Sold 5 units			
	30	Purchases	4	3,540	14,160

Required: Compute the cost of ending inventory and cost of goods sold for April to the nearest cent, using
    a.   FIFO.
    b.   LIFO.
    c.   Moving average.

P. 9-2   **Periodic inventory system.**   Maryjane Weed Farms, Inc. uses a periodic inventory system to account for its inventory of liquid fertilizer. At the beginning of planting season the farm had 16,000 gallons of fertilizer on hand which cost $13,760. Purchases and use of the fertilizer during the next 5 months were as follows:

March	used 10,000 gallons	purchased 23,000 @ $.84/gal.
April	used 17,000 gallons	purchased 11,000 @ .88/gal.
May	used 14,000 gallons	purchased 13,000 @ .90/gal.
June	used 12,000 gallons	purchased 10,000 @ .93/gal.
July	used 13,000 gallons	purchased 12,000 @ .92/gal.

Required: Calculate the cost of inventory used and the cost of ending inventory using

   a. FIFO.
   b. LIFO.
   c. Weighted average.

P. 9-3 **Perpetual and periodic inventory valuation.** Formitite Corporation has developed a process for irradiatng a special alloy used in the manufacture of spacecraft components. It buys the alloy, treats it with its process, and sells it to other manufacturers. Following is a record of the number of grams of alloy purchased and treated during July:

Date		Grams	Unit Cost
July 1	Beginning bal.	450	@ $ 90
6	Sold	220	
13	Purchased	200	94
16	Purchased	300	95
19	Sold	400	
25	Purchased	350	98
30	Sold	380	
31	Purchased	200	100

Required:

   a. Assuming the company uses a perpetual inventory system, prepare a schedule showing the valuation of inventory and calculate ending inventory and cost of goods sold using FIFO and LIFO.

   b. Assuming the company uses a periodic inventory system, prepare a schedule showing the valuation of inventory and calculate ending inventory and cost of goods sold using FIFO and LIFO.

P. 9-4 **Inventory valuation at LCM.** Renovex, Inc., values its inventory at the lower of cost or market. The following information is available as of December 31:

Product	No. of Units	Cost Per Unit	Replacement Cost	Net Realizable Value	Net Realizable Value Less Normal Profit
W	350	$3.00	$3.10	$3.15	$2.95
X	250	2.08	2.00	2.05	1.90
Y	600	1.50	1.40	1.52	1.45
Z	700	1.80	1.85	1.75	1.68

Required:

   a. Determine the amount to be used to value each product in inventory.

    b. Calculate lower of cost or market valuation for the total inventory on an item-by-item basis and for the inventory as a whole.

    c. Show how the inventory section of the balance sheet should be reported on December 31, assuming LCM applied to the inventory as a whole.

P. 9-5 **Lower of cost or market valuation.** The International Readers Company wants to determine the value of its inventory by taking a sample from each category of books that it carries. Following are results of its tests:

	Reference	Fiction	Texts	Foreign
Average cost per unit	$43	$ 9	$20	$18
Average replacement cost	45	8	16	15
Average selling price	60	10	18	20
Expected marketing expense	5	1	3	1
Normal profit	12	5	5	3
Units in inventory	500	3,000	1,000	5,000

Required:

    a. Set up a schedule similar to the one in Figure 9-6, and using lower of cost or market, calculate the value of inventory for each category of books and for the inventory as a whole.

    b. Prepare the necessary adjusting entry to record the decline in the market value of inventory, assuming valuation of separate categories.

9-6 **Gross margin inventory method.** In December 1985, the inventory of Rickel Company was destroyed by a tornado. The following information is available from the records that could be salvaged:

	1984	1985
Sales	$100,000	$125,000
Cost of goods sold	64,000	
Gross margin	36,000	
Expenses	20,000	28,000
Net income	$ 16,000	
Ending inventory	$ 29,000	
Purchases during the year	70,000	83,000

Required: Using the gross margin method, estimate the ending inventory, and prepare the income statement for 1985.

P. 9-7 **Gross margin inventory estimation.** Double-Q Company carries two types of inventories. Hard goods have a gross margin of 35 percent and soft goods have a gross margin of 45 percent. After a burglary in which a substantial amount of merchandise was stolen, the bookkeeper prepared the following estimate of ending inventory:

Double-Q Company
Estimate of Ending Inventory
May 20, 1985

Beginning inventory		$ 30,000
Add purchases		130,000
Goods available for sale		160,000
Sales	$200,000	
Average gross margin (.40 of sales)	80,000	
Average cost of goods sold (.60 of sales)		120,000
Estimated total ending inventory		40,000
Ending inventory on hand:		
Soft goods	10,500	
Hard goods	10,000	20,500
Due from insurance company		$ 19,500

In order to substantiate the insurance claim, the insurance company obtained the following additional information:

a. Soft goods represented one-third of beginning inventory
b. Purchases for the year were 40 percent soft goods
c. Sales were 35 percent soft goods and 65 percent hard goods

Required: Use the above information to obtain a correct estimate of the two types of ending inventories and determine how much the insurance company should pay for the loss.

P. 9-8   **Gross margin inventory estimation.**   The downtown store of Klausen Gem Company was broken into during the night of June 24, and many gemstones were stolen. The company collected the following data to determine the amount of the loss for income tax purposes.

	Total	Precious Stones	Semiprecious Stones
Beginning inventory	$ 60,000	65%	35%
Purchases	195,000	60	40
Sales through June 24	228,000	43	57
Gross margin		50	40
Cost of remaining gems		$7,280	$16,500

Required: Use the data provided to estimate the ending inventory of precious and semiprecious stones and determine the loss to be claimed on the company's income tax return.

P. 9-9   **Retail inventory method.**   Cardin's Patterns is a yard-goods store which uses the retail inventory method. The company prepares quarterly income statements without taking a physical count of inventory. The following information is available on September 30, 1985:

	Cost	Retail
Inventory, July 1, 1985	$360,000	$ 629,600
Purchases for the quarter	959,600	1,820,400
Freight-in	3,400	
Sales for the quarter		1,675,000

Required:
    a. Estimate the September 30, 1985, ending inventory balance.
    b. Prepare the gross margin section of the income statement for the quarter.

P. 9-10 Retail inventory method. Melmir Company, which uses the retail inventory method, collected the following data on December 31, 1985:

	Cost	Retail
Beginning inventory	$154,200	$ 223,600
Purchases	830,000	1,196,400
Freight-in	9,800	
Ending inventory physical count		246,400

Required:
    a. Estimate the cost of the ending inventory using the retail inventory method.
    b. Estimate the company's sales for the period.
    c. What can you conclude if actual sales for the period are $1,164,000?

P. 9-11 Inventory errors. Falaron Company uses a periodic inventory system. Following are account balances for selected accounts on December 31, 1985:

	Debit	Credit
Sales		$55,000
Purchases	$35,000	
Operating expenses	12,000	
Beginning inventory	3,000	

To prepare for the year-end audit, the company takes a physical count of inventory, which reveals goods on hand costing $4,000. The audit discloses the following:

    a. The ending inventory includes $300 of merchandise that had been sold for cash on December 27. The sale was recorded, but the goods were on hand because the customer wanted to pick them up on January 3, 1986.

    b. Merchandise costing $200 was sold and shipped f.o.b. destination and was still in transit on January 3, 1986. The sale of this merchandise for $380 on open account was recorded on December 27, and the goods were not included in the physical count because they were not on hand.

    c. A merchandise purchase costing $150 was in transit, shipped to the company f.o.b. shipping point on December 30. The purchase of this merchandise has not been recorded, and the goods were not included in the physical count.

    d. The purchase of $500 of merchandise in November was erroneously recorded by a debit to the Rent Expense account.

Required:
    a. Prepare the journal entries needed to correct the above errors, assuming that the books have not yet been closed.
    b. Prepare an income statement for the year 1985.

P. 9-12   **Correcting errors in income statements.** Quintal Corporation uses a periodic inventory system. The following statements were prepared prior to the company's audit:

Quintal Corporation
Income Statements
For Years Ending December 31

	1985		1984	
Sales		$98,000		$90,000
Beginning inventory	$ 8,500		$ 7,000	
Purchases	69,000		63,000	
Goods available for sale	77,500		70,000	
Ending inventory	9,800		8,500	
Cost of goods sold		67,700		61,500
Gross margin		30,300		28,500
Expenses		17,500		16,100
Income before tax		12,800		12,400
Federal income tax		3,780		3,660
Net income after tax		$ 9,020		$ 8,740

The audit discloses the following:

a. The ending inventory in 1984 was overstated by $300.

b. The beginning inventory in 1984 was understated by $200.

c. Purchases in 1985 amounting to $400 have not been recorded.

d. The physical count of inventory at the end of 1985 did not include $600 of goods on consignment with another company.

e. The company is subject to an income tax rate of 30 percent.

Required: Prepare corrected income statements for the years 1984 and 1985.

P. 9-13   **Comparison of periodic FIFO and LIFO.** Condor Company started business on July 1, 1985. A periodic inventory system is used, and the following purchases took place during July:

	No. of Units	Cost Per Unit
July 3	450	$ 9.00
7	600	9.50
14	250	10.00
24	1,000	10.10
28	500	10.40

At the end of July, a physical count of inventory revealed that 1,250 units were on hand. Sales for the month were $32,800, and operating expenses were $6,900.

The company has not given any thought to inventory valuation until now. To make an intelligent decision about adopting an inventory valuation method, the president decides to compare income statements using two valuation methods. There are 10,000 shares of common stock outstanding, and the company is subject to an income tax rate of 20 percent.

Required:

    a. Prepare two income statements for July, one using LIFO and the other using FIFO. Include earnings per share data.

    b. Write a brief report discussing the two statements and explaining the advantages and disadvantages of each.

Case 9-1 **Valuation of manufactured inventories.**

Following are data on the operations of Anderson Molded Foam Company, which has been in business for 3 years. The company manufactures molded foam packaging materials used in packaging electronic instruments and components. It uses a periodic inventory system for its finished goods. The cost of production has been rising steadily over the years, and selling prices have also risen.

	Year 3	Year 2	Year 1
Production in units	150,000	120,000	100,000
Ending inventory in units	30,000	28,000	25,000
Operating expenses	$142,350	$110,200	$95,000
Income tax rate	40%	30%	20%

Cost and Price Data

		Units Produced	Cost Per Unit	Units Sold	Selling Price
Year 1	Jan.—June	40,000	$3.00	20,000	$5.00
	July—Dec.	60,000	3.20	55,000	5.25
Year 2	Jan.—June	50,000	3.40	60,000	5.50
	July—Dec.	70,000	3.50	57,000	5.70
Year 3	Jan.—June	72,000	3.60	65,000	5.85
	July—Dec.	78,000	3.75	83,000	6.00

Required:

    a. Prepare comparative income statements for the 3 years assuming the company uses FIFO inventory valuation.

    b. Prepare comparative income statements for the 3 years assuming the company uses LIFO inventory valuation.

    c. Discuss the tax advantage of one inventory valuation method over the other. Calculate present value of the tax savings by discounting them to Year 1, using a 12 percent discount rate.

Case 9-2 **(AICPA) Inventory adjustments.**

Layne Corporation, a manufacturer of small tools, provided the following information from its accounting records for the year ended December 31, 1985:

Inventory at December 31, 1985 (based on physical
   count of goods on hand at cost) $1,750,000
Accounts payable at December 31, 1985 1,200,000
Net sales (sales less sales returns) 8,500,000

Additional information is as follows:

1. Included in the physical count were tools billed to a customer f.o.b. shipping point on December 31, 1985. These tools had a cost of $28,000 and were billed at $35,000. The shipment was on Layne's loading dock waiting to be picked up by the common carrier later in the day.

2. Goods were in transit from a vendor to Layne on December 31, 1985. The invoice cost was $50,000, and the goods were shipped f.o.b. shipping point on December 27, 1985.

3. Work in process inventory costing $20,000 was sent to an outside processor for plating on December 30, 1985.

4. Tools returned by customers and held pending inspection in the returned goods area on December 31, 1985, were not included in the physical count. On January 8, 1986, the tools, costing $26,000, were inspected and returned to inventory. Credit memos totaling $40,000 were issued to the customers on the same date.

5. Tools shipped to a customer f.o.b. destination on December 26, 1985, were in transit on December 31, 1985, and had a cost of $25,000. Upon notification of receipt by the customer on January 2, 1986, Layne issued a sales invoice for $42,000.

6. Goods with an invoice cost of $30,000, received from a vendor at 5:00 P.M. on December 31, 1985, were recorded on a receiving report dated January 2, 1986. The goods were not included in the physical count, but the invoice was included in accounts payable at December 31, 1985.

7. Goods received from a vendor on December 26, 1985, were included in the physical count. However, the related $60,000 vendor invoice was not included in the accounts payable at December 31, 1985, because the accounts payable copy of the receiving report was lost.

Required: Using the format shown below, prepare a schedule of adjustments as of December 31, 1985, to the initial amounts per Layne's accounting records. Show separately the effect, if any, of each of the seven transactions on the December 31, 1985, amounts. If a transaction has no effect on the initial amount shown, state "none."

	Inventory	**Accounts Payable**	**Net Sales**
Initial Amounts	$1,750,000	$1,200,000	$8,500,000
Increase (Decrease)			
1			
2			
•			
•			
•			
Total adjustment			
Adjusted amounts	$	$	$

Accounting for Long-Lived Assets

10

In this chapter you will study accounting for the productive assets that are used in business operations and are not held for sale. When you have completed the chapter, you should have a good understanding of:

1 What makes up the cost of fixed assets.

2 How the cost is amortized over the useful life of the assets.

3 Different methods of depreciation.

4 Accounting for asset disposals.

5 Accounting for natural resources.

6 Accounting for intangible assets.

7 The nature of goodwill.

During any single accounting period, the current assets of an entity—cash, receivables, and inventories—are used and replaced continuously. In contrast, long-lived assets such as buildings, equipment, and trade names are productive over a number of accounting periods. Long-lived assets represent the productive capacity used in the day-to-day operations of a business. In this chapter we discuss accounting for the acquisition, use, and disposal of long-lived assets. We emphasize in particular how the cost of such assets is assigned to appropriate accounting periods.

THE NATURE OF LONG-LIVED ASSETS

Long-lived assets include fixed assets, natural resources, and intangibles. **Fixed assets** are **tangibles** such as land, buildings, equipment, machinery, furniture, and fixtures. **Natural resources** are tangible assets such as mineral ores, oil deposits, timber, and other **wasting assets. Intangible assets** in-

Long-lived assets may be tangible or intangible

clude patents, copyrights, trademarks, franchises, and goodwill; they are usually classified separately from tangible assets in the balance sheet.

Long-lived assets benefit more than one accounting period. Therefore, the entire cost of a fixed asset is not an expense of the period in which the asset is acquired. Instead, the cost is capitalized and is expensed in each period in which the asset is used. To **capitalize** a cost means to record it in an asset account.

For example, a firm that buys a delivery truck with a useful life of 5 years does not view the entire $29,000 cost as an expense in the year of purchase. Instead, as the truck's productivity is used up over the 5 years, part of its cost must be **expensed**, or written off, each year. The expense matches part of the cost of the truck with the revenues earned by operating it each year. In addition to the expensed portion of the truck's cost, the cost of gasoline, oil, maintenance, insurance, and other costs of operating the truck are expensed as they occur.

Capitalized costs are usually amortized

Expensing part of the cost of a long-lived asset is called amortization. **Amortization** is a systematic writing off of an asset account in order to allocate part of the cost of the asset to each period that benefits from its use. Tangible, long-lived assets are amortized by periodic **depreciation**. A contra asset account is maintained to record accumulated depreciation. The amortization of natural resources is called **depletion**. Some companies maintain a contra asset account for accumulated depletion; others write off natural resources by crediting the asset account directly. Contra asset accounts are usually not maintained for intangible assets, and the amortization of these assets is recorded by credits to the asset account.

Items included in cost. The cost of an asset includes all expenditures necessary to acquire it and make it ready for use. For instance, when equipment is acquired, the total cost includes any freight and installation that the buyer has to pay. Any discount granted for prompt payment reduces the cost of the equipment.

For example, Comoran Company purchases equipment with a list price of $6,000 on terms 2/10, n/60. Freight on the equipment is $200, and the cost of installation is $250. Since a cash discount of $120 is available, the equipment cost should be recorded at net of discount whether or not the discount is taken. If not taken, the discount is a financing cost, and interest expense has been incurred. To record the transaction, the company may make the following entry:

Jan. 10	Equipment	5,880	
	Accounts payable		5,880
	To record purchase of equipment.		
Jan. 12	Equipment	450	
	Cash		450
	To record freight and installation of equipment.		

However the account is paid, the cost of the equipment is $5,880 plus $450. If the account is paid within the discount period, the entry is

Jan. 19	Accounts payable	5,880	
	Cash		5,880
	Paid net amount of Jan. 10 invoice.		

If the payment is made after the discount period, the entry is

Jan. 30	Accounts payable	5,880	
	Interest expense	120	
	Cash		6,000
	Paid gross amount of Jan. 10 invoice.		

Equipment purchases are only one example of fixed asset transactions. More complicated accounting problems occur with the purchase of real estate, which may include the simultaneous acquisition of several types of assets, such as land, buildings, and equipment.

Real Estate

Real estate consists of land and any improvements, such as landscaping and structures that are permanently attached to the land. The cost of land must be separated from the cost of such depreciable real estate. Land may be acquired either as an investment or for use in the business, depending on the intent of management. Land not used in business operations should be classified as an investment. If it is later put to productive use, it should be reclassified among fixed assets.

The cost of land must be separated from the cost of depreciable real estate

If property is purchased for productive use, such as building a plant, and an existing structure must first be removed from the land, the cost of removal is capitalized as part of the cost of the land. The cost of land improvements such as paving, sidewalks, or landscaping may be recorded in the Land account, but if such improvements are expected to have a limited life, they are recorded separately in an account called **Land Improvements** so that their cost may be amortized. The cost of surveys, grading and leveling, and other expenditures necessary to prepare the land for its intended use should become part of the cost of the land. On the other hand, excavation for the new construction is not part of the cost of the land but is part of the cost of the new building. Other building construction costs include architect's and engineer's fees, labor and material, building permits, legal fees, and many others. As you can see, measuring the cost of real estate can be complex and must be done carefully to ensure that the asset accounts reflect correct balances.

Basket Purchase

When several assets are acquired in a single transaction, a portion of the purchase price is assigned to each asset. Allocating the total cost of the purchase among several assets is necessary because they may have different useful lives and depreciate at different rates. The allocation may be determined on the basis of appraisals or a reasonable estimate of the assets' relative values.

Cost is allocated among several assets acquired together

For example, Fowler Corporation acquires land and a building for $60,000. The land is appraised at $16,000, and the building at $48,000. Although the appraised value is higher than cost, only the cost is recorded. The purchase price may be assigned to each asset in proportion to the fair values, as follows:

Appraised value of land	$16,000
Appraised value of building	48,000
Total appraised value	$64,000

Cost assigned to land: $\dfrac{\$16,000}{\$64,000} \times \$60,000 = \$15,000$

Cost assigned to building: $\dfrac{\$48,000}{\$64,000} \times \$60,000 = \$45,000$

The entry to record the acquisition is:

Mar. 7	Land	15,000	
	Building	45,000	
	Cash		60,000
	Bought land and building appraised at		
	$16,000 and $48,000, respectively.		

Assets Acquired for Stock

A company sometimes acquires assets by exchanging stock or other securities. The accountant must decide what value to assign to the asset. Normally the amounts to be recorded are based on the most objectively determinable value. For example, the value of common stock may be readily determined by reference to current prices in the markets in which the stock is traded. The market price is objective evidence of value because it is established by **arm's-length transactions**—that is, transactions between unrelated, independent parties.

The objectivity principle is used for recording exchanges of assets and stock

For example, Ludlow Company needed a truck and found one advertised for sale at a price of $16,000. The company offered 1,000 shares of its common stock in exchange for the truck, and the offer was accepted. The stock trades in the stock market at $15 per share. If the seller is willing to accept the stock in exchange for the truck, its cost is $15,000, not the asking price of $16,000. The transaction is recorded as follows by Ludlow Company:

May 6	Equipment	15,000	
	Capital stock		15,000
	Issued 1,000 shares of stock in exchange		
	for truck.		

Sometimes assets may be obtained in exchange for stock that does not trade in a market. When a market price of the stock does not exist, it is appropriate to obtain an appraisal of the asset's value in order to determine its cost for purposes of recording the transaction. For example, Filmore Corporation wants to acquire a parcel of land and a building for which the owner is asking $35,000. The company offers to give the owner 400 shares of preferred stock and the offer is accepted. The stock is not traded in any stock market.

The asking price for the property may be a good indication of value, but it may also be unrealistic. An independent appraiser indicates that the land is worth $10,000, and the building, $22,000. The appraisal is more objective than either the asking price or some arbitrary value that may be assigned to the preferred stock. Therefore, the transaction is recorded as follows:

Mar. 15	Land	10,000	
	Building	22,000	
	Preferred stock		32,000
	Issued 400 shares of preferred stock in		
	exchange for real estate recorded at		
	appraised value.		

If the appraised value is greater than the asking price, and objective evidence of value is lacking, the conservatism principle dictates use of the asking price to record the acquisition. As you can see, an objective cost cannot always be determined for assets. In such cases, accountants must use judgment to decide on the most appropriate amount to record in the accounts.

DEPRECIATION

Depreciation matches the cost used up with the revenue earned by using the asset

Long-lived assets benefit a business for a number of accounting periods. It is necessary to match the benefits obtained in each period with a part of the asset's cost by depreciating the asset and charging a portion of its cost to each period of its use. Depreciation expense must be determined in a systematic manner that properly matches the expense with the revenues earned each period. The cost of a long-lived asset should be prorated over the asset's useful life. The amount assigned to a particular accounting period depends on:

1. The estimate of the useful life.
2. The estimate of salvage value.
3. The choice of depreciation method.

Because depreciation is based on estimates, the expense is approximate. It should therefore be rounded at least to the nearest whole dollar. Any one of several depreciation methods may be used.

Straight-Line Depreciation

Straight-line depreciation is a time-based method

The simplest method of computing depreciation is the **straight-line method**, which we have used previously in this book. Straight-line depreciation is easy to apply and is used by many companies. The straight-line rate is calculated by dividing 1 by the asset's expected useful life. For instance, if an asset is expected to have a useful life of 5 years, the straight-line **depreciation rate** is 1/5, or 20 percent per year. If the expected useful life is 25 years, the rate is 1/25, or 4 percent per year.

Many assets are expected to have some value at the end of their useful life. This amount, known as **salvage value**, or **residual value**, must be taken into account when computing depreciation. For example, a company plans to keep its automobiles for 4 years. A car that cost $11,000 is expected to have a resale value of $1,500 after 4 years of use. Because $1,500 of the cost can be recovered by selling or exchanging the used car, only $9,500 of the cost may be depreciated. Of course, the $1,500 salvage value is estimated when the car is bought. The actual residual value may turn out to be higher or lower.

The **depreciation base** of an asset is its cost less its salvage value. The depreciation base is multiplied by the depreciation rate in order to obtain the periodic depreciation.

$$\frac{1}{\text{Number of periods of estimated useful life}} \times (\text{Cost} - \text{Salvage Value}) \quad \text{or} \quad \frac{1}{n} \times (C - S)$$

For example, Conway Company acquires a tractor for $12,000. The equipment has an estimated useful life of 10 years and a salvage value of $1,500. To apply straight-line depreciation, the company writes off 10 percent of the depreciation base of $10,500 each year. Figure 10-1 illustrates how the asset is depreciated during its useful life. The calculation is

$$\text{Annual depreciation} = \frac{1}{10} \times (\$12,000 - \$1,500) = \$1,050 \text{ per year}$$

Asset cost	$12,000
Estimated salvage value	$1,500
Estimated useful life	10 years
Depreciation base	$10,500
Depreciation rate	10% per year

Conway Company
Straight-Line Depreciation Schedule

		Depreciation Expense	Book Value
Asset cost			$12,000
Year 1	.10 × $10,500 =	$ 1,050	10,950
Year 2	.10 × 10,500 =	1,050	9,900
Year 3	.10 × 10,500 =	1,050	8,850
Year 4	.10 × 10,500 =	1,050	7,800
Year 5	.10 × 10,500 =	1,050	6,750
Year 6	.10 × 10,500 =	1,050	5,700
Year 7	.10 × 10,500 =	1,050	4,650
Year 8	.10 × 10,500 =	1,050	3,600
Year 9	.10 × 10,500 =	1,050	2,550
Year 10	.10 × 10,500 =	1,050	1,500
Total depreciation		$10,500	

Figure 10-1
Depreciation schedule with straight-line depreciation and 10-year asset life with salvage value. The amount of depreciation expense each year is the same.

At the end of each accounting period, depreciation expense is recorded with the following entry:

Dec. 31	Depreciation expense	1,050	
	Accumulated depreciation		1,050
	To record straight-line depreciation on		
	tractor.		

Accelerated Depreciation Systems

Some assets provide more service and more revenue during the early years of their life and less during their later years. For example, a machine that produces metal parts may operate with more precision and less repair time while it is relatively new. As it gets older, more of the parts it produces may have to be rejected due to lack of precision, and the machine may have more downtime for repairs and maintenance. As another example, a motel can charge higher prices and earn more revenue when it is new than when its facilities are old and outdated.

If more service or revenue is obtained from an asset in its early life, the matching concept requires charging more depreciation in earlier periods and less in later periods. Such **accelerated depreciation** may better match the cost of the asset with the revenue it produces. We now discuss two widely used methods of accelerated depreciation.

Double declining balance depreciation. One method of accelerated depreciation is the **double declining balance** method, or **DDB**. With DDB, the depreciation rate is double the straight-line rate. If the straight-line rate is 10 percent per year, the double declining balance rate is 20 percent per year. If the double rate were applied to the same depreciation base, the asset would be depreciated in 5 years instead of 10. To avoid this problem, the book value of the asset is used as the depreciation base rather than the depreciable cost minus salvage value. **Book value** is the original cost less any accumulated depreciation already recorded.

For example, the tractor bought by Conway Company has a beginning book value of $12,000 which is its cost. With the double declining balance method, the first year's depreciation is 20 percent of $12,000, or $2,400. At the end of the first year, the asset's book value is $9,600 ($12,000 − $2,400), which is the depreciation base for the second year. Since the book value each year is lower than the previous year, the depreciation rate is applied to a declining balance. The schedule in Figure 10-2 shows how the asset is depreciated over its useful life.

Asset cost		$12,000
Estimated salvage value		$1,500
Estimated useful life		10 years
Depreciation base		Book value
Depreciation rate		20% per year

**Conway Company
Double Declining Balance
Depreciation Schedule**

			Depreciation Expense	Book Value
Asset cost				$12,000
Year 1	.20 × $12,000 =		$ 2,400	9,600
Year 2	.20 ×	9,600 =	1,920	7,680
Year 3	.20 ×	7,680 =	1,536	6,144
Year 4	.20 ×	6,144 =	1,229	4,915
Year 5	.20 ×	4,915 =	983	3,932
Year 6	.20 ×	3,932 =	786	3,146
Year 7	.20 ×	3,146 =	629	2,517
Year 8	.20 ×	2,517 =	503	2,014
Year 9	.20 ×	2,014 =	403	1,611
Year 10	.20 ×	1,611* =	111	1,500
Total depreciation			$10,500	

* The calculation yields $322, which would depreciate the asset below salvage value.

**Figure 10-2
Depreciation schedule with double declining balance depreciation and 10-year asset life. Note that salvage value is not used. A constant depreciation rate is applied to a declining asset balance.**

Salvage value is ignored with the DDB method

Note that no salvage value is used, because the DDB method always leaves a residual asset value on the books. In our example, 80 percent of the previous book value is always left to be depreciated in the future. The asset can never be depreciated fully, so we assume that the remaining book value is the asset's residual value. You should keep in mind, however, that book value is not the amount for which the asset could be sold. It is merely the amount of cost left to be amortized in future years.

Although salvage value is not used with the DDB method, the asset should not be depreciated below its salvage value. In our example, depreciation for the tenth year would normally be calculated as 20 percent of $1,611, or $322. However, this would bring the book value below the $1,500 estimated salvage value. Therefore, only $111 is recorded as depreciation in the final year, thereby reducing the asset to a book value of $1,500. The salvage value can be estimated much more accurately near the end of the asset's life than at the beginning.

Sum-of-the-years'-digits depreciation.   Another accelerated depreciation method is the **sum-of-the-years'-digits method**, or **SYD**. The DDB method applies a constant depreciation rate to a decreasing depreciation base. With SYD depreciation, a decreasing rate is applied to a constant depreciation base. Each period a smaller fraction of the depreciation base is written off. The depreciation rate consists of the fraction whose numerator is the number of years remaining to be written off and whose denominator is the sum of the years' digits.

For example, if the asset is estimated to have a 5-year life, the denominator of the fraction is 15, calculated as $1 + 2 + 3 + 4 + 5$. The sum of the years' digits may be obtained by the formula

$$\frac{n(n+1)}{2}$$

where n is the number of years of estimated useful life. If the asset is expected to have a life of 5 years, the calculation of the sum of the years' digits is:

$$\text{SYD} = \frac{5(5+1)}{2} = 15$$

Salvage value must be used with SYD depreciation

The depreciation rate for the first year is 5/15; for the second year, 4/15; and so on. Because the denominator consists of the sum of the years' digits, the sum of all the fractions by the end of the fifth year is 15/15, which means 100 percent of the depreciation base is written off. Therefore it is necessary to include any estimated salvage value with this method, and the depreciation base is cost minus salvage value.

Asset cost	$12,000
Estimated salvage value	$1,500
Estimated useful life	10 years
Depreciation base	$10,500
SYD	55

Conway Company
Sum-of-the-Years'-Digits
Depreciation Schedule

		Depreciation Expense	Book Value
Asset cost			$12,000
Year 1	10/55 × $10,500 =	$ 1,909	10,091
Year 2	9/55 × 10,500 =	1,718	8,373
Year 3	8/55 × 10,500 =	1,527	6,846
Year 4	7/55 × 10,500 =	1,336	5,510
Year 5	6/55 × 10,500 =	1,145	4,365
Year 6	5/55 × 10,500 =	955	3,410
Year 7	4/55 × 10,500 =	764	2,646
Year 8	3/55 × 10,500 =	573	2,073
Year 9	2/55 × 10,500 =	382	1,691
Year 10	1/55 × 10,500 =	191	1,500
Total depreciation		$10,500	

Figure 10-3
Depreciation schedule with sum-of-the-years'-digits depreciation, a 10-year asset life, and salvage value. A declining depreciation rate is applied to a constant asset amount.

Figure 10-3 illustrates the depreciation schedule, using SYD depreciation on Conway Company's $12,000 tractor. Compare this depreciation schedule with straight-line depreciation and double declining balance. Graphs for all three methods are illustrated in Figure 10-4, which shows depreciation expense in one graph and the corresponding book value of the asset in another.

Note that with the straight-line method, depreciation expense is constant in each period. With DDB it decreases at a decreasing rate, and with SYD it decreases at a constant rate. With all three methods, the book value of the asset decreases to its salvage value by the end of the asset's useful life.

Units-of-Production Depreciation

Units-of-production depreciation does not depend on time

With some assets, it is possible to estimate accurately the number of units of service that the asset will provide. For example, a taxicab company may plan to use its automobiles for 100,000 miles before disposing of them. Federal Aviation Administration regulations require that engines of certain single-engine airplanes must be rebuilt after 1,800 hours of use. A metal press may be capable of stamping one million parts before it is discarded. Miles driven, hours of flying time, and number of parts all represent units of service, or product, available from the asset.

When the units of service for an asset can be estimated accurately,

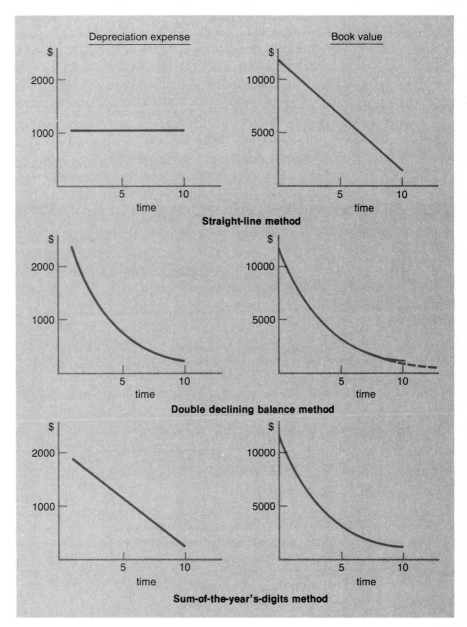

Figure 10-4
**Depreciation
expense and book
value plotted for
three depreciation
methods. The
numeric values
may be found in
Figures 10-1, 10-2,
and 10-3, from
which the plots
are derived.**

depreciation may be calculated using the **units-of-production** method. For example, if Conway Company's tractor has an expected useful life of 100,000 miles, the depreciation rate for each unit of production or service is calculated by dividing the total available units into the depreciation base, as follows:

$$\frac{\text{Cost} - \text{Salvage value}}{\text{Total estimated units}} = \frac{\$12,000 - \$1,500}{100,000 \text{ miles}} = \$.105 \text{ per mile}$$
$$\text{of production available}$$

For every mile driven, 10.5¢ of depreciation should be recorded on the tractor. If the tractor is driven 15,000 miles the first year, depreciation is $1,575 (15,000 × $.105); if it is driven 22,000 miles, depreciation is $2,310. Depreciation may also be calculated as:

$$\frac{\text{Total units produced}}{\text{Total estimated units available}} \times (C - S)$$

If the first year's mileage is substituted, depreciation is:

$$\frac{15,000 \text{ miles}}{100,000 \text{ miles}} \times (\$12,000 - \$1,500) = \$1,575$$

Depreciation for Partial Periods

A depreciation convention should be applied consistently

Sometimes depreciation must be calculated for part of the year; for example an asset might be acquired or sold in the middle of an accounting period. Because depreciation is by nature an estimate, many companies adopt a **depreciation convention**, such as recording depreciation to the nearest half year or to the nearest whole month. As long as the convention is applied consistently, the resulting total depreciation expense is reasonable. In most of our examples and problems, we assume that assets are depreciated to the nearest whole month of possession. Straight-line depreciation poses no problem. For monthly depreciation, 1/12 of the annual rate is applied to the depreciation base. With the double declining balance method, the usual procedure is to apply the annual rate to the depreciation base and use a fraction of the results for the appropriate fraction of the year.

$$\text{DDB rate} \times \text{Book value} \times \text{Fraction of year}$$

If the asset is purchased in the middle of the year, a half year's depreciation is taken in the year of acquisition. In subsequent years, a full year's depreciation is calculated on the remaining book value. For example, Conway Company would depreciate its tractor as follows if depreciation for half a year is to be recorded in the year of acquisition:

Year 1	.20 ×	$12,000 ×	1/2 =	$1,200
Year 2	.20 ×	10,800	=	2,160
Year 3	.20 ×	8,640	=	1,728

Partial-period depreciation with the SYD method is more complex to calculate. If the asset is to be depreciated for half a year in the period of acquisition and for a full year in subsequent periods, the depreciation calculations are as follows:

First half year	10/55 × $10,500 × 1/2		= $ 955

Second year $\begin{cases} 10/55 \times & 10,500 \times 1/2 = \$955 \\ 9/55 \times & 10,500 \times 1/2 = 859 \end{cases} = 1,814$

Third year $\begin{cases} 9/55 \times & 10,500 \times 1/2 = 859 \\ 8/55 \times & 10,500 \times 1/2 = 764 \end{cases} = 1,623$

Each fraction in the SYD method must be used completely. Only half of 10/55 is used in the year of acquisition, therefore the other half of the fraction must be used in the second year before the next fraction is used. Consequently each year's fraction is divided into two parts for use in consecutive years.

Changes in Depreciation

After an asset has been in use for some time, it may become evident that the useful life is going to be longer or shorter than originally estimated. For instance, a change in useful life may occur if the asset is remodeled or improved in some way. If such a change occurs, depreciation in future years should be adjusted accordingly.

Change in depreciation estimate

For example, Sillmor Corporation owns a building with an original cost of $50,000. The building was acquired 10 years ago and had an estimated useful life of 25 years with no salvage value. Straight-line depreciation is used on the building, and the Accumulated Depreciation account has a balance of $20,000. At this time the company remodels the building at a cost of $6,000. It is estimated that the remodeling will extend the useful life of the building by 9 years. The remodeling cost is capitalized, and the depreciation rate must be changed. The relevant accounts appear as follows:

Building		Accumulated Depreciation	
50,000			20,000
Remodeling 6,000			

Prior to the remodeling, the remaining useful life of the building was 15 years. The estimate is now changed to a remaining life of 24 years as a result of the remodeling. The new $36,000 book value of the building must be depreciated over the remaining life of 24 years. Depreciation for the year of remodeling, and future depreciation will be $36,000/24, or $1,500 per year.

Sometimes it is difficult to decide whether expenditures associated with an asset should be capitalized or expensed. Ordinary repairs and maintenance should be expensed. If additions or alterations change the quantity or the quality of the service provided by the asset, such costs should be capitalized. When changes in the cost of the asset require changes in depreciation, only the current and future periods' depreciation are affected.

Tax Incentives

Tax incentives are designed to stimulate business and the economy

When the U.S. economy slows down, Congress often attempts to stimulate it by providing incentives to businesses to buy fixed assets. An increase in the demand for fixed assets, and the subsequent increase in production when the assets are put to use, tends to result in economic growth. Some tax incentives allow businesses to reduce their income tax if they acquire fixed assets. Two such tax provisions are the Accelerated Cost Recovery System and the investment tax credit.

Accelerated Cost Recovery System.   The Economic Recovery Tax Act passed by Congress in 1981 requires use of the **Accelerated Cost Recovery System (ACRS)** for amortizing fixed assets for tax purposes. The ACRS allows businesses to amortize fixed assets for tax purposes over a shorter period than the assets' lives, thus allowing businesses to recover the cost of their assets relatively quickly. That is why the system is called cost recovery rather than depreciation.

ACRS classifies all assets into one of five categories and allows writing off their cost for tax purposes over periods of either 3, 5, 10, or 15 years. The 3-year class is for motor vehicles and equipment used in research and development. The 5-year class is for most other machinery and equipment. The 10-year class is primarily for public utility property, and the 15-year class is for other public utility property. Salvage value is not used with ACRS.

All real estate is amortized over 15 years using ACRS, and the percentage written off in any year depends on the month of purchase. Figure 10-5 illustrates the ACRS rates to be used for amortizing assets. Use of these rates is basically mandatory, although some modifications are permitted.

Investment tax credit.   Another tax incentive that makes the acquisition of equipment attractive is the Investment Tax Credit (ITC), which permits purchasers of qualified property to reduce their tax liability in the year of an asset purchase by a specified percentage of the asset's cost. The 1981 tax act allows a 6 percent investment tax credit for assets in the 3-year ACRS class and a 10 percent investment tax credit for 5-year assets and depreciable property other than real estate in the 10- and 15-year class. Real estate does not qualify for the investment tax credit.

If a company buys a 5-year asset for $25,000, for example, it can reduce its federal income tax payment by $2,500 in the year of purchase. The asset base for amortizing the asset using ACRS must be reduced by half of the investment tax credit, or $1,250. In other words, if a tax credit of $2,500 is claimed, the amount of asset cost that can be recovered using ACRS is $23,750 ($25,000 − $1,250). The company has an option of claim-

Asset Amortization Schedules in Percent
Under the Accelerated Cost Recovery System

Year	Equipment Class life in years				Real Estate Month asset is placed in service											
	3	5	10	15	1	2	3	4	5	6	7	8	9	10	11	12
1	25	15	8	5	12	11	10	9	8	7	6	5	4	3	2	1
2	38	22	14	10	10	10	11	11	11	11	11	11	11	11	11	12
3	37	21	12	9	9	9	9	9	10	10	10	10	10	10	10	10
4		21	10	8	8	8	8	8	8	8	9	9	9	9	9	9
5		21	10	7	7	7	7	7	7	7	8	8	8	8	8	8
6			10	7	6	6	6	6	7	7	7	7	7	7	7	7
7			9	6	6	6	6	6	6	6	6	6	6	6	6	6
8			9	6	6	6	6	6	6	6	5	6	6	6	6	6
9			9	6	6	6	6	6	5	6	5	5	5	6	6	6
10			9	6	5	6	5	6	5	5	5	5	5	5	6	5
11				6	5	5	5	5	5	5	5	5	5	5	5	5
12				6	5	5	5	5	5	5	5	5	5	5	5	5
13				6	5	5	5	5	5	5	5	5	5	5	5	5
14				6	5	5	5	5	5	5	5	5	5	5	5	5
15				6	5	5	5	5	5	5	5	5	5	5	5	5
					1	1	2	2	3	3	4	4	4	5		

Figure 10-5   **Cost recovery rates enacted by the Economic Recovery Tax Act of 1981. The depreciation rate is a specified percentage each year. Each column adds up to 100 percent. Salvage value is not used with ACRS. The 10-year and 15-year classes are for utility property only. Real estate is amortized over 15 years, with the annual percentage depending on the month it was placed in service.**

ing only an 8 percent investment tax credit on 5-year assets or a 4 percent credit on 3-year assets. In that case, the entire cost of the asset can be recovered using ACRS.

DISPOSAL OF ASSETS

Fair value is used to determine gains or losses

Assets may be disposed of by sale, exchange, or abandonment. Prior to recording disposals, it is necessary to bring depreciation up to date and to calculate the gain or loss on the disposal. The gain or loss is the difference between the book value and the fair value of the asset. The fair value of a fixed asset at any time is simply the portion of the asset that has not yet been used. If depreciation estimates were perfect, the book value and fair value would be the same. Therefore a loss or gain recorded at the time of disposal simply makes up for errors in depreciation estimates. A loss recorded on disposal means that not enough depreciation was recorded while the asset was used, so the book value is greater than fair value. A gain means that depreciation was excessive in prior years. Recording gains or losses on disposal of an asset is simply a way of adjusting for the lack of precision in depreciation estimates.

Depreciation must be brought up to date prior to recording disposals

In order to calculate the correct gain or loss, depreciation on the asset should be recorded to the date of disposal prior to recording the disposal. That way the cost of using the asset in the period of disposal is matched with the revenue of the period. For example, Marlowe Company bought a truck on January 4, 1981, and on April 29, 1985, the company decides to dispose of it. The truck had an estimated useful life of 10 years and a salvage value of $1,500. Straight-line depreciation calculated to the nearest whole month has been used.[1] At the beginning of 1985, the balances in the Equipment and Accumulated Depreciation accounts are as follows:

Equipment		Accumulated Depreciation	
12,000		1981	1,050
		1982	1,050
		1983	1,050
		1984	1,050
		Bal.	4,200

Prior to recording the disposal of the truck, the company must record depreciation to the date of sale.

Apr. 29	Depreciation expense	350	
	Accumulated depreciation		350
	To record 4 months' depreciation prior		
	to disposal of truck.		
	.10 ($12,000 − $1,500) × 4/12		

This entry brings the asset accounts up to date so that disposal may be recorded. The balance in Accumulated Depreciation is $4,550 when the entry is posted. We now use these account balances to demonstrate accounting for disposals of the asset by sale.

Disposal by Sale

Once the accumulated depreciation account has been brought up to date, the disposal of the asset can be recorded. If the asset is sold for $7,600 cash, the following entry is made:

Apr. 29	Cash	7,600	
	Accumulated depreciation	4,550	
	Equipment		12,000
	Gain on sale of equipment		150
	Sold truck for more than book value.		

---

[1] The depreciation schedule for this asset is the same as in Figure 10-1.

Both the Equipment and the Accumulated Depreciation accounts must be written off. The difference between the cash received and the asset's book value is the loss or gain. If the cash received is greater than the book value at the time of sale, there is a gain. A loss occurs when cash received is less than book value. For example, if $7,000 cash is received in exchange for the used truck, the entry to record the sale is

Apr. 29	Cash	7,000	
	Accumulated depreciation	4,550	
	Loss on sale of equipment	450	
	Equipment		12,000
	Sold truck for less than book value.		

Disposal by Exchange

FASB pronouncements[2] describe the method of accounting for the disposal of assets by exchange. The rules are complex, and we discuss only the basic aspects. Exchanges of assets can be classified into two categories. The first is the exchange of unlike assets. For example, a truck may be exchanged for an office machine, or land and buildings may be exchanged for equipment. The second category is the exchange of similar assets—a large computer is exchanged for two small ones, or an old truck is ex-

Exchanges may involve like or unlike assets

changed for a new one. When like assets are exchanged, it is assumed that the new asset is employed in the same way as the old—that is, the earning process in which the asset is used goes on as before. When unlike assets are exchanged, it is assumed that the earning process in which the old asset was used ceases, and a new earning process starts with the new asset. Consequently, exchanges of like assets are treated differently from exchanges of unlike assets.

Exchanges of unlike assets.   As you know, depreciation must be brought up to date before disposal of assets is recorded. In any exchange of unlike assets, gains or losses are calculated on the basis of the fair value of the asset given up. **Fair value** is the market value of the asset on the date of disposal. If the book value of the asset is $5,000, and its fair value is $4,500, a loss of $500 must be recorded. If the fair value is $5,800, a gain of $800 must be recorded. The fair value is often difficult to determine, because a market does not always exist for certain types of assets. In such cases it is assumed that the book value represents fair value.

For example, Colber Corporation owns a truck with a book value of $3,000—$8,000 cost and $5,000 of accumulated depreciation. The fair value of the truck is $2,400. The truck is exchanged for a new drill press with a

Exchanges resulting in losses

price listed at $4,000. The seller agrees to allow a trade-in value of $2,400 for the truck, so the company must pay the remaining balance of $1,600 in cash. The entry to record the transaction is

---

[2] APB Opinion No. 29, "Accounting for Nonmonetary Transactions," New York, AICPA, May 1973.

June 24	Equipment (drill press)	4,000	
	Accumulated depreciation (truck)	5,000	
	Loss on exchange of equipment	600	
	Equipment (truck)		8,000
	Cash		1,600
	Exchanged truck for drill press.		

In a fair exchange, each side gives up and receives an equal amount of fair value. The company gave up $1,600 in cash and a truck worth $2,400, or a total fair value of $4,000. Therefore, the equipment it received must also have a fair value of $4,000, and that is, in fact, the amount recorded for the drill press.

Exchanges resulting in gains

If, instead, the truck has a fair value of $3,200, which is allowed as trade-in value, Colber Corporation must pay $800 cash. In this case the transaction is recorded with a gain as follows:

June 24	Equipment (drill press)	4,000	
	Accumulated depreciation (truck)	5,000	
	Gain on exchange of equipment		200
	Equipment (truck)		8,000
	Cash		800
	Exchanged truck for drill press.		

Sometimes the amount allowed as a trade-in value is not the fair value of the asset given up in the exchange. The fair value must still be used to calculate the gain or loss. For example, the fair value of the truck is $2,800, but $3,100 is offered on it as a trade-in, and a cash payment of $900 is required. The calculation of the loss is

Book value of asset given up	$3,000
Fair value	2,800
Loss	$ 200

In a fair exchange, each party receives equal value

The company is giving up assets with a total fair value of $3,700. Therefore it must be receiving an equal amount of fair value in exchange. When it records the transaction, the company must record the cost of the new asset at its fair value as follows:

June 24	Equipment (drill press)	3,700	
	Accumulated depreciation (old truck)	5,000	
	Loss on exchange of equipment	200	
	Equipment (old truck)		8,000
	Cash		900
	Exchanged truck with fair value of $2,800		
	and $900 cash for drill press.		

The drill press must be overpriced; otherwise, an inflated trade-in value would not have been offered on the truck. The fair value of the drill press is recorded. Logically the fair value of the drill press must be the fair value of the assets given up in exchange for it—that is, the $2,800 truck and $900 cash.

Exchanges of like assets.   The main difference between exchanges of like and unlike assets is that with like exchanges, no gain is recorded. Losses on such exchanges are recorded, however, to satisfy the conservatism principle. Losses are calculated as the difference between the book value and the fair value of the asset given up.

To illustrate exchanges of like assets, we assume that Klimmer Corporation exchanges an old computer for a new one with an asking price of $9,000. The old computer has a cost of $10,000, accumulated depreciation of $7,000, and a fair value of $2,400. The dealer allows the fair value of $2,400 on the old computer as trade-in and requires a cash payment for the $6,600 balance. The transaction is recorded as follows:

June 24	Equipment (new computer)	9,000	
	Accumulated depreciation (old)	7,000	
	Loss on exchange of equipment	600	
	Equipment (old computer)		10,000
	Cash		6,600
	Exchanged old computer for new at a		
	loss.		

Losses on exchanges of like assets are not deductible for federal income tax purposes. If a loss occurs on the exchange, it must be used to adjust the cost of the new equipment. For tax purposes the above transaction is recorded as follows:

June 24	Equipment (new computer)	9,600	
	Accumulated depreciation (old)	7,000	
	Equipment (old computer)		10,000
	Cash		6,600
	Exchanged old computer for new; used		
	loss to adjust tax basis of new computer.		

The new asset's depreciation base for tax purposes is higher than the cost for accounting purposes. For tax purposes, depreciation expense in future years will be higher than for book purposes, and larger tax deductions will result. It is not unusual for tax laws to be inconsistent with generally accepted accounting principles. Frequently such inconsistencies require companies to maintain two sets of records, one for reporting purposes and the other for tax purposes.

Gains are realized only when the earning process culminates

If the fair value of the old computer is $3,200, there is a gain on the exchange. The gain of $200 is calculated as the difference between the fair value of $3,200 and the book value of $3,000, but the gain may not be recorded, either for accounting or for tax purposes. It is assumed that the earning process of the computer will continue, and the cost of the new computer is adjusted when the transaction is recorded. For example, if payment consists of the old computer and $5,800 cash, the entry to record the exchange is

June 24	Equipment (new computer)	8,800	
	Accumulated depreciation (old)	7,000	
	Equipment (old computer)		10,000
	Cash		5,800
	Exchanged old computer for new.		

Instead of recording the gain, the company adjusts the cost of the new computer so that the entry balances. The transaction is recorded for tax purposes exactly as above. The various examples used for exchanges of like and unlike assets are summarized in Figure 10-6.

NATURAL RESOURCES

Assets such as timber, ores, and oil reserves create special problems in assigning asset costs to accounting periods. One of the problems with accounting for natural resources is the difficulty in estimating the quantity of resource available. Although good measurements can be made of accessible resources such as timber, the amount of resources such as oil, gas, or ore deposits located underground are usually based on engineering studies and these estimates can be questionable. The salvage value of the remaining asset must also be taken into consideration. Frequently the value of the land from which the wasting asset is removed may be a large proportion of the original cost.

Removal of a natural resource causes a physical change in the asset. In some cases, such as timber, nature may add to the asset through a process known as **accretion,** which is the result of natural growth. Accretion is not recorded by accountants. Because natural resources are eventually removed, they are subject to depletion.

	Accounting Purposes		Tax Purposes	
Exchanges of Unlike Assets				
Gain:				
Equipment (new)	4,000		4,000	
Accumulated depreciation	5,000		5,000	
Gain on sale of equipment		200		200
Equipment (old)		8,000		8,000
Cash		800		800
Loss:				
Equipment (new)	4,000		4,000	
Accumulated depreciation	5,000		5,000	
Loss on sale of equipment	600		600	
Equipment (old)		8,000		8,000
Cash		1,600		1,600
Exchanges of Like Assets				
Gain:				
Equipment (new)	8,800		8,800	
Accumulated depreciation	7,000		7,000	
Equipment (old)		10,000		10,000
Cash		5,800		5,800
Loss:				
Equipment (new)	9,000		9,600	
Accumulated depreciation	7,000		7,000	
Loss on sale of equipment	600			
Equipment (old)		10,000		10,000
Cash		6,600		6,600

Figure 10-6
Summary of exchanges of like and unlike assets recorded for accounting and for tax purposes.

Depletion

Depletion is an inventoriable cost

The calculation of depletion is similar to the units-of-production method of depreciation. The depletion base is cost less salvage value of the asset. The depletion rate is calculated on the basis of total estimated units of available natural resource. Unlike depreciation, however, depletion is not recorded as an expense. Depletion is an **inventoriable** product cost that becomes an expense when the product is sold.

For example, Arkady Lumber Company owns a stand of timber that cost $270,000, of which $30,000 is the value of the land. The stand is estimated to contain three million board feet of lumber. As the lumber is cut, part of the cost of the timber stand must be amortized. During 1985 the company cuts 600,000 board feet of lumber. The depletion rate is calculated as follows:

$$\frac{\text{Depletion base}}{\text{Total estimated quantity of resource}}$$

$$\frac{\$270,000 - \$30,000}{3,000,000 \text{ board feet}} = \$.08 \text{ per board foot}$$

For 1985 depletion is $48,000 (600,000 board feet × $.08/ft), recorded as follows:

Dec. 31	Inventory of lumber	48,000	
	Timber stand (or Accumulated		
	depletion)		48,000
	To record depletion of timber stand.		

Any other costs of processing the lumber are added to the inventory account. When the lumber is sold, its cost is debited to cost of goods sold. If two-thirds of the inventory, or 400,000 board feet, is sold in 1985, two-thirds of the depletion becomes an expense, and one-third is carried forward as part of the cost of lumber inventory.

As extraction of natural resources progresses, new discoveries may be made, and the estimate of the available remaining resources may change. In this case, changes in the depletion rate are required. The remaining book value of the natural resource is written off at the new rate in the current and future years.

When equipment, buildings, or other fixed assets are necessary for mining, drilling, cutting, or other extracting operations, depreciation of such fixed assets should be calculated for the useful life of the asset, or for the duration of the extracting operations, whichever is shorter. For example, an oil field that is leased for 5 years requires construction of a building on the site to facilitate oil drilling. The building has a useful life of 30 years, but it should be written off over 5 years because it will provide services only for the duration of the lease. Such a building is a leasehold improvement rather than a fixed asset. Leasehold improvements are often reported among intangible assets. Accounting for leases is discussed in the next chapter.

INTANGIBLE ASSETS

Intangibles are assets that have no physical existence, and the precise future benefits to be derived from them may be highly uncertain and hard to measure. Intangibles, such as trademarks, trade names, goodwill, and organization costs have indefinite lives; patents and copyrights have limited lives. In either case, intangibles are subject to amortization.

Intangibles may have limited or unlimited lives

Accountants generally agree that intangibles should be recorded at their cost and carried on the books at cost less any amortization. Amortization should be based on an asset's useful life and is recorded by debiting amortization expense and crediting the intangible asset account. Some intangible assets such as organization costs and trademarks may provide benefits as long as the business continues in existence. If an intangible asset is expected to benefit the business indefinitely, accounting principles require writing off its cost over a period not exceeding 40 years.[3] Below we discuss various intangible assets.

---

[3] APB Opinion No. 17, "Intangible Assets," New York, AICPA, August 1970.

Research and development.   Intangible assets such as patents frequently result from research and development. In the past it was possible to capitalize research and development costs on the assumption that they would benefit future periods. FASB Statement No. 2 now requires expensing all such costs. While this results in low valuations of patents and other intangibles developed through research, it ensures a consistent treatment of research and development expenditures. Unfortunately, expensing all research and development can cause serious distortions in the financial statements. For example, if research results in a discovery that will benefit the company for several future periods, expensing it all in the current period understates assets and current income and overstates future income.

Patents.   A person who invents a new product or process may obtain a patent, which grants the inventor the exclusive use of the product or process for a period of 17 years. The inventor may sell the patent or may allow others to use it by selling for a fee licenses which permit buyers to make the patented product.

If a patent is purchased, the purchase price is the cost to be capitalized and amortized. If it is developed through research, the cost consists of the legal expenses and patent fees necessary to obtain the patent. The research and development costs must be written off as expenses in the period in which they are incurred.

Patents should be amortized over their legal life or over a shorter period if the benefits derived will not continue throughout the life of the patent. It is entirely possible that a patent with a legal life of 17 years will become obsolete in a much shorter period of time.

Copyrights.   A book, work of art, film, record, or other creative product may be copyrighted. A copyright lasts for the creator's lifetime plus 50 years. As with other intangibles, the period over which a copyright is amortized depends on its useful life or its legal life, whichever is shorter.

Trademarks.   Trademarks and trade names have indefinite lives. Although they often have significant value to the owner, they are written off over a period of time not exceeding 40 years.

Patents, copyrights, and trademarks provide the owner with exclusive rights, but they do not protect against infringement by others. Any infringement that occurs must usually be challenged in court. The cost of a successful lawsuit should be added to the cost of the intangible and amortized over the remaining useful life of the asset. On the other hand, if a court challenge is unsuccessful, and the judgment indicates that an intangible asset has no value, its entire cost should be written off immediately.

Leasehold improvements.   A business may use property that it does not own by leasing it and paying rent to the owner. If the lease contract is for a long term, the company may find it necessary to make improvements or modifications to the leased property. For example, a company leasing a warehouse may build partitions to divide the available space into several separate rooms. Or a company leasing grazing land may build fences on the property. If such improvements are attached to and become part of the leased asset, legally they belong to the owner of the leased property, and are called **leasehold improvements.** The company which incurred the cost of the improvement may amortize this cost over the life of the improvement or the terms of the lease, whichever is shorter.

Organization costs.   The cost of establishing a business and putting it into operation is capitalized on the assumption that such costs benefit the business as long as it is in existence. Organization costs include legal incorporation fees, promotion costs, and other costs of organizing. They do not include the expenses of operations or losses incurred in the first operating period. Organization costs may be written off over 5 years or longer for tax purposes. Although accounting theory implies that amortization over 40 years is more appropriate, most companies amortize organization costs over 5 years to avoid keeping separate tax and accounting records for this asset.

Recording amortization of intangibles

Franchises.   The privilege of operating under a specific trade name or selling a specific brand of products or services is called a franchise. Franchises are purchased for periods of time varying from a few years to perpetuity. The cost of the franchise, like other intangible asset costs, should be written off over its useful life. Intangibles are written off by debiting Amortization Expense and crediting the asset, as in the following example:

Dec. 31	Amortization expense	1,950	
	Patents		650
	Franchises		1,000
	Trademarks		300
	To amortize patents, franchises, and		
	trademarks.		

Goodwill

The term **goodwill** refers to the characteristics of a business that enable it to earn more than a normal rate of profit because of reputation, operating efficiency, location, management expertise, or other factors. Although many businesses develop a significant amount of goodwill, accountants record the value of this intangible asset only when it has been purchased as part of the purchase of an entire business. A company cannot sell its goodwill separately, and to record goodwill that has been developed over time requires subjective evaluations and is therefore not in accordance with generally accepted accounting principles.

Goodwill is recorded only if purchased

Goodwill can be approximated or measured in a number of ways in order to estimate the value of a business that is to be bought or sold. Such estimates may be useful in the bargaining process, but the amount of goodwill to be reported in the balance sheet is the difference between the fair value of the net assets acquired and the purchase price paid for the entire business. Determining the value of a business includes the process of estimating the goodwill that it may have.

Estimation of goodwill.   A business can be expected to earn a return on investment that is normal for the industry in which it operates. Any income earned by the business in excess of such a normal return is assumed to be due to goodwill. Before goodwill of a business can be estimated, however, it is necessary to measure the fair value of the assets and equities with which the business is operated.

The book value of the business is not adequate for measuring goodwill, because the fair value of the assets may be quite different from the book value. Fixed assets are carried on the books at cost less accumulated depreciation, which may be quite different from the current value. Inventories may be carried at LIFO, yet their current market value may be much higher. Investments carried at lower of cost or market may have a much higher market value than recorded in the books.

The first step in estimating goodwill is to obtain the fair value of all assets and liabilities. The fair value of total liabilities is deducted from the fair value of total assets to obtain net assets, or capital. Then the expected income of the business can be computed and compared with the company's actual history of earnings. For example, Haltom Company is for sale at an asking price of $114,500. The fair value of the company's assets and liabilities is shown in the following condensed balance sheet.

Haltom Company
Balance Sheet
October 31, 1985

Current assets	$ 20,000	Current liabilities	$ 8,000
Investments	50,000	Long-term debt	42,000
Fixed assets	80,000	Capital (net assets)	100,000
Total assets	$150,000	Total equities	$150,000

Published statistics are available on average rates of return for various industries. Such data may be used as a basis for calculating goodwill. If the normal rate of return in this company's industry is 12 percent of net assets, Haltom Company can be expected to earn a net income of $12,000 each year ($100,000 net assets × .12). For the past 5 years, the company's net income has been as follows:

1981	$11,000
1982	14,000
1983	13,000
1984	16,000
1985	15,000

Using the above figures, we determine that the average income of the company is $13,800 (total income for 5 years divided by 5). If past performance of the company is expected to continue into the foreseeable future, the company should continue to earn $1,800 per year in excess of the normal return of $12,000. There are several ways of evaluating this excess income.

Capitalizing income determines the investment needed to earn the income

Capitalization of excess earnings.   To **capitalize** earnings means to calculate how much capital must be invested at a given rate of return in order to obtain a given amount of earnings. The earnings figure is divided by the **capitalization rate**, that is, the desired rate of return, to arrive at the required capital. In the Haltom Company example, if the normal income of $12,000 is capitalized at 12 percent, the result is the fair value of existing net assets. In other words, the recorded net assets whose fair value is $100,000 are responsible for producing $12,000 of income. The excess income is therefore attributed to the existence of an unrecorded asset, which is called goodwill. If excess earnings are capitalized, the resulting figure is the amount of estimated goodwill. When excess earnings of $1,800 are capitalized at 12 percent, goodwill for the company is computed as:

$$\frac{\text{Excess earnings}}{\text{Capitalization rate}} = \frac{\$1,800}{.12} = \$15,000$$

With a net asset value of $100,000 plus the goodwill, a fair price for the company is $115,000. There is some risk in assuming that excess earnings will continue into the future. Although a normal return for this company is 12 percent, it may be reasonable to use a higher capitalization rate for estimating goodwill in order to compensate for the risk that the excess returns will not continue. If excess earnings are capitalized at 15 percent, for example, the amount of goodwill is:

$$\frac{\$1,800}{.15} = \$12,000$$

In this case a fair price for the business is $112,000—$100,000 for the fair value of the recorded assets plus $12,000 for goodwill. The choice of a capitalization rate to estimate goodwill may be totally subjective. The rate selected should be reasonable in light of the circumstances, but generally should not be lower than the normal return for the industry and usually is somewhat higher to compensate for risk.

Discounted future earnings.   It is often logical to assume that excess earnings will continue only for a limited time after the business has been sold. Any excess earnings after that time may be attributed to goodwill generated by the new owners. If excess earnings are expected to continue for a period of 10 years, they may be discounted to the present at an appropriate rate of return in order to find the amount of goodwill.

The present value of the excess earnings for the next 10 years may be found by viewing the future excess earnings as an annuity. If the earnings are to be discounted at 15 percent, we simply find the present value of an annuity of 10 rents at 15 percent. From Table IV at the end of the book, we see that the present value factor is 5.01877, and goodwill is:

$$\text{Excess earnings} \times \text{PV of annuity, } n = 10,\, i = 15\%$$

$$\$1,800 \times 5.01877 = \$9,034$$

Payback. Goodwill is sometimes estimated using the **payback** method, which is a way of determining how long it will take to recover the money invested in a business. If the asking price of $114,500 is paid for Haltom Company, at $13,800 of income each year, it will require 8.3 years to recover the asking price. The payback period is computed by dividing the asking price by average annual earnings:

Payback is the time it takes to recover an investment

$$\text{Payback} = \frac{\$114,500}{\$13,800 \text{ per year}} = 8.3 \text{ years}$$

The buyer desires a minimum payback of 8 years. In that case, the value of the entire business may be computed by multiplying average earnings by 8. Any difference between this result and net assets is estimated goodwill.

$$\text{Average earnings} \times \text{payback} = \text{Value of the firm}$$

$13,800/year × 8 years =	$110,400
Less net asset value	100,000
Estimated goodwill	$ 10,400

Accounting for goodwill. Regardless of the goodwill calculations, the actual amount of goodwill to be recorded depends on the price paid for the company. If Haltom Company is finally sold for $110,000, the buyer records the assets and liabilities at their fair market value and the goodwill as the residual amount needed to balance the entry.

Nov. 9	Current assets	20,000	
	Investments	50,000	
	Fixed assets	80,000	
	Goodwill	10,000	
	Current liabilities		8,000
	Long-term debt		42,000
	Cash		110,000

Goodwill should be amortized over its expected useful life, but not more than 40 years. If goodwill is expected to benefit the company for the next 10 years, amortization at the end of the first year is recorded as follows:

Oct. 30	Amortization expense	1,000	
	Goodwill		1,000

Sometimes a business may be purchased for less than net asset value. When this occurs, negative goodwill results which is recorded as a credit and reported among liabilities.

SUMMARY

Long-lived assets consist of real estate, equipment, natural resources, and intangible assets. The cost of such assets is **capitalized** and reported in the balance sheet. Periodic **amortization** is recorded to write off the cost of long-lived assets over their useful lives. Amortization of **fixed assets**, such as buildings, equipment, and fixtures, is called **depreciation. Natural resources**, such as timber and mineral ores, are amortized by **depletion**.

Included in the cost of fixed assets are all expenditures necessary to acquire the asset and make it ready for use. The cost of equipment includes shipping and installation. The cost of land includes removal of existing structures, surveying, and grading. If more than one type of asset is acquired in a single transaction—a **basket purchase**—the cost must be allocated to the different assets in proportion to their fair value. If assets are acquired in exchange for stock whose value can be objectively determined, their cost is the value of the stock given up. If the value of the stock cannot be determined, the fair value of the asset is used to record the transaction.

The amount of depreciation recorded on fixed assets depends on the estimate of useful life and an estimate of salvage value. It also depends on the depreciation method selected. The cost of the asset less the accumulated depreciation is the asset's **book value**.

Cost less **salvage** or **residual value** is the **depreciation base**, which is amortized in each period by applying a **depreciation rate. Straight-line** depreciation assumes an equal benefit from an asset for each period of asset use. **Accelerated depreciation** is used when more benefits are obtained during the asset's early life.

For **double declining balance** depreciation, the rate used is double the straight-line rate. This rate is multiplied by the asset's book value, which declines over time. Salvage value is disregarded when using the DDB method. The **sum-of-the-years'-digits** method is applied by multiplying cost less salvage value of the asset by a decreasing fraction.

The **units-of-production** depreciation method is based on an asset's physical use rather than on the passage of time. An estimate is made of the number of units of production available from the asset during its useful life. The percentage of units actually produced is multiplied by the depreciation base to arrive at periodic depreciation.

Depreciation for part of a year may be calculated if the asset is held for only a part of the accounting period. Whatever depreciation policy a company adopts should be fully disclosed and applied consistently. Sometimes it is necessary to revise the estimate of useful life of an asset, and this requires changes in depreciation. When depreciation rates have to be revised, the remaining book value of the asset is depreciated on the basis of its remaining useful life in the current and future periods without any prior period adjustments.

For tax purposes assets must be amortized using the **Accelerated Cost Recovery System** which provides for rapid cost recovery in order to encourage investment in fixed assets. Another tax incentive provided by tax laws is the **investment tax credit** which allows a reduction in federal income tax by a percentage of the cost of acquired fixed assets.

When assets are disposed of, depreciation is recorded to the date of disposal. Both the cost and accumulated depreciation balances must be written off when the disposal is recorded. If an asset is sold or exchanged for a dissimilar asset, a gain or loss may have to be recorded. Gains and losses on exchanges are calculated as the difference between the book value and the **fair value** of the asset given up. Assets may be exchanged for similar assets, in which case it is assumed that the earning process continues. A loss on an exchange of similar assets is recorded if one occurs, but gains are not recorded. For tax purposes, neither gains nor losses may be recorded on exchanges of like assets.

Natural resources are subject to depletion, which is calculated on the basis of estimated available resources. The percentage of resource removed or extracted is the depletion rate. Depletion is an **inventoriable cost** that increases the balance of the inventory of natural resource extracted and reduces the balance of the natural resource asset account. When the extracted inventory is sold, depletion is part of the cost of goods sold.

Intangible assets have no physical existence. Such intangibles as patents, copyrights, and some franchises have limited lives. Others, such as trademarks, organization costs, and goodwill, have unlimited lives. Intangible assets are amortized over their useful life or 40 years, whichever is shorter.

Intangibles are recorded at their cost. Some intangible assets are obtained as a result of research and development. Since it is not possible to predict whether research and development costs will yield future benefits, such costs must be expensed in the period in which they are incurred.

Goodwill may be estimated as the value of future excess earnings of a business. Such estimates may be made by using an appropriate **capitalization rate** to **capitalize** excess earnings, by finding the present value of future excess earnings, or by using the **payback** method. Goodwill may be recorded only if it is purchased in connection with the purchase of an entire business.

KEY TERMS
Accelerated Cost Recovery System
  (ACRS) *(434)*
accelerated depreciation *(427)*
accretion *(440)*
amortization *(422)*
arms'-length transaction *(424)*
book value *(428)*
capitalization rate *(446)*
capitalize *(422, 446)*
depletion *(422, 441)*
depreciation *(422)*
depreciation base *(426)*
depreciation convention *(432)*
depreciation rate *(426)*
double declining balance
  (DDB) *(428)*
fair value *(437)*

fixed assets *(421)*
goodwill *(444)*
intangible assets *(421, 442)*
investment tax credit *(434)*
leasehold improvement *(443)*
long-lived assets *(421)*
natural resources *(421, 440)*
payback *(447)*
residual value *(426)*
salvage value *(426)*
straight-line *(426)*
sum-of-the-years'-digits
  (SYD) *(429)*
tangibles *(421)*
units-of-production method *(431)*
wasting assets *(421)*

QUESTIONS

1. Some costs are capitalized whereas others are expensed when incurred. Discuss the difference between capitalizing and expensing, and explain the reasons for each treatment.

2. What is the distinction among depreciation, depletion, and amortization? To what kind of assets do these terms apply?

3. What is a basket purchase? Discuss the problems that such purchases pose for accountants.

4. When assets are acquired in exchange for stock, either the appraised value of the asset or the market value of the stock may be used to record the transaction. What is the guiding accounting principle involved in deciding which value to use?

5. What are some of the reasons that depreciation is usually rounded to whole dollars instead of computed to the nearest cent?

6. What is the justification for accelerated depreciation? What assumptions are implied in the use of straight-line depreciation?

7. Under what conditions is it appropriate to use the units-of-production depreciation method?

8. When the cost or the useful life estimate of a depreciable asset changes, how is depreciation affected? In what periods is it affected?

9. Explain the treatment of gains and losses when unlike assets are exchanged. Is the treatment the same for tax purposes?

10. Explain the treatment of gains and losses for accounting purposes and for tax purposes when exchanges of similar assets take place.

11. What is meant by depletion being an inventoriable cost? When does depletion become an expense?

12. Identify some intangible assets. Examine carefully the definition of intangible assets and decide whether some intangibles are reported in the balance sheet under a different classification.

13. The research and development efforts of Company A resulted in two patents. The research and development of Company B turned out to be fruitless. How should each company account for its research and development costs?

14. What is goodwill? Under what conditions is it recorded in the books and reported in the balance sheet?

15. A company uses several methods of estimating goodwill for a business that it wishes to purchase. When the transaction is consummated, what will finally determine the amount of goodwill?

16. What is the difference between capitalizing an expenditure and capitalizing earnings? Give examples of both types of capitalization.

EXERCISES

Ex. 10-1   Classification of expenditures.   Below is a list of transactions, all paid for in cash.

a. $25,000 for addition to old building.

b. $4,000 paid on accounts payable.

c. $1,000 for repairs of machinery damaged in accident.

d. $7,000 for new equipment.

e. $600 for accessory for new equipment.

f. $200 for equipment maintenance.

g. $300 for installation of equipment.

h. $75,000 for land.

i. $3,000 to demolish old building on land needed for new building.

j. $8,000 for 1 month's salaries.

k. $5,000 for organization of company.

l. $2,200 for modification of equipment that extends its life.

m. $14,680 for paving parking lot with a 15-year life.

n. $100,000 to retire bonds payable.

o. $17,000 for research and development which resulted in new patent.

p. $10 prize to employee for suggesting name for new product.

q. $4,000 for new fixtures and complete remodeling of showroom.

r. $160 to pay taxes payable recorded last period.

s. $1,500 for 3-year insurance policy.

Required: For each transaction, indicate with **C**, **E**, or **N** whether the cost paid should be expensed, capitalized, or neither.

Ex. 10-2 **Cost and depreciation of equipment.** On March 1, 1985, Sarah Dee Company purchased a machine listed at $10,000 on terms 2/10, n/30. Freight on the machine was $300, and the installation cost was $450, both paid in cash. The machine has an estimated useful life of 10 years with a $230 salvage value. The company uses straight-line depreciation recorded to the nearest whole month.

Required:
a. Journalize the transactions, assuming the account was paid on March 9.
b. Journalize the transactions, assuming the account was paid on March 20.
c. Journalize the depreciation entry on the machine on December 31, 1985.

Ex. 10-3 **Cost of fixed assets.** Martha Lee Company purchased land with two buildings on it for $50,000. The land was appraised at $12,000. One of the buildings was appraised at $36,000 with a 20-year life and a $2,500 salvage value. The other building was appraised at zero value. Shortly after the purchase the company had the worthless building demolished at a cost of $3,000 in order to make room for a parking lot.

Required:
a. Record this acquisition in the general journal.
b. Record the demolition of the building.
c. Record straight-line depreciation on the remaining building at the end of the first year, assuming a full year of use.

Ex. 10-4 **Exchanging stock for fixed assets.** On May 3 Quintal Corporation acquired a parcel of land in exchange for 2,000 shares of its common stock. The stock trades in the market at $12 per share. The asking price for the land was $26,500 and an appraiser said it has a value of $26,000. On the same day the company issued 200 shares of its 10 percent preferred stock in exchange for a piece of used equipment whose asking price was $16,000. The appraiser valued the equipment at $16,400. There is no market for the preferred stock. The equipment has a 5-year life and a $1,000 salvage value. The company uses straight-line depreciation computed to the nearest whole month.

Required: Record the above transaction in the general journal including depreciation expense on December 31.

Ex. 10-5 **Basket purchase in exchange for stock.** Bremsel Company is negotiating for the purchase of some real estate for which the buyer is asking $275,000. The property consists of land, two buildings, and some equipment located in one of the buildings. An appraiser has stated that the fair market value of the property on Bessemer Street is as follows:

Land	$ 30,000
Building No. 1	120,000
Building No. 2	0
Equipment	90,000

The company wants the property badly in order to expand operations, but it does not want to pay the inflated price. In a final attempt to acquire the property, the company offers $50,000 cash and 5,000 shares of its common stock. If the offer is accepted, the company plans to demolish the worthless building to make room for the construction of a water tower. The offer is accepted and the purchase is completed on March 30 when the company's stock is trading in the market at $40 per share. The company plans to use straight-line depreciation computed to the nearest whole month. The building is expected to have a useful life of 25 years and the equipment 10 years, with no salvage value. On April 18 the worthless building is demolished at a cost of $4,000.

Required: Prepare the journal entries on March 30, April 18, and December 31.

Ex. 10-6   **Amortization methods for assets.**   Below is a list of long-lived assets.

a. Land
b. Building
c. Equipment
d. Patent
e. Goodwill
f. Trademarks
g. Leasehold improvement
h. Franchise
i. License
j. Oil deposits
k. Investment in common stock

l. Timber tract
m. Fixtures
n. Land improvements
o. Copyright
p. Mineral deposit
q. Deferred charge
r. Organization costs
s. Tools
t. Furniture
u. Plant site not in use
v. Quarry

Required: For each asset, indicate the method that should be used to allocate the asset's cost to expense of the period in which the asset is used. Use the following code for the allocation methods:
D—Depreciation   **P**—Depletion   **A**—Amortization   **N**—No allocation

Ex. 10-7   **Three depreciation methods.**   Jarue Company constructed a building for $100,000. The building has a useful life of 20 years and a salvage value of $20,000.

Required: Calculate depreciation expense rounded to the nearest $10, for the first 2 years of the building's life, assuming the method of depreciation is
    a.   Straight-line.
    b.   Double declining balance.
    c.   Sum-of-the-years'-digits.

Ex. 10-8   **Five equipment depreciation methods.**   Staley Company acquired a piece of equipment in 1985 for $30,000. This equipment has a useful life of 15 years or 50,000 hours, with a salvage value of $5,000. During the first three years of ownership, the company used the equipment 4,000, 3,100 and 4,300 hours respectively. The company claimed a 10 percent investment tax credit in the year of equipment acquisition.

Required: Calculate depreciation expense for the first three years of use, assuming the depreciation method is
    a.   Straight-line.
    b.   Double declining balance.
    c.   Sum-of-the-years'-digits.
    d.   Units of production.
    e.   ACRS. (*Hint:* Use Figure 10-5)

Ex. 10-9   **Equipment depreciation with investment tax credit.**   Whatley Company's new truck cost $10,000. It has a useful life of 5 years or 90,000 miles and a salvage value of $1,000. The company claimed a 6 percent investment tax credit in the year of acquisition. During the first 3 years, the truck was used as follows:

Year	1	2	3
Miles	12,000	10,000	16,000

Required: Calculate depreciation expense and book value for each of the first 3 years using the:
- a.   Units-of-production method.
- b.   Double declining balance method.
- c.   Sum-of-the-years'-digits method.
- d.   ACRS method. (*Hint:* Use Figure 10-5)

Ex. 10-10   **Partial period depreciation with four methods.**   On July 1, 1985, Dixon Company acquired a piece of equipment for $16,000. The equipment has an estimated useful life of 5 years and a salvage value of $1,000. The company calculates depreciation to the nearest whole month at the end of each calendar year. In the year of purchase, the company claimed an 8 percent investment credit.

Required: Calculate depreciation on the equipment for 1985, 1986, and 1987, assuming depreciation is computed using the
- a.   Straight-line method.
- b.   Double declining balance method.
- c.   Sum-of-the-years'-digits method.
- d.   ACRS method. (*Hint:* Use Figure 10-5)

Ex. 10-11   **Purchase and sale of equipment.**   Robert Smith bought a machine on January 1, 1985, for $6,000. It has an estimated life of 10 years and no salvage value. Straight-line depreciation is used. On December 31, 1986, Smith sold this machine for $5,500.

Required: Prepare all journal entries to record the above events.

Ex. 10-12   **Exchange of assets.**   Freedland Company records depreciation to the nearest whole month. On December 31, 1985, its sheet metal brake had a book value of $4,000 and a cost of $9,000. It was depreciated on the straight-line basis, with a 10-year life and no salvage value. On April 30, 1986, the company exchanged the machine for a new piece of equipment whose asking price was $8,000. The fair value of the old machine was $3,900 on April 30, and the company paid $4,000 cash in the exchange.

Required:
- a.   Record the transaction, assuming the two machines were like assets.
- b.   Record the transaction, assuming the two machines were unlike assets.

Ex. 10-13   **Sale and exchange of like assets.**   Pascal Company records depreciation to the nearest whole month. On December 31, 1985, its milling machine had a book value of $4,000 and a cost of $9,000. It was depreciated on the straight-line basis, with a

10-year life and no salvage value. On April 30, when the milling machine had a fair value of $3,500, the company decided to replace it with a new machine. A similar new machine is found with a price of $10,000. The company is offered a $3,800 trade-in value on the old machine.

Required:
    a. Record the transaction, assuming the company sells its old machine for $3,500 cash and buys the new one for cash.
    b. Record the transaction, assuming the company exchanges the old machine and $6,200 cash for the new one.

Ex. 10-14 **Exchange of unlike assets.** Jensen Company owns a machine that cost $10,000 and has accumulated depreciation of $6,500. The machine is traded for a piece of land whose asking price is $10,000. The seller allows a trade-in value that is the same as the fair value. Jensen must pay the balance in cash.

Required:
    a. Record the exchange of the machine for the land assuming the fair value is $3,300.
    b. Record the exchange of the machine for the land assuming the fair value is $3,800.

Ex. 10-15 **Depletion of a mine.** Stovel Corporation acquired a silver mine for $85,000 on January 5, 1985. The mine is expected to have a salvage value of $40,000 and to yield 36,000 grams of silver over its useful life. During 1985 the company extracted 6,000 grams of silver, all of which is in inventory. The cost of operating the mine was $6,500, none of it inventoriable.

Required: Calculate depletion of the mine, and record the above in the general journal.

Ex. 10-16 **Depletion and sale of natural resource.** Everfale Company acquired a gold mine for $10,600,000 on January 4, 1985. The mine is expected to have a salvage value of $200,000 and to yield 80,000 ounces of gold over its useful life. By October 31, 1985, the company extracted 16,000 ounces of gold, all of which is in inventory. On November 15, 15,000 ounces of gold are sold for $400 per oz. The company uses a perpetual inventory system.

Required: Calculate depletion of the mine, and record the above in the general journal.

Ex. 10-17 **Acquisition and sale of patents.** Sharyl Company acquired two patents on January 2, 1985. One cost $5,000 and is expected to have a useful life of 5 years. The other cost $6,000 and is expected to have a useful life of 10 years. On June 29, 1986, the company sells the $5,000 patent for $20,000 cash.

Required:
    a. Record the acquisition of the two patents.
    b. Record the amortization of the patents on December 31, 1985.
    c. Record the disposal of the patent.

Ex. 10-18   **Excess earnings and goodwill.**   The following condensed balance sheet for Elzner Company represents the fair value of the company's net assets:

Elzner Company
Balance Sheet
December 31, 1985

Assets		Equities	
Current assets	$ 60,000	Current liabilities	$ 35,000
Investments	40,000	Long-term liabilities	60,000
Fixed assets	100,000	Capital	105,000
Total assets	$200,000	Total equities	$200,000

The normal rate of return for the industry is 15 percent of net assets. For the past 5 years, the company's net income has been as follows:

1981	$15,500
1982	15,000
1983	18,000
1984	20,000
1985	19,000

Required: Compute Elzner Company's excess earnings and estimate goodwill by capitalizing excess earnings at 20 percent.

Ex. 10-19   **Calculation of goodwill.**   Thorsen Company's net assets are $150,000. The normal rate of return in this company's industry is 12 percent of net assets. Thorsen Company's average net income is $20,000 per year.

Required: Calculate goodwill using the following assumptions:
   a.   Excess earnings are capitalized at 15 percent.
   b.   Future excess earnings are discounted at 15 percent for 12 years.
   c.   A payback of 8 years is desired.

PROBLEMS

P. 10-1   **Basket purchase.**   Bolton Company bought a manufacturing plant that included land, two buildings, and equipment. The property was appraised at $40,000 for the land, $280,000 for one building, and $80,000 for the equipment. The second building was considered worthless, and the company decided to demolish it to make room for a parking lot. The following amounts were paid in connection with the property acquisition:

Purchase price	$375,000
Land survey	600
Removal and reinstallation of equipment from building to be demolished	3,200
Demolition of building	8,000
Remodeling of remaining building	25,500

Grading and leveling of land	3,900
Salary of night guard for new property	8,400
Addition to building	53,000
Routine maintenance of equipment	5,000
Fire insurance on property	2,400

By the end of the first year the company recorded depreciation on the building of $9,000, and on the equipment, $8,200.

Required: Determine the cost of the new property, and show how the land, building, and equipment would be reported in the balance sheet at the end of the year.

P. 10-2 **Acquisition and depreciation of assets.**   On January 2, 1985, Gaylord Manufacturing Company acquired land and a building with a list price of $105,000 by exchanging 5,000 shares of its common stock. The stock is selling in the market at $20 per share. An independent appraiser valued the land at $27,000 and the building at $63,000. The building has a useful life of 20 years and a salvage value of $5,000.

On July 1, 1985, the company purchased equipment for $12,000 with a discount of 2 percent available if the invoice was paid within 10 days. The freight and installation cost of the equipment was $240. The company paid for the freight, installation, and the equipment on July 9. The equipment has a useful life of 5 years and a salvage value of $2,000. Depreciation is recorded to the nearest whole month using the straight-line method.

Required: Record the acquisition of the assets and depreciation expense on December 31, 1985.

P. 10-3 **Depreciation of equipment.**   On January 4, 1985, Esco Corporation purchased $10,000 of equipment on open account with terms 2/10, n/30. The freight and installation cost of $400 was paid in cash on January 7. The equipment has a useful life of 5 years and a salvage value of $200. The account payable is recorded at gross invoice cost and was paid on January 12.

Required:
    a. Prepare depreciation schedules similar to those found in the text figures to compute depreciation expense and book value of the equipment for its useful life, using the following methods:
        1. Straight-line
        2. Double declining balance
        3. Sum-of-the-years'-digits
    b. Prepare journal entries to record the purchase, installation, and payment, and depreciation on December 31 using the DDB method.

P. 10-4 **Accounting and tax depreciation.**   On January 4, 1984, Fletcher Company acquired a fleet of 3 identical light trucks for a total of $36,000. Each is expected to have a useful life of 4 years or 120,000 miles, and a salvage value of $1,200. The company claimed a 4 percent investment tax credit. During the next 4 years the trucks were used as follows:

Year	No. 1	No. 2	No. 3	Total Miles
1	37,000	35,000	38,000	110,000
2	30,000	29,000	29,000	89,000
3	22,000	30,000	23,000	75,000
4	32,000	23,000		55,000

On December 29, 1986, the company sold Truck No. 3 for $3,400.

Required:

a. Calculate depreciation expense for each year for the fleet using all five methods discussed in the chapter, including the 3-year ACRS.

b. Record acquisition of the trucks, depreciation for the first year, and the sale of Truck No. 3, assuming use of DDB depreciation.

P. 10-5   Depreciation on building.   Gamma Corporation completed construction of a new office building on March 31, 1985. Cost of construction was $580,000, not including the architect's fee of $40,000. On April 1 the company moved into the building. The expected useful life of the building is 25 years, and the estimated salvage value is $70,000. The company calculates depreciation to the nearest whole month.

Required:

a. Calculate depreciation on the building for the first 3 years ending December 31. Assume use of:
   1. Straight-line depreciation.
   2. Double declining balance method.
   3. Sum-of-the-years'-digits method.

b. Prepare journal entries to record depreciation expense on December 31 of 1985 and 1986, using double declining balance depreciation.

P. 10-6   Revised depreciation, sale, and exchange.   Flexifirm Company owns a piece of equipment which cost $20,000 and which has a balance of $12,000 in the Accumulated Depreciation account on December 31, 1984. The equipment was originally estimated to have a useful life of 10 years and no salvage value. Technological advances are making it necessary either to replace the machine or remodel it. The company decides on the latter course, and on January 12, 1985, spends $7,400 to modify the machine, extending its useful life by 3 years. The company uses straight-line depreciation.

On December 27, 1986, the company decides to replace the machine. A similar new machine is available at a cost of $15,000, and the company is offered $10,500 as a trade-in on its old machine with the balance of the purchase price to be paid in cash. The fair value of the remodeled machine at the end of 1986 is $10,000.

Required:

a. Record the expenditure to remodel the machine, assuming cash was paid for the work. Record depreciation expense on December 31, 1985; sale of the machine for fair value on December 27, 1986; and purchase of the new machine for cash.

b. Prepare the journal entry that would be made if the old machine were exchanged for the new one on December 27, 1986.

P. 10-7 **Depreciation and exchange of similar equipment.** H & M Farms, Inc., uses double declining balance depreciation calculated to the nearest month. On March 27, 1984, the company acquired for $10,000 a tractor with a useful life of 5 years and a salvage value of $2,000. On January 2, 1986, the company exchanged this tractor for a similar tractor listed at $12,000. The fair value of the old tractor at the time of exchange was $6,500, and the company paid $2,500 cash in addition to trading in the old tractor. The company uses the calendar year for accounting purposes.

Required: Prepare the necessary journal entries to record all the above events.

P. 10-8 **Exchange of like assets.** On January 4, 1984, Marion Corporation purchased for $18,000 a machine with a useful life of 5 years and a $3,000 salvage value. Management decided to depreciate this machine using the sum-of-the-years'-digits method. On June 29, 1987, Marion exchanged this machine for a similar machine whose asking price was $13,500. A $5,500 trade-in value was allowed on the old machine. The remaining $8,000 was paid in cash.

Required: Record this exchange of similar assets assuming the fair value of the old machine at the time of exchange was
  a. $4,300.
  b. $5,200.
  c. Record this exchange of similar assets for tax purposes.

P. 10-9 **Exchange of unlike assets.** Livorno Company owns a small crane which cost $12,000, with $8,000 of accumulated depreciation recorded by January, 1985. The company uses straight-line depreciation with a 6-year life and no salvage value, computed to the nearest whole month. On April 3, 1985, the company traded the crane for a pole trailer with a list price of $7,000. The trade-in allowance on the crane was $4,500 with the balance paid in cash.

Required: Record the exchange of unlike assets in the general journal, assuming the fair value of the crane on the date of exchange was
  a. $4,000.
  b. $3,100.

P. 10-10 **Depreciation and disposal of property.** In January of 1984, Blackwell Corporation completed building a new wing of its plant and remodeling the old building. Prior to the addition, the cost of the land was $30,000; the cost of the plant was $1,100,000, with a $100,000 salvage value and 20-year total estimated useful life; and accumulated depreciation was $500,000. The new wing and remodeling added $50,000 to the cost of the building and 10 years to the total useful life. The salvage value remained unchanged. Blackwell uses straight-line depreciation. On January 3, 1986, the entire plant and land were exchanged for a yacht with a list price of $750,000. The trade-in value allowed on the property was $710,000 and the remaining $40,000 was paid in cash.

Required:
  a. Record depreciation expense on December 31 of 1984 and 1985.
  b. Record the exchange assuming that the fair value of the property in January 1986 was $640,000.
  c. Record the exchange assuming that the fair value of the property in January 1986 was $570,000.

P. 10-11 **Depletion of timber stand.** Shelden Lumber Company owns a stand of timber with a total cost of $300,000 including land valued at $60,000. The stand contains approximately eight million board feet of lumber. In 1985 Shelden cut and processed 800,000 board feet of lumber. There was no beginning inventory in 1985. Sales of lumber in 1985 amounted to 600,000 board feet. In 1986 the company cut and processed 750,000 board feet and sold 500,000 board feet. The company incurs a processing cost of $.05 per board foot and sells its lumber at $.20 per board foot. It uses FIFO inventory valuation.

Required:
    a. Find cost of goods sold and ending inventory on:
        1. December 31, 1985.
        2. December 31, 1986.
    b. What is the book value of the timber stand on December 31, 1986?

P. 10-12 **Depletion and depreciation.** In January 1985, Golden Charm Company acquired land containing a mineral claim. Half the $600,000 purchase price is assigned to the land and half to the minerals. The company estimates that 1,250,000 tons of ore are·available from the property. A processing plant is built on the property at a cost of $60,000. The plant has a useful life of 30 years but is expected to be used only for the next 10 years, at the end of which time the minerals are expected to be depleted. During 1985 the company mined and processed 80,000 tons of ore at an operating cost of $150,000. In addition, administrative expenses amounted to $85,000. All costs except administrative are inventoriable. No processed ore was sold in 1985. In 1986 the company mined 180,000 tons of ore at an operating cost of $247,800 and administrative expenses of $90,000. During 1986, 200,000 tons were sold at $5.20 per ton. The company uses a perpetual FIFO inventory system and straight-line depreciation.

Required: Prepare journal entries to record the transactions in 1985 and 1986 including end-of-year adjustments.

P. 10-13 **Goodwill calculations.** Having saved a considerable amount of money, Sam Folsom wants to quit his job and buy a business of his own. Two companies are available that are of interest to him and within his price range. Each business is for sale for $150,000. Following are the two companies' balance sheets on December 31:

	Opticon	Geolite
Assets		
Cash	$ 40,000	$ 10,000
Accounts receivable (net)	45,000	55,000
Inventory	60,000	55,000
Fixed assets (net)	93,000	88,000
Total assets	$238,000	$208,000
Equities		
Liabilities	$ 98,000	$102,000
Capital	140,000	106,000
Total equities	$238,000	$208,000

Folsom believes that the asking price in each case is justified, but he is not sure which company represents the more favorable situation. With the permission of each company, he hires an accountant to audit the financial statements and advise him on the value of each business. During the audits the following data are disclosed:

Opticon's inventories are carried at FIFO, and current replacement cost is approximately equal to cost. The allowance for doubtful accounts needs to be increased by $5,000 due to the doubtful nature of some of the accounts re-ceivable. Fixed assets are appraised at $118,000. The average annual net income for the last 5 years is $16,200.

Geolite Company's receivables have an adequate provision for doubtful ac-counts. Inventories are carried at LIFO, and current replacement cost is about $67,000. Land with a book value of $20,000 has a market value of $32,000. The average annual net income for the last 5 years is $17,000.

Prior to the sale of the business, each owner plans to withdraw all cash from his company. All liabilities will have to be assumed by the buyer.

The annual rate of return in the industry is 12 percent. The accountant suggests estimating goodwill by capitalizing excess annual earnings at 16 percent, and discounting future excess earnings at 12 percent for 15 years. Folsom is anxious to see the resulting figure but also believes that his payback should be no more than 5 years.

Required:

a. Restate the balance sheets to reflect the current market value of each company prior to sale so that Folsom can compare the two companies.

b. Calculate the amount of goodwill, using the methods suggested by the accountant and the payback method.

c. Write a brief recommendation advising Folsom which company to acquire.

P. 10-14 **Adjusting fixed asset accounts.** Following are some transactions of Marlett Corporation during 1985 that are under examination in the year-end audit of the company's financial statements.

a. The company terminated production of a bird food that was sold under the trade name Wormling. The trade name had a book value of $20,000 and was sold to another manufacturer for $3,000. Goodwill was debited $17,000 when the cash was received and the trade name was written off.

b. Land and buildings were purchased for $75,000 on March 29, 1985, and three of the older buildings were demolished to make room for construction of a new warehouse. The demolition cost of $5,000 was debited to the building account, and the result was an increase in the book value of buildings to $55,000.

c. A truck costing $10,000 with a book value of $2,000 was sold for $3,000 cash on January 13, 1985. The entry was recorded by a debit to cash and a credit to trucks of $3,000.

d. A $10,000 addition to one of the buildings was debited to the merchandise account. Land-leveling costs of $5,000 were debited to the land account. The building addition was completed on April 3, 1985.

e. No depreciation has been recorded for the new buildings at the end of 1985. Building depreciation is normally recorded as 5 percent per year of the book value of the buildings, calculated to the nearest whole month.

Required: Prepare the entries necessary to correct the accounts and any adjusting entries needed at the end of 1985.

Case 10-1   **Interpretation of reported information.**
Owen-Gerhard Company, whose fiscal year ends on January 31, reported the following fixed assets in its 1985 annual report:

Property, Plant, and Equipment	January 31 1985 (in thousands)	1984
Land	$ 1,525	$ 1,164
Buildings and improvements	10,672	7,530
Machinery and equipment	81,366	54,215
	93,563	62,909
Less accumulated depreciation	27,511	18,677
Total	$66,052	$44,232

The company reported $11,830,000 of depreciation expense for 1985, of which $1,204,000 was for buildings. Also reported is a gain on sale of assets of $406,000 and a loss on exchange of assets of $39,000. The book value of the assets disposed of was $3,104,000 and included equipment costing $800,000 which was exchanged for land. There were no disposals of land or buildings, and the entire increase in land occurred as a result of the exchange on which the loss was recorded.

Required: Determine the cost of the equipment which was acquired in 1985, and reproduce the entry used to record the sale of equipment.

Accounting for Liabilities

11

The equity portion of the balance sheet contains a variety of equity accounts. Many of these accounts are liabilities which represent equities of the entity's creditors. When you have finished studying this chapter, you should understand:

1 Accounting for current liabilities, such as accounts payable, notes payable, payrolls, and many others.

2 Amortization of installment-type debt.

3 Two types of leases, some advantages of leasing, and lease accounting and reporting.

4 Why tax laws result in reporting of liabilities that are not owed to anyone.

5 Why some liabilities must be estimated and others are reported even if they do not exist yet.

6 How to interpret the liability section of an annual report and the related footnotes.

In this chapter we turn our attention to the liabilities of businesses, some of which have already been mentioned in previous chapters. Businesses borrow a significant portion of their resources from creditors and must account carefully for these obligations. Some liabilities, such as accounts payable, occur as a result of purchases of goods and services; others, such as notes payable, from borrowing. Taxes payable are liabilities that result from the operation of laws. And some events beyond the company's control, such as court judgments or product failures, may result in liabilities.

Although we address the salient concepts of accounting for liabilities, many of the topics in this chapter are too complex to cover in great detail. The first part of the chapter deals with current liabilities, which must be repaid within the current operating period. Next, we cover long-term liabilities except bonds, which are discussed in Chapter 12. Other liabilities, such as leases, pensions, deferred credits, and estimated obligations, are discussed in the last part of the chapter.

CURRENT LIABILITIES

Current liabilities consist of accounts payable, notes payable, deferred revenues, and accrued expenses. These liabilities are paid continuously, and new ones are created regularly in the daily course of business. You may remember from Chapter 8 and Figure 8-1 that current liabilities constitute a part of circulating capital.

Accounts Payable

Purchases of goods and services on open account result in accounts payable, and payment to creditors is required in the near future. Businesses typically incur accounts payable by signing an invoice when goods are received from a supplier, although some accounts payable are incurred when purchases are made with a credit card. Accounts payable typically must be paid in 30 to 60 days and seldom exceed 90 days. As a result, these obligations, like all current liabilities, must be paid with current assets.

Current liabilities are paid from current assets

The accountant must ensure that the balance in Accounts Payable reflects the amounts actually owed. The account should include obligations on all credit purchases even if invoices have not yet been received. Conversely, the account should not include invoices for purchases of goods to which title has not yet passed.

Short-Term Notes Payable

Short-term written promissory notes are current obligations that arise from several sources. They include:

1. Interest-bearing trade notes payable given in exchange for goods and services.
2. Short-term loans for which promissory notes are given.
3. Noninterest notes on which interest must be imputed.

Trade notes payable.   Interest-bearing trade notes payable should be reported at their face value. For example, a $12,000 purchase is made on August 15, and a 60-day 12 percent note is given to the seller. The entry is

Aug. 15	Purchases (or Merchandise)	12,000	
	Notes payable		12,000
	Obtained goods in exchange for 60-day		
	12% note.		

When the note is paid 60 days later, the entry is

Oct. 14	Notes payable	12,000	
	Interest expense	240	
	Cash		12,240
	Paid 60-day note with interest.		
	$12,000 \times .12 \times 60/360 = \$240$		

If the accounting period ends before the note matures, the interest accrued on the note should be recorded with an adjusting entry, as demonstrated in Chapter 5.

Non-interest-bearing notes may be discounted

Discounted notes payable.   A company obtains a short-term loan from a bank or other lending institution by giving the lender a non-interest-bearing note. The lender discounts the note by deducting the interest from the face amount of the note, which is also its maturity value, and pays the difference to the borrower. The borrower actually obtains less money than the face amount of the note. For example, Marcel Corporation discounted its $8,000, 90-day note with a bank. The bank, which charges a discount rate of 15 percent, calculates the discount as follows:

$$\$8,000 \times .15 \times 90/360 = \$300$$

The proceeds given to the borrower amount to $7,700 ($8,000 − $300). The company makes the following entry to record the loan:

Aug. 31	Cash	7,700	
	Discount on notes payable	300	
	Notes payable		8,000
	Discounted 90-day note with bank		
	at 15%.		

When the note matures 90 days later, the face amount of $8,000 is repaid, and the discount is written off. Writing off the discount results in recording interest expense as follows:

Nov. 29	Notes payable	8,000	
	Interest expense	300	
	Discount on notes payable		300
	Cash		8,000
	Paid discounted bank note.		

Notice that the company received only $7,700 from the bank but paid back $8,000. The difference is the interest expense. If financial statements are prepared on September 30, part of the discount is written off, and interest expense is recorded for the 30 days that the note has been outstanding, as follows:

Sept. 30	Interest expense	100	
	Discount on notes payable		100
	To amortize discount on note for 30 days.		

The discount reduces non-interest notes to their present value

Accounting principles[1] require reporting non-interest-bearing notes at their present value, rather than their face value. The discount is a contra liability account deducted from the face value of the note in the balance sheet, showing the net amount of the obligation. The note is reported in the balance sheet as follows:

Notes payable	$8,000	
Less discount on notes payable	200	$7,800

When the obligation is paid on November 29, the remaining discount is written off, and interest expense is debited. The entry is

Nov. 29	Notes payable	8,000	
	Interest expense	200	
	Discount on notes payable		8,000
	Cash		200
	Paid discounted note.		

The company pays interest calculated as 15 percent of $8,000 but actually has the use of only $7,700. Therefore the effective annual percentage rate of interest is slightly higher than 15 percent. It can be calculated as follows:

$$\text{Effective annual percentage rate} = \frac{\text{Amount of interest paid}}{\text{Amount actually borrowed}} \div \text{Time}$$

$$= \frac{\$300}{\$7,700} \div \frac{90}{360} = .15584 \text{ or } 15.584\%$$

Imputed interest on notes payable. When a note is discounted for the purpose of borrowing money, the interest rate is known and used to cal-

---

[1] APB Opinion No. 21, "Interest on Receivables and Payable," August 1971.

culate the discount. Sometimes, however, non-interest-bearing notes are given when a purchase is made, and no interest rate is stated. In that case, interest on the note must be **imputed** at a reasonable rate. The face amount of the note that will be paid on maturity includes both principal and interest, and by imputing interest and deducting it from the face amount, the note is reported at its present value.

Imputed interest is implied in the face amount of a non-interest note

For example, a company buys merchandise on August 13 by giving a $15,170, 60-day non-interest-bearing note to the seller. The actual cost of the merchandise is the present value of the $15,170 note payable. By imputing the interest and deducting it from the face amount, the company can report the note in the balance sheet at its present value and also record the merchandise at its actual cost. If 15 percent is an appropriate rate, interest for 60 days is 2.5 percent, calculated as

$$.15 \times 60/360 = .025 \text{ or } 2.5\%$$

The correct way to calculate the discount is to find the present value of the note for one period by dividing the future value of $15,170 by 1 plus the interest rate. The entry to record the note payable and the purchase of merchandise is

Aug. 13	Purchases	14,800	
	Discount on notes payable	370	
	Notes payable		15,170
	Acquired goods with noninterest note.		
	Interest imputed at 15% for 60 days.		
	$15,170/1.025 = $14,800		

Recording interest expense by writing off the discount is the same procedure used with discounted notes. The note is also reported in the balance sheet in the same manner. As time passes, interest expense is incurred on the note. If the company prepares financial statements on September 30, interest on the note is recorded to this date prior to preparing financial statements.

Sept. 30	Interest expense	296	
	Discount on notes payable		296
	To record imputed interest for 48 days.		
	$14,800 × .15 × 48/360 = $296		

When the obligation is paid on October 12, the remaining discount is written off, and interest expense is debited for $74.

Reclassification of Debt

When a long-term liability is about to mature, it should be reclassified as short-term. Sometimes management arranges to postpone the payment of short-term liabilities, and they may have to be reclassified as long-term. Such reclassifications of debt are discussed below.

Long-term debt is reclassified as short term prior to maturity

Current portion of long-term debt.   When long-term notes payable, bonds payable, or other long-term obligations fall due within 1 year, they should be reported as current liabilities. Sometimes only a part of the long-term debt matures each year, and only the part that must be repaid during the next accounting period should be reported as current. For example, Motte Company has a $45,000 mortgage payable on its building. Each year $5,000 must be repaid. The mortgage is reported as follows in the balance sheet:

Current liabilities:		
Current portion of long-term mortgage payable		$ 5,000
Long-term liabilities:		
Mortgage payable	$45,000	
Less current portion	5,000	40,000

Current liabilities to be refinanced.   In planning the repayment of debt and the financing of operations, management of a company may decide not to repay certain current liabilities when due but to arrange, instead, repayment at a later date. If repayment will take place after the end of the next accounting period, these obligations should be reported among long-term liabilities. To qualify for reporting current debt as part of long-term debt, the company must have the intention of refinancing the current obligations and must also demonstrate its ability to do so.

Two conditions must be met to reclassify short-term debt as long-term

For example, a company discounted a 90-day note with a bank. Sixty days later, management decides that it would be beneficial for the company not to repay this note for 2 years. The bank agrees to accept the company's 2-year interest-bearing note 30 days from now in exchange for the discounted note. The discounted note will not be repaid with current assets, and the company has a commitment from the bank to refinance the debt, therefore the discounted note should be removed from current liabilities and reclassified as a long-term liability.

Payrolls and Payroll Obligations

The contractual obligations that companies have with employees often involve much more than paying wages or salaries. Companies must withhold a portion of each employee's wage for the employee's income taxes and social security tax. Union dues, insurance premiums, savings bond purchases, and many other payments may also be withheld by employers. Employee benefits, sometimes called **fringe benefits**, provided by the employer include paid vacations, paid holidays, recreational programs, edu-

Payroll costs amount to more than salaries and wages alone

cational programs, and retirement plans. Even if a firm does not provide all these benefits, in many industries payroll taxes and fringe benefits may amount to as much as 40 percent of gross payroll. You can easily see why many labor disputes concern fringe benefits rather than wage rates.

In the case of income taxes and social security tax, federal laws require employers to act as agents for the federal government and withhold money from employees' paychecks. Other deductions such as bond purchase plans and union dues result from voluntary or contractual arrangements. Accounting for payrolls requires a tremendous amount of detailed record keeping. For example, employees are subject to different tax rates based on their earnings and on the number of dependents they claim. The social security tax required by the Federal Insurance Contribution Act (FICA) is levied on wages and salaries up to a specified maximum amount per year. The **FICA tax** is withheld from employees until their wages for the year reach the maximum specified. Employers must therefore maintain detailed earnings records for every employee to know when to stop withholding FICA taxes.[2]

To illustrate accounting for payrolls with a company that has three employees, we assume that the company is required to withhold 20 percent of the employees' pay for federal income taxes and 7 percent for social security tax. The cost of health insurance is shared by the company and the employees. The employees are paid monthly, and each one earns $2,000 per month.

On January 31, the payroll is computed and paid. The entry to record the payroll is:

Jan. 31	Salary expense	6,000	
	Federal income tax payable		1,200
	FICA tax payable		420
	Health insurance payable		90
	Cash		4,290
	Paid January payroll.		

The company's payroll cost for January is $6,000 even though the net amount employees receive totals $4,290. The $1,710 of withholdings are recorded as liabilities and must be paid by the company to the federal government and health insurance company. When these liabilities are paid, the employer will have paid a total of $6,000 compensation to its six employees or to others on the employees' behalf.

Payroll taxes are expenses in addition to the payroll

Payroll taxes are levied on an employer based on amounts earned by employees. The employer must match the employees' FICA tax with an equal contribution, and the employer's share of FICA tax is a significant portion of payroll costs. Another payroll cost is unemployment tax, which is levied by the state and federal governments on employers.

---

[2] FICA tax rates have been changed frequently by Congress. For simplicity we assume a 7 percent rate in this chapter.

Jan. 31	Payroll tax expense	590	
	FICA tax payable		420
	Federal unemployment tax payable		42
	State unemployment tax payable		128
	To record January payroll tax expense.		

Notice that the total FICA liability is $840, of which $420 was withheld from the employees, and $420 is the employer's expense. Below we illustrate the recording of two fringe benefits, medical insurance and a retirement plan.

Jan. 31	Payroll benefit expense	635	
	Health insurance payable		105
	Retirement fund payable		530
	To record payroll benefits for January		
	payroll.		

Payroll taxes are not accrued at year end

Most liabilities that result from the payroll are current liabilities because they must be paid within the year. Some, such as federal tax withholding, must be paid almost immediately. Retirement or pension liabilities are usually current, although some may be long term.

Payroll taxes are payable only on wages actually paid to employees. Therefore if payroll is accrued at the end of the accounting period, the employer does not also accrue the various payroll tax obligations associated with the payroll. These obligations are recorded in the next period when the payroll is paid. You can see that payrolls constitute a major record-keeping task for many businesses. Computers have been especially useful in payroll accounting applications because of the large volume of repetitive transactions and the huge quantity of records that must be maintained.

Other Current Obligations

Many other current liabilities are reported on the balance sheet. They include property taxes payable, accrued interest, income taxes payable, unearned revenues, and dividends payable. We discussed most of these liabilities in previous chapters, and they pose no new accounting problems. Accounting for dividends payable is covered in Chapter 13. The remainder of this chapter is devoted to long-term liabilities.

LONG-TERM LIABILITIES

Obligations that will not be paid during the next accounting period are classified as long-term liabilities. They include long-term installment notes and mortgages, bonds payable, notes payable, leases, and pension obligations.

Installment Notes and Mortgages Payable

Businesses as well as individuals frequently finance the purchase of real estate and other assets with installment notes or mortgages. The property purchased usually serves to secure the installment debt so that the lender is assured of receiving payment either from the borrower or from the repossession and sale of the property.

Installment notes are annuities; they are amortized over their lifetime

Installment notes and **mortgages** are obligations that require periodic payments which include interest and repayment of a portion of the principal. Such obligations are repaid over a period of time rather than in a lump sum at the end of some period.

For example, Zelda Company purchases real estate for $85,000, paying $25,000 in cash plus a $60,000, 20-year 15 percent installment note. The monthly payments on the note are $790, including interest on the remaining balance of the principal. To record the purchase, the company makes the following entry:

Feb. 1	Land	15,000	
	Building	70,000	
	Cash		25,000
	Installment notes payable		60,000
	Acquired land and building in exchange		
	for cash and 20-year 15%		
	installment note.		

Each month when the company makes the installment payment, it records interest expense and reduces the amount of the note's principal. With a beginning balance of $60,000, interest for the first month is $750, calculated as

$$\$60,000 \times .15 \times 30/360 = \$750$$

The remainder of the monthly payment reduces the principal balance, as illustrated in the following journal entry:

Mar. 1	Interest expense	750.00	
	Installment notes payable	40.00	
	Cash		790.00
	Paid installment on note, leaving a		
	principal balance of $59,960.		

Next month, with the principal reduced to $59,960, the monthly payment is recorded as

Apr. 1	Interest expense	749.50	
	Installment notes payable	40.50	
	Cash		790.00
	Paid installment on note.		
	$59,960 × .15 × 30/360 = $749.50.		

The monthly payments of $790 are the rents of an annuity whose present value is $60,000 when the property is acquired on February 1. During the early life of the loan most of the monthly payment consists of interest. Later payments will have a smaller proportion of interest as the principal is reduced. The last payment 20 years later will repay the remaining interest and principal, and the obligation will be fully repaid. The company may dispose of the property before repaying the obligation completely. Because the property secures the installment note, when the property is sold, the note must be repaid in full unless the new owner assumes the obligation to repay the balance of the note.

Mortgages and installment notes are accounted for in the same way. The difference between them is only in the legal rights that the mortgage or note holder has, and these rights vary according to state laws and individual contracts.

Leases

A **lease** is a long-term rental arrangement. The owner, or **lessor**, leases property to the **lessee**, who pays rent for the privilege of using the property. The lease agreement may contain any provisions that are suitable to the lessor and the lessee. FASB Statement No. 13 defines various types of leases and the accounting methods to be used with them. Leases are classified as those that are true rental arrangements, called **operating leases**, and those that are in reality purchase and financing arrangements, called **capital leases**.

Advantages of leasing

The advantage of an operating lease to the lessee is that no capital investment is required, and there is no expense of ownership or risk of loss. The lessor bears the risk and expense of ownership, and when the lease terminates, the property reverts to the lessor. For example, a company may decide to lease all its automobiles from an auto leasing firm. The lessee simply pays the monthly rental for the use of the cars. All maintenance is the lessor's responsibility, and when a car is worn out, obsolete, or damaged, the lessee simply obtains another from the lessor. Of course, the lessee indirectly bears the cost of maintenance, insurance, taxes, and other expenses in the form of monthly rentals but does not own the automobile. Often, however, leasing such assets rather than buying them allows a business to free its capital for other uses.

A capital lease resembles an installment note purchase. It provides a way to buy the leased property without making an initial down payment. The advantage to the lessee is the ability to finance the entire purchase price of the asset and obtain all the benefits of ownership. The lessee's rent payments actually represent the payment of interest and principal during the lease period as the lessee uses the assets. For example, a company may arrange to lease an airplane with the actual intention of using it for its entire useful life. The lessor is in effect financing the airplane with no intention of maintaining ownership after the lease terminates.

Companies sometimes construct assets to their own specifications and then sell them and lease them back from the buyer. These are called **sale-leaseback** arrangements and usually involve capital leases. For example, a retail firm may build a store in a new location to suit its needs, but it does not want to have its capital tied up in the building. It may arrange to sell the building to a company whose function is to earn income from property rentals. The retail firm recovers the investment it put into the store building and can use its money to acquire merchandise while paying periodic rent to the buyer-lessor who obtains revenue from the lease.

Accounting for operating leases.   An operating lease is one under which the lessor retains ownership of the property after the lease terminates. The periodic rent payments represent revenue to the lessor and an expense to the lessee. For example, Lassie Corporation leases a building from Bilder Company on January 1, 1985. The lease agreement calls for annual rent payments of $15,000, with a 10-year term. Lassie Corporation makes the following entry each time the rent payment is made:

Operating leases are rental agreements

Jan. 2	Rent expense	15,000	
	Cash		15,000
	Made annual payment on operating		
	lease.		

The obligation to make future payments is not recorded by the lessee, but it must be disclosed in footnotes to the financial statements.

Accounting for capital leases.   *For the lessor* a capital lease is a way to earn interest revenue on funds invested in the leased property. Legal title to the property remains with the lessor while the lease is in force, but in effect the property is owned by the lessee. The lessor removes the property from the books as if it is actually sold and capitalizes the lease.

*Capital leases
are essentially
purchase
agreements*

For the lessee the capital lease is a way of purchasing property by financing the entire purchase price. Legal title to the property remains with the lessor until the lease terminates. At that time possession of the property may revert to the lessor, or the lessee may have the right to keep the property and obtain title by making a token payment. The rent payments represent payment of interest and principal. The lessee generally assumes all the usual expenses of ownership, such as maintenance, depreciation, and property taxes. Both the property and the lease obligation are shown in the balance sheet.

The provisions of FASB Statement No. 13 on capital leases are complex. But the basic aspects of accounting for capital leases are similar to accounting for installment notes. For example, Lee Sing Corporation, the lessee, obtains equipment under a capital lease from LeSoar Company, the lessor, on January 1, 1985. LeSoar purchases the equipment for $24,000 as specified by the lessee. The equipment has an estimated useful life of 5 years. The terms of the lease are as follows:

1. The lessee is to make five annual rent payments of $6,991 at the end of each year.

2. The lessee is responsible for all maintenance and taxes on the equipment.

3. When the lease terminates, the lessee may purchase the equipment for $500.

4. The annual rental provides a rate of return to the lessor of 14 percent per year on invested capital.

To record the lease obligation, the lessee finds the present value of the future rent payments, using an appropriate interest rate. In most cases the appropriate rate is the rate at which the lessee can borrow the funds to finance the purchase of the equipment. If the lessor's interest rate is known it may be used. With the lease payments at the end of each year, and equal annual rents, the obligation is an ordinary annuity. The present value of an ordinary annuity of $1 with $n = 5$ periods and $i = 14$ percent is 3.43308. Therefore, the present value of the future lease payments is $24,000 ($6,991 × 3.43308). In fact, because the asset cost $24,000 and the lessor wants a 14 percent return, the rent of $6,991 per year was obtained by computing the rent of an ordinary annuity. The lease obligation and the leased asset should be capitalized by the lessee at $24,000, as follows:

Jan. 2,	Equipment under capital lease	24,000	
1985	Capital lease obligation		24,000
	To record present value of 5-year		
	capital lease.		

With a capital lease, the lessee depreciates the leased property

The leased asset is depreciated by the lessee over its useful life or over the life of the lease. If straight-line depreciation is used and the salvage value is $4,000, the entry to record depreciation at the end of the year is

Dec. 31,	Depreciation expense	4,000	
1985	Accumulated depreciation, leased		
	equipment		4,000
	To record depreciation for 1 year on		
	leased equipment.		

As the lease payments are made by Lee Sing Corporation, the lease obligation is reduced in the same way as an installment note. Figure 11-1 illustrates a lease amortization schedule, which shows how the interest and principal payments are calculated. From the schedule the first lease payment is recorded as follows:

Dec. 31,	Interest expense	3,360.00	
1985	Capital lease obligation	3,631.00	
	Cash		6,991.00
	To record annual payment on		
	capital lease.		

Lee Sing Corporation
Lease Amortization Schedule
Based on 14 Percent Annual Interest

Date	(1) Annual Lease Payment	(2) Interest on Principal Balance	(3) Payment on Principal	(4) Principal Balance
1/01/85				$24,000.00
12/31/85	$ 6,991.00	$ 3,360.00	$ 3,631.00	20,369.00
12/31/86	6,991.00	2,851.66	4,139.34	16,229.66
12/31/87	6,991.00	2,272.15	4,718.85	11,510.81
12/31/88	6,991.00	1,611.51	5,379.49	6,131.32
12/31/89	6,989.70*	858.38	6,131.32	0
	$34,953.70	$10,953.70	$24,000.00	

Figure 11-1
The amortization of capital leases is similar to the amortization of installment notes. The effective interest rate must be known in order to amortize the lease obligation.

Col. 2 is 14% of previous balance in col. 4.
Col. 3 is col. 1 minus col. 2.
Col. 4 is previous balance minus col. 3.
* Difference due to rounding of lease payment to whole dollar.

At the end of the second year, the asset is again depreciated, and the lease payment is recorded as follows:

Dec. 31,	Interest expense	2,851.66	
1986	Capital lease obligation	4,139.34	
	Cash		6,991.00
	To record annual payment on		
	capital lease.		

Notice that the lease obligation and the asset are not written off at the same rate. Consequently, the book value of the asset and the book value of the lease obligation are the same only at the inception of the lease. By the end of 1987 the leased asset and lease obligation are reported in the balance sheet as follows:

Fixed assets:
Equipment under capital lease	$24,000.00	
Less accumulated depreciation	8,000.00	$16,000.00

Long-term liabilities:
Capital lease obligation	$16,229.66	
Less current portion	4,718.85	$11,510.81

Capital leases may contain a bargain purchase option

When the lease terminates, Lee Sing Corporation has the option of acquiring the leased equipment for $500. If the company chooses to do so, it makes the following entry:

Jan. 2,	Equipment	24,500	
1990	Accumulated depreciation, leased		
	equipment	20,000	
	Equipment under capital lease		24,000
	Accumulated depreciation		20,000
	Cash		500
	Purchased leased equipment at		
	termination of lease.		

The equipment and its accumulated depreciation are transferred from leased equipment accounts to owned equipment accounts, and the cash payment is added to the equipment's cost. At this time the company may decide to change its estimate of the remaining useful life of the equipment if it is justified in doing so. In any case, the book value of the equipment must be written off over the remaining useful life. Sometimes the leased equipment has a useful life longer than the term of the lease. In that case depreciation is computed over the useful life.

Pensions

Many companies establish pension plans for its employees. A variety of different plans exist, and the calculation of the amount that a company must contribute to its pension plan can be complex. The amount depends on the ages of the employees, their life expectancy, their expected retirement age, the income expected to be earned by the pension fund, if any, and other factors.

Pension liabilities are current pension benefits not yet paid

Some pension plans are **unfunded**, in which case the company pays the pension benefits from its own assets. For **funded** pension plans, a separate fund is established into which the company makes periodic payments. The assets of the pension fund are invested and the investment income is used to pay pensions to retired employees. Usually the pension fund is managed by a trustee and not by the employer. Whether a company pays pension benefits directly to retired employees or to a pension fund, the entry to record pension expense is a debit to Pension Expense and a credit to Cash.

TAX ALLOCATIONS

The primary purpose of tax laws is to produce revenue for the government, but tax laws also are used to influence business behavior. For example, the government attempts to influence the course of our economy by providing tax incentives. To stimulate capital investment, the government may allow a tax reduction for businesses that acquire certain types of equipment. To reduce unemployment, the government may give tax benefits to companies that implement certain hiring practices.

Accounting income and taxable income are often different

As a result of differences between tax laws and accounting principles, what may be considered revenue or expense for accounting purposes is not necessarily revenue or expense for tax purposes. In addition, some revenues and expenses recognized in one period for accounting purposes may have to be recognized in a different period for tax purposes. Consequently, a company's accounting income and its taxable income are not always the same.

Some income is never taxed; some expenses are never tax deductible

If certain revenues are not taxed, taxable income is smaller than accounting income. If an expense is not tax deductible, taxable income is larger than the accounting income which is computed by deducting the expense. Such untaxed revenues and nondeductible expenses cause **permanent differences** between taxable income and accounting income.

If a revenue or expense is included in accounting income of one period but in the taxable income of another period, differences between taxable and accounting income occur in both periods. These are called **timing differences**. **Deferred charges** and **deferred credits** occur when timing differences make it necessary to pay income tax in one period, but the tax must be allocated or assigned to other periods for accounting purposes. Such tax allocations are often misunderstood by users of financial statements, and it is important to understand how these balance sheet accounts come about and what they mean. Below we discuss permanent differences between taxable and accounting income and then timing differences that cause tax allocations.

Permanent Differences

The Internal Revenue Code defines what kind of income is subject to taxation and also describes certain types of income that are not taxed by the federal government. It is possible for a business to report revenues for accounting purposes that are different in amount from revenues that are taxable. For example, interest earned on bonds that are issued by cities, schools, and municipalities is not subject to federal income tax. Any municipal bond interest earned by an entity is permanently excluded from income in calculating income taxes. Similarly, proceeds from life insurance policies are not subject to income tax.

On the other hand, some legitimate business expenses may not be deductible for purposes of calculating taxable income. Amortization of goodwill, for example, is not recognized by the tax code as a deductible expense. Neither are insurance premiums paid on life insurance policies, because the proceeds of such policies are not taxed. Fines and penalties resulting from law violations are also not deductible for tax purposes. Such business expenses are permanently excluded from the computation of taxable income although they enter into the computation of accounting income. Because of such permanent differences in the measurement of income for tax and accounting purposes, taxable income and accounting income may be different for a given accounting period.

When permanent differences are removed from the income statement, accounting income subject to tax is left

In order to calculate income tax expense to be deducted from the income statement, permanent differences must be excluded from revenues and expenses, and the income tax expense is calculated only on the resulting **accounting income subject to tax**. For example, Dynosonic Corporation is subject to a 20 percent tax rate on its net income. The company's income statement for accounting purposes is shown in Figure 11-2, together with the calculation of accounting income that is subject to tax. In this example, accounting income subject to tax is also taxable income, but if timing differences exist in addition to permanent differences, that is not the case. Note that taxable income or accounting income subject to tax are not reported in the income statement. Instead accounting income subject to tax is used to calculate income tax expense which is reported in the income statement.

Dynosonic Corporation's income before tax is $27,000, and the income tax expense is $4,600. Although the company is subject to a tax rate of 20 percent, the rate is applied to accounting income subject to tax, which does not include permanent differences. With $9,000 of interest revenue and $5,000 of amortization expense not used in calculating income subject to tax, the 20 percent rate is applied to $23,000 and results in a tax of $4,600, as illustrated in Figure 11-2.

Dynosonic Corporation
Income Statements
For the Year Ended December 31, 1985

	Accounting Income		Accounting Income Subject to Tax	
Service revenue		$200,000		$200,000
Interest from municipal bonds		9,000		
Total revenues		209,000		200,000
Less expenses:				
Administrative expenses	$110,000		$110,000	
Salaries and wages	55,000		55,000	
Depreciation	12,000		12,000	
Amortization of goodwill	5,000			
Total expenses		182,000		177,000
Income before tax		27,000		$ 23,000
Federal income tax expense		4,600		
Net income after tax		$ 22,400		

Alternative Calculation of Accounting Income Subject to Tax:

Total revenues		$209,000
Less municipal bond interest		9,000
Revenue subject to tax		200,000
Total expenses	$182,000	
Less amortization of goodwill	5,000	
Expenses deductible for tax purposes		177,000
Accounting income subject to tax		$ 23,000

Figure 11-2 Because of differences between accounting principles and income tax laws, accounting and taxable income are often different. This income statement contains two permanent differences which are omitted from the calculation of accounting income subject to tax. In this example accounting income subject to tax and taxable income are identical.

Timing Differences

Timing differences occur because tax laws require the recognition of certain revenues and expenses in a different period than that reported for accounting purposes. Differences in the timing of such revenues and expenses shift tax payments from one accounting period to another, but the total tax obligation over time stays the same.

When the income statement contains both permanent differences and timing differences, it is necessary to calculate accounting income subject to tax and also taxable income, both of which are different from reported income. Accounting income subject to tax includes all items reported for accounting purposes with the exception of permanent differences. **Taxable income** also excludes permanent differences, but some of the revenues and expenses used to calculate taxable income are different from those used to calculate accounting income subject to tax.

Taxable income is used to calculate the tax liability

Accounting income subject to tax is the amount of income on which **tax expense** is computed. **Taxable income** is the amount of income on which the **tax liability** is calculated.

If corporations reported tax expense as the amount of taxes actually paid in an accounting period, the financial statements could become distorted due to timing differences. A simple example illustrates the distortion that can occur.

Timing differences resulting in deferred charge.   Some revenues are recognized in the current period for tax purposes, although they are earned in a later period. Some expenses are incurred in the current period but they are deductible for tax purposes only in a later period when they are paid. The timing differences caused by such revenues and expenses result in the recording of deferred charges.

Some timing differences result in deferred charges which are reported among assets

Rent received in advance is a common example of a timing difference which causes deferred charges. For accounting purposes, rent is reported in the period earned, but for tax purposes it must be reported in the period received regardless of the period earned. Toba Company, for example, is subject to a 30 percent tax rate and earned $40,000 from operations in 1985 and 1986. In addition, in 1985 it arranged to rent part of its warehouse space to another company for 1 year. The tenant will occupy the space during 1986 and will pay $6,000 rent in advance in December 1985 and the remaining $14,000 in 1986. There are no permanent differences.

For accounting purposes, income in 1985 and 1986 is $40,000 and $60,000 respectively. For tax purposes, however, 1985 income is $46,000, and 1986 income is $54,000 because the rent must be reported in the year received. With a 30 percent tax rate, Toba Company's 1985 and 1986 income tax expense is different from its income tax liability, as shown in the following statements:

| | Accounting Income | | Taxable Income | |
	1985	1986	1985	1986
Income from operations	$40,000	$40,000	$40,000	$40,000
Rent income		20,000	6,000	14,000
Total income before tax	40,000	60,000	46,000	54,000
Income tax expense (30%)	12,000	18,000		
Net income after tax	$28,000	$42,000		
Income tax liability (30%)			$13,800	$16,200

Accounting income in 1985 is smaller than taxable income, and in 1986 accounting income is larger than taxable income. That makes the income tax expense in each year different from the income tax liability. If the company reported the tax liability as its tax expense, it would appear to be subject to different tax rates in each year, and each year's net income would be incorrect. By reporting the tax actually paid, rather than the tax expense computed as a percentage of accounting income, the company would have the following distorted figures in its income statement:

	1985	1986
Total income before tax	$40,000	$60,000
Income tax	13,800	16,200
Net income after tax	$26,200	$43,800

The tax rates appear to be 35 percent in 1985 ($13,800/$40,000) and 27 percent in 1986 ($16,200/$60,000). The total taxes and net income for the 2 years are the same in both cases, but the income statement may be misleading if the tax obligation is reported as the tax expense. To report income correctly in each year, the company should allocate the tax obligation between the 2 years so that tax expense in each year is 30 percent of pretax income even though the tax liability in the 2 years is different from the tax expense.

Allocating the tax between the two periods is accomplished easily by calculating the income tax expense as 30 percent of accounting income and income tax liability as 30 percent of taxable income. To record the expense and liability, the company should make the following entry in 1985, which results in the creation of a deferred charge:

Dec. 31,	Income tax expense	12,000	
1985	Deferred income tax	1,800	
	Income tax payable		13,800
	To record tax expense and tax liability as		
	30% of accounting and taxable income.		

Deferred charges are not real assets

Although the tax liability must be paid in full, part of it is not an expense of 1985, and the **deferred income tax** can be viewed as a prepayment of a future year's tax. The **deferred tax** charge is reported in the balance sheet among assets, but it is not really an asset. The company does not have a claim on the government for a tax refund in the amount of $1,800, because the full amount of tax paid was owed in 1985, according to tax law. The deferred tax is simply an account with a debit balance that must remain on the books as a result of timing differences.

In 1986 the entry to record income tax expense and income tax liability is again made on the basis of a 30 percent rate. This time, however, the tax expense is greater than the tax liability, and the deferred charge previously established is eliminated in order to balance the journal entry.

Dec. 31,	Income tax expense	18,000	
1986	Deferred income tax		1,800
	Income tax payable		16,200
	To record tax expense and tax liability as		
	30% of accounting and taxable income.		

Timing differences resulting in deferred credit.   Some revenues are earned in the current period but are taxed in a later period. Some expenses are deductible in the current period when paid in advance, although they will be incurred in a later period for accounting purposes. The timing differences caused by such revenues and expenses result in the recording of deferred credits.

Some timing differences result in deferred credits which are reported among liabilities

To illustrate the accounting for timing differences that result in deferred credits, we use the example of Plioscope Corporation. On January 3, 1985, the company acquires motor vehicles for $60,000 that have an expected useful life of 4 years and a $4,000 salvage value. The company decides to use straight-line depreciation for accounting purposes, and it must use ACRS depreciation for tax purposes. Depreciation under each method is calculated in Figure 11-3.

Figure 11-3
Timing differences occur between accounting income and taxable income because different accounting principles may be used in accounting for the same item. The effect of different depreciation methods is illustrated here.

Plioscope Corporation Depreciation Schedule

Asset cost		$60,000
Estimated life		4 years
Estimated salvage value		$4,000

Year	Straight-Line Depreciation	ACRS Depreciation	Difference
1	$14,000	$15,000	$1,000
2	14,000	22,800	8,800
3	14,000	22,200	8,200
4	14,000	0	(14,000)
	$56,000	$60,000	$4,000

During each of the next 4 years, the company has total revenues of $150,000 and total expenses of $70,000 not including depreciation expense. The company is subject to a tax rate of 35 percent. Its accounting income and taxable income are calculated for each of the next 4 years in Figure 11-4.

Because of timing differences in the reporting of depreciation expense, the company's tax liability in the earlier years is less than in later years. If the company reported the tax liability as its tax expense in the income statement, its income in the fourth year would appear to be taxed at a high rate, while the rate in earlier years would appear to be lower. In fact, the tax rate is identical in each year.

To allocate its income taxes to the appropriate accounting periods, the company calculates its income tax expense on the basis of its accounting income (not including permanent differences). In 1985 the company's tax expense, tax liability, and deferred tax are calculated as follows:

Plioscope Corporation
Comparative Income Statements
For Accounting Purposes

	1985	1986	1987	1988
Revenues	$150,000	$150,000	$150,000	$150,000
General expenses	(70,000)	(70,000)	(70,000)	(70,000)
Depreciation expense	(14,000)	(14,000)	(14,000)	(14,000)
Income before tax	66,000	66,000	66,000	66,000
Income tax expense (35%)	(23,100)	(23,100)	(23,100)	(23,100)
Net income after tax	$ 42,900	$ 42,900	$ 42,900	$ 42,900

Figure 11-4
Accounting income and taxable income for four consecutive years, showing the timing differences due to the use of different depreciation methods for accounting and tax purposes.

Taxable Income

	1985	1986	1987	1988
Revenues	$150,000	$150,000	$150,000	$150,000
General expenses	(70,000)	(70,000)	(70,000)	(70,000)
Depreciation expense	(15,000)	(22,800)	(22,200)	(70,000)
Taxable income	65,000	57,200	57,800	80,000
Tax liability (35% of taxable income)	(22,750)	(20,020)	(20,230)	(28,000)
Tax expense from above (35% of income before tax)	23,100	23,100	23,100	23,100
Deferred tax (cr)	$ (350)	$ (3,080)	$ (2,870)	$ 4,900

Taxable income	$65,000	
Multiply by income tax rate	.35	
Income tax liability payable currently		$22,750
Reported income before tax	66,000	
Multiply by income tax rate	.35	
Income tax expense reported currently		23,100
Deferred tax, payable in future years		$ 350

The company reports tax expense on accounting income in the amount of $23,100, but it must pay only $22,750 to the government for 1985. The remaining tax is deferred until a later period and is reported as a deferred tax credit on the liability side of the balance sheet. The entry to record tax expense and tax liability in 1985 is

Dec. 31,	Income tax expense	23,100	
1985	Deferred income tax		350
	Income tax payable		22,750
	To record tax at 35% of accounting		
	and taxable income.		

Notice that the income tax payable is a legal obligation that the company must pay within the next accounting period, and it is reported among current liabilities. On the other hand, the deferred tax credit is not an obligation. It is simply the difference between the tax paid and the tax reported as expense. The company does not owe this amount to the government. At the end of 1985, the company's balance sheet shows the deferred income tax among deferred credits in the liability section of the balance sheet. During the next 3 years, income tax expense is recorded as follows:

Deferred credits are not real liabilities

Dec. 31,	Income tax expense	23,100	
1986	Deferred income tax		3,080
	Income tax payable		20,020
Dec. 31,	Income tax expense	23,100	
1987	Deferred income tax		2,870
	Income tax payable		20,230
Dec. 31,	Income tax expense	23,100	
1988	Deferred income tax	4,900	
	Income tax payable		28,000

By the end of 1987, the credit balance in the deferred tax account is $6,300. In 1988, the tax liability calculated on the basis of taxable income is larger than the tax expense calculated on the basis of accounting income. Some of the tax deferred in earlier years must now be paid. The deferred tax credit is reduced by $4,900 to ma¹.e up the difference between tax expense and tax liability in 1988. The deferred tax account now has a credit balance of $1,400.

When the motor vehicles are sold at the end of their useful life for their salvage value of $4,000, there is no gain or loss for accounting purposes because the book value of the vehicles is $4,000. But the book value for tax purposes is zero, so there is a taxable gain of $4,000 on the sale. The tax liability on the gain is precisely the $1,400 balance in the deferred tax account ($4,000 × .35). Instead of recording a tax expense on the sale of the vehicles, the company reduces the deferred tax account to zero when it records the tax liability.

By the time the assets are disposed of at the end of 1988, the total tax paid in the 4 years is equal to the total tax expense reported in these 4 years. Although the tax expense and tax liability are the same over 4 years, however, there is a benefit from deferring the payments. The reduced tax in the early years provides the company with a larger cash flow. The money saved can be invested to earn additional revenue.

Because growing companies are usually adding and replacing assets continuously, the deferred tax credits of previous periods are being written off at the same time that new deferred credits are being added. Consequently, these deferred credits often tend to grow over the years and frequently remain in the balance sheet for long periods of time.

OTHER LIABILITY CATEGORIES

In addition to the deferred tax credits discussed above, other deferred credits sometimes occur. Deferred credits, from taxes and other sources, are usually reported among other liabilities. In addition, a company may also report estimated liabilities and contingent liabilities.

Estimated Liabilities

It is difficult to measure the amount of some liabilities because they represent obligations arising from future events. For example, when a company sells a product, it cannot determine the exact amount of liability that will arise from product warranties. Some liability surely exists. Consequently, the company must estimate and report the amount of the liability so that its financial position is not distorted.

If a future liability can be estimated, it should be reported

For example, a company that sold products for $100,000 estimates that the cost of servicing the products during the following accounting period will be 3 percent of sales. To match the expense of servicing the products with the revenue earned by selling the product and to report the estimated warranty liability, the company makes the following journal entry:

Dec. 31	Warranty expense	3,000	
	Estimated warranty liability		3,000
	To record warranties estimated at		
	3% of sales.		

In the next period, as the company uses labor and material to service products, it reduces its obligation under the warranty liability. For example, if during January the company spent $250 on warranty services, it would record this expenditure as follows:

Jan. 27	Estimated warranty liability	250	
	Cash		250
	Provided services under warranty.		

The estimated warranty expense is not deductible for tax purposes until the service is actually provided. Therefore estimated warranties cause timing differences and tax allocations.

Parsec Corporation
Liability Section of Balance Sheet
December 31, 1985

Liabilities:		
Current liabilities		
Notes payable	$11,000	
Less discount on notes payable	200	$ 10,800
Accounts payable		48,900
Taxes payable		26,600
Salaries and wages payable		12,900
Payroll taxes payable		1,600
Unearned revenues		5,300
Current portion of long-term debt		4,000
Current portion of warranty liabilities		1,200
Total current liabilities		111,300
Long-term liabilities:		
Notes payable (see Note 1)		25,000
Bonds payable, 8%, due 1993		100,000
Installment note payable	46,000	
Less current portion	4,000	42,000
Total long-term liabilities		167,000
Other liabilities:		
Employee pension obligations		23,500
Deferred income tax		7,500
Estimated warranty liabilities	5,200	
Less current portion	1,200	4,000
Total other liabilities		35,000
Total liabilities		$313,300

Note 1:   Long-term notes payable consist of a $10,000, 12.5 percent note due in November 1988 and a $15,000, 11 percent note due in May 1991.

Note 2:   The company is contingently liable on notes receivable that have been discounted with a bank. The total maturity value of such notes is $22,000. A civil suit has been filed against the company in the amount of $100,000 for patent infringement. Legal counsel believes that the action is without merit, and the company will defend itself against the suit in courts of law.

Figure 11-5
Liabilities should be reported in sufficient detail to inform users of financial statements about all obligations of the reporting entity.

An estimated liability may also arise from premium offers made to customers. The company does not know how many premiums will be redeemed but it can estimate the amount and report it. FASB Statement No. 5 requires the accrual of **estimated liabilities** if there is a probability that the liability exists and if the amount can be estimated. If the amount cannot be estimated, the liabilities are not accrued but are reported as contingencies, discussed next.

Contingent Liabilities

From time to time, future events may occur that result in a loss or a payment, but the amount cannot be estimated on the date of the balance sheet. Such future contingencies should be reported as **contingent liabilities**. An example is a note receivable discounted. If the maker of the note defaults, the company that discounted the note is liable to the bank for the money owed on the note. Until a default occurs, however, the company does not know if the liability will materialize. Another example is a lawsuit filed against the company. The outcome of the suit is not known in advance, but the possibility of loss should be disclosed in the financial statements.

If a future liability is probable but cannot be estimated, it is a contingent liability reported in footnotes

Because the amount of contingent liabilities cannot be estimated, specific amounts cannot be reported in the body of the balance sheet. Contingent liabilities are usually reported in footnotes to the financial statements, with the relevant facts described sufficiently to enable the reader to understand the situation.

ILLUSTRATIVE EXAMPLE

To illustrate some of the methods used for reporting liabilities, we show in Figure 11-5 the liability section of Parsec Corporation's balance sheet at the end of the company's accounting period. Note the different kinds of liabilities and the way they are shown in the statements.

SUMMARY

Current liabilities are obligations that must be repaid within 1 year. They include accounts payable, notes payable, payroll obligations, accrued liabilities, and the portion of long-term debt due within the next accounting period. **Accounts payable** usually require payment within 30 to 60 days. **Notes payable** are signed documents and usually require the payment of interest. If no interest is stated, it must be imputed at a reasonable rate. The **imputed interest** is recorded as a contra liability. Non-interest-bearing notes payable may be discounted with a bank, which deducts the interest in advance. The result is an interest rate slightly higher than the stated rate.

The portion of long-term debt payable within the next accounting period is reported among current liabilities. On the other hand, if some current liabilities will be refinanced and will not require the use of current assets for their payments, they may be reclassified as long-term.

Payroll accounting requires detailed record keeping. Most payroll obligations are current liabilities. In addition to paying salaries and wages, an employer must deduct a portion of each employee's earnings for the payment of individual **income taxes** and **FICA taxes**. Other deductions may be made as required by contract or voluntary arrangements with employees. The employer must pay **payroll taxes**, which are additional costs of employing personnel. All payroll deductions and employer taxes are current liabilities of the employer.

Long-term liabilities consist of notes, bonds, mortgages, installment notes, leases, pensions, and other debts. **Installment notes** and **mortgages** are repaid in installments that include the payment of interest and a portion of the principal. Ordinary notes and bonds payable, on the other hand, are usually repaid in one lump sum at some future maturity date.

Operating leases are true rental agreements whereby the **lessee** pays rent to the **lessor** for the use of property. **Capital leases** are in substance purchase agreements. The lessee reports the leased property among long-lived assets in the balance sheet and the lease obligations among long-term liabilities. Operating leases are not reported in the balance sheet. Only the periodic rent payments are reported in the income statement.

Pensions are obligations paid for the benefit of retired employees. If the pension plan is **unfunded**, the company makes payments directly to retired employees; if the pension plan is **funded**, payments are made to the pension trustee who invests the funds for the employees' benefit.

In many cases a company's accounting income and its taxable income are not the same because some revenues are not taxed, and some expenses are not deductible for tax purposes. Such differences in measurement of income are called **permanent** differences. Timing differences occur when certain revenues and expenses are reported in one period for accounting purposes and in another period for tax purposes. Tax liability is calculated from a company's **taxable income**. Tax expense is calculated from the company's **accounting income subject to tax**. The difference between tax liability and tax expense is a **deferred tax. Deferred credits** resulting from timing differences are not really liabilities since there is no legal obligation to pay them to the government. Similarly **deferred charges** resulting from timing differences are not really assets. Nevertheless, deferred taxes are permanent accounts, so they must be reported in the balance sheet.

Estimated liabilities are obligations whose exact amount is not known but can be estimated. An example is a warranty obligation. If future events will bring about liabilities whose amounts cannot be estimated, they are reported as **contingent liabilities**, which are usually disclosed in footnotes to the financial statements.

KEY TERMS

accounting income subject to
  tax *(478)*
accounts payable *(464)*
capital lease *(472)*
contingent liabilities *(487)*
deferred charges *(477, 480)*
deferred credits *(477, 482)*
deferred income tax *(481)*
estimated liabilities *(485)*
FICA tax *(469)*
fringe benefits *(468)*
funded pension plan *(477)*
imputed interest *(467)*
installment note *(471)*

lease *(472)*
lessee *(472)*
lessor *(472)*
long-term liabilities *(470)*
mortgage *(471)*
notes payable *(464)*
operating lease *(472)*
payroll taxes *(469)*
pension *(477)*
permanent differences *(477, 478)*
taxable income *(479)*
timing differences *(477, 479)*
unfunded pension plan *(477)*

QUESTIONS

1. What is the main difference between current liabilities and long-term liabilities?
2. Why is interest imputed on non-interest-bearing notes payable?
3. A note is discounted with a bank at 13 percent interest, but the effective interest rate is actually higher. Explain.
4. Explain the conditions under which long-term liabilities are reported among current liabilities and current liabilities among long-term liabilities.
5. A company's gross payroll obligation to its employees is $6,000, but it issues payroll checks in a smaller amount. Explain why there is a difference.
6. Describe the characteristics of an installment note payable.
7. What are the characteristics of operating leases and capital leases?
8. Discuss some advantages of leasing instead of buying equipment.
9. Describe the major difference between a funded pension plan and an unfunded pension plan.
10. Discuss the reasons that permanent differences occur between accounting and taxable income. Give some examples of permanent differences.
11. Discuss why timing differences between accounting and taxable income occur. Give some examples of timing differences.
12. What is a deferred credit? How does it come about?
13. What is the difference between estimated liabilities and contingent liabilities? Give some examples.

EXERCISES

Ex. 11-1 **Adjustments to accounts payable.** Starglo Corporation is undergoing an audit on November 30, the end of its fiscal year. You are assigned to examine the company's Accounts Payable Control account.

Accounts Payable, Control			
Date	Debit	Credit	Balance
10/31 Balance			2,200
11/ 4 Purchased merchandise		580	2,780
7 Purchased merchandise		900	3,680
11 Payment	1,600		2,080
20 Purchased merchandise		360	2,440
26 Payment	800		1,640
28 Purchased merchandise		450	2,090
29 Payment	950		1,140

As you examine this account, you discover that the November 28 purchase of merchandise is for goods still in transit on which title has not yet passed. The November 29 payment was for rent expense and was erroneously recorded in Accounts Payable. A purchase of $500 of merchandise has not yet been recorded because the goods are in transit, but the title has already passed.

Required:
   a. Make the appropriate adjusting entries on November 30.
   b. Calculate the correct ending balance of accounts payable.

Ex. 11-2   Accounting for note payable.   On September 1, 1985, P. D. Quemann Company purchased $10,000 of merchandise in exchange for a 90-day, 15 percent note payable. The company's accounting period ended on October 31, and it paid the note on December 1, 1985.

Required: Prepare the necessary journal entries on September 1, October 31, and December 1, 1985.

Ex. 11-3   Note payable discounted with a bank.   On September 1, Suzy discounted her $11,914, 90-day noninterest note payable with a bank that charges a discount rate of 14.4 percent. She then used the money to buy a parcel of land, paying $11,000 cash and a $35,275, 90-day noninterest note. Interest on the note is imputed at 15 percent. On November 20 Suzy sold the land for $50,000 cash, and on November 30 repaid both notes.

Required: Journalize the above transaction in the general journal.

Ex. 11-4   Imputed interest on note payable.   On May 31, 1985, the Schneider Shop purchased merchandise with a $14,760 non-interest-bearing note due July 30, 1985. The normal rate of interest for this type of note is 15 percent. The Schneider Shop prepares financial statements on June 30.

Required:
   a. Prepare the necessary journal entries on May 31, June 30, and July 30.
   b. Show how the note payable would appear in the June 30, 1985, balance sheet.

Ex. 11-5   Accounting for a noninterest note payable.   Billmore Company acquired merchandise on April 1 in exchange for a $3,672, 60-day noninterest note payable. The company normally borrows money at 12 percent. The merchandise was sold on April 9 for $6,000 cash. On May 31 the company paid the note. These transactions were recorded as follows:

Apr. 1	Merchandise	3,672	
	Note payable		3,672
	Bought merchandise with 60-day note.		
9	Cash	6,000	
	Cost of goods sold	3,672	
	Sales		6,000
	Merchandise		3,672
	Sold merchandise for cash.		
May 31	Notes payable	3,672	
	Cash		3,672
	Paid noninterest note.		

Required:

    a. Disregard the above entries, and prepare the journal entries that should have been made to record the transactions.

    b. Disregard the entries you made in part a, and prepare correcting journal entries on May 31 to correct the errors made by Billmore Company.

Ex. 11-6   **Payroll accounting.**   Wise Company has 10 employees who each receive a salary of $1,800 a month. The employer must withhold 25 percent for federal income tax, 4 percent for state income tax, and 7 percent for FICA tax from employees' salaries. The employer also must pay $35 per employee each month to a retirement fund and 2 percent of gross payroll for state unemployment taxes.

Required: Record the salaries, fringe benefits, and payroll taxes for January.

Ex. 11-7   **Mortgage note accounting and reporting.**   The balance in Brooker Company's 12 percent long-term mortgage payable account on November 1, 1985, is $46,487.06. The monthly payments of $1,204.70 are due at the end of each month. During 1986 $7,896 of the principal will be repaid.

Required:

    a. Record the November 30 and December 31 mortgage payments in the general journal.

    b. Show how the mortgage payable will be reported in the company's balance sheet on December 31, 1985.

Ex. 11-8   **Installment note accounting.**   On March 1, 1985, the Cookston Company purchased some land for $75,000, paying $20,000 in cash and a 15-year, 12 percent installment note. The monthly payments on the note are $660. On June 30 the company sold the land for $79,800 cash and repaid the mortgage.

Required: Record the purchase on March 1, 1985, the installment payments on March 31 and April 30, the sale of the land, and repayment of the debt.

Ex. 11-9   **Capital lease.**   Lotus Corporation leased equipment on January 2 from Gorum Company on a 10-year capital lease. The annual payment of $2,322 is due on December 31 of each year, and at the end of 10 years, Lotus may purchase the equipment for $200. The present value of the future lease payments at 13 percent interest is $12,600.

Required:

    a. Prepare a lease amortization schedule similar to the one in Figure 11-1 for the first 4 years of the lease.

    b. Record the acquisition of the leased equipment by Lotus, and the first lease payment.

Ex. 11-10   **Permanent differences for taxable and accounting income.**   Messing Company is subject to a 40 percent federal income tax rate. Following is the company's income statement:

Messing Company
Income Statement
For the Year Ended December 31, 1985

Sales		$200,000
Interest from municipal bonds		20,000
Total revenues		220,000
Less expenses:		
Cost of goods sold	$90,000	
Operating expenses	35,000	
Administrative expenses	19,000	
Fines for conviction on state law violations	3,000	
Depreciation expense	14,000	
Amortization of goodwill	4,000	165,000
Income before tax		$ 55,000

Required: Calculate federal income tax and net income for the company.

Ex. 11-11   **Permanent and timing differences.**   Algon Company is subject to a federal income tax rate of 40 percent. Following is the company's income statement:

Algon Company
Income Statement
For the Year Ended December 31, 1985

Sales		$200,000
Rent income		10,000
Total revenues		210,000
Less expenses:		
Cost of goods sold	$95,000	
Operating expenses	30,000	
Administrative expenses	19,000	
Depreciation expense	14,000	
Amortization of goodwill	4,000	162,000
Income before tax		$ 48,000

Last year the company collected $3,000 of this year's rent income in advance. No advance rent has been collected in 1985. For tax purposes the company claims $20,000 of depreciation expense in 1985.

Required: Calculate federal income tax and net income for the company.

Ex. 11-12   **Recording deferred taxes.**   Witkins Corporation is subject to a 40 percent income tax rate. In 1985, income before tax for accounting purposes was $80,000, but taxable income was $72,000. In 1986 accounting income before tax was $90,000 and taxable income was $94,000.

Required: Prepare the entries to record tax expense and tax liability for the company in 1985 and in 1986.

Ex. 11-13   **Interpreting deferred taxes.**   Joyful Manufacturing Company, a maker of industrial and mining equipment, reported deferred tax credits in its 1985 annual report as follows:

	1985	1984
	(thousands of dollars)	
Income taxes payable	$ 4,765	$ 5,428
Deferred income taxes	31,592	21,472

In notes to the financial statements the company provided the following information:

The provision for income tax included in the Statement of Income consists of the following:

	1985	1984
	(thousands of dollars)	
Current:		
Federal	$29,282	$25,773
State	4,127	4,135
Foreign	1,194	1,960
Total tax liability	34,603	31,868
Deferred:		
Federal	7,760	5,085
State	1,354	698
Foreign	1,006	313
Total deferred tax	10,120	6,096
Total tax expense	$44,723	$37,964

The company is subject to a federal income tax rate of 46.5 percent of taxable income, but because of deferred taxes, the effective federal tax expense was 40 percent in 1985. All year-end income tax liabilities are paid each year on April 15.

Required:
a. Determine the company's income before tax and net income as reported in the 1985 annual report.
b. Compute the company's taxable income for 1985 federal taxes.
c. Prepare the journal entry that the company made to record income taxes on December 31, 1985. Also record the tax payment on April 15, 1986.

Ex. 11-14   **Product warranties.**   Kormacki Company sold products for $50,000 during 1985 and estimated the warranty liability on these products to be 5 percent of sales. During the following year, $2,200 was spent on warranty services.

Required: Record the 1985 warranty liability and 1986 services under warranties.

Ex. 11-15   **Interpretation of various liabilities.**   Examine the financial statements of Rangaire Corporation reproduced in Chapter 5, including the notes to the company's financial statements. Using the information presented there, determine whether the following statements about the company are true or false.

a.   In 1983 most of the company's long-term debt consisted of capital leases.

b.   Part of the long-term debt in the balance sheet consists of operating leases.

c.   The minimum lease payments on operating leases for 1984 are $776,000.

d.   The company's contributory pension plan required payment for 1983 pension expense of $51,649.

e.   At the end of July 1983, the company had a noncontributory pension plan for non-union employees.

f.   The company increased its deferred income tax from 1982 to 1983.

g.   The average interest rate the company paid on short-term debt in 1983 was 17 percent.

h.   Part of the company's long-term debt is reported among current liabilities.

i.   Contingencies are reported on the balance sheet at zero, therefore the company has no contingent liabilities.

j.   All of the retained earnings balance is available for the dividend payments.

PROBLEMS

P. 11-1   **Accounting for notes payable.**   The following transactions of Rolm Company occurred during the last part of 1985 and early 1986:

a.   On September 6 the company borrowed money from a bank by discounting its $6,400, 60-day noninterest note payable at 15 percent discount.

b.   The company purchased merchandise on November 1 in exchange for a $9,315, 90-day noninterest note payable. Interest is imputed at 14 percent.

c.   On November 6 Rolm Company repaid its note to the bank.

d.   The company bought equipment on December 1, paying $2,000 cash and an $18,000, 60-day 13 percent note payable.

e.   Interest is accrued and discount is amortized on outstanding notes on December 31.

f.   On January 30 the 90-day note is paid.

g.   On January 31 the $18,000 note is paid.

Required: Journalize the above transactions in the general journal.

P. 11-2   **Accounting for notes payable.**   Some transactions of Labrede Corporation involving notes payable are described below.

a.   On August 14, 1985, the company borrowed money from its bank by discounting its $10,000, 90-day note payable at 15 percent.

b.   On September 30, the company purchased merchandise by giving a $21,000, 4-month 14 percent note payable.

c.   The company repaid the $10,000 note on November 14.

d.   An item of equipment that the company needed was available in a distress sale. Labrede purchased the equipment with a $15,450, 90-day non-interest-bearing note on December 2. A reasonable rate for imputing interest on the note is 12 percent.

e.   On December 31 interest is accrued and discount is amortized on the outstanding notes payable.

f.   The company repaid the $21,000 note on January 31, 1986.

g.   On March 1, the company paid the equipment note.

Required: Journalize the above transactions in general journal form.

P. 11-3   **Accounting for accounts and notes payable.**   Following are selected 1985 transactions of Dover Company, whose accounting period ends on December 31:

Aug. 12 Merchandise was purchased on 30-day open account for $7,800.
      27 The company purchased merchandise in exchange for a $6,901, 90-day non-interest-bearing note. A reasonable interest rate is 12 percent.
Sept. 12 The company was short of cash and could not pay for the August 12 merchandise purchase. The seller agreed to take the company's $7,800, 30-day 14 percent note payable in exchange for its account payable.
Oct. 12 The company paid the 30-day note.
Nov.   1 Dover Company purchased land for $3,000 cash and a $22,000, 90-day 12 percent note payable.
      25 Repaid the 90-day discounted note used to buy merchandise on August 27.
Dec. 16 The company discounted a $12,800, 60-day note payable with a bank that charges a 15 percent discount rate.
      31 Interest is accrued and discount is amortized on outstanding notes payable.

In 1986 the following transactions occurred:

Jan. 30 The company paid its $22,000 note.
Feb. 14 The discounted note was repaid.

Required: Record the company's transactions in the general journal.

P. 11-4   **Accounting for payrolls.**   Dukesa Company employs ten laborers and two supervisors. The laborers each earn $1,200 per month, and the supervisors earn $2,000 per month. The payroll is distributed on the last day of each month. The company deducts 20 percent of the payroll for federal income tax, 7 percent for FICA tax, and 5 percent for state income tax. In addition, $10 per month is deducted from each laborer's wages for union dues.

The company also pays 7 percent of each payroll as its own FICA contribution and 8 percent of gross pay to a retirement fund. Health insurance paid by the company for its employees amounts to $25 per employee each month. Federal tax withholdings and payroll taxes are paid to the federal government on the 10th day of the following month. The remaining payroll liabilities are paid on the 15th of each month.

Required:
    a. Record the payroll on June 30 in the general journal.
    b. Record the payment on July 10 of FICA tax and income tax withheld, and the payment on July 15 of other withholdings.

P. 11-5   **Accounting for various liabilities.**   Markwood Corporation closes its books on September 30. Following are some of the company's September transactions:

Sept. 1 Gave a $6,144, 60-day non-interest-bearing note payable in exchange for merchandise. Interest is to be imputed at 14.4 percent.

      2 Acquired land for $75,000, paying $5,000 cash giving a mortgage for the balance. The mortgage is payable at $1,000 per month, including 12 percent interest on the last day of every month.

      5 An operating lease is signed on equipment to be used for 1 year, with monthly rents of $300, the first of which is paid on this date.

    10 Borrowed money from the bank by discounting a $12,000 note payable for 30 days at 13.5 percent.

    15 Gave a 45-day 15 percent note for $8,640 in exchange for legal services performed for the company.

    30 Payroll for the month amounts to $8,000, which is subject to a 20 percent tax deduction and a 7 percent FICA tax. All payroll taxes are payable by the tenth day of the following month.

    30 Installment payment is made on the mortgage.

Required:
    a. Record the above transactions in the general journal.
    b. Prepare the necessary adjusting entries on September 30.
    c. Journalize the payment of September payroll taxes in October and all October note payments.

P. 11-6   **Capital lease.**   Woodstone Company wants to purchase a new welder at a cost of $10,000 but does not have the necessary cash. It arranges to lease the equipment from Deskoll Corporation on a 2-year capital lease with payments of $480 payable at the end of every month. Deskoll will earn a return of 13.8 percent per year, and Woodstone will be responsible for all maintenance on the equipment and will use straight-line depreciation with a 3-year life and no salvage value. At the end of the lease period, Woodstone may purchase the welder for $50. The lease is signed, and the welder delivered on May 1. Both companies close their books on July 31.

Required:
    a. Prepare the journal entries for Woodstone Company to record acquisition of the equipment, the monthly lease payments for May, June, and July, and depreciation at the end of July.

b. Show how the lease obligation and leased equipment are reported in the balance sheet on July 31, assuming that the entire lease obligation is treated as a current liability.

P. 11-7   **Accounting for a capital lease.** On January 1, 1985, Andromeda Corporation obtained equipment under a capital lease from Kimmel Company. Kimmel just bought the equipment for $27,400. The estimated useful life is 4 years with no salvage value. The terms of the lease are as follows:

1. Andromeda is to make three annual rent payments of $12,000 at the end of each year.
2. Andromeda is responsible for all maintenance and taxes on the equipment.
3. Andromeda may purchase the equipment for $600 at the end of 3 years.
4. The rate of return to Kimmel is to be 15 percent per year.

Required: Prepare the necessary journal entries to record all lease transactions in the books of Andromeda Corporation for 1985, 1986, and 1987, including double declining balance depreciation and purchase of the equipment at lease termination.

P. 11-8   **Capital lease amortization.** Belti Company entered into a capital lease agreement as lessee with Maltor Company as lessor. Under the agreement, Maltor is required to purchase a tank truck for $80,017 and lease it to Belti for 5 years at an annual rent of $22,750. The implied interest rate is 13 percent, and all lease payments are to take place at the end of each year. Belti obtains possession of the truck on January 2, 1985, and it may buy the truck at the end of the lease term for $1,000. The truck will be depreciated using straight-line depreciation over 5 years with no salvage value.

Required:
a. Prepare a schedule showing how Belti Company should amortize the lease.
b. Journalize the acquisition of the lease obligation and truck and amortization of the lease and truck depreciation in 1985 and 1986.
c. Show how the lease and truck are reported in Belti Company's balance sheet on December 31, 1986.

P. 11-9   **Computation of deferred taxes.** Conbrio Company reported the following revenues and expenses for the year ended December 31, 1985:

Sales		$87,300
Interest on municipal bonds		2,700
Total revenues		90,000
Less expenses		
Cost of goods sold	$49,000	
General expenses	11,000	
Fines and penalties	1,200	
Depreciation	3,800	
Total expenses		65,000
Income before tax		$25,000

Depreciation for tax purposes is $4,700. The fines and penalties were paid by the company for antitrust violations. In December 1985 the company arranged to rent part of its building to another company, and collected $4,000 of 1986 rent in advance. The income tax rate is 30 percent.

Required: Compute the company's taxable income and accounting income subject to tax, and prepare the entry to record the tax expense and liability for the year.

P. 11-10   **Deferred income tax.**   Below is Kalas Corporation's income statement.

Kalas Corporation
Income Statement
For the Year Ended December 31, 1985

Sales		$250,000
Rent revenue		15,000
Municipal bond interest		2,500
Total revenues		267,500
Less expenses:		
Cost of goods sold	$160,000	
Operating expenses	41,000	
Depreciation expense	4,000	205,000
Income before tax		$ 62,500

The depreciation is for a building that was purchased for $80,000 on January 3, 1985. The company uses straight-line depreciation for accounting purposes. ACRS amortization for 1985, used for tax purposes, is $7,200. Included in operating expenses are life insurance premiums of $2,000. Of the rent earned in 1985, $3,000 was collected in 1984 in advance. Rent of $1,500 for 1986, collected in advance in December, is not reported in the 1985 income statement. The company is subject to a 25 percent income tax rate.

Required: Compute the company's taxable income and accounting income subject to tax, and prepare the entry to record tax expense and tax liability for 1985.

P. 11-11   **Reporting liabilities.**   Switzer Corporation's cashier has prepared the following list of liabilities on July 31, 1985:

Accounts payable	$ 8,560
Notes payable	116,000
Salaries payable and payroll taxes	8,400
Service warranties	5,000
Legal liability	50,000
Taxes payable	9,900
Total liabilities	$197,860

In your examination of these liabilities, you discover the following:

a. All the accounts payable are due within 60 days.

b. Notes payable include a 5-year installment note with a face value of $100,000 and interest of 11 percent. In addition to the interest, $15,000 of the principal is payable within the next accounting period. Interest of $300 has accrued on this note and has not been recorded. Of the remaining notes payable, all are current, and one is a noninterest note with unamortized discount of $275. Only the face value of the note is included in the above list.

c. Accrued payroll taxes amount of $400.

d. Service warranties are correctly estimated and are considered to be long-term liabilities.

e. The legal liability results from a lawsuit in the amount of $50,000 filed against the company by a customer. The suit will come to trial in about a year, and the company's legal counsel considers it to be without merit.

f. The balance of taxes payable consists of $9,000 due in August and deferred taxes not owed at this time.

Required: Prepare the liabilities section of the company's balance sheet on July 31, 1985.

Case 11-1 **Tax deferral from capital lease.**

Bellfine Service Station is a small corporation operated by its owner, James Bellfine. The company provides automotive services, sells gasoline, and rents trailers. The company also owns an old pickup truck which it rents to customers who prefer not to rent a trailer.

Several new subdivisions have been built recently in the vicinity of the service station. The owners of the new homes have found it convenient to rent the pickup truck in order to haul trees and shrubs, building materials, topsoil, and equipment, and the demand for the truck has grown so much that Bellfine had to maintain a waiting list for his customers. In addition, the truck was old and needed frequent maintenance and repairs.

Late in 1984 Bellfine decided to meet the demand for pickup rentals by replacing the old truck with four new pickups. He made arrangements to acquire the four pickups by means of a 5-year capital lease. The lease agreement would require Bellfine to pay for all maintenance, licenses, insurance, and other costs of ownership, and title to the trucks would pass to the lessee at the end of the 5-year term. The lessor was to receive annual lease payments which would provide for a 12 percent return on the investment in the trucks, with each payment due on December 31. The lease was signed and the lessor bought the trucks for $42,248. The trucks were delivered to Bellfine on January 2, 1985.

On December 30, one day before the end of the accounting period, the owner prepared the following trial balance:

Bellfine Service Station
Trial Balance
December 30, 1985

Cash	$ 12,051	
Investment in municipal bonds	15,000	
Accounts receivable	8,600	
Merchandise and supplies inventories	72,000	
Equipment	94,800	
Accumulated depreciation		$ 28,500
Equipment under capital lease	42,248	
Accounts payable		5,198
Notes payable		40,000
Capital lease obligation		42,248
Common stock		50,000
Retained earnings		28,600
Sales and service revenue		200,000
Truck rent		16,000
Interest on municipal bonds		2,000
Cost of goods sold	133,000	
Salaries and wages	26,200	
Utilities	8,647	
Totals	$412,546	$412,546

The following events occurred on December 31, 1985, none of which are reflected in the above trial balance:

A customer who regularly rents one of the trucks approached Bellfine about the possibility of a more permanent rental arrangement in exchange for a lower fee. Bellfine agreed to do so if the customer paid rent in advance to cover a minimum number of days' rent. As a result, the customer paid $2,979 for 1986 rent which would normally cost $3,400.

Bellfine made the first payment on the company's capital lease obligation.

The company uses SYD depreciation for all equipment. Depreciation on the leased equipment has not yet been computed. Depreciation on the other equipment is $13,000 for 1985. Except for the leased trucks, all equipment was acquired prior to 1981 and depreciation for tax purposes is the same as depreciation for accounting purposes. However, the leased equipment is subject to 3-year ACRS amortization for tax purposes. (Figure 10-5, p. 435)

The company is subject to a 25 percent income tax rate. The income tax liability will be paid on April 15, 1986.

Required:
a. Prepare amortization tables for the capital lease, similar to the table in Figure 11-1. Round the lease rent to the nearest dollar. Also prepare a depreciation schedule for the leased assets, showing SYD depreciation and ACRS amortization for the assets' life.
b. Prepare journal entries to record the events which occurred on December 31, including depreciation and the entry to record the deferred tax.
c. Prepare a balance sheet and income statement for the company on December 31, 1985. Round all figures in the financial statements to the nearest dollar.

Investment by Creditors, Owners, and Businesses

Our free enterprise system depends for its strength on a vast number of large and small private businesses. Businesses, in turn, depend on private investors for their backing. Investors risk their money to invest in business ventures and businesses offer them a variety of investment alternatives, such as stocks and bonds. The money, or capital obtained from investors is used to finance business operations and the earnings of these operations are used to reward the investors with a return on their investments.

By offering different investment alternatives, businesses can attract capital from a variety of sources. Investors who prefer limited risk and an assured return may buy bonds that pay a specified rate of interest at specified times. Others may prefer a greater return and are willing to accept a greater degree of risk in order to obtain it. These investors may buy stocks that pay a return only if the business prospers.

In the next four chapters, we examine the principles and procedures used by businesses to account for their obligations to bond investors and owners, and also for their own ownership of corporate bonds and stock.

Investment by Creditors: Bonds Payable

12

Large companies frequently need large amounts of money to finance any number of projects: construction, expansion, replacement of equipment, or repayment of debt. In this chapter we explore one of the ways corporations borrow large sums of money—by issuing **bonds payable**. When you have completed this chapter, you should have a good understanding of:

---

1   Various types of bonds and their characteristics.

2   The reasons for bond discounts and premiums.

3   Accounting for bond issuance under a variety of conditions.

4   Accounting for bond interest payments.

5   How the existence of bond discount or premium affects the amount of interest expense.

6   Retirement of bonds at maturity or earlier.

Borrowed capital provides financial leverage

When a business wants a loan, it may go to a bank or other lending institution and borrow funds in exchange for notes payable, mortgages, or other debt instruments. However, if the amount of money the business requires is large, management may choose to obtain funds from the public in one of two ways: borrowing by issuing bonds payable or offering equity in the business by issuing stock. Corporate borrowing in the form of multimillion dollar bond issues may offer the advantage of financial leverage. Simply stated, **financial leverage** occurs if the borrowed money is invested to earn more income than must be paid to lenders as interest. Such a management strategy increases the return on owners' equity.

By buying bonds, investors become the corporation's creditors. Bond holders are investors who do not wish to take the risk of owning part of the business as stockholders. Instead, they prefer the assurance of earning a predetermined amount of interest on their investment and the knowledge that the money they lend will be returned. If the business is not successful and must be liquidated, creditors are always repaid before any assets are distributed to owners. Consequently, the risk of losing an investment is much less for bond holders than it is for stockholders. Corporations often obtain a large proportion of their assets by issuing bonds. In this chapter we discuss many features of bonds and the procedures used to account for bonds payable.

NATURE OF BONDS PAYABLE

Bonds may trade in markets at premiums or discounts

Corporate bonds are almost always issued in $1,000 denominations, and the **face value**, or **par value**, of the bond is $1,000. Bonds may, however, be bought or sold in bond markets above or below their face value. If the bond price is below the face value, the bonds trade at a **discount**. If the bond price is above the face value, the bonds trade at a **premium**. Bond prices are quoted as percents: A bond quoted at 101 is selling for $1,010, which is 101 percent of the face value. A bond quoted at 98½ has a price of $985, or 98.5 percent of the face value.

Bond Indenture

The conditions under which the bond is issued are known as the **bond indenture** and are usually described on the bond certificate. The indenture stipulates conditions such as the maturity date of the bond, the coupon rate of interest, and the call price, if any.

Bonds may be called in by the borrower prior to maturity

The **maturity date** of the bond is the date on which the issuing company must repay the money borrowed from the creditor. The **maturity value** of the bond is the face value. On the maturity date, the company repays $1,000 for each bond, at which time the bonds are canceled. The **coupon rate** of interest is the rate which the issuer agrees to pay on the face value of the bond. Interest is paid semiannually, and the bond indenture specifies the interest payment dates. The issuer may reserve the right to "call in" the bond and repay the debt prior to maturity. In that case a **call price** is stipulated, which is the amount the issuer must pay to redeem the bond prior to maturity. The call price is usually higher than the face value of the bond. A call price of 103 indicates that if the bond is retired early, $1,030 must be paid by the issuer in order to redeem the bond. In this example the **call premium** of $30 is the difference between the call price and face value. The call premium is paid for early redemption to compensate the investor for having to look for an alternative investment.

Types of Bonds

A variety of characteristics may be used to classify bonds into several types. The most significant of these are discussed here.

Figure 12-1   **Example of a bond certificate. The bond indenture is on the reverse side.**

Bearer and registered bonds.   Because bonds are negotiable instruments and may be traded in bond markets, a buyer of a long-term bond does not have to hold the bond until maturity. Transfer of ownership depends on whether the bonds trade as registered or bearer bonds. **Registered bonds** are issued to a particular person whose name is registered with the issuing company. When the owner sells the bond, the company cancels it and issues a new bond to the new owner, whose name appears on the bond certificate. Mere possession of a registered bond does not imply ownership. In contrast, **bearer bonds** are not identified with a particular owner, and the person who has possession of the bond, that is, the bearer, is assumed to be the owner.

Bearer bonds are not registered

Bearer bonds have coupons attached that must be clipped and sent to the bond issuer when an interest payment is due. In exchange for the coupon, the issuer pays the bond interest. As shown in Figure 12-1, registered bonds do not have coupons; the interest payments are sent directly to registered owners when due.

Secured and unsecured bonds.   Some bonds are **secured** by assets, such as real estate, owned by the bond issuing company. If the company cannot repay the debt, the secured assets may be sold to satisfy the indebtedness.

Debentures are unsecured bonds

Some bonds are **unsecured** and are backed only by the general credit of the company. Unsecured bonds are called **debentures**. Debentures of some issuers may be safer investments than secured bonds of others, because the risk of a bond depends primarily on the financial strength and credit worthiness of the issuing company.

Investors often pay a premium for the bond conversion privilege

Convertible bonds.   Bonds may have a provision allowing the bond holder to convert the bonds into a specified number of shares of the issuer's common stock. If the company is able to employ the borrowed money profitably, its common stock may increase in value. The owner of the **convertible bonds** can then exchange them for shares of common stock, whose value may be greater than the original amount paid for the bonds. A conversion privilege is attractive to bond investors who desire the safety and income provided by a bond and also the benefit of an increase in the value of the company's common stock. Accounting for the conversion of bonds is discussed in Chapter 14.

Serial bonds.   Bonds that are issued at one time but mature on a series of dates are called **serial bonds**. The issuing company obtains all of the borrowed funds when the bonds are issued, but it can spread repayment over several years. Part of the bond issue may be repaid after 5 years, another part after 6 years, and so on. Investors may choose to buy the shorter or longer maturities, depending on their investment goals.

Value of a Bond

Investors decide how much a bond is worth

To a great extent, the conditions in the bond indenture determine the value of a bond. But its value also depends on how much investors are willing to pay for it, an amount which in turn depends on the credit rating of the issuer, current interest rates, and the investment alternatives available to investors. The bond market is very sensitive to changes in interest rates. If investors are able to obtain a return of 13 percent a year from bond investments, they may not be willing to pay the full face amount of $1,000 for a bond that pays only 12 percent interest. In order to sell the bond, the issuer has to lower the price and issue the bond at a discount. On the other hand, a 14 percent bond may be very desirable in a 13 percent market. To buy the 14 percent bond, investors will bid up its price, and this bidding will cause the bond to sell at a premium.

Risk is a determinant of bond value

Bond ratings.   Although we use the term **market rate of interest**, no single market rate exists. Different levels of risk among investment alternatives create different rates of return. Investors buying government bonds believe that they have an excellent chance of getting their money back when the bond matures. They are willing to accept a relatively low interest rate in exchange for a low level of risk. A large, financially sound corporation has a better chance of repaying bonds than a medium-sized company with many other liabilities. There is a greater probability of default with the weak company than with the strong one. A bond is in **default** when its issuer is unable to pay the interest or principal when due. Investors will demand a higher interest rate from the weak company than from the strong one, because the bonds of the strong company are less risky. The greater the risk, the greater the required interest rate before investors will buy.

Bond ratings have an effect on bond yields

Financial services such as Standard & Poor's Corporation or Moody's Investors Service, Inc., evaluate bonds of most corporations and classify them according to risk and investment quality. The highest-quality bonds—those issued by the most credit-worthy companies—may be rated AAA, the next highest AA, and the next A. Bonds of less credit-worthy companies are more risky and may be rated BBB, BB, or B, with the lower ratings assigned to very risky or speculative bonds. Bonds rated CCC, CC, and C are of poor quality, with a high risk of default. Bonds that are rated DDD, DD, and D are in default, with the rating indicating the relative salvage value.

The existence of a sinking fund reduces bond risk

Bond sinking fund. Some bond indentures provide for a sinking fund that is established for the purpose of retiring the bonds. A **sinking fund** is an investment fund into which the bond issuer makes periodic cash payments in order to have sufficient money available to retire the bonds when they mature. Often the sinking fund is turned over to a trustee, who manages the fund during the life of the bonds. Money paid into the fund is invested to earn a return. The amounts paid into the fund should grow approximately to the maturity value of the bonds, taking into account the company's contributions and the expected investment income earned by the sinking fund. A bond with a sinking fund provision is considered safer than a similar bond without such a provision. Sinking funds are reported on the asset side of the balance sheet among long-term investments.

Bond Discount and Premium

A company issuing bonds in the market essentially makes two promises to its prospective creditors. It promises to:

1. Pay $1,000 for each bond on the maturity date.
2. Pay interest on $1,000 at the coupon rate of the bond every 6 months.

Investors determine the price of a bond by considering the credit rating of the issuing company and the bond rating, and by comparing the coupon rate of interest with the market rate of interest. The value of any bond depends not only on its coupon rate of interest but also on the current market rate of return for bonds of similar risk. Because bonds pay interest semiannually, investors can reinvest the interest proceeds every 6 months and obtain semiannual compounding on their investment. Therefore, it is justifiable to evaluate bonds on the basis of semiannual compounding.

Discount value of a bond.   To illustrate how bond values are determined, we use the example of Faron Corporation's new issue of 5-year 12 percent bonds. To determine these bonds' value, we assume that the market rate of interest is 14 percent. Therefore, to induce investors to buy a 12 percent bond in a 14 percent market, the corporation has to offer the bonds at a discount.

The theoretical value of a bond is based on compound interest concepts

The market price of Faron Corporation's bonds is the present value of the future cash flows the bond holders will receive from the bonds. These future cash flows are the interest and principal payments that the bond issuer will make during the life of the bonds. For each bond, Faron Corporation will pay $1,000 to the bond holder 5 years from now when the bond matures. It will also pay $60 to the bond holder every 6 months during the next 5 years. These future payments are diagrammed below.

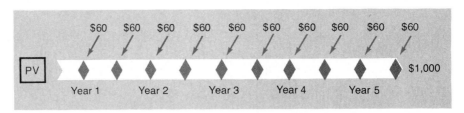

The 10 equal $60 interest payments may be viewed as an annuity. To determine the market value of the bond, we find the present value of this annuity and also the present value of the $1,000 principal payment when the bond matures. The payments are discounted at the 14 percent market rate of interest for 5 years with semiannual discounting. Therefore we use 7 percent and 10 periods and make the calculation as follows:

Present value of $1,000 at 7% for 10 periods:
.50835 × $1,000   = $508.35
Present value of annuity of $60 at 7% for 10 periods:
7.02358 × $60   =   421.41
Present value of entire bond $929.76

Yield to maturity is the actual cost of borrowing

The bond will sell in the market at $930. It will be issued at a discount because the market rate of interest is higher than the coupon rate. An investor who buys the bond and holds it to maturity will earn 14 percent interest on the investment. The 14 percent return is called **yield to maturity**.

The issuer of a bond must pay the prevailing market interest rate on borrowed money. Otherwise, no one would invest in the bonds. A company cannot borrow money for less than the market rate simply by issuing bonds with a lower interest rate. In our example, Faron Corporation is borrowing money in a 14 percent market; therefore, it must pay 14 percent interest although it is issuing 12 percent bonds. With the discount, the company is actually borrowing $930. On this loan it will pay $60 interest every 6 months, and at the end of 5 years it will pay $1,000 to the lender. Since it borrowed only $930 and is returning $1,000 on the maturity date, the company is returning $70 more than it borrowed. This $70 payment in addition to the semiannual interest payments raises the total interest cost on the loan to the market rate of interest of 14 percent.

When a company plans a bond issue, it tries to set the coupon rate at the market rate of interest. By the time the bond issue is approved, the bond certificates are printed, and the bonds reach the market, interest rates may be somewhat different than the coupon rate of the issue. For this reason the amount of premium or discount on a bond is beyond the control of the issuer, but since the difference between the market and coupon rate of interest is usually small, the premium or discount on newly issued bonds is generally not very large.

Bond values move opposite to interest rates

Premium value of a bond.   Bond values always move in the opposite direction from interest rates. If interest rates rise, bond values decline; if interest rates decline, bond values rise. Therefore, if market interest rates happen to be lower than a coupon rate of a bond, a premium on the bond develops. For example, if Faron Corporation issues its 5-year 12 percent bonds when the market interest rate is 11 percent, the market value of each bond is greater than the $1,000 face value.

To evaluate this same bond in an 11 percent market, we need to find the present value of the future payments at 11 percent semiannual discounting.

Present value of $1,000 at 5.5% for 10 periods:	
.58543 × $1,000	= $ 585.43
Present value of annuity of $60 at 5.5% for 10 periods:	
7.53763 × $60	= 452.26
Total value of bond	$1,037.69

The bond will sell at a premium of $38, and the yield to maturity will be 11 percent. The $38 premium the investor pays when the bond is issued is not repaid at maturity. By borrowing $1,038 and repaying only the face amount of $1,000, the borrower reduces the total interest cost of the debt, and the actual cost of borrowing the money is less than the coupon rate of the bonds.

ACCOUNTING FOR BONDS PAYABLE

Accounting for bonds payable is similar to accounting for other forms of debt, such as notes payable. The accountant must record the receipt of the proceeds from the sale of the bonds and the incurrence of the debt at the time the bonds are issued. If there is a premium or a discount on the bonds, it must also be recorded. The bond liability as well as the premium or discount are reported in the long-term liability section of the balance sheet. The periodic payment of interest and the accrual of interest expense at the end of the accounting period must be recorded, as well as any payments into a bond sinking fund if one exists. Interest is reported as an expense in the income statement. Finally, when the bonds are retired, either at maturity or earlier, the accountant records the cash payment to the creditors and the cancellation of the debt. Early retirement of the debt may result in a gain or loss, which must be recorded and reported in the income statement.

We now look at the accounting procedures used for bonds issued at face value and at a discount or premium. These procedures include recording the bond issuance, periodic payment and accrual of interest, and bond retirements.

Bonds Issued on Interest Payment Date

A bond issue of $5 or $6 million is small. Most corporations issue bonds in much larger amounts—$50 or $100 million, with $200 or $300 million issues not at all unusual. But to keep our numbers manageable, we deal with much smaller amounts. For example, Samson Corporation issues $100,000 of 20-year 12 percent bonds at face value on February 1, 1985. The bonds pay interest on February 1 and August 1 of each year. To record the issuance of the bonds, the company makes the following entry:

Feb. 1	Cash	100,000	
	Bonds payable		100,000
	Issued 20-year 12% bonds.		

Interest accrues on bonds as time passes

The following entries are used to record the interest expense on August 1 and to accrue interest at the end of the 1985 accounting period:

Aug. 1	Interest expense	6,000	
	Cash		6,000
	Paid semiannual interest on 12% bonds.		
	$100,000 × .12 × 6/12 = $6,000		
Dec. 31	Interest expense	5,000	
	Interest payable		5,000
	To accrue interest on 12% bonds.		
	$100,000 × .12 × 5/12 = $5,000		

The August 1 entry is for the payment of 6 months' interest expense that has accrued on the bonds since February 1. The December 31 entry is needed to record 5 months' interest that has accrued since August 1. On February 1, 1986, the next interest payment date, the following entry is made to record the interest:

Feb. 1	Interest expense	1,000	
	Interest payable	5,000	
	Cash		6,000
	Paid semiannual bond interest, part of		
	which was accrued last year.		
	$100,000 × .12 × 1/12 = $1,000		

Bonds Issued Between Interest Payment Dates

Bond investors must pay for accrued interest when they buy bonds

Corporations usually try to issue bonds close to an interest payment date, but it is not always possible to issue them exactly on the payment date. Sometimes market conditions change while a bond issue is planned, and the issuer may postpone the issue until a later time. When bonds are issued after an interest payment date, interest on them accrues and must be accounted for.

For example, if Samson Corporation issues its bonds on March 1 instead of February 1, one month's interest has already accrued on the bonds by the date of issue. On August 1 Samson Corporation will still pay the bond holder 6 months' interest even though the bonds have been outstanding for only 5 months. The payment of February's interest is avoided on August 1 by collecting the face value of $100,000 plus $1,000 of accrued interest from the purchaser when the bonds are issued. This simple but effective procedure eliminates the problem of having to pay on the first interest payment date an amount of interest different from that payable at all other times. The entry to record the bond issuance on March 1 is made as follows:

Mar. 1	Cash	101,000	
	Interest payable		1,000
	Bonds payable		100,000
	Issued $100,000, 20-year 12%		
	bonds with 1 month's accrued interest.		
	$100,000 × .12 × 1/12 year = $1,000		

When the first interest payment is made on August 1, the accrued interest is written off and 5 months' interest expense is recorded, as follows:

Aug. 1	Interest expense	5,000	
	Interest payable	1,000	
	Cash		6,000
	Paid semiannual bond interest, part of		
	which was accrued previously.		
	$100,000 × .12 × 5/12 year = $5,000		

BONDS ISSUED AT DISCOUNT OR PREMIUM

You already know that the market rate of interest determines whether a bond sells at a discount or a premium. The issuer is borrowing money at the market rate of interest, and if the coupon rate is different, it does not represent the actual cost of borrowing.

Bonds Issued at a Discount

The coupon rate of interest determines how much cash must be paid on each interest payment date. If bonds are issued at a discount, the amount of money borrowed is less than the amount that must be repaid when the bonds mature, and the effective rate of interest is higher than the coupon rate. The amount that the bond issuer pays for the use of the borrowed money is the sum of the semiannual interest payments over the life of the bonds mature, and the **effective interest** rate is higher than the coupon date of the bond. These payments are illustrated in Figure 12-2, which shows the receipts and payments for a $1,000, 3-year 12 percent bond issued at a discount of $30, providing $970 of proceeds to the issuer.

Bond discount must be amortized to satisfy the matching principle

Although the discount of $30 is paid to the lender on the bond's maturity date, it represents additional interest expense for the entire life of the bond. The matching principle requires allocating the interest expense to the periods that benefit from the use of the borrowed money. Although the discount is paid at the end of the 3-year period, it should be spread over the life of the bond so that part of it is recorded as expense in each of the 3 years. To record the actual interest expense during each period in which the borrowed money is used, we must amortize the discount over the bond's life and charge it to interest expense in each period. To **amortize** an account means to write off a portion of its balance each

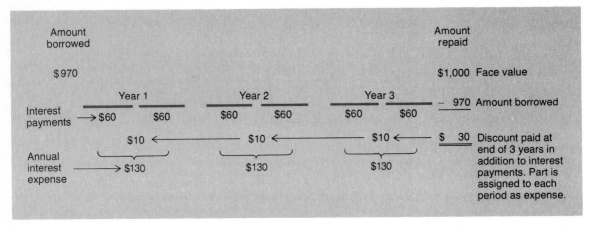

Figure 12-2   **Three-year 12 percent bond issued at a discount. The discount adds to interest expense and is amortized over the life of the bond although it is paid at bond maturity.**

period in a systematic manner. Each period's amortization reduces the discount account balance and increases interest expense. The expense caused by amortizing the bond discount is in addition to the interest actually paid. Therefore, the amount of interest expense recorded in each period is not the same as the amount of cash paid.

For example, on June 30, 1985, Grumett Corporation issues $100,000 of 5-year 11 percent bonds payable. Interest is due on June 30 and December 31. The bonds are issued for a total of $96,320 to yield 12 percent to maturity. To record the issuance, the company makes the following entry:

June 30	Cash	96,320	
	Discount on bonds payable	3,680	
	Bonds payable		100,000
	Issued $100,000, 5-year 11% bonds		
	payable to yield 12% to maturity.		

The discount on bonds payable is a **contra-liability account** related to the bonds payable account. The bonds and the discount are reported together in the balance sheet, which shows the net obligation of $96,320 on June 30, 1985, as follows:

> Bonds payable $100,000
> Less discount on bonds payable 3,680 $96,320

When discount is amortized, book value of bonds increases
As the discount is amortized, the book value of the bonds increases. At maturity the total obligation will be $100,000. At the time the bonds are retired, the entire $100,000 must be repaid even though only $96,320 was originally borrowed.

Two methods may be used to amortize the bond discount. We first discuss the straight-line method and then illustrate the effective interest method.

Straight-line amortization of bond discount.   An equal amount of bond discount is amortized in each period when the **straight-line method** of discount amortization is used, and the same amount of interest expense is recorded in each accounting period. As the discount is amortized, the remaining balance in the bond discount account becomes smaller, so the book value of the bonds becomes larger.

If Grumett Corporation amortizes the discount of its 5-year bonds by using the straight-line method, one-tenth of the discount is written off every 6 months. The entry to record the first interest payment is:

Dec. 31	Interest expense	5,868	
	Discount on bonds payable		368
	Cash		5,500
	Paid semiannual interest and amortized		
	bond discount. $3,680/10 = $368		
	$100,000 × .11 × 6/12 = $5,500		

The amount of cash paid is determined by the bond indenture and is the same on each payment date. When the discount is amortized with a credit of $368, the debit to interest expense must be equal to the total of the discount amortization and the cash payment. Therefore the interest expense is recorded as the amount of cash paid plus a portion of the discount that will be paid when the bonds mature.

The same entry is repeated with each interest payment, and each time the balance in the discount account decreases and the book value of the bonds increases. Straight-line amortization of these bonds is illustrated for the entire life of the bonds in Figure 12-3, which shows the periodic cash payment, discount amortization, interest expense, and balance of unamortized discount that is deducted from the face value of the bonds to arrive at book value. Note how book value of the bonds increases each period from the beginning amount of $96,320, which is the actual amount borrowed, to the final amount of $100,000, which is the actual amount repaid.

Amortization of Bond Discount
Straight-Line Method

$100,000, 5-year 11% bonds, with interest payable semiannually, issued at $96,320 to yield 12% to maturity

①	②	③	④	⑤	⑥	⑦
Date	Cash Payment	Discount Amortization $3,680/10	Interest Expense Cols. 2 + 3	Unamortized Discount Cols. 5 − 3	Book Value of Bonds $100,000 − Col. 5	Implied Interest (Cols. 4/6) × 2
6/30/85				$3,680	$ 96,320	
12/31/85	$ 5,500	$368	$ 5,868	3,312	96,688	12.184%
6/30/86	5,500	368	5,868	2,944	97,056	12.138
12/31/86	5,500	368	5,868	2,576	97,424	12.092
6/30/87	5,500	368	5,868	2,208	97,792	12.046
12/31/87	5,500	368	5,868	1,840	98,160	**12.001**
6/30/88	5,500	368	5,868	1,472	98,528	11.956
12/31/88	5,500	368	5,868	1,104	98,896	11.911
6/30/89	5,500	368	5,868	736	99,264	11.867
12/31/89	5,500	368	5,868	368	99,632	11.823
6/30/90	5,500	368	5,868	0	100,000	11.779
Totals	$55,000		$58,680			

Figure 12-3   **Bond discount amortization schedule using the straight-line method. Interest expense as a percentage of the bonds' book value varies from period to period although the effective interest on the bonds is actually constant. Note that the implied interest rate in column 7 is approximately equal to the effective rate on the bonds halfway in the bond term.**

The implied interest rate in column 7 of Figure 12-3 is computed by dividing the previous period's book value (column 6) into the interest expense (column 4), to obtain the semiannual rate. The annual rate is double the rate computed for 6 months. For the first interest payment, the implied annual interest rate is

$$\$5,868/\$96,320 \times 2 = .12184 \text{ or } 12.184\%$$

The implied interest rate halfway through the bonds' life is approximately equal to the effective interest rate.[1]

Straight-line amortization implies a changing interest rate

When the straight-line method of discount amortization is used, the book value of the bonds changes, but the interest expense remains the same in each period. Interest expense as a percentage of the book value of the debt is different in each period, implying that the company borrowed the money at varying interest rates although the actual cost of the debt is 12 percent. This varying interest rate, shown in column 7 of Figure 12-3, illustrates the flaw of the straight-line method of discount amortization. If the discount is large and the time to bond maturity is long, the straight-line method of discount amortization can cause a distortion in the interest rate implied by the amount of interest expense reported. In this case the more precise effective interest method of bond discount amortization should be used.

Effective interest amortization results in reporting actual interest cost

Effective interest amortization of bond discount. To reflect the *actual* cost of borrowing throughout the life of a bond issue, the effective interest method of discount amortization is used. The **effective interest method** of amortization applies the effective rate of interest to the actual amount of outstanding debt. Grumett Corporation issued its bonds when the interest rate was 12 percent; therefore 12 percent is both the cost of borrowing the money and the effective interest rate for the bond issue. The company actually borrowed $96,320 at 12 percent interest; the effective interest cost on this debt for 6 months is 6 percent of $96,320, or $5,779.20. When the interest payment is made, however, only $5,500 is paid to the bond holders, and the remainder is used to amortize the bond discount. The interest payment is recorded as follows:

Dec. 31	Interest expense	5,779.20	
	Discount on bonds payable		279.20
	Cash		5,500.00
	Paid semiannual bond interest and		
	amortized discount.		
	$ 96,320 × .12 × 6/12 = $5,779.20		
	$100,000 × .11 × 6/12 = $5,500.00		

---

[1] The effective interest rate can also be approximated by finding the mean of the first and last implied interest computation.

When the discount is amortized in this way, the book value of the bonds increases by $279.20 to $96,599.20. This is the new balance of the outstanding debt, so when the next interest payment is made, interest expense is again calculated as the book value of the bonds multiplied by 12 percent interest per year for 6 months. The second interest payment is recorded as follows:

June 30	Interest expense	5,795.95	
	Discount on bonds payable		295.95
	Cash		5,500.00
	Paid semiannual bond interest and		
	amortized discount.		
	$ 96,599.20 × .12 × 6/12 = $5,795.95		
	$100,000.00 × .11 × 6/12 = $5,500.00		

The book value of the bonds increases each period, and the amount of interest also increases accordingly. This is logical. The company initially borrowed $96,320 at 12 percent interest, so it should pay $5,779.20 interest for the first 6 month period. But it pays only $5,500 of interest. Therefore it still owes $279.20 to the lenders. This additional debt is added to the original debt; the larger debt results in more interest expense next time. Amortizing the discount is the same as borrowing additional money from the bond holders. The interest expense is always 12 percent of the outstanding debt, which is the book value of the bonds.[2]

The complete schedule of bond discount amortization using the effective interest method is shown in Figure 12-4, which illustrates the change in the book value of the bonds during their lifetime. Note that the interest expense is different in each period, whereas it is always the same with straight-line discount amortization. Over the entire life of the bond issue, however, total interest expense is the same with either method. Compare the totals of columns 2 and 3 in Figure 12-4 and you will see that interest expense consists of the cash payments made plus the entire discount.

Bonds Issued at a Premium

If bonds are issued at a premium, the actual cost of borrowing the money is less than the coupon rate of interest. Investors are willing to pay a premium for bonds that pay more than the current market rate of interest even though the premium will not be repaid when the bonds mature. The

Amortizing bond premium reduces interest expense to less than the coupon rate

---

[2] You may view the bond as an installment obligation in reverse. Instead of paying the interest and some portion of principal, the borrower pays less interest than is owed. If less interest is paid each period than the actual amount owed, the difference amounts to an additional loan which is added to the original principal. When the bond matures, the borrower owes more money than the original amount borrowed and at this time pays the interest and all of the principal, which has grown to the face value of the bonds.

Amortization of Bond Discount
Effective Interest Method

$100,000, 5-year 11% bonds, with interest payable semiannually, issued at $96,320 to yield 12% to maturity.

① Date	② Cash Payment	③ Interest Expense 6% × Col. 6	④ Discount Amortization Cols. 3 − 2	⑤ Unamortized Discount Cols. 5 − 4	⑥ Book Value of Bonds Cols. 6 + 4
6/30/85				$3,680.00	$ 96,320.00
12/31/85	$ 5,500.00	$ 5,779.20	$279.20	3,400.80	96,599.20
6/30/86	5,500.00	5,795.95	295.95	3,104.85	96,895.15
12/31/86	5,500.00	5,813.71	313.71	2,791.14	97,208.86
6/30/87	5,500.00	5,832.53	332.53	2,458.61	97,541.39
12/31/87	5,500.00	5,852.48	352.48	2,106.13	97,893.87
6/30/88	5,500.00	5,873.63	373.63	1,732.50	98,267.50
12/31/88	5,500.00	5,896.05	396.05	1,336.45	98,663.55
6/30/89	5,500.00	5,919.81	419.81	916.64	99,083.36
12/31/89	5,500.00	5,945.00	445.00	471.64	99,528.36
6/30/90	5,500.00	5,971.64*	471.64	.00	100,000.00
Totals	$55,000.00	$58,680.00			

* Computed amount is $5,971.70 and is adjusted to compensate for rounding error.

Figure 12-4   Bond discount amortization schedule using the effective interest method. Interest expense as a percentage of the bonds' book value is always the effective interest rate.

amount the bond issuer pays for the use of the borrowed money is the sum of the semiannual interest payments less the premium which is obtained from investors but which is not returned to them. These payments are illustrated in Figure 12-5, which shows the receipts and payments for a $1,000, 3-year 12 percent bond issued at a premium of $30, providing $1,030 of proceeds to the issuer.

Bond premium amortization reduces the book value of the bonds

The premium of $30 reduces interest expense over the life of the bonds. The periodic interest payments are higher than the effective interest expense on the borrowed money. When the premium is deducted from the periodic payments, the resulting interest expense is the actual cost of borrowing the money. To record the actual interest expense in each period that benefits from using the borrowed money, as required by the matching principle, we amortize the bond premium over the life of the bond.

When Hamlin Corporation issues its 11 percent bonds, for example, the bonds will sell at a premium if the market rate of interest is 10 percent. On June 30, 1985, $100,000 of 4-year 11 percent bonds payable are issued. The bonds pay interest on June 30 and December 31. They are issued for total proceeds of $103,232 to yield 10 percent to maturity. The entry to record the issuance is:

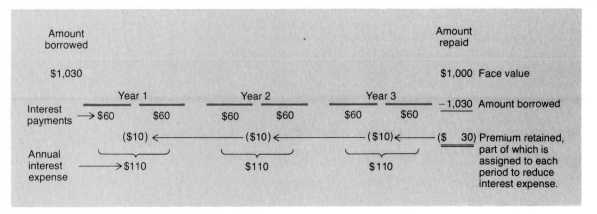

Figure 12-5   **Three-year 12 percent bond issued at a premium. The premium is not returned to the lender and therefore reduces interest expense on the bond when it is amortized over the bond's life.**

June 30	Cash	103,232	
	Bonds payable		100,000
	Premium on bonds payable		3,232
	Issued $100,000, 4-year 11% bonds		
	payable to yield 10% to maturity.		

Bond premium is an adjunct account

The bond premium is recorded in an **adjunct account**, which is similar to a contra account in every respect but one: Its balance is on the same side as the balance of the account to which it is related. The bond premium account is related to the bonds payable account. Both accounts have credit balances and appear together in the balance sheet, with their amounts added to show the book value of the bonds. The book value in our example of $103,232 is the company's obligation to the bond holders. When the bonds mature, however, the obligation will be $100,000 because the premium will not have to be repaid. On June 30, 1985, the bonds appear in the balance sheet as follows:

Bonds payable	$100,000	
Add premium on bonds payable	3,232	$103,232

To amortize the bond premium, the company records interest expense at an amount smaller than the actual cash payment made each period. The premium may be amortized by using the straight-line method or the effective interest method, as discussed below.

Straight-line amortization of bond premium.   When straight-line amortization is used, an equal amount of premium is amortized with each interest payment. The interest expense is the same for each period, but as the premium is amortized, the book value of the bonds declines with each interest payment. During the early years of bond life, the interest expense recorded is a higher percentage of book value than the effective rate, and during the later years, it is a lower percentage of book value.

Interest expense and the cash payment of interest are not always the same

When the straight-line method is used to amortize the premium over the 4-year life of the bonds, one-eighth of the premium is amortized with each interest payment. With straight-line amortization of premium, each interest payment is recorded, as follows:

Dec. 31	Interest expense	5,096	
	Premium on bonds payable	404	
	Cash		5,500
	To pay interest and amortize premium.		
	$3,232/8 = $404		
	$100,000 × .11 × 6/12 = $5,500		

Figure 12-6 illustrates straight-line amortization of bonds issued at a premium. Note that interest expense is always the same and is obtained by deducting premium amortization from the periodic cash payment. The unamortized bond premium is added to the face value of the bonds to arrive at book value, which declines with each passing period. Since interest expense is a different percentage of the bonds' book value in each

Amortization of Bond Premium
Straight-Line Method

$100,000, 4-year 11% bonds, with interest payable semiannually, issued at $103,232 to yield 10% to maturity.

① Date	② Cash Payment	③ Discount Amortization $3,232/8	④ Interest Expense Cols. 2 − 3	⑤ Unamortized Discount Cols. 5 − 3	⑥ Book Value of Bonds Col. 5 + $100,000	⑦ Implied Interest (Cols. 4/6) × 2
6/30/85				$3,232	$103,232	
12/31/85	$ 5,500	$404	$ 5,096	2,828	102,828	9.873%
6/30/86	5,500	404	5,096	2,424	102,424	9.912
12/31/86	5,500	404	5,096	2,020	102,020	9.951
6/30/87	5,500	404	5,096	1,616	101,616	9.990
12/31/87	5,500	404	5,096	1,212	101,212	10.030
6/30/88	5,500	404	5,096	808	100,808	10.070
12/31/88	5,500	404	5,096	404	100,404	10.110
6/30/89	5,500	404	5,096	0	100,000	10.151
Totals	$44,000		$40,768			

Figure 12-6   Bond premium amortization schedule using the straight-line method. The straight-line method implies a varying interest rate over the life of the bonds, although the cost of borrowing is constant at the effective rate of 10 percent. Column 7 shows that the implied interest rate is approximately equal to the effective interest rate at the halfway point in the bonds' life.

period, the company's effective interest rate appears to be changing over the life of the bonds, as indicated by column 7 in Figure 12-6. The straight-line method of amortization causes a distortion in the reported interest and may result in misleading financial statements if the bond premium is large and the time to maturity is long. For this reason FASB rules[3] require the use of the effective interest method of bond premium amortization if the straight-line method would materially distort the financial statements.

Effective interest amortization of bond premium.   When the Hamlin Corporation bonds were issued, the market rate of interest was 10 percent, and this is the cost of borrowing for the company. Initially, the net amount of indebtedness is $103,232, and 6 months' interest is 5 percent of this debt, or $5,161.60. When the interest payment is made on December 31, 1985, the entry is recorded as follows:

Effective interest amortization is necessary when the premium or discount is large

Dec. 31	Interest expense	5,161.60	
	Premium on bonds payable	338.40	
	Cash		5,500.00
	$103,232 × .10 × 6/12 = $5,161.60		
	$100,000 × .11 × 6/12 = $5,500.00		

The bond indenture requires a cash payment of $5,500, but the interest expense reflects the true cost of borrowing the money. When the premium is amortized for the first 6-month period, the book value of the bond decreases to $102,893.60. When the next interest payment is made, interest is calculated as 5 percent of the new book value, and the second interest payment is recorded as follows:

June 30	Interest expense	5,144.68	
	Premium on bonds payable	355.32	
	Cash		5,500.00
	$102,893.60 × .10 × 6/12 = $5,144.68		
	$100,000.00 × .11 × 6/12 = $5,500.00		

When premium is amortized, book value of bonds decreases

As the premium is amortized, the book value of the bonds decreases.[4] Four years after issuance, the final premium amortization leaves a book value of $100,000, the amount to be paid at maturity. The interest expense

---

[3] Accounting Principles Board Opinion No. 21, "Interest on Receivables and Payables," August 1971.

[4] This bond may be viewed as an installment obligation which is being amortized with each semiannual payment. Part of the semiannual payment is for interest on the original debt of $103,232, and the rest of the payment reduces the principal. Next time, with a smaller principal balance, less interest has to be paid, so more of the payment is used to reduce the principal. When the principal balance is reduced to $100,000, the entire principal is repaid, just as any installment note can be repaid in a lump sum before the principal is fully amortized.

Amortization of Bond Premium
Effective Interest Method

$100,000, 4-year 11% bonds, with interest payable semiannually, issued at $103,232 to yield 10% to maturity

① Date	② Cash Payment	③ Interest Expense 5% × Col. 6	④ Discount Amortization Cols. 2 − 3	⑤ Unamortized Discount Cols. 5 − 4	⑥ Book Value of Bonds Cols. 6 − 4
6/30/85				$3,232.00	$103,232.00
12/31/85	$ 5,500.00	$ 5,161.60	$338.40	2,893.60	102,893.60
6/30/86	5,500.00	5,144.68	355.32	2,538.28	102,538.28
12/31/86	5,500.00	5,126.91	373.09	2,165.19	102,165.19
6/30/87	5,500.00	5,108.26	391.74	1,773.45	101,773.45
12/31/87	5,500.00	5,088.67	411.33	1,362.12	101,362.12
6/30/88	5,500.00	5,068.11	431.89	930.23	100,930.23
12/31/88	5,500.00	5,046.51	453.49	476.74	100,476.74
6/30/89	5,500.00	5,023.26*	476.74	.00	100,000.00
Totals	$44,000.00	$40,768.00			

* Computed amount is $5,023.84 and is adjusted to compensate for rounding error.

Figure 12-7 **Bond premium amortization schedule using the effective interest method. The book value is multiplied by the effective interest rate to arrive at periodic interest expense.**

is always 10 percent per year on the outstanding balance, which is the rate at which the money was originally borrowed. The complete schedule of bond premium amortization in Figure 12-7 shows the change in the book value of the bonds over their 4-year life. Note that interest expense is different in each period, while it is always the same with the straight-line method. Over the life of the bonds, interest expense with the two methods is identical, consisting of all periodic cash payments less the entire bond premium.

Effect of Discount and Premium on Cash Flow

Cash flow and interest expense differ when bond premium or discount exists

Note carefully the difference between the amount of cash paid to service the bond indebtedness during the period and the amount of interest expense reported in the income statement. When bonds are issued at a discount, the cash outflow is **smaller** than the interest expense for the period. When they are issued at a premium, the cash outflow is **larger** than the interest expense for the period. It is important that you understand these relationships since they have a significant effect on the statement of changes in financial position discussed in Chapters 17 and 18.

BOND REDEMPTIONS

Interest must be paid to the date of retirement

When bonds payable mature, the last interest payment results in the amortization of any remaining premium or discount. The bonds are redeemed by paying to the bond holders the face value of the bonds. For example, the $100,000 of bonds issued by Hamlin Corporation on June 30, 1985, at $103,232 will mature on June 30, 1989. Figure 12-7 indicates that $476.74 of bond premium remains to be amortized with the effective interest method. On June 30, 1989, the final interest payment is made and the bonds are redeemed. The entries are

June 30	Interest expense	5,023.26	
	Premium on bonds payable	476.74	
	Cash		5,500.00
	To write off remaining premium and		
	pay interest prior to bond retirement.		
June 30	Bonds payable	100,000.00	
	Cash		100,000.00
	Retired 11% bonds at maturity.		

Early Retirement of Bonds

Refunding is the payment of one bond from the proceeds of another

The decision to retire a bond early is not necessarily made on the basis of the resulting gain or loss. A company may redeem its bonds early for many reasons. It may wish to reduce the interest burden in the future, or it may have excess cash to invest and finds it more appropriate to buy its own bonds rather than investing in other securities. The company may also decide to issue new bonds and use the proceeds to retire old ones. This may be done prior to the maturity of the old bonds if the company believes that the time is favorable for the issuance of new bonds. Issuing new bonds in order to retire old ones is known as **refunding**. One bond issue replaces another because the company perceives some advantages, such as reducing the overall interest expense in the future or extending further into the future the time that the debt must be repaid.

Gains or losses on bond retirement are extraordinary items

Because many corporations have large amounts of bonds outstanding, an early retirement of several millions of dollars of bonds may result in a gain or loss that could materially distort income from operations. For this reason FASB Statement No. 4 requires reporting gains and losses from bond retirements as extraordinary items in the income statement. This requirement separates such gains and losses from operating income or losses and ensures that users of financial statements will not be misled into believing that bond retirement gains or losses are part of normal and continuing business operations.

Examine carefully the entries below to retire bonds at a gain or loss. The gain or loss appears in the income statement and is used in the determination of net income. The amount of cash required to retire the bonds, however, is considerably different from the amount of gain or loss. In fact, while the gain is added in determining net income, there is actually a large cash outflow on the bond retirement.

Accounting for bonds retired prior to maturity.   Whether bonds are redeemed by paying the call price specified in the indenture or by purchase in the open market, interest must be paid on the bonds to the date of retirement. Let us assume that Hamlin Corporation's 4-year 11 percent bonds were issued at a premium as illustrated in Figure 12-7. Three years after the issue, the company decides to use some of its excess cash to retire the bonds. The call provision allows early retirement of the bonds at 102 during 1988 and on March 31, 1988, the bonds are called. At this time the bond liability and bond premium accounts appear as follows:

Bonds Payable	Premium on Bonds Payable
100,000	Bal. 12/31/87 1,362.12

Early retirement at call price.   The December 31, 1987, balance in the bond premium account must be amortized in order to record the correct amount of interest expense. Then any remaining balance of the premium is written off together with the bonds payable. The entry to record the payment of interest and premium amortization is

Mar. 30	Interest expense	2,534.05	
	Premium on bonds payable	215.95	
	Cash		2,750.00
	To amortize premium and pay 3 months'		
	interest prior to early bond retirement.		
	$101,362.12 \times .10 \times 3/12 = \$2,534.05$		
	$100,000.00 \times .11 \times 3/12 = \$2,750.00$		

Now a balance of $1,146.17 remains in the premium account. To record the bond retirement, the face amount of the bonds and the unamortized premium are written off as follows:

Mar. 31	Bonds payable	100,000.00	
	Premium on bonds payable	1,146.17	
	Loss on bond retirement	853.83	
	Cash		102,000.00
	Retired $100,000 of 11% bonds		
	at call price of 102.		

The cash payment of $102,000 is required by the call provision on the bonds. The loss of $853.83 is the difference between the book value of the bonds and the amount paid to retire the debt.

Early retirement at market price.   If market interest rates increased since the bonds were issued, Hamlin Corporation's bonds trade in the market at lower prices than when they were issued. The company may be able to retire these bonds not by calling them at 102, but by buying them in the open market. There is, of course, no requirement for a company to call the bonds and pay a call premium if investors are willing to sell the bonds at a discount. If the company buys the bonds at 97, it realizes a gain on the early redemption. As before, the interest must be paid to March 31, 1988, the date of redemption, and the bond premium must be amortized. The entry to record the redemption of the bonds at 97 is as follows:

Mar. 31	Bonds payable	100,000.00	
	Premium on bonds payable	1,146.17	
	Gain on bond retirement		4,146.17
	Cash		97,000.00
	Retired $100,000 of 11% bonds		
	by buying them in the market at 97.		

There is no requirement to retire the entire bond issue. Hamlin Corporation could have decided to retire $60,000 of its bonds. In that case 40 percent of the premium and $40,000 of bonds would still remain on the books, and interest on these bonds would be paid as usual on June 30 and December 31.

SUMMARY

Corporations obtain much of their borrowed funds by issuing bonds. If the interest expense on the bonds is less than the profit earned by investing the borrowed money, the company obtains **financial leverage** and increases the return on owners' equity.

The **face value** of a bond is $1,000, but the bond may be issued at a **discount** or at a **premium**. The terms of the bond, including the **maturity date**, the **coupon rate** of interest, the **call price**, interest payment dates, and other conditions are described in the **bond indenture**.

The ownership of **registered bonds** is stated on the bond certificate. **Bearer bonds** are not so identified, and the holder is presumed to be the owner. Some bonds may be **secured** by assets. **Unsecured** bonds are called **debentures**. Bonds may be **convertible** into shares of common stock, making them attractive to investors because they provide interest income and can also benefit from price increases of the common stock. Bonds that are issued at one time but mature on different dates are known as **serial bonds**. Each series has its own maturity date so that repayment of the debt may take place over several years.

Financial services rate bonds according to risk and investment quality. Low ratings are assigned to bonds with a high risk of **default**. A **sinking fund** provision of a bond requires the issuer to maintain a fund that will be used to redeem the bonds at maturity. The existence of a sinking fund reduces risk because money accumulated in the fund can be used to repay the bond.

The value of a bond depends on the interest rate available in the market for investments of similar risk, the bond coupon rate, and the term of the bond. If the market rate of interest is higher than the coupon rate of the bond, the bond sells at a **discount**, which is a price below face value. If the market rate of interest is lower than the coupon rate, the bond sells at a **premium**, which is a price above face value. As interest rates increase, bond prices decrease, and vice versa. The value of a bond may be determined by discounting the future interest and principal payments at the market rate of interest. The present value of these future payments is the market value of the bond.

The effective interest provided by the bond if it is held until maturity is known as the **yield to maturity**. It may be higher or lower than the coupon rate of interest. At maturity the bond issuer returns a principal amount that is smaller or larger than the amount originally borrowed. This difference is the premium or discount on the bond, and it affects the cost of borrowing the money.

When bonds are issued between interest payment dates, the accrued interest is collected by the issuer. Bonds pay interest every 6 months, and a full 6-months' interest is paid on each interest payment date no matter how long the bonds have been outstanding. By collecting the accrued interest when the bonds are issued, the issuer ensures that the actual amount of interest paid on the bond represents interest for the length of time that the bond has been outstanding.

When bonds are issued at a discount, interest expense during the term of the bonds is greater than the coupon rate of the bond because in addition to the interest payments, more money must be repaid than was originally borrowed. The actual interest expense is recorded by amortizing a portion of the discount each period. Amortization using the **straight-line method** results in writing off an equal amount of discount in each period. When the **effective interest method** is used, the same interest rate is applied to the book value of the bonds each period, resulting in writing off a different amount of discount in each period.

When bonds are issued at a premium, the interest expense during the life of the bonds is less than the coupon rate of interest because the premium does not have to be returned to the bond holders. Amortization of the premium ensures that the interest expense recorded in each period matches the benefits from the use of the borrowed money. Bond premium is recorded in an **adjunct account** whose balance is added to the bond liability balance in order to report the book value of the bonds in the balance sheet.

By the time bonds mature, any discount or premium is amortized, leaving the book value of the bonds equal to their face value. If bonds are retired prior to their maturity date, the remaining balance of the discount or premium account must be written off. The difference between the book value of the bond and the amount paid for its retirement is recorded as a gain or loss. Such gains or losses are classified as extraordinary items in the income statement. At the time bonds are retired, interest must be paid to the date of retirement. Bonds may be retired early either by calling them and paying the call price or by buying them in the market. A company normally chooses the least costly way of bond retirement.

KEY TERMS

adjunct account *(518)*
bearer bond *(505)*
bond indenture *(504)*
bonds payable *(503)*
call premium *(504)*
call price *(504)*
contra-liability account *(513)*
convertible bond *(506)*
coupon rate *(504)*
debenture *(506)*
default *(507)*
discount *(504)*
effective interest *(512)*
effective interest method *(515)*

face value *(504)*
financial leverage *(503)*
leverage *(503)*
maturity date *(504)*
maturity value *(504)*
par value *(504)*
premium *(504)*
registered bonds *(505)*
secured bond *(505)*
serial bonds *(506)*
sinking fund *(507)*
straight-line method *(513)*
unsecured bond *(506)*
yield to maturity *(508)*

QUESTIONS

1. Discuss the terms "bond discount" and "bond premium." Why do premiums and discounts on bonds occur?

2. What is the difference between registered bonds and bearer bonds?

3. How much money must be paid for a $1,000 face value bond selling in the market at 99 5/8? 102 3/4? 66 1/4? 122?

4. What is a sinking fund? How does the sinking fund grow in value?

5. Under what conditions does a bond sell at a discount? What conditions must exist for a bond to be issued at a premium?

6. What effect does a bond premium or discount have on the interest expense of a bond issuer?

7. Explain what happens to the market price of bonds when market interest rates increase?

8. Describe the difference between premium or discount amortization using the effective interest method and the straight-line method.

9. How does the cash outflow for interest payments differ from the interest expense reported in the income statement when bonds are issued at a discount?

10. Describe some characteristics of serial bonds.

11. How is the gain or loss from early bond retirement reported in the income statement?

EXERCISES

Ex. 12-1 **Bond issuance and partial retirement.**   On June 30, 1985, Conestoga Company issued $300,000 of 7-year 14 percent bonds at par. The bonds pay interest on June 30 and December 31. On September 30, 1986, the company's bonds were trading in the market at 98. Using some of its excess cash, the company bought $100,000 of its bonds in the market on this date and retired them.

Required: Prepare all journal entries needed to account for the company's bonds in 1985 and 1986.

Ex. 12-2 **Accounting for a bond issue.**   On October 15, 1985, Bidley Corporation issued $1,000,000 of 5-year 12 percent bonds at face value. Interest on the bonds is payable on October 15 and April 15 of each year.

Required: Prepare the journal entries associated with these bonds on:
    a. October 15, 1985.
    b. December 31, 1985, the end of the accounting period.
    c. April 15, 1986.
    d. October 15, 1986.
    e. October 15, 1990.

Ex. 12-3 **Bonds issued between interest dates.**   On April 1, 1985, Blakely Company issued $100,000 of 10-year 12 percent bonds payable at face value plus accrued interest. Interest is payable on June 1 and December 1 of each year. The company's accounting period ends on December 31.

Required: Prepare the journal entries to record bond issuance, the first three interest payments, and interest accrual at the end of the year.

Ex. 12-4 **Proceeds of a bond issue.**   Fulgen Corporation is planning to issue $500,000 face value of 16-year 12 percent bonds payable. Interest on the bonds is payable semiannually.

Required:
    a. Determine what the proceeds of the bond issue will be if the bonds are issued when the market rate of interest is 10 percent.
    b. Determine what the proceeds of the bond issue will be if the bonds are issued when the market rate of interest is 14 percent.

Ex. 12-5 **Premium and discount on bond.**   Keeley Corporation issued some 5-year 11.6 percent bonds payable. The interest on these bonds is paid semiannually.

Required: Determine the proceeds the company should receive on each $1,000 bond and the amount of discount or premium, assuming that the market rate of interest on the issue date is: **a.** 11 percent and **b.** 12 percent.

Ex. 12-6 **Finding interest payment on bond issue.**   Rozina Company issued $100,000 of 6-year bonds for total proceeds of $91,137 to yield 10 percent to maturity. The bonds pay interest semiannually and were issued on an interest payment date.

Required: Calculate the coupon rate of interest on the bonds.

Ex. 12-7 **Amortization of bond discount.** On June 30, 1985, Corruth Corporation issued $100,000 of 3-year 10 percent bonds with interest payable on June 30 and December 31. Total proceeds of the bond issue amounted to $98,740 to yield 10.5 percent to maturity. The company's accounting period ends on December 31.

Required: Record the issuance of the bonds on June 30 and the first two interest payments, assuming that bond discount is amortized using:
  a. the straight-line method.
  b. the effective interest method.

Ex. 12-8 **Amortization of bond premium.** On June 30, 1985, Sorento Corporation issued $200,000 of 12-year 10 percent bonds with interest payable on June 30 and December 31. Total proceeds of the bond issue amounted to $206,690 to yield 9.5 percent to maturity. The company's accounting period ends on December 31.

Required: Record the issuance of the bonds on June 30 and the first two interest payments, assuming that bond premium is amortized using:
  a. the straight-line method.
  b. the effective interest method.

Ex. 12-9 **Reporting bonds payable.** On June 30, 1985, Bali Corporation issued $100,000, 7-year 12 percent bonds payable at a premium of $4,788 on the issue. The bonds pay interest on June 30 and December 31, and straight-line amortization of premium is used.

Required:
  a. Record the issuance of the bonds and the first interest payment.
  b. Show how the bonds should be presented in the balance sheet on December 31, 1985.

Ex. 12-10 **Bond discount amortization table.** Flotsam Company issued $100,000 face value of 3-year 12 percent bonds payable, receiving $97,579.50 for the issue. The bonds were issued on March 31, 1985. The effective interest rate on the bonds is 13 percent. Interest payment dates are March 31 and September 30. The company uses the effective interest method to amortize bond discount.

Required: Prepare a table of bond discount amortization, similar to the one in Figure 12-4, for the company's bond issue.

Ex. 12-11 **Bond premium amortization table.** On September 30, 1985, Jetsam Company issued $100,000 face value of 3-year 12 percent bonds payable, receiving $102,497.75 for the issue. The effective interest rate on the bonds is 11 percent. Interest payment dates are March 31 and September 30. The company uses the effective interest method to amortize bond premium.

Required: Prepare a table of bond premium amortization, similar to the one in Figure 12-7, for the company's bond issue.

Ex. 12-12 **Discount amortization table with straight-line method.** The proceeds of Flojet Company's $200,000 3-year 13 percent bond issue were $191,600. The bonds were issued on February 1, 1985, and pay interest on February 1 and August 1. The company uses the straight-line method to amortize bond discount.

Required:
    a. Prepare a table of bond discount amortization, similar to the one in Figure 12-3, for the company's bond issue.
    b. Calculate the implied interest rate at each interest payment date and use these computations to estimate the effective interest rate on the bonds.

Ex. 12-13   **Early retirement of bonds.**   In the December 31, 1985, balance sheet of Rubicoff Company, bonds payable were reported as follows:

Bonds payable, 9%	$1,000,000	
Less discount on bonds payable	2,000	$998,000

The bonds pay interest on June 30 and December 31. The effective interest rate is 9.5 percent. Rubicoff Company retired these bonds early by buying them at 96 in the open market on January 31, 1986. Discount is amortized using the effective interest method.

Required:
    a. Prepare the journal entries on January 31, 1986, to pay interest and retire the bonds.
    b. Discuss briefly how the results of the bond retirement should be reported in the income statement.

Ex. 12-14   **Interest expense and cash flow.**   Clutton Company uses the straight-line method to amortize premium or discount on bonds payable. The company reported the following bonds payable in the liability section of its December 31, 1985, balance sheet:

	1985	1984
Bonds payable, 9%	$1,000,000	$1,000,000
Discount on bonds payable	(6,500)	(7,150)
Net amount	993,500	992,850
Bonds payable, 12%	3,000,000	3,000,000
Premium on bonds payable	6,900	8,050
Net amount	3,006,900	3,008,050
Total bond indebtedness	$4,000,400	$4,000,900

Interest on the bonds is payable on June 30 and December 31 of each year.

Required:
    a. Determine how much cash the company paid for bond interest in 1985.
    b. Determine how much bond interest expense the company reported on its income statement for the year ended December 31, 1985.
    c. Determine the maturity date of each bond.

Ex. 12-15   **(AICPA) Bond issuance, service, and retirement.**   Below are three independent questions from recent CPA examinations in accounting practice. Select the best answer for each question.

1. On March 1, 1985, Williams Corporation issued at 103 plus accrued interest one hundred of its 9%, $1,000 bonds. The bonds are dated January 1, 1985 and mature on January 1, 1995. Based on the information above, Williams would realize net cash receipts from the bond issuance of
   a. $101,500   b. $118,000   c. $103,000   d. $104,500

2. On January 2, 1985, a calendar-year corporation sold 5 percent bonds with a face value of $100,000. These bonds mature in 5 years, and interest is paid semiannually June 30 and December 31. The bonds were sold for $95,735 to yield 6 percent. Using the effective interest method of computing interest, how much should be charged to interest expense in 1985?
   a. $4,147   b. $4,265   c. $5,755   d. $5,853

3. On January 1, 1985, Provident Corporation issued for $1,040,000, one thousand of its 9 percent, $1,000 callable bonds. The bonds are dated January 1, 1985, and mature on January 1, 1995. Interest is payable semiannually on July 1 and January 1. The bonds can be called by the issuer at 101 at any time after December 31, 1989. On July 1, 1990, Provident called in all of the bonds and retired them. Provident uses the straight-line method of amortizing bond premium. What is the amount of gain or loss that Provident should record on this early extinguishment of debt in its income statement for the year ended December 31, 1990?
   a. $8,000 gain   b. $10,000 loss   c. $12,000 gain   d. $30,000 gain

PROBLEMS

P. 12-1   Issuance and partial retirement of bonds.   On March 31, 1985, Loubell Company issued $500,000 of 9-year 12 percent bonds payable at par. The bonds pay interest on February 28 and August 31. On October 31, 1986, when the company's bonds were trading in the market at 99, the company used its excess cash to retire $200,000 of its bonds by buying them in the market. Loubell Company's accounting period ends on December 31.

Required: Prepare journal entries to record all events associated with the company's bonds up to and including February 28, 1987.

P. 12-2   Accounting for bond issuance, interest, and retirement.   On April 30, 1985, Kipper Corporation issued $1,000,000 of 5½-year 11.4 percent bonds payable at face value. Interest is payable on February 28 and August 31. On September 30, 1986 the company retired $600,000 of its bonds by buying them in the market at 99. The accounting period ends on December 31.

Required:
   a. Prepare the necessary journal entries for these bonds from April 30, 1985 through February 28, 1987.
   b. Prepare the entry to record the bond maturity on August 31, 1990.

P. 12-3   Accounting for bonds issued at a discount.   On March 31, 1985, when the market interest rate was 11.6 percent, Gorovod Company issued $100,000 face value, 4-year 10 percent bonds payable. The issue yielded $95,008. The bonds pay interest on March 31 and September 30. The company uses the straight-line method to amortize bond discount and closes its books on December 31. On September 30, 1986, the company decided to retire the bonds and bought them in the market at 97.

Required: Prepare journal entries to record the bond issue, interest payments, interest accrual on December 31, and bond retirement.

P. 12-4   **Issuance and retirement of bonds with a discount.**   Refer to the data in Problem 12-3 on Gorovod Company's bonds, but assume that the company uses the effective interest method of amortizing bond discount.

Required: Prepare journal entries to record the bond issue, interest payments, interest accrual on December 31, and bond retirement.

P. 12-5   **Accounting for bonds issued at a premium.**   When Kogakusha Corporation issued $100,000 of its 4-year 13 percent bonds on March 31, 1985, the market rate of interest was 11.6 percent. As a result the bonds were sold at a premium of $4,368 over par value. The bonds pay interest on March 31 and September 30. The company uses the straight-line method to amortize bond premium, and it closes its books on December 31. On September 30, 1986, the company retired the bonds by buying them in the market at 99.

Required: Prepare journal entries to record issuance of the bonds, interest payments, interest accrual on December 31, and bond retirement.

P. 12-6   **Issuance and retirement of bonds with a premium.**   Refer to the data in Problem 12-5 on Kogakusha Company's bonds, but assume that the company uses the effective interest method of amortizing bond premium.

Required: Prepare journal entries to record issuance of the bonds, interest payments, interest accrual on December 31, and bond retirement.

P. 12-7   **Bond premium amortization tables.**   On December 31, 1985, Whoom Corporation issued $100,000 of 16 percent bonds at a premium of $2,023 to yield 15 percent to maturity. The bonds mature on June 30, 1988. Interest is payable on June 30 and December 31.

Required:
    a. Prepare a premium amortization table for the bonds using the effective interest method.
    b. Prepare a premium amortization table for the bonds using the straight-line method.
    c. Briefly discuss how much cash was paid for interest in 1986 and how much interest expense is recorded with each amortization method. Also compute the total interest expense over the life of the bonds with each amortization method and the implied interest rate for the first and last interest payment with each method.

P. 12-8   Bond discount amortization tables. On December 31, 1985, Yarmol Corporation issued $100,000 of 14 percent bonds payable at a discount of $2,023 to yield 15 percent to maturity. The bonds mature on June 30, 1988. Interest is payable on June 30 and December 31.

Required:
   a. Prepare a discount amortization table for the bonds using the effective interest method.
   b. Prepare a discount amortization table for the bonds using the straight-line method.
   c. Briefly discuss how much cash was paid for interest in 1986 and how much interest expense is recorded with each amortization method. Also compute the total interest expense over the life of the bonds with each amortization method and the implied interest rate for the first and last interest payment with each method.

P. 12-9   Bond discount computation and amortization table. Blue Cactus Company issued $1,000,000 of 3-year 11.6 percent bonds payable on February 28, 1985, when the market rate of interest was 12 percent. Interest on the bonds is payable on February 28 and August 31. The company's accounting period ends on December 31.

Required:
   a. Determine the total proceeds of the bond issue.
   b. Prepare a schedule of discount amortization, assuming use of the effective interest method.
   c. Record the issuance of the bonds, the first two interest payments, and interest accrual on December 31, assuming effective interest amortization of bond discount.

P. 12-10   Bond premium computation and amortization. On January 1, 1985, Salem Corporation issued $200,000 of 3-year 13.5 percent bonds when the market rate of interest was 12 percent. Interest is payable on June 30 and December 31.

Required:
   a. Determine the total proceeds of the bond issue.
   b. Prepare a schedule of premium amortization, assuming use of the effective interest method.
   c. Record the issuance of the bonds and the first two interest payments, assuming effective interest amortization of bond premium.

P. 12-11   Amortizing and reporting bond discount. On January 1, 1985, Garrett and Sons, Inc. issued $100,000 of 5-year 9 percent bonds payable to yield 10 percent to maturity. Proceeds were $96,140.

Required:
   a. Record the issuance of the bonds.
   b. Record interest payments on June 30 and December 31 using straight-line amortization of bond discount. Also show how the bonds are reported on the balance sheet on December 31, 1985.

c. Record interest payments on June 30 and December 31, 1985, using effective interest amortization of bond discount. Also show how the bonds are reported on the balance sheet on December 31, 1985.

P. 12-12   **Discounted bonds issued between interest dates.** On March 31, 1985, Fordee Company issued $100,000 face value of 10.2 percent bonds payable. The bonds pay interest on February 28 and August 31, and mature on February 28, 1990. Proceeds of the issue were $92,920, plus accrued interest. The company decided to use the straight-line method of discount amortization. The company closes its books on December 31. On May 31, 1986, the company retired its bonds by buying them in the market at 95.

Required: Record issuance of the bonds, interest payments in 1985 and 1986, interest accrual on December 31, and the bond retirement.

P. 12-13   **Bond premium amortization table and early retirement.** Rossini, Finkelstein, & Wong, Inc. issued $100,000 of 9-year 15 percent bonds payable on April 30, 1985. The bonds pay interest on April 30 and October 31, and were sold to yield 14 percent to maturity. The company uses the effective interest method to amortize bond premium. Its accounting period ends on December 31. On October 31, 1987, the company retires $40,000 of its bonds by buying them in the market at 98.

Required:
a. Determine the proceeds of the bond issue.
b. Prepare a table of bond premium amortization for the first 3 years of the bond's life.
c. Journalize the issuance of the bonds, interest payments through April 1986, and the bond retirement on October 31, 1987.
d. State how the gain or loss from the bond retirement should be reported in the financial statements in 1987.

Case 12-1   **Interpreting bonds on a balance sheet.**
Molaska Public Power Company reported the following bonds payable among its long-term debt:

	December 31	
	1985	**1984**
Pollution control bonds, 10%, due 2002	$45,000,000	
First mortgage bonds payable, 8.4%	60,000,000	$60,000,000
Discount on 8.4% bonds	(112,000)	(126,000)
Subordinated debentures, 7%, due 1989	40,000,000	40,000,000
Premium on 7% debentures	276,111	334,349

The pollution control bonds issued June 1, 1985 have $375,000 interest accrued at year end. There are no interest accruals on other bonds at year end. The company amortized the discount on its 8.4 percent bonds using the straight-line method, and the premium on its 7 percent debentures is amortized using the effective interest method with an effective yield of 6.8 percent per year. All bonds pay interest semiannually. The company's term debt agreements contain various restrictions on dividend payments and incurring additional debt. As of December

31, 1985, $110,000,000 of retained earnings were not available for dividend payments, and the company could incur additional indebtedness of approximately $83,520,000.

Required:
   a. What is the maturity date of the 8.4 percent bonds?
   b. What are the interest payment dates of the 10 percent bonds?
   c. How much bond interest expense did the company report for 1985?
   d. How much cash did the company pay for bond interest in 1985?

Case 12-2   **Bond refunding.**

Sparkle Corporation has outstanding $2,000,000 of 20-year 7.2 percent bonds payable issued in 1969. The bonds were originally issued for $2,024,000, and the company has accounted for premium amortization using the straight-line method. Interest on the bonds is payable on April 30 and October 31, and they are callable at 103 until October 31, 1986, at which time the call price declines to 102. The December 31, 1984 balance sheet reported the bonds with a premium of $5,200, and interest payable of $24,000.

   Interest rates on bonds had been as high as 17 percent in the early 1980s, and the company had postponed needed plant construction because of the high cost of borrowing. Then the rate declined to 11 percent. Economists predicted an increase in rates from current levels, however, so the company considered issuing another bond to finance new construction and at the same time to refund the 7.2 percent bonds. The 7.2 percent bonds were trading in the market at 87.

   After some deliberation at the March 1985 board of directors meeting, the decision was made to issue $5,000,000 of 10-year 11 percent bonds on June 30. Interest on the bonds will be payable on June 30 and December 31.

   By the time the April 30 interest payment arrived, the bond prospectus was ready for submission to the SEC and negotiations were in progress with an underwriter. The bonds were issued on June 30 as planned, but interest rates had increased by then and the effective interest cost of the borrowing to the company was 12 percent. The company's accountant informed the board of directors that the bonds would have to be accounted for using the effective interest method, in accordance with FASB pronouncements.

   The company placed an order with a broker to acquire as many of the old bonds as possible at the market price, and on July 31 it was successful in buying $1,000,000 of the bonds at 85. On August 31 another $500,000 of the old bonds were bought at 89. Bond holders did not offer more bonds for sale, so the company called the remaining bonds on the October 31 interest payment date.

Required:
   a. Compute the proceeds of the new bond issue and prepare a discount amortization schedule for the first 3 or 4 years of the bonds' life.
   b. Prepare journal entries to record the April 30 interest payment on the 7.2 percent bonds, the bond retirements, and interest payments on the new bonds.
   c. Determine how much of the new bond issue proceeds is available for new plant construction.
   d. Discuss the advisability of the refunding.

Investment by Owners: Business Capital

13

This chapter covers basic but important and interesting material about owners' equity of proprietorships, partnerships, and corporations. When you have finished the chapter, you should have a good understanding of:

1   Accounting for the capital of a sole proprietorship.

2   Accounting for partnership income distributions.

3   Statements of capital for partnerships and sole proprietorships.

4   How a partner is admitted to or retired from a partnership.

5   Characteristics of corporations.

6   Different types of capital stock.

7   Accounting for retained earnings and dividends.

The three basic forms of business entities—sole proprietorships, partnerships, and corporations—have distinct characteristics. Each requires a different set of accounting procedures for owners' equity.

Accounting for the capital of proprietorships and partnerships is relatively simple compared with accounting for the capital of corporations. Setting up business as a sole proprietorship is a fairly easy process. The owner can be flexible in arranging business affairs and accounting for capital investment. As soon as there is more than one owner, the situation becomes more complicated because two or more individuals must agree on their method of operations.

Whether the business is a sole proprietorship or a partnership, the owners of the business are personally responsible to creditors. Their responsibility is not limited by the amount of the capital accounts of the business. For this reason, there are no restrictions on accounting for proprietorship or partnership capital. On the other hand, the owners of a corporation are not personally liable for the debts of the business entity. Because the owners' liability is limited, accounting for corporate capital must include some safeguards for creditors. Corporations are complex business entities, and accounting for their capital is more complex than accounting for the capital of unincorporated businesses.

In this chapter we first deal with capital of unincorporated business, starting with sole proprietorships and partnerships. The last half of this chapter, however, and all of Chapter 14 are devoted to owners' equity of corporations.

SOLE PROPRIETORSHIP

Three activities affect the capital account of a sole proprietor: the investment of assets in the business by the owner, the earning of net income or net loss by the business, and the withdrawal of assets from the business by the owner. When a proprietor invests in a business by contributing cash or other assets, the assets of the business increase, and the corresponding increase in owners' equity is recorded in a **capital account**. The purpose of investing in business is to earn income which benefits the owner. Net income of the proprietorship therefore increases the balance of the capital account. If the business is not successful and incurs a loss, the loss reduces the capital account. The owner may withdraw cash or other assets from the firm for personal use, thereby reducing his equity in the business. Such withdrawals may take place whether or not the business earns any income.

A sole proprietorship is an accounting entity, but it is not a legal entity. The income earned by the business legally belongs to the owner, who must report it on his personal tax return together with any other income. Therefore, the business entity does not pay any taxes on its income, and the financial statements of a sole proprietorship do not report income tax expense or income tax payable. The owner must pay the income tax whether or not the income is withdrawn from the business.

Sole proprietorships do not pay income taxes; their owners do

Capital Investment

Assets invested in the business by the owner are recorded at their fair value with a debit, and Capital is credited. For example, on March 3 Albert invests $10,000 cash and $20,000 of equipment to start a new business. The entry to record the investment is

Mar. 3	Cash	10,000	
	Equipment	20,000	
	Capital, Albert		30,000
	Invested cash and equipment in		
	business.		

Any additional investments are recorded in the same manner. On the other hand, when the owner withdraws assets from the business, the Capital account is usually not debited. Because withdrawals may take place frequently during an accounting period, they are usually recorded in a temporary account which is described below.

Drawings.   The owner may withdraw cash or other assets from the business during the accounting period. The amounts withdrawn during the period may be more or less than the net income earned by the business. Income not withdrawn remains invested in the business. If more is withdrawn than is earned, capital invested previously is reduced.

A temporary account called **drawings** is used to maintain a record of the owner's withdrawals of assets during the accounting period. The Drawings account is closed at the end of the accounting period by transferring its balance to the Capital account. The Capital account then reflects all changes resulting from earnings, investments, and withdrawals of the period.

The owner may withdraw assets for living expenses or other personal use, but it is incorrect to call the owner's withdrawals "salary" because any assets taken from the business by the owner are not expenses of operating the business. Drawings do not reduce the amount of net income earned. Nevertheless, it may be convenient for managerial purposes to view some or all of the owner's drawings as salary in order to enable comparisons of the business with other similar businesses. The owner who manages his own business may wish to measure the performance of the business as if a salary were paid to a manager. Such analyses for managerial purposes are discussed in the managerial volume of this series. For financial purposes any "salary" withdrawn by the owner is recorded as drawings and not as an expense of operating the business.

Proprietor's drawings are not expenses

Withdrawals are recorded by debits to the Drawings account and credits to an asset account. For example, Albert withdraws $1,200 cash from his business on April 15. The entry is

Apr. 15	Drawings, Albert	1,200	
	Cash		1,200
	Withdrew cash for personal use.		

If assets other than cash, such as equipment or merchandise, are withdrawn by the owner, the cost of the asset is removed from the asset accounts. At the end of the accounting period, the drawings account is closed directly to the Capital account. Revenues and expenses are closed to Income Summary, which in turn is closed to the Capital account. For example, Albert's capital accounts appear as follows at the end of the first accounting period:

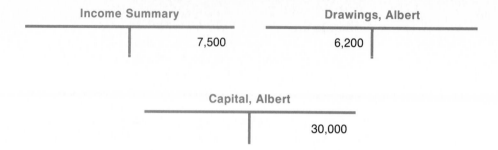

Income Summary		Drawings, Albert	
	7,500	6,200	

Capital, Albert	
	30,000

The entries to close the Drawings and Income Summary accounts leave a credit balance of $31,300 in the Capital account.

Dec. 31	Income summary	7,500	
	Capital, Albert		7,500
	To close income summary.		
	Capital, Albert	6,200	
	Drawings, Albert		6,200
	To close drawings account.		

Statement of Capital

At the end of the accounting period, a **statement of owners' equity**, also called the **statement of capital**, is prepared to explain the change in owners' equity for the period. This statement is similar to the statement of retained earnings of a corporation. The statement of capital for Albert Company is illustrated in Figure 13-1. Often this statement is not prepared separately but is included in its entirety in the capital section of the balance sheet.

Albert Company
Statement of Capital
For the 10 Months Ended December 31, 1985

Capital, 3/03/85	$30,000
Add net income	7,500
	37,500
Less drawings	6,200
Capital, 12/31/85	$31,300

Figure 13-1   **A statement of capital for a proprietorship is similar to a retained earnings statement of a corporation. It shows how capital of the proprietorship changed during the accounting period.**

PARTNERSHIP CAPITAL

A **partnership** is a business with two or more owners. The partners are bound by a partnership agreement and by provisions of the Uniform Partnership Act, which has been adopted by most states. In the absence of a specific written or verbal agreement on profit sharing, all partners are assumed to have an equal share in profits and losses. Partners may, of course, agree to share profits and losses in any manner. A written partnership agreement is not necessary but it is highly desirable, so that all partners clearly understand their duties, obligations, and privileges.

The partnership agreement may limit the amount of assets any individual partner may withdraw, and may also specify a minimum required amount of capital that each partner must maintain. The agreement may also impose restrictions on the partners' ability to enter into contracts without consulting the other partners. It may specify the conditions under which a partner may withdraw from the business or how a new partner will be accepted into the business.

Each partner has a capital account

Separate capital accounts and drawings accounts are maintained for each partner. When a partner invests in the business by contributing assets, that partner's capital account is credited. Any withdrawals by partners are recorded as debits in the appropriate drawings accounts. The balances of the partners' capital accounts represent the partners' respective interest in the business. Because partners may invest and withdraw varying amounts, each partner's interest in the business is not necessarily in the same proportion as the profit and loss sharing ratio.

Partners' Investments

To illustrate accounting for partnership capital, we use the example of Oliver, Pratt, and Quillen, who formed the OPQ Company. Oliver invests $20,000, Pratt invests land and a building valued at $10,000 and $30,000, respectively, and Quillen invests $10,000 cash and equipment valued at $10,000.

To record the original investment, the company makes the following entry:

Jan. 5	Cash	30,000	
	Land	10,000	
	Buildings	30,000	
	Equipment	10,000	
	Capital, Oliver		20,000
	Capital, Pratt		40,000
	Capital, Quillen		20,000
	To record partners' investment.		

By the end of the first year of operations, the partnership capital accounts have the following balances:

Capital, Oliver		Drawings, Oliver	
	20,000	4,200	
	5,000		
Bal.	25,000		

Capital, Pratt		Drawings, Pratt	
	40,000	3,800	

Capital, Quillen		Drawings, Quillen	
	20,000	4,500	

Oliver's capital account shows that an additional investment was made during the year. When the business needs additional money, partners often make additional investments if they decide this is more desirable than borrowing the needed funds. Sometimes partners lend money to the business, and the partnership records a liability to the partner.

Profit-Sharing Arrangements

Partners' salaries are not expenses

Partners may agree on any formula for sharing profits and losses. Sometimes one partner devotes more time to the operation of the business than the others and therefore receives a greater share of profits. The partners may decide that an additional share of profits may be allowed in the form of a salary to the more active partner. The salary is part of the profit-sharing agreement and is not an expense of the business. Partners may also agree to credit each capital account with interest at some specified rate. Again the interest is not an expense but simply a method of dividing the profits. Below we discuss a variety of profit-sharing agreements.

Profits divided among partners.   Oliver, Pratt, and Quillen have decided to share profits and losses in the ratio of 1:2:1, respectively. If by the end of the first year of operations the partnership has earned $24,000, this net income is divided among the partners in the profit-sharing ratio with the following entry when the books are closed:

Dec. 31	Income summary	24,000	
	Capital, Oliver		6,000
	Capital, Pratt		12,000
	Capital, Quillen		6,000
	To allocate net income to partners'		
	capital in profit-sharing ratio.		

If the partnership incurs a loss, the capital accounts are debited in the profit-sharing ratio when income summary is closed.

Salary agreements.   When the profit-sharing agreement is more complex, a schedule may be prepared for the calculation of the amounts to be credited to each partner's capital account. For example, the OPQ Company profit-sharing agreement states that Quillen is to be allowed a salary of $9,000 per year with the remaining profits divided in the ratio of 1:2:1. With a net income of $24,000, the allocation to the partners' capital accounts is made in accordance with the schedule in Figure 13-2. Note that the salary is first allocated to Quillen, then the remaining profit is divided among the three partners in the agreed ratio. The total of the last column in the schedule must always equal the balance in the income summary account.

The entry to close the income summary account is

Dec. 31	Income summary	24,000	
	Capital, Oliver		3,750
	Capital, Pratt		7,500
	Capital, Quillen		12,750
	To allocate net income to partners'		
	capital in accordance with profit-		
	sharing agreement as per schedule.		
	[Figure 13-2]		

OPQ Company
Schedule of Profit Distribution
For the Year Ended December 31, 1985

	Oliver	Pratt	Quillen	Total
Salary			$ 9,000	$ 9,000
Balance divided 1:2:1	$3,750	$7,500	3,750	15,000
Total	$3,750	$7,500	$12,750	$24,000

Figure 13-2   **Amounts designated as partners' salaries are distributions of net income to the partners' capital accounts. The salary is not an expense of operating the partnership business.**

OPQ Company
Schedule of Profit Distribution
For the Year Ended December 31, 1985

	Oliver	Pratt	Quillen	Total
Salary			$9,000	$9,000
Balance divided 1:2:1	$(1,000)	$(2,000)	(1,000)	(4,000)
Total	$(1,000)	$(2,000)	$8,000	$5,000

Figure 13-3 **If a profit-sharing agreement requires crediting a partner's account with salary, the agreement must be followed whether or not sufficient income has been earned to cover the salary amount.**

If the partners have agreed to allow salaries to one or more partners, such salaries must be credited whether or not the business earns enough profit to make up the full amount of the salary. For example, if the OPQ Company earned $5,000 for the year, and Quillen is to be allowed a salary of $9,000, the allocation of net income is made according to the schedule in Figure 13-3.

The $4,000 shortage that occurs because the salary allowance is larger than net income must be divided among the partners in the agreed-upon ratio for sharing profits and losses. Here, the entry to close the Income Summary account is

Dec. 31	Income summary	5,000	
	Capital, Oliver	1,000	
	Capital, Pratt	2,000	
	Capital, Quillen		8,000
	To allocate net income to partners'		
	capital in accordance with profit-sharing		
	agreement as per schedule. [Figure 13-3]		

Even if the partnership incurs a loss, the agreement on salary allowances must be followed. For example, if the company incurred a net loss of $11,000 in the first year of operations, the allocation of this loss is made in accordance with the schedule in Figure 13-4. Notice that the requirement to allow a $9,000 salary to Quillen makes it necessary to divide a $20,000 debit among the partners to equal the $11,000 debit balance of the Income Summary account.

Figure 13-4
Even if a partnership incurs a loss, the profit-sharing agreement must be followed when the loss is distributed to the partners' capital accounts.

OPQ Company
Schedule of Profit Distribution
For the Year Ended December 31, 1985

	Oliver	Pratt	Quillen	Total
Salary			$9,000	$ 9,000
Balance divided 1:2:1	$(5,000)	$(10,000)	(5,000)	(20,000)
Total	$(5,000)	$(10,000)	$4,000	$(11,000)

Interest on capital balances.   When the partnership agreement states that interest is to be allowed on the partners' capital balances, the interest must be allocated whether or not the partnership has earned enough profit to cover it. The partnership agreement may combine allocations of both interest and salaries. Figure 13-5 illustrates the allocation of 10 percent interest on the balance of each capital account, $9,000 salary to Quillen, and the remainder divided in the 1:2:1 ratio. Net income for the period in this example is $26,000. Remember that during the period, Oliver made an additional investment of $5,000, which increased his capital balance. To avoid an unfair allocation of interest on capital invested during the period, interest is often credited on the weighted average capital rather than on the beginning or ending balance. Interest may also be allocated after drawings are deducted from the capital accounts.

Interest on capital balances is not an expense

OPQ Company
Schedule of Profit Distribution
For the Year Ended December 31, 1985

	Oliver	Pratt	Quillen	Total
Capital balances	$25,000	$40,000	$20,000	$85,000
Interest at 10%	2,500	4,000	2,000	8,500
Salary to Quillen			9,000	9,000
Balance divided 1:2:1	2,125	4,250	2,125	8,500
Total	$ 4,625	$ 8,250	$13,125	$26,000

Figure 13-5   **Partners may establish any type of profit-sharing agreement. Here interest is credited to all partners and salary to one partner prior to distributing the remaining income or loss to the partners' capital accounts in an agreed-upon ratio.**

Closing Partnership Temporary Accounts

Drawings accounts are closed at year-end

When the allocation of income has been determined, the Income Summary and Drawings accounts are closed. Assuming drawing account balances as illustrated before and income distributions as in Figure 13-5, the closing entries are as follows:

Dec. 31	Income summary	26,000	
	Capital, Oliver		4,625
	Capital, Pratt		8,250
	Capital, Quillen		13,125
	To close income summary account and		
	allocate net income in accordance with		
	schedule. [Figure 13-5]		
Dec. 31	Capital, Oliver	4,200	
	Capital, Pratt	3,800	
	Capital, Quillen	4,500	
	Drawings, Oliver		4,200
	Drawings, Pratt		3,800
	Drawings, Quillen		4,500
	To close partners' drawings accounts.		

Statement of partners' capital. A statement of partners' capital, explaining the change in the capital account balances, is usually prepared at the end of the accounting period. The OPQ Company statement, based on the profit-sharing schedule in Figure 13-5, appears in Figure 13-6. This statement may be made a part of the capital section of the partnership balance sheet. Notice that the partners' ending capital balances are not in the profit and loss sharing ratio because partners may invest or withdraw various amounts during the period. As with sole proprietorships, the financial statements of partnerships do not report income tax expense because partnerships are not taxable entities.

OPQ Company
Statement of Partners' Capital
For the Year Ended December 31, 1985

	Oliver	Pratt	Quillen	Total
Balances, 1/05/85	$20,000	$40,000	$20,000	$ 80,000
Additional investment	5,000			5,000
Add net income*	4,625	8,250	13,125	26,000
Total	29,625	48,250	33,125	111,000
Less drawings	4,200	3,800	4,500	12,500
Balances, 12/31/85	$25,425	$44,450	$28,625	$ 98,500

* See Figure 13-5.

Figure 13-6 **The statement of partners' capital is often made a part of the capital section of the balance sheet. It shows the change in each partner's capital as well as the change in total capital.**

Admission of New Partner into the Business

From a legal point of view, when a partnership gains or loses a partner, the old entity is dissolved and a new one is created. From an accounting point of view, however, the entity continues in existence but changes take place in its **capital structure**. A partnership may admit a new partner into the business only if all partners agree. The new partner may acquire an interest by buying all or part of an existing partners' interest or by investing directly in the partnership.

Buying an existing interest from a partner. Kelly and Lorin are partners sharing profits and losses equally. Each has a capital account of $100,000. With Kelly's approval, Lorin decides to sell one half of his interest in the partnership to Merrill for $70,000. The exchange of money between Lorin and Merrill is a private transaction and is not reflected on the partnership books. But the capital structure of the partnership changes, and so does the profit-sharing ratio.

To record the admission of Merrill into the partnership, one half of Lorin's capital is transferred to Merrill. The entry is

	Capital, Lorin	50,000	
	Capital, Merrill		50,000
	To transfer half of Lorin's capital to		
	new partner.		

Note that Merrill paid $70,000 for a $50,000 interest in the business. Lorin has a gain on the sale, but that is part of his personal affairs and does not affect the partnership books. If Merrill had bought Lorin's entire interest, Lorin would retire from the partnership, and Kelly and Merrill would continue the business as partners. Alternatively, Merrill could also join the partnership by buying a portion of each partner's interest. For example, Merrill could agree to pay each partner $40,000 for a 30 percent interest in the partnership. The cash payment is a private transaction; the partnership records the change in capital as follows:

	Capital, Kelly	30,000	
	Capital, Lorin	30,000	
	Capital, Merrill		60,000
	To transfer 30 percent interest to new		
	partner.		

Investing in the Partnership

When a partner acquires an interest in a partnership by investing assets rather than by buying an existing interest, the partnership receives assets. There are several ways to account for the admission of a new partner who makes an investment. The simplest is to record the increase in assets and credit the new partner's capital account. For example, Kelly and Lorin agree to admit Merrill as a partner with a one-third interest in the business if Merrill invests $100,000 in the business. The entry to record Merrill's investment is

	Cash	100,000	
	Capital, Merrill		100,000
	To record investment by new partner.		

Just because Merrill has a one-third interest in the business does not mean that he has to have a one-third interest in the profits. The partners may share profits and losses in any ratio upon which they agree.

A new partner may find an existing partnership to be a very desirable investment and may be willing to pay a premium for the privilege of joining the firm. Alternatively, a partnership may find the investment of a new partner so desirable that it allows him to acquire an interest at a discount. There are several ways to account for the admission of a new partner when the amount invested is not the same as the amount credited to the new partner's capital account:

1. Bonus allowed to old partners
2. Goodwill allowed to old partners
3. Bonus allowed to new partner

Admitting a new partner may increase old partners' capital

Bonus allowed to old partners.   Kelly and Lorin are willing to admit Merrill to a 25 percent interest in the partnership for a $100,000 investment in the firm. In this case the entire $100,000 invested by Merrill is not credited to his capital account. Instead, Merrill's capital account is credited for 25 percent of the total capital after he makes the investment.

Total capital (net assets) prior to Merrill's investment	$200,000
Cash invested by Merrill	100,000
Total capital	300,000
Multiply by Merrill's interest	.25
Merrill's capital	$ 75,000

The remainder of Merrill's investment is credited as a **bonus** to the existing partners in their profit-sharing ratio. The entry is

	Cash	100,000	
	Capital, Merrill		75,000
	Capital, Kelly		12,500
	Capital, Lorin		12,500
	To record the admission of Merrill to a		
	25 percent interest in the business, with		
	bonus allowed to old partners.		

Goodwill allowed to old partners.   If Merrill is willing to invest $100,000 for a 25 percent interest, there is an implication that his share will be 25 percent of the fair value of the new partnership. If his $100,000 investment is 25 percent of the value, then the old partners must be contributing the remaining 75 percent. The assumption is that the fair value of the existing partnership includes goodwill which was not previously recorded in the books of the partnership. The amount of goodwill is calculated as follows:

Goodwill may be recorded when a new partner is admitted

Merrill's investment		$100,000
Divide by Merrill's interest in the business		.25
Implied value of the entire business		400,000
Owners' equity of existing business	$200,000	
Merrill's investment	100,000	
Net tangible assets		300,000
Goodwill		$100,000

The goodwill is credited to the existing partners in their profit-sharing ratio. To record Merrill's investment using the **goodwill** method, the following entry is made:

	Cash	100,000	
	Goodwill	100,000	
	Capital, Kelly		50,000
	Capital, Lorin		50,000
	Capital, Merrill		100,000
	To recognize goodwill on admission of		
	new partner.		

Note the difference between the bonus and goodwill methods. When a bonus is credited to the old partners, the new partner's capital account is smaller than his investment. When the goodwill method is used, the new partner's capital account is equal to his investment.

Bonus allowed to the new partner.   If Kelly and Lorin are anxious to admit Merrill into the partnership, they may offer him an interest greater than his investment by offering him a bonus. For example, the partnership offers Merrill a 40 percent interest in the business and a 40 percent share of profits if he invests $100,000. Merrill's capital account is credited for 40 percent of the total capital of the new partnership.

Admitting a new partner may decrease old partners' capital

Total capital (net assets) prior to Merrill's investment	$200,000
Cash invested by Merrill	100,000
Total capital	300,000
Multiply by Merrill's interest	.40
Merrill's capital	$120,000

The entry to record Merrill's admission to the partnership is

Cash		100,000	
Capital, Kelly		10,000	
Capital, Lorin		10,000	
Capital, Merrill			120,000
To record investment with bonus allowed			
to new partner.			

Retirement of a Partner

A partner may retire by selling his interest, either to a new partner or to the existing ones, in a personal transaction as already illustrated. A partner may also retire by having the partnership make a payment in exchange for the retiring partner's capital. If the payment is equal to the capital account, an entry is required debiting capital and crediting cash for the amount of the payment. The payment may be larger or smaller than the capital balance, resulting in a bonus either to the retiring or the remaining partners.

The partnership buys the capital of a retiring partner

Bonus allowed to retiring partner.   Davis, Engle, and Faris are partners sharing profits and losses equally. Each has a capital balance of $60,000. Davis and Engle are anxious to operate the business without Faris, so they offer her a bonus if she agrees to retire. Faris agrees to retire if the partnership pays her $80,000 for her capital balance. The entry to record the retirement is

Capital, Davis		10,000	
Capital, Engle		10,000	
Capital, Faris		60,000	
Cash			80,000
To record payment of bonus to retiring			
partner.			

Bonus allowed to remaining partners.   If Faris is anxious to retire from the business, she may be willing to accept less than her capital balance. In this case the remaining partners are credited with a bonus. For example, Faris agrees to retire from the partnership for a cash payment of $50,000. The entry to record the retirement is

Capital, Faris		60,000	
Capital, Davis			5,000
Capital, Engle			5,000
Cash			50,000
To record payment to retiring partner			
with bonus to remaining partners.			

Death of a partner.   If a partner dies, the partnership is automatically dissolved, just as when a partner retires. Typically, the business will continue to operate as a new partnership or a sole proprietorship. To ensure a fair settlement with the dead partner's estate or heirs, the partnership agreement should stipulate how the interest of the deceased is to be handled.

The death of a partner usually requires an audit of the partnership and the preparation of financial statements in order to credit all partners with their share of profits or losses up to the time of death. The assets may have to be appraised to determine if there is any unrecorded goodwill or declines in net asset value so that the estate may be paid an amount that represents fairly the deceased partner's share of the business.

The partnership may also carry life insurance on each partner. The insurance proceeds may be used to pay the estate of the dead partner without depleting the assets of the business so that the remaining partners may continue in operation.

OWNERS' EQUITY OF CORPORATIONS

A corporation is an artificial person

Corporations are both accounting entities and legal entities. They are artificial persons with rights and obligations granted by the state in which they are organized. State corporation laws vary, but some general requirements must be met to incorporate. The incorporators who wish to organize the corporation prepare **articles of incorporation** and submit them to the state for approval. The articles of incorporation include the name and purpose of the corporation, the names of the incorporators, and the number of shares of capital stock that the corporation may issue. When the state approves the articles, they become the **corporate charter**.

Characteristics of Corporations

A **public corporation** is one whose shares are publicly owned and may be traded in stock markets. A **closely held corporation** is one whose stock is privately owned by a small number of shareholders and is not traded. The shareholders elect a **board of directors** whose members represent the owners and direct the affairs of the corporation. The board of directors may consist of three or more members, and some large corporations have boards of over 20 directors. The board of directors appoints officers, some of whom may be board members, to manage the corporation.

Corporations obtain assets from equity investors by issuing shares of stock to them. Most corporations issue only **common stock**, but other classes, such as **preferred stock**, may be issued in addition. Common stock is the **residual equity** of a corporation, that is, the owners' interest in **net assets** and income remaining after all other equity obligations have been satisfied.

Preferred stock represents a limited type of ownership that entitles shareholders to a specified but limited portion of net income and to certain rights and preferences that must be satisfied before any assets are distributed to common shareholders. In some cases preferred stock may be **convertible** to common stock at the option of the preferred shareholder.

The **corporate charter** describes each type of stock a corporation may issue to investors and the number of shares authorized. The number of **authorized shares** is the total number of shares of each type of stock that a corporation can issue. When the corporation sells shares to investors, the stock is said to be **issued** and **outstanding**. Any shares authorized but not issued are available to be issued at the discretion of the board of directors.

The concept of par value stock

Corporations may assign to each share of stock an arbitrary value called **par value**, or **stated value**. If no such value is assigned, the company is said to have **no-par** stock. Many corporations assign common stock a par value of $1, 25 cents, or some other small amount. Par or stated value has no impact on the market price of the stock and has no significance other than to determine the amount to be recorded in the capital stock account. Accounting for capital stock has more to do with satisfying state laws than with satisfying accounting theory.

If a par or stated value is assigned, the total authorized **capitalization** of the corporation is the par or stated value times the number of shares authorized. For example, a corporation that is authorized to issue 2 million shares of $2 par common stock has a total authorized capitalization of $4,000,000.

The par or stated value has no influence on the amount of money the stock sells for at the time it is issued. Most stock is issued at a premium, that is, at a price higher than par, and issuing stock at a price below par, at a discount, is illegal. Prior to issuing any capital stock, the corporation must obtain a permit from the state or approval from the Securities and Exchange Commission. Usually fewer than the total authorized number of shares are issued.

Stock certificates are evidence of ownership

When investors buy stock, the corporation issues to them stock certificates, such as the one illustrated in Figure 13-7, as evidence of ownership. Stock certificates of public corporations are negotiable instruments and may be traded in the stock market or on stock exchanges. When one investor sells some shares to another, the stock certificates representing those shares are returned to the corporation, which issues new shares. The new investor's name is recorded on the stock certificate, and the corporation keeps records of its owners' share holdings.

The amount paid for stock by an investor is the maximum amount that the investor can lose. Unlike a partner or a sole proprietor, the owner of corporate stock is not liable for any debts of the corporation. This **limited liability** is one of the advantages of the corporate form of business. The ability of capital stock to trade freely in markets and the limited liability of owners are the primary reasons why corporations are able to raise large amounts of capital through stock issues.

Accounting for Common Stock

Corporations must account for the issuance of stock, the distribution of earnings to shareholders, any portion of earnings retained by the corporation, and the reacquisition of stock.

Figure 13-7   **Negotiable stock certificates are issued to shareholders of a corporation. When a shareholder sells stock, a new certificate is issued to the new owner and the old certificate is canceled.**

Par value or stated value stock.   Accounting for par value and stated value stock is identical; only the terminology is different. To illustrate, we use the example of Howell Corporation's issuance of 10,000 shares of $2 par common stock at $20 per share on February 15. The receipt of cash in exchange for the stock is recorded as follows:

Feb. 15	Cash	200,000	
	Common stock, $2 par		20,000
	Paid-in capital in excess		
	of par on common stock		180,000
	Issued 10,000 shares of common stock		
	at $20 per share.		

Corporate capital is divided into several accounts

The above entry has several important characteristics. The common stock account is always credited for the par value of the stock, which is the number of shares issued multiplied by the par value per share. This amount is the **legal capital** of the corporation in many states. Any money received for the stock in excess of par or stated value is recorded in a separate account called **Paid-in Capital in Excess of Par on Common Stock**. The terms **Additional Paid-in Capital** or **Premium on Common Stock** also are used sometimes.

Legal capital may not be reduced by dividends

Together the Common Stock and the Additional Paid-in Capital accounts make up **contributed capital**, which represents the amount of assets contributed by shareholders. In some states, legal capital consists of all contributed capital rather than the par or stated capital. The legal capital of a corporation may be reduced only under very limited circumstances, such as corporate liquidation. The assets contributed by shareholders and represented by legal capital may not be returned to them. Therefore, payments of dividends to shareholders are limited to assets that the company obtains from earnings. Legal capital can be viewed as a safety cushion that protects creditors and employees from losses. The company can incur some losses and still have sufficient assets to repay its debts. Such a safety cushion is necessary, because if the corporation cannot pay its obligations, creditors may not look to shareholders for payment.

Stock without par or stated value.   If Howell Corporation's common stock has neither a par value nor a stated value, the entire amount of contributed capital is recorded in the Common Stock account. A separate paid-in capital account does not exist. The entry to record the issuance of no-par common stock is

Feb. 15	Cash	200,000	
	Common stock		200,000
	Issued 10,000 shares of no-par common		
	stock at $20 per share.		

Stock issued for other than cash.   Sometimes stock is issued for assets other than cash, as discussed in Chapter 10. For example, Howell Corporation issues 5,000 shares of its $2 par common stock in exchange for equipment valued at $90,000. The entry is

Feb. 19	Equipment	90,000	
	Common stock		10,000
	Additional paid-in capital		80,000
	Issued 5,000 shares common stock in		
	exchange for equipment valued at		
	$90,000.		

If the stock trades in a market and has a readily available price, it may be more appropriate to use the market value of the stock to record the cost of the equipment. The choice depends on which value can be determined more objectively.

After the initial issues of stock and the stock issued in exchange for equipment, Howell Corporation now has the following capital structure:

Common stock $2 par, 15,000 shares issued and outstanding	$ 30,000
Paid-in capital in excess of par on common stock	260,000

Dividend Distributions

Corporations do not have to pay dividends

A **dividend** is a distribution of cash or other assets to shareholders of the corporation. Dividend distributions provide shareholders with a return on their investment. There is, however, no obligation on the part of a corporation to pay dividends, and many corporations retain all their earnings in order to grow and to expand their business. The board of directors decides whether a dividend shall be paid and in what amount. Many corporations have a policy of paying dividends regularly, and investors who want steady dividend income buy the stock of such companies. Some investors prefer to buy the stock of companies that pay no dividends in order to benefit from the growth of the company. Investors expect to benefit from the increase in the value of their shares that may occur as the company expands its operations by investing all the income it retains.

Dividend payments reduce assets with a corresponding reduction of capital. Contributed capital normally may not be reduced, however, so the payment of dividends is recorded as a reduction in cash and a corresponding reduction in retained earnings. This can be done only if the retained earnings account has a credit balance.

Dates associated with dividends

When the board of directors votes to pay a dividend, it announces the amount, the date of record, and the date of payment. The **declaration date** is the date on which the dividend is announced by the board of directors and recorded by the corporation. On this date the dividend becomes a current liability of the corporation, payable to its shareholders. Once the dividend is declared, the board of directors cannot change its mind and decide not to pay it. Like any other current liability, the dividend must be paid when it comes due.

The **date of record** is the date on which a shareholder must own the stock in order to be entitled to the dividend. If the stock is actively traded in the stock market, several days may be necessary for the company to receive notification that a particular investor has bought or sold shares of the company's stock. To ensure that all records are up to date when the dividend is paid, the stock exchange establishes an **ex-dividend date** 3 days prior to the date of record. The ex-dividend date is the date on which the stock trades without the dividend, and an investor buying the stock is not entitled to receive the dividend that has been declared. The 3 days between the ex-dividend date and the date of record give the company time to adjust its records so that it can pay the dividend to the owner of the stock. On the **payment date**, dividend checks are sent to shareholders, eliminating the dividend liability.

To demonstrate the payment of dividends, we assume that Howell Corporation has operated profitably during 1985, and by the end of July has earned in excess of $100,000. The company may legally pay dividends to its shareholders only from its earnings.

Cash dividends.   The most common type of dividend, and the only kind paid on preferred stock, is a **cash dividend**. For example, Howell Corporation's board of directors votes to pay a cash dividend of $3 per share on the common stock. The common dividend is declared on July 5, payable on August 9, with a date of record of July 31. The entry on the declaration date is

July 5	Dividends, common	45,000	
	Dividends payable		45,000
	Declared $3 per share cash dividend,		
	on common stock, payable on		
	August 9.		

The Dividends account, often called **Dividend Declared**, is a temporary account that is closed directly to retained earnings at the end of the accounting period. The Dividends Payable account is a current liability reported in the balance sheet if financial statements are prepared prior to the payment of the dividend. On the payment date, the dividend is paid and the liability is eliminated as follows:

Aug. 9	Dividends payable	45,000	
	Cash		45,000
	Paid cash dividend to shareholders with		
	July 31 date of record.		

If both common and preferred shares are outstanding, the common shareholders may not receive a dividend unless the preferred dividend is also paid in the same year.

Dividends in kind.   Just after repeal of the prohibition amendment to the United States Constitution, a distillery distributed liquor to its shareholders as a **dividend in kind**. Such dividends, paid with assets other than cash, are also called **property dividends**, but they are rare because most assets are not readily divisible into parts that can be distributed to shareholders in proportion to their ownership.

Stock dividends.   A corporation that has accumulated a large credit balance in its retained earnings account may wish to pay a dividend but may want or need to retain its cash for operations or expansion. In such a case, the board of directors may declare a **stock dividend** and distribute additional shares to the owners in proportion to the shares they already own. A 5 percent stock dividend means that a shareholder who owns 100 shares of common stock receives an additional 5 shares, while one who owns 1,000 shares receives an additional 50 shares.

Stock dividends do not involve asset distributions

A stock dividend does not alter the percentage of ownership of any shareholder. It also has no effect on assets. Like other dividends, however, it does reduce retained earnings. The reduction in the retained earnings account is offset by a corresponding increase in other capital accounts. The amount of retained earnings reduction resulting from a stock dividend depends on the **market value** of the stock that is distributed to shareholders. For example, the market price of Howell Corporation's common stock is $40 per share, and there are 15,000 shares of $2 par stock outstanding. The company declares a 10 percent common stock dividend and issues 1,500 new shares to its shareholders. Based on the current market price, the total value of 1,500 shares is $60,000. To record the stock dividend, the company makes the following entry:

Sept.17	Retained earnings	60,000	
	Common stock		3,000
	Additional paid-in capital		57,000
	Issued 1,500 shares new common stock		
	as 10% stock dividend.		

Retained earnings are capitalized by stock dividends

Pay close attention to this entry: No cash or other assets are distributed to shareholders, so there is no reduction in owners' equity. Instead, there is a decrease in retained earnings and a corresponding increase in contributed capital. The effect is to **capitalize** permanently part of the retained earnings balance; that is, a portion of retained earnings is converted to contributed capital and is no longer available for the payment of dividends. There is no change in **total** stockholders' equity, but the individual capital balances are different. Obviously, a stock dividend can be distributed only if the retained earnings account has a sufficiently large credit balance.

After the stock dividend, Howell Corporation's contributed capital accounts have the following balances:

Common stock, $2 par, 16,500 shares	$ 33,000
Paid in capital in excess of par on common stock	317,000

There are several benefits from stock dividends. From the investors point of view, a cash dividend is subject to personal income tax, but a stock dividend is not. A shareholder can obtain cash from the stock dividend by selling the additional shares. Of course, selling stock reduces a shareholder's percentage of ownership, but most people are not concerned about owning a specific percentage of a corporation.

For the company, it makes sense to capitalize a portion of retained earnings by increasing contributed capital with a stock dividend. A company that wants to pay dividends regularly can continue declaring dividends during periods of cash shortages by paying stock dividends. When a company is growing and expanding operations, most of its earnings are invested in productive resources. With the earnings already invested in fixed assets, they cannot be distributed as dividends.

Accounting for Preferred Stock

Holders of preferred shares have limited rights as owners. Usually they do not have voting privileges and are entitled only to a limited share of the company's earnings. In exchange for such limitations, holders of preferred stock obtain certain preferences with regard to dividends and asset distributions in case of a liquidation.

If common dividends are paid, preferred dividends must be paid too

Dividend preferences entitle preferred shareholders to a dividend at a stated dollar amount or a stated rate of par value. If the company does not pay the preferred dividend in any one year, it may not distribute any income to common shareholders. A preference for asset distribution means that if the company is liquidated, any proceeds from the sale of assets that are left after the payment of liabilities must first be paid to the holders of preferred shares, usually to the extent of par value. The holders of common shares are entitled to the remainder, if any.

Preferred stock usually has a par value, most often $100. Recording the issuance of preferred stock is similar to recording the issuance of common stock. For example, Howell Corporation is authorized to issue 100,000 shares of $100 par preferred stock. On August 23, it issues 1,000 shares at $110 each. The entry is

Aug. 23	Cash	110,000	
	Preferred stock, $100 par		100,000
	Paid-in capital in excess		
	of par on preferred stock		10,000
	Issued 1,000 shares of 9% preferred		
	stock at $110 per share.		

The account name Premium on Preferred Stock is also sometimes used to record amounts received in excess of par. Now the contributed capital structure of the corporation is as follows:

Preferred stock, $100 par, 1,000 shares	$100,000
Paid-in capital in excess of par on preferred stock	10,000
Common stock, $2 par, 16,500 shares	33,000
Paid-in capital in excess of par on common stock	317,000
Total contributed capital	$460,000

Dividend preferences.   A dividend preference is the right of a preferred shareholder to receive an annual dividend at the rate specified for the preferred stock. Dividends on preferred stock may be expressed as a dollar amount, such as $6 preferred or $7.50 preferred, or they may be expressed as a percentage of par value. For example, a 6 percent, $100 par preferred stock pays $6 per year in dividends, and a 6 percent $50 par preferred stock pays $3 per year. Howell Corporation has 1,000 shares of $100 par 9 percent preferred stock outstanding. When a dividend on the preferred stock is declared the following entry is made:

Dec. 6	Dividends, preferred	9,000	
	Dividends payable		9,000
	Declared preferred dividend of $9 per		
	share.		

A dividend preference does not entitle the preferred shareholder to payment unless a dividend is declared by the board of directors. When a preferred dividend is not declared it is said to be **passed**. Corporations may pass a dividend if they do not have sufficient cash to pay it, or if they cannot pay it because of a retained earnings debit balance.

Dividend preferences may be classified into several types, each determining the manner and amount of dividend payments to holders of preferred shares. The classifications are: cumulative or noncumulative; and participating or nonparticipating.

Passed dividends may accumulate on preferred stock

If the dividend on a **cumulative preferred stock** is not declared in any one year, that dividend accumulates on the stock. This means that before the company can pay a common dividend, it must pay the previously unpaid dividends on the preferred shares. Passed dividends on cumulative preferred stock are said to be **dividends in arrears**.

For example, in 1984 a corporation did not declare a dividend on its $6 preferred stock nor on its common stock. In 1985 the company wishes to pay a dividend on its common stock. It cannot do so until it declares the dividend in arrears and also the **current dividend** on its preferred stock. Each preferred share must receive $12 of dividends before the holders of common shares are entitled to a dividend distribution.

When a company is incurring losses or needs to retain its earnings for expansion, it may declare no dividends for several years in a row. The cumulative dividend preference ensures that the holders of preferred shares will get their past *and* current dividends before dividends are paid to common shareholders. Otherwise the board of directors could favor the holders of common shares by omitting dividends for several years in a row and then declaring only the current dividends.

Noncumulative preferred stock is entitled to a dividend only in the current year. Passed dividends do not accumulate and are lost to preferred shareholders. Consequently, such stock is not very popular with investors, and few companies issue noncumulative preferred shares.

A **participating preferred stock** is entitled to its regular dividend when declared and participates with common stock in additional dividends as well. Such stock may be **fully participating** or **partially participating**.

For example, a corporation has outstanding 2,000 shares of 6 percent, fully participating, $100 par preferred stock. When dividends are declared, each preferred share is entitled to its $6 dividend as long as the common dividend is 6 percent of par value or less. If the common dividend is larger than 6 percent of par value, the preferred shares are also entitled to the larger percentage. If preferred shares are partially participating, there is an upper limit beyond which the preferred dividend percentage may not rise. For example, the 6 percent preferred stock may participate in dividends with common up to an additional 3 percent but not beyond. Participating preferences are not often found in preferred stock, and most preferred stock is nonparticipating.

Schedule of Dividend Distributions
10,000 Shares, $2 Par Common
1,000 Shares, $100 Par 6% Preferred

Year Paid	Total Dividends Declared	Total Paid to Preferred	Paid to Preferred Per Share	Total Paid to Common	Paid to Common Per Share	% of Common Par
If the preferred dividend is cumulative:						
1985	$ 6,000	$ 6,000	$ 6	—	—	—
1986	7,000	6,000	6	$1,000	$.10	5%
1987	—	—	—	—	—	—
1988	14,400	12,000	12	2,400	.24	12%
1989	3,000	3,000	3	—	—	—
1990	12,600	9,000	9	3,600	.36	18%
1991	13,000	6,000	6	7,000	.70	35%
If the preferred dividend is not cumulative:						
1985	$ 6,000	$6,000	$6	—	—	—
1986	7,000	6,000	6	$1,000	$.10	5%
1987	—	—	—	—	—	—
1988	14,400	6,000	6	8,400	.84	42%
1989	3,000	3,000	3	—	—	—
1990	12,600	6,000	6	6,600	.66	33%
1991	13,000	6,000	6	7,000	.70	35%
If the preferred dividend is cumulative and participating up to 10%:						
1985	$ 6,000	$ 6,000	$ 6	—	—	—
1986	7,000	6,000	6	$1,000	$.10	5%
1987	—	—	—	—	—	—
1988	14,400	13,000	13[1]	1,400	.14	7%
1989	3,000	3,000	3	—	—	—
1990	12,600	11,000	11[2]	1,600	.16	8%
1991	13,000	10,000	10[3]	3,000	.30	15%

[1] 6% in arrears + 7% participating.
[2] 3% in arrears + 8% participating.
[3] 10% maximum participating.

Figure 13-8   **Dividend distributions for a 7-year period, with comparison of dividend preferences for cumulative, noncumulative, and participating preferred stock.**

Figure 13-8 illustrates the distributions of dividends for a company under several preference assumptions. Note that the common shares receive no dividends unless the preferred stock dividend requirements are satisfied.

Stock Splits

Stock splits have no effect on retained earnings

A company's stock may be difficult to sell because its price is too high. Some investors have psychological barriers against buying stock in price ranges of $70 or above. They prefer stock that trades in the $20 to $50 price range. To maintain the marketability of its stock, a company may find a **stock split** desirable. A 2-for-1 stock split means that for every share outstanding, the company issues an additional share. In a 3-for-1 stock split, the company issues two new shares for every share outstanding. A shareholder who owns 100 shares prior to a 3-for-1 stock split owns 300 shares after the 3-for-1 split.

As the number of shares increases, the price in the market decreases. If stock is trading at $90 per share, a 3-for-1 stock split should cause the market price to decline to about $30 per share. Obviously, the total value of a shareholder's stock remains about the same, but the shares can be traded more easily at the lower price, and the increased demand for the shares may cause the market price to rise above $30 per share.

A stock split usually does not affect the accounting records of the company, and a journal entry is not required. But there is a change in the par value of the stock and in the number of shares authorized and issued. A 2-for-1 stock split has the effect of reducing the par or stated value of the stock to half the original amount. The number of authorized, issued, and outstanding shares is doubled. Often a memorandum entry is made in the journal to describe the stock split, but no account balances are affected. If Howell Corporation effects a 2-for-1 stock split on December 10, 1985, it might make the following memorandum entry in its journal:

Dec. 10	Effected 2-for-1 stock split on common		
	stock by issuing 16,500 additional		
	shares and reducing the par		
	value to $1 per share.		

Now the capital stock accounts appear as follows:

Preferred stock, $100 par, 11,000 shares	$100,000
Paid-in capital in excess of par on preferred stock	10,000
Common stock, $1 par, 33,000 shares	33,000
Paid-in capital in excess of par on common stock	317,000

At this point we summarize the capital transactions that Howell Corporation had made during its 1985 operating period, as described up to now.

Jan.   5   Authorized 1,000,000 shares $2 par common stock and 10,000 shares $100 par convertible preferred stock.
Feb. 15   Issued 10,000 shares common at $20 per share.
Feb. 19   Issued 5,000 shares common in exchange for equipment.
July   5   Declared $3 per share cash dividend on common.
Aug. 23   Issued 1,000 shares preferred at $110 per share.
Sept. 17   Distributed 1,500 shares of common as 10 percent stock dividend.
Dec.   6   Declared $9 per share cash dividend on preferred.
Dec. 10   Issued 16,500 shares common in 2-for-1 stock split. Par value reduced to $1 and authorized shares increased to 2,000,000.
Dec. 31   Credited $145,000 net income to retained earnings.

Retained Earnings

The retained earnings account is part of capital

Like other capital accounts, the Retained Earnings account represents a portion of the owners' interest in the assets of the corporation. Owners' equity of a corporation usually increases in one of two ways: through the sale of stock to investors, which increases the capital stock accounts, or

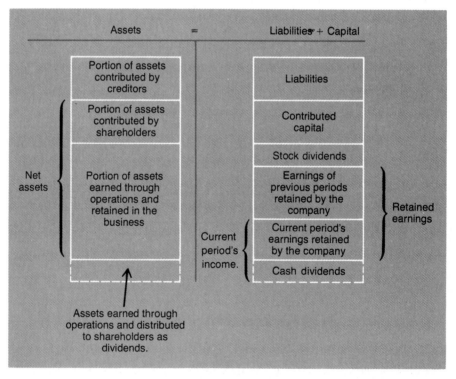

Figure 13-9   **The relationship between assets and equities. Net assets are the portion represented by owners' equity, part of which is contributed capital and part retained earnings. Assets contributed by investors provide a safety cushion to protect creditors from excessive risk. Assets earned through operations may be distributed as dividends. Stock dividends have no effect on assets; they merely shift retained earnings to contributed capital.**

through the earning of profits, which increases the Retained Earnings account. If the company incurs losses, the Retained Earnings account may have a debit balance. A debit balance in retained earnings is known as a **deficit**.

Retained earnings are not assets. Rather, they represent an ownership interest in assets. It is often said that dividends are paid from retained earnings, but dividends are cash payments. When cash is credited for the payment of dividends, ownership interest is reduced by debiting retained earnings. Earnings retained by a business are seldom held as cash; instead they are invested in earning assets such as merchandise, equipment, and buildings. Therefore the amount of cash available for dividend payment may be far smaller than the credit balance in the Retained Earnings account. Figure 13-9 illustrates the relationship between assets and capital accounts and shows that a distribution of assets to shareholders occurs when cash dividends reduce retained earnings. A stock dividend, on the other hand, does not reduce assets but simply shifts a portion of total capital from retained earnings to contributed capital.

Retained earnings statement.   A corporation's annual report usually includes a **statement of retained earnings**, which explains the change in the retained earnings balance from one period to the next. Figure 13-10 illustrates the retained earnings statement of Howell Corporation at the end of the 1985 accounting period, for which the company reported net income of $145,000. Because the company started operations in 1985, there is no beginning balance in retained earnings. Pay particular attention to the way the cash and stock dividends are reported.

The balance sheet reports owners' equity in detail, describing each capital account completely. When the capital structure of a company requires reporting many accounts, a company may report only total capital in the balance sheet and provide the detail in a **statement of capital**. Figure 13-11 shows Howell Corporation's statement of capital on December 31, 1985.

Figure 13-10
Retained earnings statement showing dividend distributions on two classes of stock, and a stock dividend.

Howell Corporation **Statement of Retained Earnings** **For the Year Ended December 31, 1985**		
Retained earnings, 1/1/85		$ 0
Add net income		145,000
		145,000
Less dividends declared		
On preferred stock, $9 per share	$ 9,000	
On common stock, $3 per share	45,000	
Stock dividends	60,000	114,000
Retained earnings, 12/31/85		$ 31,000

Howell Corporation
Statement of Capital
December 31, 1985

Preferred stock, $100 par, 9% cumulative, 100,000 shares authorized, 1,000 shares issued and outstanding, each convertible into 11 shares of common stock	$100,000
Paid-in capital in excess of par on preferred stock	10,000
Common stock, $1 par, 4,000,000 shares authorized, 33,000 shares issued and outstanding	33,000
Paid-in capital in excess of par on common stock	317,000
Retained earnings	31,000
Total capital	$491,000

Figure 13-11   **Each capital account of a corporation is described in detail when reported in financial statement. Total capital represents the company's net assets.**

SUMMARY

The owners' equity accounts of sole proprietorships and partnerships consist of a **capital account** and a **drawings account** for each owner. The capital account increases when an owner invests assets in the business. Any withdrawals of assets are recorded as debits in the drawings accounts, which are closed to capital at the end of the accounting period. A **statement of capital** prepared at the end of the accounting period explains the changes in owners' equity for the period.

Partnerships and sole proprietorships are not subject to income taxes. Each owner's share of the business income is treated as personal income for tax purposes. In the absence of an agreement, partners share profits and losses equally, but they may also agree on different profit and loss ratios and on salary or interest allowances to be allocated to the capital accounts. Such agreements do not result in recording salary or interest expense but are used merely to determine how the net income is distributed to the partners' capital accounts.

A partnership may admit a new partner who acquires an interest from the existing partners or who invests assets in the partnership. A **bonus to the existing partners** is recognized if the new partner's capital balance is smaller than the amount invested. Alternatively, the partnership may decide to record **goodwill** which is credited to the old partners' capital accounts when a new partner invests in the business. A **bonus to the new partner** is recognized when the amount credited to his capital account is larger than the amount of assets invested.

When a partner retires, the existing partners may buy his interest in a private transaction, or the partnership may distribute assets in exchange for the retiring partner's capital. A bonus to the retiring partner or to the remaining partners may be recorded, depending on the amount of assets distributed.

Corporations are legal entities or artificial persons subject to income taxes. A **public corporation** is one whose shares are publicly traded; a **closely held corporation** is one whose shares are privately held and not traded. A corporation is organized by preparing **articles of incorporation** which become a **corporate charter** when approved by the state. A corporation may be **capitalized** with common and preferred stock to which a **par value**, or **stated value**, may be assigned. The number of **authorized** shares of stock times their assigned value is the total **capitalization** of the corporation. Some of the authorized shares are **issued** to shareholders, who elect a **board of directors** to manage the affairs of the corporation.

The amount received from shareholders for the par or stated value of the issued shares is known as **legal capital**. Amounts received above the par or stated value are recorded in an account called **Paid-in Capital in Excess of Par**. The total amount paid by shareholders to the corporation for their stock is known as **contributed capital**. In most states legal and contributed capital may not be reduced by the payment of dividends.

Holders of common shares are the voting owners of the company who take most of the business risk and own the **residual equity** of the corporation. Dividends on common stock are paid only if **declared** by the board of directors. They are announced on the **declaration date** and paid on the **payment date** to owners who held the stock on the **date of record**. The **ex-dividend date** is set by the stock exchange to indicate to investors that the stock is being traded but the declared dividend is not available to them.

Cash dividends are most common, but dividends **in kind**, or **property dividends**, may also be distributed. **Stock dividends** reduce retained earnings by the market value of the shares distributed. Assets and total capital are not affected by a stock dividend, but retained earnings are permanently **capitalized**. A **stock split** increases the number of shares **authorized, issued,** and **outstanding**, and the split reduces the par or stated value of each share, leaving total capital unchanged.

In contrast to common shareholders, preferred shareholders do not vote, and the return on their investment is limited to the amount of dividend specified for their shares. Preferred dividends are always in cash, and they may be **cumulative** or **noncumulative**, and **participating** or **nonparticipating**. When a cumulative dividend is not paid, it is said to be **passed** or **in arrears**.

All earnings of the corporation are credited to the Retained Earnings account, whose balance shows the legal amount of assets the corporation may distribute as dividends. Dividends may not be distributed by a corporation with a **deficit** in retained earnings. The **statement of retained earnings** reports the change in the retained earnings balance as a result of net income of the period, cash dividends paid on common and preferred stock, and stock dividends distributed.

KEY TERMS

additional paid-in capital *(552)*	goodwill *(547)*
articles of incorporation *(549)*	issued shares *(550)*
authorized shares *(550)*	legal capital *(551)*
board of directors *(549)*	limited liability *(550)*
bonus *(546)*	net assets *(549)*
capital structure *(545)*	noncumulative preferred
capitalization *(550)*	stock *(557)*
capitalized retained	no-par stock *(550)*
earnings *(555)*	outstanding shares *(550)*
cash dividend *(554)*	paid-in capital in excess of par *(552)*
closely held corporation *(549)*	par value *(550)*
common stock *(549)*	participating preferred
contributed capital *(552)*	stock *(557)*
convertible preferred stock *(550)*	passed dividend *(557)*
corporate charter *(549)*	payment date *(553)*
cumulative preferred stock *(557)*	preferred stock *(549)*
date of record *(553)*	property dividend *(554)*
declaration date *(553)*	public corporation *(549)*
deficit *(561)*	residual equity *(549)*
dividend in arrears *(557)*	stated value *(550)*
dividend in kind *(554)*	statement of capital *(538)*
drawings *(537)*	stock dividend *(554)*
ex-dividend date *(553)*	stock split *(559)*

QUESTIONS

1. Compare and contrast the capital accounts of a corporation, a partnership, and a sole proprietorship.

2. A sole proprietor pays herself a salary each month. How should this salary be accounted for?

3. A partnership agreement indicates that partners are to share profits and losses equally after the allocation of a salary to one partner and interest on partners' capital. Describe how the interest and salary enter into the distribution of partnership profits.

4. Two partners share profits and losses equally after allowing $8,000 salary to Partner A. In 1985 the partnership incurred a loss of $2,000. Partner B says, "Looks like each of our capital accounts will be reduced by $1,000 since there was no money earned to pay your salary." As Partner A, you are to explain to Partner B why she is wrong.

5. Explain why a new partner would agree to invest more money in an existing partnership than is credited to his capital account. Why should existing partners agree to recognize a bonus to a new partner by crediting his capital account for more than his investment?

6. What is the difference between authorized shares of capital stock and shares that are issued and outstanding?

7. What is the difference between a public corporation and a closely held corporation?

8. Briefly describe and define legal capital and contributed capital.

9. What is the difference between cumulative and noncumulative preferred stock?

10. Discuss the dates associated with the issuance of a cash dividend.

11. What is a stock dividend, and how does it affect the capital section of a balance sheet? Why does a corporation issue stock dividends?

12. What is the purpose of a stock split, and how does a stock split affect the accounting records?

EXERCISES

Ex. 13-1 **Capital of sole proprietor.** B. A. Payne is a dentist operating as a sole proprietor. At the beginning of 1985 his capital account had a credit balance of $20,000. During 1985 Payne withdrew $2,500 per month from his practice, recording each withdrawal in a Drawings account. Revenues for the year of $84,000 and expenses of $51,000 are summarized in the Income Summary account.

Required:
a. Prepare journal entries to record one monthly withdrawal by Payne, and to close the Income Summary and Drawings accounts at year end.
b. Prepare a statement of capital for the proprietorship.

Ex. 13-2 **Partnership capital.** Jay and Kaye are partners sharing profits in the ratio 2:3, respectively. Jay's beginning capital balance was $16,000, and Kaye's was $22,000. During the year Jay withdrew $7,000, and Kaye withdrew $9,000. Net income of the Jay & Kaye Company for the year ending December 31, 1985, was $30,000.

Required: Prepare a statement of partners' capital on December 31, 1985.

Ex. 13-3 **Partnership capital and income distribution.** Lowrey, Miller, and Norris are partners operating as LMN company. They share profits in the ratio 2:3:5, respectively. Their respective beginning capital balances were $40,000, $80,000, and $100,000. During the year Lowrey withdrew $7,000 from the partnership, Miller withdrew $10,000, and Norris withdrew $8,000. For the year ended December 30, 1985, the LMN Company had a net loss of $65,000. Miller and Norris are entitled to salaries of $5,000 and $10,000 respectively.

Required:
a. Prepare a schedule of partnership income distribution for the year.
b. Prepare a statement of partners' capital on December 31, 1985.

Ex. 13-4 **Income distribution for a partnership.** Alberg, Benson, Cosly, and Davis own the Albecoda Company. They share profits and losses equally after allowing 10 percent interest on beginning capital balances to all partners and salaries of $17,000 and $20,000 to Benson and Cosly, respectively. On December 31, 1985, prior to closing the books, the capital account balances are as follows:

	Debit	Credit
Capital, Alberg		$25,000
Drawings, Alberg	$6,000	
Capital, Benson		30,000
Drawings, Benson	5,000	
Capital, Cosly		40,000
Drawings, Cosly	4,800	
Capital, Davis		20,000
Drawings, Davis	4,000	
Income Summary		46,300

Required:
    a. Prepare a schedule of income distribution for the partnership.
    b. Prepare the entries to close the books on December 31, 1985.

Ex. 13-5   **Admission of a partner.**   Abdul Efreet and Isaac Feingold are partners sharing profits and losses equally. Each has a capital account with a $90,000 credit balance. They agree to admit Boris Gorki to the partnership with a one-third interest in the business. The partners will share profits and losses equally.

Required: Record the admission of Gorki in the partnership books under the following independent assumptions:
    a. Gorki pays each partner $50,000 for his interest in the business.
    b. Gorki pays the partnership $120,000 for his interest in the business, and a bonus is allowed.
    c. Gorki pays the partnership $120,000 for his interest and goodwill is recognized.
    d. Gorki pays the partnership $52,000 for his interest and a bonus is allowed.

Ex. 13-6   **Retirement of a partner.**   Harris, Inman, and Jaye are partners sharing profits equally, with capital balances of $200,000 each. Harris decides to retire from the partnership.

Required: Record the retirement in the partnership books under the following independent assumptions:
    a. Inman and Jaye agree to buy Harris' share by paying $120,000 each from personal funds.
    b. The partnership agrees to pay Harris $230,000 cash.
    c. Harris agrees to accept $180,000 cash for her share of the partnership.

Ex. 13-7   **Issuance of stock.**   Palmer Corporation has authorized 100,000 shares of $10 par common stock and 10,000 shares of $100 par, 7 percent preferred stock. The following events occurred in 1985:

    a. Issued 1,000 shares common stock at $35 per share.
    b. Issued 1,000 shares of preferred stock at $106 per share.
    c. Issued 500 shares of common stock in exchange for land valued at $20,000.
    d. Net income for 1985 is $16,000.

Required: Record the stock issuance and close the Income Summary account in the general journal.

Ex. 13-8   **Current and passed dividends.**   On July 19, 1985, Bigmet Corporation's board of directors declared total dividends of $60,000 on the company's preferred and common stock. The company has outstanding 50,000 shares of common and 2,000 shares of $5 cumulative preferred stock. The dividends are payable on August 30 to shareholders whose date of record is August 9, 1985.

Required:

    a. Record the declaration of the dividends assuming that no dividends are in arrears.

    b. Record the declaration of the dividends assuming that dividends on the preferred stock are in arrears for 1984.

    c. Record payment of the dividends declared in part **b**.

Ex. 13-9   **Common and preferred dividends.**   Frummer Corporation has outstanding 1,000 shares of $100 par, 8 percent preferred stock and 10,000 shares of $5 par common stock. On August 15, 1985, the board of directors declares a cash dividend of $62,000, payable on September 20. The company has paid dividends regularly each year except 1984, when all dividends were passed because of a large, extraordinary loss.

Required:

    a. Record the declaration and payment of the dividends, assuming the preferred stock is cumulative.

    b. Record the declaration and payment of the dividends, assuming the preferred stock is noncumulative.

Ex. 13-10   **Stock dividend and capital.**   Slocum Corporation has authorized 1 million shares of $5 par common stock, of which 100,000 were outstanding at the beginning of 1985. The stock was originally issued for $20 per share. On November 5, when the retained earnings balance was $2,000,000, the company distributed a 6 percent stock dividend. The common stock traded in the market at $28 per share on that date.

Required:

    a. Record the distribution of the stock dividend.

    b. Show the capital section of the balance sheet immediately after the stock dividend has been distributed.

Ex. 13-11   **Stock and cash dividend.**   Collin Corporation has outstanding 200,000 shares of $10 par common stock. On July 12 it issued a 10 percent stock dividend when the market price of the stock was $40 per share. On September 2 when the market price of the stock was $49 per share, the company declared a cash dividend of $.25 per share, payable on September 30.

Required: Record the above transactions in the general journal.

Ex. 13-12   **Statement of retained earnings.**   Danforth Company's retained earnings balance on December 31, 1984, was $485,000. During 1985 the company earned net income of $205,000 and paid a cash dividend of $60,000. A stock dividend was also issued, which decreased retained earnings by $30,000.

Required: Prepare a retained earnings statement on December 31, 1985.

PROBLEMS

P. 13-1   **Proprietorship capital.**   Don Carlos owns a sole proprietorship whose capital balance on January 1, 1985, was $70,000. During the year the following events took place:

a. Don Carlos invested an additional $40,000 on January 20, 1985.

b. On February 22, Don Carlos withdrew merchandise costing $2,500 from the business for his personal use.

c. On July 31, the owner withdrew $22,400 cash from the business.

d. Net income for the year was $36,000.

Required:
  a. Journalize the above transactions and close the Income Summary and Drawings accounts on December 31, 1985.
  b. Prepare a statement of capital for the business on December 31, 1985.

P. 13-2   **Capital of a sole proprietorship.**   For several years Robert Greene worked for a shoe manufacturer. Then he decided to open his own shoe repair shop. The following events occurred during 1985:

a. On January 3 Robert started the business by depositing $12,000 cash in a bank to open the Greene Shoe Repairs bank account. He also invested personal tools and equipment with a market value of $5,000.

b. In order to acquire more equipment later, Robert invested an additional $4,000 on March 22.

c. On April 30 Robert withdrew $10,000 from the business for his personal use.

d. Robert withdrew $8,000 from the business on October 5.

e. Net income for the year was $26,400.

Required:
  a. Journalize the above transactions, including entries to close the Income Summary and Drawings accounts.
  b. Prepare a statement of capital for the year.

P. 13-3   **Partnership distribution of income.**   Yung and Prettie are partners sharing profits and losses in the ratio 2:3 respectively. Yung, who does not work in the partnership, is entitled to 10 percent interest on her capital balance. Prettie manages the business and is entitled to a salary of $15,000. The salary and interest are to be distributed to the partners prior to the division of any remaining income. Yung's capital balance is $70,000 and Prettie's is $90,000.

Required:
  a. Prepare a schedule of income distribution for the partnership, assuming that net income for the year ending December 31, 1985, is $47,000. Then prepare the entry to close the Income Summary account.
  b. Prepare a schedule of income distribution for the partnership, assuming that net income for the year is $2,000. Then prepare the entry to close the Income Summary account.

P. 13-4   **Partnership distribution of income.**   Janet Chane and George Ball operate the Ball and Chane Company as a partnership. The profit sharing agreement states that partners are to be credited with 15 percent interest on capital balances, and Chane is to be credited with $20,000 of salary prior to distributing the remaining profit or loss equally. Chane's capital balance is $60,000 and Ball's is $80,000.

Required:
   a.   Prepare a schedule of income distribution for the partnership, assuming that net income for the year ending December 31, 1985 is $71,000. Then prepare the entry to close the Income Summary account.
   b.   Prepare a schedule of income distribution for the partnership, assuming that net income for the year is $11,000. Then prepare the entry to close the Income Summary account.

P. 13-5   **Partnership capital.**   The condensed balance sheet of James Lind Company on June 30, 1985, appears below.

James Lind Company
Balance Sheet
June 30, 1985

Assets		Equities	
Cash	$ 3,000	Liabilities	$20,000
Other assets	47,000	Capital, Lind	30,000
Total assets	$50,000	Total equities	$50,000

On July 1 James agrees to accept Charlie Berg as a partner. The company is short of working capital, and Charlie is willing to invest $30,000 for a 50 percent share of the business.

The partners agree that Lind will continue to operate the business and will be entitled to a salary of $20,000 per year. All remaining profits are to be shared equally.

The business prospers and by June 30, 1986, the Lindberg Company earns a net income of $48,000. Lind withdrew $26,000 and Berg withdrew $9,000 from the business during the fiscal year.

Required:
   a.   Journalize Berg's investment in the business.
   b.   Prepare a schedule of income distribution for the partnership.
   c.   Prepare a statement of partners' capital for the 6-month period.
   d.   Prepare journal entries to close the partners' drawings accounts and the Income Summary account.

P. 13-6   **Accounting for partnership capital.**   John Wend and Arnold Gorman operated Vega Company as a partnership for a number of years. Wend is active in management and entitled to a salary of $20,000 per year, with the remaining profits divided equally between the partners. By the end of the December 31, 1985, operating year, the business had earned a net income of $32,000. Wend's capital and drawing accounts had balances of $21,000 and $22,000 respectively, and Gorman's capital and drawings had balances of $31,000 and $7,000. The partners were not satisfied with the performance of the business and realized that they needed more capital in order to continue competing successfully with other businesses in their field. They offered their friend, Roger Upton, a 50 percent share in the partnership in exchange for a $45,000 cash investment with a bonus allowed to the new partner. Upton agreed to invest the money and become a partner effective January 1, 1986.

The partners agreed to allow Wend a salary of $25,000 per year and Upton a consulting fee of $10,000 per year, with the balance of profits and losses shared in proportion to their January 1, 1986, capital balances. By the end of 1986 Upton, Wend, and Gorman had withdrawn $30,000, $29,000, and $10,000 respectively, and the business had net income of $85,000.

Required:
  a. Prepare a schedule of income distribution and a statement of capital for Vega Company on December 31, 1985.
  b. Close the Income Summary and Drawings accounts of the Vega Company on December 31, 1985, and record Upton's investment on January 1, 1986.
  c. Prepare a schedule of income distribution and a statement of capital for Vega Company on December 31, 1986.

P. 13-7   Partnership capital and retirement of partner.   Olson, Piney, and Quand have a partnership agreement that calls for sharing profits and losses in the ratio 5:2:3 respectively after allowing a salary of $10,000 to Olson and $25,000 to Piney. On December 31, 1985, the following account balances are found in the company's trial balance:

Capital, Olson		70,000
Capital, Piney		20,000
Capital, Quand		45,000
Drawings, Olson	30,000	
Drawings, Piney	30,000	
Drawings, Quand	15,000	
Income summary		75,000

Quand has expressed a desire to retire from the partnership. After some negotiations, the partners agree that Quand should be allowed to retire at the end of 1985, and that the partnership should pay him $59,000 for his interest in the business.

Required:
  a. Prepare a schedule of income distribution for the partnership on December 31, 1985, and a statement of capital on the same date.
  b. Prepare journal entries to close the partnership books and to record Quand's retirement.

P. 13-8   Capital transactions and statements.   On December 31, 1984, the capital section of BCM Corporation's balance sheet appeared as follows:

Preferred stock, $100 par, 7 percent cumulative, 20,000 shares
  authorized, 1,000 shares issued and outstanding[1] $100,000
Paid-in capital in excess of par on preferred stock   3,000
Common stock, $4 par, 50,000 shares authorized, 5,000 shares issued
  and outstanding   20,000
Paid-in capital in excess of par on common stock   80,000
Retained earnings[1]   265,000
Total capital $468,000

[1] Dividends for 1984 are in arrears on the preferred stock.

The following events occurred during 1985:

Jan. 11 Issued 2,000 shares of common stock in exchange for equipment. Market price of stock on this date was $30 per share.
Feb. 25 Effected a 2-for-1 stock split on the common shares.
June 28 Distributed 5 percent stock dividend on common stock. Market value of stock was $32 per share on this date.
Oct. 17 Declared cash dividends of $28,700, payable on November 8.
Nov. 8 Paid cash dividends.
Dec. 31 Net income for the year was $138,500.

Required:
    a. Journalize the above transactions.
    b. Prepare a statement of retained earnings.
    c. Prepare the capital section of the balance sheet on December 31, 1985.

P. 13-9 **Capital transactions and statements.** On January 3, 1985, Norbert Corporation obtained its corporate charter, which provided for a capitalization of 300,000 $3 par common shares and 50,000 $100 par, $8.50 cumulative preferred shares. During 1985 the following transactions took place.

Jan.   9 Issued 10,000 shares common stock for $65 cash per share.
Jan. 18 Issued 400 shares of preferred stock in exchange for equipment with a market value of $47,000.
Feb. 20 The company issued 3,000 shares of common stock in exchange for land valued at $20,000 and building valued at $140,000.
July 31 The company effected a 3-for-1 stock split of common shares.
Aug.   2 Operations for the first half of the year were profitable, so the company declared a cash dividend of $8.50 on the preferred stock and $1 per share on the common stock, payable on September 6 to holders of record on September 1.
Sept. 6 Paid cash dividends.
Oct. 16 The company distributed a 5 percent stock dividend on its common stock which traded in the market at $25 per share.
Dec. 31 Net income for the year was $194,100.

Required:
    a. Journalize the transactions in the general journal.
    b. Prepare a statement of retained earnings on December 31, 1985.
    c. Prepare the capital section of the balance sheet for the company on December 31, 1985.

P. 13-10   **Capital transactions and statements.**   The capital accounts of Cobalt Corporation had the following balances on December 31, 1985:

Preferred stock, $100 par, $8 cumulative, 50,000 shares authorized, 2,000 shares issued and outstanding	$200,000
Paid-in capital in excess of par on preferred	10,000
Common stock, $12 par, 50,000 shares authorized, 10,000 shares issued and outstanding	120,000
Paid-in capital in excess of par on common	600,000
Retained earnings	900,000

The following took place during 1985:

Feb. 25 Issued 5,000 shares of common stock at the market price of $180 per share.

Mar. 19 Issued 1,000 shares of preferred stock in exchange for land. The stock traded in the market on this date at $120 per share.

June 12 Effected a 3-for-1 stock split on the common shares to reduce the market price. The stock traded at $190 per share prior to the split.

Sept. 19 Declared cash dividends, $8 per share on preferred and $2 per share on common, payable on October 10.

Oct. 10 Paid the cash dividend declared on September 19.

Nov.   1 Declared and distributed a 10 percent stock dividend on the common stock which traded in the market at $70 per share.

Nov. 29 Declared an extra $1 per share cash dividend on common stock, payable on January 6 of next year.

Dec. 31 Net income for the year was $560,000 after taxes.

Required:
a. Journalize the above transactions.
b. Prepare a statement of retained earnings for the year.
c. Show how the capital accounts should be reported in the balance sheet on December 31, 1985.

Case 13-1   **Partnership accounting.**
Charlie Dole and John Ebling are locksmiths. Their partnership has been profitable and has grown over the years from a two-man shop to an operation with five employees and annual sales of $700,000. The competition in the field is keen, however, and when the company bids on new construction projects, it is usually successful in getting contracts only on about 10 percent of the projects on which it bids.

Near the end of 1985, the partnership had bids outstanding on seven construction projects. The partners needed at least one contract in order to keep their employees working. As luck would have it, three of the bids were accepted, including one on a very large new office building, and the company was suddenly faced with more work than it could handle. The primary problem was a shortage of working capital, but interest rates were high, and the partners' financial position was not strong enough to enable them to get bank financing.

John Ebling had a friend, Harry Fox, who had in the past expressed an interest in quitting his job with a manufacturing company and going into business for himself. Charlie and John approached Fox about joining the partnership, and Fox agreed if an acceptable arrangement could be made. Fox wanted to see the partnership books before further discussions.

Dole and Ebling share profits and losses in the ratio 5:3 respectively after allowing 10 percent interest on beginning capital balances. The end-of-year condensed trial balance of the partnership is shown below:

Dole, Ebling, and Company
Trial Balance
December 31, 1985

Assets	$340,000	
Liabilities		$100,000
Capital, Dole		123,000
Capital, Ebling		77,000
Drawings, Dole	25,300	
Drawings, Ebling	18,700	
Income summary		84,000
Totals	$384,000	$384,000

After examining the books, Fox agreed to invest $50,000 cash for a 20 percent interest in the business and a 20 percent share of profits and losses. However, because he would start working in the partnership and would have to give up his current $25,000 salary, he also wanted his share of the first year's profits to include a salary. The partners then agreed that interest would no longer be credited on beginning capital balances, Fox would be credited $16,000 salary only for the first 2 years of operations, and the profit-sharing ratio for Dole, Ebling, and Fox would be 5:3:2 respectively. On January 2, 1986, Fox gave a check to the partnership for $50,000, and his capital account was credited for 20 percent of total capital of the newly named DEF Company.

At the end of 1986, Fox expressed dissatisfaction with the large amount of work that was expected of each partner. The partnership had earned a net income of $98,000 in 1986, and Dole, Ebling, and Fox had withdrawn $27,000, $30,000, and $35,000 respectively from the business. Fox wanted to retire from the partnership despite the urging of his partners to stay and participate in the growth of the company, which seemed assured. Finally he said, "I put $50,000 into the business last year and took out $35,000. I'm willing to get out if you pay me another $25,000 for my share." The partners agreed that Fox could retire with a $25,000 payment from partnership assets.

Required:
    a. Close the books for 1985. Support your entries with a schedule of profit distribution. Prepare a statement of capital at the end of 1985, and prepare the entry to admit Fox into the partnership.
    b. Close the books for 1986. Support your entries with a schedule of profit distribution. Prepare a statement of capital at the end of 1986, and prepare the entry to record Fox's retirement.
    c. Assess Fox's decision to retire from the partnership.

Additional Corporate Capital Issues

14

Many of the challenges of operating large corporations are illustrated by the methods used to account for corporate capital. This chapter describes aspects of corporate capital that pertain primarily to complex corporate organizations. It will give you an insight into

1 Accounting for convertible securities.

2 Treasury stock transactions.

3 Restrictions and adjustments of retained earnings.

4 The meaning of book value of stock.

5 The calculation of earnings per share.

The basic capital transactions involving the issuance of stock and payment of dividends are carried on by all corporations. Some of the larger corporate entities, however, have evolved into even more complex organizations whose capital transactions go beyond the material covered in Chapter 13. If corporations issue convertible bonds or preferred stock, they must account for the possible conversion of these securities into common stock. In order to have shares available for conversion, companies sometimes buy their own stock in the market. They must account for such purchases and subsequent sales of their own stock. Corporations that have convertible securities outstanding must report two earnings per share figures whose calculation can be complicated. We discuss these topics by illustrating some operations of a complex corporation.

CONVERTIBLE SECURITIES

Some corporations issue preferred stock or bonds payable that are **convertible** into a specified number of shares of common stock. Investors like the guaranteed income from bond interest or preferred dividends and, at the same time, like to be able to benefit from price increases of the common stock. Because conversion privileges are valuable, investors are frequently willing to pay a premium for convertible securities. A corporation is usually able to issue bonds or preferred stock with lower interest or dividend provisions by making them convertible into common stock. Another advantage to the corporation of issuing convertible bonds is that after conversion, the money borrowed by issuing the bonds does not have to be repaid.

The conversion ratio determines conversion value

The **conversion ratio** is the number of common shares into which a single bond or share of preferred stock can be converted. Conversion ratios are set so that at the time the convertible security is issued, its value is greater than the value of the common shares to which it is convertible. For example, if the conversion ratio of a $1,000 bond is 25:1, the bond may be converted to 25 shares of common stock. If the common stock is trading at $30 per share, there is no incentive to convert the bond, because the shares obtained in exchange are worth only $750. Therefore the bonds are not converted immediately after they are issued and the conversion privilege becomes valuable only if the company uses the borrowed money successfully to increase earnings which in turn increase the market value of the common stock. In this example the conversion privilege becomes valuable only when the price of the stock exceeds $40 per share. When the stock price is $45 per share, for example, the conversion privilege makes the bonds worth $1,125 ($45 per share × 25 shares for each bond).

Convertible securities are protected against dilution caused by stock dividends or stock splits. For example, a preferred stock that was convertible into 8 shares prior to a 3-for-1 stock split automatically becomes convertible into 24 shares after the split. If subsequently the company pays a 10 percent stock dividend, the conversion ratio increases by 10 percent. Each preferred share becomes convertible into 26.4 shares of common stock. Of course, fractional shares of stock cannot be issued by a corporation. If the conversion of bonds or preferred stock includes a fractional share of common stock, the corporation pays cash instead of the fractional share. The market value of common stock on the date of conversion is used to determine the amount of cash payment.

To illustrate the conversion of preferred stock and convertible bonds, we use the debt and capital structure of Braxton Corporation, illustrated in Figure 14-1. On December 31, 1984, the company had outstanding some convertible bonds, 1,000 shares of convertible preferred stock, and 50,000 shares of common stock. Each $1,000 bond payable is convertible into 50 shares of common stock, and each share of preferred stock is convertible into 11 shares of common stock.

Braxton Corporation Statement of Capital December 31, 1984	
Preferred Stock, $100 par, 9% cumulative, 100,000 shares authorized, 1,000 shares issued and outstanding, each convertible into 11 shares of common stock	$100,000
Paid-in capital in excess of par on preferred stock	10,000
Common stock, $1 par, 4,000,000 shares authorized, 50,000 shares issued and outstanding	50,000
Paid-in capital in excess of par on common stock	400,000
Retained earnings	75,000
Total capital	$635,000

Figure 14-1
Each capital account of a corporation is described in detail in financial statements. The final figure equals the company's net assets.

Conversion of Preferred Stock

The conversion of preferred stock into common stock requires canceling of the preferred shares submitted for conversion and issuing new common stock in exchange for them. The convertible preferred stock of Braxton Corporation was originally issued at $110 per share, so there is paid-in capital of $10 recorded for each preferred share in addition to the $100 par value. On September 7, 1985, when 100 shares of preferred stock are submitted to the company for conversion into common stock, the preferred stock is canceled by writing off the par value and premium, and new common shares are issued. The conversion is recorded as follows:

Sept. 7	Preferred stock	10,000	
	Paid-in capital on preferred stock	1,000	
	Common stock, $1 par		1,100
	Additional paid-in capital		9,900
	Issued 1,100 common shares in		
	exchange for 100 shares of convertible		
	preferred.		

After the conversion, the capital structure of the company is as follows:

Preferred stock, $100 par, 900 shares	$ 90,000
Paid-in capital in excess of par on preferred stock	9,000
Common stock, $1 par, 51,100 shares	51,100
Paid-in capital in excess of par on common stock	409,900
Retained earnings	75,000

Conversion of Bonds Payable

When bonds payable are converted into common stock, the converted bonds and any premium or discount must be written off. Let us examine the background of Braxton Corporation's convertible bonds. They were issued on September 30, 1984, when the company's common stock was trading at $17 per share. The company issued $100,000 of 10-year 10 percent convertible bonds payable at 106½ to yield 9 percent to maturity. The bond issue was recorded as follows in 1984:

Sept. 30	Cash	106,500	
	Bonds payable		100,000
	Premium on bonds payable		6,500
	Issued $100,000, 10-year 10%		
	convertible bonds at 106½. Conversion		
	ratio is 50:1.		

At the time this entry was made in 1984, there was no incentive to convert the bonds into common stock. Fifty shares of common stock had a market value of $850, so the conversion value of each bond was less than the $1,065.00 that investors paid for each bond. The **conversion value** of a convertible security is the market value of the common stock into which the security can be converted.

Today Braxton Corporation's common stock is trading at $28 per share. Therefore the conversion value of each bond is $1,400 ($28 × 50 shares), and the bonds trade in the market at 145. It is not unusual for convertible securities to trade at a premium above conversion value if investors believe that there is a potential for further increases in value.

Convertible securities often trade at a premium above conversion value

When bonds are submitted for conversion, the company must pay the accrued interest and amortize the appropriate amount of premium or discount, just as with any early bond retirement. By September 30, 1985, after Braxton Corporation paid the interest on its bonds, the Bonds Payable and Bond Premium accounts appeared as follows:

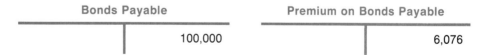

Bonds Payable		Premium on Bonds Payable	
	100,000		6,076

Holders of $25,000 face value of bonds decide to convert their bonds into common stock on September 30, 1985. Braxton Corporation must accept the bonds and issue 1,250 new common shares in exchange. The book value of the converted bonds is written off by debiting Bonds Payable $25,000 and Premium on Bonds Payable $1,519, which is 25 percent of each bond account. The issuance of stock is recorded by crediting Common Stock $1,250 (1,250 shares × $1 par) and crediting Additional Paid-in Capital for the remainder. The entry is:

Oct. 1	Bonds payable	25,000	
	Premium on bonds payable	1,519	
	Common stock, $1 par		1,250
	Additional paid-in capital		25,269
	Converted $25,000 face value of 10%		
	bonds into 1,250 shares common stock.		

Although the market value of the new common shares is $35,000 (1,250 × $28 per share), the capital accounts are credited for $25,269, the amount recorded as the book value of the converted bonds which have been canceled. There is no gain or loss on the conversion for Braxton Corporation. Some of the bondholders have become stockholders, and the company has simply capitalized part of its long-term debt. Now the company's debt and capital structure is:

Bonds payable	$ 75,000
Premium on bonds payable	4,557
Preferred stock, $100 par, 900 shares	90,000
Paid-in capital in excess of par on preferred stock	9,000
Common stock, $1 par, 52,350 shares	52,350
Paid-in capital in excess of par on common stock	435,169
Retained earnings	75,000

TREASURY STOCK

Treasury stock is issued but not outstanding

Shares of stock that are issued and in the hands of shareholders are **outstanding shares**. Frequently the number of shares **issued** and the number of shares outstanding are the same. Sometimes a corporation may reacquire some of its outstanding shares by buying them in the market. Typically, reacquired stock is not canceled but is instead held in the treasury awaiting some disposition. Stock that has been reacquired by the corporation is classified as **treasury stock**, which consists of shares that are issued but not outstanding. The company may reissue treasury stock without obtaining a permit from the state or SEC. When treasury shares are reissued by the corporation, they become issued and outstanding once more.

Stock that is not outstanding has no owner, therefore cash or stock dividends cannot be paid on treasury stock. On the other hand, all authorized stock of a company, whether issued or not, is affected by stock splits.

Acquisition of Treasury Stock

Treasury stock purchases are made for many reasons. A company may wish to have some stock available for the conversion of convertible securities. Some corporations establish employee stock purchase plans and stock option plans, which enable employees to obtain shares of stock below market value. Treasury shares may be used to satisfy the provisions of such incentive plans. A company's own stock may be a better investment of idle cash than the securities of other companies. Occasionally corporations buy their own stock in order to change their status from public to closely-held companies.

Treasury stock is not an asset

A corporation cannot own itself; therefore, shares of its own stock may not be recorded as investments or carried as assets. When treasury stock is acquired, a Treasury Stock account is debited, and Cash is credited. For example, Braxton Corporation's $1 par common stock is trading in the market at $30 per share. The company purchases 1,000 shares of treasury stock on October 4, 1985, and records the purchase as follows:

Oct. 4	Treasury stock	30,000	
	Cash		30,000
	Acquired 1,000 shares of treasury stock		
	at $30 per share.		

The treasury stock is recorded at cost.[1] The Treasury Stock account has a debit balance, but it is a capital account, therefore it reduces total owners' equity.

Sale of Treasury Stock

Gains or losses are never recorded on sales of treasury stock

When treasury stock is reissued, the corporation may receive more or less than it paid for the shares. However, a corporation cannot record gains or losses as a result of capital transactions, and any issuance or acquisition of stock by the company is a capital transaction between the company and its owners. What is done with the difference between the cost of the stock and the proceeds from its sale? This depends on whether the stock is sold for more or less than the cost.

On October 30, 1985, when the market price of Braxton Corporation's stock is $27 per share, the company reissues 200 shares of its treasury stock. The entry to record the sale at a price below cost is:

Oct. 30	Cash	5,400	
	Retained earnings	600	
	Treasury stock		6,000
	Reissued 200 shares of treasury stock at		
	$27 per share.		

Keep in mind that the par value of the treasury stock was not removed from the Common Stock account nor was the additional paid-in capital reduced when the treasury stock was acquired. In the above transaction,

---

[1] Treasury stock may also be recorded at par value. The par value method is somewhat more complex and is not discussed in this book.

the new owner of the shares contributed less than the previous owner, but the previous contributed capital cannot be reduced. By buying the stock for $30 per share and reissuing it for $27 per share, the company in effect made a distribution of assets of $3 per share on the 200 sold shares. This reduction in assets must be recorded by a corresponding reduction of retained earnings, which is the only capital account that may be used to distribute assets to shareholders.

Because treasury stock transactions may result in asset distributions, state laws do not permit corporations to buy their own stock unless the retained earnings account has a credit balance at least as large as the cost of the stock. In addition, as soon as treasury stock is purchased, a portion of retained earnings becomes restricted and cannot be distributed as dividends. Such restrictions are discussed shortly.

Treasury stock causes a restriction of retained earnings

When treasury stock is sold at a price above its cost, the company obtains more capital from the new owner than it paid to the previous owner. For example, on November 14, 1985, Braxton Corporation sells 300 shares of its treasury stock at the market price of $31 per share. The journal entry is

Nov. 14	Cash	9,300	
	Treasury stock		9,000
	Additional paid-in capital		300
	Reissued 300 shares of treasury stock at		
	$31 per share.		

Additional Paid-in Capital is credited with the excess of the sales price above cost of the stock. This is because that excess is an investment made by the new owner of the stock in addition to the investment made by the previous owner and already recorded as contributed capital. Amounts paid by shareholders for common stock may not be returned to them, therefore they are recorded as part of contributed capital. Retained earnings cannot be credited because money obtained by a corporation in exchange for stock is not earned.

RETAINED EARNINGS RESTRICTIONS AND ADJUSTMENTS

The retained earnings statement of a corporation sometimes reports more information than illustrated previously in this book. There may be times when all of the retained earnings balance is not available for dividend distributions. In addition, adjustments may be needed to retained earnings for errors made in previous accounting periods.

Retained Earnings Restrictions

The credit balance in the retained earnings account is the total amount that a corporation may legally pay to shareholders as dividends. Occasionally the corporation may have to limit the amount of retained earnings available for distribution to shareholders. Such limitations may be contractual or a result of the operation of state laws. When part of retained earnings is not available for the payment of dividends, that portion is **restricted** or **appropriated**.

Restricted retained earnings cannot be used for dividend payments

An example of a contractual limitation on retained earnings is an agreement with a lender to restrict the retained earnings balance. A corporation may borrow money from a bank and agree to restrict retained earnings in an amount equal to the debt or to refrain from paying dividends until the debt is repaid.

A legal restriction occurs when a corporation purchases treasury stock. By purchasing treasury stock, the company is returning to some shareholders the money they invested. But distributions of contributed capital to the company's owners are illegal. To avoid reducing contributed capital, the distribution of assets must be accompanied by a corresponding reduction of retained earnings. The company must restrict a portion of retained earnings. The amount restricted is equal to the cost of the treasury stock, making that amount of retained earnings unavailable for dividends.

Remember that the purchase of treasury stock does not reduce the balances of either contributed capital accounts nor the retained earnings account. The balance of the treasury stock account is simply deducted from total capital in the balance sheet. The restriction of retained earnings tells financial statement readers that the entire retained earnings balance reported in the balance sheet is not available for dividend distributions. State laws do not permit corporations to buy their own stock unless the retained earnings account has a credit balance, and the balance must be at least as large as the cost of the treasury stock.

Restricted retained earnings are usually reported by means of a footnote as illustrated in Figure 14-2. Restrictions of retained earnings often have no real effect on dividends, because the amount of retained earnings is usually far larger than the dividends a corporation would usually pay, or the amount of cash available for dividends.

Figure 14-2

Retained earnings statement with prior period adjustment, dividend distributions on two classes of stock, and restriction described by a footnote.

Braxton Corporation
Statement of Retained Earnings
For the Year Ended December 31, 1985

Retained earnings, 12/31/84		$ 75,000
Less prior period adjustment: Understatement of depreciation expense in 1984		(9,000)
Retained earnings as adjusted		66,000
Add net income		172,000
		238,000
Less dividends declared:		
On preferred stock, $9 per share	$ 9,000	
On common stock, $2 per share	104,700	(113,700)
Less reduction from sale of treasury stock for less than cost		(600)
Retained earnings, 12/31/85 (see Note)		$123,700

Note: Retained earnings are restricted in the amount of $15,000 for the cost of treasury stock.

Prior Period Adjustments

Prior period adjustments are required when accounting errors made in past periods are discovered in the current period

If an error in the accounting records or financial statements occurs in a prior accounting period and is discovered in a subsequent period, the correction of the error is a **prior period adjustment**. A prior period adjustment is recorded in the Retained Earnings account and reported in the retained earnings statement. For example, in 1984, Braxton Corporation failed to record depreciation expense of $9,000, and the error is discovered in 1985. The error caused depreciation expense in 1984 to be understated, which overstated 1984 net income. That means the retained earnings balance is now overstated, and accumulated depreciation is understated. The entry to correct the error is

Dec. 16	Retained earnings	9,000	
	Accumulated depreciation		9,000
	To correct depreciation of prior period.		

When a prior period adjustment such as the above is made, it is reported in the retained earnings statement separately, as shown in Figure 14-2. FASB Statement No. 16 limits prior period adjustments to correction of accounting errors. All other changes in owners' equity resulting from operating the company must be reported in the income statement.

Retained earnings statement.   The retained earnings statement in Figure 14-2 shows a beginning balance of $75,000, which was the ending balance in 1984. The prior period adjustment is shown separately and is used to arrive at adjusted retained earnings. Note how the reduction in retained earnings from the sale of treasury stock is reported. Note also the treasury stock restriction described in the footnote to the statement. At the end of 1985, the company still holds 500 shares of treasury stock costing $30 per share, requiring a $15,000 retained earnings restriction.

Figure 14-3 illustrates Braxton Corporation's balance sheet on December 31, 1985. To emphasize the capital section of the statement, the assets and liabilities are condensed into single figures. Observe the reporting of treasury stock as a reduction from total capital. Although treasury shares are not outstanding, the common stock account balance includes the par value of treasury shares because they are issued. Note also that the capital stock accounts in the financial statements describe fully all information about each class of stock, including the par value, number of shares authorized and outstanding, and any other characteristics that may be of importance to the user of the statement.

BOOK VALUE OF STOCK

The market value of stock is important to shareholders as a measure of the value of their investment. It also affects accounting for issuance of stock,

Braxton Corporation
Balance Sheet
December 31, 1985

Total assets	$1,294,500
Total liabilities	$ 598,981
Capital	
Preferred stock, $100 par, 9% cumulative, 100,000 shares author- ized, 900 shares issued and outstanding, each convertible into 11 shares of common stock	90,000
Paid-in capital in excess of par on preferred stock	9,000
Common stock, $1 par, 2,000,000 shares authorized, 52,350 shares issued, 51,850 outstanding	52,350
Paid-in capital in excess of par on common stock	435,469
Retained earnings	123,700
Total	710,519
Less treasury stock, 500 shares at cost	15,000
Total capital	695,519
Total liabilities and capital	$1,294,500

Figure 14-3
Each capital account of a corporation is described in detail in financial statements. Total capital is equal to net assets.

distributions of stock dividends, and treasury stock transactions. The total market value of all shares outstanding is the market value of the entire company.

Another measure of stock value is the **book value** of stock, which represents **net assets**, or total assets less total liabilities, as recorded on the books of the company. Book value of the entire company is not as significant as the book value of individual shares, especially if more than one type of stock is outstanding. The book value per share and the market value per share are seldom the same because book value is based on the recorded value of assets as reported in the balance sheet, and market value is based on investors' assessment of the fair value of assets and of company performance.

Net assets are equal to book value of the company

The calculation of book value is quite simple. If the company is capitalized only with common stock the entire capital is divided by the number of shares of stock outstanding. If the company is capitalized with more than one kind of stock, the preferred stock account balances must be deducted from total capital before the book value of common stock can be calculated.

Book value per share is an important measure

At the end of 1985, the balance sheet of Braxton Corporation in Figure 14-3 shows that the total book value of the company is $695,519, of which $99,000 belongs to preferred shareholders. The book value per share of preferred stock is obtained from the two preferred stock accounts as follows:

$$\frac{\text{Book value of preferred stock}}{\text{No. of preferred shares outstanding}} = \frac{\$99,000}{900 \text{ shares}} = \$110 \text{ per share}$$

Although 52,350 shares of common stock have been issued, only 51,850 are outstanding; there are 500 shares of treasury stock. The book value per share of common stock is:

$$\frac{\text{Book value of common stock}}{\text{No. of common shares outstanding}} = \frac{\$695,519 - \$99,000}{51,850 \text{ shares}}$$

$$= \$11.50 \text{ per share}$$

The computation of book value per share is based on the assumption that all of the retained earnings belong to common shareholders. If, however, dividends are in arrears on preferred stock, then a portion of the retained earnings belongs to the preferred shareholders, because they are entitled to receive the dividends in arrears which are included in the retained earnings balance. With dividends in arrears, calculating the book value per share of common stock requires deducting from retained earnings that portion belonging to preferred shareholders.

EARNINGS PER SHARE

A very important figure reported in financial statements is the earnings per share figure. Because so much emphasis is placed on this figure, the rules for calculating it are extremely complex. We cover only basic concepts in this book, including earnings per share for companies with simple capital structures, and also companies with complex capital structures.

Simple Capital Structure

A company with a simple capital structure has no convertibles

A corporation is said to have a **simple capital structure** if it has no convertible securities outstanding. For such companies, the calculation of earnings per share is relatively simple. Earnings per share is the net income earned for each share of common stock outstanding. The concept of **earnings per share (EPS)** is that the net income of a corporation is earned for the benefit of shareholders, and shareholders are therefore interested in the amount of income earned for their share of ownership. Such information is expressed as the net income earned for a single share of common stock. For example, if a company earns net income of $275,000 and has 100,000 common shares outstanding, net income per share of common stock is $2.75, calculated as:

$$\text{EPS} = \frac{\text{Net income}}{\text{No. of common shares}} = \frac{\$275,000}{100,000 \text{ shares}} = \$2.75 \text{ per share}$$

Even with a simple capital structure, several factors can complicate the computation of earnings per share. First, a company may have preferred as well as common stock outstanding. Second, the number of common shares may change during the accounting period.

EPS with preferred stock outstanding.   Preferred shareholders are entitled to their dividend prior to any distribution of income to holders of common shares. Therefore the current preferred dividend requirement has to be deducted from net income before EPS can be calculated. It does not matter whether or not the preferred dividend has b en paid, because the payment or nonpayment of the dividend does not determine the amount of income earned.

For example, Leider Corporation has outstanding 5,000 shares of $100 par, 6 percent cumulative preferred stock, and 100,000 shares of $1 par common stock. Net income is $175,000, of which $30,000 is required to pay the preferred dividend. Even if the preferred dividend is not declared, the common shareholders are not entitled to this portion of the net income because the dividend is cumulative. It is therefore necessary to deduct the preferred dividend requirement from net income in order to calculate EPS. The calculation is as follows:

$$\text{EPS} = \frac{\text{Net income} - \text{Preferred dividend requirement}}{\text{Weighted average number of common shares}}$$

$$= \frac{\$175,000 - \$30,000}{100,000 \text{ shares}} = \$1.45 \text{ per share}$$

Number of shares for EPS calculations.   FASB rules for calculating earnings per share state that the weighted average number of common shares outstanding is to be used as the denominator in the EPS calculation. Shares of stock issued near the end of the year should not influence the EPS calculation as heavily as those that have been outstanding all year. This is because the assets contributed by the shares issued late in the year were available for a shorter time and could not earn as much income as assets available for the entire year.

The weighted average number of shares is used for calculating EPS

For example, a corporation had 100,000 shares outstanding on January 1, 1985. On June 30, the corporation issued 60,000 shares of common stock, and on September 30, 20,000 shares were reacquired as treasury stock. On December 31, the corporation has outstanding a total of 140,000 common shares, but because all the shares had not been outstanding for the full year, the weighted average number of shares is smaller. The shares outstanding from the beginning of the year are assigned their full weight. The shares outstanding for half a year are weighted by one-half. The weighted average number of shares is easily computed as follows by multiplying the number of shares outstanding by the portion of the period they are outstanding.

Jan. 1 to June 30	100,000 shares	×	6/12 =	50,000
June 30 to Sept. 30	160,000 shares	×	3/12 =	40,000
Sept. 30 to Dec. 31	140,000 shares	×	3/12 =	35,000
Weighted average number of shares			12/12	125,000 shares

Complex Capital Structures

Convertible securities make a complex capital structure

The same weighted average shares computation that applies to corporations with simple capital structures also applies to companies with complex capital structures. A corporation that has convertible securities outstanding has a **complex capital structure.** The owners of convertible stocks or bonds have the privilege of converting their securities into common stock at any time, thus increasing the number of common shares outstanding. The increase in the number of common shares means less income for each share. The company must, therefore, inform its shareholders of the potential **dilution,** or decrease in earnings per share, that results from the conversion of convertible securities.

Convertible securities are classified into two types for EPS purposes: Those that are common stock equivalents and those that are not common stock equivalents. **Common stock equivalents** are convertible securities that investors acquire primarily because they are convertible into common stock and secondarily for the interest or dividend income they yield. Convertible securities that are purchased by investors primarily for the income they yield are not common stock equivalents. The cash yield produced by a convertible stock or bond at the time it is issued determines whether or not the security is a common stock equivalent.[2]

Two earnings per share figures exist with complex capital structures

With two types of convertible securities, corporations with complex capital structures are required to report two earnings per share figures. The two EPS figures are called primary earnings per share and fully diluted earnings per share. The **primary earnings per share** figure is reported on the assumption that all common stock equivalents have been converted into common stock. The denominator for calculating this EPS figure is the weighted average number of common shares outstanding, plus the weighted average number of shares into which the common stock equivalents can be converted. Primary earnings per share take into account the potential dilution of earnings caused by the conversion of common stock equivalents into common stock.

The **fully diluted earnings per share** figure is calculated on the assumption that **all convertible securities,** whether or not they are common stock equivalents, have been converted into common stock. The denominator in the EPS calculation is the largest possible number of common shares after all conversions take place. Fully diluted earnings per share is the smallest possible figure, taking into account all possible conversions.

If a convertible security is **actually** converted into common stock during the accounting period, the convertible security no longer exists at the end of the year when the EPS calculation is made. It is only with outstanding convertible securities that the accountant must make assumptions in order to calculate EPS. For EPS calculations, all convertible securities are assumed to be converted at the beginning of the accounting period.

---

[2] A convertible security is a common stock equivalent if, at the time it is issued, its cash yield is less than ⅔ of the average yield of AA rated bonds.

Assumed conversions cause many complications

Complexities occur when the assumption is made that securities have been converted into common stock. If a convertible preferred stock is assumed to be converted, it is also necessary to assume that the dividend on this preferred stock need not be paid. Therefore dividends on preferred stock assumed converted should not be deducted from net income in the EPS calculation. Similarly, if a convertible bond is assumed converted, it is also necessary to assume that interest on the bond is not paid. This means that income must be increased by the amount of interest normally paid on the bond. But if income is larger because the interest expense is assumed not to exist, the income tax is also larger. The net-of-tax interest saving of a convertible bond is added to net income in the EPS calculation if the bond is assumed to be converted into common stock.

Illustrative EPS Example

To illustrate the calculation of earnings per share for a company with a complex capital structure, we use the example of Falten Corporation, whose debt and capital structure is illustrated in Figure 14-4. The company's convertible bonds are common stock equivalents, and its convertible preferred shares are not common stock equivalents. The company is subject to an income tax rate of 30 percent of net pretax income. Net income after tax is $214,000.

Figure 14-4
A corporation with a complex capital structure has convertible securities outstanding. These may or may not be common stock equivalents.

Debt and Capital Structure of Falten Corporation

Long-term debt	
Bonds payable, 10%, due 1990, each $1,000 bond convertible into 50 shares of stock	$ 200,000
Owners' equity	
Preferred stock, $100 par, $6 cumulative, 5,000 shares authorized, issued, and outstanding, each convertible into 5 shares of common stock	$ 500,000
Common stock, $1 par, 1,000,000 shares authorized, 100,000 shares issued and outstanding	100,000
Paid-in capital in excess of par on common stock	800,000
Retained earnings	1,300,000
Total owners' equity	$2,700,000

Net income is calculated by deducting bond interest as an expense in the income statement to arrive at income before tax. Then the income tax is deducted to arrive at net income after tax. Dividends are not expenses and are not tax deductible. They do not affect the computation of income tax or net income.

Earnings per share calculated without considering the dilution caused by convertible securities is $1.84 per share, as shown on the following page.

$$EPS = \frac{\text{Net income} - \text{Preferred dividends}}{\text{Weighted average number of common shares}}$$

$$= \frac{\$214,000 - \$30,000}{100,000 \text{ shares}} = \$1.84 \text{ per share}$$

Primary earnings per share.   The $1.84 per share figure should not be reported because it does not take into account the dilution of earnings, but having this figure enables us to see the extent of the dilution that would be caused if holders of convertible stocks and bonds decide to convert their securities into common stock. To obtain primary earnings per share, we must assume that the convertible bonds, which are common stock equivalents, are converted into common stock.

The assumed conversion of bonds requires the issuance of 10,000 common shares, because each $1,000 bond is convertible into 50 shares, and there are 200 bonds outstanding. If the bonds are assumed converted, interest on them does not have to be paid. The total annual interest on the bonds is 10 percent of $200,000, or $20,000. Income before tax is assumed to be $20,000 greater, and the income tax is assumed to be $6,000 greater (30 percent of $20,000). Therefore, net income after tax is $14,000 greater if the bonds are assumed converted.

Given the above assumptions, we can calculate primary earnings per share of $1.80, as follows:

$$EPS = \frac{\text{Net income} - \text{Preferred dividends} + \text{Net-of-tax interest saving}}{\text{Common shares} + \text{Common shares from conversion of bonds}}$$

$$= \frac{\$214,000 - \$30,000 + (\$20,000 - \$6,000)}{100,000 + 10,000 \text{ shares}} = \frac{\$198,000}{110,000 \text{ shares}}$$

$$= \$1.80 \text{ per share}$$

Comparing the primary EPS of $1.80 per share with the earlier computation of $1.84 per share shows that the conversion of the bonds would dilute earnings by 4 cents per share.

Fully diluted earnings per share.   The smallest possible EPS figure is reported on the assumption that all convertible securities are converted. The preferred stock can be converted into a total of 25,000 common shares. Assuming that the securities are converted, the preferred dividend would not have to be paid. It is therefore necessary to add 25,000 shares to the denominator in the EPS calculation, and the preferred dividend is not deducted from net income in the numerator. The convertible bond is also assumed to be converted as before. The calculation of fully diluted earnings per share results in EPS of $1.69, obtained as follows:

$$\text{EPS} = \frac{\text{Net income } + \text{ Net-of-tax interest saving}}{\text{Common shares } + \text{ Common shares from bond conversion}} \\ \text{+ Shares from conversion of other convertible securities}$$

$$= \frac{\$214,000 \ + \ \$14,000}{100,000 \ + \ 10,000 \ + \ 25,000 \text{ shares}} = \frac{\$228,000}{135,000 \text{ shares}}$$

$$= \$1.69$$

Again we can compare the fully diluted EPS of $1.69 with the $1.84 calculated without any conversions, and we see that the earnings can be diluted by 15 cents if all convertible securities are converted into common stock.

Keep in mind that if there is preferred stock outstanding that is not convertible, its dividends must still be deducted from net income in all EPS calculations. Net income in the income statement includes income earned for both preferred and common shareholders. Earnings per share figures, on the other hand, are computed for common shares only. The income statement of the company reports primary earnings of $1.80 per share and fully diluted earnings of $1.69 per share.

Many complications can develop in computing earnings per share. Special types of convertibles called options and warrants pose problems that are beyond the scope of this book. Convertible securities sometimes cause the EPS figure to increase when their conversion is assumed because the numerator in the calculation may increase by a higher percentage than the denominator. Such securities are said to be **antidilutive** and may not be used in the calculation of EPS. Numerous other problems exist that can be discussed only in more advanced textbooks. If you understand the basic situation described above, you have a better knowledge of earnings per share than most readers of financial statements.

SUMMARY   Corporations sometimes issue bonds or preferred stocks that are **convertible** into common stock at the option of the owner. All account balances associated with the convertible stocks or bonds are written off when the securities are converted, and common stock is issued by crediting the Common Stock account for the par value and Additional Paid-in Capital for any difference.

When corporations buy their own shares from stockholders, such shares are called **treasury stock**, which are no longer **outstanding** although it is still **issued**. Treasury stock may be reissued below or above its cost. If treasury shares are sold for less than their cost, the Retained Earnings account is debited for the difference between the cost and the proceeds. If the shares are sold for more than their cost, Additional Paid-in Capital is credited for the difference.

Retained earnings are **restricted**, or **appropriated**, for the cost of treasury stock, as long as the stock is held. Retained earnings restrictions may also take place as a result of contractual agreements with lenders. Restricted retained earnings may not be used for dividend distributions. Restrictions are reported in footnotes to the financial statements. The retained earnings statement may report **prior period adjustments** resulting from accounting errors made in previous financial statements.

The **book value** of a company is the recorded net asset value, or the amount of total capital. The **book value per share** of stock is each share's proportionate interest in total capital.

The capital section of a corporation's balance sheet usually contains detailed descriptions of each capital account, including the number of shares of each type of stock authorized, issued, and outstanding, additional paid-in capital on each type of stock, retained earnings, treasury stock as a deduction from total assets, and any restrictions on retained earnings.

One of the most widely used items of accounting information is the **earnings per share (EPS)** figure, calculated by dividing net income by the weighted average number of common shares outstanding. If preferred stock is outstanding, the preferred dividend must be deducted from net income before EPS is calculated.

A corporation that has no convertible securities outstanding has a **simple capital structure** and reports one earnings per share figure. A corporation that has convertible securities outstanding has a **complex capital structure** and must report two EPS figures. Some convertible securities are classified as **common stock equivalents** for EPS calculations. **Primary earnings per share** is calculated by assuming that all common stock equivalents have been converted into common stock. **Fully diluted earnings per share** is calculated by assuming that **all** convertible securities have been converted. When conversion of securities is assumed, it must also be assumed that preferred dividends or bond interest on those securities are not paid. Primary and fully diluted earnings per share inform shareholders of the potential **dilution** in earnings that may occur if holders of convertible securities decide to exercise their conversion privilege.

KEY TERMS

appropriated retained
 earnings *(581)*
book value *(583)*
common stock equivalent *(586)*
complex capital structure *(586)*
conversion ratio *(575)*
convertible security *(575)*
dilution of earnings *(586)*
fully diluted earnings per
 share *(586)*

issued shares *(578)*
outstanding shares *(578)*
primary earnings per share *(586)*
prior period adjustment *(582)*
restricted retained earnings *(581)*
simple capital structure *(584)*
treasury stock *(578)*

QUESTIONS

1. What benefits are available to owners of convertible securities? How does a corporation benefit from issuing convertible securities?

2. Describe a situation that requires the restriction of retained earnings. What is the effect of such a restriction?

3. What is a prior period adjustment, and how does it affect the retained earnings statement?

4. What is treasury stock? How is the difference between cost and the selling price of treasury stock accounted for when treasury stock is reissued?

5. What is the book value of a company? Of a share of stock?

6. What is meant by the weighted average number of common shares? How is this number used in financial reporting?

7. What is meant by complex capital structure of a corporation? How does a corporation with a complex capital structure report earnings per share?

8. Describe the difference between primary earnings per share and fully diluted earnings per share.

9. What is the basis for differentiating between convertible securities that are common stock equivalents and those that are not?

EXERCISES

Ex. 14-1   **Conversion of preferred stock.**   The capital section of Yoshitamo Company, Inc. had the following account balances on June 30, 1985:

Preferred stock, $100 par, $8.30 cumulative convertible, 25,000 shares authorized, 5,000 shares issued, conversion ratio 12:1	$500,000
Paid-in capital in excess of par on preferred stock	25,000
Common stock, $4 par, 100,000 shares authorized, 40,000 shares issued and outstanding	160,000
Paid-in capital in excess of par on common stock	385,000
Retained earnings	726,000

On July 20, 1985, shareholders submitted 1,000 shares of preferred stock for conversion.

Required:
a. Prepare the entry to record conversion of the preferred stock.
b. Prepare the capital section of the balance sheet immediately after the conversion.

Ex. 14-2   **Bond conversion.**   Lee Kie Container Corporation has outstanding $1 million of 9 percent bonds payable with a book value of $979,000 on December 31, 1985. Interest is payable on June 30 and December 31 of each year. The company amortizes $12,000 of bond discount each year using the straight-line method. Each $1,000 bond is convertible into 15 shares of the company's $1 par common stock.

On July 31, 1985, $10,000 face value of bonds were submitted to the company for conversion.

Required: Prepare journal entries to record interest expense and discount amortization to the date of conversion and to convert the bonds.

Ex. 14-3   **Treasury stock.**   Mellors Corporation has outstanding 80,000 shares of $7 par common stock. On February 15 the company bought 1,000 shares of its own stock in the market at $32 per share.

On July 19 the company sold 300 shares of its treasury stock at $28 per share, and on August 23 it sold 400 shares at $36 per share.

Required: Record the acquisition and sales of treasury stock.

Ex. 14-4   **Retained earnings statement.**   Jennisonic Corporation's retained earnings balance on December 31, 1984, was $180,000. During the year 1985, the company paid a cash dividend of $20,000 on its common stock and a 5 percent stock dividend that reduced retained earnings by $40,000. The company's internal auditor also discovered that the company failed to record a $10,000 gain on sale of securities in 1980. Net income for 1985 was $95,000.

Required: Prepare a retained earnings statement for the year 1985.

Ex. 14-5   **Statement of retained earnings.**   Balforth Company's retained earnings balance on December 31, 1984, was $485,000. The company holds treasury stock that cost $20,000. During 1985 it earned net income of $150,000 and paid a cash dividend of $60,000. A stock dividend was also issued, which decreased retained earnings by $30,000. In 1985 the company agreed to restrict $100,000 of retained earnings until it repays a newly negotiated bank loan.

Required: Prepare a retained earnings statement on December 31, 1985, including appropriate footnotes.

Ex. 14-6   **Capital and book value.**   Morro Corporation has outstanding 10,000 shares of $100 par, $8 preferred stock, originally issued at $107 per share. Also outstanding are 150,000 shares of $2 par common stock issued at $40 per share. Retained earnings amount to $2,775,000. No dividends are in arrears.

Required:
  a.   Prepare the capital section of the balance sheet.
  b.   Calculate the book value of the preferred and common shares.

Ex. 14-7   **Weighted average shares.**   On January 1, 1985, Slindy Corporation had outstanding 200,000 shares of common stock. On March 31, the company issued an additional 50,000 shares. On June 30 the company acquired 10,000 shares of treasury stock, and it sold 3,000 of its treasury shares on September 1.

Required: Determine the weighted average number of shares for calculating earnings per share on December 31, 1985.

Ex. 14-8   **Calculating weighted average shares.**   Ulmar Company had 200,000 shares of common stock outstanding on January 1, 1985. On April 1 it issued an additional 70,000 shares. On July 31 the company issued 60,000 shares of common stock. On September 30 it acquired 20,000 shares of treasury stock which it still holds on December 31, 1985.

Required: Calculate the weighted average number of shares for the 1985 EPS computation.

Ex. 14-9   **EPS with simple capital structure.**   Kaudler Industries, Inc., has outstanding 60,000 shares of common stock and 5,000 shares of $8 preferred stock. Net income for 1985 was $400,000. The preferred dividend was paid in 1985, but there was no common dividend.

Required: Calculate earnings per share for 1985.

Ex. 14-10   **EPS and weighted average shares.**   Gleemor Corporation had outstanding 3,725 shares of $6 preferred stock and 60,000 shares of common stock on January 1, 1985. On June 1, 1985, the company issued 6,000 new shares of common stock, and on July 31 it acquired 3,000 shares of treasury stock. Net income for the year was $196,650.

Required: Calculate earnings per share for 1985.

Ex. 14-11   **EPS with complex capital structure.**   Jezebel Corporation has outstanding 2,000 shares of $8 preferred stock. Each share is convertible into 14 shares of common stock. There are 120,000 shares of common stock outstanding. Net income for the year was $376,000. There are no common stock equivalents outstanding.

Required: Calculate the primary and fully diluted earnings per share.

Ex. 14-12   **Complex capital structure and weighted average shares.**   Flamis Corporation has outstanding $100,000, 9 percent bonds payable. Each $1,000 bond is convertible into 36 shares of common stock. The bonds are not common stock equivalents. The company also had outstanding 60,000 shares of common stock on January 1, 1985. On June 1, 1985, the company issued 12,000 new shares of common stock, and on July 31 it acquired 3,000 shares of treasury stock. Net income for the year was $170,950. The company's income tax rate is 40 percent.

Required: Calculate earnings per share for 1985.

PROBLEMS

P. 14-1   **Capital transactions and retained earnings statement.**   The capital accounts of Lombay Corporation had the following balances on December 31, 1984:

Preferred stock, $100 par, $8 cumulative, 50,000 shares authorized, 2,000 shares issued and outstanding, each share convertible into 2 shares common	$200,000
Paid-in capital in excess of par on preferred stock	10,000
Common stock, $12 par, 50,000 shares authorized, 10,000 shares issued and outstanding	120,000
Paid-in capital in excess of par on common stock	600,000
Retained earnings	900,000

The following took place during 1985:

Feb. 25 Acquired 2,000 common shares of treasury stock at $90 per share.
Mar. 19 100 shares of preferred stock were converted into common.
Apr. 26 Sold 800 shares of treasury stock at $86 per share.
Sept. 19 Declared cash dividends, $8 per share on preferred and $4 per share on common, payable on October 10.
Oct. 10 Paid the cash dividend declared on September 19.
Oct. 18 Sold 700 shares of treasury stock at $93 per share.
Nov. 15 Discovered that depreciation expense was understated in 1983 by $4,000. Depreciation in later years is correct.
Dec. 31 Net income for the year was $360,000 after taxes.

Required:
  a. Journalize the above transactions.
  b. Prepare a statement of retained earnings for the year.

P. 14-2 **Capital transactions and statements.** Neurotti Corporation has outstanding 2,000 shares of $100 par, $9 cumulative preferred stock, each share of which is convertible into 10 shares of common stock. The preferred stock was issued at $102 per share. The company also has outstanding 25,000 shares of $1 par common stock. Paid-in capital in excess of par on common has a credit balance of $50,000, and retained earnings has a credit balance of $100,000 on December 31, 1984. Following are selected transactions for 1985:

May 15 Preferred shareholders converted 400 shares of their stock into common stock.
June 6 The company declared and paid a 5 percent common stock dividend. The market value of the common shares on this date was $15 per share.
Sept. 3 The company declared the annual dividend on its preferred stock, payable on September 30.
Oct. 5 The company declared a cash dividend of $.50 per share on common stock, payable on November 8.
Dec. 16 The company acquired 500 shares of treasury stock at $20 per share.
Dec. 31 Net income for the year was $93,400.

Required:
  a. Journalize the above transactions, including dividend payments.
  b. Prepare the retained earnings statement for the year.
  c. Prepare the capital section of the company's balance sheet on December 31, 1985.

P. 14-3 **Capital transactions and reporting.** Clark Corporation has authorized 10,000 shares of $100 par, 8 percent cumulative preferred stock and 100,000 shares of $10 par common stock. The company obtained its charter on December 28, 1984. During 1985 the following events took place:

Jan. 2 Issued 12,000 shares common stock at $40 per share.
Jan. 11 Issued 1,000 shares of preferred stock for land and buildings. The land is appraised at $30,000, and the building at $80,000.
Apr. 30 Issued 6,000 shares of common stock at 45 per share.
Sept. 2 Acquired 1,500 shares of treasury stock at $50 per share to have available for employee stock purchase plan.
Dec. 31 Net income for the year amounted to $129,900. No dividends were paid.

Required:
  a. Journalize the above transactions.
  b. Prepare the capital section of the company's balance sheet on December 31, 1985.
  c. Calculate earnings per share for the year.

P. 14-4 **Capital transactions, statement, and EPS.** Sofia Corporation has 100,000 shares of common stock authorized, with a par value of $5 per share. Also authorized are 10,000 shares of $100 par, $7.50 cumulative preferred shares. The company has outstanding 10,000 shares of common, issued at $20 each. No preferred stock has been issued. The retained earnings balance on December 31, 1984, is $80,000. Following are selected transactions for the year 1985:

Jan.	4	Issued 1,000 shares preferred stock at $102 per share.
Jan.	31	Declared and distributed a 10 percent stock dividend, on the common stock. The market price of the stock was $32 per share on this date.
Apr.	19	Declared a cash dividend of $.50 per share on common stock, payable on May 15 to shareholders whose date of record is May 4.
May	15	Paid the common dividend.
June	28	Acquired 2,000 shares of treasury stock at $31 per share.
Oct.	1	Issued 5,000 shares of common stock at $35 per share. These are new shares and do not involve treasury stock.
Oct.	23	Declared a $7.50 per share cash dividend on preferred stock, payable on November 15 to shareholders whose date of record is November 5.
Nov.	5	Paid the preferred dividend.
Dec.	31	Net income for the year is $80,625 after tax.

Required:
a. Journalize the above transactions.
b. Prepare the capital section of the company's balance sheet on December 31, 1985.
c. Calculate earnings per share for 1985.

P. 14-5   Primary and fully diluted EPS.   Following are the capital accounts of Palmera Corporation on December 31, 1985:

Preferred stock, $100 par, 10% cumulative convertible, 100 shares outstanding, each convertible into 5 shares of common stock	$ 10,000
Preferred stock, $60 par, 8%, 1,000 shares outstanding, each convertible into 4 shares of common stock	60,000
Paid-in capital on 8% preferred stock	8,000
Common stock, $10 par, 2,000 shares outstanding	20,000
Paid-in capital on common stock	60,000
Retained earnings	73,000
Total capital	$231,000

In 1985 the company earned $36,400 net income after tax. The 8 percent preferred stock is a common stock equivalent, and the 10 percent preferred is not.

Required: Calculate primary and fully diluted earnings per share for 1985.

P. 14-6   EPS for a complex capital structure.   Following is the capital section of Kerrie Corporation's balance sheet on December 31, 1985:

Preferred stock, $100 par, 9% cumulative convertible, 100 shares outstanding, each convertible into 5 shares of common stock	$ 10,000
Preferred stock, $60 par, 7% cumulative convertible, 1,000 shares outstanding, each convertible into 4 shares of common stock	60,000
Paid-in capital on 7% preferred stock	9,000
Common stock, $10 par, 4,000 shares outstanding	40,000
Paid-in capital on common stock	290,000
Retained earnings	300,000
Total capital	$709,000

In 1985 the company reported net income after tax of $24,990. The 9 percent preferred shares are common stock equivalents, and the 7 percent preferred shares are not.

Required: Calculate primary and fully diluted earnings per share for 1985.

P. 14-7   **EPS with convertible bonds.**   Following are the bond and capital accounts of Tetra Corporation on December 31, 1985:

Convertible bonds payable, 10%, each $1,000 bond convertible into
  45 shares of common stock $100,000
Preferred stock, $100 par, $9 cumulative, 1,000 shares outstanding   100,000
Common stock, $10 par, 10,000 shares outstanding   100,000
Retained earnings   100,000

In 1985 the company earned $65,800 net income after tax. The tax rate is 30 percent. The company's convertible bonds are not common stock equivalents.

Required: Calculate the primary and fully diluted earnings per share for 1985.

P. 14-8   **EPS with convertible bonds and preferred.**   Following are the bonds payable and capital accounts of Microgiant Corporation on December 31, 1985:

Convertible bonds payable, 9%, each $1,000 bond convertible into
  50 shares of common stock $100,000
Preferred stock, $100 par, 8% convertible, 1,000 shares outstanding,
  each convertible into 6 shares of common stock   100,000
Common stock, no par, 15,000 shares outstanding   200,000
Retained earnings   300,000

In 1985 the company earned $62,200 net income after tax. The tax rate is 40 percent. The bonds are common stock equivalents, and the preferred shares are not.

Required: Calculate the primary and fully diluted earnings per share for 1985.

P. 14-9   **Complex EPS with two convertible preferred stocks.**   Following are the capital accounts of Urex Corporation on December 31, 1985:

Preferred stock, $100 par, 10%, cumulative convertible, 1,000 shares
  outstanding, each convertible into 12 shares of common stock $ 100,000
Paid-in capital on 10% preferred stock   10,000
Preferred stock, $100 par, $9, 2,000 shares outstanding, each
  convertible into 10 shares of common stock   200,000
Common stock, $2 par, 100,000 shares outstanding   200,000
Paid-in capital on common stock   860,000
Retained earnings   73,000
Total capital $1,443,000

In 1985 the company earned $247,900 net income after tax.

Required:
  a. Calculate primary and fully diluted earnings per share for 1985, assuming

the 10 percent preferred stock is a common stock equivalent, and the $9 preferred is not.

b. Calculate primary and fully diluted earnings per share for 1985, assuming the $9 preferred stock is a common stock equivalent, and the 10 percent preferred is not.

Case 14-1   **Equipment financing with convertibles.**

Poorley Company has outstanding 100,000 shares of $1 par common stock originally issued at $7 per share, and now trading in the market at $15 per share. The company has operated profitably, but management is not satisfied because operations are limited to a fairly small scale. For the year ending December 31, 1985, the results were as follows:

Sales	$1,500,000
Cost of goods sold	690,000
Gross margin	810,000
Operating expenses	(490,000)
Depreciation	(8,000)
Interest	(2,000)
Income before tax	310,000
Tax	124,000
Net income	$ 186,000

If the company acquires equipment for $200,000, management believes profitability would improve substantially. Sales for 1985 are expected to increase to $2,000,000 with the new equipment, and cost of goods sold will remain the same percentage of sales as in 1985. Operating expenses are expected to increase by $100,000 in addition to depreciation on new equipment based on a 5-year life and use of straight-line depreciation with no salvage value. Depending on how the equipment is financed, interest expense may also increase.

The company can finance its acquisition of equipment by issuing either $200,000 of 10 percent convertible bonds or $200,000 of $10 preferred convertible stock. Each $1,000 bond would be convertible into 50 shares of common stock. Each share of preferred stock would be convertible into 5 shares of common stock. The company expects that the bonds or the preferred stock could be sold at par value. Neither the bonds nor the preferred stock would be common stock equivalents for EPS computations. The company expects its income tax rate to remain unchanged. It plans to issue the bonds or preferred stock and acquire the new equipment in the first week of January 1986.

Required:

a. Determine what the expected results of operations will be if the company acquires the new equipment with proceeds from each type of convertible security.

b. Compute the expected primary and fully diluted earnings per share for each alternative method of financing the equipment purchase.

c. Calculate the market price that the company's common stock would have to exceed in order to induce holders of convertible securities to convert to common stock.

d. Explain which type of security would provide the greater benefit for the company's shareholders.

Long-Term Investments by Businesses

15

Businesses frequently invest in the stocks and bonds issued by other businesses, often with the intent of holding such investments for a long time. The discussion of long-term investments in this chapter should enable you to understand:

---

1 Why businesses make long-term investments.

2 How long-term bond investments are accounted for.

3 How premiums and discounts on bond investments are treated.

4 Several classifications of stock investments.

5 The lower-of-cost-or-market method of accounting for equity investments.

6 How long-term investments are reported in financial statements.

7 The equity method of accounting for equity investments.

Businesses, like individuals, invest in securities that they intend to hold for a long time. Businesses buy bonds primarily to earn interest income, but the income is not always a primary objective. A corporation may buy a bond issue of one of its suppliers in order to provide the supplier with necessary financing and thereby ensure a stable source of supply. Funds not needed for current operations may be invested in bonds so that money will be available in the future for projects such as planned plant expansion or the payment of pension obligations.

Businesses buy the stock of other corporations because the stock may be a good investment that provides dividend income and the opportunity for gains from increasing stock prices. A company may, however, buy the common stock of other corporations primarily to gain some control over their operations. By having sufficient stock to elect one or more members to the board of directors, a company may exert considerable influence over the operations of a supplier of needed resources. A company may also buy stock of a corporation that buys its products, thereby ensuring that its customer has sufficient financial resources to maintain continuous operations. Companies whose stock is owned by other corporations may also benefit from their owners' management experience, credit rating, financing ability, and access to markets.

A company or person investing in bonds and stocks of other companies is an **investor**. The issuer of the bonds or stocks is called an **investee**. In this chapter we discuss how corporations account for their long-term investments in bonds and stocks of other corporations. We draw heavily on the discussion of investments in Chapter 8 and the discussion of bonds in Chapter 12.

LONG-TERM BOND INVESTMENTS

Bond investors must pay for accrued interest

Bonds issued by governments and corporations make suitable long-term investments if they satisfy the risk and return requirements of the investor. Bonds bought as an investment may be newly-issued bonds or they may have been outstanding for some time. A bond investment may be purchased at a discount or a premium, and if the bonds are acquired between interest payment dates, the investor must pay for the accrued interest.

The type and importance of bond yield varies with the investor's objectives

You may remember from the discussion in Chapter 12 that the amount of discount or premium depends on the riskiness of the bond and the market interest rate, as well as the coupon interest rate of the bond. **Yield to maturity** is of primary interest to investors who intend to hold their bond investments until maturity. Short-term bond investors are interested primarily in **current yield**, explained in Chapter 8.

The discount or premium on bond investments has a significant effect on the yield of the bonds when they are held for a long time or until maturity. Bonds purchased at a discount provide a yield to maturity that is greater than the current yield because when the bond matures, the full face value will be paid by the bond issuer. The purchase price of the bonds is less than face value, so the discount received at maturity is income in addition to the periodic interest payments. The opposite is true of bonds acquired at a premium. Any amount paid for the bonds in excess of face value will not be recovered when the bond matures. The lost premium is, in effect, a reduction in the total interest received from the bond over its holding period.

Discount or premium on long-term bond investments is amortized

With temporary investments, any discounts or premiums are ignored in the measurement of interest income because there is no intent to hold the bonds to maturity. If the intent is to hold bonds as a long-term investment, however, the discount or premium should be amortized so that the interest income reflects the actual interest earned over the bonds' holding periods.

Bonds Acquired at a Premium

To illustrate the acquisition of a long-term bond investment at a premium, we use the example of Spencer Company's purchase of $10,000 face value of 13.8 percent bonds on May 31, 1985. The bonds pay interest on May 31 and November 30 of each year and mature on November 30, 1988. The company paid $10,444 for the bonds and a commission of $60, for a yield to maturity of 12 percent. To record the acquisition of the bonds, the company prepares the following journal entry:

May 31	Investment in bonds	10,504	
	Cash		10,504
	Bought $10,000 face value 13.8%		
	bonds for $10,444 plus $60 commission		
	for a yield to maturity of 12%.		

The full cost of bonds is recorded in the investment account

Notice that the commission is not recorded separately but becomes part of the cost of the bonds. Also note that the entire cost is recorded in one account. Bond investors typically do not record bond premium in a separate account, as they do for bonds payable discussed in Chapter 12.

When the bonds mature, the company will collect $10,000 from the issuer. The $504 premium will not be repaid to the investor. The investor is willing to pay the premium because at the time of purchase, the interest income from the bonds is greater than the market rate of interest on bonds of similar risk.

Every 6 months the investor receives $690 of interest. Over the remaining 3½-year life of the bonds, the total interest received will be $4,830, but the interest actually earned will be $4,326 ($4,830 − $504 of premium). To recognize the correct amount of interest income in each accounting period, the investor amortizes the bond premium. Either straight-line or effective interest amortization may be used.

Straight-line amortization of premium.   If the premium on bond investments is amortized by the straight-line method, an equal amount of premium is written off in each period. In our example, there are 42 months from the date of purchase to the date of maturity. Dividing the $504 premium by 42 months, we find that $12 of premium should be amortized each month. On November 30, 1985, when the company receives its first interest payment, 6 months have passed since bond acquisition; therefore, the amount to be amortized is $72 ($12 × 6 months). The entry to record interest income is

Nov. 30	Cash	690	
	Investment in bonds		72
	Interest income		618
	Received semiannual interest on 13.6%		
	bonds and amortized premium for 6		
	months at $12 per month.		

Amortization of premium reduces investment book value

The bond investment account is credited whenever bond premium is amortized, which reduces the book value of the bond investment. If the company's accounting period ends on December 31, an adjusting entry is needed to accrue the interest on the bond investment and to amortize one month's premium. The entry is

Dec. 31	Interest receivable	115	
	Investment in bonds		12
	Interest income		103
	To accrue interest and amortize bond		
	premium for 1 month.		
	$10,000 × .138 × 1/12 = $115		

At the rate of $12 per month, the entire premium will be amortized by the end of 42 months when the bonds mature. A schedule of premium amortization is given in Figure 15-1, which shows an equal amount of premium amortization every 6 months.

When the final interest payment is received on November 30, 1988, the last of the premium is amortized, and the balance of the bond investment account is $10,000. On this date the bonds are redeemed by the

Amortization of Bond Premium
Straight-Line Method

$10,000, 13.8 percent bond investment with interest payable semiannually, maturing on November 30, 1988, acquired on May 31, 1985, at $10,504, to yield 12 percent to maturity.

1 Date	2 Cash Received	3 Interest Income 2 − 4	4 Premium Amortization $504/7	5 Book Value of Bonds 5 − 4	6 Implied Annual Interest Rate
5/31/85				$10,504	
11/30/85	$ 690	$ 618	$72	10,432	11.77%
5/31/86	690	618	72	10,360	11.85
11/30/86	690	618	72	10,288	11.93
5/31/87	690	618	72	10,216	12.01
11/30/87	690	618	72	10,144	12.10
5/31/88	690	618	72	10,072	12.18
11/30/88	690	618	72	10,000	12.27
	$4,830	$4,326			

Figure 15-1   **Bond premium amortization schedule using the straight-line method. The book value of the investment decreases, but the same amount of interest revenue is recorded in each period; therefore, the interest revenue is a changing percentage of the book value of the investment. The semiannual interest rate is obtained by dividing $618 by the previous book value. This rate is multiplied by 2 to obtain the annual interest rate in column 6.**

issuer. Spencer Company records the receipt of the final interest payment and the bond redemption in 1988 as follows:

Nov. 30	Cash	690	
	Investment in bonds		72
	Interest income		618
	Received semiannual interest on 13.8%		
	bonds and amortized premium for		
	6 months at $12 per month.		
30	Cash	10,000	
	Investment in bonds		10,000
	To record redemption of bond		
	investment.		

The above entries may, of course, be recorded as one compound journal entry.

Effective interest amortization of premium. The straight-line method and effective interest method of premium amortization result in the recognition of the same amount of interest income over the life of the bonds. However, the two methods recognize revenue at a different rate. With the straight-line method, the same amount of interest is recorded in each period. The effective interest method recognizes more interest when the book value of the bonds is higher and less when the book value is lower. The book value of the bonds is identical under the two methods only until the first receipt of interest and at the bond maturity date.

Yield to maturity is the effective interest rate

The effective interest method is based on the concept that interest income recorded in each period should be the effective yield on the investment. Therefore, each time interest revenue is recorded, it should be the same percentage of the bond investment's book value. To use the effective interest method, you must know the effective interest rate which is the yield to maturity on the bond. To calculate the periodic interest income, the yield to maturity is multiplied by the book value of the bond.

The difference between the interest income and the cash received is the amount of amortization. For example, the yield to maturity on Spencer Company's bond investment is 12 percent. When the first interest income is received on November 30, 1985, the bonds have been held for 6 months; therefore, the calculation of interest income is

Book value of bonds × Effective interest rate × Time

$10,504 × .12 × 6/12 year = $630.24

To record the interest income and premium amortization, the investor makes the following entry:

Nov. 30	Cash	690.00	
	Investment in bonds		59.76
	Interest income		630.24
	Received semiannual interest on 13.8%		
	bonds yielding 12% to maturity.		

Notice that the amount required to balance the journal entry amortizes the bond premium and reduces the book value of the bond investment. Unlike the straight-line method, the effective interest method amortizes a different amount of premium each time, but it results in recording the same percentage rate of interest on the balance in the bond investment account. In our example the yield to maturity is given as 12 percent. Bond tables are available from which the yield to maturity can be obtained for bonds with various maturities and interest rates.

Figure 15-2 shows the interest to be recorded on each payment date when the effective interest method is used. It also illustrates the decline in the book value of the bond investment account as the premium is amortized, until the maturity date when the book value and face value are equal.

Amortization of Bond Premium
Effective Interest Method

$10,000, 13.8 percent bond investment with interest payable semiannually, maturing on November 30, 1988, acquired on May 31, 1985, at $10,504, to yield 12 percent to maturity.

1 Date	2 Cash Received	3 Interest Income (12% of 5)/2	4 Premium Amortization 2 − 3	5 Book Value of Bonds 5 − 4	6 Annual Interest
5/31/85				$10,504.00	
11/30/85	$ 690.00	$ 630.24	59.76	10,444.24	12.0%
5/31/86	690.00	626.65	63.35	10,380.89	12.0
11/30/86	690.00	622.85	67.15	10,313.74	12.0
5/31/87	690.00	618.82	71.18	10,242.56	12.0
11/30/87	690.00	614.55	75.45	10,167.11	12.0
5/31/88	690.00	610.03	79.97	10,087.14	12.0
11/30/88	690.00	602.86	87.14	10,000.00	12.0
	$4,830.00	$4,326.00			

Figure 15-2   **Bond premium amortization schedule using the effective interest method. The interest income is always the same percentage of the investment's book value. The difference between the total cash received and total interest income is the $504 premium. Compare this figure with Figure 15-1. Over the life of the bonds the same amount of cash is received and the same amount of interest earned, regardless of the amortization method used.**

If the accounting period ends on December 31, 1985, the entry to record the accrual of interest is

Dec. 31	Interest receivable	115.00	
	Investment in bonds		10.56
	Interest income		104.44
	To accrue interest for 1 month.		
	$10,000.00 × .138 × 1/12 = $115.00		
	$10,444.24 × .12 × 1/12 = $104.44		

To record the next receipt of interest on May 31, the same book value is used for the calculation of interest income, to complete amortization for the 6-month period of which only 1 month has been amortized by the above entry. The May 31, 1986 entry is

May 31	Cash	690.00	
	Interest receivable		115.00
	Investment in bonds		52.79
	Interest income		522.21
	To record semiannual interest, including		
	interest accrued at end of last year.		
	$10,444.24 × .12 × 5/12 = $522.21		

The interest income for 1 month recorded in December, plus the interest income recorded for 5 months in this entry, is equal to the interest income of $626.65 shown in the amortization table in Figure 15-2. This is also true of premium amortization in the two entries.

Bonds Acquired at a Discount

During the 1960s when interest rates were relatively low, many companies issued long-term bonds with interest rates of 6 to 7 percent. Now interest rates are much higher, and these bonds trade in the bond market at very low prices. Often they are referred to as **deep-discount bonds**. As these bonds approach maturity, their market values approach the face value of the bond. With long maturities, however, it is not uncommon to find such bonds trading as low as 45 to 50 percent of their face value. There are, of course, many bonds that trade at small discounts.

We illustrate accounting for bond discounts with Spencer Company's acquisition of $10,000 face value 7 percent deep-discount bonds on June 30, 1985. The bonds were originally issued in 1960, mature on June 30, 1991, and pay interest on June 30 and December 31. The total cost is

$7,900, including commission, yielding 12 percent to maturity. To record the purchase, the company makes the following entry:

June 30	Investment in bonds	7,900	
	Cash		7,900
	Acquired $10,000 face value of 7%		
	bonds to yield 12% to maturity.		

The semiannual interest payment on these bonds is only $350, but $2,100 of bond discount must be amortized over the next 6 years, which results in effective interest income that is much larger than the cash receipt.

Straight-line amortization of discount.   With 72 months until maturity, amortization of $2,100 of bond discount requires writing off $29.17 of discount every month, or a total of $175 every 6 months. To record the receipt of the first interest income on December 31, 1985, the company makes the following entry:

Dec. 31	Cash	350	
	Investment in bonds	175	
	Interest income		525
	Received semiannual interest on 7%		
	bonds and amortized discount for 6		
	months at $29.17 per month.		

Discount amortization increases investment book value

Notice that the total income recorded consists of the cash received now plus a portion of the cash that will be received when the bonds mature. As the discount is amortized, the book value of the bonds increases until at maturity it equals the face value. Because amortizing the discount requires adding to the bond account, discount amortization is also known as **discount accumulation.**

Straight-line amortization can distort income on long-term deep-discount bonds

When the discount is very large, and the time to maturity quite long, the straight-line method of discount amortization can result in a significant distortion of reported interest income. Even with the short maturity in our example, the reported yield implies an interest rate that varies considerably from the early periods to the later periods during which the bond investment is held. Figure 15-3 shows the discount amortization table for this investment if the straight-line method is used, and column 6 in the table shows the change in reported interest over the 6 years. Because of the distortion in income caused by the straight-line method, the effective interest method is often preferred for deep-discount bond investments.

Amortization of Bond Discount
Straight-Line Method

$10,000, 7 percent bond investment with interest payable semiannually, maturing on June 30, 1991, acquired on June 30, 1985, at $7,900, to yield 12 percent to maturity.

1 Date	2 Cash Received	3 Interest Income 2 + 4	4 Discount Amortization $2,100/12	5 Book Value of Bonds 5 + 4	6 Implied Annual Interest Rate
6/30/85				$ 7,900	
12/31/85	$ 350	$ 525	$175	8,075	13.29%
6/30/86	350	525	175	8,250	13.00
12/31/86	350	525	175	8,425	12.73
6/30/87	350	525	175	8,600	12.46
12/31/87	350	525	175	8,775	12.21
6/30/88	350	525	175	8,950	11.97
12/31/88	350	525	175	9,125	11.73
6/30/89	350	525	175	9,300	11.51
12/31/89	350	525	175	9,475	11.29
6/30/90	350	525	175	9,650	11.08
12/31/90	350	525	175	9,825	10.88
6/30/91	350	525	175	10,000	10.69
	$4,200	$6,300			

Figure 15-3 **Bond discount amortization table using the straight-line method. The straight-line method produces a variable yield on book value over the life of the investment. Column 6 is computed as $525 divided by the previous book value and multiplied by 2 to yield the annual interest rate.**

Effective interest amortization of discount.   As with bond premiums, the effective interest method is applied by multiplying the book value of the bond investment by the yield to maturity to obtain periodic interest income. On December 31, 1985, the book value of the investment is $7,900, and the calculation of the first 6 months' interest is

Book value of bonds × Effective interest rate × Time

$7,900 × .12 × 6/12 year = $474.00

To record the December 31, 1985, interest income and bond discount amortization, the entry is

Dec. 31	Cash	350.00	
	Investment in bonds	124.00	
	Interest income		474.00
	Received semiannual interest on 7%		
	bonds and recorded income at		
	12% yield to maturity for 6 months.		

Amortization of Bond Discount
Effective Interest Method

$10,000, 7 percent bond investment with interest payable semiannually, maturing on June 30, 1991, acquired on June 30, 1985, at $7,900, to yield 12 percent to maturity.

1 Date	2 Cash Received	3 Interest Income (12% of 5)/2	4 Discount Amortization 3 − 2	5 Book Value of Bonds 5 + 4	6 Effective Interest Rate
6/30/85				$ 7,900.00	
12/31/85	$ 350.00	$ 474.00	$124.00	8,024.00	12.0%
6/30/86	350.00	481.44	131.44	8,155.44	12.0
12/31/86	350.00	489.33	139.33	8,294.77	12.0
6/30/87	350.00	497.69	147.69	8,442.46	12.0
12/31/87	350.00	506.55	156.55	8,599.01	12.0
6/30/88	350.00	515.94	165.94	8,764.95	12.0
12/31/88	350.00	525.90	175.90	8,940.85	12.0
6/30/89	350.00	536.45	186.45	9,127.30	12.0
12/31/89	350.00	547.64	197.64	9,324.94	12.0
6/30/90	350.00	559.50	209.50	9,534.44	12.0
12/31/90	350.00	572.07	222.07	9,756.51	12.0
6/30/91	350.00	593.49	243.49	10,000.00	12.0
	$4,200.00	$6,300.00			

Figure 15-4   **Bond discount amortization table using the effective interest method. Interest income is a constant percentage of the investment's book value. Compare this figure with Figure 15-3. Total interest earned over the life of the bonds is total cash received plus the $2,100 discount.**

A discount amortization table using the effective interest method is illustrated in Figure 15-4.

According to the table in Figure 15-4, the June 30, 1986 receipt of interest income is recorded as follows:

June 30	Cash	350.00	
	Investment in bonds	131.44	
	Interest income		481.44
	Received semiannual interest.		
	$10,000 × .07 × 6/12 = $350.00		
	$8,024 × .12 × 6/12 = $481.44		

Illustrative Example

It is not necessary to amortize bond discount or premium every time an interest payment is received, as shown above. Investors often credit interest income for the amount of cash received without amortizing the discount or premium, then make one adjusting entry at the end of the year to record the amortization. This method of amortization is used here.

Bond investors sometimes dispose of their investments prior to maturity, an action that requires recording gains or losses on the disposal. Accounting for discount amortization at year-end and accounting for gains and losses on disposals are illustrated with the following bond investment purchased by Spencer Company:

a. Bonds with face value of $10,000 are purchased on January 31, 1985, for $9,410 plus a commission of $50. The coupon rate of interest is 9 percent, and interest is payable on April 30 and October 31.

b. The bonds mature on April 30, 1987, and the company intends to hold them until maturity.

c. The company's accounting period ends on December 31, and it uses straight-line discount amortization.

d. On May 31, 1986, the bond investment is sold for $9,975 plus accrued interest, less a commission of $60.

The above bond investment and the discussion that follows are illustrated graphically in Figure 15-5.

Recording bond acquisition.   When bonds are acquired between interest payment dates, the buyer must pay for the accrued interest on the bonds in addition to the bond price and commissions. On the next interest payment date, the investor receives a full 6 months' interest. On January 31, 1985, when the bonds are purchased by Spencer Company, 3 months' interest is accrued. The acquisition is recorded as follows:

Jan. 31	Investment in bonds	9,460	
	Interest receivable	225	
	Cash		9,685
	Acquired $10,000 face value of 9%		
	bonds plus 3 months' accrued interest.		
	$10,000 × .09 × 3/12 = $225		

The commission becomes part of the cost of the bond. The interest accrued on the bond is debited to the Interest Receivable account.

The bonds have a remaining life of 27 months from the date of purchase to maturity. Using the straight-line method of discount amortization, the company should amortize $20 of bond discount for each month that the bonds are held, calculated as follows:

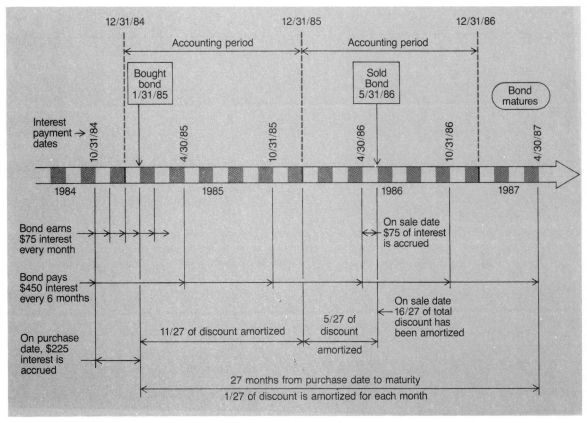

Figure 15-5   **Anatomy of a bond investment. The life of a $10,000, 9 percent bond is broken down into monthly periods to illustrate interest accrual, discount amortization, and interest collection, from the purchase date to the date of sale of the investment.**

$$\frac{\text{Total discount}}{\text{No. of months}} = \frac{\$540}{27} = \$20 \text{ per month}$$

Recording interest receipts.   On April 30, 1985, when the company receives its first interest income, the receipt of cash is recorded without amortizing any discount, as follows:

Apr. 30	Cash	450	
	Interest receivable		225
	Interest income		225
	Received semiannual interest on 9%		
	bonds, which were held 3 months.		
	$10,000 × .09 × 6/12 = $450		

Premium or discount may be amortized at year-end rather than on interest payment dates

No discount is amortized at this time; an adjustment at the end of the year will be made to record the amortization. At this point the bond investment accounts of the company appear as shown below.

Investment in Bonds				Interest Receivable			
1/31/85	9,460			1/31/85	225	4/30/85	225

Interest Income	
	4/30/85	225

On October 31, interest is again received on the bond and is recorded as follows:

Oct. 31	Cash	450	
	Interest income		450
	Received semiannual interest on 9%		
	bonds.		

Again the discount is not amortized. Amortization is left as a separate entry after all interest has been recorded. At the end of the company's accounting period, it is necessary to prepare an adjusting entry to account for the accrued interest on the bonds. The entry is

Dec. 31	Interest receivable	150	
	Interest income		150
	To accrue interest for 2 months.		
	$10,000 × .09 × 2/12 = $150		

When the next interest payment is received, part of it will be the collection of the receivable, and part will be interest income for the first 4 months of 1986.

Recording periodic amortization.   In addition to the interest accrual at the end of the accounting period, another adjusting entry is prepared to amortize the bond discount for the entire period. The bond investment has been held for 11 months; consequently, 11/27, or $220 of the bond discount, must be amortized. The entry adjusts the Interest Income and the Bond Investment accounts.

Dec. 31	Investment in bonds	220	
	Interest income		220
	To amortize bond discount for 11 months		
	at $20 per month.		

After the above entry is posted the bond accounts appear as follows:

Investment in Bonds

1/31/85	9,460	
12/31/85	220	
Bal.	9,680	

Interest Receivable

1/31/85	225	4/30/85	225
12/31/85	150		
Bal.	150		

Interest Income

	4/30/85	225
	10/31/85	450
	12/31/85	150
	12/31/85	220
	Bal.	1,045

On April 30, 1986, interest is again received and recorded without amortizing the bond discount.

Apr. 30	Cash	450	
	Interest receivable		150
	Interest income		300
	Received semiannual interest, of which		
	$150 was earned and accrued last year.		

Recording bond disposal. On May 31, 1986, Spencer Company sells its bond investment at 99¾ less $60 commission for a total of $9,915 ($9,975 − $60). In addition to the sales price, Spencer will collect the accrued interest from the buyer. Prior to recording the sale, the company must bring the bond-related accounts up to date. No bond discount has been amortized as yet in 1986, and this is now done for all 5 months that the bond has been held in 1986.

May 31	Investment in bonds	100	
	Interest income		100
	To amortize bond discount for 5 months		
	at $20 per month prior to disposal of		
	bonds.		

At this point the bond account appears as follows:

Investment in Bonds

1/31/85	9,460	
12/31/85	220	
Bal.	9,680	
5/31/86	100	
Bal.	9,780	

The sale of the bond is now recorded, including the receipt of 1 month's interest accrued to the date of sale.

Nov. 30	Cash	9,990	
	Interest income		75
	Investment in bonds		9,780
	Gain on sale of bond investment		135
	Sold $10,000 face value of 9%		
	bonds for $9,915 plus accrued interest		
	of $75 for 1 month.		
	$10,000 × .09 × 1/12 = $75		

The Interest Income account now appears as follows:

Interest Income

	4/30/86	300
	5/31/86	100
	5/31/86	75

The net result in the financial statements is the same whether the discount is amortized monthly, annually, or when interest payments are received.

LONG-TERM STOCK INVESTMENTS

Corporations may acquire a small amount of another company's stock as a long-term investment or they may acquire all of the outstanding stock of another corporation as a means of expanding their own business operations. It is not unusual for a corporation to own all the stock of another company that supplements or complements its business.

Classification of Long-Term Stock Investments

The method of accounting for long-term stock investments depends on the amount of stock held by the investor and the resulting control that the investor has over the operations of the investee. Control is determined by the percentage of the investee's outstanding common stock owned by the investor. Three classifications are used:

1. The investor owns less than 20 percent of the investee's stock.
2. The investor owns 20 to 50 percent of the investee corporation.
3. The investor owns more than 50 percent of the investee corporation.

Stock investments classification depends on the percentage of common stock owned

For each of the above classifications, an assumption of control is made that determines the accounting method to be used in accounting for the long-term stock investment.

1. With less than 20 percent ownership, the investor is assumed to have little or no control over the investee's operations, and the investment is accounted for at **lower of cost or market** value.
2. With 20 to 50 percent ownership, the investor is assumed to have significant control over the operations of the investee corporation, and the investment is accounted for by using the **equity method**.
3. With more than 50 percent ownership, the investor is assumed to have full control of the investee corporation's operations, and the investment is **consolidated**.

Controlling Interest in Stock of Investee

Parent and subsidiary statements are consolidated into a single annual report

When a corporation owns more than 50 percent of the outstanding common stock of another corporation, the investor corporation is known as the **parent company**, and the investee corporation is known as the **subsidiary company**. In most cases of parent and subsidiary relationships, the financial statements of the two companies are **consolidated** into a single set of financial statements and reported as if the parent and its subsidiaries were one accounting entity. Since consolidated financial statements are covered in Chapter 16, we limit our discussion in this chapter to long-term investments that are not consolidated.

Accounting for Stock Investments at Lower of Cost or Market

Classification of investments depends on management's intent

There is only a slight difference between accounting for long-term and short-term stock investments at lower of cost or market. Whether investments in equity securities are classified as temporary or long-term depends entirely on the **intent** of management. Short-term, or temporary equity investments are discussed in Chapter 8, and the discussion is not repeated here; however, we do point out the main difference between the two investment classifications.

Equity investments are normally carried at cost, but if the market value is less than cost, the investment is reported at market value to satisfy the conservatism principle. To reduce the investment to market value, the company credits an allowance account, and in the case of temporary investments, the company debits a loss account and reports the loss in the income statement in the period of the market decline. If the investments are classified as long-term, however, an **unrealized loss** account is debited, but it is **not** reported in the income statement. Instead, the unrealized loss is reported in the capital section of the balance sheet as a deduction from total capital.

For example, a company owns long-term equity investments acquired at a cost of $30,000. At the end of the year, the market value of these investments is $27,200. To record the decline in market value, the company makes the following entry:

Dec. 31	Unrealized loss in market value		
	of equity investment	2,800	
	Allowance for decline in market		
	value of equity investment		2,800
	To reduce long-term investment to		
	market value that is lower than		
	original cost.		

The allowance account is reported in the balance sheet as a deduction from the cost of the long-term investment, reducing the cost to market value. The unrealized loss account is reported as a deduction from the total capital of the company. A partial balance sheet is illustrated in Figure 15-6 to show the reporting of these accounts.

If the market value of the long-term investment subsequently increases, the allowance account is debited, and the unrealized loss account is credited for the increase. These entries increase the book value of the investment. The amount recorded for the investment, however, may never exceed the original cost.

Assets		
Long-term investment in marketable equity securities at cost	$ 30,000	
Less allowance for decline in market value	2,800	$27,200

Capital		
Common stock	$ 50,000	
Paid-in capital	250,000	
Retained earnings	248,000	
	548,000	
Less unrealized loss in market value of long-term equity investment	2,800	
Total capital	$545,200	

Figure 15-6   By using an allowance account, the company preserves the cost of equity investments when the investment is reported at market. The unrealized loss in long-term equity investments is reported in the capital section of the balance sheet rather than in the income statement, as with temporary equity investments.

The aggregate portfolio is valued at cost or market, whichever is lower

When a company owns several different stocks in its long-term equity portfolio, the market value of all of them together is used to determine the aggregate market value of the portfolio. Therefore, it is possible for the portfolio to increase in value even if some of the stocks declined.

Dividends on stock investments.   When the investor receives a cash dividend on the stock investment, cash is debited and dividend income is credited. If a stock dividend is received, no revenue is recognized, and the new shares simply become part of the investment portfolio. For example, an investor owns 1,000 shares of common stock purchased for $20,000, or $20 per share. When a 4 percent stock dividend is paid on this stock the investor receives an additional 40 shares. The total portfolio cost is unchanged, but the cost of each share becomes different, as follows:

A stock dividend changes the cost per share of equity investments

$$\frac{\text{Cost of original shares}}{\text{Total shares after stock dividend}} = \frac{\$20,000}{1,040 \text{ shares}} = \$19.23 \text{ per share}$$

If all or part of the investment is sold after the stock dividend is received, the gain or loss must be calculated on the basis of the new cost of $19.23 per share.

Disposal of long-term investments.   When an investor disposes of long-term investments by sale or exchange, a gain or loss is recorded, calculated as the difference between the proceeds of the sale and the book value of the investment. If the sold investments were acquired at different times and different prices, the gain is calculated by assuming that the securities bought earliest are sold first. This FIFO assumption is required by tax laws unless the investor can specifically identify the sold securities and their purchase dates, in which case specific identification is permitted.

Accounting for Stock Investments at Equity

When a corporation owns 20 percent or more of the common stock of another company, it usually can exert significant influence over the operations of the investee. Such influence is possible because the remaining common stock of the investee usually is held by many stockholders, none of whom alone significantly influences the company. Many shareholders, in fact, vote by **proxy**; that is, they assign their voting privilege to members of management who vote on behalf of the individual investors to elect members of the board of directors or adopt new corporate policies. Therefore, a holder with as much as 20 percent of the common stock usually has significant control over the selection of members of the board of directors and consequently the company's operations.

An investment in any amount of preferred stock is accounted for at cost, because preferred stock has no voting privileges and does not convey any control over the investee.

With the **equity method** of accounting for investments, the investor's common stock should be carried at an amount representing the investor's **equity interest** in the investee corporation rather than the investor's cost of the securities. The investor's equity interest is the underlying book value of the common stock held by the investor, which is the book value as recorded on the investee's books. To illustrate, Figure 15-7 portrays the balance sheets of two companies. In this example, Senior Corporation owns 30 percent of the common stock of Junior Corporation. The stock investment is therefore carried as an asset whose book value is 30 percent of the book value of Junior Corporation's total capital.

The investor records equity changes reported by the investee

The capital of Junior Corporation increases as a result of net income and decreases as a result of net losses or the payment of dividends. With the equity method of accounting for stock investments, when changes in the book value of capital are recorded by Junior Corporation, Senior Corporation also records changes in its common stock investment. The stock investment is maintained at an amount that reflects the proportion of owners' equity of Junior Corporation owned by Senior Corporation. We illustrate these accounting concepts below.

Purchase of common stock investment. Senior Corporation acquired its 30 percent ownership in 1985 by buying outstanding shares of Junior Corporation's common stock at book value. The acquisition of these shares for cash is recorded as follows:

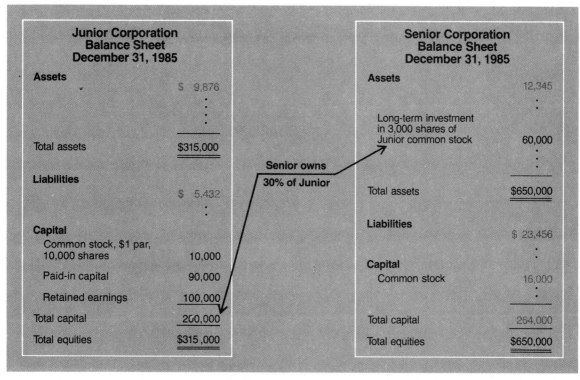

Junior Corporation Balance Sheet December 31, 1985		Senior Corporation Balance Sheet December 31, 1985	
Assets	$ 9,876	**Assets**	12,345
	·		·
	·	Long-term investment in 3,000 shares of Junior common stock	60,000
	·		·
Total assets	$315,000		
		Total assets	$650,000
Liabilities	$ 5,432		
	·	**Liabilities**	$ 23,456
			·
Capital Common stock, $1 par, 10,000 shares	10,000	**Capital** Common stock	16,000
Paid-in capital	90,000		·
Retained earnings	100,000		
Total capital	200,000	Total capital	264,000
Total equities	$315,000	Total equities	$650,000

Senior owns
30% of Junior

Figure 15-7   **When the investment in equity securities is a significant portion of the investee's equity, the equity method should be used to account for the investment.**

Dec. 31	Investment in common stock	60,000	
	Cash		60,000
	Acquired 30% interest in Junior		
	Corporation by purchasing 3,000 shares		
	of common stock at $20 per share.		

Increase in book value of investment.   Whenever the book value of Junior Corporation's common stock changes, Senior Corporation records a corresponding change in its investment account. Junior Corporation's accounting period ends on December 31, and for 1986 the company reports net income of $40,000. The increase in owners' equity of Junior Corporation must be reflected in the investment account of Senior Corporation, which has a 30 percent interest in the net income of Junior. To record the increase in its share of owners' equity, Senior Corporation prepares the following entry on December 31:

Dec. 31	Investment in common stock	12,000	
	Investment income		12,000
	To record 30% of income earned by		
	Junior Corporation.		

Income earned is not the same as cash received

Note that income is credited although Senior Corporation received nothing from Junior Corporation. The entry reflects the fact that the owners' equity of the investor has increased because the company whose stock is owned has earned net income.

Receipt of dividend from investee.   When Junior Corporation pays a dividend to its shareholders, it reduces assets and records a corresponding reduction in retained earnings. The total capital of the company decreases, so it is necessary for Senior Corporation to reflect this decrease in the book value of its investment. For example, Junior Corporation declares a cash dividend of $15,000 on its common stock and pays it to shareholders on March 15, 1987. To record the receipt of the dividend and the reduction of its ownership interest in Junior Corporation, Senior Corporation makes the following entry:

Mar. 15	Cash	4,500	
	Investment in common stock		4,500
	Received cash dividend from Junior		
	Corporation and reduced book value of		
	investment.		

Cash received as dividends is not always income

Although cash is received, Senior Corporation does not record dividend income. Receipt of the dividend is merely the exchange of one asset, investment in stock, for another asset, cash. Senior's portion of Junior's net income was already recorded as revenue on December 31. The receipt of the dividend is credited to the common stock investment account so that the investment is maintained at 30 percent of the book value of Junior Corporation's total capital. At this point, Senior's investment account appears as follows:

Investment in Common Stock

12/31/85	60,000	3/15/87	4,500
12/31/86	12,000		

Loss reported by investee. During the year ending December 31, 1987, Junior Corporation incurred a $20,000 net loss from operations. The loss reduces total owners' equity of Junior Corporation, and the investment account of Senior Corporation must also be reduced. When Junior Corporation reports the loss from operations for 1987, Senior Corporation makes the following entry to maintain its investment at equity:

Dec. 31	Investment loss	6,000	
	Investment in common stock		6,000
	To record 30% of loss reported by		
	Junior Corporation.		

The investment income or investment loss is reported in the investor's income statement among other revenues and expenses. The amounts reported as investment income or investment loss do not represent money actually received from the investee. The cash collected in the form of dividends is not income. It is simply a transfer of assets and therefore is not reported in the income statement. Now the investment account appears below and the two companies' balance sheets are shown in Figure 15-8.

Investment in Common Stock

12/31/85	60,000	3/15/87	4,500
12/31/86	12,000	12/31/87	6,000
12/31/87	61,500		

You can see from the above discussion that income is not synonymous with cash flow, yet both net income and cash flow are important accounting concepts. Many users of financial statements mistakenly believe that net income is the amount of money received by a business. Differentiating between net income and cash flow is necessary in your understanding of cash flows discussed in later chapters.

Goodwill and the equity method. When an investor buys an investee's common stock in the stock market, it is unlikely that the purchase price will equal the book value of the stock. In most cases the market price of the stock exceeds the investee's book value, although it is also possible for the market price of the stock to be less than the investee's book value. The discrepancy between the book value of stock and its market value occurs for many reasons. Some of the assets of the company may be undervalued, or the company may have a considerable amount of unrecorded

Market value and book value are often different

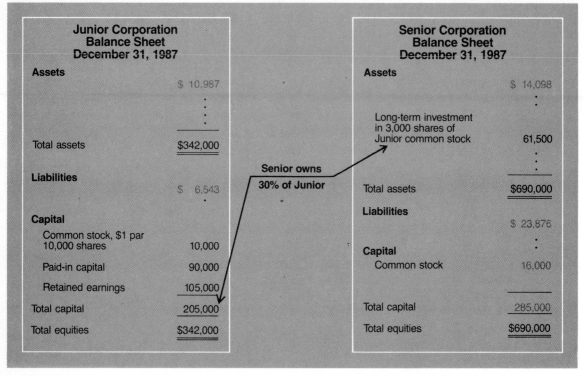

Figure 15-8 **When the equity method is used, the investor's long-term equity investment changes as the owners' equity of the investee changes.**

goodwill resulting from such things as choice location, good reputation, and good customer relations. Investors who trade the stock in the market are aware that the economic value of a company is often different from the book value.

When an investment is accounted for using the equity method, the original purchase of the investment is recorded at the actual cost to the investor. If the cost differs from the book value of the investment, the difference should be amortized until the recorded value of the investment is the same as book value.

Part of the cost of equity investments may have to be amortized

For example, suppose that Senior Corporation originally paid $70,000 for its 30 percent interest in Junior Corporation, instead of the $60,000 book value. There is a $10,000 **excess of cost over book value**, which is attributed to goodwill. The investment is recorded at its cost of $70,000 when the stock is acquired. Senior Corporation decides to amortize the excess of cost over book value over a period of 10 years. On December 31, 1986, when Junior Corporation reports net income of $40,000, Senior Corporation makes the following entries to record its share of the income and to amortize 10 percent of the excess of cost over book value.

Dec. 31	Investment in common stock	12,000	
	Investment income		12,000
	To recognize 30% of income		
	reported by Junior Corporation.		
	Investment income	1,000	
	Investment in common stock		1,000
	To reduce investment income and com-		
	mon stock investment by amortizing		
	excess of cost over book value.		

On December 31, 1987, a similar amortization entry is made, but instead of reducing the income account, the investor increases the loss account because the investee reported a net loss that year. The entries for 1987 are as follows:

Mar. 15	Cash	4,500	
	Investment in common stock		4,500
	Received cash dividend from Junior.		
Dec. 31	Investment loss	7,000	
	Investment in common stock		7,000
	To record 30% of $20,000 loss reported		
	by Junior Corporation and amortize		
	$1,000 of excess of cost over book value.		

The December 31, 1987 entry combines the recording of the investment loss and the amortization; of course, these events can be recorded separately.

If the stock of the investee is acquired for less than book value, the entry to amortize the **excess of book value over cost** would require a debit to the investment account and a credit to the income or loss account, which would bring the investment balance closer to book value.

Disposal of long-term equity investments.   The sale of long-term equity investments carried at equity is accounted for the same as when the investment is carried at cost. The gain or loss on the sale is the difference between the proceeds and the book value of the sold shares.

Disposal of stock may require a change from the equity method to the cost method

The sale of a part of equity investments may reduce a company's holding to the point where the investment can no longer be accounted for using the equity method. In this case the remaining stock investment is maintained in the accounts at its book value, but it is accounted for at lower of cost or market.

For example, on December 31, 1987, Senior Corporation's investment in Junior common stock consists of 3,000 shares with a book value of $69,500. On January 2, 1988, Senior sells 1,800 shares, or 60 percent, of its Junior common shares at $27 per share. The entry is

Jan. 2	Cash	48,600	
	Gain on sale of investment		6,900
	Investment in common stock		41,700
	Sold 1,800 shares of Junior common at		
	$27 per share.		
	60% of $69,500 book value = $41,700		

The remaining investment of 1,200 shares, with a book value of $27,800 (40 percent of $69,500), is less than 20 percent of Junior Corporation's outstanding stock. Therefore the investment is no longer accounted for using the equity method.

Accounting for investments by the equity method can be more complicated than discussed here, but any further discussion is beyond the scope of this book.

Comparison of Cost and Equity Methods

To illustrate the difference between the cost and equity method of accounting for marketable securities, we present the following example of two investments owned by Destra Corporation:

  a. On December 30, 1985, Destra Company purchased 1,000 shares of Ester Corporation common stock and 1,000 shares of Coster Corporation common stock. The cost of each investment was $25,000. Ester Corporation has a total of 4,000 shares of common stock outstanding with a book value of $25 per share; Coster has a total of 20,000 shares outstanding with a book value of $15 per share.

  b. On September 30, 1986, Ester Company and Coster Company each pay a cash dividend of $.50 per share.

  c. On December 31, 1986, each company reports net income of $2 per share. On this date the two companies' shares are trading in the market at $27 per share.

  d. On December 31, 1987, each company reports a net loss of $1 per share. On this date the two companies' shares are trading in the market at $22 per share.

The Ester Corporation stock investment is 25 percent of the investee's equity, and the equity method must be used. The Coster Corporation stock investment should be accounted for at cost or market value. The entries

Investment Recorded at Equity			Investment Recorded at Cost or Market Value		

12/30/85	Investment in common stock
	  Cash
	To record purchase of 25% interest in common stock of Ester Corporation.
		25,000	25,000	12/30/85	Investment in common stock
					  Cash
					To record purchase of 1,000 shares of common stock of Coster Corp.
						25,000	25,000

9/30/86	Cash
	  Investment in common stock
	To record receipt of $.50 per share cash dividend on stock accounted for at equity.
		500	500	9/30/86	Cash
					  Dividend income
					To record receipt of $.50 per share cash dividend on common stock investment.
						500	500

12/31/86	Investment in common stock Investment income To record increase in equity of common stock investment reported as income by Ester Corporation.	2,000	2,000	12/31/86	No entry		

12/31/87	Investment loss
	  Investment in common stock
	To record decrease in equity of common stock investment reported as net loss by Ester Corporation.
		1,000	1,000	12/31/87	Unrealized loss from decline in market value
					  Allowance for decline in market value
					To record decline in market value of common stock investment to $22 per share.
						3,000	3,000

Figure 15-9   **Comparison of journal entries for investments carried at equity and at cost.**

to record the above transaction in the books of Destra Corporation are illustrated in Figure 15-9 in a parallel listing so that they are easy to compare.

OTHER LONG-TERM INVESTMENTS

In addition to stock and bond investments, a company may invest in other types of assets. For example, land may be held as an investment for future sale at a profit or for future use. While it is unused, a land investment should be classified among long-term investments. When it is put to use, the land should be transferred to fixed assets.

Life Insurance

Companies frequently purchase life insurance on their executives because the unexpected death of a key decision maker may disrupt operations and require considerable expense to replace the executive. Some life insurance policies accumulate a **cash surrender value**, which is the amount that can be obtained by canceling the policy. The cash surrender value builds up with each payment of the insurance premium, so only part of the premium should be accounted for as an expense of the period. For example, if a $1,200 insurance premium is paid, and it increases the cash surrender value of the insurance policy by $500, the entry to record the payment is

July 19	Insurance expense	700	
	Cash surrender value of life insurance	500	
	Cash		1,200
	Paid annual life insurance premium.		

The cash surrender value of life insurance is usually reported among long-term investments in the balance sheet.

Funds

The term "funds" has many meanings

Corporations often set aside cash for specific uses such as future plant expansion, employee pension funds, and bond sinking funds. Such **funds** are usually invested in stocks or bonds to earn income while the funds are waiting to be used. Often the funds are turned over to a trustee, who manages the fund and reports to the company on the fund's earnings. To transfer money to a fund, the company may make the following entry:

Nov. 6	Plant expansion fund cash	100,000	
	Cash		100,000
	Invested in fund for future plant		
	expansion.		

The company may maintain separate records for the fund and keep the fund investments separate from its other long-term investments. For example, if some of the fund cash is used to buy investments, the entries to record the purchase and subsequent receipt of interest income are:

Nov. 19	Plant expansion fund investments	70,000	
	Plant expansion fund cash		70,000
	Bought bonds for plant expansion fund.		
Dec. 15	Plant expansion fund cash	8,000	
	Plant expansion fund income		8,000
	Received interest on plant expansion		
	fund bond investments.		

SUMMARY   Businesses may acquire bonds and stock of corporations with the intent of holding the investments for a long time. The **investor**, who buys the securities issued by the **investee**, may wish to earn income from such securities, provide funds to the investee, or obtain some degree of control over the investee's operations.

When long-term bond investments are acquired at a premium or discount, the entire cost of the bonds, including any commission paid, is recorded in the Bond Investment account. The premium or discount is amortized over the life of the bond investment in order to measure properly the amount of interest income earned. Either straight-line or effective interest amortization may be used to amortize bond premium or discount.

Deep-discount bonds selling at very low prices because of low coupon interest rates should be amortized using the effective interest method because the straight-line method may distort the reported interest income. Bond discount amortization is sometimes called **discount accumulation** because the amounts amortized are added to the bond investment account. By the time investments mature, the discount or premium is amortized, and the investment account balance is the same as the face value of the bonds. If bond investments are sold prior to maturity, a gain or loss may have to be recorded on the sale.

The method used to account for long-term stock investments depends on the percentage of the investee's stock owned by the investor. With less than 20 percent ownership, the investment is accounted for at **lower of cost or market**. If the investor owns between 20 and 50 percent of the investee's outstanding common stock, the investment should be accounted for by the **equity method**. With more than 50 percent ownership, the investor has control of the investee, and the investment should be **consolidated**.

Long-term investments of less than 20 percent of the outstanding stock of the investee are accounted for in the same way as temporary equity investments except for losses from decline in market value. Declines in market value are recorded in the period in which they occur, but instead of reporting a loss in the income statement, the investor reports **unrealized losses** in the capital section of the balance sheet where they are deducted from total capital. Subsequent recoveries of unrealized losses reduce the capital deduction, but increases in market value above cost are not recorded. Cash dividends are recorded as dividend income. Stock dividends are not income, and when they are received, the cost per share of stock declines. Gains or losses on subsequent sales of stock on which stock dividends have been received are calculated on the basis of cost adjusted for the stock dividend.

The **equity method** of accounting for long-term investments is based on the assumption that the investor has significant influence over the operations of the investee. The investment is initially recorded at cost but should be carried at an amount equal to the ownership percentage times the book value recorded by the investee. If cost is not the same as the amount of underlying book value, any **excess of cost over book value** or **excess of book value over cost** is amortized. When the investee reports net income, the investor increases the investment account by his share of the reported income and records **investment income**. When the investee reduces owners' equity by paying a dividend, the investor reduces the investment account when the dividend is received. As the investee's capital balance changes, the investor's investment account also changes so that its balance always reflects the investor's percentage interest in the owners' equity of the investee.

Other long-term investments of corporations include investment in assets such as land, **cash surrender value of life insurance**, and **funds**, such as bond sinking funds and other funds established for specific purposes.

KEY TERMS

cash surrender value of life
  insurance *(623)*
consolidation *(613)*
current yield *(599)*
deep discount bonds *(604)*
discount accumulation *(605)*
equity method *(613, 616)*
excess of book value over
  cost *(621)*
excess of cost over book
  value *(620)*

funds *(624)*
investee *(599)*
investor *(599)*
lower of cost or market *(613)*
parent *(613)*
proxy *(616)*
subsidiary *(613)*
unrealized loss from decline in
  market value *(614)*
yield to maturity *(599)*

QUESTIONS

1. Explain the difference between coupon yield, current yield, and yield to maturity on bond investments.

2. What determines whether an investment is classified as temporary or long-term?

3. Why are investors willing to pay more than face value for some bond investments?

4. Explain the characteristics of a deep-discount bond.

5. Describe three classifications of equity investments based on the percentage of ownership.

6. Parent Corporation owns all the preferred stock of another company. What method should be used to account for this investment?

7. What is the main difference between accounting for temporary and long-term equity investments at lower of cost or market? What determines whether equity investments are classified as temporary or long-term?

8. What is meant by the term excess of cost over book value of stock investment?

9. Describe briefly the basic procedures of accounting for common stock investments by using the equity method.

10. What is cash surrender value of life insurance?

11. A company holds 30 percent of the outstanding common stock of another corporation as an investment in its bond sinking fund. How should this investment be accounted for?

12. (AICPA) A company's long-term portfolio of marketable equity securities consists of the common stock of one company. At the end of the prior year the market value of the security was 50 percent of original cost, and the effect was properly reflected in a valuation allowance account. However, at the end of the current year the market value of the security had appreciated to twice the original cost. The security is still considered long-term at year end. What is the effect of the price increase upon classification, book value, and current year earnings in this situation?

EXERCISES

Ex. 15-1 **Bond premium with straight-line amortization.**   On April 1, 1985, Stanley Company acquired $100,000 of 14 percent bonds as a long-term investment for $102,070. The bonds pay interest on April 1 and October 1, yield 13 percent to maturity, and mature on September 30, 1987. The company's accounting period ends on December 31, and it uses the straight-line method of bond premium amortization.

Required: Record the purchase of the bonds, receipt of interest in October, interest accrual on December 31, and interest receipt on April 1, 1986.

Ex. 15-2 **Bond premium with effective interest amortization.**   Refer to the data in Exercise 15-1 on Stanley Corporation's purchase of bonds, but assume that the company uses the effective interest method of bond premium amortization.

Required: Record the purchase of the bonds, receipt of interest in October, interest accrual on December 31, and interest receipt on April 1, 1986.

Ex. 15-3 **Bond discount with straight-line amortization.**   On May 31, 1985, Gilkie Company acquired $200,000 of 12 percent bonds as a long-term investment for $195,176. The bonds pay interest on May 31 and November 30, yield 13 percent to maturity, and mature on May 31, 1988. The company's accounting period ends on December 31, and it uses the straight-line method of bond discount amortization.

Required: Record the purchase of the bonds, receipt of interest in November, interest accrual on December 31, and interest receipt on May 31, 1986.

Ex. 15-4 **Bond discount with effective interest amortization.**   Refer to the data in Exercise 15-3 on Gilkie Corporation's purchase of bonds, but assume that the company uses the effective interest method of bond discount amortization.

Required: Record the purchase of the bonds, receipt of interest in November, interest accrual on December 31, and interest receipt on May 31, 1986.

Ex. 15-5   **Premium amortization table.**   On October 31, 1985, Fental Company acquired $10,000 face value of 12 percent bonds at 101¾, to yield 11 percent to maturity. The bonds pay interest on April 30 and October 31, and mature on October 31, 1987. The company uses the effective interest method of bond premium amortization.

Required:
   a.   Prepare a table of bond premium amortization for the life of the bonds.
   b.   Record the bond acquisition, interest accrual on December 31, 1985, and interest receipt during 1986.

Ex. 15-6   **Bonds acquired at premium between interest payment dates.**   On January 15, 1985, Kevin & Kline, Inc., acquired $100,000 face value, 15 percent bonds at 110¼ plus accrued interest as a long-term investment. The bonds pay interest on May 31 and November 30 and mature on May 31, 1989. They yield 12 percent to maturity. The company uses the effective interest method of premium amortization.

Required: Record the acquisition of the bonds and the receipt of interest in May and November of 1985.

Ex. 15-7   **Bond investment at discount.**   On April 1, 1985, Plover Company acquired $10,000 face value, 11.3 percent bonds as a long-term investment at the market price of 97 to yield 12.3 percent to maturity. The bonds pay interest on April 1 and October 1 and mature on April 1, 1989.

Required:
   a.   Record the purchase of the bonds.
   b.   Record the collection of interest in October and interest accrual on December 31, 1985, assuming straight-line amortization of discount.
   c.   Record the collection of interest in October and interest accrual on December 31, 1985, assuming effective interest amortization of discount.

Ex. 15-8   **Sale of bond investments.**   On July 1, 1985 Polovino Corporation owned $300,000 of National Electronics 11 percent debentures. The book value of the bonds and their purchase dates are as follows:

	Book Value
$100,000 bought July 19, 1981	$ 97,200
100,000 bought February 24, 1983	98,600
100,000 bought June 8, 1984	101,000

The bonds mature in 1996 and pay interest on July 1 and December 31. On July 1, 1985, after receiving the interest on the bonds, Polovino sold $160,000 face value of its bonds at 99, delivering all the bonds bought on June 8, 1984, and part of those bought on February 24, 1983.

Required:
   a.   Record the sale of the bonds, assuming specific identification of investments.
   b.   Record the sale of the bonds, using a FIFO assumption.

Ex. 15-9   **Purchase and partial sale of bonds.**   On January 31, 1985, Aloha Corporation acquired $100,000 of 12 percent bonds at 97 as a long-term investment. The bonds pay interest on January 31 and July 31 and mature on January 31, 1995. The company uses straight-line amortization of bond discount.

On September 30, 1985, Aloha Corporation needed cash and sold $40,000 of its bond investment at 99 plus accrued interest.

On October 31, 1985, the company sold the remaining $60,000 of its bond investment at 96.

Required:
  a. Record the purchase of the bonds, receipt of interest in July, and sale of the bonds.
  b. Discuss what happened to market interest rates between the purchase date of the bond, the first sale, and the second sale.

Ex. 15-10   **Correction of errors in bond accounting.**   On April 30, 1985, Juliett Company bought $10,000 of 9 percent bonds as a long-term investment for $7,984. The bonds pay interest on April 30, and October 31, mature on April 30, 1991, and yield 14 percent to maturity. On October 31, when the company received interest on the bonds it failed to amortize the discount and recorded interest income at $450. On December 31, 1985, the company sold its bonds at 85 plus accrued interest and made the following entry to record the sale:

Cash	8,650	
Gain on sale of bonds		516
Investment in bonds		7,984
Interest income		150

Required:
  a. Prepare the entries needed to correct the errors made by Juliett Company assuming the company uses straight-line discount amortization.
  b. Prepare the entries needed to correct the errors made by Juliett Company assuming the company uses effective interest amortization.

Ex. 15-11   **Purchase and sale of equity securities.**   Kolinar Company had the following transactions in its long-term equity securities portfolio during the year:

July 1 Purchased 1,000 shares Fumm Corporation common stock for cash at $40 per share and paid a commission of $180.
     31 Received a dividend of $.80 per share on the Fumm stock.
Sept. 3 Sold 600 shares of Fumm common for $42.50 per share and paid a commission of $100.
Dec. 31 At the end of the accounting period, Fumm common stock is trading in the market at $39.50 per share.

Required:
  a. Record the above transactions in the general journal.

    b. Prepare the necessary adjusting entry on December 31.

    c. Show how the investment related accounts should be reported in the balance sheet on December 31.

Ex. 15-12   **Valuation of equity securities.**   Soretti Company's long-term investment portfolio of equity securities contains the stocks of two corporations, whose costs and market prices per share are as follows:

		Market Value Per Share on December 31		
	Cost	**1985**	**1986**	**1987**
200 shares Gleam Corp.	$2,600	$12.00	$11.50	$16.00
400 shares Flitt Corp.	5,450	15.00	15.75	14.25
Total cost	$8,050			

Required: Prepare adjusting entries on December 31, 1985, 1986, and 1987.

Ex. 15-13   **Stock dividend on long-term investment.**   Smoley Company owns 500 shares of Burky Photo Corporation common stock which it acquired several years ago at $89.25 per share as a long-term investment. During the current year the following occurred:

    a. Burky Photo declared and paid a cash dividend of $4 per share in March.

    b. In May Burky Photo issued a 5 percent stock dividend.

    c. Smoley sold 100 shares of its Burky Photo common stock at $90 per share in August.

    d. Burky Photo declared and paid a cash dividend of $4 per share in November.

    e. On December 31, Burky Photo common stock is trading in the market at $87 per share.

Required: Prepare the journal entries needed on the books of Smoley Company to reflect the above events.

Ex. 15-14   **Accounting method for equity investments.**   Below are descriptions of various long-term investments, their acquisition cost, and their current market value.

    a. 10,000 shares of common stock acquired at $25 per share. Market value is $32 per share, and the investee has 1,000,000 shares outstanding.

    b. 40,000 shares of common stock acquired at $30 per share. Market value is $28 per share. The investee has outstanding 100,000 shares of common and 80,000 shares of preferred.

    c. 20,000 shares of common stock acquired at $50 per share. Market value is $60 per share, and 75,000 shares are outstanding.

    d. 80 percent of the outstanding preferred shares of a corporation acquired at $101 per share. Market value is $93 per share.

    e. 40,000 shares of common stock acquired at $45 per share. Market value is $37 per share, and 50,000 shares are outstanding.

f.   5,000 shares of common stock acquired at $39 per share. Market value is $44 per share, and there are 40,000 shares outstanding. The investor just sold another 5,000 shares, and until now carried the investment at equity.

g.   A portfolio containing 10 different common and preferred stocks, each representing less than 5 percent of the outstanding stock of its issuer. Total cost of the portfolio is $75,000, and the market value is $73,400. Six of the stocks in the portfolio have increased in value, and four have decreased since the purchase date.

h.   All the outstanding stock of a small corporation that has only common stock issued. The cost is $80 per share, and there is no market value.

i.   10,000 shares of common stock acquired at $19 per share. Market value is $12 per share. The investee has outstanding 80,000 shares of common and 35,000 shares of preferred.

j.   45,000 shares of common stock, which was acquired in three purchases of 15,000 shares each at a total cost of $1,400,000. Market value is $30 per share, and there are 100,000 shares outstanding.

k.   10,000 shares bought at $5 per share, 10,000 at $8 per share, and 10,000 at $6 per share. Market value is $7 per share, and the investee has 300,000 shares outstanding.

l.   100,000 shares acquired at a cost of $22.50 per share. Market value is $24.75 per share. The issuer has outstanding 150,000 shares of common stock and no preferred stock.

Required: Set up a table as illustrated and list vertically the letters **a** to **l**. For each type of investment, place a check mark in the table to indicate the proper accounting method for reporting the investment.

	Consolidated	Equity Method	Cost	Market
a.				

Ex. 15-15   **Investment in common stock.**   On January 3 Faust Corporation acquired 20,000 shares of the common stock of Lucifer Corporation at $40 per share which is the stock's book value. On September 6 Lucifer declared and paid a cash dividend of $1.20 per share on its common stock. On December 31 when Lucifer common stock traded in the market at 37 per share, the company reported net income of $400,000.

Required:
a.   Record the above long-term investment transactions of Faust Corporation, assuming Lucifer has 800,000 shares outstanding.
b.   Record the above long-term investment transactions of Faust Corporation, assuming Lucifer has 80,000 shares outstanding.

Ex. 15-16   **Equity method with excess of cost over book value.**   On February 1, 1985, Winner Company purchased 25 percent of the outstanding common stock of Leiser Corporation for $120,000 as a long-term investment. Leiser has outstanding 40,000 shares with a book value of $10 per share. Winner amortizes the excess of cost over book value of its investment over 20 years.

On December 31, Leiser reported a net loss of $48,000 for the year. It paid no dividends in 1985, but on March 10, 1986, the company paid a dividend of $.50 per share, and at the end of 1986 reported net income of $60,000.

Required: Prepare the journal entries for Winner to reflect the above facts.

Ex. 15-17 **Life insurance and funds.** Sure-Life Corporation carries life insurance on its president. The insurance policy has a cash surrender value of $8,300. On June 3 the company pays the annual premium of $900, which increases the cash surrender value by $430. On July 2 the company transferred $30,000 cash into a fund for future equipment replacement. On July 15 the equipment replacement fund, which is managed by the company, invested $20,000 in 400 shares of common stock and $10,000 in 11 percent bonds, both carried as long-term investments.

Required: Record the payment of the insurance premium, investment in the fund, and investment by the fund.

PROBLEMS

P. 15-1 **Purchase and sale of bonds at discount.** Slidder Company acquired $80,000 of 9 percent bonds for $77,000 as a long-term investment on April 30, 1985, to yield 10 percent to maturity. The bonds pay interest on April 30 and October 31 and mature on April 30, 1990. The company uses the straight-line method to amortize bond discount. Its accounting period ends on December 31. On October 31, 1986, Slidder Company sold its bond investment at 98.

Required: Record the purchase of the bonds, the receipt of interest and interest accrual in 1985 and 1986, and the sale of the bonds.

P. 15-2 **Purchase and sale of discounted bonds.** Refer to the data on Slidder Company's bond investment in Problem 15-1, and assume that the company uses the effective interest method to amortize discount on bond investments.

Required: Record the purchase of the bonds, the receipt of interest and interest accrual in 1985 and 1986, and the sale of the bonds.

P. 15-3 **Accounting for bonds acquired at a premium.** Belrose Company acquired $50,000 of 12 percent bonds for $51,710 plus accrued interest as a long-term investment on April 15, 1985. The bonds pay interest on May 31 and November 30 and mature on May 31, 1992. The effective yield on these bonds is 11 percent.

On June 30, 1986, the company sold the bond investment at 99½. The company uses the straight-line method to amortize bond premium. Its accounting period ends on December 31.

Required: Record the acquisition of the bonds, the receipt of interest and interest accrual from the date of purchase to the date of sale, and the sale of the bonds.

P. 15-4 **Bond discount amortization table.** On January 31, 1985, Tefra Corporation acquired as a long-term investment $100,000 face value of 9 percent bonds for

$91,689 to yield 13 percent to maturity. The bonds pay interest on January 31 and July 31 and mature on July 31, 1987. The company uses the effective interest method to amortize bond discount.

Required:
    a. Prepare a bond discount amortization table for the remaining life of the bond investment.
    b. Journalize the bond purchase and the receipt of the first interest payment.

P. 15-5   **Bond premium amortization table.**   Local 696 of the United Retailers Union bought $100,000 face value of 12.6 percent bonds as a long-term investment for its pension trust on January 31, 1985. The cost of the investment was $102,548, to yield 11.4 percent to maturity. The bonds pay interest on January 31 and July 31 and mature on July 31, 1987. The pension trust uses the effective interest method to amortize bond premium.

Required:
    a. Prepare a bond premium amortization table for the remaining life of the bond investment.
    b. Journalize the bond purchase and the receipt of the first interest payment.

P. 15-6   **Effective interest accounting for bonds acquired at a premium.**   On April 15, 1985, Frumius Company acquired $50,000 of 12 percent bonds for $51,710 as a long-term investment. The bonds pay interest on April 15 and October 15 and mature on October 15, 1992. The effective yield on these bonds is 11 percent. The company uses the effective interest method to amortize bond premium.

    On December 1, 1986, the company sold the bond investment at 99½. The company's accounting period ends on December 31.

Required: Record the acquisition of the bonds, the receipt of interest and interest accrual from the date of purchase to the date of sale, and the sale of the bonds.

P. 15-7   **Investment in equity securities.**   The long-term stock portfolio of Chan Hu Li Company consists of the following equity securities carried at cost on December 31, 1985:

    700 shares Lee-King Wok Company common, $55,650
    500 shares Ki Lee Corporation common,   10,000

During 1986 the following transactions took place:

Jan. 14 Bought 200 shares of Finkelstein Imports, Inc., common at $50 per share.
Mar. 15 Sold 200 shares Lee-King Wok at $74 per share.
Apr. 30 Received $.50 per share cash dividend on Ki Lee stock.
July   9 Received 6 percent stock dividend on Lee-King Wok stock.
Oct. 28 Sold 200 shares Lee-King Wok stock at $79 per share.
Dec. 31 Market price per share of stocks on this date is

        Lee-King Wok $77.00
        Ki Lee   17.50
        Finkelstein   51.00

Required:

   a. Journalize the above transactions, including any year-end adjustments, if necessary.
   b. Show how the relevant information should be reported in the balance sheet on December 31, 1985.

P. 15-8   **Investments in common stock.**   Freemore Corporation had the following long-term investment transactions during the current accounting period:

Jan.   4 Acquired 10,000 of Falco Corporation common stock at $47.25 per share. Falco has outstanding 200,000 shares of stock with a book value of $15 per share.

       11 Acquired 15,000 shares of Driwel Oil Corporation common stock at $25 per share. Driwel has outstanding 60,000 shares of stock with a book value of $20 per share. The excess of cost over book value is attributable to goodwill with a 5-year life.

Feb.   8 Acquired 5,000 shares of Byt Industries, Inc. common stock at $50 per share from one of the owners of this closely held company. Byt has outstanding 15,000 shares of stock with a book value of $50 per share.

May   7 Received $1 per share cash dividend on Falco stock.

Oct.   3 Sold 4,000 shares of Falco Corporation stock at $50 per share.

Oct.   22 Received 5 percent stock dividend on Falco common. The stock is trading in the market at $48 per share.

Nov.   9 Received $1.50 per share cash dividend on Driwel common.

Dec.   5 Sold 1,000 shares of Falco common at $47 per share.

Dec.   31 Driwel reported net income of $160,000 for the year ending December 31. Byt reported a net loss of $45,000 for the same period. The market value of Driwel common is $24 per share, and the market value of Falco common is $43.75 per share. Byt stock does not trade in the market.

Required: Prepare journal entries on the books of Freemore Corporation to reflect all of the above events.

P. 15-9   **Investment carried at equity.**   On January 14, 1985, Elmira Company acquired 4,000 shares of Mullin Company common stock at $90 per share as a long-term investment. Mullin has 10,000 shares of stock outstanding, with a book value of $75 per share. On June 12, 1985, Mullin Company paid a cash dividend of $.25 per share on its common stock, and on November 15, 1985, it paid another cash dividend of $.30 per share.

   On December 31, 1985, Mullin Company reported net income of $80,000 for the year. During 1986 no cash dividends were paid, but on March 5 Mullin distributed a 10 percent stock dividend, and on December 31, 1986, reported a net loss of $30,000 for the year. Elmira Company accounts for its investment in Mullin stock on the equity basis and amortizes any excess of cost over book value of shares over a period of 10 years.

Required: Record the above events in the general journal of Elmira Company.

P. 15-10   **Investment in common stock at equity.**   On January 7, 1985, Miller Company acquired 15,000 shares of Elmer Company's common stock, which represents 30 percent of the outstanding shares of Elmer. The book value of the shares is $40, but Miller paid $48 per share and plans to amortize the excess over a period of 10 years. On December 31, 1985, Elmer Company reported a net loss of $90,000 for the year. Next year's operations were better, however, and Elmer paid a dividend of $.25 per share on July 14, 1986. For the year ending December 31, 1986, Elmer reported net income of $150,000.

Miller Company sold 1,000 shares of its stock investment on January 16, 1987, to Elmer Company for $50 per share, to be held as treasury stock.

Required: Journalize the above events in the books of Miller Company.

P. 15-11   **Investment accounted for at equity and cost.**   On January 3, 1985, Martine Company acquired a 40 percent interest in the common stock of Rachel Corporation, by buying 4,000 shares in the market at $32 per share. The book value of Rachel stock is $30 and the excess of cost over book value is attributed to goodwill with a 10-year life. On September 4, 1985, Rachel paid a cash dividend of $.75 per share, and on December 31 reported net income of $40,000.

On January 8, 1986, Martine Company sold 3,000 shares of its Rachel Corporation common stock at $38 per share. On August 15, 1986, Rachel paid a cash dividend of $1 per share and reported net income of $50,000 on December 31. At the end of 1986 Rachel Corporation common stock was selling in the market at $40 per share.

Required: Journalize the above events on the books of Martine Company.

P. 15-12   **Change from equity method to LCM.**   On February 6, 1985, Tory Company acquired 35,000 shares of Calt Corporation common stock at $15 per share as a long-term investment. Calt has outstanding 100,000 common shares with a total book value of $1,200,000. On October 3 Calt paid a dividend of $1.60 per share on its common stock, and on December 31, 1985, it reported net income of $250,000. Tory Company attributes the excess of cost over book value of its investment to goodwill with a 10-year life.

On January 6, 1986, Calt paid a cash dividend of $2.00 per share on its common stock. Tory Company needed funds for a new project and sold 30,000 shares of its Calt common stock at $20 per share on February 18, 1986. Calt paid another cash dividend of $2 per share on October 10, 1986, and reported net income of $285,000 for the year ended December 31, 1986. At the end of 1986 Calt common was selling at $18 per share.

Required: Prepare the necessary journal entries to reflect the above facts on the books of Tory Company.

CASES

Case 15-1   **Investment portfolio.**
Until last year, Teasdale Construction Company was a large, closely held corporation which had been in business for ten years. In 1985 the company had its first public offering of stock, and it now requires an audit of its books so that it can issue its annual report. The company has always maintained an extensive portfolio of stock and bond investments, and you are assigned to audit its investments and determine what amounts are to be reported. The company's controller provides you with the following information:

Date Bought	Company Name	Shares or Face Value	Cost	12/31/85 Mkt. Price	Date Sold	Sale Proceeds
3/19/83	Alpha Co. common	3,000	$ 90,000	$ 28.25		
6/24/83	Bravo Corp. pfd.	1,200	122,100	103.50		
4/30/84	Charlie Co. 9% bonds	$10,000	9,600	94		
8/16/84	Delta Co. common	800	36,800	54.00	2/17/85	$40,800
10/31/84	Echo, Inc. common	1,000	24,000	24.75		
1/3/85	Foxtrot Co. common	10,000	150,000	18.75		
4/30/85	Golf Co. 12% bonds	$25,000	25,540	101		
5/31/85	Hot-L Co. 11% bonds	$15,000	14,625	97	11/30/85	13,625
7/11/85	India Inc. common	2,000	32,000	14.00	8/30/85	34,500
7/20/85	Juliet Co. common	1,500	30,000	18.50		
12/28/85	U.S. Treasury bills	$20,000	19,760	98.8		

After examining the data and additional documents, and asking some questions, you ascertain the following:

The costs, market prices, and proceeds of sold securities are correct as listed. Management intends to keep the Echo, India, and Juliet common stock, and the Charlie bonds and U.S. Treasury bills as temporary investments.

Management intends to keep the remaining securities as long-term investments, and of these, Foxtrot common represents a 25 percent interest in the stock of Foxtrot Company. At the time the Foxtrot stock was bought, Foxtrot Company had a book value of $600,000.

The company recorded interest income of $3,725 on its bond investments, including year-end accruals. However, no premium or discount was amortized on any of the bonds. A loss of $1,000 was recorded on the sale of Hot-L Company bonds.

The Charlie Company bonds mature on April 30, 1986. The Golf Company bonds mature on October 31, 1989. Both pay interest on April 30 and October 31. The Hot-L Company bonds mature on November 30, 1987, and pay interest on May 31 and November 30. The company amortizes discount or premium using the straight-line method.

The company recorded dividend income of $16,500 for 1985. Cash dividends per share were received as follows: Bravo preferred, $7.50; Echo common, $1; Foxtrot common, $.60; and Juliet common, $.25. Foxtrot Company reported net income of $120,000 for 1985.

Required: Determine the correct amounts to be reported by the company for the following asset accounts:

> Marketable Debt Securities
> Marketable Equity Securities
> Long-Term Bond Investments
> Long-Term Stock Investments
> Investments in Stock Accounted for at Equity

Determine the appropriate amounts of interest, dividend, and investment income to be reported on the income statement, and the correct amounts to be reported as gains or losses associated with the investment portfolios.

Prepare adjusting entries as needed to correct any incorrect account balances associated with the investment portfolios.

Consolidations

16

A parent company that owns more than 50 percent of the voting stock of a subsidiary company has control over the subsidiary, and typically prepares consolidated financial statements which report the combined operations of both businesses. This chapter explains how the financial statements of several companies can be combined into a single set of consolidated financial statements. When you have finished the chapter, you should understand:

1 The purpose of mergers and consolidations.

2 Several different types of business combinations.

3 The difference between the purchase of a subsidiary and the pooling of interests of two companies.

4 The reporting of the minority interest that arises when one company buys less than 100 percent of another.

5 How to prepare consolidated financial statements for a purchase.

6 How to prepare consolidated financial statements for a pooling of interests.

7 How to consolidate companies when minority interest exists.

8 How to prepare consolidated financial statements on a date subsequent to the original merger.

When a corporation owns more than 50 percent of the outstanding stock of another company, it usually issues **consolidated financial statements** that report the combined operations of the companies. Businesspeople should understand some of the basic principles underlying the preparation of consolidated financial statements because the financial reports of most large corporations are consolidated statements. Accounting for consolidated operations can be complex, and we can discuss only the fundamentals of consolidated financial statements. This chapter provides a back-

$27+3|+3|+28$

ground for understanding and preparing simple consolidated financial statements. More comprehensive aspects of consolidations are covered in advanced accounting courses.

TYPES OF BUSINESS COMBINATIONS

Business combinations are described as mergers, acquisitions, reorganizations, and consolidations. In general a **merger** or **reorganization** is the combining of two separate businesses into one new legal entity. **Acquisitions** and **consolidations** generally describe the combining of the economic interests of two or more business entities, with each maintaining its separate legal corporate status. Whatever the method of business combination, if two or more separate corporations join together but maintain their separate legal status, the term **consolidation** describes the accounting procedures used to prepare financial reports for the combination. Financial statements of two or more corporations are combined into a single financial report when one corporation has a controlling interest in the other, and their businesses are sufficiently similar to be considered economically compatible. Consolidated financial statements report the combined operations of the affiliated companies as if they were one economic business entity although they remain separate legal entities.

Business combinations are classified into several types according to the relationship between the combined businesses. The term **vertical combination** describes several companies in related industries that complement the activities of one another. For example, a lumber company may own a corporation that operates timber tracts and lumber mills, and it may also own a company that builds houses. Such a combination involves the processing of raw materials, the sale of finished lumber to users, and the use of lumber in the final product sold to consumers.

A **horizontal combination** consists of several companies in a similar line of business. For example, a lumber company may own a paint distributor and a company that sells building equipment. In this case all three businesses sell goods to building contractors, but each specializes in a different type of material. Finally, a corporation may own a number of unrelated businesses, in which case it is called a **conglomerate**. An example is a corporation that sells electronic equipment and that also owns controlling investments in an apparel company, a sporting goods company, and a film processing company.

Parent-subsidiary relationships are called affiliates and their financial statements are usually consolidated

Sometimes corporations are formed primarily for the purpose of holding the stock of other companies. Such corporations are known as **holding companies**, and their operations typically consist only of the management and financing of the various businesses whose stock they own. Companies that are combined in a vertical, horizontal, conglomerate, or holding-company relationship are known as **affiliated** companies. The operations and financial position of such affiliated companies are usually combined and reported in a single set of consolidated financial statements, in order to enable users of the statements to evaluate the operation of the entire group of companies.

Sometimes a corporation owns a controlling interest in another company but does not consolidate the other company's operations in its financial reports because the affiliate's business is not related to the parent's operations. For example, a manufacturing company may own several manufacturing affiliates whose financial statements are consolidated. The parent company would probably not consolidate its controlling interest in an insurance business because the businesses are not similar enough or economically compatible. Such an investment is reported in the balance sheet as an investment in an unconsolidated subsidiary and is accounted for by using the equity method discussed in Chapter 15. However, when several dissimilar businesses are combined, they become a conglomerate whose operations are consolidated.

It would be difficult for decision makers to evaluate a business if much of its resources and earning power were reported as equity investments of corporations whose separate financial statements are available only to the parent company. Therefore the parent company prepares consolidated financial statements to enable users of accounting information to evaluate the operations of related businesses as if they were a single company.

Parent-Subsidiary Affiliations

In a parent-subsidiary affiliation, the acquired company maintains its legal existence

A business combination occurs when one company, usually called a **parent corporation**, acquires control of another company, usually called a **subsidiary**. The companies are said to be **affiliated**, but they remain separate legal entities. Each corporation prepares separate financial statements, but the parent corporation issues consolidated financial statements to its shareholders.

When the parent company owns 100 percent of the outstanding common stock of the subsidiary corporation, the subsidiary is said to be **wholly owned**. When the parent owns less than 100 percent of the outstanding stock of the subsidiary, the subsidiary is **partially owned**. In addition to the parent company which is a majority owner, other owners exist, called minority shareholders whose **minority interest** must be reported in the consolidated financial statements.

The basic idea behind consolidations is simple, namely to combine the information from the separate financial statements of the parent and subsidiary into a single set of financial statements. The assets of the subsidiary are added to the assets of the parent and are reported together in the consolidated balance sheet as the assets of a single entity. Similarly the liabilities of each company are added and reported in the consolidated statement as if they were all owed by a single entity to the creditors of the separate companies. The capital accounts of the separate companies, however, cannot simply be added together because the consolidated entity would then report capital that represented, in part at least, its ownership of itself.

To understand the basic concepts of consolidations it is helpful to look at a very simple illustration and examine the various ways that two companies can be consolidated. In Figures 16-1 through 16-5 we show graphically how a consolidated balance sheet is constructed from the separate balance sheets of two companies. Two methods of effecting the business combination, each with and without minority interests, are discussed, together with the accounting problems associated with such combinations. Finally we demonstrate actual accounting procedures for preparing consolidated financial statements for a variety of different business combinations.

REPORTING OF CONSOLIDATIONS

To understand the concept of consolidations, you must first understand the parent-subsidiary relationship and the way that relationship can be presented in the financial statements as if the two firms are a single accounting entity. We use the financial statements of the two companies illustrated in Figure 16-1 to demonstrate various parent-subsidiary combinations.

Sam Company has no liabilities, and all its stock is owned by Sam Smith, who formed the company by investing a patent that he developed. Pam Corporation is a publicly owned company with $60,000 of assets. Pam Corporation offers to acquire the patent owned by Sam Company, and Smith agrees to sell it for $10,000. There are several ways of handling the transaction.

Figure 16-1
Graphic illustration of the separate balance sheets of two corporations prior to a business combination. Pam Corporation can buy the patent from Sam Company, purchase the stock of Sam Company from the owner, or exchange its own stock for the stock of Sam Company.

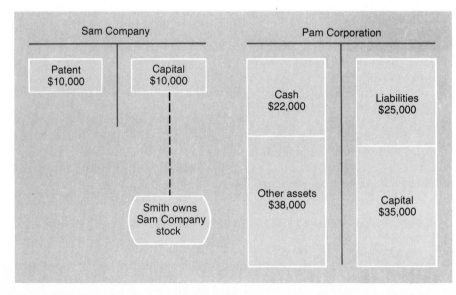

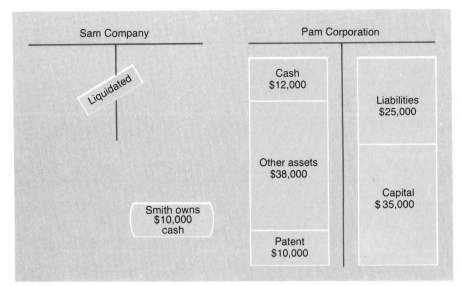

Figure 16-2   **Pam Corporation has purchased the patent from Sam Company for $10,000 cash. Smith has liquidated his company, but there is no reason why he could not leave the cash invested and have Sam Company continue its existence as a separate business entity. No parent-subsidiary relationship occurs in this example.**

Purchase of Assets

Pam Corporation pays $10,000 cash for the patent, whereupon Smith liquidates his corporation by taking the cash and canceling the stock. The result is illustrated in Figure 16-2. Smith has $10,000, and Pam Corporation still has $60,000 of assets, having exchanged its cash for the patent. Sam Company no longer exists. In this situation consolidated statements are not prepared because only a single company remains, and even if Sam Company still existed, Pam Corporation would have no relationship with it.

Purchase of Stock

An alternative to purchasing Sam Company's patent is for Pam Corporation to pay $10,000 directly to Smith in exchange for his stock of Sam Company. The result is that Smith again has $10,000 and no stock, and Pam Corporation still has $60,000 of assets, part of which consists of the $10,000 investment in stock. Since Pam Corporation now owns Sam Company, it has control over the patent it needed. The situation is illustrated in Figure 16-3.

Pam Corporation has the use of the patent regardless of the way it is acquired. But because it does not own the patent directly, but rather owns the stock which represents an interest in the patent, Pam must consolidate

Figure 16-3
Pam Corporation has acquired an interest in the patent by purchasing the entire company that owns it. Pam paid $10,000 to Smith for all the stock of Sam Company. The separate balance sheets of the two companies are combined into one balance sheet as if the two companies were a single economic entity. Pam Corporation owns no more than if it had purchased the patent outright; therefore, the capital accounts of Sam and the investment account of Pam are eliminated in the consolidation. Compare the consolidated balance sheet with the balance sheet of Pam Corporation in Figure 16-2.

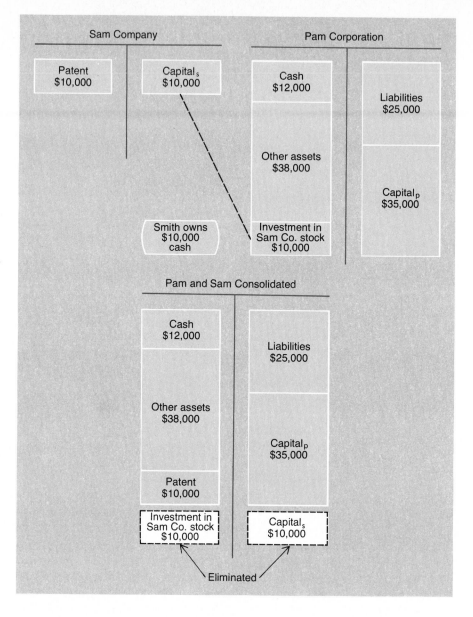

In a consolidation, the parent's and subsidiary's capital balances cannot be added together

its wholly-owned subsidiary's financial statements with its own in order to report its ownership of Sam's assets.

If Pam Corporation consolidates the statements of the two companies simply by combining the separate assets and equities in one statement, the consolidated balance sheet would report assets of $70,000, consisting of Pam's $60,000 of assets and Sam's $10,000 patent. But that does not make sense because Pam Corporation's investment in Sam Company stock represents ownership of the patent; therefore, reporting both the stock investment and the patent as different assets in the balance sheet means reporting the same thing twice. If Pam Corporation paid $10,000 for the patent itself, it would report only $60,000 of assets. It cannot create another $10,000 of assets by buying an indirect ownership in the same patent for the same price. Consequently, when the two companies' balance sheets are consolidated, the double counting of the patent and its ownership interest must be eliminated.

Eliminating the investment account avoids double counting of assets

In the separate balance sheet of the subsidiary, owners' equity is reported as outstanding stock. This same stock is reported as the investment asset in the separate balance sheet of the parent, as shown in Figure 16-3. Because Sam Company's capital account represents Pam Corporation's interest in Sam's assets, the stock owned by the parent company represents an indirect ownership of the patent. Consequently, when the two balance sheets are combined into a consolidated statement, the capital of the subsidiary and the investment account of the parent offset each other and are not included in the consolidated balance sheet. The stock and the patent are one and the same, and by reporting only the patent, there is no double counting. The consolidated balance sheet in Figure 16-3 shows the combined assets of the parent and subsidiary with the parent's investment in stock and the subsidiary's capital account eliminated.

The consolidated company still owns $60,000 of assets, and the consolidated statement is the same as if the patent instead of the stock had been purchased outright. Note that Smith has no financial interest in the consolidated entity.

Pooling of Interests

Pam Corporation can also acquire control over the assets of Sam Company by issuing shares of its own stock in exchange for the stock of Sam Company. In this case, Smith receives Pam Corporation stock with a market value of $10,000. As illustrated in Figure 16-4, Smith becomes a shareholder of Pam Corporation. Pam, which now has $10,000 more of its own shares outstanding, acquires an investment in Sam Company stock. Smith's original interest in Sam Company has now been **pooled** with the interest of the other shareholders of Pam Corporation. Pam Corporation did not use any of its assets to acquire the investment in Sam Company stock, therefore there was no purchase. When the pooling of interests took place, Pam Corporation's assets and owners' equity each increased by $10,000.

When two companies pool their interests and start operating jointly, neither has acquired the other

When the financial statements of Pam Corporation and Sam Company are consolidated as a pooling of interests, the consolidated balance sheet shows that the consolidated entity owns the asset of the subsidiary as well as the assets owned by the parent. Neither company has acquired the other. Their ownership interest has simply been pooled into one company, so their assets and liabilities are pooled also. The investment account of the parent is eliminated together with the capital account of the subsidiary to avoid double counting of assets. Compare this consolidation with the previous one in Figure 16-4. The consolidated company now has $10,000 more assets, and Smith became a shareholder of the consolidated entity.

Up to now we have discussed consolidations involving a wholly-owned subsidiary. When the parent company does not acquire a 100 percent interest in the subsidiary, the consolidated entity must report the interest of the minority of shareholders still holding some shares of the subsidiary.

Figure 16-4
Acquisition by parent of a subsidiary through a pooling of interests. Pam Corporation obtained Sam Company's stock from Smith by issuing its own voting stock in exchange. Smith is now a shareholder of the consolidated entity.

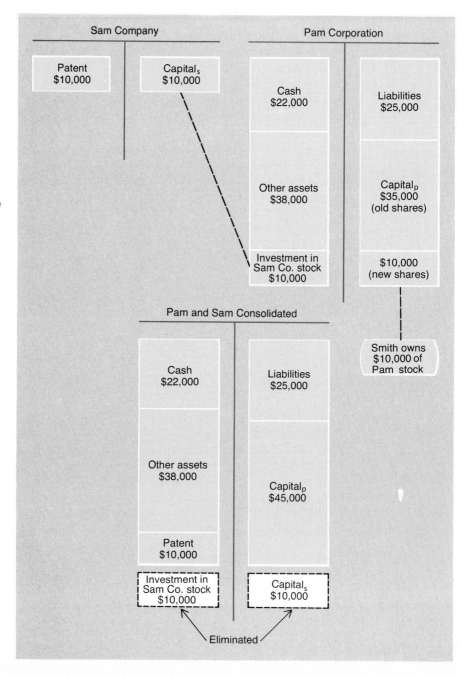

Consolidation with Minority Interest

Figure 16-5 shows the separate balance sheets of two companies and their consolidated balance sheet. S Company has $20,000 of capital stock outstanding, $15,000 of which is owned by P Corporation as a long-term investment, and the remaining $5,000 is held by a minority of shareholders. In the consolidated balance sheet, the assets of S Company are added to the assets of P Corporation to report the combined assets of the consolidated entity, but as usual the investment in S Company stock owned by P Corporation is eliminated to avoid double counting. Similarly the liabilities of S Company and P Corporation are combined to report the combined liabilities of the combined entity. P Corporation holds only 75 percent of S Company stock, so only 75 percent of the capital of S Company is eliminated, and the remaining 25 percent is left to be reported as a **minority interest** in the consolidated financial statement.

Minority shareholders have no interest in the consolidated entity

Minority shareholders are owners of the subsidiary company only and do not own an interest in the consolidated corporation. Their interest is reported between the liabilities and capital sections of the consolidated balance sheet and is viewed as a liability, based on the assumption that part of the assets of the consolidated corporation have been borrowed from the minority shareholders. The minority shareholders do not receive the consolidated financial statements of the parent company but instead are provided with the financial statements prepared by the subsidiary as a separate entity.

Two Ways of Accounting for Consolidations

The examples of purchases and pooling of interests just illustrated are deliberately simple in order to explain the concept of eliminating the parent's investment in stock and the subsidiary's capital when the two companies are consolidated. It is unlikely, however, that an investment can always be obtained at the book value of the subsidiary's stock. Later in the chapter, we explain how to account for acquisitions above and below book value.

Although business combinations may take many forms and may be referred to as mergers, acquisitions, or consolidations, they are all accounted for either as **purchases** or **poolings of interests**.

Purchase.   If one corporation purchases the assets or shares of another, the business combination is accounted for as a purchase. When a **purchase** takes place, the owners of the subsidiary company give up their interest, and the owners of the parent company obtain an interest in the combined business. The shareholders of the subsidiary who sold their stock no longer have an interest in either the subsidiary or the consolidated entity.

One method of consolidating is by means of a purchase

If the subsidiary is obtained by purchase, the investment in subsidiary stock is accounted for by the parent using either the cost or equity methods

Figure 16-5
Graphic illustration of consolidation of a parent and a partially owned subsidiary. The portion of the subsidiary's stock now owned by the parent is shown in the consolidated balance sheet as minority interest.

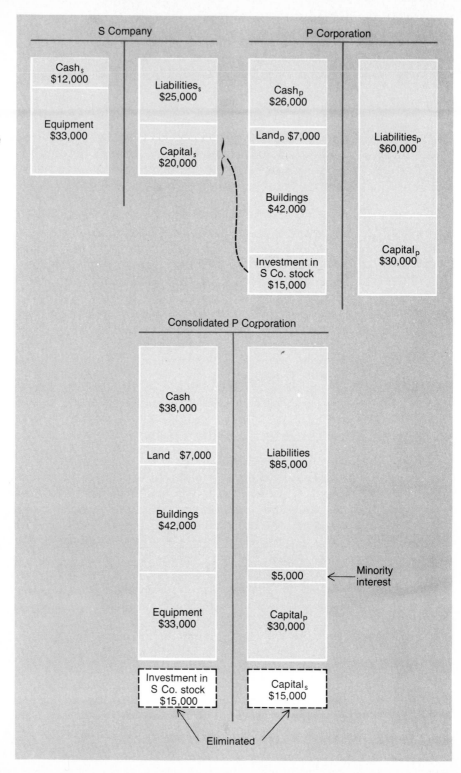

discussed in Chapter 15. The choice depends on the parent's preference. Whether the cost or equity method is used, the consolidated statements are the same.

Pooling of interests.   If two businesses decide to merge their operations into one, and the shareholders of both become the shareholders of the combined entity, a **pooling of interests** has taken place. Voting stock of the parent company is issued to the shareholders of the subsidiary company in exchange for their shares. The shareholders of the subsidiary become the shareholders of the parent. No purchase has taken place, so there is no change in the book value of assets or equities. The parent company therefore carries its investment in subsidiary stock at the book value recorded by the subsidiary for its shares. When the companies are consolidated, the account balances are merely pooled in one statement without any adjustments in asset values. A pooling consolidation results in a larger consolidated entity than the purchase consolidation because no assets are used by the parent to acquire a pooled company, and the issuance of new stock increases total capital.

Another method of consolidating is by means of a pooling of interests

CRITERIA FOR POOLINGS OF INTERESTS

In the history of United States business, there are several periods characterized by large numbers of consolidations. One such wave of business combinations took place during the 1960s when a large number of businesses merged, and the resulting financial statements focused attention on some serious difficulties in reporting adequately the results of consolidated business operations. Few accounting rules had been developed for reporting consolidations, and companies often had to resort to their own ingenuity to decide how to prepare consolidated statements.

To prevent the inconsistencies in reporting that were taking place, the Financial Accounting Standards Board issued several pronouncements.[1] They describe the conditions under which a business combination should be accounted for as a pooling of interest or as a purchase, and also the methods of accounting for intangible assets, notably goodwill that results when a business combination takes place as a purchase.

To qualify as a pooling of interests, a business combination must satisfy certain rigid criteria. If any of these criteria is not satisfied, the combination **must** be accounted for as a purchase. If the criteria are satisfied, the combination **must** be accounted for as a pooling. Among the **criteria for a pooling of interests** are the following:

---

[1] APB Opinion No. 16, "Business Combinations," August 1970, discusses the accounting rules for purchases and poolings of interests. APB Opinion No. 17, "Intangible Assets," August 1970, describes the rules for accounting for goodwill that arises from consolidations.

Criteria for a pooling of interests

1. The combining companies are independent and autonomous, and neither was a subsidiary of another corporation for the past 2 years.
2. The combination is effected in a single business transaction.
3. The parent corporation must issue only common voting stock in exchange for the stock of the subsidiary.
4. The parent corporation must acquire substantially all the voting stock of the subsidiary. This has been interpreted to mean 90 percent or more of the outstanding common shares.
5. The shareholders of the subsidiary acquire the same voting rights as the shareholders of the parent when the combination takes place. Their voting rights may not be restricted in any way.
6. The combined corporation does not make an agreement with any shareholders to reacquire shares issued to them in the combination or to enter into any other financial arrangements for the benefit of the former shareholders of the subsidiary.
7. The combined corporation does not intend to dispose of a significant part of the acquired assets within 2 years.

Again, if stock is issued in an acquisition but one of the pooling criteria is not satisfied, the acquisition must be accounted for as a purchase. It is, therefore, possible to have a combination accounted for as a purchase, although no assets are paid for the acquired company. When stock is issued in a pooling of interests, it is recorded on the parent company's books at the **book value** of the assets acquired. When stock is issued in a purchase, however, it is recorded at the **fair value** of the assets acquired, or the **market value** of the stock, whichever can be more objectively determined. For example, on March 15, Noah Company's common stock trades in the market at $25 per share. On that date Noah Company acquires a controlling interest in Ark Company for $50,000 cash and 10,000 shares of Noah's $1 par common stock. The acquisition is recorded as follows:

Mar. 15	Investment in common stock	84,000	
	Cash		50,000
	Common stock		10,000
	Paid-in capital in excess of par		24,000
	Acquired controlling interest in Ark		
	Company, to be accounted for as a		
	purchase.		

ACCOUNTING FOR CONSOLIDATIONS OF WHOLLY OWNED SUBSIDIARIES

To illustrate accounting for consolidations, we discuss the acquisition by P of 100 percent of S Corporation's common stock as a purchase and also a pooling of interests by P and S Corporations. Figure 16-6 shows the financial statements of P and S Corporations prior to the merger.

	P Corporation	S Corporation
Financial Statements of P and S Corporations Prior to Merger		
Income and Retained Earnings		
Sales	$ 950,000	$ 90,000
Cost of goods sold	500,000	40,000
Administrative expenses	192,000	22,000
Depreciation expense	42,000	9,000
Other expenses	86,000	11,000
Net income	130,000	8,000
Retained earnings, beginning balance	230,000	35,000
	360,000	43,000
Less dividends	60,000	3,000
Retained earnings, ending balance	$ 300,000	$ 40,000
Balance Sheets		
Current assets	$ 374,000	$ 40,000
Receivable from S Corporation	6,000	
Fixed assets	1,295,000	180,000
Accumulated depreciation	(175,000)	(30,000)
Total assets	$1,500,000	$190,000
Current liabilities	$ 140,000	$ 14,000
Payable to P Corporation		6,000
Long-term debt	560,000	70,000
Common stock, $1 par	100,000	10,000
Additional paid-in capital	400,000	50,000
Retained earnings	300,000	40,000
Total equities	$1,500,000	$190,000
Market price of stock	$22 per share	$13 per share

Figure 16-6
Financial statements of P Corporation and S Corporation prior to acquisition of S by P.

Wholly Owned Subsidiary Investment—Purchase

Consolidated financial statements are prepared in a consolidation worksheet, which is used to **eliminate** the appropriate accounts and to combine the remaining accounts. Keep in mind that each corporation issues its own independent financial statements. The data from the separate financial statements are entered into the worksheet and then used by the accountant to prepare consolidated statements.

Past operations are not consolidated in a purchase

When a consolidation is accounted for as a purchase, only the balance sheet can be consolidated on the date of acquisition, because the separate income statements report the results of separate company operations prior to the acquisition. The operations of the combined entities can be consolidated only after the two companies have operated as affiliates. Subsequent to the date of acquisition, all financial statements are consolidated.

P Corporation paid $130,000 cash in order to acquire all the stock of S Corporation. The acquisition is recorded by P with the following journal entry:

Mar. 31	Investment in subsidiary	130,000	
	Cash		130,000
	Purchased 100 percent of outstanding		
	stock of S Corporation.		

Excess of cost over book value is assigned to assets

In keeping with generally accepted accounting principles, the purchase is recorded at cost, which is the fair value of the net assets acquired. The book value of S Corporation stock is $100,000, consisting of $10,000 of common stock, $50,000 of paid-in capital, and $40,000 of retained earnings; therefore, the cost is greater than the book value in this case. The **excess of cost over book value** must be assigned to specific assets that are acquired so that these assets are reported in the consolidated financial statements at their fair value, which is their cost to the parent company. Any amounts that cannot be attributed to specific assets are treated as goodwill, normally called the **excess of cost over fair value** of assets.

The excess of cost over book value assigned to depreciable assets or goodwill is amortized over the remaining useful life of these assets by the consolidated entity. In our example the excess of cost over book value is $30,000, of which $20,000 is attributed to fixed assets that are carried on the books of S Corporation at cost and which have a remaining useful life of 20 years. The $20,000 amount is arrived at by means of an appraisal which indicates that the fair value of certain assets is $20,000 greater than their book value. The remaining $10,000 cannot be attributed to any recorded assets, therefore it is assumed to consist of goodwill. This goodwill will be amortized over the next 10 years in our example.

Consolidation at date of acquisition.   The worksheet for consolidating the balance sheets of P and S Corporations is shown in Figure 16-7. The first two columns contain the statements of the two companies, the next two columns are used for eliminations and adjustments of various accounts, and the last column is the consolidated statement. The income and retained earnings statements are not consolidated, so they are not included in the worksheet.

Consolidation Worksheet for P and S Corporations
100%-Owned Subsidiary Accounted for as a Purchase at Date of Acquisition

	P. Corp.	S. Corp.	Eliminations		Consolidated
Current assets	244,000*	40,000			284,000
Receivable from S	6,000		**c.** 6,000		
Investment in S stock	130,000		**a.** 100,000		
			b. 30,000		
Fixed assets	1,295,000	180,000	**b.** 20,000		1,495,000
Accumulated depreciation	(175,000)	(30,000)			(205,000)
Excess of cost over fair					
value (goodwill)			**b.** 10,000		10,000
Total assets	1,500,000	190,000			1,584,000
Current liabilities	140,000	14,000			154,000
Payable to P		6,000	**c.** 6,000		
Long-term debt	560,000	70,000			630,000
Common stock, $1 par	100,000	10,000	**a.** 10,000		100,000
Additional paid-in capital	400,000	50,000	**a.** 50,000		400,000
Retained earnings	300,000	40,000	**a.** 40,000		300,000
Total equities	1,500,000	190,000	136,000	136,000	1,584,000

* $374,000 less $130,000 paid for investment in S stock.

a. To eliminate investment and capital accounts.
b. To assign excess of cost over book value to fixed assets and goodwill.
c. To eliminate intercompany debt.

Figure 16-7 **Consolidation worksheet on the date of purchase by P of 100 percent of S stock for $130,000. Note that the purchase price is greater than the book value of the subsidiary company.**

The parent's investment account and the subsidiary's capital accounts must be eliminated to avoid double counting. With 100 percent ownership, all the capital of S is eliminated by debiting each capital account for the amount of its credit balance. These debits are coded with the small letter a in the elimination columns. A $100,000 credit is entered to eliminate part of the investment account and to balance the debits. Since there was a $30,000 excess of cost over book value of the subsidiary, all the investment account is not eliminated yet. The excess must be eliminated by assigning it to the appropriate assets.

Excess of cost over fair value is goodwill

Entry **b** eliminates the remainder of P's investment account with a credit of $30,000, and the debit part of the entry assigns $20,000 of this amount to fixed assets and the remaining $10,000 to goodwill, which is usually called **excess of cost over fair value of assets.** Now the assets of S Corporation have been increased to reflect their cost to the **parent** company instead of the book values recorded in the **subsidiary's** books.

Intercompany obligations are eliminated

The balance sheets of the two companies indicate that S Corporation owes $6,000 to P Corporation. The receivable and payable must be eliminated, because the consolidated company should not report an asset and a liability that do not exist when the two companies' statements are combined. The consolidated company in effect owes the money to itself. By eliminating the receivable and payable, only liabilities owed to outsiders are reported. Entry **c** eliminates this $6,000 **intercompany debt**.

The elimination entries are summarized below in journal entry form.

a.	Common stock, S Corporation	10,000	
	Paid-in capital, S Corporation	50,000	
	Retained earnings, S Corporation	40,000	
	Investment in S Corporation		100,000
	To eliminate the capital accounts of S Corporation and the investment in S Corporation stock.		
b.	Fixed assets	20,000	
	Goodwill	10,000	
	Investment in S Corporation		30,000
	To eliminate excess of cost over book value and assign it to undervalued assets.		
c.	Payable to P Corporation	6,000	
	Receivable from S Corporation		6,000
	To eliminate intercompany debt.		

Consolidation entries are not recorded in the books

These journal entries are **not** recorded in the books of either company. They are used only in the worksheet to arrive at consolidated financial statements. When all the eliminations have been entered in the elimination columns, the balance sheet accounts are extended to the consolidated balance sheet column. Note that the consolidated balance sheet contains the assets and liabilities of both corporations and the capital of only the parent company. The double counting of subsidiary stock and investment has been eliminated.

Consolidation subsequent to acquisition date.   Following the date of acquisition, the operations of the parent and subsidiary companies are consolidated and reported as if the two companies were one. Therefore, the income statement and the retained earnings statement must be consolidated, as well as the balance sheet.

When all financial statements are to be consolidated, the process is more easily learned if pre-closing trial balances are used instead of the income statement and balance sheet. The result is a consolidated trial balance which is then used to prepare consolidated financial statements.

In practice, accountants prefer to consolidate the individual financial statements. Whether you consolidate individual statements or pre-closing trial balances, the result is the same. Note that when only the balance sheet is consolidated, as in Figure 16-7, it contains nothing more than the balances in the post-closing trial balance.

Intercompany dividends are eliminated in a consolidation

In Figure 16-8 we present the consolidation worksheet for P and S Corporations 1 year after the acquisition of all of S Corporation's stock by P. Examine the first two columns, showing the separate trial balances of the two companies. Both companies have paid dividends, but because P owns 100 percent of S, P has received all the dividends paid by S. This intercompany income must be eliminated because dividends are the payment to P of part of S Corporation's earnings. The earnings of the two companies are consolidated, so the portion paid out as dividends should

Consolidation Worksheet for P and S Corporations
100%-Owned Subsidiary Accounted for as a Purchase
One Year after Acquisition

	P Corp.	S Corp.	Eliminations		Consolidated
Current assets	304,200	58,800			363,000
Receivable from S	5,000			**b.** 5,000	
Investment in S	130,000			**c.** 30,000	
				e. 100,000	
Fixed assets	1,350,000	180,000	**c.** 20,000		1,550,000
Accumulated depreciation	(220,000)	(39,000)		**d.** 1,000	(260,000)
Goodwill			**c.** 10,000	**d.** 1,000	9,000
Current liabilities	(165,000)	(15,000)			(180,000)
Payable to P		(5,000)	**b.** 5,000		
Long-term debt	(530,000)	(75,000)			(605,000)
Common stock, $1 par	(100,000)	(10,000)	**e.** 10,000		(100,000)
Additional paid-in capital	(400,000)	(50,000)	**e.** 50,000		(400,000)
Retained earnings, Jan. 1	(300,000)	(40,000)	**e.** 40,000		(300,000)
Dividends	60,000	4,200		**a.** 4,200	60,000
Sales	(1,056,000)	(98,000)			(1,154,000)
Dividend income	(4,200)		**a.** 4,200		
Cost of goods sold	600,000	43,000			643,000
Administrative expenses	196,000	25,000			221,000
Depreciation expense	45,000	9,000	**d.** 1,000		55,000
Other expenses	85,000	12,000	**d.** 1,000		98,000
Totals	0	0	141,200	141,200	0

a. To eliminate intercompany dividends.
b. To eliminate intercompany debt.
c. To assign excess of cost over book value to fixed assets and goodwill.
d. To amortize excess of cost over book value.
e. To eliminate investment and capital accounts.

Figure 16-8   Consolidation worksheet of 100-percent-owned subsidiary 1 year after acquisition by parent. The permanent and temporary accounts are consolidated.

not be counted twice—once as net income of S and again as dividend income of P. The elimination of intercompany dividends is made by entry **a** in the consolidation worksheet elimination columns.

Entry **b** eliminates the intercompany debt. The only difference between this entry and the same elimination at the date of acquisition is the amount of the debt, part of which was repaid by S during the year. Entry **c** is the same as entry **b** in Figure 16-7. It assigns to fixed assets and goodwill the excess of cost over book value paid by P Corporation for its investment in S Corporation stock. This entry is made each time a consolidation worksheet is prepared, as long as the assets are on the books of S.

Excess of cost over book value is amortized

A year has gone by since the acquisition took place, however, and the excess of cost over book value must now be amortized. Assuming straight-line amortization and depreciation, $1,000 of goodwill must be amortized ($10,000/10 years), and $1,000 of the excess assigned to fixed assets ($20,000/20 years) must be depreciated in addition to the depreciation of original cost already recorded for its assets by S Corporation. Entry **d** debits depreciation expense and amortization expense for $1,000 each, and the corresponding credits increase accumulated depreciation and decrease the book value of goodwill.

Elimination of the capital accounts is slightly different now than on the date of acquisition. The remaining $100,000 of the investment account must be eliminated against common stock, paid-in capital, and the original balance of retained earnings. Any addition to retained earnings from income earned by S Corporation since it was acquired belongs to the consolidated entity and is not eliminated. In this case the net income has not yet been added to retained earnings, and entry **e** eliminates the $40,000 beginning retained earnings balance of S. The rest of the capital accounts of S are also eliminated by entry **e** in Figure 16-8, which corresponds to entry **a** in Figure 16-7.

After the worksheet is extended to the consolidated column, the resulting trial balance can be used to prepare consolidated financial statements. The consolidated balance sheet reports the assets at their cost to the parent less any amortization or depreciation. The cost to the parent of fixed assets and goodwill is greater than the subsidiary's book value of these assets. Therefore the total depreciation and amortization expense for the consolidated entity is greater than the sum of the amortization and depreciation expense accounts of the separate entities.

Consolidated expenses are greater than the separate expenses of the consolidated companies because of additional amortization

In addition to depreciation recorded by the separate companies, additional depreciation is reported in the consolidated statement for the excess of cost over book value paid by the parent. Also, goodwill, which does not exist in the separate books of either company, is reported in the consolidated balance sheet and is amortized. Any intercompany transactions have been eliminated to avoid double counting of assets, liabilities, revenues, or expenses. Our example contains only the simplest types of intercompany transactions. Many more complicated eliminations are encountered in practice, but their study must be deferred for more advanced accounting courses.

Wholly Owned Subsidiary Investment—Pooling of Interests

Poolings of interests are recorded at book values

When a consolidation is accounted for as a pooling of interests, the separate operations of the two companies are pooled into one operation. Because only stock is exchanged in a pooling, no assets are acquired or given up by either company. Therefore, there is no change in the book values of the accounts of either company. The consolidated financial statements report the continuing operations of both companies as a single entity, and there is no assumption that a new organization has emerged from the pooling. Rather, the assumption is that two continuing businesses have pooled their interests and now report their operations as if they were always one entity. Consequently, on the date of the pooling, all financial statements are consolidated.

Consolidating only the balance sheets but not the income statement would imply that the parent corporation acquired the subsidiary. However, since there is no acquisition but merely a merging of two existing companies into one, implied by a pooling of interests, the consolidated income statement must report the continuing operations of both companies, not just the parent.

The financial statements of both companies, just prior to the pooling of interests, are shown in Figure 16-6, used previously to illustrate a purchase. On the date of the pooling, P Corporation issued 6,000 shares of its common stock to the shareholders of S Corporation in exchange for all the shares of S. The shareholders of S become the shareholders of the pooled companies and receive consolidated financial statements. To record the acquisition of its investment, P Corporation makes the following journal entry:

Mar. 31	Investment in subsidiary	100,000	
	Common stock, $1 par		6,000
	Paid-in capital from consolidation		94,000
	Issued 6,000 shares common stock in		
	exchange for 100 percent of S		
	Corporation shares.		

There is no goodwill in a pooling of interests

The investment is recorded at the book value of the stock acquired by P, consisting of S Corporation's Common Stock, Paid-in Capital, and Retained Earnings account balances. The value in excess of par of the stock newly issued by P is credited to a new Paid-in Capital account as shown above. Notice that Figure 16-6 indicates that the common stock of P and S Corporations trades in the market at $22 and $13 per share, respectively.

The 6,000 shares of P Corporation issued to the owners of S Corporation have a market value of $132,000. The owners, of course, are not willing to give up their 10,000 shares of S Corporation stock for less than its market value of $130,000. On the contrary, they often require a premium above market value. In this case the management of P Corporation recognized that undervalued assets exist in S Corporation, and they were willing to pay accordingly. But the excess of cost over book value is not recorded in a pooling of interests, and assets are not written up when the financial statements of the two companies are consolidated. The fair value of the two companies assets is reflected in the market value of their stock, but the stock and assets remain recorded at book value.

Past operations are consolidated in a pooling

Consolidation at date of acquisition.   The worksheet in Figure 16-9 illustrates the consolidation of the two companies' financial statements on the date of acquisition. Note the difference in the trial balances in Figures 16-7 and 16-9. In Figure 16-7, the acquisition was made by a payment of cash. In Figure 16-9, the acquisition was made by the issuance of stock. Therefore P's Cash account in Figure 16-9 is larger, and its capital accounts reflect the new stock issued in exchange for the investment.

With excess of cost over book value not recorded, fewer elimination entries are required. The intercompany transactions that took place during the past year must be eliminated. In our example, however, S Corporation paid its dividends to its own shareholders in the past year, so these are not eliminated because they were paid to outsiders and not to P Corporation. The intercompany debt of $6,000 is eliminated with entry **a** as before.

When a consolidation is accounted for as a purchase, all the subsidiary's capital accounts are eliminated. This is not the case with a pooling of interest. With no excess of cost over book value in a pooling, the entire investment account is eliminated with a credit of $100,000, shown as entry **b**. The amount of capital eliminated in a pooling of interests depends on the par or stated value of the stock issued in exchange for the investment, and on the structure of the subsidiary's capital account. Generally, only part of the capital accounts is eliminated in a pooling of interests, and the eliminations take place in a specific order. First, the Common Stock account of the subsidiary is eliminated with the $10,000 debit of entry **b** in Figure 16-9. Next, the Paid-in Capital from Consolidation is eliminated. In this example, a debit of $90,000 is sufficient to complete entry **b**. But sometimes the elimination of the entire balance of Paid-in Capital from Consolidation may not be enough to complete the elimination entry. If more debit eliminations are required in order to equal the credit to the Investment account, part or all of the subsidiary's Additional Paid-in Capital is eliminated.

The Retained Earnings account of the subsidiary is eliminated last, but in most cases the other capital accounts have sufficient balances so that the retained earnings balance does not have to be eliminated. In these cases, the retained earnings balance of the subsidiary is combined with the retained earnings of the parent in the consolidated balance sheet. In our example, only the common stock and part of paid-in capital from consolidation must be eliminated. This leaves $4,000 of paid-in capital

Consolidation Worksheet for P and S Corporations
100%-Owned Subsidiary Accounted for as a Pooling of Interests on Date of Acquisition

	P Corp.	S Corp.	Eliminations		Consolidated
Current assets	374,000	40,000			414,000
Receivable from S	6,000		**a.** 6,000		
Investment in S	100,000		**b.** 100,000		
Fixed assets	1,295,000	180,000			1,475,000
Accumulated depreciation	(175,000)	(30,000)			(205,000)
Current liabilities	(140,000)	(14,000)			(154,000)
Payable to P		(6,000)	**a.** 6,000		
Long-term debt	(560,000)	(70,000)			(630,000)
Common stock, $1 par	(106,000)	(10,000)	**b.** 10,000		(106,000)
Additional paid-in capital	(400,000)	(50,000)			(450,000)
Paid-in capital from consolidation	(94,000)		**b.** 90,000		(4,000)
Retained earnings, Jan. 1	(230,000)	(35,000)			(265,000)
Dividends	60,000	3,000			63,000
Sales	(950,000)	(90,000)			(1,040,000)
Cost of goods sold	500,000	40,000			540,000
Administrative expenses	192,000	22,000			214,000
Depreciation expense	42,000	9,000			51,000
Other expenses	86,000	11,000			97,000
	0	0	106,000	106,000	0

a. To eliminate intercompany debt.
b. To eliminate investment and related capital accounts.

Figure 16-9   Consolidation worksheet on the date of acquisition by P of 100 percent of S stock in a pooling of interests. P issued 6,000 shares of its common stock, whose market value is greater than the book value of S. However, the issued stock is recorded at the book value of S and not at its market value. In a pooling of interests, all statements are consolidated on the acquisition date.

from consolidation to be reported in the consolidated balance sheet, as shown in Figure 16-9.

Consolidation subsequent to acquisition date.   As in the case of purchases, the consolidated financial statements prepared subsequent to the business combination must take into account the combined operations of the two companies. The consolidation worksheet illustrated in Figure 16-10 shows the elimination of intercompany dividends paid by S Corporation to its parent during the first year of pooled operations. This is shown as elimination entry **a**. Elimination entry **b** treats the intercompany debt as before, and entry **c** eliminates the investment account and the capital accounts. There is neither a write-up of assets nor goodwill, so there is no additional amortization or depreciation to be recorded. As you can see, pooling of interests consolidations are simpler than purchase consolidations. However, there are more complicated situations than those shown here.

Consolidation Worksheet for P and S Corporations
100%-Owned Subsidiary Accounted for as a Pooling of Interests
One Year after Date of Acquisition

	P Corp.	S Corp.	Eliminations		Consolidated
Current assets	434,200	58,800			493,000
Receivable from S	5,000		**b.** 5,000		
Investment in S	100,000		**c.** 100,000		
Fixed assets	1,350,000	180,000			1,530,000
Accumulated depreciation	(220,000)	(39,000)			(259,000)
Current liabilities	(165,000)	(15,000)			(180,000)
Payable to P		(5,000)	**b.** 5,000		
Long-term debt	(530,000)	(75,000)			(605,000)
Common stock, $1 par	(106,000)	(10,000)	**c.** 10,000		(106,000)
Additional paid-in capital	(400,000)	(50,000)			(450,000)
Paid-in capital from consolidation	(94,000)		**c.** 90,000		(4,000)
Retained earnings, Jan. 1	(300,000)	(40,000)			(340,000)
Dividends	60,000	4,200		**a.** 4,200	60,000
Sales	(1,056,000)	(98,000)			(1,154,000)
Dividend income	(4,200)		**a.** 4,200		
Cost of goods sold	600,000	43,000			643,000
Administrative expenses	196,000	25,000			221,000
Depreciation expense	45,000	9,000			54,000
Other expenses	85,000	12,000			97,000
Totals	0	0	109,200	109,200	0

a. To eliminate intercompany dividends.
b. To eliminate intercompany debt.
c. To eliminate investment and related capital accounts.

Figure 16-10 **Consolidation worksheet of 100-percent-owned subsidiary accounted for as a pooling of interests, prepared 1 year after acquisition.**

Comparison of Purchase and Pooling Results

Figure 16-11 shows the consolidated financial statements resulting from P Corporation's acquisition of S Corporation, with the acquisition accounted for both as a purchase and as a pooling of interest. The statements are taken from the consolidated trial balances in Figures 16-6 and 16-9. The differences between the two methods are also illustrated.

Pooling results in higher earnings than a purchase

The difference in the income and retained earnings statements is obvious because these statements are not consolidated on the date of acquisition in a purchase, and they are consolidated in a pooling. The significant differences, therefore, occur only in the balance sheet. Because cash is used to acquire the subsidiary by purchase, and stock is used to acquire it by a pooling, the current asset balance is much greater with a pooling. On the other hand, there is no goodwill, and assets are not written up to their fair values in a pooling of interests, which means that future

Comparison of Financial Statements for Purchase and Pooling on Date of Acquisition

	Purchase	Pooling	Differences
Income Statements			
Sales	$ 950,000	$1,040,000	$ 90,000
Less expenses	820,000	902,000	82,000
Net income	130,000	138,000	8,000
Retained earnings, Jan. 1	230,000	265,000	35,000
	360,000	403,000	43,000
Dividends	60,000	63,000	3,000
Retained earnings, Dec. 31	$ 300,000	$ 340,000	$ 40,000
Balance Sheets			
Current assets	$ 284,000	$ 414,000	$130,000
Fixed assets	1,495,000	1,475,000	(20,000)
Accumulated depreciation	(205,000)	(205,000)	0
Goodwill	10,000		(10,000)
Total assets	$1,584,000	$1,684,000	$100,000
Current liabilities	$ 154,000	$ 154,000	0
Long-term debt	630,000	630,000	0
Common stock, $1 par	100,000	106,000	$ 6,000
Additional paid-in capital	400,000	450,000	50,000
Paid-in capital from consolidation		4,000	4,000
Retained earnings	300,000	340,000	40,000
Total equities	$1,584,000	$1,684,000	$100,000

Figure 16-11   **Accounting for a consolidation as a purchase or a pooling of interests yields different results. Net income is usually larger for a pooling. Current assets are larger and fixed assets smaller in a pooling, whereas total assets and total capital are usually smaller in a purchase.**

amortization and depreciation expenses will be smaller in a pooling and will leave more reported net income.

The larger amount of assets resulting from a pooling is balanced by a larger amount of capital, because new stock was issued by P Corporation. The newly issued stock is reflected in the consolidated balance sheet. In addition, the retained earnings accounts are combined in a pooling of interests, but in a purchase the retained earnings balance of the subsidiary is eliminated.

Figure 16-12 shows the consolidated financial statements 1 year after the acquisition, taken from the consolidated trial balances in Figures 16-8 and 16-10. Here you see that expenses are greater for the purchase method because more amortization and depreciation is recorded as a result of the subsidiary's assets having been written up to their fair value. Net income is therefore greater with a pooling of interests.

Comparison of Financial Statements for Purchase and Pooling One Year after Acquisition

	Purchase	Pooling	Differences
Income Statements			
Sales	$1,154,000	$1,154,000	0
Less expenses	1,017,000	1,015,000	$ (2,000)
Net income	137,000	139,000	2,000
Retained earnings, beginning	300,000	340,000	40,000
	437,000	479,000	42,000
Dividends	60,000	60,000	0
Retained earnings, ending	$ 377,000	$ 419,000	$ 42,000
Balance Sheets			
Current assets	$ 363,000	$ 493,000	$130,000
Fixed assets	1,550,000	1,530,000	(20,000)
Accumulated depreciation	(260,000)	(259,000)	1,000
Goodwill	9,000		(9,000)
Total assets	$1,662,000	$1,764,000	$102,000
Current liabilities	$ 180,000	$ 180,000	0
Long-term debt	605,000	605,000	0
Common stock, $1 par	100,000	106,000	$ 6,000
Additional paid-in capital	400,000	450,000	50,000
Paid-in capital from consolidation		4,000	4,000
Retained earnings	377,000	419,000	42,000
Total equities	$1,662,000	$1,764,000	$102,000

Figure 16-12 **One year after acquisition differences in income occur between a purchase and a pooling of interests due to additional amortization and depreciation recorded in a purchase. These additional expenses also have an effect on balance sheet items.**

Current assets are still $130,000 greater when the pooling method is used, but the $30,000 that was added to fixed assets and goodwill in the purchase method now amounts to only $28,000, because $2,000 of the original amount has been amortized. Therefore, total assets are $102,000 greater when the pooling method is used. Capital is also greater in a pooling because stock was issued. The retained earnings balances are increased by the net income that has been added less any dividends paid by P Corporation to its shareholders.

The reason managers prefer the pooling of interest method over the purchase method should be clear: Net income, assets, and capital are greater, and the company appears in a much more favorable light to shareholders.

ACCOUNTING FOR CONSOLIDATIONS OF PARTIALLY OWNED SUBSIDIARIES

When the parent corporation acquires less than 100 percent of the outstanding voting stock of a subsidiary, the consolidated financial statements must report the minority interest in subsidiary income and its capital. To illustrate accounting for minority interest, we continue with the example of P and S Corporations, whose financial statements just prior to acquisition are presented in Figure 16-6.

Purchase of 95 Percent of Subsidiary Investment

As we said earlier, on the date of acquisition of a subsidiary by purchase, only the balance sheet can be consolidated. When P Corporation acquires 95 percent of the outstanding stock of S Corporation by purchasing the shares from the owners, P pays the fair market value for these shares, regardless of the book value recorded by S Corporation. The acquisition of 9,500 shares for cash is recorded as follows:

Mar. 31	Investment in stock of subsidiary	123,500	
	Cash		123,500
	Purchased 95% of outstanding		
	shares of S Corporation.		

Minority interest may result from a consolidation

Payment of $123,500 for 95 percent of the stock implies that the entire company has a fair value of $130,000, calculated as

$$\$123,500 = .95 \times \text{Fair value}$$
$$\text{Fair value} = \$123,500/.95$$
$$= \$130,000$$

The purchase price of a majority interest of the company implies a fair value for the entire company

The book value of the subsidiary's total net assets, or capital, is $100,000, and the difference between book value and fair market value of $130,000 is attributed to undervalued assets. As in the previous example, we assume that $20,000 is attributed to fixed assets, and $10,000 to goodwill. However, the parent company acquired only 95 percent of the subsidiary, therefore only 95 percent of $20,000 can be assigned to fixed assets and 95 percent of $10,000 to goodwill. The cost concept does not allow writing up assets above their cost, and the cost of the assets belonging to the minority interest is not changed. The amount of excess to be assigned to fixed assets and goodwill is obtained as follows:

Fair value of company	$130,000
Book value of company	100,000
Excess of fair value over book value	30,000
Multiply by parent's interest	.95
Excess to be assigned to assets	28,500
Assign ⅔ to fixed assets	19,000
Goodwill	$ 9,500

Consolidation at date of acquisition. The worksheet in Figure 16-13 contains only balance sheet accounts because the income statements of the two companies cannot be consolidated at the date of acquisition. Eliminations can take place in any order, and we start by eliminating the $6,000 intercompany debt with entry **a**. Again we remind you that the elimination entries are not entered in the books of either company but are used only in the worksheet.

Consolidation Worksheet for P and S Corporations
95%-Owned Subsidiary Accounted for as a Purchase on Date of Acquisition

	P Corp.	S Corp.	Eliminations		Consolidated
Current assets	250,500	40,000			290,500
Receivable from S	6,000		**a.**	6,000	
Investment in S	123,500		**b.**	95,000	
			c.	28,500	
Fixed assets	1,295,000	180,000	**c.** 19,000		1,494,000
Accumulated depreciation	(175,000)	(30,000)			(205,000)
Goodwill			**c.** 9,500		9,500
Total assets	1,500,000	190,000			1,589,000
Current liabilities	140,000	14,000			154,000
Payable to P		6,000	**a.** 6,000		
Long-term debt	560,000	70,000			630,000
Minority interest				**b.** 5,000	5,000
Common stock, $1 par	100,000	10,000	**b.** 10,000		100,000
Additional paid-in capital	400,000	50,000	**b.** 50,000		400,000
Retained earnings, Jan. 1	300,000	40,000	**b.** 40,000		300,000
Total equities	1,500,000	190,000	134,500	134,500	1,589,000

a. To eliminate intercompany debt.
b. To eliminate investment and capital accounts and create minority interest.
c. To write up assets to fair value.

Figure 16-13 **The purchase of less than 100 percent of a subsidiary results in minority interest reported on the consolidated balance sheet. Only the balance sheet is consolidated on the date of acquisition.**

When the investment and capital accounts of the subsidiary are eliminated, it is necessary to keep in mind that a part of owners' equity belongs to the minority shareholders. In this example the minority owners hold 5 percent of the subsidiary corporation's stock, and their interest therefore amounts to $5,000 (5 percent of $100,000 total capital). The entry to establish the minority interest and eliminate the capital and investment accounts is

b.	Common stock of S	10,000	
	Paid-in capital of S	50,000	
	Retained earnings of S	40,000	
	Investment in S stock		95,000
	Minority interest		5,000

This entry is entered in the worksheet as entry **b**, and you should note that the entry eliminates only $95,000 of the Investment account, leaving a balance of $28,500 ($123,500 cost − $95,000). The excess must also be eliminated, and this is accomplished with entry **c**. The amount added to Goodwill and Fixed Assets to bring their balances to the fair value paid by P is 95 percent of $30,000, or $28,500. In general journal form, entry **c** appears as follows:

A percentage of the subsidiary's total capital is assigned to minority interest

c.	Fixed assets	19,000	
	Goodwill	9,500	
	Investment in S stock		28,500

Consolidation Subsequent to Acquisition Date

Accounting for minority interest subsequent to date of acquisition is not illustrated because it can become quite complicated due to the additional concepts that need to be introduced. For example, part of the subsidiary dividends are paid to minority shareholders, who are also entitled to a portion of current income as well as to a portion of retained earnings and capital. Intercompany transactions involving revenue or expense may have to be eliminated by assigning a part of the revenue or expense to the minority interests. This situation may arise if the subsidiary sells merchandise to the parent at a profit or pays interest on bonds issued by the subsidiary and purchased by the parent. Such transactions are too complex for an introductory textbook.

Partially Owned Subsidiaries—Pooling of Interests

According to the criteria established for poolings, the exchange of voting stock must result in the parent company acquiring substantially all the

Minority interest is small with poolings

stock of the subsidiary company. This has been interpreted to mean that at least 90 percent or more of the voting stock of the subsidiary must be acquired by the parent. If less than 90 percent is acquired, the acquisition must be accounted for as a purchase. Most poolings result in the parent acquiring 100 percent of the subsidiary stock, so that minority interest seldom exists after a pooling of interests, and if it does exist, it is very small. In contrast, the minority interest can be quite large in the case of a purchase, as it is, for example, if the parent acquires just over 50 percent of the subsidiary. Because poolings of interest with minority interest are rare, we do not discuss the accounting for such situations.

SUMMARY

When one corporation owns more than 50 percent of the voting stock of another corporation, the operations of the two are usually reported in **consolidated financial statements**. The two corporations maintain their separate legal entities, but the consolidated statements report their operations as if they were one economic unit.

A **vertical combination** is the merger of companies in several related industries, such as mining of iron ore, smelting of steel, and manufacturing of steel products. A **horizontal combination** involves several companies in the same industry, such as manufacturing or retailing. A combination consisting of several companies in unrelated industries is called a **conglomerate**. Companies organized for the purpose of holding the stock of other companies as their primary assets are called **holding companies**.

The investor company is usually called the **parent** company, and the investee company is called the **subsidiary**. Companies with parent-subsidiary relationships are called **affiliated** companies. Each prepares separate financial statements, which are then consolidated for issuance to the parent's shareholders. A subsidiary may be **wholly owned** or **partially owned**. In the latter case, the **minority interest** must be reported in the consolidated financial statements.

Consolidations may be accounted for as purchases or as poolings of interests. A **purchase** occurs when the parent company pays cash or other assets for the voting stock of the subsidiary, and the owners who sell their stock no longer have an interest in either company. The parent records the investment at its cost, which may include an **excess of cost over book value**. Such excess is the amount paid for goodwill and the fair value of the assets of the subsidiary company in excess of the recorded values carried on the subsidiary's books.

A **pooling of interests** takes place when the parent company issues its own voting stock in exchange for substantially all the subsidiary's voting stock. The owners of the subsidiary become the owners of the parent company when they exchange their shares. The investment in the subsidiary stock is recorded by the parent at the book value of the net assets of the subsidiary company, and there is no recognition of goodwill or write-up of assets to their fair value. No purchase or sale has occurred, the account balances of the two companies are carried forward at their recorded values when they are combined in the consolidated financial statements.

The FASB has issued several pronouncements to clarify the rules for consolidations. They include criteria for purchases and poolings of interest and for the measurement and reporting of intangible assets resulting from business combinations.

At the date of acquisition by purchase, only the balance sheet can be consolidated, because the combined business entity does not have any previous joint operations to be reported. If the combination is a pooling of interests, however, all financial statements are consolidated because there is not a purchase of one business by another, but merely the pooling of two continuing businesses' operations. The parent's investment account and the capital accounts of the subsidiary must be eliminated prior to consolidating the remaining account balances in order to avoid double counting. In addition, any intercompany transactions and debts must be eliminated so that transactions that the combined entity has with itself or debts that it owes to itself will not be reported.

When the investment and capital accounts are eliminated in a combination accounted for as a purchase, **excess of cost over fair value** of assets, or goodwill, often emerges, and some assets of the subsidiary may be written up to their fair values. Subsequent to the date of acquisition, the goodwill and write-ups of assets must be amortized. In a pooling of interests, no write-ups or goodwill are recorded, so there is no additional amortization in subsequent periods. Pooling of interests usually results in higher reported net income and earnings per share, greater amounts of cash and capital, and smaller amounts of long-lived assets than in combinations accounted for as purchases.

KEY TERMS

acquisition (638)
affiliated companies (638)
business combination (638)
conglomerate (638)
consolidated financial statements (637)
consolidation (638)
excess of cost over book value of assets (650)
excess of cost over fair value of assets (650)
holding company (638)

horizontal combination (638)
intercompany debt (652)
merger (638)
minority interest (639)
parent corporation (639)
partially owned subsidiary (639)
pooling of interests (645)
purchase (645)
subsidiary (639)
vertical combination (638)
wholly owned subsidiary (639)

QUESTIONS

1. Under what circumstances should the financial statements of two corporations be consolidated?
2. Discuss the concepts of legal and accounting entities in connection with consolidated financial statements.
3. What is meant by the parent-subsidiary relationship?
4. What conditions usually exist when a controlling interest in a subsidiary is not consolidated by the parent corporation? How is such an interest reported in the parent's financial statements?
5. What conditions exist that require the reporting of minority interest in consolidated financial statements? How is minority interest reported?
6. Describe the conditions that require a business combination to be accounted for as a purchase; as a pooling of interests.
7. What amount is recorded in the investment account of a parent corporation in a business combination effected by a purchase? What amount is usually recorded in the investment account of a parent corporation in a business combination effected by a pooling of interests?
8. Why are investment and capital account balances eliminated when consolidated financial statements are prepared?
9. Why is dividend income received by a parent corporation from its subsidiary not reported in the parent's consolidated financial statements?
10. What happens to asset values when the separate balances of the parent's and subsidiary's assets are combined in a consolidated financial statement prepared on a purchase basis? How does this differ from a consolidation based on a pooling of interests?
11. What are some reasons for higher income and higher asset values reported in consolidated statements prepared as a pooling of interests as compared with statements prepared on a purchase basis?
12. What is the status of the former shareholders of a corporation that has been acquired by a purchase? What is their status in a pooling of interests?
13. Discuss some conditions that must be satisfied in order for businesses to effect a pooling of interests.

EXERCISES

Ex. 16-1 Classification of acquisitions. Below are descriptions of various situations involving business combinations. Using the following codes, indicate whether the parent corporation should consolidate the acquisition as a purchase, a pooling, or not at all: **1**—Purchase; **2**—Pooling; or **3**—Not consolidated.

a. P acquires 100 percent of S common stock for cash.
b. P acquires 90 percent of S common stock in exchange for its voting stock.
c. P acquires 100 percent of S common stock in exchange for its own preferred shares and a note payable.
d. P acquires 40 percent of S stock in exchange for cash and notes.

e. P manufactures appliances and owns an apparel store and a television station that are consolidated. P acquires 100 percent of a shipping line, paying $10 cash and one share of its own voting stock for each share of S stock.

f. P manufactures tractors and owns an electronics manufacturer and a boat manufacturer that are consolidated. P acquires 60 percent of a bank for cash.

g. P is a loan company and owns an insurance company and a bank that are consolidated. P acquires 100 percent of the preferred stock of a finance company in exchange for some of its own common stock.

h. S common stock is trading at $20 per share. P Common stock is trading at $40 per share. P issues two shares in exchange for every three shares of S common stock, acquiring all outstanding shares of S.

i. P owns 100 percent of S stock, which is consolidated as a pooling. It sells 60 percent of this investment for cash.

j. P owned 35 percent of S Company common stock that had been acquired for cash, and acquires the remaining 65 percent in exchange for its own voting stock.

k. P acquires 75 percent of S common stock in exchange for its own voting stock.

l. P acquires 100 percent of S common stock in exchange for its own voting stock. S has 40 percent of its assets invested in land and marketable securities that P wants to sell within a few months.

m. P acquires 100 percent of S common stock in exchange for its own common shares and agrees to purchase its own shares from the former shareholders of S at their option during the next 12 months.

Ex. 16-2   **Consolidation by purchase at book value.**   The condensed trial balances of Paul Company and Saul Corporation on December 31, 1985, are presented below.

Balances Prior to Merger

	Paul	Saul
Current assets	$280,000	$ 50,000
Fixed assets (net)	600,000	170,000
Liabilities	(360,000)	(70,000)
Common stock, $10 par	(450,000)	(100,000)
Retained earnings	(55,000)	(45,000)
Revenues	(700,000)	(90,000)
Expenses	685,000	85,000
Totals	$ 0	$ 0

Paul Company stock trades in the market at $30 per share. Saul Corporation stock trades at $14 per share. On January 2, 1986, Paul Company acquired all of the outstanding shares of Saul Corporation.

Required: Prepare a consolidation worksheet for Paul Company and Saul Corporation, assuming that Paul paid $15 per share in cash for its investment in Saul stock.

Ex. 16-3   **Consolidation by pooling of interests.**   Refer to the data in Exercise 16-2 on Paul Company and Saul Corporation.

Required: Prepare a consolidation worksheet for Paul Company and Saul Corporation, assuming that Paul issued 1 share of its common stock in exchange for every two shares of Saul common in a pooling of interests.

Ex. 16-4   Goodwill in an acquisition. On January 1, 1985, the balance sheets of P and S Corporations appeared as follows prior to P Corporation's acquisition of 100 percent of S Corporation's stock. The market prices of P and S stock on January 2, 1985, were $25 and $20 per share, respectively.

Balances Prior to Merger

	P Corp.	S Corp.
Current assets	$130,000	$ 30,000
Fixed assets (net)	100,000	80,000
Total assets	$230,000	$110,000
Liabilities	$ 90,000	$ 30,000
Common stock, $10 par	100,000	50,000
Retained earnings	40,000	30,000
Total equities	$230,000	$110,000

An appraisal discloses that the fixed assets of S Corporation have a fair value of $85,000. On January 2, 1985, P Corporation paid $105,000 cash for the stock of S Corporation.

Required:
   a.   As a shareholder of S stock, determine the least amount of cash you should accept for your stock. Explain.
   b.   Calculate the amount of goodwill implied by the market price of S stock.
   c.   Calculate the amount of goodwill implied by the price paid by P for S stock.
   d.   Prepare the journal entry for P to record the acquisition.
   e.   Was the acquisition a purchase or a pooling of interests? Explain.

Ex. 16-5   Consolidation with goodwill. Refer to the data in Exercise 16-4 for P and S Corporations.

Required:
   a.   Prepare a consolidation worksheet on the date of business combination on the purchase basis.
   b.   What expenses, if any, not reported by either of the separate companies, should be included in the consolidated income statement one year after the business combination? Explain.

Ex. 16-6   Consolidation worksheet. The common stock of Slinkie Company traded in the market at $20 per share on June 1, 1985. The company had 3,000 shares outstanding, and on this date Pinkie Corporation acquired all 3,000 shares. Immediately after the acquisition, the separate balance sheets of the two companies appeared as follows:

	Pinkie	Slinkie
Cash	$ 50,000	$14,000
Receivable from Slinkie	9,000	
Merchandise	51,000	19,000
Investment in Slinkie stock	60,000	
Fixed assets	130,000	45,000
Accumulated depreciation	(25,000)	(8,000)
Total assets	$275,000	$70,000
Liabilities	$ 49,000	$21,000
Payable to Pinkie		9,000
Common stock, no par	180,000	30,000
Retained earnings	46,000	10,000
Total equities	$275,000	$70,000

Required:

    a. Is the acquisition accounted for as a pooling of interests or a purchase? Explain.

    b. Prepare the journal entry for P Corporation to record the acquisition.

    c. Prepare a consolidation worksheet on June 1.

Ex. 16-7 **Consolidation worksheet.** On March 31, 1985, S Company stock traded in the market at $20 per share. On this date P Company acquired all 3,000 shares of the outstanding stock of S. The separate balance sheets of the two companies immediately after the acquisition are shown below.

	P	S
Cash	$ 75,000	$10,000
Receivable from S	12,000	
Merchandise	63,000	32,000
Investment in S stock	40,000	
Fixed assets	180,000	60,000
Accumulated depreciation	(50,000)	(30,000)
Total assets	$320,000	$72,000
Liabilities	$ 60,000	$20,000
Payable to P Corp.		12,000
Common stock, no par	200,000	30,000
Retained earnings	60,000	10,000
Total equities	$320,000	$72,000

Required:

    a. Is the acquisition accounted for as a pooling of interests or a purchase? Explain.

    b. Prepare the journal entry for P Company to record the acquisition.

    c. Prepare a consolidation worksheet on March 31.

Ex. 16-8 **Consolidation one year after acquisition.** On January 2, 1985, Phil Company acquired all 4,000 shares of Sandra Company common stock for $70,000 cash. The stock had a book value of $60,000, and the excess of cost over book value paid by Phil was attributed to goodwill of Sandra Company with a remaining life of 10 years. On December 31, 1985, the separate trial balances of Phil and Sandra Companies appeared as follows:

	Phil	Sandra
Cash	$ 65,000	$ 20,000
Receivable from Sandra	5,000	
Merchandise	50,000	30,000
Investment in Sandra stock	70,000	
Fixed assets (net)	140,000	90,000
Goodwill		
Liabilities	(90,000)	(55,000)
Payable to Phil		(5,000)
Common stock, no par	(140,000)	(50,000)
Retained earnings	(60,000)	(10,000)
Operating revenue	(400,000)	(100,000)
Operating expenses	360,000	80,000
Totals	$ 0	$. 0

Required: Prepare a consolidation worksheet on December 31, 1985.

Ex. 16-9 **Interpreting a consolidation worksheet.** Carefully examine the following worksheet for P and S Corporations on December 31.

	P Corp. dr (cr)	S Corp. dr (cr)	Eliminations dr	Eliminations cr	Consolidated dr (cr)
Cash	78,000	31,000			109,000
Receivable from S	9,000			a. 9,000	
Accounts receivable	157,000	95,000			252,000
Investment in S stock	175,000			c. 150,000	
				d. 25,000	
Fixed assets	159,000	90,000	d. 20,000		269,000
Accumulated depreciation	(40,000)	(28,000)		e. 2,000	(70,000)
Goodwill			d. 5,000	f. 1,000	4,000
Liabilities	(75,000)	(12,000)			(87,000)
Payable to P		(9,000)	a. 9,000		
Common stock	(100,000)	(20,000)	c. 20,000		(100,000)
Additional paid-in capital	(200,000)	(90,000)	c. 90,000		(200,000)
Retained earnings, Jan. 1	(120,000)	(40,000)	c. 40,000		(120,000)
Dividends paid		10,000		b. 10,000	
Service revenue	(400,000)	(125,000)			(525,000)
Revenue from investment	(10,000)		b. 10,000		
Expenses (aggregated)	330,000	85,000			415,000
Depreciation expense	12,000	5,000	e. 2,000		19,000
Amortization expense			f. 1,000		1,000
Income tax expense	25,000	8,000			33,000
	0	0	197,000	197,000	0

Required:
a. Is the business combination accounted for as a pooling of interests or as a purchase? Explain.
b. Is this worksheet prepared on or subsequent to the date of acquisition? Explain.
c. Explain the reason for each of the elimination entries.

Ex. 16-10 **Statements from consolidated trial balance.** Refer to the consolidation worksheet in Exercise 16-9.

Required: Use the consolidated trial balance to prepare consolidated financial statements for P Corporation in good accounting form.

Ex. 16-11   **Interpreting a consolidation worksheet.**   Carefully examine the following consolidation worksheet for P and S Corporations on December 31.

	P Corp. dr (cr)	S Corp. dr (cr)	Elimination dr	Elimination dr	Consolidated dr (cr)
Cash	205,000	36,000			241,000
Receivable from S	11,000			a. 11,000	
Accounts receivable	157,000	85,000			242,000
Investment in S stock	150,000			b. 150,000	
Fixed assets	159,000	90,000			249,000
Accumulated depreciation	(40,000)	(28,000)			(68,000)
Goodwill		6,000			6,000
Liabilities	(75,000)	(12,000)			(87,000)
Payable to P		(11,000)	a. 11,000		
Common stock	(100,000)	(20,000)	b. 20,000		(100,000)
Additional paid-in capital	(200,000)	(90,000)	b. 26,000		(264,000)
Paid-in capital from consolidation	(104,000)		b. 104,000		
Retained earnings	(120,000)	(40,000)			(160,000)
Dividends distributed		10,000		c. 10,000	
Service revenue	(400,000)	(125,000)			(525,000)
Dividend income	(10,000)		c. 10,000		
Expenses (aggregated)	330,000	85,000			415,000
Depreciation expense	12,000	5,000			17,000
Amortization expense		1,000			1,000
Income tax expense	25,000	8,000			33,000
	0	0	171,000	171,000	0

Required:
a.   Is the business combination accounted for as a pooling of interests or a purchase? Explain.
b.   Is this worksheet prepared on or subsequent to the date of acquisition? Explain.
c.   Explain the reason for each of the elimination entries.

Ex. 16-12   **Financial statement from a consolidation worksheet.**   Refer to the consolidation worksheet in Exercise 16-11.

Required: Use the consolidated trial balance to prepare a consolidated balance sheet and income statement for P Corporation on December 31.

Ex. 16-13   **Consolidation worksheet with minority interest.**   On January 3, 1985, Plinkie Company acquired 80 percent of the outstanding common stock of Slindy Company for $38,000 in a combination which is to be accounted for as a purchase. The excess of cost over book value is attributed to goodwill with a 10-year life. The separate balance sheets of the two companies immediately after the acquisition are shown on the following page.

	Plinkie	Slindy
Cash	$ 72,000	$12,000
Receivable from Slindy	15,000	
Merchandise	65,000	13,000
Investment in Slindy stock	38,000	
Fixed assets (net)	200,000	50,000
Total assets	$390,000	$75,000
Liabilities	$100,000	$20,000
Payable to Plinkie Corp.		15,000
Common stock, no par	200,000	30,000
Retained earnings	90,000	10,000
Total equities	$390,000	$75,000

Required: Determine the amount of goodwill to be recorded in the consolidation and prepare a consolidation worksheet on the date of acquisition.

PROBLEMS

P. 16-1   **Consolidation of a purchased subsidiary.**

	Plugg	Stomp	Plugg	Stomp
	December 31, 1985		December 31, 1986	
Cash	$ 50,000	$ 32,500	$ 57,000	$ 32,000
Accounts receivable	108,000	40,000	132,000	50,400
Receivable from Stomp	4,500		3,000	
Investment in Stomp	160,000		160,000	
Land	28,000	12,000	54,000	12,000
Buildings	180,000		180,000	
Equipment	318,000	220,000	340,000	248,000
Accumulated depreciation	(138,000)	(48,000)	(162,000)	(64,000)
Notes payable	(17,500)	(22,000)	(12,000)	(14,400)
Payable to Plugg		(4,500)		(3,000)
Long-term debt	(240,000)	(90,000)	(216,000)	(89,000)
Common stock	(48,000)	(60,000)	(48,000)	(60,000)
Additional paid-in capital	(192,000)		(192,000)	
Retained earnings	(213,000)	(80,000)	(213,000)	(80,000)
Dividends			21,000	6,400
Sales			(354,000)	(128,000)
Dividend income			(6,400)	
Administrative expense			232,400	73,600
Depreciation expense			24,000	16,000
Totals	$ 0	$ 0	$ 0	$ 0

The December 31, 1985, trial balances of Plugg and Stomp Companies are presented above, immediately after Plugg acquired a 100 percent interest in Stomp by buying all of its outstanding common stock for $160,000 cash. The excess of cost over book value of net assets is attributable $10,000 to equipment and the remainder to goodwill.

Required: Prepare a consolidation worksheet for Plugg and Stomp Companies on December 31, 1985, on the purchase basis.

P. 16-2   **Purchased consolidation one year after acquisition.**   Refer to the data on Plugg Company and Stomp Company in Problem 16-1, which shows the trial balances of the two companies immediately after the acquisition and one year later. The excess of cost over book value of net assets is attributable $10,000 to equipment with a 5-year life and the remainder to goodwill with a 10-year life. Straight-line depreciation and amortization are used.

Required: Prepare a consolidation worksheet for Plugg and Stomp Companies on December 31, 1986, 1 year after acquisition.

P. 16-3   **Consolidation of pooled subsidiary.**   Below are the trial balances of Plum and Sugar Corporations.

	January 2, 1985		December 31, 1985	
	Plum	Sugar	Plum	Sugar
Cash	$ 89,000	$ 52,500	$138,800	$ 47,300
Accounts receivable	126,000	30,000	142,400	49,000
Receivable from Sugar	5,400		3,700	
Investment in Sugar	200,000		200,000	
Land		22,000		22,000
Buildings		65,000		65,000
Equipment	398,000	184,900	433,000	206,400
Accumulated depreciation	(112,000)	(46,000)	(140,000)	(58,000)
Notes payable	(26,400)	(18,000)	(23,900)	(14,000)
Payable to Plum		(5,400)		(3,700)
Long-term debt	(160,000)	(85,000)	(145,000)	(94,000)
Common stock	(95,000)	(70,000)	(95,000)	(70,000)
Additional paid-in capital	(130,000)	(50,000)	(130,000)	(50,000)
Paid-in capital from consolidation	(115,000)		(115,000)	
Retained earnings	(117,000)	(40,000)	(180,000)	(80,000)
Dividends	18,000	8,000	25,000	35,000
Revenues	(342,000)	(98,000)	(372,000)	(120,000)
			(35,000)	
Operating expenses	261,000	50,000	293,000	65,000
Totals	$ 0	$ 0	$ 0	$ 0

On January 2, 1985, Plum Corporation acquired 100 percent of the outstanding stock of Sugar Corporation in a pooling of interests.

Required: Prepare a consolidation worksheet on January 2, 1985, for the pooling of interests.

P. 16-4   **Consolidation of pooled subsidiary after acquisition.**   Refer to the data on Plum and Sugar Corporations presented in Problem 16-3.

Required: Prepare a consolidation worksheet on December 31, 1985, for the pooling of interests.

P. 16-5   **Consolidation of a partially owned purchased subsidiary.**   The December 31, 1985, trial balances of Plaid and Stripe Companies are presented below, immediately after Plaid acquired 90 percent of the Stripe Company common stock by purchasing it in the market for $151,200 cash. The excess of cost over book value of net assets is attributed $15,200 to equipment and the remainder to goodwill.

Trial Balances
December 31, 1985

	Plaid	Stripe
Cash	$ 75,000	$ 26,000
Accounts receivable	110,000	40,000
Receivable from Stripe	2,500	
Investment in Stripe	151,200	
Land		32,000
Buildings		100,000
Equipment	430,000	210,500
Accumulated depreciation	(115,000)	(48,000)
Goodwill		
Notes payable	(18,700)	(23,000)
Payable to Plaid		(2,500)
Long-term debt	(240,000)	(195,000)
Common stock	(100,000)	(80,000)
Additional paid-in capital	(200,000)	
Retained earnings	(95,000)	(60,000)
Totals	$ 0	$ 0

Required: Prepare a consolidation worksheet for Plaid and Stripe Companies on December 31, 1985, on the purchase basis.

P. 16-6 **Consolidation of purchased subsidiary.** The trial balances of Plume and Silke Companies are presented below. On December 31, 1985, Plume acquired all the outstanding common stock of Silke for $220,000 cash. Of the excess of cost over book value of net assets, $20,000 is attributable to equipment with a 10-year life and the remainder to goodwill with a 5-year life. Straight-line depreciation and amortization are used.

	Trial Balances Prior to Acquisition December 31, 1985		Trial Balances One Year after Acquisition December 31, 1986	
	Plume	Silke	Plume	Silke
Cash	$310,000	$ 38,000	$ 95,000	$ 40,000
Accounts receivable	180,000	50,000	230,000	63,000
Receivable from Plume		7,000		5,000
Investment in Silke			220,000	
Land	47,000		90,000	
Buildings	300,000		300,000	
Equipment	580,000	290,000	630,000	340,000
Accumulated depreciation	(230,000)	(60,000)	(270,000)	(80,000)
Notes payable	(25,000)	(15,000)	(20,000)	(18,000)
Payable to Silke	(7,000)		(5,000)	
Long-term debt	(400,000)	(120,000)	(360,000)	(120,000)
Common stock	(80,000)	(90,000)	(80,000)	(90,000)
Additional paid-in capital	(320,000)		(320,000)	
Retained earnings	(240,000)	(60,000)	(355,000)	(100,000)
Dividends	37,000	6,000	35,000	8,000
Sales	(540,000)	(144,000)	(590,000)	(160,000)
Dividend income			(8,000)	
Administrative expense	354,000	83,000	368,000	92,000
Depreciation expense	34,000	15,000	40,000	20,000
Totals	$ 0	$ 0	$ 0	$ 0

Required: Prepare a consolidation worksheet for Plume and Silke Companies on December 31, 1985, on the purchase basis.

P. 16-7 **Consolidation one year after purchase.**   Refer to the data and 1986 trial balances in Problem 16-6. Plume paid $220,000 cash to acquire Silke, which was $30,000 above book value, with $20,000 attributed to equipment and $10,000 to goodwill.

Required: Prepare a consolidation worksheet for Plume and Silke Companies on December 31, 1986.

P. 16-8 **Pooling of interests on date of acquisition.**   The trial balances of Pepper and Salte Corporations are presented below. Pepper has outstanding 80,000 shares of $1 par common stock, and Salte has outstanding 10,000 shares of no-par common stock. On December 31, 1985, Pepper acquired all the outstanding shares of Salte stock in a pooling of interests by issuing three new shares of its common stock in exchange for each share of Salte common.

	Trial Balances Prior to Acquisition December 31, 1985		Trial Balances One Year after Acquisition December 31, 1986	
	Pepper	**Salte**	**Pepper**	**Salte**
Cash	$310,000	$ 38,000	$285,000	$ 40,000
Accounts receivable	180,000	50,000	230,000	63,000
Receivable from Pepper		7,000		5,000
Investment in Salte	190,000		190,000	
Land	47,000		90,000	
Buildings	300,000		300,000	
Equipment	580,000	290,000	630,000	340,000
Accumulated depreciation	(230,000)	(60,000)	(270,000)	(80,000)
Notes payable	(25,000)	(15,000)	(20,000)	(18,000)
Payable to Salte	(7,000)		(5,000)	
Long-term debt	(400,000)	(120,000)	(360,000)	(120,000)
Common stock	(110,000)	(90,000)	(80,000)	(90,000)
Additional paid-in capital	(320,000)		(320,000)	
Paid-in capital from consolidation	(160,000)		(160,000)	
Retained earnings	(240,000)	(60,000)	(355,000)	(100,000)
Dividends	37,000	6,000	35,000	8,000
Sales	(540,000)	(144,000)	(590,000)	(160,000)
Dividend income			(8,000)	
Administrative expense	354,000	83,000	368,000	92,000
Depreciation expense	34,000	15,000	40,000	20,000
Totals	$ 0	$ 0	$ 0	$ 0

Required: Prepare a consolidation worksheet for Pepper and Salte Corporations on December 31, 1985.

P. 16-9 **Pooling of interests 1 year after acquisition.**   Refer to the trial balances and other data in Problem 16-8. On December 31, 1985, Pepper Corporation acquired Salte Corporation in a pooling of interests. The two companies have operated jointly for 1 year since the merger.

Required: Prepare a consolidation worksheet for Pepper and Salte Corporations on December 31, 1986.

P. 16-10 **Consolidation at acquisition and 1 year later (purchase).** On January 2, 1985, Pelt Company acquired all 3,000 shares of Skinn Company common stock for $100,000 cash. The excess of cost over book value paid by Pelt is attributable to fixed assets of Skinn Company with a remaining life of 10 years. The separate trial balances of Pelt and Skinn Companies appeared as follows immediately after the acquisition and 1 year later:

	Pelt Company		Skinn Company	
	1/2/85	12/31/85	1/2/85	12/31/85
Cash	$ 65,000	$ 69,000	$ 24,000	$ 22,000
Receivable from Skinn	10,000	8,000		
Merchandise	50,000	57,000	36,000	31,000
Investment in Skinn stock	100,000	100,000		
Fixed assets	120,000	140,000	85,000	92,000
Accumulated depreciation	(40,000)	(50,000)	(15,000)	(20,000)
Liabilities	(95,000)	(94,000)	(40,000)	(27,000)
Payable to Pelt			(10,000)	(8,000)
Common stock, no par	(150,000)	(150,000)	(60,000)	(60,000)
Retained earnings	(60,000)	(60,000)	(20,000)	(20,000)
Dividends		10,000		5,000
Operating revenues		(500,000)		(170,000)
Dividend income		(5,000)		
Operating expenses		475,000		155,000
Totals	$ 0	$ 0	$ 0	$ 0

Required: Prepare a consolidation worksheet on January 2, 1985, and also on December 31, 1985.

P. 16-11 **Consolidation at acquisition and 1 year later (pooling).** On December 31, 1985, Pitt Company acquired all outstanding shares of Stone Company common stock by issuing its own common stock in a pooling of interests. The separate trial balances of Pitt and Stone Companies appeared as follows immediately after the acquisition and 1 year later:

	Pitt Company		Stone Company	
	12/31/85	12/31/86	12/31/85	12/31/86
Cash	$ 54,500	$ 89,000	$ 29,000	$ 32,000
Receivable from Stone	13,500	8,000		
Merchandise	52,000	57,000	36,000	31,000
Investment in Stone stock	90,000	90,000		
Fixed assets	130,000	165,000	97,500	102,000
Accumulated depreciation	(40,000)	(50,000)	(25,000)	(30,000)
Liabilities	(55,000)	(74,000)	(34,000)	(37,000)
Payable to Pitt			(13,500)	(8,000)
Common stock, no par	(140,000)	(140,000)	(60,000)	(60,000)
Paid-in capital from consolidation	(40,000)	(40,000)		
Retained earnings	(34,000)	(65,000)	(18,000)	(30,000)
Dividends	8,000	10,000	5,000	15,000
Operating revenue	(476,000)	(500,000)	(141,000)	(170,000)
Dividend income		(15,000)		
Operating expenses	437,000	465,000	124,000	155,000
Totals	$ 0	$ 0	$ 0	$ 0

Required: Prepare a consolidation worksheet on December 31, 1985, and also on December 31, 1986.

Case 16-1 Consolidation of two purchased subsidiaries.

Below are the trial balances of Poole, Sinck, and Swimme Companies on May 31, 1985, prepared just prior to the acquisition by Poole of all the outstanding common stock of Sinck and Swimme Companies. On this date Poole purchased the stock of Sinck for $25,000 and the stock of Swimme for $20,000 cash. The accumulated depreciation account of Sinck Company is understated by $1,000 and the remainder of the excess of cost over book value is attributed to goodwill. The excess of cost over book value of Swimme Company is attributed to undervalued land. All three companies close their books on May 31, and the books of Swimme Company have already been closed.

Poole, Sinck, and Swimme Companies
Trial Balances
May 31, 1985

	Poole	Sinck	Swimme
Cash	$58,400	$ 3,800	$ 1,900
Accounts receivable	18,000	5,000	2,100
Receivable from Poole		700	
Receivable from Sinck			900
Land	6,100		6,800
Buildings	30,000		18,400
Equipment	58,000	29,000	
Accumulated depreciation	(23,000)	(6,000)	(2,600)
Notes payable	(3,300)	(1,600)	(2,000)
Payable to Sinck	(700)		
Payable to Swimme		(900)	
Long-term debt	(48,000)	(11,000)	(9,500)
Common stock	(8,000)	(9,000)	(1,000)
Additional paid-in capital	(52,000)		(6,000)
Retained earnings	(27,800)	(5,000)	(9,000)
Dividends	3,000		
Sales	(90,000)	(58,000)	
Cost of goods sold	52,000	29,000	
Operating expenses	27,300	24,000	
Totals	$ 0	$ 0	$ 0

Required: Prepare a single consolidation worksheet to consolidate the three companies on May 31. Enter each trial balance in a separate column and use a single pair of elimination columns in your worksheet.

The Synthesis of Financial Accounting

part 4

The basic principles, concepts, and procedures used in the preparation of financial statements are examined in the first part of this book. The next two parts cover in detail the components of financial statements in order to give you a deeper understanding of asset and equity valuation and income measurement. Now the pieces are brought together into a coherent whole as all the information you have gained is used to evaluate the financial position of a business and the results of its operations.

The material contained in the balance sheet, income statement, and statement of retained earnings is used to construct the statement of changes in financial position discussed in Chapters 17 and 18. The four statements together make up a complete financial report of a business organization. The next two chapters are devoted to the statement of changes. Chapter 19 describes the analytical tools used by financial analysts and other decision makers to interpret the data in financial statements in order to evaluate a business and make decisions about it. Chapter 20 deals with the issues posed by inflation and shows how accounting attempts to explain the effect of inflation on the financial statements.

Statement of Changes in Financial Position

The statement of changes in financial position is one of the basic financial statements found in the annual report of a company. It reports on the way funds flow in and out of the business. When you complete study of this chapter, you should understand:

---

1 How financing and investing activities affect businesses, and the way the results of these activities are reported in the statement of changes.

2 Two definitions of funds that may be used in the preparation of the statement of changes.

3 The difference between net income earned and the amount of funds provided by operations.

4 What is meant by sources of funds and uses of funds.

5 How sources and uses of funds are reported in the statement of changes.

6 What is meant by the concept of all financial resources, and the way the concept affects the statement of changes.

7 How the statement of changes is used in decision making.

Your study of accounting up to this point has focused on the measurement of revenues and expenses and the valuation of assets, liabilities, and owners' equity. These measures provide the basis for determining net income from operations and for presenting financial position. However, the income statement and the balance sheet do not provide adequate information on the amount of cash flowing in and out of a business. Many internal and external decision makers require cash flow information.

In this book we frequently point out transactions in which the amount of income or expense recorded is not the same as the amount of cash received or paid. The inflow and outflow of funds is so important that it warrants the preparation of another separate financial statement. FASB pronouncements require corporations to include in each annual report a statement of changes in financial position.

The **statement of changes in financial position**, often referred to as the **funds flow statement**, describes the financing and investing activities of a business enterprise. **Financing activities** are transactions that result in a flow of financial resources **into** the business. Examples are borrowing money or selling merchandise, both of which result in a business receiving funds. **Investing activities** are transactions that result in the flow of financial resources **out** of a business. Examples include the purchase of equipment or the repayment of debt, both of which result in cash outflows. The financial resources, or **funds**, obtained from financing activities are used to pay for investing activities.

Financing activities are sources of funds— investing activities are uses of funds

The statement of changes reports the **sources** from which funds were obtained and the **uses** to which funds were put during an accounting period. In addition, it explains why the amount of funds on hand at the end of the accounting period is different from the amount of funds on hand at the beginning of the period. The purpose of this chapter is to discuss the nature of the statement of changes and the type of information it conveys.

THE NATURE OF CHANGES IN FINANCIAL POSITION

Funds may be defined in several ways. Before the statement of changes in financial position can be prepared, it is necessary to understand which definition is being used. Two definitions are commonly used:

1. **Funds are defined as cash.**
2. **Funds are defined as working capital.**

Two definitions of funds: Cash and working capital

The form of the statement of changes in financial position depends on the definition used. When funds are defined as cash, the statement of changes explains the amount of cash that various financing activities provided, the amount of cash used for various investing activities, and the resulting change in the cash balance from the beginning of the accounting period to the end as shown in the balance sheet. When funds are defined as working capital, the statement of changes explains how much working capital the financing and investing activities provided and used, and how working capital changed from the amount available at the beginning of the accounting period to the amount available at the end of the period.

Funds are usually defined as working capital for external users

Funds are usually defined as working capital in statements prepared for external users. Investors, shareholders, financial analysts, and other external users are usually not interested in the detailed operations that are disclosed by cash flow information. They need a broad view of fund flows in order to determine the general well-being of the company and its ability to generate funds.

Funds are often defined as cash for managers

The statement of changes with funds defined as cash is of interest primarily to internal managers. Managers need information on the day-to-day operations of the business, and must manage the flow of cash carefully. To monitor current operations and control the flow of current assets and liabilities, they must have detailed information on each component of working capital including cash.

Sources and Uses of Funds

All financing and investing activities can be divided into a small number of categories. There are four types of financing activities that provide funds, however funds are defined:

1. Operations that generate net income are the primary source of funds for most businesses.
2. Capital contributions by owners during the accounting period are a major source of funds.
3. Borrowing from financial institutions or from the public is a significant source of funds.
4. The sale of assets normally not held for sale is a source of funds, although usually not a major source.

The funds made available by financing activities are used for making investments. There are four types of investing activities that require the use of funds. They are:

1. The acquisition of fixed assets in order to expand the business.
2. Repayment of debt to creditors.
3. Reacquisition of capital stock.
4. The payment of dividends to shareholders.

If a business obtains more funds from financing activities than it needs for investing activities, the unused funds increase the company's working capital or cash. This situation is described algebraically as follows, with hypothetical figures used to illustrate the equation:

$$\text{Sources} - \text{Uses} = \text{Increase in funds}$$

$$\$100,000 - \$90,000 = \$10,000 \text{ increase}$$

If the business obtains less funds from financing activities than it needs for investing, cash or working capital must be reduced to provide the balance of the funds used in investing activities. In that case, the situation is described algebraically as follows:

$$\text{Sources} - \text{Uses} = \text{Decrease in funds}$$

$$\$92,000 - \$100,000 = \$8,000 \text{ decrease}$$

The statement of changes in financial position reports all of the sources and uses of funds and is frequently prepared showing the change in funds as the difference between the sources and uses, as follows:

Sources	$ 92,000
Uses	100,000
Decrease in funds	$ 8,000

This form is used in Figures 17-6 and 17-8. Some accountants prefer to prepare the statement in balanced form, with the change in funds viewed as if it were itself a source or use of funds, so that the algebraic representation becomes:

$$\text{Sources} = \text{Uses}$$

When the statement is viewed as a balanced equation, an increase in cash or working capital is reported together with the uses of funds, and a decrease is reported together with the sources. The first example, with an increase in funds, appears in the balanced form as follows:

$$\text{Sources} = \qquad\qquad \text{Uses}$$

$$\$100,000 = \$90,000 + \$10,000 \text{ increase in funds}$$

The second example, with a decrease in funds, appears in the balanced form as:

$$\text{Sources} \qquad\qquad = \text{Uses}$$

$$\$92,000 + \$8,000 \text{ decrease in funds} = \$100,000$$

The balanced form of the statement of changes in financial position is prepared as follows:

Sources	$ 92,000
Decrease in funds	8,000
Total	$100,000
Uses	$100,000

Figure 17-10, on page 705, illustrates the balanced form of the statement of changes. It does not matter which form is used, so long as you understand that the difference between total sources and total uses of funds is the change in funds for the period.

How sources and uses of funds change the balance sheet.   A business employs its assets to operate in order to earn more assets. Operations are the primary source of funds that are used to repay debts, acquire new assets, and pay dividends. A company also obtains funds by selling fixed or other assets, by issuing new stock, and by incurring new debts. Each source of funds and each use of funds causes a change in the balance sheet. Although some of the changes are obvious, it helps to examine what accounts change in the balance sheet as various financing and investing activities occur.

Financing and investing activities cause balance sheet changes

1. Funds provided by operations change the balance of retained earnings. This change occurs when the books are closed and the temporary account balances are transferred to the retained earnings account.

2. Funds provided by issuing stock increase the contributed capital accounts, such as preferred stock, common stock, and paid-in capital.

3. Funds provided by borrowing increase long-term liability accounts such as bonds payable, mortgages payable, and capital lease obligations.

4. Funds provided by the sale of assets decrease the fixed asset accounts such as land, buildings, and equipment.

5. Funds used to pay dividends decrease the retained earnings account.

6. Funds used to repay debt decrease long-term liability accounts.

7. Funds used to reacquire stock decrease capital accounts such as preferred stock, or increase the treasury stock account which is also a decrease in capital.

8. Funds used to acquire assets increase fixed asset accounts.

Each of these sources and uses of funds increases and decreases cash or working capital. The statement of changes reports all sources, all uses, and the net change in funds, which is the difference between total sources and total uses.

In Figure 17-1, we illustrate how the statement of changes is related to the other three statements. As its name implies, the statement reports the **changes** in financial position that occurred between the beginning and ending balance sheets.

The statement of changes covers one accounting period

Of the four statements that make up the annual report, only the balance sheet is a static statement; it reports financial position at a specific point in time. The income statement, the statement of retained earnings, and the statement of changes in financial position are dynamic statements that report changes occurring during one accounting period.

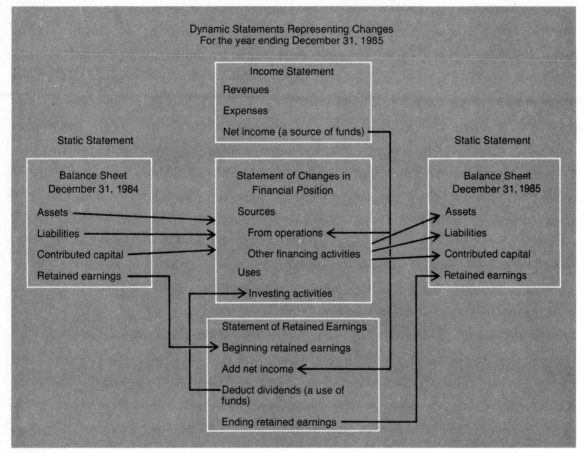

Figure 17-1   **Relationship between static balance sheet that report financial position and dynamic statements that report changes. The statement of changes in financial position describes the financing and investing activities of the business.**

A look at a simple example.   If we know how sources and uses of funds change balance sheet accounts, then we can look at changes in balance sheet accounts and decide what type of source or use of funds caused the change. If we see that bonds payable increased from one year to the next, we know that funds were provided by borrowing. If we see that land increased, we know that funds were probably used to acquire land. If we see that retained earnings decreased, we might assume that funds were used to pay dividends. The dividend payments can be verified by looking at the statement of retained earnings. The beginning and ending balance sheets and the statements of income and retained earnings provide the information needed to prepare the statement of changes in financial position.

Basic Corporation
Comparative Balance Sheets
December 31, 1985 and 1984

Assets	1985	1984	Liabilities and Capital	1985	1984
Current assets:			Current liabilities:		
Cash	$ 69	$ 74	Salaries payable	$125	$110
Accounts receivable	191	150	Long-term liabilities:		
Total current assets	260	224	Mortgage note payable	215	260
Fixed assets:			Total liabilities	340	370
Land	187	200	Capital:		
Buildings	500	500	Common stock	400	400
Accumulated depreciation	(50)	(40)	Retained earnings	157	114
Total fixed assets	637	660			
Total assets	$897	$884	Total liabilities and capital	$897	$884

Basic Corporation
Income Statement
For the Year Ended December 31, 1985

Sales		$550
Less expenses:		
Salaries	$470	
Depreciation	10	
Interest	18	498
Net income		$ 52

Figure 17-2
Annual reports present comparative financial statements such as the balance sheets shown here. The statement of changes in financial position is prepared from the data in this figure. It explains the change from one balance sheet to the next.

Basic Corporation
Statement of Retained Earnings
For the Year Ended December 31, 1985

Retained earnings, 12/31/84	$114
Add net income	52
	166
Less dividends	9
Retained earnings, 12/31/85	$157

To illustrate how changes in financial position are reported, we use the comparative balance sheets, income statement, and statement of retained earnings of Basic Company, presented in Figure 17-2. The statement of changes that we develop will explain the change from one balance sheet to the next. It will show all sources and uses of funds.

Working capital = Current assets − Current liabilities

The cash balance of Basic Corporation changed from $74 on December 31, 1984, to $69 at the end of 1985. The statement of changes must explain this $5 decrease if funds are defined as cash. Working capital is the difference between current assets and current liabilities. Basic Corporation's working capital on December 31, 1984, was $114 (current assets of $224 less current liabilities of $110), and at the end of 1985 working capital was $135 ($260 − $125). If funds are defined as working capital, the statement of changes must explain the $21 increase in working capital.

First we discuss the statement of changes with funds defined as cash. Later we use the same example to show the statement of changes with funds defined as working capital. The last part of the chapter illustrates a more elaborate set of financial statements, including a more complete statement of changes in financial position that is developed fully in Chapter 18.

CHANGE IN FINANCIAL POSITION—FUNDS DEFINED AS CASH

Why did cash decrease by $5 between 1984 and 1985? To explain this change in funds, which we now define as cash, we analyze the changes that took place in each balance sheet account from the end of 1984 to the end of 1985. Figure 17-3 shows the differences computed between the comparative balance sheets, indicating the increases or decreases in asset and equity accounts from one year to the next.

Cash decreased by $5 from the beginning of the period to the end. Therefore it is evident that total financing activities provided $5 less funds than was used to pay for total investing activities. The difference required a reduction in the cash account in order to finance the additional $5 investment not financed from other sources. The statement of changes in financial position must show the nature and amount of the financing and investing activities and thereby explain the change in the cash balance.

The decrease in Cash is denoted by a $5 credit in Figure 17-3. Increases in assets are shown as debits. Increases in liabilities and capital are credits, and decreases are debits. There was no change in the Common Stock account, but Retained Earnings increased by $43, shown as a credit. Because the debits and credits in each balance sheet are equal, the debit and credit changes also balance.

Some transactions are financing or investing activities— others have no effect on funds

To record a transaction in a journal we analyze its effect on the accounting equation. We can also analyze a transaction's effect on sources and uses of funds to see how the statement of changes explains the financing and investing activities. By examining journal entries, including adjusting entries and closing entries, you can see that some entries include financing and investing activities that must be reported in the statement of changes and others have no effect on funds, although they affect the income statement or the balance sheet.

Basic Corporation
Comparative Balance Sheets
December 31, 1985 and 1984

	1985	1984	Changes	
			dr	cr
Assets				
Cash	$ 69	$ 74		5
Accounts receivable	191	150	41	
Land	187	200		13
Buildings	500	500		
Accumulated depreciation	(50)	(40)		10
Total assets	$897	$884		
Equities				
Salaries payable	$125	$110		15
Mortgage note payable	215	260	45	
Common stock	400	400		
Retained earnings	157	114		43
Total equities	$897	$884	86	86

Figure 17-3
Changes in balance sheet amounts that must be explained by the statement of changes in financial position are shown as debits and credits. Generally, debits are uses of funds and credits are sources.

Operations are a major source of funds. We therefore first examine all transactions affecting the income statement, which is a summary of business operations for one accounting period. Most of the net income has been received in the form of cash, but income is measured in accordance with the accrual concept and matching principle, rather than on the cash basis. Therefore net income does not report exactly how much cash was collected from operations, and the net income figure must be converted to a cash inflow figure by appropriate adjustments.

Transactions that affect the income statement also affect the balance sheet, so an examination of business operations should explain some of the balance sheet changes calculated in Figure 17-3. Any other balance sheet changes are the result of other financing and investing activities, many of which have no effect on the income statement.

Cash Provided by Operations

Operations are a major source of funds

The income statement in Figure 17-2 shows sales revenue of $550 less total expenses of $498, leaving a net income of $52 which increased the Retained Earnings balance. The change in Retained Earnings, however, is only $43 because the company paid $9 of cash dividends during the year, as reported in the statement of retained earnings in Figure 17-2.

Now we look in detail at the transactions that occurred in 1985 as a result of operations. Note that these transactions were recorded during the year as they occurred. The journal entries are reproduced here to explain cash flows. Many identical transactions are aggregated into a single entry so that the overall effect on cash may be seen. From the income statement, we know that sales were $550, recorded as follows:

Accounts receivable	550	
Sales		550

All revenues are not cash inflows

Operations provided $550 of sales revenue, but only $509 of cash was collected from customers. This is evident from an examination of accounts receivable, which increased by $41. The beginning balance in Accounts Receivable was $150, and $550 was added as a result of the current year's sales. If the ending balance is $191, only $509 of accounts receivable was collected during the year. The collection of receivables is recorded as follows:

Cash	509	
Accounts receivable		509

The above two entries are posted in the account below.

Accounts Receivable

Bal. 12/31/84	150	1985 collections	509
1985 sales	550		
Bal. 12/31/85	191		

Given the beginning balance of $150, credit sales of $550, and the ending balance of $191, the credit to Accounts Receivable must have been $509. Therefore if accounts receivable increased during the period, cash collections are less than sales revenue. Conversely, if the balance of receivable decreased, the company must have collected more than its credit sales for the year. We can compute cash collections as follows:

Sales revenue	$550
Less increase in accounts receivable	41
Cash collected from customers[1]	$509

The journal entries to record expenses are given below. The payment of salaries includes not only the current year's salaries paid in cash, but also the payment of Salaries Payable accrued at the end of the previous year.

---

[1] The result is the same if all sales are not on credit.

Salaries payable	110	
Salaries expense	345	
Cash		455
To pay current salaries and beginning		
balance of Salaries Payable.		

The adjusting entry at the end of 1985 records salary expenses that have not yet been paid but which are accrued at the end of the year.

Salaries expense	125	
Salaries payable		125
To accrue salaries at end of 1985.		

Salaries Payable

1985 payments	110	Bal. 12/31/84	110
		12/31/85 accrual	125
		Bal. 12/31/85	125

All expenses are not cash outflows

The $455 of cash used to pay salaries during 1985 is clearly not the same as the amount of salaries expense reported in the 1985 income statement. Cash paid for salaries is less than the reported expense of $470 because the company increased its liability to its employees by $15 from $110 at the end of 1984 to $125 at the end of 1985.

Some expenses are not paid with funds— they are nonfund items

Depreciation expense reported on the income statement does not require the use of either cash or working capital, because no current assets or liabilities are affected by the recording of depreciation. Depreciation is therefore known as a **nonfund item** on the income statement; it neither provides nor uses funds.

| Depreciation expense | 10 | |
| Accumulated depreciation | | 10 |

The payment of interest resulted in the use of $18 of cash. No accrued interest is reported in the balance sheet, so the amount of cash paid is the same as the amount of interest expense reported.

| Interest expense | 18 | |
| Cash | | 18 |

Of the above six entries that affected the 1985 income statement, three affected cash. Collection of sales revenue caused a cash debit of $509, and payments of salaries and interest caused cash credits of $455 and $18, for a net cash increase from operation of $36. These changes in the cash account resulting from operations are shown below.

Cash

Bal. 12/31/84	74	Payment of salaries	455
Collection of receivables	509	Payment of interest	18

Schedule of Cash Provided by Operations

The $36 of cash provided by operations can be reported in the statement of changes by showing how each amount reported in the income statement is converted to a cash flow. A schedule of **cash provided by operations** is shown in Figure 17-4. The sales revenue of $550 is converted to a cash inflow by deducting the increase in accounts receivable, leaving a net cash inflow of $509. From this inflow we deduct the cash outflows. The cash paid for salaries is calculated by deducting from the salaries expense of $470 the $15 increase in salaries payable, leaving $455 cash used to pay salaries during 1985. Interest of $18 was paid in cash. Depreciation expense did not require the use of cash. Cash flow from depreciation is zero so it is not included in the schedule. Total cash deductions from revenue are $473. The result of operations was a net income of $52, but an increase in cash of $36.

Figure 17-4

Cash provided by operations is not the same as net income. This schedule explains how each item in the income statement is modified to reflect cash inflows and outflows.

Basic Corporation
Schedule of Cash Provided by Operations
For the Year Ended December 31, 1985

Revenues		$550
Less increase in accounts receivable		41
Cash collected from customers		509
Deduct expenses:		
Salaries	$470	
Less increase in salaries payable	15	
Salaries paid in cash	455	
Interest expense	18	473
Cash provided by operations		$ 36

There are two ways of converting net income to cash provided by operations

An alternative calculation of cash provided by operations is shown in Figure 17-5. Here the net income figure of $52 is adjusted by adding back those items that did not require the use of cash but were deducted to arrive at net income.

Basic Corporation
Schedule of Cash Provided by Operations
For the Year Ended December 31, 1985

Net income		$52
Add items not requiring use of cash:		
Depreciation expense	$10	
Increase in salaries payable	15	25
Deduct items not providing cash:		
Increase in accounts receivable		(41)
Cash provided by operations		$36

Figure 17-5
Another version of a schedule of cash provided by operations. Here the net income figure is adjusted to arrive at the amount of net cash inflows from operations.

Current assets and current liabilities are used in operations

Examine again the changes calculated for the comparative balance sheets in Figure 17-3. We now know how operations changed the balances in Accounts Receivable and Salaries Payable. Typically, the current assets and current liabilities are used in operations. Operating the business causes changes in current account balances, and these changes are aggregated and reported in the statement of changes as the single amount called funds provided by operations. In addition to funds provided by operations, there are three other types of sources of funds and four types of uses of funds that change the balances of noncurrent accounts—those not used in the day-to-day operations of the business.

Other Sources and Uses of Cash

The change in Accumulated Depreciation is explained as a nonfund item used in the computation of funds provided by operations. The $10 increase in this account was caused by reporting depreciation expense in the income statement, and depreciation expense, being a nonfund item, was added back to net income in Figure 17-5 to arrive at funds provided by operations. Changes in the Land, Mortgage, and Retained Earnings accounts must still be explained. The transactions that changed these accounts are the sale of land, repayment of the mortgage note, and payment of cash dividends.

Selling assets is a source of funds

The sale of land did not result in a gain or loss, because no gain or loss is reported on the income statement. Therefore the following transaction may have been recorded:

Cash		13	
Land			13

It is possible that the company exchanged the land for some cash and a note, or for a note only. Since a note receivable does not appear on the balance sheet, if one was received it was also collected prior to the end of the year. Therefore, regardless of how the land was sold, the transaction yielded $13 of cash. If land was exchanged for a note, the transactions would be recorded as follows:

Notes receivable		13	
Land			13
Cash		13	
Notes receivable			13

Paying debts is a use of funds

The reduction of the mortgage note and the payment of dividends required the use of cash.

Mortgage note payable		45	
Cash			45

Paying dividends is a use of funds which decreases retained earnings

The land and mortgage transactions explain all of the remaining changes in the balance sheet, except for changes in the Retained Earnings account. The change in retained earnings is explained by recording the payment of dividends and closing the temporary accounts.

Dividends		9	
Cash			9

All the transactions affecting cash are posted below to show the net decrease in cash of $5 for the year.

Cash

Bal. 12/31/84	74	Payment of salaries	455
Collection of receivables	509	Payment of interest	18
Sale of land	13	Payment of mortgage	45
		Payment of dividends	9
Bal. 12/31/85	69		

The entries below illustrate that closing the books does not affect assets or liabilities. Closing the Income Summary account increases retained earnings by $52, and closing the Dividends account reduces retained earnings by $9, resulting in a net increase of $43 in the Retained Earnings account.

Revenues	550	
Income summary		550
Income summary	498	
Salaries expense		470
Interest expense		18
Depreciation expense		10
Income summary	52	
Retained earnings		52
Retained earnings	9	
Dividends		9

Retained Earnings

1985 dividends	9	Bal. 12/31/84	114
		Net income for 1985	52
		Bal. 12/31/85	157

The Statement of Changes

The statement of changes in financial position, with funds defined as cash, can be constructed from the information discussed above. This statement is shown in Figure 17-6. Because the example is very simple, it shows only two sources and two uses of cash. Although funds are defined as cash, **the statement also reports the change in working capital**. This is required by FASB pronouncements. A more elaborate statement of changes in financial position is illustrated later in this chapter.

The uses of cash during the accounting period were greater than the sources obtained in the same period, so the difference had to come from the cash already on hand at the beginning of the period. Therefore, cash decreased by $5 during the period.

Basic Corporation
Statement of Changes in Financial Position
For the Year Ended December 31, 1985

Sources of Cash

From operations (see schedule in Figure 16-4 or 16-5)	$36	
Other sources of cash:		
Sale of land	13	
Total sources		$49

Uses of Cash

Payment of dividends	9	
Repayment of long-term debt	45	
Total uses		54
Decrease in cash		$(5)

Schedule of Changes in Working Capital

	Increase (decrease)
Cash decreased	$ (5)
Accounts receivable increased	41
Salaries payable increased	(15)
Working capital increased	$ 21

Figure 17-6
A simple statement of changes in financial position with funds defined as cash. Note the three distinct parts of the statement: sources, uses, and the change in working capital.

CHANGE IN FINANCIAL POSITION—FUNDS DEFINED AS WORKING CAPITAL

Operations change the balances in working capital accounts

When funds are defined as working capital, the funds flow statement must explain the net change in working capital during the accounting period. The change in working capital occurs as a result of operations and other financing activities, and also from investing activities. Three types of transactions are reflected in the statement of changes with funds defined as working capital:

1. Transactions that affect only working capital accounts.
2. Transactions that affect both working capital accounts and noncurrent accounts.
3. Transactions that do not affect working capital accounts.

Transactions That Affect Only Working Capital

When a transaction affects only current assets and current liabilities, **the amount of working capital does not change.** Only the components change. For example, the payment of a current liability does not change the amount of working capital. Cash decreases, and a payable decreases by the same amount, leaving working capital unchanged. The **purchase** of merchandise on account increases current assets and current liabilities by the same amount, leaving working capital unchanged. The collection of receivables increases cash, but decreases receivables by the same amount. Consequently, such transactions have no effect on the funds flow statement when funds are defined as working capital.

Transactions That Affect Both Current and Noncurrent Accounts

Unlike the purchase of merchandise, the **sale** of merchandise usually increases working capital, because the selling price is greater than cost. The transaction affects working capital and owners' equity. The sales revenue includes gross margin, so the increase in cash or receivables is greater than the decrease in merchandise. Other transactions that occur in daily business operations also affect only working capital and owners' equity accounts. For example, the payment of a short-term note payable reduces a current liability, reduces cash, and reduces owners' equity in the form of interest expense. The decrease in working capital is equal to the interest expense.

Expenses reduce working capital whether they are paid or accrued

Most adjusting entries affect working capital and the income statement. When salaries are accrued, the salary expense is equal to the decrease in working capital resulting from the increase in salaries payable. When interest receivable is accrued, working capital increases by the amount of interest income that is recorded.

Some transactions affect working capital and noncurrent assets or liabilities. These are always financing or investing activities **other than from operations**. Such transactions may also affect owners' equity, because they may result in gains or losses which are reported as nonfund items in the income statement. The sale of fixed assets, the payment of long-term debt, the acquisition of long-lived assets, and the declaration of cash dividends all change working capital. The effects of such transactions must, therefore, be reported in the funds flow statement. As indicated previously, these transactions are some of the main sources and uses of funds. The difference between such sources and uses is the net change in working capital for the period.

Transactions That Do Not Affect Working Capital Accounts

Certain exchanges must be included in the funds flow statement although they do not have any effect on working capital. For example, equipment acquired in exchange for common stock or a mortgage exchanged for a parcel of land are transactions that do not affect funds. Such exchanges must be disclosed in the funds flow statement to satisfy the concept of funds as all financial resources, which is discussed later in this chapter.

CHANGE IN WORKING CAPITAL

We now return to the Basic Corporation example and define funds as working capital. Working capital, defined as current assets minus current liabilities, is calculated below for December 31, 1984 and 1985. The calculation shows that working capital increased by $21.

	1985	1984	Change	
Current assets	$260	$224	dr	$36
Less current liabilities	125	110	cr	15
Working capital	$135	$114	dr	$21

The $21 increase in working capital can also be obtained by netting the changes in the individual components of working capital. In our example, these include the changes in Cash, Accounts Receivable, and Salaries Payable as shown in Figure 17-3 on page 689. Because these three changes are made up of a $5 credit, a $41 debit, and a $15 credit, the change in working capital is a $21 debit, indicating an increase from one year to the next. In the comparative balance sheets in Figure 17-7, the current assets and current liabilities are combined into working capital, making it easy to calculate the $21 change.

Figure 17-7
When funds are defined as working capital the statement of changes explains the change in working capital rather than the change in cash. These comparative balance sheets have been modified to show the change in working capital rather than all the working capital components.

Basic Corporation
Comparative Balance Sheets
December 31, 1985 and 1984

	1985	1984	Changes dr	Changes cr
Debits:				
Working capital	$135	$114	21	
Land	187	200		13
Buildings	500	500		
Total debits	$822	$814		
Credits:				
Accumulated depreciation	$ 50	$ 40		10
Mortgage notes payable	215	260	45	
Common stock	400	400		
Retained earnings	157	114		43
Total credits	$822	$814	66	66

Working Capital Provided by Operations

With funds defined as working capital, most of the items presented in the income statement are increases or decreases in funds. The entry to record the sales reported in Basic Corporation's income statement in Figure 17-2 on page 687 is reproduced here.

	Accounts receivable	550	
	Sales		550

Most revenues and expenses are increases and decreases in working capital

Sales provide working capital whether goods are sold for cash or on open account, because both cash and accounts receivable are components of working capital. Whether or not the accounts receivable are collected during the period, Basic Corporation's sales increased working capital by $550. Similarly, salaries require the use of working capital whether paid in cash or accrued as current liabilities.

	Salaries payable	110	
	Salaries expense	345	
	Cash		455
	Payment of current and accrued salaries.		
	Salaries expense	125	
	Salaries payable		125
	Accrual of salaries at year-end.		

The effect of the salary transactions on working capital is shown below. The two transactions reduced working capital by $470, precisely the amount reported as salaries expense in the income statement in Figure 17-2.

Working Capital

Salaries payable	110	Cash (for salaries)	455
		Salaries payable	125
		Net change	470

Depreciation expense has no effect on funds but interest expense reduces working capital, as shown in the following entries.

	Depreciation expense	10	
	Accumulated depreciation		10
	Interest expense	18	
	Cash		18

The effects of all the above transactions on working capital are summarized below to show the amount of funds provided by operations.

Working Capital

Accounts receivable	550	Cash (for salaries)	455
Salaries payable	110	Salaries payable	125
		Cash (for interest)	18
From operations	62		

Nonfund items on the income statement neither use nor provide funds

Altogether working capital increased by $62 as a result of operations, although net income was only $52, according to Figure 17-2. The net income figure can be converted to working capital provided by operations by adjusting it for **nonfund items**—that is, items, such as depreciation expense, which do not provide or use working capital.

The simplest way of converting net income to funds provided by operations is to add back to net income those nonfund items that were deducted in the income statement, and deduct from net income those nonfund items that were added in the income statement. Depreciation expense was deducted in arriving at net income, so it is necessary to add it back in order to convert net income to working capital provided by operations, as illustrated below.

Net income	$52
Add depreciation expense	10
Working capital provided by operations	$62

Other Sources and Uses of Working Capital

The changes in balance sheet accounts shown in Figure 17-7 indicate that land was sold and the sale provided $13 of working capital. The change in the Mortgage Note Payable account indicates that $45 of working capital was used to repay some of the long-term debt. We know from the statement of retained earnings that $9 was used to pay cash dividends. The payments of dividends and mortgage note are the total uses of working capital. Funds from operations and the sale of land are the total sources of working capital. All of the uses and sources are summarized below, showing that working capital increased by $21 during 1985.

Working Capital

Accounts receivable	550	Cash (for salaries)	455
Salaries payable	110	Salaries payable	125
		Cash (for interest)	18
From operations	62	Cash (for mortgage)	45
Cash (from land)	13	Cash (for dividends)	9
Increase	21		

The Statement of Changes

Figure 17-8 shows the statement of changes in financial position with funds defined as working capital. The statement reports that the sources of working capital exceeded the uses, and excess funds remained on hand, resulting in an increase of $21 in working capital. This statement is in the form Sources − Uses = Working capital. Later the balanced form, Sources = Uses, is illustrated. Regardless of the format, the statement of changes in financial position also explains the change in the working capital components. One form of the schedule of changes in working capital is illustrated in the lower portion of Figure 17-8. Another form is shown later in this chapter.

Basic Corporation
Statement of Changes in Financial Position
For the Year Ended December 31, 1985

Sources of Working Capital		
From operations:		
Net income	$52	
Add depreciation	10	
Total provided by operations	62	
Other sources:		
Sale of land	13	
Total sources		$75
Uses of Working Capital		
Payment of dividends	9	
Repayment of long-term debt	45	
Total uses		54
Increase in working capital		$21

Schedule of Changes in Working Capital

	Balance Dec. 31 1985	Balance Dec. 31 1984	Working Capital Increase (decrease)
Cash	$ 69	$ 74	$ (5)
Accounts receivable	191	150	41
Salaries payable	(125)	(110)	(15)
Working capital	$135	$114	$ 21

Figure 17-8
A simple statement of changes in financial position with funds defined as working capital. Note the three parts of the statement: sources, uses, and changes in working capital.

ADDITIONAL FUND FLOW CONCEPTS

The deliberately simple Basic Corporation example illustrates clearly the basic concepts underlying the statement of changes in financial position. Now we turn to a more complete illustration and discuss some additional concepts. For this purpose, we present the comparative balance sheets, the income statement, and the statement of retained earnings of Phoenix Corporation in Figure 17-9. The statement of changes in financial position, with funds defined as working capital, is shown in Figure 17-10. During the year 1985, the transactions listed on the next page took place.

Phoenix Corporation
Comparative Balance Sheets
December 31, 1985 and 1984

	1985	1984
Assets		
Cash	$ 165	$ 67
Accounts receivable (net)	127	90
Merchandise	78	95
Total current assets	370	252
Land	60	60
Buildings	1,000	987
Equipment	841	800
Less accumulated depreciation	(706)	(660)
Total fixed assets	1,195	1,187
Long-term investments	100	125
Patents	33	37
Total other assets	133	162
Total assets	$1,698	$1,601
Liabilities		
Accounts payable	$ 92	$ 74
Salaries payable	21	30
Income taxes payable	20	13
Dividends payable	10	
Total current liabilities	143	117
Notes payable, due 1989	44	
Bonds payable, due 1994	450	450
Premium on bonds payable	16	18
Total long-term liabilities	510	468
Total liabilities	653	585
Capital		
Preferred stock		48
Common stock $1 par	510	500
Paid-in capital on common	260	220
Retained earnings	275	248
Total capital	1,045	1,016
Total liabilities and capital	$1,698	$1,601

Fixed assets that cost $25 and had a book value of $11 at the time of sale were sold for $8 cash.

A 2 percent stock dividend was distributed on the common stock in addition to the cash dividend.

Preferred stock was redeemed at its book value and retired.

New equipment was purchased for $22 cash and a $44 long-term note payable.

Phoenix Corporation
Income Statement
For the Year Ended December 31, 1985

Sales		$2,340
Less cost of goods sold:		
Beginning inventory	$ 95	
Add purchases	1,387	
Goods available for sale	1,482	
Less ending inventory	78	
Cost of goods sold		1,404
Gross margin		936
Less expenses:		
Administrative	317	
Salaries	306	
Depreciation	60	
Amortization of patent	4	
Interest	38	
Total expenses		725
Income from operations		211
Other income:		
Gain on sale of investments	5	
Loss on sale of equipment	(3)	2
Income before tax		213
Less income tax expense		96
Net income		$ 117

Figure 17-9
The income statement, statement of retained earnings, and the comparative balance sheets shown here are accompanied by the statement of changes in financial position in Figure 17-10 to make up a complete annual report.

Phoenix Corporation
Statement of Retained Earnings
For the Year Ended December 31, 1985

Retained earnings, 12/31/84		$ 248
Add net income		117
		365
Deduct dividends:		
Cash dividends	$ 40	
2% stock dividend	50	90
Retained earnings, 12/31/85		$ 275

Examine carefully the financial statements and the statement of changes to see how the sources and uses of funds are reported. The statement of changes in financial position consists of three distinct parts: sources of funds, uses of funds, and a schedule of changes in working capital. The statement in Figure 17-10 is in the form Sources = Uses, with the increase in working capital shown among the uses of funds.

Funds Provided by Operations

Net income measured under the accrual concept is not the same as the amount of funds obtained from operations. Some expenses and losses are deducted from revenues to arrive at net income, although they did not require the use of funds. Depreciation expense is an obvious example. Other nonfund deductions include amortization of intangibles, losses, deferred taxes, and amortization of bond discount. To convert the net income figure to a figure representing fund inflows from operations, such nonfund deductions must be added back to net income.

The income statement also contains items that are added in arriving at net income but that did not provide funds. Amortization of premium on bonds payable, gains, and income from stock investments accounted for by the equity method are examples. Because such nonfund items are not fund inflows, they must be deducted from net income to convert the net income figure to a fund inflow from operations. Some of these nonfund additions and deductions are explained below.

Depreciation and amortization.   You already know that depreciation does not require the use of funds. No one writes a check to pay for depreciation expense. Amortization of intangible assets and depletion of natural resources similarly do not require the use of funds. Because such items are added back to income in the funds flow statement, many users of financial statements mistakenly believe that depreciation is a source of funds. Some people believe, in fact, that accumulated depreciation is a fund accumulated for the purpose of acquiring new assets when the old ones need to be replaced. Such misconceptions arise from a lack of understanding of fund flow concepts. Revenue, which results in reporting of net income on the income statement, is the source of funds. Depreciation is simply a nonfund expense which makes revenue smaller than the fund inflow. To show the fund inflow, depreciation is simply added back to income.

Depreciation is neither a source nor a use of funds

Premium on bonds payable.   When bond discount or premium is amortized, the amount of interest expense reported in the income statement is not the same as the amount of cash paid for bond interest. You may remember from Chapter 12 that interest expense on bonds issued at a premium is smaller than the required interest payments. Phoenix Corpora-

Phoenix Corporation
Statement of Changes in Financial Position
For the Year Ended December 31, 1985

Sources of Working Capital

Funds provided by operations:		
Net income		$117
Add items not requiring use of working capital:		
Depreciation expense	$ 60	
Amortization of patent	4	
Loss on sale of equipment	3	67
Less items not providing working capital:		
Amortization of bond premium		(2)
Gain on sale of investments		(5)
Working capital provided by operations		177
Other sources:		
Sale of equipment		8
Sale of long-term investments		30
Long-term borrowing used to finance purchase of new equipment		44
Total sources of working capital		$259

Uses of Working Capital

Payment of dividends	$ 40
Retirement of preferred stock	48
Addition to buildings	13
Purchase of new equipment, partly financed by new long-term borrowing	66
Increase in working capital	92
Total uses of working capital	$259

Schedule of Changes in Working Capital

	Working Capital Increase	Decrease
Increase in cash	$ 98	
Increase in accounts receivable	37	
Decrease in merchandise		$ 17
Increase in accounts payable		18
Decrease in salaries payable	9	
Increase in income taxes payable		7
Increase in dividends payable		10
Total changes	144	52
Net increase in working capital		92
Total	$144	$144

Figure 17-10
Statement of changes in financial position with funds defined as working capital. Compare the schedule of changes in working capital with the same schedule in Figure 17-8 and note the different format used in the two schedules.

tion's interest expense is $38, and on the balance sheet you see that premium on bonds payable changed from $18 to $16 because $2 of bond premium was amortized. Therefore, the entries to record interest expense must have been:

Interest expense	40	
Cash		40

Cash paid to bond holders was $40, but the income statement reports only $38 of interest expense because at the end of the year interest expense was adjusted and reduced to $38 when bond premium was amortized.

Premium on bonds payable	2	
Interest expense		2

Bond premium or discount amortization is a nonfund item

The $40 outflow of working capital for the payment of interest was greater than the $38 of interest expense deducted to arrive at net income. The difference, caused by $2 of bond premium amortization, is therefore a nonfund item that must be deducted from net income in order to convert the net income figure to funds obtained from operations.

If bond discount had been amortized instead of bond premium, the amortization of the discount is added back to net income to arrive at funds provided by operations. A similar treatment is necessary for discount or premium amortization on long-term bond investments, because the amount of interest income recorded is not the same as the amount of cash received.

Gains and losses. When transactions result in gains or losses, the gain or loss reported in the income statement is only the net effect on owners' equity, and not the entire amount of funds obtained from the transaction. The fund flow effects of such transactions are quite different from the amount of gain or loss. Transactions that result in gains or losses may be either financing or investing activities. For example, the sale of fixed assets is a financing activity that may result in a gain or a loss. On the other hand, the early retirement of bonds payable is an investing activity that may result in a gain or loss.

A transaction resulting in a gain or a loss has an impact on fund flows which is usually greater than the gain or loss reported in the income statement. In addition, such transactions have nothing to do with the daily operations of a business, and therefore their effect on funds should not be part of funds provided by operations.

Gains and losses are nonfund items

If we examine the entry to record the sale of an asset, we see that the gain or loss is only a part of the entire transaction. It would be incorrect to show a part of the transaction as the fund flow. The entire amount of funds provided by the sale should be reported in the statement of changes, whereas only the gain or loss portion is shown in the income statement. Such gains or losses are nonfund items that must be added back to, or deducted from, net income to convert the net income figure to a number representing fund flows from operations.

For example, Phoenix Corporation sold equipment costing $25 and having a book value of $11. The sale of this fixed asset for $8 cash was recorded as follows:

Cash	8	
Accumulated depreciation	14	
Loss on sale of fixed assets	3	
Equipment		25

Deducting a loss in the income statement has the same effect on net income as deducting an expense for which a check was issued. The $3 loss is neither an inflow or outflow of funds. The transaction actually provided $8 of cash because there was a transfer of $8 from fixed assets to current assets. Because equipment with a book value of $11 was exchanged for the cash, the difference is reported as a loss. But the company is not in the business of selling fixed assets, and this transaction does not belong in the category of sources of funds from operations, even though the loss is reported in the income statement. Therefore, the loss must be added back to net income in the funds flow statement, and the entire proceeds from the sale of the asset are reported among sources of funds from the sale of fixed assets.

If gains occur from sales of assets, they must be deducted from income to arrive at funds from operations. The gain itself is not an increase in funds, because the increase occurred from the entire proceeds of the sale.

Other Nonfund Transactions

Changes sometimes occur in capital accounts that appear to be sources or uses of funds when in fact they are not. The issuance of new stock provides a source of funds if assets are received when the stock is issued. However, if stock is issued as a result of a stock split, there is no effect on funds. Changes from stock splits do not appear on the statement of changes in financial position. Similarly, the issuance of a stock dividend neither provides nor uses funds. Therefore, the 2 percent stock dividend distributed by Phoenix Corporation is not disclosed in the funds flow statement although it appears in the statement of retained earnings.

The Concept of All Financial Resources

Transactions that do not affect cash or working capital may take place during an accounting period. For example, common stock may be issued in exchange for land and buildings. Or a new 10-year bond payable may be issued in exchange for an old bond payable which is about to mature. Although such transactions do not affect funds, they nevertheless involve resource changes that must be disclosed in the statement of changes in financial position.

The statement of changes should report all financial resources

The ability of a company to issue additional common stock is an important resource. The acquisition of new land and buildings in exchange for the stock is an important use of the company's resources although it did not affect funds. To ensure that all such resources are disclosed, the concept of **all financial resources** requires the reporting of the financing and investing aspects of exchanges.

An example of the way exchanges are treated is the acquisition of new equipment by Phoenix Corporation in exchange for cash and a long-term note payable. The cost of the equipment was $66 and Phoenix paid $22 cash. The transaction was recorded as follows:

Equipment		66	
Cash			22
Notes payable			44

Exchanges include both sources and uses

Only $22 of working capital was needed to acquire the new equipment. The company was able to obtain $44 of long-term financing for the acquisition of these assets. Although the note payable did not provide working capital, it does indicate the ability to borrow funds. Also, the purchase of assets represents $66 of investing activities, not just $22 represented by the use of cash.

If only the $22 of working capital effects of the above transaction were disclosed in the funds flow statement, the result would be to hide part of the company's investing and financing activities. Instead, as illustrated in Figure 17-10, such activities are reported and described in the statement to indicate that they do not involve working capital. Among sources of funds, the long-term borrowing is described as an exchange for equipment. Among the uses of funds, the acquisition of equipment is described as being partly financed by funds (the $22 cash payment) and partly by long-term borrowing.

Use of the Funds Flow Statement

Phoenix Corporation's statement of changes in financial position illustrated in Figure 17-10 shows that most of the company's funds were provided by business operations. A relatively small amount came from the sale of fixed assets, indicating that the business did not depend on such sales for its major source of funds. At the same time, the disposal of old assets and investment in new ones shows that the business is updating its plant and equipment and expanding its operations. The sale of long-term investments and the retirement of preferred stock may also indicate that management is revising its asset and equity structure to meet changing business conditions.

The increase in working capital seems to be rather large. A well-managed company normally does not maintain excessively large working capital balances to avoid inefficient operations. The increases in working capital may be necessary if a larger volume of business is expected in the future. By examining the detailed changes in working capital, we see that funds have become much more liquid, with cash, temporary investments, and receivables increasing and less liquid assets, such as merchandise and prepayments, decreasing. The company is therefore in a good position to improve its current ratio by repaying current liabilities, to finance expansion by new long-term investments, and to increase the volume of current operations, thereby possibly improving future profits.

Defining funds as working capital is useful to financial analysts

Financial analysts examine the statement of changes together with the other financial statements to assess the overall condition and performance of a business. They may, for example, find a company to be a rather undesirable investment if it is paying cash dividends while it is obtaining more funds from the sale of fixed assets than from operations. The above discussions are only brief examples of the type of information that may be obtained from the statement of changes. A more complete discussion of financial statement analysis is found in Chapter 19. At this point, however, you should try to learn the relationships among the numbers disclosed in the funds flow statement.

Use of the Cash Flow Statement

Managers are especially interested in the funds flow statement prepared with funds defined as cash. They need information on cash flows in order to maintain good control over business operations and current resources and to maintain working capital at an appropriate level.

Cash from operations.   Figure 17.11 illustrates Phoenix Corporation's **cash flow statement**, with cash provided by operations shown in a separate schedule in Figure 17-12. It is convenient to prepare a separate schedule when the calculation of funds provided by operations is elaborate.

Phoenix Corporation
Statement of Changes in Financial Position
For the Year Ended December 31, 1985

Sources of Cash

Cash provided by operations (see schedule, Figure 17-12)	$173
Other sources of cash:	
Sale of equipment	8
Sale of long-term investments	30
Long-term borrowing used to finance	
purchase of new equipment	44
Total sources of cash	$255

Uses of Cash

Payment of dividends	$ 30
Retirement of preferred stock	48
Addition to buildings	13
Purchase of equipment, financed partly by	
new long-term borrowing	66
Increase in cash balance	98
Total uses of cash	$255

Schedule of Changes in Working Capital

	Working Capital Increase	Decrease
Increase in cash	$ 98	
Increase in accounts receivable	37	
Decrease in merchandise		$ 17
Increase in accounts payable		18
Decrease in salaries payable	9	
Increase in income taxes payable		7
Increase in dividends payable		10
Total changes	144	52
Net increase in working capital		92
	$144	$144

Figure 17-11
Statement of changes in financial position with funds defined as cash. When the cash from operations requires elaborate explanations, a separate schedule may be prepared in which the details are shown.

Most working capital accounts change as a result of business operations; therefore, their effect on cash is shown as part of funds from operations. An exception is dividends payable, which is not related to the operations of the business but is nevertheless a component of working capital. Note that increases in current liabilities are added back to net income to arrive at cash provided by operations. The increase in dividends payable, however, is not included in the schedule, because the increase in this current liability has nothing to do with operating the company.

Phoenix Corporation
Schedule of Cash Provided by Operations
For the Year Ended December 31, 1985

Net income	$117
Add items not requiring use of cash:	
Decrease in merchandise	17
Increase in accounts payable	18
Increase in income taxes payable	7
Depreciation expense	60
Amortization of patent	4
Loss on sale of fixed assets	3
Total additions	226
Less items not providing cash:	
Increase in accounts receivable	37
Decrease in salaries payable	9
Gain on sale of investments	5
Amortization of bond premium	2
Total deductions	53
Total sources of cash from operations	$173

Figure 17-12
The schedule of cash provided by operations may be shown separately if it is elaborate as this one.

Other cash sources and uses.   Except for funds provided by operations, the other sources and uses of cash shown in the statement are not different from those shown in the previous statement, in which funds are defined as working capital. Generally, the way funds are defined affects only sources from operations, as explained in the beginning of this chapter. Therefore the analysis of sources and uses from other than operations is the same with either definition of funds. Again the exception is the amount of cash used for payment of dividends. Part of the dividends declared have not been paid and are still listed among dividends payable. When funds are defined as working capital, the entire amount of dividends declared is a use of funds. When funds are defined as cash, only the dividends paid are reported in the funds flow statement. Dividends are usually paid shortly after their declaration, so we know that part of the cash balance will soon be used by management to discharge the dividend obligation.

Defining funds as cash is useful to managers

FASB rules require the statement of changes to report the changes in working capital even if funds are defined as cash. This schedule therefore always is a part of the statement of changes.

SUMMARY

The **statement of changes in financial position** reports the **financing activities** and **investing activities** of a business. Such activities are inflows and outflows of **funds**, which may be defined either as **cash** or as **working capital**. Financing activities are sources of funds. They include business operations, the sale of fixed assets, issuance of capital stock, and borrowing of money. Funds obtained from financing activities are used for investment in noncurrent assets, for the repayment of debts, and for the distribution of assets to shareholders in the form of dividends or by the reacquisition of capital stock. The difference between total sources and total uses of funds is the change in cash or in working capital.

The statement of changes in financial position is also known as a **funds flow statement**. It is a **cash flow statement** if funds are defined as cash. In either case, the funds flow statement must be prepared in accordance with the concept of **all financial resources**. This means that certain exchanges that do not affect funds must be reported in the statement of changes of financial position because they involve financial resources about which statement users should be aware. The statement of changes consists of three distinct parts: sources of funds, uses of funds, and a schedule of changes in working capital. The sources and uses sections of the statement may be prepared in balanced form, or one part may be shown as a deduction from the other, with the difference explaining the change in funds.

Business operations are an important source of funds. Income is not the same as **funds provided by operations**, because the income statement includes some expenses, revenues, and other deductions and additions that do not use or provide funds. Such **nonfund items** include depreciation and amortization expense, gains and losses, amortization of bond premium and discount, and tax deferrals. The net income figure must be modified to convert it to a figure representing fund flows from operations. For this reason the amount of funds from operations is shown in considerable detail in the funds flow statement.

In most annual reports, the funds flow statement is based on changes in working capital. External users of the statement analyze the relationships among the various sources and uses of funds to determine the effectiveness of management's investing and financing activities. For managerial purposes, it is more useful to define funds as cash, because managers are interested in the more detailed day-to-day operations of the business. The components of working capital and the way they affect cash from operations are of more interest to management than is working capital as a whole.

KEY TERMS

all financial resources *(708)*

cash *(682)*

cash flow statement *(709)*

cash provided by operations *(692)*

financing activities *(682)*

funds *(682)*

funds flow statement *(682)*

funds provided by operations *(704)*

investing activities *(682)*

nonfund items *(691, 700)*

sources of funds *(682, 685)*

statement of changes in financial position *(682)*

uses of funds *(682)*

working capital *(682)*

QUESTIONS

1. What are the four major categories of financing activities? What are the four major categories of investing activities?

2. What is the effect on funds if the amount available from financing activities is greater than the amount needed for investing activities?

3. Why is depreciation added back to net income in order to arrive at cash generated by operations? Why not do the same with other expenses such as salary expense?

4. Define working capital.

5. Explain why sales usually provide cash and working capital in different amounts. Under what circumstances do sales provide an equal amount of cash and working capital?

6. A company sold fixed assets at a loss. Describe the fund flow aspects of such a transaction, and explain why the loss is added back to net income in the funds flow statement.

7. What is meant by the concept of all financial resources? Describe a transaction that illustrates the concept.

8. Why does an increase in long-term notes payable affect working capital while an increase in short-term notes payable does not?

9. Explain why a purchase of merchandise on open account does not affect working capital, but a sale of merchandise on open account does.

10. A company issues 1,000 shares of common stock in exchange for land. What is the effect on funds, and how is this transaction reported on the statement of changes in financial position?

EXERCISES

Ex. 17-1   **Change in working capital.**   The current asset and current liability account balances of Billco Corporation at the beginning and end of the accounting year were as follows:

	Beginning	Ending
Cash	$1,360	$2,110
Accounts receivable	3,050	3,490
Merchandise	7,510	6,790
Supplies	370	420
Accounts payable	2,300	2,490
Notes payable	1,980	1,710
Salaries payable	2,400	2,730
Taxes payable	1,530	1,500

Required: Calculate the change in working capital for the year.

Ex. 17-2   **Effect of operations on funds and income.**   Below is a list of independent transactions or events, each of which may have an effect on cash, working capital, or income.

   a.   Sold merchandise costing $500 from perpetual inventory for $900 on open account.
   b.   Purchased merchandise on open account for $1,780 for perpetual inventory.
   c.   Paid $1,000, 30-day 12 percent note payable.
   d.   Used supplies costing $35 bought on open account last month.
   e.   Wrote off $750 uncollectible account against allowance for bad debts.
   f.   Paid $980 of accounts payable recorded at gross amount of $1,000 and recorded discount taken.
   g.   Received $1,000 cash and a $3,000, 30-day note from a customer in exchange for her $4,000 account receivable.
   h.   Sold temporary investment with a cost of $10,000 for $13,500 cash.
   i.   Paid $7,000 semiannual interest on long-term bonds payable and amortized discount of $120. None of the interest had been recorded as an accrual.
   j.   Recorded $900 of bad debt expense at end of year based on aging of accounts receivable.
   k.   Accrued $650 of interest receivable on bond investment at end of year.

   Required: On a sheet of paper list the letters **a** through **k** and headings as shown below. For each item indicate whether it caused cash, working capital, and income to increase or decrease, and by how much. Use a minus sign to show decreases. The first item is solved below as an example.

	Cash	**Working Capital**	**Income**
a.	0	$400	$400

Ex. 17-3   **Effect of nonfund transactions on funds and income.**   Below is a list of independent transactions or events, each of which may have an effect on cash, working capital, or income.

   a.   Bought equipment for $1,000 cash and a $6,000, 12 percent 90-day note payable.
   b.   Sold equipment for $3,500 cash and a $5,000, 60-day note receivable. The equipment had a book value of $7,500.
   c.   Sold land with a book value of $2,500 for $8,500 cash.
   d.   Sold land with a book value of $9,000 for $4,000 cash and a $10,000 mortgage note.
   e.   Sold a patent with a book value of $5,000 for $3,200 cash.
   f.   Exchanged equipment with a book value of $3,200 for new equipment with a fair value of $3,000.
   g.   Retired long-term bonds payable with a book value of $10,300 for $9,800 cash.
   h.   Sold treasury stock that cost $5,000 for $4,750 cash.
   i.   Declared a cash dividend of $9,500 payable next month.

j. Sold long-term bond investment with a book value of $7,000 for $6,500 cash.

k. Paid the $9,500 dividend payable declared earlier this year.

Required: On a sheet of paper list the letters **a** through **k** and headings as shown below. For each item indicate whether it caused cash, working capital, and income to increase or decrease, and by how much. Use a minus sign to show decreases. The first item is solved below as an example.

	Cash	Working Capital	Income
a.	− $1,000	− $7,000	0

Ex. 17-4   **Calculating funds from operations.**   Following are data from a company's income statement and changes in its working capital accounts. Also given is the only nonfund item reported in the income statement.

		Definition of Funds	
		Cash	Working Capital
	Reported net income	$30,000	$30,000
a.	Depreciation expense, $4,000	4,000	4,000
b.	Decrease in accounts receivable, $1,600.	1,600	0
c.	Increase in merchandise, $3,500.	_____	_____
d.	Increase in prepaid expenses, $700.	_____	_____
e.	Decrease in interest receivable, $200.	_____	_____
f.	Increase in accounts payable, $2,100.	_____	_____
g.	Decrease in wages payable, $1,200.	_____	_____
h.	Increase in taxes payable, $500.	_____	_____
i.	Funds provided by operations.	$_____	$_____

Required: For each item, indicate whether the increase or decrease is added to net income, subtracted from net income, or neither, in order to calculate the amount of cash or working capital provided by operations. The solutions for the first two items are given as examples.

Ex. 17-5   **Calculating funds from operations.**   Brooks Company reported net income of $40,000 for the year ending December 31, 1985. The income statement included depreciation expense of $3,500 and a gain on sale of land of $2,000. From the beginning to the end of the accounting period cash increased $1,500, accounts receivable increased $1,000, merchandise decreased $1,200, and current liabilities increased by $800.

Required:
   a. Determine how much cash was provided by operations during 1985.
   b. Determine how much working capital was provided by operations during 1985.

Ex. 17-6 **Calculation of net income from cash flows.** For the year ended December 31, 1985, Conn-Fuse Company, a maker of electrical connectors and fuses, had $75,000 of cash provided by operations. Depreciation expense for the year was $7,500 and the company incurred a loss of $1,000 on the sale of equipment. The cash flow statement prepared for management reported total uses of funds of $245,860. Following are data on the company's current asset and liability account balances:

	12/31/1985	12/31/1984
Cash	$36,800	$33,940
Accounts receivable	49,000	40,000
Merchandise	63,000	64,500
Prepaid expenses	19,460	19,460
Accounts payable	59,800	56,800
Accrued expenses	37,500	40,500
Taxes payable	29,750	29,750

Required: Calculate the company's net income for 1985, and the amount of cash provided from sources other than operations.

Ex. 17-7 **Cash receipts and payments.** Gyneth Company had sales of $12,000 and cost of goods sold of $7,500 in 1985. Working capital account balances were as follows:

	Beginning	Ending
Cash	$9,000	$9,800
Accounts receivable	4,600	4,000
Merchandise	6,300	6,000
Accounts payable	3,200	3,000

Required:
   a. Calculate how much cash was collected from customers in 1985.
   b. Calculate how much was paid for merchandise in 1985.

Ex. 17-8 **Cash collection and payments.** Slinger Company's fee revenue amounted to $28,000 in 1985. Salary expenses were $18,600, and supplies expenses were $1,700. Working capital balances were as follows:

	Beginning	Ending
Cash	$1,250	$1,760
Accounts receivable	2,150	2,830
Supplies	890	780
Accounts payable	1,180	1,050
Salaries payable	1,340	1,560

Required:
   a. Calculate the amount of cash collected from clients in 1985.
   b. Calculate the amount of cash paid for salaries and supplies in 1985, assuming that all accounts payable are owed for supplies.

Ex. 17-9   **Interpretation of statement of changes.**   Examine carefully the following statement of changes.

Corion Company
Statement of Changes in Financial Position
For the Year Ended December 31, 1985

Sources of Funds
   From operations:
      Net loss $(3,000)
      Add depreciation expense   12,000
      Add loss on sale of fixed assets   2,000

Total		$ 11,000
Other sources:		
New 2-year note payable		15,000
Sale of land		30,000
Sale of equipment		10,000
Change in funds		9,000
Total sources		$ 75,000

Uses of Funds

Repayment of mortgage	$ 40,000
Payment of dividends	8,000
Purchase of new equipment	27,000
Total uses	$ 75,000

Changes in Funds

Cash decrease	$(23,000)
Accounts receivable increase	8,000
Merchandise increase	16,000
Accounts payable increase	(15,000)
Notes payable decrease	5,000
Change in funds	$ (9,000)

Required:
  a. What is the definition of funds? Explain.
  b. Did funds increase or decrease and by how much?
  c. What was the company's main source of funds?
  d. Explain how operations produced $11,000 of funds when the company operated at a loss.
  e. What was the company's main use of funds?
  f. What problems do you perceive with the composition of liabilities? The composition of working capital? The company's ability to generate funds in the future?
  g. Discuss the soundness of the decision to pay a dividend.

Ex. 17-10 **Interpretation of funds from operations.** Examine the following schedule prepared by Knubble Corporation.

Knubble Corporation
Schedule of Funds Provided by Operations
For the Year Ended July 31, 1985

Sales		$32,760	
Add decrease in notes receivable		1,000	
Less increase in accounts receivable		(626)	
Inflow from operating revenues			$33,134
Cost of goods sold	$18,588		
Less decrease in merchandise	(212)		
Add decrease in trade payables	81	18,457	
Wages and salaries	5,284		
Less increase in wages payable	(12)	5,272	
Administrative expenses	3,066		
Add increase in prepaid expenses	11	3,077	
Property taxes		428	
Interest expense	532		
Add bond premium amortization	20	552	
Outflows from operating expenses			27,786
From operations			5,348
Rent income		207	
Add increase in unearned rent		3	210
Total			5,558
Federal income tax		1,330	
Less increase in deferred tax		50	1,280
Funds from operations			$ 4,278

Required:
   a. What is the definition of funds?
   b. What amount was reported as gross margin on the income statement?
   c. How much rent was collected during the year?
   d. How much rent was actually earned during the year?
   e. How much cash was collected from customers?
   f. As a result of changes in merchandise, did working capital increase or decrease and by what amount?
   g. How much tax had to be paid to the federal government on the year's income?
   h. What was the amount of tax expense reported on the income statement?

Ex. 17-11 **Interpretation of statement of changes.** Examine the following statement prepared by Faron Company's new treasurer.

Faron Company
Statement of Changes in Financial Position
December 31, 1985

Sources:

Net income from income statement	$ 3,000
Accounts receivable decrease	6,000
Merchandise increase	(9,000)
Accounts payable increase	2,000
Depreciation	7,000
Total	9,000
Cost of land sold at loss of $4,000	24,000
New 3-year note payable	10,000
Change in funds	8,000
Total	$51,000

Uses:

Debt	$30,000
Equipment	12,000
Dividends	9,000
Total	$51,000

Required:

a. Does the statement present information adequately? Explain.
b. What is the definition of funds? Explain.
c. Did funds increase or decrease and by how much?
d. What was the company's main source of funds?
e. What amount of funds was actually provided by the sale of land? Where should the loss on the sale appear?
f. What amount of funds was actually provided by operations? Explain how funds from operation can be so much greater than net income?
g. Does the statement indicate that current assets are becoming more or less liquid? Explain.
h. What was the main use of funds?
i. Does the decision to pay dividends appear to be sound?
j. Does the statement indicate the presence of potential problems for the company? Explain.

Ex. 17-12 **Recasting a statement of changes.**   Examine the statement of changes in financial position presented in Exercise 17-11 and note any deficiencies in the presentation.

Required: Recast the statement in its proper form assuming it covers a 1-year period.

Ex. 17-13 **Interpretation of statement of changes.**   Examine the consolidated statement of changes in financial position of Rangaire Corporation illustrated on page 202. Respond to the following statements by indicating for each statement whether it is true or false.

a. The company defines funds as working capital.

b. The company obtained more working capital from long-term debt in 1983 than it used to repay long-term debt.

c. Deferred income taxes reported on the income statement are considered to be nonfund items.

d. Of all the sources of funds in 1983 and 1982, operations were by far the largest source.

e. A major investment of funds in 1983 was the acquisition of a subsidiary.

f. Working capital decreased by over $3 million between July 1982 and July 1983.

g. Issuance of common stock did not provide funds but is reported as a source of funds under the all financial resources concept.

h. The change in the current portion of long-term debt increased working capital in 1982 and decreased working capital in 1981 and 1983.

i. Prepaid expenses increased from $163,220 in 1982 to $792,536 in 1983.

j. The company consistently obtains a large amount of its funds from the sale of assets.

PROBLEMS

P. 17-1   Funds provided by operations.   The income statement of Hermetica Corporation is provided below.

Hermetica Corporation
Income Statement
For the Year Ended December 31, 1985

Sales		$175,000
Less cost of goods sold		103,200
Gross margin		71,800
Less expenses:		
Salaries	$28,900	
Administrative	19,700	
Depreciation	5,800	
Amortization of patent	1,500	
Other	4,600	60,500
Operating income		11,300
Other income and expenses:		
Rent income	1,000	
Loss on sale of equipment	(300)	700
Income before tax		12,000
Less income tax		5,100
Income before extraordinary item		6,900
Extraordinary gain on bond redemption (net of tax)		600
Net income		$ 7,500

Required: Prepare a schedule showing the amount of working capital provided by operations.

P. 17-2 Change in working capital. Comparative trial balances of Danbrooks Corporation are presented below.

Danbrooks Corporation **Comparative Trial Balances** **December 31, 1985 and 1984**		
	1985	**1984**
Cash	$ 2,180	$ 1,160
Temporary investments	3,200	3,350
Accounts receivable	3,390	3,150
Merchandise	6,520	6,760
Prepaid expenses	860	950
Equipment	11,670	11,580
Accumulated depreciation	(4,450)	(3,500)
Accounts payable	(2,370)	(2,210)
Taxes payable	(880)	(1,060)
Salaries payable	(3,720)	(3,500)
Unearned revenue	(1,710)	(1,980)
Dividends payable	(5,000)	(5,100)
Bonds payable	(5,000)	(5,000)
Common stock	(3,200)	(3,000)
Retained earnings	(1,490)	(1,600)
	$ 0	$ 0

Required: Prepare a schedule of changes in working capital similar to the one shown at the bottom of Figure 17-10.

P. 17-3 Statement of changes, working capital basis. Following is a list of transactions and their amounts as collected by Fleximat Company's internal auditor from data in the company's books for the year ended December 31, 1985.

Transactions	Amount
Total revenues	$300,000
Depreciation expense	21,000
Other expenses	177,000
Amortization of patents	3,000
Increase in inventory	4,000
Purchase of land	40,000
Decrease in receivables	7,000
Increase in payables	9,000
Redemption of bonds payable	35,000
Sale of equipment at book value	22,000
Issuance of common stock	23,000
Purchase of building	85,000
Increase in cash	20,000

Required: Prepare a statement of changes in financial position for 1985, with funds defined as working capital.

P. 17-4 **Statement of changes, cash basis.** Use the data provided for Fleximat Company in Problem 17-3 to prepare a statement of changes in financial position for 1985, with funds defined as cash.

P. 17-5 **Simple statement of changes.** Comparative financial statements of Mars Company are provided below. Net income for the year was $3,980, and the company declared and paid $5,000 of dividends.

Mars Company
Comparative Balance Sheets
December 31, 1985 and 1984

	1985	1984
Assets:		
Cash	$ 680	$ 500
Accounts receivable	1,440	1,250
Merchandise	2,070	2,130
Land	7,700	5,600
Buildings	15,200	15,200
Accumulated depreciation	(5,300)	(4,100)
Total assets	$21,790	$20,580
Equities:		
Accounts payable	$ 1,160	$ 930
Bonds payable, due 1999	10,000	8,000
Common stock	5,000	5,000
Retained earnings	5,630	6,650
Total equities	$21,790	$20,580

Required: Prepare a statement of changes in financial position for the company, with funds defined as working capital.

P. 17-6 **Simple cash flow statement.** Use the data in Problem 17-5 to prepare a statement of changes in financial position for Mars Company, with funds defined as cash.

P. 17-7 **Statement of changes using working capital.** Listed on the following page are changes in account balances for Venus Company calculated from the December 31, 1984 and 1985 balance sheets. During 1985, the company had a net loss of $390, the owner withdrew $630, and land was sold at a gain of $300.

	Changes dr (cr)
Cash	$ (180)
Accounts receivables	(190)
Merchandise	60
Land	(2,100)
Plant and equipment	360
Accumulated depreciation	(1,200)
Accounts payable	230
Mortgage payable	2,000
Capital, Venus	1,020
	$ 0

Required: Prepare a statement of changes in financial position for the company, with funds defined as working capital.

P. 17-8 Simple cash flow statement. Use the data in Problem 17-7 to prepare a statement of changes of financial position for Venus Company, with funds defined as cash.

P. 17-9 Interpreting a statement of changes. Examine the partial statement of changes shown below, as taken from the annual report of Jojoba Industries.

Jojoba Industries
Statement of Changes in Financial Position
For the Year Ended December 31, 1985

Sources of Funds		
From operations:		
Net income	$28,000	
Add depreciation	3,200	
Loss on sale of land	1,000	
Less increase in deferred tax	(500)	$31,700
Other sources:		
Issuance of bonds		10,000
Sale of land		19,000
Total sources		$60,700
Uses of Funds		
Payment of dividends		$15,000
Acquisition of plant		22,400
Retirement of preferred stock		18,500
Change in funds		4,800
Total uses		$60,700

Required:

a. What is the definition of funds?

b. Did funds increase or decrease and by how much?

    c. What was the book value of the sold land?

    d. What was the change in retained earnings?

    e. Was the amount of tax expense more or less than the tax liability, and by how much?

    f. Was the deferred tax account debited or credited, and by how much?

    g. Was the preferred stock account debited or credited, and by how much?

P. 17-10   **Recasting a statement of changes.** The following statement was prepared by Burble Company on December 31, 1985.

Burble Company
Funds Flow Statement
For the Year 1985

Funds provided:		
Net income		$26,860
Depreciation		1,530
Amortization		600
Accounts receivable decrease		120
Accounts payable increase		150
Bond discount amortization		90
Sale of land		1,880
Sale of investments		1,090
Sale of stock		4,000
Total		$36,320
Funds applied:		
Dividends		$15,000
Merchandise increase		430
Notes payable, current, decrease		200
Gain on sale of land	$480	
Less loss of sale of investments	210	270
New buildings		16,100
New equipment		4,100
Change in cash		220
Total		$36,320

CASH PROJ POR 29,450

Required: Recast the above statement, using proper accounting terminology and form, with funds defined as working capital.

P. 17-11   **Recasting a statement of changes.** Refer to the statement provided by Burble Company in Problem 17-10.

Required: Recast the statement, using proper accounting terminology and form, with funds defined as cash.

P. 17-12   Interpreting a statement of changes.   Examine the statement below taken from the annual report of Nikita Corporation.

Nikita Corporation
Statement of Changes in Financial Position
For the Year Ended December 31, 1985

Sources of funds		
From operations:		
Net income	$120,000	
Add depreciation	84,000	
Amortization of patents	36,000	
Increase in accounts payable	26,400	
Decrease in inventories	33,600	
Loss on sale of investments	28,800	
Less increase in accounts receivable	(10,800)	
Decrease in wages payable	(7,200)	
Gain on sale of equipment	(18,000)	$ 288,000
Other sources:		
Sale of equipment		696,000
Sale of investments		120,000
Issuance of stock		360,000
Total sources of funds		$1,468,800
Uses of funds		
Payment of dividends		$ 540,000
Retirement of bonds		780,000
Building improvements		132,000
Change in funds		16,800
Total uses of funds		$1,468,800

Required:
a. What definition of funds was used to prepare the statement?
b. What was the major source of funds?
c. Did funds increase or decrease and by how much?
d. What was the book value of the sold equipment?
e. What was the book value of the sold investment?
f. What was the book value of the retired bonds?
g. How much cash was required to retire bonds?
h. Discuss the source of funds provided by operations.
i. Assess the soundness of the dividend.
j. Do you perceive any problems with this company? Explain.
k. Prepare the schedule missing from the statement.

Case 17-1   **Interpreting and recasting a statement of changes.**
Following is a statement prepared by White Company.

White Company
Statement of Fund Flows
December 31, 1985

Net income		$112,800
Add items not requiring use of funds:		
Depreciation expense	$ 24,000	
Amortization of patents	4,500	
Loss on sale of investments	3,000	
Book value of land sold at $300 gain	67,500	
Proceeds from sale of investments	45,000	
Bank loan	30,000	174,000
		286,800
Less items not providing funds:		
New equipment	126,600	
Withdrawn by owner	43,200	
Cash paid for new building	105,000	274,800
Change in funds		$ 12,000

Change in Funds	**Increase (decrease)**
Increase in cash	$ 1,800
Decrease in notes receivable	(5,250)
Increase in accounts receivable	6,300
Increase in merchandise	9,750
Increase in notes payable	(5,400)
Decrease in accounts payable	2,850
Decrease in wages payable	3,450
Increase in unearned rent	(1,500)
Net change in funds	$ 12,000

Required:
a. What definition of funds is implied by the statement?
b. What was the book value of the sold investments?
c. What were the proceeds from the sale of land?
d. Is the entity a corporation, partnership, or sole proprietorship?
e. Recast the schedule above into a statement of changes, with funds defined as cash. You may omit the schedule of changes in working capital from your statement.

Statement of Changes in Financial Position: Technical Aspects

18

This chapter is an extension of the material you learned in Chapter 17. It discusses the technical aspects of preparing statements of changes in financial position. When you complete your study of this chapter, you should understand:

1   Nonfund items and how they are used to convert net income to fund flows.

2   The T-account approach to preparing the statement of changes with funds defined as working capital.

3   The T-account approach to preparing the statement of changes with funds defined as cash.

4   The use of working papers in preparing the statement of changes.

Now that you have some understanding of the concepts behind the statement of changes in financial position, we can proceed to a discussion of the procedures and techniques used to prepare the statement. This chapter should strengthen your comprehension of the statement of changes and enhance your appreciation of the wealth of information it contains.

As you already know, the statement of changes in financial position is prepared from information found in comparative balance sheets and income statements and from other financial data. But the information on income and financial position must be transformed into information on fund inflows and outflows. Two common techniques used to perform this task are the **T-account method** and the **worksheet method**. The T-account approach is typically the easiest and fastest way of preparing a statement of changes, and is used in this chapter. The worksheet method is illustrated in an appendix to this chapter.

You will find it easiest to learn the techniques for preparing the statement of changes if you understand the nature of changes that are reported in the statement. We therefore start by illustrating why debits can be viewed as uses of funds and credits may be viewed as sources of funds. We also further explain the nature of nonfund items that are frequently found in the income statement.

THE NATURE OF BALANCE SHEET CHANGES

The financial statements of Phoenix Corporation presented in Chapter 17 are used in this chapter to illustrate the technical aspects of preparing the statement of changes in financial position. The resulting funds flow statements are the same as illustrated in Chapter 17, but now we show in detail specifically how they are derived. To review briefly the concept of sources and uses of funds, examine the comparative balance sheet in Figure 18-1 and the income statement in Figure 18-2.

Debits and Credits as Uses and Sources of Funds

The changes in the balance sheet accounts are calculated and shown in Figure 18-1 in the two columns headed Uses and Sources. The headings of these two columns also indicate that debits are uses of funds and credits are sources of funds. Why should this be the case? The reason is explained by reference to a change in a long-term liability or a fixed asset.

For example, Figure 18-1 shows that Phoenix Corporation did not have long-term notes payable outstanding in 1984 but does have them outstanding in 1985. It is therefore clear that the company borrowed money by issuing notes payable. When it did so the following entry was made:

Cash	44	
Notes payable		44

Credits are sources of funds

Issuing the note is a **financing activity** which **provides funds** and requires crediting a liability. The note payable is the **source** of the funds received, and it is recorded by a **credit**. If, instead, a liability had been reduced, it would have required the **use of funds**, and the decrease in the liability would be recorded as a **debit**. Therefore, credits represent sources of funds and debits represent uses of funds.

The same reasoning applies to a change in a fixed asset. Phoenix Corporation acquired buildings in 1985, resulting in the following entry:

Buildings		13	
Cash			13

Phoenix Corporation
Comparative Balance Sheets
December 31, 1985 and 1984

			Changes	
			Uses	Sources
	1985	1984	dr	cr
Assets				
Cash	$ 165	$ 67	98	
Accounts receivable (net)	127	90	37	
Merchandise	78	95		17
Total current assets	370	252		
Land	60	60		
Buildings	1,000	987	13	
Equipment	841	800	41	
Less accumulated depreciation	(706)	(660)		46
Total fixed assets	1,195	1,187		
Long-term investments	100	125		25
Patents	33	37		4
Total other assets	133	162		
Total assets	$1,698	$1,601		
Liabilities				
Accounts payable	$ 92	$ 74		18
Salaries payable	21	30	9	
Income taxes payable	20	13		7
Dividends payable	10			10
Total current liabilities	143	117		
Notes payable, due 1989	44			44
Bonds payable, due 1994	450	450		
Premium on bonds payable	16	18	2	
Total long-term liabilities	510	468		
Total liabilities	653	585		
Capital				
Preferred stock		48	48	
Common stock $1 par	510	500		10
Paid-in capital on common	260	220		40
Retained earnings	275	248		27
Total capital	1,045	1,016		
Total liabilities and capital	$1,698	$1,601	248	248

Figure 18-1
Comparative
balance sheets
with changes
calculated in
preparation for
constructing a
statement of
changes in
financial position.

Phoenix Corporation
Income Statement
For the Year Ended December 31, 1985

Sales		$2,340
Less cost of goods sold:		
Beginning inventory	$ 95	
Add purchases	1,387	
Goods available for sale	1,482	
Less ending inventory	78	
Cost of goods sold		1,404
Gross margin		936
Less expenses:		
Administrative	317	
Salaries	306	
Depreciation	60	
Amortization of patent	4	
Interest	38	
Total expenses		725
Income from operations		211
Other income:		
Gain on sale of investments	5	
Loss on sale of equipment	(3)	2
Income before tax		213
Less income tax expense		96
Net income		$ 117

Figure 18-2
Income statement and statement of retained earnings to be used for preparing a statement of changes in financial position. Information on nonfund items and retained earnings changes is obtained from these statements.

Phoenix Corporation
Statement of Retained Earnings
For the Year Ended December 31, 1985

Retained earnings, 12/31/84		$ 248
Add net income		117
		365
Deduct dividends:		
Cash dividends	$ 40	
2% stock dividend	50	90
Retained earnings, 12/31/85		$ 275

Debits are uses of funds

Funds were **used** to acquire the buildings whose increase is recorded with a **debit**. Therefore debits are uses of funds. Similarly, selling a fixed asset **provides funds**. The decrease in the asset account is a credit, so credits are sources of funds. This logic works with long-term liabilities and fixed assets. Do not use it on current accounts because those accounts **are** funds. The idea is to differentiate between funds and their sources and uses. Borrowing is the source which provides cash, or funds. The increase in the building account is the use, which decreases cash.

The Concept of Nonfund Items

Operating a business is the most important source of funds. **Revenues are sources and are recorded by credits; expenses are uses and are recorded by debits.** In the statement of changes in financial position, we do not detail all sources and uses from operations. Instead we report the net source, which is the difference between revenue sources and expense uses.

Nonfund items are used to convert net income to fund flows

Net income includes a number of nonfund items. Therefore to convert net income to a **net source of funds**, the net income figure must be adjusted to eliminate the effects of the nonfund items and to **reflect only sources and uses of funds from operations.** The adjustments required to convert net income to net fund flows from operations is simple and logical. If a nonfund item, such as depreciation expense, was included in the income statement so that it reduced net income, that item is added back. If a nonfund item, such as a gain, was included in the income statement so that it increased net income, that item is deducted. Adjustments are needed for the following nonfund items commonly found in income statements:

Nonfund items that reduce reported net income but do not actually use funds and therefore must be added back to net income include:

Depreciation of fixed assets
Depletion of natural resources
Amortization of intangibles
Discount amortization on bonds payable
Premium amortization on bond investments
Increases in deferred tax credits
Decreases in deferred tax charges
Losses

Nonfund items that increase reported net income but do not actually provide funds and therefore must be deducted from net income include:

Premium amortization on bonds payable
Discount amortization on bond investments
Decreases in deferred tax credits
Increases in deferred tax charges
Income from investments carried at equity
Gains

DATA FOR STATEMENT PREPARATION

The comparative balance sheets, income statement, and retained earnings statement are the primary sources of information for preparing the statement of changes. Additional data from the accounting records may also be used to analyze the way specific transactions affect funds. As discussed in Chapter 17, the following relevant transactions occurred during 1985.

Fixed assets that cost $25 and had a book value of $11 were sold for $8 cash.

A 2 percent stock dividend was paid on the common stock in addition to the cash dividend.

Preferred stock was redeemed at its book value and retired.

New equipment was purchased for $22 cash and a $44 long-term note payable.

Working papers are used to prepare the statement of changes

The statement of changes is prepared by means of a series of mechanical steps. They are designed to convert the information available above and in the company's financial statements into a statement of changes in financial position. You cannot become entirely familiar with these procedures merely by reading about them; you must use them in order to comprehend them. The procedure consists of preparing working papers either as a set of T accounts or as a columnar worksheet. Entries are made in these working papers so that information is organized into a form from which the formal statement of changes in financial position may be prepared.

The entries used to prepare the statement of changes do not become part of the accounting records of the company. They are made in the working papers only, not in the books of account. The purpose of these entries is to enable the accountant to examine transactions that were recorded in the books previously. But now these transactions are examined to see their effect on funds rather than their effect on the accounting equation.

The changes in the balance sheet accounts, which the statement of changes explains, occurred as a result of transactions that were recorded in the books during the past accounting period. When the transactions were originally recorded, they were analyzed to determine their effect on the accounting equation. Now we need to analyze these same transactions to determine their effect on fund flows. The easiest way to analyze each transaction is to reproduce the journal entry that describes it and enter it into the working papers. As each entry is entered, it explains some of the changes in the account balances. When the change in each account in the working papers has been explained, sufficient information is accumulated to prepare the statement of changes.

T accounts make statement preparation fast and easy

First we illustrate the T-account method with funds defined as working capital. Next we use the same method with funds defined as cash. The techniques employed for preparing the statement of changes depend on the definition of funds. With either definition, the concept of all financial resources is used.

FUNDS DEFINED AS WORKING CAPITAL

In the statement of changes that we are about to prepare, funds are defined as working capital. The statement will report the amount of working capital provided by operations and other sources of working capital. It will also show how working capital was used in investing activities, and the changes in working capital and its components.

Steps in Preparing the Statement of Changes

A step-by-step T-account procedure is used to prepare the statement of changes in financial position. Keep in mind that these are mechanical procedures, the logic of which becomes clear only after some proficiency is developed.

Setting Up the Working T Accounts

The first four steps are procedures to organize the working papers, enter the available data in them, and calculate the change in working capital. When these steps are completed, we are ready to start the analysis of income statement and balance sheet data.

Step 1. The changes in balance sheet accounts are calculated and entered in the two columns of changes as shown in Figure 18-1. Increases in assets from the previous year to the current year are debits; decreases are credits. The opposite is the case for equities. The change in each account must be calculated. Before you proceed to the next step, add up the two columns to ensure that debits equal credits. Do not proceed further until the sources and uses balance.

Posting backward wipes out a change previously recorded

Step 2. A T account is established for every balance sheet account that changed. In each T account, the amount of the change is entered as the beginning balance. If the change in an account is a debit, it is entered in the T account as a credit; if the change is a credit, it is entered as a debit. By entering all the changes **backward**, we are undoing these changes in the T accounts. There is no special significance to entering the changes backward; this just makes the preparation of the statement of changes easier.

You may view this backward entry as the amount needed to change the account from its beginning balance to the ending balance. For example, the ending balance of cash is $165 shown in the T account below as a debit. The beginning balance of $67 is shown as a credit because this cash has been used up. The change of $98 is the amount that has to be added to the beginning balance to bring the cash account to its ending balance.

Instead of showing the beginning balance, ending balance, and change in each T account, as done below, in the working papers we show only the change.

Cash

Ending bal.	165	Beginning bal.	67
		change	98

If you compare the balance sheet changes shown in Figure 18-1 with the T accounts in Figure 18-3, you can see how each change is entered in the working papers. You should not proceed further until you are sure this step is done properly.

Funds provided by operations are accumulated in Operating Summary

Step 3.   Two additional T accounts are established, one labeled **Operating Summary** and the other labeled **Funds Flow Summary**. These two accounts are needed to accumulate the information that is used later to prepare the statement of changes. As each change in the T accounts is analyzed, its effect on funds is classified either as funds from operations in the Operating Summary account or as other sources and uses of funds in the Funds Flow Summary account.

Initially the Operating Summary and Funds Flow Summary accounts are empty, as shown in Figure 18-3. The beginning balances in the other accounts are the balance sheet changes that must be explained in the statement of changes, and they may be viewed as signals that indicate how a change is to be analyzed.

Remember that all of the balance sheet changes have been undone by entering them backward. Now by analyzing transactions that caused these changes, we can determine whether the transaction affected funds. If a particular transaction affects funds from operations, it is recorded in the Operating Summary account; if it affects other sources or uses of funds, it is recorded in the Funds Flow Summary account. These two accounts conveniently and systematically accumulate information that makes up the statement of changes in financial position.

Other sources and uses are accumulated in Funds Flow Summary

The figures that will accumulate in the Operating Summary and Funds Flow Summary accounts explain the effect of various transactions on funds. The entries to be posted in the other T accounts will restore the balance sheet changes that were wiped out by entering backward. When all of the accounts have zero balances, the change originally entered into each account has been fully explained. The process will become clearer as it is demonstrated in the following steps.

Step 4.   The fourth step in the process is to calculate the change in working capital as a single number. This figure will be reported in the statement of changes, therefore it must appear in the Funds Flow Summary account.

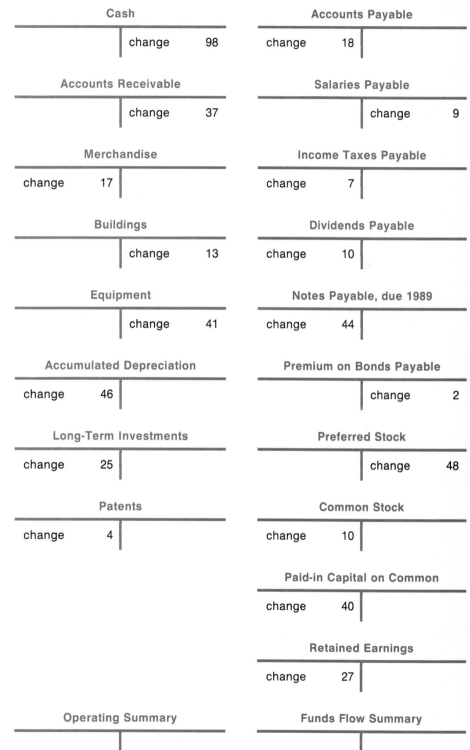

Figure 18-3
Working T accounts at the start of the process of preparing a funds flow statement. An account is established for every balance sheet account that changed, and the change is entered in the T account backward. Debit changes are entered as credits and credit changes as debits. Two summary accounts are also established.

Cash			Accounts Payable		
	change	98	change	18	

Accounts Receivable			Salaries Payable		
	change	37		change	9

Merchandise			Income Taxes Payable		
change	17		change	7	

Buildings			Dividends Payable		
	change	13	change	10	

Equipment			Notes Payable, due 1989		
	change	41	change	44	

Accumulated Depreciation			Premium on Bonds Payable		
change	46			change	2

Long-Term Investments			Preferred Stock		
change	25			change	48

Patents			Common Stock		
change	4		change	10	

Paid-in Capital on Common		
change	40	

Retained Earnings		
change	27	

Operating Summary	Funds Flow Summary

The change in working capital must be calculated

The change in working capital is placed into the Funds Flow Summary account by eliminating all of the changes found in the T accounts that make up working capital—the current asset and current liability accounts. Changes in those accounts are transferred to the Funds Flow Summary account by entering a debit in each current account that has a credit change and a corresponding credit in the Funds Flow Summary. Similarly, the debit change in each current account is transferred to Funds Flow Summary. The following entries, journalized in the working papers, eliminate the changes in current asset and current liability accounts when they are entered in the working paper T accounts.

1.	Cash	98	
	Funds flow summary		98
2.	Accounts receivable	37	
	Funds flow summary		37
3.	Funds flow summary	17	
	Merchandise		17
4.	Funds flow summary	18	
	Accounts payable		18
5.	Salaries payable	9	
	Funds flow summary		9
6.	Funds flow summary	7	
	Income taxes payable		7
7.	Funds flow summary	10	
	Dividends payable		10

When these entries are entered in the working paper T accounts, the current asset and current liability accounts all have zero balances. We can calculate the change in working capital by finding the balance in the Funds Flow Summary account. The net change in working capital appears as a credit of $92. We can verify the accuracy of this amount by calculating the change directly from the balance sheets.

	1985	**1984**	**Change**
Current assets	$370	$252	$118 increase
Current liabilities	143	117	26 increase
Working capital	$227	$135	$ 92 increase

When funds are defined as working capital, current account changes are transferred to Funds Flow Summary

Figure 18-4 shows no current accounts; they are unnecessary because their changes have been summarized in Funds Flow Summary. Why did we establish current accounts first when it would be simpler to enter the changes in working capital accounts directly to Funds Flow Summary initially? We handled each account separately because the procedure later helps to illustrate statement preparation with funds defined as cash. Step 4 is, in fact, the major difference in procedures between funds defined as working capital and funds defined as cash.

Figure 18-4
Working T accounts with working capital accounts eliminated. The net change in working capital (WC) is entered in the Funds Flow Summary account. Funds are defined as working capital.

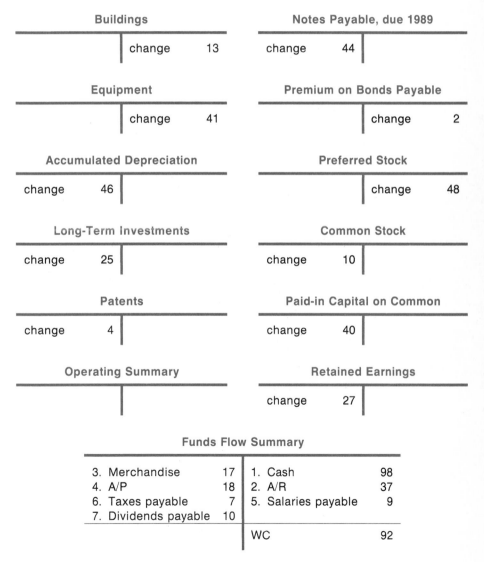

Buildings			Notes Payable, due 1989		
	change	13	change	44	

Equipment			Premium on Bonds Payable		
	change	41		change	2

Accumulated Depreciation			Preferred Stock		
change	46			change	48

Long-Term Investments			Common Stock		
change	25		change	10	

Patents			Paid-in Capital on Common		
change	4		change	40	

Operating Summary			Retained Earnings		
			change	27	

Funds Flow Summary

3. Merchandise	17	1. Cash	98
4. A/P	18	2. A/R	37
6. Taxes payable	7	5. Salaries payable	9
7. Dividends payable	10		
		WC	92

Examination of Income Statement

The purpose of the next two steps is to determine the amount of funds provided by operations. Operations generate net income, which changes retained earnings. But because net income is not the same as net fund inflows from operations, the net income figure must be converted to fund inflows by eliminating nonfund items that appear in the income statement.

Net income goes into the Operating Summary account

Step 5. With this step, we use the net income figure to see how it changed the retained earnings account balance. The procedure results in entering net income in the Operating Summary account, where it is ready to be converted to funds provided by operations.

How does net income change the balance sheet? The change is in the Retained Earnings account, and it occurs when the books are closed and the balance in the Income Summary account is transferred to retained earnings. Remember that we undid all the balance sheet changes by posting them backward. Having undone the changes, we now record them again, in the working papers, in order to observe their effect on funds as they are posted into the T accounts that make up our working papers. From the net income reported in the income statement, we know that the entry to close the Income Summary account was as follows:

a.	Income summary	117	
	Retained earnings		117

Entering this entry to the working paper T accounts would seem to require a debit in Income Summary, and we do not have such an account in Figure 18-4. The T account approach to preparing the statement of changes does **not** require the addition of new accounts to our working papers. Any part of an entry that cannot be entered in an existing T account is placed either in Operating Summary or Funds Flow Summary. Indeed, the debit in our entry is the net income that will eventually be converted to funds provided by operations. Sources from operations are accumulated in the Operating Summary account, so the above entry is entered as follows:

Retained Earnings				Operating Summary		
change	27	a.	117	a. Net income	117	

The $117 debit in the Operating Summary account is the first component of funds provided by operations. The Retained Earnings account is credited, as it was when the books were originally closed, changing the balance in Retained Earnings. Because this credit to retained earnings does not eliminate the retained earnings change in the T account, other transactions must have affected this account. We shall deal with them shortly.

As we examine transactions that caused changes in funds, it is necessary to accumulate the fund flows from these transactions in the Operating Summary or Funds Flow Summary accounts. Therefore it helps to know how a transaction should be entered in these accounts. You will always enter each transaction into the working papers correctly if you remember the following simple rules:

Rules for posting T accounts

1. All temporary accounts are entered in Operating Summary.
2. Permanent accounts are entered in their respective T accounts if a T account exists in the working papers.
3. Permanent accounts that do not have a T account in the working papers are fund flows and are entered in Funds Flow Summary.

You can see that these rules were followed with entry **a**. Income summary is a temporary account and is therefore entered in Operating Summary.

Step 6.   Now we turn our attention to the rest of the income statement and examine each account reported in it to determine if there are any nonfund items that must be removed from income in order to convert net income to funds provided by operations.

The income statement is examined for nonfund items

Most revenues are inflows of working capital and most expenses are outflows of working capital. With funds defined as working capital, the net inflow from these revenues and expenses is already reflected in net income. Therefore we need only look for nonfund items. Starting at the top of the income statement, we note that sales are inflows of funds, and cost of goods sold are outflows of funds. Neither contains any nonfund items. Similarly administrative expenses and salaries are outflows of funds which are already reflected in the net income figure.

An obvious nonfund item is depreciation expense. As soon as we find a nonfund item in the income statement, we can reproduce the journal entry that was originally used to record this item. The entry in our working papers to record depreciation is:

b.	Depreciation exp. (Operating summary)	60	
	Accumulated depreciation		60

Accumulated Depreciation			Operating Summary	
change	46	b. 60	a. Net income 117	
			b. Depreciation 60	

Because Depreciation Expense is a temporary account, it is entered in Operating Summary as a debit. Depreciation expense is a nonfund item that must be added back to net income to convert the net income figure to a cash inflow; therefore, both net income and depreciation expense appear on the same side of the Operating Summary account. The credit is placed in the Accumulated Depreciation T account in our working papers. It eliminates more than the $46 change originally entered in this account. This means that another transaction occurred that changed accumulated depreciation.

Returning to the income statement we find amortization of patents, another expense that does not require the use of funds, as can be seen when amortization expense is recorded. The entry to amortize the patent is

c.	Amortization exp. (Operating summary)	4	
	Patents		4

This entry eliminates the change in the Patents account and adds back the amortization expense to net income in the Operating Summary account. The principle is the same as for depreciation expense.

Patents					**Operating Summary**		
change	4	c.	4	a. Net income	117		
				b. Depreciation	60		
				c. Amortization	4		

A nonfund item may be hidden in interest expenses

The next item in the income statement is interest expense. When interest expense is paid, an outflow of funds occurs, but the amount of interest expense reported on the income statement is not necessarily the amount of cash used to pay the interest. A nonfund item may be hidden in the interest expense. This is because a year-end adjustment to amortize bond discount or premium may have affected the interest expense. In fact, there is a premium on bonds payable on the balance sheet, and it was reduced by $2 during the year. Therefore the amount of interest paid was not $38 as reported in the income statement, but $40. The payment of interest is normally recorded as follows:

	Interest expense	40	
	Cash		40

The cash payment was an outflow of working capital, and interest expense appears on the income statement as a deduction, so we do not need to do anything with this entry, just as there is no need to make an adjustment for the payment of salaries or rent. However, at the end of the accounting period, the following adjusting entry was made to record the amortization of premium on bonds payable:

d.	Premium on bonds payable	2	
	Interest exp. (Operating summary)		2

Now we see that the $38 of interest expense reported in the income statement is smaller than the $40 of cash actually paid by the company for interest. Less was deducted as interest expense than was actually paid, so now the $2 difference must be deducted from net income. Entry **d** adds $2 to the credit side of Operating Summary, reducing funds from operations by $2. The debit of $2 is placed in the Premium on Bonds Payable account, eliminating its change as shown below.

Premium on Bonds Payable				**Operating Summary**			
d.	2	change	2	a. Net income	117	d. Bond premium	2
				b. Depreciation	60		
				c. Amortization	4		

Proceeding further in our examination of the income statement, we find that a gain on sale of investments of $5 was recorded. Although this gain was added to arrive at net income, the inflow of cash from the sale of investments was not $5. Moreover, selling investments is not a part of usual business operations.

How do we know the amount of investments sold? The working papers provide a clue. The Long-Term Investments account in the working papers has a debit balance of $25. It requires a credit of $25 in order to eliminate its change. The sale of long-term investments, therefore, must have been recorded as follows:

e.	Cash (Funds flow summary)	30	
	Gain (Operating summary)		5
	Long-term investments		25

Gains and losses are nonfund items

The sale of long-term investments is not part of operations. It is a different type of financing activity. Selling investments increased working capital by $30. Therefore, the $30 inflow will appear in the Funds Flow Summary account as a debit. The $5 gain originally added in the income statement is a nonfund item which did not provide any working capital; it is placed on the credit side of Operating Summary, automatically reducing funds from operations. The $25 credit eliminates the change in Long-Term Investments.

Long-Term Investments		
change	25	e. 25

Funds Flow Summary		
e. Investments	30	WC[1] 92

Operating Summary

a. Net income	117	d. Bond premium	2
b. Depreciation	60	e. Gain	5
c. Amortization	4		

The next item on the income statement is the loss on sale of equipment. Losses are nonfund items, and the sale of equipment does not provide funds from operations; it is one of the other categories of fund sources. The description of this equipment sale on page 732 says that the proceeds of the sale were $8 and the sold equipment had a cost of $25 and a book value of $11. If the sale resulted in a loss of $3, as reported in the income statement, it must have been recorded with the following entry:

f.	Cash (Funds flow summary)	8	
	Accumulated depreciation	14	
	Loss (Operating summary)	3	
	Equipment		25

The sale of equipment resulted in an $8 inflow of funds, but on the income statement there is a deduction of $3 for the loss. Clearly, the $3 loss did not result in an outflow of funds, yet $3 was deducted to arrive at net income. To convert the net income figure to the amount of funds flowing into the company as a result of operations, we add this loss back to net income. The loss, a nonfund item, is automatically added to net income in the Operating Summary account when the entry is made.

Equipment	
change	41
f.	25

Accumulated Depreciation		
change	46	b. 60
f.	14	

Operating Summary			
a. Net income	117	d. Bond premium	2
b. Depreciation	60	e. Gain	5
c. Amortization	4		
f. Loss	3		

Funds Flow Summary		
e. Investments	30	WC 92
f. Equipment	8	

[1] To simplify the presentation, we show only the change in working capital in the Funds Flow Summary account, and omit the detail of working capital components shown in Figure 18-4.

The $14 debit to Accumulated Depreciation eliminates the remaining balance of that account. But the $25 credit to Equipment does not eliminate the balance in the Equipment T account. This means that there is yet another transaction to be analyzed to determine the overall change in equipment.

Deferred taxes are nonfund items sometimes hidden in tax expense

The last expense reported in the income statement is federal income tax. We must decide whether the entire $96 expense was an outflow of funds, or whether more or less tax was actually paid. Tax expense and the tax payment are not the same if a deferred tax account was debited and credited. Deferred taxes are nonfund items that may be hidden in the tax expense, but in this case there is no deferred tax account whose balance changed in the balance sheet. Therefore nothing has to be done with tax expense.

We have now completed our examination of the income statement, and all nonfund items are entered in the Operating Summary account in a way that converts the net income figure to funds provided by operations.

Examination of Retained Earnings Statement

The next step is the analysis of transactions that affected the retained earnings statement. The change caused by income from operations is already in the Retained Earnings T account.

Operations and dividends change the retained earnings account

Step 7. The retained earnings statement in Figure 18-2 shows that net income was earned and dividends were paid in 1985. The $117 change caused by operations is already in the Operating Summary account and in the Retained Earnings account in our working papers. Therefore we can proceed directly to the dividends.

The cash dividend of $40 used working capital when it was declared. The entry is reproduced below. It eliminates part of the balance still remaining in the Retained Earnings account. The dividend declaration used $40 of working capital, which is entered in Funds Flow Summary. When dividends are declared the Dividends Payable account is credited—$40 in this case. But the balance of dividends payable is $10, so cash must have been used to reduce the dividends payable liability from $40 to $10. Since both cash and dividends payable are components of working capital, the entire $40 is an outflow of funds.

g.	Retained earnings	40	
	Dividends payable (Funds flow		
	summary)		40

Retained Earnings				Funds Flow Summary				
change	27	a.	117	e. Investments	30	WC	92	
g.	40			f. Equipment	8	g. Dividends	40	

The 2 percent stock dividend reported in the statement of retained earnings reduced retained earnings by $50. Originally 500 shares of $1 par common stock were outstanding, as shown in the 1984 balance sheet, and an additional 10 shares were issued as a stock dividend, as reported in the retained earnings statement and shown by the $510 ending common stock balance in the 1985 balance sheet. The entry to record the stock dividend is reproduced below.

h.	Retained earnings	50	
	Common stock		10
	Additional paid-in capital		40

Common Stock				**Paid-in Capital on Common**		
change	10	h.	10	change	40	h.	40

Retained Earnings		
change	27	a.	117
g.	40		
h.	50		

Stock dividends have no effect on funds

The payment of a stock dividend has no effect on funds. When the entry is posted in the working papers, it eliminates the changes in the Common Stock and Paid-in Capital accounts, as well as in the Retained Earnings account.

Examination of Remaining Transactions

We have now completed the analysis of both the income statement and the retained earnings statement. This analysis enabled us to explain several of the balance sheet changes. There is no need to analyze the comparative balance sheets, because the changes in which we are interested are already in our working papers.

The remaining T accounts with balances are eliminated

Step 8.   In this step we complete the elimination of all remaining balance sheet T accounts in our working papers. At this point we are left with two of the four transactions described on page 732: the retirement of preferred stock and the acquisition of equipment. Each of them must be analyzed to determine its effect on fund flows.

To find out the amount of preferred stock that was retired, we look for a clue in the working capital T accounts, where we see that the Preferred Stock account has a credit change of $48. To eliminate this account we must debit it. The acquisition and retirement of preferred stock at its book value is recorded as follows:

i.	Preferred stock	48	
	Cash (Funds flow summary)		48

Preferred Stock				**Funds Flow Summary**			
i.	48	change	48	e. Investments	30	WC	92
				f. Equipment	8	g. Dividends	40
						i. Preferred	48

The change in preferred stock was originally entered backward as a credit, so the debit of $48 to the Preferred Stock account eliminates the change in that account. The original credit change in this account is merely there to tell us that there is nothing more to explain about preferred stock changes because now there is no balance left in the account. The $48 credit in entry **i** is a fund outflow and is posted to the Funds Flow Summary account representing funds used to retire the preferred stock.

The all financial resources concept applied   The acquisition of equipment in exchange for cash and a note payable is an application of the **all financial resources** concept. Originally the transaction was recorded as follows, as described on page 732:

j.	Equipment	66	
	Cash		22
	Notes payable		44

If this transaction were entered as journalized above, Equipment would be debited $66, eliminating its balance, and the Notes Payable change would be eliminated by the $44 credit, but Funds Flow Summary would be credited only $22. If the statement of changes is to report **all financial resources**, the company's ability to borrow funds for the purpose of acquiring assets must be fully disclosed. We therefore separate the above transaction into two components: one to record the source of funds from borrowing and the other to record the use of funds for buying equipment. The two component transactions are

j.	Cash (Funds flow summary)	44	
	Notes payable		44
	Equipment	66	
	Cash (Funds flow summary)		66

When these two entries are made, they have the same effect on the Equipment and Notes Payable accounts as the first version of entry **j**. But now the Funds Flow Summary account shows all financial resources obtained and used in this transaction.

Equipment			Notes Payable, due 1989		
j.	66	change 41 f. 25	change 44	j.	44

Funds Flow Summary			
e. Investments	30	WC	92
f. Equipment	8	g. Dividends	40
j. Notes payable	44	i. Preferred	48
		j. Equipment	66

Only the Buildings account still has a change to be explained. With access to the accounting records, the accountant can easily find out why the Building account changed. Even if we do not look at the underlying records, however, it is clear what occurred. To eliminate the Buildings account change, a debit of $13 is needed. This implies that buildings were acquired or additions were made to existing buildings, and such transactions required the use of funds. The change in the Buildings account is eliminated with the following entry:

k.	Buildings		13	
	Funds flow summary			13

Buildings			Funds Flow Summary		
k.	13	change 13	e. Investments 30	WC	92
			f. Equipment 8	g. Dividends	40
			j. Notes payable 44	i. Preferred	48
				j. Equipment	66
				k. Buildings	13

Any other accounts remaining with unexplained changes are treated similarly. For example, if a mortgage had been repaid, a mortgage account would exist whose change, entered as a credit, would have to be eliminated with a debit. Debiting the mortgage account would imply the use of funds to repay the debt. Any remaining changes in the T accounts can usually be eliminated simply by debiting or crediting the account. The corresponding credit or debit part of the entry is usually a funds flow item.

Preparation of the Statement of Changes

The only T accounts with balances in our working papers are the Operating Summary account and the Funds Flow Summary account. The last two steps consist of balancing the working papers and preparing the statement of changes.

Step 9. To check the accuracy of our work, we need to find the balances of the Operating Summary and Funds Flow Summary accounts. Operating Summary summarizes all of the funds provided by operations, including net income and the adjustments needed to convert net income to net working capital inflows. Operating Summary has a debit balance of $177 representing total funds provided by operations.

When all accounts have zero balances, the statement of changes may be prepared

The Funds Flow Summary account contains all of the fund inflows and outflows not related to operations. To check on the accuracy of journalizing and posting, the Operating Summary balance is transferred to Funds Flow Summary with the following entry, which simultaneously causes both accounts to have zero balances, proving that the equality of debits and credits has been maintained throughout the problem:

l.	Funds flow summary	177	
	Operating summary		177

Operating Summary

a. Net income	117	d. Bond premium	2
b. Depreciation	60	e. Gain	5
c. Amortization	4		
f. Loss	3		
Bal.	177	l. Transfer	177

Funds Flow Summary

3. Merchandise	17	1. Cash	98
4. A/P	18	2. A/R	37
6. Taxes payable	7	5. Salaries payable	9
7. Dividends payable	10		
e. Investments	30	WC	92
f. Equipment	8	g. Dividends	40
j. Notes payable	44	i. Preferred	48
l. Operations	177	j. Equipment	66
		k. Buildings	13

Step 10. The data in the Operating Summary and Funds Flow Summary accounts are used to prepare a formal statement of changes in financial position. The Operating Summary account contains the details necessary

to report the amount of working capital provided by operations, which may be shown in a separate schedule or included in the statement of changes as in Figure 18-5.

Phoenix Corporation
Statement of Changes in Financial Position
For the Year Ended December 31, 1985

Sources of Working Capital

Funds provided by operations:		
Net income		$117
Add items not requiring use of working capital:		
Depreciation expense	$ 60	
Amortization of patent	4	
Loss on sale of equipment	3	67
Less items not providing working capital:		
Amortization of bond premium		(2)
Gain on sale of investments		(5)
Working capital provided by operations		177
Other sources:		
Sale of equipment		8
Sale of long-term investments		30
Long-term borrowing used to finance purchase		
of new equipment		44
Total sources of working capital		$259

Uses of Working Capital

Payment of dividends	$ 40
Retirement of preferred stock	48
Addition to buildings	13
Purchase of new equipment, partly financed by	
new long-term borrowing	66
Increase in working capital	92
Total uses of working capital	$259

Schedule of Changes in Working Capital

	Working Capital	
	Increase	Decrease
Increase in cash	$ 98	
Increase in accounts receivable	37	
Decrease in merchandise		$ 17
Increase in accounts payable		18
Decrease in salaries payable	9	
Increase in income taxes payable		7
Increase in dividends payable		10
Total changes	144	52
Net increase in working capital		92
	$144	$144

Figure 18-5
Complete statement of changes in financial position with funds defined as working capital, using the concept of all financial resources.

The top portion of the Funds Flow Summary account contains all the working capital components whose changes are shown in the schedule at the bottom of the statement of changes. The lower portion of Funds Flow Summary contains all sources and uses of funds, including $177 of funds provided by operations, and the $92 increase in working capital which is the difference between total sources and total uses of funds. Because the debits and credits were initially reversed, the sources of funds are now found on the debit side of the Funds Flow Summary account and the uses on the credit side.

FUNDS DEFINED AS CASH

When funds are defined as cash, the statement of changes in financial position is somewhat more complex because reporting cash provided by operations requires more detail than reporting working capital provided by operations. The procedures, however, are not more difficult.

Every change in the balance sheet, including changes in current assets and current liabilities, must be explained to show the effect on cash. Changes in the current asset and current liability accounts affect cash primarily through operations. The change in accounts receivable affects the amount of cash provided by sales. Similarly, changes in accounts payable and merchandise affect the amount of cash used to pay for the goods sold.

Not all changes in current accounts are related to the operations of the company. For example, if equipment is purchased on open account, the increase in accounts payable is due to the purchase of fixed assets rather than the purchase of merchandise. A careful analysis of current accounts is necessary to determine if some of their changes result from nonoperating transactions. In general, however, you can assume that all changes in current accounts are due to operations. Therefore, current assets and liabilities are handled as follows in converting the net income from operations to a cash flow figure:

Items added to net income:	Items deducted from net income:
Decreases in current assets	Increases in current assets
Increases in current liabilities	Decreases in current liabilities

In addition, nonfund items such as depreciation expenses and gains are added or deducted as already illustrated.

Steps in Preparing the Statement of Changes

Steps 1 to 3.   The T-account approach is ideal for the preparation of the statement of changes with funds defined as cash. Steps 1, 2, and 3 are identical to the first three steps for funds defined as working capital. They result in the working T accounts illustrated in Figure 18-3. Step 4 is the major difference between the working capital and cash approaches.

Setting Up the Working T Accounts

Step 4. Changes in current assets and current liabilities affect the amount of cash provided by operations. In Figure 18-4, the changes in these accounts were used to determine the net change in working capital. Now, instead of transferring all these current account changes to Funds Flow Summary, we follow a somewhat different procedure.

With funds defined as cash, the change in cash is the difference between total sources and total uses of funds. The change in the Cash T account is therefore transferred to the Funds Flow Summary account. This change in cash will appear on the statement of changes as the difference between total sources and total uses of cash. Another way of looking at this change in cash is to see it as the balancing item that makes sources of cash from all financing activities equal to uses of cash for all investing activities reported in the statement of changes.

1.	Cash	98	
	Funds flow summary		98

With funds defined as cash, current accounts are transferred to Operating Summary

We transfer the remaining current account changes, except the change in Dividends Payable, to the Operating Summary account. We do this because these changes affect the amount of funds provided by operations when funds are defined as cash. Proceeding with the accounts shown in Figure 18-3, the balances in the operating current accounts are eliminated with the following entries in our working papers:

2.	Accounts receivable	37	
	Operating summary		37
3.	Operating summary	17	
	Merchandise		17
4.	Operating summary	18	
	Accounts payable		18
5.	Salaries payable	9	
	Operating summary		9
6.	Operating summary	7	
	Income taxes payable		7

The only remaining current account is Dividends Payable. The change in this account is not transferred to Operating Summary because dividends have nothing to do with operations.

Dividends payable are treated as noncurrent when funds are defined as cash

Figure 18-6 shows the result of entering the above six entries. Compare the T accounts in this figure with those in Figure 18-4. The Funds Flow Summary account contains the change in cash, and the Operating Summary account contains the changes of the current asset and current liability accounts that affect operations. Dividends Payable, a current account that does not affect operations, still contains its change and must be eliminated. When funds are defined as cash, the Dividends Payable account is treated simply as if it is not part of working capital. The increase in this account means that the amount of cash used for the payment of dividends, which is an investing activity, was less than the total amount of dividends declared.

Figure 18-6
Working T accounts with most working capital balances transferred to Operating Summary, and cash transferred to Funds Flow Summary. Note that Dividends Payable is the only current account which has a balance remaining.

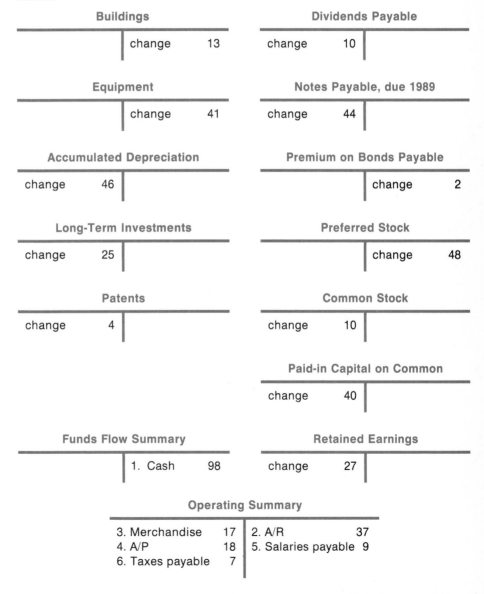

Now you see the main difference in the preparation of the statement of changes in financial position between the two definitions of funds. The difference lies in the treatment of current accounts. When funds are defined as working capital, all of the current account changes are transferred to Funds Flow Summary to provide the change in working capital. When funds are defined as cash, only the change in cash is transferred to Funds Flow Summary.

Aside from these differences, the rest of the procedure is the same as described for funds defined as working capital. We proceed through the entire example again with explanations only where they are necessary to illustrate the differences between the two approaches. Remember that the entries made at this time are not recorded in the books. They are simply reproduced in the working papers in order to analyze their effect on funds. Making each entry in the working papers eliminates all balance sheet T accounts and accumulates all funds flows in the Operating Summary and Funds Flow Summary accounts.

Examination of Income Statement

Step 5. The Income Summary account is closed in order to transfer net income to retained earnings.

a.	Income summary (Operating summary)	117	
	Retained earnings		117

Step 6. The income statement is examined for any nonfund items needed to convert the net income figure to a cash flow figure. Depreciation and amortization expense do not result in an outflow of cash and are added back to net income.

b.	Depreciation exp. (Operating summary)	60	
	Accumulated depreciation		60
c.	Amortization exp. (Operating summary)	4	
	Patents		4

Interest expense includes a nonfund item resulting from amortization of bond premium. The change in the bond premium account is transferred to the Operating Summary account, to adjust for premium amortization.

d.	Premium on bonds payable	2	
	Interest exp. (Operating summary)		2

The sale of investments provided a $30 cash inflow. The gain added in the income statement must be deducted from net income because it is not an inflow of cash.

e.	Cash (Funds flow summary)	30	
	Gain (Operating summary)		5
	Long-term investments		25

The loss on sale of equipment is a nonfund item. The entry to record the transaction is reproduced in the working papers.

f.	Cash (Funds flow summary)	8	
	Accumulated depreciation	14	
	Loss (Operating summary)	3	
	Equipment		25

Examination of Retained Earnings Statement

Step 7. The payment of cash dividends is recorded with the following sequence of entries:

g.	Retained earnings	40	
	Dividends payable		40
	Dividends payable	30	
	Cash (Funds flow summary)		30

Making these two entries eliminates the change in the Dividends Payable account. Now the Funds Flow Summary account indicates that $30 of cash was used to pay dividends. Look closely at the treatment of dividends here as compared to the previous example. When funds are defined as working capital, nothing has to be done with the Dividends Payable account because it is one of the working capital components that determines the change in working capital. When funds are defined as cash, however, we have to treat the Dividends Payable account separately. Not all dividend declarations result in cash outflows. Entry **g** ensures that only the amount of cash paid as dividends is reported in the statement of changes as a use of cash.

A 2 percent stock dividend is declared and paid, and there is no effect on cash.

h.	Retained earnings	50	
	Common stock		10
	Additional paid-in capital		40

Examination of Remaining Transactions

Step 8.   Preferred stock is acquired and retired.

i.	Preferred stock	48	
	Cash (Funds flow summary)		48

The purchase of equipment for cash and a long-term note payable is recorded using the concept of all financial resources, which means the transaction is split into two components, one showing a source of funds and the other a use of funds.

j.	Cash (Funds flow summary)	44	
	Notes payable		44
	Equipment	66	
	Cash (Funds flow summary)		66

The Buildings account still contains a change that has not been explained yet. The following entry eliminates the change in the Buildings account:

k.	Buildings	13	
	Funds flow summary		13

Preparation of the Statement of Changes

Step 9.   The balance in Operating Summary is the amount of cash provided by operations. This is transferred to Funds Flow Summary leaving both accounts with zero balances.

l.	Funds flow summary	173	
	Operating summary		173

Step 10.   All of the above entries are illustrated in the T accounts in Figure 18-7. Preparation of the cash flow statement is a matter of using the information in the Operating Summary and the Funds Flow Summary accounts to make up the formal report shown in Figure 18-8. When cash provided by operations is a fairly complex computation as in this example, it is reported in a separate schedule with a reference in the statement of changes in financial position.

Figure 18-7
**Working T
accounts used to
prepare the
statement of
changes with
funds defined as
cash. All account
balances have
been eliminated.**

Buildings

| k. | 13 | change | 13 |

Equipment

| j. | 66 | change | 41 |
| | | f. | 25 |

Accumulated Depreciation

| change | 11 | b. | 60 |
| f. | 14 | | |

Long-Term Investments

| change | 25 | e. | 25 |

Patents

| change | 4 | c. | 4 |

Retained Earnings

change	27	a.	117
g.	40		
h.	50		

Dividends Payable

| change | 10 | g. | 40 |
| g. | 30 | | |

Notes Payable

| change | 44 | j. | 44 |

Premium on Bonds Payable

| d. | 2 | change | 2 |

Preferred Stock

| i. | 48 | change | 48 |

Common Stock

| change | 10 | h. | 10 |

Additional Paid-in Capital

| change | 40 | h. | 40 |

Operating Summary

3. Merchandise	17	2. A/R	37
4. A/P	18	5. Salaries payable	9
6. Taxes payable	7		
a. Net income	17	d. Bond premium	2
b. Depreciation	60	e. Gain	5
c. Amortization	4		
f. Loss	3	l. Transfer	173

Funds Flow Summary

e. Investments	30	1. Cash	98
f. Equipment	8	g. Dividends	30
j. Notes	44	i. Preferred	48
l. Operations	173	j. Equipment	66
		k. Buildings	13

Phoenix Corporation
Statement of Changes in Financial Position
For the Year Ended December 31, 1985

Sources of Cash

Cash provided by operations (see schedule, Figure 18-9)	$173
Other sources of cash:	
Sale of equipment	8
Sale of long-term investments	30
Long-term borrowing used to finance purchase	
of new equipment	44
Total sources of cash	$255

Uses of Cash

Payment of dividends	$ 30
Retirement of preferred stock	48
Addition to buildings	13
Purchase of new equipment, partly financed by	
new long-term borrowing	66
Increase in cash balance	98
Total uses of cash	$255

Schedule of Changes in Working Capital

	Working Capital Increase	Decrease
Increase in cash	$ 98	
Increase in accounts receivable	37	
Decrease in merchandise		$ 17
Increase in accounts payable		18
Decrease in salaries payable	9	
Increase in income taxes payable		7
Increase in dividends payable		10
Total changes	144	52
Net increase in working capital		92
	$144	$144

Figure 18-8

Statement of changes in financial position, with funds defined as cash, prepared from accounts in Figure 18-7. Note the reference to a separate schedule of cash provided by operations.

Look closely at the schedule of cash provided by operations shown in Figure 18-9, and compare it with a similar schedule in Figure 17-12 in the previous chapter. In Figure 18-9 net income is adjusted first for nonfund items, resulting in working capital provided by operations. Then this figure is adjusted for working capital items that affect cash from operations, yielding cash provided by operations. This approach illustrates the difference and the similarity between the two definitions of funds.

Phoenix Corporation
Schedule of Cash Provided by Operations
For the Year Ended December 31, 1985

Net income		$117
Add depreciation expense	$ 60	
Amortization of patent	4	
Loss on sale of fixed assets	3	
Less gain on sale of investments	(5)	
Amortization of bond premium	(2)	60
Working capital provided by operations		177
Add decrease in merchandise	17	
Increase in accounts payable	18	
Increase in income taxes payable	7	
Less increase in accounts receivable	(37)	
Decrease in salaries payable	(9)	(4)
Total cash provided by operations		$173

Figure 18-9   **This schedule of cash provided by operations shows net income adjusted for nonfund items to isolate working capital provided by operations. This amount is further adjusted for changes in working capital accounts to arrive at cash provided by operations. Compare the form of this schedule with the same schedule in Figure 17-12.**

SUMMARY

Your ability to use and interpret the statement of changes in financial position is enhanced if you understand the technical aspects of preparing the statement. A first step in such understanding is knowing clearly why specific transactions result in sources and uses of funds. In addition, the nature of nonfund items found in the balance sheet must be understood.

Debit changes in balance sheet accounts are **uses** of funds. **Credit** changes are **sources** of funds. The source from operations is the net result of revenue credits and expense debits. Sources of funds from operations are of major interest to managers and investors and should be reported in sufficient detail to explain how the net income figure is adjusted for nonfund items and converted to a figure representing net inflows of funds from operations.

The T account approach enables you to isolate funds provided by operations in an **Operating Summary** account. Other sources and uses of funds, and the change in funds, are accumulated in the **Funds Flow Summary** account. These two accounts contain all the information needed for the preparation of the formal statement of changes.

When funds are defined as working capital, all of the current asset and current liability account **changes** are netted into one figure which explains the net change in working capital. When funds are defined as cash, most of the working capital accounts affect cash flows through operations. Dividends payable do not affect business operations and are treated separately. With funds defined as cash, current assets and current liability changes are entered into the Operating Summary account, and only the change in cash goes into the Funds Flow Summary account. This way, net income from operations is automatically converted to cash flows from operations.

Exchanges do not usually affect funds. To disclose fully a company's ability to obtain and use funds, the statement of changes must report such transactions using the concept of **all financial resources**. In the preparation of the funds flow statement, such transactions may be divided into two components. One component shows financial resources provided by the transaction, and the other shows financial resources used. The source and use of financial resources is then reported in the funds flow statement as if the transaction had provided and used funds.

The chapter describes ten steps that can be used systematically to prepare the statement of changes with either definition of funds. When you have learned these ten steps, you will understand that they can be summarized into the following procedures:

Establish the working papers with working capital entered into the Funds Flow Summary account or the Operating Summary account, depending on the definition of funds used.

Examine the income statement to identify the nonfund items that must be used to convert net income to funds provided by operations.

Examine the retained earnings statement to find the sources and uses that changed the retained earnings balance.

Examine other available data, including the remaining T accounts, to complete the worksheet.

Prepare the statement of changes from the information accumulated in the Operating Summary and Funds Flow Summary accounts.

APPENDIX: WORKSHEET APPROACH FOR PREPARING THE STATEMENT OF CHANGES

Preparing a funds flow statement by means of a worksheet is not much different from preparing one using T accounts. The worksheet is more compact, but it is not as easy to see when a change in an account has been fully explained. To illustrate use of the worksheet, we again use the statements and transactions of the Phoenix Corporation. The explanations below are based on the assumption that you have studied the material and are familiar with the procedures discussed in this chapter.

Funds Defined as Working Capital

A four-column worksheet is established with beginning balance sheet accounts in the first column and ending balances in the last column. When funds are defined as working capital, it is convenient to enter the beginning and ending balances of working capital rather than all current asset and liability accounts. Figure 18-10 shows a completed worksheet for the working capital approach.

Phoenix Corporation
Worksheet for Statement of Changes in Financial Position
For the Year Ended December 31, 1985

Debits				
Working capital	135	1. 92		227
Land	60			60
Buildings	987	k. 13		1,000
Equipment	800	j. 66	f. 25	841
Long-term investments	125		e. 25	100
Patents	37		c. 4	33
Totals	2,144			2,261
Credits				
Accumulated depreciation	660	f. 14	b. 60	706
Notes payable, due 1989	—		j. 44	44
Bonds payable, due 1994	450			450
Premium on bonds payable	18	d. 2		16
Preferred stock	48	i. 48		—
Common stock $1 par	500		h. 10	510
Paid-in capital on common	220		h. 40	260
Retained earnings	248	g. 40	a. 117	275
		h. 50		
Totals	2,144	325	325	2,261
Sources of working capital from operations:				
Net income		a. 117		
Depreciation of equipment		b. 60		
Amortization of patent		c. 4		
Amortization of bond premium			d. 2	
Gain on sale of investments			e. 5	
Loss on sale of equipment		f. 3		
Other sources of working capital				
Sale of long-term investments		e. 30		
Sale of equipment		f. 8		
Increase in long-term debt		j. 44		
Uses of working capital				
Payment of dividends			g. 40	
Retirement of preferred stock			i. 48	
Purchase of equipment			j. 66	
Addition to buildings			k. 13	
Increase in working capital			1. 92	
Totals		266	266	

Figure 18-10   **Worksheet used to prepare the statement of changes in Figure 18-5, with funds defined as working capital. The entries are coded to the discussion in the text and are the same as those used with the T-account approach.**

The beginning balances come directly from the beginning and ending balance sheet in Figure 18-1. Setting up the worksheet and filling in beginning and ending account balances is equivalent to completing steps 1 and 2 discussed in the chapter.

The two middle columns in the worksheet are used to eliminate account changes and to record sources and uses of funds. The lower portion of the worksheet is divided into three sections: one for sources from operations, one for other sources, and one for uses of funds. Setting up these work areas is equivalent to completing step 3.

The procedures for completing the worksheet are the same as with the T-account approach. The calculation of working capital is already completed, and we perform step 4 by transferring the $92 difference between beginning and ending working capital to the bottom of the worksheet. A $92 debit is needed to change working capital from the beginning balance of $135 to the ending balance of $227. This debit, labeled 1, is matched by the corresponding credit at the bottom of the worksheet.

We proceed with step 5 as before, by examining the income statement. Net income is credited to retained earnings with entry **a**. The debit part of the entry is recorded under sources from operations. You may view this part of the worksheet as the Operating Summary account used in the T-account approach. Next we look for nonfund items in the income statement. Entries **b** and **c** are debited as sources from operations in the worksheet, and credited to accumulated depreciation and patents respectively.

Interest expense in the income statement contains a hidden nonfund item consisting of amortization of bond premium. As we know from the discussion on page 740, this is handled simply with entry **d** by transferring the change in the bond premium account to funds from operations.

Gains and losses are best analyzed by reproducing the transaction in journal entry form before entering it in the worksheet. Entries **e** and **f** in the worksheet are based on the following transactions:

e.	Cash (Fund flows)	30	
	Gain on sale of investments		5
	Long-term investments		25
f.	Cash (Fund flows)	8	
	Accumulated depreciation	14	
	Loss on sale of equipment	3	
	Equipment		25

The fund inflows from the sale of assets are entered under sources of funds. The gain and loss are temporary accounts and are entered under funds from operations. The remaining parts of these entries adjust the permanent accounts in the upper part of the worksheet. The portion of the worksheet in which other sources and uses are entered may be viewed as the Funds Flow Summary account used with the T-account approach.

Examination of the retained earnings statement provides the information necessary to explain the change in retained earnings from dividend distributions. The payment of cash dividends is recorded with entry **g**. Entry **h**, for the 2 percent stock dividend distribution, explains the remaining change in retained earnings as well as the changes in the common stock and paid-in capital accounts. The stock dividend has no effect on funds, so no part of this entry appears in the lower portion of the worksheet.

The remaining changes in balance sheet accounts represent sources and uses of funds and are handled with entries **i** for the retirement of preferred stock; **j** for the purchase of equipment (using the all financial resources concept); and **k** for the purchase of building.

At this point it is a good idea to find the totals for the top and bottom parts of the two middle columns in the worksheet. If the columns balance, as in Figure 18-10, the lower part of the worksheet can be used to prepare the formal statement of changes illustrated in Figure 18-5.

Funds Defined as Cash

With funds defined as cash, the preparation of the statement of changes is somewhat more elaborate, as you saw earlier with the T-account approach. All balance sheet accounts are entered in the worksheet as in Figure 18-11. Step 4 requires transferring only the change in cash to the bottom of the worksheet. Changes in the remaining current asset and liability account balances, with the exception of Dividends Payable, are transferred to sources from operations. This is accomplished with the entries numbered from 1 to 6.

The rest of the process is the same as just described. All of the entries in the worksheet are coded to match the transactions discussed in the main body of the chapter. Note the way the change in Dividends Payable is handled with entry **g**. You should compare the worksheet with the T-account example.

Phoenix Corporation
Worksheet for Statement of Changes in Financial Position
For the Year Ended December 31, 1985

	Beginning Balances 12/31/84	Balance Sheet Changes dr	Balance Sheet Changes cr	Ending Balances 12/31/85
Debits				
Cash	67	1. 98		165
Accounts receivable (net)	90	2. 37		127
Merchandise	95		3. 17	78
Land	60			60
Buildings	987	k. 13		1,000
Equipment	800	j. 66	f. 25	841
Long-term investments	125		e. 25	100
Patents	37		c. 4	33
Totals	2,261			2,404
Credits				
Accounts payable	74		4. 18	92
Salaries payable	30	5. 9		21
Income taxes payable	13		6. 7	20
Dividends payable	—	g. 30	g. 40	10
Accumulated depreciation	660	f. 14	b. 60	706
Notes payable, due 1989	—		j. 44	44
Bonds payable, 1994	450			450
Premium on bonds payable	18	d. 2		16
Preferred stock	48	i. 48		—
Common stock $1 par	500		h. 10	510
Paid-in capital on common	220		h. 40	260
Retained earnings	248	g. 40	a. 117	275
		h. 50		
Totals	2,261	407	407	2,404
Sources of cash from operations:				
Net income		a. 117		
Increase in accounts receivable			2. 37	
Decrease in merchandise		3. 17		
Increase in accounts payable		4. 18		
Decrease in salaries payable			5. 9	
Increase in income taxes payable		6. 7		
Depreciation of equipment		b. 60		
Amortization of patent		c. 4		
Amortization of bond premium			d. 2	
Gain on sale of investments			e. 5	
Loss on sale of equipment		f. 3		
Other sources of cash:				
Sale of long-term investments		e. 30		
Sale of equipment		f. 8		
Increase in long-term debt		j. 44		
Uses of cash:				
Payment of dividends			g. 30	
Retirement of preferred stock			i. 48	
Purchase of equipment			j. 66	
Addition to buildings			k. 13	
Increase in cash balance			1. 98	
Totals		308	308	

Figure 18-11   Worksheet used to prepare the statement of changes in Figure 18-8 with funds defined as cash.

QUESTIONS

1. An increase in the Land account means that funds were used to acquire land. Is the same true about an increase in the Cash account? Explain.

2. List some of the nonfund items that must be added back to net income in order to arrive at funds from operations. List some of the nonfund items that must be deducted from net income in order to arrive at funds from operations.

3. What sort of data are accumulated in the T account labeled Operating Summary? What sort of data are accumulated in Funds Flow Summary?

4. A company had temporary investments that cost $1,000 which it sold for $1,250. What is the effect of this transaction on the accounting equation, on cash, and on working capital? What would the effect be if the investment were long-term?

5. Equipment with a cost of $1,600 and a book value of $600 is sold for $250 cash and a $500 short-term note receivable. Describe the effect of this transaction on the accounting equation. Describe the effect on funds with funds defined as cash and also with funds defined as working capital.

6. During the year a company declared dividends of $2,000. Of this amount, $500 remains unpaid at the end of the accounting period. What is the effect of the dividend on the accounting equation, on cash, and on working capital?

7. (AICPA) The statement of changes in financial position is normally a required basic financial statement for each period for which an earnings statement is presented. The reporting entity has the flexibility in form, content, and terminology of this statement to meet the objectives of differing circumstances. For example, the concept of "funds" may be interpreted to mean, among other things, cash or working capital. However, the statement should be prepared based on the all financial resources concept. What is the all financial resources concept? What are two types of financial transactions that would be disclosed under the all financial resources concept that would not be disclosed without this concept?

8. (AICPA) What effect, if any, would each of the following five items have upon the preparation of a statement of changes in financial position prepared in accordance with generally accepted accounting principles with funds defined as cash?
    a. Accounts receivable
    b. Depreciation
    c. Issuance of long-term debt in payment for a building
    d. Paying off a current debt
    e. Sale of a fixed asset resulting in a loss

EXERCISES

Ex. 18-1   **Recognizing nonfund items.**   Certain nonfund items must be added to or deducted from net income to convert it to fund inflows from operations. Below is a list of items, some of which may have to be used to convert net income to fund flows.

a.   Increase in bonds payable

b.   Depreciation expense

   c.   Amortization of discount on bond investment

   d.   Gain on sale of land

   e.   Loss on redemption of bonds payable

   f.   Issuance of common stock

   g.   Amortization of intangibles

   h.   Retirement of preferred stock

   i.   Amortization of discount on bonds payable

   j.   Dividend income from temporary equity investments

   k.   Decrease in deferred tax credits

   l.   Loss on sale of equipment

   m.   Increase in deferred tax charges

   n.   Amortization of premium on bonds payable

   o.   Purchase of land

   p.   Income from investment carried on equity basis

   q.   Depletion of natural resources

   r.   Acquisition of treasury stock

Required: Code each item in the list to indicate whether it should be added to net income, deducted from net income, or does not affect funds from operations. Use the following codes:

0   No effect. Neither add to nor deduct from net income.

+   Add to net income to arrive at fund flows.

−   Deduct from net income to arrive at fund flows.

Ex. 18-2   **Converting income to cash flows.**   Certain changes in current assets and liabilities must be added to or deducted from net income to convert it to cash inflows from operations. Below is a list of independent items, some of which may affect cash provided by operations.

   a.   Increase in accounts receivable

   b.   Decrease in supplies

   c.   Decrease in accounts payable

   d.   Increase in long-term debt

   e.   Increase in merchandise inventory

   f.   Increase in payroll taxes payable

   g.   Decrease in dividends payable

   h.   Decrease in land

   i.   Decrease in accounts receivable

   j.   Increase in cash

   k.   Increase in prepaid expenses

   l.   Decrease in salaries payable

   m.   Increase in interest payable

n. Decrease in interest receivable −

o. Increase in retained earnings 0

Required: Code each item in the list to indicate whether it should be added to net income, deducted from net income, or does not affect the amount of cash provided by operations. Use the following codes:

0   No effect. Neither add to nor deduct from net income.
+   Add to net income to arrive at cash flows.
−   Deduct from net income to arrive at cash flows.

Ex. 18-3 **Interpreting summary accounts.**   After completing the working papers for the preparation of a funds flow statement on December 31, 1985, P. T. Barney had the following two T accounts:

Operating Summary

Net income	47,000	Gain on sale of land	4,000
Depreciation	5,900	Bond premium	300
Deferred tax	1,500		
Balance	50,100	Transfer to FFS	50,100

Funds Flow Summary

Land	20,200	Funds	6,800
Bonds payable	25,000	Dividends	20,000
Common stock	10,000	Equipment	73,500
Operations	50,100	Preferred stock	5,000

Required:
a. What definition of funds was used to prepare these two accounts? Explain.
b. What was the cost of the land that was sold?
c. Was the amount of interest expense reported in the income statement greater or smaller than the amount actually paid to bond holders? Explain.
d. Which stock was issued, and which stock was retired? Explain.

Ex. 18-4 **Using summary accounts.**   Refer to the Funds Flow Summary and Operating Summary accounts presented in Exercise 18-3.

Required: Use the data in the two accounts to prepare a statement of changes in financial position, working capital basis, omitting the details of changes in working capital.

Ex. 18-5   **Interpreting summary accounts.**   After completing the working papers for the preparation of a funds flow statement on December 31, 1985, Jolly Roger Company had the following T accounts:

Operating Summary

Net income	52,000	Accounts payable	2,000
Depreciation	7,200	Accounts receivable	2,700
Merchandise	1,500	Prepaid expenses	800
Notes payable	1,200	Gain on bond redemption	1,300
Loss on sale of equipment	900		
Balance	56,000	Transfer to FFS	56,000

Funds Flow Summary

Preferred stock	60,000	Funds	11,300
Equipment	16,300	Buildings	19,000
Operations	56,000	Bonds payable	30,000
		Investment in subsidiary	60,000
		Dividends	12,000

Required:
  a. What definition of funds is used in these accounts? Explain.
  b. Is it possible to determine from the above data the cost of the equipment that was sold? Is it possible to determine its book value? Explain.
  c. Was preferred stock issued or retired? Explain.
  d. Calculate the change in working capital.

 Ex. 18-6   **Using summary accounts with funds defined as cash.**   Refer to the Funds Flow Summary and Operating Summary accounts presented in Exercise 18-5.

Required: Use the data in the two accounts to prepare a statement of changes in financial position, with funds defined as cash.

Ex. 18-7   **Conversion from cash to working capital definition.**   Refer to the Funds Flow Summary and Operating Summary accounts of Jolly Roger Company presented in Exercise 18-5. The two accounts were prepared with funds defined as cash.

Required: Use the data in the two accounts to prepare a statement of changes in financial position with funds defined as working capital.

Ex. 18-8   **Working papers with funds defined as working capital.**   Following are account balances of Simplitica Company, which reported $10,000 of net income for the year ended June 30, 1985:

	1985	1984
Cash	$ 7,200	$ 5,500
Accounts receivable	5,300	6,000
Equipment	59,000	54,000
Accumulated depreciation	(11,500)	(10,500)
Total assets	$60,000	$55,000
Accounts payable	$ 6,000	$ 7,800
Long-term debt	20,000	17,200
Capital	34,000	30,000
Total equities	$60,000	$55,000

During the fiscal year, the owner withdrew $6,000 from the business.

Required: Set up working papers for the preparation of a statement of changes in financial position with funds defined as working capital. Complete the working papers, using either the T-account or the worksheet approach.

Ex. 18-9   **Working papers with funds defined as cash.**   Refer to the data for Simplitica Company in Exercise 18-8.

Required: Set up working papers for the preparation of a statement of changes in financial position with funds defined as cash. Complete the working papers, using either the T-account or the worksheet approach.

*Ex. 18-10 **Interpreting a funds flow worksheet.** The controller of Elmer Corporation prepared the following worksheet on December 31, 1985:

	Beginning Balance	Changes		Ending Balance
		dr	cr	
Debits:				
Working capital	$ 200	g. 20		$ 220
Fixed assets	2,800	f. 581	b. 35	3,346
Long-term investments	1,500			1,500
Totals	$4,500			$5,066
Credits:				
Accumulated depreciation	400		c. 23	423
Long-term debt	1,000			1,000
Common stock	2,000		d. 400	2,400
Retained earnings	1,100	e. 17	a. 160	1,243
Totals	$4,500	618	618	$5,066
Sources and uses of funds:				
Net income		a. 160		
Gain on sale of fixed assets			b. 5	
Depreciation		c. 23		
Sales of fixed assets		b. 40		
Common stock issued		d. 400		
Dividends			e. 17	
Fixed assets acquired			f. 581	
Change in working capital			g. 20	
Totals		623	623	

Required:
a. What definition of funds is used in this worksheet? Explain.
b. Is it possible to determine the cost of the sold assets from the above data? Is it possible to determine the book value? Explain.
c. Did funds increase or decrease and by how much?
d. What was the amount of funds provided by operations?

*Ex. 18-11 **Use of funds flow worksheet.** Refer to the worksheet of Elmer Corporation presented in Exercise 18-10.

Required: Use the data in the worksheet to prepare a statement of changes in financial position with funds defined as working capital. Omit the schedule of working capital changes.

---

* Exercises and problems marked with an asterisk refer to material in the appendix of the chapter.

*Ex. 18-12   **Interpretation of funds flow worksheet.**   Bleekey Company's internal auditor prepared the following worksheet on June 30, 1985:

	Beginning Balance	Changes dr	Changes cr	Ending Balance
Debits				
Cash	$ 1,200	m. 48		$ 1,248
Accounts receivable	1,900		a. 73	1,827
Merchandise	2,300	b. 105		2,405
Fixed assets	5,900	j. 332	c. 170	6,062
Patents	1,600		f. 10	1,590
Total debits	12,900			13,132
Credits				
Accumulated depreciation	1,800		d. 72	1,872
Accounts payable	1,600		e. 30	1,630
Long-term debt (net)	2,500	l. 150	g. 5	2,355
Preferred stock	2,300	i. 300		2,000
Common stock	3,000		h. 400	3,400
Retained earnings	1,700	k. 40	x. 215	1,875
Total credits	12,900	975	975	13,132
Sources of funds				
Net income		x. 215		
Accounts receivable		a. 73		
Merchandise			b. 105	
Gain on sale of land			c. 5	
Depreciation		d. 72		
Accounts payable		e. 30		
Amortization of patents		f. 10		
Bond discount		g. 5		
Land		c. 175		
Common stock		h. 400		
Uses of funds				
Preferred stock			i. 300	
Equipment			j. 332	
Dividends			k. 40	
Bonds			l. 150	
Cash			m. 48	
Totals		980	980	

Required:

a.   What definition of funds is used in this worksheet? Explain.

b.   What was the cost of the land that was sold? What was the selling price? Explain.

c.   Which stock was retired, and which stock was issued during the period? Explain.

d.   Was the amount of interest expense reported on the income statement greater or smaller than the amount actually paid to bond holders? Explain.

e.   Calculate the change in working capital.

*Ex. 18-13 **Use of funds flow worksheet.** Examine the worksheet presented for Bleekey Company in Exercise 18-12.

Required: Use the data in the worksheet to prepare a statement of changes in financial position with funds defined as cash.

*Ex. 18-14 **Change of funds definition.** Examine the worksheet presented for Bleekey Company in Exercise 18-12, which is prepared with funds defined as cash.

Required: Use the data in the worksheet to prepare a statement of changes in financial position but with funds defined as working capital.

PROBLEMS

P. 18-1 **Working capital basis statement of changes.** Comparative financial statements of Mars Company are provided below. Net income for the year was $3,980, and the company declared and paid $5,000 of dividends.

Mars Company
Comparative Balance Sheets
December 31, 1985 and 1984

	1985	1984
Assets:		
Cash	$ 680	$ 500
Accounts receivable	1,440	1,250
Merchandise	2,070	2,130
Land	7,700	5,600
Buildings	15,200	15,200
Accumulated depreciation	(5,300)	(4,100)
Total assets	$21,790	$20,580
Equities:		
Accounts payable	$ 1,160	$ 930
Bonds payable, due 1999	10,000	8,000
Common stock	5,000	5,000
Retained earnings	5,630	6,650
Total equities	$21,790	$20,580

Required: Prepare a statement of changes in financial position for the company with funds defined as working capital.

P. 18-2 **Cash basis statement of changes.** Use the data in Problem 18-1 to prepare a statement of changes in financial position for Mars Company with funds defined as cash.

P. 18-3 **Statement of changes, working capital basis.** On the following page are the financial statements of Bronwyn Company prepared by the controller at the end of the accounting period. During the year the company constructed a building, part of which it financed by a new mortgage. The company also acquired some new equipment in exchange for new shares of preferred stock.

Bronwyn Company
Balance Sheets
December 31

	1985	1984
Cash	$ 13,600	$ 10,500
Accounts receivable	17,300	16,400
Merchandise	27,500	28,900
Land	28,000	56,000
Buildings	120,000	55,000
Equipment	241,600	226,600
Accumulated depreciation	(44,000)	(36,000)
Patents	21,000	22,000
Total assets	$425,000	$379,400
Accounts payable	$ 25,400	$ 23,600
Salaries payable	1,600	2,800
Mortgage payable	40,000	
Bonds payable	55,000	75,000
Preferred stock	15,000	
Common stock	50,000	50,000
Paid-in capital	150,000	150,000
Retained earnings	88,000	78,000
Total equities	$425,000	$379,400

Bronwyn Company
Statement of Income and Retained Earnings
For the Year Ended December 31, 1985

Sales revenue		$101,000
Less expenses:		
Administrative	$ 17,000	
Salaries	39,000	
Interest expense	6,000	
Depreciation	8,000	
Amortization of patent	1,000	71,000
Operating income		30,000
Gain on sale of land		2,000
Income before tax		32,000
Income tax expense		12,000
Net income		20,000
Add retained earnings, 12/31/84		78,000
		98,000
Less dividends		10,000
Retained earnings, 12/31/85		$ 88,000

Required: Use the data presented in the statements to prepare a statement of changes in financial position with funds defined as working capital.

P. 18-4   Statement of changes, cash basis.   Refer to the financial statements and other data of Bronwyn Company as presented in Problem 18-3.

Required: Use the data presented to prepare a statement of changes in financial position with funds defined as cash.

P. 18-5   **Funds defined as working capital.**   The comparative financial statements of Venus Corporation are presented below. During 1985 the company issued new shares of its common stock in exchange for new equipment. The company declared and paid $16,140 in cash dividends in 1985.

Venus Corporation
Comparative Balance Sheets
December 31, 1985 and 1984

	1985	1984
Assets:		
Cash	$ 1,120	$ 900
Accounts receivable	2,710	2,830
Merchandise	5,180	4,750
Long-term investments	7,700	9,000
Land	6,000	7,400
Buildings	27,800	21,600
Equipment	21,340	17,340
Accumulated depreciation	(10,890)	(9,360)
Patents	5,000	5,600
Total	$65,960	$60,060
Equities:		
Notes payable	$ 1,800	$ 2,000
Accounts payable	2,310	2,160
Bonds payable	30,000	30,000
Discount on bonds payable	(660)	(750)
Common stock	14,000	10,000
Retained earnings	18,510	16,650
Total	$65,960	$60,060

Venus Corporation
Comparative Income Statements
For the Years Ended December 31, 1985 and 1984

	1985	1984
Sales	$82,520	$77,740
Gain on sale of land	480	
Total revenues	83,000	77,740
Administrative	18,400	18,980
Salaries and wages	21,660	20,900
Depreciation of fixed assets	1,530	1,420
Amortization of patents	600	600
Loss on sale of investments	210	
Interest expense	4,000	3,840
Income taxes	18,600	15,400
Total expenses	65,000	61,140
Net income	$18,000	$16,600

Required: Prepare a statement of changes in financial position for the company with funds defined as working capital.

P. 18-6   **Funds defined as cash.**   The comparative financial statements of Venus Corporation and other data on the company's operations are presented in Problem 18-5.

Required: Prepare a statement of changes in financial position for the company with funds defined as cash.

P. 18-7   **Statement of changes.**   Below are the changes in account balances taken from the December 31, 1984 and 1985, balance sheets of Cusip Company.

	Changes dr (cr)
Cash	$ (560)
Accounts receivable	240
Merchandise	(860)
Land	(12,000)
Buildings	4,000
Equipment	7,550
Accumulated depreciation	(7,000)
Patents	900
Notes payable	(400)
Accounts payable	300
Mortgage payable	3,500
Bonds payable	(5,000)
Premium on bonds payable	180
Common stock	0
Retained earnings	9,150
	$ 0

The income statement reported $7,000 depreciation expense, $500 amortization of patent, a loss of $2,000 on the sale of land, and a net loss of $8,700 for the year ending December 31, 1985. Dividends in the amount of $450 were declared and paid in 1985.

Required: Prepare a statement of changes in financial position for Cusip Company with funds defined as working capital.

P. 18-8   **Statement of changes.**   Use the data in Problem 18-7 to prepare a statement of changes in financial position for Cusip Company with funds defined as cash.

P. 18-9   **Statement of changes, working capital basis.**   On the following page are the comparative balance sheets and the 1985 income statement of Neptune Company. During 1985 the company sold equipment with a book value of $2,000 and a cost of $3,000. It issued new shares of its common stock in exchange for new equipment. The company declared $12,000 in cash dividends in 1985.

Neptune Company
Comparative Balance Sheets
December 31, 1985 and 1984

	1985	1984
Assets:		
Cash	$ 2,100	$ 2,870
Accounts receivable	5,700	4,230
Merchandise	5,200	6,000
Land	10,000	17,400
Buildings	87,000	58,600
Equipment	81,500	76,500
Accumulated depreciation	(30,000)	(26,000)
Patents	9,000	7,500
Total assets	$170,500	$147,100
Equities:		
Accounts payable	$ 3,800	$ 3,630
Salaries payable	2,300	3,200
Dividends payable		120
Bonds payable	50,000	50,000
Discount on bonds payable	(2,000)	(2,250)
Common stock	12,000	10,000
Paid-in capital	45,900	39,900
Retained earnings	58,500	42,500
Total equities	$170,500	$147,100

Neptune Company
Comparative Income Statements
For the Year Ended December 31, 1985

Sales		$120,300
Gain on sale of land		2,700
Total revenues		123,000
Less expenses:		
Administrative	$ 22,190	
Salaries and wages	31,660	
Depreciation of fixed assets	5,000	
Amortization of patents	500	
Interest expense	6,750	
Loss on sale of equipment	800	
Income taxes	28,100	95,000
Net income		$ 28,000

Required: Prepare a statement of changes in financial position for the company with funds defined as working capital.

P. 18-10   **Statement of changes, cash basis.**   The comparative balance sheets and the 1985 income statement of Neptune Company are presented in Problem 18-9, together with additional data on the company's operations.

Required: Prepare a statement of changes in financial position for the company with funds defined as cash.

P. 18-11   **Funds defined as working capital.**   The financial statements of Saturn Corporation are presented below. During the year, the company sold a parcel of land that had a cost of $2,000. It also sold equipment with a book value of $400 and a cost of $490 for $300 cash. In 1985 the company declared cash dividends of $358.

Saturn Corporation
Comparative Balance Sheets
December 31, 1985 and 1984

	1985	1984	Changes dr (cr)
Assets:			
Cash	$ 1,586	$ 2,064	(478)
Accounts receivable (net)	3,676	2,980	696
Merchandise inventory	1,688	1,960	(272)
Prepaid expenses	149	138	11
Property plant and equipment	29,582	26,670	2,912
Accumulated depreciation	(10,710)	(9,870)	(840)
Total assets	$25,971	$23,942	
Liabilities and capital:			
Notes payable	$ 990	$ 919	(71)
Accounts payable	2,147	2,190	43
Dividends payable	37	28	(9)
Bonds payable	5,000	3,000	(2,000)
Mortgage note payable	3,000	3,500	500
Common stock	8,000	8,000	
Retained earnings	7,797	6,305	(1,492)
Treasury stock	(1,000)		1,000
Total liabilities and capital	$25,971	$23,942	

Saturn Corporation
Income Statement
For the Year Ended December 31, 1985

Sales		$39,290
Less expenses:		
Cost of goods sold	$25,347	
Selling and administrative	5,360	
Wages and salaries	4,025	
Depreciation	930	
Interest	520	36,182
Operating income		3,108
Gain on sale of land	72	
Loss on sale of equipment	(100)	(28)
Income before tax		3,080
Federal income tax		1,230
Net income		$ 1,850

Required: Prepare a statement of changes in financial position, working capital basis for Saturn Corporation for 1985.

P. 18-12   **Funds defined as cash.**   The comparative balance sheets and the 1985 income statement of Saturn Corporation are presented in Problem 18-11, together with additional data on the company's operations.

Required: Prepare a statement of changes in financial position with funds defined as cash.

P. 18-13   **Statement of changes in financial position.**   The 1985 financial statements of Pluto Corporation are provided below. The following information is also available:

a.   The company declared and paid a cash dividend of $1,250 during 1985.

b.   In June, 1985, the company issued 100 shares of common stock at $37.50 per share.

c.   During the year, the company sold land and building for $1,960. The land was carried at a cost of $630. The building was carried at a cost of $1,800 and a book value of $1,250.

Pluto Corporation
Income Statement
For the Year Ended December 31, 1985

Sales		$49,140
Less cost of goods sold:		
Beginning inventory	$ 2,250	
Purchases	29,150	
Goods available for sale	31,400	
Less ending inventory	1,930	
Cost of goods sold		29,470
Gross margin		19,670
Less expenses:		
Wages and salaries	7,920	
Selling and administrative	4,590	
Depreciation	1,260	
Property taxes	640	
Interest expense	790	15,200
Income from operations		4,470
Other income and expenses:		
Rent income	310	
Gain on sale of fixed assets	80	
Loss on sale of investments	(60)	330
Income before tax		4,800
Federal income tax		2,000
Net income		$ 2,800

Pluto Corporation
Comparative Balance Sheets
December 31, 1985 and 1984

	1985	1984	Changes dr (cr)
Assets			
Current assets:			
Cash	$ 2,070	$ 1,290	780
Notes receivable	300	1,800	(1,500)
Accounts receivable (net)	3,300	2,370	930
Merchandise	1,930	2,250	(320)
Prepaid expenses	70	50	20
Total current assets	7,670	7,760	
Fixed assets:			
Land	2,220	2,850	(630)
Plant and equipment	43,650	37,150	6,500
Accumulated depreciation	(15,510)	(14,800)	(710)
Total fixed assets	30,360	25,200	
Investments:			
Sinking fund	2,470	2,100	370
Common stock of subsidiaries	600	690	(90)
Total investments	3,070	2,790	
Total assets	$41,100	$35,750	
Liabilities and Capital			
Current liabilities:			
Notes payable	$ 750	$ 600	(150)
Accounts payable	1,790	1,920	130
Wages and salaries payable	460	440	(20)
Unearned rent income		30	30
Total current liabilities	3,000	2,990	
Long-term liabilities:			
Bond payable	9,750	9,750	
Premium on bonds payable	300	330	30
Deferred income taxes	1,420	1,350	(70)
Total long-term liabilities	11,470	11,430	
Total liabilities	14,480	14,420	
Capital:			
Common stock $10 par	13,500	12,000	(1,500)
Paid-in capital in excess of par	6,600	4,350	(2,250)
Retained earnings	6,530	4,980	(1,550)
Total capital	26,630	21,330	
Total liabilities and capital	$41,100	$35,750	

Required: Prepare a statement of changes in financial position for Pluto Corporation with funds defined as working capital.

P. 18-14   **Statement of changes in financial position.**   The 1985 financial statements of Pluto Corporation and additional data on the company's operations are provided in Problem 18-13.

Required: Prepare a statement of changes in financial position with funds defined as cash.

Case 18-1   **Reconstruction of lost records.**

Mr. Simkins has been waiting anxiously for the financial statements of Nebula Corporation, which he must present tomorrow to the board of directors of his company, Galaxie Enterprises. Galaxie has been negotiating for the acquisition of Nebula, and the statements are needed to support the company's offer to purchase the outstanding stock. Simkins is therefore relieved when he opens his mail and finds Nebula Corporation's materials. The enclosed letter states in part:

> You will be pleased to know that we completed the addition to our building for which the contractor agreed to accept 100 shares of our common stock as payment. In addition we were able to dispose of old equipment costing $3,000 permitting us to replace it with more modern equipment, putting us into a much better competitive position.

On close examination of the reports, Simkins notes with dismay that the balance sheet and retained earnings statements had been inadvertently omitted from the materials. He quickly reports the problem to his superior, Mrs. Brooks, and points out that it is not possible to obtain the missing reports in the time remaining before the board meeting.

"No problem," says Mrs. Brooks. "We have their annual report from last year." Going to a file, she retrieves the annual report which includes the 1984 balance sheet. "Here you are. You can use this balance sheet and the material you have to reconstruct the 1985 balance sheet. Any minor discrepancies will not matter for the purposes of this board meeting."

Simkins takes the annual report, returns to his office, and begins to review the following information in order to derive the missing report:

Nebula Corporation
Balance Sheet
December 31, 1984

Assets

Cash	$10,280
Notes receivable	4,800
Accounts receivable (net)	2,370
Merchandise	2,050
Prepaid expenses	150
Land	12,000
Plant and equipment	42,150
Accumulated depreciation	(11,800)
Common stock of subsidiary	4,000
Total assets	$66,000

Liabilities and Capital

Notes payable	$ 900
Accounts payable	6,050
Wages and salaries payable	240
Bond payable	18,000
Discount on bonds payable	(550)
Deferred income taxes	1,150
Common stock $30 par	10,000
Paid-in capital in excess of par	20,000
Retained earnings	10,210
Total liabilities and capital	$66,000

Nebula Corporation
Income Statement
For the Year Ended December 31, 1985

Sales		$90,380
Income from subsidiary carried at equity		800
Gain on sale of fixed assets		400
Total revenues		91,580
Less expenses:		
Cost of goods sold	$39,400	
Wages and salaries	19,550	
Selling and administrative	14,590	
Depreciation	4,720	
Interest expense	1,350	
Federal income tax	5,000	84,610
Net income		$ 6,970

Nebula Corporation
Statement of Changes in Financial Position
For the Year Ended December 31, 1985

Sources of working capital

From operations:

Net income		$ 6,970
Add depreciation	$ 4,720	
Bond discount amortization	50	
Increase in deferred tax	470	
Less gain on sale of fixed assets	(400)	
Income from subsidiary	(800)	4,040
Working capital provided by operations		11,010
Other sources:		
Stock issued in exchange for building addition		9,000
Sale of fixed assets		2,400
Total sources		$22,410

Uses of working capital

Payment of dividends	2,800
Building construction financed by stock issuance	9,000
Purchase of fixed assets	5,500
Retirement of bonds payable	4,000
Increase in working capital	1,110
Total uses	$22,410

Changes in working capital

	Increase	Decrease
Increase in cash		$ 8,210
Decrease in notes receivable	$ 1,200	
Increase in accounts receivable	2,930	
Decrease in merchandise	3,880	
Increase in prepaid expenses	1,120	
Increase in notes payable		850
Decrease in accounts payable	1,260	
Increase in wages and salaries payable		220
	10,390	9,280
Increase in working capital		1,110
	$10,390	$10,390

After several attempts at reconstructing the 1985 balance sheet, Mr. Simkins realizes that he is hopelessly lost. He therefore comes to you and asks you to do the job.

Required: Use the available data to construct the December 31, 1985 balance sheet for Nebula Corporation.

Case 18-2   **(AICPA) Statement of changes.**
Presented below are comparative statements of financial position of Kenwood Corporation as of December 31, 1985, and December 31, 1984, respectively and the company's income statement.

Kenwood Corporation
Statement of Financial Position

	December 31, 1985	December 31, 1984	Increase (Decrease)
Assets			
Current assets:			
Cash	$ 100,000	$ 90,000	$ 10,000
Accounts receivable (net)	210,000	140,000	70,000
Inventories	260,000	220,000	40,000
Total current assets	570,000	450,000	120,000
Land	325,000	200,000	125,000
Plant and equipment	580,000	633,000	(53,000)
Less accumulated depreciation	(90,000)	(100,000)	10,000
Patents	30,000	33,000	(3,000)
Total assets	$1,415,000	$1,216,000	$199,000
Liabilities and Shareholders' Equity			
Current liabilities:			
Accounts payable	$ 260,000	$ 200,000	$ 60,000
Accrued expenses	200,000	210,000	(10,000)
Total current liabilities	460,000	410,000	50,000
Deferred income taxes	140,000	100,000	40,000
Long-term bonds (due 1990)	130,000	168,000	(38,000)
Total liabilities	730,000	678,000	52,000
Shareholders' equity:			
Common stock, par value $5	250,000	210,000	40,000
Additional paid-in capital	233,000	170,000	63,000
Retained earnings	202,000	158,000	44,000
Total shareholders' equity	685,000	538,000	147,000
Total liabilities and shareholders' equity	$1,415,000	$1,216,000	$199,000

Kenwood Corporation
Income Statement
For the Year Ended December 31, 1985

Sales	$1,000,000
Expenses:	
Cost of sales	560,000
Salary and wages	190,000
Depreciation	20,000
Amortization	3,000
Loss on sale of equipment	4,000
Interest	16,000
Miscellaneous	8,000
Total expenses	801,000
Income before income taxes	199,000
Income taxes	
Current	50,000
Deferred	40,000
Provision for income taxes	90,000
Net income	$ 109,000
Earnings per share:	$2.21

Additional information:

• On February 2, 1985, Kenwood issued a 10% stock dividend to shareholders of record on January 15, 1985. The market price per share of the common stock on February 2 was $15.

• On March 1 Kenwood issued 3,800 shares of common stock for land. The common stock and land had current market values of approximately $40,000 on March 1.

• On April 15 Kenwood repurchased long-term bonds with a face value of $38,000 with no gain or loss.

• On June 30 Kenwood sold equipment costing $53,000, with a book value of $23,000, for $19,000 cash.

• On September 30 Kenwood declared and paid a $.04 per share cash dividend to shareholders of record August 1.

• On October 10 Kenwood purchased land for $85,000 cash.

• Deferred income taxes represent timing differences relating to the use of accelerated depreciation methods for income tax reporting and straight-line depreciation methods for financial statement reporting.

Required: Using the working-capital concept of funds, prepare a statement of changes in financial position of Kenwood Corporation for the year ended December 31, 1985. (Do not prepare a schedule of changes in working capital.)

Financial Statement Analysis

19

By drawing on a knowledge of accounting, finance, economics, and other related fields, financial statements can be used to evaluate the financial condition and performance of a business. This chapter is a synthesis of the many concepts, principles, and procedures you have studied. It will enable you to understand:

---

1 The meaning of financial analysis.

2 How to perform horizontal and vertical analyses of financial statements.

3 How to perform a ratio analysis of financial statements.

4 What tests you can perform to learn about the liquidity and solvency of a business organization.

5 Several measures of business profitability.

6 The purpose of market tests used by investors and analysts.

7 That a real appreciation and understanding of the value of accounting information requires a good knowledge of accounting and considerable experience with financial statement analysis.

By the time many corporations issue their annual report, thousands of transactions involving millions of dollars have taken place. The history of the transactions is recorded in voluminous journals and ledgers, but is reported in four brief, highly condensed, general-purpose statements. The balance sheet presents the financial condition of the entity. The income statement tells what was accomplished as a result of operations. A retained

earnings statement explains the change in the earned portion of o
equity. And a statement of changes in financial position describ
financing and investing activities of the business.

Each statement provides essential information, but the four statements
together present a total picture which is complete only when the information in any one statement is **related** to the information in all the others.

Decision makers analyze financial statements in order to take future
action. How can financial statements, which report on past history,
help analysts to make decisions about the future? Often the best indicators of future conditions and events are data about the immediate past.
Reading financial statements provides a considerable amount of information, but making good decisions requires a thorough analysis of the
statements.

Financial analysis requires experience

A single chapter on **financial statement analysis** can only introduce
the topic and discuss some of the information that emerges when financial
statements are thoroughly analyzed. The integration of such information
into a complete, coherent analysis can be accomplished only after much
experience and more study of this and related topics.

Comparative figures enhance the analysis

The usefulness of most data in financial statements is enhanced significantly when statements of the current period can be compared with
statements of previous accounting periods. Such comparisons may reveal
trends and highlight important relationships that are not evident from the
financial information of a single period. Therefore corporations provide
annual reports with **comparative** financial statements—that is, reports that
contain statements for at least two consecutive accounting periods. In
addition, annual reports contain a great deal of information in the notes
that accompany the financial statements.

The notes explain many aspects of business operations that cannot be
shown clearly in the figures alone. This includes several types of information required by the full disclosure principle. For example, the report
discloses whether FIFO or LIFO is used for inventory valuation and
whether depreciation is based on the straight-line or accelerated methods.
Items that may be shown as a single figure in the statements, such as
contributed capital or funds provided by operations, are reported in detailed schedules. Various contingencies, such as pending lawsuits, are
disclosed and any other data necessary to make the report complete are
included.

Management is responsible for providing financial statements to users
who need the information, but management cannot anticipate how the
information will be used. Therefore the analysis of the information is left
to the individual users, who must suit their investigation to their specific
needs. Financial analysts develop a comprehensive picture of the financial
status and future prospects of a firm by performing horizontal, vertical, and
ratio analyses. To illustrate these three types of analysis, we use the financial statements of Megatrix Corporation for 1984 and 1985, shown in Figure
19-1.

HORIZONTAL ANALYSIS

Absolute and percentage changes are needed

Horizontal analysis is the comparison of figures reported in financial statements of two or more consecutive accounting periods. The analyst calculates the absolute changes—the difference between the figures of one year and the next—and also the percentage change from one year to the next, using the earlier year as the base period. Much additional information is obtained from financial statements in this manner. For example, in Figure 19-1, 1985 net income of $95,300 is a significant item of information. It becomes more significant, however, when it is seen as an increase of $7,700, or 8.8 percent, over the previous year, because it shows an upward trend. The information says even more about the performance of the com-

Megatrix Corporation
Income Statements
For Years Ended December 31, 1985 and 1984

	1985	1984	Increase (decrease) Amount	%
Sales	$1,210,000	$1,251,400	$ (41,400)	(3.3)
Less cost of goods sold	666,500	713,800	(47,300)	(6.6)
Gross margin	543,500	537,600	5,900	1.1
Less expenses:				
Selling	142,800	158,100	(15,300)	(9.7)
Administrative	150,700	155,400	(4,700)	(3.0)
Other expenses	69,900	67,500	2,400	3.6
Interest expense	33,500	21,800	11,700	53.7
Total expenses	396,900	402,800	(5,900)	(1.5)
Income before tax	146,600	134,800	11,800	8.8
Income tax	51,300	47,200	4,100	8.7
Net income	$ 95,300	$ 87,600	$ 7,700	8.8
Earnings per common share	$9.53	$8.76	$.77	8.8

Megatrix Corporation
Statement of Retained Earnings
For Years Ended December 31, 1985 and 1984

	1985	1984	Increase (decrease) Amount	%
Retained earnings, Jan. 1	$ 139,600	$ 96,000	$ 43,600	45.4
Add net income	95,300	87,600	7,700	8.8
	234,900	183,600	51,300	27.9
Less dividends:				
Preferred	(3,000)	(3,000)	0	—
Common	(45,500)	(41,000)	(4,500)	11.0
Retained earnings, Dec. 31	$ 186,400	$ 139,600	$ 46,800	33.5

pany when we see that the 8.8 percent increase in earnings was achieved with a 3.3 percent decrease in total sales. This indicates that operations were more efficient in 1985 than in 1984, because cost of goods sold and operating expenses were a smaller percentage of sales than before.

Megatrix Corporation
Balance Sheets
December 31, 1985 and 1984

	1985	1984	Increase (decrease) Amount	%
Assets				
Current assets:				
Cash	$ 38,570	$ 33,500	$ 5,070	15.1
Temporary investments	18,000	5,600	12,400	221.4
Accounts receivable (net)	91,280	79,700	11,580	14.5
Merchandise inventory	78,300	68,100	10,200	15.0
Prepaid expenses	9,350	18,200	(8,850)	(48.6)
Total current assets	235,500	205,100	30,400	14.8
Investments:				
Bond sinking fund	42,000	36,000	6,000	16.7
Investments in securities	182,000	181,300	700	.4
Total investments	224,000	217,300	6,700	3.1
Long-lived assets:				
Land	30,000	30,000	0	0
Buildings	330,000	280,000	50,000	17.9
Equipment	670,700	526,300	144,400	27.4
Less accumulated depreciation	(427,900)	(376,200)	(51,700)	13.7
Intangible assets	40,200	44,700	(4,500)	(10.1)
Total long-lived assets	643,000	504,800	138,200	27.4
Total assets	$1,102,500	$ 927,200	$175,300	18.9
Liabilities and Capital				
Current liabilities:				
Notes payable	$ 23,000	$ 30,000	$ (7,000)	(23.3)
Accounts payable	42,100	53,200	(11,100)	(20.9)
Taxes payable	12,600	10,700	1,900	17.8
Unearned revenues	38,400	43,700	(5,300)	(12.1)
Total current liabilities	116,100	137,600	(21,500)	(15.6)
Bonds payable, 9%, due 1997	350,000	200,000	150,000	75.0
Total liabilities	466,100	337,600	128,500	38.1
Capital:				
6% preferred stock, $100 par	50,000	50,000	0	0
Common stock, $10 par	100,000	100,000	0	0
Paid-in capital	300,000	300,000	0	0
Retained earnings	186,400	139,600	46,800	33.5
Total capital	636,400	589,600	46,800	7.9
Total liabilities and capital	$1,102,500	$ 927,200	$175,300	18.9

**Figure 19-1
Horizontal
analysis of
financial
statements. The
difference
between one year
and the next for
each item is
computed both as
an absolute and
as a percentage
change.**

The earlier year is usually the base period for calculating percentage changes. For example, Figure 19-1 shows that cash increased from 1984 to 1985 by $5,070. The percent increase is calculated as follows:

$$\frac{\text{Most recent value} - \text{Base period value}}{\text{Base period value}} = \text{Percentage change}$$

$$\frac{\$38,570 - \$33,500}{\$33,500} = \frac{\$5,070}{\$33,500} = .151, \text{ or } 15.1\%$$

The absolute changes and the percentage changes between reported amounts must be interpreted carefully to prevent unusual circumstances from causing inappropriate conclusions. For example, if the base period amount is very small, the percentage change may appear extremely large although the absolute change is not especially significant. An example is the change in temporary investments in Megatrix Corporation's balance sheet, which shows an absolute change of $12,400. Although the change of 221.4 percent appears large, the amount of temporary investments in either year is not unusual for a corporation with assets of over $1 million. The percent change cannot be calculated if the base year amount is zero.

Trends are disclosed by analyses of several accounting periods

Horizontal analysis can provide an indication of significant **trends** in financial statement items. For this reason, corporations often provide comparative data for longer periods of time, such as 5 or 10 years, so that a number of year-to-year comparisons can be made. Note that horizontal analysis is not performed on the statement of changes because that statement already shows changes from one period to another.

Long-term comparisons are often more significant than comparisons for only two accounting periods, because more time periods can indicate the presence of trends in the figures. A change from one period to the next is not necessarily part of a longer trend, because it could be caused by unusual economic conditions or a few transactions that cannot be expected to recur. For example, a company experiences a sharp increase in earnings per share as a result of a profitable sale of investments which were acquired several years ago. The same surge in earnings cannot occur again once the investments are sold. Comparing only the past year's earnings with the current year's earnings might imply a sharp earnings uptrend. But comparing the past five years of earnings may indicate that the sharp upturn of earnings in the current year is not typical of the company's usual performance.

In addition to data for long-term comparisons, summaries of items such as total sales, total expenses, net income, earnings per share, and other important figures may be supplied in tables or graphs in the annual report to highlight the company's operations. Graphic presentations often illustrate financial relationships that are difficult to perceive by reading the statements alone. In addition, graphs can convey a large amount of information at a glance. Some examples of graphic illustrations are shown for Megatrix Corporation in Figure 19-2. Note the obvious presence of upwards trends in sales and income and the corresponding trend in earnings and dividends per share.

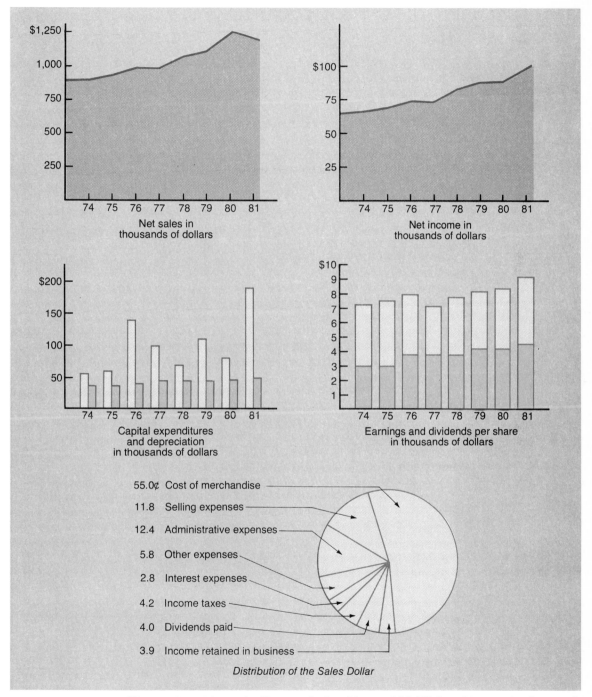

$1,250
1,000
750
500
250
74 75 76 77 78 79 80 81
Net sales in
thousands of dollars

$100
75
50
25
74 75 76 77 78 79 80 81
Net income in
thousands of dollars

$200
150
100
50
74 75 76 77 78 79 80 81
Capital expenditures
and depreciation
in thousands of dollars

$10
9
8
7
6
5
4
3
2
1
74 75 76 77 78 79 80 81
Earnings and dividends per share
in thousands of dollars

55.0¢ Cost of merchandise
11.8   Selling expenses
12.4   Administrative expenses
5.8   Other expenses
2.8   Interest expenses
4.2   Income taxes
4.0   Dividends paid
3.9   Income retained in business

Distribution of the Sales Dollar

Figure 19-2   **Many significant relationships and highlights of important financial data can be shown graphically in annual reports to supplement financial statements. The graphs shown here are only a small sample of the ways information can be presented.**

VERTICAL ANALYSIS

Statements can be converted to common units

Comparing figures in the financial statements of a single period is known as **vertical analysis**. All figures in a statement are converted to a common unit by expressing them as a percentage of a key figure in the statement, such as total sales in the income statement or total assets in a balance sheet. Figure 19-3 shows the income statement of Megatrix Corporation with each item expressed in dollars and as a percentage of sales. The statement of changes is expressed as a percentage of total sources or uses of funds, except for the schedule of working capital changes.

The individual percentages may reveal important proportional relationships among income statement items for each year or between the two years' figures. For instance, cost of goods sold as a percentage of sales decreased from 57 percent in 1984 to 55 percent in 1985. Total expenses increased from 32.2 to 32.8 percent. Net income as a percentage of sales was 7.9 percent in 1985 compared to 7.0 percent in 1984; thus despite a decrease in net sales, the company earned a higher net income primarily by reducing product expense. The implication is that management is controlling operating and product costs carefully to counteract an adverse sales trend, which may be the result of temporary economic conditions.

Balance sheet items are usually expressed as percentages of total assets, as shown in Figure 19-4 for Megatrix Corporation. The component percentages indicate that current assets in 1985 are 21.4 percent of the total assets, whereas current liabilities are only 10.5 percent of the total. A comparison of the current asset components in the years 1984 and 1985

Megatrix Corporation
Income Statement
For Years Ended December 31, 1985 and 1984

	1985	%	1984	%
Sales	$1,210,000	100.0	$1,251,400	100.0
Less cost of goods sold	666,500	55.1	713,800	57.0
Gross margin	543,500	44.9	537,600	43.0
Less expenses:				
Selling	142,800	11.8	158,100	12.6
Administrative	150,700	12.4	155,400	12.4
Other expenses	69,900	5.8	67,500	5.4
Interest expense	33,500	2.8	21,800	1.7
Total expenses	396,900	32.8	402,800	32.2
Income before tax	146,600	12.1	134,800	10.8
Income tax	51,300	4.2	47,200	3.8
Net income	$ 95,300	7.9	$ 87,600	7.0

shows that the company reduced both receivables and inventories as a percentage of total assets. Although long-term investments increased in 1985, they are a smaller percentage of total assets than in 1984. The company is relying more heavily on creditors for its financing in 1985 than it did in 1984, with total liabilities increasing from 40.7 percent to 42.3 percent of total equities. But the company has shifted toward more long-term financing, as indicated by a decrease in the percentage of current liabilities. Reducing current assets as a percentage of total assets is con-

Figure 19.3
Vertical analysis of the income statement and statement of changes in financial position. The items in the income statement are reduced to a percentage of sales. In the statement of changes they are reduced to a percentage of total sources or working capital. The percentages are common units that facilitate comparisons within a statement and between statements.

Megatrix Corporation
Statement of Changes in Financial Position
For Years Ended December 31, 1985 and 1984

	1985	%	1984	%
Sources of Working Capital				
From operations:				
Net income	$ 95,300	31.6	$ 87,600	42.3
Add Depreciation	51,700	17.1	49,800	24.1
Amortization	4,500	1.5	4,500	2.2
Working capital from operations	151,500	50.2	141,900	68.6
Other sources:				
Issuance of bonds payable	150,000	49.8	–	
Issuance of preferred stock	–		50,000	24.2
Sale of investments	–		15,000	7.2
Total sources of working capital	$ 301,500	100.0	$ 206,900	100.0
Uses of Working Capital				
Dividends	$ 48,500	16.1	$ 44,000	21.3
Purchase of equipment	144,400	47.9	125,500	60.7
Addition to buildings	50,000	16.6	–	
Purchase of investments	6,700	2.2	–	
Increase in working capital	51,900	17.2	37,400	18.1
Total uses of working capital	$ 301,500	100.0	$ 206,900	100.0
Increase (Decrease) in Working Capital				
Cash increased	$ 5,070	9.8	$ 8,680	23.2
Temporary investments	12,400	23.9	(5,800)	(15.5)
Accounts receivable	11,580	22.3	7,500	20.1
Merchandise inventory	10,200	19.7	9,600	25.7
Prepaid expenses	(8,850)	(17.1)	(1,250)	(3.3)
Notes payable	7,000	13.5	(5,000)	(13.4)
Accounts payable	11,100	21.4	12,650	33.8
Taxes payable	(1,900)	(3.7)	3,800	10.2
Unearned revenues	5,300	10.2	7,220	19.3
Increase in working capital	$ 51,900	100.0	$ 37,400	100.0

Megatrix Corporation
Balance Sheets
December 31. 1985 and 1984

	1985	%	1984	%
Assets				
Current assets:				
Cash	$ 38,570	3.5	$ 33,500	3.6
Temporary investments	18,000	1.6	5,600	.6
Accounts receivable (net)	91,280	8.3	79,700	8.6
Merchandise inventory	78,300	7.1	68,100	7.3
Prepaid expenses	9,350	.8	18,200	2.0
Total current assets	235,500	21.4	205,100	22.1
Investments:				
Bond sinking fund	42,000	3.8	36,000	3.9
Investments in securities	182,000	16.5	181,300	19.6
Total investments	224,000	20.3	217,300	23.5
Long-lived assets:				
Land	30,000	2.7	30,000	3.2
Buildings	330,000	29.9	280,000	30.2
Equipment	670,700	60.8	526,300	56.8
Less accumulated depreciation	(427,900)	(38.8)	(376,200)	(40.6)
Intangible assets	40,200	3.6	44,700	4.8
Total long-lived assets	643,000	58.3	504,800	54.4
Total assets	$1,102,500	100.0	$ 927,200	100.0
Liabilities and Capital				
Current liabilities:				
Notes payable	$ 23,000	2.1	$ 30,000	3.2
Accounts payable	42,100	3.8	53,200	5.7
Taxes payable	12,600	1.1	10,700	1.2
Unearned revenues	38,400	3.5	43,700	4.7
Total current liabilities	116,100	10.5	137,600	14.8
Bonds payable, 9%, due 1997	350,000	31.7	200,000	21.6
Total liabilities	466,100	42.3	377,600	36.4
Capital:				
6% preferred stock, $100 par	50,000	4.5	50,000	5.4
Common stock, $10 par	100,000	9.1	100,000	10.8
Paid-in capital in excess of par	300,000	27.2	300,000	32.4
Retained earnings	186,400	16.9	139,600	15.1
Total capital	636,400	57.7	589,600	63.6
Total liabilities and capital	$1,102,500	100.0	$ 927,200	100.0

Figure 19-4
**Vertical analysis
of balance sheets.
Each item is
reduced to a
percentage of
total assets.**

sistent with the reduction in sales and shows careful management of working capital, which should lessen with declining sales. A shift to longer-term liabilities will preserve working capital and may improve financial leverage.

A change in a particular percentage may occur from a change in the individual item or a change in the total of several items. For example, if an asset increases from $100 to $120 while total assets increase from $1,000 to $1,500, the percentage change in the asset shows a decrease as follows:

	Current Year	%	Base Year	%	Actual Change
Supplies	$120	8	$100	10	$20 increase
.	.	.	.	.	.
.	.	.	.	.	.
Total assets	$1,500	100	$1,000	100	$500 increase

Percentage changes require careful analysis

The asset decreased from 10 percent of the total to 8 percent of the total although it increased in absolute terms. Often a change in an item or its percentage may indicate that further analysis is necessary to determine if there is a potential problem or potential improvement in future operations. Therefore, percentages should be used together with absolute values in any analysis.

RATIO ANALYSIS

A ratio is a number expressing the relationship between two other numbers. **Ratio analysis** is the examination of various ratios in order to learn something about the statements being analyzed. Both vertical and horizontal analyses produce ratios, because a percentage is a ratio obtained by dividing one figure into another. But ratio analysis typically includes measures that do not fall into either the vertical or horizontal category.

Different ratios are useful to different users

In earlier chapters we discussed measures such as the current ratio and the price-earnings ratio, and we indicated that they provide information useful for management and for financial analysis. Information is a personal thing, however. Data useful to one decision maker may be of little interest to another person who is making the same type of decision but who places primary emphasis on other types of data. One analyst may view the current ratio as important in an analysis while another decides that it is of minor consequence. Therefore, the selection of the most meaningful ratios depends on the individual user of the information and on the type of decision or analysis being made.

For example, long-term creditors are interested in the solvency of the corporation, whereas short-term creditors are more interested in liquidity. In either case, they want to know something about the company's ability to repay its debts when they mature. Shareholders and potential investors are interested primarily in the company's profitability and in the way the company's stock behaves in the stock market. Managers want to know all aspects of business operations to ensure that the financial statements reflect results that will be viewed favorably by creditors, shareholders, and potential investors. By maintaining adequate liquidity and an appropriate balance between assets, liabilities, and owners' equity, managers attempt to keep the company solvent and profitable over a long period of time. As a history of profitable operations develops, investors tend to view the company favorably, and their views are reflected in the market price of the company's stock. How do all these users of financial information measure solvency, liquidity, and profitability?

Ratio analysis can be useful to each class of decision makers for making such measurements. Ratios can be classified into four general categories, although there is some overlap. A specific ratio may fit into more than one category. The four categories are:

Tests of liquidity
1. Current ratio, also called the working capital ratio
2. Acid test ratio, also called the quick ratio
3. Receivables turnover, also called average collection period
4. Inventory turnover, also called average days' supply

Tests of solvency
5. Times interest earned
6. Debt-equity ratio
7. Debt ratio
8. Equity ratio
9. Funds flow to debt ratio

Tests of profitability
10. Return on sales, or profit margin
11. Return on total assets
12. Return on owners' equity
13. Financial leverage
14. Earnings per share (EPS)

Market tests
15. Book value per share
16. Price-earnings (P/E) ratio
17. Dividend yield
18. Dividend payout

Other ratios can be calculated as required for specific situations. Those listed above are discussed in connection with our analysis of Megatrix Corporation for the year 1985. A more complete analysis requires the calculation of comparative ratios so that trends can be examined as well as the ratios themselves. Our purpose, however, is not to perform an analysis but to show how each ratio is calculated and used. Our calculations are rounded to one decimal place as more precision is usually not warranted.

Tests of Liquidity

Liquidity is a measure of a company's ability to convert assets to cash to meet its current obligations. Current assets are used for current debt repayment, therefore measures of liquidity focus on the components of working capital.

1. **Current ratio.**   The number of times that current assets could be used to repay current liabilities is called the **current ratio**. For Megatrix Corporation, the current ratio, or **working capital ratio**, is calculated as follows:

$$\text{Current ratio} = \frac{\text{Current assets}}{\text{Current liabilities}}$$

$$= \frac{\$235,500}{\$116,100} = 2.0 \text{ times}$$

Adequate values of ratios depend on the type of company and industry

The ratio shows that there are enough current assets to repay the current liabilities twice. For some businesses, this may be an adequate current ratio; for others it may be too high or too low. In evaluating the appropriateness of financial ratios, much depends on the nature of the business. If the current ratio is quite low, such as 1.2, sufficient cash may not be available to pay current liabilities. Not all current assets are readily convertible into cash to pay debts. For example, prepaid expenses are not converted to cash but instead are used in operations. Inventories are usually converted to receivables before the receivables can be converted to cash. Therefore, some of the current assets are considerably less liquid than others.

If the current ratio is high, such as 4.6, the company may have an excessive investment in current assets that do not produce a significant return. How does the current ratio in 1984 compare with the 1985 ratio calculated above?

2. **Acid test ratio.**   To test the company's **immediate ability** to meet its current obligations, the **acid test ratio**, or **quick ratio**, is computed by omitting the less liquid current assets. The liquid, or quick, assets include cash and other assets that can be converted to cash quickly, such as temporary investments, notes receivable, and accounts receivable. In our example, merchandise inventory and prepaid expenses are excluded to obtain quick assets for 1985 ($235,500 of current assets − $78,300 of merchandise − $9,350 of prepaid expenses = $147,850 of quick assets).

$$\text{Acid test ratio} = \frac{\text{Liquid assets}}{\text{Current liabilities}}$$

$$= \frac{\$147,850}{\$116,100} = 1.3 \text{ times}$$

Many analysts believe that an acid test ratio of 1 indicates an adequate ability to satisfy current obligations, but you should beware of such general rules because they do not apply to all situations. A more significant evaluation is obtained by comparing the current and acid test ratios.

The adequacy of ratios depends on the industry in which the company operates

As an example, a company whose current and acid test ratios are 2.3 and 1.5, respectively, is much more liquid than one whose ratios are 2.3 and 1.1; but whether the former or the latter is in a more favorable situation depends on many other factors. The industry in which the business operates, or the type of credit terms it grants and receives, may require more or less liquid positions. A company that grants credit terms of 30 days but is allowed 60 days to pay its accounts payable does not need as high an acid test ratio as one that grants 60-day terms but must pay its own debts within 30 days. The former company collects its accounts faster and can get by with less cash on hand than the latter.

3. Receivables turnover.   Another measure of liquidity is receivables turnover, which indicates how quickly accounts receivable are converted into cash. **Receivables turnover** is the time required for one complete cycle: from the time receivables are recorded through collection to the time new receivables are recorded. The faster the cycle is completed, the more quickly receivables are converted into cash. Receivables result directly from credit sales, and their turnover depends in part on the credit terms granted to customers. Ideally only credit sales should be used to calculate receivables turnover. However, this information often is not available in the financial statements, and net sales must be used instead. For Megatrix Corporation the calculation is as follows:

$$\text{Receivables turnover} = \frac{\text{Net sales}}{\text{Average receivables}}$$

$$= \frac{\$1,210,000}{(91,280 + \$79,700)/2}$$

$$= \frac{\$1,210,000}{\$85,490} = 14.2 \text{ times}$$

Average balance sheet figures are compared with income statement data

Notice the use of average receivables in the calculation rather than the ending balance of receivables. This is because the ratio relates income statement data to balance sheet data. Income statement information covers an entire accounting period, but balance sheet data are for a point in time. For the relationship to be meaningful, the balance sheet information should cover the same period as the income statement information. Therefore it is averaged in order to represent the entire accounting period as well. Calculating receivables turnover for 1984 would require use of the 1983 ending balance of accounts receivable, which is not available in Megatrix Corporation's statements.

The use of the beginning and ending balances to calculate averages may not provide the best average figure. Year-end balances may not be representative of account balances during most of the year due to seasonal variation in business volume. Therefore, when available, the current year's monthly or quarterly data should be used to calculate averages.

The liquidity of receivables is sometimes measured as the number of days' sales contained in the accounts receivable balance. The number of **days' sales in receivables**, also called the **average age of receivables** or the **average collection period**, is determined by calculating the average day's sales and then dividing the result into average receivables as follows:

$$\text{Average day's sales} = \frac{\text{Net Sales}}{\text{Number of days in period}}$$

$$= \frac{\$1,210,000}{360 \text{ days}} = \$3,361 \text{ per day}$$

$$\text{Days' sales in receivables} = \frac{\text{Average receivables}}{\text{Average day's sales}}$$

$$= \frac{\$85,490}{\$3,361 \text{ per day}} = 25.4 \text{ days}$$

These calculations show that the receivables are held on the average for about 25 days before collection. If the company grants credit terms of n/30, this ratio indicates that customers are paying their accounts well within the credit period. In general, days' sales in receivables would indicate a collection problem if it exceeded the 30-day credit terms by a significant amount, such as 20 or 30 days. A collection problem caused by excessive delinquent accounts could in turn lead to a liquidity problem.

The same calculation can be made by dividing the receivables turnover into the number of days in the accounting period.

$$\text{Days' sales in receivables} = \frac{\text{Number of days in period}}{\text{Receivables turnover}}$$

$$= \frac{360 \text{ days}}{14.2} = 25.4 \text{ days}$$

We use 360 days in the calculation, but it is also possible to use 365 days or a 300-day business year, which excludes Sundays and holidays. The figure selected should be used consistently so that the resulting ratios are comparable.

4. Inventory turnover. The liquidity of inventories is measured by the number of times that average inventory is replaced during the period. **Inventory turnover** may be calculated by dividing average inventory into cost of goods sold. Average inventory is obtained by adding the beginning and ending inventory balance and dividing by 2. The inventory turnover for Megatrix Corporation is determined as follows:

$$\text{Inventory turnover} = \frac{\text{Cost of goods sold}}{\text{Average inventory}}$$

$$= \frac{\$666,500}{(\$78,300 + \$68,100)/2}$$

$$= \frac{\$666,500}{\$73,200} = 9.1 \text{ times}$$

A high turnover is generally more desirable than a low turnover, because each time merchandise is sold a profit is usually realized. However, too high a turnover may mean that sufficient goods are not on hand to satisfy customer needs; in that case the company may be losing some sales if merchandise is out of stock. Conversely, a low turnover may mean that merchandise is lying idle, and is an unproductive resource.

If inventory turns over slowly, gross margin must be higher than with rapid turnovers

Whether a particular turnover figure is too high or too low depends on the type of business. Inventory turnover rates vary tremendously by the types of merchandise that a business sells. Perishable merchandise requires a higher turnover than durable goods. To induce customers to buy perishable merchandise quickly, profit margins are kept to a minimum. Consequently, businesses that sell perishable merchandise usually have lower profit margins on each item. A high turnover compensates for a lower margin on each item, producing a normal profit for the business. On the other hand, a business that sells slow-moving goods must make up for the low turnover by a higher profit margin on each item sold. For example, a grocer may charge $1 for an item that cost $.90, but a jeweler may charge $100 for an item that cost $45. However, the jeweler may have to hold the $100 item for a year before it is sold.

The liquidity of inventories may also be measured by the average number of days' supply of merchandise in the inventory balance. The **days' supply of inventory** is the number of days required to sell the average inventory on hand. The calculation for Megatrix Corporation is shown below.

$$\text{Average day's cost of goods sold} = \frac{\text{Cost of goods sold}}{\text{Number of days in period}}$$

$$= \frac{\$666,500}{360 \text{ days}} = \$1,851 \text{ per day}$$

$$\text{Days' supply of inventory} = \frac{\text{Average inventory}}{\text{Average day's CGS}}$$

$$= \frac{\$73,200}{\$1,851 \text{ per day}} = 39.5 \text{ days}$$

The company requires approximately 40 days to sell the inventory it normally keeps on hand. Whether this is good or bad depends on the type of inventory, industry standards, and management policy. The average days' supply of inventory can also be calculated by dividing the inventory turnover into the number of days in the period as follows:

$$\text{Days' supply of inventory} = \frac{\text{Number of days in period}}{\text{Inventory turnover}}$$

$$= \frac{360 \text{ days}}{9.1} = 39.6^{1} \text{ days}$$

Liquidity ratios are affected by the nature of the business, credit terms granted by the company, management policies, and the accounting method used. Analysts must be aware of each of these and allow for them when performing analyses or comparing the statements of several companies. A company using LIFO inventory valuation, for example, can be expected to have a lower current ratio than one using FIFO. The LIFO inventory may be undervalued, and may appear to have a higher turnover.

Tests of Solvency

An insolvent company cannot pay its bills

Liquidity is a measure of a company's ability to pay its current debts. **Solvency** refers to a company's ability to pay all of its debts as they come due, whether current or noncurrent. **Tests of solvency** focus on the company's ability to satisfy its long-term creditors. In order to service its bond indebtedness, a company must not only earn sufficient income to pay its interest expense in addition to paying all other expenses, it must also have a sufficient cash flow to service the debt. When the bonds payable mature, the company must have the ability to repay the debt from its own funds or from newly borrowed funds. The ability to obtain and to repay a long-term debt often depends on the firm's ability to obtain capital from shareholders. Therefore, the relationship between shareholders' equity and creditors' equity is evaluated.

5. Times interest earned.   A company earns revenue from which it pays its expenses; any remainder is net income. If it earns only enough revenue to pay expenses, there is no income, but still the expenses are paid. The company that earns only enough to pay its interest and other expenses, with little or nothing left for net income, is less solvent than a company that can pay all its expenses and have a large net income. Analysts measure solvency by calculating how many times a company could pay its interest expense. The number of **times interest is earned** is calculated by dividing interest expense into earnings available for payment of interest expense.

---

[1] The difference between the first and second calculation of average days' supply of inventory is due to rounding of inventory turnover.

Interest is paid with before-tax dollars— therefore the cost of interest is less than the interest rate

Interest expense is first added back to income before tax, because the interest paid has also been earned in addition to the remaining income. Interest is a tax-deductible expense, so the before-tax figure is used because it is the maximum that could be paid as interest. For Megatrix Corporation, times interest earned for 1985 is calculated as follows:

$$\text{Times interest earned} = \frac{\text{Income before tax} + \text{Interest expense}}{\text{Interest expense}}$$

$$= \frac{\$146,600 + \$33,500}{\$33,500} = \frac{\$180,100}{\$33,500} = 5.4 \text{ times}$$

Income before tax plus interest expense is abbreviated as **EBIT**, derived from **E**arnings **B**efore **I**nterest and **T**axes. EBIT is used frequently in financial analysis.

6. Debt-equity ratio.   Businesses obtain assets from owners and from creditors. The larger the portion provided by owners, the less risk is assumed by creditors. Liabilities expressed as a percentage of owners' equity is a ratio that indicates how much capital is provided by creditors compared to that provided by owners. If this ratio is 1, or 100%, each group provided an equal amount of capital. As the ratio increases, the amount of risk assumed by creditors increases, because the ratio indicates decreasing solvency. In our example, the ratio is as follows:

$$\text{Debt-equity ratio} = \frac{\text{Total liabilities}}{\text{Total owners' equity}}$$

$$= \frac{\$466,100}{\$636,400} = .732, \text{ or } 73.2\%$$

Owners provided more of the equities of Megatrix Corporation than creditors. Debt-equity ratios vary widely across industries. Financial institutions, such as banks or brokerage houses, typically have much higher debt-equity ratios than manufacturing companies or retail merchandisers. The relative amounts of debt and equity are also measured by the debt ratio or the equity ratio, as indicated below.

7. Debt ratio.   Dividing total liabilities by total equities indicates the percentage of total assets provided by creditors. In our example the calculation is as follows:

$$\text{Debt ratio} = \frac{\text{Total liabilities}}{\text{Total equities}}$$

$$= \frac{\$466,100}{\$1,102,500} = .423, \text{ or } 42.3\%$$

8. Equity ratio. Subtracting the debt ratio of 42.3 percent from 100 percent yields 57.7 as the percent of assets provided by owners. The ratio can, of course, be calculated as follows:

$$\text{Equity ratio} = \frac{\text{Total owners' equity}}{\text{Total equities}}$$

$$= \frac{\$636,400}{\$1,102,500} = .577, \text{ or } 57.7\%$$

The relationship between owners' equity and liabilities is an indication of the company's use of financial leverage. The more debt, the more leverage the company has. Leverage is an indication of the use a company makes of borrowed funds to increase the return on owners' equity. If the borrowed money can be invested to return a yield higher than the interest rate paid on the borrowed money, the difference increases the profit for the owners. However, interest expense must be paid whether or not the company earns a profit, and with large amounts of debt, the company runs a greater risk of not having enough income to service the debt.

9. Funds flow to debt ratio. Liabilities are repaid with cash, and operations are the main source of cash for a business. The company's ability to generate cash from operations is reported in the statement of changes in *Debt is paid with cash, not with earnings* financial position. External reports typically define funds as working capital, but for analytical purposes, it is assumed that working capital is a good surrogate for cash. After all, no one expects a company to repay all its debts at one time; the analyst only wants to assess its ability to do so. The ratio of **funds flow to debt** is calculated as follows:

$$\text{Funds flow to debt} = \frac{\text{Funds provided by operations}}{\text{Average total liabilities}}$$

$$= \frac{\$151,500}{(\$466,100 + \$337,600)/2}$$

$$= \frac{\$151,500}{\$401,850} = .377, \text{ or } 37.7\%$$

As with other calculations that involve both income statement and balance sheet figures, average balance sheet data are used. Megatrix Company generated enough funds from operations to repay about a third of its debt. Whether this is sufficient depends on the amount of debt that is ready to mature, and the company's ability to refinance the debt from sources other than operations. As with all other ratios, the analyst evaluates this one by reference to other information, such as the average funds flow to debt ratio for the industry. Some analysts like to include preferred stock in the denominator of the ratio, viewing preferred shares as debt rather than capital. Analysts sometimes use net income plus depreciation expense as the numerator of the ratio, on the assumption that other nonfund items in the income statement are usually not significant.

Tests of Profitability

In order to attract capital, businesses must earn enough profits to yield a satisfactory return to investors. If the profits do not materialize, a business will not be able to continue attracting capital from owners or creditors. The long-range survival of a business depends on its ability to earn enough revenue to satisfy all obligations and still provide a return on the owners' investment. Several **tests of profitability** are available to measure the adequacy of income.

The basic calculation of return relates the amount of income earned to the amount of investment used to earn that income. Return is expressed as a percentage rate and is calculated as follows:

$$\text{Rate of return} = \frac{\text{Income earned on investment}}{\text{Amount of investment}}$$

Several different rates of return can be calculated, each using a different definition of income and investment.

10. Return on sales. The amount of net income earned on an average dollar of sales revenue is called the **return on sales**, or **profit margin**. Return on sales is calculated as a percentage of net sales as follows:

$$\text{Return on sales} = \frac{\text{Net income}}{\text{Net sales}}$$

$$= \frac{\$95,300}{\$1,210,000} = .079, \text{ or } 7.9\%$$

High profit margins compensate for high risk

Each dollar of sales earned $.079, or about 8 cents of profit. Whether this profit margin is adequate depends on the type of business the company operates, and on the amount of assets invested in the business. If the assets turn over rapidly, the return on sales is usually lower than for businesses with slow turnovers. A business that holds slow-moving assets assumes more risk that those assets will become obsolete, more costly to replace, or less productive. In addition, assets tied up in one activity might earn a higher return if invested in another activity. The results obtained from assets with a high turnover are easier to predict, and holding such assets involves less risk. To compensate for high risk, businesses must earn higher returns.

11. Return on total assets.   Income is earned by using assets productively. The more efficiently assets are used, the more profitable the business. Assets perform their function whether they are obtained from borrowed money or from owners; therefore, the return on assets should be calculated before deducting interest expense. If interest is not deducted, income taxes should not be deducted either because taxes are calculated on income after interest deductions. Consequently, EBIT is usually used to measure the return on assets.

Assets work the same whether they are acquired with debt or equity capital

$$\text{Return on total assets} = \frac{\text{Earnings before interest and taxes (EBIT)}}{\text{Average total assets}}$$

$$= \frac{\$146{,}600 + \$33{,}500}{(\$1{,}102{,}500 + \$927{,}200)/2}$$

$$= \frac{\$180{,}100}{\$1{,}014{,}850} = .177, \text{ or } 17.7\%$$

On the average, every dollar of assets earned 17.7 cents of income from which interest and taxes must be paid. When interest expense and tax data are not available because condensed statements are presented, the analyst has no choice but to calculate return on total assets by using net income instead of EBIT.

12. Return on owners' equity.   The profit earned for the owners of a business is called **return on owners' equity** or **return on investment**. Return on owners' equity is an indication of the company's profitability because it shows how well the company is doing with the investment contributed by its owners. For Megatrix Corporation, return on total owners' equity is calculated as follows:

$$\text{Return on owners' equity} = \frac{\text{Net income}}{\text{Average owners' equity}}$$

$$= \frac{\$95{,}300}{(\$636{,}400 + \$589{,}600)/2}$$

$$= \frac{\$95{,}300}{\$613{,}000} = .155, \text{ or } 15.5\%$$

Net income is not shared equally by common and preferred shareholders. The return to preferred shareholders is limited to their preferred dividend—$3,000 per year for the Megatrix 6 percent preferred stock (6% of $50,000). All remaining income belongs to the common shareholders, whether or not it is paid to them in the form of dividends. For the common shareholders, therefore, return on investment should be calculated separately by excluding from total owners' equity the book value of preferred stock. Common equity therefore consists of total capital less $50,000 of preferred equity. Return on common equity for Megatrix is 16.4 percent, calculated as follows:

$$\text{Return on common equity} = \frac{\text{Net income} - \text{Preferred dividend requirement}}{\text{Average common equity}}$$

$$= \frac{\$95,300 - \$3,000}{(\$586,400 + \$539,600)/2}$$

$$= \frac{\$92,300}{\$563,000} = .164, \text{ or } 16.4\%$$

Leverage is the benefit obtained by using borrowed money

13. Financial leverage.   If all of the assets of the business were contributed by shareholders, the entire return on these assets would belong to owners. If a business can borrow funds at an interest cost that is lower than the rate of return on assets, the owners can benefit from the borrowing. The benefit of borrowing money and investing at a rate higher than the cost of the funds is called **financial leverage.** For example, return on assets for a corporation is 12 percent, and the company issued 10 percent bonds. The bond proceeds can be invested at 12 percent, leaving 2 percent of the return for owners after paying the 10 percent interest. The same 12 percent return on assets now provides a greater return on owners' equity than without the use of borrowed money.

Precisely how much the return on common equity is increased by leverage depends on the proportion of assets borrowed, the interest rate, the rate of return on assets, and the income tax rate. For example, let us assume a company has $20,000 of assets, no liabilities, income before tax of $4,000, and a 40 percent income tax rate, leaving a net income of $2,400. With no liabilities or interest expense, return on total assets is calculated on net income rather than on EBIT. We call this the **net return on assets,** and when there is no debt, net return on assets is the same as return on owners' equity, because total assets equal total owners' equity.

$$\text{Net return on assets} = \frac{\text{Net income}}{\text{Average total assets}} = \frac{\$2,400}{\$20,000} = .12, \text{ or } 12\%$$

$$\text{Return on common equity} = \frac{\text{Net income}}{\text{Common equity}} = \frac{\$2,400}{\$20,000} = .12, \text{ or } 12\%$$

Now we assume the company's equities consist of $10,000 of common stock and $10,000 of 10 percent bonds payable. The assets still earn $4,000 before tax, but $1,000 of this must be paid as interest, leaving $3,000 of income subject to the 40 percent tax. This means that net income after tax is $1,800 and return on common owners' equity is

$$\text{Return on common equity} = \frac{\text{Net income}}{\text{Common equity}} = \frac{\$1,800}{\$10,000} = .18, \text{ or } 18\%$$

By borrowing half of its assets, the company added 6 percent more return on owners' equity, although the assets earned the same amount of income. Notice, however, that net income is smaller because of the need to pay interest. But it is not $1,000 smaller because less income also means less income tax. In fact, net income is smaller by the cost of interest less the tax saving created by the interest expense. The net-of-tax interest cost is only $1,000 − .4(1,000), or $600.

To measure financial leverage, we have to find the difference between return on common equity when all assets are contributed by owners and return on common equity when part of the assets are contributed by creditors. Leverage is the difference between the return on owners' equity and the net return on assets. But to find net return on assets when interest expense exists, we divide total assets into **net income plus the net-of-tax interest expense**. This way, net return on assets is precisely the same return the common stock would earn if all assets had been contributed by owners.

$$\text{Net return on assets} = \frac{\text{Net income} + \text{Net-of-tax interest expense}}{\text{Average total assets}}$$

$$= \frac{\$1,800 + \$600}{\$20,000} = \frac{\$2,400}{\$20,000} = .12, \text{ or } 12\%$$

$$\text{Financial leverage} = \text{Return on common equity} - \text{Net return on assets}$$
$$= .18 - .12 = .06 \text{ or } 6\%$$

Leverage can be positive or negative

In this example leverage is positive, providing 6 percent more return on common equity than would have been earned if the company had not made use of borrowed funds. However, if the net return on assets happens to be lower than the net-of-tax interest cost, leverage can be negative, often leaving shareholders with a smaller return or larger loss than would occur without borrowing. Once funds are borrowed, the company cannot simply stop paying interest if sales decline or costs increase. For this reason, managers must be careful not to increase owners' risk excessively by too much borrowing.

To illustrate negative leverage, suppose that EBIT of the company in our example decreases from $4,000 to $1,800. This 55 percent decrease in EBIT would be accompanied by a 73 percent decrease in return on common equity, from 18 percent to 4.8 percent, because the net return on assets would be less than the net-of-tax interest rate on debt. The calculations are shown below.

Net income before interest and tax (EBIT)	$1,800
Less interest expense	1,000
Income before tax	800
Less income tax at 40 percent	320
Net income	$ 480

$$\text{Return on assets} = \frac{\text{EBIT}}{\text{Average total assets}} = \frac{\$1,800}{\$20,000} = .090, \text{ or } 9.0\%$$

$$\text{Net return on assets} = \frac{\text{Net income} + \text{Net-of-tax interest expense}}{\text{Average total assets}}$$

$$= \frac{\$480 + \$600}{\$20,000} = \frac{\$1,080}{\$20,000} = .054, \text{ or } 5.4\%$$

$$\text{Return on common equity} = \frac{\text{Net income}}{\text{Common equity}}$$

$$= \frac{\$480}{\$10,000} = .048, \text{ or } 4.8\%$$

$$\text{Leverage} = \text{Return on common equity} - \text{Net return on assets}$$
$$= 4.8\% - 5.4\% = -.6\%$$

Now we return to our analysis of Megatrix Corporation for which we can calculate financial leverage. We already know the return on common equity is 16.4 percent. Net income and interest expense are available from the financial statements, and the income tax rate is calculated as 34.99 percent ($51,300/$146,600). This can be rounded to 35 percent for purposes of financial analysis. Below we calculate the net-of-tax interest expense and net return on assets:

Interest expense	$33,500
Less 35 percent tax	11,725
Net-of-tax interest expense	$21,775

The same calculation can be obtained as follows:

$$\text{Net of tax interest expense} = \text{Interest expense} \times (1 - \text{Tax rate})$$
$$= \$33,500 \,(1 - .35)$$
$$= \$21,775$$

$$\text{Net return on assets} = \frac{\text{Net income} + \text{Net-of-tax interest expense}}{\text{Average total assets}}$$

$$= \frac{\$95,300 + \$21,775}{(\$1,102,500 + \$927,200)/2}$$

$$= \frac{\$117,075}{\$1,014,850} = .115, \text{ or } 11.5\%$$

$$\text{Leverage} = \text{Return on common equity} - \text{Net return on assets}$$
$$= 16.4\% - 11.5\% = 4.9\%$$

Megatrix Corporation's financial leverage is positive, providing 4.9 percent more return on owners' equity than would have been earned if the company had not made use of borrowed funds.

The existence of preferred stock can also provide leverage, because the preferred dividend is the same no matter how much or how little the company earns. When interest and tax data are not available, leverage is computed by using return on assets calculated on the basis of net income alone.

14. Earnings per share (EPS).   You have already studied earnings per share in Chapter 14, and know that its calculation can be complicated. EPS is one of the most important indicators of profitability because it can easily be compared to previous EPS figures and to the EPS figures of other companies. In addition, investors find it convenient to see the amount earned for a single share of stock. Interpreting this ratio properly requires a good understanding of how primary and fully diluted earnings per share are calculated. Since Megatrix Corporation does not have a complex capital structure, the calculation of earnings per share is simple.

$$\text{Earnings per share} = \frac{\text{Net income} - \text{Preferred dividend}}{\text{Weighted average no. of common shares}}$$

$$= \frac{\$95,300 - \$3,000}{10,000 \text{ shares}} = \frac{\$92,300}{10,000 \text{ shares}} = \$9.23$$

As with all ratios, the absolute value of EPS for the year is not as significant as the change from previous years. Therefore, financial analysis should include calculations of ratios for comparative statements.

The analyst should be aware of the effect on profitability ratios of alternative accounting methods and management policies. A company using accelerated depreciation, for instance, typically has a smaller asset base than it would have with straight-line depreciation, making the return on assets appear larger. A company that leases a large proportion of its assets may have a larger proportion of long-term liabilities than a company that buys its assets. A firm that uses operating leases extensively will seem to have a smaller amount of assets than it actually uses in its operations. Financial statements disclose a large amount of information in footnotes which must be examined carefully in order to interpret the ratios computed from the figures in the main body of the statements.

Market Tests

Investors and shareholders are usually interested in the market price of a company's common stock, and in ratios that describe the stock's market performance. An investor has to pay the market price for a share of stock, therefore most market tests are based on the current price of the stock. Megatrix Corporation's common stock sells in the market at $70 per share.

15. Book value per share.   As you learned in Chapter 14, book value of a company often has little relationship to its market value. For companies with large amounts of financial assets, such as insurance companies, loan companies, and savings institutions, book value may be significant because a large portion of assets such as stock, bond, and mortgage investments and savings deposits usually has a book value that is close to market value. In that case, a comparison of book value and market value of the company's stock may reveal that a financial company's stock is trading in the market at bargain prices or at excessive prices.

Book value of stock is usually lower than market value

For most industrial companies with large amounts of fixed assets and inventories recorded at cost, book value of stock is often significantly below market value. Nevertheless, a comparison of book value and market value of stock sometimes gives an indication of how investors view the company. If market value is higher than book value, investors are attributing goodwill to the company or they are paying for undervalued assets, and their assessment of the company's asset value is reflected in the price of the stock. Book value may be calculated for preferred and common stock, but it is typically relevant only for common shares. Book value per common share is calculated by dividing total common equity (total capital − preferred equity) by the number of common shares. For Megatrix Corporation the calculation is:

$$\text{Book value per common share} = \frac{\text{Total common equity}}{\text{Number of common shares}}$$

$$= \frac{\$636,400 - \$50,000}{10,000 \text{ shares}} = \$58.64 \text{ per share}$$

With a market price of $70 per share, investors believe that the company's net assets are undervalued. The high returns on assets and on owners' equity provide justification for their assessment of the company's value.

16. Price-earnings (P/E) ratio. The price of a stock alone does not indicate whether or not the stock is expensive. A $60 stock may be a better buy than a $25 stock. To estimate value, the price should be related to the amount of income the company earns. The price-earnings (P/E) ratio reduces the stock to a common unit of measure for comparison with other stocks. It indicates how many dollars are required to buy $1 worth of earnings. In our example, the calculation is as follows:

The P/E ratio tells how expensive a stock is

$$\text{Price-earnings (P/E) ratio} = \frac{\text{Price per share}}{\text{Earnings per share}}$$

$$= \frac{\$70}{\$9.23} = 7.58 \text{ times}$$

This calculation shows that to buy $1 of Megatrix Corporation's annual earnings an investor must pay about 7.6 times that amount. Typically companies whose earnings exhibit a rapid rate of growth have higher P/E ratios than those whose earnings are stable. Investors are willing to pay more for current earnings if they anticipate that future earnings will be higher. There is a very wide range of P/E ratios in the stock market. The average in the past few years has been between 6 and 12, but P/E ratios of over 100 occasionally occur.

Dividend yield is a rate of return

17. Dividend yield.   Some investors buy common stock in order to earn dividend income. Others are more interested in the growth of their shares' market value. **Dividend yield** is one measure of rate of return on the investor's stock investment. It is calculated as follows:

$$\text{Dividend yield} = \frac{\text{Dividend per share}}{\text{Price per share}}$$

$$= \frac{\$4.55}{\$70} = .065, \text{ or } 6.5\%$$

If the company has a policy of paying regular dividends, the investor can expect a yield of 6.5 percent on an investment in the common stock of Megatrix Corporation. There is, of course, no guarantee that the company will continue to pay dividends. Many companies, however, try to maintain a stable dividend and to increase the dividend when possible, so that investors can depend on receiving a steady income from their shareholdings. Some companies, on the other hand, pay little or no dividend, because they attempt to grow by retaining and investing their earnings. Investors buy the stocks of such companies for their growth rather than for their dividend yield. Megatrix Corporation's dividend history, illustrated in Figure 19-2, indicates that current dividend rates will probably continue into the future.

18. Dividend payout.   **Dividend payout** is the percentage of net income distributed by the company; it is an indication of the proportion of net income distributed to common shareholders and the proportion retained by the business.

$$\text{Dividend payout} = \frac{\text{Total dividend}}{\text{Net income}}$$

$$= \frac{\$48,500}{\$95,300} = .51, \text{ or } 51\%$$

Slightly more than half of the income was distributed as dividends. The dividend payout can also be calculated from the point of view of common shareholders, by relating common dividends to net income less preferred dividends. The calculation may be made on the basis of total dividends and income, or on a per-share basis as follows:

$$\text{Dividend payout} = \frac{\text{Common dividend per share}}{\text{Earnings per share}}$$

$$= \frac{\$4.55}{\$9.23} = .49, \text{ or } 49\%$$

The portion of net income not paid to shareholders as dividends is retained by the company for the purpose of financing growth and expansion. Retained earnings do not provide a direct yield to the shareholder, but the shareholder can benefit from this portion of the company's income through growth in the market value of stock caused by the growth in retained earnings. With approximately half of its income retained, Megatrix Corporation is providing for its future growth and increased earnings.

All of the ratios discussed above are summarized in Figure 19-5, which shows how the ratios are calculated and their interpretation.

INTERPRETATION AND USE OF FINANCIAL RATIOS

The ratios presented in this chapter are some of the more common ones used by managers and financial analysts to assess the performance and future potential of a business. Other ratios can be calculated, and some of those presented may be calculated differently than shown here. Sometimes it is necessary to calculate only a small number of ratios in order to arrive at a decision about a business. More important than calculating the ratios is interpreting them. Evaluating ratios allows the analyst to determine whether specific areas of a business warrant further investigation.

An adequate financial analysis involves more than an understanding and interpretation of each of the individual ratios. An insight into the meaning of the interrelationships among the ratios and financial data in the statements is also needed. Gaining such an insight and understanding requires considerable experience in the analysis and interpretation of financial statements. Moreover, even experienced analysts cannot apply their skill equally well to all financial statements. Every industry has its own characteristics with which analysts must be familiar, and it is not possible for any one individual to understand all industries equally well.

Several financial services compile data and provide information on American industry and business corporations. Standard & Poor's *Corporation Records*, Moody's *Manual of Investments*, and Arnold Bernhard's *Value Line Investment Survey* are publications that provide large amounts of financial data, ratios, and financial analyses to help decision makers evaluate businesses. Dun & Bradstreet compiles lists of ratios that represent averages for many industries. Published industry averages, ratios, and financial analyses can be helpful, but the individual analyst must still rely on skill, insight, and even intuition in order to interpret the financial statements of a corporation and arrive at a decision. A comparison of historical ratios for a single company may indicate important trends, and may be more useful than published averages that obscure significant variations among companies.

In addition to the analysis of financial statements, analysts often use other available information about a company or an industry. The backlog of orders a company has, the new government contract it has just signed, or the successful test of a newly developed product, all can have a significant impact on future earnings. The analyst continuously seeks information to supplement the financial data available in accounting reports. What is the impact on a chemical company from legislation that prohibits use of certain pesticides because they pollute the environment? How will the auto industry be affected if Congress mandates that all cars must withstand a 5 mph crash without damage? What will happen to the earnings of domestic amateur movie camera makers when a foreign company introduces a low-priced color video camera for the amateur market? These and many other questions cannot be answered by reading the financial statements. But answers to such questions are of little value if they cannot be related to information in accounting reports.

Economic, social, and political factors enter into an analysis

In their search for information, financial analysts look to many sources. Information about new legislation, technological developments, foreign relations, and the state of the economy all can be relevant to an analysis of a single company. When necessary, an analyst will go directly to the company and ask questions. Financial analysts have also been instrumental in bringing about changes in the way accounting data are reported. For example, the statement of changes in financial position was not a part of the annual report of corporations until financial analysts began to demand that it be provided.

More recently financial analysts have been requesting that corporations publish forecasts and projections of future operations. Such **pro forma** financial statements are available only to management, and companies have been reluctant to provide them to external users. Managers prepare pro forma statements by adjusting the data in the current period's financial statements to reflect expected or planned changes. For example, if sales are $100,000 currently and management expects a 15 percent increase in sales, the pro forma income statement shows sales of $115,000. Other figures are similarly obtained from estimates, projections, budgets, and educated guesses. Pro forma statements can obviously prove to be quite different from actual results, but they are extremely useful to managers for planning operations and controlling business activities.

Financial forecasts may be included in future annual reports

Financial analysts would obviously find managements' projections useful in their assessment of future business performance. But the accounting profession is concerned about the way that pro forma statements should be verified and certified. There is a danger that forecasts could be viewed as actual expectations by external users, who may feel misled if the forecasted performance is not achieved. Nevertheless, in the future we may see annual reports containing pro forma financial statements in addition to historical data.

Name of Ratio	Method of Calculation	Interpretation
Tests of Liquidity		
Current (working capital) ratio	$\dfrac{\text{Current assets}}{\text{Current liabilities}}$	Ability to pay current debts from current assets
Acid test (quick) ratio	$\dfrac{\text{Liquid assets}}{\text{Current liabilities}}$	Immediate ability to pay current debts from liquid assets
Receivables turnover	$\dfrac{\text{Net sales}}{\text{Average receivables}}$	Ability to convert receivables to cash measured by the number of collection cycles
Days' sales in receivables	$\dfrac{\text{Number of days in period}}{\text{Receivables turnover}}$	Effectiveness of credit terms measured by average age of receivables, or average collection period
Inventory turnover	$\dfrac{\text{Cost of goods sold}}{\text{Average inventory}}$	Ability to sell inventories measured by the number of purchase and sales cycles
Days' supply in inventory	$\dfrac{\text{Number of days in period}}{\text{Inventory turnover}}$	Time required to sell average inventory measured by average age of merchandise on hand
Tests of Solvency		
Times interest earned	$\dfrac{\text{Earnings before interest and taxes (EBIT)}}{\text{Interest expense}}$	Ability to service long-term debt
Debt-equity ratio	$\dfrac{\text{Total liabilities}}{\text{Total owners' equity}}$	Proportion of assets provided by creditors compared with that provided by owners
Debt ratio	$\dfrac{\text{Total liabilities}}{\text{Total equities}}$	Proportion of total assets provided by creditors
Equity ratio	$\dfrac{\text{Total owners' equity}}{\text{Total equities}}$	Proportion of total assets provided by owners
Fund flows to debt ratio	$\dfrac{\text{Funds from operations}}{\text{Average total liabilities}}$	Ability to repay debts from funds generated by business operations
Test of Profitability		
Return on sales	$\dfrac{\text{Net income}}{\text{Net sales}}$	Profit margin earned on each dollar of sales
Return on total assets	$\dfrac{\text{Earnings before interest and taxes (EBIT)}}{\text{Average total assets}}$	Efficiency with which managers use total assets to operate the business
Return on owners' equity	$\dfrac{\text{Net income}}{\text{Average owners' equity}}$	Rate of return earned by owners on their investment.
Net return on assets	$\dfrac{\text{Net income + Net-of-tax interest expense}}{\text{Average total assets}}$	Return on assets after tax and without interest, used for leverage calculations.
Leverage	Return on common equity − Net return on assets	Advantage to owners from using borrowed funds to earn a higher return on investment
Earnings per share (EPS)	$\dfrac{\text{Net income − Preferred dividend}}{\text{Weighted average no. of common shares}}$	Amount of net income earned by each common share
Market Tests		
Book value per common share	$\dfrac{\text{Total common equity}}{\text{Number of common shares}}$	Amount of owners' equity in each share of stock
Price-earnings (P/E) ratio	$\dfrac{\text{Price per share}}{\text{Earnings per share}}$	Number of dollars required to buy $1 of earnings
Dividend yield	$\dfrac{\text{Dividend per share}}{\text{Price per share}}$	Return to owner on the investment required to buy one share of stock
Dividend payout	$\dfrac{\text{Common dividends}}{\text{Net income}}$ or $\dfrac{\text{Common dividend per share}}{\text{Earnings per share}}$	Proportion of earnings distributed as dividends

Figure 19-5   Summary of financial ratios discussed in the chapter.

SUMMARY

Analysis of financial statements requires a thorough understanding of the accounting principles and concepts used for measuring and reporting of financial data, and of alternative accounting methods that may be selected by managers to present historical information. An adequate analysis requires the comparison of at least two accounting periods, and data on several consecutive periods are needed in order to perceive trends in the figures presented. A complete financial analysis may involve horizontal, vertical, and ratio analysis.

Horizontal analysis is the calculation of differences between account balances in the statements of two accounting periods. Such differences are computed in absolute and in percentage amounts and, if calculated for several accounting periods, may indicate significant trends in the figures. **Vertical analysis** is the comparison of figures within a financial statement of one period. The figures are expressed in common terms by converting them to a percentage of a significant value. In the income statement, all amounts are usually converted to a percentage of sales. In the balance sheet, amounts are usually converted to a percentage of total assets.

Ratio analysis is the calculation of the relationship between two figures which may come from the same statement or from two different statements. Ratios may be classified into tests of **liquidity, solvency, profitability,** and **market tests**. The most common of these ratios are summarized in Figure 19-5.

The interpretation of financial statements requires skills and insight which can be achieved only through experience. Published ratios and analyses may be helpful but they form only a part of the input that is needed to assess the past performance and future potential of a business.

KEY TERMS

acid test ratio   *(795)*
average age of receivables   *(797)*
average collection period   *(797)*
current ratio   *(795)*
days' sales in receivables   *(797)*
day's supply in inventory   *(798)*
debt-equity ratio   *(800)*
debt ratio   *(800)*
dividend payout   *(809)*
dividend yield   *(809)*
EBIT   *(800)*
equity ratio   *(801)*
financial leverage   *(804)*
financial statement analysis   *(785)*
funds flow to debt ratio   *(801)*
horizontal analysis   *(786)*
inventory turnover   *(797)*
leverage   *(804)*
liquidity   *(794)*
market tests   *(807)*

net return on assets   *(804)*
price-earnings (P/E) ratio   *(808)*
pro forma statements   *(811)*
profit margin   *(802)*
profitability ratios   *(802)*
quick ratio   *(795)*
ratio analysis   *(793)*
receivables turnover   *(796)*
return on owners' equity   *(803)*
return on sales   *(802)*
return on total assets   *(803)*
solvency   *(799)*
tests of liquidity   *(794)*
tests of profitability   *(802)*
tests of solvency   *(799)*
times interest earned   *(799)*
trends   *(788)*
vertical analysis   *(790)*
working capital ratio   *(795)*

QUESTIONS

1. Discuss what is meant by external and internal decision makers, and the purposes for which they use financial statements.

2. What are the main purposes of analyzing financial statements?

3. What are some of the reasons for presenting comparative financial statements in annual reports?

4. Explain the main difference between horizontal and vertical analysis of financial statements.

5. Describe what is meant by ratio analysis of financial statements. What kind of tests can be performed with ratio analysis?

6. What advantage is offered by presenting financial statements of the past 5 to 10 years compared with presenting financial statements for only the current year and previous year?

7. Discuss the concept of financial leverage. What advantage can be derived by owners from financial leverage? What are the risks involved?

8. Stock A trades in the market at $60 per share. Stock B trades in the market at $20 per share. The price-earnings ratio of A is 9 and the price-earnings ratio of B is 12. While talking to his stock broker, Mr. Smith said, "I can't afford Stock A. It's too expensive. Buy 100 shares of Stock B." Discuss Mr. Smith's statement.

9. You are analyzing the financial statements of two companies which have virtually the same equity structure and net income. Company A uses FIFO inventory valuation and straight-line depreciation for its fixed assets. Company B uses LIFO inventory valuation and double-declining-balance depreciation. What are some of the differences you expect to find in the ratios of the two companies, and which ratios do you expect to differ?

10. Jack said to his friend Bill, "I just bought the stock of BDM Company at $50 per share. The dividend payout of 50 percent provides me with a yield of 10 percent on my investment and a chance for some growth." "That's nothing," replied Bill. "Six years ago I bought shares of UMS Company for $50 per share. The stock is now selling for $130 and the $10 dividend gives me a 20 percent return. I need a high return on my investments, because I depend on the dividends for half my income." "In that case you have better alternatives," suggested Jack. What are EPS and dividend per share on the BDM stock? Is Bill calculating return correctly? What does Jack mean by better alternatives?

EXERCISES

Ex. 19-1   **Using ratios to reconstruct financial data.**   The annual report of Mattrix Company included the president's letter to shareholders, which stated: "Return on sales this year increased to 9 percent from 7.5 percent last year. The company's net income was $1,134,000 this year, up 8 percent over last year.

Required: Determine the percentage increase or decrease in sales from last year to the current year.

Ex. 19-2   **Using ratios to obtain financial data.**   The current ratio of a company is 1.6, and working capital is $30,000. The company uses $8,000 of cash to repay a short-term note payable.

Required: Determine the amount of current assets, current liabilities, and the current ratio after the payment of the note.

Ex. 19-3   **Measures of liquidity.**   Simian Company's current ratio is 2, and its quick ratio is 1.2. Listed below are several independent events or transactions, some of which affect the company's liquidity.

a.   Delivered merchandise costing $6,000 to a customer in exchange for $500 cash and a patent worth $5,500.
b.   Purchased merchandise on open account.
c.   Declared a cash dividend payable next month.
d.   Changed from terms of n/60 to 3/10, n/30 on accounts receivable.
e.   Purchased equipment on open account.
f.   Reduced selling price of merchandise and advertised special sale, thereby increasing volume of sales.
g.   Paid account payable.
h.   Sold merchandise for cash.
i.   Changed from FIFO to LIFO inventory method because prices are rising.
j.   Wrote off uncollectible account against allowance for bad debts.
k.   Collected account receivable.
l.   Paid dividend previously declared.
m.   Issued stock in exchange for land.
n.   Sold temporary investment at a profit.
o.   Added new line of durable goods to present line of perishable goods.

Required: Set up a table as shown below. For each item indicate what effect it will have on the company's current ratio, quick ratio, receivables turnover, and inventory turnover. Use a + to show an increase in the ratio, − to show a decrease, and 0 if the ratio is not affected or the effect cannot be determined. The first item is solved as an example.

Item	Current Ratio	Quick Ratio	Receivables Turnover	Inventory Turnover
a.	−	+	0	+

Ex. 19-4 **Measures of solvency and profitability.** Below is a list of independent trans-actions or events, each followed by some measures of solvency or profitability.

a. Issued capital stock for cash.
1. Debt-equity ratio
2. Return on sales
3. Debt ratio

b. Declared and paid cash dividend.
1. Equity ratio
2. Return on owners' equity
3. Debt-equity ratio

c. Notified by the city of a decrease in property taxes.
1. Return on sales
2. Fund flows to debt
3. Leverage

d. Bond holders converted bonds into common stock.
1. Leverage
2. Return on total assets
3. Fund flows to debt

e. Inventory turnover increased with no change in costs or selling prices.
1. Return on sales
2. Return on total assets
3. Times interest earned

f. Operating income increased 15 percent; interest expense increased 5 percent.
1. Return on owners' equity
2. Times interest earned
3. Leverage

Required: Indicate what effect each transaction would have on the ratios that follow it. Use a + or − to show an increase or decrease in the ratio, and a 0 to show that there is no change or the effect on the ratio cannot be determined.

Ex. 19-5 **Profitability and leverage.** Lancer Company has total assets of $3,000,000 and owners' equity of $1,200,000. Income after interest and before tax is $200,000, and interest expense is $80,000. The company is subject to a tax rate of 40 percent.

Required: Calculate the following ratios:
a. Times interest earned.
b. Return on total assets.
c. Return on equity.
d. Financial leverage.

Ex. 19-6   **Effects on market measures.**   Below is a list of independent transactions or events, some of which affect market ratios of Bylo Company.

a. Issued 10 percent stock dividend followed by the regular quarterly cash dividend which had always been $1 per share.

b. Declared regular quarterly cash dividend.

c. Issued common stock for cash at market price, which is double the book value.

d. Effected a 2-for-1 stock split.

e. Won large court award in patent infringement suit.

f. Declared and issued 5 percent stock dividend.

g. Acquired profitable subsidiary in a pooling of interests. Prior to acquisition P/E ratio was 20 for Bylo stock and 6 for subsidiary stock.

h. The board of directors declared an increased dividend, payable next month.

i. Return on assets is 15 percent. Issued 12 percent bonds at par.

j. Net income increased, but the market price of the stock remained unchanged.

k. Earnings increased 20 percent, dividend payout remained unchanged.

l. Sales decreased, and return on sales is unchanged. Market price of stock remains the same.

Required: Set up a table as shown below. For each item indicate what effect it will have on the company's book value per share, earnings per share, price-earnings ratio, and dividend yield. Use a + or − to show an increase or decrease, and a 0 if there is no change or the change cannot be determined. The first item is solved as an example.

Book Value per Share	EPS	P/E	Dividend Yield
−	−	0	+

Ex. 19-7   **Turnover ratios.**   Below are financial data taken from the records of Paemore Company.

Sales	$385,000
Cost of goods sold	170,000
Gross margin	215,000
Beginning inventory	19,950
Ending inventory	22,550
Beginning receivables	26,220
Ending receivables	28,780

Required: Calculate the following ratios:
  a. Inventory turnover.
  b. Receivables turnover.
  c. Days' supply of inventory.
  d. Days' sales in receivables.

Ex. 19-8   Horizontal analysis. Following are comparative financial statements of Kamasuto Corporation in condensed form:

**Kamasuto Corporation
Statements of Income and Retained Earnings
For the Years Ended December 31, 1985 and 1984**

	1985	1984
Sales	$270,000	$252,000
Less cost of goods sold	156,000	153,600
Gross margin	114,000	98,400
Operating expenses	(60,960)	(56,160)
Depreciation expense	(10,800)	(9,600)
Interest expense	(6,240)	(6,240)
Income before taxes	36,000	26,400
Income taxes	10,800	7,680
Net income	25,200	18,720
Add beginning retained earnings	19,200	9,600
	44,400	28,320
Less dividends	20,400	9,120
Retained earnings ending balance	$ 24,000	$ 19,200

**Kamasuto Corporation
Balance Sheets
December 31, 1985 and 1984**

	1985	1984
Cash	$ 14,400	$ 19,200
Accounts receivable (net)	22,800	27,600
Inventories	55,200	51,600
Fixed assets (net)	96,000	84,000
Total assets	$188,400	$182,400
Current liabilities	$ 30,000	$ 28,800
Bonds payable, 10 percent	62,400	62,400
Common stock 6,000 shares	72,000	72,000
Retained earnings	24,000	19,200
Total equities	$188,400	$182,400
Year-end market price of stock	$37.75	$30.00

Required: Perform a horizontal analysis of Kamasuto Corporation's financial statements by completing two additional columns, one for the amount of increase or decrease for 1985 over 1984, and the other for the percentage increase or decrease.

Ex. 19-9   Vertical analysis.

> **Required:** Refer to the financial statements of Kamasuto Corporation in Exercise 19-8. Perform a vertical analysis of these statements by converting the statements to common units. Convert the income and retained earnings statement to percentages of sales. Convert the balance sheet to percentages of total assets.

Ex. 19-10   Ratio analysis.

> **Required:** Refer to the financial statements of Kamasuto Corporation in Exercise 19-8. Perform a ratio analysis for the company for 1985, by calculating each of the ratios discussed in the text.

Ex. 19-11   Profitability and leverage.   Lumpie Company had total assets of $900,000 at the beginning of the year and $1,100,000 at the end of the year. Net income before tax was $200,000, the tax rate is 40 percent, and the company paid $100,000 of interest expense. Average common equity for the year is $600,000 and return on sales was 8 percent.

> **Required:** Calculate the return on total assets, return on common equity, leverage, and sales for the year.

Ex. 19-12   Understanding profitability and solvency.   The rate of return on average total assets is 20 percent for Ypsilon Company. Its return on average common equity is 16 percent. The company is subject to an income tax rate of 40 percent, and its interest rate on average debt is 10 percent. There is no preferred stock outstanding. Average total assets are $3,200,000.

> **Required:** Calculate average equity, debt, interest expense, times interest earned, and the debt ratio.

Ex. 19-13   Measuring liquidity.   The current portions of the balance sheets of Blount Tool Corporation and Obtoose Cutlery Company are shown below.

	Blount	Obtoose
Current assets:		
Cash	$ 2,610	$ 2,370
Temporary investments	3,000	1,560
Notes receivable	1,470	1,170
Accounts receivable	4,140	3,450
Merchandise inventory	2,340	6,420
Prepaid expenses	750	2,850
Total current assets	$14,310	$17,820
Current liabilities:		
Notes payable	$ 1,740	$ 1,410
Taxes payable	900	960
Accounts payable	2,790	4,080
Salaries payable	2,520	2,910
Total current liabilities	$ 7,950	$ 9,360

Required:
  a. Calculate the current ratio and working capital for each company.
  b. Compare the current ratios and working capital for the two companies and discuss each company's ability to meet current obligations.
  c. Calculate the acid test ratio for each company.
  d. Explain each company's liquidity in terms of the acid test ratio.
  e. What additional information did you gain by calculating the acid test ratio?

Ex. 19-14   **Understanding market tests.**   Adrianne Company's stock trades in the market at $54 per share with a price-earnings ratio of 9. The company's dividend payout is 72 percent. It has 100,000 shares of common stock outstanding, and no preferred stock. Book value per share is $42.

Required: Calculate earnings per share, net income, dividends per share, dividend yield, and return on common equity.

Ex. 19-15   **Understanding profitability and solvency ratios.**   Drubbing Company's return on total assets is 22 percent and its return on owners' equity is 16 percent. Average total assets for the year are $3,000,000 and beginning owners' equity is $2,070,000. The company is subject to a 40 percent income tax rate. There were no capital transactions during the year and no dividends were paid. Interest expense for the year was $60,000. There is no preferred stock outstanding and liabilities at the end of the year are the same as at the beginning.

Required: Calculate the debt-equity ratio for Drubbing Company at the end of the accounting period.

Ex. 19-16   **Understanding liquidity ratios.**   Puzzel Company operates 360 days per year. Following are some data calculated from its financial statements.

  a. There are 18 days' supply in ending inventory.
  b. Cost of goods sold for the year was $1,296,000 which is 60 percent of sales.
  c. There are 24 days' sales in ending accounts receivable.
  d. Inventory and accounts receivable ending balances are the same as beginning balances.
  e. The current ratio is 2.4 and the quick ratio is 1.86.
  f. Current assets consist of cash, accounts receivable, and merchandise.

Required: Find the ending balance of each of the current assets.

PROBLEMS

P. 19-1 **Horizontal analysis.** The condensed financial statements of Gutierez Company, a sole proprietorship, are presented below for the years ending December 31, 1983, 1984, and 1985.

	1985	1984	1983
Income statements:			
Sales	$60,000	$60,000	$63,000
Less cost of goods sold	22,500	25,500	27,000
Gross margin	37,500	34,500	36,000
Operating expenses	(19,950)	(19,050)	(20,550)
Depreciation expense	(7,800)	(7,650)	(7,500)
Interest expense	(2,250)	(1,800)	(1,950)
Net income	$ 7,500	$ 6,000	$ 6,000
Balance sheets:			
Current assets	$22,275	$18,900	$12,000
Investments	13,500	11,250	16,200
Fixed assets (net)	39,225	37,350	34,800
Total assets	$75,000	$67,500	$63,000
Current liabilities	$10,125	$10,500	$ 7,500
Long-term debt	18,000	15,000	16,500
Capital, Gutierez	46,875	42,000	39,000
Total equities	$75,000	$67,500	$63,000

Required:
  a. Perform a horizontal analysis of the statements.
  b. Explain any trends that appear to be significant.
  c. Do you perceive any significant improvement in operations or financial position over the years presented? Explain.

P. 19-2 **Vertical analysis.** Refer to the financial statements of Gutierez Company in Problem 19-1.

Required:
  a. Perform a vertical analysis for each of the three years.
  b. Do you perceive any significant changes in the statements over the years presented? Explain.
  c. What seems to be the primary reason for the increase in net income?

P. 19-3 **Ratio analysis.** Refer to the financial statements of Gutierez Company in Problem 19-1.

Required:
  a. Calculate the following financial ratios for 1985 and 1984.
      1. Times interest earned
      2. Debt-equity ratio

3. Debt ratio
4. Equity ratio
5. Funds flow to debt ratio
6. Return on sales
7. Return on total assets
8. Return on owners' equity
9. Leverage

b. Do you perceive any significant trend in the rates of return? Explain.
c. Do the solvency measures indicate any significant trends? Explain.
d. Has the book value of the company increased faster or slower than net income over the past 2 years? Explain.

P. 19-4   **Horizontal analysis.**   The condensed financial statements of Trendix Company are presented below for 3 years ending January 31.

	1985	1984	1983
Income statements:			
Sales	$ 80,000	$ 85,000	$ 83,000
Less cost of goods sold	38,000	40,000	37,000
Gross margin	42,000	45,000	46,000
Operating expenses	(6,900)	(8,325)	(7,350)
Depreciation	(3,000)	(2,700)	(2,800)
Interest	(4,600)	(4,600)	(4,600)
Income tax	(5,500)	(5,875)	(6,250)
Net income	$ 22,000	$ 23,500	$ 25,000
Balance sheets:			
Current assets	$103,500	$ 90,000	$ 72,000
Fixed assets (net)	126,000	112,500	108,000
Intangibles	40,500	42,750	45,000
Total	$270,000	$245,250	$225,000
Current liabilities	$ 63,000	$ 51,750	$ 38,250
Bonds payable, due 2001	90,000	90,000	90,000
Common stock $10 par	60,000	60,000	60,000
Retained earnings	57,000	43,500	36,750
Total	$270,000	$245,250	$225,000

Required:
a. Perform a horizontal analysis of the statements.
b. Discuss any trends that appear to be significant and any significant changes in operations or financial position over the years presented.

P. 19-5   **Vertical analysis.**   Refer to the financial statements of Trendix Company in Problem 19-4.

Required:
a. Perform a vertical analysis for each of the 3 years.
b. Do you perceive any significant changes in the statements over the years presented? Explain.
c. What seems to be the primary reason for the decline in net income?

P. 19-6 **Ratio analysis.** Refer to the financial statements of Trendix Company in Problem 19-4.

Required:
    a. Calculate the following financial ratios for each of the two latest years:
        1. Times interest earned
        2. Debt-equity ratio
        3. Debt ratio
        4. Equity ratio
        5. Fund flows to debt ratio
        6. Return on sales
        7. Return on total assets
        8. Return on owners' equity
        9. Financial leverage
       10. Current ratio
    b. Explain any significant trends that you perceive in the ratios.
    c. Is the book value increasing faster or slower than net income? Explain.

P. 19-7 **Market tests.** Refer to the financial statements of Trendix Company in Problem 19-4. The company paid cash dividends in 1984 and 1985 but not in 1983. The year-end market price per share of the company's stock was $36.75 in 1985, $35.25 in 1984, and $39.63 in 1983.

Required:
    a. Calculate the amount of dividends paid by the company in 1984 and 1985.
    b. Calculate the following ratios for each of the 3 years:
        1. Earnings per share
        2. Price-earnings ratio
        3. Dividend payout
        4. Dividend yield
    c. Do you perceive any significant trends in the ratios you calculated? Explain.

P. 19-8 **Complete financial analysis.** Provided below and on the following page are the comparative income statements and balance sheets of Niblix Company for 1985 and 1984.

Niblix Company
Income Statements
For the Years Ended December 31, 1985 and 1984

	1985	1984
Sales	$240,000	$210,000
Cost of goods sold	114,000	102,000
Gross margin	126,000	108,000
Operating expenses	(58,000)	(52,000)
Depreciation expense	(10,000)	(9,600)
Interest expense	(5,000)	(5,900)
Income tax expense	(21,200)	(16,200)
Net income	$ 31,800	$ 24,300

Niblix Company
Balance Sheet
December 31, 1985 and 1984

	1985	1984
Assets:		
Cash	$ 13,800	$ 17,000
Temporary investments	9,000	9,600
Accounts receivable	35,400	38,200
Merchandise	30,000	4,600
Prepaid expenses	1,800	2,400
Fixed assets	144,000	120,000
Accumulated depreciation	(48,000)	(42,000)
Total assets	$186,000	$170,600
Equities:		
Accounts payable	$ 34,200	$ 33,000
Accrued expenses	13,800	14,400
Long-term debt	36,000	48,000
Common stock	60,000	60,000
Retained earnings	42,000	15,200
Total equities	$186,000	$170,600

Required:

a. Perform a vertical analysis on the 1985 statements and a horizontal analysis comparing the 1985 statements with those of 1984.

b. Calculate the following ratios for 1985:
1. Current ratio
2. Acid test ratio
3. Inventory turnover
4. Days' supply of inventory
5. Receivables turnover
6. Days' sales in receivables
7. Return on sales
8. Return on total assets
9. Return on owners' equity
10. Financial leverage
11. Times interest earned
12. Debt-equity ratio
13. Gross margin percentage
14. Funds flow to debt ratio
15. Dividend payout ratio

P. 19-9   (CMA) Financial analysis.   The 1985 financial statements for Johanson Company are reproduced on the following page.

Johanson Company
Statement of Financial Position
December 31, 1985 and 1984
($000 omitted)

	1985	1984
Assets		
Current assets:		
Cash and temporary investments	$ 400	$ 380
Accounts receivable (net)	1,700	1,500
Inventories	2,200	2,120
Total current assets	4,300	4,000
Long-term assets:		
Land	500	500
Building and equipment (net)	4,700	4,000
Total long-term assets	5,200	4,500
Total assets	$9,500	$8,500
Liabilities and Capital		
Current liabilities:		
Accounts payable	$1,400	$ 700
Current portion of long-term debt	1,000	500
Total current liabilities	2,400	1,200
Long-term debt	3,000	4,000
Total liabilities	5,400	5,200
Stockholders' equity:		
Common stock	3,000	3,000
Retained earnings	1,100	300
Total stockholders' equity	4,100	3,300
Total liabilities and capital	$9,500	$8,500

Johanson Company
Statement of Income and Retained Earnings
For the Year Ended December 31, 1985
($000 omitted)

Net sales		$28,800
Less cost of goods sold	$15,120	
Selling expenses	7,180	
Administrative expenses	4,100	
Interest	400	
Income taxes	800	27,600
Net income		1,200
Retained earnings January 1		300
Subtotal		1,500
Cash dividends declared and paid		400
Retained earnings December 31		$ 1,100

Required: Select the best answer for each of the following questions:

1. The acid test ratio for 1985 is closest to
   a. 1.1 to 1   b. .9 to 1   c. 1.8 to 1   d. .2 to 1   e. .17 to 1

2. The average number of days' sales in receivables in 1985 is
   a. 18 days   b. 360 days   c. 20 days   d. 4.4 days   e. 80 days

3. Times interest earned ratio in 1985 is
   a. 3.0 times   b. 1.0 times   c. 72 times   d. 2.0 times   e. 6.0 times

4. The return on assets in 1985 is
   a. 26.7%   b. 13.3%   c. 25.3%   d. 12.6%   e. 23.1%

5. The inventory turnover in 1985 is
   a. 13.6 times   b. 12.5 times   c. .9 times   d. 7.0 times   e. 51.4 times

6. The return on sales in 1985 is
   a. 3.8%   b. 47.5%   c. 52.5%   d. 95.8%   e. 4.3%

7. The dividend payout ratio in 1985 is
   a. 33.3%   b. 36%   c. 20%   d. 8.8%   e. 100%

8. The return on owners' equity in 1985 is
   a. 12.6%   b. 32.4%   c. 29.3%   d. 9.8%   e. 10.8%

P. 19-10   **Horizontal, vertical, and ratio analysis.**   The comparative balance sheets of Sylphia Company and its income statements for 1985 and 1984 are presented below and on the following page.

Sylphia Company
Balance Sheets
October 31, 1985 and 1984

	1985	1984
Cash	$ 4,000	$ 9,500
Accounts receivable	13,500	11,500
Merchandise	36,000	52,500
Prepaid expenses	2,500	2,500
Fixed assets	90,000	100,000
Accumulated depreciation	(32,000)	(35,000)
Total assets	$114,000	$141,000
Accounts payable	$ 20,000	$ 37,000
Accrued expenses	15,000	19,000
Notes payable, due 1989–1992	39,000	32,000
Capital, Sylvia	21,500	27,900
Capital, Sophia	18,500	25,100
Total equities	$114,000	$141,000

Sylphia Company
Income Statements
For the Years Ended October 31, 1985 and 1984

	1985	1984
Sales	$500,000	$505,000
Cost of goods sold	354,000	360,000
Operating expenses	112,380	106,500
Depreciation expense	8,120	9,200
Interest expense	5,500	5,300
Total expenses	480,000	481,000
Net income	$ 20,000	$ 24,000

Required:

a. Perform a vertical analysis of the 1985 statements and horizontal analysis comparing 1985 with 1984.

b. Calculate the following ratios for 1985:

  1. Current ratio
  2. Acid test ratio
  3. Inventory turnover
  4. Days' supply of inventory
  5. Receivables turnover
  6. Days' sales in receivables
  7. Return on sales
  8. Return on total assets
  9. Return on owners' equity
  10. Leverage
  11. Times interest earned
  12. Debt-equity ratio
  13. Cash flow to debt ratio

P. 19-11 **Reconstruction of balance sheet.** The December 31, 1984, balance sheet of Erika Company, and its statement of changes in financial position for the year ending December 31, 1985 are presented below and on the following page.

Erika Company
Balance Sheet
December 31, 1984

Cash	$ 530	Accounts payable	$ 2,140
Accounts receivable	1,300	Bonds payable, due 1990	7,000
Merchandise inventory	2,370	Preferred stock	2,500
Land	9,800	Common stock	6,000
Equipment	12,200	Retained earnings	6,560
Accumulated depreciation	(2,000)		
Total assets	$24,200	Total equities	$24,200

Erika Company
Statement of Changes in Financial Position
For the Year Ended December 31, 1985

Sources		Uses	
From operations		Paid cash dividends	$ 360
Net income	$1,200	Retired preferred stock	2,500
Depreciation	600	Retired bonds payable	1,400
Gain on sale of land	(80)	Purchased equipment	3,000
Total from operations	1,720	Increase in working capital	340
Issued common stock	4,000		
Sold land	1,880		
Total sources	$7,600	Total uses	$7,600

Erika Company had the following financial ratios at the end of 1985:

Current ratio	2.20
Acid test ratio	.80
EBIT	$1,968
Return on average total assets	.08
Return on sales	.03
Turnover of average receivables	32.00
Dividend payout	.30

Required: Prepare the December 31, 1985, balance sheet for Erika Company without adding any new accounts.

P. 19-12   **Reconstruction of financial statements.**   Following is the balance sheet of Detrex Company on December 31, 1984:

Detrex Company
Balance Sheet
December 31, 1984

Cash	$ 600	Accounts payable	$11,580
Accounts receivable	3,000	Bonds payable	30,000
Merchandise	11,000	Common stock, $10 par	10,000
Prepaid expenses	230	Additional paid-in capital	30,000
Fixed assets	110,000	Retained earnings	13,250
Accumulated depreciation	(30,000)		
Total assets	$ 94,830	Total equities	$94,830

The company did not buy or sell any fixed assets nor issue any stock during 1985. On December 31, 1985, the company's accountant obtained the following ratios and other data based on the 1985 operations:

Current ratio	2.0 times
Acid test ratio	.8 times
Inventory turnover	5.0 times
Receivables turnover	25.0 times
Equity ratio	58.8%
Debt ratio	41.2%
Times interest earned	6.0 times
Return on sales	7.0%
Gross margin percentage	52.0%
Book value per share	$58.80
Market price per share	$64.00
Earnings per share	$ 8.75
Dividend yield	5.0%
Federal income tax rate	30.0%
Depreciation rate	4.0%

Required: Use the above data to prepare the company's balance sheet on December 31, 1985 and income statement for the year ending December 31, 1985. The following form is suggested for the income statement:

Detrex Company
Income Statement
For the Year Ended December 31, 1985

Sales
Less cost of goods sold
Gross margin
Less expenses
   Depreciation expense
   Interest expense
   Other expense
Total expenses
Income before tax
Federal income tax
Net income

Case 19-1   **Analysis of pro forma statements.**
On the following page are the financial statements of Alexander Corporation. The company was established 6 years ago, and based on market studies and demand for the company's products, management has decided that it is time for a major expansion. To accomplish the expansion, the company needs a $100,000 infusion of capital. Two alternatives are considered by management. The company can issue additional common stock for $100,000 or it can obtain the same amount by issuing 12 percent bonds. The funds are to be used to buy new equipment for $70,000 and to increase working capital. The company pays no dividends and is subject to a 40 percent income tax rate. The stock or bonds are to be issued in early December 1985.

Alexander Corporation
Balance Sheet
November 30, 1985

Current assets	$ 25,000	Current liabilities	$ 14,000
Fixed assets	115,000	Note payable, 11%, 1988	30,000
Accumulated depreciation	(40,000)	Common stock, $10 par	40,000
		Retained earnings	16,000
Total assets	$100,000	Total equities	$100,000

Alexander Corporation
Income Statement
For the Year Ended November 30, 1985

Sales		$112,500
Selling and administrative expenses	$88,700	
Depreciation expense	5,500	
Interest expense	3,300	
Federal income tax	6,000	
Total expenses		97,500
Net income		$ 9,000

The following projections are made for the next year of operations:

a. The old equipment includes a fully depreciated machine that cost $10,000. This will be discarded as it has no salvage value. The remaining equipment is depreciated at an annual rate of 5 percent.

b. The new equipment will be depreciated at 10 percent per year with no salvage value. The equipment will be acquired in December 1985.

c. Sales are expected to increase by 40 percent and selling and administrative expenses by 30 percent over the current year.

d. Interest expense will remain the same if the stock is issued. If the bonds are issued, interest expense will increase.

e. Current liabilities are expected to increase by $30,000 by November 30, 1986.

Required:
    a. Prepare pro forma financial statements for the year ending November 30, 1986 for each alternative method of financing the expanded operations.
    b. Perform as complete a ratio analysis as possible on the 1985 statements and on the pro forma statements.
    c. Recommend which alternative you prefer. Support your recommendation with the findings in your analysis.

Accounting for the Effects of Inflation

20

This chapter discusses the accounting profession's attempt to deal with distortions in financial statements caused by inflation. When you have finished studying the chapter, you should understand:

1 Why inflation causes distortions in financial statements.

2 How price indexes can be used to show the effect that inflation has on financial figures.

3 The use of current cost data for restating financial figures to account for the effects of inflation.

4 The manner in which companies report the effects of inflation in their annual reports.

5 Advantages and disadvantages of inflation accounting.

Financial statements prepared in accordance with the accounting concepts and principles presented in this book have served decision makers well. Nevertheless, accountants constantly search for ways to improve the information provided by accounting systems by improving the measurement and reporting of accounting information.

One issue in financial reporting that has interested the accounting profession for years, especially recently, is the effect of inflation on financial statements. This chapter is devoted to the topic of accounting for price-level changes and the effects changing price levels have on financial statements.

ACCOUNTING FOR THE EFFECTS OF INFLATION

*Inflation
reduces the
purchasing
power of money*

Money is used as the common unit of measure in financial statements. The assumption is that the value of money remains constant over time. This is the **stable dollar assumption** of accounting, discussed in Chapter 2. But the value of money is not constant. The value of money—that is, its **purchasing power**—is measured by the quantity of goods and services that can be acquired with a given amount of money. During periods of inflation, a dollar buys smaller and smaller quantities of goods and services as prices rise. During periods of deflation, a dollar buys larger quantities of goods and services. We therefore say that **inflation** is a period of rising prices and **deflation** is a period of declining prices.

Inflation in the United States

The United States economy has experienced some inflation for more than 35 years. The problem became more critical during the 1970s, when the rate of inflation increased well above any rate the country had experienced previously. For example, a three-bedroom home that cost $20,000 in 1965 carries a price tag of over $90,000 today. Many automobiles could be bought in 1975 for $5,000. Today it is difficult to find a similar new car selling for less than $10,000. The purchasing power of the dollar has declined over time, but in accounting, we assume that it remains stable. A dollar used to acquire land in 1965 is assumed to be equal in value to a dollar used to pay salaries in 1982 or to repay bonds in 1984. Figure 20-1 illustrates the value of $1.00 in the beginning of 1967 declining to $.34 by the end of 1983. Another way of describing the decline in the purchasing power of the dollar is to say that about $3.00 was required at the end of 1983 to buy as much as $1.00 would have bought at the beginning of 1967.

Compared with such countries as Argentina, Brazil, and Israel, the United States has experienced only mild inflation during its history. Annual inflation rates of 100 percent, 300 percent, or higher are common in some parts of the world.

For many years, accountants have been concerned about the distortion in financial statements caused by changing price levels. In 1969, after numerous studies, the rule-making body of the accounting profession recommended, but did not require, publication of financial statements adjusted for changes in the purchasing power of money as supplements to conventional financial statements. Very few companies followed the recommendation, partly because of the additional cost involved, and partly because inflation was not viewed as a serious problem in the United States at that time. In addition, there is disagreement in the business community and in the accounting profession about the proper method of adjusting financial data for price level changes and about the value of such data.

*Businesses
account for
inflation using
two methods*

In response to increased inflation in the late 1970s, the Financial Accounting Standards Board issued Statement No. 33 in 1979, requiring the use of two methods of reporting the effects of inflation in financial

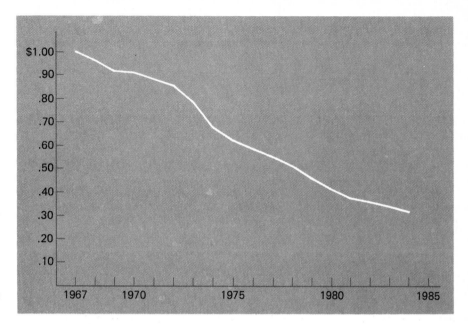

Figure 20-1
Decline in the purchasing power of the dollar, based on the Consumer Price Index, with 1967 as the base year. The 1984 data are estimated.

statements of businesses that meet specific size criteria.[1] One method, called **constant dollar accounting**, uses a price index to report the effects of inflation on income; the other method, called **current cost accounting**, converts the historical cost of specific assets and expenses to their replacement cost. Information must be presented using both methods. The information produced does not replace the basic financial statements in the annual report. Instead it is reported in the form of **supplementary financial statements**. Most companies present the inflation data in notes to the financial statements.[2]

Constant dollar accounting.   By reporting income and financial position in terms of constant purchasing power, the effects of inflation are eliminated from the figures. One way to accomplish this is to use a price index to restate all dollar amounts in financial statements and report them in terms of the same purchasing power—that is, in terms of constant dollars. In addition to restating income statement and balance sheet items in terms of constant dollars, the gains or losses from holding certain liabilities or assets during periods of changing prices are also calculated using a price index.

---

[1] Reporting on the effects of changing prices is required for companies with either: (a) inventories and plant, property, and equipment (before deducting accumulated depreciation, depletion, and amortization) amounting in aggregate to more than $125 million; or (b) total assets amounting to more than $1 billion (after deducting accumulated depreciation),

[2] At the time this book went to press, the FASB was reviewing its inflation reporting requirements to determine if they should remain in effect or if they should be discontinued.

Price indexes measure the purchasing power of money

Price indexes are measures of the dollar's purchasing power. A **general price index** consists of the aggregate prices of a variety of goods and services generally purchased and sold in an economy. Examples are the Consumer Price Index and the Gross National Product (GNP) Implicit Price Deflator. The **Consumer Price Index (CPI)** is constructed from the prices of a variety of goods typically purchased by American consumers. It measures the change in the general purchasing power of money. The **GNP Implicit Price Deflator** is a broad-based index made up of the prices of all goods and services produced in this country. The FASB decided that the consumer price index should be used to convert financial statements to constant dollars.

The CPI is used to convert financial statements to constant dollars

Current cost accounting.   Inflation does not affect all financial statement items equally. The prices of some assets may increase faster than the prices of others, and even during periods of inflation, prices of some items may decline. So adjustments using a general price index cannot eliminate all effects of inflation. Current cost accounting is an attempt to account for the effects of inflation by reporting the replacement cost of assets on hand and of assets expensed during the period. Instead of reporting assets and expenses on the basis of historical cost, these resources are restated to the amount of money required to replace them. Such restatements can be accomplished by reference to current price lists or vendors' price quotations, or by using a specific price index.

A **specific price index** consists of the aggregate prices of specific types of goods, such as industrial equipment or farm commodities. An example is the Construction Cost Index, which measures the cost of building construction in the United States. Specific price indexes are used to measure the change in the dollar's power to buy specific types of goods. The United States government compiles numerous indexes for the purpose of measuring the purchasing power of money in general or specific terms.

To illustrate the process of reporting the effects of changes in price levels, we use the example of Leida Company, whose financial statements are presented in Figure 20-2. Leida Company started operations in January of Year 1, at which time it acquired its land and building. Equipment was purchased late in December of Year 1 and was used during Year 2.

We first discuss constant dollar accounting using a general price index, and later we use the same example to illustrate current cost accounting.

CONSTANT DOLLAR ACCOUNTING

To convert historical cost dollars to dollars of current purchasing power, that is, to constant dollars, it is necessary to know the current value of the general price index and also the value of the index at the time when the transaction took place and the original amount was recorded. For example,

Leida Company
Comparative Balance Sheets
December 31

	Year 2	Year 1
Cash	$ 17,500	$11,800
Accounts receivable	7,500	8,200
Merchandise	6,000	5,000
Land	10,000	10,000
Building	50,000	50,000
Accumulated depreciation, building	(4,000)	(2,000)
Equipment	15,000	
Accumulated depreciation, equipment	(1,500)	
Total assets	$100,500	$83,000
Accounts payable	$ 6,500	$ 4,000
Notes payable, long-term	8,000	8,000
Common stock	65,000	65,000
Retained earnings	21,000	6,000
Total equities	$100,500	$83,000

Figure 20-2
Financial statements prepared on a historical cost basis for use in the main body of the annual report. Some of the data from these statements must be restated to constant dollars and to current costs and reported as supplementary information in the footnotes of the annual report.

Leida Company
Income Statement
For the Year Ended December 31, Year 2

Sales		$74,000
Less cost of goods sold		34,000
Gross margin		40,000
Depreciation expense	$ 3,500	
Other expenses	20,500	24,000
Income from operations		$16,000

we assume that the following values of the general price index are used for converting the statements of Leida Company:

Date	Index
January Year 1	95
December Year 1	100
December Year 2	120

The **base period** is the date for which the index is 100—December Year 1 in this case. In January Year 1, prices in general were 5 percent lower than base period prices and by December Year 2, they were 20 percent higher than base period prices. Leida Company paid $10,000 to acquire land in January Year 1. To report the cost of the land in December

Year 2 dollars, the $10,000 cost has to be restated because the index increased. The purchasing power of the dollar decreased, so it takes more dollars to buy a given quantity of goods than was required earlier. Therefore, the cost of goods acquired in earlier periods is **restated** to the purchasing power of dollars prevailing at **the date of restatement**. To make the restatement, we multiply the cost of the land by the following fraction:

$$\frac{\text{Price Index at time of restatement}}{\text{Index at time of original transaction}}$$

In December Year 1 dollars, the land has a restated cost of $10,526, calculated as follows:[3]

$$\$10,000 \times \frac{100}{95} = \$10,526$$

In terms of December Year 2 dollars, the land has the following restated cost:

$$\$10,000 \times \frac{120}{95} = \$12,632$$

What do restated figures show?

What is the significance of the $12,632 figure? It is the cost of land measured in terms of the current purchasing power of the dollar. By restating the cost of the land in today's dollars, we see the number of dollars needed now to provide the same purchasing power as the number of dollars with which the land was acquired.

Monetary and Nonmonetary Items

Not all figures in the financial statements are converted by means of indexes because they are already expressed in constant dollars. These are known as **monetary items**, and they include cash and all assets and liabilities that are expressed in fixed amounts of dollars due to their contractual nature. For example, a $1,000, 60-day 12 percent note receivable will result in the collection of $1,020 at maturity no matter how much prices have changed. Similarly, accounts receivable and payable, notes payable, bonds, and preferred stock are all contracts that stipulate repayment of a specific amount. All other assets and equities are **nonmonetary items**.

---

[3] All figures in this chapter are rounded to the nearest whole dollar.

During inflation, debtors gain purchasing power

Monetary items are **not** adjusted for price-level changes, but that does not mean that they do not affect the purchasing power of their owner. In periods of inflation, a company that holds money or other monetary assets loses purchasing power because prices of goods and services are rising and a given amount of money held declines in value. A firm with $10,000 at the beginning of a year loses purchasing power by holding the money when the price index rises 15 percent. By the time the price index has changed that much, $11,500 is required to purchase the same quantity of goods. On the other hand, a firm that owes money during a period of rising prices gains in purchasing power because the debt will be repaid with cheaper dollars. Consequently, when financial statements are converted to constant dollars, it is necessary to calculate the gain or loss from holding monetary items.

Holding monetary items causes purchasing power gains or losses

To determine whether gains or losses occurred from holding monetary items, it is necessary to calculate the net amount of monetary assets and monetary liabilities. **Net monetary assets** are held if monetary assets exceed monetary liabilities; **net monetary liabilities** are held if monetary liabilities exceed monetary assets.

A company with net monetary assets incurs **purchasing power losses** during periods of inflation. If a company holds net monetary liabilities, it incurs **purchasing power gains**. When financial statements are restated to reflect changes in the general price level, gains and losses from holding **net monetary items** are reported in the constant dollar income statement.

Restating Income to Constant Dollars

Cost of goods sold and depreciation expense are restated using the CPI

The Financial Accounting Standards Board requires companies to report the current year's income statement information on a constant dollar basis and to include in the report the purchasing power gain or loss from holding net monetary items during the current year. However, it is necessary to convert only cost of goods sold and depreciation and amortization expense to constant dollars. Revenues earned and expenses incurred are already stated in current period dollars. Depreciation, amortization, and part of cost of goods sold, on the other hand, are the expirations of assets acquired in earlier periods; they must be restated to current period dollars so that all items in the income statement are in constant dollars.

All restatements are made using the average index of the year

To convert the income statement to constant dollars, it is necessary to know the current value of the Consumer Price Index as well as the CPI value for periods in which various transactions, such as asset acquisitions, took place. The portion of cost of goods sold consisting of inventory acquired in the current year is not converted because it is already stated in current dollars. Cost of goods sold consisting of inventory acquired in previous periods is converted using the average CPI of the current year and the CPI at the time the inventory was originally acquired. Similarly, depreciation and amortization are converted using the average CPI for the current year and the CPI when the assets were acquired. To demonstrate the conversion process, we use the indexes relevant for Leida Company, shown on page 835.

The average index for the current year is calculated from the beginning and ending indexes. With a beginning general price level index of 100 and an ending index of 120, the average index for Year 2 is 110, calculated as (100 + 120)/2. This average index is used to convert cost of goods sold to constant dollars. Any of the merchandise bought and sold during the current period is already reflected as cost of goods sold in constant dollars. We need to know, therefore, how much of the $34,000 cost of goods sold figure is sales of merchandise acquired in earlier periods.

Restating cost of goods sold.   Leida Company uses FIFO inventory valuation and had a beginning inventory or $5,000, all of which was acquired at the end of Year 1 when the general index was 100. Total purchases during Year 2 were $35,000, of which $6,000 remains in ending inventory. Therefore $29,000 of current year purchases was sold in addition to the beginning inventory. To restate cost of goods sold to constant dollars, the following calculation is made:

$$\text{Cost of beginning inventory} \qquad \$5,000 \times \frac{110}{100} = \$\ 5,500$$

Cost of current purchases sold	29,000
Cost of goods sold, restated	$34,500

Restating depreciation.   Depreciation expense is converted using the average general index for Year 2 and the index at the time the depreciated assets were acquired. From the comparative balance sheets in Figure 20-2, we see that accumulated depreciation on the building increased from $2,000 to $4,000. Therefore depreciation expense for the current year is $2,000. The remainder of the $3,500 depreciation expense reported on the income statement is for equipment. The building was acquired when the general index was 95, and the equipment was acquired when it was 100. Therefore, depreciation on the building is converted using the index value of 95, and the equipment is converted using the index value of 100. The figures are then added together to arrive at total depreciation expense for the year. Depreciation expense is converted to constant dollars as follows:

$$\text{Depreciation on building} \qquad \$2,000 \times \frac{110}{95} = \$2,316$$

$$\text{Depreciation on equipment} \qquad \$1,500 \times \frac{110}{100} = \ 1,650$$

Total depreciation, restated	$3,966

Once cost of goods sold and depreciation expense have been restated, they are used to restate operating income to constant dollars. In addition to restated operating income, the restated income statement must also report the purchasing power gain or loss from holding net monetary items, as discussed next.

Purchasing Power Gain or Loss

The beginning and ending balances of monetary assets and monetary liabilities are used to calculate the purchasing power gain or loss from holding net monetary items. To make the calculation, we use the general price index at the beginning and end of the year, as well as the average index. Leida Company's net monetary items are calculated as follows:

	December 31	
	Year 2	Year 1
Monetary assets:		
Cash	$17,500	$11,800
Accounts receivable	7,500	8,200
Total monetary assets	25,000	20,000
Less monetary liabilities:		
Accounts payable	6,500	4,000
Notes payable	8,000	8,000
Total monetary liabilities	14,500	12,000
Net monetary assets	$10,500	$ 8,000

The net monetary position at the end of the year is restated to average figures for the year

At the beginning of Year 2, the company had net monetary assets of $8,000 which increased to $10,500 by the end of the year. To calculate the loss from holding net monetary assets during a period of inflation, the beginning amount, the change during the year, and the ending amount are all compared. The FASB suggests using the average index for the current year to calculate the purchasing power gain or loss. Using the average index results in calculating the purchasing power in the middle of the year rather than at the end. This is consistent with using the average index to convert income statement items to constant dollars.

The beginning and average indexes are used to restate the beginning balance. Any change during the year is assumed to be stated in terms of average purchasing power for the year. And the average and ending indexes are used to restate the ending balance. The calculation of the purchasing power loss is made as follows:

Net monetary assets at beginning, restated to current amount	$ 8,000 \times \dfrac{110}{100} =$	$ 8,800
Add increase during the year	2,500	2,500
Total		11,300
Less net monetary assets at end, restated to current amount	$10,500 \times \dfrac{110}{120} =$	9,625
Loss from holding net monetary items		$ 1,675

What do these calculations show? Leida Company would need $8,800 in net monetary assets in the middle of Year 2 in order to have the same purchasing power as the $8,000 balance at the beginning of the year. To have the same purchasing power in the middle of Year 2 as it had at the end, the company would need $9,625. This amount in the middle of the year is equal in purchasing power to the $10,500 ending balance of net monetary assets.

In this calculation, the beginning and average indexes **increase** the beginning balance to constant dollars in the middle of the year. The increase in net monetary items that occurred is already stated in constant dollars; it is added to the beginning constant dollar amount to arrive at the constant dollar amount at the middle of the year. The ending and average indexes **reduce** the ending balance to constant dollars in the middle of the year. The difference between the two amounts is the gain or loss in purchasing power. This calculation is illustrated graphically in Figure 20-3.

If a decrease in net monetary assets had occurred during the year, it would be deducted from the restated beginning amount rather than added. Similar calculations are made if the company has net monetary liabilities, but during periods of rising prices, a holding gain occurs.

The loss in purchasing power from holding net monetary assets is reported in the restated income statement as shown in Figure 20-4. Notice that the loss is not made part of operating income but is simply shown on the statement as a separate item.

Index:	100		110		120
	12/31/Year 1				12/31/Year 2

	$\times$ (110/100) $\longrightarrow$ $ 8,800		
$8,000			$10,500
	Added during year 2,500	(110/120) $\times$	
	11,300		
	9,625		
	Purchasing power loss $ 1,675		

Beginning Balance					Ending Balance
$8,000	+	$ 2,500		=	$10,500

Figure 20-3 Net monetary asset position of Leida Company for Year 2. The beginning balance is converted to its equivalent of purchasing power in the middle of the year, using the beginning and average index. The addition to net monetary assets during the year is assumed to be in constant dollars. The ending balance is converted to its equivalent of purchasing power in the middle of the year, using the average and ending index. The difference is the average purchasing power gain or loss for the year.

Leida Company
Income Statement
For the Year Ended December 31, Year 2

	Historical Cost	Constant Dollars
Sales	$74,000	$74,000
Less cost of goods sold	34,000	34,500
Gross margin	40,000	39,500
Depreciation expense	3,500	3,966
Other expenses	20,500	20,500
Total expenses	24,000	24,466
Income from operations	$16,000	$15,034
Loss from holding net monetary items		$ (1,675)

Figure 20-4   **The historical cost of goods sold and depreciation expense are restated to common dollars using a general price index to show the effect of inflation on the purchasing power of the company. Note the difference in net income. The loss from holding monetary items is not included in the calculation of constant dollar income but is reported separately.**

CURRENT COST ACCOUNTING

To illustrate current-cost accounting, we continue with the example of Leida Company, whose financial statements are presented in Figure 20-2. The FASB requires companies to disclose the following:

Current cost reporting requirements

1. Income from continuing operations on a current cost basis.
2. The current cost of inventory and property, plant, and equipment at the end of the reporting period.
3. The holding gain or loss in merchandise and property, plant, and equipment net of inflation.

Current Costs on the Balance Sheet

Before income from continuing operations can be reported in terms of current costs, it is necessary to determine the current costs of balance sheet items. The current cost of assets can be obtained by means of specific price indexes, vendor quotations or price lists, appraisals, or estimates of the cost required to reproduce the assets.

There are many ways to find replacement costs

The ending inventory of merchandise has a replacement cost of $6,000, obtained from price quotations of dealers. This is unchanged from historical cost because all the inventory was acquired at the end of Year 2.

A specific price index may be used to find current cost of assets

Leida Company has decided to use a specific price index to restate its land to current **replacement cost**—the amount that would have to be paid today to replace the asset. Based on increases in land values, and using 100 as the index at the time the land was acquired, the specific index for land is 115 at the end of Year 1 and 128 at the end of Year 2. To find the change in current cost for the year, it is necessary to calculate the current cost of the land at the beginning and end of Year 2. Using the specific price index, the calculations are as follows:

$$\text{Replacement cost of land at end of Year 1} = \$10,000 \times \frac{115}{100} = \$11,500$$

$$\text{Replacement cost of land at end of Year 2} = \$10,000 \times \frac{128}{100} = \$12,800$$

The building, which originally cost $50,000, is valued at $64,000 at the end of Year 2, based on an estimate of what it would cost to reproduce it. In order to calculate current cost depreciation expense on the building, it is necessary to know the current cost of the building at the beginning of the year as well as the ending current cost. Depreciation is then calculated for each year on the average of these two values. At the beginning of Year 2, for example, the current cost of the building was $58,000. Therefore the average current cost of the building for Year 2 is ($58,000 + $64,000)/2, or $61,000.

Depreciation is calculated on the average current cost of assets

Now we can calculate current cost depreciation on the building since its acquisition. Current cost depreciation is based on the same method and rate as cost-based depreciation, but it is calculated on the average current cost of the building instead of original cost. With a 25-year life and the straight-line method, current cost depreciation each year on the building is average current cost divided by 25 years. The calculation of depreciation for Year 1 and Year 2 based on the current costs shown below is as follows:

	Current Cost	Average Current Cost	Depreciation Expense
Acquisition in January 1	$50,000	$54,000/25 =	$2,160
December Year 1	58,000	61,000/25 =	2,440
December Year 2	64,000		
Accumulated depreciation after 2 years			$4,600

Equipment is valued at the current cost of similar assets available in the market, and is shown at $19,000 in the replacement cost balance sheet. With a 10-year life, and 1 year of use for the equipment, accumulated depreciation is 10 percent of the equipment's average replacement cost of $17,000 (Original replacement cost of $15,000 + Current replacement cost of $19,000 divided by 2). Therefore replacement cost depreciation of equipment is $1,700 for Year 2.

Current Costs on the Income Statement

Reading down the current cost income statement, cost of goods sold is the first figure that is different from the original income statement. For this example, we assume that the current cost of goods sold is $36,900, obtained by valuing the sold merchandise at the amount it would cost to replace at the time of sale. Sales revenue in the replacement cost income statement is the same as in the historical cost income statement. Therefore deducting a larger cost of goods sold figure in the replacement cost income statement yields a $2,900 smaller gross margin. This does not mean, however, that the company obtained less money from selling the inventory. It simply means that the total difference between the original cost of the merchandise and its selling price is classified into two parts: current cost gross margin and the **holding gain**—the gain from holding merchandise while prices are rising. This holding gain is reported elsewhere in the current cost income statement and is discussed later.

Cost of goods sold and depreciation expense are reported at current cost in the income statement

Depreciation expense is reported on the basis of the replacement cost of fixed assets as already calculated for balance sheet reporting. The sum of the Year 2 replacement cost depreciation on the building and equipment is $4,140 ($2,440 for the building plus $1,700 for the equipment). Therefore replacement cost depreciation expense is $640 greater than historical cost depreciation expense.

Other operating expenses, such as salaries, rents, and taxes incurred during the period are reported in the replacement cost income statement in the same amount as in the historical cost income statement. When expenses are deducted from revenues, the result is **income from continuing operations**, or simply **income from operations**. A comparison of historical cost net income and replacement cost income from operations is shown in Figure 20-5. But holding gains and losses, not shown in Figure 20-5, are also reported in the replacement cost income statement.

Figure 20-5
Income statement prepared on historical cost basis and also on current cost basis. The current cost statement shows cost of goods sold and depreciation expense restated to current costs.

Leida Company
Income Statement
For the Year Ended December 31, Year 2

	Historical Cost	Current Cost
Sales	$74,000	$74,000
Cost of goods sold	34,000	36,900
Gross margin	40,000	37,100
Depreciation expense	3,500	4,140
Other expenses	20,500	20,500
Total expenses	24,000	24,640
Income from operations	$16,000	$12,460

Calculation of Holding Gains and Losses

If an item of merchandise is bought for $100 and sold for $130, on a historical cost basis, gross margin of $30 has been earned. Suppose, however, that a company buys an item of merchandise for $100 and cannot sell it right away. One month later, prices have increased and the company buys another identical item for $110. Then it sells both items for $140. With historical cost accounting, the gross margin is $40 on the first item and $30 on the second. Total gross margin for the two items is $70:

	Item 1	Item 2	Total
Selling price	$140	$140	$280
Cost of merchandise	100	110	210
Gross margin	$ 40	$ 30	$ 70

Current cost accounting looks at gross margin differently. Instead of deducting historical cost from sales revenue, the replacement cost of merchandise is deducted. At the time of sale, the replacement cost of the first item of merchandise is $110, therefore the gross margin on the first item of merchandise is $30, the same as on the second. What happens to the other $10 the company received from the sale of the first item?

Holding gains or losses result from specific price changes

By buying an item of merchandise for $100 and waiting a month to sell it, the company earned $10 of profit simply as a result of holding the item while prices were rising. This holding gain is realized when the item is sold. Using replacement cost accounting, we can make the following calculation:

	Item 1	Item 2	Total
Selling price	$140	$140	$280
Replacement cost of merchandise	110	110	220
Gross margin	30	30	60
Replacement cost at time of sale	110	110	220
Less historical cost	100	110	210
Holding gain	10	0	10
Total	$ 40	$ 30	$ 70

Holding gains and losses are separated from operating profits

You can see that current cost gross margin plus the holding gain is equal to the historical cost gross margin. Why should the holding gain be separated in the current cost income statements? Some accountants argue that the holding gain is not really income. If the company distributed its income and the holding gain to shareholders, it could not replace the inventory item because prices have increased. Therefore the holding gain should not be viewed as income because it is needed to maintain the company's real capital intact.

Part of the holding gain may be due to general price changes.

Holding gains and losses net of inflation. Why did the holding gain occur? It occurred partly because prices in general have been rising since the first item was bought, and partly because the price of this specific type of merchandise was also rising. Let us assume that during the 1-month holding period, the general price index rose 7 percent, to 214 from 200 a month earlier. In that case we would expect the cost of a $100 item to increase to $107. Instead, the cost of the inventory item increased to $110. Therefore $7 of the holding gain is due to inflation in general, and $3 of holding gain is due to the change in specific prices of this type of merchandise. The gain of $3 is the **holding gain net of inflation**.

Holding gains may be realized or unrealized

Holding gains or losses also can occur on items that are not sold during the period. Merchandise held in ending inventory may have a holding gain which is not yet realized by selling the goods. For example, an item bought for $100 is held in ending inventory at the end of the year. Replacement cost is $113, and the general price index has risen 15 percent—from 200 to 230—since the item was bought. In this case, the **unrealized holding gain** of $13 consists of a general inflation component of $15 and a **holding loss net of inflation** of $2 due to changes in specific prices:

Increase in specific prices ($113 − $100)	$13
Effect of general price change ($100 × 200/230 − $100)	15
Holding loss net of inflation	$ (2)

Figure 20-6 illustrates graphically the above examples of holding gains and losses. In the first example, there is a holding gain net of inflation, calculated as the excess of the specific price increase over the general price increase. In the second example, there is a holding loss net of inflation, calculated as the excess of the general price increase over the specific price increase.

Figure 20-6
Holding gains and losses net of inflation are calculated as the difference between the total actual holding gain and the gain that could be expected given the change in general prices. The specific price change in one item exceeded the rate of inflation; the specific price change of the other was less than the rate of inflation.

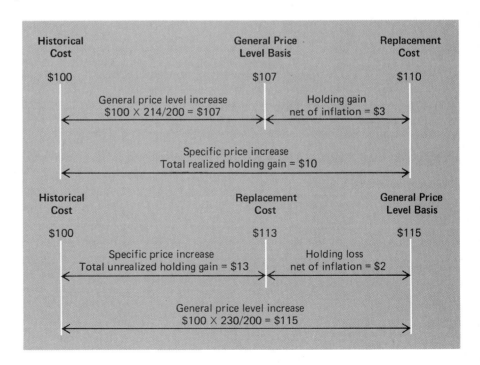

We can now apply these same principles to the assets of Leida Company, including the assets that were sold or used during the year. We want to find the change in the current cost of assets from the beginning of the year to the end and determine how much of that change is due to general inflation and how much is due to changes in specific prices of the assets.

FASB rules define holding gains and losses for a period as the change in current costs during the current accounting period. The portion of this gain net of inflation is calculated using the average general price index for the period. Leida Company's ending inventory is already stated at current cost and constant dollars because it was acquired at the end of Year 2. Therefore there is no holding gain or loss on the ending inventory.

Unrealized holding gains on land.   The holding gain on fixed assets is calculated as the difference between the current cost book value at the beginning of the period and the current cost book value at the end of the period. Land had a current cost of $11,500 at the end of Year 1 and a current cost of $12,800 at the end of Year 2, as calculated earlier. To find the current cost increase net of inflation, we have to determine how much of the increase was the result of general price changes. The calculations are as follows:

Increase in specific prices of land:		
Current cost of land at end of year	$12,800	
Current cost at beginning of year	11,500	
Total increase in current cost for 1985		$1,300
Increase in general prices:		
Current cost of land at beginning of year converted to constant dollars $11,500 × 110/100	12,650	
Current cost at beginning of year	11,500	
Increase in current cost due to inflation		1,150
Excess of specific price increase of land over general price increase		$ 150

This calculation tells us that the total increase in the current cost of the land was $1,300 during Year 2, of which $1,150 was due to inflation and $150 is the unrealized gain from holding land during a period when specific prices of land increased more than the general price index. The FASB refers to holding gains adjusted for inflation as the **excess of specific price increase over general price increase.**

Unrealized holding loss on depreciable assets.   A holding gain or loss on the building and equipment can be calculated in a similar way by finding the change in the current cost net of depreciation from the beginning to the end of the year that we could expect from inflation. The beginning and the average price indexes for Year 2 are used to adjust for inflation.

Increase in specific prices of building:		
Current cost of building at end of year	$64,000	
Less current cost accumulated depreciation (as calculated on page 842)	4,600	$59,400
Current cost of building at beginning of year	58,000	
Less current cost accumulated depreciation (as calculated on page 842)	2,160	55,840
Total increase in current cost for Year 2		3,560
Increase in general prices:		
Net current cost at beginning of year converted to constant dollars $55,840 × 110/100	61,424	
Net current cost at beginning of year	55,840	
Increase in current cost due to inflation		5,584
Excess of general price increase over specific price increase		$ (2,024)

Holding gains on fixed assets are calculated net of current cost depreciation

Realized holding gains on fixed assets are reflected in depreciation expense

A similar calculation using the equipment's current cost net of depreciation at the beginning and end of the year yields a specific price increase of $2,300, a general price increase of $1,500, and an unrealized holding gain net of inflation of $800.

Study the above figures and calculations carefully and note that the increases in specific prices and in general prices are calculated on the book value of the assets—that is, on the part of the assets not yet used up. Therefore the gain or loss is the **unrealized holding gain or loss**. Holding gains on inventory are realized through sale of the goods. But holding gains or losses on fixed assets are realized through use rather than through sale. Use of the assets is reflected in depreciation expense. We now proceed to a calculation of **realized holding gains or losses** on sold merchandise and fixed assets used during the period.

Realized holding loss on merchandise.   The company's cost of goods sold consists of beginning inventory which was stated at current cost at the beginning of the period plus purchases made during the period. The historical cost of the goods sold is therefore the same as beginning current cost. Cost of goods sold had a historical cost of $34,000, as seen in the income statement in Figure 20-2. These same goods had a replacement cost at the time of sale of $36,900, obtained by valuing the goods throughout the accounting period. The total holding gain is therefore $2,900. Based on the average change in the general price index from 100 to 110, we could expect the sold merchandise to increase in cost from $34,000 to $37,400. Therefore the company experienced a holding loss net of inflation of $500. The computations are as follows:

Increase in specific prices of goods sold:
Current cost of goods sold	$36,900	
Less historical cost of goods sold	34,000	$2,900

Increase in general prices:
Constant dollars ($34,000 × 110/100)	37,400	
Less historical cost of goods sold	34,000	3,400

Excess of general price increase over specific price increase of merchandise		$ (500)

When the effect of inflation is taken out of a holding gain, it may become a holding loss

    When the increase in cost of goods sold is adjusted for inflation, we see that the company incurred a net holding loss because the sold inventory did not increase in value as rapidly as prices in general. The FASB refers to holding losses adjusted for inflation as the **excess of general price increases over specific price increases.**

Realized holding gains on fixed assets.   The realized holding gain on fixed assets for the current period is the difference between historical cost depreciation expense and current cost depreciation expense. Therefore the realized holding gain on the building and equipment for Year 2 is $640. To find the holding gain net of inflation, we make the following calculation:

Increase in specific prices:
Current cost depreciation expense	$4,140	
Less historical cost depreciation expense	3,500	$640

Increase in general prices:
Constant dollars ($3,500 × 110/100)	3,850	
Less historical cost depreciation expense	3,500	350

Excess of general price increase over specific price increase		$290

    We now combine all the data from this and earlier calculations as follows:

	Increase in Specific Prices	Increase in General Prices	Holding Gain or (Loss) Net of Inflation
Ending inventory	$ 0	$ 0	$ 0
Land	1,300	1,150	150
Building	3,560	5,584	(2,024)
Equipment	2,300	1,500	800
Unrealized holding loss			(1,074)
Cost of goods sold	2,900	3,400	(500)
Depreciation expense	640	350	290
Realized holding loss			(210)
Totals	$10,700	$11,984	$(1,284)

Reporting of Holding Gains and Losses

Holding gains or losses are separated from operating income

FASB rules require reporting of holding gains of losses net of inflation. The gain or loss from specific price changes is reported first. Then the portion of the gain or loss caused by general price changes is deducted to arrive at the difference between specific and general price changes. Figure 20-7 shows how Leida Company reports this supplementary information in its annual report.

In addition to the constant dollar and current cost information shown in Figure 20-7, FASB rules require companies to report certain restated income, dividend, and asset data in summary form for the past 5 years. Figure 20-8 shows how General Motors reported the 5-year summary data and information on 1983 figures adjusted for changing prices.

Leida Company
Income Statement Adjusted for Changing Prices
For the Year Ended December 31, Year 2

	As Reported in Primary Statements	Adjusted for General Inflation	Adjusted for Changes in Specific Prices (Current Cost)
Sales	$74,000	$74,000	$74,000
Less cost of goods sold	34,000	34,500	36,900
Gross margin	40,000	39,500	37,100
Depreciation expense	3,500	3,966	4,140
Other expenses	20,500	20,500	20,500
Total expenses	24,000	24,466	24,640
Income from operations	$16,000	$15,034	$12,460
Loss from decline in purchasing power of monetary items owned		$ (1,675)	$ (1,675)
Increase in specific prices (current cost) of inventory, property, plant, and equipment held during the year.			$10,700
Effect of increase in general price level			11,984
Excess of increase in general prices over increase in specific price level			$ 1,284
Current cost of inventory at December 31, Year 2			$ 6,000
Current cost of property, plant, and equipment net of accumulated depreciation at December 31, Year 2			$89,500

Figure 20-7
Reporting of constant dollar and current cost information in accordance with FASB requirements. Note that changes in the purchasing power of monetary items and holding gains or losses are not included as part of income from operations.

SCHEDULE A

Comparison of Selected Data Adjusted for Effects of Changing Prices
(Dollars in Millions Except Per Share Amounts)
Historical cost data adjusted for general inflation (constant dollar) and changes in specific prices (current cost). (A)

	1983	1982	1981	1980	1979
Net Sales—as reported	$74,581.6	$60,025.6	$62,698.5	$57,728.5	$66,311.2
—in constant 1967 dollars	24,993.8	20,762.9	23,017.1	23,390.8	30,501.9
Net Income (Loss)—as reported	$ 3,730.2	$ 962.7	$ 333.4	($ 762.5)	$ 2,892.7
—in constant 1967 dollars	1,199.2(B)	(38.9)	(305.8)	(1,023.8)	817.0
—in current cost 1967 dollars	1,144.0(B)	71.7	(252.8)	(829.5)	829.5
Net income (loss) as a percent of sales—as reported	5.0%	1.6%	0.5%	(1.3%)	4.4%
—in constant 1967 dollars	4.8	(0.2)	(1.3)	(4.4)	2.7
—in current cost 1967 dollars	4.6	0.3	(1.1)	(3.5)	2.7
Earnings (Loss) per share of common stock—as reported	$11.84	$3.09	$1.07	($2.65)	$10.04
—in constant 1967 dollars	3.80(B)	(0.14)	(1.04)	(3.52)	2.83
—in current cost 1967 dollars	3.63(B)	0.22	(0.86)	(2.86)	2.87
Dividends per share of common stock—as reported	$2.80	$2.40	$2.40	$2.95	$5.30
—in constant 1967 dollars	0.94	0.83	0.88	1.20	2.44
Net assets at year-end—as reported	$20,766.6	$18,287.1	$17,721.1	$17,814.6	$19,179.3
—in constant 1967 dollars	11,059.5	10,153.9	10,247.2	10,887.6	12,163.4
—in current cost 1967 dollars	10,635.1	9,818.3	10,450.9	11,377.2	12,982.7
Accumulated foreign currency translation adjustments					
—as reported	($ 661.8)				
—in constant 1967 dollars	(109.3)				
—in current cost 1967 dollars	(129.8)				
Unrealized gain from decline in purchasing power of dollars of net amounts owed	$ 86.5	$ 130.5	$ 241.3	$ 182.3	$ 83.8
Excess of increase in general price level over increase in specific prices of inventory and property	$ 78.4	$ 861.2	$ 619.0	$ 689.2	$ 221.8
Market price per common share at year-end—unadjusted	$74.38	$62.38	$38.50	$45.00	$50.00
—in constant 1967 dollars	24.93	21.58	14.13	18.23	23.00
Average Consumer Price Index	298.4	289.1	272.4	246.8	217.4

(A) Adjusted data have generally been determined by applying the Consumer Price Index—Urban to the data with 1967 (CPI-100) as the base year. Depreciation has been determined on a straight-line basis for this calculation.

(B) These amounts will differ from those shown for constant dollar and current cost in Schedule B because a different base year (1983) has been used in Schedule B in order to illustrate the effect of changing prices in an alternative form.

SCHEDULE B

Schedule of Income Adjusted for Changing Prices
For the Year Ended December 31, 1983
(Dollars in Millions Except Per Share Amounts)

	As Reported in the Financial Statements (Historical Cost)	Adjusted for General Inflation (1983 Constant Dollar)	Adjusted for Changes in Specific Prices (1983 Current Cost)
Net Sales	$74,581.6	$74,581.6	$74,581.6
Cost of sales	60,718.8	60,870.7	60,767.0
Depreciation and amortization expense (A)	5,119.6	5,025.8	5,387.9
Other operating and nonoperating items—net	2,789.2	2,789.2	2,789.2
United States and other income taxes	2,223.8	2,223.8	2,223.8
Total costs and expenses	70,851.4	70,909.5	71,167.9
Net Income	$ 3,730.2	$ 3,672.1(B)	$ 3,413.7(B)
Earnings per share of common stock	$11.84	$11.66(B)	$10.83(B)
Accumulated foreign currency translation adjustments	($ 661.8)	($ 462.4)	($ 387.5)
Unrealized gain from decline in purchasing power of dollars of net amounts owed		$ 258.0	$ 258.0
Excess of increase in general price level over increase in specific prices of inventory and property			$ 233.9(C)

(A) The recent high level of expenditures for property (including special tools), coupled with the use of accelerated methods for computing historical cost depreciation and amortization, causes the historical cost amounts to approximate constant dollar and current cost depreciation and amortization which are calculated using the straight-line method.

(B) These amounts will differ from those shown for constant dollar and current cost in Schedule A because a different base year (1967) has been used in Schedule A in order to illustrate the effect of changing prices in an alternative form.

(C) At December 31, 1983, current cost of inventory was $8,658.8 million and current cost of property (including special tools), net of accumulated depreciation and amortization, was $28,096.4 million.

Figure 20-8   Constant dollar and current cost information as reported in the notes of General Motors Corporation's 1983 annual report.

ADVANTAGES AND DISADVANTAGES OF PRICE-LEVEL ADJUSTMENTS

Restating financial statements to reflect changes in price levels, using index numbers and current cost, has both advantages and disadvantages. We discuss some of these below.

Use of Index Numbers

Proponents of price-level-adjusted financial statements claim that such statements enhance comparability between firms and between statements of different periods, and also make trend analysis more useful. The figures are objectively determined and eliminate piecemeal approaches to measuring the effects of inflation on financial reports. There is no deviation from the original cost figures, which are maintained in the statements and are simply restated to reflect the changing value of money.

There are still many flaws in accounting for the effects of inflation

Opponents of restating financial reports using indexes point out that the restated amounts do not reflect current market value, replacement cost, net realizable value, appraisals, or original cost. The value of any one item may have changed more or less than the index used to adjust the item's historical cost. Therefore the restated figures only approximate specific purchasing power or value changes. Presenting multiple sets of statements may confuse users and restating the original amounts does not eliminate the flaws inherent in cost figures. The additional cost of preparing supplementary statements is not warranted. The gains and losses from monetary items may be misleading. For instance, the gains do not provide funds for dividends, expansion, or replacement of assets.

Use of Current Cost Data

Replacement cost financial statements eliminate some of the disadvantages of historical cost figures. Assets are stated in terms of current replacement prices, making the assessment of operations and financial statement comparisons potentially more meaningful. Reporting current cost of assets indicates how much capital is required on the balance sheet date to maintain the company's operations at the capacity that existed prior to the change in prices. The current cost of assets is not obscured by the use of general price indexes which may restate assets' costs more or less than the actual change in value.

Current cost accounting has several disadvantages. Numerous methods of estimating current costs exist, and no standards have been developed for measuring current costs. Consequently, different companies using different methods of arriving at current cost produce statements that are not comparable. The current cost figures lack objectivity and are expensive to obtain.

SUMMARY   During periods of **inflation**, the **purchasing power** of money declines as prices of goods and services increase relative to the value of the dollar. More dollars are required than before to purchase the same amount of real goods. **Deflation** has the opposite effect. A **general price index measures the change in aggregate** prices of a bundle of general goods and services. The rate of inflation is measured by one of several general price indexes, such as the **Consumer Price Index** or the **GNP Implicit Price Deflator.** A **specific price index** measures changes in a bundle of a specific kind of goods, such as farm commodities. In an attempt to eliminate the distortion in financial statements caused by inflation, the accounting profession has explored several alternative methods for reporting the effects of changing price levels.

FASB Statement No. 33 requires certain large corporations to report the effects of changing prices as **supplementary information** with their annual financial statements. **Constant dollar** accounting is accomplished by restating cost of goods sold, depreciation expense, and amortization expense to dollars of constant purchasing power using the Consumer Price Index. **Current cost** accounting is accomplished by restating inventories, property, plant, and equipment, as well as cost of goods sold, depreciation, and amortization in terms of current costs. Current costs may be obtained by means of specific price indexes, appraisals, price quotations, or replacement cost. The restated figures also must show the gain or loss from holding net monetary items and gains or losses from holding nonmonetary items.

Monetary items are assets and liabilities whose amount is expressed in a fixed number of dollars to be paid or received in the future, regardless of the way prices change. Holding **net monetary assets** during periods of inflation results in incurring **purchasing power losses**. Holding **net monetary liabilities** results in **purchasing power gains**.

Nonmonetary items are assets or equities that change in value with changing price levels. Holding nonmonetary items during periods of inflation generally prevents losses in purchasing power. However, not all prices change at the same rate. A general price level index measures changes in **aggregate** prices, whereas prices of specific goods may change more or less than the general index. A business may experience gains or losses from holding nonmonetary assets during periods of rising prices. Such **holding gains or losses** are realized by selling or using the asset, or they are unrealized if the asset is still held at the end of the accounting period. The FASB requires reporting the effects of holding gains and losses. Gains or losses must be divided into the portion resulting from changes in general price levels and the portion resulting from changes in specific prices. Companies are required to report the **excess of general price changes over specific price changes** for inventories and fixed assets.

KEY TERMS

base period *(835)*
constant dollar accounting *(833)*
Consumer Price Index (CPI) *(834)*
current cost accounting *(833)*
deflation *(832)*
excess of general price changes
    over specific price changes *(848)*
excess of specific price changes
    over general price changes *(846)*
GNP Implicit Price Deflator *(834)*
general price index *(834)*
holding gain or loss *(843)*
holding gain or loss net of
    inflation *(845)*
income from operations *(843)*
inflation *(832)*

monetary assets *(837)*
monetary items *(836)*
monetary liabilities *(837)*
net monetary items *(837)*
nonmonetary items *(836)*
purchasing power *(832)*
purchasing power gains or
    losses *(837)*
realized holding gains or
    losses *(847)*
replacement cost *(842)*
restated figures *(836, 838)*
specific price index *(834)*
stable dollar assumption *(832)*
supplementary statements *(833)*
unrealized holding gain or
    loss *(845)*

QUESTIONS

1. What is meant by the purchasing power of the dollar?

2. What is a general price index? How does it differ from a specific price index?

3. What are monetary items? Name some monetary assets and liabilities.

4. What are nonmonetary items? Name some nonmonetary assets and equities.

5. Mrs. Brown bought a house in 1965 for $30,000, paying $5,000 cash and a mortgage for the balance. If prices have been rising steadily for the past 20 years, what is the effect on Mrs. Brown's purchasing power as a result of this transaction?

6. Mr. Green inherited some money in 1970 and immediately invested it in 5 percent long-term bonds. Fifteen years later when the bonds have matured, the price level has doubled. Describe the effect of these events on Mr. Green's purchasing power.

7. What is the primary purpose of restating the income statement to constant dollars? What does such a statement report? How does it differ from current cost statements?

8. Describe the FASB requirements for reporting constant dollar and current cost financial information.

9. What are some of the advantages and disadvantages of constant dollar and current cost financial information?

10. What is meant by unrealized and realized holding gains or losses? How are these items reported? Why are they not included in operating income?

EXERCISES

Ex. 20-1 **Use of index numbers.** Following are values of a general price index for selected dates and some transactions that occurred during Year 2:

January Year 1	90	March Year 2	104
June Year 1	96	April Year 2	105
December Year 1	100	December Year 2	116

a. Equipment bought in January Year 1 for $8,000.

b. Land bought in June Year 1 for $12,000.

c. Building erected on new land completed in March Year 2 at a cost of $45,000.

d. Equipment purchased in April Year 2 for $14,500.

e. Accumulated depreciation on equipment purchased in Year 1 is $1,500 at the end of Year 2.

f. Depreciation expense on building for Year 2 is $2,000.

g. Cash reported on the December 31, Year 2 balance sheet is $7,200.

h. Periodic LIFO inventory beginning balance in Year 2 was $2,000, ending balance is $3,000.

Required: For each item, indicate in whole dollars the amount of constant dollars to which each item should be restated on December 31, Year 2.

Ex. 20-2 **Cost of goods sold restatement with FIFO and LIFO.** Babcock Company uses a periodic inventory system. Its inventory turns over 25 times per year. Beginning inventory was $10,000, acquired when the general price index was 103. Total purchases during the year were $190,000. Ending inventory is $14,000 if FIFO is used and $11,000 if LIFO is used. The average index is 108.

Required:
 a. Restate cost of goods sold to constant dollars, assuming the company uses FIFO inventory valuation.
 b. Restate cost of goods sold to constant dollars, assuming the company uses LIFO inventory valuation.

Ex. 20-3 **Constant dollar inventory with FIFO and LIFO.** Conwell Company uses a periodic inventory system. Cost of goods sold for the year is $300,000. Beginning inventory was $21,000, acquired when the general price index was 102. Ending inventory is $17,000. The general price index was 106 at the beginning of the year and 114 at the end of the year.

Required:
 a. Show the amount of ending inventory and cost of goods sold to be reported in constant dollars in the end-of-year financial statements, assuming the company uses FIFO inventory valuation.
 b. Repeat a assuming LIFO inventory valuation.

Ex. 20-4   **Constant dollar depreciation.**   The fixed asset ledger of Dukesa Company contains the following information:

Date Acquired	Item	Cost	Estimated Life	Depreciation Method	Salvage Value
12/27/Y1	Building	59,000	20	St. line	None
1/12/Y2	Desk computers	22,000	5	St. line	None
6/30/Y4	Metal brake	7,800	5	St. line	$1,000
1/ 4/Y5	Lathe	17,000	5	St. line	3,200

The general price index had the following values on the dates the equipment was acquired and at the end of Year 5:

December Year 1	132	June Year 4	155
January Year 2	137	January Year 5	166
January Year 3	143	December Year 5	174

Required: Determine the amount of constant dollar depreciation expense that should be reported in the Year 5 financial statements.

Ex. 20-5   **Net monetary items.**   Below are the current assets and liabilities of Elfin Company, taken from the company's balance sheets. The company has no long-term monetary assets. There is no long-term debt and the company is capitalized entirely with common stock. The general price index was 180 at the end of Year 1 and 196 at the end of Year 2.

	December 31 Year 2	Year 1
Current assets:		
Cash	$ 44,300	$ 29,400
Accounts receivable	40,980	35,320
Merchandise	37,800	31,900
Prepaid expenses	3,680	4,220
Total current assets	$126,760	$100,840
Current liabilities:		
Accounts payable	$ 26,500	$ 24,000
Notes payable	8,000	6,000
Interest payable	3,600	4,100
Total current liabilities	$ 38,100	$ 34,100

Required: Compute the gain or loss from holding net monetary items during Year 2.

Ex. 20-6   **Decrease in net monetary items.**   Below are the monetary assets and monetary liabilities taken from the balance sheets of Finogle Company. The general price index was 170 at the end of Year 1 and 188 at the end of Year 2.

	December 31 Year 2	Year 1
Monetary assets:		
Cash	$25,000	$19,000
Accounts receivable	19,500	21,200
Notes receivable	31,300	28,700
Total monetary assets	$75,800	$68,900
Monetary liabilities:		
Accounts payable	$16,500	$18,000
Notes payable	23,000	6,100
Bonds payable	30,000	30,000
Total monetary liabilities	$69,500	$54,100

Required: Compute the gain or loss from holding net monetary items during Year 2.

Ex. 20-7   **Change in net monetary items.**   Below are the totals of monetary assets and monetary liabilities as reported by Grunkle Company in its Year 2 annual report. The general price index was 145 at the end of Year 1 and 165 at the end of Year 2.

	December 31 Year 2	Year 1
Total monetary assets	$45,200	$32,400
Total monetary liabilities	52,500	54,100

Required: Compute the gain or loss from holding net monetary items during Year 2.

Ex. 20-8   **Current cost depreciation.**   Below are the book values and current costs of Hollerite Company's building since its acquisition:

	Book Value	Current Cost
February 4, Year 1	$100,000	$100,000
December 31, Year 1	95,000	104,000
December 31, Year 2	90,000	110,000
December 31, Year 3	85,000	116,000
December 31, Year 4	80,000	116,000

Required: Calculate current cost depreciation expense for each year and show the amounts for fixed assets and depreciation expense that should be reported at current cost in notes to the Year 4 financial statements.

Ex. 20-9   **Holding gains on cost of goods sold.**   Jimminex Company's cost of goods sold of $136,600 had a replacement cost of $156,542 at the time of sale. During the year the general price index increased from 135 at the beginning of the year to 159 at the end of the year.

Required: Calculate the realized holding gain for the company.

Ex. 20-10   **Finding the general price index.**   Kilopot Company's cost of goods sold of $180,000 had a replacement cost of $229,500 at the time of sale. The company realized holding gains on sold merchandise of $12,000. The general price index at the beginning of the year was 120.

Required: Find the general price index at the end of the year.

Ex. 20-11   **Holding gains on fixed assets.**   Indiplex Corporation reported the following current cost data in its December 31, Year 2 annual report:

	Year 2	Year 1
Equipment	$50,000	$44,600
Accumulated depreciation	(21,000)	(18,000)
Total fixed assets	$29,000	$26,600

Historical cost depreciation expense reported in the Year 2 income statement is $2,500. Current cost depreciation expense is $3,000 for Year 2. The general price index at the end of Year 1 was 120; it was 140 at the end of Year 2.

Required: Calculate the excess of specific price increase over the general price increase (holding gain net of inflation) for the equipment at the end of Year 2.

Ex. 20-12   **Realized holding gain on fixed asset.**   Refer to the data in Exercise 20-11 on the depreciation on Indiplex Corporation's equipment.

Required: Calculate the realized holding gain net of inflation as reflected in the equipment's depreciation expense.

PROBLEMS

P. 20-1   **Monetary items.**   The condensed comparative balance sheets of Belinda Company are presented on the following page. The change in monetary items occurred evenly over the year. The general price index at the beginning of the year was 130 and at the end of the year it was 140.

Belinda Company
Balance Sheet
December 31

	Current Year	Last Year
Cash	$ 5,500	$ 4,500
Accounts receivable	6,000	5,000
Notes receivable	3,000	2,000
Merchandise	9,490	10,000
Fixed assets (net)	24,500	23,500
Total assets	$48,490	$45,000
Notes payable	$ 3,000	$ 2,800
Accounts payable	7,700	6,700
Taxes payable	1,300	300
Bonds payable	4,000	4,000
Common stock	20,000	20,000
Retained earnings	12,490	11,200
Total equities	$48,490	$45,000

Required: Calculate the gain or loss from holding monetary items.

P. 20-2   Monetary items.   Following are condensed comparative balance sheets for Winner Company:

Winner Company
Balance Sheet
December 31

	Year 2	Year 1
Cash	$ 40,000	$ 34,000
Accounts receivable	60,000	45,000
Notes receivable	10,000	10,000
Merchandise	105,000	100,000
Fixed assets	110,000	105,000
Total assets	$325,000	$294,000
Notes payable	—	$ 10,000
Accounts payable	$ 67,000	43,000
Taxes payable	3,000	2,000
Bonds payable	20,000	30,000
Common stock	200,000	200,000
Retained earnings	35,000	9,000
Total equities	$325,000	$294,000

The company repaid its note payable and part of its bonds on June 30, Year 2. The change in remaining monetary assets occurred evenly during the year. Values of the general price index for Year 2 were 100 on January 1 and 116 on December 31.

Required: Calculate the gain or loss from holding monetary items.

P. 20-3　**Holding gains on fixed assets.**　Mollynex Corporation reported the following current cost data in its December 31, Year 2 annual report:

	Year 2	Year 1
Land	$ 9,800	$ 8,000
Building	87,500	77,000
Accumulated depreciation	(47,000)	(41,000)
Total fixed assets	$38,510	$40,000

Historical cost depreciation expense reported in the Year 2 income statement is $4,800. Current cost depreciation expense is $6,000 for Year 2. The general price index at the end of Year 1 was 120; it was 144 at the end of Year 2.

Required:
    a. Calculate the excess of specific price increase over the general price increase (holding gain net of inflation) for the fixed assets at the end of Year 2.
    b. Calculate the realized holding gain net of inflation as reflected in the building's depreciation expense.

P. 20-4　**Constant dollar reporting.**　The financial statements of Ludlow Company are presented below and on the following page. The company uses LIFO inventory valuation. The beginning inventory for 1985 was acquired when the general price index was 150. The ending inventory was purchased in December 1985. The company purchased its equipment in early 1982 when the general price index was 130. New equipment was purchased for $20,000 in late December 1985. All equipment has a useful life of 5 years with no salvage value. Straight-line depreciation is used. The general price index was 160 at the beginning of 1985 and 170 at the end.

Ludlow Company
Comparative Balance Sheets
December 31, 1985 and 1984

	1985	1984
Cash	$ 9,000	$13,000
Accounts receivable	12,000	11,000
Merchandise	16,000	12,000
Equipment	70,000	50,000
Accumulated depreciation	(40,000)	(30,000)
Total assets	$67,000	$56,000
Accounts payable	$12,000	$10,000
Bonds payable	16,000	16,000
Common stock	20,000	20,000
Retained earnings	19,000	10,000
Total equities	$67,000	$56,000

Ludlow Company
Income Statement
For the Year Ended December 31, 1985

Sales		$85,000
Less cost of goods sold		50,000
Gross margin		35,000
Depreciation expense	$10,000	
Other expenses	16,000	26,000
Net income		$ 9,000

Required: Show how the company should report the results of operations in a constant dollar income statement.

P. 20-5   **Current cost reporting.**   Refer to the data in Problem 20-4, which shows the financial statements of Ludlow Company and other information. Following is current cost information for the company:

	December 31			
	1985	**1984**	**1983**	**1982**
Equipment, old	$69,000	$62,000	$58,000	$53,000
Equipment, new	10,000			
Cost of goods sold	52,495			
Merchandise, beginning	14,950	12,000		
Merchandise purchases	4,000			

Required: Show how the company should report the results of operations in a current cost income statement.

P. 20-6   **Reporting constant dollar data.**   On the following page are trial balances of Korble Company at the end of Year 2 and Year 1. The company uses a FIFO inventory system, and all ending inventory was acquired in late December. The beginning inventory was acquired when the general price index was 150, which was its value at the end of Year 1. In January Year 2, the company purchased equipment for $13,000. All of the other equipment was acquired in early Year 1 when the general price index was 130. All the equipment has a useful life of 5 years with no salvage value. Straight-line depreciation is used. The company's land was acquired in early Year 1 when the general price index was 140. The index was 160 at the end of Year 2.

Korble Company
Trial Balance
December 31

	Year 2	Year 1
Cash	$15,000	$13,000
Accounts receivable	14,000	12,000
Merchandise	11,000	9,000
Land	20,000	20,000
Equipment	73,000	60,000
Accumulated depreciation	(38,000)	(24,000)
Accounts payable	(17,000)	(10,000)
Bonds payable	(13,000)	(30,000)
Common stock	(40,000)	(40,000)
Retained earnings, 12/31/Y1	(10,000)	(10,000)
Sales	(90,000)	
Cost of goods sold	50,000	
Depreciation expense	14,000	
Other expenses	11,000	
Totals	$ 0	$ 0

Required: Show how the company should report the results of operations in a constant dollar income statement.

P. 20-7 **Reporting current cost data.** Refer to the trial balances and other data of Korble Company in Problem 20-6. Given below are current cost data for the company:

	December 31		
	Year 2	Year 1	Year 0
Cost of goods sold	$55,000		
Merchandise	11,000	$ 9,000	
Land	30,000	26,000	
Equipment, old	75,000	67,000	$63,000

Required: Show how the company should report the results of operations in a current cost income statement.

P. 20-8   **Interpreting inflation accounting data.**   Following is information provided by Jones and Jones in its 1985 annual report:

Statement of Earnings Adjusted for Changing Prices

For the Year Ended January 2, 1986 In Average 1985 Dollars (Dollars in Millions)	As Reported in the Primary Statements	Adjusted for Specific Costs (Current Costs)	Amount Increase (Decrease)
Sales to customers and other revenues	$5,899	$5,899	—
Cost of products sold (excluding depreciation)	2,332	2,365	33
Depreciation and amortization	176	223	47
Other operating expenses (excluding depreciation)	2,604	2,604	—
Provision for taxes on income	264	264	—
Earnings before extraordinary charge	$ 523	$ 443	(80)

Five Year Selected Financial Data Adjusted for Changing Prices

Current Cost Data in Average 1985 Dollars (Dollars in Millions Except Per Share Figures)	1985	1984	1983	1982	1981
Sales and other revenues—as reported	$5,899	5,506	4,914	4,278	3,543
—in average 1985 dollars	5,899	5,842	5,756	5,687	5,240
Earnings before extraordinary charge—as reported	523	468	401	352	299
—in current costs	443	393	377	384	310
Earnings per share before extraordinary charge—as reported	2.79	2.51	2.17	1.92	1.67
—in current costs	2.36	2.11	2.04	2.09	1.73
Dividends per share—as reported	1.00	.85	.74	.67	.57
—in average 1985 dollars	1.00	.90	.87	.89	.84
Net assets at year-end—as reported	2,800	2,528	2,269	1,987	1,701
—in current costs	3,572	3,404	3,449	3,449	2,788
Translation adjustment—in current costs	(187)	(213)	(201)	(167)	(143)
(Loss) from decline in general purchasing power of net monetary assets held	(12)	(30)	(47)	(57)	(39)
Current cost increases of inventories and net property, plant and equipment greater (less) than the increase in general price level	98	(64)	(144)	(99)	(78)
Market price per share at year-end—as reported	50.00	37.13	33.38	26.63	24.63
—in average 1985 dollars	49.45	38.13	37.27	33.47	35.02
Average price index (1967 = 100)	289.0	272.4	246.8	217.4	195.4
Annual percent increase in average index	6.0	10.4	13.5	11.3	7.7

(1) The current cost of net property, plant and equipment at the end of 1985 was $2,237 million and was established based on several methods, including indexing and unit pricing. Potential technological improvements and efficiencies which might be associated with actual replacement of assets have not been reflected.
(2) At the end of 1985, the current cost of inventories was $1,110 million estimated on the FIFO or actual cost method.
(3) Cost of goods sold for current costs approximates a LIFO basis.
(4) Depreciation and amortization was computed using the straight-line method. In the primary financial statements, accelerated methods are generally used for domestic assets and the straight-line method for international assets.
(5) The increase in the general price level of inventories and net property, plant and equipment for 1985 was $115 million. The effect of increases in current costs for those assets was $213 million.
(6) 1983–1981 market price per common share data is adjusted for the 1984 three-for-one stock split.

Supplementary Information on the Effects of Changing Prices

Introduction

Financial Accounting Standard (FAS) No. 33 as amended by FAS No. 70 requires the disclosure of supplementary income calculations based on two methods of accounting: constant dollar accounting, which adjusts inventory and property, plant and equipment for general inflation using a general price index, and current cost accounting, which adjusts for specific price changes of inventories and property, plant and equipment.

FAS No. 70, however, exempts the presentation of the constant dollar method when a significant part of a company's operations is measured in functional currencies other than the U.S. dollar. Since this is the case for the Company, constant dollar data have been omitted.

The current cost information which is presented has been calculated by the translate-restate option available under FAS No. 70, which requires the translation of the foreign currency data in accordance with FAS No. 52 and restatement of the current cost data based on the general price index.

Summary Results

The adjustments to cost of products sold for current costs are not significant because of frequent inventory turnover, use of LIFO inventory valuation and current exchange rates that reflect a strong U.S. dollar, all of which reduce the effects of inflation on reported earnings. The accelerated methods of depreciation used in the primary financial statements partially allow for expected price changes. For this reason, the current cost adjustment was computed using the straight-line method. This difference in method has the effect of reducing the amount of the adjustment. Also, FAS No. 33 specifically prohibits the restatement of income tax expense, thus illustrating that effective tax rates increase as inflation erodes earnings.

The Five Year Selected Financial Data Adjusted for Changing Prices presents current cost information adjusted to average 1985 dollars to make the years comparable.

Management also believes that the current cost method is not a good predictor of future cash flows. Jones and Jones is a growth-oriented company and future cash flows are substantially affected by management's strategy in pursuing new markets, further developing technology and increasing productivity. Future cash flows, therefore, cannot be properly assessed solely by evaluating existing assets.

Required: Indicate whether the following statements are true or false after examining carefully the information provided:

1. Constant dollar information is provided by the company in another part of its annual report.

2. The replacement cost of sold inventories generally was higher at the time of sale than the original cost.

3. The company held net monetary liabilities during 1985.

4. The company's inventory and fixed assets increased at a higher rate than the general price level during the year.

5. The company reports its inflation data in accordance with FASB Statement No. 52 rather than Statement No. 33.

6. FASB Statement No. 70 exempts certain companies from presenting constant dollar financial figures.

7. The company uses FIFO inventory valuation and its inventory turnover is about 7.

8. The amount of 1985 earnings that the company can distribute as dividends is no more than $443 million.

9. Company management believes that the current cost information is a good predictor of future cash flows.

Case 20-1   Inflation reporting.

Account balances taken from the ledger of Mullinah Company are presented below, together with current cost data for inventory and equipment. The company uses FIFO inventory valuation. The beginning inventory was acquired when the general price index was 140. The ending inventory was purchased in December 1985. The company purchased its equipment in early 1983 when the general price index was 120. New equipment was purchased for $16,000 in late December 1985. All equipment has a useful life of 5 years and no salvage value. Straight-line depreciation is used. The general price index was 140 at the beginning of 1985 and 150 at the end.

	December 31 1985	December 31 1984
Cash	$ 9,000	$10,000
Accounts receivable	14,000	11,000
Merchandise	15,000	12,000
Equipment	76,000	60,000
Accumulated depreciation	(36,000)	(24,000)
Accounts payable	(12,000)	(10,000)
Bonds payable	(25,000)	(20,000)
Common stock	(20,000)	(20,000)
Retained earnings	(19,000)	(19,000)
Dividends	2,000	
Sales	(75,000)	
Cost of goods sold	40,000	
Depreciation expense	12,000	
Other expenses	19,000	
Totals	$ 0	$ 0

Current Costs on December 31

	1985	1984	1983
Equipment, old	$72,000	$66,000	$63,000
Equipment, new	16,000		
Cost of goods sold	48,000		
Merchandise	15,000	12,000	

Required:

a. Show how the company should report the results of operations in a constant dollar and current cost income statement in accordance with FASB Statement No. 33.

b. Discuss briefly the significance of the restated net income and other figures in the statements.

Case 20-2   Interpreting an inflation accounting report.
Following is the consolidated statement of income adjusted for changing prices for the year ended September 30, 1982, in thousands of dollars (except for per share data) reported by Staley Company in its 1982 annual report:

	As Reported in Primary Statements (Historical Costs)	Adjusted for General Inflation (Constant Dollars)	Adjusted for Change in Specific Prices (Current Cost)
Net Sales	$1,588,114	$1,588,114	$1,588,114
Costs and expenses:			
Cost of products sold	1,428,716	1,429,534	1,428,352
Selling and administrative expenses	79,444	79,444	79,444
Depreciation	47,944	71,448	71,402
Interest expense	7,303	7,303	7,303
Total costs and expenses	1,563,407	1,587,729	1,586,501
Earnings before income taxes	24,707	385	1,613
Income taxes (credits)	(31,445)	(31,445)	(31,445)
Earnings before share of equity companies' net earnings	56,152	31,830	33,058
Share of equity companies' net earnings	6,460	6,460	6,460
Net Earnings	$ 62,612	$ 38,290	$ 39,518
Per common share	$2.75	$1.64	$1.69
Other Information			
Common shareholders' equity at September 30, 1982	$ 514,669	$ 750,151	$ 728,109
Per common share	$23.19	$33.80	$32.81
Gain from decline in purchasing power of net amounts owed		$ 21,990	$ 21,990
Increase in specific prices of inventories and property and equipment held during year			$ 8,014
Effect of increase in general price level			52,685
Decrease in specific prices vs. general prices			$ 44,671

Required: Respond to the following questions after you have examined carefully the reported information. In all cases state your reasons for the answer.

    a. What are the reasons for the differences among the three figures reported for cost of products sold?

    b. Did the company hold net monetary assets or net monetary liabilities during the reporting period?

    c. How was the constant dollar depreciation expense calculated?

    d. How was current cost depreciation expense calculated?

    e. Explain the $44,671 decrease in specific prices versus general prices.

    f. What do the net earnings figures tell you?

Glossary

The numbers in parentheses following each term refer to the chapters in which the terms are defined and discussed.

Accelerated cost recovery system (ACRS) (10) A method of accelerated depreciation required for tax purposes for assets acquired after 1980.

accelerated depreciation (10) A method of depreciation that writes off more of the asset's cost in earlier years than in later years. *See* double declining balance, sum-of-the-years'-digits, and Accelerated Cost Recovery System.

account (2) A record used for collecting financial data for a specific category or classification of assets, liabilities, or owners' equity. To provide a reckoning, to report financial events.

account balance (2) The sum total of what has been recorded in an account. The ending amount remaining in the account at any time.

accounting (1) The practice of providing financial information to decision makers, including the measurement and communication of such information, and its analysis and interpretation.

accounting cycle (5) The process that takes place during one accounting period, including the maintenance of accounting records and end-of-period accounting procedures. It includes journalizing transactions, posting ledger accounts, preparing trial balances, making adjusting and closing entries, preparing financial statements at the end of the period, and making reversing entries at the beginning of the following period.

accounting equation (2) The equation $A = E$, indicating the equality of assets and equities. The accounting identity, also expressed as $A = L + C$ or $A - L = C$.

accounting income subject to tax (11) All revenue and expenses reported in the income statement for external reporting that are taxable or tax deductible, not including revenues and expenses consisting of permanent differences, which are not taxable or tax deductible.

accounting period (3) A period of time, usually 1 year, at the end of which financial statements are prepared. The accounting period of companies on a calendar year ends on December 31. If the accounting period ends on some other date, the company is said to be on a fiscal year.

accounting system (2) The combination of records and procedures used to collect, record, and classify accounting data so that they may be summarized and reported as financial information.

accounts payable (11) Accounts maintained by a business of its suppliers from whom it purchases goods and services on credit. Also known as trade accounts and open accounts.

accounts receivable (8) Accounts maintained by a business of its customers who purchase goods and services on credit. Also known as trade accounts and open accounts.

accretion (10) A physical increase in an asset due to natural growth.

accrual (4) The accounting concept that requires revenues to be recorded when earned regardless of the time money is received, and expenses to be recorded when incurred regardless of the time money is paid. **(5)** The accumulation of revenue and expense that has been earned or incurred but has not yet been recorded because no payment has been received or made. Accruals require adjusting entries at the end of the accounting period.

accumulated depreciation (10) A contra asset account used to record the portion of fixed asset costs that has been allocated to past accounting periods, reducing the book value of the asset.

accumulation of discount (15) *See* discount accumulation.

acid test ratio (18) The ratio of liquid assets to current liabilities, used as a measure of liquidity. Also called the quick ratio.

acquisition (15) *See* business combination.

additional paid-in capital (13) *See* paid-in capital in excess of par.

adjunct account (12) One of a set of related accounts reported together on the balance sheet, with their balances added to arrive at book value. An example is the premium on bonds payable.

adjusted trial balance (5) A trial balance taken after adjusting entries have been made.

adjusting entry (5) A journal entry made at the end of the accounting period to record an accrual, deferral, or allocation and thereby to bring an account balance to its proper amount.

affiliated companies (16) Companies that are related because one owns all or most of the stock of the other, resulting in a parent-subsidiary relationship.

aging of receivables (8) A technique used to estimate the amount of bad debts expense and uncollectible accounts.

all financial resources (17) The concept of reporting all financing and investing activities in the statement of changes of financial position, including those that do not affect cash or working capital, such as exchanges of stock or long-term debt for fixed assets.

allocation (5) Assigning of asset costs to the periods that benefit from the use of assets whose life extends over several accounting periods. Allocations require adjusting entries at the end of the accounting period.

allowance for uncollectible accounts (3, 5, 8) A contra account to accounts receivable used for reporting receivables at net realizable value.

American Accounting Association (AAA) (1) An organization of persons interested in accounting, consisting mostly of university professors. The AAA promotes research in accounting.

American Institute of Certified Public Accountants (AICPA) (1) An organization whose members are accountants certified by individual states for the practice of public accounting. The AICPA is the largest accounting organization in the United States.

amortization (10) A systematic writing off of an account balance, such as the cost of an asset or the discount of a bond payable.

amount (7) See future value.

amount of annuity (7) See future value of annuity.

annual report (5) A report prepared by a business entity and provided to its owners at the end of each accounting period. Annual reports include a complete set of financial statements.

annuity (7) A series of equal periodic payments, called rents, with each payment taking place at a compounding period.

appropriated retained earnings (14) A portion of the retained earnings account which has been restricted, making it unavailable for dividend distributions.

arms'-length transaction (10) A transaction between unrelated independent parties.

articles of incorporation (13) The document prepared by a corporation describing its purposes, capitalization, place of business, and other characteristics. The document is submitted to the state and becomes the corporate charter when it is approved by the state incorporating the business.

asset (2) A valuable economic resource from which future benefits can be obtained by its owner, consisting of tangible or intangible property.

audit trail (4) The cross-referencing of business records and documents that allow an accountant to trace a transaction to its origin.

auditing (1) The practice of examining financial statements of an organization for the purpose of verifying that they are fair and reliable and expressing an opinion about them.

authorized shares (13) The number of shares of each class of stock a corporation may issue to its shareholders. The number of shares authorized is usually larger than the number of shares issued.

average age of receivables (19) See days' sales in receivables.

average collection period (19) See days' sales in receivables.

average cost (9) The cost assigned to inventory items when the weighted average method or moving average method of inventory valuation is used.

average days' supply in inventory (19) A ratio used to measure liquidity, calculated by dividing inventory turnover into the number of days in the accounting period.

bad debts (8) Expenses arising from granting credit to poor credit risks, resulting in the inability to collect accounts receivable.

balance sheet (2) A financial report showing the financial condition at a point in time for a specific accounting entity. Also called statement of financial position.

bank reconciliation (8) A schedule prepared to identify discrepancies between the bank statement and the cash record in the ledger.

base period (20) The time period when a price index is established with a value of 100, with which other index values may be compared.

bearer bond (12) A bond that is not registered in the name of an owner but is instead deemed to be owned by its possessor.

board of directors (13) A group of individuals elected by the shareholders of a corporation to represent them in overseeing the operations of the business. The board of directors appoints officers who manage business operations.

bond discount (12) See discount.

bond indenture (12) The written contract describing the conditions under which a bond is issued, including such terms as the coupon interest rate, interest payment dates, maturity date, and call prices.

bonds (12) Negotiable financial instruments representing the indebtedness of a business or government.

bonds payable (12) The long-term liability account reporting the face value of outstanding bond obligations.

book of original entry (4) See journal.

book value (3, 10, 14) The net amount reported for an item on the balance sheet, such as accounts receivable less allowance for doubtful accounts, equipment less accumulated depreciation, or bonds payable less bond discount. Also known as carrying value. When referring to an entire business, book value is the amount of net assets or total capital as reported in the company's balance sheet (19) Book value per share is total capital divided by the number of common shares outstanding.

bookkeeping (1) The routine clerical task of recording accounting information in journals and ledgers, often performed by a computer.

books of account (4) The set of accounting records, consisting of journals and ledgers, in which all accounting transactions are recorded.

budget (8) A plan of future operations, expressed in quantitative terms for a specific entity and time period, such as a cash budget detailing the expected receipts and disbursements of cash.

business combination (16) The acquisition by one business entity of a controlling interest of another, resulting in a new entity or a consolidation of two separate entities. Also called acquisition or merger. *See* consolidation.

call premium (12) The difference between the face value of a bond and its call price.

call price (12) The price that must be paid by a corporation in order to reacquire and retire bonds outstanding prior to their maturity date.

capital (2) Owners' equity, or the rights to the benefits available from ownership of assets. A representation of the wealth of an individual. The amount invested in a business by owners. The residual left when liabilities are deducted from assets.

capital lease (11) An arrangement for leasing equipment or other property, which is in substance a purchase agreement, with the lessee responsible for all expenses of ownership and the lessor providing financing for the purchase.

capital stock (3, 13) Owners' equity of a corporation represented by shares of common or preferred stock.

capital structure (13) The combination of common stock preferred stock, paid in capital and retained earnings, which together make up owners' equity of a business.

capital transactions (4) Transactions between a business and its owners that result in changes in owners' equity, such as payment of dividends or issuance of stock to shareholders.

capitalization (10) The determination of the amount of capital required at a given rate of interest in order to obtain a given amount of earnings. **(13)** In reference to a corporation, the total amount of authorized capital stock multiplied by its par or stated value.

capitalization rate (10) The interest rate at which a business must be capitalized in order to yield a specific return on investment.

capitalize (10) To record an expenditure in a permanent account as contrasted to expensing it. The cost of an asset is capitalized when the asset is acquired and expensed as the asset is used. To determine how much capital is required at a given rate of interest in order to obtain a given amount of earnings. **(13)** To establish a corporation by authorizing a specific number of shares of capital stock.

capitalized retained earnings (13) The amount of retained earnings that has been transferred to contributed capital and is no longer available for the payment of cash dividends.

carrying value (3) *See* book value.

cash (8) Medium of exchange normally held in the form of currency, coin, demand deposits, and time deposits. Checks and money orders may also be considered cash. **(17, 18)** One of the definitions of funds, used in the preparation of the statement of changes in financial position.

cash basis (4) The accounting system in which revenues and expenses are recorded at the time they are received or paid rather than when earned or incurred. The cash basis of accounting is used by most individuals and some small businesses.

cash disbursements journal (6) A special journal designed for recording all cash payments.

cash discount (6) A reduction of the amount due on an invoice, offered as an inducement for early payment. The cash discount usually represents a high interest rate if the invoice is not paid within the discount period.

cash dividend (13) A distribution of cash paid out of earnings to the shareholders of a corporation.

cash flow statement (17) The statement of changes in financial position with funds defined as cash; primarily used for internal decision making.

cash provided by operations (17) The portion of financing activities obtained by operating the business, reported under sources of funds in the statement of changes in financial resources.

cash receipts journal (6) A special journal designed to record the receipt of cash from cash sales and other sources.

cash short or over (8) An account in which an entity records differences between the actual amount of cash and the cash balance in the books.

cash surrender value of life insurance (15) The amount of money that can be obtained from an insurance company by surrendering a life insurance policy on which cash surrender value accumulates, thereby canceling the policy. Also known as loan value.

Certificate in Management Accounting (CMA) (1) A certificate granted by the Institute of Management Accounting to candidates who have successfully completed a rigorous professional examination administered by the institute.

certified public accountant (CPA) (1) A professional accountant who has passed a professional examination, obtained practical experience, and satisfied other requirements and is certified by a state to practice public accounting, including the auditing of financial statements of organizations and expressing an opinion on the fairness of the statements.

charge (2) Debit.

circulating capital (8) The current assets and current liabilities of a business used in daily business operations. *See also* working capital.

closely held corporation (13) A corporation whose shares are held by a small number of individuals and are not traded among the public.

closing entries (5) Journal entries prepared at the end of an accounting period in order to transfer the balances of temporary accounts to the retained earnings account, leaving the temporary accounts with a zero balance.

common stock (13) The residual equity account of the owners of a corporation who are the primary risk takers, recorded on the books at par or stated value. The stock certificates issued to the owners of a corporation as evidence of their ownership.

common stock equivalent (14) A security, such as a preferred stock or bond payable, which is convertible into a given number of shares of common stock and which was acquired by its owners primarily for the conversion privilege and secondarily for the dividend or interest revenue which it yields.

complex capital structure (14) The capital structure of a corporation that has convertible securities outstanding, requiring the reporting of primary and fully diluted earnings per share.

compound discount (7) The interest rate used to find the present value of future payments, assuming that compounding takes place at periodic intervals. The accumulated interest that is deducted from a future payment in order to arrive at its present value.

compound interest (7) The interest rate used to find the future value of future payments, assuming that compounding takes place at periodic intervals. The accumulated interest added to the original investment in order to arrive at its future value.

compound journal entry (4) A journal entry resulting from a transaction that affects more than two accounts.

conglomerate (16) A corporation that owns a number of other companies in a variety of unrelated industries.

conservatism (4) The accounting principle requiring the selection of the accounting method which is least likely to overstate income and financial position.

consignee (9) A firm or a person who holds consigned inventory belonging to another firm or person, for the purpose of selling that inventory and earning a commission. The consignee does not take title to the inventory held for sale.

consignment (9) Merchandise in the hands of a consignee, held for the purpose of sale but not owned by the holder.

consignor (9) A person or firm that has consigned merchandise to another person or firm for the purpose of having it sold. The consignor does not possess the merchandise but owns the goods until they have been sold.

consistency (4, 9) The accounting principle requiring that an accounting or reporting method, once selected, is used from one period to another in order to make financial statements of different periods comparable. The consistency principle requires a change in accounting methods to be disclosed in the financial statements.

consolidation (15, 16) The combination of two or more corporate accounting entities into a single new entity.

The combining of several entities' financial statements into one set of financial statements representing the combined operations of the several entities.

constant dollar accounting (20) Reporting of financial information adjusted for the effects of inflation by use of a price index, so as to show all figures in dollars of equal purchasing power.

Consumer Price Index (20) A general index compiled by the Bureau of Labor Statistics, representing the price of a general basket of consumer goods and used for measuring the purchasing power of the dollar.

contingent liability (8, 11) A liability that may materialize in the future but whose amount is not owed at the time financial statements are prepared and cannot be estimated. Usually reported in footnotes to the financial statements. Not a legal obligation.

continuity (3) See going concern.

contra asset (3) An account related to another asset account, but having a credit balance, such as accumulated depreciation or allowance for doubtful accounts.

contra account (6, 12) An account whose balance is on the opposite side of the account to which it is related. Examples include accumulated depreciation, which is a contra asset; sales discounts, which is a contra revenue; purchases returns, which is a contra expense; and discount on bonds payable, which is a contra liability.

contra expense accounts (6) An account related to an expense account but having a credit balance, whose balance is deducted from the expense account to arrive at the net expense.

contra revenue accounts (6) An account related to a revenue account but having a debit balance, whose balance is deducted from the revenue account to arrive at the net revenue.

contributed capital (3, 13) The total amount of owners' equity of a corporation that has been contributed by its shareholders, as contrasted to capital that has been earned by operations of the corporation.

control account (6) An account whose balance is the total of all balances in the separate accounts of a related subsidiary ledger. Accounts receivable is the control account for the individual subsidiary accounts of customers.

controlling interest (15, 16) The ownership of more than 50 percent of the outstanding common stock of a corporation.

convertible bond (12) A bond that may be converted into common stock of the issuer at the option of the bond holder.

convertible preferred stock (13) Preferred stock that may be converted into the common stock of the issuer at the option of the preferred shareholder.

convertible security (12, 14) A security, such as a bond or preferred stock, that may be converted into a given number of shares of common stock at the option of the owner.

copyright (10) An intangible asset representing the right to exclusive reproduction and distribution of creative works such as books, manuscripts, or art works.

corporate charter (1, 13) The document approved by the state creating the corporation as an artificial person.

corporation (1) A business entity created by state law and characterized by having legal existence as an artificial person.

correcting entry (5) A journal entry prepared in order to correct an error that has been made in the books of account.

cost (2) The amount or fair value in terms of money or other resources given up to acquire goods or services. The amount recorded for assets when they are first acquired. Also referred to as historical cost.

cost accounting (1) The branch of accounting dealing with the measurement of costs of manufactured products and the reporting of cost information.

cost concept (2) The accounting rule that requires recording assets at their cost rather than some other value.

cost of goods sold (CGS) (6) The expense recorded when merchandise is sold, consisting of the original cost of the merchandise. The expense account whose balance is deducted from net sales to arrive at gross margin on the income statement. In a periodic inventory system, the cost of goods sold account does not exist; instead the expense is calculated and the account is created at the end of the accounting period.

coupon rate (12) The interest rate, expressed in the bond indenture as a percentage of the face value of the bond, that determines the amount of the periodic interest payment.

CPA (1) *See* certified public accountant.

credit (2) The right side of a T account. An entry that decreases an asset account or increases an equity account. To make an entry on the right side of a T account. **(17)** In connection with fund flows, a source of funds.

creditor (1) An individual or organization that provides resources to other individuals or organizations in the form of loans.

cumulative preferred stock (13) Preferred stock whose dividends accumulate if they are not paid in any given year and must be paid in a subsequent year prior to any distribution of dividends to common shareholders.

current assets (3) An asset classification that contains all assets that a company uses in operations during one accounting period.

current cost accounting (20) The method of reporting financial information in terms of replacement costs or market values existing on the reporting date, rather than in terms of historical cost, in order to avoid the distortions in financial information caused by changing price levels.

current liabilities (3) A liability classification that contains all liabilities that a company expects to repay or discharge during one accounting period.

current ratio (3, 19) Measure of liquidity obtained by dividing current assets by current liabilities.

current value accounting (20) *See* current cost accounting.

current yield (8) The return on an investment for a single period, usually a year, calculated by dividing the income from the investment by its cost.

date of record (13) The date on which the corporation stock ownership records are checked to determine who receives the dividend that has been declared.

days' sales in receivables (19) A ratio used to measure liquidity, calculated by dividing the receivables turnover into the number of days in the accounting period.

debenture (12) An unsecured bond whose security consists only of the credit worthiness of the issuer.

debit (2) The left side of a T account. An entry that increases an asset account or decreases an equity account. To make an entry on the left side of a T account. To charge an account.

debt-equity ratio (19) A measure of solvency calculated by dividing total liabilities by total owners' equity.

debt ratio (19) A measure of solvency calculated by dividing total liabilities by total equities, indicating the percentage of equities provided by creditors.

declaration date (13) The date when a dividend is announced by the board of directors, creating an obligation by the corporation to its shareholders.

deep discount bonds (15) Bonds trading in bond markets at prices far below their face value, usually due to a coupon rate of interest that is far lower than the current market rate of interest.

default (8) Failure to pay a debt when it is due.

deferral (5) Adjustment needed at the end of the accounting period to ensure that transactions previously recorded as a result of exchanges of assets are now brought up to date so that all of the current period's expenses and revenues are recorded and any expenses and revenues of future periods are deferred by recording them as assets or liabilities.

deferred charge (11) Account with a debit balance reported on the asset side of the balance sheet, usually resulting from timing differences between accounting and taxable income. Deferred charges are not really assets in that they do not constitute claims or future benefits.

deferred credit (11) Account with a credit balance reported in the liability section of the balance sheet, usually resulting from timing differences between accounting and taxable income. Deferred credits are not true liabilities because the amounts are not owed to anyone.

deferred tax (11) Deferred charge or deferred credit resulting from timing differences between accounting and taxable income.

deficit (13) A debit balance in the retained earnings account.

deflation (20) An economic condition during which

prices of goods and services are generally declining and the purchasing power of money is increasing.

demand deposit (8) Bank deposits on which checks may be drawn, ordering the bank to make payment to the payee on behalf of the payor.

depletion (10) The using up of natural resources. The amortization of natural resources.

depreciation (3, 10) The systematic writing off of the cost of fixed assets, converting part of their cost to an expense in the periods benefiting from use of the asset. The expense resulting from the using up of long-lived assets.

depreciation base (10) The amount of a fixed asset's cost that is subject to depreciation over its lifetime.

depreciation convention (10) A policy adopted by an entity for determining how to depreciate assets that are used for less than a whole accounting period.

depreciation rate (10) The rate at which a fixed asset is depreciated or amortized, expressed as a decimal or a percentage of the depreciation base.

dilution of earnings (14) The potential decrease in earnings and earnings per share that can result if convertible securities are converted into common stock.

disclosure (9) *See* full disclosure.

discount (7) The reduction in the value of a future payment to some present value. To calculate the present value of a future payment. Discount is the opposite of interest and causes a decrease in value rather than growth. (8, 12)   The amount below face value at which a debt security trades in the market. The reduction in the face value of a security. The balance in the contra asset account which reduces the book value of a bond payable. (6)   The amount that may be deducted from an invoice if it is paid within a stipulated period of time. *See* purchase discounts and sales discounts.

discount accumulation (15) Same as discount amortization. The term refers to the increase in the book value of a bond investment that occurs as the discount on the bond is amortized.

discounted security (8) Short-term securities that trade in the market below their face value and on which no interest rate is expressed, such as treasury bills. The interest on discounted securities is the difference between their face value and their present value.

discounts lost (6) An interest expense resulting from failure to take cash discounts offered on purchases. The account in which discounts lost are recorded.

dividend (3, 13) Distributions of assets by a corporation to its owners, resulting in the reduction of retained earnings. Dividends may not reduce contributed capital and can be paid only if the corporation has a credit balance in retained earnings.

dividend in arrears (13) A dividend on cumulative preferred stock that has been passed by the board of directors and accumulates so that it must be paid in the future prior to any dividend distributions to common shareholders.

dividend in kind (13) A dividend paid in the form of assets other than cash.

dividend payout (19) A ratio indicating what percentage of net income is paid by a corporation in the form of dividends, calculated by dividing dividends per share by earnings per share.

dividend yield (19) The rate of return on common stock, calculated as the dividend per share divided by the price per share of stock.

double declining balance (DDB) (10) An accelerated depreciation method using a depreciation rate that is twice the straight-line rate and not taking into account any residual value of the asset.

double-entry system (3) An accounting system that requires recording the dual aspects of every business transaction. Each transaction affects at least two accounts and requires recording an equal dollar amount of debits and credits.

doubtful accounts (8) *See* uncollectible accounts.

drawings (3, 13) Distributions of assets to owners of an unincorporated business, resulting in the reduction of owners' equity.

earnings per share (EPS) (4, 14, 19) The amount of net income earned in one period for each share of common stock.

EBIT (19) Earnings before interest and taxes.

effective interest (12) The actual interest cost resulting from the issuance of bonds payable at a premium or a discount. The interest rate which expresses yield to maturity of a bond.

electronic data processing (EDP) (4) The use of computers to record financial and other data, to manipulate the data, and to report information.

entity (1) An economic unit whose financial affairs are reported in financial statements. Accounting entities may encompass any economic activity and therefore may include entire nations, businesses, parts of businesses, and individuals.

equity (2) The rights of owners or creditors to the assets of an accounting entity. Creditors' equities are called liabilities and owners' equity is called capital.

equity method (15) A method of accounting for stock investments by maintaining their book value at the same amount as the book value recorded on the investee's books.

equity ratio (19) A measure of solvency calculated by dividing total owners' equity by total equities, indicating the percentage of equities contributed by shareholders.

equity security (8) Securities, such as common and preferred stock, representing owners' equity of a corporation.

estimated liabilities (11) Obligations whose exact amount is not known but can be estimated, such as product warranties.

excess of book value over cost (15) The difference between the amount paid for a stock investment and the underlying book value recorded for the stock on the issuer's books.

excess of cost over book value of assets (15) The amount paid for a stock investment in excess of the underlying book value recorded on the stock issuer's books. **(16)** The amount in excess of the recorded book value of net assets paid by a company for its investment in the stock of a subsidiary. It is the amount that must be assigned to specific assets and to goodwill in a consolidation accounted for as a purchase.

excess of cost over fair value of assets (16) The amount of goodwill resulting in a consolidation that is accounted for as a purchase. It is the portion of the excess of cost over the book value of subsidiary assets that cannot be assigned to specific assets.

excess of general price changes over specific price changes (20) The net realized and unrealized holding losses net of inflation reported in current cost financial statements, occurring as a result of changing prices and measured as the difference between holding gains or losses computed on a historical cost basis and holding gains or losses adjusted for changes in the general price level.

excess of specific price changes over general price changes (20) The net realized and unrealized holding gains net of inflation reported in current cost financial statements, occurring as a result of changing prices and measured as the difference between holding gains or losses computed on a historical cost basis and holding gains or losses adjusted for changes in the general price level.

ex-dividend date (13) The date, three days prior to the dividend record date, when a stock trades in the market with the buyer not entitled to receive the dividend that has been declared.

expenditure (4) The use of cash to pay for an expense, for the acquisition of an asset, for the repayment of a debt, or for any other business purpose.

expense (2) The reduction of owners' equity or capital resulting from the using up of goods or services.

external reports (1) Financial accounting reports prepared primarily for users of accounting information outside of the business organization.

extraordinary items (4) A classification of the income statement used for reporting the effects of events that are both unusual and nonrecurring.

face value (12) The value expressed on the face of a security. Also known as par value.

factor (8) A person or a business that purchases accounts receivable. To sell accounts receivable to a factor.

fair presentation (5) The reporting of financial position and the results of operations in a way that is not misleading and discloses fully all pertinent information.

fair value (10) The market value at which an asset may be disposed of by sale or exchange.

fee revenue (4) Revenue earned by performing services rather than by selling goods.

FICA tax (11) Social security tax required by the Federal Insurance Contribution Act; part of the tax is deducted from employees' wages and a portion is paid by employers.

fiduciary (1) A person entrusted with money or property of others and charged with the safeguarding and management of such property.

financial accounting (1) Accounting for the financial affairs of entities for the purpose of reporting such affairs to those outside of the entity. *See* external reports.

Financial Accounting Standards Board (FASB) (1) An independent rule-making body of the accounting profession, charged with issuing accounting rules known as standards.

financial analysis (19) The interpretation of financial statements for the purpose of assessing past business performance, evaluating present business conditions, and predicting future potential for business success.

financial leverage (12, 19) The benefit obtained by borrowing money at one rate of interest and investing it at a higher rate of interest so that the return on the investor's equity is greater than it would be without borrowing.

financial position (2, 3) *See* balance sheet.

financing activities (17) Business activities that provide funds, reported in the statement of changes in financial position. Examples include operations that generate net income, investment by owners, borrowing, and sale of noncurrent assets.

first in, first out (FIFO) (9) The inventory valuation method which assumes that the inventory acquired earliest is the first to be sold. The method refers to the flow of costs rather than to the physical flow of goods.

fiscal year (3) An accounting period that ends on a date other than December 31.

fixed assets (3, 10) A classification of assets that a company expects to use for a number of accounting periods. Also called long-lived assets.

f.o.b. destination (9) Terms of shipment for goods, indicating that title to the goods is transferred as soon as the goods are delivered at their destination by the common carrier.

f.o.b. shipping point (9) Terms of shipment for goods, indicating that title to the goods is transferred at the time the goods are placed on the common carrier at their shipping point.

franchise (10) An intangible asset representing the privilege of using another entity's name, trademark, patent, or product, and of selling another entity's goods or services under a licensing agreement.

freight-in (6) The cost of shipping purchased merchandise from the supplier to the buyer. The account in which freight-in is recorded, and whose balance is added to purchases at the end of the period in order to arrive at cost of goods sold.

freight-out (6) An expense account in which the cost of

shipping merchandise to customers is recorded. It is usually classified as a selling expense on the income statement.

fringe benefits (11) Payments made by an employer in addition to wages and salaries, providing employees with benefits such as pensions, paid vacations, and insurance.

full disclosure (5, 9) The accounting principle that requires financial reports to disclose fully all relevant information that may be used by a decision maker reading the financial statements.

fully diluted earnings per share (14) Earnings per share of a corporation with a complex capital structure, calculated by assuming that all convertible securities have been converted into common stock, thus yielding the smallest possible earnings per share figure.

funded pension plan (11) A retirement plan whereby the employer contributes funds into a formally established plan, which invests the funds for the purpose of providing retirement benefits to employees.

funds (15) Long-term investments maintained for special purposes such as future bond retirements or planned expansions. **(17)** Cash or working capital whose change is reported in the statement of changes of financial position.

funds flow statement (17) *See* statement of changes in financial position.

funds provided by operations (17) The amount of cash or working capital provided by operating the business rather than from other sources, generally consisting of net income adjusted for nonfund items and reported in the statement of changes in financial position.

future value (7) The amount to which an investment will grow at a given interest rate with compounding for a given number of periods. The sum that will accumulate at some date in the future as a result of growth of a single payment or investment today. Also known as amount.

future value of annuity (7) The amount that will accumulate as a result of periodic payments into an investment that pays interest at a given rate with compounding occurring at the time when each periodic payment is made. The amount that will accumulate in the future as a result of the growth of periodic payments, allowed to earn interest. Also known as amount of annuity.

gain (4) The net effect on owners' equity of transactions that are not a normal part of business operations, such as the sale for more than book value of assets normally not held for sale.

general journal (4) *See* journal.

general ledger (4) *See* ledger.

general price index (20) An index representing the general purchasing power of a dollar, consisting of the value of a large variety of goods and services rather than the value of specific goods.

generally accepted accounting principles (GAAP) (3) The conventions, rules, and procedures that define ac-

counting practice and financial reporting and have substantial authoritative support.

GNP Implicit Price Deflator (20) A broad-based price index made up of the prices of all goods and services produced in the United States. Compiled by the Department of Commerce and published quarterly.

going-concern concept (3) An accounting concept based on the assumption that a business will continue to exist indefinitely. Also known as the continuity assumption.

goods available for sale (6) The total amount of goods available for sale during an accounting period. It consists of the beginning balance of merchandise and any purchases made during the period. When the balance of ending inventory is deducted from goods available for sale, the result is cost of goods sold.

goodwill (10) The intangible asset consisting of the excess earning power of a business. A favorable attitude toward a business by its customers. Recorded in the books only if purchased. **(15)** The excess of cost over book value of assets that cannot be assigned to specific assets. Also known as excess of cost over fair value.

gross invoice method (6) The accounting procedure of recording purchases or sales merchandise at the gross amount shown on the invoice without deducting any cash discounts offered.

gross margin (6) The difference between net sales and cost of goods sold. Also known as gross profit.

gross margin method (9) A method of inventory estimation based on the past gross margin experienced by the business.

gross margin percentage (9) Gross margin expressed as a percentage of sales.

gross margin ratio (9) *See* gross margin percentage.

gross profit (6) *See* gross margin.

historical cost (19) *See* cost.

holding company (16) A corporation whose primary function is to hold the stock of other companies and provide them with financing and management but that does not operate a business.

holding gain or loss (20) The increase or decrease in the value of assets resulting from changes in specific price levels and reported in financial statements prepared on the current cost basis.

horizontal analysis (19) Financial analysis involving the comparison of figures in financial statements of two or more consecutive accounting periods.

horizontal combination (16) A combination of several companies, each operating in a related line of business but not competing directly with one another.

imputed interest (8, 11) The interest on non-interest-bearing notes that is implied in the face value of the note and must be extracted in order to record the note at its present value.

income (4) The result of operations measured as the difference between revenues and expenses. *See* net income.

income statement (4) A financial report that describes the results of operations for one accounting period.

income summary (4) A temporary account created during the closing process for the purpose of accumulating all revenue and expense account balances. The income summary account is closed to retained earnings. Also known as profit and loss.

income tax (4) The tax imposed by federal, state, and other governments on the income earned by an entity.

independent accountant (1) *See* certified public accountant.

inflation (20) The economic condition during which prices of goods and services are rising and the purchasing power of money is declining.

insolvent (8) The condition of inability to pay obligations as they come due.

installment note (11) An obligation that is repaid in periodic installments that typically include interest on the remaining balance of the obligation and repayment of a portion of the principal.

intangible assets (10) Assets that have no tangible existence and consist of rights and privileges, such as those granted by patents, copyrights, franchises, and trademarks. Intangibles also include organization costs and goodwill.

intercompany debt (16) Debt that exists between affiliated companies and that must be eliminated in consolidation.

interest (2, 7) Payment required of a borrower for the use of borrowed money. Usually calculated on the basis of an annual percentage rate. The price paid for the use of borrowed money or the price received for lending money. Lending money implies a sacrifice because the money cannot be used until it is repaid. Interest is compensation for this sacrifice and also for bearing risk.

interim report (5) Financial statements prepared for a part of an accounting year, such as a month or quarter.

internal control (8) The system of rules and procedures established to ensure that all assets of an entity are used properly for business purposes.

internal reports (1) Managerial accounting reports prepared primarily for users of accounting information concerned with the management of the accounting entity.

inventoriable cost (9) A cost that is properly assigned to goods in inventory and which becomes an expense only when the inventory is sold.

inventory (3) A current asset consisting of merchandise held for sale. In manufacturing operations inventory includes raw materials, work in process, and finished goods.

inventory profits (9) The portion of profits reported when cost of inventory acquired in an earlier period, when lower costs prevailed, is matched with current revenue.

inventory shrinkage (6) The loss of inventory due to spoilage, breakage, theft, and other similar causes.

inventory turnover (19) A measure of liquidity calculated by dividing cost of goods sold for a period by average inventory of the same period.

investee (15) The entity issuing securities that are acquired by investors.

investing activities (17) Business activities that require the use of funds, such as acquisition of assets, repayment of debt, payment of dividends, and reacquisition of stock.

investment tax credit (10) A tax incentive consisting of a direct reduction of federal income tax liability by some percentage of the cost of equipment acquired in the tax period.

investor (15) The entity acquiring securities for purposes of keeping them as investments.

issued shares (13) Shares of capital stock of a corporation that have been issued to the public and may be outstanding or may be held as treasury shares by the corporation.

journal (4) An accounting record in which businesses' transactions are recorded in chronological order as they occur. Also known as the book of original entry.

journal entry (4) A systematic record of a business transaction showing the accounts affected and the amounts of debits and credits and containing sufficient other information to describe the transaction completely.

journalize (4) To record a transaction in a journal.

last in, first out (LIFO) (9) Inventory valuation method based on the assumption that the goods purchased most recently are the first ones sold. The method refers to the flow of inventory costs and not to the physical flow of the goods.

lease (11) A long-term rental agreement. *See* capital lease or operating lease.

leasehold improvements (10) Intangible assets consisting of improvements made by a lessee to leased property that will eventually revert back to the lessor.

ledger (4) The collection of all permanent and temporary accounts of a business in which information contained in the journal is recorded by a process called posting.

legal capital (13) The amount of contributed capital of a corporation that may not be returned to the shareholders in the form of dividends. In most states, legal capital is the same as contributed capital.

lessee (11) The entity that rents assets from a lessor under a lease agreement.

lessor (11) The entity that owns assets which it leases to a lessee.

leverage (12, 19) *See* financial leverage.

liability (2) Creditors' equity. Obligation of an accounting entity to its creditors. The rights of creditors to be repaid.

limited liability (13) The characteristic of ownership of corporations that limits the owners' loss to the amount invested because the owners are not liable for the debts of the corporation.

liquidity (3, 19) The speed with which assets can be converted to cash. The ability of an entity to pay its current debts as they mature.

loan value of insurance (14) *See* cash surrender value.

long-lived assets (3, 10) *See* fixed assets.

long-term liabilities (3, 11) Liabilities that will be repaid beyond the next accounting period.

loss (4) The net reduction of owners' equity resulting from a transaction that is not a normal part of business, such as sale of a fixed asset for less than book value or destruction of an asset by a disaster.

lower of cost or market (LCM) (8, 9) The accounting rule requiring marketable equity securities and inventories to be recorded at their market value if the market value is below their cost.

management advisory services (1) Services performed by CPAs for their clients, involving advice on many aspects of business management.

managerial accounting (1) Accounting and reporting of information to managers of entities as contrasted to reporting to outsiders. *See* internal reports.

market price (8, 19) The price at which an item trades in the market and for which it may be bought or sold. The fair price of an item.

market tests (19) That part of financial analysis that involves the calculation of financial ratios, such as dividend yield, price-earnings ratio, and others derived from stock market data.

market value (8, 15) The fair value of an item at which it trades in the market. The value of securities as determined by market prices.

marketable debt security (8) Investment securities that consist of debt obligations of their issuers, such as corporate or government bonds, treasury bills, and certificates of deposit.

marketable equity security (8) Investment securities consisting of common or preferred stock of corporations, representing a direct ownership of the investee company.

matching (4) The accounting principle that requires recognition of expenses in the same period in which the related revenues were earned.

maturity (12) The expiration of debt. The point in time when a debt obligation, such as a bond or a note payable must be repaid.

maturity date (12) The date at which a bond or other obligation matures and must be repaid by the borrower.

maturity value (8) The amount that will be paid for an obligation, such as a bond or note, at the time the obligation matures. Maturity value may include the principal of the obligation plus accumulated interest.

merger (15) *See* business combination.

minority interest (16) The portion of a partially owned subsidiary corporation that does not belong to the parent company but represents stock held by outsiders consisting of a minority of owners' equity.

monetary assets (20) Assets such as cash, notes receivable, and bond investments, whose amount is expressed in a fixed number of dollars.

monetary items (20) Monetary assets and monetary liabilities.

monetary liabilities (20) Liabilities, such as notes payable, bonds payable, and preferred stock, whose amount is expressed in a fixed number of dollars.

money measurement concept (2) The accounting concept requiring all financial transactions to be expressed in terms of money.

mortgage (11) An obligation, usually secured by real estate, typically repayable in installments that include interest and a portion of the principal.

moving average (9) A method of measuring the cost of inventory in a perpetual inventory system in which the cost of new acquisitions is added to the total cost of previous acquisitions not yet sold and the sum divided by the number of units of inventory on hand.

multiple-step income statement (4) Form of the income statement in which revenues, expenses, gains, and losses are classified into specific categories.

National Association of Accountants (NAA) (1) Organization of management accountants interested primarily in internal reporting.

natural resources (3, 10) Assets consisting of mineral deposits, ores, timber, and other naturally occurring materials, generally subject to depletion. Also known as wasting assets.

net assets (2) Total assets less total liabilities. Net assets are equal in amount to owners' equity.

net income (2, 3, 4) The excess of revenues over expenses. The net increase in owners' equity resulting from business transactions taking place during a specified period of time. The net result of operations for one period of time, reported as the bottom line of the income statement, just prior to earnings per share.

net invoice method (6) The accounting procedure of recording purchases or sales or merchandise at the net amount expected to be paid or received. Calculated as the gross amount shown on the invoice less any cash discounts offered.

net loss (2, 3, 4) The excess of expenses over revenues. The net decrease in owners' equity resulting from business transactions taking place during a specified period of time. Reported as the bottom line of the income statement, just above loss per share.

net monetary items (20) The net difference between monetary assets and monetary liabilities held during a period by an accounting entity and used to calculate the gain or loss in purchasing power from holding monetary items during periods of changing prices.

net purchases (6) The cost of merchandise purchased during the year, calculated as the invoice cost less any purchase discounts and purchase returns and allowances.

net realizable value (9) The net amount that can be realized from the liquidation of an asset. Net realizable value of inventory is usually the selling price less any cost of marketing the goods. Net realizable value of receivables is the portion that can be collected, not including the uncollectible accounts.

net sales (6) Total sales for a period reduced by any sales discounts and sales returns and allowances.

net worth (2) Capital, owners' equity. The term is becoming obsolete.

nominal account (4) *See* temporary account.

noncumulative preferred stock (13) Preferred stock on which a dividend does not accumulate if it is not paid in any specific year.

nonfund items (17) Those expenses, revenues, gains, and losses reported in the income statement that do not provide or use cash or working capital. Items that are added to or deducted from net income to arrive at funds from operations.

non-interest-bearing notes (8) Promissory notes on which no interest is expressed whose payment at maturity consists only of the face value of the note. Interest on such notes must be imputed.

nonmonetary items (20) Assets and liabilities other than monetary, whose amounts are not expressed in a fixed number of dollars to be paid or received in the future, such as equipment, land, equity securities, deferred credits, unearned revenues, and common stock.

no-par stock (13) Stock that does not have a par or stated value assigned to its shares.

notes payable (11) Liabilities consisting of promissory notes, which are signed documents promising to pay at some future date a specific amount of money including principal and interest.

notes receivable (8) Promissory notes from customers consisting of signed documents promising to pay a specific amount of money at a specific future time, and often including the payment of interest, held as assets.

not-for-profit organization (1) An entity operating for purposes other than for earning a profit, such as a government, hospital, university, church, or charity.

NSF check (8) A check returned by a bank to the payee because the payor's demand deposit did not have sufficient funds to cover payment.

objectivity (4) The accounting principle that requires financial information to be unbiased so as not to favor any individual user or class of users.

open accounts (8) *See* accounts receivables or accounts payable.

operating cycle (3) The time required for current assets to be converted to cash, or 1 year, whichever is longer.

operating expense (4) The classification of expenses related to the normal operations of a business.

operating income (4) The result of normal operations of a business, calculated by deducting operating expenses from operating revenues.

operating lease (11) A rental agreement whereby the lessee obtains use of property in exchange for periodic rent payments and the lessor retains ownership of the property.

operating revenue (4) The classification of revenues earned in the normal operations of a business.

opinion of auditor (1) The report prepared by a certified public accountant at the completion of an audit, expressing an opinion on the fairness of the financial statements of the audited entity.

ordinary annuity (7) A series of equal periodic payments with each payment occurring at the end of the period at which compounding takes place.

organization costs (10) An intangible asset made up of the costs required to organize a corporation, usually amortized over a period of 5 years.

outstanding shares (13) The number of shares of capital stock which are in the hands of shareholders.

owners' equity (2) *See* capital.

paid-in capital in excess of par (13) The capital account in which is recorded the amount of contributed capital in excess of the par or stated value of common or preferred stock.

par value (12) The face value of a bond. (13) An arbitrary figure assigned to a share of capital stock and used for recording the stock in the books of the issuing corporation.

parent corporation (16) A corporation that owns subsidiary companies.

partially owned subsidiary (16) A corporation that is less than 100 percent owned by its parent company, having some minority stockholders.

participating preferred stock (13) Preferred stock that participates with common stock in dividend distributions beyond the amount normally payable to the preferred shareholders if the company distributes a dividend to common shareholders that is greater than a stated amount.

partnership (1, 13) A business entity having two or more owners who have agreed to operate the business as co-owners.

passed dividend (13) A dividend which has not been declared and is consequently not going to be paid by a corporation. *See* dividend in arrears.

patent (10) An intangible asset consisting of a privilege granted by the patent office to produce and distribute, on an exclusive basis, an original design, device, or invention for a period of 17 years.

payback (10) The time required to recover the cost of an investment, typically measured in years.

payment date (13) The date when a previously declared dividend is distributed to shareholders of record.

payout ratio (19) *See* dividend payout.

payroll taxes (11) *See* FICA taxes.

pension (11) A plan or a fund established for the purpose

of paying retirement benefits to retired employees of an organization.

period cost (9) A cost that cannot be associated with a specific product but is associated with a particular period of operation and is expensed in that period and matched with the revenues earned in the same period.

periodic inventory system (6) The system of accounting for merchandise inventory used for merchandise consisting of diverse goods for which it is not practical to record cost of goods sold as sales take place. A physical count of goods at the end of the accounting period is required to allow calculation of cost of goods sold.

periodicity concept (3) The accounting concept that requires preparation of financial statements at specified intervals of time, dividing the life of a going concern into discrete accounting periods.

permanent account (4) Ledger accounts whose balances are reported on the balance sheet, including asset, liability, and owners' equity accounts. Also known as real accounts.

permanent differences (11) Differences between accounting and taxable income caused by revenues that are not taxable or expenses that are not deductible for tax purposes.

perpetual inventory system (6) A system of accounting for merchandise whose cost is removed from the merchandise account and recorded as cost of goods sold at the time of sale. A periodic inventory count is used to verify the balance of the merchandise account.

petty cash (8) A cash fund established for the payment of small amounts of cash for which writing checks is not warranted.

pledge (8) The security given in exchange for a loan. To designate property as security for a loan.

pooling of interests (16) A business combination consisting of the mergers of the operations of two companies into one, with the shareholders of both becoming the owners of the combined entity.

portfolio (8) The collection of investments held by an investor, such as the colleciton of equity or debt securities.

post-closing trial balance (4) A trial balance prepared after the books have been closed at the end of an accounting period.

posting (4) The process of transferring information from the journal to ledger accounts.

pre-closing trial balance (4) A trial balance taken prior to closing the books of account at the end of an accounting period.

preferred stock (3, 13) Capital stock of a corporation whose owners are entitled to certain preferences, such as a specified amount of annual dividends.

premium (8, 12) The amount above face value of a security at which the security trades in a market. The amount added to the face value of a security to arrive at its market price. The balance in the bond payable ad-

junct account which is added to the face value of the bonds to arrive at book value on the balance sheet. The portion of a long-term bond investment that must be amortized over the bonds' life. **(13)** Obsolete term for paid-in capital in excess of par value of stock, still sometimes used for preferred stock.

prepaid expense (3, 5) The category of current assets consisting of goods or services that have been paid for in advance and will be used during the next accounting period. Prepaid expenses are normally not converted into cash.

present value (7) The value today of a sum of money to be received or paid in the future. The present value is lower than the future sum because the future sum includes the accumulation of interest.

present value of annuity (7) The present value of a series of future payments discounted to the present at a given interest rate with compounding assumed to take place at the time of each payment.

price-earnings ratio (19) The ratio calculated by dividing the market price of a stock by its earnings per share.

price-level adjustment (20) The conversion of recorded account balances to amounts representing the purchasing power of money rather than the actual amount of dollars recorded in the account. Used for reporting financial statement information in constant dollars.

primary earnings per share (14) The earnings per share figure of a corporation with a complex capital structure, calculated on the assumption that all common stock equivalents have been converted into common stock.

principal (7) Money invested to earn interest. The original capital invested in order to have it grow.

prior period adjustment (14) An adjustment to the beginning balance of retained earnings, resulting from an error that occurred in a previous period but was discovered in the current accounting period.

product cost (9) A cost that can be associated with a specific product and is recorded as an asset. Inventoriable cost. Product costs become expenses when the product is sold.

pro forma statements (19) Financial statements of future accounting periods, consisting of expected future account balances prepared on the basis of projections and expectations of future events.

profit and loss summary (4) *See* income summary.

profit margin (19) *See* return on sales.

profitability ratios (19) *See* test of profitability.

promissory notes (8) *See* notes receivable or notes payable.

property dividend (13) *See* dividend in kind.

proprietorship (2) Capital, owners' equity. The term is obsolete.

public corporation (13) A corporation whose shares are held by the public and traded in stock markets.

purchase (16) In respect to a business combination, the

acquisition by one company of the assets or shares of another, with the previous shareholders of the acquired company no longer having an interest in the combined business.

purchase discounts (6) A contra purchases account maintained in the periodic inventory system, used for recording cash discounts. The balance of purchase discounts is deducted from purchases to arrive at net purchases. This account exists when the gross invoice method of recording purchases is used.

purchase discounts lost (6) *See* discounts lost.

purchase returns and allowances (6) A contra purchases account used for recording goods returned to vendors or the allowances made by vendors to reduce the purchase price of goods. The balance of this account is deducted from purchases in the calculation of net purchases and cost of goods sold.

purchases (6) A temporary account maintained in a periodic inventory system and used for recording all purchases of merchandise made during the accounting period.

purchases journal (6) A special journal used exclusively for recording purchases of goods and services.

purchasing power (20) The value of money measured by the quantity of goods and services that can be acquired with it.

purchasing power gains or losses (20) The gains or losses resulting from holding net monetary items during periods of changing prices.

quick ratio (19) *See* acid test ratio.

ratio analysis (19) A method of analyzing financial statements by calculating ratios between specific items of data presented in the statements for the purpose of obtaining measures of liquidity, solvency, and profitability.

real account (4) *See* permanent account.

realization (4) *See* revenue realization.

realized holding gains or losses (20) The difference between historical cost of assets sold and their replacement cost at the time of sale, occurring as a result of changes in price levels of specific assets.

receivables turnover (19) A measure of liquidity calculated by dividing net sales by average accounts receivable, indicating the speed with which receivables are collected and converted to cash.

registered bonds (12) Bonds that are issued to a specific entity whose name is recorded in the bond issuer's records and also on the bond certificate indicating the owner of the bond.

regulated business (1) A business such as a public utility, which is subject to substantial regulation of its operations by a government agency that controls the prices charged by the business.

rent (7) The periodic payment of an annuity occurring at the same time that compounding of interest takes place.

replacement cost (9, 20) The market price that must be paid by a business in order to replace an asset that it now holds.

replacement cost accounting (20) *See* current cost accounting.

residual equity (2, 13) Capital, owners' equity, or shareholders' equity. It is a residual because it is derived as the difference between assets and liabilities.

residual value (10) *See* salvage value.

restated figures (20) Amounts converted to constant dollars or current cost, reported in financial statements that show the effects of inflation.

restricted retained earnings (14) Retained earnings that are not available for the payment of dividends as a result of a legal or contractual restriction. Also called appropriated retained earnings.

retail inventory method (9) A method of estimating the cost of inventories using the ratio of the products' cost to their selling price.

retained earnings (3) Owners' equity account of a corporation consisting of amounts earned from business operations and retained by the business. The amount of owners' equity available for dividend distributions.

return on owners' equity (19) A measure of profitability calculated by dividing net income by average owners' equity.

return on sales (19) A measure of profitability calculated by dividing net income by net sales.

return on total assets (19) A measure of profitability calculated by dividing net income before interest and taxes by total average assets.

revenue (2) The increase in owners' equity or capital resulting from earnings generated by selling goods and performing services.

revenue and expense summary (4) *See* income summary.

revenue realization (4) The accounting principle requiring revenue to be recognized when a service is performed or goods are delivered.

reversing entry (5) A journal entry that cancels a previous entry. Usually used after the closing process in order to make the accounts ready for the next period's transactions.

sales (6) The revenue account in which the sale of merchandise is recorded.

sales discounts (6) A contra revenue account used for recording cash discounts taken by customers for early payment of sales invoices. The balance of this account is deducted from sales in order to arrive at net sales.

sales returns and allowances (6) A contra revenue account used for recording amounts paid to customers for goods returned or for goods on which the sales price is reduced. The balance of this account is deducted from sales in order to arrive at net sales.

sales revenue (4) Revenue earned by selling merchandise.

salvage value (10) The amount that can be realized from

an asset at the end of its useful life. Salvage value is generally estimated and deducted from asset costs to arrive at the depreciation base. Also called residual value.

secured bond (12) A debt instrument issued by a corporation, with some corporate assets serving as security for the obligation. If the issuer cannot repay the bond, the assets may be sold and the proceeds used to pay the debt.

Securities and Exchange Commission (SEC) (1) A regulatory body of the United States government charged with overseeing the operation of stock markets and regulation of public corporations.

serial bonds (12) Bonds that are issued at the same time but have varying maturity dates.

shareholder (1) Owner of a corporation whose ownership interest is represented by shares of stock issued by the corporation.

short-term investments (8) See temporary investments.

simple capital structure (14) The capital structure of a corporation that has no convertible securities outstanding, requiring the reporting of a single earnings per share figure.

simple interest (7) Interest calculated without compounding for a single period of time, usually for 1 year or a fraction of a year.

single-step income statement (4) Form of the income statement in which all revenues and gains are shown first and all expenses and losses are deducted to arrive at net income, without any classification of accounts into various categories.

sinking fund (12) An investment into which periodic payments are made by a borrower for the purpose of having sufficient money available to retire bonds on their maturity date.

sole proprietorship (1) A business entity having an individual as an owner.

solvency (19) The ability to repay all debts and obligations as they come due.

source document (4) Any document, such as a check, invoice, purchase order, or other business paper, from which information is obtained for the preparation of journal entries.

sources of funds (17, 18) Financing activities reported on the statement of changes in financial position.

special journals (6) Books of original entry designed for recording specific types of transactions such as purchases or sales. The form of the journal is designed to handle specific types of transactions efficiently but it cannot handle all types of transactions.

specific identification method (9) The accounting procedure in a perpetual inventory system for goods whose cost can be specifically identified and recorded at the time of sale.

specific price index (20) A price index made up of the value of specific goods or services, such as industrial machinery or buildings, showing the change in the purchasing power of money for those types of goods.

stable dollar (2, 20) An accounting concept based on the assumption that the value of the dollar does not change and all transactions can be recorded as if each dollar is worth as much as any other dollar in the past or in the future.

stated value (13) An arbitrary value assigned to capital stock and used to record the capital stock on the books of the company.

statement of changes in financial position (17) One of the basic financial statements presented in annual reports, describing the financing and investing activities of a business enterprise. Also called funds flow statement or cash flow statement.

statement of financial position (2) See balance sheet.

statement of retained earnings (4, 14) A financial statement reporting the change in retained earnings from the beginning of the period to the end of the period.

stewardship (1) The function of safeguarding and proper management of the property of others, or the performance of such function.

stock certificate (1) Document representing ownership of shares of a corporation, issued by the corporation to its owners. May be traded in stock markets among investors who buy and sell stocks of corporations.

stock dividend (13) A dividend distributed in the form of shares of stock rather than cash. A stock dividend permanently capitalizes a portion of retained earnings.

stock split (13) The issuance of additional shares to current shareholders for the purpose of increasing the number of shares outstanding by a factor of 2, 3, or some other multiple and reducing the par or stated value of the stock.

straight-line method (10) A method of depreciation or amortization which amortizes an equal amount of an account every accounting period.

subsidiary (15, 16) A corporation that is wholly or partially owned by another company referred to as its parent.

subsidiary account (6) An individual account of a customer or supplier. The total of all balances of one type of subsidiary account makes up the balance of their related control account.

subsidiary ledger (6) A book of accounts containing subsidiary accounts of a particular type, such as subsidiary accounts payable.

sum-of-the-years'-digits (SYD) (10) An accelerated method of depreciation that amortizes the depreciation base of an asset using a decreasing fraction in each period.

supplementary statements (20) Financial statements provided in addition to those usually reported in order to present supplementary information such as price level adjustments.

T account (2) An account in the form of the letter T,

with debts recorded on the left side and credits on the right side.

tangibles (10) Long-lived assets, consisting of tangible property such as equipment, land, and buildings.

tax accounting (1) Accounting services provided by CPAs and others, involving tax planning and reporting.

taxable income (11) The income of a corporation that is used for calculating the income tax liability. Taxable income does not include any permanent differences and differs from accounting income because of timing differences.

temporary account (4) A ledger account that is closed at the end of the accounting period. It is a temporary subdivision of the retained earnings account, used to record revenues, expenses, gains, losses, and dividends for one accounting period. Nominal account.

temporary investments (8) Investments in marketable equity or debt securities that are intended to be held for a short period of time and which can be converted to cash easily and quickly.

terms of invoice (6) The description on an invoice of the time which the customer can wait to pay the invoice amount. The terms may include cash discounts.

tests of liquidity (19) That portion of financial analysis that involves the calculation of ratios, such as the current ratio, quick ratio, and various turnovers, that provide an indication of a company's liquidity.

tests of profitability (19) That portion of financial analysis that involves the calculation of ratios, such as rates of return, that provide information on the profitability of a business.

tests of solvency (19) That portion of financial analysis that involves the calculation of ratios, such as the debt-equity ratio, and other tests that provide an indication of a company's ability to pay its debts as they mature.

time deposit (8) Bank deposits consisting of savings accounts that earn interest.

times interest earned (19) A measure of solvency calculated as net income before interest and taxes divided by the required interest expense.

timing differences (11) Differences between accounting and taxable income caused by revenues and expenses that are reported in one period for accounting purposes and in another period for tax purposes.

trade accounts (8, 11) *See* accounts receivable and accounts payable.

trade discount (6) The reduction from the retail price of an item allowed to a customer, expressed as a percentage of the price. Trade discounts are used so that a single price list may be provided to all customers.

transaction (1) An economic event measurable in terms of money, usually involving an exchange between two entities.

treasury bills (8) Short-term discounted securities issued by the federal government and often acquired by investors as temporary investments.

treasury stock (14) Capital stock of a corporation that has been issued and then reacquired by the corporation and is held in the treasury for future use. Treasury stock is not outstanding.

trend analysis (19) Analysis of financial statements for the purpose of measuring trends in sales, earnings, or other aspects of business performance.

trial balance (3) A list of accounts and their balances, used to verify that the total dollar amount of debits equals the total dollar amount of credits.

uncollectible accounts (8) An estimate of the amount of accounts receivable expected not to be collectible in the future. The amount so estimated is recorded as a contra asset account. Also known as doubtful accounts.

unearned revenue (3, 11) A liability account used for recording revenues collected in advance that will be earned in a future accounting period.

unfunded pension plan (11) A pension plan that does not operate as an investment fund but involves payment of pension benefits to retired employees from the general assets of the entity that has established the plan.

units-of-production method (10) A method of depreciation based on the productive output or activity of an asset rather than on the passage of time.

unrealized holding gain or loss (20) Difference between the historical cost of an asset not yet sold and the replacement cost of the asset, showing the change in asset value due to changes in specific price levels.

unrealized loss from decline in market value (16) Decline in market value of equity securities held as long-term investments, reported in the capital section of the balance sheet rather than in the income statement.

unrestricted retained earnings (14) The portion of retained earnings available for the payment of dividends, usually the entire balance of retained earnings except when a portion has been restricted. Also called unappropriated retained earnings.

unsecured bond (12) A bond obligation not secured by specific assets whose repayment is guaranteed only by the general credit worthiness of the bond issuer.

uses of funds (17) Investing activities reported on the statement of changes in financial position.

usury (1) Excessive interest charged on borrowed money.

vendor (6) A supplier of goods. One who sells goods.

vertical analysis (19) Financial analysis that involves the comparison of figures within a financial statement or between financial statements of a single period.

vertical combination (16) A combination of several companies in related industries that complement one another's activities.

voucher (8) A document used to ensure a high degree of control of cash disbursements, requiring approval for each expenditure.

voucher register (8) A journal used for recording

amounts in vouchers and the payments of the amounts approved in a voucher.

voucher system (8) A system of cash control requiring the approval of all expenditures by recording them in a voucher before checks are approved and issued in payment.

wasting assets (10) *See* natural resources.

wealth (2) Economic well-being characterized by the possession of property that has economic value.

weighted average (9) A method of measuring the cost of inventory in a periodic inventory system in which the total cost of all items acquired during the period is divided by the total number of items.

wholly owned subsidiary (16) A corporation whose stock is 100 percent owned by its parent company.

working capital (3) The net current assets of a business not required for the payment of current liabilities, calculated as current assets minus current liabilities. (17, 18) One of the definitions of funds, used in the preparation of the statement of changes in financial position.

worksheet (5) An accounting tool used with end-of-period procedures to find adjusted account balances and prepare financial statements without disturbing the books of account. Worksheets are also used for many other accounting purposes.

yield to maturity (12) The effective interest rate on a bond. The actual interest rate paid by a bond if it is held until it matures.

TABLE I.
Future Value of $1

n	.5%	1%	1.5%	2%	2.5%	3%	3.5%	4%	4.5%	n
1	1.00500	1.01000	1.01500	1.02000	1.02500	1.03000	1.03500	1.04000	1.04500	1
2	1.01003	1.02010	1.03023	1.04040	1.05062	1.06090	1.07123	1.08160	1.09203	2
3	1.01508	1.03030	1.04568	1.06121	1.07689	1.09273	1.10872	1.12486	1.14117	3
4	1.02015	1.04060	1.06136	1.08243	1.10381	1.12551	1.14752	1.16986	1.19252	4
5	1.02525	1.05101	1.07728	1.10408	1.13141	1.15927	1.18769	1.21665	1.24618	5
6	1.03038	1.06152	1.09344	1.12616	1.15969	1.19405	1.22926	1.26532	1.30226	6
7	1.03553	1.07214	1.10984	1.14869	1.18869	1.22987	1.27228	1.31593	1.36086	7
8	1.04071	1.08286	1.12649	1.17166	1.21840	1.26677	1.31681	1.36857	1.42210	8
9	1.04591	1.09369	1.14339	1.19509	1.24886	1.30477	1.36290	1.42331	1.48610	9
10	1.05114	1.10462	1.16054	1.21899	1.28008	1.34392	1.41060	1.48024	1.55297	10
11	1.05640	1.11567	1.17795	1.24337	1.31209	1.38423	1.45997	1.53945	1.62285	11
12	1.06168	1.12683	1.19562	1.26824	1.34489	1.42576	1.51107	1.60103	1.69588	12
13	1.06699	1.13809	1.21355	1.29361	1.37851	1.46853	1.56396	1.66507	1.77220	13
14	1.07232	1.14947	1.23176	1.31948	1.41297	1.51259	1.61869	1.73168	1.85194	14
15	1.07768	1.16097	1.25023	1.34587	1.44830	1.55797	1.67535	1.80094	1.93528	15
16	1.08307	1.17258	1.26899	1.37279	1.48451	1.60471	1.73399	1.87298	2.02237	16
17	1.08849	1.18430	1.28802	1.40024	1.52162	1.65285	1.79468	1.94790	2.11338	17
18	1.09393	1.19615	1.30734	1.42825	1.55966	1.70243	1.85749	2.02582	2.20848	18
19	1.09940	1.20811	1.32695	1.45681	1.59865	1.75351	1.92250	2.10685	2.30786	19
20	1.10490	1.22019	1.34686	1.48595	1.63862	1.80611	1.98979	2.19112	2.41171	20
21	1.11042	1.23239	1.36706	1.51567	1.67958	1.86029	2.05943	2.27877	2.52024	21
22	1.11597	1.24472	1.38756	1.54598	1.72157	1.91610	2.13151	2.36992	2.63365	22
23	1.12155	1.25716	1.40838	1.57690	1.76461	1.97359	2.20611	2.46472	2.75217	23
24	1.12716	1.26973	1.42950	1.60844	1.80873	2.03279	2.28333	2.56330	2.87601	24
25	1.13280	1.28243	1.45095	1.64061	1.85394	2.09378	2.36324	2.66584	3.00543	25
26	1.13846	1.29526	1.47271	1.67342	1.90029	2.15659	2.44596	2.77247	3.14068	26
27	1.14415	1.30821	1.49480	1.70689	1.94780	2.22129	2.53157	2.88337	3.28201	27
28	1.14987	1.32129	1.51722	1.74102	1.99650	2.28793	2.62017	2.99870	3.42970	28
29	1.15562	1.33450	1.53998	1.77584	2.04641	2.35657	2.71188	3.11865	3.58404	29
30	1.16140	1.34785	1.56308	1.81136	2.09757	2.42726	2.80679	3.24340	3.74532	30
31	1.16721	1.36133	1.58653	1.84759	2.15001	2.50008	2.90503	3.37313	3.91386	31
32	1.17304	1.37494	1.61032	1.88454	2.20376	2.57508	3.00671	3.50806	4.08998	32
33	1.17891	1.38869	1.63448	1.92223	2.25885	2.65234	3.11194	3.64838	4.27403	33
34	1.18480	1.40258	1.65900	1.96068	2.31532	2.73191	3.22086	3.79432	4.46636	34
35	1.19073	1.41660	1.68388	1.99989	2.37321	2.81386	3.33359	3.94609	4.66735	35
36	1.19668	1.43077	1.70914	2.03989	2.43254	2.89828	3.45027	4.10393	4.87738	36
37	1.20266	1.44508	1.73478	2.08069	2.49335	2.98523	3.57103	4.26809	5.09686	37
38	1.20868	1.45953	1.76080	2.12230	2.55568	3.07478	3.69601	4.43881	5.32622	38
39	1.21472	1.47412	1.78721	2.16474	2.61957	3.16703	3.82537	4.61637	5.56590	39
40	1.22079	1.48886	1.81402	2.20804	2.68506	3.26204	3.95926	4.80102	5.81636	40
41	1.22690	1.50375	1.84123	2.25220	2.75219	3.35990	4.09783	4.99306	6.07810	41
42	1.23303	1.51879	1.86885	2.29724	2.82100	3.46070	4.24126	5.19278	6.35162	42
43	1.23920	1.53398	1.89688	2.34319	2.89152	3.56452	4.38970	5.40050	6.63744	43
44	1.24539	1.54932	1.92533	2.39005	2.96381	3.67145	4.54334	5.61652	6.93612	44
45	1.25162	1.56481	1.95421	2.43785	3.03790	3.78160	4.70236	5.84118	7.24825	45
46	1.25788	1.58046	1.98353	2.48661	3.11385	3.89504	4.86694	6.07482	7.57442	46
47	1.26417	1.59626	2.01328	2.53634	3.19170	4.01190	5.03728	6.31782	7.91527	47
48	1.27049	1.61223	2.04348	2.58707	3.27149	4.13225	5.21359	6.57053	8.27146	48
49	1.27684	1.62835	2.07413	2.63881	3.35328	4.25622	5.39606	6.83335	8.64367	49
50	1.28323	1.64463	2.10524	2.69159	3.43711	4.38391	5.58493	7.10668	9.03264	50

n	5%	5.5%	6%	6.5%	7%	7.5%	8%	9%	10%	n
1	1.05000	1.05500	1.06000	1.06500	1.07000	1.07500	1.08000	1.09000	1.10000	1
2	1.10250	1.11302	1.12360	1.13423	1.14490	1.15563	1.16640	1.18810	1.21000	2
3	1.15763	1.17424	1.19102	1.20795	1.22504	1.24230	1.25971	1.29503	1.33100	3
4	1.21551	1.23882	1.26248	1.28647	1.31080	1.33547	1.36049	1.41158	1.46410	4
5	1.27628	1.30696	1.33823	1.37009	1.40255	1.43563	1.46933	1.53862	1.61051	5
6	1.34010	1.37884	1.41852	1.45914	1.50073	1.54330	1.58687	1.67710	1.77156	6
7	1.40710	1.45468	1.50363	1.55399	1.60578	1.65905	1.71382	1.82804	1.94872	7
8	1.47746	1.53469	1.59385	1.65500	1.71819	1.78348	1.85093	1.99256	2.14359	8
9	1.55133	1.61909	1.68948	1.76257	1.83846	1.91724	1.99900	2.17189	2.35795	9
10	1.62889	1.70814	1.79085	1.87714	1.96715	2.06103	2.15892	2.36736	2.59374	10
11	1.71034	1.80209	1.89830	1.99915	2.10485	2.21561	2.33164	2.58043	2.85312	11
12	1.79586	1.90121	2.01220	2.12910	2.25219	2.38178	2.51817	2.81266	3.13843	12
13	1.88565	2.00577	2.13293	2.26749	2.40985	2.56041	2.71962	3.06580	3.45227	13
14	1.97993	2.11609	2.26090	2.41487	2.57853	2.75244	2.93719	3.34173	3.79750	14
15	2.07893	2.23248	2.39656	2.57184	2.75903	2.95888	3.17217	3.64248	4.17725	15
16	2.18287	2.35526	2.54035	2.73901	2.95216	3.18079	3.42594	3.97031	4.59497	16
17	2.29202	2.48480	2.69277	2.91705	3.15882	3.41935	3.70002	4.32763	5.05447	17
18	2.40662	2.62147	2.85434	3.10665	3.37993	3.67580	3.99602	4.71712	5.55992	18
19	2.52695	2.76565	3.02560	3.30859	3.61653	3.95149	4.31570	5.14166	6.11591	19
20	2.65330	2.91776	3.20714	3.52365	3.86968	4.24785	4.66096	5.60441	6.72750	20
21	2.78596	3.07823	3.39956	3.75268	4.14056	4.56644	5.03383	6.10881	7.40025	21
22	2.92526	3.24754	3.60354	3.99661	4.43040	4.90892	5.43654	6.65860	8.14027	22
23	3.07152	3.42615	3.81975	4.25639	4.74053	5.27709	5.87146	7.25787	8.95430	23
24	3.22510	3.61459	4.04893	4.53305	5.07237	5.67287	6.34118	7.91108	9.84973	24
25	3.38635	3.81339	4.29187	4.82770	5.42743	6.09834	6.84848	8.62308	10.83471	25
26	3.55567	4.02313	4.54938	5.14150	5.80735	6.55572	7.39635	9.39916	11.91818	26
27	3.73346	4.24440	4.82235	5.47570	6.21387	7.04739	7.98806	10.24508	13.10999	27
28	3.92013	4.47784	5.11169	5.83162	6.64884	7.57595	8.62711	11.16714	14.42099	28
29	4.11614	4.72412	5.41839	6.21067	7.11426	8.14414	9.31727	12.17218	15.86309	29
30	4.32194	4.98395	5.74349	6.61437	7.61226	8.75496	10.06266	13.26768	17.44940	30
31	4.53804	5.25807	6.08810	7.04430	8.14511	9.41158	10.86767	14.46177	19.19434	31
32	4.76494	5.54726	6.45339	7.50218	8.71527	10.11745	11.73708	15.76333	21.11378	32
33	5.00319	5.85236	6.84059	7.98982	9.32534	10.87625	12.67605	17.18203	23.22515	33
34	5.25335	6.17424	7.25103	8.50916	9.97811	11.69197	13.69013	18.72841	25.54767	34
35	5.51602	6.51383	7.68609	9.06225	10.67658	12.56887	14.78534	20.41397	28.10244	35
36	5.79182	6.87209	8.14725	9.65130	11.42394	13.51154	15.96817	22.25123	30.91268	36
37	6.08141	7.25005	8.63609	10.27864	12.22362	14.52490	17.24563	24.25384	34.00395	37
38	6.38548	7.64880	9.15425	10.94675	13.07927	15.61427	18.62528	26.43668	37.40434	38
39	6.70475	8.06949	9.70351	11.65829	13.99482	16.78534	20.11530	28.81598	41.14478	39
40	7.03999	8.51331	10.28572	12.41607	14.97446	18.04424	21.72452	31.40942	45.25926	40
41	7.39199	8.98154	10.90286	13.22312	16.02267	19.39756	23.46248	34.23627	49.78518	41
42	7.76159	9.47553	11.55703	14.08262	17.14426	20.85237	25.33948	37.31753	54.76370	42
43	8.14967	9.99668	12.25045	14.99799	18.34435	22.41630	27.36664	40.67611	60.24007	43
44	8.55715	10.54650	12.98548	15.97286	19.62846	24.09752	29.55597	44.33696	66.26408	44
45	8.98501	11.12655	13.76461	17.01110	21.00245	25.90484	31.92045	48.32729	72.89048	45
46	9.43426	11.73851	14.59049	18.11682	22.47262	27.84770	34.47409	52.67674	80.17953	46
47	9.90597	12.38413	15.46592	19.29441	24.04571	29.93628	37.23201	57.41765	88.19749	47
48	10.4013	13.06526	16.39387	20.54855	25.72891	32.18150	40.21057	62.58524	97.01723	48
49	10.9213	13.78385	17.37750	21.88421	27.52993	34.59511	43.42742	68.21791	106.7190	49
50	11.4674	14.54196	18.42015	23.30668	29.45703	37.18975	46.90161	74.35752	117.3909	50

TABLE I.
Future Value of $1 (continued)

n	11%	12%	13%	14%	15%	16%	17%	18%	19%	n
1	1.11000	1.12000	1.13000	1.14000	1.15000	1.16000	1.17000	1.18000	1.19000	1
2	1.23210	1.25440	1.27690	1.29960	1.32250	1.34560	1.36890	1.39240	1.41610	2
3	1.36763	1.40493	1.44290	1.48154	1.52087	1.56090	1.60161	1.64303	1.68516	3
4	1.51807	1.57352	1.63047	1.68896	1.74901	1.81064	1.87389	1.93878	2.00534	4
5	1.68506	1.76234	1.84244	1.92541	2.01136	2.10034	2.19245	2.28776	2.38635	5
6	1.87041	1.97382	2.08195	2.19497	2.31306	2.43640	2.56516	2.69955	2.83976	6
7	2.07616	2.21068	2.35261	2.50227	2.66002	2.82622	3.00124	3.18547	3.37932	7
8	2.30454	2.47596	2.65844	2.85259	3.05902	3.27841	3.51145	3.75886	4.02139	8
9	2.55804	2.77308	3.00404	3.25195	3.51788	3.80296	4.10840	4.43545	4.78545	9
10	2.83942	3.10585	3.39457	3.70722	4.04556	4.41144	4.80683	5.23384	5.69468	10
11	3.15176	3.47855	3.83586	4.22623	4.65239	5.11726	5.62399	6.17593	6.77667	11
12	3.49845	3.89598	4.33452	4.81790	5.35025	5.93603	6.58007	7.28759	8.06424	12
13	3.88328	4.36349	4.89801	5.49241	6.15279	6.88579	7.69868	8.59936	9.59645	13
14	4.31044	4.88711	5.53475	6.26135	7.07571	7.98752	9.00745	10.14724	11.41977	14
15	4.78459	5.47357	6.25427	7.13794	8.13706	9.26552	10.53872	11.97375	13.58953	15
16	5.31089	6.13039	7.06733	8.13725	9.35762	10.74800	12.33030	14.12902	16.17154	16
17	5.89509	6.86604	7.98608	9.27646	10.76126	12.46768	14.42646	16.67225	19.24413	17
18	6.54355	7.68997	9.02427	10.57517	12.37545	14.46251	16.87895	19.67325	22.90052	18
19	7.26334	8.61276	10.19742	12.05569	14.23177	16.77652	19.74838	23.21444	27.25162	19
20	8.06231	9.64629	11.52309	13.74349	16.36654	19.46076	23.10560	27.39303	32.42942	20
21	8.94917	10.80385	13.02109	15.66758	18.82152	22.57448	27.03355	32.32378	38.59101	21
22	9.93357	12.10031	14.71383	17.86104	21.64475	26.18640	31.62925	38.14206	45.92331	22
23	11.02627	13.55235	16.62663	20.36158	24.89146	30.37622	37.00623	45.00763	54.64873	23
24	12.23916	15.17863	18.78809	23.21221	28.62518	35.23642	43.29729	53.10901	65.03199	24
25	13.58546	17.00006	21.23054	26.46192	32.91895	40.87424	50.65783	62.66863	77.38807	25
26	15.07986	19.04007	23.99051	30.16658	37.85680	47.41412	59.26966	73.94898	92.09181	26
27	16.73865	21.32488	27.10928	34.38991	43.53531	55.00038	69.34550	87.25980	109.5893	27
28	18.57990	23.88387	30.63349	39.20449	50.06561	63.80044	81.13423	102.9666	130.4112	28
29	20.62369	26.74993	34.61584	44.69312	57.57545	74.00851	94.92705	121.5005	155.1893	29
30	22.89230	29.95992	39.11590	50.95016	66.21177	85.84988	111.0647	143.3706	184.6753	30
31	25.41045	33.55511	44.20096	58.08318	76.14354	99.58586	129.9456	169.1774	219.7636	31
32	28.20560	37.58173	49.94709	66.21483	87.56507	115.5196	152.0364	199.6293	261.5187	32
33	31.30821	42.09153	56.44021	75.48490	100.6998	134.0027	177.8826	235.5626	311.2073	33
34	34.75212	47.14252	63.77744	86.05279	115.8048	155.4432	208.1226	277.9638	370.3366	34
35	38.57485	52.79962	72.06851	98.10018	133.1755	180.3141	243.5035	327.9973	440.7006	35
36	42.81808	59.13557	81.43741	111.8342	153.1519	209.1643	284.8991	387.0368	524.4337	36
37	47.52807	66.23184	92.02428	127.4910	176.1246	242.6306	333.3319	456.7034	624.0761	37
38	52.75616	74.17966	103.9874	145.3397	202.5433	281.4515	389.9983	538.9100	742.6506	38
39	58.55934	83.08122	117.5058	165.6873	232.9248	326.4838	456.2981	635.9139	883.7542	39
40	65.00087	93.05097	132.7816	188.8835	267.8636	378.7212	533.8687	750.3783	1051.668	40
41	72.15096	104.2171	150.0432	215.3272	308.0431	439.3165	624.6264	885.4465	1251.484	41
42	80.08757	116.7231	169.5488	245.4730	354.2495	509.6072	730.8129	1044.827	1489.266	42
43	88.89720	130.7299	191.5901	279.8392	407.3870	591.1443	855.0511	1232.896	1772.227	43
44	98.67589	146.4175	216.4968	319.0167	468.4950	685.7274	1000.410	1454.817	2108.950	44
45	109.5302	163.9876	244.6414	363.6791	538.7693	795.4438	1170.479	1716.684	2509.651	45
46	121.5786	183.6661	276.4448	414.5941	619.5847	922.7148	1369.461	2025.687	2986.484	46
47	134.9522	205.7061	312.3826	472.6373	712.5224	1070.349	1602.269	2390.311	3553.916	47
48	149.7970	230.3908	352.9923	538.8066	819.4007	1241.605	1874.655	2820.567	4229.160	48
49	166.2746	258.0377	398.8814	614.2395	942.3108	1440.262	2193.346	3328.269	5032.701	49
50	184.5648	289.0022	450.7359	700.2330	1083.657	1670.704	2566.215	3927.357	5988.914	50

n	20%	21%	22%	23%	24%	25%	26%	28%	30%	n
1	1.20000	1.21000	1.22000	1.23000	1.24000	1.25000	1.26000	1.28000	1.30000	1
2	1.44000	1.46410	1.48840	1.51290	1.53760	1.56250	1.58760	1.63840	1.69000	2
3	1.72800	1.77156	1.81585	1.86087	1.90662	1.95312	2.00038	2.09715	2.19700	3
4	2.07360	2.14359	2.21533	2.28887	2.36421	2.44141	2.52047	2.68435	2.85610	4
5	2.48832	2.59374	2.70271	2.81531	2.93163	3.05176	3.17580	3.43597	3.71293	5
6	2.98598	3.13843	3.29730	3.46283	3.63522	3.81470	4.00150	4.39805	4.82681	6
7	3.58318	3.79750	4.02271	4.25928	4.50767	4.76837	5.04190	5.62950	6.27485	7
8	4.29982	4.59497	4.90771	5.23891	5.58951	5.96046	6.35279	7.20576	8.15731	8
9	5.15978	5.55992	5.98740	6.44386	6.93099	7.45058	8.00451	9.22337	10.60450	9
10	6.19174	6.72750	7.30463	7.92595	8.59443	9.31323	10.08569	11.80592	13.78585	10
11	7.43008	8.14027	8.91165	9.74891	10.65709	11.64153	12.70796	15.11157	17.92160	11
12	8.91610	9.84973	10.87221	11.99116	13.21479	14.55192	16.01204	19.34281	23.29809	12
13	10.69932	11.91818	13.26410	14.74913	16.38634	18.18989	20.17516	24.75880	30.28751	13
14	12.83918	14.42099	16.18220	18.14143	20.31906	22.73737	25.42071	31.69127	39.37376	14
15	15.40702	17.44940	19.74229	22.31396	25.19563	28.42171	32.03009	40.56482	51.18589	15
16	18.48843	21.11378	24.08559	27.44617	31.24259	35.52714	40.35792	51.92297	66.54166	16
17	22.18611	25.54767	29.38442	33.75879	38.74081	44.40892	50.85097	66.46140	86.50416	17
18	26.62333	30.91268	35.84894	41.52331	48.03860	55.51115	64.07223	85.07059	112.4554	18
19	31.94800	37.40434	43.73577	51.07368	59.56786	69.38894	80.73100	108.8904	146.1920	19
20	38.33760	45.25926	53.35764	62.82062	73.86415	86.73617	101.7211	139.3797	190.0496	20
21	46.00512	54.76370	65.09632	77.26936	91.59155	108.4202	128.1685	178.4060	247.0645	21
22	55.20614	66.26408	79.41751	95.04132	113.5735	135.5253	161.4924	228.3596	321.1839	22
23	66.24737	80.17953	96.88936	116.9008	140.8312	169.4066	203.4804	292.3003	417.5391	23
24	79.49685	97.01723	118.2050	143.7880	174.6306	211.7582	256.3853	374.1444	542.8008	24
25	95.39622	117.3909	144.2101	176.8593	216.5420	264.6978	323.0455	478.9049	705.6410	25
26	114.4755	142.0429	175.9364	217.5369	268.5121	330.8723	407.0373	612.9982	917.3333	26
27	137.3706	171.8719	214.6424	267.5704	332.9550	413.5903	512.8670	784.6377	1192.533	27
28	164.8447	207.9651	261.8637	329.1116	412.8642	516.9879	646.2124	1004.336	1550.293	28
29	197.8136	251.6377	319.4737	404.8072	511.9516	646.2349	814.2276	1285.550	2015.381	29
30	237.3763	304.4816	389.7579	497.9129	634.8199	807.7936	1025.927	1645.505	2619.996	30
31	284.8516	368.4228	475.5046	612.4328	787.1767	1009.742	1292.668	2106.246	3405.994	31
32	341.8219	445.7916	580.1157	753.2924	976.0991	1262.177	1628.761	2695.995	4427.793	32
33	410.1863	539.4078	707.7411	926.5496	1210.363	1577.722	2052.239	3450.873	5756.130	33
34	492.2235	652.6834	863.4441	1139.656	1500.850	1972.152	2585.821	4417.118	7482.970	34
35	590.6682	789.7470	1053.402	1401.777	1861.054	2465.190	3258.135	5653.911	9727.860	35
36	708.8019	955.5938	1285.150	1724.186	2307.707	3081.488	4105.250	7237.006	12646.22	36
37	850.5623	1156.269	1567.883	2120.748	2861.557	3851.860	5172.615	9263.367	16440.08	37
38	1020.675	1399.085	1912.818	2608.520	3548.330	4814.825	6517.495	11857.11	21372.11	38
39	1224.810	1692.893	2333.638	3208.480	4399.930	6018.531	8212.044	15177.10	27783.74	39
40	1469.772	2048.400	2847.038	3946.430	5455.913	7523.164	10347.18	19426.69	36118.86	40
41	1763.726	2478.564	3473.386	4854.110	6765.336	9403.955	13037.44	24866.16	46954.52	41
42	2116.471	2999.063	4237.531	5970.555	8389.011	11754.94	16427.18	31828.69	61040.88	42
43	2539.765	3628.866	5169.788	7343.782	10402.37	14693.68	20698.24	40740.72	79353.15	43
44	3047.718	4390.928	6307.141	9032.852	12898.94	18367.10	26079.78	52148.12	103159.1	44
45	3657.262	5313.023	7694.712	11110.41	15994.69	22958.87	32860.53	66749.59	134106.8	45
46	4388.714	6428.757	9387.549	13665.80	19833.42	28698.59	41404.26	85439.48	174338.9	46
47	5266.457	7778.796	11452.81	16808.94	24593.44	35873.24	52169.37	109362.5	226640.5	47
48	6319.749	9412.344	13972.43	20674.99	30495.86	44841.55	65733.41	139984.0	294632.7	48
49	7583.698	11388.94	17046.36	25430.24	37814.87	56051.94	82824.10	179179.6	383022.5	49
50	9100.438	13780.61	20796.56	31279.20	46890.43	70064.92	104358.4	229349.9	497929.2	50

TABLE II.
Present Value of $1

n	.5%	1%	1.5%	2%	2.5%	3%	3.5%	4%	4.5%	n
1	.99502	.99010	.98522	.98039	.97561	.97087	.96618	.96154	.95694	1
2	.99007	.98030	.97066	.96117	.95181	.94260	.93351	.92456	.91573	2
3	.98515	.97059	.95632	.94232	.92860	.91514	.90194	.88900	.87630	3
4	.98025	.96098	.94218	.92385	.90595	.88849	.87144	.85480	.83856	4
5	.97537	.95147	.92826	.90573	.88385	.86261	.84197	.82193	.80245	5
6	.97052	.94205	.91454	.88797	.86230	.83748	.81350	.79031	.76790	6
7	.96569	.93272	.90103	.87056	.84127	.81309	.78599	.75992	.73483	7
8	.96089	.92348	.88771	.85349	.82075	.78941	.75941	.73069	.70319	8
9	.95610	.91434	.87459	.83676	.80073	.76642	.73373	.70259	.67290	9
10	.95135	.90529	.86167	.82035	.78120	.74409	.70892	.67556	.64393	10
11	.94661	.89632	.84893	.80426	.76214	.72242	.68495	.64958	.61620	11
12	.94191	.88745	.83639	.78849	.74356	.70138	.66178	.62460	.58966	12
13	.93722	.87866	.82403	.77303	.72542	.68095	.63940	.60057	.56427	13
14	.93256	.86996	.81185	.75788	.70773	.66112	.61778	.57748	.53997	14
15	.92792	.86135	.79985	.74301	.69047	.64186	.59689	.55526	.51672	15
16	.92330	.85282	.78803	.72845	.67362	.62317	.57671	.53391	.49447	16
17	.91871	.84438	.77639	.71416	.65720	.60502	.55720	.51337	.47318	17
18	.91414	.83602	.76491	.70016	.64117	.58739	.53836	.49363	.45280	18
19	.90959	.82774	.75361	.68643	.62553	.57029	.52016	.47464	.43330	19
20	.90506	.81954	.74247	.67297	.61027	.55368	.50257	.45639	.41464	20
21	.90056	.81143	.73150	.65978	.59539	.53755	.48557	.43883	.39679	21
22	.89608	.80340	.72069	.64684	.58086	.52189	.46915	.42196	.37970	22
23	.89162	.79544	.71004	.63416	.56670	.50669	.45329	.40573	.36335	23
24	.88719	.78757	.69954	.62172	.55288	.49193	.43796	.39012	.34770	24
25	.88277	.77977	.68921	.60953	.53939	.47761	.42315	.37512	.33273	25
26	.87838	.77205	.67902	.59758	.52623	.46369	.40884	.36069	.31840	26
27	.87401	.76440	.66899	.58586	.51340	.45019	.39501	.34682	.30469	27
28	.86966	.75684	.65910	.57437	.50088	.43708	.38165	.33348	.29157	28
29	.86533	.74934	.64936	.56311	.48866	.42435	.36875	.32065	.27902	29
30	.86103	.74192	.63976	.55207	.47674	.41199	.35628	.30832	.26700	30
31	.85675	.73458	.63031	.54125	.46511	.39999	.34423	.29646	.25550	31
32	.85248	.72730	.62099	.53063	.45377	.38834	.33259	.28506	.24450	32
33	.84824	.72010	.61182	.52023	.44270	.37703	.32134	.27409	.23397	33
34	.84402	.71297	.60277	.51003	.43191	.36604	.31048	.26355	.22390	34
35	.83982	.70591	.59387	.50003	.42137	.35538	.29998	.25342	.21425	35
36	.83564	.69892	.58509	.49022	.41109	.34503	.28983	.24367	.20503	36
37	.83149	.69200	.57644	.48061	.40107	.33498	.28003	.23430	.19620	37
38	.82735	.68515	.56792	.47119	.39128	.32523	.27056	.22529	.18775	38
39	.82323	.67837	.55953	.46195	.38174	.31575	.26141	.21662	.17967	39
40	.81914	.67165	.55126	.45289	.37243	.30656	.25257	.20829	.17193	40
41	.81506	.66500	.54312	.44401	.36335	.29763	.24403	.20028	.16453	41
42	.81101	.65842	.53509	.43530	.35448	.28896	.23578	.19257	.15744	42
43	.80697	.65190	.52718	.42677	.34584	.28054	.22781	.18517	.15066	43
44	.80296	.64545	.51939	.41840	.33740	.27237	.22010	.17805	.14417	44
45	.79896	.63905	.51171	.41020	.32917	.26444	.21266	.17120	.13796	45
46	.79499	.63273	.50415	.40215	.32115	.25674	.20547	.16461	.13202	46
47	.79103	.62646	.49670	.39427	.31331	.24926	.19852	.15828	.12634	47
48	.78710	.62026	.48936	.38654	.30567	.24200	.19181	.15219	.12090	48
49	.78318	.61412	.48213	.37896	.29822	.23495	.18532	.14634	.11569	49
50	.77929	.60804	.47500	.37153	.29094	.22811	.17905	.14071	.11071	50

n	5%	5.5%	6%	6.5	7%	7.5	8%	9%	10%	n
1	.95238	.94787	.94340	.93897	.93458	.93023	.92593	.91743	.90909	1
2	.90703	.89845	.89000	.88166	.87344	.86533	.85734	.84168	.82645	2
3	.86384	.85161	.83962	.82785	.81630	.80496	.79383	.77218	.75131	3
4	.82270	.80722	.79209	.77732	.76290	.74880	.73503	.70843	.68301	4
5	.78353	.76513	.74726	.72988	.71299	.69656	.68058	.64993	.62092	5
6	.74622	.72525	.70496	.68533	.66634	.64796	.63017	.59627	.56447	6
7	.71068	.68744	.66506	.64351	.62275	.60275	.58349	.54703	.51316	7
8	.67684	.65160	.62741	.60423	.58201	.56070	.54027	.50187	.46651	8
9	.64461	.61763	.59190	.56735	.54393	.52158	.50025	.46043	.42410	9
10	.61391	.58543	.55839	.53273	.50835	.48519	.46319	.42241	.38554	10
11	.58468	.55491	.52679	.50021	.47509	.45134	.42888	.38753	.35049	11
12	.55684	.52598	.49697	.46968	.44401	.41985	.39711	.35553	.31863	12
13	.53032	.49856	.46884	.44102	.41496	.39056	.36770	.32618	.28966	13
14	.50507	.47257	.44230	.41410	.38782	.36331	.34046	.29925	.26333	14
15	.48102	.44793	.41727	.38883	.36245	.33797	.31524	.27454	.23939	15
16	.45811	.42458	.39365	.36510	.33873	.31439	.29189	.25187	.21763	16
17	.43630	.40245	.37136	.34281	.31657	.29245	.27027	.23107	.19784	17
18	.41552	.38147	.35034	.32189	.29586	.27205	.25025	.21199	.17986	18
19	.39573	.36158	.33051	.30224	.27651	.25307	.23171	.19449	.16351	19
20	.37689	.34273	.31180	.28380	.25842	.23541	.21455	.17843	.14864	20
21	.35894	.32486	.29416	.26648	.24151	.21899	.19866	.16370	.13513	21
22	.34185	.30793	.27751	.25021	.22571	.20371	.18394	.15018	.12285	22
23	.32557	.29187	.26180	.23494	.21095	.18950	.17032	.13778	.11168	23
24	.31007	.27666	.24698	.22060	.19715	.17628	.15770	.12640	.10153	24
25	.29530	.26223	.23300	.20714	.18425	.16398	.14602	.11597	.09230	25
26	.28124	.24856	.21981	.19450	.17220	.15254	.13520	.10639	.08391	26
27	.26785	.23560	.20737	.18263	.16093	.14190	.12519	.09761	.07628	27
28	.25509	.22332	.19563	.17148	.15040	.13200	.11591	.08955	.06934	28
29	.24295	.21168	.18456	.16101	.14056	.12279	.10733	.08215	.06304	29
30	.23138	.20064	.17411	.15119	.13137	.11422	.09938	.07537	.05731	30
31	.22036	.19018	.16425	.14196	.12277	.10625	.09202	.06915	.05210	31
32	.20987	.18027	.15496	.13329	.11474	.09884	.08520	.06344	.04736	32
33	.19987	.17087	.14619	.12516	.10723	.09194	.07889	.05820	.04306	33
34	.19035	.16196	.13791	.11752	.10022	.08553	.07305	.05339	.03914	34
35	.18129	.15352	.13011	.11035	.09366	.07956	.06763	.04899	.03558	35
36	.17266	.14552	.12274	.10361	.08754	.07401	.06262	.04494	.03235	36
37	.16444	.13793	.11579	.09729	.08181	.06885	.05799	.04123	.02941	37
38	.15661	.13074	.10924	.09135	.07646	.06404	.05369	.03783	.02673	38
39	.14915	.12392	.10306	.08578	.07146	.05958	.04971	.03470	.02430	39
40	.14205	.11746	.09722	.08054	.06678	.05542	.04603	.03184	.02209	40
41	.13528	.11134	.09172	.07563	.06241	.05155	.04262	.02921	.02009	41
42	.12884	.10554	.08653	.07101	.05833	.04796	.03946	.02680	.01826	42
43	.12270	.10003	.08163	.06668	.05451	.04461	.03654	.02458	.01660	43
44	.11686	.09482	.07701	.06261	.05095	.04150	.03383	.02255	.01509	44
45	.11130	.08988	.07265	.05879	.04761	.03860	.03133	.02069	.01372	45
46	.10600	.08519	.06854	.05520	.04450	.03591	.02901	.01898	.01247	46
47	.10095	.08075	.06466	.05183	.04159	.03340	.02686	.01742	.01134	47
48	.09614	.07654	.06100	.04867	.03887	.03107	.02487	.01598	.01031	48
49	.09156	.07255	.05755	.04570	.03632	.02891	.02303	.01466	.00937	49
50	.08720	.06877	.05429	.04291	.03395	.02689	.02132	.01345	.00852	50

TABLE II.
Present Value of $1 (continued)

n	11%	12%	13%	14%	15%	16%	17%	18%	19%	n
1	.90090	.89286	.88496	.87719	.86957	.86207	.85470	.84746	.84034	1
2	.81162	.79719	.78315	.76947	.75614	.74316	.73051	.71818	.70616	2
3	.73119	.71178	.69305	.67497	.65752	.64066	.62437	.60863	.59342	3
4	.65873	.63552	.61332	.59208	.57175	.55229	.53365	.51579	.49867	4
5	.59345	.56743	.54276	.51937	.49718	.47611	.45611	.43711	.41905	5
6	.53464	.50663	.48032	.45559	.43233	.41044	.38984	.37043	.35214	6
7	.48166	.45235	.42506	.39964	.37594	.35383	.33320	.31393	.29592	7
8	.43393	.40388	.37616	.35056	.32690	.30503	.28478	.26604	.24867	8
9	.39092	.36061	.33288	.30751	.28426	.26295	.24340	.22546	.20897	9
10	.35218	.32197	.29459	.26974	.24718	.22668	.20804	.19106	.17560	10
11	.31728	.28748	.26070	.23662	.21494	.19542	.17781	.16192	.14757	11
12	.28584	.25668	.23071	.20756	.18691	.16846	.15197	.13722	.12400	12
13	.25751	.22917	.20416	.18207	.16253	.14523	.12989	.11629	.10421	13
14	.23199	.20462	.18068	.15971	.14133	.12520	.11102	.09855	.08757	14
15	.20900	.18270	.15989	.14010	.12289	.10793	.09489	.08352	.07359	15
16	.18829	.16312	.14150	.12289	.10686	.09304	.08110	.07078	.06184	16
17	.16963	.14564	.12522	.10780	.09293	.08021	.06932	.05998	.05196	17
18	.15282	.13004	.11081	.09456	.08081	.06914	.05925	.05083	.04367	18
19	.13768	.11611	.09806	.08295	.07027	.05961	.05064	.04308	.03670	19
20	.12403	.10367	.08678	.07276	.06110	.05139	.04328	.03651	.03084	20
21	.11174	.09256	.07680	.06383	.05313	.04430	.03699	.03094	.02591	21
22	.10067	.08264	.06796	.05599	.04620	.03819	.03162	.02622	.02178	22
23	.09069	.07379	.06014	.04911	.04017	.03292	.02702	.02222	.01830	23
24	.08170	.06588	.05323	.04308	.03493	.02838	.02310	.01883	.01538	24
25	.07361	.05882	.04710	.03779	.03038	.02447	.01974	.01596	.01292	25
26	.06631	.05252	.04168	.03315	.02642	.02109	.01687	.01352	.01086	26
27	.05974	.04689	.03689	.02908	.02297	.01818	.01442	.01146	.00912	27
28	.05382	.04187	.03264	.02551	.01997	.01567	.01233	.00971	.00767	28
29	.04849	.03738	.02889	.02237	.01737	.01351	.01053	.00823	.00644	29
30	.04368	.03338	.02557	.01963	.01510	.01165	.00900	.00697	.00541	30
31	.03935	.02980	.02262	.01722	.01313	.01004	.00770	.00591	.00455	31
32	.03545	.02661	.02002	.01510	.01142	.00866	.00658	.00501	.00382	32
33	.03194	.02376	.01772	.01325	.00993	.00746	.00562	.00425	.00321	33
34	.02878	.02121	.01568	.01162	.00864	.00643	.00480	.00360	.00270	34
35	.02592	.01894	.01388	.01019	.00751	.00555	.00411	.00305	.00227	35
36	.02335	.01691	.01228	.00894	.00653	.00478	.00351	.00258	.00191	36
37	.02104	.01510	.01087	.00784	.00568	.00412	.00300	.00219	.00160	37
38	.01896	.01348	.00962	.00688	.00494	.00355	.00256	.00186	.00135	38
39	.01708	.01204	.00851	.00604	.00429	.00306	.00219	.00157	.00113	39
40	.01538	.01075	.00753	.00529	.00373	.00264	.00187	.00133	.00095	40
41	.01386	.00960	.00666	.00464	.00325	.00228	.00160	.00113	.00080	41
42	.01249	.00857	.00590	.00407	.00282	.00196	.00137	.00096	.00067	42
43	.01125	.00765	.00522	.00357	.00245	.00169	.00117	.00081	.00056	43
44	.01013	.00683	.00462	.00313	.00213	.00146	.00100	.00069	.00047	44
45	.00913	.00610	.00409	.00275	.00186	.00126	.00085	.00058	.00040	45
46	.00823	.00544	.00362	.00241	.00161	.00108	.00073	.00049	.00033	46
47	.00741	.00486	.00320	.00212	.00140	.00093	.00062	.00042	.00028	47
48	.00668	.00434	.00283	.00186	.00122	.00081	.00053	.00035	.00024	48
49	.00601	.00388	.00251	.00163	.00106	.00069	.00046	.00030	.00020	49
50	.00542	.00346	.00222	.00143	.00092	.00060	.00039	.00025	.00017	50

n	20%	21%	22%	23%	24%	25	26%	28%	30%	n
1	.83333	.82645	.81967	.81301	.80645	.80000	.79365	.78125	.76923	1
2	.69444	.68301	.67186	.66098	.65036	.64000	.62988	.61035	.59172	2
3	.57870	.56447	.55071	.53738	.52449	.51200	.49991	.47684	.45517	3
4	.48225	.46651	.45140	.43690	.42297	.40960	.39675	.37253	.35013	4
5	.40188	.38554	.37000	.35520	.34111	.32768	.31488	.29104	.26933	5
6	.33490	.31863	.30328	.28878	.27509	.26214	.24991	.22737	.20718	6
7	.27908	.26333	.24859	.23478	.22184	.20972	.19834	.17764	.15937	7
8	.23257	.21763	.20376	.19088	.17891	.16777	.15741	.13878	.12259	8
9	.19381	.17986	.16702	.15519	.14428	.13422	.12493	.10842	.09430	9
10	.16151	.14864	.13690	.12617	.11635	.10737	.09915	.08470	.07254	10
11	.13459	.12285	.11221	.10258	.09383	.08590	.07869	.06617	.05580	11
12	.11216	.10153	.09198	.08339	.07567	.06872	.06245	.05170	.04292	12
13	.09346	.08391	.07539	.06780	.06103	.05498	.04957	.04039	.03302	13
14	.07789	.06934	.06180	.05512	.04921	.04398	.03934	.03155	.02540	14
15	.06491	.05731	.05065	.04481	.03969	.03518	.03122	.02465	.01954	15
16	.05409	.04736	.04152	.03643	.03201	.02815	.02478	.01926	.01503	16
17	.04507	.03914	.03403	.02962	.02581	.02252	.01967	.01505	.01156	17
18	.03756	.03235	.02789	.02408	.02082	.01801	.01561	.01175	.00889	18
19	.03130	.02673	.02286	.01958	.01679	.01441	.01239	.00918	.00684	19
20	.02608	.02209	.01874	.01592	.01354	.01153	.00983	.00717	.00526	20
21	.02174	.01826	.01536	.01294	.01092	.00922	.00780	.00561	.00405	21
22	.01811	.01509	.01259	.01052	.00880	.00738	.00619	.00438	.00311	22
23	.01509	.01247	.01032	.00855	.00710	.00590	.00491	.00342	.00239	23
24	.01258	.01031	.00846	.00695	.00573	.00472	.00390	.00267	.00184	24
25	.01048	.00852	.00693	.00565	.00462	.00378	.00310	.00209	.00142	25
26	.00874	.00704	.00568	.00460	.00372	.00302	.00246	.00163	.00109	26
27	.00728	.00582	.00466	.00374	.00300	.00242	.00195	.00127	.00084	27
28	.00607	.00481	.00382	.00304	.00242	.00193	.00155	.00100	.00065	28
29	.00506	.00397	.00313	.00247	.00195	.00155	.00123	.00078	.00050	29
30	.00421	.00328	.00257	.00201	.00158	.00124	.00097	.00061	.00038	30
31	.00351	.00271	.00210	.00163	.00127	.00099	.00077	.00047	.00029	31
32	.00293	.00224	.00172	.00133	.00102	.00079	.00061	.00037	.00023	32
33	.00244	.00185	.00141	.00108	.00083	.00063	.00049	.00029	.00017	33
34	.00203	.00153	.00116	.00088	.00067	.00051	.00039	.00023	.00013	34
35	.00169	.00127	.00095	.00071	.00054	.00041	.00031	.00018	.00010	35
36	.00141	.00105	.00078	.00058	.00043	.00032	.00024	.00014	.00008	36
37	.00118	.00086	.00064	.00047	.00035	.00026	.00019	.00011	.00006	37
38	.00098	.00071	.00052	.00038	.00028	.00021	.00015	.00008	.00005	38
39	.00082	.00059	.00043	.00031	.00023	.00017	.00012	.00007	.00004	39
40	.00068	.00049	.00035	.00025	.00018	.00013	.00010	.00005	.00003	40
41	.00057	.00040	.00029	.00021	.00015	.00011	.00008	.00004	.00002	41
42	.00047	.00033	.00024	.00017	.00012	.00009	.00006	.00003	.00002	42
43	.00039	.00028	.00019	.00014	.00010	.00007	.00005	.00002	.00001	43
44	.00033	.00023	.00016	.00011	.00008	.00005	.00004	.00002	.00001	44
45	.00027	.00019	.00013	.00009	.00006	.00004	.00003	.00001	.00001	45
46	.00023	.00016	.00011	.00007	.00005	.00003	.00002	.00001	.00001	46
47	.00019	.00013	.00009	.00006	.00004	.00003	.00002	.00001	.00000	47
48	.00016	.00011	.00007	.00005	.00003	.00002	.00002	.00001	.00000	48
49	.00013	.00009	.00006	.00004	.00003	.00002	.00001	.00001	.00000	49
50	.00011	.00007	.00005	.00003	.00002	.00001	.00001	.00000	.00000	50

TABLE III.
Future Value of Annuity of $1

n	.5%	1%	1.5%	2%	2.5%	3%	3.5%	4%	4.5%	n
1	1.00000	1.00000	1.00000	1.00000	1.00000	1.00000	1.00000	1.00000	1.00000	1
2	2.00500	2.01000	2.01500	2.02000	2.02500	2.03000	2.03500	2.04000	2.04500	2
3	3.01503	3.03010	3.04523	3.06040	3.07562	3.09090	3.10623	3.12160	3.13703	3
4	4.03010	4.06040	4.09090	4.12161	4.15252	4.18363	4.21494	4.24646	4.27819	4
5	5.05025	5.10101	5.15227	5.20404	5.25633	5.30914	5.36247	5.41632	5.47071	5
6	6.07550	6.15202	6.22955	6.30812	6.38774	6.46841	6.55015	6.63298	6.71689	6
7	7.10588	7.21354	7.32299	7.43428	7.54743	7.66246	7.77941	7.89829	8.01915	7
8	8.14141	8.28567	8.43284	8.58297	8.73612	8.89234	9.05169	9.21423	9.38001	8
9	9.18212	9.36853	9.55933	9.75463	9.95452	10.15911	10.36850	10.58280	10.80211	9
10	10.22803	10.46221	10.70272	10.94972	11.20338	11.46388	11.73139	12.00611	12.28821	10
11	11.27917	11.56683	11.86326	12.16872	12.48347	12.80780	13.14199	13.48635	13.84118	11
12	12.33556	12.68250	13.04121	13.41209	13.79555	14.19203	14.60196	15.02581	15.46403	12
13	13.39724	13.80933	14.23683	14.68033	15.14044	15.61779	16.11303	16.62684	17.15991	13
14	14.46423	14.94742	15.45038	15.97394	16.51895	17.08632	17.67699	18.29191	18.93211	14
15	15.53655	16.09690	16.68214	17.29342	17.93193	18.59891	19.29568	20.02359	20.78405	15
16	16.61423	17.25786	17.93237	18.63929	19.38022	20.15688	20.97103	21.82453	22.71934	16
17	17.69730	18.43044	19.20136	20.01207	20.86473	21.76159	22.70502	23.69751	24.74171	17
18	18.78579	19.61475	20.48938	21.41231	22.38635	23.41444	24.49969	25.64541	26.85508	18
19	19.87972	20.81090	21.79672	22.84056	23.94601	25.11687	26.35718	27.67123	29.06356	19
20	20.97912	22.01900	23.12367	24.29737	25.54466	26.87037	28.27968	29.77808	31.37142	20
21	22.08401	23.23919	24.47052	25.78332	27.18327	28.67649	30.26947	31.96920	33.78314	21
22	23.19443	24.47159	25.83758	27.29898	28.86286	30.53678	32.32890	34.24797	36.30338	22
23	24.31040	25.71630	27.22514	28.84496	30.58443	32.45288	34.46041	36.61789	38.93703	23
24	25.43196	26.97346	28.63352	30.42186	32.34904	34.42647	36.66653	39.08260	41.68920	24
25	26.55912	28.24320	30.06302	32.03030	34.15776	36.45926	38.94986	41.64591	44.56521	25
26	27.69191	29.52563	31.51397	33.67091	36.01171	38.55304	41.31310	44.31174	47.57064	26
27	28.83037	30.82089	32.98668	35.34432	37.91200	40.70963	43.75906	47.08421	50.71132	27
28	29.97452	32.12910	34.48148	37.05121	39.85980	42.93092	46.29063	49.96758	53.99333	28
29	31.12439	33.45039	35.99870	38.79223	41.85630	45.21885	48.91080	52.96629	57.42303	29
30	32.28002	34.78489	37.53868	40.56808	43.90270	47.57542	51.62268	56.08494	61.00707	30
31	33.44142	36.13274	39.10176	42.37944	46.00027	50.00268	54.42947	59.32834	64.75239	31
32	34.60862	37.49407	40.68829	44.22703	48.15028	52.50276	57.33450	62.70147	68.66625	32
33	35.78167	38.86901	42.29861	46.11157	50.35403	55.07784	60.34121	66.20953	72.75623	33
34	36.96058	40.25770	43.93309	48.03380	52.61289	57.73018	63.45315	69.85791	77.03026	34
35	38.14538	41.66028	45.59209	49.99448	54.92821	60.46208	66.67401	73.65222	81.49662	35
36	39.33610	43.07688	47.27597	51.99437	57.30141	63.27594	70.00760	77.59831	86.16397	36
37	40.53279	44.50765	48.98511	54.03425	59.73395	66.17422	73.45787	81.70225	91.04134	37
38	41.73545	45.95272	50.71989	56.11494	62.22730	69.15945	77.02889	85.97034	96.13820	38
39	42.94413	47.41225	52.48068	58.23724	64.78298	72.23423	80.72491	90.40915	101.4644	39
40	44.15885	48.88637	54.26789	60.40198	67.40255	75.40126	84.55028	95.02552	107.0303	40
41	45.37964	50.37524	56.08191	62.61002	70.08762	78.66330	88.50954	99.82654	112.8467	41
42	46.60654	51.87899	57.92314	64.86222	72.83981	82.02320	92.60737	104.8196	118.9248	42
43	47.83957	53.39778	59.79199	67.15947	75.66080	85.48389	96.84863	110.0124	125.2764	43
44	49.07877	54.95272	61.68887	69.50266	78.55232	89.04841	101.2383	115.4129	131.9138	44
45	50.32416	56.48107	63.61420	71.89271	81.51613	92.71986	105.7817	121.0294	138.8500	45
46	51.57578	58.04589	65.56841	74.33056	84.55403	96.50146	110.4840	126.8706	146.0982	46
47	52.83366	59.62634	67.55194	76.81718	87.66789	100.3965	115.3510	132.9454	153.6726	47
48	54.09783	61.22261	69.56522	79.35362	90.85958	104.4084	120.3883	139.2632	161.5879	48
49	55.36832	62.83483	71.60870	81.94059	94.13107	108.5407	125.6019	145.8337	169.8594	49
50	56.64516	64.46318	73.68283	84.57940	97.48435	112.7969	130.9979	152.6671	178.5030	50

n	5%	5.5%	6%	6.5%	7%	7.5	8%	9%	10%	n
1	1.00000	1.00000	1.00000	1.00000	1.00000	1.00000	1.00000	1.00000	1.00000	1
2	2.05000	2.05500	2.06000	2.06500	2.07000	2.07500	2.08000	2.09000	2.10000	2
3	3.15250	3.16802	3.18360	3.19923	3.21490	3.23063	3.24640	3.27810	3.31000	3
4	4.31013	4.34227	4.37462	4.40717	4.43994	4.47292	4.50611	4.57313	4.64100	4
5	5.52563	5.58109	5.63709	5.69364	5.75074	5.80839	5.86660	5.98471	6.10510	5
6	6.80191	6.88805	6.97532	7.06373	7.15329	7.24402	7.33593	7.52333	7.71561	6
7	8.14201	8.26689	8.39384	8.52287	8.65402	8.78732	8.92280	9.20043	9.48717	7
8	9.54911	9.72157	9.89747	10.07686	10.25980	10.44637	10.63663	11.02847	11.43589	8
9	11.02656	11.25626	11.49132	11.73185	11.97799	12.22985	12.48756	13.02104	13.57948	9
10	12.57789	12.87535	13.18079	13.49442	13.81645	14.14709	14.48656	15.19293	15.93742	10
11	14.20679	14.58350	14.97164	15.37156	15.78360	16.20812	16.64549	17.56029	18.53117	11
12	15.91713	16.38559	16.86994	17.37071	17.88845	18.42373	18.97713	20.14072	21.38428	12
13	17.71298	18.28680	18.88214	19.49981	20.14064	20.80551	21.49530	22.95338	24.52271	13
14	19.59863	20.29257	21.01507	21.76730	22.55049	23.36592	24.21492	26.01919	27.97498	14
15	21.57856	22.40866	23.27597	24.18217	25.12902	26.11836	27.15211	29.36092	31.77248	15
16	23.65749	24.64114	25.67253	26.75401	27.88805	29.07724	30.32428	33.00340	35.94973	16
17	25.84037	26.99640	28.21288	29.49302	30.84022	32.25804	33.75023	36.97370	40.54470	17
18	28.13238	29.48120	30.90565	32.41007	33.99903	35.67739	37.45024	41.30134	45.59917	18
19	30.53900	32.10267	33.75999	35.51672	37.37896	39.35319	41.44626	46.01846	51.15909	19
20	33.06595	34.86832	36.78559	38.82531	40.99549	43.30468	45.76196	51.16012	57.27500	20
21	35.71925	37.78608	39.99273	42.34895	44.86518	47.55253	50.42292	56.76453	64.00250	21
22	38.50521	40.86431	43.39229	46.10164	49.00574	52.11897	55.45676	62.87334	71.40275	22
23	41.43048	44.11185	46.99583	50.09824	53.43614	57.02790	60.89330	69.53194	79.54302	23
24	44.50200	47.53800	50.81558	54.35463	58.17667	62.30499	66.76476	76.78981	88.49733	24
25	47.72710	51.15259	54.86451	58.88768	63.24904	67.97786	73.10594	84.70090	98.34706	25
26	51.11345	54.96598	59.15638	63.71538	68.67647	74.07620	79.95442	93.32398	109.1818	26
27	54.66913	58.98911	63.70577	68.85688	74.48382	80.63192	87.35077	102.7231	121.0999	27
28	58.40258	63.23351	68.52811	74.33257	80.69769	87.67931	95.33883	112.9682	134.2099	28
29	62.32271	67.71135	73.63980	80.16419	87.34653	95.25526	103.9659	124.1354	148.6309	29
30	66.43885	72.43548	79.05819	86.37486	94.46079	103.3994	113.2832	136.3075	164.4940	30
31	70.76079	77.41943	84.80168	92.98923	102.0730	112.1544	123.3459	149.5752	181.9434	31
32	75.29883	82.67750	90.88978	100.0335	110.2182	121.5659	134.2135	164.0370	201.1378	32
33	80.06377	88.22476	97.34316	107.5357	118.9334	131.6834	145.9506	179.8003	222.2515	33
34	85.06696	94.07712	104.1838	115.5255	128.2588	142.5596	158.6267	196.9823	245.4767	34
35	90.32031	100.2514	111.4348	124.0347	138.2369	154.2516	172.3168	215.7108	271.0244	35
36	95.83632	106.7652	119.1209	133.0970	148.9135	166.8205	187.1022	236.1247	299.1268	36
37	101.6281	113.6373	127.2681	142.7483	160.3374	180.3320	203.0703	258.3760	330.0395	37
38	107.7096	120.8873	135.9042	153.0269	172.5610	194.8569	220.3160	282.6298	364.0434	38
39	114.0950	128.5361	145.0585	163.9736	185.6403	210.4712	238.9412	309.0665	401.4478	39
40	120.7998	136.6056	154.7620	175.6319	199.6351	227.2565	259.0565	337.8825	442.5926	40
41	127.8398	145.1189	165.0477	188.0480	214.6096	245.3008	280.7810	369.2919	487.8518	41
42	135.2318	154.1005	175.9505	201.2711	230.6322	264.6983	304.2435	403.5281	537.6370	42
43	142.9933	163.5760	187.5076	215.3537	247.7765	285.5507	329.5830	440.8457	592.4007	43
44	151.1430	173.5727	199.7580	230.3517	266.1209	307.9670	356.9497	481.5218	652.6408	44
45	159.7002	184.1192	212.7435	246.3246	285.7493	332.0645	386.5056	525.8587	718.9048	45
46	168.6852	195.2457	226.5081	263.3357	306.7518	357.9694	418.4261	574.1860	791.7953	46
47	178.1194	206.9842	241.0986	281.4525	329.2244	385.8171	452.9002	626.8628	871.9749	47
48	188.0254	219.3684	256.5645	300.7469	353.2701	415.7533	490.1322	684.2804	960.1723	48
49	198.4267	232.4336	272.9584	321.2955	378.9990	447.9348	530.3427	746.8657	1057.190	49
50	209.3480	246.2175	290.3359	343.1797	406.5289	482.5300	573.7702	815.0836	1163.909	50

TABLE III.
Future Value of Annuity of $1 (continued)

n	11%	12%	13%	14%	15%	16%	17%	18%	19%	n
1	1.00000	1.00000	1.00000	1.00000	1.00000	1.00000	1.00000	1.00000	1.00000	1
2	2.11000	2.12000	2.13000	2.14000	2.15000	2.16000	2.17000	2.18000	2.19000	2
3	3.34210	3.37440	3.40690	3.43960	3.47250	3.50560	3.53890	3.57240	3.60610	3
4	4.70973	4.77933	4.84980	4.92114	4.99337	5.06650	5.14051	5.21543	5.29126	4
5	6.22780	6.35285	6.48027	6.61010	6.74238	6.87714	7.01440	7.15421	7.29660	5
6	7.91286	8.11519	8.32271	8.53552	8.75374	8.97748	9.20685	9.44197	9.68295	6
7	9.78327	10.08901	10.40466	10.73049	11.06680	11.41387	11.77201	12.14152	12.52271	7
8	11.85943	12.29969	12.75726	13.23276	13.72682	14.24009	14.77325	15.32700	15.90203	8
9	14.16397	14.77566	15.41571	16.08535	16.78584	17.51851	18.28471	19.08585	19.92341	9
10	16.72201	17.54874	18.41975	19.33730	20.30372	21.32147	22.39311	23.52131	24.70886	10
11	19.56143	20.65458	21.81432	23.04452	24.34928	25.73290	27.19994	28.75514	30.40355	11
12	22.71319	24.13313	25.65018	27.27075	29.00167	30.85017	32.82393	34.93107	37.18022	12
13	26.21164	28.02911	29.98470	32.08865	34.35192	36.78620	39.40399	42.21866	45.24446	13
14	30.09492	32.39260	34.88271	37.58107	40.50471	43.67199	47.10267	50.81802	54.84091	14
15	34.40536	37.27971	40.41746	43.84241	47.58041	51.65951	56.11013	60.96527	66.26068	15
16	39.18995	42.75328	46.67173	50.98035	55.71747	60.92503	66.64885	72.93901	79.85021	16
17	44.50084	48.88367	53.73906	59.11760	65.07509	71.67303	78.97915	87.06804	96.02175	17
18	50.39594	55.74971	61.72514	68.39407	75.83636	84.14072	93.40561	103.7403	115.2659	18
19	56.93949	63.43968	70.74941	78.96923	88.21181	98.60323	110.2846	123.4135	138.1664	19
20	64.20283	72.05244	80.94683	91.02493	102.4436	115.3798	130.0329	146.6280	165.4180	20
21	72.26514	81.69874	92.46992	104.7684	118.8101	134.8405	153.1385	174.0210	197.8474	21
22	81.21431	92.50258	105.4910	120.4360	137.6316	157.4150	180.1721	206.3448	236.4385	22
23	91.14788	104.6029	120.2048	138.2970	159.2764	183.6014	211.8013	244.4869	282.3618	23
24	102.1742	118.1552	136.8315	158.6586	184.1678	213.9776	248.8076	289.4945	337.0105	24
25	114.4133	133.3339	155.6196	181.8708	212.7930	249.2140	292.1049	342.6035	402.0425	25
26	127.9988	150.3339	176.8501	208.3327	245.7120	290.0883	342.7627	405.2721	479.4306	26
27	143.0786	169.3740	200.8406	238.4993	283.5688	337.5024	402.0323	479.2211	571.5224	27
28	159.8173	190.6989	227.9499	272.8892	327.1041	392.5028	471.3778	566.4809	681.1116	28
29	178.3972	214.5828	258.5834	312.0937	377.1697	456.3032	552.5121	669.4475	811.5228	29
30	199.0209	241.3327	293.1992	356.7869	434.7452	530.3117	647.4391	790.9480	966.7122	30
31	221.9132	271.2926	332.3151	407.7370	500.9569	616.1616	758.5038	934.3186	1151.387	31
32	247.3236	304.8477	376.5161	465.8202	577.1005	715.7475	888.4494	1103.496	1371.151	32
33	275.5292	342.4295	426.4632	532.0350	664.6655	831.2671	1040.486	1303.125	1632.670	33
34	306.8374	384.5210	482.9034	607.5199	765.3654	965.2698	1218.368	1538.688	1943.877	34
35	341.5896	431.6635	546.6808	693.5727	881.1702	1120.713	1426.491	1816.652	2314.214	35
36	380.1644	484.4631	618.7493	791.6729	1014.346	1301.027	1669.995	2144.649	2754.914	36
37	422.9825	543.5987	700.1867	903.5071	1167.498	1510.191	1954.894	2531.686	3279.348	37
38	470.5106	609.8305	792.2110	1030.998	1343.622	1752.822	2288.225	2988.389	3903.424	38
39	523.2667	684.0102	896.1985	1176.338	1546.166	2034.274	2678.224	3527.299	4646.075	39
40	581.8261	767.0914	1013.704	1342.025	1779.090	2360.757	3134.522	4163.213	5529.829	40
41	646.8269	860.1424	1146.486	1530.909	2046.954	2739.478	3668.391	4913.591	6581.496	41
42	718.9779	964.3595	1296.529	1746.236	2354.997	3178.795	4293.017	5799.038	7832.981	42
43	799.0655	1081.083	1466.078	1991.709	2709.247	3688.402	5023.830	6843.865	9322.247	43
44	887.9627	1211.813	1657.668	2271.548	3116.633	4279.547	5878.881	8076.760	11094.47	44
45	986.6386	1358.230	1874.165	2590.565	3585.129	4965.274	6879.291	9531.577	13203.42	45
46	1096.169	1522.218	2118.806	2954.244	4123.898	5760.718	8049.770	11248.26	15713.07	46
47	1217.747	1705.884	2395.251	3368.838	4743.482	6683.433	9419.231	13273.95	18699.56	47
48	1352.700	1911.590	2707.633	3841.475	5456.005	7753.782	11021.50	15664.26	22253.48	48
49	1502.497	2141.981	3060.626	4380.282	6275.406	8995.387	12896.16	18484.83	26482.64	49
50	1668.771	2400.018	3459.507	4994.521	7217.716	10435.65	15089.50	21813.09	31515.34	50

n	20%	21%	22%	23%	24%	25%	26%	28%	30%	n
1	1.00000	1.00000	1.00000	1.00000	1.00000	1.00000	1.00000	1.00000	1.00000	1
2	2.20000	2.21000	2.22000	2.23000	2.24000	2.25000	2.26000	2.28000	2.30000	2
3	3.64000	3.67410	3.70840	3.74290	3.77760	3.81250	3.84760	3.91840	3.99000	3
4	5.36800	5.44566	5.52425	5.60377	5.68422	5.76562	5.84798	6.01555	6.18700	4
5	7.44160	7.58925	7.73958	7.89263	8.04844	8.20703	8.36845	8.69991	9.04310	5
6	9.92992	10.18299	10.44229	10.70794	10.98006	11.25879	11.54425	12.13588	12.75603	6
7	12.91590	13.32142	13.73959	14.17077	14.61528	15.07349	15.54575	16.53393	17.58284	7
8	16.49908	17.11892	17.76231	18.43004	19.12294	19.84186	20.58765	22.16343	23.85769	8
9	20.79890	21.71389	22.67001	23.66895	24.71245	25.80232	26.94043	29.36919	32.01500	9
10	25.95868	27.27381	28.65742	30.11281	31.64344	33.25290	34.94495	38.59256	42.61950	10
11	32.15042	34.00131	35.96205	38.03876	40.23787	42.56613	45.03063	50.39847	56.40535	11
12	39.58050	42.14158	44.87370	47.78767	50.89495	54.20766	57.73860	65.51005	74.32695	12
13	48.49660	51.99132	55.74591	59.77883	64.10974	68.75958	73.75063	84.85286	97.62504	13
14	59.19592	63.90949	69.01001	74.52796	80.49608	86.94947	93.92580	109.6117	127.9126	14
15	72.03511	78.33049	85.19221	92.66940	100.8151	109.6868	119.3465	141.3029	167.2863	15
16	87.44213	95.77989	104.9345	114.9834	126.0108	138.1086	151.3766	181.8677	218.4722	16
17	105.9306	116.8937	129.0201	142.4295	157.2534	173.6357	191.7345	233.7907	285.0139	17
18	128.1167	142.4413	158.4045	176.1883	195.9942	218.0446	242.5855	300.2521	371.5180	18
19	154.7400	173.3540	194.2535	217.7116	244.0328	273.5558	306.6577	385.3227	483.9734	19
20	186.6880	210.7584	237.9893	268.7853	303.6006	342.9447	387.3887	494.2131	630.1655	20
21	225.0256	256.0176	291.3469	331.6059	377.4648	429.6809	489.1098	633.5927	820.2151	21
22	271.0307	310.7813	356.4432	408.8753	469.0563	538.1011	617.2783	811.9987	1067.280	22
23	326.2369	377.0454	435.8608	503.9166	582.6298	673.6264	778.7707	1040.358	1388.464	23
24	392.4842	457.2249	532.7501	620.8174	723.4610	843.0330	982.2511	1332.659	1806.003	24
25	471.9811	554.2422	650.9551	764.6055	898.0916	1054.791	1238.636	1706.803	2348.803	25
26	567.3773	671.6330	795.1653	941.4647	1114.634	1319.489	1561.682	2185.708	3054.444	26
27	681.8528	813.6759	971.1016	1159.002	1383.146	1650.361	1968.719	2798.706	3971.778	27
28	819.2233	985.5479	1185.744	1426.572	1716.101	2063.952	2481.586	3583.344	5164.311	28
29	984.0680	1193.513	1447.608	1755.683	2128.965	2580.939	3127.798	4587.680	6714.604	29
30	1181.882	1445.151	1767.081	2160.491	2640.916	3227.174	3942.026	5873.231	8729.985	30
31	1419.258	1749.632	2156.839	2658.404	3275.736	4034.968	4967.953	7518.735	11349.98	31
32	1704.109	2118.055	2632.344	3270.836	4062.913	5044.710	6260.620	9624.981	14755.98	32
33	2045.931	2563.847	3212.460	4024.129	5039.012	6306.887	7889.382	12320.98	19183.77	33
34	2456.118	3103.254	3920.201	4950.678	6249.375	7884.609	9941.621	15771.85	24939.90	34
35	2948.341	3755.938	4783.645	6090.334	7750.225	9856.761	12527.44	20188.97	32422.87	35
36	3539.009	4545.685	5837.047	7492.111	9611.279	12321.95	15785.58	25842.88	42150.73	36
37	4247.811	5501.279	7122.197	9216.297	11918.99	15403.44	19890.83	33079.88	54796.95	37
38	5098.374	6657.547	8690.080	11337.05	14780.54	19255.30	25063.44	42343.25	71237.03	38
39	6119.048	8056.632	10602.90	13945.57	18328.87	24070.12	31580.94	54200.36	92609.14	39
40	7343.858	9749.525	12936.54	17154.05	22728.80	30088.66	39792.98	69377.46	120392.9	40
41	8813.629	11797.93	15783.57	21100.48	28184.72	37611.82	50140.16	88804.15	156511.7	41
42	10577.36	14276.49	19256.96	25954.59	34950.05	47015.77	63177.60	113670.3	203466.3	42
43	12693.83	17275.55	23494.49	31925.14	43339.06	58770.72	79604.77	145499.0	264507.2	43
44	15233.59	20904.42	28664.28	39268.92	53741.43	73464.40	100303.0	186239.7	343860.3	44
45	18281.31	25295.35	34971.42	48301.77	66640.38	91831.50	126382.8	238387.8	447019.4	45
46	21938.57	30608.37	42666.13	59412.18	82635.07	114790.4	159243.3	305137.4	581126.2	46
47	26327.29	37037.13	52053.68	73077.98	102468.5	143489.0	200647.6	390576.9	755465.1	47
48	31593.74	44815.92	63506.49	89886.92	127061.9	179362.2	252817.0	499939.5	982105.6	48
49	37913.49	54228.27	77478.92	110561.9	157557.8	224203.8	318550.4	639923.5	1276738.3	49
50	45497.19	65617.20	94525.28	135992.2	195372.6	280255.7	401374.5	819103.1	1659760.7	50

TABLE IV.
Present Value of Annuity of $1

n	.5%	1%	1.5%	2%	2.5%	3%	3.5%	4%	4.5%	n
1	0.99502	0.99010	0.98522	0.98039	0.97561	0.97087	0.96618	0.96154	0.95694	1
2	1.98510	1.97040	1.95588	1.94156	1.92742	1.91347	1.89969	1.88609	1.87267	2
3	2.97025	2.94099	2.91220	2.88388	2.85602	2.82861	2.80164	2.77509	2.74896	3
4	3.95050	3.90197	3.85438	3.80773	3.76197	3.71710	3.67308	3.62990	3.58753	4
5	4.92587	4.85343	4.78264	4.71346	4.64583	4.57971	4.51505	4.45182	4.38998	5
6	5.89638	5.79548	5.69719	5.60143	5.50813	5.41719	5.32855	5.24214	5.15787	6
7	6.86207	6.72819	6.59821	6.47199	6.34939	6.23028	6.11454	6.00205	5.89270	7
8	7.82296	7.65168	7.48593	7.32548	7.17014	7.01969	6.87396	6.73274	6.59589	8
9	8.77906	8.56602	8.36052	8.16224	7.97087	7.78611	7.60769	7.43533	7.26879	9
10	9.73041	9.47130	9.22218	8.98259	8.75206	8.53020	8.31661	8.11090	7.91272	10
11	10.67703	10.36763	10.07112	9.78685	9.51421	9.25262	9.00155	8.76048	8.52892	11
12	11.61893	11.25508	10.90751	10.57534	10.25776	9.95400	9.66333	9.38507	9.11858	12
13	12.55615	12.13374	11.73153	11.34837	10.98318	10.63496	10.30274	9.98565	9.68285	13
14	13.48871	13.00370	12.54338	12.10625	11.69091	11.29607	10.92052	10.56312	10.22283	14
15	14.41662	13.86505	13.34323	12.84926	12.38138	11.93794	11.51741	11.11839	10.73955	15
16	15.33993	14.71787	14.13126	13.57771	13.05500	12.56110	12.09412	11.65230	11.23402	16
17	16.25863	15.56225	14.90765	14.29187	13.71220	13.16612	12.65132	12.16567	11.70719	17
18	17.17277	16.39827	15.67256	14.99203	14.35336	13.75351	13.18968	12.65930	12.15999	18
19	18.08236	17.22601	16.42617	15.67846	14.97889	14.32380	13.70984	13.13394	12.59329	19
20	18.98742	18.04555	17.16864	16.35143	15.58916	14.87747	14.21240	13.59033	13.00794	20
21	19.88798	18.85698	17.90014	17.01121	16.18455	15.41502	14.69797	14.02916	13.40472	21
22	20.78406	19.66038	18.62082	17.65805	16.76541	15.93692	15.16712	14.45112	13.78442	22
23	21.67568	20.45582	19.33086	18.29220	17.33211	16.44361	15.62041	14.85684	14.14777	23
24	22.56287	21.24339	20.03041	18.91393	17.88499	16.93554	16.05837	15.24696	14.49548	24
25	23.44564	22.02316	20.71961	19.52346	18.42438	17.41315	16.48151	15.62208	14.82821	25
26	24.32402	22.79520	21.39863	20.12104	18.95061	17.87684	16.89035	15.98277	15.14661	26
27	25.19803	23.55961	22.06762	20.70690	19.46401	18.32703	17.28536	16.32959	15.45130	27
28	26.06769	24.31644	22.72672	21.28127	19.96489	18.76411	17.66702	16.66306	15.74287	28
29	26.93302	25.06579	23.37608	21.84438	20.45355	19.18845	18.03577	16.98371	16.02189	29
30	27.79405	25.80771	24.01584	22.39646	20.93029	19.60044	18.39205	17.29203	16.28889	30
31	28.65080	26.54229	24.64615	22.93770	21.39541	20.00043	18.73628	17.58849	16.54439	31
32	29.50328	27.26959	25.26714	23.46833	21.84918	20.38877	19.06887	17.87355	16.78889	32
33	30.35153	27.98969	25.87895	23.98856	22.29188	20.76579	19.39021	18.14765	17.02286	33
34	31.19555	28.70267	26.48173	24.49859	22.72379	21.13184	19.70068	18.41120	17.24676	34
35	32.03537	29.40858	27.07559	24.99862	23.14516	21.48722	20.00066	18.66461	17.46101	35
36	32.87102	30.10751	27.66068	25.48884	23.55625	21.83225	20.29049	18.90828	17.66604	36
37	33.70250	30.79951	28.23713	25.96945	23.95732	22.16724	20.57053	19.14258	17.86224	37
38	34.52985	31.48466	28.80505	26.44064	24.34860	22.49246	20.84109	19.36786	18.04999	38
39	35.35309	32.16303	29.36458	26.90259	24.73034	22.80822	21.10250	19.58448	18.22966	39
40	36.17223	32.83469	29.91585	27.35548	25.10278	23.11477	21.35507	19.79277	18.40158	40
41	36.98729	33.49969	30.45896	27.79949	25.46612	23.41240	21.59910	19.99305	18.56611	41
42	37.79830	34.15811	30.99405	28.23479	25.82061	23.70136	21.83488	20.18563	18.72355	42
43	38.60527	34.81001	31.52123	28.66156	26.16645	23.98190	22.06269	20.37079	18.87421	43
44	39.40823	35.45545	32.04062	29.07996	26.50385	24.25427	22.28279	20.54884	19.01838	44
45	40.20720	36.09451	32.55234	29.49016	26.83302	24.51871	22.49545	20.72004	19.15635	45
46	41.00219	36.72724	33.05649	29.89231	27.15417	24.77545	22.70092	20.88465	19.28837	46
47	41.79322	37.35370	33.55319	30.28658	27.46748	25.02471	22.89944	21.04294	19.41471	47
48	42.58032	37.97396	34.04255	30.67312	27.77315	25.26671	23.09124	21.19513	19.53561	48
49	43.36350	38.58808	34.52468	31.05208	28.07137	25.50166	23.27656	21.34147	19.65130	49
50	44.14279	39.19612	34.99969	31.42361	28.36231	25.72976	23.45562	21.48218	19.76201	50

n	5%	5.5%	6%	6.5%	7%	7.5%	8%	9%	10%	n
1	0.95238	0.94787	0.94340	0.93897	0.93458	0.93023	0.92593	0.91743	0.90909	1
2	1.85941	1.84632	1.83339	1.82063	1.80802	1.79557	1.78326	1.75911	1.73554	2
3	2.72325	2.69793	2.67301	2.64848	2.62432	2.60053	2.57710	2.53129	2.48685	3
4	3.54595	3.50515	3.46511	3.42580	3.38721	3.34933	3.31213	3.23972	3.16987	4
5	4.32948	4.27028	4.21236	4.15568	4.10020	4.04588	3.99271	3.88965	3.79079	5
6	5.07569	4.99553	4.91732	4.84101	4.76654	4.69385	4.62288	4.48592	4.35526	6
7	5.78637	5.68297	5.58238	5.48452	5.38929	5.29660	5.20637	5.03295	4.86842	7
8	6.46321	6.33457	6.20979	6.08875	5.97130	5.85730	5.74664	5.53482	5.33493	8
9	7.10782	6.95220	6.80169	6.65610	6.51523	6.37889	6.24689	5.99525	5.75902	9
10	7.72173	7.53763	7.36009	7.18883	7.02358	6.86408	6.71008	6.41766	6.14457	10
11	8.30641	8.09254	7.88687	7.68904	7.49867	7.31542	7.13896	6.80519	6.49506	11
12	8.86325	8.61852	8.38384	8.15873	7.94269	7.73528	7.53608	7.16073	6.81369	12
13	9.39357	9.11708	8.85268	8.59974	8.35765	8.12584	7.90378	7.48690	7.10336	13
14	9.89864	9.58965	9.29498	9.01384	8.74547	8.48915	8.24424	7.78615	7.36669	14
15	10.37966	10.03758	9.71225	9.40267	9.10791	8.82712	8.55948	8.06069	7.60608	15
16	10.83777	10.46216	10.10590	9.76776	9.44665	9.14151	8.85137	8.31256	7.82371	16
17	11.27407	10.86461	10.47726	10.11058	9.76322	9.43396	9.12164	8.54363	8.02155	17
18	11.68959	11.24607	10.82760	10.43247	10.05909	9.70601	9.37189	8.75563	8.20141	18
19	12.08532	11.60765	11.15812	10.73471	10.33560	9.95908	9.60360	8.95011	8.36492	19
20	12.46221	11.95038	11.46992	11.01851	10.59401	10.19449	9.81815	9.12855	8.51356	20
21	12.82115	12.27524	11.76408	11.28498	10.83553	10.41348	10.01680	9.29224	8.64869	21
22	13.16300	12.58317	12.04158	11.53520	11.06124	10.61719	10.20074	9.44243	8.77154	22
23	13.48857	12.87504	12.30338	11.77014	11.27219	10.80669	10.37106	9.58021	8.88322	23
24	13.79864	13.15170	12.55036	11.99074	11.46933	10.98297	10.52876	9.70661	8.98474	24
25	14.09394	13.41393	12.78336	12.19788	11.65358	11.14695	10.67478	9.82258	9.07704	25
26	14.37519	13.66250	13.00317	12.39237	11.82578	11.29948	10.80998	9.92897	9.16095	26
27	14.64303	13.89810	13.21053	12.57500	11.98671	11.44138	10.93516	10.02658	9.23722	27
28	14.89813	14.12142	13.40616	12.74648	12.13711	11.57338	11.05108	10.11613	9.30657	28
29	15.14107	14.33310	13.59072	12.90749	12.27767	11.69617	11.15841	10.19828	9.36961	29
30	15.37245	14.53375	13.76483	13.05868	12.40904	11.81039	11.25778	10.27365	9.42691	30
31	15.59281	14.72393	13.92909	13.20063	12.53181	11.91664	11.34980	10.34280	9.47901	31
32	15.80268	14.90420	14.08404	13.33393	12.64656	12.01548	11.43500	10.40624	9.52638	32
33	16.00255	15.07507	14.23023	13.45909	12.75379	12.10742	11.51389	10.46444	9.56943	33
34	16.19290	15.23703	14.36814	13.57661	12.85401	12.19295	11.58693	10.51784	9.60857	34
35	16.37419	15.39055	14.49825	13.68696	12.94767	12.27251	11.65457	10.56682	9.64416	35
36	16.54685	15.53607	14.62099	13.79057	13.03521	12.34652	11.71719	10.61176	9.67651	36
37	16.71129	15.67400	14.73678	13.88786	13.11702	12.41537	11.77518	10.65299	9.70592	37
38	16.86789	15.80474	14.84602	13.97921	13.19347	12.47941	11.82887	10.69082	9.73265	38
39	17.01704	15.92866	14.94907	14.06499	13.26493	12.53899	11.87858	10.72552	9.75696	39
40	17.15909	16.04612	15.04630	14.14553	13.33171	12.59441	11.92461	10.75736	9.77905	40
41	17.29437	16.15746	15.13802	14.22115	13.39412	12.64596	11.96723	10.78657	9.79914	41
42	17.42321	16.26300	15.22454	14.29216	13.45245	12.69392	12.00670	10.81337	9.81740	42
43	17.54591	16.36303	15.30617	14.35884	13.50696	12.73853	12.04324	10.83795	9.83400	43
44	17.66277	16.45785	15.38318	14.42144	13.55791	12.78003	12.07707	10.86051	9.84909	44
45	17.77407	16.54773	15.45583	14.48023	13.60552	12.81863	12.10840	10.88120	9.86281	45
46	17.88007	16.63292	15.52437	14.53543	13.65002	12.85454	12.13741	10.90018	9.87528	46
47	17.98102	16.71366	15.58903	14.58725	13.69161	12.88794	12.16427	10.91760	9.88662	47
48	18.07716	16.79020	15.65003	14.63592	13.73047	12.91902	12.18914	10.93358	9.89693	48
49	18.16872	16.86275	15.70757	14.68161	13.76680	12.94792	12.21216	10.94823	9.90630	49
50	18.25593	16.93152	15.76186	14.72452	13.80075	12.97481	12.23348	10.96168	9.91481	50

TABLE IV.
Present Value of Annuity of $1

n	11%	12%	13%	14%	15%	16%	17%	18%	19%	n
1	0.90090	0.89286	0.88496	0.87719	0.86957	0.86207	0.85470	0.84746	0.84034	1
2	1.71252	1.69005	1.66810	1.64666	1.62571	1.60523	1.58521	1.56564	1.54650	2
3	2.44371	2.40183	2.36115	2.32163	2.28323	2.24589	2.20958	2.17427	2.13992	3
4	3.10245	3.03735	2.97447	2.91371	2.85498	2.79818	2.74324	2.69006	2.63859	4
5	3.69590	3.60478	3.51723	3.43308	3.35216	3.27429	3.19935	3.12717	3.05763	5
6	4.23054	4.11141	3.99755	3.88867	3.78448	3.68474	3.58918	3.49760	3.40978	6
7	4.71220	4.56376	4.42261	4.28830	4.16042	4.03857	3.92238	3.81153	3.70570	7
8	5.14612	4.96764	4.79877	4.63886	4.48732	4.34359	4.20716	4.07757	3.95437	8
9	5.53705	5.32825	5.13166	4.94637	4.77158	4.60654	4.45057	4.30302	4.16333	9
10	5.88923	5.65022	5.42624	5.21612	5.01877	4.83323	4.65860	4.49409	4.33893	10
11	6.20652	5.93770	5.68694	5.45273	5.23371	5.02864	4.83641	4.65601	4.48650	11
12	6.49236	6.19437	5.91765	5.66029	5.42062	5.19711	4.98839	4.79322	4.61050	12
13	6.74987	6.42355	6.12181	5.84236	5.58315	5.34233	5.11828	4.90951	4.71471	13
14	6.98187	6.62817	6.30249	6.00207	5.72448	5.46753	5.22930	5.00806	4.80228	14
15	7.19087	6.81086	6.46238	6.14217	5.84737	5.57546	5.32419	5.09158	4.87586	15
16	7.37916	6.97399	6.60388	6.26506	5.95423	5.66850	5.40529	5.16235	4.93770	16
17	7.54879	7.11963	6.72909	6.37286	6.04716	5.74870	5.47461	5.22233	4.98966	17
18	7.70162	7.24967	6.83991	6.46742	6.12797	5.81785	5.53385	5.27316	5.03333	18
19	7.83929	7.36578	6.93797	6.55037	6.19823	5.87746	5.58449	5.31624	5.07003	19
20	7.96333	7.46944	7.02475	6.62313	6.25933	5.92884	5.62777	5.35275	5.10086	20
21	8.07507	7.56200	7.10155	6.68696	6.31246	5.97314	5.66476	5.38368	5.12677	21
22	8.17574	7.64465	7.16951	6.74294	6.35866	6.01133	5.69637	5.40990	5.14855	22
23	8.26643	7.71843	7.22966	6.79206	6.39884	6.04425	5.72340	5.43212	5.16685	23
24	8.34814	7.78432	7.28288	6.83514	6.43377	6.07263	5.74649	5.45095	5.18223	24
25	8.42174	7.84314	7.32998	6.87293	6.46415	6.09709	5.76623	5.46691	5.19515	25
26	8.48806	7.89566	7.37167	6.90608	6.49056	6.11818	5.78311	5.48043	5.20601	26
27	8.54780	7.94255	7.40856	6.93515	6.51353	6.13636	5.79753	5.49189	5.21513	27
28	8.60162	7.98442	7.44120	6.96066	6.53351	6.15204	5.80985	5.50160	5.22280	28
29	8.65011	8.02181	7.47009	6.98304	6.55088	6.16555	5.82039	5.50983	5.22924	29
30	8.69379	8.05518	7.49565	7.00266	6.56598	6.17720	5.82939	5.51681	5.23466	30
31	8.73315	8.08499	7.51828	7.01988	6.57911	6.18724	5.83709	5.52272	5.23921	31
32	8.76860	8.11159	7.53830	7.03498	6.59053	6.19590	5.84366	5.52773	5.24303	32
33	8.80054	8.13535	7.55602	7.04823	6.60046	6.20336	5.84928	5.53197	5.24625	33
34	8.82932	8.15656	7.57170	7.05985	6.60910	6.20979	5.85409	5.53557	5.24895	34
35	8.85524	8.17550	7.58557	7.07005	6.61661	6.21534	5.85820	5.53862	5.25122	35
36	8.87859	8.19241	7.59785	7.07899	6.62314	6.22012	5.86171	5.54120	5.25312	36
37	8.89963	8.20751	7.60872	7.08683	6.62881	6.22424	5.86471	5.54339	5.25472	37
38	8.91859	8.22099	7.61833	7.09371	6.63375	6.22779	5.86727	5.54525	5.25607	38
39	8.93567	8.23303	7.62684	7.09975	6.63805	6.23086	5.86946	5.54682	5.25720	39
40	8.95105	8.24378	7.63438	7.10504	6.64178	6.23350	5.87133	5.54815	5.25815	40
41	8.96491	8.25337	7.64104	7.10969	6.64502	6.23577	5.87294	5.54928	5.25895	41
42	8.97740	8.26194	7.64694	7.11376	6.64785	6.23774	5.87430	5.55024	5.25962	42
43	8.98865	8.26959	7.65216	7.11733	6.65030	6.23943	5.87547	5.55105	5.26019	43
44	8.99878	8.27642	7.65678	7.12047	6.65244	6.24089	5.87647	5.55174	5.26066	44
45	9.00791	8.28252	7.66086	7.12322	6.65429	6.24214	5.87733	5.55232	5.26106	45
46	9.01614	8.28796	7.66448	7.12563	6.65591	6.24323	5.87806	5.55281	5.26140	46
47	9.02355	8.29282	7.66768	7.12774	6.65731	6.24416	5.87868	5.55323	5.26168	47
48	9.03022	8.29716	7.67052	7.12960	6.65853	6.24497	5.87922	5.55359	5.26191	48
49	9.03624	8.30104	7.67302	7.13123	6.65959	6.24566	5.87967	5.55389	5.26211	49
50	9.04165	8.30450	7.67524	7.13266	6.66051	6.24626	5.88006	5.55414	5.26228	50

n	20%	21%	22%	23%	24%	25%	26%	28%	30%	n
1	0.83333	0.82645	0.81967	0.81301	0.80645	0.80000	0.79365	0.78125	0.76923	1
2	1.52778	1.50946	1.49153	1.47399	1.45682	1.44000	1.42353	1.39160	1.36095	2
3	2.10648	2.07393	2.04224	2.01137	1.98130	1.95200	1.92344	1.86844	1.81611	3
4	2.58873	2.54044	2.49364	2.44827	2.40428	2.36160	2.32019	2.24097	2.16624	4
5	2.99061	2.92598	2.86364	2.80347	2.74538	2.68928	2.63507	2.53201	2.43557	5
6	3.32551	3.24462	3.16692	3.09225	3.02047	2.95142	2.88498	2.75938	2.64275	6
7	3.60459	3.50795	3.41551	3.32704	3.24232	3.16114	3.08331	2.93702	2.80211	7
8	3.83716	3.72558	3.61927	3.51792	3.42122	3.32891	3.24073	3.07579	2.92470	8
9	4.03097	3.90543	3.78628	3.67310	3.56550	3.46313	3.36566	3.18421	3.01900	9
10	4.19247	4.05408	3.92318	3.79927	3.68186	3.57050	3.46481	3.26892	3.09154	10
11	4.32706	4.17692	4.03540	3.90185	3.77569	3.65640	3.54350	3.33509	3.14734	11
12	4.43922	4.27845	4.12737	3.98524	3.85136	3.72512	3.60595	3.38679	3.19026	12
13	4.53268	4.36235	4.20277	4.05304	3.91239	3.78010	3.65552	3.42718	3.22328	13
14	4.61057	4.43170	4.26456	4.10816	3.96160	3.82408	3.69485	3.45873	3.24867	14
15	4.67547	4.48901	4.31522	4.15298	4.00129	3.85926	3.72607	3.48339	3.26821	15
16	4.72956	4.53637	4.35673	4.18941	4.03330	3.88741	3.75085	3.50265	3.28324	16
17	4.77463	4.57551	4.39077	4.21904	4.05911	3.90993	3.77052	3.51769	3.29480	17
18	4.81219	4.60786	4.41866	4.24312	4.07993	3.92794	3.78613	3.52945	3.30369	18
19	4.84350	4.63460	4.44152	4.26270	4.09672	3.94235	3.79851	3.53863	3.31053	19
20	4.86958	4.65669	4.46027	4.27862	4.11026	3.95388	3.80834	3.54580	3.31579	20
21	4.89132	4.67495	4.47563	4.29156	4.12117	3.96311	3.81615	3.55141	3.31984	21
22	4.90943	4.69004	4.48822	4.30208	4.12998	3.97049	3.82234	3.55579	3.32296	22
23	4.92453	4.70251	4.49854	4.31063	4.13708	3.97639	3.82725	3.55921	3.32535	23
24	4.93710	4.71282	4.50700	4.31759	4.14281	3.98111	3.83115	3.56188	3.32719	24
25	4.94759	4.72134	4.51393	4.32324	4.14742	3.98489	3.83425	3.56397	3.32861	25
26	4.95632	4.72838	4.51962	4.32784	4.15115	3.98791	3.83670	3.56560	3.32970	26
27	4.96360	4.73420	4.52428	4.33158	4.15415	3.99033	3.83865	3.56688	3.33054	27
28	4.96967	4.73901	4.52810	4.33462	4.15657	3.99226	3.84020	3.56787	3.33118	28
29	4.97472	4.74298	4.53123	4.33709	4.15853	3.99381	3.84143	3.56865	3.33168	29
30	4.97894	4.74627	4.53379	4.33909	4.16010	3.99505	3.84240	3.56926	3.33206	30
31	4.98245	4.74898	4.53590	4.34073	4.16137	3.99604	3.84318	3.56973	3.33235	31
32	4.98537	4.75122	4.53762	4.34205	4.16240	3.99683	3.84379	3.57010	3.33258	32
33	4.98781	4.75308	4.53903	4.34313	4.16322	3.99746	3.84428	3.57039	3.33275	33
34	4.98984	4.75461	4.54019	4.34401	4.16389	3.99797	3.84467	3.57062	3.33289	34
35	4.99154	4.75588	4.54114	4.34472	4.16443	3.99838	3.84497	3.57080	3.33299	35
36	4.99295	4.75692	4.54192	4.34530	4.16486	3.99870	3.84522	3.57094	3.33307	36
37	4.99412	4.75779	4.54256	4.34578	4.16521	3.99896	3.84541	3.57104	3.33313	37
38	4.99510	4.75850	4.54308	4.34616	4.16549	3.99917	3.84556	3.57113	3.33318	38
39	4.99592	4.75909	4.54351	4.34647	4.16572	3.99934	3.84569	3.57119	3.33321	39
40	4.99660	4.75958	4.54386	4.34672	4.16590	3.99947	3.84578	3.57124	3.33324	40
41	4.99717	4.75998	4.54415	4.34693	4.16605	3.99957	3.84586	3.57128	3.33326	41
42	4.99764	4.76032	4.54438	4.34710	4.16617	3.99966	3.84592	3.57132	3.33328	42
43	4.99803	4.76059	4.54458	4.34723	4.16627	3.99973	3.84597	3.57134	3.33329	43
44	4.99836	4.76082	4.54473	4.34734	4.16634	3.99978	3.84601	3.57136	3.33330	44
45	4.99863	4.76101	4.54486	4.34743	4.16641	3.99983	3.84604	3.57138	3.33331	45
46	4.99886	4.76116	4.54497	4.34751	4.16646	3.99986	3.84606	3.57139	3.33331	46
47	4.99905	4.76129	4.54506	4.34757	4.16650	3.99989	3.84608	3.57140	3.33332	47
48	4.99921	4.76140	4.54513	4.34762	4.16653	3.99991	3.84610	3.57140	3.33332	48
49	4.99934	4.76149	4.54519	4.34766	4.16656	3.99993	3.84611	3.57141	3.33332	49
50	4.99945	4.76156	4.54524	4.34769	4.16658	3.99994	3.84612	3.57141	3.33333	50

Key Figures

P. **5-5** Net income, $7,500; Total assets $45,000

P. **5-6** Net income, $2,530

P. **5-9** Cash inflow from operations, $29,000; Total assets, $57,000

P. **5-10** Net income, $15,100; Total assets, $41,700

P. **5-11** Net income, $15,000

P. **5-12** Total assets, $24,450

P. **5-13** Net income, $43,800; Total assets, $370,530

P. **5-14** Net income, $13,010; Total assets, $26,990

Case **5-2** Net income, $10,000; Total assets, $184,750

CHAPTER 6

Ex. **6-3** Gross margin, $162,933

Ex. **6-4** Gross margin, $79,310

Ex. **6-7** Gross margin, $222,210

Ex. **6-8** Gross margin, $1,377,700

Ex. **6-9** Gross margin, $1,558,000

Ex. **6-10** Cost of goods sold, $460,000

Ex. **6-18** Accounts receivable control, $34,125

P. **6-1** Net income, $80,000

P. **6-6** Gross margin, $3,510

P. **6-7** Gross margin, $5,360

P. **6-8** Net loss, $950

P. **6-9** Net income, $2,500

P. **6-10** Net income, $7,000

P. **6-11** Net income, $10,000

P. **6-12** Net income, $16,000

P. **6-14** Total accounts payable, $3,700

Case **6-1** Net income, $9,000; Total assets, $218,260

CHAPTER 7

Ex. **7-3** b. 13 percent

Ex. **7-13** a. 8 years

Ex. **7-15** b. 8 deposits

Ex. **7-19** Term of 6 percent mortgage, 3 years.

P. **7-1** b. 11 percent; c. 75 days

P. **7-3** b. $9,330.84

P. **7-4** $105,972

P. **7-5** $70,042.78

P. **7-6** Present value of alternative b, $803,760

P. **7-7** Present value of alternative b, $1,836,143

P. **7-8** b. $176.94; c. $3,992.33

P. **7-9** $11,821.46

P. **7-10** $84,591.90

P. **7-11** $253,558.27

P. **7-12** $418,467

P. **7-13** a. $460,014.50

P. **7-14** $44,666.74

P. **7-15** c. $50,000 and $100,521.46

P. **7-16** b. $35,122.62

Case **7-1** a. $15,938.03; c. 11 percent

CHAPTER 8

Ex. **8-3** Adjusted bank balance, $10,327

Ex. **8-6** b. Gain, $1,290

Ex. **8-7** b. Book value, $15,800

Ex. **8-8** 1986 recovery of loss, $200

Ex. **8-10** March 1 gain, $90

Ex. **8-11** Dec. 31 interest income, $1,875

Ex. **8-12** July 25 interest income, $900

Ex. **8-13** Jan. 30 interest income, $43.75

Ex. **8-16** 14 percent

Ex. **8-17** c. Interest income, $482.76

Ex. **8-18** Oct. 10 interest income, $426.98

P. **8-1** Corrected book balance, $13,955

P. **8-2** Balance per books, $5,520.02

P. **8-3** b. Book value, $21,575

P. **8-4** 1987 recovery of loss, $250

P. **8-5** Sept. 30 loss, $105

P. **8-6** Dec. 31 loss, $1,115

P. **8-9** b. 3 percent

P. **8-10** June 30 bad debts expense, $440

P. **8-11** b. Bad debts expense, $246

Case **8-1** June 30, Loss from decline, $320; Bad debts expense, $529; Total current assets, $109,200

CHAPTER 9

Ex. **9-1** July sales, $47,000

Ex. **9-2** April sales, $35,700

Ex. **9-3** Ending inventory: FIFO, $255.50; LIFO, $235.00

Ex. **9-4** Cost of goods sold: FIFO, $457; LIFO, $460

Ex. **9-5** CGS: FIFO, $3,099; LIFO, $3,267; Average, $3,200.76

Ex. **9-6** LIFO ending inventory: a. $2,000; b. $2,020

Ex. **9-7** Ending inventory, $3,080

Ex. **9-11** Ending inventory, $55,250

Ex. **9-12** Inventory loss, $6,077

Ex. **9-13** Net income: 1984, $50,000; 1985, $42,000

Ex. **9-14** Ending inventory, $50,400

Ex. **9-15** Weighted average ending inventory $19,702

P. **9-1** Ending inventory: a. $28,160; b. $26,960; c. $27,675.38

P. **9-2** Ending inventory: a. $17,550; b. $16,280; c. $16,720

P. **9-3** CGS: a. FIFO, $92,700; LIFO, $94,820; b. LIFO, $96,900

P. **9-4** Allowance for decline, $85

Ex. 13-5   c. Capital, F, credit $30,000;
d. Capital, F, debit $4,000

Ex. 13-10   Total capital, $4,000,000

Ex. 13-12   Retained earnings ending balance, $600,000

P. 13-1   Capital, 12/31/85, $121,100

P. 13-2   Capital, ending $29,400

P. 13-3   Share of profits, Yung: a. $17,000; b. ($1,000)

P. 13-4   Share of profits: a. Ball, $27,000; b. Chane, $14,000

P. 13-5   Ending capital, Lind, $38,000

P. 13-6   c. Share of profits, Upton, $35,000; ending capital, Wend, $29,750

P. 13-7   Quand's capital on retiring, $42,000

P. 13-8   b. Retained earnings, ending, $352,400; Capital, $637,800

P. 13-9   Retained earnings, ending, $102,950; Total capital, $1,008,700

P. 13-10   Retained earnings, ending, $981,500; Total capital, $3,246,500

Case 13-1   Capital, Dec. 31, 1986: D, $164,000; E, $84,600; F, $55,400

CHAPTER 14

Ex. 14-1   Total capital, $1,796,000

Ex. 14-4   Retained earnings, ending balance, $225,000

Ex. 14-5   Retained earnings, ending balance, $545,000

Ex. 14-6   a. Total capital, $9,845,000; b. Book value of common, $58.50

Ex. 14-7   Weighted average shares, 233,500

Ex. 14-8   Weighted average shares, 272,500

Ex. 14-9   EPS, $6

Ex. 14-10   EPS, $2.80

Ex. 14-11   Primary EPS, $3.00; fully diluted, $2.54

Ex. 14-12   Primary EPS, $2.60; fully diluted, $2.54

P. 14-1   Retained earnings, ending, $1,201,600

P. 14-2   Retained earnings, ending, $142,025; Capital, $432,775

P. 14-3   Capital, $914,900; EPS, $7.80

P. 14-4   Capital, $562,625; EPS, $6.50

P. 14-5   Primary EPS, $5.90; Fully diluted, $5.60

P. 14-6   Primary EPS, $4.62; Fully diluted, $2.94

P. 14-7   Primary EPS, $5.68; Fully diluted, $4.40

P. 14-8   Primary EPS, $2.98; Fully diluted, $2.60

P. 14-9   b. Primary EPS, $1.92; Fully diluted, $1.85

Case 14-1   Net income and primary EPS: With preferred stock, $264,000, $2.44; With bonds, $252,000, $2.52

CHAPTER 15

Ex. 15-2   April 1 amortization, $194.60

Ex. 15-4   May 31 interest income, $10,609.22

Ex. 15-5   October 31, 1986 interest income, $557.40

Ex. 15-6   November 30 amortization, $924.82

Ex. 15-7   Interest income Dec. 31: b. $301.25; c. $299.25

Ex. 15-8   b. Gain, $2,040

Ex. 15-9   Oct. 31 loss on sale of bonds, $735

Ex. 15-10   b. Debit gain, $147.71

Ex. 15-11   Dec. 31 unrealized loss, $272

Ex. 15-12   Unrealized gain at end of 1987, $50; debit allowance, $250

P. 15-1   Oct. 31 gain, $500

P. 15-2   Oct. 31 gain, $611.87

P. 15-3   June 30, 1986 loss on sale, $1,670

P. 15-6   Dec. 1 1986 loss on sale, $1,420.17

P. 15-7   Unrealized loss, $390

P. 15-8   Dec. 31 unrealized loss, $6,250

P. 15-10   Jan. 16, 1986 gain on sale, $2,650

P. 15-11   Jan. 8, 1986 gain, $8,850

P. 15-12   Feb. 18 gain on sale, $192,000

Case 15-1   Interest income, $3,720; Dividend income, $10,500; Unrealized loss, $2,900

CHAPTER 16

Ex. 16-4   c. Goodwill, $20,000

Ex. 16-5   Goodwill, $20,000

Ex. 16-7   Total consolidation assets, $296,000

Ex. 16-8   Goodwill, $9,000

Ex. 16-10   Consolidated net income, $57,000; Total assets, $564,000

Ex. 16-12   Consolidated net income, $59,000; Total assets, $670,000

Ex. 16-13   Goodwill, $6,000; Minority interest, $8,000

P. 16-1   Goodwill, $10,000

P. 16-2   Goodwill, $9,000; Net income, $133,000

P. 16-4   Consolidated net income, $134,000

P. 16-5   Goodwill, $10,000; Minority interest, $14,000

P. 16-6   Excess of cost over book value, $30,000

P. 16-7   Goodwill, $8,000; Net income, $226,000

P. 16-8   Consolidated net income, $198,000

P. 16-9   Consolidated net income, $230,000

P. 16-10   Total assets, Jan. 2, $345,000; Consolidated income, Dec. 31, $38,000
P. 16-11   Consolidated net income, 12/31/85, $56,000; 12/31/85, $50,000
Case 16-1   Goodwill, $7,000; Total assets, $170,900

CHAPTER 17

Ex. 17-1   Working capital increase, $300
Ex. 17-4   Cash from operations, $33,000
Ex. 17-5   Cash provided by operations, $42,500
Ex. 17-6   Net income, $74,000
Ex. 17-7   Cash collected, $12,600; Cash paid, $7,400
Ex. 17-8   Cash collected, $27,320; Cash paid, $20,100
Ex. 17-12   Total uses of cash, $51,000
P. 17-1   Working capital provided by operations, $14,500
P. 17-2   Working capital increase, $950
P. 17-3   Total sources, $168,000
P. 17-4   Sources from operations, $135,000; Total sources $180,000
P. 17-5   Total sources, $7,180
P. 17-6   Total sources, $7,280
P. 17-7   Total uses, $2,990
P. 17-8   Total uses, $2,990
P. 17-10   Working capital from operations, $28,810; Total sources, $35,780
P. 17-11   Cash from operations, $28,450; Total sources, $35,420
P. 17-12   Working capital decrease, $25,200
Case 17-1   Cash from operations, $133,800; Total sources of cash, $276,600

CHAPTER 18

Ex. 18-4   Sources of working capital, $105,300
Ex. 18-5   Working capital increase, $14,100
Ex. 18-6   Sources of cash, $132,300
Ex. 18-7   Sources of working capital, $135,100
Ex. 18-8   Funds from operations, $11,000
Ex. 18-9   Funds from operations, $9,900
*Ex. 18-11 Sources of working capital, $618
*Ex. 18-12 Increase in working capital, $50
*Ex. 18-13 Sources of cash, $870
*Ex. 18-14 Sources of working capital, $872
P. 18-1   Sources of working capital, $7,180
P. 18-2   Sources of cash, $7,280
P. 18-3   Sources of working capital, $112,000
P. 18-4   Sources of cash, $113,100
P. 18-5   Sources of working capital, $26,920
P. 18-6   Cash provided by operations, $19,590; Sources of cash, $26,560
P. 18-7   Uses of working capital, $16,900
P. 18-8   Cash provided by operations, $1,340; Uses of cash, $16,900

P. 18-9   Sources of working capital, $51,150
P. 18-10   Cash provided by operations, $30,450; Uses of cash, $50,520
P. 18-11   Sources of working capital, $7,180
P. 18-12   Cash provided by operations, $2,401; Sources of cash, $6,773
P. 18-13   Uses of working capital, $9,920
P. 18-14   Cash provided by operations, $4,960; Sources of cash, $10,700
Case 18-1   Total assets, $75,500
Case 18-2   Sources of working capital, $235,000

CHAPTER 19

Ex. 19-1   Increase in sales, 10 percent
Ex. 19-2   Current ratio after note payment, 1.7 times
Ex. 19-5   Leverage, 4.4 percent
Ex. 19-7   Days' supply of inventory, 45; Days' sales in receivables, 25.7
Ex. 19-10   Times interest earned, 6.8; Leverage, 11.2%; P/E ratio, 9
Ex. 19-11   Return on equity, 20%; Leverage, 2%
Ex. 19-12   Times interest earned, 9; Debt ratio 25%
Ex. 19-14   Dividend yield, 8%; Return on equity, 14.3%
Ex. 19-15   Debt-equity ratio, 31 percent
Ex. 19-16   Inventory, $64,800; Receivables, $144,000; Cash, $79,200
P. 19-3   1985 ratios: Return on assets, .137; Return on equity, .169
P. 19-6   1985 ratios: Times interest earned, 5.78; Return on equity, .19
P. 19-7   1985 ratios: P/E, 10; Dividend payout, .39
P. 19-8   Receivables turnover, 6.5; Return on equity, .359; Leverage, .164
P. 19-10   Inventory turnover, 8; Leverage, .23; Funds flow to debt, .35
P. 19-11   Total assets, $25,000; Cash, $400; Retained earnings, $7,400
P. 19-12   Net income, $8,750; Cash, $2,760; Retained earnings, $18,800
Case 19-1   Net inome: With stock $17,550; With bonds, $13,230.   Total assets: With stock $207,500;   with bonds $203,230

CHAPTER 20

Ex. 20-2   CGS, a. $186,485; b. $179,000
Ex. 20-3   CGS, a. $300,792; b. $300,314
Ex. 20-4   Total depreciation, $14,452
Ex. 20-5   Loss, $3,287
Ex. 20-6   Loss, $1,086
Ex. 20-7   Gain, $1,939
Ex. 20-8   Accumulated depreciation, $21,900
Ex. 20-9   Holding gain, $7,800

Ex. 20-10   Ending price index, 170
Ex. 20-11   Holding gain, $183
Ex. 20-12   Holding gain, $292
P.   20-1   Purchasing power gain, $142
P.   20-2   Purchasing power loss, $1,699
P.   20-3   a. Gain on building, $900;   b. $720
P.   20-4   Constant dollar income from operations, $6,308;   Gain on monetary items, $269

P.   20-5   Current cost income from operations, $3,405;   Net holding loss, $5,045

P.   20-6   Constant dollar income from operations, $11,705;   Gain on monetary items, $531

P.   20-7   Current cost income from operations, $9,800;   Net holding gain, $182

Case 20-1   Income: Constant dollar, $1,500; Current cost, $4,200;   Gain on monetary items, $454;   Net holding loss, $10,629

Index